Dear NFT User,

Welcome to the 2006 edition of the NFT Guide to Los Angeles.

We hope that here you find something to make your day-to-day life easier and more pleasurable in a city that is both topographically and culturally rich, as well as fundamentally unwieldy.

Because of this excess of richness and size, every Angeleno inhabits his or her own unique city—one defined by habit, commute, default, and sometimes by accident. Invariably, in each individual Los Angeles, there are gaps in the map. These are the places that we sail through at 40 mph, or overlook, literally, as we sit on the freeway, waiting for the Sigalert to clear.

Though any map can tell you where you are, no map can give you the context you need to transform these in-between places into meaningful, useful, and even treasured parts of your city.

That's where we step in. Our Neighborhood Editors have worked not just to give information, but also to give meaning, to where you are. For 2006, we have fresh perspectives on neighborhoods, and have expanded our Shopping, Restaurant, Hotel, and Movie Theater listings. We have brand new sections on MOCA, Zuma Beach, San Pedro, and Sports. And to get you where you are going quickly and safely, we have expanded the section on shortcuts and driving tips.

If there is anything that you would like to see in the next edition of NFT Los Angeles, please visit our website at www.notfortourists.com and let us know. Your feedback is vital.

We thank our Neighborhood Editors for their expert insight. And we especially thank the NFT staff for their hard work. Their passion for what they do transforms raw information into the beautiful tool you hold in your hands.

Here's hoping you find more than you were looking for.

Yours Truly,

Jess, Jean, Jane, Rob, and Diana

The Valley

42 Chatsworth
43 Granada Hills/ Northridge
44 Mission Hills/ North Hills

45 Canoga Park/ Woodland Hills
46 Reseda
47 Van Nuys
48 North Hollywood
49 Burbank
50 Burbank East/ Glendale West

52 Tarzana/ Woodland Hills
53 Encino
54 Sherman Oaks West
55 Sherman Oaks East
56 Studio City/ Valley Village
57 Toluca Lake
51 Glendale South

405
170
101
5
134
2
210
21
110
10

Griffith Park
PAGE 246

East Side & Pasade...

33 Eagle Rock/ Highland Park
34 Pasadena
35 Pasadena East/ San Marino
36 Mt Washington
37 Lincoln Heights
38 El Sereno
39 Alhambra
40 Boyle Heights
41 City Terrace/ East LA

West Side & the Beach

17 Bel Air/ Holmby Hills
1 Beverly Hills
16 Brentwood
20 Westwood/ Century City
15 Pacific Palisades
19 West LA
18 Santa Monica
23 Rancho Park/ Palms
22 Mar Vista
21 Venice
24 Culver City
25 Marina Del Rey/ Westchester West
26 Westchester/ Fox Hills/ Ladera Heights/ LAX

2 West Hollywood
3 Hollywood
4 Los Feliz
5 Silver Lake/ Echo Park/ Atwater
6 Miracle Mile/ Mid-City
7 Hancock Park
8 Korea Town
9 Downtown
10 Baldwin Hills
11 South Central West
12 South Central East
13 Inglewood
14 Inglewood East/ Morningside Park

Central LA

LAX PAGE 306

27 El Segundo/ Manhattan Beach
28 Hawthorne
29 Hermosa Beach/ Redondo Beach North
30 Torrance North
31 Redondo Beach
32 Torrance South

105
710
5
405

Pacific Ocean

South Bay

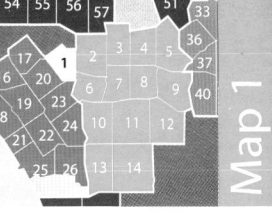

This is what the rest of the world pictures when they think of Los Angeles: palm-lined, broad avenues of beautiful people, their beautiful homes and cars, and fancy retail. In some spots, it does retain a thrilling nosebleed-prices charm. Though the holiday decorations are lovely, traffic is thick on Wilshire Boulevard six days a week. Take Olympic Boulevard or Burton Way to Little Santa Monica Boulevard if you're passing through, or enjoy two hours of free parking during the times you are not.

$ Banks

- **Bank of America** · 460 N Beverly Dr
- **Bank of America** · 9461 Wilshire Blvd
- **Bank of the West** · 9401 Wilshire Blvd
- **California National** · 9100 Wilshire Blvd
- **Citibank** · 9059 W Sunset Blvd
- **Citibank** · 9401 Wilshire Blvd
- **City National** · 400 N Roxbury Dr
- **City National** · 9229 W Sunset Blvd
- **Comerica** · 9757 Wilshire Blvd
- **First Bank & Trust** · 9145 Wilshire Blvd
- **First Republic** · 9593 Wilshire Blvd
- **Manufacturers** · 9777 Wilshire Blvd
- **Pacific Western** · 9454 Wilshire Blvd
- **Union** · 9460 Wilshire Blvd
- **United National** · 450 N Roxbury Dr
- **US** · 9595 Wilshire Blvd
- **Washington Mutual** · 9245 Wilshire Blvd
- **Wells Fargo** · 9354 Wilshire Blvd
- **Wells Fargo** · 9600 Santa Monica Blvd
- **Western Financial** · 9107 Wilshire Blvd

Car Rental

- **Budget** · 9815 Wilshire Blvd

Car Washes

- **Aqua Carwash** · 9601 Wilshire Blvd

Gas Stations

- **76** · 427 N Crescent Dr
- **76** · 9460 W Olympic Blvd

Landmarks

- **Academy of Motion Pictures Arts & Sciences** · 8949 Wilshire Blvd
- **Beverly Hills Civic Center** · Rexford Dr & Santa Monica Blvd
- **Beverly Hills Hotel** · 9641 Sunset Blvd
- **Greystone Park** · 905 Loma Vista Dr
- **Museum of Television and Radio** · 465 N Beverly Dr
- **Prada Store** · 469 N Rodeo Dr
- **Regent Beverly Wilshire Hotel** · 9500 Wilshire Blvd
- **The Witch's House** · 516 Walden Dr

Libraries

- **Beverly Hills Public Library** · 444 N Rexford Dr · 310-288-2220

Pharmacies

- **Rite-Aid** · 463 N Bedford Dr · 310-247-0843
- **Rite-Aid (24 hrs)** · 300 N Canon Dr · 310-273-3561
- **Sav-On** · 9045 Wilshire Blvd · 310-273-5252

Police

- **Beverly Hills Police** · 464 N Rexford Dr · 310-550-4951

Post Offices

- 312 S Beverly Dr · 310-247-3470
- 323 N Crescent Dr ·
- 325 N Maple Dr · 310-247-3400

Schools

- **Beverly Hills Preparatory** · 9250 Olympic Blvd
- **Beverly Vista Elementary** · 200 S Elm Dr
- **Good Shepherd Catholic** · 148 S Linden Dr
- **Hawthorne Elementary** · 624 N Rexford Dr
- **West Hollywood Elementary** · 970 N Hammond St

Supermarkets

- **Pavilions** · 9467 W Olympic Blvd
- **Whole Foods Market** · 239 N Crescent Dr

Map 1 · Beverly Hills

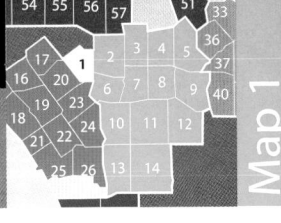
Rodeo Drive is a theme park—albeit a very glossy one. It is not a reliable place to see the beau monde (unless you cruise N Bedford Drive, the plastic surgery capital of the world). Head to Beverly Drive south of Wilshire Boulevard for a more down-to-earth experience: a supermarket, small shops, nail salons, bakeries, cafes, an inspiring newsstand, places to grab lunch or an afternoon yoga class, and a friendly post office.

 Coffee

- **Aloha Island Coffee Company** · 153 S Beverly Dr
- **Coffee Bean & Tea Leaf** · 233 S Beverly Dr
- **Coffee Bean & Tea Leaf** · 445 N Beverly Dr
- **Euro Caffe** · 9559 Santa Monica Blvd
- **Graffeo Coffee Roasting** · 315 N Beverly Dr
- **It's Coffee Lovers Time** · 468 N Camden Dr
- **Peet's Coffee & Tea** · 258 S Beverly Dr
- **Seletoo** · 433 N Camden Dr
- **Splurge** · 9595 Wilshire Blvd
- **Starbucks** · 202 S Beverly Dr
- **Starbucks** · 428 N Beverly Dr
- **Starbucks** · 9844 Wilshire Blvd
- **Urth Caffe** · 267 S Beverly Dr

Copy Centers

- **Keystone Copy** · 9877 Santa Monica Blvd · 310-553-5697
- **Kinko's** · 9334 Wilshire Blvd · 310-271-1258
- **Mail Boxes Etc** · 269 S Beverly Dr · 310-274-7721
- **Mail Boxes Etc** · 9663 Santa Monica Blvd · 310-858-7122
- **Printcraft Printing** · 9301 Wilshire Blvd · 310-247-0234

Farmer's Markets

- **Beverly Hills** · 200 N Canon Dr

Gyms

- **Sports Club LA** · 9601 Wilshire Blvd · 310-888-8100

Hardware Stores

- **Pioneer & Lucerne Hardware** · 315 N Crescent Dr · 310-276-1167

Liquor Stores

- **Wine Merchant** · 9467 Santa Monica Blvd
- **Wine Shop** · 350 N Canon Dr

 Nightlife

- **Bar Noir in Maison 140** · 140 S Lasky Dr · 310-281-4000
- **Belvedere at the Peninsula Hotel** · 9882 Santa Monica Blvd · 310-551-2888
- **Blue on Blue** · 9400 W Olympic Blvd · 310-277-5221
- **Larry Flynt's Supper Cabaret** · 424 Beverly Dr · 310-275-8511
- **Regent Beverly Wilshire** · 9500 Wilshire Blvd · 310-275-5200
- **Trader Vic's** · 9876 Wilshire Blvd · 310-276-6345
- **Writer's Bar at L'Ermitage Hotel** · 9291 Burton Wy · 310-278-3344

Pet Stores

- **Elite Animals** · 9040 Santa Monica Blvd · 310-888-0115
- **Petco** · 508 N Doheny Dr · 310-275-6012

 Restaurants

- **Baja Fresh** · 475 N Beverly Dr · 310-858-6690
- **Barney Greengrass** · 9570 Wilshire Blvd · 310-777-5877
- **Basic Bites** · 443 N Beverly Blvd · 310-247-9673
- **The Belvedere** · 9882 Little Santa Monica Blvd · 310-788-2306
- **Blowfish Sushi** · 9229 Sunset Blvd · 310-887-3848
- **Blue on Blue** · 9400 W Olympic Blvd · 310-277-5221
- **BOE** · 403 N Crescent Dr · 310-247-0505
- **Brighton Coffee Shop** · 9600 Brighton Wy · 310-276-7732
- **Café Talesai** · 9198 W Olympic Blvd · 310-271-9345
- **Crustacean** · 9646 Little Santa Monica Blvd · 310-205-8990
- **Da Pasquale** · 9749 Little Santa Monica Blvd · 310-859-3884
- **Dan Tana's** · 9071 Santa Monica Blvd · 310-275-9444
- **El Torito Grill** · 9595 Wilshire Blvd · 310-550-1599
- **Farm of Beverly Hills** · 439 N Beverly Dr · 310-273-5578
- **Ginza Sushi-Ko** · 218 N Rodeo Dr · 310-247-8939
- **The Grill** · 9560 Dayton Wy · 310-276-0615
- **Joss** · 9255 Sunset Blvd · 310-276-1886
- **Kate Mantilini** · 9101 Wilshire Blvd · 310-278-3699
- **La Scala** · 434 N Canon Dr · 310-275-0579
- **Le Pain Quotidien** · 9630 Little Santa Monica Blvd · 310-859-1100
- **Maple Drive** · 345 N Maple Dr · 310-274-9800
- **Mastro** · 246 N Canon Dr · 310-888-8782
- **Mulberry Street Pizzeria** · 240 S Beverly Dr · 310-247-8100
- **Mulberry Street Pizzeria** · 347 N Canon Dr · 310-247-8998
- **Nate 'n Al's** · 414 N Beverly Dr · 310-274-0101
- **Nic's** · 453 N Canon Dr · 310-550-5707
- **Polo Lounge** · 9641 Sunset Blvd · 310-276-2251
- **Real Food Daily** · 242 S Beverly Dr · 310-858-0880
- **Regent Beverly Wilshire** · 9500 Wilshire Blvd · 310-275-5200
- **Trader Vic's** · 9876 Wilshire Blvd · 310-276-6345
- **Xi'an** · 362 N Canon Dr · 310-275-3345

Shopping

- **Anthropologie** · 320 N Beverly Dr · 310-385-7390
- **Barney's New York** · 9570 Wilshire Blvd · 310-276-4400
- **Cheese Store of Beverly Hills** · 419 N Beverly Dr · 310-278-2855
- **Geary's of Beverly Hills** · 351 N Beverly Dr · 310-273-4741
- **Mrs Beasley's/Miss Grace Lemon Cake Co** · 255 1/2 S Beverly Dr · 310-276-6516
- **Prada Epicenter** · 343 N Rodeo Dr · 310-278-8661
- **Saks Fifth Avenue** · 9600 Wilshire Blvd · 310-275-4211
- **The Taschen Store** · 354 N Beverly Dr · 310-274-4300

 Video Rental

- **Video Collection** · 470 N Doheny Dr · 310-273-7700

Map 2 • West Hollywood

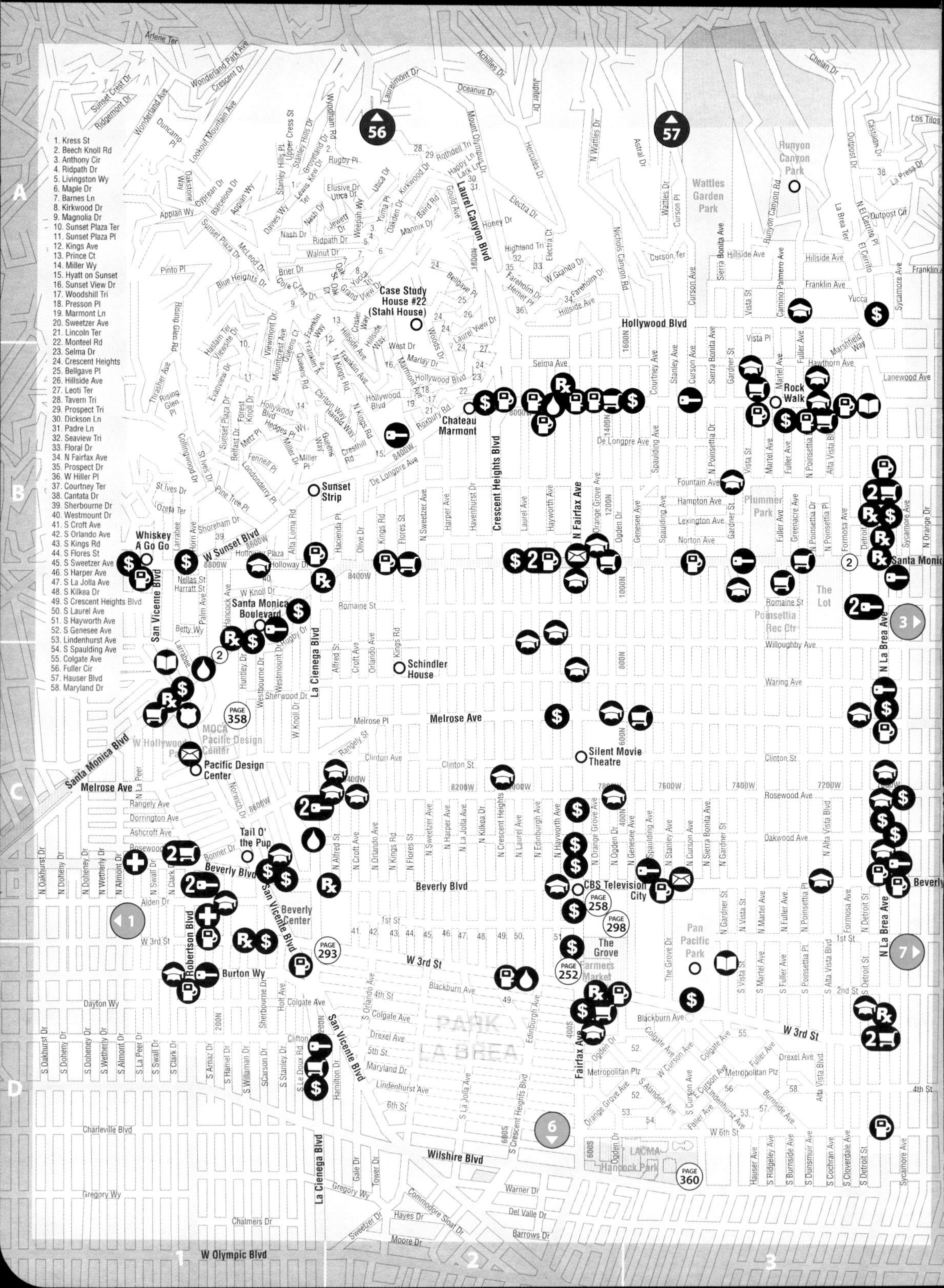

1. Kress St
2. Beech Knoll Rd
3. Anthony Cir
4. Ridpath Dr
5. Livingston Wy
6. Maple Dr
7. Barnes Ln
8. Kirkwood Dr
9. Magnolia Dr
10. Sunset Plaza Ter
11. Sunset Plaza Pl
12. Kings Ave
13. Prince Ct
14. Miller Wy
15. Hyatt on Sunset
16. Sunset View Dr
17. Woodshill Tri
18. Presson Pl
19. Marmont Ln
20. Sweetzer Ave
21. Lincoln Ter
22. Monteel Rd
23. Selma Dr
24. Crescent Heights
25. Bellgave Pl
26. Kings Ave
27. Leoti Ter
28. Tavern Tri
29. Prospect Tri
30. Dickson Ln
31. Padre Ln
32. Seaview Tri
33. Floral Dr
34. N Fairfax Ave
35. Prospect Dr
36. W Hiller Pl
37. Courtney Ter
38. Cantata Dr
39. Sherbourne Dr
40. Westmount Dr
41. S Croft Ave
42. S Orlando Ave
43. S Kings Rd
44. S Flores St
45. S Sweetzer Ave
46. S Harper Ave
47. S La Jolla Ave
48. S Kilkea Dr
49. S Crescent Heights Blvd
50. S Laurel Ave
51. S Hayworth Ave
52. S Genesee Ave
53. Lindenhurst Ave
54. S Spaulding Ave
55. Colgate Ave
56. Fuller Cir
57. Hauser Blvd
58. Maryland Dr

56

57

Runyon Canyon Park

Wattles Garden Park

Case Study House #22 (Stahl House)

Chateau Marmont

Sunset Strip

Whiskey A Go Go

Rock Walk

Plummer Park

The Lot

Poinsettia Rec Ctr

Santa Monica Boulevard

Schindler House

PAGE 358

MOCA Pacific Design Center

Pacific Design Center

Silent Movie Theatre

Melrose Ave

Tail O' the Pup

Beverly Center

CBS Television City

Pan Pacific Park

PAGE 258

PAGE 298

PAGE 293

The Grove

Farmers Market

PAGE 252

PARK LA BREA

6

PAGE 360

LACMA Hancock Park

W Olympic Blvd

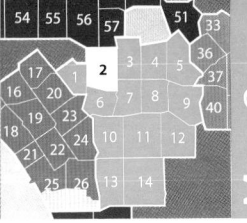
The City of West Hollywood is its own progressive, leafy municipality, with both rent control and some of the most complex parking restrictions on the planet. It is also home to a vibrant and varied population—gay, Russian, urban professional, Orthodox Jewish, and former real estate agent-turned-yoga teacher, to name a few. Every Halloween, the big party—multi-generational, multi-ethnic, and fabulous—is on Santa Monica Boulevard between La Cienega and San Vicente Boulevards.

💲Banks
- **Bank of America** • 9021 W Sunset Blvd
- 7800 W Sunset Blvd • 7900 Melrose Ave
- 8025 Santa Monica Blvd • 8655 Beverly Blvd
- 8921 Santa Monica Blvd • 466 N La Brea Ave
- **California National** • 145 S Fairfax Ave
- **California National** • 736 N La Brea Ave
- **California National** • 8601 Santa Monica Blvd
- **Citibank** • 300 S Fairfax Ave
- **Citibank** • 7257 W Sunset Blvd
- **Citibank** • 8900 Santa Monica Blvd
- **First Federal** • 400 N La Brea Ave
- **First Federal** • 464 N Fairfax Ave
- **First Federal** • 8653 Beverly Blvd
- **First Regional** • 7083 Hollywood Blvd
- **Gilmore** • 7929 W 3rd St
- **US** • 8901 Santa Monica Blvd
- **Washington Mutual** • 310 N Fairfax Ave
- **Washington Mutual** • 449 N La Brea Ave
- **Washington Mutual** • 6120 W 3rd St
- **Washington Mutual** • 8150 W Sunset Blvd
- **Wells Fargo** • 8625 W 3rd St
- 100 N La Cienega Blvd • 137 N Fairfax Ave
- 8571 Santa Monica Blvd • 1233 N La Brea Ave

🚗Car Rental
- **Advantage Rent-a-Car** • 737 N La Brea Ave
- **Affordable Car Rental** • 1040 N La Brea Ave
- **Annex Enterprises** • 200 N La Cienega Blvd
- **Avon Rent-A-Car** • 7080 Santa Monica Blvd
- **Black & White Rent-a-Car** • 8800 Burton Wy
- **Enterprise** • 265 N Robertson Blvd
- **Enterprise** • 463 N La Cienega Blvd
- **Enterprise** • 7100 Beverly Blvd
- **Enterprise** • 8367 W Sunset Blvd
- **Enterprise** • 8583 Santa Monica Blvd
- **Enterprise** • 943 N La Brea Ave
- **Hertz** • 361 N La Brea Ave
- **Hertz** • 450 N La Cienega Blvd
- **Priceless Rent-a-Car** • 7415 Santa Monica Blvd
- **West Hollywood Rent-a-Car** •
  7610 W Sunset Blvd

💧Car Washes
- **Majestic Car Wash** • 8017 W 3rd St
- **Medison Car Wash** • 7617 Santa Monica Blvd
- **Royal Car Wash** • 431 N La Cienega Blvd
- **Santa Palm Car Wash** • 8787 Santa Monica Blvd
- **Sunset Car Wash** • 7955 Sunset Blvd

⛽Gas Stations
- **76** • 5436 W 6th St
- **76** • 7751 Beverly Blvd
- **76** • 7960 Santa Monica Blvd
- **76** • 7979 W Sunset Blvd
- **76** • 8755 W 3rd St
- **Arco** • 7564 Santa Monica Blvd
- **Arco** • 7901 W Sunset Blvd
- **Chevron** • 1107 N La Cienega Blvd
- **Chevron** • 7020 Beverly Blvd
- **Chevron** • 7100 Melrose Ave
- **Chevron** • 7955 W Sunset Blvd
- **Chevron** • 8017 W 3rd St
- **Chevron** • 8101 W Sunset Blvd
- **Exxon** • 391 S Robertson Blvd

- **Exxon** • 8020 Santa Monica Blvd
- **Independent** • 8906 W Sunset Blvd
- **Mobil** • 307 N La Brea Ave
- **Mobil** • 7100 W Sunset Blvd
- **Mobil** • 7865 W Sunset Blvd
- **Mobil** • 8380 Santa Monica Blvd
- **Mobil** • 8489 Beverly Blvd
- **Shell** • 1309 N La Brea Ave
- **Texaco** • 7318 W Sunset Blvd

➕Hospitals
- **Cedars-Sinai Medical Center** •
  8700 Beverly Blvd

⭕Landmarks
- **Case Study House #22 (Stahl House)** •
  1636 Woods Dr
- **CBS Television City** • Beverly Blvd &
  N Fairfax Ave
- **Chateau Marmont** • 8221 Sunset Blvd
- **Pacific Design Center** • Melrose Ave &
  San Vicente Blvd
- **Pan Pacific Park** • 7600 Beverly Blvd
- **Rock Walk** • 7435 Sunset Blvd
- **Runyon Canyon Park** • Franklin Ave & Fuller Dr
- **Santa Monica Blvd** • b/w La Cienega Blvd &
  Robertson Blvd
- **Schindler House** • 833 N Kings Rd
- **Silent Movie Theatre** • 611 N Fairfax Ave
- **Sunset Strip** • Sunset Blvd b/w N Doheny Dr
  & N Fairfax Ave
- **Tail O' the Pup** • 329 N San Vicente Blvd
- **Whiskey A Go Go** • 8901 Sunset Blvd

📖Libraries
- **Fairfax Branch Library** • 161 S Gardner St •
  323-936-6191
- **West Hollywood** • 715 N San Vicente Blvd •
  310-652-5340
- **Will & Ariel Durant Branch** •
  7140 W Sunset Blvd • 323-876-2741

℞Pharmacies
- **CVS/ProCare** • 8635 W 3rd St • 310-652-1080
- **Longs Drugs (24 hours)** • 8490 Beverly Blvd
  • 323-653-4616
- **Pavilions** • 8969 Santa Monica Blvd •
  310-273-5126
- **PharmaCare** • 8607 Santa Monica Blvd •
  310-659-9810
- **Ralphs** • 1233 N La Brea Ave • 323-876-5651
- **Ralphs** • 260 S La Brea Ave • 323-937-9383
- **Rite-Aid** • 7900 W Sunset Blvd • 323-876-4466
- **Rite-Aid** • 1130 N La Brea Ave • 323-463-8539
- **Sav-On** • 8491 W Santa Monica Blvd •
  310-360-7306
- **Sav-On (24 hrs)** • 6360 W 3rd St •
  323-937-3030
- **Target** • 7100 Santa Monica Blvd •
  323-603-0005

👮Police
- **Los Angeles County Sheriff's Dept—West
  Hollywood Station** • 720 N San Vicente Blvd
  • 310-855-8850

✉Post Offices
- 1125 N Fairfax Ave •
- 7610 Beverly Blvd •
- 820 N San Vicente Blvd • 310-652-2345

🎓Schools
- **Bais Tzivia for Girls** • 7269 Beverly Blvd
- **Bais Yaakov for Girls** • 461 N La Brea Ave
- **Center for Early Education** • 563 N Alfred St
- **Cheder of Los Angeles** • 348 N La Brea Ave
- **Cheerful Helpers Therapeutic School** •
  8730 Alden Dr
- **Daniel Murphy Catholic High** •
  241 S Detroit St
- **Emanuel Academy** • 8844 Burton Wy
- **Fairfax Senior High** • 7850 Melrose Ave
- **Fountain Day** • 1128 N Orange Grove Ave
- **Gardner St Elementary** • 7450 Hawthorn Ave
- **Hancock Park Elementary** • 408 S Fairfax Ave
- **Laurel EEC** • 8023 Willoughby Ave
- **Laurel Elementary** • 925 N Hayworth Ave
- **Maimonides Academy** • 310 N Huntley
- **Melrose Ave Elementary** • 731 N Detroit St
- **Ofman Learning Center** • 812 N Fairfax Ave
- **Pacific Hills** • 8628 Holloway Dr
- **Perutz Jacob Hebrew Academy** •
  7951 Melrose Ave
- **Rosewood Ave Elementary** • 503 N Croft Ave
- **Rosewood EEC** • 510 N Alfred St
- **Temple Israel Day** • 7300 Hollywood Blvd
- **West Hollywood Children's Academy** •
  1031 N Vista St
- **West Hollywood Community Day** •
  1049 N Fairfax Ave
- **Whitman Continuation** • 7795 Rosewood Ave
- **Yeshiva Ohr Elchonon Chabad** •
  7215 Waring Ave
- **Yeshiva Rav Isaacsohn** • 540 N La Brea Ave
- **Young Hollywood** • 1434 N Poinsettia Pl

🛒Supermarkets
- **Bristol Farms** • 7880 W Sunset Blvd
- **Bristol Farms** • 9039 Beverly Blvd
- **Gelson's Markets** • 8330 Santa Monica Blvd
- **Jons Marketplace** • 1234 N La Brea Ave
- **Pavilions** • 8969 Santa Monica Blvd
- **Ralphs** • 100 N La Cienega Blvd
- **Ralphs** • 1233 N La Brea Ave
- **Ralphs** • 260 S La Brea Ave
- **Ralphs** • 7257 Sunset Blvd
- **Ralphs** • 9040 Beverly Blvd
- **Smart & Final** • 1041 N Fuller Ave
- **Smart & Final** • 7720 Melrose Ave
- **Trader Joe's** • 263 S La Brea Ave
- **Trader Joe's** • 7304 Santa Monica Blvd
- **Trader Joe's** • 8611 Santa Monica Blvd
- **Whole Foods Market** • 6350 W 3rd St
- **Whole Foods Market** •
  7871 Santa Monica Blvd

Map 2 • West Hollywood

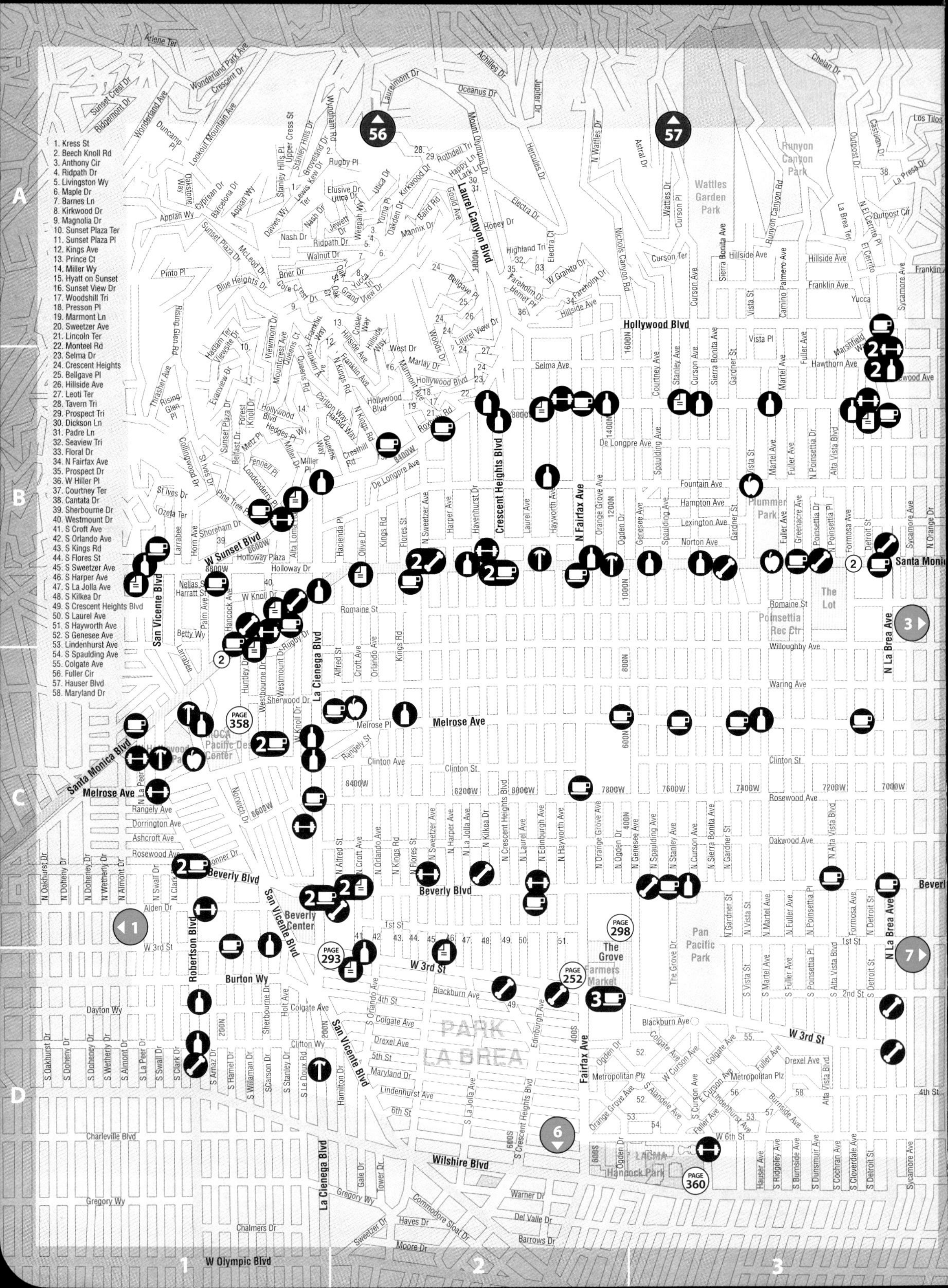

N
1. Kress St
2. Beech Knoll Rd
3. Anthony Cir
4. Ridpath Dr
5. Livingston Wy
6. Maple Dr
7. Barnes Ln
8. Kirkwood Dr
9. Magnolia Dr
10. Sunset Plaza Ter
11. Sunset Plaza Pl
12. Kings Ave
13. Prince Ct
14. Miller Wy
15. Hyatt on Sunset
16. Sunset View Dr
17. Woodshill Trl
18. Presson Pl
19. Marmont Ln
20. Sweetzer Ave
21. Lincoln Ter
22. Monteel Rd
23. Selma Dr
24. Crescent Heights
25. Bellgave Pl
26. Hillside Ave
27. Leoti Ter
28. Tavern Trl
29. Prospect Trl
30. Dickson Ln
31. Padre Ln
32. Seaview Trl
33. Floral Dr
34. N Fairfax Ave
35. Prospect Dr
36. W Hiller Pl
37. Courtney Ter
38. Cantata Dr
39. Sherbourne Dr
40. Westmount Dr
41. S Croft Ave
42. S Orlando Ave
43. S Kings Rd
44. S Flores St
45. S Sweetzer Ave
46. S Harper Ave
47. S La Jolla Ave
48. S Kilkea Dr
49. S Crescent Heights Blvd
50. S Laurel Ave
51. S Hayworth Ave
52. S Genesee Ave
53. Lindenhurst Ave
54. S Spaulding Ave
55. Colgate Ave
56. Fuller Cir
57. Hauser Blvd
58. Maryland Dr
56
57
A
B
C
D
1
2
3
Laurel Canyon Blvd
Hollywood Blvd
W Sunset Blvd
Santa Monica Blvd
Melrose Ave
Beverly Blvd
W 3rd St
Wilshire Blvd
W Olympic Blvd
La Cienega Blvd
Crescent Heights Blvd
N Fairfax Ave
Fairfax Ave
N La Brea Ave
San Vicente Blvd
Robertson Blvd
Runyon Canyon Park
Wattles Garden Park
Plummer Park
The Lot
Poinsettia Rec Ctr
Pan Pacific Park
The Grove
Farmers Market
PARK LA BREA
Beverly Center
LACMA
Hancock Park
PAGE 358
PAGE 298
PAGE 293
PAGE 252
PAGE 360

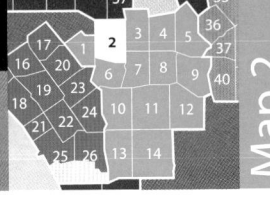
The area boasts some of the most cohesive and walkable micro-neighborhoods in town (try Third Street west of Fairfax Avenue, the changes in demographic along Melrose Avenue from Doheny Drive east to La Brea Avenue, or Fairfax Avenue north of Beverly Boulevard). This does make the installation of The Grove shopping mall, with its faux-village atmosphere, a little ironic. (Though in fairness, the dancing fountains are delightful, and the Farmer's Market food and tchotchke stalls have been left just as perfect as they ever were.)

Coffee

- **African Red Tea** · 533 N Fairfax Ave
- **At Coffee Shop** · 7200 Melrose Ave
- **Basix Coffee** · 8333 Santa Monica Blvd
- **Bob's Coffee & Donuts** · 6333 W 3rd St
- **Buzz Coffee** · 7623 Beverly Blvd
- **Café Marco** · 8200 Santa Monica Blvd
- **Chris Michael's Café** · 8687 Melrose Ave
- **Coffee Bean & Tea Leaf**
  - · 6333 W 3rd St
  - · 7502 Melrose Ave
  - · 8500 Beverly Blvd
  - · 8735 Santa Monica Blvd
  - · 7235 Beverly Blvd
  - · 7915 W Sunset Blvd
  - · 8591 W Sunset Blvd
  - · 8793 Beverly Blvd
- **Coffee Corner** · 6333 W 3rd St
- **Cyber Java Internet Store** · 7080 Hollywood Blvd
- **Daily Grind** · 7801 Melrose Ave
- **Dialog Coffee & Bakery** · 8766 Holloway Dr
- **Dukes Tropicana Coffee Shop** · 8909 W Sunset Blvd
- **Ramma Geni Café** · 8500 Melrose Ave
- **Royal Coffee & Tea** · 8151 Santa Monica Blvd
- **Sam's Coffee** · 7310 Santa Monica Blvd
- **Starbucks**
  - · 6333 W 3rd St
  - · 7100 Santa Monica Blvd
  - · 7624 Melrose Ave
  - · 8363 NE Sunset Blvd
  - · 8949 Santa Monica Blvd
  - · 164 N Robertson Blvd
  - · 7055 Sunset Blvd
  - · 7122 Beverly Blvd
  - · 7901 Santa Monica Blvd
  - · 8595 Santa Monica Blvd
  - · Beverly Center, 8500 Beverly Center
- **Swingers** · 8020 Beverly Blvd
- **Tully's Coffee** · 8631 W 3rd St
- **Urth Caffe** · 8565 Melrose Ave

Copy Centers

- **A Plus Printing & Copy** · 8424 Santa Monica Blvd · 323-656-8061
- **Alpha Print & Copy** · 9030 W Sunset Blvd · 310-273-9460
- **Kinko's** · 7630 W Sunset Blvd · 323-845-4501
- **Kinko's** · 8471 Beverly Blvd · 323-782-6905
- **Mail Boxes Etc** · 8391 Beverly Blvd · 323-655-9980
- **Mail Boxes Etc** · 8581 Santa Monica Blvd · 310-289-5952
- **New Image Printing** · 7109 W Sunset Blvd · 323-876-1102
- **Pacific Instant Printing** · 8239 W 3rd St · 323-651-4964
- **Printop Copy Center** · 8539 W Sunset Blvd · 310-854-0403
- **Sharp-Print** · 8426 W 3rd St · 310-300-9228
- **Sir Speedy** · 8730 Santa Monica Blvd · 310-657-7210
- **UPS Store** · 8033 W Sunset Blvd · 323-848-8300

Farmer's Markets

- **Melrose Place** · Melrose Pl & N Croft Ave
- **Plummer Park** · 7377 Santa Monica Blvd
- **West Hollywood** · 647 N San Vicente Blvd
- **West Hollywood** · Plummer Park, N Vista St & Fountain Ave

Gyms

- **24-Hour Fitness** · 8612 Santa Monica Blvd · 310-652-7440
- **Beverly Hills Health & Fitness** · 8301 Beverly Blvd · 323-658-6999
- **Boulevard Health** · 120 N Robertson Blvd · 310-659-5002
- **Crunch** · 8000 W Sunset Blvd · 323-654-4550
- **Curves** · 415 Westmount Dr · 310-854-4428
- **Curves** · 7125 1/2 W Sunset Blvd · 323-851-2878
- **Easton Gym** · 8053 Beverly Blvd · 323-651-3636
- **Emerson Health & Fitness** · 8816 Melrose Ave · 310-858-6812

- **Equinox** · 8590 W Sunset Blvd · 310-289-1900
- **Fitness Factory** · 650 N La Peer Dr · 310-358-1838
- **Groove Fitness** · 1626 N La Brea Ave · 323-960-0660
- **Hollywood Gym** · 1551 N La Brea Ave · 323-845-1420

Hardware Stores

- **Anawalt Lumber** · 641 N Robertson Blvd · 310-652-6202
- **Koontz True Value** · 8914 Santa Monica Blvd · 310-652-0123
- **Laurel Hardware** · 7984 Santa Monica Blvd · 323-656-9605
- **Tashman Screens & Hardware** · 7769 Santa Monica Blvd · 323-656-7028

Liquor Stores

- **Almor Liquors** · 7855 W Sunset Blvd
- **Bicentennial 13** · 7613 Beverly Blvd
- **Carmel Liquor** · 8200 Santa Monica Blvd
- **Consumers Liquor** · 7151 W Sunset Blvd
- **Crown Liquor** · 130 N Robertson Blvd
- **Du Vin Wine & Spirits** · 540 N San Vicente Blvd
- **Fountain Liquor** · 7952 Fountain Ave
- **Gil Turner's Fine Wine & Spirits** · 9101 W Sunset Blvd
- **Golden Rule Liquor** · 7753 Santa Monica Blvd
- **Greenblatt's Deli & Fine Wines** · 8017 W Sunset Blvd
- **John & Pete's Liquor** · 621 N La Cienega Blvd
- **Lee's Liquor** · 8572 W 3rd St
- **Limelite Liquors** · 1649 N La Brea Ave
- **Liquor Locker** · 8161 W Sunset Blvd
- **Liquor Time** · 7873 Santa Monica Blvd
- **Mel & Rose Liquor & Cigars** · 8344 Melrose Ave
- **Melrose Liquors** · 7435 Melrose Ave
- **Monaco Liquor** · 8513 Santa Monica Blvd
- **Mr S Liquor** · 7580 W Sunset Blvd
- **Pink Dot Market Deli/Grocery** · 8495 W Sunset Blvd
- **Robert Burns Liquor** · 157 N Robertson Blvd
- **Roman's Liquor** · 1529 N La Brea Ave
- **S&S Liquor** · 7600 Santa Monica Blvd
- **St Regis Liquors** · 8401 W 3rd St
- **Sun Bee Food & Liquor** · 8860 W Sunset Blvd
- **Sunset Plaza Liquor** · 7365 W Sunset Blvd

Pet Stores

- **Amazon Rainforest Pet Shop** · 7505 Santa Monica Blvd · 323-969-8382
- **Animal Crackers** · 8023 Beverly Blvd · 310-659-1919
- **Animal Farm Pet Shop** · 8270 Santa Monica Blvd · 323-650-7772
- **Centinela Feed & Pet Supplies** · 331 N Robertson Blvd · 310-246-0367
- **Chateau Marmutt** · 8128 W 3rd St · 323-653-2062
- **Collar & Leash Pet Food & Supply** · 8555 Santa Monica Blvd · 310-657-6638
- **For Birds Only** · 8273 Santa Monica Blvd · 323-848-8361
- **For Pets Only** · 310 S La Brea Ave · 323-934-8303
- **Omar's Exotic Birds** · 8729 Santa Monica Blvd · 310-659-6552
- **Oranda Aquarium** · 7320 Santa Monica Blvd · 323-876-5059
- **Pet Love** · 131 N La Cienega Blvd · 310-659-8490
- **Petco** · 200 S La Brea Ave · 323-934-8444
- **Pour La Pooch** · 7617 Beverly Blvd · 323-934-0940

Map 2 • West Hollywood

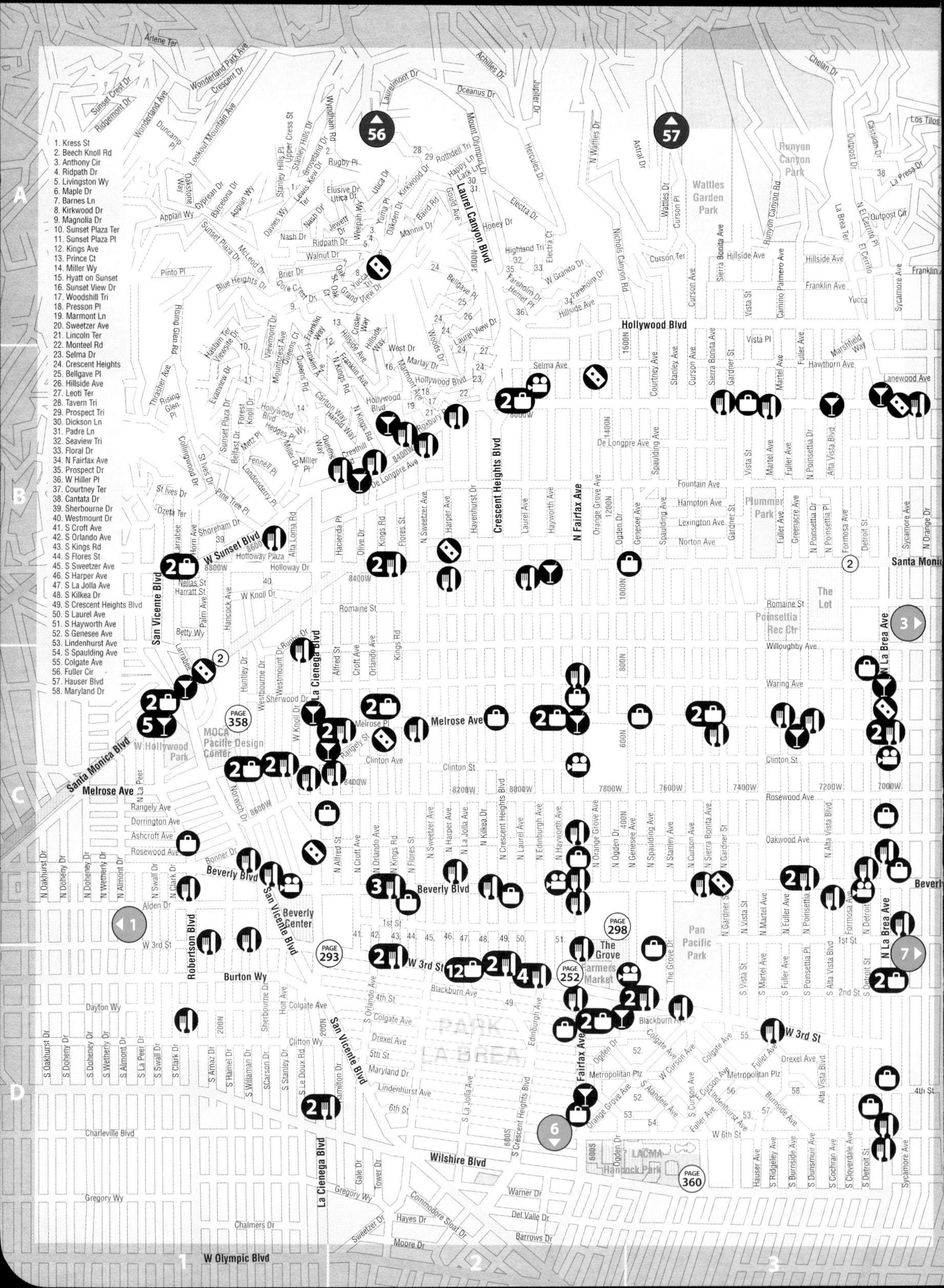

1. Kress St
2. Beech Knoll Rd
3. Anthony Cir
4. Ridpath Dr
5. Livingston Wy
6. Maple Dr
7. Barnes Ln
8. Kirkwood Dr
9. Magnolia Dr
10. Sunset Plaza Ter
11. Sunset Plaza Pl
12. Kings Ave
13. Prince Ct
14. Miller Wy
15. Hyatt on Sunset
16. Sunset View Dr
17. Woodshill Trl
18. Presson Pl
19. Marmont Ln
20. Sweetzer Ave
21. Lincoln Ter
22. Monteel Rd
23. Selma Dr
24. Crescent Heights
25. Bellgave Pl
26. Hillside Ave
27. Leoti Ter
28. Tavern Trl
29. Prospect Trl
30. Dickson Ln
31. Padre Ln
32. Seaview Trl
33. Floral Dr
34. N Fairfax Ave
35. Prospect Dr
36. W Hiller Pl
37. Courtney Ter
38. Cantata Dr
39. Sherbourne Dr
40. Westmount Dr
41. S Croft Ave
42. S Orlando Ave
43. S Kings Rd
44. S Flores St
45. S Sweetzer Ave
46. S Harper Ave
47. S La Jolla Ave
48. S Kilkea Dr
49. S Crescent Heights Blvd
50. S Laurel Ave
51. S Hayworth Ave
52. S Genesee Ave
53. Lindenhurst Ave
54. S Spaulding Ave
55. Colgate Ave
56. Fuller Cir
57. Hauser Blvd
58. Maryland Dr
Laurel Canyon Blvd
Hollywood Blvd
W Sunset Blvd
Santa Monica Blvd
Melrose Ave
Beverly Blvd
W 3rd St
Wilshire Blvd
W Olympic Blvd
San Vicente Blvd
La Cienega Blvd
Crescent Heights Blvd
N Fairfax Ave
N La Brea Ave
Robertson Blvd
Burton Wy
Runyon Canyon Park
Wattles Garden Park
Plummer Park
The Lot
Poinsettia Rec Ctr
W Hollywood Park
MOCA Pacific Design Center
Beverly Center
The Grove
Farmers Market
Pan Pacific Park
PARK LA BREA
LACMA
Hancock Park
PAGE 358
PAGE 298
PAGE 293
PAGE 252
PAGE 360

If Los Angeles were a high school, this area would be straight-up the most popular kid on campus, beloved by jocks, geeks, brains, stoners, preppies, and the entire pep squad. That it is so much to so many makes it both good and bad. Meantime, the available inventory is impressive. Velvet rope? Check. Art-house cinemas? Check. Sidewalk café tables? Check. Celebrity gawking? Check. Are you with us? Good. Now go out and make some new friends.

Movie Theaters

- **Laemmle Fairfax 3** • 7907 Beverly Blvd • 323-655-4010
- **Laemmle Sunset 5** • 8000 W Sunset Blvd • 323-848-3500
- **Loews Beverly Center 13** • 8522 Beverly Blvd • 310-652-7760
- **New Beverly Cinema** • 7165 Beverly Blvd • 323-938-4038
- **Pacific's The Grove Stadium 14** • 189 The Grove Dr • 323-692-0829
- **Regent Showcase Theatre** • 614 N La Brea Ave • 323-934-2944
- **Silent Movie Theatre** • 611 N Fairfax Ave • 323-655-2520

Nightlife

- **The Abbey** • 692 N Robertson Blvd • 310-289-8410
- **The Bar at the Four Seasons Hotel** • 300 S Doheny Dr • 310-273-2222
- **Bar at the Standard** • 8300 W Sunset Blvd • 323-650-9090
- **Bar Marmont** • 8221 W Sunset Blvd • 323-650-0575
- **Barney's Beanery** • 8447 Santa Monica Blvd • 323-654-2287
- **Bel Age Hotel** • 1020 N San Vicente Blvd • 310-854-1111
- **Bliss** • 650 N La Cienega Blvd • 310-659-0999
- **Club 7969** • 7969 Santa Monica Blvd • 323-654-0280
- **Dominick's** • 8715 Beverly Blvd • 310-652-2335
- **El Carmen Tequila & Taco Bar** • 8138 W 3rd St • 323-852-1552
- **El Coyote** • 7312 Beverly Blvd • 323-939-2255
- **The Factory/Ultra Suede** • 661 N Robertson Blvd • 310-659-4551
- **Falcon** • 7213 W Sunset Blvd • 323-850-5350
- **Fenix Lounge** • 8385 W Sunset Blvd • 323-654-7100
- **Formosa Café** • 7156 Santa Monica Blvd • 323-850-9050
- **Garden of Eden** • 7080 Hollywood Blvd • 323-465-3336
- **Genghis Cohen** • 740 N Fairfax Ave • 323-653-0640
- **Here** • 696 N Robertson Blvd • 310-360-8455
- **House of Blues** • 8430 Sunset Blvd • 323-848-5100
- **Jones** • 7205 Santa Monica Blvd • 323-850-1727
- **La Plaza** • 739 N La Brea Ave • 323-939-0703
- **Largo** • 432 N Fairfax Ave • 323-852-1073
- **Lava Lounge** • 1533 N La Brea Ave • 323-876-6612
- **Lola's** • 945 N Fairfax Ave • 213-736-5652
- **Molly Malone's** • 575 S Fairfax Ave • 323-935-1577
- **Monsieur Marcel** • 6333 W 3rd St • 323-939-7792
- **Pearl** • 665 N Robertson Blvd • 310-358-9191
- **Prey** • 643 N La Cienega Blvd • 310-652-2012
- **Rage** • 8911 Santa Monica Blvd • 310-652-7055
- **The Rainbow** • 9015 Sunset Blvd • 310-278-4232
- **Roxy** • 9009 Sunset Blvd • 310-276-2222
- **The Ruby** • 7070 Hollywood Blvd • 323-467-7070
- **Saddle Ranch Chop House** • 8371 W Sunset Blvd • 323-656-2007
- **The Skybar** • 8440 W Sunset Blvd • 323-650-8999
- **Snake Pit Ale House** • 7529 Melrose Ave • 323-653-2011
- **Tower Bar at the Argyle Hotel** • 8358 Sunset Blvd • 323-654-7100
- **The Troubadour** • 9081 Santa Monica Blvd • 310-276-6168
- **Viper Room** • 8852 Sunset Blvd • 310-358-1880
- **Whiskey Bar** • 1200 N Alta Loma Rd • 310-657-0611
- **Whisky A Go Go** • 8901 Sunset Blvd • 310-652-4202

Restaurants

- **AOC** • 8022 W 3rd St • 323-653-6359
- **Ago** • 8478 Melrose Ave • 323-655-6333
- **Amalfi** • 143 N La Brea Ave • 323-938-2504
- **Angeli Caffe** • 7274 Melrose Ave • 323-936-9086
- **Angelini Osteria** • 7313 Beverly Blvd • 323-297-0070
- **Authentic Café** • 7605 Beverly Blvd • 323-939-4626
- **Balboa** • The Grafton Hotel, 8462 W Sunset Blvd • 323-650-8383
- **Barefoot Bar & Grill** • 8722 W 3rd St • 310-276-6223
- **Basix Café** • 8333 Santa Monica Blvd • 323-848-2460
- **Benito's Taco Shop** • 7912 Beverly Blvd • 323-938-7427
- **Bistro 21** • 846 N La Cienega Blvd • 310-967-0021
- **Bossa Nova** • 685 N Robertson Blvd • 310-657-5070
- **Café Angelino** • 8735 W 3rd St • 310-246-1177
- **Café Med** • 8615 Sunset Blvd • 310-652-0445
- **Campanile** • 624 S La Brea Ave • 323-938-1447
- **Canter's Deli** • 419 N Fairfax Ave • 323-651-2030
- **Chameau** • 339 N Fairfax Ave • 323-951-0039
- **Chateau Marmont** • 8221 W Sunset Blvd • 323-656-1010
- **Chaya Brasserie** • 8741 Alden Dr • 310-859-8833
- **Cheebo** • 7533 W Sunset Blvd • 323-850-7070
- **Chipotle** • 121 N La Cienega Blvd • 310-855-0371
- **Cynthia's** • 8370 W 3rd St • 323-658-7851
- **Daily Grill** • 100 N La Cienega Blvd • 310-659-3100
- **Dolce Enoteca** • 8284 Melrose Ave • 323-852-7174
- **Doughboys** • 8136 W 3rd St • 323-651-4202
- **East India Grill** • 345 N La Brea Ter • 323-936-8844
- **Eat Well** • 8252 Santa Monica Blvd • 323-656-1383
- **Ed's Coffee Shop** • 460 N Robertson Blvd • 310-659-8625
- **El Compadre** • 7408 W Sunset Blvd • 323-874-7924
- **Farm of Beverly Hills** • 189 The Grove Dr • 323-525-1699
- **Fish Grill** • 7226 Beverly Blvd • 323-937-7162
- **Flora Kitchen** • 460 S La Brea Ave • 323-931-9900
- **French Quarter Market Place** • 7985 Santa Monica Blvd • 323-654-0898
- **Genghis Cohen** • 740 N Fairfax Ave • 323-653-0640
- **Gumbo Pot** • 6333 W 3rd St • 323-933-0358
- **Hirozen** • 8385 Beverly Blvd • 323-653-0470
- **House of Blues** • 8430 Sunset Blvd • 323-848-5100
- **Hugo's** • 8401 Santa Monica Blvd • 323-654-3993
- **In-N-Out Burger** • 7009 W Sunset Blvd • 800-786-1000
- **The Ivy** • 113 N Robertson Blvd • 310-274-8303
- **JAR** • 8225 Beverly Blvd • 323-655-6566
- **King's Road Café** • 8361 Beverly Blvd • 323-655-9044
- **Kokomo** • Inside Farmer's Market, 3rd St & Fairfax Ave • 323-933-0773
- **Le Pain Quotidien** • 8607 Melrose Ave • 310-854-3700
- **Loteria Grill** • 6333 W 3rd St • 323-930-2211
- **Lucques** • 8474 Melrose Ave • 323-655-6277
- **Mandarette** • 8386 Beverly Blvd • 323-655-6115
- **Newsroom Café** • 120 N Robertson Blvd • 310-652-4444
- **Noura Café** • 8479 Melrose Ave • 323-651-4581
- **The Pig** • 612 N La Brea Ave • 323-935-1116
- **Pink's Famous Chili Dogs** • 709 N La Brea Ave • 323-931-4223
- **Quality Food & Beverage** • 8030 W 3rd St • 323-658-5959
- **Real Food Daily** • 414 N La Cienega Blvd • 310-289-9910
- **Saddle Ranch Chop House** • 8371 Sunset Blvd • 323-656-2007
- **The Standard** • 8300 Sunset Blvd • 323-650-9090
- **Surya India** • 8048 W 3rd St • 323-653-5151
- **Susina** • 7122 Beverly Blvd • 323-934-7900
- **Sweet Lady Jane** • 8360 Melrose Ave • 323-653-7145
- **Swingers** • 8020 Beverly Blvd • 323-653-5858
- **Tail O' the Pup** • 329 N San Vicente Blvd • 310-652-4517
- **Trattoria Amici** • 469 N Doheny Dr • 310-858-0271
- **Urth Caffé** • 8565 Melrose Ave • 310-659-0628
- **Yabu** • 521 N La Cienega Blvd • 310-854-0400

Shopping

- **Aardvark's Odd Ark** • 7579 Melrose Ave • 323-655-6769
- **Agent Provocateur** • 7961 Melrose Ave • 323-653-0229
- **American Apparel** • 104 N Robertson Blvd • 310-274-6292
- **American Rag** • 150 S La Brea Ave • 323-935-3154
- **Apple Store** • 189 The Grove Dr • 323-965-8400
- **The Bodhi Tree** • 8585 Melrose Ave • 310-659-1733
- **Book Soup** • 8818 Sunset Blvd • 310-659-3110
- **Button Store** • 8344 W 3rd St • 323-658-5473
- **Centerfold Newsstand** • 716 N Fairfax Ave • 323-651-4822
- **Chado Tea Room** • 8422 1/2 W 3rd St • 323-655-2056
- **Chateau Marmutt** • 8128 W 3rd St • 323-653-2062
- **The Cook's Library** • 8373 W 3rd St • 323-655-3141
- **Cost Plus World Market** • 6333 W 3rd St • 323-935-5530
- **Denim Doctor** • 8044 W 3rd St • 323-852-0171
- **Doggie Bag** • 8568 1/2 Melrose Ave • 310-855-9990
- **Ethel** • 8235 1/2 W 3rd St • 323-658-8602
- **Flight 001** • 8235 3rd St • 323-966-0001
- **Fred Segal** • 8100 Melrose Ave • 323-651-4129
- **Futurama** • 446 N La Brea Ave • 323-937-4522
- **Golden Apple** • 7711 Melrose Ave • 323-658-6047
- **Guitar Center** • 7425 Sunset Blvd • 323-874-1060
- **I Martin** • 8330 Beverly Blvd • 323-653-6900
- **Jet Rag** • 825 N La Brea Ave • 323-939-0528
- **Joan's on Third** • 8350 W 3rd St • 323-655-2285
- **Koontz Hardware** • 8914 Santa Monica Blvd • 323-652-0123
- **Liz's Antique Hardware** • 453 S La Brea Ave • 323-939-4403
- **Maison Midi** • 148 S La Brea Ave • 323-935-3157
- **Mani's Bakery** • 519 S Fairfax Ave • 323-938-8800
- **Marc Jacobs** • 8400 Melrose Pl • 323-653-5100
- **Marc Jacobs Accessories** • 8401 Melrose Pl • 323-653-0100
- **Mr Marcel's** • 6333 W 3rd St (Farmers Market) • 323-935-9451
- **Plastica** • 8405 W 3rd St • 323-655-1051
- **Pleasure Chest** • 7733 Santa Monica Blvd • 323-650-1022
- **Pulp** • 452 S La Brea Ave • 323-937-3505
- **Restoration Hardware** • 131 N La Cienega Blvd • 310-360-9651
- **Room Service** • 8115 3rd St • 323-653-4242
- **Sam Ash Music** • 8000 Sunset Blvd • 323-654-4922
- **Samy's Camera** • 431 S Fairfax Ave • 323-938-4400
- **Satine** • 8117 3rd St • 323-655-2142
- **Solomon's** • 447 N Fairfax Ave • 323-653-9045
- **Soolip** • 8646 Melrose Ave • 310-360-0545
- **Splash Bath & Body** • 8934 Santa Monica Blvd • 877-664-7627
- **Storyopolis** • 116 N Robertson Blvd • 310-358-2500
- **Susina Bakery** • 7122 Beverly Blvd • 323-934-7900
- **Tower Records** • 8801 W Sunset Blvd • 310-657-7300
- **Trashy Lingerie** • 402 La Cienega Blvd • 310-652-4543
- **Traveler's Bookcase** • 8375 W 3rd St • 310-665-0575
- **Twentieth** • 8057 Beverly Blvd • 323-904-1200
- **Virgin Megastore** • 8000 W Sunset Blvd • 323-650-8666
- **Zipper** • 8316 W 3rd St • 323-951-0620

Video Rental

- **20-20 Video** • 7064 W Sunset Blvd • 323-957-2020
- **20-20 Video** • 7515 Beverly Blvd • 323-965-2020
- **20-20 Video** • 8208 Santa Monica Blvd • 323-656-2300
- **Blockbuster** • 1508 N Orange Grove Ave • 323-851-2688
- **Blockbuster** • 330 N La Cienega Blvd • 310-659-8366
- **Movies & More** • 8320 Melrose Ave • 323-658-5151
- **Rocket Video** • 726 N La Brea Ave • 323-965-1100
- **Top One Video** • 901 N Fairfax Ave • 323-654-0434
- **Video West** • 805 Larrabee St • 310-659-5762

Map 3 • Hollywood

1. Timmons Trl
2. Macal Pl
3. Bryn Mawr Ct
4. Fink Pl
5. San Marco Cir
6. Lorenzo Dr
7. Whitley Ter
8. Fairfield Ave
9. Watsonia Ct
10. High Tower Dr
11. Los Altos Pl
12. Yeager Pl
13. Rockledge Rd
14. Woodland Wy
15. Paramount Dr
16. Bella Vista Wy
17. Holly Hill
18. Wilcox Ave
19. Hollyridge Pl
20. W Allview Ter
21. E Allview Ter
22. Manola Wy
23. Argosy Wy
24. Tuxedo Ter
25. High Oak Dr

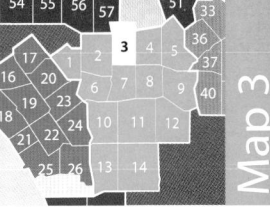
Despite the fluorescent Times Square-style circus at Hollywood & Highland, and the steroidal inflammation at Sunset and Vine, the place remains resolutely trashy around the edges. There just aren't enough places left in the world to buy thigh-high red patent leather boots. Thank you, Hollywood, for that. Look out for slow but steady gentrification of homes between Sunset Boulevard and Melrose Avenue.

Banks
- **Bank of America** · 6300 Sunset Blvd
- **California National** · 6922 Hollywood Blvd
- **Washington Mutual** · 1500 Vine St
- **Wells Fargo** · 6320 W Sunset Blvd

Car Rental
- **Basic Car Rental** · 1819 N Cahuenga Blvd
- **Budget** · 6822 Hollywood Blvd
- **Enterprise** · 1770 Ivar Ave
- **Enterprise** · 990 N Vine St
- **Hertz** · 1755 N Highland Ave
- **Hollywood Rent A Car** · 6421 Selma Ave

Car Washes
- **Celebrity Car Wash** · 901 Vine St
- **Cook's Corner Smog** · 5925 Melrose Ave
- **Paramount Car Wash** · 1411 N Highland Ave

Gas Stations
- **76** · 4700 Beverly Blvd
- **76** · 5890 Hollywood Blvd
- **76** · 6051 Franklin Ave
- **76** · 6537 Melrose Ave
- **76** · 6678 Santa Monica Blvd
- **Arco** · 5175 Melrose Ave
- **Arco** · 6100 Franklin Ave
- **Chevron** · 1255 N Highland Ave
- **Chevron** · 1787 N Highland Ave
- **Chevron** · 1934 N Cahuenga Blvd
- **Mobil** · 1051 N Highland Ave
- **Mobil** · 5700 Hollywood Blvd
- **Mobil** · 5857 W Sunset Blvd
- **Mobil** · 6228 Franklin Ave
- **Mobil** · 6301 Santa Monica Blvd
- **Mobil** · 6601 Melrose Ave
- **Shell** · 5657 W Sunset Blvd
- **Shell** · 6420 Franklin Ave
- **Valero** · 655 N Rossmore Ave

Landmarks
- **Capitol Records Building** · 1750 N Vine St
- **Crossroads of the World** · 6671 Sunset Blvd
- **Egyptian Theater** · 6712 Hollywood Blvd
- **The Erotic Museum** · 6741 Hollywood Blvd
- **Frederick's of Hollywood Lingerie Museum** · 6608 Hollywood Blvd
- **Grauman's Chinese Theatre** · 6925 Hollywood Blvd
- **Hollywood Bowl** · 2301 N Highland Ave
- **Hollywood Forever Cemetery** · 6000 Santa Monica Blvd
- **Hollywood & Highland Mall** · 6801 Hollywood Blvd
- **Hollywood Roosevelt Hotel** · 7000 Hollywood Blvd
- **Hollywood Walk of Fame** · Hollywood Blvd from N Gower St to La Brea Ter
- **Hollywood Wax Museum** · 6767 Hollywood Blvd
- **Magic Castle of Hollywood** · 7025 Franklin Ave
- **Pantages Theatre** · 6233 Hollywood Blvd
- **Paramount Studios** · 5555 Melrose Ave
- **Pig 'n Whistle Restaurant** · 6714 Hollywood Blvd
- **Ripley's Believe It or Not** · 6780 Hollywood Blvd

Libraries
- **John C Fremont Branch** · 6145 Melrose Ave · 323-962-3521

Pharmacies
- **Pavilions** · 727 N Vine St · 323-466-7158
- **Rite-Aid** · 6130 W Sunset Blvd · 323-467-4201
- **Sav-On** · 1747 N Cahuenga Blvd · 323-463-7900
- **Sav-On** · 861 N Vine St · 323-466-7697

Police
- **Los Angeles Police Dept** · 1358 Wilcox Ave · 213-972-2971

Post Offices
- 1425 N Cherokee Ave
- 1615 Wilcox Ave
- 6457 Santa Monica Blvd

Schools
- **ABC Educational Center** · 1129 Cole Ave
- **Blessed Sacrament** · 6641 W Sunset Blvd
- **Booth High** · 2670 Griffin Ave
- **Cheder Menachem** · 5120 Melrose Ave
- **Cheremoya Avenue Elementary** · 6017 Franklin Ave
- **Christ the King Elementary** · 617 N Arden Blvd
- **Frances Blend Special Education** · 5210 Clinton St
- **Grant EEC** · 1559 N St Andrews Pl
- **Grant Elementary** · 1530 N Wilton Pl
- **Hollywood Little Red School House** · 1248 N Highland Ave
- **Hollywood Senior High** · 1521 N Highland Ave
- **Hubert Howe Bancroft Middle** · 929 N Las Palmas Ave
- **Joseph le Conte Middle** · 1316 N Bronson Ave
- **Learning Connection** · 2528 Canyon Dr
- **Oaks** · 6817 Franklin Ave
- **Page Private** · 565 N Larchmont Blvd
- **Santa Monica Blvd Community Charter** · 1022 N Van Ness Ave
- **Selma Ave Elementary** · 6611 Selma Ave
- **Soledad Enrichment Action** · 1717 N Gramercy Pl
- **Tca Arshag Dickranian Armenian** · 1200 N Cahuenga Blvd
- **Van Ness Ave Elementary** · 501 N Van Ness Ave
- **Vine EEC** · 6312 Eleanor Ave
- **Vine St Elementary** · 955 Vine St
- **Wagon Wheel** · 653 N Cahuenga Blvd

Supermarkets
- **Mayfair Market** · 5877 Franklin Ave
- **Pavilions** · 727 Vine St
- **Stop N Shop** · 1123 Vine St

Map 3 · Hollywood

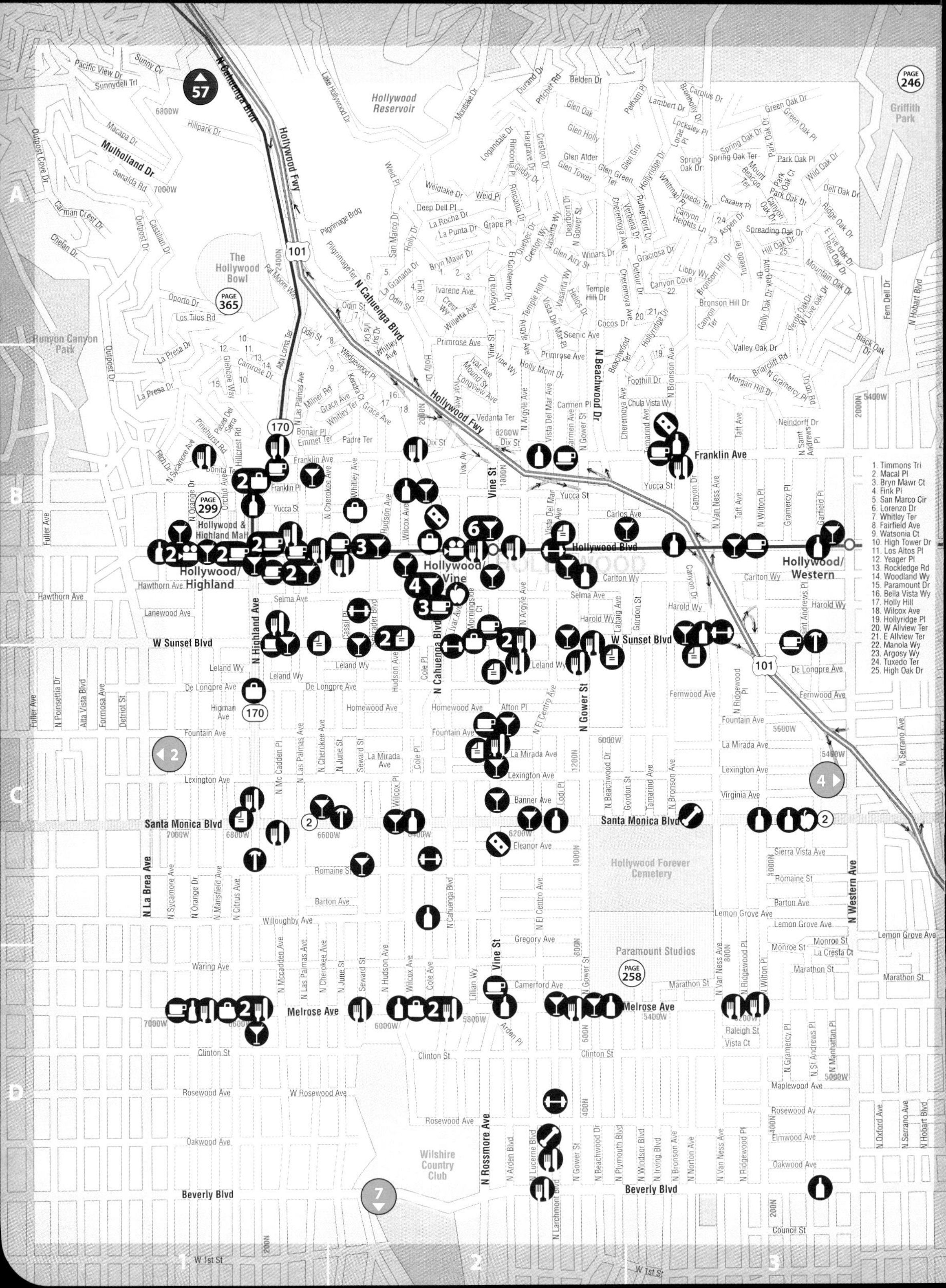

1. Timmons Trl
2. Macal Pl
3. Bryn Mawr Ct
4. Fink Pl
5. San Marco Cir
6. Lorenzo Dr
7. Whitley Ter
8. Fairfield Ave
9. Watsonia Ct
10. High Tower Dr
11. Los Altos Pl
12. Yeager Pl
13. Rockledge Rd
14. Woodland Wy
15. Paramount Dr
16. Bella Vista Wy
17. Holly Hill
18. Wilcox Ave
19. Hollyridge Pl
20. W Allview Ter
21. E Allview Ter
22. Manola Wy
23. Argosy Wy
24. Tuxedo Ter
25. High Oak Dr

You know an old neighborhood has undergone a transformation when it gets a nickname you've never heard uttered in conversation. Hence, the "Cahuenga Corridor"—formerly needle exchanges and pawn shops, now home to a strip of nightclubs. The Hotel Cafe is an intimate little acoustic lounge hidden amid the megaclubs on Cahuenga. Farther from the fray, La Buca on Melrose may be the only hole-in-the-wall destination restaurant we know of. Go for the martinis at Musso & Frank, the worthy Pantages Theater, and the homey Farmers' Market every Sunday morning on Selma and Ivar Avenues.

Coffee

- **101 Coffee Shop** • 6145 Franklin Ave
- **Bliss Art House Café** • 1249 Vine St
- **Bourgeois Pig** • 5931 Franklin Ave
- **Coffee Bean & Tea Leaf** • 6255 W Sunset Blvd
- **Coffee Bean & Tea Leaf** • 6922 Hollywood Blvd
- **Goldberg's Famous Coffee Bar** • 6767 W Sunset Blvd
- **Green Room** • 6752 Hollywood Blvd
- **Karma Coffeehouse** • 1544 N Cahuenga Blvd
- **Kelly's Coffee & Fudge** • 6801 Hollywood Blvd
- **Lithium Café** • 5634 Hollywood Blvd
- **Starbucks** • 1900 N Highland Ave
- **Starbucks** • 5615 Sunset Blvd
- **Starbucks** • 6102 W Sunset Blvd
- **Starbucks** • 6745 Hollywood Blvd
- **Starbucks** • 6801 Hollywood Blvd
- **Starbucks** • Pavilions, 727 N Vine St
- **Stir Crazy Coffee Shop** • 6917 Melrose Ave

Copy Centers

- **Command Print + Graphics** • 6832 Santa Monica Blvd • 323-871-1811
- **Copy Central** • 6464 W Sunset Blvd • 323-461-1222
- **Davco Printing** • 5825 W Sunset Blvd • 323-466-9591
- **Kinko's** • 1440 Vine St • 323-871-1300
- **Nonstop Printing** • 6140 Hollywood Blvd • 323-464-1640
- **Office Depot** • 1240 Vine St • 323-957-1274
- **Rush Copy** • 6095 W Sunset Blvd • 323-462-3196
- **Sir Speedy** • 6660 W Sunset Blvd • 323-469-0327
- **Staples** • 6450 W Sunset Blvd • 323-467-2155

Farmer's Markets

- **Hollywood** • Ivar Ave & Selma Ave b/w Hollywood Blvd & W Sunset Blvd
- **Sears Parking Lot-Hollywood** • 5601 Santa Monica Blvd

Gyms

- **24-Hour Fitness** • 6380 W Sunset Blvd • 323461-2024
- **Bally Total Fitness** • 1628 N El Centro Ave • 323-461-0227
- **Curves** • 527 N Larchmont Blvd • 323-465-4652
- **Curves** • 5825 W Sunset Blvd • 323-467-8101
- **Gold's Gym** • 1016 Cole Ave • 323-462-7012
- **Hollywood YMCA** • 1553 N Schrader Blvd • 323-467-4161

Hardware Stores

- **Anawalt Lumber** • 1001 N Highland Ave • 323-464-1600
- **Home Depot** • 5600 W Sunset Blvd • 323-461-3303
- **Stock Building Supply** • 6641 Santa Monica Blvd • 323-469-1951

Liquor Stores

- **Al's Liquor Store** • 5550 Melrose Ave
- **Bogie's Liquor** • 5753 Melrose Ave
- **Carlton Liquor** • 1610 N Gower St
- **Highland Liquor** • 1770 N Highland Ave
- **Hollywood Liquors** • 7040 Hollywood Blvd
- **Howie's Liquor** • 5645 Santa Monica Blvd
- **Hudson Liquor & Deli** • 6023 Melrose Ave
- **Liquor & Food Mart** • 4657 Beverly Blvd
- **Liquor To Go Go** • 5901 Hollywood Blvd
- **P&J Liquor** • 6170 Santa Monica Blvd
- **P&J Liquor & Deli** • 6480 Santa Monica Blvd
- **Pla-Boy Liquor** • 6435 Yucca St
- **Quaker State Liquor** • 6901 Melrose Ave
- **Quik Stop Liquor** • 6223 Franklin Ave
- **St Andrew's Liquor** • 5566 Hollywood Blvd
- **Sunset Market & Liquor** • 5825 W Sunset Blvd
- **Tony's Liquor** • 5707 Santa Monica Blvd
- **Victor's Liquor & Deli** • 1915 N Bronson Ave

Movie Theaters

- **ArcLight Hollywood/Cinerama Dome** • 6360 W Sunset Blvd • 323-464-1465
- **Cinespace** • 6356 Hollywood Blvd • 323-817-3456
- **Egyptian Theater** • 6712 Hollywood Blvd • 323-466-3456
- **Grauman's Chinese Theatre** • 6925 Hollywood Blvd • 323-464-6266
- **Mann Chinese 6** • 6801 Hollywood Blvd • 323-461-9624
- **Pacific El Capitan** • 6838 Hollywood Blvd • 323-467-7674
- **Vine Theatre** • 6321 Hollywood Blvd • 323-463-6819

Nightlife

- **AD** • 836 N Highland Ave • 323-467-3000
- **ArcLight Café Bar & Balcony** • 6360 W Sunset Blvd • 323-464-1478
- **Avalon** • 1735 Vine St • 323-462-8900
- **The Bar** • 5851 Sunset Blvd • 323-468-9154
- **Beauty Bar** • 1638 N Cahuenga Blvd • 323-464-7676
- **Birds** • 5925 Franklin Ave • 323-465-0175
- **Blu Monkey** • 5521 Hollywood Blvd • 323-465-0115
- **Boardner's** • 1642 N Cherokee Ave • 323-462-9621
- **Burgundy Room** • 1621 1/2 Cahuenga Blvd • 323-465-7530
- **The Cat & Fiddle** • 6530 Sunset Blvd • 323-468-3800
- **Catalina Bar & Grill** • 6725 Sunset Blvd • 323-466-2210
- **The Cinegrill** • 7000 Hollywood Blvd • 323-466-7000
- **Cinespace** • 6356 Hollywood Blvd • 323-817-3456
- **Circus Disco** • 6655 Santa Monica Blvd • 323-462-1291
- **Daddy's Bar & Lounge** • 1610 N Vine St • 323-463-7777
- **Dragonfly** • 6510 Santa Monica Blvd • 323-466-6111
- **El Centro** • 6202 Santa Monica Blvd • 323-957-1066
- **El Floridita** • 1253 N Vine St • 323-871-8612
- **Element** • 1642 Las Palmas Ave • 323-460-4632
- **Forty Deuce** • 5574 Melrose Ave • 323-465-4242
- **Frolic Room** • 6245 Hollywood Blvd • 323-462-5890
- **Henry Fonda Music Box** • 6126 Hollywood Blvd • 323-464-0808
- **The Highlands** • 6801 Hollywood Blvd • 323-461-9800
- **Hollywood Athletic Club** • 6525 Sunset Blvd • 323-462-6262
- **Hollywood Billiards** • 5750 Hollywood Blvd • 323-465-0115
- **Hollywood Canteen** • 1006 N Seward St • 323-465-0961
- **Hollywood Palladium** • 6215 Hollywood Blvd • 323-962-7600
- **The Hotel Café** • 1623 1/2 N Cahuenga Blvd • 323-461-2040
- **Ivar** • 6356 Hollywood Blvd • 323-465-4827
- **Joseph's** • 1775 Ivar Ave • 323-462-8697
- **King King** • 6555 Hollywood Blvd • 323-960-5765
- **Knitting Factory** • 7021 Hollywood Blvd • 323-463-0204
- **La Velvet Margarita Cantina** • 1612 N Cahuenga Blvd • 323-469-2000
- **The Larchmont** • 5657 Melrose Ave • 323-467-4068
- **Las Palmas** • 1714 N Las Palmas Ave • 323-464-0171
- **M-Bar** • 1253 Vine St • 323-856-0036
- **Montmartre Lounge** • 6757 Hollywood Blvd • no phone
- **Mood** • 6623 Hollywood Blvd • 323-464-6663
- **Musso & Frank Grill Bar** • 6667 Hollywood Blvd • 323-467-5123
- **Nacional** • 1645 Wilcox Ave • 323-962-7712
- **The Room** • 1626 N Cahuenga Blvd • 323-462-7196
- **Spider Club at the Avalon** • 1735 Vine St • 323-462-8270
- **Star Shoes** • 6364 Hollywood Blvd • 323-462-7827
- **Teddy's at the Roosevelt Hotel** • 7000 Hollywood Blvd • 323-466-7000
- **Three of Clubs** • 1123 N Vine St • 323-462-6441
- **The Vanguard** • 6021 Hollywood Blvd • 323-463-3331
- **Vine** • 1235 Vine St • 323-960-0800
- **Vine Street Lounge** • 1708 Vine St • 323-464-0404
- **The Well** • 6255 W Sunset Blvd • 323-467-9355
- **White Horse** • 1532 N Western Ave • 323-462-8088
- **White Lotus** • 1743 N Cahuenga Ave • 323-463-0060
- **Xes** • 1716 N Cahuenga Blvd • 323-481-8190
- **Xiomara** • 6101 Melrose Ave • 323-461-0601

Pet Stores

- **Barking Lot** • 336 N Larchmont Blvd • 323-464-3031
- **Yo Aquarium** • 5846 Santa Monica Blvd • 323-871-2730

Restaurants

- **Ammo** • 1155 N Highland Ave • 323-871-2666
- **Astro Burger** • 5601 Melrose Ave • 323-469-1924
- **Benito's Taco Shop** • 6751 Santa Monica Blvd • 323-466-9333
- **California Chicken Café** • 6805 Melrose Ave • 323-935-5877
- **Chan Dara** • 310 N Larchmont Blvd • 323-467-1052
- **Cinespace** • 6356 Hollywood Blvd • 323-817-3456
- **Fabiolus Café** • 6270 W Sunset Blvd • 323-467-2882
- **Fabiolus Café** • 5255 Melrose Ave • 323-464-5857
- **Geisha House** • 6633 Hollywood Blvd • 323-460-6300
- **Hola Fresh Mexican Grill** • 1807 N Cahuenga Blvd • 323-466-0000
- **Hollywood and Vine** • 6263 Hollywood Blvd • 323-464-2345
- **La Buca** • 5210 Melrose Ave • 323-462-1900
- **La Poubelle** • 5907 Franklin Ave • 323-465-0807
- **Larchmont Deli** • 5210 Beverly Blvd • 323-466-1193
- **Miceli's** • 1646 N Las Palmas Ave • 323-466-3438
- **Musso & Frank Grill** • 6667 Hollywood Blvd • 323-467-7788
- **Off Vine** • 6263 Leland Wy • 323-962-1900
- **Patina** • Walt Disney Concert Hall, 141 S Grand Ave • 213-972-3331
- **Pig 'n Whistle** • 6714 Hollywood Blvd • 323-463-0000
- **Roscoe's House of Chicken n' Waffles** • 1514 N Gower St • 323-466-7453
- **Yamakasa** • 1900 N Highland Ave • 323-882-6524
- **Yamashiro** • 1999 N Sycamore Ave • 323-466-5125

Shopping

- **Amoeba Music** • 6400 Sunset Blvd • 310-245-6400
- **Aron's Records** • 1150 N Highland Ave • 323-469-4700
- **Cahuenga World News** • 1652 N Cahuenga Blvd • 323-465-4357
- **Conservatory Florist** • 1900 N Highland Ave • 323-851-6290
- **Counterpoint Records and Books** • 5911 Franklin Ave • 323-957-7965
- **Espíritu de Vida** • 5913 Franklin Ave • 323-463-0281
- **Half-Off Clothing** • 660 N Larchmont Blvd • 323-463-6613
- **Hollywood Hills Beauty Center and Spa** • 1915 N Highland Ave • 323-874-5159
- **Larry Edmunds Cinema and Theater Bookshop** • 6644 Hollywood Blvd • 323-463-3273
- **Pom Pom** • 6819 Melrose Ave • 323-938-6286
- **Ray the Retoucher** • 1330 N Highland Ave • 323-463-0555
- **Vine American Party Store** • 5969 Melrose Ave • 323-467-7124

Video Rental

- **SKG Video Rental** • 1051 Vine St • 323-465-4005
- **Video Hut** • 1931 N Bronson Ave • 323-461-4190
- **Yucca Video** • 1817 N Cahuenga Blvd • 323-465-2376

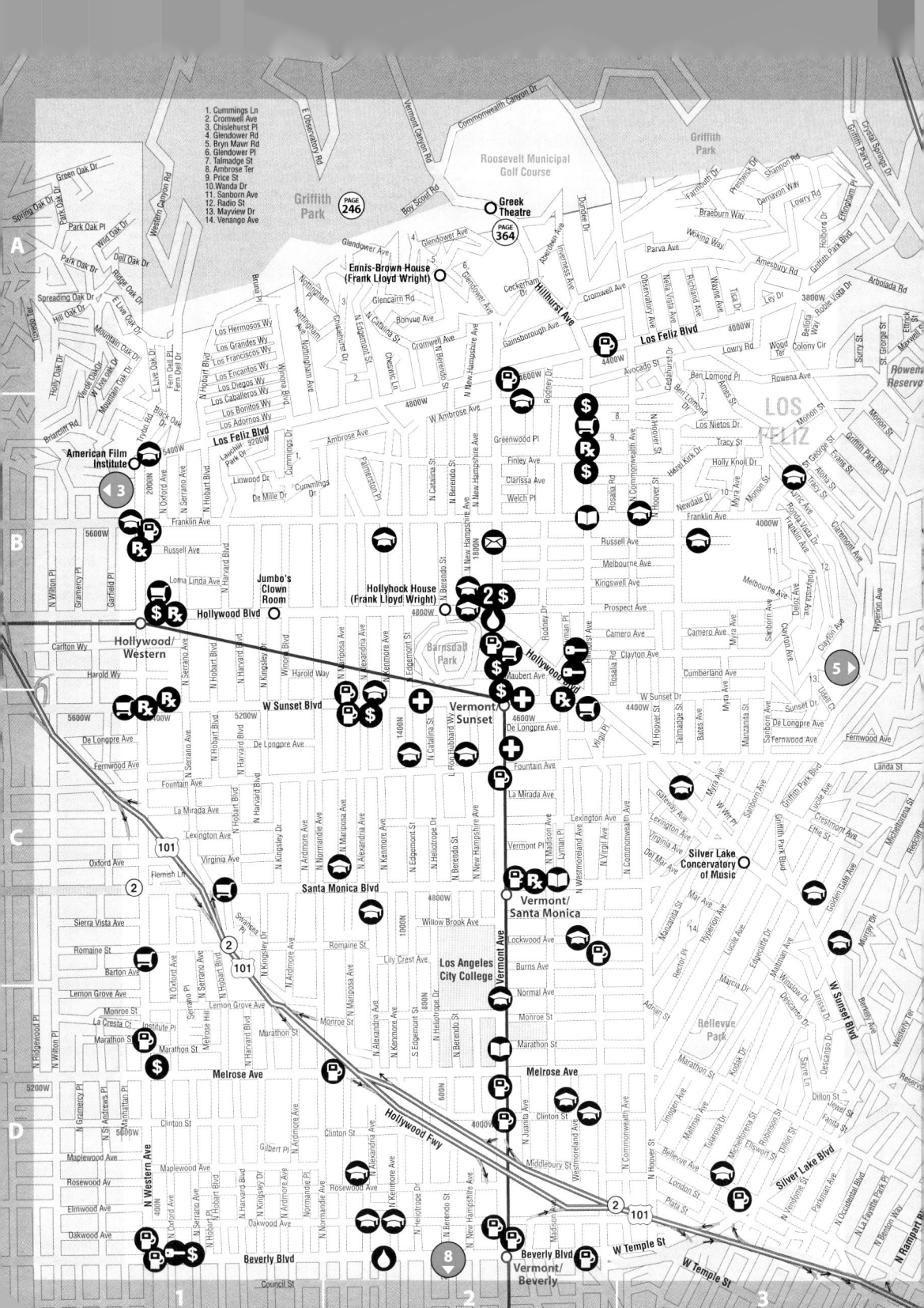

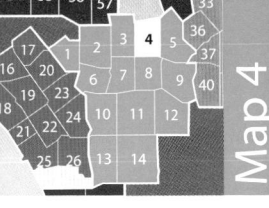

Map 4

Los Feliz perseveres despite the burden of being America's most hyped neighborhood. It continues to have ample room for everyone—from grannies wearing old cardigans, to hipsters wearing...old cardigans. You'll find multimillion-dollar playpens on the hill, as well as crowded studio apartment buildings lining Vermont and Hillhurst Avenues. There's a wealth of creativity in this little hamlet east of Hollywood—from Frank Lloyd Wright homes to tiny shops selling Che tees and feather boas.

$ Banks

- **Bank of America** · 1715 N Vermont Ave
- **Bank of America (Albertsons)** · 2035 Hillhurst Ave
- **Bank of America** · 4975 Melrose Ave
- **California National** · 1702 N Vermont Ave
- **California National** · 4500 W Beverly Blvd
- **Citibank** · 1965 N Hillhurst Ave
- **Citibank** · 5000 Sunset Blvd
- **US** · 5454 Hollywood Blvd
- **Washington Mutual** · 1600 N Vermont Ave
- **Wells Fargo** · 1534 N Vermont Ave

Car Rental

- **Enterprise** · 1608 Hillhurst Ave
- **Enterprise** · 4550 Beverly Blvd
- **U-Haul** · 4550 Hollywood Blvd

Car Washes

- **Beverly Catalina Car Wash** · 4000 Beverly Blvd
- **Hollymont Car Wash & Detail** · 1666 N Vermont Ave

Gas Stations

- **76** · 1270 N Vermont Ave
- **76** · 1300 N Western Ave
- **76** · 304 N Vermont Ave
- **76** · 4456 Los Feliz Blvd
- **76** · 4600 Melrose Ave
- **76** · 800 N Western Ave
- **Arco** · 5025 W Sunset Blvd
- **Chevron** · 1868 N Western Ave
- **Chevron** · 2134 N Vermont Ave
- **Chevron** · 4590 Melrose Ave
- **Chevron** · 4666 Santa Monica Blvd
- **Chevron** · 591 N Vermont Ave
- **Independent** · 5007 W Sunset Blvd
- **Independent** · 655 N Western Ave
- **Independent** · 924 N Virgil Ave
- **Mobil** · 4605 Beverly Blvd
- **Mobil** · 515 Silver Lake Blvd
- **Mobil** · 657 N Vermont Ave
- **Shell** · 1630 N Vermont Ave
- **Shell** · 341 N Vermont Ave

Hospitals

- **Children's** · 4650 W Sunset Blvd
- **Hollywood Presbyterian** · 1300 N Vermont Ave
- **Kaiser Foundation** · 4867 W Sunset Blvd

Landmarks

- **American Film Institute** · 2021 N Western Ave
- **Ennis-Brown House (Frank Lloyd Wright)** · 2607 Glendower Ave
- **Greek Theatre** · 2700 N Vermont Ave
- **Hollyhock House (Frank Lloyd Wright)** · 4800 Hollywood Blvd
- **Jumbo's Clown Room** · 5153 Hollywood Blvd
- **Silverlake Conservatory of Music** · 3920 Sunset Blvd

Libraries

- **Cahuenga Branch** · 4591 Santa Monica Blvd · 323-664-6418
- **Los Angeles Main Branch-Braille Institute Library** · 741 N Vermont Ave · 800-808-2555
- **Los Feliz Branch** · 1874 Hillhurst Ave · 323-913-4710

Pharmacies

- **Ralphs** · 5429 Hollywood Blvd · 323-957-6830
- **Rite-Aid** · 1637 N Vermont Ave · 323-664-9854
- **Rite-Aid** · 1841 N Western Ave · 323-461-6136
- **Rite-Aid** · 4633 Santa Monica Blvd · 323-666-6125
- **Sav-On** · 5510 W Sunset Blvd · 323-464-2172
- **Sav-On (Albertsons)** · 2035 Hillhurst Ave · 323-660-0687
- **Vons** · 4520 W Sunset Blvd · 323-662-2121
- **Walgreens (24 hrs)** · 5451 W Sunset Blvd · 323-860-7970

Post Offices

- 1825 N Vermont Ave ·

Schools

- **Alexandria Ave Elementary** · 4211 Oakwood Ave
- **Alexandria EEC** · 4304 Rosewood Ave
- **American Montessori** · 1313 N Edgemont St
- **Bellevue Primary** · 610 N Micheltorena St
- **Dayton EEC** · 3917 Clinton St
- **Dayton Heights Elementary** · 607 N Westmoreland Ave
- **Franklin Ave Elementary** · 1910 N Commonwealth Ave
- **Hollywood Los Feliz Corners** · 1839 N Kenmore Ave
- **Hollywood Lutheran Child Development** · 1733 N New Hampshire Ave
- **Immaculate Heart** · 5515 Franklin Ave
- **Immaculate Heart Mary** · 1055 N Alexandria Ave
- **John Marshall Senior High** · 3939 Tracy St
- **Lockwood Ave Elementary** · 4345 Lockwood Ave
- **Los Angeles City College** · 855 N Vermont Ave
- **Los Feliz Elementary** · 1740 N New Hampshire Ave
- **Lycee International de Los Angeles** · 4155 Russell Ave
- **Mary's Schoolhouse** · 1334 L Ron Hubbard Wy
- **Micheltorena St Elementary** · 1511 Micheltorena St
- **Our Mother of Good Counsel** · 4622 Ambrose Ave
- **Ramona Elementary** · 1133 N Mariposa Ave
- **Rose Alex Pilibos Arm** · 1615 N Alexandria Ave
- **Silverlake Los Feliz Jewish County** · 1110 Bates Ave
- **St Casimir** · 2714 St George St
- **St Francis of Assisi** · 1550 Maltman Ave
- **Thomas Starr King Junior High** · 4201 Fountain Ave

Supermarkets

- **Albertsons** · 2035 Hillhurst Ave
- **Food 4 Less** · 5420 W Sunset Blvd
- **Jons Marketplace** · 1601 N Vermont Ave
- **Jons Marketplace** · 5315 Santa Monica Blvd
- **Ralphs** · 5429 Hollywood Blvd
- **Smart & Final** · 939 N Western Ave
- **Vons** · 4520 W Sunset Blvd

Map 4 • Los Feliz

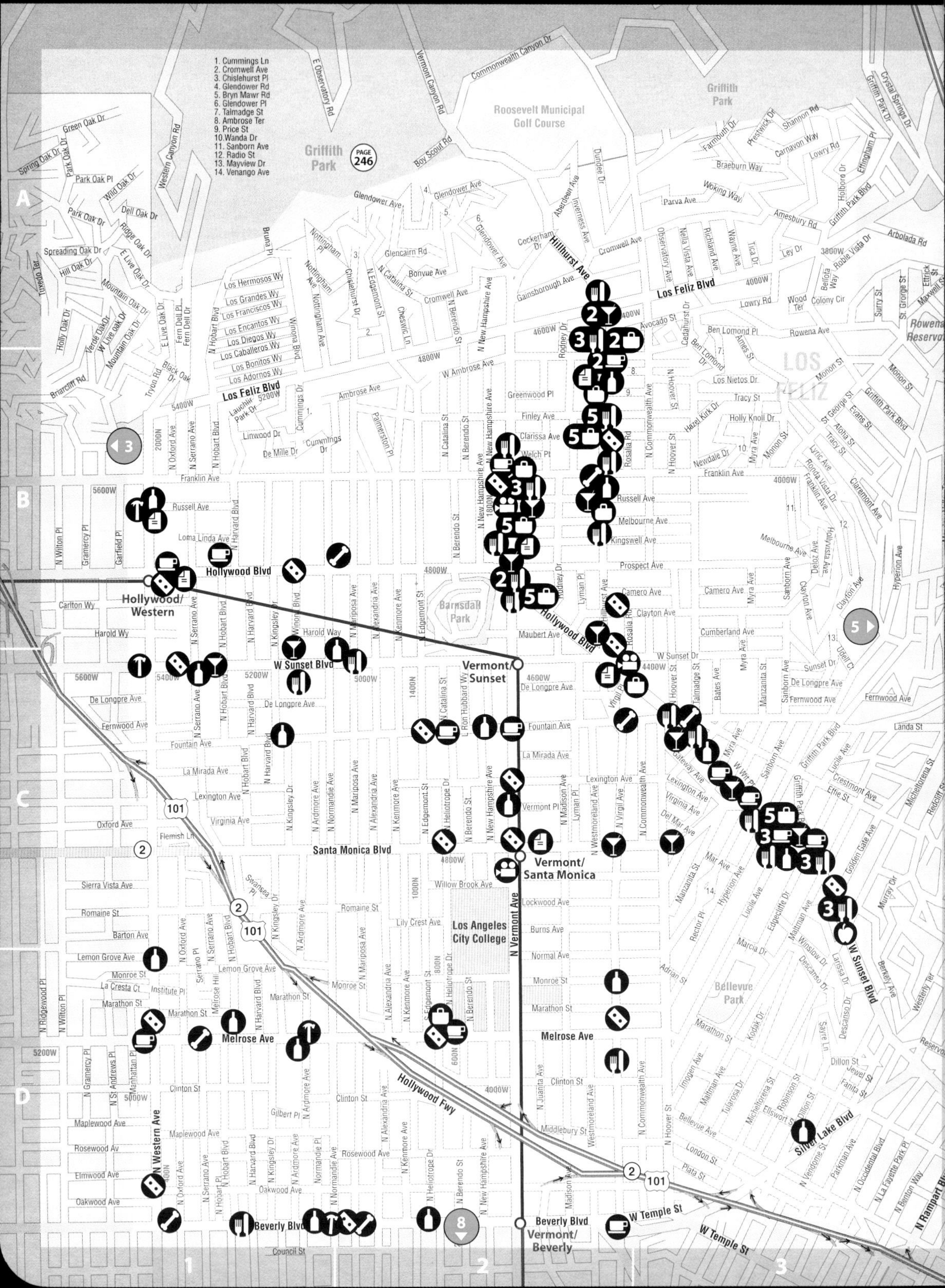

N
1. Cummings Ln
2. Cromwell Ave
3. Chislehurst Pl
4. Glendower Rd
5. Bryn Mawr Rd
6. Glendower Pl
7. Talmadge St
8. Ambrose Ter
9. Price St
10. Wanda Dr
11. Sanborn Ave
12. Radio St
13. Mayview Dr
14. Venango Ave
Griffith Park
PAGE 246
Roosevelt Municipal Golf Course
Commonwealth Canyon Dr
Vermont Canyon Rd
E Observatory Rd
Boy Scout Rd
Western Canyon Rd
Glendower Ave
Los Feliz Blvd
Hillhurst Ave
Hollywood Blvd
Hollywood/ Western
Vermont/ Sunset
Vermont/ Santa Monica
Vermont/ Beverly
W Sunset Blvd
Santa Monica Blvd
Melrose Ave
Beverly Blvd
W Temple St
Hollywood Fwy
Barnsdall Park
Los Angeles City College
Bellevue Park
Los Feliz
Silver Lake Blvd
N Vermont Ave
N Western Ave
Franklin Ave
Fountain Ave
Russell Ave
Prospect Ave
Griffith Park Blvd
Rowena Reservoir
101
2
3
5
8
A
B
C
D
1
2
3

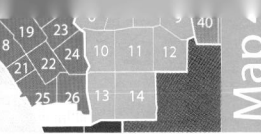

While much has changed in this neighborhood in the last few years, the corporate commerce stops pretty much at Starbucks and 7-11. Yuca's is still making award-winning tacos in their tiny Hillhurst locale. The Dresden Room and The Derby have weathered the swing craze and remain reliable lounges to throw back a few martinis. Don't miss: the zacatecana sauce at Mexico City, the brunch scene on the patio at the Alcove, or the burlesque shows at Tangier Lounge.

Coffee
- **Café Los Feliz** • 2118 N Hillhurst Ave
- **Café Stella** • 3932 W Sunset Blvd
- **Casbah Café** • 3900 W Sunset Blvd
- **Coffee Bean & Tea Leaf** • 2081 Hillhurst Ave
- **Lollicup** • 4716 Fountain Ave
- **Lollicup** • 5259 Hollywood Blvd
- **Mailbox Café** • 4845 Fountain Ave
- **Melrose Café & Bakery** • 5003 Melrose Ave
- **Mornings Nights** • 1523 Griffith Park Blvd
- **Night in Tunisia** • 710 N Heliotrope Dr
- **Prasadam** • 3818 W Sunset Blvd
- **Psychobabble** • 1866 N Vermont Ave
- **Starbucks** • 1700 N Vermont Ave
- **Starbucks** • 5453 Hollywood Blvd
- **Tsunami Coffee House** • 4019 W Sunset Blvd

Copy Centers
- **Copies Unlimited** • 1823 N Western Ave • 323-462-5532
- **Copy Cat** • 2044 Hillhurst Ave • 323-913-0360
- **Staples** • 4641 Santa Monica Blvd • 323-669-7583
- **UPS Store** • 4470 W Sunset Blvd • 323-644-2621
- **UPS Store** • 5419 Hollywood Blvd • 323-460-6323

Farmer's Markets
- **Silver Lake Farmer's Market** • 3700 W Sunset Blvd

Gyms
- **Curves** • 1761 Vermont Ave • 323-644-9898

Hardware Stores
- **B&M Hardware** • 4226 Beverly Blvd • 213-388-7655
- **Orchard Supply Hardware** • 5525 W Sunset Blvd • 323-871-1707
- **True Value** • 1801 N Western Ave • 323-467-2129
- **True Value** • 4583 Melrose Ave • 323-663-7232

Liquor Stores
- **Beverly Mart Liquors** • 4003 Beverly Blvd
- **Big Mac's Liquor** • 3735 W Sunset Blvd
- **Bill's Liquor** • 5334 W Sunset Blvd
- **Fountain Liquor** • 4711 Fountain Ave
- **Grand Liquor** • 4669 Melrose Ave
- **Hillhurst Liquor** • 2060 Hillhurst Ave
- **Ink Cigarettes & Liquor** • 5063 W Sunset Blvd
- **JB Liquor** • 1185 N Vermont Ave
- **John & Pat's Fountain Liquor** • 5203 Fountain Ave
- **Liquor Center** • 861 N Western Ave
- **Melrose Market** • 4803 Melrose Ave
- **Michael's Liquor** • 4323 W Sunset Blvd
- **Mikron Liquor** • 631 Silver Lake Blvd
- **Pacific Liquors** • 4228 Beverly Blvd
- **Pink Elephant Liquors** • 1836 N Western Ave
- **Robin's Liquor** • 5102 Hollywood Blvd
- **Village Liquor** • 1859 Hillhurst Ave
- **Virgil Liquors** • 780 N Virgil Ave

Movie Theaters
- **Five Star Theaters Los Feliz 3** • 1822 N Vermont Ave • 323-668-9004
- **Vista Theatre** • 4473 Sunset Blvd • 323-660-6639

Nightlife
- **4100 Club** • 4100 W Sunset Blvd • 323-666-4460
- **Akbar** • 4356 W Sunset Blvd • 323-665-6810
- **The Derby** • 4500 Los Feliz Blvd • 323-663-8979
- **Drawing Room** • 1800 Hillhurst Ave • 323-665-0135
- **The Dresden Room** • 1760 N Vermont Ave • 323-665-4294
- **Figaro Café** • 1802 N Vermont Ave • 323-662-1587
- **Gauntlet II** • 4219 Santa Monica Blvd • 323-669-9472
- **Good Luck Bar** • 1514 Hillhurst Ave • 323-664-3524
- **Jumbo's Clown Room** • 5153 Hollywood Blvd • 323-666-1187
- **Little Temple** • 4519 Santa Monica Blvd • 323-660-4540
- **Malo** • 4326 W Sunset Blvd • 323-664-1011
- **Tangier Lounge** • 2138 Hillhurst Ave • 323-666-8666
- **Tantra Bar** • 3705 W Sunset Blvd • 323-663-9090
- **Tiki Ti** • 4427 W Sunset Blvd • 323-669-9381
- **Vermont Bar** • 1714 N Vermont Ave • 323-661-6163
- **Ye Rustic Inn** • 1831 Hillhurst Ave • 323-662-5757

Pet Stores
- **Beverly & Normandie Pets** • 4152 Beverly Blvd • 213-382-9314
- **Bird Kingdom & Pet Shop** • 4562 Beverly Blvd • 323-461-5538
- **Collar & Leash** • 4327 W Sunset Blvd • 323-665-2215
- **Fish on the Wall** • 4901 Melrose Ave • 323-468-0103
- **Fish Tale** • 4364 Fountain Ave • 323-665-0350
- **For Pets Only** • 1903 Hillhurst Ave • 323-664-4211
- **J's Dog & Cat Grooming** • 5065 Hollywood Blvd • 323-667-1255
- **Kim's Pets & Fish** • 1187 N Vermont Ave • 323-664-3338
- **Young's Tropical Fish** • 1953 1/2 Hillhurst Ave • 323-663-5665

Restaurants
- **Alcove Bakery & Café** • 1929 Hillhurst Ave • 323-644-0100
- **Alegria on Sunset** • 3510 W Sunset Blvd • 323-913-1422
- **Café Los Feliz** • 2081 N Hillhurst Ave • 323-664-7111
- **Café Stella** • 3932 Sunset Blvd • 323-666-0265
- **Casbah Café** • 3900 W Sunset Blvd • 323-664-7000
- **Cha Cha Cha** • 656 N Virgil Ave • 323-664-7723
- **Cliff's Edge** • 3626 W Sunset Blvd • 323-666-6116
- **Cobras and Matadors** • 4655 Hollywood Blvd • 323-669-3922
- **Eat Well** • 3916 E Sunset Blvd • 323-664-1624
- **El Conquistador** • 3701 Sunset Blvd • 323-666-5136
- **Electric Lotus** • 4656 Franklin Ave • 323-953-0040
- **Farfalla Trattoria** • 1978 Hillhurst Ave • 323-661-7365
- **Fred 62** • 1850 N Vermont Ave • 323-667-0062
- **Home** • 1760 Hillhurst Ave • 323-669-0211
- **House of Pies** • 1869 N Vermont Ave • 323-666-9961
- **The Kitchen** • 4348 Fountain Ave • 323-664-3663
- **La Belle Epoque** • 2129 Hillhurst Ave • 323-669-7640
- **Madame Matisse** • 3536 W Sunset Blvd • 323-662-4862
- **Malo** • 4326 W Sunset Blvd • 323-664-1011
- **Mexico City** • 2121 Hillhurst Ave • 323-661-7227
- **Millie's** • 3524 Sunset Blvd • 323-664-0404
- **Mustard Seed Café** • 1948 Hillhurst Ave • 323-660-0670
- **Palermo** • 1858 N Vermont Ave • 323-663-1178
- **Paru's** • 5140 W Sunset Blvd • 323-661-7600
- **Prasadam** • 3818 W Sunset Blvd • 323-644-0068
- **Shin** • 1972 Hillhurst Ave • 323-664-1891
- **Tantra** • 3705 W Sunset Blvd • 323-663-8268
- **Vermont** • 1714 N Vermont Ave • 323-661-6163
- **Vida** • 1930 Hillhurst Ave • 323-662-1248
- **Yuca's** • 2056 Hillhurst Ave • 323-662-1214
- **Zankou Chicken** • 5065 W Sunset Blvd • 323-665-7845

Shopping
- **American Apparel** • 4665 Hollywood Blvd • 323-661-1407
- **Atmosphere** • 1728 N Vermont Blvd • 323-666-8420
- **The Bicycle Kitchen** • 706 N Heliotrope Dr • 323-NO-CARRO
- **Blue Rooster Art Supplies** • 1718 N Vermont Ave • 323-661-9471
- **Camille Hudson** • 4685 Hollywood Blvd • 323-953-0377
- **Casbah Café** • 3900 W Sunset Blvd • 323-664-7000
- **Cheese Store of Silver Lake** • 3926 W Sunset Blvd • 323-644-7511
- **Eastside Records** • 1813 Hillhurst Ave • 323-913-7461
- **Glory** • 4659 Hollywood Blvd • 323-644-5679
- **Golden Needle Tailoring** • 2044 Hillhurst Ave • 323-666-3365
- **Gypsy** • 3915 W Sunset Blvd • 323-660-2556
- **Half-Off Clothing** • 1748 N Vermont Ave • 323-665-1526
- **LS** • 2120 Hillhurst Ave • 323-913-1444
- **Mishka** • 3820 W Sunset Blvd • 323-664-8778
- **Moss House** • 1936 Hillhurst Ave
- **Naturemart & Bulk Bin** • 2080 Hillhurst Ave • 323-667-1677
- **Oou** • 1764 N Vermont Ave • 323-665-6263
- **Ozzie Dots** • 4641 Hollywood Blvd • 323-663-2867
- **Rosetta Stone** • 1958 Hillhurst Ave • 323-913-0369
- **Serifos** • 3814 W Sunset Blvd • 323-660-7467
- **Skylight Books** • 1818 Vermont Ave • 323-660-1175
- **Squaresville** • 1800 N Vermont Ave • 323-669-8464
- **Steinberg & Sons** • 4712 Franklin Ave • 323-660-0294
- **Uncle Jer's** • 4459 W Sunset Blvd • 323-662-6710
- **Village Gourmet** • 1927 Hillhurst Ave • 323-660-3803
- **Wacko** • 4633 Hollywood Blvd • 323-663-0122
- **White Trash Charms** • 1951 Hillhurst Ave • 323-666-9585
- **Y Que Trading Post** • 1770 Vermont Ave • 323-664-0021
- **Zoe & Sage** • 2134 Hillhurst Ave • 323-906-1874

Video Rental
- **20-20 Video** • 5420 W Sunset Blvd • 323-467-2020
- **Blockbuster** • 4470 Sunset Blvd • 323-661-0791
- **Blockbuster** • 5445 Hollywood Blvd • 323-467-0481
- **Deme A-1 Video** • 1100 N Vermont Ave • 323-669-1230
- **Five Star Video (Thai)** • 5155 Hollywood Blvd • 323-665-9547
- **Hollywood Video** • 1075 N Western Ave • 323-464-0294
- **Jerry's Video Room** • 1904 N Hillhurst Ave • 323-666-7471
- **LA Video** • 720 N Western Ave • 323-465-0705
- **LA Video & Music** • 711 N Virgil Ave • 323-663-0116
- **Mondo Video A-Go-Go** • 4328 Melrose Ave • 323-953-8896
- **Super Videoland** • 1189 N Vermont Ave • 323-661-2583
- **Video Hot** • 4207 Beverly Blvd • 323-668-1616
- **Video Hut** • 1864 N Vermont Ave • 323-661-4680
- **Video Market** • 3607 W Sunset Blvd • 323-663-6000
- **Video Universal Rental** • 1306 N Edgemont St • 323-660-2169
- **Winn Video** • 4855 Santa Monica Blvd • 323-953-9732

23

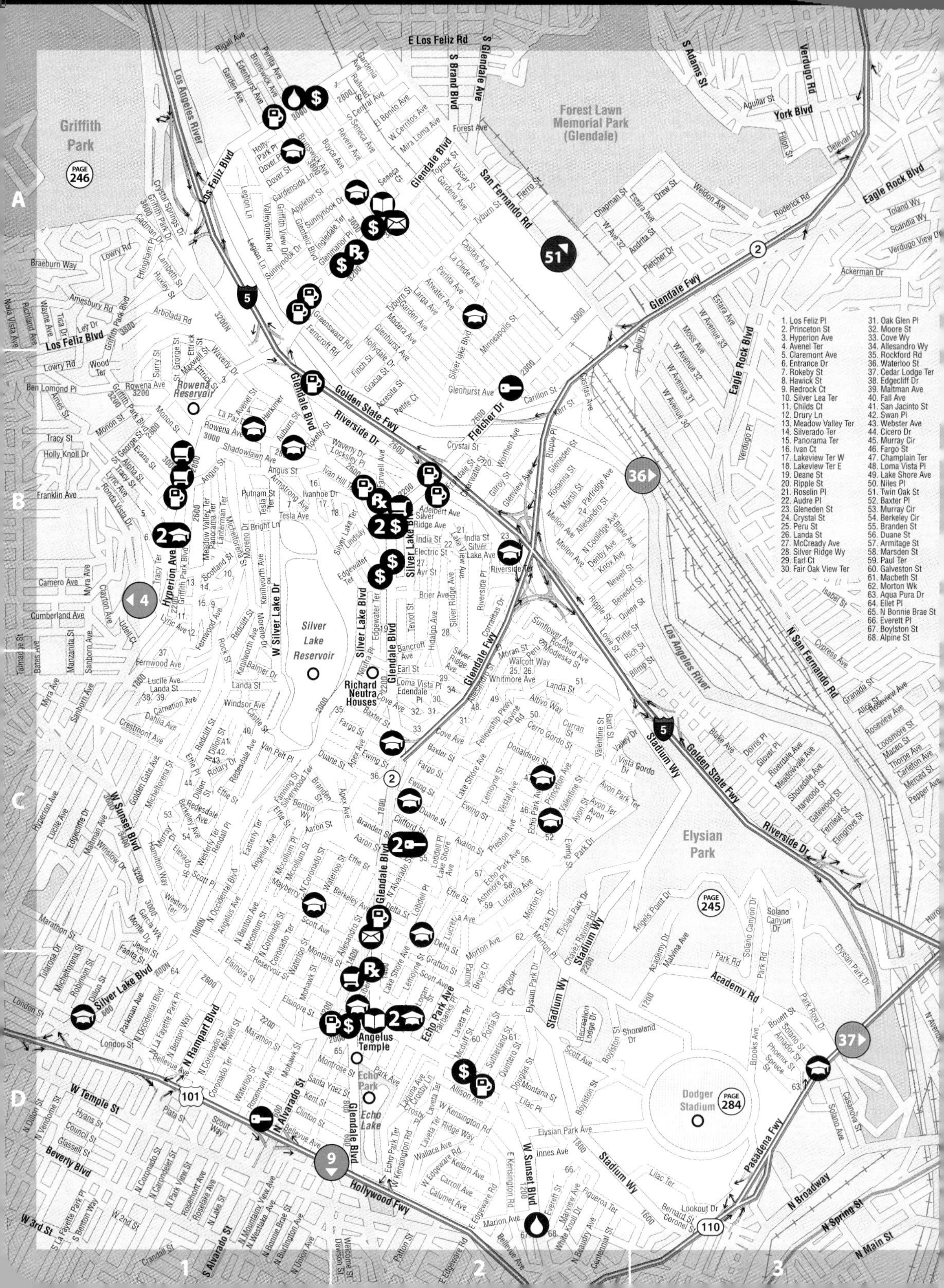

Map 5 • Silve

Griffith Park

PAGE 246

Forest Lawn Memorial Park (Glendale)

York Blvd

Eagle Rock Blvd

Glendale Fwy

51

Griffith Park

Los Angeles River

Los Feliz Blvd

Rowena Reservoir

Golden State Fwy

Riverside Dr

Silver Lake Reservoir

Richard Neutra Houses

36

Elysian Park

PAGE 245

PAGE 284

Dodger Stadium

Angelus Temple

Echo Park

Echo Lake

Silver Lake Blvd

Glendale Blvd

W Sunset Blvd

Stadium Wy

Academy Rd

Riverside Dr

Golden State Fwy

37

9

Hollywood Fwy

Beverly Blvd

W Temple St

101

1. Los Feliz Pl
2. Princeton St
3. Hyperion Ave
4. Avenel Ter
5. Claremont Ave
6. Entrance Dr
7. Rokeby St
8. Hawick St
9. Redrock Ct
10. Silver Lea Ter
11. Childs Ct
12. Drury Ln
13. Meadow Valley Ter
14. Silverado Ter
15. Panorama Ter
16. Ivan Ct
17. Lakeview Ter W
18. Lakeview Ter E
19. Deane St
20. Ripple St
21. Roselin Pl
22. Audre Pl
23. Gleneden St
24. Crystal St
25. Peru St
26. Landa St
27. McCready Ave
28. Silver Ridge Wy
29. Earl Ct
30. Fair Oak View Ter

31. Oak Glen Pl
32. Moore St
33. Cove Wy
34. Allesandro Wy
35. Rockford Rd
36. Waterloo St
37. Cedar Lodge Ter
38. Edgecliff Dr
39. Maltman Ave
40. Fall Ave
41. San Jacinto St
42. Swan Pl
43. Webster Ave
44. Cicero Dr
45. Murray Cir
46. Fargo St
47. Champlain Ter
48. Loma Vista Pl
49. Lake Shore Ave
50. Niles St
51. Twin Oak St
52. Baxter St
53. Murray Cir
54. Berkeley Ave
55. Branden St
56. Duane St
57. Armitage St
58. Marsden St
59. Paul Ter
60. Galveston St
61. Macbeth St
62. Morton Wk
63. Aqua Pura St
64. Eilet Pl
65. N Bonnie Brae St
66. Everett Pl
67. Boylston St
68. Alpine St

2

4

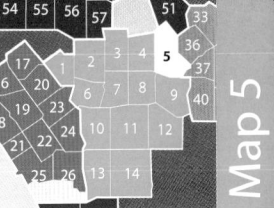
A few years ago, Silver Lake was an insider's playground, and Echo Park was known as home to folkie (and now fallen angel) Elliott Smith. Today, housing prices have quadrupled, and the area (once predominantly Hispanic) is changing in ways familiar to veterans of San Francisco's Mission District. The Sunset Junction street fair in August unites all the locals in the area for a weekend of music, art, food, and bad-ass tattoo smackdowns.

$ Banks

- **Bank of America** · 1572 W Sunset Blvd
- **Bank of America** · 2420 Glendale Blvd
- **Citibank** · 1900 Sunset Blvd
- **Citibank** · 2450 Glendale Blvd
- **East West** · 2496 Glendale Blvd
- **Union** · 3355 Glendale Blvd
- **Wells Fargo** · 2933 Los Feliz Blvd
- **Wells Fargo** · 3250 Glendale Blvd

Car Rental

- **AAA Value Rent A Car** · 1728 Glendale Blvd
- **Alpha Rent A Car** · 1750 Glendale Blvd
- **U-Haul** · 2111 Bellevue Ave
- **U-Haul** · 2671 Fletcher Dr

Car Washes

- **Best Way Hand Car Wash** · 1185 W Sunset Blvd
- **Coin-Op Car Wash** · 3128 W Sunset Blvd
- **Los Feliz Car Wash** · 3000 Los Feliz Blvd

Gas Stations

- **76** · 2035 W Sunset Blvd
- **76** · 2580 Glendale Blvd
- **76** · 2635 Hyperion Ave
- **76** · 3053 Los Feliz Blvd
- **76** · 3070 Glendale Blvd
- **Arco** · 1605 Glendale Blvd
- **Arco** · 2466 Riverside Dr
- **Chevron** · 2427 Fletcher Dr
- **Gas Express** · 1467 W Sunset Blvd
- **Independent** · 3047 Glendale Blvd
- **Shell** · 3053 Los Feliz Blvd
- **Valero** · 2918 Riverside Dr

o Landmarks

- **Angelus Temple** · 1100 Glendale Blvd
- **Dodger Stadium** · 1000 Elysian Park Ave
- **Echo Park** · Glendale Blvd & Park Ave
- **Richard Neutra Houses** · 2200 Silver Lake Blvd
- **Rowena Reservoir** · Corner of Hyperion Ave & Rowena Ave
- **Silver Lake Reservoir** · Silverlake Blvd & Duane St

Libraries

- **Atwater Branch** · 3379 Glendale Blvd · 323-664-1353
- **Edendale Branch** · 2011 W Sunset Blvd · 213-207-3000

Pharmacies

- **CVS/ProCare** · 3224 Glendale Blvd · 323-663-6231
- **Rite-Aid** · 1433 Glendale Blvd · 213-483-3468
- **Sav-On (24 hrs)** · 2530 Glendale Blvd · 323-666-6555

Post Offices

- 1525 N Alvarado St
- 3370 Glendale Blvd

Schools

- **Allesandro Elementary** · 2210 Riverside Dr
- **Atwater Avenue Elementary** · 3271 Silver Lake Blvd
- **Baxter Montessori** · 2101 Echo Park Ave
- **Berkeley EEC** · 1814 Berkeley Ave
- **Clifford St Elementary** · 2150 Duane St
- **Elysian Heights Elementary** · 1562 Baxter St
- **Glenfeliz Blvd Elementary** · 3955 Glenfeliz Blvd
- **Glenfeliz EEC** · 3745 Dover Pl
- **Golden West Christian** · 1310 Liberty St
- **Happyland School** · 2132 Hyperion Ave
- **Holy Trinity** · 3716 Boyce Ave
- **Ivanhoe Elementary** · 2828 W Herkimer St
- **Kids' World** · 2442 Hyperion Ave
- **LA International Christian** · 2301 Bellevue Ave
- **Learning Kingdom** · 2772 Rowena Ave
- **Logan EEC** · 1712 Montana St
- **Logan St Elementary** · 1711 Montana St
- **Mayberry St Elementary** · 2414 Mayberry St
- **Solano Ave Elementary** · 615 Solano Ave
- **St Teresa of Avila** · 2215 Fargo St

Supermarkets

- **Gelson's Markets** · 2725 Hyperion Ave
- **Ralphs** · 2520 Glendale Blvd
- **Trader Joe's** · 2738 Hyperion Ave
- **Vons** · 1342 N Alvarado St

Map 5 • Silver Lake / Echo Park / Atwater

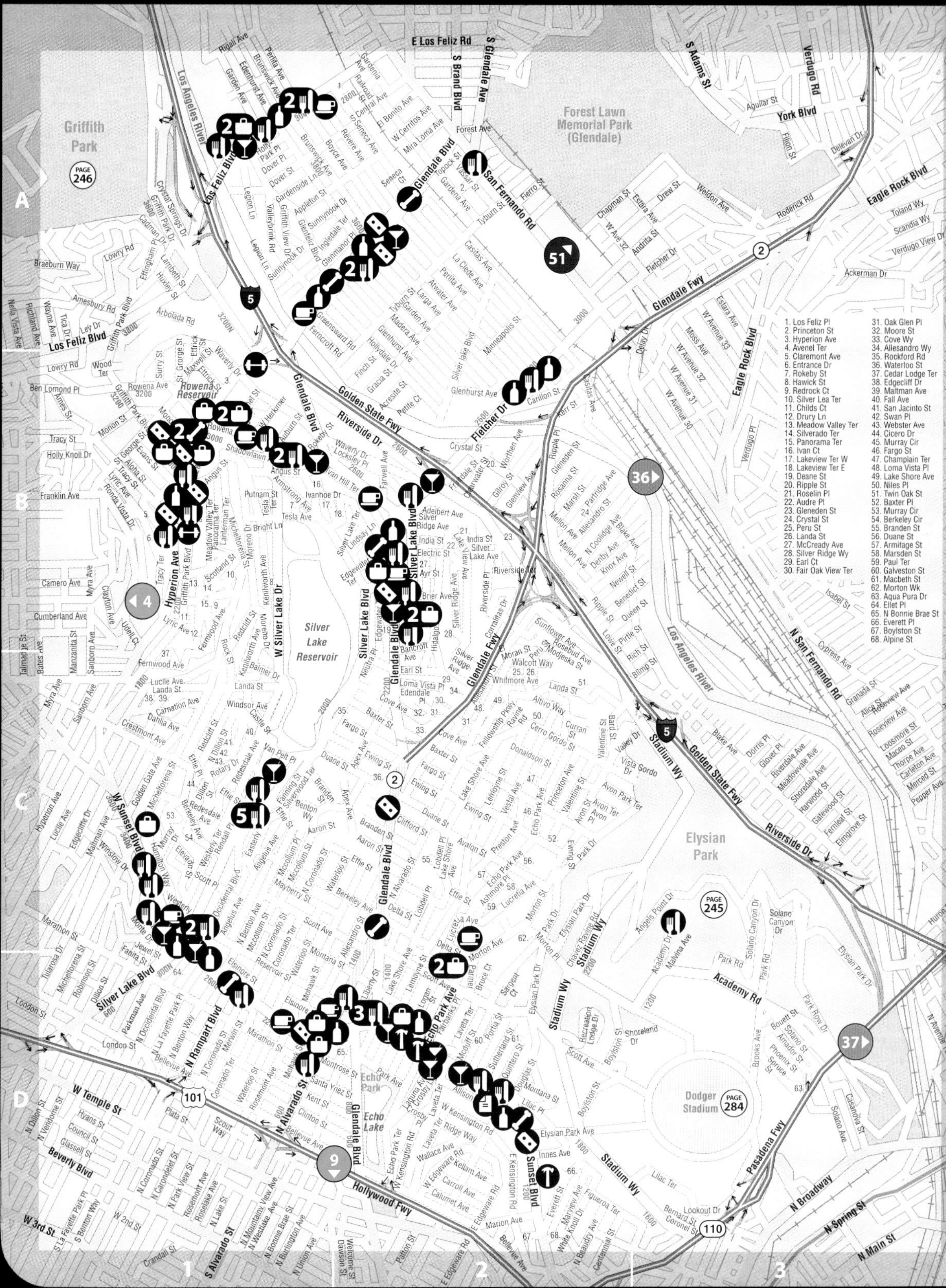
N
Griffith Park
PAGE 246
Forest Lawn Memorial Park (Glendale)
Silver Lake Reservoir
Rowena Reservoir
Echo Park
Echo Lake
Elysian Park
PAGE 245
Dodger Stadium
PAGE 284
Los Angeles River
Golden State Fwy
Glendale Fwy
Hollywood Fwy
Pasadena Fwy
E Los Feliz Rd
Los Feliz Blvd
S Brand Blvd
S Glendale Ave
San Fernando Rd
Glendale Blvd
Riverside Dr
Fletcher Dr
Hyperion Ave
Silver Lake Blvd
W Silver Lake Dr
Sunset Blvd
W Sunset Blvd
N Alvarado St
Echo Park Ave
Stadium Wy
Eagle Rock Blvd
York Blvd
Verdugo Rd
S Adams St
W Temple St
Beverly Blvd
W 3rd St
N Broadway
N Spring St
N Main St
1. Los Feliz Pl
2. Princeton St
3. Hyperion Ave
4. Avenel Ter
5. Claremont Ave
6. Entrance Dr
7. Rokeby St
8. Hawick St
9. Redrock Ct
10. Silver Lea Ter
11. Childs Ct
12. Drury Ln
13. Meadow Valley Ter
14. Silverado Ter
15. Panorama Ter
16. Ivan Ct
17. Lakeview Ter W
18. Lakeview Ter E
19. Deane St
20. Ripple St
21. Roselin Pl
22. Audre Pl
23. Gleneden St
24. Crystal St
25. Peru St
26. Landa St
27. McCready Ave
28. Silver Ridge Wy
29. Earl Ct
30. Fair Oak View Ter
31. Oak Glen Pl
32. Moore St
33. Cove Wy
34. Allesandro Wy
35. Rockford Rd
36. Waterloo St
37. Cedar Lodge Ter
38. Edgecliff Dr
39. Maltman Ave
40. Fall Ave
41. San Jacinto St
42. Swan Pl
43. Webster Ave
44. Cicero Dr
45. Murray Cir
46. Fargo St
47. Champlain Ter
48. Loma Vista Pl
49. Lake Shore Ave
50. Niles Pl
51. Twin Oak St
52. Baxter Pl
53. Murray Cir
54. Berkeley Cir
55. Branden St
56. Duane St
57. Armitage St
58. Marsden St
59. Paul Ter
60. Galveston St
61. Macbeth St
62. Morton Wk
63. Aqua Pura Dr
64. Ellet Pl
65. N Bonnie Brae St
66. Everett Pl
67. Boylston St
68. Alpine St
A
B
C
D
1
2
3

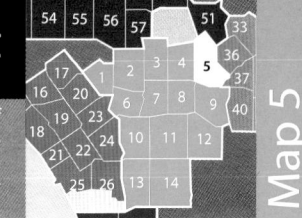
Best described as low-key and local, the area can be a true (and pleasant) surprise to those whose experience of Los Angeles is limited to the Westside. By day, the real entertainment is people-watching in the cafés and shops along Hyperion, Sunset, Rowena, Silver Lake, and Glendale. By night, the action moves indoors to hotspots such as Spaceland, the Echo, and the Silverlake Lounge. For late-night entertainment, we recommend the gender-bending after-hours parade in and around the Astro Family Restaurant and Rudolpho's.

Coffee
- **Chango** • 1559 Echo Park Ave
- **The Downbeat Café** • 1202 N Alvarado St
- **Kaldi Coffee & Tea** • 3147 Glendale Blvd
- **Silverlake Coffee** • 2388 Glendale Blvd
- **Starbucks** • 2134 Sunset Blvd
- **Starbucks** • 2560 Glendale Blvd
- **Starbucks** • 2919 Los Feliz Blvd

Copy Centers
- **ER Copies** • 1439 W Sunset Blvd • 213-482-3804

Gyms
- **Body Builders Gym** • 2516 Hyperion Ave • 323-668-0802
- **Curves** • 2724 Griffith Park Blvd • 323-912-9205

Hardware Stores
- **Reliable Do It Center** • 1229 W Sunset Blvd • 213-250-3970
- **True Value** • 2505 Hyperion Ave • 323-665-4149

Liquor Stores
- **Bill's Liquor** • 3150 Glendale Blvd
- **Bogie's Liquor** • 2560 Hyperion Ave
- **House of Spirits** • 1314 Echo Park Ave
- **King Liquors** • 2105 W Sunset Blvd
- **Kopper Keg Liquors** • 3237 Glendale Blvd
- **Liquor Royale** • 1508 W Sunset Blvd
- **Los Feliz Liquor** • 3006 Los Feliz Blvd
- **M&W Liquor** • 2801 Fletcher Dr
- **Plaza Liquors** • 2829 W Sunset Blvd
- **Ray's Liquor** • 2730 Fletcher Dr
- **Silver Glen Liquor** • 2474 Glendale Blvd
- **Silversun Liquor** • 2901 W Sunset Blvd

Nightlife
- **Bigfoot Lodge** • 3172 Los Feliz Blvd • 323-662-9227
- **Club Tee Gee** • 3210 Glendale Blvd • 323-669-9631
- **The Echo** • 1822 W Sunset Blvd • 213-413-8200
- **Gold Room** • 1558 W Sunset Blvd • 213-482-5259
- **Johnny's Bar** • 2939 W Sunset Blvd • 323-660-2276
- **Little Joy** • 1477 W Sunset Blvd • 213-250-3417
- **Mixville Bar** • 2838 Rowena Ave • 323-666-2000
- **Red Lion Tavern** • 2366 Glendale Blvd • 323-662-5337
- **The Roost** • 3100 Los Feliz Blvd • 323-664-7272
- **Rudolpho's** • 2500 Riverside Dr • 323-669-1226
- **Short Stop** • 1455 W Sunset Blvd • 213-482-4942
- **Silverlake Lounge** • 2906 Sunset Blvd • 323-666-2407

- **Spaceland** • 1717 Silver Lake Blvd • 323-661-4380
- **The Tam O'Shanter** • 2980 Los Feliz Blvd • 323-664-0228

Pet Stores
- **Catts & Doggs Pet Boutique** • 2833 1/2 Hyperion Ave • 323-953-8383
- **Jimmy's Pet Store** • 1548 Glendale Blvd • 213-413-8013
- **LA Tropical Fish Pet & Supplies** • 1371 W Sunset Blvd • 213-482-9131
- **Pampered Birds** • 3183 Glendale Blvd • 323-662-7807
- **Pet Express** • 2472 Glendale Blvd • 323-668-2255
- **Pets Lover** • 3400 Glendale Blvd • 323-913-3368
- **Tiffany's Pet Food** • 2854 W Sunset Blvd • 323-662-7173

Restaurants
- **Astro Family Restaurant** • 2300 Fletcher Dr • 323-663-9241
- **Baracoa Cuban Café** • 3175 Glendale Blvd • 323-665-9590
- **Blair's** • 2903 Rowena Ave • 323-660-1882
- **Brite Spot Family Restaurant** • 1918 W Sunset Blvd • 213-484-9800
- **Café Tropical** • 2900 W Sunset Blvd • 323-661-8391
- **Caffe Capri** • 2547 Hyperion Ave • 323-644-7906
- **The Downbeat Café** • 1202 N Alvarado St • 213-483-3955
- **Dusty's** • 3200 W Sunset Blvd • 323-906-1018
- **Edendale Grill** • 2838 Rowena Ave • 323-666-2000
- **Gingergrass** • 2396 Glendale Blvd • 323-644-1600
- **Hard Times Pizza Co** • 2664 Griffith Park Blvd • 323-661-5656
- **India Sweets and Spices** • 3126 Los Feliz Blvd • 323-345-0360
- **La Parrilla** • 3129 W Sunset Blvd • 323-661-8055
- **Leela Thai** • 1737 Silver Lake Blvd • 323-660-6100
- **Mae Ploy** • 2606 W Sunset Blvd • 213-353-9635
- **Masa** • 1800 W Sunset Blvd • 213-989-1558
- **Michelangelo Pizzeria** • 1637 Silver Lake Blvd • 323-660-4843
- **Mimi's Café** • 2925 Los Feliz Blvd • 323-668-1715
- **Netty's** • 1700 Silver Lake Blvd • 323-662-8655
- **Nicky D's Wood-Fired Pizza** • 2764 Rowena Ave • 323-664-3333
- **Osteria Nonni** • 3219 Glendale Blvd • 323-666-7133
- **Pho' Café** • 2841 W Sunset Blvd • 213-413-0888
- **Police Academy Café** • 1880 Academy Dr • 323-221-5222
- **Rambutan Thai** • 2835 W Sunset Blvd • 213-273-8424

- **Red Lion Tavern** • 2366 Glendale Blvd • 323-662-5337
- **Taix** • 1911 W Sunset Blvd • 323-484-1265
- **Tam O'Shanter** • 2980 Los Feliz Blvd • 323-664-0228
- **Thai Mix Grill** • 2728 Fletcher Dr • 323-664-1812

Shopping
- **American Apparel** • 2111 W Sunset Blvd • 213-484-6464
- **Bittersweet Butterfly** • 1406 Micheltorena St • 323-660-4303
- **Edna Harte & Fay** • 2941 Rowena Blvd • 323-661-4070
- **Grometville** • 2876 Rowena Ave • 323-665-5524
- **Island LS** • 3038 Rowena Blvd • 323-665-7454
- **The Kids Are Alright** • 2201 W Sunset Blvd • 213-413-4104
- **Le Pink** • 1545 Echo Park Ave • 213-250-0265
- **mini MELT** • 3151 Los Feliz Blvd • 323-668-1212
- **Panty Raid** • 2378 Glendale Blvd • 323-668-1888
- **Pot-ted** • 3158 Los Feliz Blvd • 323-665-3801
- **Rockaway Records** • 2395 Glendale Blvd • 323-664-3232
- **Say Cheese** • 2800 Hyperion Ave • 323-665-0545
- **Sea Level Records** • 1716 W Sunset Blvd • 213-989-0146
- **Show Pony** • 1543 Echo Park Ave • 213-482-7676
- **Silverlake Wine** • 2395 Glendale Blvd • 323-662-9024
- **Video Journeys** • 2730 Griffith Park Blvd • 323-663-5857

Video Rental
- **20-20 Video** • 2522 Glendale Blvd • 323-665-2020
- **50 50 Video** • 1717 W Sunset Blvd • 213-353-0406
- **Asian Star Video (Chinese & Thai)** • 1498 W Sunset Blvd • 213-481-2896
- **Blockbuster** • 2656 Griffith Park Blvd • 323-665-6764
- **Cookie Video Rental** • 2501 W Sunset Blvd • 213-484-2317
- **Go Video** • 2147 W Sunset Blvd • 213-413-0860
- **Silverlake Video** • 3206 Glendale Blvd • 323-666-5570
- **Video Active** • 2522 Hyperion Ave • 323-669-8544
- **Video Channel** • 1501 W Sunset Blvd • 213-481-8218
- **Video House** • 1864 Glendale Blvd • 323-663-9175
- **Video Hut** • 2732 Hyperion Ave • 323-660-1166
- **Video Journeys** • 2730 Griffith Park Blvd • 323-663-5857
- **VideoCzar** • 3332 Glendale Blvd • 323-661-2978

27

Map 6 • **Miracle Mile / Mid-City**

N

PAGE 360

LACMA West

LA County Museum of Art

La Brea Tar Pits

George C Page Museum of La Brea Discoveries

Petersen Auto Museum

Hancock Park

Craft & Folk Art Museum

Lula Washington Dance Theatre

La Cienega Park

BEVERLY HILLS

National Blvd

Ballona Creek

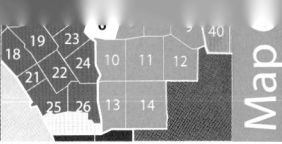

"Miracle Mile" refers to the stretch of Wilshire Boulevard between La Brea and Fairfax Avenues, once a snappy, Art Deco-influenced shopping destination. The Art Deco is still there, mercifully, even if the retail doesn't stand up to scrutiny. But it is home to many of the city's major museums, including the soon to be Renzo Piano-ed LA County Museum of Art, the La Brea Tar Pits, the Peterson Automotive Museum, and the Los Angeles Craft & Folk Art Museum.

 Banks

- **Bank Leumi USA** · 8383 Wilshire Blvd
- **Bank of America** · 5304 Wilshire Blvd
- **Bank of America** · 8381 Wilshire Blvd
- **Bank of America** · 8501 W Pico Blvd
- **Bank of America** · 8760 Wilshire Blvd
- **California Bank & Trust** ·
  6500 Wilshire Blvd
- **Citibank** · 5660 Wilshire Blvd
- **Citibank** · 8485 Wilshire Blvd
- **City National** · 6100 Wilshire Blvd
- **Washington Mutual** · 8500 Wilshire Blvd
- **Wells Fargo** · 5601 Wilshire Blvd
- **Wells Fargo** · 6245 Wilshire Blvd

Car Rental

- **Aviv Rent A Car** · 8946 W Pico Blvd
- **Dollar** · 732 S La Brea Ave
- **Edson Luxury Car Rental** ·
  5455 Wilshire Blvd
- **Enterprise** · 1234 S La Brea Ave
- **Enterprise** · 1435 S La Cienega Blvd
- **Enterprise** · 5406 Wilshire Blvd
- **Enterprise** · 800 S La Brea Ave
- **Horizon** · 5226 W Pico Blvd
- **Premier Car Rental** · 5651 W Pico Blvd
- **U-Haul** · 964 S La Brea Ave
- **Universal Rent-a-Car** · 920 S La Brea Ave

Car Washes

- **Expert Car Wash** · 900 S La Brea Ave
- **La Cienega Car Wash** ·
  1907 S La Cienega Blvd
- **Oasis Hand Wash & Detail** ·
  5700 Wilshire Blvd

Gas Stations

- **76** · 1004 S La Cienega Blvd
- **76** · 1515 S La Brea Ave
- **76** · 1701 S Robertson Blvd
- **Arco** · 5301 W Olympic Blvd
- **Arco** · 5420 Venice Blvd
- **Arco** · 8770 W Olympic Blvd
- **Chevron** · 1865 S La Brea Ave
- **Chevron** · 2065 S La Cienega Blvd
- **Exxon** · 1460 S La Cienega Blvd
- **Global Oil** · 5801 W Pico Blvd
- **Mobil** · 2305 S La Cienega Blvd
- **Mobil** · 8567 Wilshire Blvd
- **Shell** · 1502 S Robertson Blvd
- **Shell** · 2339 S La Brea Ave
- **Shell** · 5164 W Washington Blvd
- **Shell** · 6101 W Olympic Blvd
- **Shell** · 8500 W Pico Blvd

 Hospitals

- **Kaiser Foundation** · 6041 Cadillac Ave
- **Olympic Medical Center** ·
  5900 W Olympic Blvd

Landmarks

- **Craft & Folk Art Museum** ·
  5800 Wilshire Blvd
- **George C Page Museum of La Brea Discoveries** · 5801 Wilshire Blvd
- **La Brea Tar Pits** · Wilshire Blvd & S Curson Ave
- **LA County Museum of Art** ·
  5905 Wilshire Blvd
- **LACMA West (former May Co Building)** ·
  6067 Wilshire Blvd
- **Lula Washington Dance Theatre** ·
  5041 W Pico Blvd
- **Petersen Automotive Museum** ·
  6060 Wilshire Blvd

Libraries

- **Goethe Institute-Los Angeles** ·
  5750 Wilshire Blvd · 323-525-3388
- **LACMA Visual Resource Center** ·
  5905 Wilshire Blvd · 323-857-6116
- **Robertson Branch** · 1719 S Robertson Blvd · 310-840-2147

Pharmacies

- **Ralphs** · 5601 Wilshire Blvd ·
  323-936-0050
- **Rite-Aid** · 1843 S La Cienega Blvd ·
  310-559-1402
- **Rite-Aid** · 5575 Wilshire Blvd ·
  323-954-7193
- **Sav-On** · 5985 W Pico Blvd · 323-965-9161
- **Walgreens** · 5467 Wilshire Blvd ·
  323-525-0311
- **Walgreens (24 hrs)** · 8770 W Pico Blvd ·
  310-275-1344

Post Offices

- 1270 S Alfred St
- 4960 W Washington Blvd
- 5350 Wilshire Blvd
- 8383 Wilshire Blvd

Schools

- **Aloha** · 5042 Venice Blvd
- **Bais Chana** · 9041 W Pico Blvd
- **Bais Chaya Mushka** · 9051 W Pico Blvd
- **Carthay Center Elementary** ·
  6351 W Olympic Blvd
- **Cathedral Chapel** · 755 S Cochran Ave
- **Crescent Heights Blvd Elementary** ·
  1661 S Crescent Heights Blvd
- **Crescent Heights EEC** · 1700 Alvira St
- **Donna Ro** · 4946 W 20th St
- **Frances Hatch** · 4930 Venice Blvd
- **Hillel Hebrew Academy** ·
  9120 W Olympic Blvd
- **Holy Spirit Elementary** ·
  1418 S Burnside Ave
- **Horace Mann Elementary** ·
  8701 Charleville Blvd
- **Joannes Taylor** · 1372 S Cochran Ave
- **Kabbalah Center** · 1062 S Robertson Blvd
- **Kabbalah Children's Academy** ·
  1046 S Robertson Blvd
- **Los Angeles Center for Enriched Studies** · 5931 W 18th St
- **Marvin Ave Children's Center** ·
  2341 S Curson Ave
- **Marvin Elementary** · 2411 Marvin Ave
- **Netan Eli High** · 1445 S Robertson Blvd
- **Ohr Haemet Institute for Girls** ·
  1030 S Robertson Blvd
- **Page Private** · 419 S Robertson Blvd
- **Rabbi Jacob Pressman Academy** ·
  1055 S La Cienega Blvd
- **Rejoice in Jesus Christian** ·
  1304 S Cochran Ave
- **Saturn St Elementary** · 5360 Saturn St
- **Savoy Junior Academy** ·
  5211 Venice Blvd
- **Shalhevet High** · 910 S Fairfax Ave
- **Shenandoah St Elementary** ·
  2450 S Shenandoah St
- **St Mary Magdalen** · 1223 S Corning St
- **Torat Hayim Hebrew Academy** ·
  1210 S La Cienega Blvd
- **Yeshiva Gedolah of Los Angeles** ·
  5444 W Olympic Blvd
- **Yeshiva University High of Los Angeles** · 1619 S Robertson Blvd

 Supermarkets

- **Ralphs** · 5601 Wilshire Blvd
- **Smart & Final** · 1835 S La Cienega Blvd
- **Smart & Final** · 5555 Wilshire Blvd
- **Vons** · 1430 S Fairfax Ave

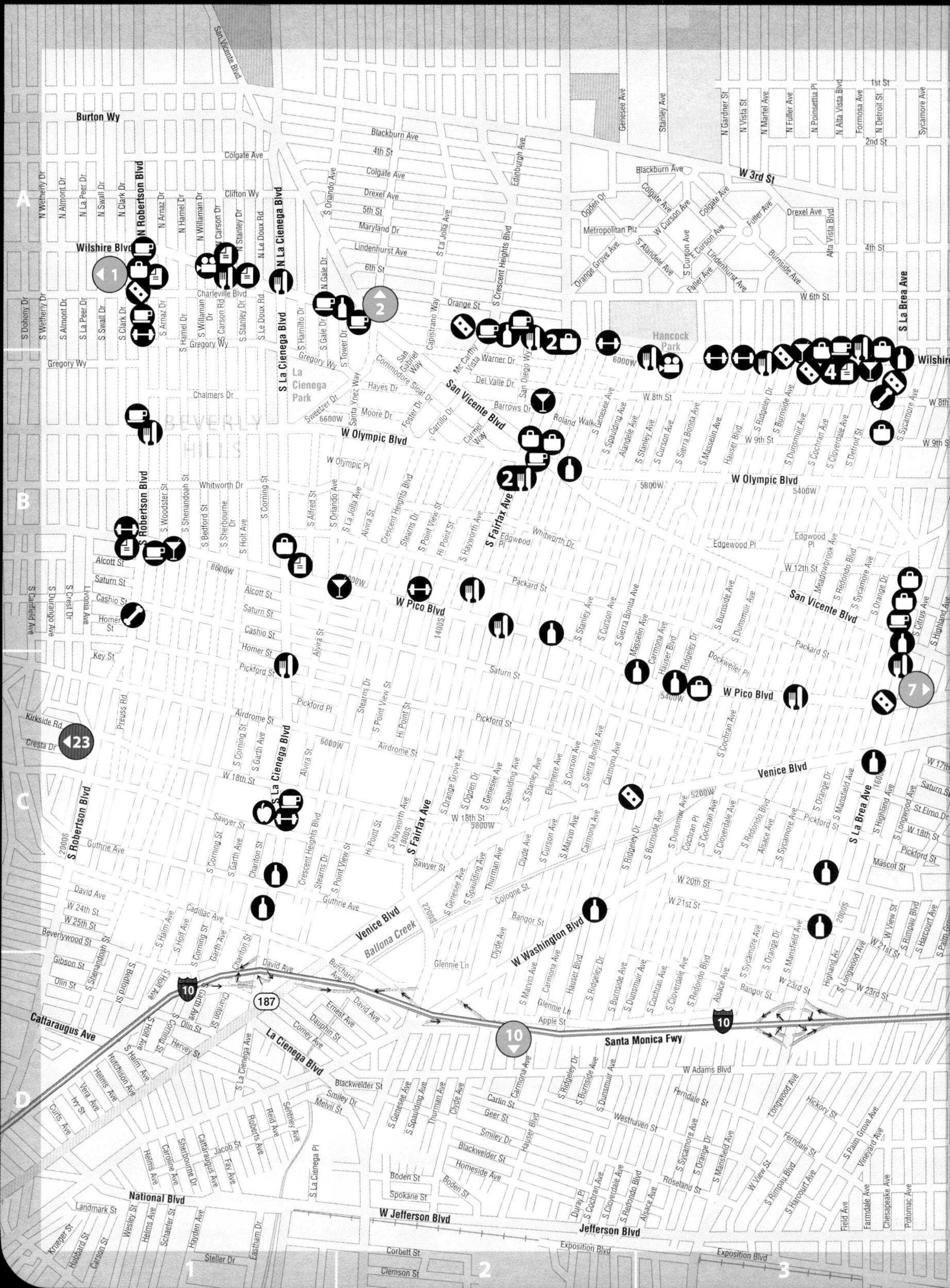

Map 6 • **Miracle Mile / Mid-City**

N

1

2

7

123

10

187

10

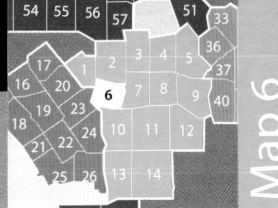
After something of a slump, Mid-City and Miracle Mile are on the upswing. The gluttonous state of the real estate market has generated passionate interest in the single-family homes in the neighborhoods south of Olympic Boulevard (a handful of which remain affordable options in a city otherwise studded with $800,000 cottages). A lively Ethiopian community is blooming on Fairfax Avenue below San Vicente Boulevard, and good Irish coffee (and great neon!) can be found nearby at Tom Bergin's Tavern.

☕Coffee
- **Backdoor Boba** · 5484 Wilshire Blvd
- **Café Latte** · 6254 Wilshire Blvd
- **Coffee Bean & Tea Leaf** · 1845 S La Cienega Blvd
- **Coffee Bean & Tea Leaf** · 8328 Wilshire Blvd
- **La Peer Coffee Shop** · 8920 Wilshire Blvd
- **Mio's Café** · 265 S Robertson Blvd
- **Starbucks** · 1258 S La Brea Ave
- **Starbucks** · 257 S La Cienega Blvd
- **Starbucks** · 6066 W Olympic Blvd
- **Starbucks** · 8783 W Pico Blvd
- **Starbucks** · 9049 W Olympic Blvd
- **Taistee Coffee Shop** · 6200 Wilshire Blvd

🖨Copy Centers
- **Copy Copy** · 8621 Wilshire Blvd · 310-659-8171
- **Easy Copy** · 8582 Wilshire Blvd · 310-657-7777
- **Kinko's** · 5500 Wilshire Blvd · 323-937-0126
- **Moonlight Printing** · 137 S Robertson Blvd · 310-657-7528
- **Office Depot** · 5570 Wilshire Blvd · 323-939-0186
- **Staples** · 1833 La Cienega Blvd · 310-202-5343
- **Staples** · 5407 Wilshire Blvd · 323-965-5240
- **UPS Store** · 5482 Wilshire Blvd · 323-939-6001
- **UPS Store** · 8807 W Pico Blvd · 310-860-0856

🛒Farmer's Markets
- **La Cienega Farmer's Market** · 1801 La Cienega Blvd

🏋Gyms
- **Bolder Fitness** · 8810 W Pico Blvd · 310-276-5505
- **Curves** · 5945 W Pico Blvd · 323-931-5940
- **LA Fitness Sports Club** · 1833 La Cienega Blvd · 310-202-6823
- **LA Fitness Sports Club** · 5950 Wilshire Blvd · 323-934-6150
- **Meridian Sports Club** · 5750 Wilshire Blvd · 323-933-5875
- **Quick's Fitness Center** · 473 S Robertson Blvd · 310-271-7933

🍸Liquor Stores
- **Beverly Hills Beverage** · 8318 Wilshire Blvd
- **Century Liquor** · 5431 W Pico Blvd
- **Community Market** · 5390 W Washington Blvd
- **L&E Liquors** · 1298 S La Brea Ave
- **La Brea Liquor** · 1617 S La Brea Ave
- **La Brea Liquor** · 718 S La Brea Ave
- **Le Chateau Wines & Spirits** · 6252 Wilshire Blvd
- **Liquorama Liquor Store** · 4979 W Washington Blvd
- **Midtown Liquor** · 5956 W Olympic Blvd
- **Okay Liquor** · 5500 W Pico Blvd
- **PM Liquor** · 1976 S La Cienega Blvd
- **Sunshine Liquor** · 5677 W Pico Blvd
- **Teddy's Liquor** · 2112 S La Brea Ave
- **Thriftown Liquor** · 2043 S La Cienega Blvd
- **Vendome Wines & Spirits** · 9153 W Olympic Blvd

🎬Movie Theaters
- **Bing Theater at LACMA** · 5905 Wilshire Blvd · 323-857-6000
- **Laemmle Music Hall 3** · 9036 Wilshire Blvd · 310-274-6869
- **Landmark Cecchi Gori Fine Arts Theatre** · 8556 Wilshire Blvd · 310-281-8223

🍸Nightlife
- **Conga Room** · 5364 Wilshire Blvd · 323-938-1696
- **El Rey** · 5515 Wilshire Blvd · 323-936-4790
- **The Joint** · 8771 W Pico Blvd · 310-275-2619
- **The Mint** · 6010 Pico Blvd · 323-954-9630
- **Tom Bergin's** · 840 S Fairfax Ave · 323-936-7151

🐾Pet Stores
- **Pet Club** · 778 S La Brea Ave · 323-933-8811
- **Petco** · 1475 S Robertson Blvd · 310-282-8166

🍴Restaurants
- **Benito's Taco Shop** · 1544 S La Cienega Blvd · 310-360-7386
- **Black Dog Coffee** · 5657 Wilshire Blvd · 323-933-1976
- **Caffé Latte** · 6254 Wilshire Blvd · 323-936-5213
- **Cobra Lily** · 8442 Wilshire Blvd · 323-651-5051
- **Crazy Fish** · 9105 W Olympic Blvd · 310-550-8547
- **La Boca del Conga Room** · 5364 Wilshire Blvd · 323-938-1696
- **Lucy's** · 1371 S La Brea Ave · 323-938-4337
- **Luna Park** · 672 S La Brea Ave · 323-934-2110
- **Natalee Thai** · 998 S Robertson Blvd · 310-855-9380
- **Nyala Ethiopian Cuisine** · 1076 S Fairfax Ave · 323-936-5918
- **Rosalind's** · 1044 S Fairfax Ave · 323-936-2486
- **Roscoe's Chicken & Waffles** · 5006 W Pico Blvd · 323-934-4405
- **Versailles** · 1415 S La Cienega Blvd · 310-289-0392
- **Wi Jammin** · 5103 Pico Blvd · 323-965-9809

🛍Shopping
- **99 Cent Store** · 6121 Wilshire Blvd · 323-939-9991
- **Ace Gallery** · 5514 Wilshire Blvd · 323-935-4411
- **Albertson Wedding Chapel** · 5318 Wilshire Blvd · 323-937-4919
- **Bang a Drum** · 1255 S La Brea Ave · 800-495-1109
- **City Spa** · 5325 Pico Blvd · 323-933-5954
- **Feldman Watch** · 9000 W Pico Blvd · 310-274-8016
- **Hansen's Cakes** · 1072 S Fairfax Ave · 323-936-4332
- **Kitson** · 115 S Robertson Blvd · 310-859-2652
- **Marinello Beauty School** · 6111 Wilshire Blvd · 323-938-2005
- **Miauhaus** · 1201 S La Brea Ave · 323-933-6150
- **Oh My Nappy Hair!** · 805 S La Brea Ave · 323-939-3999
- **Pearl Art and Craft Supplies** · 1250 S La Cienega Blvd · 310-854-4900
- **Tom Bergin's** · 840 S Fairfax Ave · 323-936-7151
- **Up Health Merchants** · 6051 San Vicente Blvd · 323-935-3020

🎬Video Rental
- **20-20 Video** · 6161 W Pico Blvd · 310-551-2020
- **Blockbuster** · 270 S Robertson Blvd · 310-854-0991
- **Blockbuster** · 6340 Wilshire Blvd · 323-782-9733
- **Calis Video** · 5411 Venice Blvd · 323-936-9688
- **Hollywood Video** · 3939 Crenshaw Blvd · 323-293-5762
- **Hollywood Video** · 5522 Wilshire Blvd · 323-937-5647
- **La Brea Video** · 752 S La Brea Ave · 323-936-1274
- **Top Video** · 4972 W Pico Blvd · 323-935-6960

Map 7 · Hancock Park

The tree-lined oasis of Hancock Park has long been one of the city's most discreetly lovely residential neighborhoods. Architecturally speaking, it's a big candy store. This is where the studio moguls from Hollywood's Golden Age used to live, and in fact Nat King Cole broke the color line here when he purchased his home. No time for a lazy stroll in the shade? Then definitely take a drive through at Christmastime—the decorations range from Rockwell to straight-from-hell.

$ Banks

- **Bank of America** · 100 N Larchmont Blvd
- **Bank of America** · 4077 W Washington Blvd
- **Bank of America** · 4649 Venice Blvd
- **Broadway Federal** · 4800 Wilshire Blvd
- **Broadway Federal** · 4835 Venice Blvd
- **California National** · 157 N Larchmont Blvd
- **Hanmi** · 3737 W Olympic Blvd
- **Washington Mutual** · 101 N Larchmont Blvd
- **Washington Mutual** · 4333 Wilshire Blvd
- **Wells Fargo** · 245 N Larchmont Blvd
- **Wilshire State** · 3832 Wilshire Blvd

Car Rental

- **Enterprise** · 3412 W Pico Blvd

Car Washes

- **Car Wash** · 2345 Crenshaw Blvd
- **Olympic Car Wash** · 3554 W Olympic Blvd

Gas Stations

- **76** · 2121 Arlington Ave
- **76** · 3477 W Olympic Blvd
- **76** · 3481 W Olympic Blvd
- **76** · 4176 Venice Blvd
- **Chevron** · 1009 Crenshaw Blvd
- **Chevron** · 1907 Arlington Ave
- **Independent** · 4169 Venice Blvd
- **Mobil** · 1925 Crenshaw Blvd
- **Mobil** · 3950 W Olympic Blvd

Landmarks

- **Getty House (Mayor's official residence)** · 605 S Irving Blvd
- **Los Altos Apartments** · 4121 Wilshire Blvd
- **Wilshire Ebell Theatre & Club** · 4401 W 8th St
- **Wiltern LG** · 3780 Wilshire Blvd

Libraries

- **Memorial Branch** · 4625 W Olympic Blvd · 323-938-2732
- **Washington Irving Branch** · 4117 W Washington Blvd · 323-734-6303
- **Wilshire Library** · 149 N St Andrews Pl · 323-957-4550

Rx Pharmacies

- **Rite-Aid** · 226 N Larchmont Blvd · 323-467-1366
- **Rite-Aid** · 959 Crenshaw Blvd · 323-939-7911
- **Sav-On** · 4707 W Venice Blvd · 323-938-9001

Police

- **Los Angeles Police Dept** · 4849 W Venice Blvd · 213-473-0277
- **Los Angeles Police Dept** · 4861 W Venice Blvd · 213-473-0476

Post Offices

- 4040 W Washington Blvd ·

Schools

- **3rd St Elementary** · 201 S June St
- **Academic** · 4001 Venice Blvd
- **Alta Loma Elementary** · 1745 Vineyard Ave
- **Arlington Heights Elementary** · 1717 7th Ave
- **John Burroughs Middle** · 600 S McCadden Pl
- **King Learning Academy** · 2250 Crenshaw Blvd
- **Los Angeles Senior High** · 4650 W Olympic Blvd
- **Marlborough** · 250 S Rossmore Ave
- **Mount Vernon Middle** · 4066 W 17th St
- **Pio Pico Elementary** · 1512 S Arlington
- **Queen Anne EEC** · 1191 S Lucerne Blvd
- **Queen Anne Pl Elementary** · 1212 Queen Anne Pl
- **Roennes** · 4701 W Washington Blvd
- **St Gregory Nazianzen** · 911 S Norton Ave
- **St James** · 625 S St Andrews Pl
- **St Paul Elementary** · 1908 S Bronson Ave
- **Wilshire Crest Elementary** · 5241 W Olympic Blvd
- **Wilshire Elementary** · 4900 Wilshire Blvd
- **Wilton Pl Elementary** · 745 S Wilton Pl
- **Wilton Place EEC** · 4030 Leeward Ave
- **Yavneh Hebrew Academy** · 5353 W 3rd St

Supermarkets

- **Ralphs** · 4760 W Pico Blvd

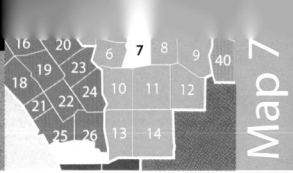

Larchmont Village nesters with huge strollers and/or designer dogs and private school kids slurping smoothies in the late afternoon. Though you could go to that New York bagel chain up the street, note that the egg-and-cheese bagels at Sam's cure hangovers, and the pastrami sandwich at Larchmont Deli can't be beat. The Sunday Farmer's Market is convivial, and the oenophile staff at Larchmont Village Wine & Cheese will recommend the perfect vintage if you let them know what's for dinner.

Coffee

- **Café Americano** · 4001 Wilshire Blvd
- **Coffee Bean & Tea Leaf** · 135 N Larchmont Blvd
- **Coffeecana** · 3959 Wilshire Blvd
- **Expresso Roma** · 124 N Larchmont Blvd
- **Hwa Sun Ji Tea & Coffee** · 3960 Wilshire Blvd
- **Le Petite** · 4055 Wilshire Blvd
- **Sam's Bagels** · 150 N Larchmont Blvd
- **Starbucks** · 206 N Larchmont Blvd
- **Starbucks** · 5020 Wilshire Blvd

Farmer's Markets

- **Larchmont Farmers Market** · Larchmont Blvd b/w W 1st St & Beverly Blvd

Gyms

- **Century Sports Club** · 4120 W Olympic Blvd · 323-954-1020
- **Curves** · 5001 Wilshire Blvd · 323-937-8767

Hardware Stores

- **Orchard Supply Hardware** · 4801 Venice Blvd · 323-930-6060
- **True Value** · 152 N Larchmont Blvd · 323-463-5783

Liquor Stores

- **Grand Prize Liquor & Deli** · 4555 W Washington Blvd
- **Jack's Cigars** · 3720 W Olympic Blvd
- **L&J Liquor** · 4111 Venice Blvd
- **LA Liquor** · 4816 W Washington Blvd
- **Larchmont Village Wine & Cheese** · 223 N Larchmont Blvd
- **Midway Liquor** · 3186 W Pico Blvd
- **Olympic Liquors** · 3533 W Olympic Blvd
- **Relay Liquor Store** · 3230 W Washington Blvd
- **Showplace Liquors** · 3401 Venice Blvd
- **Sixth Avenue Liquor** · 3526 W Washington Blvd
- **Three Jays Liquor** · 2333 W Washington Blvd
- **Tony's Liquor** · 4485 W Pico Blvd
- **Victoria Plaza Liquors** · 4226 W Pico Blvd

Nightlife

- **Jewel's Catch One** · 4067 W Pico Blvd · 323-737-1159
- **Mixed Nuts Comedy Club** · 4000 W Washington Blvd · 323-735-6622

Pet Stores

- **Fumi's Tropical Fish** · 4158 W Pico Blvd · 323-731-5255
- **Kyoto Aquarium** · 3952 Wilshire Blvd · 213-487-7302

Restaurants

- **Girasole** · 225 1/2 N Larchmont · 323-464-6978
- **Kiku Sushi** · 246 N Larchmont Blvd · 323-464-1200
- **La Bottega Marino** · 203 N Larchmont · 323-962-1325
- **La Luna** · 113 N Larchmont Blvd · 323-962-2130
- **Larchmont Village Pizzeria** · 131 N Larchmont Blvd · 323-465-5566
- **Le Petit Greek** · 127 N Larchmont Blvd · 323-464-5160
- **Prado** · 244 N Larchmont Blvd · 323-467-3871
- **Z Pizza** · 123 N Larchmont · 323-466-6969

Shopping

- **Absolute Tickets** · 144 N Larchmont Blvd · 323-957-6699
- **Center for Yoga** · 230-1/2 N Larchmont Blvd · 323-464-1276
- **Cottage Antiques** · 107 N Larchmont Blvd · 323-469-6444
- **Earl Jean** · 141-1/2 N Larchmont Blvd · 323-463-1556
- **Hans Custom Optik** · 212 N Larchmont Blvd · 323-462-5195
- **Kicks Sole Provider** · 143 N Larchmont Blvd · 323-468-9794
- **Landis Department Store** · 138 N Larchmont Blvd · 323-465-7998
- **Larchmont Beauty Center** · 208 N Larchmont Blvd · 323-461-0162
- **Larchmont News Stand** · 230 N Larchmont Blvd ·
- **Larchmont Village Wine & Cheese** · 223 N Larchmont Blvd · 323-856-8699
- **Leonidas Belgian Chocolates** · 201 N Larchmont Blvd · 323-860-7966
- **Picket Fences** · 214 N Larchmont · 323-467-2140

Video Rental

- **Blockbuster** · 147 N Larchmont Blvd · 323-461-3341
- **No 1 Video** · 4409 W Pico Blvd · 323-932-6299
- **Oscar Video (Korean)** · 4001 Wilshire Blvd · 213-384-7770
- **Video 21** · 4020 W Washington Blvd · 323-730-8927

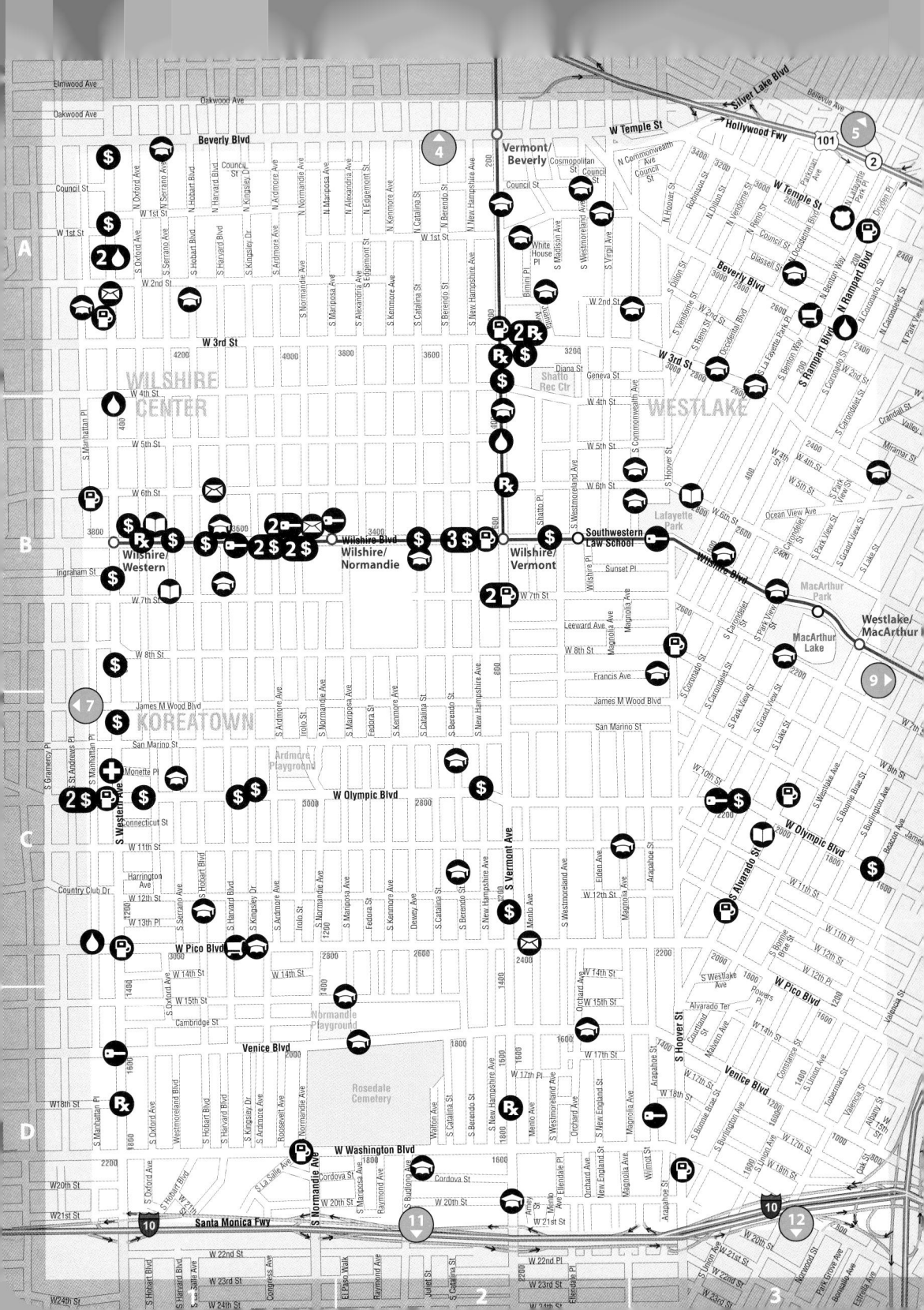

Map 3

You know you're in Korea Town when Wilshire Boulevard recedes into the horizon, none of the signs are in English, and the green Wiltern LG looms large overhead. There's lots to do, from warbling "My Way" at Orchid Karaoke Club to browsing shops like Beautiful Tonight at the unique Koreatown Plaza on Western Avenue.

Banks

- **Banco Popular** · 3360 W Olympic Blvd
- **Bank of America** · 1232 S Vermont Ave
- **Bank of America** · 3045 Wilshire Blvd
- **Bank of America** · 3320 W Olympic Blvd
- **Bank of America** · 3442 Wilshire Blvd
- **Bank of the West** · 3347 Wilshire Blvd
- **California Bank & Trust** · 3250 Wilshire Blvd
- **California Center** · 2222 W Olympic Blvd
- **California Center** · 253 N Western Ave
- **California Center** · 3435 Wilshire Blvd
- **California Center** · 3525 W 8th St
- **California Korea** · 3099 W Olympic Blvd
- **California Korea** · 3530 Wilshire Blvd
- **Citibank** · 270 N Vermont Ave
- **Citibank** · 3530 Wilshire Blvd
- **City National** · 1730 W Olympic Blvd
- **First Federal** · 351 S Vermont Ave
- **Hanmi** · 120 S Western Ave
- **Hanmi** · 3099 W Olympic Blvd
- **Hanmi** · 3255 W Olympic Blvd
- **Hanmi** · 3660 Wilshire Blvd
- **Hanmi** · 928 S Western Ave
- **Hanmi** · 933 S Vermont Ave
- **Nara** · 2727 W Olympic Blvd
- **Nara** · 3680 Wilshire Blvd
- **Nara** · 3701 Wilshire Blvd
- **US** · 3461 W 3rd St
- **Washington Mutual** · 3731 Wilshire Blvd
- **Wells Fargo** · 3550 Wilshire Blvd
- **Wells Fargo** · 670 S Western Ave
- **Wilshire State** · 3200 Wilshire Blvd
- **Wilshire State** · 841 S Western Ave

Car Rental

- **Allied Rent-a-Car** · 3540 Wilshire Blvd
- **Budget** · 3600 Wilshire Blvd
- **Dollar** · 2320 W Olympic Blvd
- **Dollar** · 3515 Wilshire Blvd
- **Enterprise** · 3435 Wilshire Blvd
- **Midway Car Rental** · 2926 Wilshire Blvd
- **U-Haul** · 1600 S Western Ave
- **U-Haul** · 1836 Arapahoe St

Car Washes

- **4th & Western Car Wash** · 401 S Western Ave
- **Auto Spa Hand Car Wash** · 128 S Western Ave
- **Narys Car Wash** · 2570 Beverly Blvd
- **Pico Car Wash** · 3131 W Pico Blvd
- **Silverlake Car Wash** · 3595 Beverly Blvd
- **Wilshire Car Wash** · 505 S Vermont Ave

Gas Stations

- **76** · 1000 S Vermont Ave
- **76** · 3501 W 3rd St
- **76** · 4000 W 6th St
- **76** · 801 S Hoover St
- **76** · 801 S Western Ave
- **Arco** · 1205 S Alvarado St
- **Chevron** · 2503 W Pico Blvd
- **Chevron** · 3325 W 6th St
- **Chevron** · 3625 Beverly Blvd
- **Chevron** · 3817 W 3rd St
- **Mobil** · 1904 W Washington Blvd
- **Mobil** · 1940 S Hoover St
- **Mobil** · 2608 W Temple St
- **Mobil** · 3309 W Olympic Blvd
- **Mobil** · 958 S Alvarado St
- **Shell** · 1303 S Western Ave
- **Shell** · 270 S Western Ave
- **Shell** · 3201 Wilshire Blvd
- **Shell** · 700 S Vermont Ave

Landmarks

- **MacArthur Park** · Wilshire Blvd & S Alvarado St
- **Southwestern Law School** · 3050 Wilshire Blvd

Libraries

- **Felipe De Neve Branch** · 2820 W 6th St · 213-384-7676
- **Pico Union Branch** · 1030 S Alvarado St · 213-368-7545
- **Pio Pico Koreatown Branch** · 694 S Oxford Ave · 213-368-7647

Pharmacies

- **Ralphs (24 hrs)** · 3410 W 3rd St · 213-480-3112
- **Rite-Aid** · 1815 S Vermont Ave · 323-735-0774
- **Rite-Aid (24 hrs)** · 334 S Vermont Ave · 213-381-5257
- **Sav-On** · 1701 S Western Ave · 323-731-8819
- **Sav-On** · 3751 Wilshire Blvd · 213-385-5030
- **Vons** · 3461 W 3rd St · 213-382-5971
- **Walgreens (24 hrs)** · 3201 W 6th St · 213-251-0078

Police

- **Los Angeles Police Dept** · 2710 W Temple St · 213-485-4061

Post Offices

- 2390 W Pico Blvd ·
- 265 S Western Ave ·
- 3450 Wilshire Blvd · 213-738-9714
- 3751 W 6th St ·

Schools

- **Berendo Middle** · 1157 S Berendo St
- **Berkeley Hall** · 16000 Mulholland Dr
- **The Beverly Academy** · 224 N Serrano Ave
- **Bishop Conaty–Our Lady of Love** · 2900 W Pico Blvd
- **Cahuenga Elementary** · 220 S Hobart Blvd
- **Camino Nuevo Charter Academy** · 635 S Harvard Blvd
- **Camino Nuevo HS** · 631 S Commonwealth Ave
- **Central City Value** · 221 N Westmoreland Ave
- **Commonwealth Ave Elementary** · 215 S Commonwealth Ave
- **First Lutheran** · 3119 W 6th St
- **Green Pastures Academy** · 600 S Lafayette Park Pl
- **Hobart Blvd Elementary** · 980 S Hobart Blvd
- **Hobart EEC** · 982 S Serrano Ave
- **Hoover St Elementary** · 2726 Francis Ave
- **Korean Baptist Church** · 975 S Berendo St
- **La Fayette Park Primary Center** · 310 S La Fayette Park Pl
- **LA Leadership Academy** · 668 S Catalina St
- **Leo Politi Elementary** · 2481 W 11th St
- **Linden Center West** · 2706 Wilshire Blvd
- **Los Angeles Christian** · 2001 S Vermont Ave
- **Los Angeles Elementary** · 1211 S Hobart Blvd
- **Loyola High** · 1901 Venice Blvd
- **MacArthur Park PC** · 2300 W 7th St
- **Magnolia Ave Elementary** · 1626 Orchard Ave
- **McAlistar High** · 155 N Occidental Blvd
- **Mid-Wilshire Christian** · 221 S Juanita Ave
- **New Covenant Academy** · 691 S Harvard Blvd
- **New Horizon** · 434 S Vermont Ave
- **Phillip's Academy** · 3404 W 1st St
- **Pilgrim** · 540 S Commonwealth Ave
- **Precious Blood** · 307 S Occidental Blvd
- **Salvin Special Ed Center** · 1925 S Budlong Ave
- **St Brendan** · 238 S Manhattan Pl
- **St Thomas Apostle Elementary** · 2632 W 15th St
- **Virgil Middle** · 152 N Vermont Ave
- **White Elementary** · 2401 Wilshire Blvd
- **White House Primary Center** · 108 S Bimini Pl

Supermarkets

- **Food 4 Less** · 1091 S Hoover St
- **Food 4 Less** · 1717 S Western Ave
- **Jons Supermarket** · 3334 W 8th St
- **Jons Supermarket** · 3667 W 3rd St
- **Jons Supermarket** · 840 S Alvarado St
- **Ralphs** · 3410 W 3rd St
- **Ralphs** · 670 S Western Ave
- **Smart & Final** · 2720 Beverly Blvd
- **Smart & Final** · 2949 W Pico Blvd
- **Vons** · 3461 W 3rd St

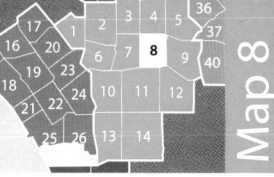
K-town is home to one of the most interactive and group-friendly dining experiences in Los Angeles: Korean Barbecue. If you don't mind cooking your own meat and the lingering smell of campfire on your clothes, head to Soot Bull Jeep on the cheap side, or Dong Il Jang on the plush end, and be sure to take a bunch of friends. Mexican restaurant El Cholo is an LA institution, serving tacos and burritos in the same location for over 70 years.

Coffee
- **Baristar** · 698 S Vermont Ave
- **Boba Loca** · 610 1/2 S Western Ave
- **Café Aristo** · 664 S Catalina St
- **Coffee House Cona** · 425 S Western Ave
- **Coffee World** · 3500 Wilshire Blvd
- **Coffee Zone** · 3240 Wilshire Blvd
- **Donuts & Coffee Shop** · 207 N Western Ave
- **Essence Coffee** · 3458 1/2 Wilshire Blvd
- **Lollicup** · 3805 W 6th St
- **New Seoul Hotel Coffee House** · 2666 W Olympic Blvd
- **Starbucks** · 3680 Wilshire Blvd
- **Starbucks (Vons)** · 3461 W 3rd St
- **Sunshine Café** · 2500 Wilshire Blvd
- **Vienna Coffee** · 2716 W Olympic Blvd

Copy Centers
- **Color & Copy** · 3460 Wilshire Blvd · 213-381-0077
- **Copy Express LA** · 3321 Wilshire Blvd · 213-380-0062
- **Copy USA** · 3377 Wilshire Blvd · 213-384-8184
- **Just Fill** · 3435 Wilshire Blvd · 213-738-8116
- **Saver Office Supplies** · 143 N Western Ave · 323-469-8401
- **Universal Reprographics** · 2706 Wilshire Blvd · 213-365-7750

Gyms
- **24-Hour Fitness** · 3699 Wilshire Blvd · 213-388-2700
- **Curves** · 126 S Vermont Ave · 213-383-9111
- **Natura Sports Health Club** · 3240 Wilshire Blvd · 213-637-9640

Hardware Stores
- **Ace** · 513 S Western Ave · 213-389-6529
- **Ace** · 915 S Alvarado St · 213-382-1305
- **Callahan True Value** · 139 S Western Ave · 213-387-3336
- **Catalina Hardware & Paint** · 3615 W 3rd St · 213-384-3059
- **D&D Hardware** · 2831 James M Wood Blvd · 213-386-6220
- **J&C Hardware** · 1426 W Pico Blvd · 213-748-1530
- **LA Hardware** · 4027 W 3rd St · 213-388-4644
- **Orlando's Key Shop & Hardware** · 2026 W Washington Blvd · 323-737-5017
- **Pico Building Supply** · 2595 W Pico Blvd · 213-388-5102
- **Villanueva's Hardware** · 3030 W Pico Blvd · 323-737-1099

Liquor Stores
- **3rd St Liquors** · 4023 W 3rd St
- **8 OK Liquors** · 749 S Western Ave
- **A&A Liquors** · 111 S Vermont Ave
- **Albert's Liquors** · 3088 W Pico Blvd
- **Amigos Liquor** · 2601 W 7th St
- **Ardmore Liquor** · 4056 W 3rd St
- **Ashibi Liquor** · 4376 W 3rd St
- **Bengal Liquor** · 3600 W 3rd St
- **Catalina Liquor** · 3130 W 8th St
- **Cheyenne Liquor Store** · 1611 S Vermont Ave
- **Crest Liquors** · 2543 W 3rd St
- **Dick's Beverage House** · 3315 W 6th St
- **El Serrano Liquor** · 3833 W 6th St
- **Garden Liquor** · 1479 W Washington Blvd
- **Gary's Liquors** · 2171 Venice Blvd
- **Gourmet Liquors** · 826 S Alvarado St
- **Hiro's Liquor & Groceries** · 2340 W Pico Blvd
- **Hobart Liquor** · 4212 W 3rd St
- **Hope Liquor** · 687 S Hoover St
- **Imperial Liquor** · 1602 W Pico Blvd
- **J&F Liquor** · 1512 W Pico Blvd
- **J&H Liquors** · 1154 Venice Blvd
- **Jeff's Liquor** · 1683 W 11th St
- **Jons Market** · 3334 W 8th St
- **Kumano Liquor** · 2801 W Pico Blvd
- **LA Pit Stop** · 2571 W Olympic Blvd
- **Ladd Liquor** · 4217 W 3rd St
- **Lawrence Liquor** · 2301 W James M Wood Blvd
- **Lucky Liquor** · 2201 W Pico Blvd
- **Nadee's Liquor** · 863 S Vermont Ave
- **Occidental Liquor** · 2755 Beverly Blvd
- **Ocean Liquor** · 760 S Alvarado St
- **Olympic Liquor** · 3060 W Olympic Blvd
- **Oxford Mini Mart** · 3502 W 8th St
- **Park Liquor** · 3554 Beverly Blvd
- **Service Liquor House** · 3803 W 3rd St
- **Silver Liquor & Deli** · 2717 W 3rd St
- **Superior Liquor** · 2700 W Pico Blvd
- **Tighi Liquor** · 2701 W 8th St
- **Topper Liquor** · 3061 W 8th St
- **West Seven Liquor** · 707 S Western Ave
- **Western Liquor** · 553 S Western Ave
- **Westmoreland Market** · 2800 James M Wood Blvd

Nightlife
- **Barcade** · 4366 2nd St · no phone
- **Brass Monkey** · 659 Mariposa Ave · 213-381-7047
- **HMS Bounty** · 3357 Wilshire Blvd · 213-385-7275
- **La Fonda De Los Camperos** · 2501 Wilshire Blvd · 213-380-5055
- **Orchid Karaoke Club** · 3900 W 6th St, 2nd Fl · 213-251-8886
- **The Prince** · 3198 7th St · 213-389-1586

Pet Stores
- **Hobby Life Center** · 533 S Western Ave · 323-262-9999
- **Western Pet Center** · 533 S Western Ave · 213-381-3435
- **World Pet Shop & Bonsai** · 151 N Western Ave · 323-469-9977

Restaurants
- **Dong Il Jang** · 3455 W 8th St · 213-383-5757
- **El Cholo** · 1121 S Western Ave · 323-734-2773
- **El Farolito** · 2737 W Pico Blvd · 323-731-4329
- **M Grill** · 3832 Wilshire Blvd · 213-389-2770
- **Soot Bull Jeep** · 3136 W 8th St · 213-387-3865
- **Taylor's Prime Steaks** · 3361 W 8th St · 213-382-8449
- **Tommy's** · 2575 Beverly Blvd · 213-389-9060

Shopping
- **Beautiful Tonight Lingerie** · 928 S Western Ave · 213-736-5844
- **Picholine** · 3360 W 1st St · 213-252-8722

Video Rental
- **20-20 Video** · 142 S Vermont Ave · 213-380-0202
- **20-20 Video** · 1720 S Vermont Ave · 323-734-2020
- **3rd Street Video (Korean)** · 3559 W 3rd St · 213-739-5935
- **50 50 Video** · 2411 W Olympic Blvd · 213-384-4585
- **A&T Video Center** · 272 S Rampart Blvd · 213-387-6161
- **ABC Video (Filipino)** · 4031 W 3rd St · 213-380-3575
- **Blockbuster** · 2190 W Washington Blvd · 323-373-2082
- **Blockbuster** · 2377 W Pico Blvd · 213-383-2927
- **Blockbuster** · 4005 W 3rd St · 213-252-3133
- **CALA Video** · 3801 W 3rd St · 213-388-3744
- **Central Video (Korean)** · 3072 W 8th St · 213-389-2111
- **Chung's Video (Korean only)** · 244 S Oxford Ave · 213-384-9900
- **Cinema Story** · 401 S Vermont Ave · 213-383-6211
- **Corner Video (Korean)** · 2528 W Olympic Blvd · 213-388-2255
- **El Chasis Video** · 2980 W 8th St · 213-385-4702
- **Excalibur Video** · 1724 S Western Ave · 323-731-1801
- **Han Nam Video (Korean)** · 2716 W Olympic Blvd · 213-487-1225
- **Hollywood Video** · 650 S Western Ave · 213-385-7233
- **J&J Video** · 3101 Beverly Blvd · 213-380-4169
- **Korea Town Plaza Video (Korean)** · 928 S Western Ave · 213-480-8080
- **Korean Video Store (Korean)** · 401 S Vermont Ave · 213-386-7116
- **LA Korean Video (Korean)** · 326 S Western Ave · 213-389-4989
- **Lucky Video (Korean)** · 124 N Western Ave · 323-460-4398
- **Mickey Video (Korean)** · 3134 W Olympic Blvd · 323-732-8399
- **Opaane Video Store** · 3967 W 6th St · 213-427-9855
- **P&J (Korean)** · 549 S Western Ave · 213-380-6699
- **Planet Video** · 2026 W Pico Blvd · 213-381-1884
- **Super Video (Korean)** · 3388 W 8th St · 213-380-0550
- **Video Target** · 3128 W 8th St · 213-487-6035
- **Video Tek (Korean only)** · 849 S Western Ave · 213-382-0714
- **Virgil Video** · 2161 Venice Blvd · 323-734-6007
- **Westside Video** · 2709 W 6th St · 213-384-4725

Map 9 · Downtown

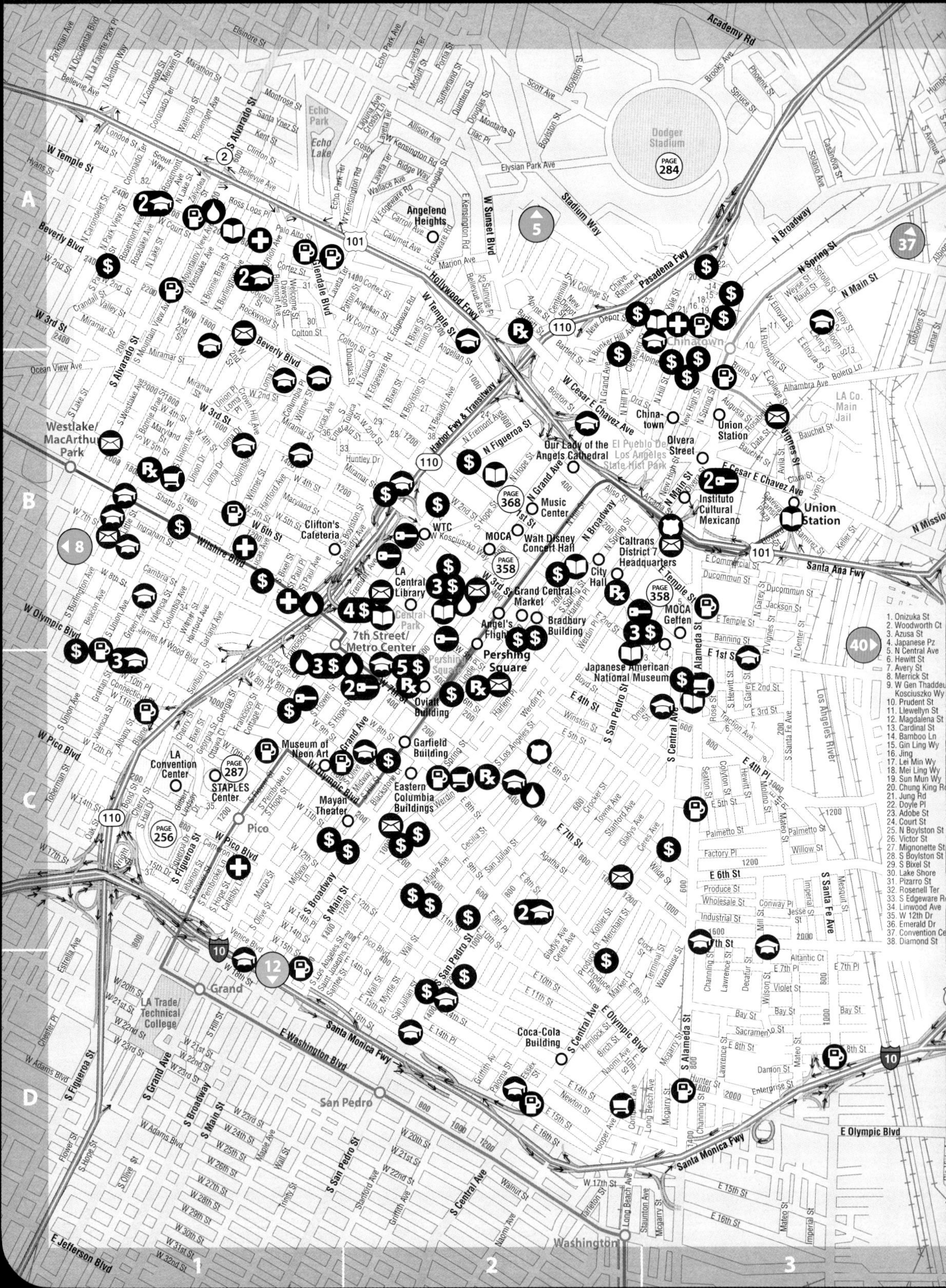

N

1. Onizuka St
2. Woolworth Ct
3. Azusa St
4. Japanese Pz
5. N Central Ave
6. Hewitt St
7. Avery St
8. Merrick St
9. W Gen Thaddeus Kosciuszko Wy
10. Prudent St
11. Llewellyn St
12. Magdalena St
13. Cardinal St
14. Bamboo Ln
15. Gin Ling Wy
16. Jing
17. Lei Min Wy
18. Mei Ling Wy
19. Sun Mun Wy
20. Chung King Rd
21. Jung Rd
22. Doyle Pl
23. Adobe St
24. Court St
25. N Boylston St
26. Victor St
27. Mignonette St
28. S Boylston St
29. S Bixel St
30. Lake Shore
31. Pizarro St
32. Rosenell Ter
33. S Edgeware Rd
34. Linwood Ave
35. W 12th Dr
36. Emerald Dr
37. Convention Ct
38. Diamond St

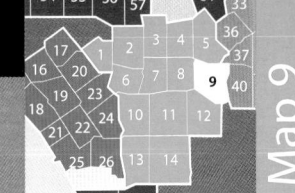

Downtown LA is evolving into the city's cultural center, with the Gehry-designed Disney Hall and surrounding venues drawing a steady crowd of music, dance and theatre lovers. Art fans tour the Chinatown galleries and visit two of the Museum of Contemporary Art's more spacious locations to find the latest West Coast wunderkinds. In the summer months, locals load up their picnic baskets at Grand Central Market and head up the hill for free evening concerts at the California Plaza Watercourt.

$ Banks

- **Banco Popular** · 354 S Spring St
- **Bank of America**
  - 100 S Broadway
  - 1551 Wilshire Blvd
  - 2101 W 6th St
  - 550 S Hill St
  - 600 Wilshire Blvd
  - 850 N Broadway
  - 333 S Alameda St
  - 1127 S Hill St
  - 1625 W Olympic Blvd
  - 333 S Hope St
  - 590 S Central Ave
  - 735 S Figueroa St
  - 300 S Grand Ave
  - 601 S Figueroa St
- **California Bank & Trust** · 101 S San Pedro St
- **California Bank & Trust** · 550 S Hope St
- **California Center** · 1059 S San Pedro St
- **California Center** · 1205 S Broadway
- **California Credit Union** · 333 S Beaudry Ave
- **California Credit Union** · 420 N Rosenall Ter
- **California National** · 221 S Figueroa St
- **Cathay** · 777 N Broadway
- **Cathay** · 800 W 6th St
- **Citibank** · 324 E 1st St
- **Citibank** · 787 W 5th St
- **Citibank** · 800 N Hill St
- **City National** · 555 S Flower St
- **City National** · 606 S Olive St
- **Comerica** · 110 E 9th St
- **Comerica** · 201 N Figueroa St
- **East West** · 624 S Grand Ave
- **East West** · 942 N Broadway
- **Far East National** · 350 S Grand Ave
- **Far East National** · 977 N Broadway
- **First Bank & Trust** · 711 W College St
- **First Republic** · 901 W 7th St
- **Hanmi** · 726 E 12th St
- **Hanmi** · 950 S Los Angeles St
- **International Bank of California** · 2323 Beverly Blvd
- **International Bank of California** · 888 S Figueroa St
- **Manufacturers** · 200 S San Pedro St
- **Manufacturers** · 515 S Figueroa St
- **Nara** · 1122 S Wall St
- **Preferred** · 601 S Figueroa St
- **Union** · 120 S San Pedro St
- **Union** · 445 S Figueroa St
- **Union** · 900 S Main St
- **United Commercial** · 767 N Hill St
- **US** · 633 W 5th St
- **Washington Mutual** · 400 S Hope St
- **Washington Mutual** · 725 S Figueroa St
- **Washington Mutual** · 855 S Hill St
- **Wells Fargo**
  - 1200 Wilshire Blvd
  - 333 S Grand Ave
  - 707 Wilshire Blvd
  - 1244 E 8th St
  - 333 S Spring St
  - 988 N Hill St
- **Wilshire State** · 1122 Maple Ave
- **Wilshire State** · 1300 S San Pedro St

Car Rental

- **Avis** · 888 S Figueroa St
- **Budget** · 800 N Alameda St
- **Enterprise** · 404 S Figueroa St
- **Enterprise** · 530 S Olive St
- **Enterprise** · 718 Wilshire Blvd
- **Hertz** · 333 S Figueroa St
- **Hertz** · 711 S Hope St
- **Hertz** · 800 N Alameda St
- **Sakura Rent-a-Car** · 248 E 1st St

Car Washes

- **Daisy Shell** · 400 N Alvarado St
- **Downtown Car Wash** · 811 W Olympic Blvd
- **Joe's Car Wash** · 400 E 7th St
- **Leo's Car Wash** · 700 S Flower St
- **Mario's Hand Wash & Detailing** · 1000 Wilshire Blvd
- **Valet Car Wash** · 355 S Grand Ave
- **Valet Car Wash** · 948 W 8th St

Gas Stations

- **76** · 1307 W 6th St
- **76** · 1800 E Olympic Blvd
- **Arco** · 1045 Blaine St
- **Arco** · 2041 Beverly Blvd
- **Arco** · 2106 W Temple St
- **Chevron** · 1516 S Main St
- **Chevron** · 1600 W Olympic Blvd
- **Chevron** · 501 Glendale Blvd
- **Chevron** · 811 W Olympic Blvd
- **Chevron** · 901 N Alameda St
- **Independent** · 812 S Main St
- **Independent** · 900 N Hill St
- **Shell** · 1520 Santa Fe Ave
- **Shell** · 1541 S Central Ave
- **Shell** · 400 N Alvarado St
- **Shell** · 504 W Olympic Blvd
- **Texaco** · 500 S Alameda St

Hospitals

- **California Hospital Medical** · 1338 S Hope St
- **City of Angels** · 1711 W Temple St
- **Good Samaritan** · 1225 Wilshire Blvd
- **Pacific Alliance** · 531 W College St

o Landmarks

- **Angel's Flight** · W 4th St & Hill St
- **Angeleno Heights** · Carroll/Kellam/W Kensington Aves
- **Bradbury Building** · 304 S Broadway
- **Caltrans District 7 Headquarters** · 100 N Main St
- **Chinatown** · 700-1000 N Broadway
- **City Hall** · 200 N Spring St
- **Clifton's Cafeteria** · 648 S Broadway
- **Coca-Cola Building** · 1334 S Central Ave
- **Eastern Columbia Buildings** · 849 S Broadway
- **Garfield Building** · 403 W 8th St
- **Grand Central Market** · 317 S Broadway
- **Instituto Cultural Mexicano** · 125 Paseo de la Plz
- **Japanese American National Museum** · 369 E 1st St
- **LA Central Library** · 630 W 5th St
- **LA Convention Center** · 1201 S Figueroa St
- **Mayan Theater** · 1038 S Hill St
- **MOCA** · 250 S Grand Ave
- **MOCA at the Geffen Contemporary** · 152 N Central Ave
- **Museum of Neon Art** · 501 W Olympic Blvd
- **Music Center** · 135 N Grand Ave
- **Olvera Street** · Olvera St
- **Our Lady of Angels Cathedral** · 555 W Temple St
- **Oviatt Building** · 617 S Olive St
- **STAPLES Center** · 1111 S Figueroa St
- **Union Station** · 800 N Alameda St
- **Walt Disney Concert Hall** · 141 S Grand Ave
- **World Trade Center** · 350 S Figueroa St

Libraries

- **Chinatown Branch** · 639 N Hill St · 213-620-0925
- **Echo Park Library** · 1410 W Temple St · 213-250-7808
- **Franklin D Murphy Library (Temporarily Closed)** · 244 S San Pedro St · 213-628-2725
- **LA County Law Library** · 301 W 1st St · 213-629-3531
- **Little Tokyo Branch** · 244 S Alameda St · 213-612-0525
- **Los Angeles Central Library** · 630 W 5th St · 213-228-7000
- **MTA Library** · 1 Gateway Plz · 213-922-4859
- **Water & Power Library** · 111 N Hope St · 213-367-1995

Rx Pharmacies

- **Rite-Aid** · 700 S Los Angeles St · 213-614-9574
- **Rite-Aid** · 1744 W 6th St · 213-413-2458
- **Rite-Aid** · 501 S Broadway · 213-623-5820
- **Rite-Aid** · 600 W 7th St · 213-896-0083
- **Sav-On** · 1050 Sunset Blvd · 213-975-1165
- **Sav-On** · 201 N Los Angeles St · 213-620-1491

Police

- **Los Angeles Police Dept** · 251 E 6th St · 213-485-3294
- **Los Angeles Police Dept - Administrative Office** · 150 N Los Angeles St · 213-485-3205

Post Offices

- 100 W Olympic Blvd · 213-627-6412
- 1055 N Vignes St
- 1122 E 7th St
- 1660 Beverly Blvd
- 1808 W 7th St
- 2005 W 6th St · 213-483-4098
- 300 N Los Angeles St
- 350 S Grand Ave
- 505 S Flower St
- 508 S Spring St

Schools

- **10th St Elementary** · 1000 Grattan St
- **9th St Elementary** · 820 Towne Ave
- **Ann St Elementary** · 126 E Bloom St
- **Belmont Senior High** · 1575 W 2nd St
- **Betty Plasencia Elementary** · 1321 Cortez St
- **Camino Nuevo Charter Academy** · 697 S Burlington Ave
- **Camino Nuevo Charter Middle** · 653 S Burlington Ave
- **Castelar Elementary** · 840 Yale St
- **Central Adult HS** · 211 W 17th St
- **City of Angels Independent Study** · 1449 S San Pedro
- **Citylife Downtown Charter** · 700 Wilshire Blvd
- **Cruz EEC** · 1020 Valencia St
- **DBM/Electronic Information Magnet** · 1081 W Temple St
- **Elementary Community Day** · 333 S Beaudry Ave
- **Esperanza Elementary** · 680 Little St
- **Evelyn Thurman Gratts Elementary** · 309 Lucas Ave
- **Immaculate Conception** · 830 Green Ave
- **Jardin D La Infancia** · 307 E 7th St
- **LA Trade/Technical College** · 400 W Washington Blvd
- **LA Unified Alternative Education** · 450 N Grand Ave
- **Lanterman** · 820 Towne Ave
- **Los Angelitos EEC** · 400 W 9th St
- **Lumbini Child Development Center** · 505 E 3rd St
- **Metropolitan Continuation** · 727 Wilson St
- **New Academy for Science & Arts** · 379 Loma Dr
- **Newmark HS** · 134 Witmer St
- **Nishi Hongwanji Child Development Center** · 815 E 1st St
- **Our Lady of Lorette Academy** · 258 N Union Ave
- **Our Lady of Loretto** · 250 N Union Ave
- **Para Los Ninos Charter** · 1617 E 7th St
- **Rosemont Ave Elementary** · 421 Rosemont Ave
- **Rosemont EEC** · 430 Rosemont Ave
- **St Nicholas Primary** · 2300 W 3rd St
- **St Turibius Elementary** · 1524 Essex St
- **Tri-C Community Day** · 716 E 14th St
- **Union Ave Elementary** · 150 S Burlington Ave

Supermarkets

- **Food 4 Less** · 1700 W 6th St
- **Rons** · 805 S Main St
- **Smart & Final** · 1216 Compton Ave

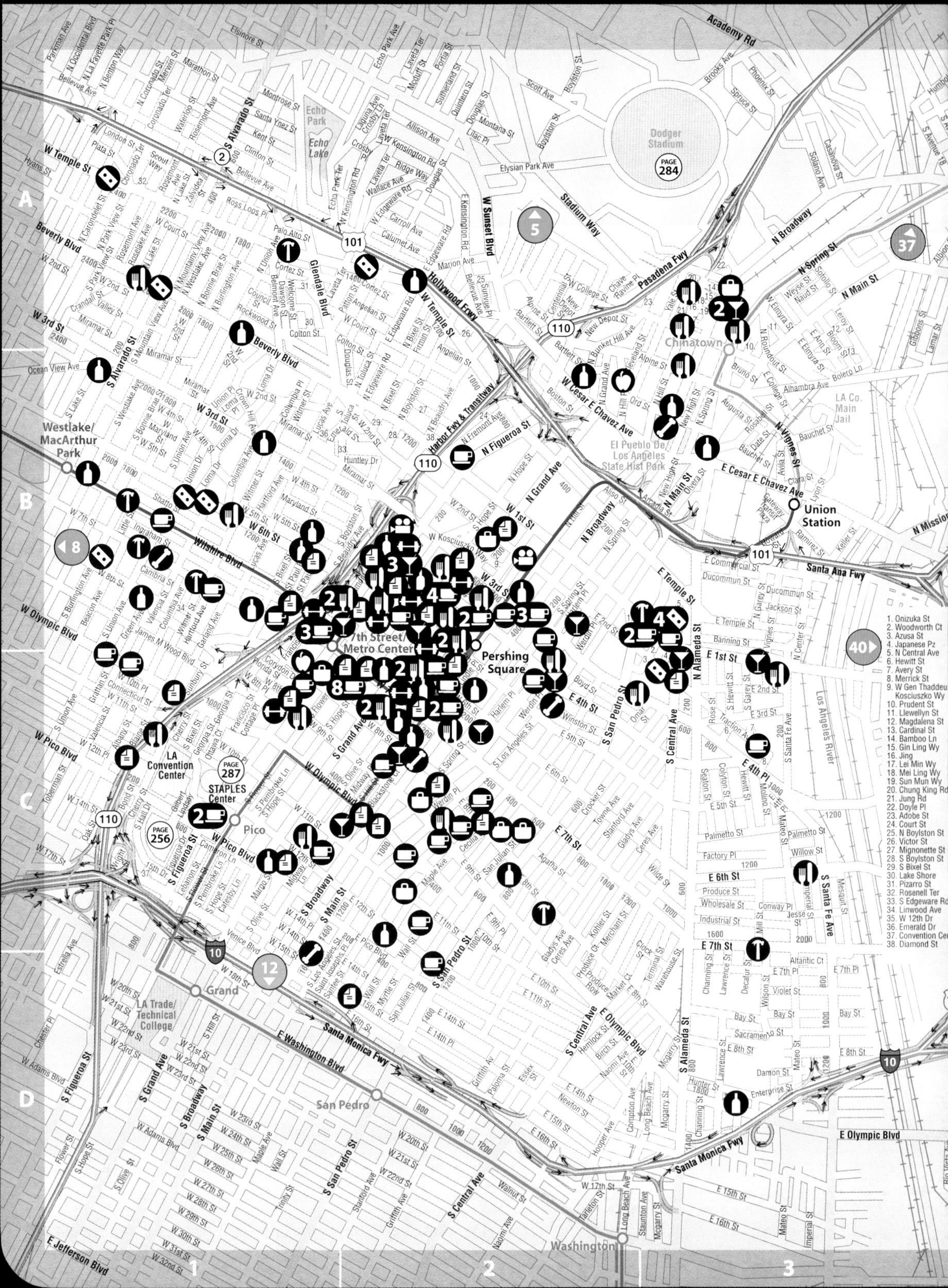

Map 9 • Downtown

1. Onizuka St
2. Woodworth Ct
3. Azusa St
4. Japanese Pz
5. N Central Ave
6. Hewitt St
7. Avery St
8. Merrick St
9. W Gen Thaddeus Kosciuszko St
10. Prudent St
11. Llewellyn St
12. Magdalena St
13. Cardinal St
14. Bamboo Ln
15. Gin Ling Wy
16. Jing
17. Lei Min Wy
18. Mei Ling Wy
19. Sun Mun Wy
20. Chung King Rd
21. Jung Rd
22. Doyle Pl
23. Adobe St
24. Court St
25. S Boylston St
26. Victor St
27. Mignonette St
28. S Boylston St
29. S Bixel St
30. Lake Shore
31. Pizarro St
32. Rosenell Ter
33. S Edgeware Rd
34. Linwood Ave
35. W 12th Dr
36. Emerald Dr
37. Convention Center
38. Diamond St

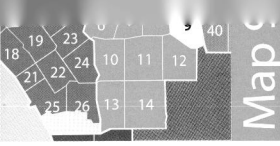

The heart of Los Angeles plays host to an impressive array of restaurant choices. Our favorites are the pan-Latin Ciudad for its cool atmosphere and cheap happy-hour tapas and Philippe for the French-dip sandwiches. If you are making a night of it, go to the Standard for the bar scene, or head to the funky, kinda-Moorish, kinda-colonial Figueroa Hotel, whose tiny pool is an oasis of calm and—more importantly—sensibly priced drinks.

Coffee

- Banquette Café • 400 S Main St
- Blue Diamond • 631 S Hill St
- Boba Loca • 623 E 12th St
- Café Take 5 • 328 E 1st St
- Caffe Bellagio • 1149 S Hill St
- Coffee Bean & Tea Leaf • 210 E Olympic Blvd
- Coffee Bean & Tea Leaf • 801 W 7th St
- Coffee Shop • 915 Wilshire Blvd
- Coffee Sin • 1125 Wall St
- Corner Bakery Café • 801 S Figueroa St
- Emerson's Café • 606 S Olive St
- Gourmet Coffee & Nuts • 505 S Flower St
- Groundworks Downtown • 811 Traction Ave
- Happy Time Snack • 819 Santee St
- Harlls Café • 317 S Broadway
- Jolt-Bar Café • 1055 W 7th St
- Larry's Cookie • 221 N Figueroa St
- Lollicup • 821 S Cecilia St
- Lollicup • 988 N Hill St
- Marie Café • 733 W 7th St
- Moose's Juices • 444 S Flower St
- Park Central Coffee Shop • 412 W 6th St
- Pasquini Imports • 1501 W Olympic Blvd
- Poirier & Co • 550 S Hope St
- Primo's Expresso Americana • 333 S Spring St
- Quality Coffee Shop • 1238 W 7th St
- Ric's Café • 350 S Grand Ave
- Starbucks
  - 10925 Atlantic Ave • 1201 S Figueroa St (South Hall)
  - 138 S Central Ave • 1201 S Figueroa St (West Hall)
  - 1601 Wilshire Blvd • 217 N Hill St
  - 300 E 9th St • 330 S Hope St
  - 333 S Hope St • 350 S Grand Ave
  - 400 S Hope St • 445 S Figueroa St
  - 555 W 5th St • 633 W 5th St
  - 695 S Figueroa St • 735 S Figueroa St
- Time Snack • 1541 W Olympic Blvd
- Tokyo Café • 116 Judge John Aiso St
- Trimana Restaurant • 615 W 6th St

Copy Centers

- 101 Printing • 820 S Main St • 213-489-5050
- Ace Copy Center • 1001 S Hill St • 213-746-0222
- Ace Reprographics • 811 Wilshire Blvd • 213-680-1932
- Color & Copy • 1300 W Olympic Blvd • 213-736-5550
- Columbia Printing • 1055 Wilshire Blvd • 213-738-7406
- Concord Document Services • 1321 W 12th St • 213-680-1114
- Copy LA • 1001 S Broadway • 213-746-3391
- Copy Star • 1515 Maple Ave • 213-744-1738
- Copy Vision • 123 S Grand Ave • 213-687-9994
- Copypage • 330 S Hope St • 213-617-4040
- Copypage • 865 S Figueroa St • 213-439-9656
- Downtown Reprographics • 640 S Olive St • 213-488-3332
- Graphic Copy • 727 W 7th St • 213-627-3083
- Kinko's • 835 Wilshire Blvd • 213-892-1700
- LA Best Copies • 621 W 6th St • 213-622-1622
- LA Reprographics • 601 W 5th St • 213-673-4460
- Office Depot • 401 E 2nd St • 213-628-5000
- Ready Reproductions • 1212 S Olive St • 213-749-2041
- Unlimited Copy • 1111 W 6th St • 213-250-8951
- Unlimited Reprographics • 444 S Flower St • 213-892-9000

Farmer's Markets

- Los Angeles-7th & Figueroa • 735 S Figueroa St
- Los Angeles-Chinatown • 727 N Hill St

Gyms

- 24-Hour Fitness • 505 S Flower St • 213-683-1400
- Bally Total Fitness • 700 S Flower St • 213-624-3933
- Curves • 350 S Grand Ave • 213-851-2878
- Gold's Gym • 735 S Figueroa St • 213-688-1441
- Los Angeles Athletic Club • 431 W 7th St • 213-625-2211
- Millennium Biltmore Hotel Health • 506 S Grand Ave • 213-612-1567

Hardware Stores

- 7th & Union Hardware • 1622 W 7th St • 213-483-5138
- Anzen Hardware • 309 E 1st St • 213-628-2068
- Cooper Ace Hardware • 1645 W Temple St • 213-483-3353
- Douglas Hardware • 1811 E 7th St • 213-622-4666
- Home Depot • 1675 Wilshire Blvd • 213-273-8464
- Terminal Hardware • 824 E 8th St • 213-624-4078

Liquor Stores

- Bixel Liquor • 467 S Bixel St
- Duke's Liquor • 818 S San Pedro St
- Esquire Liquor & Deli • 619 S Olive St
- French Kitchen • 404 S Figueroa St
- Friendly Liquor • 1553 W 8th St
- George's Liquor • 1300 W Temple St
- George's Liquor • 700 N Broadway
- Gourmet Liquors • 1476 W 3rd St
- Gourmet Wines & Spirits • 626 Wilshire Blvd
- Grand Central Public Market • 317 S Broadway
- Hope Liquor • 1216 W 7th St
- Jack's Market • 520 E 5th St
- Jo's Liquor • 333 W Pico Blvd
- Macy Liquor • 111 W Cesar E Chavez Ave
- Mark's Liquor • 1259 W 6th St
- OT Liquor • 1920 E Olympic Blvd
- Pete's Liquor • 1234 Maple Ave
- Reads Liquor Store • 308 S Alvarado St
- Sam's Liquor • 2001 W 6th St
- Sorrento Liquor • 801 W Cesar E Chavez Ave
- Union Liquor Store • 1703 Beverly Blvd

Movie Theaters

- Laemmle Grande 4 • 349 S Figueroa St • 213-617-0268
- REDCAT • 631 W 2nd St • 213-237-2800

Nightlife

- Bonaventure Brewing Co at the Bonaventure Hotel • 404 Figueroa St • 213-236-0802
- BonaVista at the Bonaventure Hotel • 404 Figueroa St • 213-624-1000
- Ciudad • 445 S Figueroa St • 213-486-5171
- Gallery Bar at the Millennium Biltmore Hotel • 506 S Grand Ave • 213-624-1011
- The Golden Gopher • 417 W 8th St • 213-614-2001
- Hop Louie • 950 Mei Ling Wy • 213-628-4244
- Little Pedro's • 901 E 1st St • 213-687-3766
- Mayan • 1040 S Hill St • 213-746-4287
- Mountain Bar • 473 Ging Ling Wy • 213-625-7500
- Oiwake • 122 Japanese Village Plz Mall • 213-628-2678
- Pete's Café & Bar • 400 S Main St • 213-617-1000
- Point Moorea Lounge (Wilshire Grand Hotel) • 930 Wilshire Blvd • 213-833-5100
- Roof Bar at the Standard Downtown • 550 S Flower St • 213-892-8080
- The Smell • 247 S Main St • no phone
- Stock Exchange • 618 S Spring St • 213-489-3877

Pet Stores

- Al's Pet Supplies • 430 S Los Angeles St • 213-622-1215
- Liberty Fish & Pet Shop • 665 N Broadway • 213-628-9664
- Trinity Animal Hospital • 1504 S Main St • 530-623-5757

Restaurants

- Brooklyn Bagel • 2217 Beverly Blvd • 213-413-4114
- Café Pinot • 700 W 5th St • 213-239-6500
- California Roll & Sushi Fish • 727 W 7th St • 213-489-0238
- Checkers • 535 S Grand Ave • 213-624-0000
- Cicada • 617 S Olive St • 213-488-9488
- Ciudad • 445 S Figueroa St • 213-486-5171
- Clifton's Cafeteria • 648 S Broadway • 213-627-1673
- Emerson's • 606 S Olive St • 213-623-3006
- Emerson's • 862 S Los Angeles St • 213-623-8807
- Empress Pavillion • 988 N Hill St • 213-617-9898
- Engine Co No 28 • 644 S Figueroa St • 213-624-6996
- Mrs Beasley's • 735 S Figueroa St • 213-228-0227
- Nick & Stef's Steakhouse • 330 S Hope St • 213-680-0330
- Noe • 251 S Olive St • 213-356-4100
- NY Pizza • 518 W 6th St • 213-614-1100
- Original Pantry Café • 877 S Figueroa Ave • 213-972-9279
- Pacific Dining Car • 1310 W 6th St • 213-483-6000
- Pete's Café & Bar • 400 S Main St • 213-617-1000
- Philippe, the Original • 1001 N Alameda St • 213-628-3781
- Plum Tree Inn • 937 W Hill St • 213-613-1819
- R-23 • 923 E 2nd St • 213-687-7178
- Seoul Jung Korean • 930 Wilshire Blvd • 213-688-7880
- Soul Folks Café • 613 Imperial St • 213-613-0381
- The Standard Downtown Restaurant & Lounge • 550 S Flower St • 213-892-8080
- Water Grill • 544 S Grand Ave • 213-891-0900
- Yang Chow • 819 N Broadway • 213-625-0811

Shopping

- 7 + Fig at Ernst & Young Plaza • 735 S Figueroa St • 213-955-7150
- American Apparel • 374 E 2nd St • 213-687-0467
- California Market Center • 110 E 9th St • 213-630-3600
- Grand Central Market • 317 S Broadway • 213-625-5006
- LA Flower Market • 766 Wall St • 213-622-1966
- MOCA Store • 250 S Grand Ave • 213-621-1710
- Moskatel's • 733 San Julian St • 213-689-4590
- Munky King • 441 Gin Ling Wy • 213-620-8787
- Santee Alley • midway b/w Santee St & Maple Ave, from 12th St to Olympic Blvd • 213-488-1153

Video Rental

- B&C Video Rental • 1416 W 6th St • 213-484-5383
- Blockbuster • 1830 W 8th Ave • 213-250-1292
- Gemini Video • 2424 W Temple St • 213-389-2030
- J Wave • 319 E 2nd St • 213-687-9920
- Tokyo Market (Japanese) • 339 E 1st St • 213-620-0033
- Video Hot • 2110 Beverly Blvd • 213-413-5433
- Video Paradise (Japanese) • 321 E 1st St • 213-625-2671
- Video Rental • 1509 W 6th St • 213-353-9086
- Video Z • 1460 W Temple St • 213-481-0996

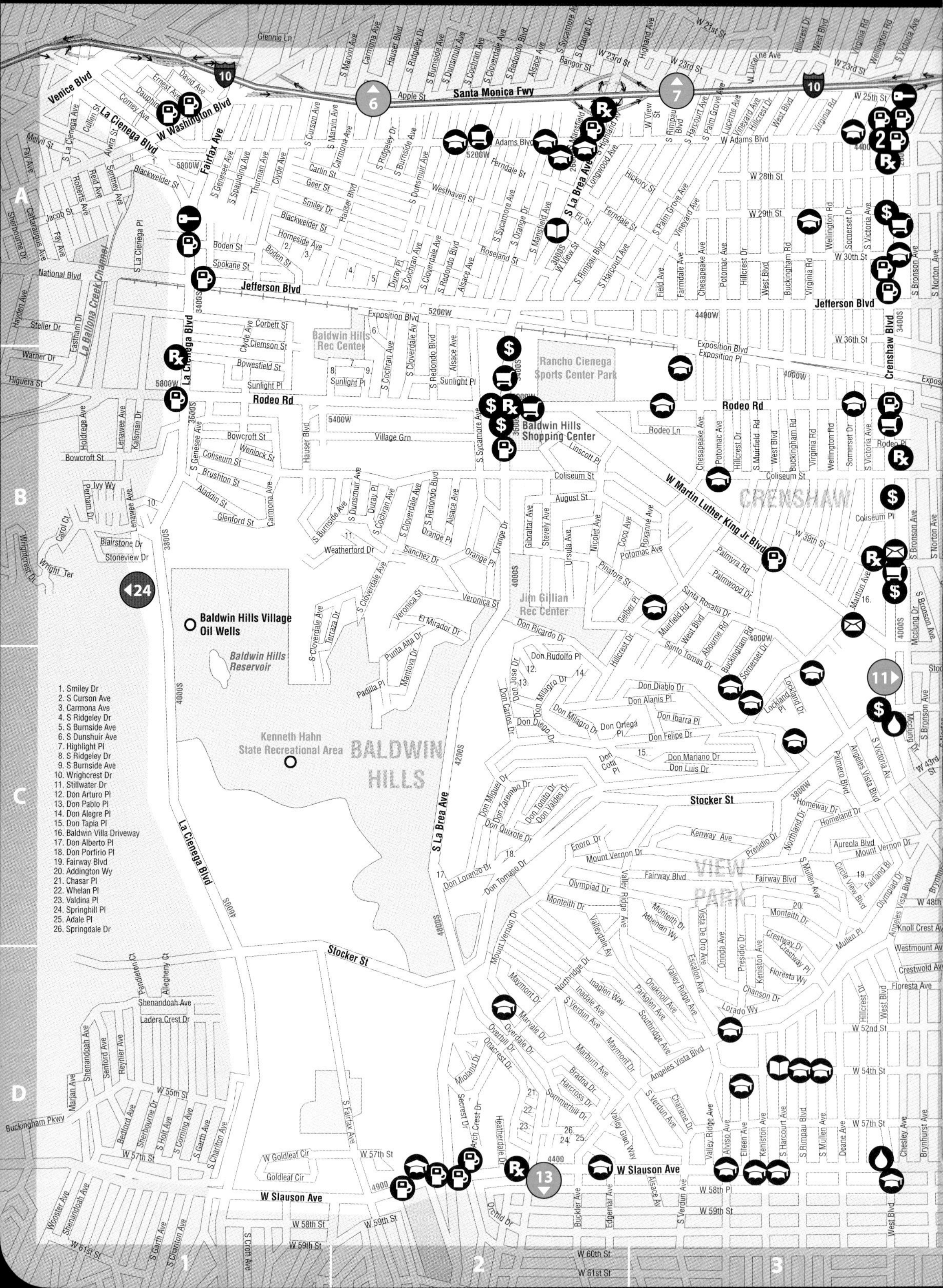

Map 10 · **Baldwin Hills**

N

Venice Blvd
Santa Monica Fwy
10

Baldwin Hills Rec Center

Rancho Cienega Sports Center Park

Baldwin Hills Shopping Center

Rodeo Rd

CRENSHAW

Jefferson Blvd

Jim Gillian Rec Center

24

Baldwin Hills Village Oil Wells

Baldwin Hills Reservoir

Kenneth Hahn State Recreational Area

BALDWIN HILLS

Stocker St

VIEW PARK

1. Smiley Dr
2. S Curson Ave
3. Carmona Ave
4. S Ridgeley Dr
5. S Burnside Ave
6. S Dunshuir Ave
7. Highlight Pl
8. S Ridgeley Dr
9. S Burnside Ave
10. Wrighcrest Dr
11. Stillwater Dr
12. Don Arturo Pl
13. Don Pablo Pl
14. Don Alegre Pl
15. Don Tapia Pl
16. Baldwin Villa Driveway
17. Don Alberto Pl
18. Don Porfirio Pl
19. Fairway Blvd
20. Addington Wy
21. Chasar Pl
22. Whelan Pl
23. Valdina Pl
24. Springhill Pl
25. Adale Pl
26. Springdale Dr

Stocker St

W Slauson Ave

W Slauson Ave

13

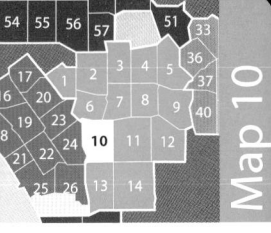
Baldwin Hills is a wealthy, predominantly African-American community whose first claim to fame was hosting the world's first Olympic Village in 1932. A year later, the Los Angeles Sentinel newspaper was founded. The newspaper is today the largest and most influential black-owned newspaper on the West Coast, and is headquartered on the neighborhood's historic main drag, Crenshaw Boulevard.

$ Banks

- **Bank of America** · 2907 Crenshaw Blvd
- **Bank of America** · 3615 S La Brea Ave
- **Bank of America** · 3945 Crenshaw Blvd
- **California Bank & Trust** · 3810 Crenshaw Blvd
- **US** · 3605 S La Brea Ave
- **Wells Fargo** · 3480 S La Brea Ave
- **Wells Fargo** · 3649 Stocker St

Car Rental

- **Enterprise** · 3318 S La Cienega Blvd
- **U-Haul** · 2451 Crenshaw Blvd

Car Washes

- **Crenshaw Car Wash** · 4220 Crenshaw Blvd
- **Slauson Hand Car Wash** · 3615 W Slauson Ave

Gas Stations

- **76** · 4856 W Slauson Ave
- **76** · 5100 W Jefferson Blvd
- **Arco** · 3412 Crenshaw Blvd
- **Arco** · 4406 Adams Blvd
- **Arco** · 4661 W Slauson Ave
- **Arco** · 5884 Washington Blvd
- **Chevron** · 2538 Crenshaw Blvd
- **Chevron** · 2546 S La Brea Ave
- **Chevron** · 3063 Crenshaw Blvd
- **Chevron** · 3742 S La Brea Ave
- **Chevron** · 4701 W Slauson Ave
- **Independent** · 3300 S La Cienega Blvd
- **Mobil** · 3950 W Martin Luther King Jr Blvd
- **Mobil** · 4380 W Adams Blvd
- **Mobil** · 5776 Washington Blvd
- **Shell** · 2545 S Crenshaw Blvd
- **Shell** · 3645 Crenshaw Blvd
- **Shell** · 4660 W Slauson Ave

Landmarks

- **Baldwin Hills Village Oil Wells** · East of La Cienega Blvd
- **Kenneth Hahn State Recreation Area** · 4100 S La Cienega Blvd

Libraries

- **Baldwin Hills Branch** · 2906 S La Brea Ave · 323-733-1196
- **View Park** · 3854 W 54th St · 323-293-5371

Pharmacies

- **Rite-Aid** · 3550 S La Brea Ave · 323-293-9397
- **Rite-Aid** · 3566 Rodeo Pl · 323-295-3323

- **Sav-On** · 3741 Crenshaw Blvd · 323-298-5595
- **Sav-On** · 4501 W Slauson Ave · 323-292-4114
- **Sav-On** · 5101 W Rodeo Dr · 323-936-0279
- **Sav-On (Albertsons)** · 3901 Crenshaw Blvd · 323-295-1919
- **Target** · 3535 La Cienega Blvd · 310-895-1132

Post Offices

- 3650 W Martin Luther King Jr Blvd ·
- 3894 Crenshaw Blvd ·

Schools

- **54th St Elementary** · 5501 Eileen Ave
- **Alpha Elementary** · 5252 W Adams Blvd
- **Applied Learning Academy** · 3855 W Slauson Ave
- **Ascension Lutheran** · 5820 West Blvd
- **Baldwin Hills Elementary** · 5421 Rodeo Rd
- **CCDC of Little Angels** · 3808 W 54th St
- **Cienega Elementary** · 2611 S Orange Dr
- **Cleophas Oliver Learning Center** · 4449 W Adams Blvd
- **Coliseum St Elementary** · 4400 Coliseum St
- **Communion Christian Academy (second location)** · 4729 W Slauson Ave
- **Ebony Learning Tree** · 3906 W Slauson Ave
- **Foundation for the Junior Blind** · 5300 Angeles Vista Blvd
- **Hillcrest Dr Elementary** · 4041 Hillcrest Dr
- **Marlton Elementary** · 4000 Santo Tomas Dr
- **New Designs (MS)** · 3770 Santa Rosalia Dr
- **Progressive Education Entrepreneurial Charter School** · 2600 S La Brea Ave
- **Slausen Learning Center** · 4000 W Slauson Ave
- **Southern California Prep Academy** · 4300 W Slauson Ave
- **St Bernadette Elementary** · 4196 Marlton Ave
- **Stella Middle Charter** · 2636 Mansfield Ave
- **Susan Miller Dorsey Senior High** · 3537 Farmdale Ave
- **View Park Continuation** · 4701 Rodeo Rd
- **View Park Preparatory Accelerated Charter** · 3751 W 54th St
- **View Park Preparatory Accelerated Middle** · 5753 Rodeo Rd
- **Virginia Rd Elementary** · 2925 Virginia Rd
- **West Angeles Christian Academy** · 3010 S Crenshaw Blvd
- **Wilkerson Academy of Learning** · 3740 Don Felipe Dr
- **Windsor Hills Math & Science Elementary** · 5215 Overdale Dr

Supermarkets

- **Albertsons** · 3480 S La Brea Ave
- **Albertsons** · 3901 Crenshaw Blvd
- **Ralphs** · 3670 Crenshaw Blvd
- **Ralphs** · 5080 Rodeo Rd
- **Ranch Market** · 5212 W Adams Blvd
- **Smart & Final** · 2929 Crenshaw Blvd

Map 10 • Baldwin Hills

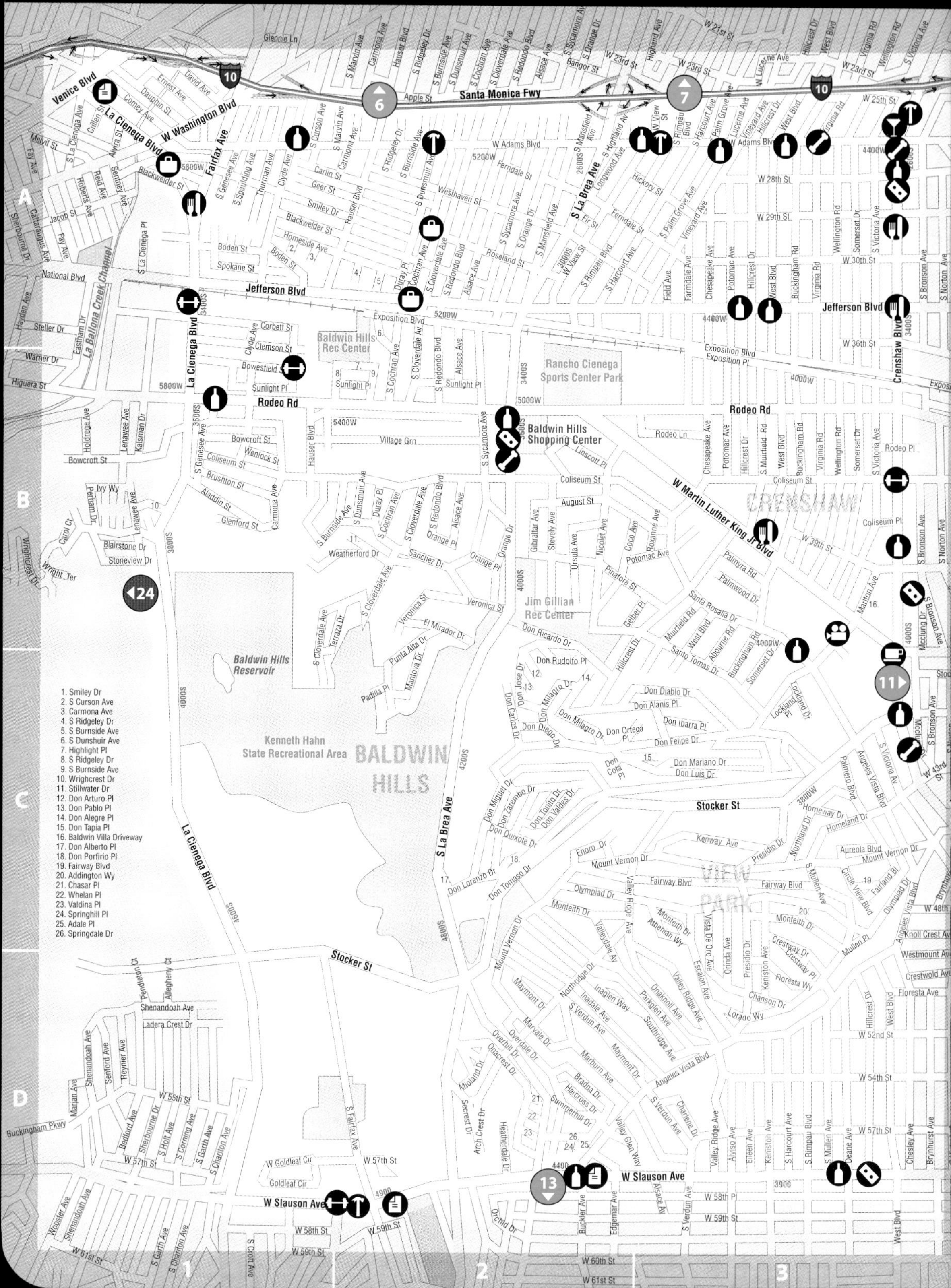

N

1. Smiley Dr
2. S Curson Ave
3. Carmona Ave
4. S Ridgeley Dr
5. S Burnside Ave
6. S Dunshuir Ave
7. Highlight Pl
8. S Ridgeley Dr
9. S Burnside Ave
10. Wrighcrest Dr
11. Stillwater Dr
12. Don Arturo Pl
13. Don Pablo Pl
14. Don Alegre Pl
15. Don Tapia Pl
16. Baldwin Villa Driveway
17. Don Alberto Pl
18. Don Porfirio Pl
19. Fairway Blvd
20. Addington Wy
21. Chasar Pl
22. Whelan Pl
23. Valdina Pl
24. Springhill Pl
25. Adale Pl
26. Springdale Dr

BALDWIN
HILLS

Kenneth Hahn
State Recreational Area

Baldwin Hills
Reservoir

CRENSHAW

VIEW PARK

Baldwin Hills
Rec Center

Rancho Cienega
Sports Center Park

Baldwin Hills
Shopping Center

Jim Gillian
Rec Center

Perched atop Baldwin Hills, Kenneth Hahn State Recreation Area flies under the radar of even longtime Angelenos. But its five miles of hiking trails, many playgrounds, and stocked fishing pond get heavy use on weekends. The surrounding oil fields will become part of the park when the wells dry up—estimated to be in about 2030.

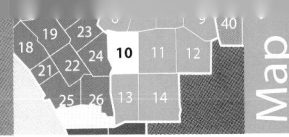

Coffee

- **Krispy Kreme Doughnuts** · 4034 Crenshaw Blvd

Copy Centers

- **Copies Plus** · 4401 W Slauson Ave · 323-296-1470
- **Efiximage** · 2632 S La Cienega Blvd · 310-559-2200
- **UPS Store** · 4859 W Slauson St · 323-291-4800

Gyms

- **24-Hour Fitness** · 5045 W Slauson Ave · 323-293-2481
- **Curves** · 3485 La Cienega Blvd · 310-558-0912
- **Curves** · 3737 S Crenshaw Blvd · 323-295-3737

Hardware Stores

- **Ace** · 2620 Crenshaw Blvd · 323-733-9157
- **Home Depot** · 4925 W Slauson Ave · 323-298-1155
- **Slater Hardware** · 5365 W Adams Blvd · 323-932-1942
- **Sonora Hardware** · 4860 W Adams Blvd · 323-766-1396

Liquor Stores

- **Adam's Liquor** · 4620 W Adams Blvd
- **Arcade Liquor** · 4431 W Slauson Ave
- **Baldwin Hills Liquor** · 3629 S La Brea Ave
- **Bell's Liquor** · 3869 Santa Rosalia Dr
- **Bottle Bar Liquors** · 2642 Crenshaw Blvd
- **Cabin Liquor Store** · 5633 W Adams Blvd
- **Gubby's Liquor** · 4800 W Adams Blvd
- **Holiday Liquor** · 4966 W Adams Blvd
- **Janet's Liquor** · 4028 W Jefferson Blvd
- **Liquor, Bank & Deli** · 3600 Stocker St
- **PG's Liquor** · 4407 W Jefferson Blvd
- **T&D Liquor** · 3860 W Slauson Ave
- **Tag's Liquor** · 3866 Crenshaw Blvd
- **Wine Cellar** · 5747 Rodeo Rd

Movie Theaters

- **Loews Magic Johnson Theatre 15** · 4020 Marlton Ave · 323-290-5900

Nightlife

- **Café Club Fais Do-Do** · 5257 W Adams Blvd · 323-954-8080
- **The Living Room** · 2636 Crenshaw Blvd · 323-735-8748

Pet Stores

- **James' Tropical Fish** · 4273 Crenshaw Blvd · 323-294-6490
- **Pets Planet** · 3651 S La Brea Ave · 323-293-1212
- **Tokyo Aquarium** · 4600 W Adams Blvd · 323-735-7553

Restaurants

- **Stevie's Creole Café** · 3403 Crenshaw Blvd · 323-734-6975
- **Tasty Q** · 2959 Crenshaw Blvd · 323-735-8325

Shopping

- **Bebere Imports** · 3049 S La Cienega Blvd · 310-842-3842
- **Graphaids** · 3030 S La Cienega Blvd · 310-204-1212
- **Normandie Pate** · 3022 S Cochran Ave · 323-939-5528

Video Rental

- **Home Video Club** · 2803 Crenshaw Blvd · 323-730-1322
- **LA Hit Video** · 3653 S La Brea Ave · 323-290-1655
- **Rick's Video** · 3608 W Slauson Ave · 323-299-2950
- **Video Club** · 4130 Crenshaw Blvd · 323-294-8997

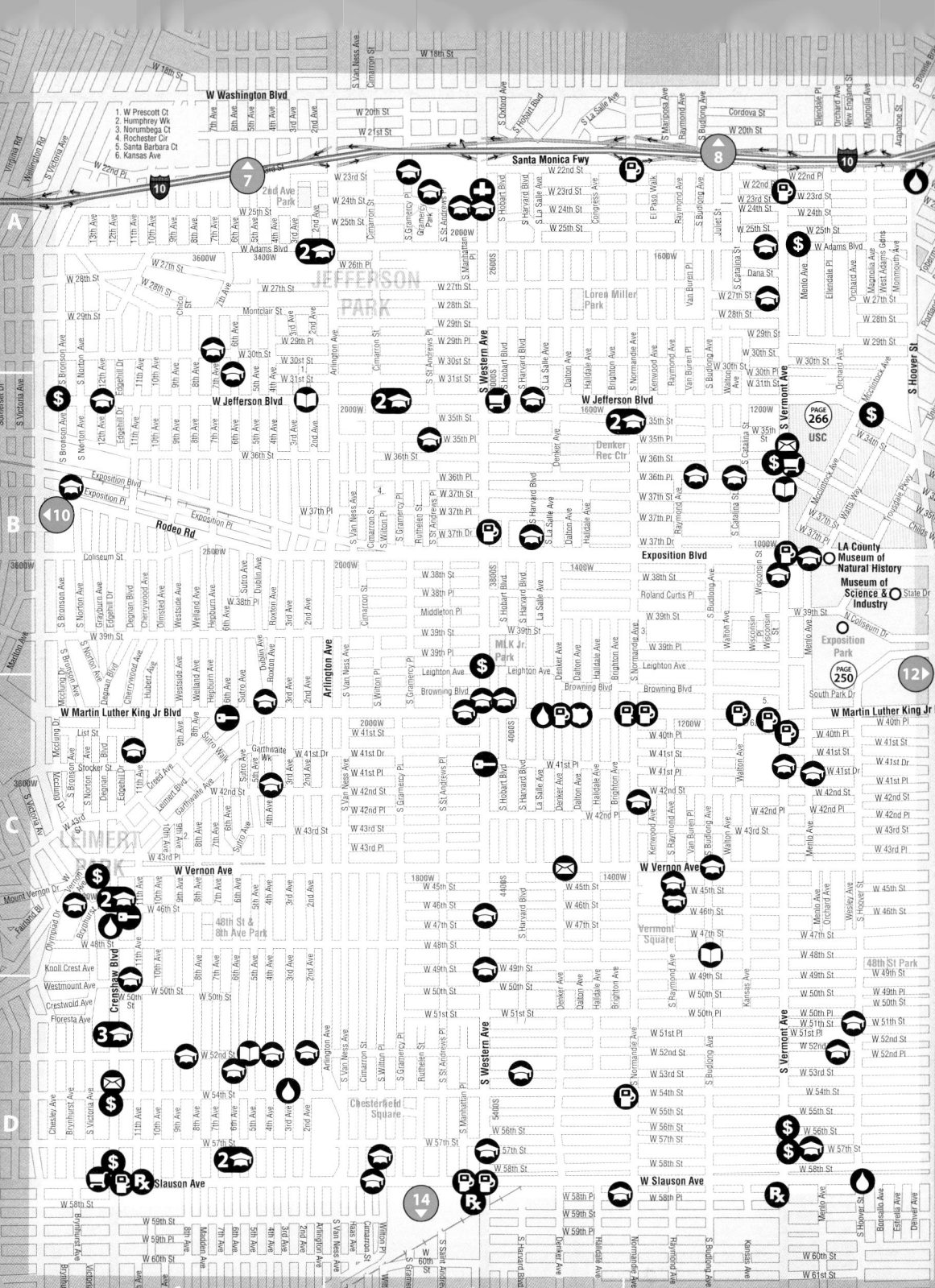

This area is home to USC. If you've never visited, you may find the lovely architecture (abundant red brick) and landscaping to be a bit of a surprise. Check local listings for on-campus concerts, lectures, and sporting events (many of which are free). And, lest we forget: go Trojans.

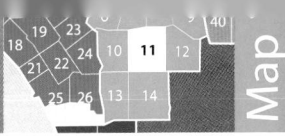
$ Banks
- **Bank of America** • 4103 S Western Ave
- **Bank of America** • 5471 Crenshaw Blvd
- **Bank of America** • 5700 S Vermont Ave
- **Bank of America** • 985 W Jefferson Blvd
- **Citibank** • 3615 S Vermont Ave
- **Downey Savings & Loan** • 2600 S Vermont Ave
- **Union** • 3501 W Jefferson Blvd
- **US** • 5760 Crenshaw Blvd
- **Washington Mutual** • 4401 Crenshaw Blvd
- **Washington Mutual** • 5717 S Vermont Ave

Car Rental
- **Enterprise** • 4610 Crenshaw Blvd
- **Trouble Free** • 2814 W Martin Luther King Jr Blvd
- **U-Haul** • 4167 S Western Ave

Car Washes
- **A Moment's Notice Hand Carwash** • 4727 Crenshaw Blvd
- **Red Carpet Carwash** • 1620 W Martin Luther King Jr Blvd
- **V&A Car Wash** • 5845 S Hoover St

Gas Stations
- **76** • 3774 S Western Ave
- **76** • 5816 S Western Ave
- **Arco** • 1355 W Martin Luther King Jr Blvd
- **Arco** • 3775 S Vermont St
- **Arco** • 5407 S Normandie Ave
- **Arco** • 5804 Crenshaw Blvd
- **Chevron** • 1100 W Martin Luther King Jr Blvd
- **Chevron** • 2202 S Vermont Ave
- **Independent** • 1515 W Martin Luther King Jr Blvd
- **Shell** • 1010 W Martin Luther King Jr Blvd
- **Shell** • 1404 W Martin Luther King Jr Blvd
- **Valero** • 2217 S Normandie Ave

Landmarks
- **Exposition Park** • Menlo Ave & S Park Dr
- **LA County Museum of Natural History** • 900 Exposition Blvd
- **Museum of Science & Industry** • 700 State Dr

Libraries
- **Angeles Mesa** • 2700 W 52nd St • 323-292-4328
- **Exposition Park Branch** • 3665 S Vermont Ave • 323-732-0169
- **Jefferson Branch** • 2211 W Jefferson Blvd • 323-734-8573
- **Vermont Square Branch** • 1201 W 48th St • 323-290-7405

Pharmacies
- **Rite-Aid** • 3230 W Slauson Ave • 323-295-9661
- **Sav-On** • 5822 S Vermont Ave • 323-750-5222
- **Walgreens** • 1800 W Slauson Ave • 323-292-1941

Police
- **Los Angeles Police Dept** • 1546 W Martin Luther King Jr Blvd • 213-485-2582

Post Offices
- 1515 W Vernon Ave
- 3585 S Vermont Ave
- 5472 Crenshaw Blvd

Schools
- **24th St EEC** • 2101 W 24th St
- **24th St Elementary** • 2055 W 24th St
- **36th St EEC** • 3556 S St Andrews Pl
- **37th St Children** • 1204 W 36th Pl
- **42nd St Elementary** • 4231 4th Ave
- **52nd St EEC** • 901 W 52nd St
- **52nd St Elementary** • 816 W 51st St
- **6th Ave EEC** • 3124 7th Ave
- **Al Madinah** • 3510 Exposition Pl
- **Angeles Mesa Elementary** • 2611 W 52nd St
- **Ashanti Christian Academy** • 2801 W 54th St
- **Audubon Middle** • 4120 11th Ave
- **Believers Christian Academy** • 3500 S Normandie Ave
- **Birdielee V Bright Elementary** • 1771 W 36th St
- **Breckenridge** • 1216 W Vernon Ave
- **Burton Green** • 3787 S Vermont Ave
- **Cecil L Murray Educational Center** • 2400 S Western Ave
- **College-Ready Academy High** • 1729 W Martin Luther King Jr Blvd
- **Community Harvest Charter** • 3202 W Adams Blvd
- **Crenshaw Arts-Technology High** • 4625 Crenshaw Blvd
- **Crenshaw Arts-Technology HS** • 5125 Crenshaw Blvd
- **Crenshaw Montessori Academy** • 4914 Crenshaw Blvd
- **Crenshaw Senior High** • 5010 11th Ave
- **Crenshaw Tot Academy** • 5150 Crenshaw Blvd
- **Culture & Language Academy** • 5760 6th Ave
- **Dorothy Brown** • 3502 S Normandie Ave
- **Foshay Learning Center** • 3751 S Harvard Blvd
- **Golden Day** • 4476 Crenshaw Blvd
- **Holy Name of Jesus Elementary** • 1955 W Jefferson Blvd
- **Joseph Pomeroy Widney High** • 2302 S Gramercy Pl
- **Lenicia B Weemes Elementary** • 1260 W 36th Pl
- **Leon Garr Learning Institute** • 5101 S Western Ave
- **Lewis Metropolitan Christian** • 4900 S Western Ave
- **Little Citizens Westside Academy** • 4256 S Western Ave
- **Little Lamb–Lamb of God Christ** • 5720 S Wilton Pl
- **Little Scholars** • 1712 W Jefferson Blvd
- **Manual Arts Senior High** • 4131 S Vermont Ave
- **Marcus Garvey** • 5760 6th Ave
- **Marie Fegan** • 2069 W Slauson Ave
- **Martin Luther King Jr Elementary** • 3989 S Hobart Blvd
- **Menlo Ave Elementary** • 4156 Menlo Ave
- **Mid-City Magnet** • 3150 W Adams Blvd
- **Nativity** • 943 W 57th St
- **Normandie Ave Elementary** • 4505 S Raymond Ave
- **Normandie EEC** • 4407 S Raymond Ave
- **Owens Community Day** • 2400 W 54th St
- **Parks/Huerta Primary** • 1020 W 58th Pl
- **Perry-Meadows Learning Center** • 1986 W Jefferson Blvd
- **Sixth Ave Elementary** • 3109 6th Ave
- **St Agnes Elementary** • 1428 W Adams Blvd
- **St Cecilia Elementary** • 4224 S Normandie Ave
- **Testimonial Christian** • 5701 S Western Ave
- **Today's Fresh Start** • 4470 Crenshaw Blvd
- **Transfiguration** • 4020 Roxton Ave
- **United World Christian Educational Center** • 5125 Crenshaw Blvd
- **University of Southern California** • Trousdale Pkwy
- **Vermont Ave Elementary** • 1435 W 27th St
- **West Adams Academy** • 900 Exposition Blvd
- **Western Ave Elementary** • 1724 W 53rd St
- **Westside Academy / Little Citizens** • 3411 12th Ave
- **Whitney Young Continuation** • 3051 W 52nd St

Supermarkets
- **Food 4 Less** • 1748 S Jefferson Blvd
- **Food 4 Less** • 1820 W Slauson Ave
- **Ralphs** • 2600 S Vermont Ave
- **Ralphs** • 3300 W Slauson Ave
- **Ralphs** • 4030 S Western Ave
- **Smart & Final** • 3607 S Vermont Ave

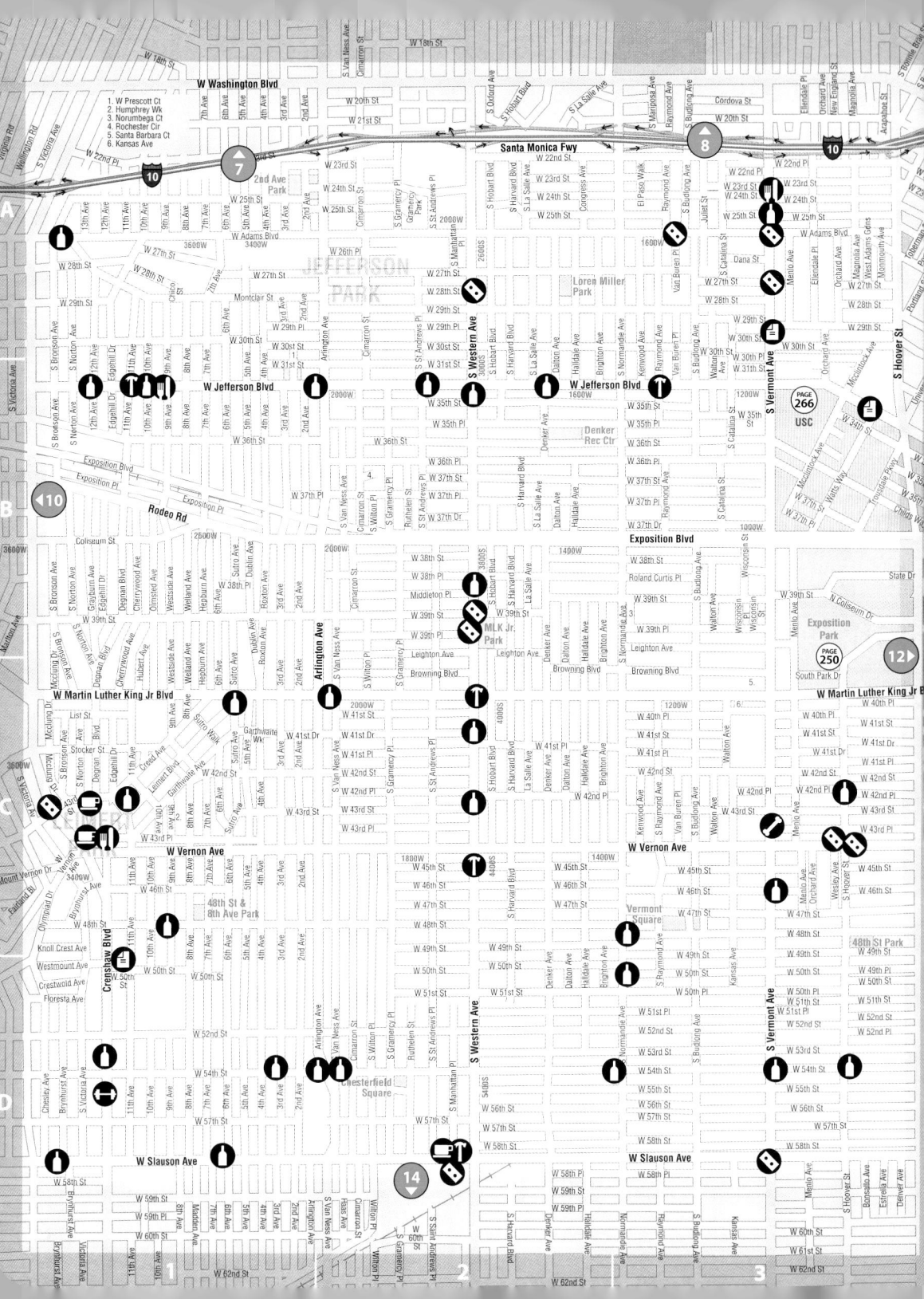

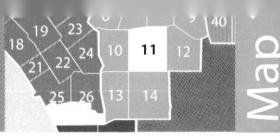

Harold & Belle's Restaurant may have the best Cajun and Creole cooking this side of the Mississippi: go for the gumbo. Leimert Park Village (bordered by Vernon Avenue, Crenshaw Boulevard, 43rd Street, and Leimert Boulevard) is a shopping and arts district with an emphasis on African-American culture. If you check the area out, you'll find awesome jazz clubs, sidewalk chess games, and terrific soul food. Adjacent to USC, Exposition Park features an admirable rose garden, and the Natural History Museum does a fine job making things interesting for the kids.

# Coffee

- **Lucy Florence Coffee House** • 4305 Degnan Blvd
- **Starbucks** • 1850 W Slauson Ave
- **Sunny's Spott** • 3349 W 43rd Pl

# Copy Centers

- **Awesome Print Copy & Graphic Design** • 4936 Crenshaw Blvd • 323-292-0352
- **Copies Ink** • 907 W Jefferson Blvd • 213-744-1511
- **SC College Printing & Stationery** • 2928 S Vermont Ave • 323-732-8055

Farmer's Markets

- **St Agnes Catholic Church** • 1432 W Adams

Gyms

- **Black Diamond Fitness** • 5436 Crenshaw Blvd • 323-291-0294

Hardware Stores

- **Bravo's Hardware** • 1439 W Jefferson Blvd • 323-735-3777
- **Home Depot** • 1830 W Slauson Ave • 323-292-1397
- **J&J Hardware** • 1755 W Martin Luther King Jr Blvd • 323-290-0909
- **Peterson's True Value** • 4823 S Western Ave • 323-292-5310
- **RPM Hardware & Lumber** • 3001 W Jefferson Blvd • 323-737-6282
- **Tak's Hardware** • 3318 W Jefferson Blvd • 323-732-6966
- **True Value** • 2929 S Vermont Ave • 323-734-4477

# Liquor Stores

- **7 Kings Liquor** • 4051 Leimert Blvd
- **ABIC Liquor** • 3115 S Western Ave
- **Century Liquor** • 2115 W Jefferson Blvd
- **Century Liquor** • 2301 W 54th St
- **Century Liquor** • 3894 S Western Ave
- **F&J Liquor** • 5360 Crenshaw Blvd
- **Fairway Liquor** • 5400 S Hoover St
- **Fifty-Fourth Van Ness** • 2201 W 54th St
- **Ford's Liquor & Deli** • 4629 S Western Ave
- **G&I Liquor** • 3504 W Slauson Ave
- **Gee-Gee Liquors** • 5028 S Normandie Ave
- **Hubert's Liquor** • 4307 Leimert Blvd
- **Jesse's Liquor** • 2527 W 54th St
- **John's Liquor** • 2428 S Vermont Ave
- **Kenny's Liquor** • 3104 W 48th St
- **LA Liquor** • 1403 W 54th St
- **Lucky Liquor** • 2109 W Martin Luther King Jr Blvd
- **Marvin's Liquor & Deli** • 1650 W Jefferson Blvd
- **Saki Liquor** • 3300 W Jefferson Blvd

- **Slauson Liquor** • 2825 W Slauson Ave
- **St Andrew's Liquor** • 1894 W Jefferson Blvd
- **T's Liquor** • 3019 W Jefferson Blvd
- **Two & One Liquor** • 4829 S Normandie Ave
- **West-Vern Liquor** • 4381 S Western Ave
- **Wine Barrel Liquors** • 4250 S Hoover St

# Movie Theaters

- **California Science Center IMAX** • 700 State Dr • 213-748-6321

Nightlife

- **Babe's Ricky Inn** • 4339 Leimert Blvd • 323-295-9112

Pet Stores

- **Tong's Tropical Fish & Pets** • 4327 S Vermont Ave • 323-235-4370

# Restaurants

- **Harold & Belle's** • 2920 W Jefferson Blvd • 323-735-3376
- **La Barca** • 2414 S Vermont Ave • 323-735-6567
- **Phillip's Barbecue** • 4307 Leimert Blvd • 323-292-7613

Video Rental

- **Alpha Video** • 807 W Vernon Ave • 323-233-8930
- **Blockbuster** • 1852 W Slauson Ave • 323-290-7691
- **Blockbuster** • 4299 Crenshaw Blvd • 323-295-7233
- **Blockbuster** • 728 W Vernon Ave • 323-238-0146
- **Cocos Video** • 3951 S Western Ave • 323-299-9386
- **Echo Video & Mini Mart** • 2701 S Western Ave • 323-735-7411
- **Johnny's Video** • 2709 S Vermont Ave • 323-733-0862
- **Omni Video** • 5862 S Vermont Ave • 323-759-7100
- **Video World** • 2604 S Vermont Ave • 323-733-1877

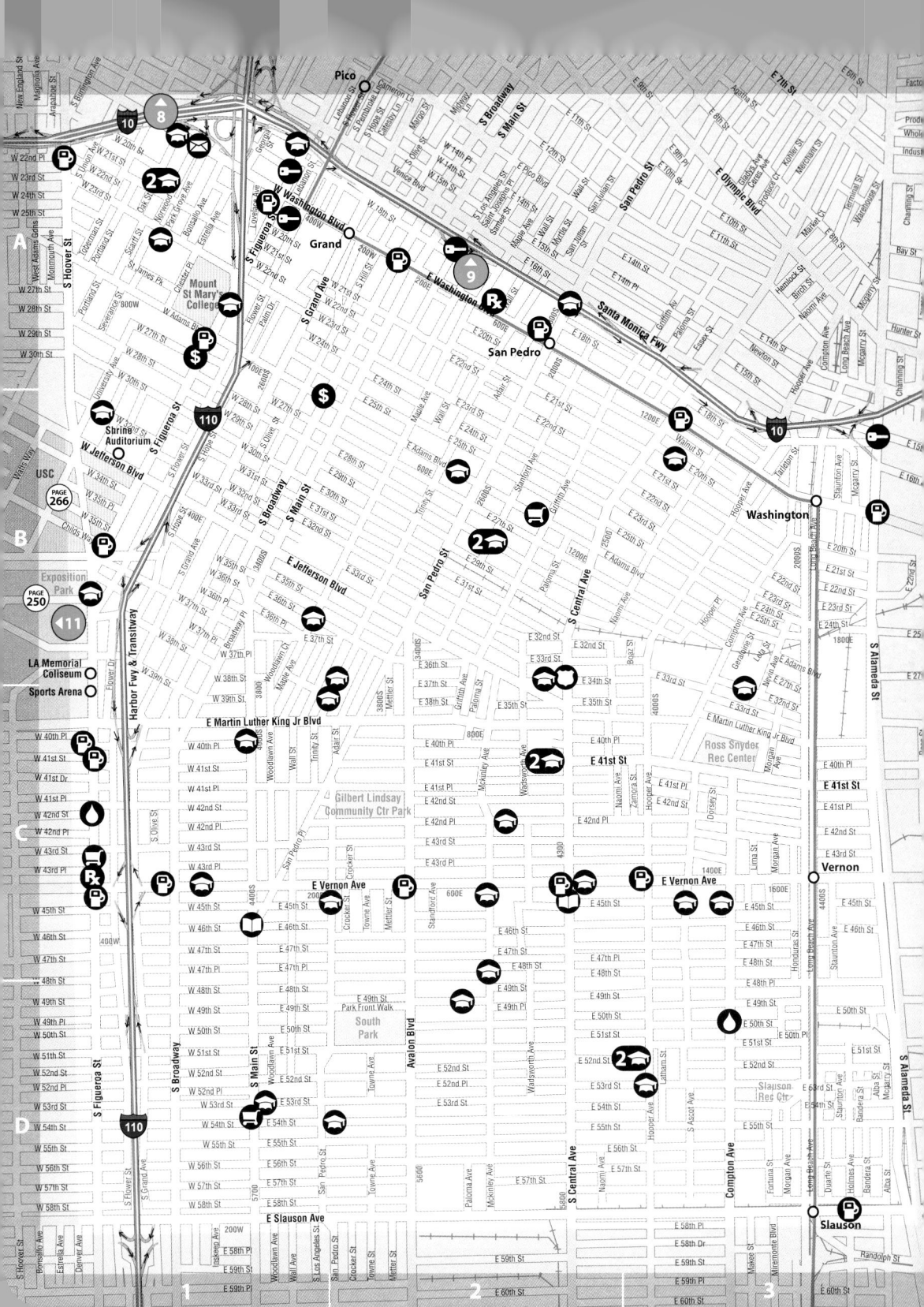

Most Angelenos are familiar with this area for one reason: the Shrine Auditorium, which frequently hosts film industry events, along with the occasional rock concert. It may surprise many to know that the Shrine Auditorium is used most often by the Shriners (go figure!). The Shrine's vast size and unique appearance, which resembles a mosque, make it a great landmark when navigating the area or giving directions.

$ Banks
- **Bank of America** · 2703 S Figueroa St
- **Broadway Federal** · 4001 S Figueroa St
- **Wells Fargo** · 141 W Adams Blvd

Car Rental
- **Downtown Rent-a-Car** · 1740 S Los Angeles St
- **Enterprise** · 1801 S Figueroa St
- **Enterprise** · 1944 S Figueroa St
- **Ryder Truck Rental** · 1508 S Alameda St

Car Washes
- **Figueroa Car Wash** · 4200 S Figueroa St
- **Martinez Hand Car Wash** · 5000 Compton Ave

Gas Stations
- **76** · 1900 S Broadway
- **76** · 505 W Vernon Ave
- **Arco** · 1800 E Slauson Ave
- **Arco** · 2211 S Hoover St
- **Arco** · 4424 S Central Ave
- **Arco** · 4442 S Avalon Blvd
- **Chevron** · 3584 S Figueroa St
- **Chevron** · 4000 S Figueroa St
- **Chevron** · 525 W Washington Blvd
- **Chevron** · 650 E Washington Blvd
- **Mobil** · 1690 S Alameda St
- **Mobil** · 2620 S Figueroa St
- **Mobil** · 315 W Vernon Ave
- **Shell** · 1285 E Vernon Ave
- **Shell** · 1317 E Washington Blvd
- **Shell** · 4403 S Figueroa St

Landmarks
- **LA Memorial Coliseum** · 3911 S Figueroa St
- **Shrine Auditorium** · 665 W Jefferson Blvd
- **Sports Arena** · 3939 S Figueroa St

Libraries
- **Junipero Serra Branch** · 4607 S Main St · 323-234-1685
- **Vernon Branch** · 4504 S Central Ave · 323-234-9106

Pharmacies
- **Rite-Aid** · 4322 S Figueroa St · 323-235-3535
- **Rite-Aid** · 446 E Washington Blvd · 213-747-9581

Police
- **Los Angeles Police Dept** · 3400 S Central Ave · 323-846-6524

Post Offices
- 819 W Washington Blvd

Schools
- **20th St Elementary** · 1353 E 20th St
- **28th St EEC** · 747 E 28th St
- **28th St Elementary** · 2807 Stanford Ave
- **49th St Elementary** · 750 E 49th St
- **Accelerated School** · 116 E Martin Luther King Jr Blvd
- **Arco Iris Primary Center** · 4504 Ascot Ave
- **Ascot Ave Elementary** · 1447 E 45th St
- **Central Continuation** · 644 W 17th St
- **Downtown Value** · 950 W Washington Blvd
- **Dr Theodore T Alexander Jr Science Center** · 3737 S Figueroa St
- **George Washington Carver Middle** · 4410 McKinley Ave
- **Hooper Ave Elementary** · 1225 E 52nd St
- **Hooper EEC** · 1224 E 52nd St
- **Jefferson New Elementary** · 899 E 42nd St
- **Jefferson New PC #6** · 3601 Maple Ave
- **John Adams Middle** · 151 W 30th St
- **Johnson Community Day** · 333 E 54th St
- **La Senda Antigua Charter** · 631 E Adams Blvd
- **Lanterman High** · 2328 St James Pl
- **Los Angeles Academy Middle** · 644 E 56th St
- **Main St Elementary** · 129 E 53rd St
- **Mount St Mary's College–Doheny Campus** · 10 Chester Pl
- **Nevin Ave Elementary** · 1569 E 32nd St
- **Norwood EEC** · 855 W 21st St
- **Norwood St Elementary** · 2020 Oak St
- **Page Multicultural Learning Academy** · 216 W Vernon Ave
- **Roberti EEC** · 1156 E Vernon Ave
- **San Pedro St Elementary** · 1635 S San Pedro St
- **Solid Front for Unity** · 425 E Vernon Ave
- **St Odilia** · 5300 Hooper Ave
- **St Vincent Elementary** · 2333 S Figueroa St
- **Synergy Charter** · 1010 E 34th St
- **Temple Baptist Church Star Charter** · 2120 Estella Ave
- **Thomas Jefferson Senior High** · 1319 E 41st St
- **Trinity EEC** · 3816 Trinity St
- **Trinity St Elementary** · 3736 Trinity St
- **University of Southern California** · Trousdale Pkwy
- **USC Performing Arts** · 822 W 32nd St
- **Victory Baptist Day** · 4802 McKinley Ave
- **Wadsworth Ave Elementary** · 981 E 41st St
- **Wadsworth EEC** · 1047 E 41st St
- **West Vernon Ave Elementary** · 4312 S Grand Ave

Supermarkets
- **Food 4 Less** · 5318 S Main St
- **Jons Supermarket** · 1011 E Adams Blvd
- **Ralphs** · 4360 S Figueroa St

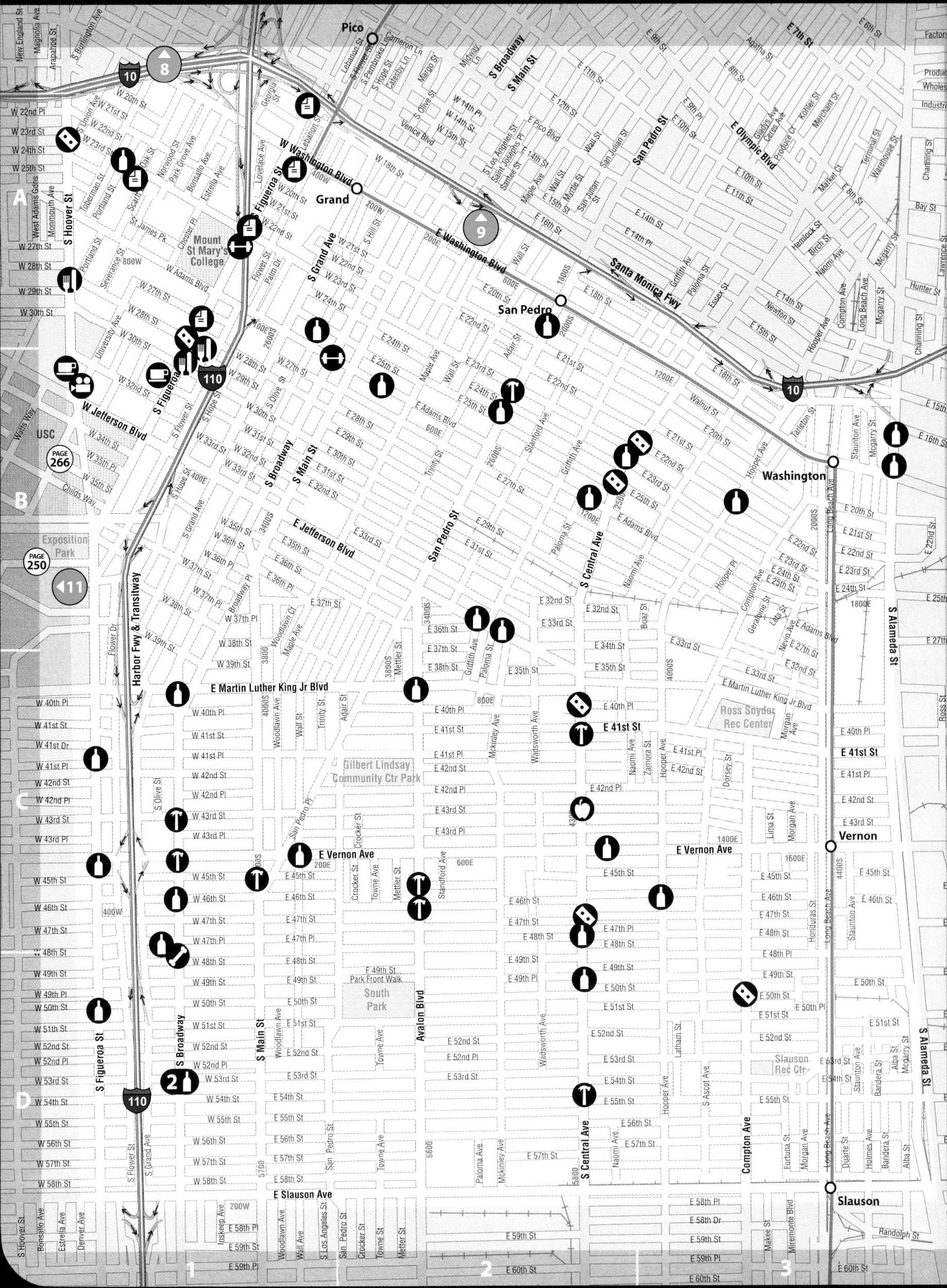

Map 12 · **South Central East**

Pico

W 22nd Pl
W 23rd St
W 24th St

New England St
Arapahoe St
S Burlington Ave
Magnolia Ave

10 **8**

W Washington Blvd

A

Grand

S Hoover St
Monmouth Ave
West Adams Gdns
Toberman St
Portland St
Scarff St

W 27th St
W 28th St
W 29th St
W 30th St

Figueroa Ln
Lovelace Ave

W 18th St

W 20th St

Mount
St Mary's
College

Grand

S Grand Ave
S Hope St

E Washington Blvd

Santa Monica Fwy

S Broadway
S Main St
E 11th St

E 12th St
E 14th St
E 15th St

Pico Blvd

Wall St

San Pedro St
San Julian St
Maple Ave

E Olympic Blvd

Long Beach Ave
Compton Ave
Mogarry St

9

San Pedro

E 21st St
E 22nd St

Washington

10

E 15th St
E 16th St

USC

W Jefferson Blvd

Watts St

B

Exposition
Park

PAGE
266

PAGE
250

11

E Jefferson Blvd

San Pedro St

S Central Ave

Hooper Ave

Long Beach Ave
Staunton Ave

S Alameda St

E 32nd St
E 33rd St
E 34th St
E 35th St

Ross Snyder
Rec Center

Gilbert Lindsay
Community Ctr Park

Harbor Fwy & Transitway

E Martin Luther King Jr Blvd

E 40th Pl

E 41st St

Vernon

C

Griffith Ave
Paloma Ave

E Vernon Ave

E Vernon Ave

South
Park

Avalon Blvd

S Central Ave

Compton Ave

Slauson
Rec Ctr

D

110

21

S Figueroa St
S Broadway
S Main St
Woodlawn Ave

E Slauson Ave

Slauson

1 **2** **3**

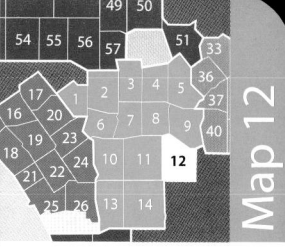

Following a controversial name change in 2003—dropping the "Central" in "South Central"—the newly monikered South LA is vying for your business. Try the 29th Street Café for weekend brunch, or tour this old LA neighborhood on the Metro where it goes overground.

Coffee

- **Coffee Factory** · 3014 S Figueroa St
- **Starbucks** · 3303 S Hoover St

Copy Centers

- **Kinko's** · 2723 S Figueroa St · 213-747-8341
- **Office Depot** · 2020 Figueroa St · 213-741-0576
- **Sir Speedy** · 900 W 23rd St · 310-212-6162
- **Staples** · 1701 S Figueroa St · 213-746-6330
- **UPS Store** · 2202 S Figueroa St · 213-749-1249

Farmer's Markets

- **Los Angeles Central Ave** · 43rd St & Central Ave

Gyms

- **Curves** · 2268 Figueroa St · 213-383-9111
- **Trojan Iron Work Weight Gym** · 158 W Adams Blvd · 213-746-9683

Hardware Stores

- **Avalon Tools & Supplies** · 4514 Avalon Blvd · 323-232-6516
- **Barbara's Hardware** · 4609 Avalon Blvd · 323-232-4514
- **Flores Hardware** · 4121 S Central Ave · 323-234-3623
- **Garcia Hardware** · 2414 S San Pedro St · 213-749-0992
- **Jalisco Hardware** · 5423 S Central Ave · 323-231-3340
- **Los Perritos Tools** · 4752 S Broadway · 323-232-1602
- **Main Building Materials** · 4308 S Broadway · 323-235-6253
- **Marce's** · 4500 S Main St · 323-233-9320

Liquor Stores

- **A&D Mini-Mart** · 4006 Avalon Blvd
- **A&J Liquors** · 200 E Vernon Ave
- **A&J Liquors** · 2527 S Hill St
- **Ace Liquors** · 2525 Griffith Ave
- **Bestway Liquors** · 4157 S Figueroa St
- **C&C Liquor** · 4606 S Broadway
- **Central Liquor** · 5000 S Central Ave
- **Express Liquor** · 1601 S Alameda St
- **Gordon's Liquors & Wines** · 842 E Jefferson Blvd
- **Harry's Corner** · 2315 S Central Ave
- **JKO Liquor** · 255 E Adams Blvd
- **Johnny's Liquor** · 4000 S Broadway
- **Jons Market** · 1011 E Adams Blvd
- **Kimbo Liquor** · 1161 E Vernon Ave
- **Koko's Liquor** · 5029 S Figueroa St
- **Lee's Liquor** · 936 W 23rd St
- **Los Altos Liquor** · 4625 Hooper Ave
- **Louie's Liquor** · 908 E Jefferson Blvd
- **Maple Liquor** · 2401 S San Pedro St
- **Peewee Liquor** · 5323 S Broadway
- **Reggie's Liquor & Junior Market** · 4426 S Figueroa St
- **Steve's Liquor** · 1501 E 22nd St
- **Toni's Liquor & Deli** · 5955 West Blvd
- **Wally's Liquor** · 1955 S San Pedro St
- **Webb's Liquor Store & Sundries** · 4762 S Central Ave

Movie Theaters

- **Flagship University Village 3** · 3323 S Hoover St · 213-748-6321

Pet Stores

- **Maria's Pet Shop** · 4757 S Broadway · 323-234-7887

Restaurants

- **29th Street Café** · 2827 S Hoover St · 213-746-2929
- **Chano's Drive-In** · 3000 S Figueroa St · 213-747-3944
- **Pasta Roma** · 2827 S Figueroa St · 213-742-0303

Video Rental

- **Central Video** · 2204 S Central Ave · 213-749-7716
- **Compton Video** · 5035 Compton Ave · 323-233-2822
- **Danny Boy Video** · 2506 S Central Ave · 323-234-4412
- **Eve's Video** · 4068 S Central Ave · 323-234-0473
- **Hernandez Video** · 4754 S Central Ave · 323-231-0213
- **Little Hollywood Video** · 1105 W 23rd St · 213-741-1303
- **Video Hits** · 2813 S Figueroa St · 213-748-2928

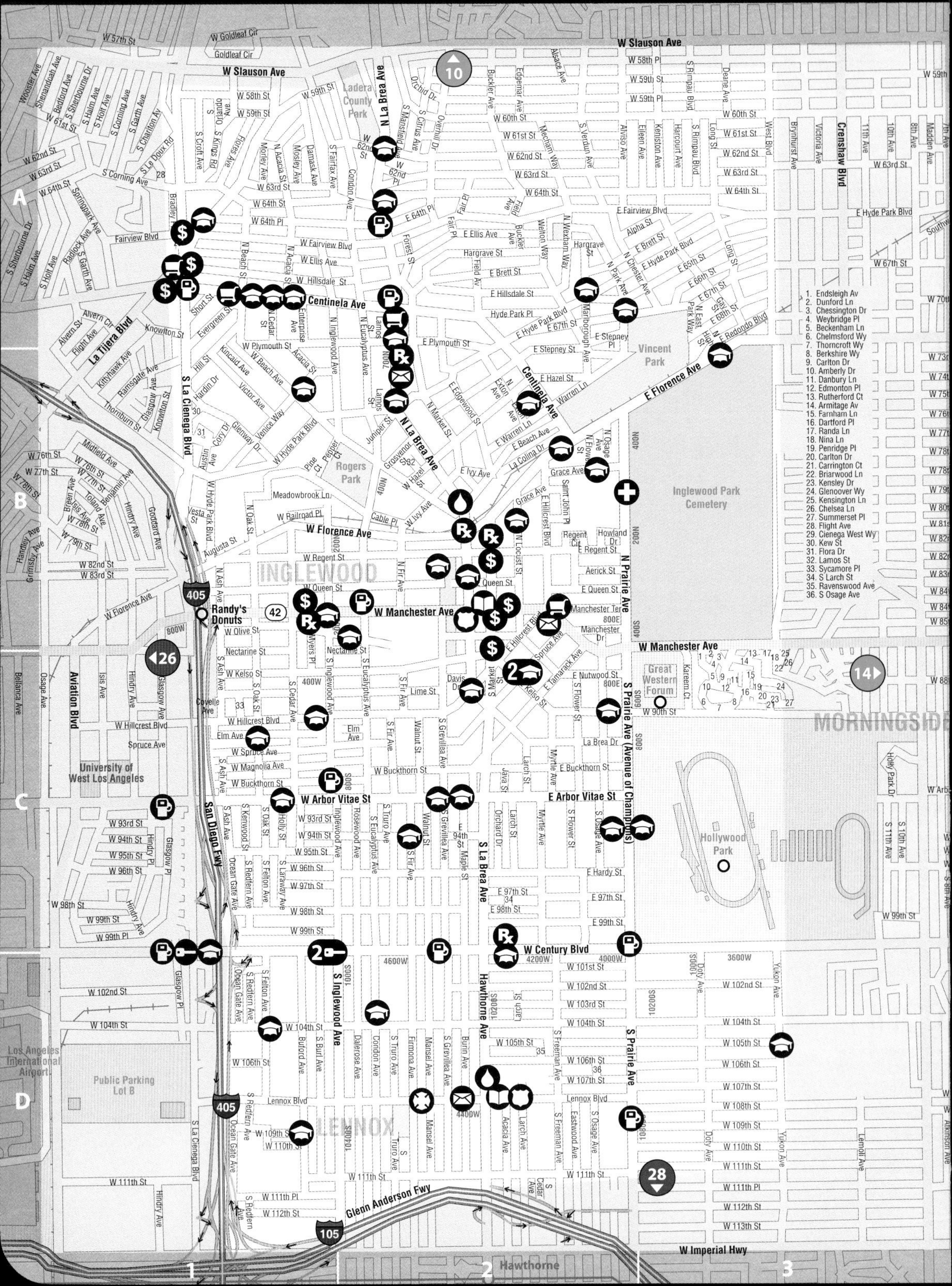

Map 13 · Inglewood

Street index:

1. Endsleigh Av
2. Dunford Ln
3. Chessington Dr
4. Weybridge Pl
5. Beckenham Ln
6. Chelmsford Wy
7. Thorncroft Wy
8. Berkshire Wy
9. Carlton Dr
10. Amberly Dr
11. Danbury Ln
12. Edmonton Pl
13. Rutherford Ct
14. Armitage Av
15. Farnham Ln
16. Dartford Pl
17. Rands Ln
18. Nina Ln
19. Penridge Pl
20. Carrington Ct
21. Carrington Ct
22. Briarwood Ln
23. Kensley Dr
24. Glenoover Wy
25. Kensington Ln
26. Chelsea Ln
27. Summerset Pl
28. Flight Av
29. Cienega West Wy
30. Kew St
31. Flora Dr
32. Lamos St
33. Sycamore St
34. S Larch St
35. Ravenswood Av
36. S Osage Av

W Slauson Ave
Ladera County Park
Rogers Park
Vincent Park
Inglewood Park Cemetery
INGLEWOOD
Randy's Donuts
405
26
42
University of West Los Angeles
San Diego Fwy
W Manchester Ave
W Arbor Vitae St
E Arbor Vitae St (Avenue of Champions)
Great Western Forum
MORNINGSIDE
14
Hollywood Park
W Century Blvd
Los Angeles International Airport
Public Parking Lot B
LENNOX
405
28
105
Glenn Anderson Fwy
W Imperial Hwy
Hawthorne

1   2   3

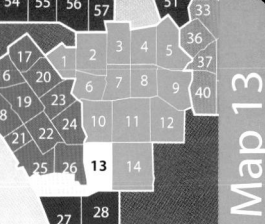
While north Inglewood's charming tree-lined avenues played stunt double for the Yourtown Midwest locale of Wayne's World, the rest of the city's grittiness reflects the loss of its adored Lakers. But if former Laker Magic Johnson has his way, Inglewood will gentrify yet. Magic gets the assist for bringing to the 'hood several Starbucks, 24-Hour Fitness, and assorted snazzy shopping centers.

$ Banks

- **Bank of America** · 330 E Manchester Blvd
- **Bank of America** · 6611 La Cienega Westway St
- **Broadway Federal** · 170 N Market St
- **Downey Savings & Loan** · 5245 Centinela Ave
- **Union** · 6719 La Tijera Blvd
- **US** · 500 E Manchester Blvd
- **Washington Mutual** · 355 E Manchester Blvd
- **Wells Fargo** · 400 S Market St

Car Rental

- **GA Car Rental** · 4840 W Century Blvd
- **Priceless Car Rental** · 4831 W Century Blvd

Car Washes

- **Inglewood Car Wash** · 320 N La Brea Ave
- **Lennox Car Wash** · 10709 Hawthorne Blvd

Gas Stations

- **76** · 400 W Arbor Vitae
- **76** · 4520 W Century Blvd
- **76** · 633 W Manchester Blvd
- **Arco** · 4130 W Century
- **Chevron** · 4015 W Century Blvd
- **Independent** · 1430 N La Brea Ave
- **Independent** · 145 E Manchester Blvd
- **Mobil** · 1007 N La Brea Ave
- **Mobil** · 1244 S Inglewood Ave
- **Mobil** · 5215 W Centinela Ave
- **Shell** · 10800 S Prairie Blvd

✚ Hospitals

- **Centinela** · 555 E Hardy St
- **Daniel Freeman Memorial** · 333 N Prairie Ave

o Landmarks

- **Great Western Forum** · Manchester Ave & Prairie Ave
- **Hollywood Park** · 1050 S Prairie Ave
- **Randy's Donuts** · 805 W Manchester Blvd

Libraries

- **Inglewood Public Library** · 101 W Manchester Blvd · 310-412-5380
- **Lennox** · 4359 Lennox Blvd · 310-674-0385

Rx Pharmacies

- **Sav-On** · 4345 W Century Blvd · 310-672-6072
- **Sav-On (24 hrs)** · 222 Market St · 310-671-0441
- **The Medicine Shoppe** · 923 N La Brea Ave · 310-412-6088
- **Vons** · 500 E Manchester Blvd · 310-677-0501
- **Walgreens (24 hrs)** · 230 N La Brea Ave · 310-671-2049

Police

- **Inglewood Police Dept** · 1 W Manchester Blvd · 310-412-5111
- **Los Angeles County Sheriff's Dept-Lennox Station** · 4331 W Lennox Blvd · 310-617-7531

✉ Post Offices

- 300 E Hillcrest Blvd
- 4443 Lennox Blvd
- 811 N La Brea Ave

Schools

- **Academy for Early Learning** · 1020 N Park Ave
- **AF Williams Christian Academy** · 1437 W Centinela Ave
- **Amino Inglewood Charter High** · 304 E Spruce Ave
- **Basics Plus Learning Academy** · 4323 W Century Blvd
- **Buelah Payne Elementary** · 215 W 94th St
- **Buford Elementary** · 4919 W 109th St
- **Centinela Elementary** · 1123 Marlborough Ave
- **Claude Hudnall Elementary** · 331 Olive St
- **Communion Christian Academy** · 6201 S La Brea Ave
- **Coporate Preparatory Academy** · 101 N La Brea Ave
- **The Extraordinary Place** · 421 Centinela Ave
- **Felton Elementary** · 10417 Felton Ave
- **Frank D Parent Elementary** · 5354 W 64th St
- **George W Crozier Junior High** · 151 N Grevillea Ave
- **Good Shepherd Lutheran** · 901 Maple Ave
- **Higher Learning Academy** · 534 W Arbor Vitae St
- **Highland Elementary** · 430 Venice Wy
- **Hillcrest High** · 441 W Hillcrest Blvd
- **Inglewood Ave Kindergarten** · 215 S Inglewood Ave
- **Inglewood Christian** · 215 E Hillcrest Blvd
- **Inglewood High** · 231 S Grevillea Ave
- **Jefferson Elementary** · 10322 Condon Ave
- **K Anthony's Middle** · 1003 S Prairie Ave
- **Kids' Castle Child Care Center** · 745 N La Brea Ave
- **La Tijera Elementary** · 1415 S La Tijera Blvd
- **The Learning Zone** · 901 E Redondo Blvd
- **Morningside High** · 10500 Yukon Ave
- **Oak St Elementary** · 633 S Oak St
- **Saluson Learning Center** · 260 N Locust St
- **St John Chrysotom Elementary** · 530 E Florence Ave
- **St Mary's Academy** · 701 Grace Ave
- **Tender Care Kindergarten** · 336 E Spruce Ave
- **University of Children** · 1518 Centinela Ave
- **Wilder's Preparatory Academy Charter** · 830 N La Brea Ave
- **WIlliam H Kelso Elementary** · 809 E Kelso St
- **Wiz** · 121 W Arbor Vitae
- **Worthington Elementary** · 11101 Yukon Ave

Supermarkets

- **Ralphs** · 5245 W Centinela Ave
- **Ralphs** · 950 N La Brea Ave
- **Smart & Final** · 1575 Centinela Ave
- **Vons** · 500 E Manchester Blvd

Map 13 • Inglewood

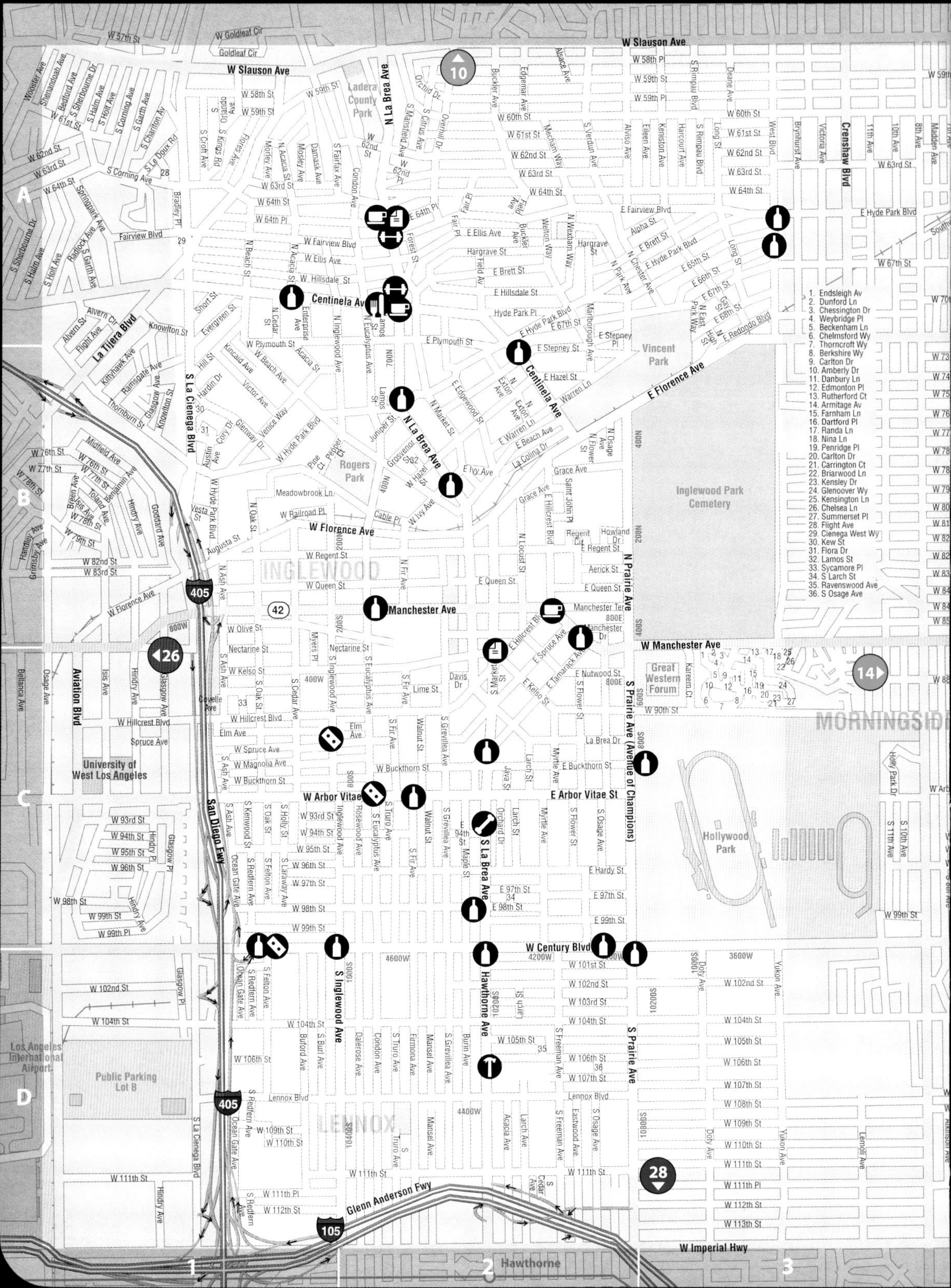

N

W 57th St
W Goldleaf Cir
Goldleaf Cir
W Slauson Ave
W Slauson Ave
W 58th Pl
W 58th St
W 59th St
W 58th St
W 59th St
W 59th St
W 59th St

Ladera
County
Park
W 60th St
W 61st St
W 60th St
W 61st St
W 61st St
W 62nd St
W 62nd St
W 62nd St
W 63rd St
W 62nd St
W 63rd St
W 63rd St
W 63rd St
W 63rd St

Fairview Blvd
W 64th St
W 64th St
E Fairview Blvd
E Hyde Park Blvd
W 64th Pl
W 64th St
W 64th Pl

W Fairview Blvd
E Ellis Ave
E Brett St
E Hyde Park Blvd
E 65th St
E 66th St
E Hyde Park Blvd

W Ellis Ave
Hargrave St
E Brett St
E 67th St
E 66th St
E Hyde Park Blvd
Centinela Ave
W Hilldale St
E Hillsdale St
E 67th St
E 67th St
E 66th St
E Redondo Blvd

Hyde Park Pl
E Hyde Park Blvd
E 67th St

W Plymouth St
E Plymouth St
E Stepney St

Vincent
Park

Centinela Ave
E Stepney St
E Hazel St
E Florence Ave
E Edgewood Ln
E Warren Ln
E Warren St
E Beach Ave
N Osage Ave
La Cana Ave

Rogers
Park
Grace Ave
Grace Ave
Saint John Pl
Hillcrest Blvd
Inglewood Park
Cemetery

Meadowbrook Av
Cable St
W Florence Ave
Regent
Howland Dr

INGLEWOOD
W Regent St
E Queen St
E Queen St
N Prairie Ave
W Manchester Ave
Manchester Ave
Manchester Ter
Manchester Dr
E Manchester
E Spruce Ave
Great
Western
Forum

Nectarine St
Nectarine St
Davis
Dr
E Nutwood St.
W 90th St
MORNINGSIDE

W Kelso St
Lime St
E Kelso St
La Brea Dr

Elm Ave
Walnut St
E Buckthorn St

W Arbor Vitae
Truro Ave
Walnut St
E Arbor Vitae St (Avenue of Champions)
Hollywood
Park

W 93rd St
W 94th St
W 94th St
W 95th St
E 94th St
E 97th St
E 99th St
W 99th St

W Century Blvd
W 101st St
W 102nd St
W 103rd St
W 105th St
Lennox Blvd

Public Parking
Lot B
LENNOX
W 109th St
W 110th St
W 111th St
W 111th Pl
W 112th St
Glenn Anderson Fwy
Hawthorne
W Imperial Hwy

1. Endsleigh Av
2. Dunford Ln
3. Chessington Dr
4. Weybridge Ln
5. Beckenham Ln
6. Chelmsford Wy
7. Thorncroft Wy
8. Berkshire Wy
9. Carlton Dr
10. Amberly Dr
11. Danbury Ln
12. Edmonton Pl
13. Rutherford Ct
14. Armitage Av
15. Farnham Ln
16. Dartford Pl
17. Randa Ln
18. Nina Ln
19. Penridge Pl
20. Carlton Dr
21. Carrington Ct
22. Briarwood Ln
23. Kensley Dr
24. Glenoover Wy
25. Kensington Ln
26. Chelsea Ln
27. Summerset Pl
28. Flight Ave
29. Cienega West Wy
30. Kew St
31. Flora Dr
32. Lamos St
33. Sycamore Pl
34. S Larch St
35. Ravenswood Ave
36. S Osage Ave

Downtown Inglewood's pedestrian-friendly Market Street offers a step back in time with mom-and-pop establishments you won't find amid most chain-saturated mega-malls. It has a way to go before it exudes the charm of an Anytown USA Main Street, but the surrounding area's booming real estate market bodes well for Market Street's future.

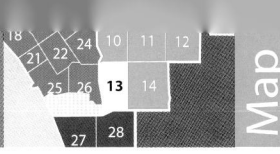

Coffee

- **A Cultural Affair Coffee House** • 1330 N La Brea Ave
- **Starbucks** • 941 N La Brea Ave
- **Starbucks (Vons)** • 500 E Manchester Blvd

Copy Centers

- **D'Menace Copies & Communications** • 1401 N La Brea Ave • 310-677-1683
- **Postal Plus Business Copy** • 309 E Hillcrest Blvd • 310-672-9097

Gyms

- **Curves** • 979 N La Brea Ave • 310-673-9043
- **Huff N Puff Gym** • 1321 N La Brea Ave • 310-672-5055

Hardware Stores

- **Inglewood True Value** • 10600 Hawthorne Blvd • 323-678-6261

Liquor Stores

- **Airport Liquors & Groceries** • 420 N La Brea Ave
- **Andy's Liquors** • 440 W Manchester Blvd
- **Banks of Scotland Liquor** • 5014 W Century Blvd
- **Century Discount Liquor** • 4082 W Century Blvd
- **Forum Liquors** • 801 S Prairie Ave
- **Happy Time Liquors** • 730 N La Brea Ave
- **Hyde Park Liquor** • 622 Centinela Ave
- **JR's Liquor** • 10025 S Inglewood Ave
- **Liquorette** • 1400 Centinela Ave
- **Martino's Liquor** • 706 E Manchester Blvd
- **Mr B's Liquor** • 10025 S Prairie Ave
- **Nelson's Liquor** • 1435 N 64th St
- **Speedy Spot Liquor** • 1190 S La Brea Ave
- **Tran's Liquor** • 10021 Hawthorne Blvd
- **Will's Liquor** • 6513 West Blvd

Pet Stores

- **Distributors Feed** • 4435 Lennox Blvd • 310-677-0200
- **Inglewood Pet Shop** • 979 S La Brea Ave • 310-677-2225

Restaurants

- **Caribbean Treehouse** • 1226 Centinela Ave • 310-330-1170

Video Rental

- **Carrousel Video** • 911 S Inglewood Ave • 310-677-1888
- **Hollywood Video** • 425 E Manchester Blvd • 310-677-6510
- **Starr Video** • 313 W Arbor Vitae St • 310-680-7325
- **Video Vision** • 5008 W Century Blvd • 310-674-0004

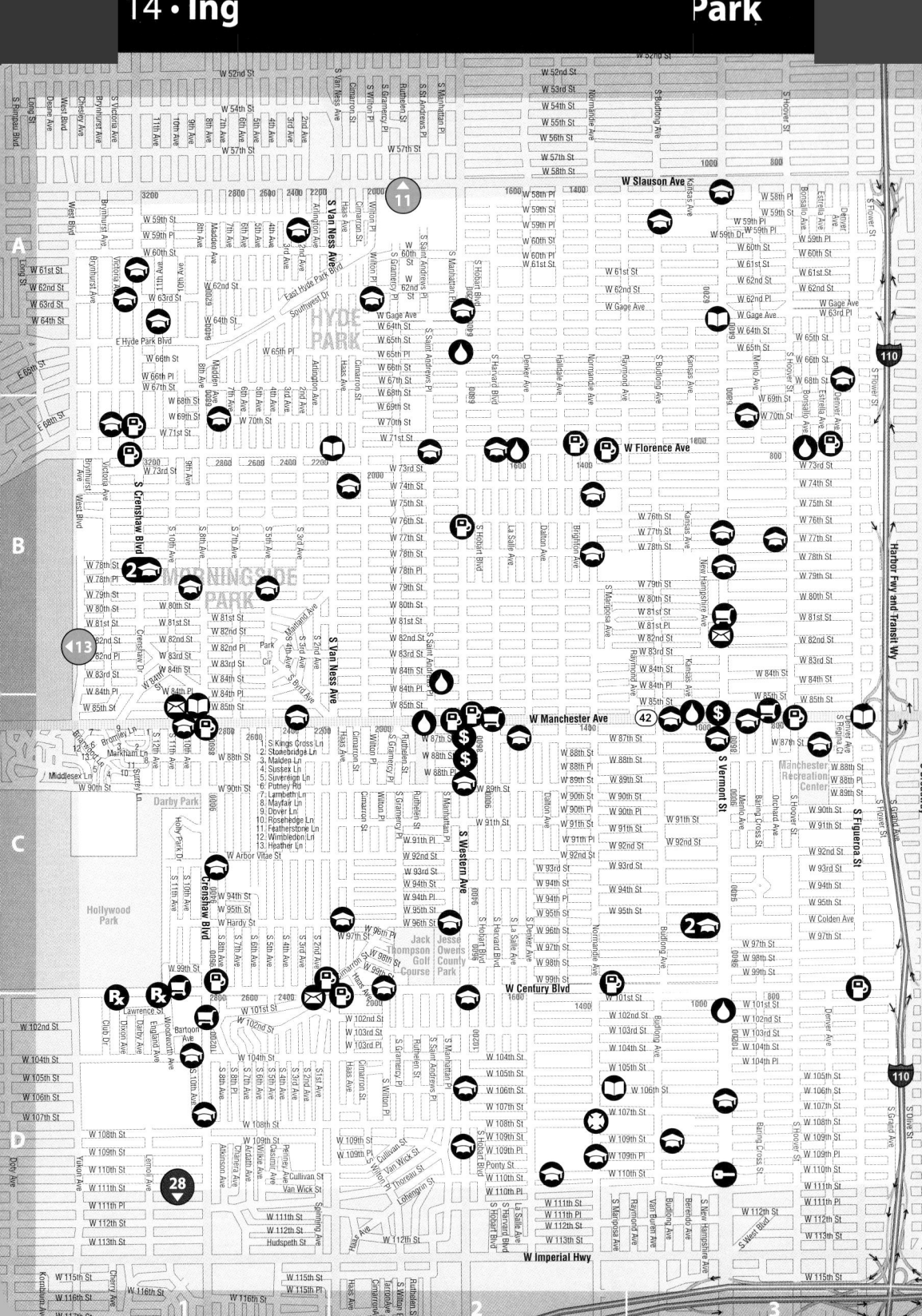

Although mostly known as South Central, the area west of the 10 and north of the 105 boasts pockets of domestic pride surprising to the passer-through. Morningside Park claims blocks of manicured, vintage houses quietly celebrating community amid an otherwise rough-edged neighborhood.

$ Banks

- **Bank of America** • 8701 S Western Ave
- **Union** • 8811 S Western Ave
- **Washington Mutual** • 1027 W Manchester Ave

Car Rental

- **U-Haul** • 11020 S Vermont Ave

Car Washes

- **EJ Hand Car Wash** • 2320 W Manchester Ave
- **Magic Car Wash** • 1923 W Manchester Ave
- **Manchester Car Wash** • 1111 W Manchester Ave
- **Mike's Hand Car Wash** • 10135 S Vermont Ave
- **Moore's Car Wash** • 6522 S Western Ave
- **Personal Touch Hand Car Wash** • 1624 W Florence Ave
- **Spot Car Wash** • 701 W Florence Ave

Gas Stations

- **76** • 10000 S Figueroa St
- **76** • 1350 W Florence Ave
- **76** • 9830 S Crenshaw Blvd
- **Arco** • 1403 Century Blvd
- **Arco** • 3411 W Florence Ave
- **Arco** • 615 W Florence Ave
- **Arco** • 7600 S Western Ave
- **Arco** • 800 W Manchester Ave
- **Mobil** • 1400 W Florence Ave
- **Mobil** • 1803 W Manchester Ave
- **Mobil** • 3016 W Century Blvd
- **Mobil** • 7130 Crenshaw Blvd
- **Shell** • 2138 W Century Blvd
- **Shell** • 3100 W Manchester Ave
- **Shell** • 9920 S Hoover St
- **Valero** • 1359 W Century Blvd

Libraries

- **Hyde Park–Miriam Matthews Branch** • 2205 W Florence Ave • 323-750-7241
- **John Muir Branch** • 1005 W 64th St • 323-789-4800
- **Mark Twain Branch** • 9621 S Figueroa St • 323-755-4088
- **Morningside Park Branch** • 3202 W 85th St • 310-412-5400
- **Woodcrest** • 1340 W 106th St • 323-757-9373

Rx Pharmacies

- **Target** • 3471 W Century Blvd • 310-677-5937
- **Walgreens** • 3331 W Century Blvd • 310-671-1043

Post Offices

- 2200 W Century Blvd
- 3212 W 85th St
- 8200 S Vermont Ave

Schools

- **59th St Elementary** • 5939 2nd Ave
- **68th St Elementary** • 612 W 68th St
- **74th St Elementary** • 2112 W 74th St
- **95th St EEC** • 1027 W 96th St
- **95th St Elementary** • 1109 W 96th St
- **Albert F Monroe Junior High** • 10711 S 10th Ave
- **Aloha** • 6206 S Wilton Pl
- **Bret Harte Middle** • 9301 S Hoover St
- **Budlong Ave Elementary** • 5940 S Budlong Ave
- **Cavalry Christian** • 2400 W 85th St
- **Century Park Elementary** • 10935 Spinning Ave
- **Children's Enrichment Center** • 3209 W Manchester Ave
- **Cleophas Oliver Learning Academy** • 1902 W Florence Ave
- **Clyde Woodworth Elementary** • 3200 W 104th St
- **Cornerstone Prep** • 10963 S Western Ave
- **Daniel Freeman Elementary** • 2602 W 79th St
- **Duke Ellington High** • 1541 W 110th St
- **Faith Children's Center** • 2057 W Century Blvd
- **Faith Lutheran** • 3320 W 85th St
- **First Church of God** • 2941 W 70th St
- **Frederick KC Price** • 7901 S Vermont Ave
- **Fresh Starts Child Enrichment** • 7867 Crenshaw Blvd
- **George Washington Preparatory High** • 10860 S Denker Ave
- **Horace Mann Middle** • 7001 S St Andrews Pl
- **Hyde Park Blvd Elementary** • 3140 Hyde Park Blvd
- **Hyde Park EEC** • 6428 11th Ave
- **John Muir Middle** • 5929 S Vermont Ave
- **Kipp Academy of Opportunity** • 3127 W 79th St
- **La Salle Ave Elementary** • 8715 La Salle Ave
- **Little Rainbow Children's Center** • 7419 S Normandie Ave
- **Los Angeles Christian Faith** • 8862 S Western Ave
- **Manchester Ave Elementary** • 661 W 87th St
- **Manhattan Pl Elementary** • 1850 W 96th St
- **Mikes EEC** • 7720 S Vermont Ave
- **Miller Elementary** • 830 W 77th St
- **Nelson Christian** • 10531 S Western Ave
- **New West Technical Academy** • 10513 S Vermont Ave
- **Nikka Tiffany** • 7112 S Victoria Ave
- **Normandie Christian** • 6306 S Normandie Ave
- **Puente Charter** • 10000 S Western Ave
- **Raymond Ave Elementary** • 7511 Raymond Ave
- **San Pedro Academy** • 1145 W Manchester Ave
- **St Eugene** • 9521 Haas Ave
- **St John the Evangelist** • 6028 Victoria Ave
- **St John the Evangelist** • 6103 Crenshaw Blvd
- **St Michael's Elementary** • 1027 W 87th St
- **St Raphael's Elementary** • 924 W 70th St
- **Stafford-Ford Christian Academy** • 1641 W Florence Ave
- **Toddler Technical University** • 7861 S Normandie Ave
- **Warren Lane Elementary** • 9330 S 8th Ave
- **Woodcrest Elementary** • 1151 W 109th St
- **Woodcrest Nazarene** • 10926 S Normandie Ave
- **Youth Opportunities Unlimited** • 915 W Manchester Ave

Supermarkets

- **Food 4 Less** • 3200 W Century Blvd
- **Ralphs** • 1730 W Manchester Ave
- **Ralphs** • 8620 Orchard Ave
- **Smart & Final** • 10100 Crenshaw Blvd
- **Smart & Final** • 8137 S Vermont Ave

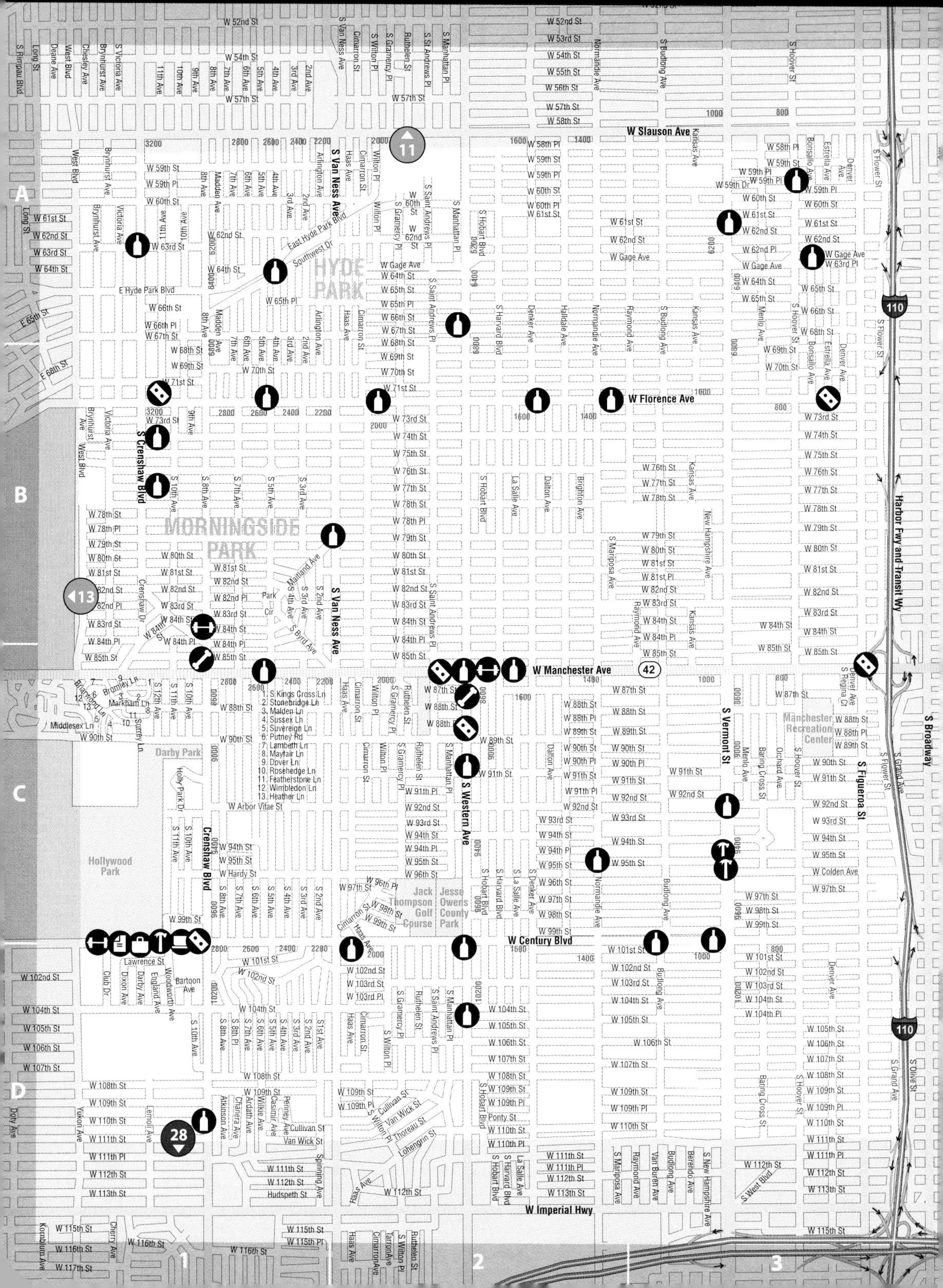

Map 14 • Inglewood East / Morningside Park

HYDE PARK

MORNINGSIDE PARK

Hollywood Park

Darby Park

Jack Thompson Golf Course

Jesse Owens County Park

Manchester Recreation Center

1. S Kings Cross Ln
2. Stonehedge Ln
3. Malden Ln
4. Sussex Ln
5. Sovereign Ln
6. Putney Rd
7. Lambeth Ln
8. Mayfair Ln
9. Dover Ln
10. Rosehedge Ln
11. Featherstone Ln
12. Wimbledon Ln
13. Heather Ln

Shedding its inner-city vibe and getting more in tune with its south bay neighbors, Inglewood and environs to the east now include super-retailers like Costco anchoring shopping centers usually more prevalent in the outer reaches of suburbia. Local flavor remains in the newly retro-cool Hollywood Park horse-racing track and casino.

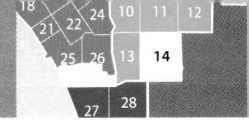

Coffee
- **Starbucks** · 3351 W Century Blvd

Copy Centers
- **Staples** · 3451 W Century Blvd · 310-673-6800

Gyms
- **Bally Total Fitness** · 3531 W Century Blvd · 310-672-6002
- **Curves** · 8409 8th Ave · 323-971-1382

Hardware Stores
- **Ferreteria Lemus Supply** · 9510 S Vermont Ave · 323-418-8041
- **Home Depot** · 3363 Century Blvd · 310-677-1944

Liquor Stores
- **All Star Liquor & Market** · 6300 Crenshaw Blvd
- **Bufkin Liquor** · 2063 W Florence Ave
- **Comet Liquor Store** · 714 W Gage Ave
- **Dave's Liquors** · 9317 S Vermont Ave
- **Florence Liquor** · 1534 W Florence Ave
- **Gin's Liquor Store** · 11001 Crenshaw Blvd
- **Holiday Liquor** · 9150 S Western Ave
- **J's Liquor** · 1005 W Century Blvd
- **M&J Liquor** · 7405 Crenshaw Blvd
- **Maple Liquor** · 10421 S Western Ave
- **Mr Spirit's Liquor** · 6818 S Western Ave
- **Ralph's Drive-In Liquor** · 2130 W Century Blvd
- **Red's Liquor** · 1201 W Century Blvd
- **Red's Liquor** · 2600 Southwest Dr
- **San's Liquor** · 7911 S Van Ness Ave
- **Shyrea's Liquor** · 1753 W Century Blvd
- **Silver Dollar Liquor** · 1650 W Manchester Ave
- **SMB's Liquors** · 9467 S Normandie Ave
- **Sunshine Liquor** · 2619 W Florence Ave
- **Susie's Liquor** · 5953 S Hoover St
- **Vee's Liquor** · 7707 Crenshaw Blvd
- **Vermont Liquor** · 6107 S Vermont Ave

Pet Stores
- **James' Tropical Fish** · 8519 Crenshaw Blvd · 323-758-4406

Shopping
- **Costco** · 3560 W Century Blvd · 310-242-2774

Video Rental
- **A&N Video** · 519 W Manchester Ave · 323-971-6249
- **Blockbuster** · 3111 W Century Blvd · 310-330-1193
- **Blockbuster** · 3330 W Florence Ave · 323-789-7991
- **Blockbuster** · 8811 S Western Ave · 323-750-2947
- **Estreollita Video** · 645 W Florence Ave · 323-751-1750

A

B

C

D

Topanga
State Park

PAGE
260

Will Rogers
State Historic Park

Pacific
Ocean

Will Rogers
State Beach

Pacific Coast Hwy

Will Rogers
State Beach

PACIFIC
PALISADES

Lake Shrine
Temple

Santa Monica
Steps

Riviera
Country
Club

1. Drift Wood Dr
2. Drift Wood Pl
3. Terrace Pl
4. West View Ln
5. Ocean Vw
6. Pacific Pl
7. Kontiki Wy
8. Coco Pl
9. Kiki Pl
10. Haney Pl
11. Dobbins Pl
12. Channel Ln
13. Short St
14. La Cruz Dr

16

18

3
7 $
3

1

2

3

Made up of streets winding continuously through the hills with endless ocean views, the Palisades are one of LA's most beautiful areas, home to many celebs and movie moguls—as the lavish homes might suggest. A very steep hike at the end of Paseo Miramar off Sunset is worth it for the spectacular panoramic ocean views. Though technically in Santa Monica, the 4th Street Steps are a popular place for people-watching as well as an excellent workout.

$ Banks

- **Bank of America** · 15314 W Sunset Blvd
- **California National** · 15305 W Sunset Blvd
- **Citibank** · 15215 Sunset Blvd
- **First Federal** · 15135 W Sunset Blvd
- **US** · 15245 W Sunset Blvd
- **Washington Mutual** · 15200 W Sunset Blvd
- **Wells Fargo** · 1012 Swarthmore Ave

Car Washes

- **Palisades Car Wash** · 890 Alma Real Dr

Gas Stations

- **76** · 15400 W Sunset Blvd
- **Mobil** · 15281 W Sunset Blvd
- **Shell** · 15401 W Sunset Blvd

Landmarks

- **Santa Monica Steps** · 4th St & Adelaide Dr
- **Self Realization Fellowship Lake Shrine Temple** · Sunset Blvd near Palisades Dr
- **Will Rogers State Historic Park** · Sunset Blvd

Libraries

- **Pacific Palisades Branch** · 861 Alma Real Dr · 310-459-2754

Post Offices

- **US Post Office** · 15209 W Sunset Blvd
- **US Post Office** · 15243 La Cruz Dr

Schools

- **Canyon Elementary** · 421 Entrada Dr
- **Corpus Christi** · 890 Toyopa Dr
- **Marquez Elementary** · 16821 Marquez Ave
- **Pacific Palisades Elementary** · 800 Via De La Paz
- **Palisades Charter High** · 15777 Bowdoin St
- **St Matthew's Episcopal** · 1031 Bienveneda Ave
- **Temescal Canyon High** · 777 Temescal Canyon Rd
- **Village** · 780 Swarthmore Ave

Supermarkets

- **Gelson's Markets** · 15424 W Sunset Blvd
- **Ralphs** · 15120 W Sunset Blvd

A

B

C

D

Topanga
State Park

PAGE
260

Will Rogers
State Historic Park

16

PACIFIC
PALISADES

W Sunset Blvd

W Sunset Blvd

9

2

5

Temescal Canyon
Park

Palisades
Park

Rustic
Canyon
Rec Center

Riviera
Country
Club

Pacific Coast Hwy

Will Rogers
State Beach

Palisades
Park

18

Lincoln Blvd

1. Drift Wood Dr
2. Drift Wood Pl
3. Terrace Pl
4. West View Ln
5. Ocean Vw
6. Pacific Pl
7. Kontiki Wy
8. Coco Pl
9. Kiki Pl
10. Haney Pl
11. Dobbins Pl
12. Channel Ln
13. Short St
14. La Cruz Dr

Montana Ave

Pacific
Ocean

Palisades Beach Rd

1

2

3

Amenities in the Palisades are generally limited to the village, just off Sunset Boulevard, along Swarthmore Avenue. But Santa Monica is just a short hop down the PCH, as long as mudslides or flooding don't interfere—forcing a longer, and sometimes hazardous, drive along the more serpentine Sunset Boulevard.

Coffee

- **Coffee Bean & Tea Leaf** • 15278 Antioch St
- **Starbucks** • 15300 Sunset Blvd

Farmer's Markets

- **Farmer's Market** • Swarthmore Ave & W Sunset Blvd

Gyms

- **Curves** • 881 Alma Real Dr • 310-459-1003
- **Spectrum Club** • 17383 Sunset Blvd • 310-459-2582

Hardware Stores

- **Norris True Value** • 15140 W Sunset Blvd • 310-454-4116

Liquor Stores

- **State Beach Liquor** • 14801 Pacific Coast Hwy

Nightlife

- **Pearl Dragon** • 15229 Sunset Blvd • 310-459-9790

Restaurants

- **A La Tarte Bistrot** • 1037 Swarthmore Ave • 310-459-6635
- **Dante Palisades Restaurant** • 1032 Swarthmore Ave • 310-459-7561
- **Giorgio Baldi** • 114 W Channel Rd • 310-573-1660
- **Kay 'n Dave's** • 15246 W Sunset Blvd • 310-459-8118
- **Marix Tex Mex Café** • 118 Entrada Dr • 310-459-8596
- **Mort's Deli** • 1035 Swarthmore Ave • 310-454-5511
- **Patrick's Roadhouse** • 106 Entrada Dr • 310-459-4544
- **Pure Energy Café** • 17383 W Sunset Blvd • 310-573-4105
- **Robek's Juice** • 15280 Antioch St • 310-230-3991
- **Terry's** • 1028 Swarthmore Ave • 310-454-6467

Shopping

- **Benton's Sporting Goods** • 1038 Swarthmore Ave • 310-459-8451
- **Gelson's Market** • 15424 Sunset Blvd • 310-459-4483
- **Gift Garden Antiques** • 15266 Antioch St • 310-459-4114
- **Ivy Greene for Kids** • 1020 Swarthmore Ave • 310-230-0301
- **Palisades Playthings** • 1041 Swarthmore Ave • 310-454-8648
- **The Prince's Table** • 1051 Swarthmore Ave • 310-573-3667
- **Village Books** • 1049 Swarthmore Ave • 310-454-4063
- **Vivian's Boutique** • 970 Monument St • 310-573-1326
- **Whispers** • 1013 Swarthmore Ave • 310-454-5582

Video Rental

- **Blockbuster** • 970 Monument St • 310-230-3002
- **Palisades Video Plus** • 542 Palisades Dr • 310-230-1688

67

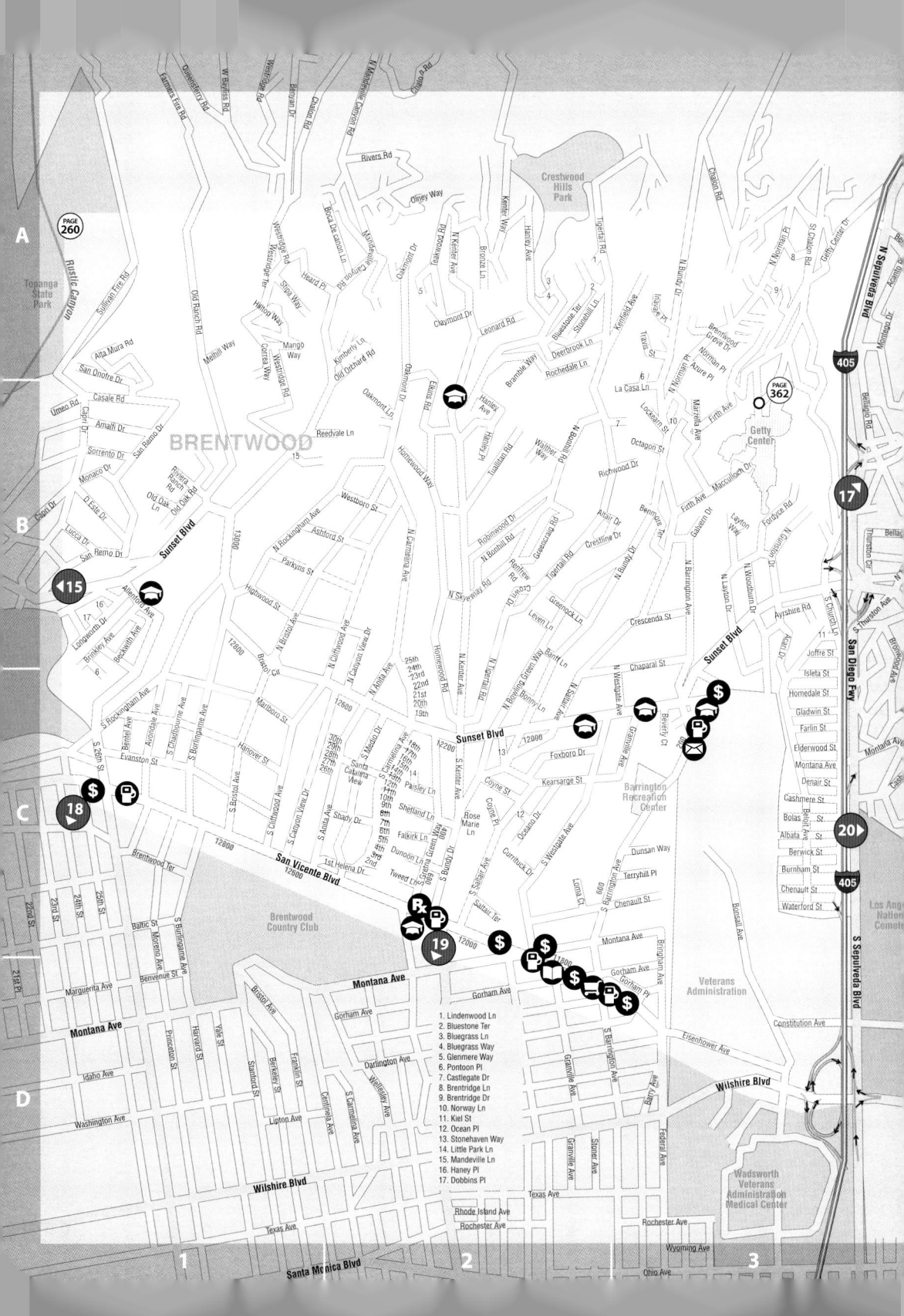

O.J. Simpson put Brentwood on most Americans' radar, but this neighborhood is back to being the quietly affluent place it once was. San Vicente Boulevard serves as a shady and pleasant place for a jog or bike ride (complete with a bicycle lane), and is the scene of the annual Kickin' Cancer 5K run (www.kickincancer.com). Many young professionals prefer the rent over here compared to neighboring Santa Monica, but parking can be a nightmare.

$ Banks
- **Bank of America** · 11911 San Vicente Blvd
- **California National** · 11777 San Vicente Blvd
- **Union** · 11661 San Vicente Blvd
- **Washington Mutual** · 226 26th St
- **Wells Fargo** · 11836 San Vicente Blvd
- **Wells Fargo** · 143 S Barrington Pl

Gas Stations
- **76** · 12037 San Vicente Blvd
- **76** · 13060 San Vicente Blvd
- **Chevron** · 110 S Barrington Ave
- **Chevron** · 11852 San Vincente Blvd
- **Independent** · 11811 San Vicente Blvd

o Landmarks
- **Getty Center** · 1200 Getty Center Dr

Libraries
- **Donald Bruce Kaufman** · 11820 San Vicente Blvd · 310-575-8273

Rx Pharmacies
- **Longs Drugs (24 hours)** · 11941 San Vicente Blvd · 310-440-4162

Post Offices
- **US Post Office** · 200 S Barrington Ave

Schools
- **Archer School for Girls** · 11725 W Sunset Blvd
- **Brentwood** · 100 S Barrington Pl
- **Brentwood Science** · 740 Gretna Green Wy
- **Kenter Canyon Elementary** · 645 N Kenter Ave
- **Paul Revere Middle** · 1450 Allenford Ave
- **St Martin of Tours Elementary** · 11955 W Sunset Blvd

Supermarkets
- **Whole Foods Market** · 11737 San Vicente Blvd

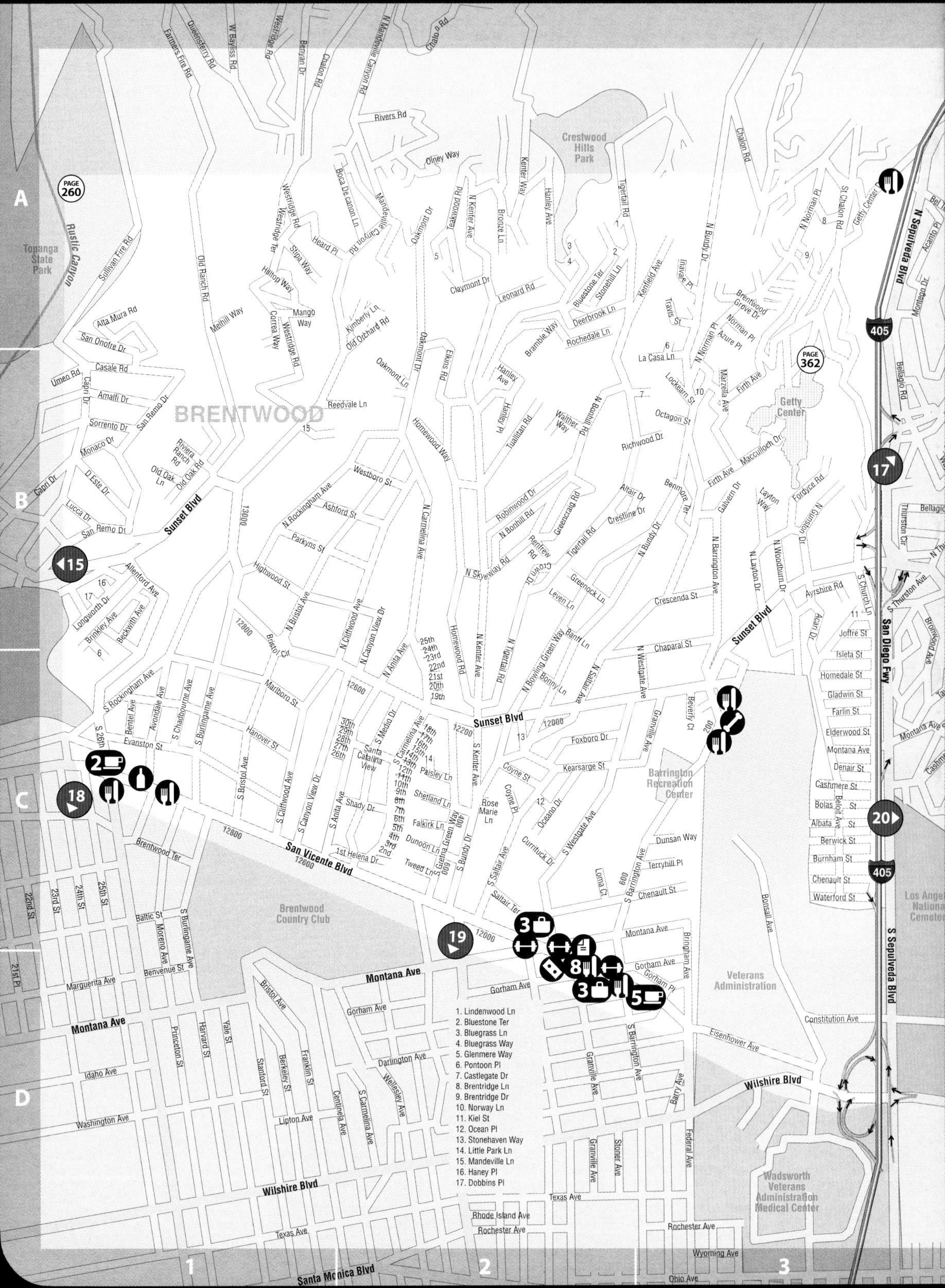

Map 16 • Brentwood

Brentwood

Topanga State Park
Rustic Canyon
Crestwood Hills Park
Getty Center
Brentwood Country Club
Barrington Recreation Center
Veterans Administration
Wadsworth Veterans Administration Medical Center
Los Angeles National Cemetery

1. Lindenwood Ln
2. Bluestone Ter
3. Bluegrass Ln
4. Bluegrass Way
5. Glenmere Way
6. Pontoon Pl
7. Castlegate Dr
8. Brentridge Ln
9. Brentridge Dr
10. Norway Ln
11. Kiel St
12. Ocean Pl
13. Stonehaven Way
14. Little Park Ln
15. Mandeville Ln
16. Haney Pl
17. Dobbins Pl

PAGE 260
PAGE 362

Sunset Blvd
San Vicente Blvd
Montana Ave
Wilshire Blvd
Santa Monica Blvd
San Diego Fwy
S Sepulveda Blvd
Getty Center Dr
N Sepulveda Blvd
405
17
15
20
18
19
2
3
5
8

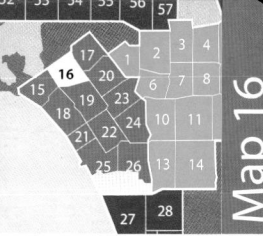

Map 16

San Vicente Boulevard seems to have an outpost of every major chain restaurant, from Chin Chin to Ben & Jerry's, but there are a few independent restaurants that are worth noting. We love the pastas at Pizzicotto and Coral Tree Café offers a perfect study or first-date atmosphere. Brentwood is home to one of LA's best independent booksellers, Dutton's—it has an impressive selection and an atmosphere geared toward serious readers.

Coffee

- **Brew-N-Beans** · 11911 San Vicente Blvd
- **Coffee Bean & Tea Leaf** · 11698 San Vicente Blvd
- **Coral Tree Café** · 11645 San Vicente Blvd
- **Mart Coffee & Juice Bar** · 225 26th St
- **Peet's Coffee & Tea** · 11750 San Vicente Blvd
- **Starbucks** · 11700 Barrington Ct
- **Starbucks** · 11707 San Vicente Blvd
- **Starbucks** · 13050 San Vicente Blvd

Copy Centers

- **Brentwood Printing** · 11726 San Vicente Blvd · 310-826-1011

Gyms

- **Curves** · 11777 San Vicente Blvd · 310-571-2422
- **Great Shape** · 11980 San Vicente Blvd · 310-820-6602
- **Pro Gym** · 11920 San Vicente Blvd · 310-826-6624

Liquor Stores

- **Briggs Wines & Spirits** · 13038 San Vicente Blvd

Pet Stores

- **Petspot** · 11720 Barrington Ct · 310-471-8169

Restaurants

- **A Votre Sante** · 13016 San Vicente Blvd · 310-451-1813
- **The Brentwood** · 148 S Barrington Ave · 310-476-3511
- **Cheesecake Factory** · 11647 San Vicente Blvd · 310-826-7111
- **Chin Chin** · 11740 San Vicente Blvd · 310-826-2525
- **Daily Grill** · 11677 San Vicente Blvd · 310-442-0044
- **Gaucho Grill** · 11754 San Vicente Blvd · 310-447-7898
- **La Scala Presto** · 11740 San Vicente Blvd · 310-826-6100
- **Le Pain Quotidien** · 11702 Barrington Ct · 310-476-0969
- **Pizzicotto** · 11758 San Vicente Blvd · 310-442-7188
- **Reddi Chick BBQ** · 225 26th St · 310-393-5238
- **Toscana** · 11633 San Vicente Blvd · 310-820-2448
- **Vincenti** · 11930 San Vicente Blvd · 310-207-0127

Shopping

- **Dutton's Brentwood** · 11975 San Vicente Blvd · 310-476-6263
- **Falconhead** · 11911 San Vicente Blvd · 310-471-7075
- **PJ London** · 11661 San Vicente Blvd · 310-826-4649
- **Porta Bella** · 11715 San Vicente Blvd · 310-820-2550
- **Terra Cotta** · 11922 San Vicente Blvd · 310-826-7878
- **Whole Foods Market** · 11737 San Vicente Blvd · 310-826-4433

Video Rental

- **Blockbuster** · 11770 San Vicente Blvd · 310-207-3837

Map 17 • **Bel Air / Holmby Hills**

1. S Sepulveda Blvd
2. Taro Wy
3. Cecina Wy
4. Tione Rd
5. Duluth Ln

BEL AIR ESTATES

Stone Canyon Reservoir

Beverly Hillbillies' House

Bel Air Country Club

UCLA
PAGE 264

Los Angeles Country Club

A B C D

1 2 3

Both of these neighborhoods are almost completely residential. The nosy can purchase star maps on the street that will direct you to celebrity homes, or rather a tour of their 15-foot tree barrier fencing. The roads are confusing and it's easy to get lost in Bel Air, but the homes you *can* see are so stunning to look at that you may not mind.

Gas Stations

- **76** · 800 N Sepulveda Blvd
- **Chevron** · 670 N Sepulveda Blvd

Landmarks

- **Beverly Hillbillies' House** · 700 Bel Air Rd

Schools

- **Community Magnet Center** · 11301 Bellagio Rd
- **Harvard-Westlake (second location)** · 700 N Faring Rd
- **John Thomas Dye** · 11414 Chalon Rd
- **Marymount High** · 10643 W Sunset Blvd

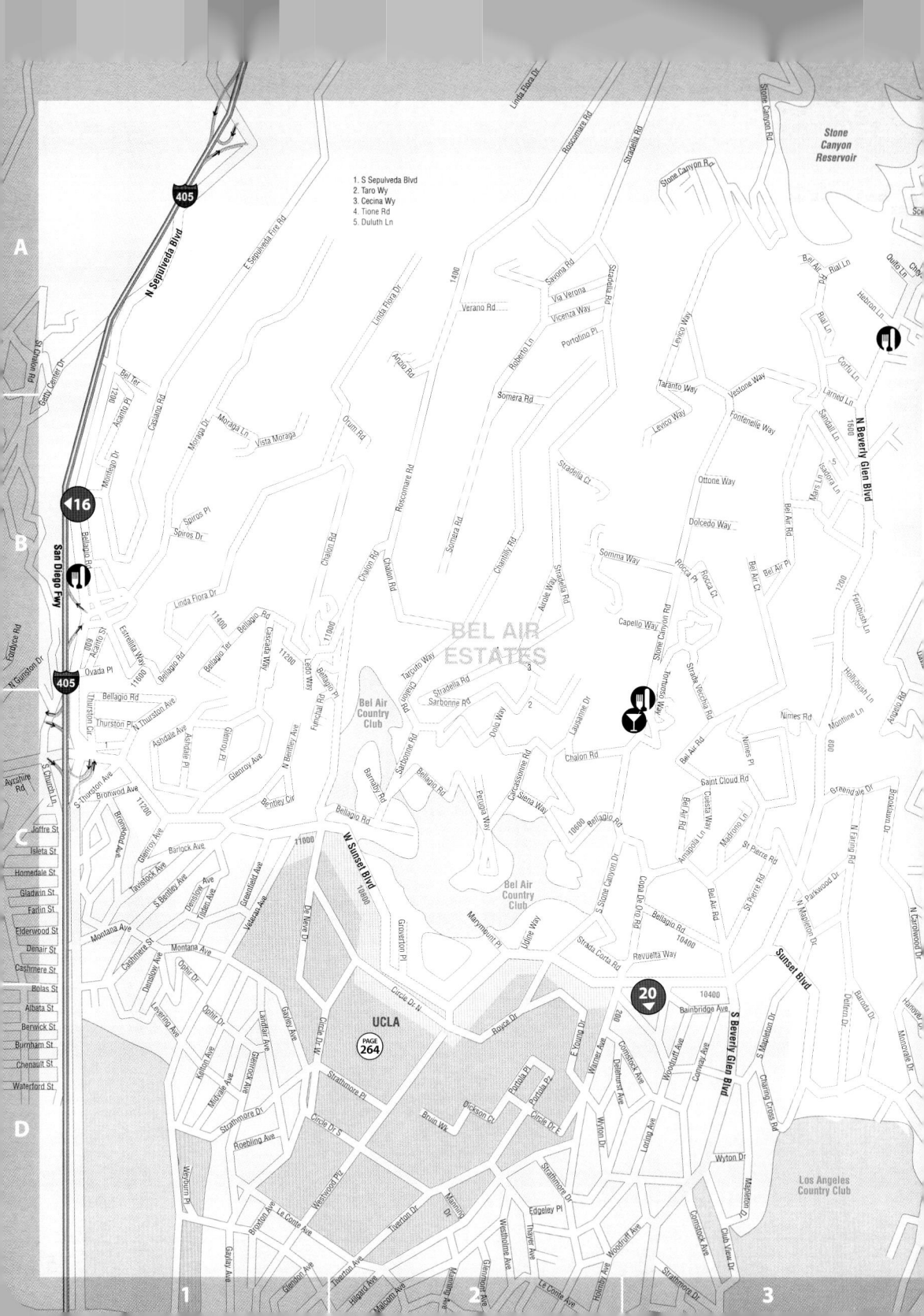

The Hotel Bel Air might be Los Angeles County's most beautiful hotel. The grounds are exquisitely maintained, and it's easy to understand why so many couples wed here, and why Oscar nominees take up temporary residence here for a little calm and serenity before the awards.

Nightlife

- **Hotel Bel Air Lounge** · 701 Stone Canyon Rd · 310-472-1211

Restaurants

- **Bel Air Bar & Grill** · 662 N Sepulveda Blvd · 310-440-5544
- **Four Oaks** · 2181 N Beverly Glen Blvd · 310-470-2265
- **Hotel Bel Air Dining Room** · 701 Stone Canyon Rd · 310-472-1211

Map 18 · **Santa Monica**

1. Esparta Way
2. Foxtail Dr
3. Larkin Pl
4. Winnett Pl
5. Arroyo Vista Dr
6. Seaside Ter
7. Seaview Ter
8. Pacific Ter
9. Vicente Ter
10. Arcadia Ter
11. Pacific Ter
12. Marine Ter
13. Moss Ave
14. Goldsmith St
15. Ruskin St
16. Bentley Ct
17. Marine Pl N
18. Lincoln Ct
19. Longfellow St

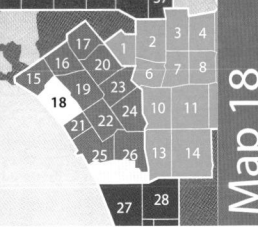
Resting along the country's edge, Santa Monica continuously multiplies with families, young professionals, artists, and tourists. Strolling 3rd Street Promenade remains a favorite pastime, next to wheeling down the beach bike path and shopping along cozy Main Street. The Hotel Casa Del Mar offers beach-view afternoon tea, while Santa Monica College boasts the best public swimming pool in the county.

$ Banks
- **Bank of America** · 1301 4th St
- **Bank of America** · 1430 Wilshire Blvd
- **Bank of the West** · 407 Colorado Ave
- **California Bank & Trust** · 100 Wilshire Blvd
- **California National** · 201 Santa Monica Blvd
- **Citibank** · 1505 Montana Ave
- **Citibank** · 501 Santa Monica Blvd
- **First Federal** · 1630 Montana Ave
- **First Federal** · 1750 Ocean Park Blvd
- **First Federal** · 2827 Main St
- **First Federal** · 401 Wilshire Blvd
- **First Regional** · 501 Santa Monica Blvd
- **Pacific Western** · 120 Wilshire Blvd
- **Preferred** · 524 Wilshire Blvd
- **Union** · 1101 Montana Ave
- **Union** · 2001 Wilshire Blvd
- **Union** · 429 Santa Monica Blvd
- **US** · 1401 Wilshire Blvd
- **US** · 2221 Santa Monica Blvd
- **US** · 400 Wilshire Blvd
- **Washington Mutual** · 1333 4th St
- **Wells Fargo** · 1300 4th St
- **Wells Fargo** · 2444 Wilshire Blvd
- **World Savings & Loan** · 729 Montana Ave

Car Rental
- **Ava's** · 842 11th St
- **Enterprise** · 1695 Santa Monica Blvd
- **Enterprise** · 2487 Lincoln Blvd
- **Enterprise** · 2700 Lincoln Blvd
- **Hertz** · 101 Wilshire Blvd
- **Hertz** · 1426 Santa Monica Blvd
- **Hertz** · 1700 Ocean Ave
- **Midway Car Rental** · 1901 Ocean Ave
- **National-Alamo** · 1027 Broadway
- **U-Haul** · 1747 Lincoln Blvd

Car Washes
- **Bonus Car Wash & Auto Detail** · 2800 Lincoln Blvd
- **Lincoln Blvd Car Wash** · 1624 Lincoln Blvd
- **Wilshire West Detail & Car Wash** · 2320 Wilshire Blvd

Gas Stations
- **76** · 1402 Santa Monica Blvd
- **76** · 1944 Pico Blvd
- **76** · 2120 Lincoln Blvd
- **Arco** · 2555 Lincoln Blvd
- **Arco** · 332 Pico Blvd
- **Chevron** · 1330 Santa Monica Blvd

- **Chevron** · 1732 Lincoln Blvd
- **Chevron** · 432 Wilshire Blvd
- **Exxon** · 1801 Lincoln Blvd
- **Mobil** · 731 Santa Monica Blvd
- **Shell** · 1866 Lincoln Blvd

Hospitals
- **St John's** · 2130 Santa Monica Blvd

o Landmarks
- **3rd Street Promenade** · 3rd St b/w Broadway & Wilshire
- **Heritage Square** · Main St & Ocean Park Blvd
- **Santa Monica Civic Auditorium/Civic Center** · 1855 Main St
- **Santa Monica Pier** · Ocean Ave & Colorado Ave

Libraries
- **LA County Law Library–Santa Monica** · 1725 Main St · 310-260-3644
- **Santa Monica Fairview Branch** · 2101 Ocean Park Blvd · 310-450-0443
- **Santa Monica Montana Avenue Branch** · 1704 Montana Ave · 310-829-7081
- **Santa Monica Ocean Park Branch** · 2601 Main St · 310-392-3804
- **Santa Monica Public Library (Temporarily Closed)** · 1343 6th St · 310-458-8600
- **Santa Monica Public Main Library (Temporary Location)** · 1324 5th St · 315-458-8600

Rx Pharmacies
- **Ralphs** · 1644 Cloverfield Blvd · 310-582-3915
- **Rite-Aid** · 1331 Wilshire Blvd · 310-458-0731
- **Rite-Aid (24 hrs)** · 1808 Wilshire Blvd · 310-829-3951
- **Sav-On** · 1411 Lincoln Blvd · 310-319-1318
- **Walgreens (24 hrs)** · 1932 Wilshire Blvd · 310-829-6813

Police
- **Santa Monica Police Headquarters** · 1685 Main St · 310-395-9931

Post Offices
- **US Post Office** · 1025 Colorado Ave
- **US Post Office** · 1217 Wilshire Blvd
- **US Post Office** · 1248 5th St
- **US Post Office** · 2720 Neilson Wy

Schools
- **Carlthorp** · 438 San Vicente Blvd
- **Concord High** · 1831 Wilshire Blvd
- **Crossroads Elementary** · 1714 21st St
- **Delphi Academy** · 1730 Wilshire Blvd
- **Franklin Elementary** · 2400 Montana Ave
- **FSG Lighthouse** · 1220 20th St
- **Garden of Angels** · 1009 18th St
- **John Adams Middle** · 2425 16th St
- **John Muir Elementary** · 2526 6th St
- **Lincoln Middle** · 1501 California Ave
- **McKinley Elementary** · 2401 Santa Monica Blvd
- **New Path Montessori** · 1962 20th St
- **New Roads** · 1238 Lincoln Blvd
- **Newbridge** · 1512 Pearl St
- **Olympic High** · 721 Ocean Park Blvd
- **Pilgrim Lutheran** · 1730 Wilshire Blvd
- **Pluralistic** · 1454 Euclid St
- **Roosevelt Elementary** · 801 Montana Ave
- **Santa Monica Alternative** · 2525 5th St
- **Santa Monica College** · 1900 Pico Blvd
- **Santa Monica First Methodist Kindergarten** · 1008 11th St
- **Santa Monica High** · 601 Pico Blvd
- **Santa Monica Montessori** · 1909 Colorado Ave
- **Soledad Enrichment Action** · 141 S Fetterly Ave
- **St Anne** · 1519 20th St
- **St John** · 1339 20th St
- **St Monica Elementary** · 1039 7th St
- **St Monica's High** · 1030 Lincoln Blvd
- **Westside Waldorf** · 1229 4th St
- **Will Rogers Elementary** · 2401 14th St

Supermarkets
- **Albertsons** · 2627 Lincoln Blvd
- **Pavilions** · 820 Montana Ave
- **Ralphs** · 1644 Cloverfield Blvd
- **Vons** · 1311 Wilshire Blvd
- **Vons** · 710 Broadway
- **Whole Foods Market** · 2201 Wilshire Blvd
- **Wild Oats** · 1425 Montana Ave
- **Wild Oats** · 500 Wilshire Blvd

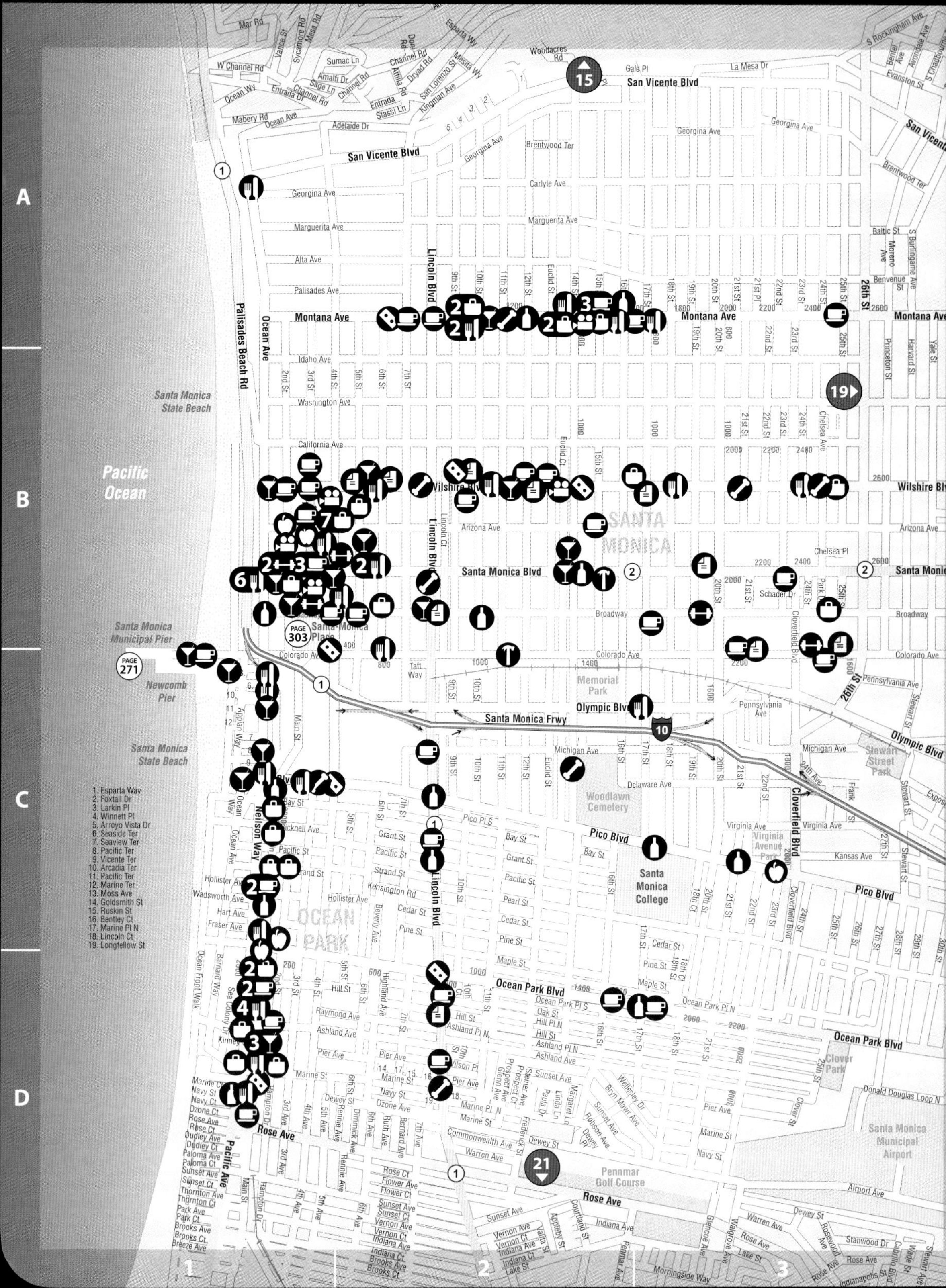

Map 18 · **Santa Monica**

1. Esparta Way
2. Foxtail Dr
3. Larkin Pl
4. Winnett Pl
5. Arroyo Vista Dr
6. Seaside Ter
7. Seaview Ter
8. Pacific Ter
9. Vicente Ter
10. Arcadia Ter
11. Pacific Ter
12. Marine Ter
13. Moss Ave
14. Goldsmith St
15. Ruskin St
16. Bentley Ct
17. Marine Pl N
18. Lincoln Ct
19. Longfellow St

Pacific Ocean

Santa Monica State Beach

Palisades Beach Rd

San Vicente Blvd

Montana Ave

Wilshire Blvd

SANTA MONICA

Santa Monica Blvd

Broadway

Colorado Ave

Santa Monica Frwy

Olympic Blvd

Pico Blvd

Ocean Park Blvd

Rose Ave

OCEAN PARK

Santa Monica College

Woodlawn Cemetery

Memorial Park

Virginia Avenue Park

Stewart Street Park

Clover Park

Pennmar Golf Course

Santa Monica Municipal Airport

Newcomb Pier

Santa Monica Municipal Pier

PAGE 271

PAGE 303

A day in Santa Monica might start at the Omelette Parlor. For celebrity viewing and a $200 T-shirt, there's Fred Segal. We like the Powerhouse Theater (3116 2nd St); check out its *SNL*-style show, Skit-so-phrenia, which pushes the limit on shocking humor (www.skitsola.com).

Coffee
- **18th Street Coffee House** · 1725 Broadway
- **Amelia's** · 2645 Main St
- **Café Bolivar** · 1741 Ocean Park Blvd
- **Café Promenade** · 1260 3rd St Prom
- **Caffe Divine** · 500 Broadway
- **Charlie's Coffee** · 2425 Colorado Ave
- **Coffee Bean & Tea Leaf** · 1312 3rd St Prom
  - 1426 Montana Ave   · 1804 Lincoln Blvd
  - 2901 Main St   · 200 Santa Monica Blvd
  - 829 Wilshire Blvd   · 380 Santa Monica Pier
- **Coffee Cup Bakery** · 321 Santa Monica Blvd
- **Cutting Board** · 1260 15th St
- **Diedrich Coffee** · 732 Montana Ave
- **Hear Music** · 1429 3rd St Prom
- **Infuzion Café** · 1149 3rd St
- **Ive's Dream Coffee Bar** · 1324 Wilshire Blvd
- **Krispy Kreme Doughnuts** · 1231 Wilshire Blvd
- **Mystic Joe** · 2311 Santa Monica Blvd
- **Pane Dolce** · 1627 Montana Ave
- **Peet's Coffee & Tea** · 1401 Montana Ave
- **Peet's Coffee & Tea** · 2439 Main St
- **Starbucks**   · 1356 3rd St Prom
  - 1426 Montana Ave   · 2200 Colorado Ave
  - 2671 Main St   · 3020 Lincoln Blvd
  - 308 Wilshire Blvd   · 3110 Main St
  - 701 Montana Ave   · Albertsons, 2627 Lincoln Blvd
- **Talking Stick** · 1630 Ocean Park Blvd
- **Urth Caffe** · 2327 Main St
- **Velocity Café** · 2127 Lincoln Blvd

Copy Centers
- **Copypage** · 2450 Colorado Ave · 310-453-3600
- **Image Square** · 2200 Colorado Ave · 310-998-8687
- **Kinko's** · 601 Wilshire Blvd · 310-576-7710
- **Printing Palace** · 513 Wilshire Blvd · 310-451-5151
- **Santa Monica Copy Printing** · 924 Wilshire Blvd · 310-319-1341
- **Sir Speedy** · 1909 Santa Monica Blvd · 310-829-3022
- **Staples** · 1501 Lincoln Blvd · 310-577-6740
- **Staples** · 1610 Wilshire Blvd · 310-828-7779
- **UPS Store** · 1223 Wilshire Blvd · 310-458-6878
- **UPS Store** · 2633 Lincoln Blvd · 310-396-5707

Farmer's Markets
- **Farmers' Market** · Arizona Ave & 2nd St
- **Santa Monica** · 2300 Pico Blvd
- **Santa Monica** · Arizona Ave & 3rd St Prom
- **Santa Monica** · Ocean Park Blvd & Main St

Gyms
- **24-Hour Fitness** · 1415 2nd St · 310-255-0008
- **Club at Colorado** · 2425 Colorado Ave · 310-829-2227
- **Curves** · 1335 4th St · 310-917-1371
- **Curves** · 1919 Broadway · 310-582-9181
- **Easton Gym** · 1233 3rd St Prom · 310-395-4441
- **Equinox** · 201 Santa Monica Blvd · 310-593-8888

Hardware Stores
- **Ace** · 1521 Santa Monica Blvd · 310-395-1158
- **True Value** · 1636 11th St · 310-450-6556

Liquor Stores
- **A&E Liquor Mart** · 2116 Pico Blvd
- **Bill's Liquor** · 2202 Lincoln Blvd
- **Davey Jones Liquor Locker** · 63 Navy St
- **Duck Blind** · 1102 Montana Ave
- **Ed's Liquor** · 825 Pico Blvd
- **Fireside Liquors** · 1421 Montana Ave
- **Frank's Liquor** · 115 Broadway
- **Hank's Liquor** · 1436 Santa Monica Blvd
- **Ladd Liquor** · 1011 Broadway
- **Marty's Liquor** · 1736 Ocean Park Blvd
- **Moore's Liquors** · 1711 Pico Blvd
- **Star Liquor** · 1929 Main St
- **Surf Liquor** · 2522 Main St

Movie Theaters
- **Aero Theater** · 1328 Montana Ave · 310-260-1528
- **AMC Santa Monica 7 Plex** · 1310 3rd St Prom · 310-395-3030
- **Laemmle Monica 4** · 1332 2nd St · 310-394-9741
- **Landmark NuWilshire Theatre** · 1314 Wilshire Blvd · 310-394-8099
- **Loews Broadway Cinemas 4** · 1441 3rd St Prom · 310-458-3924
- **Mann Criterion 6** · 1313 3rd St Prom · 310-395-1599

Nightlife
- **14 Below** · 1348 14th St · 310-451-5040
- **Bar Copa** · 2810 Main St · 310-452-2445
- **Big Dean's Café** · 1615 Ocean Front Wk · 310-393-2666
- **Cameo Bar at The Viceroy Hotel** · 1819 Ocean Ave · 310-451-8711
- **Casa del Mar** · 1910 Ocean Wy · 310-581-5533
- **Circle Bar** · 2926 Main St · 310-450-0508
- **Cock N' Bull Pub** · 2947 Lincoln Blvd · 310-399-9696
- **Fairmont Miramar Hotel / Grill Restaurant** · 101 Wilshire Blvd · 310-576-7777
- **Father's Office** · 1018 Montana Ave · 310-393-2337
- **Harvelle's** · 1432 4th St · 310-395-1676
- **The Library Ale House** · 2911 Main St · 310-314-4855
- **Loews Santa Monica Beach Hotel** · 1700 Ocean Ave · 310-458-6700
- **Lounge 217** · 217 Broadway · 310-394-6336
- **O'Brien's** · 2941 Main St · 310-396-4725
- **Renee's Courtyard** · 522 Wilshire Blvd · 310-451-9341
- **The Room SM** · 1323 Santa Monica Blvd · 310-458-0707
- **Rusty's Surf Ranch** · 256 Santa Monica Pier · 310-393-7437
- **Shutters** · 1 Pico Blvd · 310-458-0030
- **Sugar** · 814 Broadway · 310-899-1989
- **Temple Bar** · 1026 Wilshire Blvd · 310-393-6611
- **Voda** · 1449 2nd St · 310-394-9774
- **Ye Olde King's Head** · 116 Santa Monica Blvd · 310-451-1402
- **Zanzibar** · 1301 5th St · 310-451-2221

Pet Stores
- **Animal Kingdom** · 300 Pico Blvd · 310-392-4074
- **Aquarium & Pet Center** · 826 Wilshire Blvd · 310-395-1009
- **Centinela Feed & Pet Supplies** · 1448 Lincoln Blvd · 310-451-7140
- **Consolidated Pet Supplies** · 1840 14th St · 310-393-9393
- **Pet Affaire** · 3013 Lincoln Blvd · 310-396-0804
- **Pets of Wilshire** · 2102 Wilshire Blvd · 310-453-7676
- **Wagging Tail** · 1123 Montana Ave · 310-656-9663
- **Wilshire Animal Hospital** · 2421 Wilshire Blvd · 310-828-4587

Restaurants
- **17th Street Café** · 1610 Montana Ave · 310-453-2771
- **Babalu** · 1002 Montana Ave · 310-395-2500
- **Blueberry** · 510 Santa Monica Blvd · 310-394-7766
- **Border Grill** · 1445 4th St · 310-451-1655
- **Broadway Deli** · 1457 3rd St Prom · 310-451-0616
- **Buffalo Club** · 1520 Olympic Blvd · 310-450-8600
- **Café Montana** · 1534 Montana Ave · 310-829-3990
- **California Chicken Café** · 2401 Wilshire Blvd · 310-453-0477
- **Cha Cha Chicken** · 1906 Ocean Ave · 310-581-1684
- **Chaya Venice** · 110 Navy St · 310-396-1179
- **Chez Jay** · 1657 Ocean Ave · 310-395-1741
- **Chinois on Main** · 2709 Main St · 310-392-9025
- **Dhaba** · 2104 Main St · 310-399-9452
- **El Cholo** · 1025 Wilshire Blvd · 310-899-1106
- **Falafel King** · 1315 3rd St Prom · 310-587-2551
- **Finn McCool's** · 2702 Main St · 310-452-1734
- **Fritto Misto** · 601 Colorado Ave · 310-458-2829
- **Fromin's Delicatessen** · 1832 Wilshire Blvd · 310-829-5443
- **Library Ale House** · 2911 Main St · 310-314-4855
- **The Lobster** · 1602 Ocean Ave · 310-458-9294
- **Lula** · 2720 Main St · 310-392-5711
- **Mani's** · 2507 Main St · 310-396-7700
- **Michael D's Café & Catering** · 234 Pico Blvd · 310-452-8737
- **Newsroom Café** · 530 Wilshire Blvd · 310-319-9100
- **Ocean Ave Seafood** · 1401 Ocean Ave · 310-394-5669
- **Ocean Park Omelette Parlor** · 2732 Main St · 310-399-7892
- **Sushi Roku** · 1401 Ocean Ave · 310-458-4771
- **Trastavere** · 1360 3rd St Prom · 310-319-1985
- **Tudor House** · 1403 2nd St · 310-451-4107
- **World Café** · 2820 Main St · 310-392-1661
- **Ye Olde King's Head** · 116 Santa Monica Blvd · 310-451-1402
- **Yu Restaurant and Lounge** · 1323 Montana Ave · 310-395-4727

Shopping
- **Acorn Store** · 1220 5th St · 310-451-5845
- **Apple Store** · 1248 3rd St Prom · 310-576-1011
- **Continental Shop** · 1619 Wilshire Blvd · 310-453-8655
- **Eames Office** · 2665 Main St · 310-396-5991
- **Fred Segal** · 500 Broadway · 310-393-3940
- **Hear Music** · 1429 3rd St Prom · 310-319-9527
- **Helen's Cycles** · 2501 Broadway · 310-829-1836
- **Herb King** · 2305 Main St · 310-399-4470
- **Horizons West** · 2011 Main St · 310-392-1122
- **Kiehl's** · 1516 Montana Ave · 310-255-0055
- **Le Sanctuaire** · 2710 Main St · 310-581-8999
- **London Sole** · 1331 Montana Ave · 310-255-0937
- **Midnight Special Bookstore** · 1318 3rd St Prom · 310-393-2923
- **Number One Beauty Supply** · 1426 Montana Ave · 310-394-6968
- **One Life Natural Foods** · 3001 Main St · 310-392-4501
- **Palmetto** · 1034 Montana Ave · 310-395-6687
- **Pump Station** · 2415 Wilshire Blvd · 310-826-5774
- **Puzzle Zoo** · 1413 3rd St Prom · 310-393-9201
- **Santa Monica Farms** · 2015 Main St · 310-396-4069
- **Splash Bath & Body** · 2823 Main St · 310-581-4200
- **Step!** · 1004 Montana Ave · 310-899-4409
- **Tao Healing Arts Center** · 2309 Main St · 310-396-4877
- **Tiffany & Jax** · 1244 3rd St Prom · 310-260-8656
- **Tudor House** · 1403 2nd St · 310-451-4107

Video Rental
- **50 50 Video** · 920 Wilshire Blvd · 310-393-5402
- **Blockbuster** · 1402 Wilshire Blvd · 310-394-7792
- **Blockbuster** · 180 Pier Ave · 310-452-4243
- **Blockbuster** · 2602 Lincoln Blvd · 310-392-3228
- **Blockbuster** · 625 Montana Ave · 310-393-5131
- **Vidiots** · 302 Pico Blvd · 310-392-8508

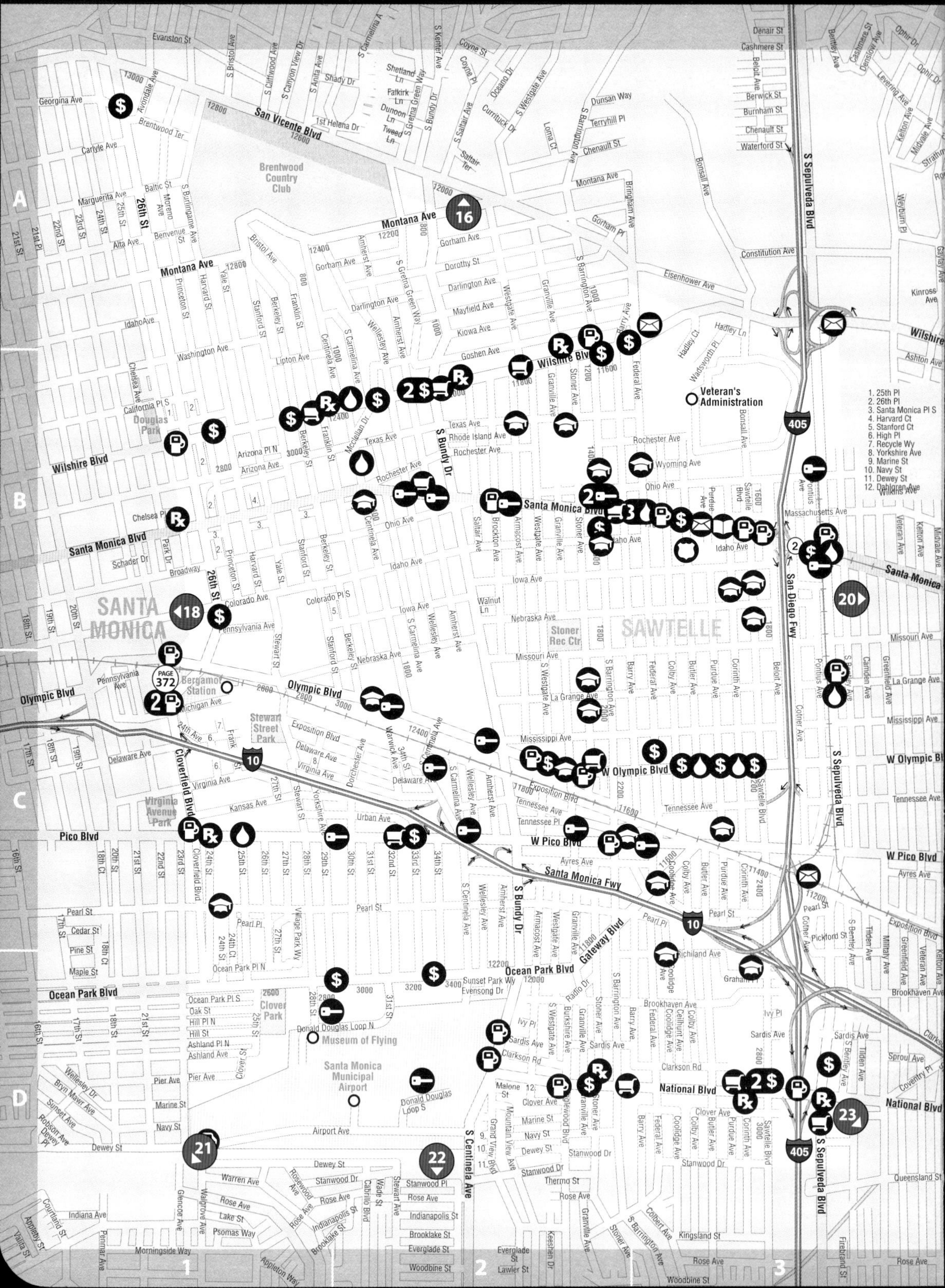

Map 19 • West LA / Santa Monica East

Often referred to as "The Westside," West LA/Santa Monica East is the city's version of limbo—not as posh as the beach, but tamer than the Eastside. Most residents of the area will agree that the proximity to the beach (and the accompanying air quality), wealth of shopping and dining options, and easy access to the 10 and 405 freeways make it a great place to live.

$ Banks

- **Bank of America** · 11501 Santa Monica Blvd
- **Bank of America** · 287 26th St
- **Bank of America** · 2930 S Sepulveda Blvd
- **Bank of America** · 3320 Ocean Park Blvd
- **Bank of America Mortgage** · 3032 Wilshire Blvd
- **California Bank & Trust** · 11345 W Olympic Blvd
- **City National** · 11500 W Olympic Blvd
- **City National** · 1620 26th St
- **First Bank & Trust** · 11835 W Olympic Blvd
- **First Federal** · 11310 National Blvd
- **First Federal** · 12401 Wilshire Blvd
- **Guaranty Bank of California** · 12301 Wilshire Blvd
- **Pacific Western** · 11150 W Olympic Blvd
- **US** · 12100 Wilshire Blvd
- **US** · 3302 Pico Blvd
- **Washington Mutual** · 11285 National Blvd
- **Washington Mutual** · 11766 Wilshire Blvd
- **Washington Mutual** · 2701 Wilshire Blvd
- **Wells Fargo** · 11377 W Olympic Blvd
- **Wells Fargo** · 11727 W Olympic Blvd
- **Wells Fargo** · 2940 Ocean Park Blvd
- **World Savings & Loan** · 11601 Wilshire Blvd

Car Rental

- **Avis** · 11901 Santa Monica Blvd
- **Buddy Trucks** · 11700 Santa Monica Blvd
- **California Rent-a-Car** · 11725 Santa Monica Blvd
- **Dreamboats Rent-a-Car** · 2929 Pico Blvd
- **Enterprise** · 11151 W Olympic Blvd
- **Enterprise** · 11779 W Pico Blvd
- **Enterprise** · 12101 Olympic Blvd
- **Enterprise** · 12207 Santa Monica Blvd
- **Hertz** · 3223 Donald Douglas Loop S
- **Midway Car Rental** · 1800 S Sepulveda Blvd
- **Midway Car Rental** · 2828 Donald Douglas Loop N
- **OK Rent a Car** · 12301 Santa Monica Blvd
- **Penske Truck Rental** · 2270 S Centinela Ave
- **Rapid Rent-a-Car** · 11590 W Pico Blvd
- **Rent-a-Wreck** · 12333 W Pico Blvd
- **U-Haul** · 3250 Olympic Blvd

Car Washes

- **All By Hand** · 11111 Santa Monica Blvd
- **Auto Beauty Spa** · 1346 S Centinela Ave
- **Blue Wave Car Wash** · 11602 Santa Monica Blvd
- **Mr Detail Auto Waxing** · 11500 W Olympic Blvd
- **Santa Monica Car Wash & Detail** · 2510 Pico Blvd
- **Sepulveda West Car Wash** · 2001 S Sepulveda Blvd
- **Shell** · 11574 Santa Monica Blvd
- **Shine for Show** · 11755 Wilshire Blvd
- **West LA Car Wash** · 11350 W Olympic Blvd

Gas Stations

- **76** · 11280 National Blvd
- **76** · 11305 Santa Monica Blvd
- **76** · 11675 W Pico Blvd
- **76** · 11954 Santa Monica Blvd
- **76** · 2001 S Sepulveda Blvd
- **76** · 2601 Wilshire Blvd
- **76** · 2876 S Bundy Dr
- **Arco** · 11748 W Olympic Blvd
- **Arco** · 1819 Cloverfield Blvd
- **Chevron** · 11261 Santa Monica Blvd
- **Chevron** · 11951 W Olympic Blvd
- **Chevron** · 2501 Airport Ave
- **Exxon** · 1770 Cloverfield Blvd
- **Mobil** · 11666 Wilshire Blvd
- **Mobil** · 1660 S Sepulveda Blvd
- **Shell** · 11574 Santa Monica Blvd
- **Shell** · 11944 W Olympic Blvd
- **Shell** · 1802 Cloverfield Blvd
- **Shell** · 2876 S Bundy Dr

○ Landmarks

- **Bergamot Station** · 2525 Michigan Ave
- **Museum of Flying** · 2772 Donald Douglas Loop N
- **Santa Monica Municipal Airport** · 3223 Donald Douglas Loop S
- **Veteran's Administration** · Federal Ave & S Sepulveda Blvd

Libraries

- **West Los Angeles Regional** · 11360 Santa Monica Blvd · 310-575-8323

Rx Pharmacies

- **Longs Drugs** · 3202 Wilshire Blvd · 310-829-5523
- **Pavilions** · 11750 Wilshire Blvd · 310-473-6138
- **Ralphs** · 11727 W Olympic Blvd · 310-444-0603
- **Rite-Aid** · 11321 National Blvd · 310-479-5729
- **Rite-Aid** · 2412 Pico Blvd · 310-450-7624
- **Sav-On** · 12015 W Wilshire Blvd · 310-479-6500
- **Sav-On (24 hrs)** · 2505 Santa Monica Blvd · 310-828-6056
- **Sav-On (24 hrs)** · 3010 S Sepulveda Blvd · 310-478-9821

Police

- **Los Angeles Police Dept** · 1663 Butler Ave · 310-575-8402

Post Offices

- **US Post Office** · 11270 Exposition Blvd
- **US Post Office** · 11301 Wilshire Blvd
- **US Post Office** · 11420 Santa Monica Blvd

Schools

- **Brockton Ave Elementary** · 1309 Armacost Ave
- **Daniel Webster Middle** · 11330 W Graham Pl
- **Edison Elementary** · 2425 Kansas Ave
- **Grant Elementary** · 2368 Pearl St
- **Indian Springs Continuation** · 1441 S Barrington Ave
- **New Horizon** · 1819 Sawtelle Blvd
- **New Roads** · 3131 Olympic Blvd
- **New West Charter Middle** · 11625 W Pico Blvd
- **Nora Sterry Elementary** · 1730 Corinth Ave
- **Park Century** · 2040 Stoner Ave
- **Poseidon** · 11811 W Pico Blvd
- **Richland Ave Elementary** · 11562 Richland Ave
- **Richland EEC** · 2623 Coolidge Ave
- **Southern California Montessori** · 1430 Centinela Ave
- **St Joan of Arc Elementary** · 11561 Gateway Blvd
- **St Sebastian** · 1430 Federal Ave
- **Sterry EEC** · 1747 Sawtelle Blvd
- **University Senior High** · 11800 Texas Ave
- **West LA Baptist** · 1609 Barrington Ct
- **Westview** · 2000 Stoner Ave
- **Wildwood** · 11811 W Olympic Blvd

Supermarkets

- **Albertsons** · 3105 Wilshire Blvd
- **Pavilions** · 11750 Wilshire Blvd
- **Ralphs** · 11361 National Blvd
- **Ralphs** · 11727 W Olympic Blvd
- **Ralphs** · 12057 Wilshire Blvd
- **Smart & Final** · 11221 W Pico Blvd
- **Smart & Final** · 12210 Santa Monica Blvd
- **Trader Joe's** · 3212 Pico Blvd
- **Vons** · 11674 Santa Monica Blvd
- **Vons** · 3118 S Sepulveda Blvd
- **Whole Foods Market** · 11666 National Blvd

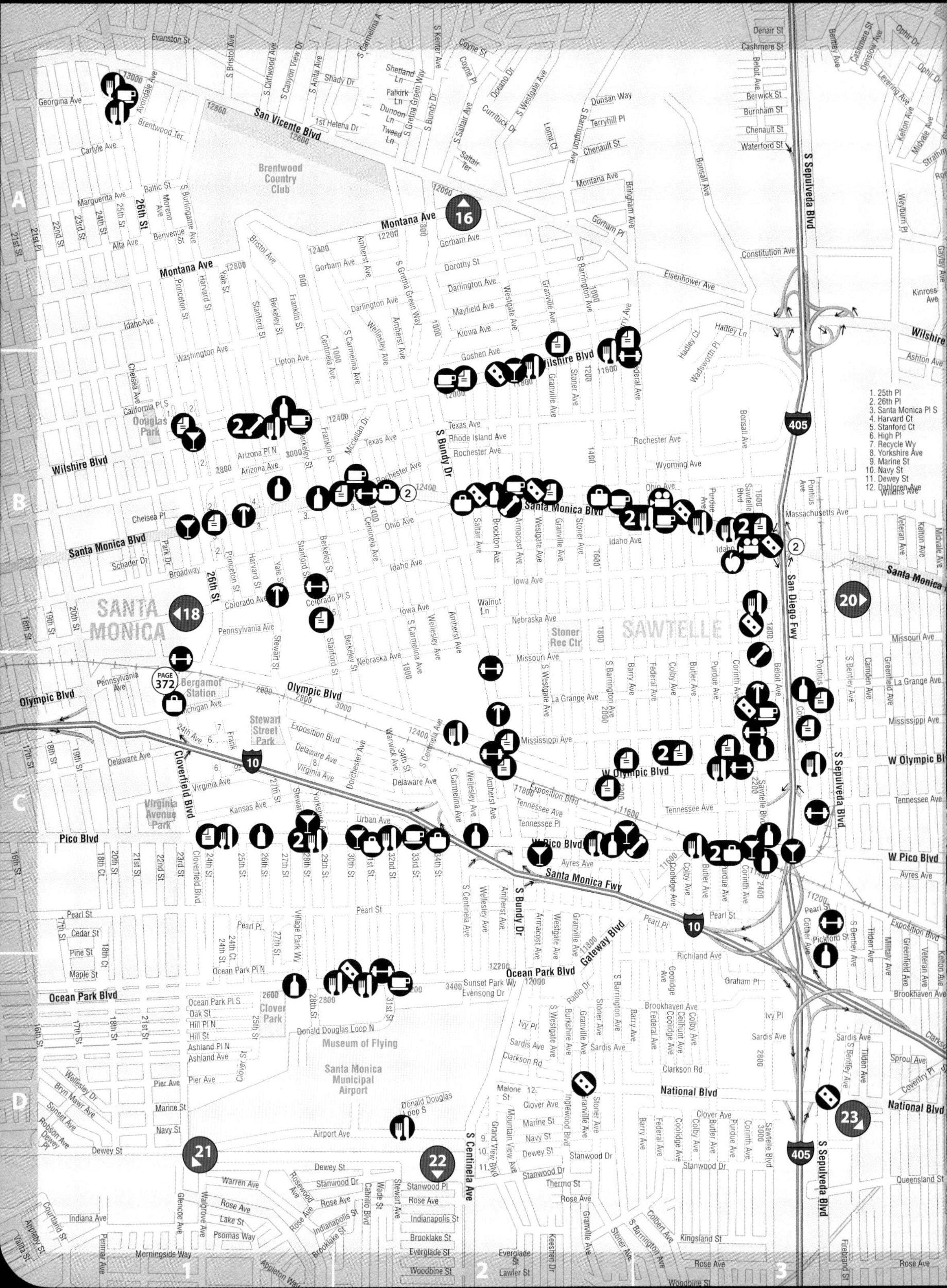
SANTA MONICA
SAWTELLE
Wilshire Blvd
Santa Monica Blvd
Olympic Blvd
Pico Blvd
Ocean Park Blvd
National Blvd
S Sepulveda Blvd
San Diego Fwy
Santa Monica Fwy
S Bundy Dr
Montana Ave
San Vicente Blvd
Brentwood Country Club
Douglas Park
Bergamot Station
Stewart Street Park
Virginia Avenue Park
Clover Park
Stoner Rec Ctr
Museum of Flying
Santa Monica Municipal Airport
PAGE 372
1. 25th Pl
2. 26th Pl
3. Santa Monica Pl S
4. Harvard Ct
5. Stanford Ct
6. High Pl
7. Recycle Wy
8. Yorkshire Ave
9. Marine St
10. Navy St
11. Dewey St
12. Dahlgren Ave

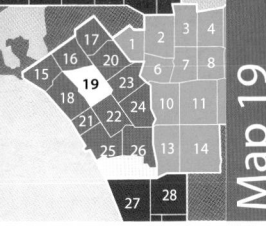

For services, your best bets are along the east-west arteries. The exception: karaoke is to be found along Sepulveda/Sawtelle Boulevards. A variety of restaurants and cuisines illustrate the neighborhood's diversity. The Arsenal serves up great tunes and cocktails in a near-pitch dark atmosphere. The independent movie theater reigns in this neighborhood: both the NuArt and Royal Theatres are hopping all weekend.

Coffee

- **Balcony** · 12431 Rochester Ave
- **Cacao Coffee House** · 11609 Santa Monica Blvd
- **Coffee Bean & Tea Leaf** · 3150 Ocean Park Blvd
- **Literati Café** · 12081 Wilshire Blvd
- **Starbucks** · 11155 Santa Monica Blvd
- **Starbucks** · 11280 W Olympic Blvd
- **Starbucks** · 11705 National Blvd
- **Starbucks** · 12100 Santa Monica Blvd
- **Starbucks** · 2525 Wilshire Blvd
- **Starbucks** · 2901 Ocean Park Blvd
- **Starbucks (Albertsons)** · 3105 Wilshire Blvd
- **Tanner's Coffee Company** · 11901 Santa Monica Blvd
- **The Office** · 256 26th St
- **Unurban** · 3301 Pico Blvd
- **Volcano Tea** · 2111 Sawtelle Blvd

Copy Centers

- **Advance Graphics & Printing** · 2233 Barry Ave · 310-473-7002
- **Blair Graphics** · 1740 Stanford St · 310-829-4621
- **Copy Central** · 11988 Wilshire Blvd · 310-207-5952
- **Copy Depot & Printing** · 1635 Sawtelle Blvd · 310-473-5152
- **Copy Impress** · 12041 Wilshire Blvd · 310-312-0809
- **Copyco Printing** · 11555 W Olympic Blvd · 310-478-1776
- **Image Square** · 1627 Stanford St · 310-586-2333
- **Kinko's** · 11819 Wilshire Blvd · 310-477-7756
- **Kinko's** · 2139 S Bundy Dr · 310-826-8122
- **Mail Boxes Etc** · 1158 26th St · 310-453-4111
- **Office Depot** · 2231 S Barrington Ave · 310-478-7103
- **Phantom Lithography** · 11279 Santa Monica Blvd · 310-478-4667
- **Pip Printing** · 2612 Santa Monica Blvd · 310-315-9625
- **Printers Company** · 11601 Wilshire Blvd · 310-477-8818
- **Quality Digital Solutions** · 11159 Mississippi Ave · 310-914-7606
- **Reliable Graphics** · 3212 Santa Monica Blvd · 310-453-7991
- **Sir Speedy** · 11660 W Olympic Blvd · 310-473-9256
- **Staples** · 2052 Bundy Dr · 310-826-0442
- **Super Fast Copying & Binding Systems** · 2358 Pico Blvd · 310-452-3352
- **Universal Reprographics** · 2043 Pontius Ave · 310-458-3523
- **UPS Store** · 11301 W Olympic Blvd · 310-445-4014
- **UPS Store** · 11870 Santa Monica Blvd · 310-207-1530
- **West LA Print & Copy** · 11577 Olympic Blvd · 310-473-5620

Farmer's Markets

- **West LA Civic** · 1645 Corinth Ave

Gyms

- **24-Hour Fitness** · 2929 31st St · 310-450-4464
- **Bally Total Fitness** · 1914 S Bundy Dr · 310-820-7571
- **Bodies In Motion** · 12100 Olympic Blvd · 310-836-8000
- **Curves** · 2130 Sawtelle Blvd · 310-444-8805
- **Joe's Gym** · 11601 Wilshire Blvd · 310-966-1999
- **Powerhouse Gym** · 11400 W Olympic Blvd · 310-914-5120
- **Spectrum Club** · 2425 Olympic Blvd · 310-829-4995
- **Sports Club LA** · 1835 S Sepulveda Blvd · 310-473-1447

Hardware Stores

- **George's Hardware & Garden Supply** · 2060 Sawtelle Blvd · 310-479-1280
- **Hardware Express** · 2834 Colorado Ave · 310-829-1184
- **Orchard Supply Hardware** · 2020 S Bundy Dr · 310-571-3838
- **Tool Power** · 2828 Santa Monica Blvd · 310-453-2012

Liquor Stores

- **2020 Wine Company** · 2020 Cotner Ave
- **Barrington Liquor** · 1166 S Barrington Ave
- **Brockton Liquor** · 11932 Santa Monica Blvd
- **Hai's Liquor** · 11701 W Pico Blvd
- **In & Out Liquor** · 2130 Sawtelle Blvd
- **Jan's Liquors** · 12300 W Pico Blvd
- **Jerry's Liquor** · 2923 Wilshire Blvd
- **King Liquor** · 3100 Santa Monica Blvd
- **Mark's International Wines** · 2311 Cotner Ave
- **Signiture Wines & Spirits** · 2717 Ocean Park Blvd
- **Sunset Plaza Liquor** · 2602 Pico Blvd
- **Wine Expo** · 2933 Santa Monica Blvd

Movie Theaters

- **Landmark NuArt Theatre** · 11272 Santa Monica Blvd · 310-478-6379
- **Laemmle Royal** · 11523 Santa Monica Blvd

Nightlife

- **The Arsenal** · 12012 W Pico Blvd · 310-575-5511
- **The Joker** · 2827 Pico Blvd · 310-828-9235
- **Liquid Kitty** · 11780 W Pico Blvd · 310-473-3707
- **McCabe's** · 3101 Pico Blvd · 310-828-4403
- **Plan B** · 11637 W Pico Blvd · 310-312-3633
- **Q's Billiards** · 11835 Wilshire Blvd · 310-477-7550
- **Sonny McLean's** · 2615 Wilshire Blvd · 310-828-9839
- **The Shack** · 2518 Santa Monica Blvd · 310-449-1171

Pet Stores

- **Elaine's Pet Shop** · 2919 Wilshire Blvd · 310-828-4545
- **LA Aquarium & Pet Supplies** · 11662 W Pico Blvd · 310-477-1928
- **Petco** · 2910 Wilshire Blvd · 310-586-1963
- **Pets Salon** · 12243 Santa Monica Blvd · 310-207-0838

Restaurants

- **Asakuma** · 11701 Wilshire Blvd · 310-826-0013
- **Bandera** · 11700 Wilshire Blvd · 310-477-3524
- **Benito's Taco Shop** · 11614 Santa Monica Blvd · 310-442-9924
- **Bombay Café** · 12021 W Pico Blvd · 310-473-3388
- **Chez Mimi** · 246 26th St · 310-393-0558
- **Hide Sushi** · 2040 Sawtelle Blvd · 310-477-7242
- **Il Forno** · 2901 Ocean Park Blvd · 310-450-1241
- **Il Moro** · 11400 W Olympic Blvd · 310-575-3530
- **Javan** · 11500 Santa Monica Blvd · 310-207-5555
- **Josie Restaurant** · 2424 Pico Blvd · 310-581-9888
- **Kay 'n Dave's** · 262 26th St · 310-260-1355
- **La Bottega Marino** · 11363 Santa Monica Blvd · 310-477-7777
- **Lares** · 2909 Pico Blvd · 310-829-4550
- **Le Saigon** · 11611 Santa Monica Blvd · 310-312-2929
- **Rae's Restaurant** · 2901 Ocean Park Blvd · 310-828-7937
- **Royal Star Seafood** · 3001 Wilshire Blvd · 310-828-8812
- **Sushi Sasabune** · 11300 Nebraska Ave · 310-268-8380
- **Tlapazola Grill** · 11676 Gateway Blvd · 310-477-1577
- **Typhoon** · 3221 Donald Douglas Loop S · 310-390-6565
- **Valentino** · 3115 Pico Blvd · 310-829-4313
- **Vito** · 2807 Ocean Park Blvd · 310-450-4999
- **Yabu** · 11820 W Pico Blvd · 310-473-9757
- **Zabies** · 3003 Ocean Park Blvd · 310-392-9036

Shopping

- **Any Occasion Balloons** · 12009 W Pico Blvd · 310-473-9963
- **California Map & Travel** · 3312 Pico Blvd · 310-396-6277
- **Graphaids** · 12400 Santa Monica Blvd · 310-820-0445
- **Hiromi Paper International** · Bergamot Station, 2525 Michigan Ave · 310-998-0098
- **McCabe's Guitar Shop** · 3101 Pico Blvd · 310-828-4497
- **Musicians' Supply Shop** · 12010 Ohio Ave · 310-478-7836
- **Record Surplus** · 11609 W Pico Blvd · 310-478-4217
- **Utrecht Arts Supplies** · 11677 Santa Monica Blvd · 310-478-5775

Video Rental

- **20-20 Video** · 11550 Santa Monica Blvd · 310-478-2020
- **20-20 Video** · 3000 S Sepulveda Blvd · 310-836-2020
- **Blockbuster** · 11700 National Blvd · 310-391-8233
- **Blockbuster** · 12112 Santa Monica Blvd · 310-447-2481
- **Cinefile Video** · 11280 Santa Monica Blvd · 310-312-8836
- **Galaxy Video & 28-Minute Photo** · 2901 Ocean Park Blvd · 310-450-0900
- **Hollywood Video** · 11870 Santa Monica Blvd · 310-207-1485
- **Odyssey Video** · 11910 Wilshire Blvd · 310-477-2523
- **Video Addict (Asian)** · 1818 Sawtelle Blvd · 310-312-5083
- **Video One (Japanese only)** · 2011 Sawtelle Blvd · 310-479-4992

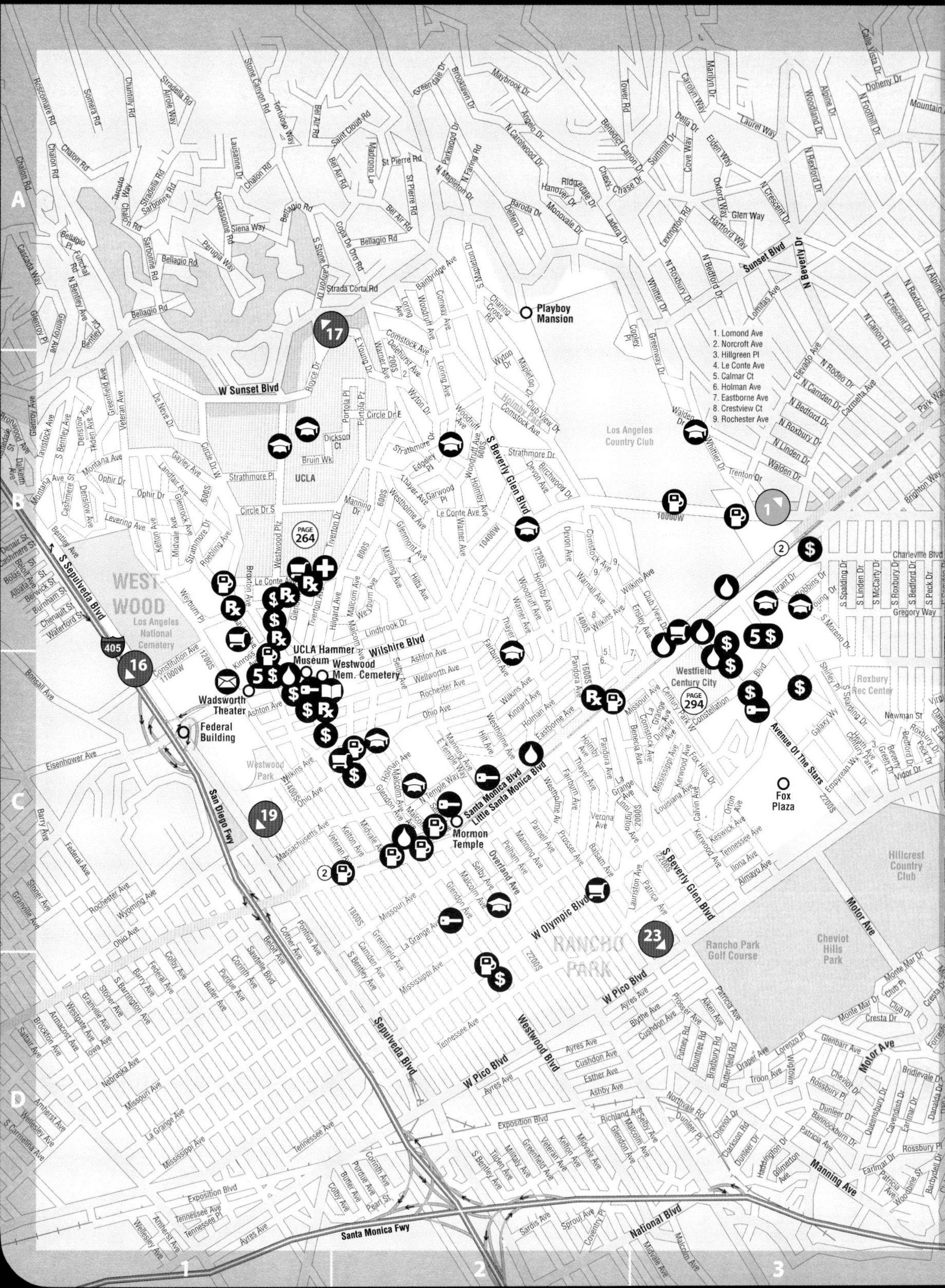

Map 20 · **Westwood / Century City**

A

B

C

D

1 2 3

WEST WOOD

Los Angeles National Cemetery

UCLA

Bruin Wlk

PAGE 264

UCLA Hammer Museum
Westwood Mem. Cemetery

Wadsworth Theater

Federal Building

Westwood Park

Playboy Mansion

Los Angeles Country Club

1. Lomond Ave
2. Norcroft Ave
3. Hillgreen Pl
4. Le Conte Ave
5. Calmar Ct
6. Holman Ave
7. Eastborne Ave
8. Crestview Ct
9. Rochester Ave

Westfield Century City
PAGE 294

Fox Plaza

Roxbury Rec Center

Hillcrest Country Club

Cheviot Hills Park

Rancho Park Golf Course

RANCHO PARK

Mormon Temple

W Sunset Blvd

Wilshire Blvd

Santa Monica Blvd
Little Santa Monica Blvd

W Olympic Blvd

W Pico Blvd

Santa Monica Fwy

National Blvd

San Diego Fwy

405

16

17

19

23

5

Avenue Of The Stars

Century City is mostly office buildings and becomes a virtual ghost town at night—with the exception of the Century City Mall and ABC Entertainment Center. Westwood, however, is always brimming with UCLA students, film-goers, and sports fans. As a result, street parking is a game of chance and a test of one's patience. Don't miss the LA Times Festival of Books on-campus every April.

$ Banks

- **Bank of America** • 10960 Wilshire Blvd
- **Bank of America** • 2049 Century Park E
- **Bank of America** • 930 Westwood Blvd
- **Bank of the West** • 10929 Wilshire Blvd
- **California Bank & Trust** • 1940 Century Park E
- **California Commerce** • 2029 Century Park E
- **California Credit Union** • 2215 Westwood Blvd
- **California National** • 1460 Westwood Blvd
- **California National** • 1800 Avenue of the Stars
- **Citibank** • 1072 Westwood Blvd
- **Citibank** • 1801 Avenue of the Stars
- **City National** • 10889 Wilshire Blvd
- **City National** • 1800 Century Park E
- **City National** • 1950 Avenue of the Stars
- **City National** • 2029 Century Park E
- **Comerica** • 10900 Wilshire Blvd
- **East West** • 1900 Avenue of the Stars
- **First Regional** • 1801 Century Park E
- **First Republic** • 1888 Century Park E
- **Preferred** • 1801 Century Park E
- **Union** • 10900 Wilshire Blvd
- **Union** • 1901 Avenue of the Stars
- **US** • 10866 Wilshire Blvd
- **Washington Mutual** • 10901 Wilshire Blvd
- **Washington Mutual** • 1550 Westwood Blvd
- **Washington Mutual** • 1925 Century Park E
- **Wells Fargo** • 10920 Wilshire Blvd
- **Wells Fargo** • 1801 Avenue of the Stars

Car Rental

- **Avis** • 1234 Westwood Blvd
- **Basic Car Rental** • 10687 Santa Monica Blvd
- **Eli's Rent a Car** • 2021 Westwood Blvd
- **Enterprise** • 10799 Santa Monica Blvd
- **Hertz** • 2025 Avenue of the Stars

Car Washes

- **Blue Auto Spa** • 10250 Santa Monica Blvd
- **Blue Wave Car Wash** • 10850 Santa Monica Blvd
- **Century City** • 1800 Avenue of the Stars
- **Mario's Hand Car Wash** • 10940 Wilshire Blvd
- **Mario's Hand Wash & Auto Detailing** • 10100 Santa Monica Blvd
- **Mr Polish** • 1901 Avenue of the Stars
- **Schic Detailing & Hand Car Wash** • 10585 Santa Monica Blvd

Gas Stations

- **76** • 10389 Santa Monica Blvd
- **76** • 1157 W Gayley Ave
- **76** • 9988 Wilshire Blvd
- **Chevron** • 10867 Santa Monica Blvd
- **Chevron** • 10984 Le Conte Ave
- **Exxon** • 10991 Santa Monica Blvd
- **Mobil** • 10857 Santa Monica Blvd
- **Mobil** • 10863 W Olympic Blvd
- **Mobil** • 1465 Glendon Ave
- **Thrifty** • 10801 Santa Monica Blvd

Hospitals

- **UCLA Medical Center** • 10833 Le Conte Ave

o Landmarks

- **Federal Building** • Wilshire Blvd & Sepulveda Blvd
- **Fox Plaza (AKA the** *Die Hard* **building)** • 2121 Avenue of the Stars
- **Mormon Temple** • 10777 Santa Monica Blvd
- **Playboy Mansion** • 10236 Charing Cross Rd
- **UCLA Hammer Museum** • 10889 Wilshire Blvd
- **Wadsworth Theater** • 11000 Wilshire Blvd
- **Westwood Memorial Cemetery** • 1218 Glendon Ave

Libraries

- **Westwood Branch** • 1246 Glendon Ave • 310-474-1739

Pharmacies

- **CVS** • 1001 Westwood Blvd • 310-209-9141
- **Longs Drugs** • 10861 Weyburn Ave • 310-209-1652
- **Ralphs** • 10861 Le Conte Ave • 310-824-5994
- **Rite-Aid** • 1101 Westwood Blvd • 310-209-0708
- **Sav-On** • 10889 Wellworth Ave • 310-474-2152
- **Walgreens** • 10407 Santa Monica Blvd • 310-481-7174

Post Offices

- **US Post Office** • 11000 Wilshire Blvd

Schools

- **Beverly Hills High** • 241 S Moreno Dr
- **Beverly Hills Montessori** • 1105 N Laurel Ave
- **El Rodeo Elementary** • 605 N Whittier Dr
- **Fairburn Ave Elementary** • 1403 Fairburn Ave
- **Moreno High** • 214 Moreno Dr
- **Ralph Waldo Emerson Middle** • 1650 Selby Ave
- **Sinai Akiba Academy** • 10400 Wilshire Blvd
- **St Paul the Apostle** • 1536 Selby Ave
- **UCLA** • 405 Hilgard Ave
- **UCLA Neuropsychiatric Hospital** • 760 Westwood Plz
- **Warner Ave Elementary** • 615 Holmby Ave
- **Westwood Elementary** • 2050 Selby Ave

Supermarkets

- **Bristol Farms** • 1515 Westwood Blvd
- **Gelson's Markets** • 10250 Santa Monica Blvd
- **Ralphs** • 10309 W Olympic Blvd
- **Ralphs** • 10861 Le Conte Ave
- **Whole Foods Market** • 1050 S Gayley Ave

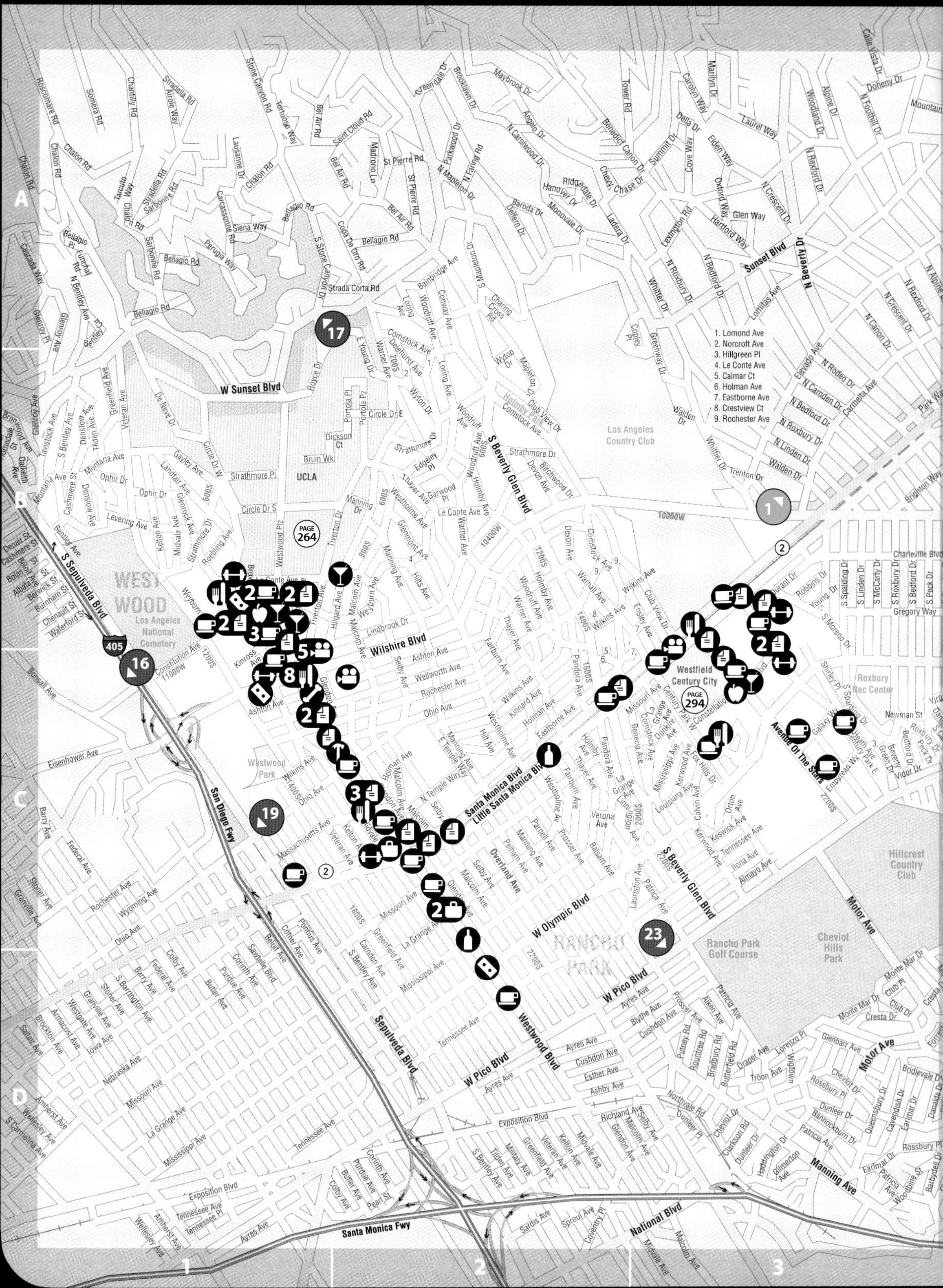

Map 20 · **Westwood / Century City**

N

PAGE 264

PAGE 294

1. Lomond Ave
2. Norcroft Ave
3. Hillgreen Pl
4. Le Conte Ave
5. Calmar Ct
6. Holman Ave
7. Eastborne Ave
8. Crestview Ct
9. Rochester Ave

Los Angeles
Country Club

WEST
WOOD

Los Angeles
National Cemetery

UCLA

Westfield
Century City

Roxbury
Rec Center

Hillcrest
Country Club

Cheviot
Hills
Park

Rancho Park
Golf Course

RANCHO
PARK

Westwood
Park

Wilshire Blvd

W Sunset Blvd

W Olympic Blvd

W Pico Blvd

W Pico Blvd

Santa Monica Blvd
Little Santa Monica Blvd

Santa Monica Fwy

National Blvd

Avenue Of The Stars

S Sepulveda Blvd

San Diego Fwy

Sepulveda Blvd

Westwood Blvd

S Beverly Glen Blvd

S Beverly Glen Blvd

Motor Ave

Sunset Blvd

N Beverly Dr

Because of the symbiotic relationship Westwood has with UCLA, there are many unhealthy, inexpensive, and delicious places to eat: Stan's Donuts; Diddy Riese Cookies (a quarter a cookie); and Falafel King (which deserves its name, serving some of the best baba ghanoush in town). With some of the best and oldest remaining one-screen movie houses in town, Westwood is a great place to take in a movie.

Coffee
- **Bolee's Gourmet** · 10100 Santa Monica Blvd
- **City Bean** · 2121 Avenue of the Stars
- **City Bean Coffee** · 10911 Lindbrook Dr
- **Coffee Bean & Tea Leaf** · 1001 Gayley Ave
- **Coffee Bean & Tea Leaf** ·
  10401 Santa Monica Blvd
- **Coffee Bean & Tea Leaf** ·
  11049 Santa Monica Blvd
- **Coffee Bean & Tea Leaf** · 1500 Westwood Blvd
- **Coffee Bean & Tea Leaf** ·
  1940 Century Park E
- **Coffee Bean & Tea Leaf** · 950 Westwood Blvd
- **Coffee Zinio** · 1731 Westwood Blvd
- **Down to Earth** · 10887 Weyburn Ave
- **Habibi Café** · 923 Broxton Ave
- **Kelly's Coffee & Fudge** ·
  10250 Santa Monica Blvd
- **Lollicup** · 10948 Weyburn Ave
- **Peet's Coffee & Tea** · 1154 Westwood Blvd
- **Peet's Coffee & Tea** · 1854 Westwood Blvd
- **Starbucks** · 10955 W Weyburn Ave
- **Starbucks** · 1161 Westwood Blvd
- **Starbucks** · 1875 Century Park E
- **Starbucks** · 1898 Westwood Blvd
- **Starbucks** · 1999 Avenue of the Stars
- **Starbucks** · 2049 Century Park E
- **Starbucks** · 2215 Westwood Blvd

Copy Centers
- **ABC Copy & Print** · 1557 Westwood Blvd ·
  310-473-2813
- **Budget Printing & Copy** ·
  1718 Westwood Blvd · 310-444-1478
- **Concord Document Services** ·
  1900 Avenue of the Stars · 310-820-7876
- **Copy Central** · 925 Westwood Blvd ·
  818-824-5276
- **Copy Express** · 1609 Westwood Blvd ·
  310-478-1131
- **Copy To Go Printing** · 1311 Westwood Blvd
  · 310-478-5455
- **Copytron & Printing** · 1377 Westwood Blvd
  · 310-473-0773
- **Doggie Logic** · 10100 Santa Monica Blvd ·
  310-556-7751
- **Kinko's** · 10924 Weyburn Ave · 310-443-5502
- **Kinko's** · 1520 Westwood Blvd ·
  310-475-0789
- **Kinko's** · 1875 Century Park E · 310-277-0686
- **LA Reprographics** · 1940 Century Park E ·
  310-300-0193
- **Mail Boxes Etc** · 1875 Century Park E ·
  310-286-1875
- **Mail Boxes Etc** · 914 Westwood Blvd ·
  310-208-5022
- **Next Print** · 1632 Westwood Blvd ·
  310-441-5999
- **Print Run Services** · 952 Gayley Ave ·
  310-824-5150
- **Repro Solutions** · 10780 Santa Monica Blvd
  · 310-441-4333
- **Staples** · 10830 Santa Monica Blvd ·
  310-441-1734
- **Summitt Reprographics** ·
  1801 Avenue of the Stars · 310-788-3481

- **Sunshine Instant Printing** ·
  10900 Wellworth Ave · 310-479-5939
- **Unlimited Reprographics** · 1880 Century
  Park E · 310-282-0202
- **Westside Reprographics** · 10390 Santa
  Monica Blvd · 310-552-3252
- **Westwood Copies** · 1001 Gayley Ave ·
  310-208-3233

Farmer's Markets
- **Farmers' Market - Century City** ·
  Constellation Blvd & Avenue of the Stars
- **Westwood Village** · Weyburn Ave &
  Westwood Blvd

Gyms
- **Better Body Maker** ·
  10936 Santa Monica Blvd · 310-473-4302
- **Curves** · 10966 Le Conte Ave · 310-443-9044
- **LA Fitness Sports Clubs** ·
  10921 Wilshire Blvd · 310-209-5002
- **Meridian Sports Club** · 1950 Century Park E
  · 310-789-1111

Hardware Stores
- **Boulevard Hardware** · 1456 Westwood Blvd
  · 310-475-0795

Liquor Stores
- **Frank's Liquor** · 10559 Santa Monica Blvd
- **Wally's Wines & Liquors** ·
  2107 Westwood Blvd

Movie Theaters
- **AMC Avco Center Cinemas** ·
  10840 Wilshire Blvd · 310-475-0711
- **AMC Century 14** · 10250 Santa Monica Blvd
  · 310-553-8900
- **Landmark Regent Theatre** ·
  1045 Broxton Ave · 310-208-3259
- **Majestic Crest Theatre** ·
  1262 Westwood Blvd · 310-474-7866
- **Mann Bruin** · 948 Broxton Ave ·
  310-208-8998
- **Mann National Theatre** · 10925 Lindbrook
  Dr · 310-208-4366
- **Mann Village Theatre Westwood** ·
  961 Broxton Ave · 310-208-5576
- **UCLA Film & TV Archive** · 1409 Melnitz Bldg
  · 310-206-8422

Nightlife
- **The Century Club** · 10131 Constellation Blvd
  · 310-553-6000
- **Westwood Brewing Company** ·
  1097 Glendon Ave · 310-209-2739
- **Whiskey Blue (W Hotel)** · 930 Hilgard Ave ·
  310-208-8765

Pet Stores
- **Katie's Pet Depot** · 1278 Westwood Blvd ·
  310-441-4122

Restaurants
- **Big Chill** · 10850 Olympic Blvd ·
  310-441-0643
- **Clementine** · 1751 Ensley Ave ·
  310-552-1080
- **Diddy Riese Cookies** · 926 Broxton Ave ·
  310-208-0448
- **Earth, Wind & Flour** · 1776 Westwood Blvd ·
  310-470-2499
- **Falafel King** · 1059 Broxton Ave ·
  310-208-4444
- **Gardens on Glendon** · 1139 Glendon Ave ·
  310-824-1818
- **In-N-Out Burger** · 922 Gayley Ave ·
  800-786-1000
- **Johnnie's NY Pizzeria** · 10251 Santa Monica
  Blvd · 310-553-1188
- **La Bruschetta** · 1621 Westwood Blvd ·
  310-477-1052
- **La Cachette** · 10506 Santa Monica Blvd ·
  310-470-4992
- **Matteo's Hoboken** · 2323 Westwood Blvd ·
  310-474-1109
- **Napa Valley Grille** · 1100 Glendon Ave ·
  310-824-3322
- **Stan's Donuts** · 10948 Weyburn Ave ·
  310-208-8660
- **Tengu** · 10853 Lindbrook Dr · 310-209-0071

Shopping
- **Bristol Farms** · 1515 Westwood Blvd ·
  310-481-0100
- **Cost Plus World Market** ·
  10860 Santa Monica Blvd · 310-441-5115
- **Restoration Hardware** · 10250 Santa
  Monica Blvd · 310-551-4995
- **Rhino Records** · 2028 Westwood Blvd ·
  310-474-8685
- **The Writer's Store** · 2040 Westwood Blvd ·
  310-441-5151

Video Rental
- **Blockbuster** · 10917 Weyburn Ave ·
  310-824-5235
- **Hollywood Video** · 2201 Westwood Blvd ·
  310-475-0636

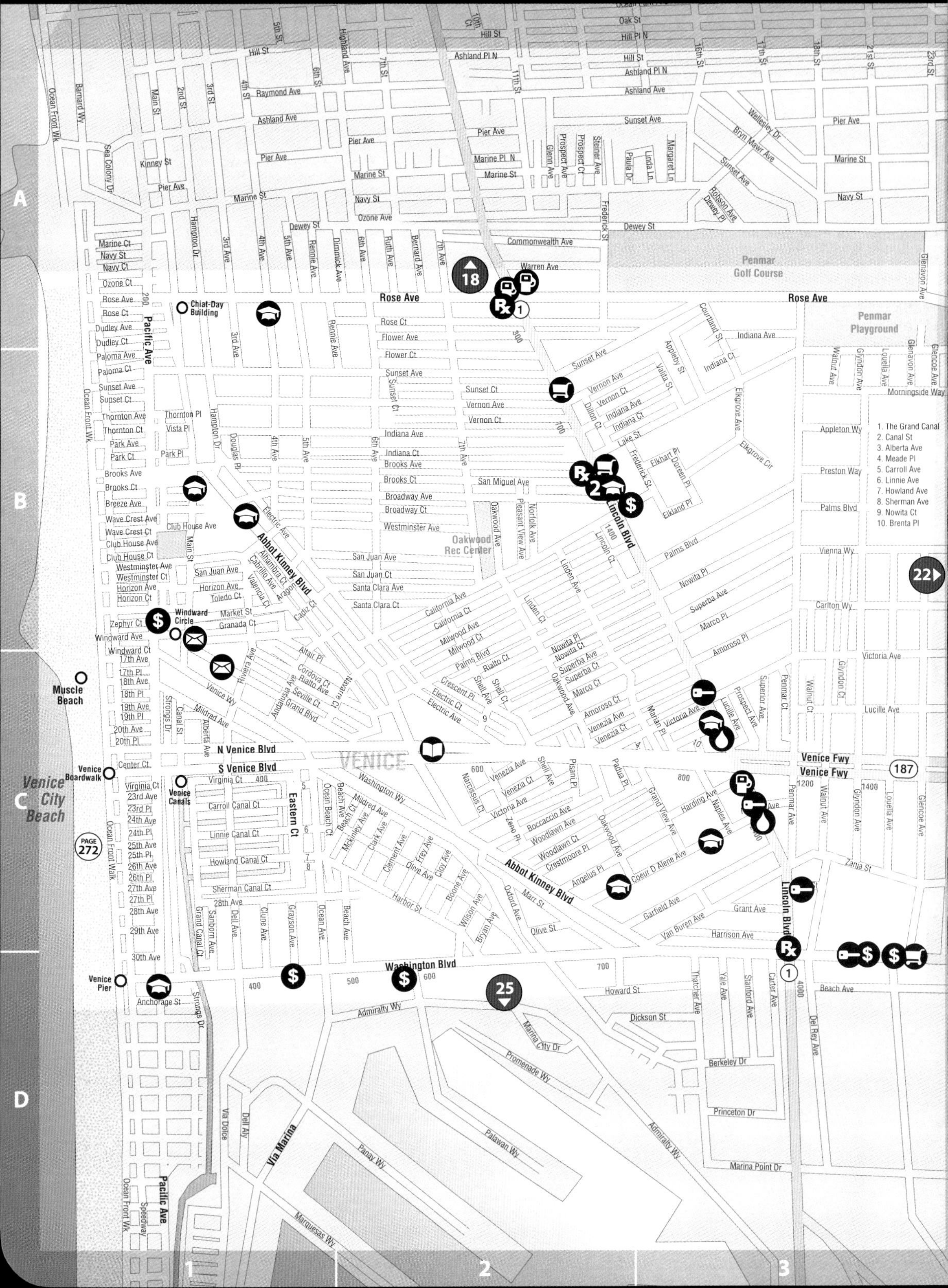

Map 21 · Venice

Penmar
Golf Course

Penmar
Playground

1. The Grand Canal
2. Canal St
3. Alberta Ave
4. Meade Pl
5. Carroll Ave
6. Linnie Ave
7. Howland Ave
8. Sherman Ave
9. Nowita Ct
10. Brenta Pl

VENICE

Venice
City
Beach

Muscle
Beach

Venice
Boardwalk

Venice
Canals

Venice
Pier

Chiat-Day
Building

Windward
Circle

Oakwood
Rec Center

PAGE
272

18

22

25

187

1
2
3

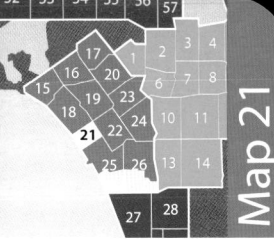
Venice has somehow survived the ravages of history—from the smuggling of alcohol to beachfront hotels during Prohibition, to the economic devastation of the Depression, to the arrival of the art dealers in the '70s. But in an increasingly generic world, Venice stands apart, as if to say to one and all: "it's your thing, do what you wanna do." For proof, just take a Sunday stroll on one of Venice's main drags—Abbot Kinney Boulevard or Ocean Front Walk.

$ Banks

- **Bank of America** · 121 Windward Ave
- **Downey Savings & Loan** · 13401 Washington Blvd
- **Downey Savings & Loan** · 8824 S Sepulveda Blvd
- **First Coastal** · 590 Washington Blvd
- **First Federal** · 13405 Washington Blvd
- **Washington Mutual** · 1415 Lincoln Blvd
- **Wells Fargo** · 13400 Washington Blvd
- **Wells Fargo** · 480 Washington Blvd

Car Rental

- **Bayview Rent-a-Car** · 2124 Lincoln Blvd
- **California Rent-a-Car** · 2423 Lincoln Blvd
- **Hertz** · 2519 Lincoln Blvd
- **Rent $ Less** · 13464 Washington Blvd

Car Washes

- **Lincoln Millennium Car Wash** · 2454 Lincoln Blvd
- **Marina Car Wash** · 2305 Lincoln Blvd

Gas Stations

- **76** · 300 Lincoln Blvd
- **Arco** · 251 Lincoln Blvd
- **Chevron** · 2400 Lincoln Blvd

o Landmarks

- **Chiat-Day Building** · 340 Main St
- **Muscle Beach** · 1817 Ocean Front Wk
- **Venice Boardwalk** · Ocean Front Wk
- **Venice Canals** · Venice Blvd & Pacific Ave
- **Venice Pier** · Far west end of Washington Blvd
- **Windward Circle** · Main St & Windward Ave

Libraries

- **Venice Branch** · 501 S Venice Blvd · 310-821-1769

Pharmacies

- **Rite-Aid** · 888 Lincoln Blvd · 310-396-2838
- **Sav-On** · 219 Lincoln Blvd · 310-392-3983
- **Walgreens (24 hrs)** · 4009 Lincoln Blvd · 310-823-7152

Post Offices

- **US Post Office** · 1601 Main St
- **US Post Office** · 313 Grand Blvd

Schools

- **Animo Venice Charter High** · 1015 Lincoln Blvd
- **Broadway Elementary** · 1015 Lincoln Blvd
- **Coeur D'Alene Ave Elementary** · 810 Coeur D'Alene Ave
- **Cornerstone Prep Charter** · 2232 Lincoln Blvd
- **First Lutheran** · 815 Venice Blvd
- **St Mark's Elementary** · 912 Coeur D'Alene Ave
- **Venice Skills Center** · 611 5th Ave
- **Westminster Ave Elementary** · 1010 Abbot Kinney Blvd
- **Westminster EEC** · 1010 Main St
- **Westside Leadership Magnet** · 104 Anchorage St

Supermarkets

- **Albertsons** · 13401 Washington Blvd
- **Ralphs** · 910 Lincoln Blvd
- **Smart & Final** · 604 Lincoln Blvd

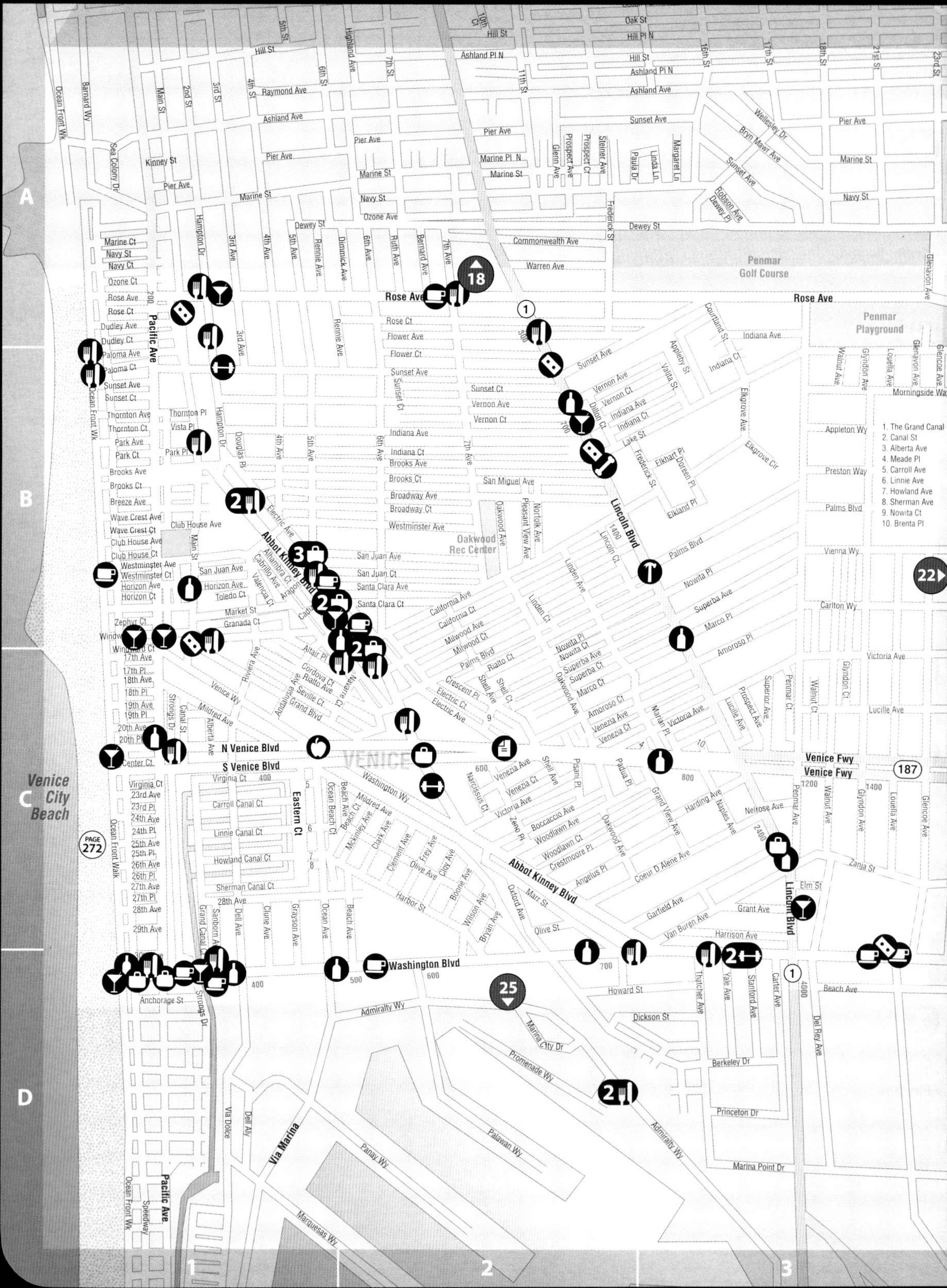

Map 21 · Venice

1. The Grand Canal
2. Canal St
3. Alberta Ave
4. Meade Pl
5. Carroll Ave
6. Linnie Ave
7. Howland Ave
8. Sherman Ave
9. Nowita Ct
10. Brenta Pl

Penmar Golf Course

Penmar Playground

Venice City Beach

VENICE

PAGE 272

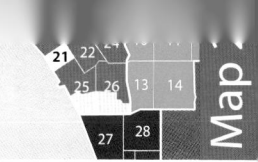

When Abbot Kinney conceived of Venice, CA, he envisioned it as an American replica of Venice, Italy—complete with canals. But the canals proved to be impractical after the automobile gained popularity, so most of the canals were filled in and turned to roads in 1929. Just six canals remain, and they were refurbished in 1994. The houses that line the canals are gorgeous in their own right, and the area is definitely worth a visit.

Coffee
- **Abbot's Habit** · 1401 Abbot Kinney Blvd
- **The Cow's End** · 34 Washington Blvd
- **Groundwork Coffee Company** · 3 Westminster Ave
- **Groundwork Coffee Company** · 671 Rose Ave
- **Jin Patisserie** · 1202 Abbot Kinney Blvd
- **Joni's Coffee Roaster Café** · 552 Washington Blvd
- **Starbucks** · 100 Washington Blvd
- **Starbucks** · 13431 Washington Blvd
- **Starbucks** · Albertsons, 13401 Washington Blvd

Copy Centers
- **Graphic Details** · 660 Venice Blvd · 310-823-2679

Farmer's Markets
- **Venice** · Venice Blvd & Venice Wy

Gyms
- **Curves** · 1733 Abbot Kinney Blvd · 310-301-9933
- **Gold's Gym** · 360 Hampton Dr · 310-392-6004
- **World Gym** · 3205 Washington Blvd · 310-827-8019

Hardware Stores
- **True Value** · 1609 Lincoln Blvd · 310-821-1027

Liquor Stores
- **Alan's Market** · 339 Washington Blvd
- **Bob's Liquor** · 727 Lincoln Blvd
- **Day & Night Liquor & Market** · 1002 Venice Blvd
- **Joe's Liquor** · 1901 Lincoln Blvd
- **Lincoln Liquor Locker** · 2498 Lincoln Blvd
- **Lucky Stop** · 1360 Abbot Kinney Blvd
- **Marina Del Rey Liquormart** · 753 Washington Blvd
- **Munis Liquor** · 2022 Pacific Ave
- **Nick's Liquor** · 11 Washington Blvd
- **Trading Post Liquor** · 1313 Main St
- **Wolf's Liquor** · 536 Washington Blvd

Nightlife
- **Baja Cantina** · 311 Washington Blvd · 310-821-2252
- **The Brig** · 1515 Abbot Kinney Blvd · 310-399-7537
- **Firehouse** · 213 Rose Ave · 310-396-6810
- **James' Beach** · 60 Venice Blvd · 310-823-5396
- **Red Garter** · 2536 Lincoln Blvd · 310-306-8300
- **Roosterfish** · 1302 Abbot Kinney Blvd · 310-392-2123
- **The Town House** · 52 Windward Ave · 310-392-4040
- **Venice Whaler Bar & Grill** · 10 Washington Blvd · 310-821-8737

Pet Stores
- **Allan's Aquarium & Pet Center** · 845 Lincoln Blvd · 310-399-5464

Restaurants
- **Abbot's Pizza** · 1407 Abbot Kinney Blvd · 310-396-7334
- **Amuse Café** · 796 Main St · 310-450-1956
- **Baja Cantina Restaurant** · 311 Washington Blvd · 310-821-2252
- **Beechwood** · 822 Washington Blvd · 310-448-8884
- **The Brick House** · 826 Hampton Dr · 310-581-1639
- **C&O Trattoria** · 3016 Washington Blvd · 310-301-7278
- **C&O Trattoria** · 31 Washington Blvd · 310-823-9491
- **Café 50's** · 838 Lincoln Blvd · 310-399-1955
- **Canal Club** · 2025 Pacific Ave · 310-823-3878
- **Casablanca** · 220 Lincoln Blvd · 310-392-5751
- **Figtree's Café** · 429 Ocean Front Wk · 310-392-4937
- **Hal's Bar & Grill** · 1349 Abbot Kinney Blvd · 310-396-3105
- **Hama Sushi** · 213 Windward Ave · 310-396-8783
- **Jer-ne** · 4375 Admiralty Wy · 323-574-4333
- **Jin Patisserie** · 1202 Abbot Kinney Blvd · 310-399-8801
- **Joe's** · 1023 Abbot Kinney Blvd · 310-399-5811
- **Killer Shrimp** · 523 Washington Blvd · 310-578-2293
- **La Cabana Restaurant and Bar** · 738 Rose Ave · 310-392-7973
- **Rose Café** · 220 Rose Ave · 310-399-0711
- **Tony P's Dockside Grill** · 4445 Admiralty Wy · 310-823-4534
- **Wabi-Sabi** · 1635 Abbot Kinney Blvd · 310-314-2229

Shopping
- **Brick Lane** · 1132 Abbot Kinney Blvd · 310-392-2525
- **Cabana Joe's** · 1415 Abbot Kinney Blvd · 310-452-2343
- **Daisy Arts** · 1312 Abbot Kinney Blvd · 310-396-8463
- **DNA** · 411 Rose Ave · 310-399-0341
- **Green House Smoke Shop** · 1428 Abbot Kinney Blvd · 310-450-6420
- **Helen's Cycles** · 2472 Lincoln Blvd · 310-306-7843
- **Hydro Lab** · 1140 Abbot Kinney Blvd · 310-450-7221
- **Johnny B Wood** · 1108 Abbot Kinney Blvd · 310-709-4189
- **Samy's Camera** · 585 Venice Blvd · 310-450-4551
- **The Starting Line** · 114 Washington Blvd · 310-827-3035
- **Venice Bike & Skate** · 21 Washington Blvd · 310-301-4011
- **Waraku** · 1225 Abbot Kinney Blvd · 310-452-5300

Video Rental
- **Jungle Video** · 423 Lincoln Blvd · 310-314-7777
- **Main St Video** · 1600 Main St · 310-821-7838
- **Red Hot Video** · 835 Lincoln Blvd · 310-399-4289

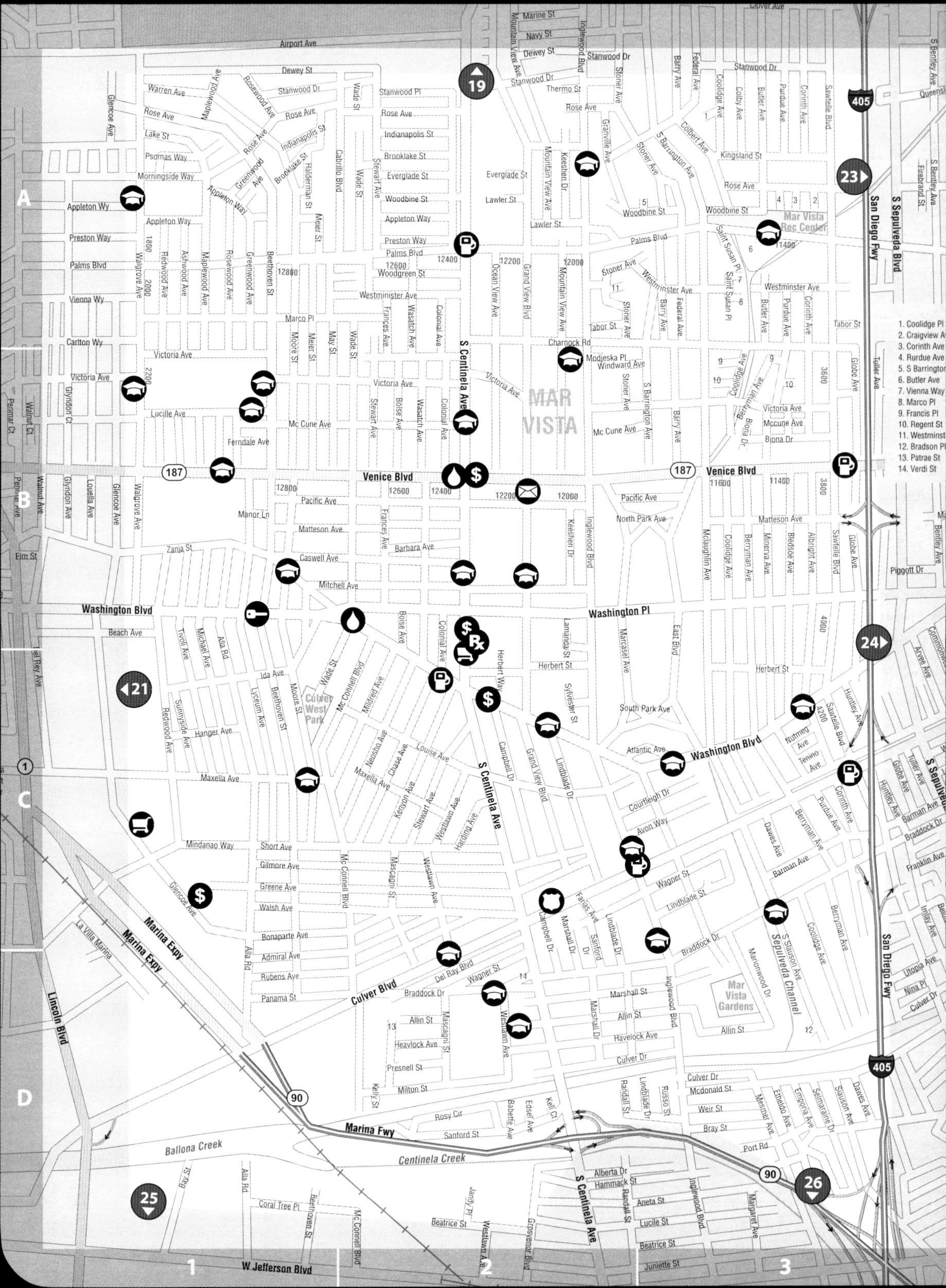

Map 22 · **Mar Vista**

19
23
24
21
25
26

405

MAR
VISTA

Mar Vista
Rec Center

Mar Vista
Gardens

1. Coolidge Pl
2. Craigview A
3. Corinth Ave
4. Rurdue Ave
5. S Barrington
6. Butler Ave
7. Vienna Way
8. Marco Pl
9. Francis Pl
10. Regent St
11. Westminst
12. Bradson Pl
13. Patrae St
14. Verdi St

You may be driving too fast along Centinela Avenue or Venice Boulevard to notice the traces of mid-century Los Angeles that still linger in Mar Vista, but even at 40 mph, they are there. Plenty of formica-and-vinyl diners, excellent signage, and a bowling alley. What more do you need? On a practical note: during rush hour, Venice Boulevard is an east-west alternative to the 10 freeway; Palms Boulevard to the north is fairly speedy as well.

Banks

- **Bank of America** · 12316 W Washington Blvd
- **Citibank** · 4375 Glencoe Ave
- **Union** · 4032 S Centinela Ave
- **Washington Mutual** · 12335 Venice Blvd

Car Rental

- **Marathon Rent-A-Car** · 12903 W Washington Blvd

Car Washes

- **Car Wash Coin Op** · 12415 Venice Blvd
- **Handy J Car Wash** · 12681 W Washington Blvd

Gas Stations

- **76** · 11305 Culver Blvd
- **Arco** · 12000 Culver Blvd
- **Arco** · 12332 W Washington Blvd
- **Chevron** · 3500 S Centinela Ave
- **Independent** · 11284 Venice Blvd

Libraries

- **Mar Vista Branch** · 12006 Venice Blvd · 310-390-3454

Pharmacies

- **Rite-Aid** · 4046 S Centinela Ave · 310-391-0255

Police

- **Los Angeles Police Dept** · 12312 Culver Blvd · 310-482-6334

Post Offices

- **US Post Office** · 3826 Grand View Blvd

Schools

- **Beethoven EEC** · 12939 Lucille Ave
- **Beethoven St Elementary** · 3711 Beethoven St
- **Braddock Dr Elementary** · 4711 Inglewood Blvd
- **Culver Christian** · 11312 Washington Blvd
- **Culver City Adventist** · 11828 W Washington Blvd
- **Grand View Blvd Elementary** · 3951 Grand View Blvd
- **James J McBride** · 3960 Centinela Ave
- **Mar Vista Elementary** · 3330 Granville Ave
- **Marina del Rey Middle** · 12500 Braddock Dr
- **Marina EEC** · 4908 Westlawn Ave
- **Mark Twain Middle** · 2224 Walgrove Ave
- **Montessori Learning Center** · 11363 Washington Blvd
- **Ocean Charter** · 12606 Culver Blvd
- **Pacifica Montessori** · 3734 Centinela Ave
- **Phoenix Continuation** · 12971 Zanja St
- **Shining Path Montessori** · 11500 Culver Blvd
- **Short Ave Elementary** · 12814 Maxella Ave
- **St Gerard Majella Elementary** · 4451 Inglewood Blvd
- **Stoner Ave Elementary** · 11735 Braddock Dr
- **Summit View West** · 12101 W Washington Blvd
- **Tom Bradley Environmental Science & Humanities** · 3875 Dublin Ave
- **Venice Senior High** · 13000 Venice Blvd
- **Walgrove Ave Elementary** · 1630 Walgrove Ave
- **Windward** · 11350 Palms Blvd

Supermarkets

- **Vons** · 4030 S Centinela Ave
- **Vons** · 4365 Glencoe Ave

Map 22 • **Mar Vista**

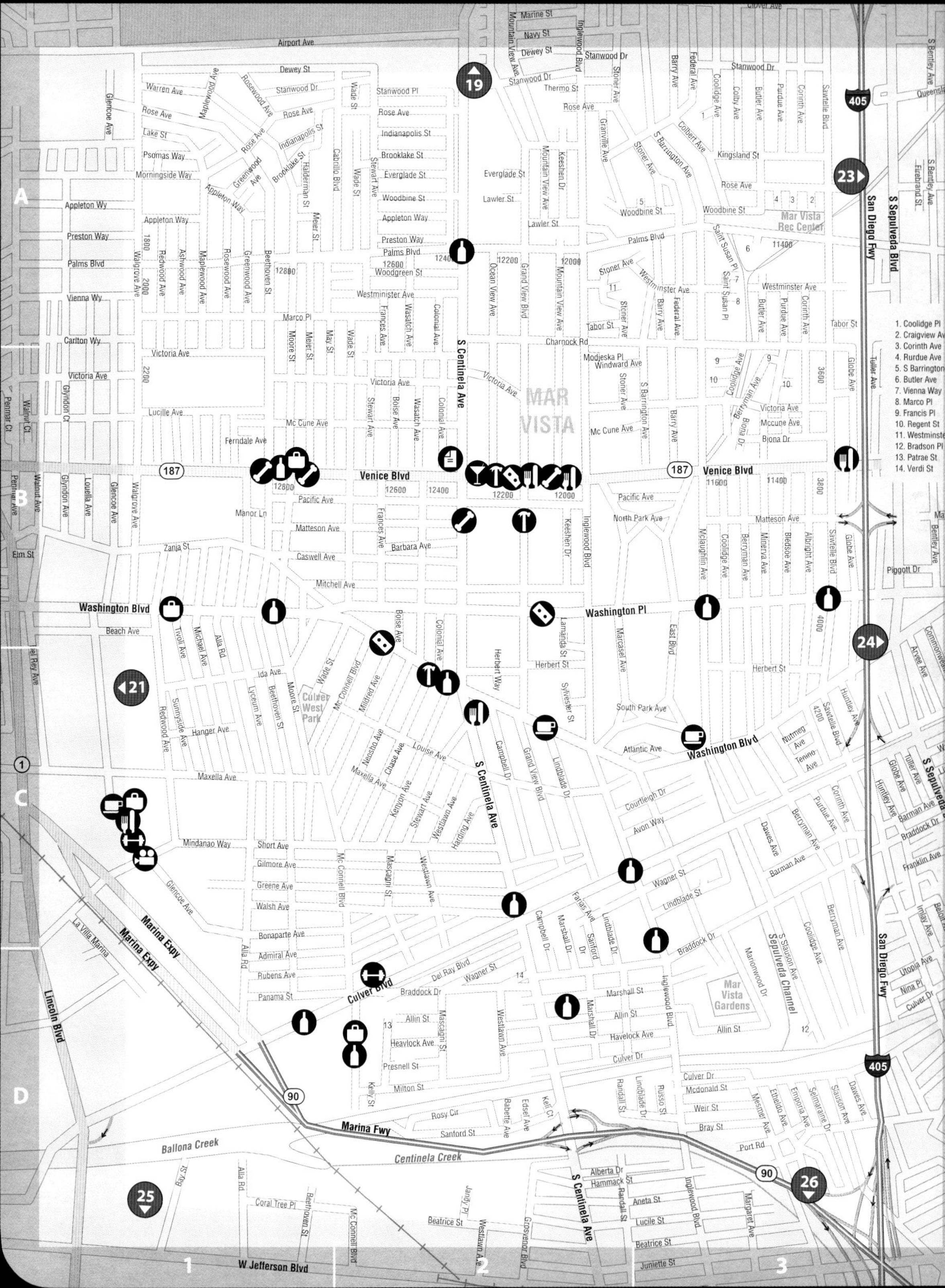

What is there to do for fun in Mar Vista? Go bowling! The Mar Vista Bowl (12125 Venice Boulevard) is a throwback to the '60s, decorated with a psychedelic galaxy theme. Do wear your sharpest bowling shirt.

Coffee

- **Panini Coffee & Café** · 4325 Glencoe Ave
- **Rumor Mill** · 11739 W Washington Blvd
- **Rutts Hawaiian Café** · 12114 W Washington Blvd

Copy Centers

- **UPS Store** · 12405 Venice Blvd · 310-915-6580

Gyms

- **Boditron Fitness Academy** · 4371 Glencoe Ave · 310-574-8785
- **Curves** · 12740 Culver Blvd · 310-301-6733

Hardware Stores

- **Ace** · 12450 W Washington Blvd · 310-390-9413
- **Dick's True Value** · 12216 Venice Blvd · 310-397-3220
- **Stock Building Supply** · 3860 Grand View Blvd · 310-390-3621

Liquor Stores

- **A&M Liquors** · 11700 Washington Pl
- **Beverage Warehouse** · 4935 McConnell Ave
- **Bill's Liquor** · 11700 Culver Blvd
- **Dicoteca Licorerea La Mexicana** · 4513 Inglewood Blvd
- **Happy Corner Liquors** · 4584 S Centinela Ave
- **Jay's Liquor** · 11305 Washington Pl
- **Los Angeles Wine Company** · 4935 McConnell Ave
- **Rajmohan's Liquors** · 12815 Venice Blvd
- **Sun Liquor Shop** · 12827 W Washington Blvd
- **Super Liquor & Deli** · 4704 Inglewood Blvd
- **US Liquors** · 12403 W Washington Blvd
- **Westside Liquor** · 3501 S Centinela Ave

Movie Theaters

- **United Artists Marina del Rey 6** · 4335 Glencoe Ave · 310-823-3959

Nightlife

- **Dear John's** · 11208 Culver Blvd · 310-397-0276
- **Good Hurt** · 12249 Venice Blvd · 310-390-1076

Pet Stores

- **Aquarium** · 12807 Venice Blvd · 310-398-9920
- **Centinela Feed & Pet Supplies** · 3860 S Centinela Ave · 310-398-2134
- **Dogromat** · 12926 Venice Blvd · 310-306-8885
- **Kirby's Pet Depot** · 12112 Venice Blvd · 310-313-1801

Restaurants

- **Aunt Kizzy's Back Porch** · 4325 Glencoe Ave · 310-578-1005
- **Empanada's Place** · 3811 Sawtelle Blvd · 310-391-0888
- **Paco's Tacos** · 4141 Centinela Ave · 310-391-9616
- **Pepy's Galley** · 12125 Venice Blvd · 310-390-0577
- **Venus of Venice** · 12034 Venice Blvd · 310-391-7674

Shopping

- **A Mano Yarn Center** · 12808 Venice Blvd · 310-397-7170
- **The Los Angeles Wine Company** · 4935 McConnell Ave · 310-306-9463
- **Prebica Coffee** · 4325 Glencoe Ave · 310-823-4446
- **Vanity Room** · 13217 Washington Blvd · 310-306-3336

Video Rental

- **Grand View Video** · 12131 Washington Pl · 310-572-6200
- **La Mexicana Video Rental (Mexican)** · 12612 W Washington Blvd · 310-390-9691
- **Video Exhibition** · 12200 Venice Blvd · 310-737-0053

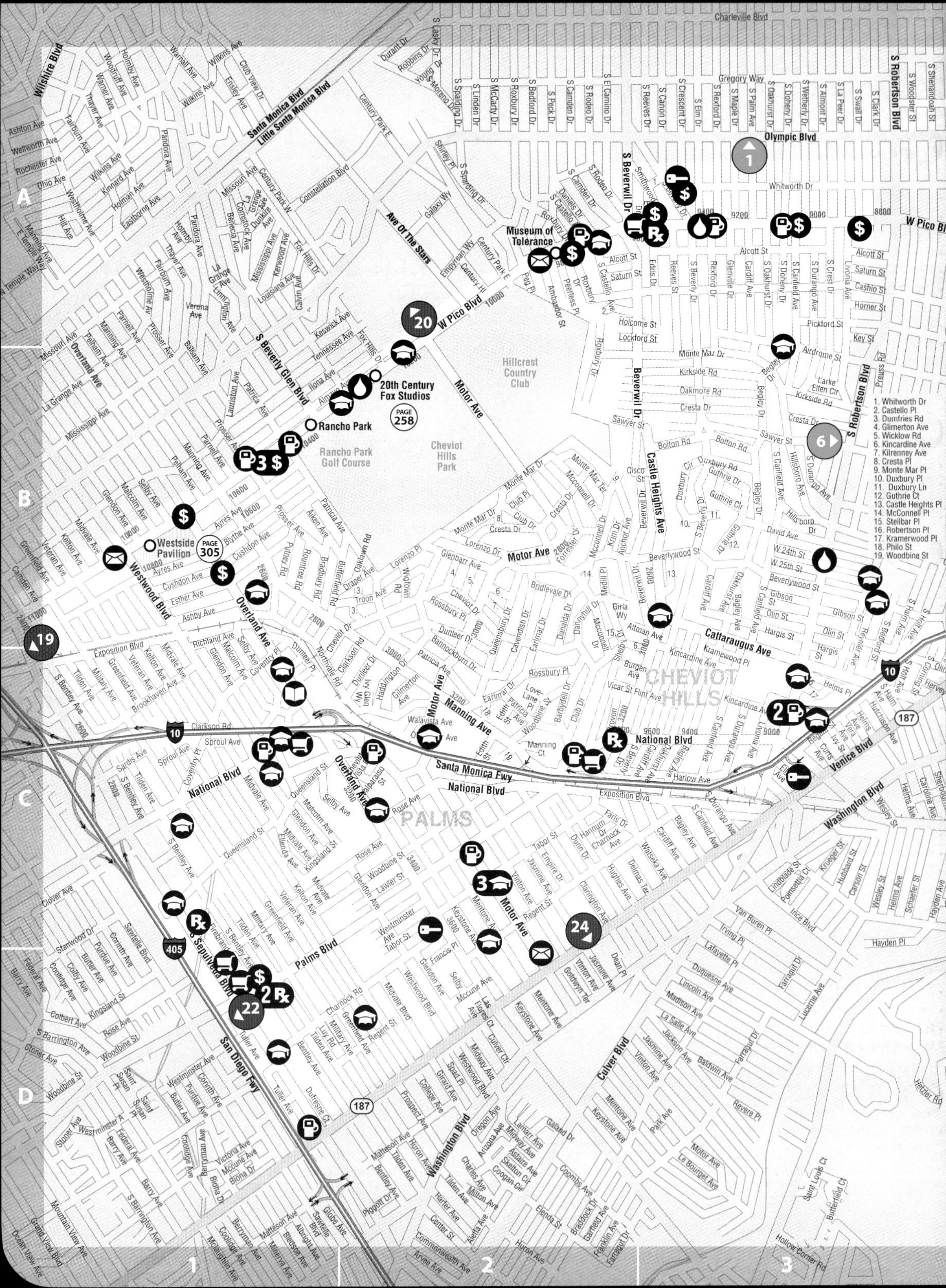

Map 23 • **Rancho Park / Palms**

Index of streets (right side panel):

1. Whitworth Dr
2. Castello Pl
3. Dumfries Rd
4. Glimerton Ave
5. Wicklow Rd
6. Kincardine Ave
7. Kilrenney Ave
8. Cresta Pl
9. Monte Mar Pl
10. Duxbury Pl
11. Duxbury Ln
12. Guthrie Ct
13. Castle Heights Pl
14. McConnell Pl
15. Stellbar Pl
16. Robertson Pl
17. Kramerwood Pl
18. Philo St
19. Woodbine St

20th Century Fox Studios
PAGE 258

Rancho Park

Rancho Park Golf Course

Cheviot Hills Park

Hillcrest Country Club

Westside Pavilion
PAGE 305

Museum of Tolerance

CHEVIOT HILLS

PALMS

The Rancho Park Golf Course is reportedly the busiest in the world. It's located at the Cheviot Hills Recreation Center, which also contains tennis courts, basketball hoops, ball diamonds, and more. Motor Avenue is a nifty way to cut across town from Pico to Venice Boulevard.

$ Banks

- **Bank of America** · 10731 W Pico Blvd
- **California National** · 2566 Overland Ave
- **Citibank** · 10680 W Pico Blvd
- **Citibank** · 1180 S Beverly Dr
- **Citibank** · 2566 Overland Ave
- **First Federal** · 9618 W Pico Blvd
- **Washington Mutual** · 10701 W Pico Blvd
- **Washington Mutual** · 9080 W Pico Blvd
- **Washington Mutual** · 9800 W Pico Blvd
- **Wells Fargo** · 10789 W Pico Blvd
- **Wells Fargo** · 11116 Palms Blvd
- **Wells Fargo** · 8901 W Pico Blvd

Car Rental

- **City Rent-a-Car** · 3638 Overland Ave
- **Downtown Car Rental** · 8919 Ellis Ave
- **Midway Car Rental** · 1150 S Beverly Dr

Car Washes

- **Century West Car Wash** · 9500 W Pico Blvd
- **Crown Car Wash** · 10399 W Pico Blvd
- **Robertson Car Wash** · 2460 S Robertson Blvd

Gas Stations

- **76** · 9081 W Pico Blvd
- **76** · 9779 W Pico Blvd
- **76** · 9930 National Blvd
- **Arco** · 3479 Motor Ave
- **Chevron** · 3029 S Robertson Blvd
- **Chevron** · 3775 S Sepulveda Blvd
- **Exxon** · 10691 W Pico Blvd
- **Mobil** · 10611 National Blvd
- **Mobil** · 3071 S Robertson Blvd
- **Mobil** · 9448 W Pico Blvd
- **Shell** · 10564 Pico Blvd
- **Shell** · 10815 National Blvd

Landmarks

- **20th Century Fox Studios** · 10201 Pico Blvd
- **Museum of Tolerance** · 9786 W Pico Blvd
- **Rancho Park** · W Pico Blvd & S Beverly Glen Blvd
- **Westside Pavilion** · 10800 W Pico Blvd

Libraries

- **Palms-Rancho Park Branch** · 2920 Overland Ave · 310-840-2142

Rx Pharmacies

- **Longs Drugs** · 9618 W Pico Blvd · 310-858-1855
- **Longs Drugs (24 hours)** · 3458 S Sepulveda Blvd · 310-839-9055
- **The Medicine Shoppe** · 11126 Palms Blvd · 310-837-1030
- **Rite-Aid** · 9864 National Blvd · 310-836-0623
- **Sav-On (Albertsons)** · 3443 S Sepulveda Blvd · 310-390-7857

Post Offices

- **US Post Office** · 10850 W Pico Blvd
- **US Post Office** · 3751 Motor Ave
- **US Post Office** · 9911 W Pico Blvd

Schools

- **Adat Shalom Preschool/Kindergarten** · 3030 Westwood Blvd
- **Alexander Hamilton Senior High** · 2955 Robertson Blvd
- **Canfield Ave Elementary** · 9233 Airdrome St
- **Castle Heights Elementary** · 9755 Cattaraugus Ave
- **Charnock Rd Elementary** · 11133 Charnock Rd
- **Cheviot Hills Continuation** · 9200 Cattaraugus Ave
- **Clover Ave Elementary** · 11020 Clover Ave
- **Julia Ann Singer Center** · 3200 Motor Ave
- **Le Lycee Francais de LA** · 10361 W Pico Blvd
- **Le Lycee Francais de LA** · 3261 Overland Ave
- **Mel-O-Dee Montessori Center** · 3659 Motor Ave
- **New World Montessori** · 10520 Regent St
- **Notre Dame Academy Elementary** · 2911 Overland Ave
- **Notre Dame Academy Girls High** · 2851 Overland Ave
- **Overland Ave Elementary** · 10650 Ashby Ave
- **Pacifica Community Charter** · 3754 Dunn Dr
- **Palms Elementary** · 3520 Motor Ave
- **Palms Middle** · 10860 Woodbine St
- **Palms Tiny Tot Preschool/Kindergarten** · 3614 Motor Ave
- **Redeemer Baptist Elementary** · 10792 National Blvd
- **Shenandoah EEC** · 8861 Beverlywood St
- **St Timothy** · 10479 W Pico Blvd
- **University Village CCC** · 3233 S Sepulveda Blvd
- **Vista** · 3200 Motor Ave
- **Yeshiva University High** · 9760 W Pico Blvd

Supermarkets

- **Albertsons** · 3443 S Sepulveda Blvd
- **Ralphs** · 9616 W Pico Blvd
- **Trader Joe's** · 10850 National Blvd
- **Trader Joe's** · 3456 S Sepulveda Blvd
- **Vons** · 9860 National Blvd

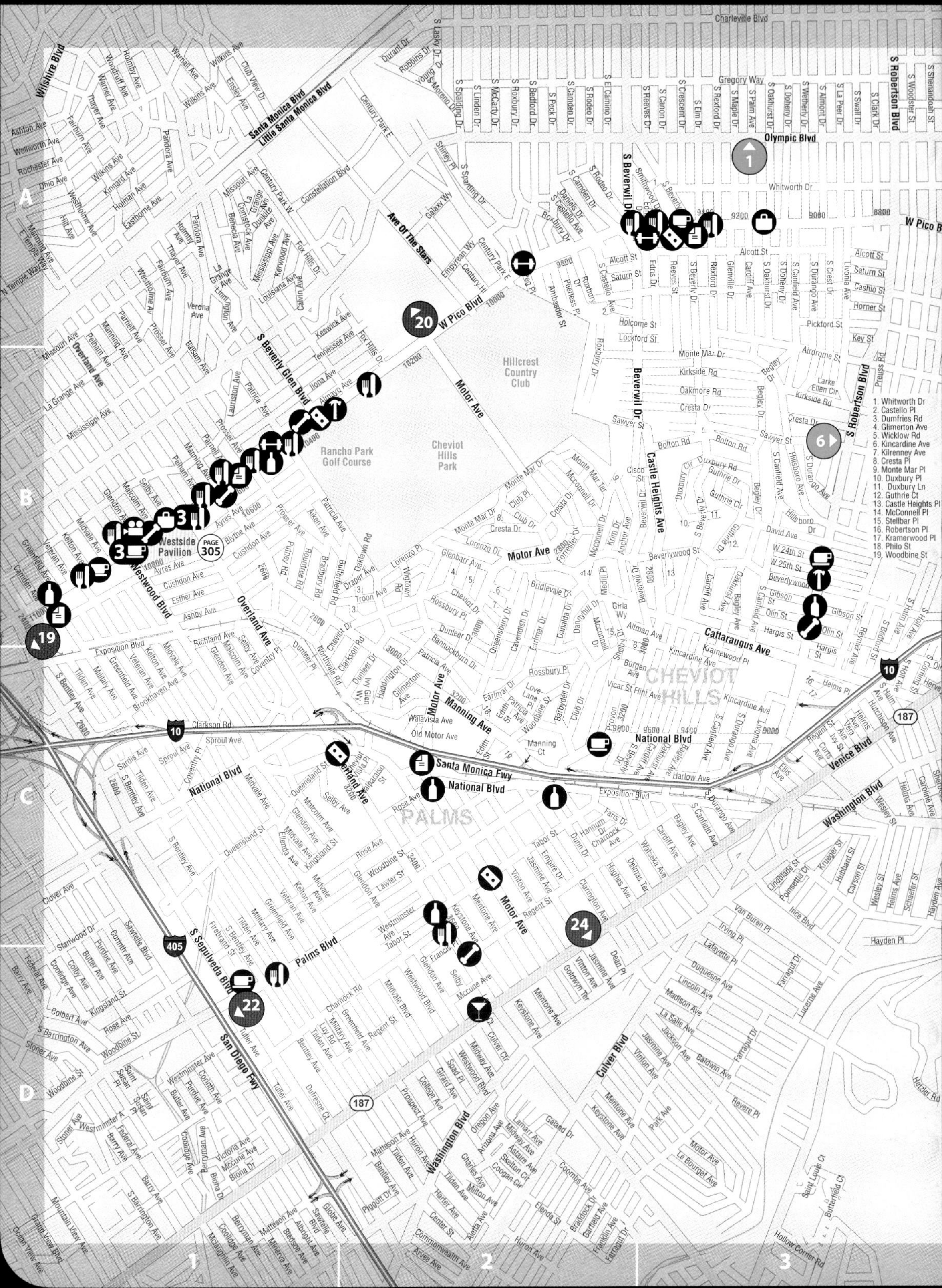

Map 23 • **Rancho Park / Palms**

Americans love to shop, and they love to eat—and what screams red, white, and blue more than a hamburger and a slice of apple pie? Do your patriotic duty by jostling for a counter seat at the legendary Apple Pan on Pico Boulevard; afterward, get some exercise and do your part to stimulate the economy with a walk through the Westside Pavilion.

Coffee

- **Coffee Bean & Tea Leaf** · 10800 W Pico Blvd
- **Coffee Bean & Tea Leaf** · 10897 W Pico Blvd
- **Coffee Bean & Tea Leaf** · 3470 S Sepulveda Blvd
- **Coffee Bean & Tea Leaf** · 9541 W Pico Blvd
- **Miss Donuts** · 2520 S Robertson Blvd
- **Starbucks** · 10911 Pico Blvd
- **Starbucks** · 9824 National Blvd
- **Ugo an Italian Café** · 10915 W Pico Blvd

Copy Centers

- **Ford Graphics** · 2435 Military Ave · 310-477-6501
- **Office Depot** · 9527 W Pico Blvd · 910-551-3006
- **Printex** · 3272 Motor Ave · 310-278-0008
- **UPS Store** · 10573 W Pico Blvd · 310-474-7383

Gyms

- **24-Hour Fitness** · 9911 W Pico Blvd · 310-553-7600
- **Curves** · 10522 W Pico Blvd · 310-836-3050
- **Curves** · 9618 W Pico Blvd · 310-858-7546

Hardware Stores

- **Anawalt Lumber** · 11060 W Pico Blvd · 310-478-0324
- **Emil's Hardware** · 2525 S Robertson Blvd · 310-839-8571

Liquor Stores

- **Bob's Food Mart & Liquors** · 10000 National Blvd
- **Dave's Liquors** · 2704 S Robertson Blvd
- **Hillis Liquors** · 3308 Motor Ave
- **Joseph Liquor** · 11304 W Pico Blvd
- **Overland Liquor** · 3585 Overland Ave
- **Rancho Park Liquors** · 10526 W Pico Blvd

Movie Theaters

- **Landmark Westside Pavilion Cinemas** · 10800 W Pico Blvd · 310-475-0202

Nightlife

- **Zabumba** · 10717 Venice Blvd · 310-841-6525

Pet Stores

- **Centinela Feed & Pet Supplies** · 11055 W Pico Blvd · 310-473-5099
- **Many Paws** · 2730 S Robertson Blvd · 310-837-1710
- **Westside Pet Stop** · 10588 W Pico Blvd · 310-202-1076

Restaurants

- **Apple Pan** · 10801 W Pico Blvd · 310-475-3585
- **Bourbon Street Shrimp** · 10928 W Pico Blvd · 310-474-0007
- **Delmonico's Seafood Grille** · 9320 W Pico Blvd · 310-550-7737
- **Factor's Famous Deli** · 9420 W Pico Blvd · 310-278-9175
- **Guelaguetza** · 11127 Palms Blvd · 310-837-1153
- **Gyu-kaku** · 10925 W Pico Blvd · 310-234-8641
- **Hop Li** · 10974 W Pico Blvd · 310-441-3708
- **Jack Sprat's** · 10668 W Pico Blvd · 310-837-6662
- **John O'Groat's** · 10516 W Pico Blvd · 310-204-0692
- **Junior's Deli** · 2379 Westwood Blvd · 310-475-5771
- **La Serenata Gourmet** · 10924 W Pico Blvd · 310-441-9667
- **Lot 1224** · 1224 S Beverlywil Dr · 310-277-2800
- **Milky Way** · 9108 W Pico Blvd · 310-859-0004
- **Overland Café** · 3601 Overland Ave · 310-559-9999

Shopping

- **Adventure 16** · 11161 Pico Blvd · 310-473-4574
- **Delmarus Lox** · 9340 W Pico Blvd · 310-273-3004

Video Rental

- **Blockbuster** · 3101 Overland Ave · 310-842-9110
- **Blockbuster** · 9618 W Pico Blvd · 310-858-3822
- **Laser Blazer** · 10587 W Pico Blvd · 310-475-4788
- **Pro Video** · 10401 Tabor St · 310-202-1508

Map 24 · **Culver City**

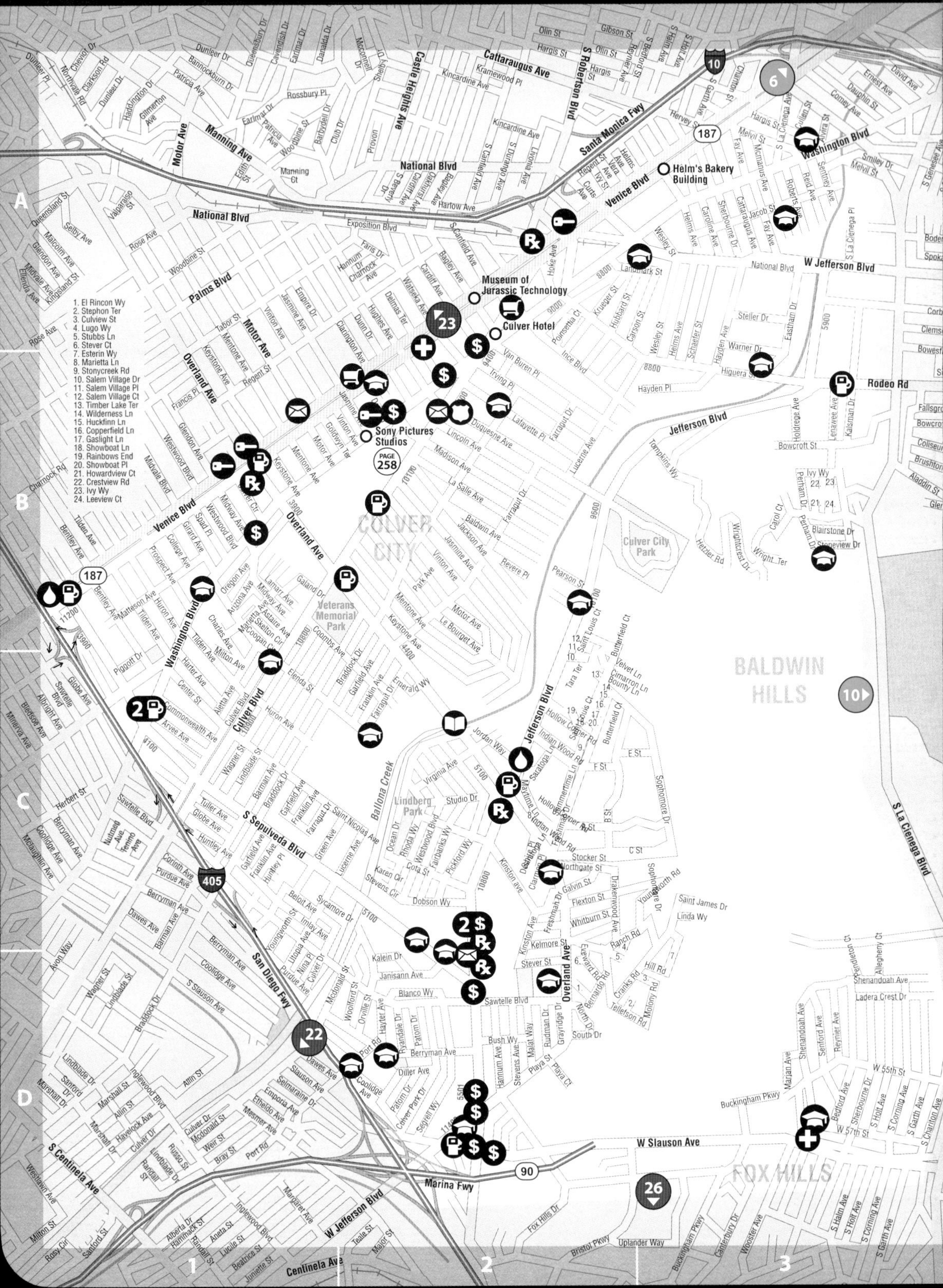

1. El Rincon Wy
2. Stephon Ter
3. Culview St
4. Lugo Wy
5. Stubbs Ct
6. Stever Ct
7. Esterin Wy
8. Marietta Ln
9. Stonycreek Rd
10. Salem Village Dr
11. Salem Village Pl
12. Salem Village Ct
13. Timber Lake Ter
14. Wilderness Ln
15. Huckfinn Ln
16. Copperfield Ln
17. Gaslight Ln
18. Showboat Ln
19. Rainbows End
20. Showboat Pl
21. Howardview Ct
22. Crestview Rd
23. Ivy Wy
24. Leeview Ct

Helm's Bakery Building

Museum of Jurassic Technology

Culver Hotel

Sony Pictures Studios

PAGE 258

CULVER CITY

Veterans Memorial Park

Lindberg Park

BALDWIN HILLS

Culver City Park

FOX HILLS

They used to make bread and baked goods at the Helm's Bakery Building, but it's now home to an assortment of furniture stores—both high-end and relatively affordable. The Art Deco-style building also houses the Jazz Bakery, a non-profit performance space that has hosted Woody Allen and Mose Allison. And yes, you can order dessert at the Bakery.

$ Banks

- **Bank of America** · 3809 Culver Ctr
- **Bank of America** · 5541 S Sepulveda Blvd
- **Bank of America** · 9453 Culver Blvd
- **Bank of the West** · 9735 Washington Blvd
- **Citibank** · 5700 S Sepulveda Blvd
- **First Federal** · 10784 Jefferson Blvd
- **First Federal** · 5573 S Sepulveda Blvd
- **US** · 5399 S Sepulveda Blvd
- **Washington Mutual** · 10970 Jefferson Blvd
- **Washington Mutual** · 5670 Sepulveda Blvd
- **Washington Mutual** · 9801 Washington Blvd
- **Wells Fargo** · 10011 Washington Blvd
- **Wells Fargo** · 11030 Jefferson Blvd

Car Rental

- **Enterprise** · 10757 Venice Blvd
- **Enterprise** · 8949 Venice Blvd
- **G&R Car Rental** · 10620 Venice Blvd
- **Hertz** · 11201 Washington Blvd

Car Washes

- **Bubble Machine Car Wash** · 10649 Jefferson Blvd
- **Shine & Brite Hand Car Wash** · 11166 Venice Blvd

Gas Stations

- **76** · 10638 Culver Blvd
- **Arco** · 10646 Venice Blvd
- **Arco** · 11181 W Washington Blvd
- **Arco** · 5851 Rodeo Rd
- **Arco** · 6300 W Slauson Ave
- **Chevron** · 10649 Jefferson Blvd
- **Chevron** · 11197 Washington Pl
- **Shell** · 10332 Culver Blvd
- **Shell** · 3801 Sepulveda Blvd
- **Shell** · 3801 Sepulveda Blvd

Hospitals

- **Brotman** · 3828 Delmas Ter

Landmarks

- **Culver Hotel** · 9400 Culver Blvd
- **Helm's Bakery Building** · 3233 Helms Ave
- **Museum of Jurassic Technology** · 9341 Venice Blvd
- **Sony Pictures Studios** · 10202 W Washington Blvd

Libraries

- **Culver City Julian Dixon** · 4975 Overland Ave · 310-559-1676

Rx Pharmacies

- **Pavilions** · 11030 Jefferson Blvd · 310-398-1945
- **Rite-Aid** · 11096 Jefferson Blvd · 310-397-3931
- **Rite-Aid** · 3802 Culver Center St · 310-837-2122
- **Sav-On** · 8985 Venice Blvd · 310-838-1049
- **Target** · 10820 Jefferson Blvd · 310-836-7087

Police

- **Culver City Police Dept** · 4040 Duquesne Ave · 310-837-1221

Post Offices

- **US Post Office** · 11111 Jefferson Blvd ·
- **US Post Office** · 9942 Culver Blvd ·

Schools

- **City Honors High** · 4800 Freshman Dr, West LA College
- **Culver City Independent Study** · 11450 Port Rd
- **Culver City Middle** · 4601 Elenda St
- **Culver City Senior High** · 4401 Elenda St
- **Culver Park Continuation** · 5303 Berryman Ave
- **Echo Horizon** · 3430 McManus Ave
- **El Marino Elementary** · 11450 Port Rd
- **El Rincon Elementary** · 11177 Overland Ave
- **Eras Center** · 5350 Machado Ln
- **Extraordinary Place** · 5707 Shenandoah Ave
- **Farragut Elementary** · 10820 Farragut Dr
- **La Ballona Elementary** · 10915 Washington Blvd
- **Linwood E Howe Elementary** · 4100 Irving Pl
- **Ohr Eliahu Academy** · 5950 Stoneview
- **Play Mountain Place** · 6063 Hargis St
- **St Augustine Elementary** · 3819 Clarington Ave
- **STAR Academy** · 10101 Jefferson Blvd
- **Temple Akiba** · 5249 S Sepulveda Blvd
- **Turningpoint** · 8780 National Blvd
- **Venture** · 11477 Jefferson Blvd
- **West Los Angeles College** · 9000 Overland Ave
- **Willows Community** · 8509 Higuera St

Supermarkets

- **Albertsons** · 8985 Venice Blvd
- **Pavilions** · 11030 Jefferson Blvd
- **Ralphs** · 10772 Jefferson Blvd
- **Ralphs** · 3827 Culver Ctr
- **Smart & Final** · 10113 Venice Blvd
- **Trader Joe's** · 9290 Culver Blvd

1. El Rincon Wy
2. Stephon Ter
3. Culver St
4. Lugo Wy
5. Stubbs Ln
6. Stever Ct
7. Esterin Wy
8. Marietta St
9. Stonycreek Rd
10. Salem Village Dr
11. Salem Village Pl
12. Salem Village Ct
13. Timber Lake Ter
14. Wilderness Ln
15. Huckfinn Ln
16. Copperfield Ln
17. Gaslight Ln
18. Showboat Ln
19. Showboat Pl
20. Showboat Pl
21. Howardview Ct
22. Crestview Rd
23. Ivy Wy
24. Leeview Ct

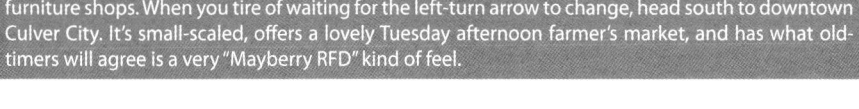

Venice Boulevard offers Brazilian food, Cuban food, Thai food, and a whole bunch of discount furniture shops. When you tire of waiting for the left-turn arrow to change, head south to downtown Culver City. It's small-scaled, offers a lovely Tuesday afternoon farmer's market, and has what old-timers will agree is a very "Mayberry RFD" kind of feel.

Coffee

- **Conservatory for Coffee** · 10117 Washington Blvd
- **Cubby's Coffee House** · 4455 Overland Ave
- **Kings Café** · 5508 Sawtelle Blvd
- **Starbucks** · 10705 W Washington Blvd
- **Starbucks** · 10820 Jefferson Blvd
- **Starbucks** · 8985 Venice Blvd
- **Starbucks** · 9718 Washington Blvd
- **Starbucks (Safeway)** · 11030 Jefferson Blvd
- **Tanner's Coffee** · 4342 Sepulveda Blvd
- **Teaforest** · 8686 Washington Blvd
- **Wanna Bagel** · 10780 Jefferson Blvd

Copy Centers

- **Copymax** · 8985 Venice Blvd · 310-836-5244
- **Kinko's** · 5575 Sepulveda Blvd · 310-313-2578
- **Office Depot** · 5640 Sepulveda Blvd · 310-390-4023
- **Pip Printing** · 9401 Venice Blvd · 310-837-6151
- **Reprographics** · 4215 Sepulveda Blvd · 310-391-0416
- **UPS Store** · 10401 Venice Blvd · 310-287-2269
- **UPS Store** · 10736 Jefferson Blvd · 310-558-4778

Farmer's Markets

- **Culver City** · Culver Blvd & Main St

Gyms

- **Bally Total Fitness** · 3827 Overland Ave · 310-204-2030
- **Curves** · 3861 Hughes Ave · 310-202-8653
- **Liberty Fitness** · 11409 Jefferson Blvd · 310-572-9356

Hardware Stores

- **A-1 Hardware** · 11119 Washington Blvd · 310-559-9594
- **Ace** · 5429 Sepulveda Blvd · 310-398-1251
- **Stellar True Value** · 3833 Main St · 310-558-4507
- **Tools to Go** · 10248 Culver Blvd · 310-815-8555

Liquor Stores

- **Albert's Liquors** · 5565 Sepulveda Blvd
- **Big Seven Liquors** · 10217 Venice Blvd
- **Crest Jr Market & Liquor** · 11127 Venice Blvd
- **Culver Liquor** · 10548 Culver Blvd
- **Liquor Barrel** · 3923 Sepulveda Blvd
- **Palm Tree Liquor** · 10425 Venice Blvd
- **R&Z Liquor** · 6142 Washington Blvd
- **R&Z Liquor** · 8582 Washington Blvd
- **Studio Village Liquor** · 10725 Jefferson Blvd
- **Taylor Liquors** · 11156 Washington Blvd

Movie Theaters

- **Mann Culver Plaza 6** · 9919 Washington Blvd · 310-841-2993

Nightlife

- **Jazz Bakery** · 3238 Helms Ave · 310-271-9039

Pet Stores

- **Apex Aquariums** · 4338 Sepulveda Blvd · 310-391-0305
- **The Aquarium** · 5403 Sepulveda Blvd · 310-390-1240
- **Centinela Feed & Pet Supplies** · 5299 Sepulveda Blvd · 310-572-6107
- **Petco** · 5347 S Sepulveda Blvd · 310-390-7255

Restaurants

- **Bamboo** · 10835 Venice Blvd · 310-287-0668
- **Café Brasil** · 10831 Venice Blvd · 310-837-8957
- **Conservatory for Coffee** · 10117 Washington Blvd · 310-558-0436
- **In-N-Out Burger** · 9245 W Venice Blvd · 800-786-1000
- **Johnnie's Pastrami** · 4017 Sepulveda Blvd · 310-397-6654
- **Natalee Thai** · 10101 Venice Blvd · 310-202-7003
- **Petrelli's Steakhouse** · 5615 S Sepulveda Blvd · 310-397-1438
- **S&W Country Diner** · 9748 Washington Blvd · 310-204-5136
- **Tito's Tacos** · 11222 Washington Pl · 310-391-5780
- **Versailles** · 10319 Venice Blvd · 310-558-3168

Shopping

- **Allied Model Trains** · 4411 Sepulveda Blvd · 310-313-9353
- **Civilization** · 8884 Venice Blvd · 310-202-8883
- **Culver City Home Brewing Supply** · 4358 1/2 Sepulveda Blvd · 310-397-3453
- **Dovetail** · 8918 Venice Blvd · 310-559-9431
- **HD Buttercup Mart** · 3225 Helms Ave · 310-558-8900
- **Last Chance** · 8712 Washington Blvd · 310-287-2333
- **Surfas** · 8825 National Blvd · 310-559-4770

Video Rental

- **Blockbuster** · 5359 Sepulveda Blvd · 310-915-1192
- **Blockbuster** · 9201 Venice Blvd · 310-837-1286
- **Hollywood Video** · 8985 Venice Blvd · 310-559-4942

103

Map 25 · **Marina del Rey / Westchester West**

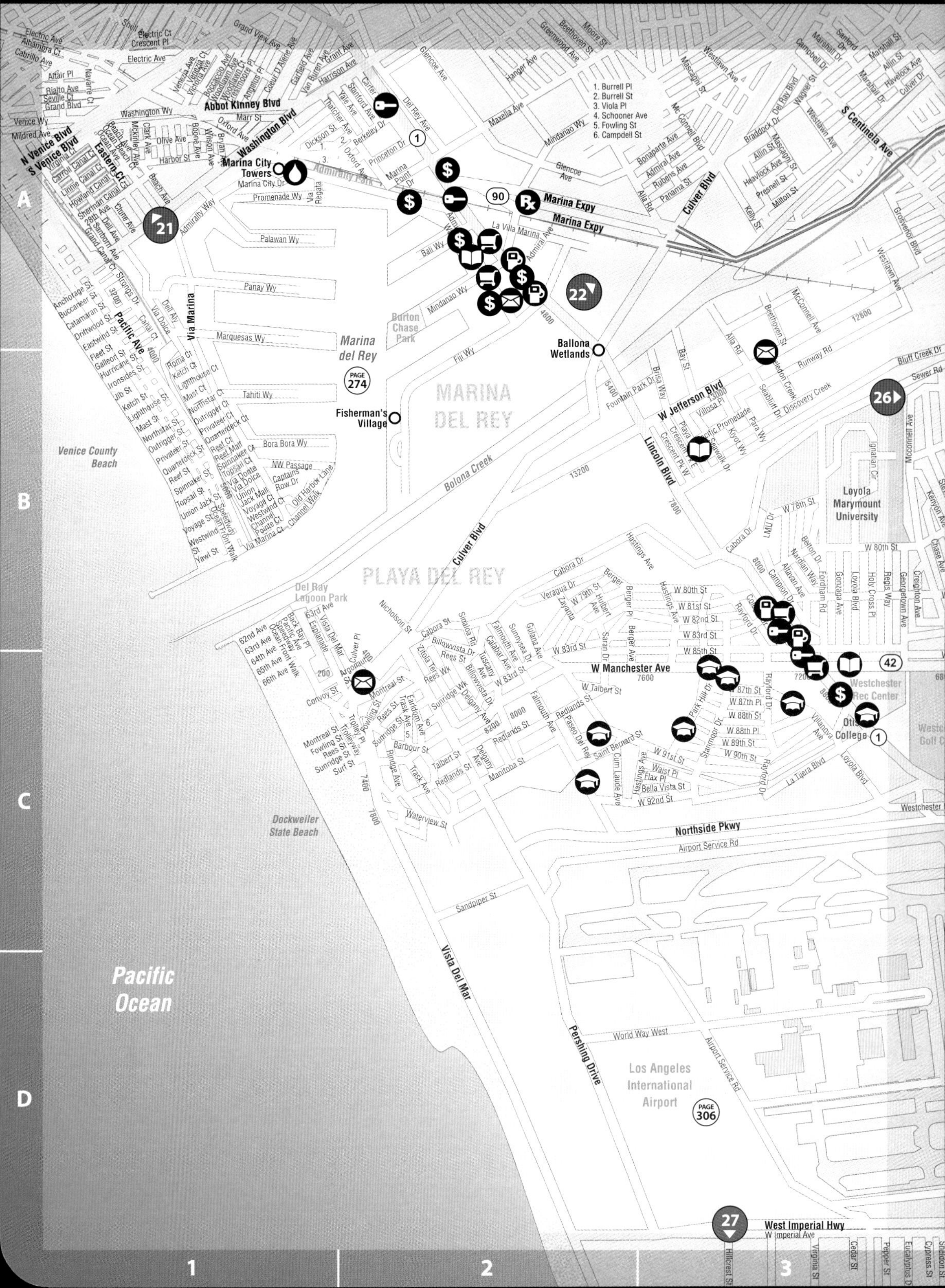

Electric Ave
Crescent Pl
Cabrillo Ave
Grand View Ave
Shell Ave
Electric Ct
Electric Ave
Greenwood Ave
Moor St
Westlawn Ave
Campbell Dr
Marshall St
Sanford St
Alla St

Rialto Ave
Venice Wy
N Venice Blvd
S Venice Blvd
Mildred Ave

Abbot Kinney Blvd

Washington Blvd
Washington Wy

Marina City Towers
Marina City Dr
Promenade Wy

21

Admiralty Way

Via Marina
Panay Wy
Marquesas Wy
Tahiti Wy

Marina del Rey

PAGE 274

Fisherman's Village

Venice County Beach

1. Burrell Pl
2. Burrell St
3. Viola Pl
4. Schooner Ave
5. Fowling St
6. Campdell St

Marina Expy
Marina Expy

90
Rx

22

Ballona Wetlands

S Centinela Ave

Culver Blvd

W Jefferson Blvd

Lincoln Blvd

26

Loyola Marymount University

W 78th St
W 80th St

MARINA DEL REY

Bolona Creek

PLAYA DEL REY

Del Rey Lagoon Park

Culver Blvd

Cabora Dr
Veragua Dr
Berger Pl
Hastings Ave

W 79th St
W 80th St
W 81st St
W 82nd St
W 83rd St
W 85th St

W Manchester Ave
7600

W Talbert St
W 87th St
W 88th Pl
W 89th Pl
W 90th St

42

Westchester Rec Center

Otis College
1

62nd Ave
63rd Ave
64th Ave
65th Ave
66th Ave

Dockweiler State Beach

Northside Pkwy
Airport Service Rd

Sandpiper St

Vista Del Mar

Pacific Ocean

Pershing Drive

World Way West

Los Angeles International Airport

PAGE 306

27
West Imperial Hwy
W Imperial Ave

A

B

C

D

1

2

3

Built around the largest man-made harbor in the world, Marina del Rey is home to over 6,000 boats (yachts too!). The marina provides LA with an easily accessible port for amateur and professional sailors alike (not to mention a great view for drinks at sunset!).

Map 25

$ Banks

- **Bank of America** · 4754 Admiralty Wy
- **Bank of America** · 9001 Lincoln Blvd
- **Downey Savings & Loan** · 4311 Lincoln Blvd
- **First Bank & Trust** · 4519 Admiralty Wy
- **US** · 4700 Lincoln Blvd
- **Washington Mutual** · 4676 Admiralty Wy

Car Rental

- **Budget** · 4363 Lincoln Blvd
- **Hertz** · 4100 Admiralty Wy
- **LAX Rent-a-Car** · 7115 W Manchester Ave
- **Penske Truck Rental** · 4500 Lincoln Blvd
- **Rocket Rent A Car** · 8601 Lincoln Blvd

Car Washes

- **Mr Polish** · 4333 Admiralty Wy

Gas Stations

- **76** · 4300 Lincoln Blvd
- **76** · 8300 Lincoln Blvd
- **Arco** · 8007 W Manchester Ave
- **Chevron** · 4680 Lincoln Blvd
- **Mobil** · 449 W Manchester
- **Shell** · 4770 Lincoln Blvd
- **Shell** · 8126 Lincoln Blvd

o Landmarks

- **Ballona Wetlands** · around Ballona Creek
- **Fisherman's Village** · 13755 Fiji Wy
- **Marina City Towers** · 4333 Admiralty Wy

Libraries

- **Lloyd Taber** · 4533 Admiralty Wy · 310-821-3415
- **Playa Vista Branch** · 6400 Playa Vista Dr · 310-437-6680
- **Westchester Branch** · 7114 W Manchester Ave · 310-348-1096

Pharmacies

- **Ralphs** · 4311 Lincoln Blvd · 310-821-4993
- **Sav-On (24 hrs)** · 13171 Mindanao Wy · 310-821-8908

Police

- **Los Angeles County Sheriff's Dept–Marina del Rey Station** · 13851 Fiji Wy · 310-823-7762

Post Offices

- **US Post Office** · 13031 W Jefferson Blvd
- **US Post Office** · 215 Culver Blvd
- **US Post Office** · 4766 Admiralty Wy

Schools

- **Del Rey Continuation** · 8701 Park Hill Dr
- **Loyola Marymount Univeristy** · 1 LMU Dr
- **Loyola Village Elementary** · 8821 Villanova St
- **Otis College of Art & Design** · 9045 Lincoln Blvd
- **Paseo del Rey Elementary** · 7751 Paseo Del Rey
- **St Anastansia Elementary** · 8631 S Stanmoor Dr
- **St Bernard High** · 9100 Falmouth Ave
- **Westchester Senior High** · 7400 W Manchester Ave

Supermarkets

- **Albertsons** · 8448 Lincoln Blvd
- **Gelson's Markets** · 13455 Maxella Ave
- **Ralphs** · 4311 Lincoln Blvd
- **Ralphs** · 4700 Admiralty Wy
- **Ralphs** · 8701 Lincoln Blvd

Map 25 · **Marina del Rey / Westchester West**

Electric Ct
Crescent Pl
Electric Ave
Shell Ave
Electric Ave
Grand View Ave
Alfair Pl
Rialto Ave
Seville Ct
Grand Blvd
Cabrillo Ave
Alhambra Ct
Afair Pl

Abbot Kinney Blvd
Washington Blvd

N Venice Blvd
S Venice Blvd
Mildred Ave
Venice Wy

Marina del Rey

PAGE 274

MARINA
DEL REY

PLAYA DEL REY

Venice County Beach

Pacific Ocean

Del Rey Lagoon Park

Dockweiler State Beach

Marina Expy
Marina Expy
La Villa Marina Ave

Burton Chase Park

Bolona Creek

Culver Blvd

Loyola Marymount University

W Jefferson Blvd
Lincoln Blvd

W Manchester Ave
7600

Northside Pkwy
Airport Service Rd

Los Angeles International Airport

PAGE 306

Westchester Rec Center

Otis College

Westchester Golf Course

1. Burrell Pl
2. Burrell St
3. Viola Pl
4. Schooner Ave
5. Fowling St
6. Campdell St

S Centinela Ave
Culver Blvd

21 **22** **26** **42** **90** **27** **1** **2**

West Imperial Hwy
W Imperial Ave

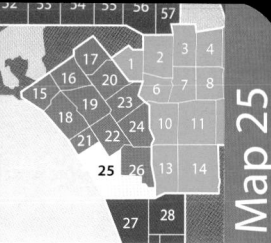

Map 25

Because of a large storm drain that flows throughout the year, Mothers Beach has not always gotten a high score when local water has been tested for bacterial pollution. But Mothers Beach was singled out as a "Best Beach for Kids" by Sunset Magazine. There are no waves—the beach lies in a quiet cove—and lifeguards are especially attentive. We guess it's a trade-off.

Coffee

- **Coffee Bean & Tea Leaf** · 13420 Maxella Ave
- **KC's Café** · 8320 Lincoln Blvd
- **Starbucks** · 4264 Lincoln Blvd
- **Tanner's Coffee** · 200 Culver Blvd

Copy Centers

- **Kinko's** · 4350 Lincoln Blvd · 310-827-2297
- **UPS Store** · 13428 Maxella Ave · 310-827-4000
- **UPS Store** · 322 Culver Ave · 310-448-1218
- **UPS Store** · 4712 Admiralty Wy · 310-827-9002

Gyms

- **Angel City Fitness** · 4144 Glencoe Ave · 310-578-2272
- **Curves** · 8327 Lincoln Blvd · 310-670-2517
- **LA Fitness Sports Clubs** · 13455 Maxella Ave · 310-827-0904
- **Marina City Club** · 4333 Admiralty Wy · 310-822-0611
- **Marina Fitness Center** · 14045 Panay Wy · 310-821-1662

Hardware Stores

- **Ace** · 7280 W Manchester Ave · 310-670-0652
- **Home Depot** · 12975 W Jefferson Blvd · 310-822-3330

Liquor Stores

- **Century Marina Liquors** · 8526 Lincoln Blvd
- **Del Rey Liquors** · 8367 W Manchester Ave
- **Marina Liquor** · 4148 Via Marina
- **Sandune Liquor** · 317 Culver Blvd

Movie Theaters

- **Loews Marina Marketplace Cinemas** · 13455 Maxella Ave · 310-827-2883

Nightlife

- **Brennan's** · 4089 Lincoln Blvd · 310-821-6622
- **Marina Lounge at the Furama Hotel** · 8601 Lincoln Blvd · 310-670-8111

Pet Stores

- **Housecat Premiere** · 8180 Manitoba St · 310-577-9956

Restaurants

- **Alejo's** · 4002 Lincoln Blvd · 310-822-0095
- **Alejo's** · 8343 Lincoln Blvd · 310-670-6677
- **Antica Pizzeria** · 13455 Maxella Ave · 310-577-8182
- **Ballona Fish Market** · 13455 Maxella Ave · 310-822-8979
- **Café Del Rey** · 4451 Admiralty Wy · 310-823-6395
- **Caffe Pinguini** · 6935 Pacific Ave · 310-306-0117
- **Casa Escobar** · 14160 Palawan Wy · 310-822-2199
- **Chan Dara** · 13490 Maxella Ave · 310-301-1004
- **Chloe** · 333 Culver Blvd · 310-305-4505
- **The Shack** · 185 Culver Blvd · 310-823-6222
- **Shanghai Red's** · 13813 Fiji Wy · 310-823-4522
- **The Warehouse** · 4499 Admiralty Wy · 310-823-5451

Video Rental

- **Blockbuster** · 8101 Manchester Blvd · 310-578-2243
- **Odyssey Video** · 4240 Lincoln Blvd · 310-823-2780
- **Video Café** · 8416 Pershing Dr · 310-306-4335

Map 26 • Westchester / Fox Hills / Ladera Heights / LAX

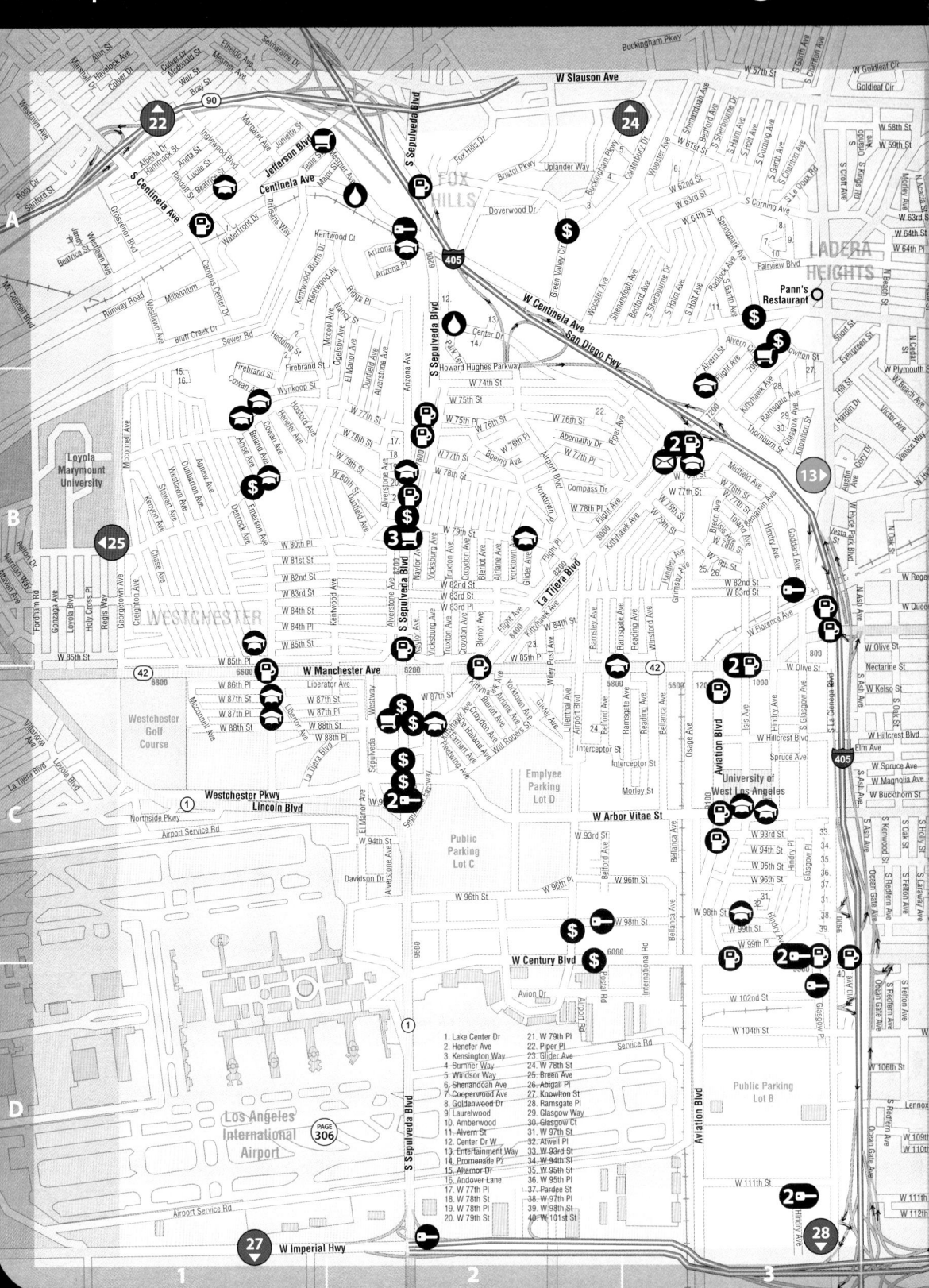

1. Lake Center Dr
2. Henefer Ave
3. Kensington Way
4. Sumner Way
5. Windsor Way
6. Shenandoah Ave
7. Cooperwood Ave
8. Goldenwood Dr
9. Laurelwood
10. Amberwood
11. Alvern St
12. Center Dr W
13. Entertainment Way
14. Promenade Pz
15. Altamor Dr
16. Andover Lane
17. W 77th Pl
18. W 78th St
19. W 78th Pl
20. W 79th St

21. W 79th Pl
22. Piper Ave
23. Glider Ave
24. W 78th St
25. Breen Ave
26. Abigail Pl
27. Knowlton St
28. Ramsgate Pl
29. Glasgow Way
30. Glasgow Ct
31. W 97th St
32. Atwell Pl
33. W 94th St
34. W 94th St
35. W 95th St
36. W 95th Pl
37. Pardee St
38. W 97th Pl
39. W 98th Pl
40. W 101st St

La Tijera Boulevard, which runs through this neighborhood, is the best shortcut to LAX that we know. It's accessible from La Cienega Boulevard, and is never congested. Just don't tell anyone else about it…

Banks

- **Bank of America** • 8946 S Sepulveda Blvd
- **Citibank** • 8800 S Sepulveda Blvd
- **Citibank** • 9841 Airport Blvd
- **City National** • 6033 W Century Blvd
- **First Federal** • 8750 S Sepulveda Blvd
- **Washington Mutual** • 8915 S Sepulveda Blvd
- **Wells Fargo** • 5377 W Centinela Ave
- **Wells Fargo** • 5899 Green Valley Cir
- **Wells Fargo** • 8814 S Sepulveda Blvd

Car Rental

- **A-One Rent-a-Car** • 6502 Arizona Ave
- **Ace Rent-a-Car** • 11101 Hindry Ave
- **Ace Rent-a-Car** • 9142 S Sepulveda Blvd
- **Advantage Rent-a-Car** • 1030 W Manchester Blvd
- **Aero Stars Car Rental** • 11220 Hindry Ave
- **Alamo** • 9020 Aviation Blvd
- **All States Car Rental** • 8705 La Tijera Blvd
- **Allied Rent-a-Car** • 5250 W Century Blvd
- **Allied Rent-a-Car** • 5280 W Century Blvd
- **Ariana Rent-a-Car** • 6201 W 87th St
- **Atlas Rent-a-Car** • 8924 Bellanca Ave
- **Atwest Rent-a-Car** • 5777 W 98th St
- **Avis** • 9217 Airport Blvd
- **Beverly Hills Rent-a-Car** • 9220 S Sepulveda Blvd
- **Budget** • 9775 Airport Blvd
- **Dollar** • 5630 W Arbor Vitae St
- **Easy Rent-a-Car** • 9142 S Sepulveda Blvd
- **Enterprise** • 8734 Bellanca Ave
- **Global Rent-a-Car** • 5249 W Century Blvd
- **Hertz** • 5711 W Century Blvd
- **Hertz** • 5855 W Century Blvd
- **Hertz** • 9000 Airport Blvd
- **Los Angeles Rent-a-Car** • 8911 Bellanca Ave
- **Lucky Rent-a-Car** • 8620 Airport Blvd
- **Midway Car Rental** • 6201 W Imperial Hwy
- **Midway Car Rental** • 6225 W Century Blvd
- **National** • 9020 Aviation Blvd
- **Payless Car Rental** • 10121 Glasgow Pl
- **Ritz Rent-a-Car** • 9100 S Sepulveda Blvd
- **Ryder Truck Rental** • 5366 W 83rd St
- **Sakura Rent-a-Car** • 5250 W Century Blvd
- **Sunrise Rent-a-Car** • 9204 Airport Blvd
- **Super Cheap Car Rental** • 10212 S La Cienega Blvd
- **Thrifty** • 5440 W Century Blvd
- **U-Save** • 941 W Manchester Blvd
- **United Rent-a-Car** • 5250 W Century Blvd

Car Washes

- **Howard Hughes Handwash** • 6080 Center Dr
- **Playa Vista Car Care** • 6900 S Centinela Ave

Gas Stations

- **76** • 12401 W Jefferson Blvd
- **76** • 5552 W Century Blvd
- **76** • 7400 La Tijera Blvd
- **76** • 8525 S Sepulveda Blvd
- **Arco** • 1110 W Manchester Blvd
- **Arco** • 5201 Century Blvd
- **Arco** • 7370 La Tijera Blvd
- **Arco** • 9200 Aviation Blvd
- **Chevron** • 5156 W Century Blvd
- **Chevron** • 6101 W Manchester Ave
- **Chevron** • 6900 S Centinela Ave
- **Chevron** • 7360 La Tijera Blvd
- **Exxon** • 9131 Aviation Blvd
- **Mobil** • 6100 Sepulveda Blvd
- **Mobil** • 6600 W Manchester Ave
- **Mobil** • 7601 S Sepulveda Blvd
- **Mobil** • 8307 S La Cienega Blvd
- **Shell** • 804 W Manchester Blvd
- **Texaco** • 5551 W Century Blvd

Landmarks

- **Pann's Restaurant** • 6710 La Tijera Blvd

Pharmacies

- **Longs Drugs** • 8900 Sepulveda Westway • 310-258-0265
- **Sav-On** • 5399 W Centinela Ave • 310-670-3335
- **Sav-On** • 5748 Messmer Ave • 310-915-9652
- **Sav-On** • 6299 S Bristol Pkwy • 310-641-3901
- **Sav-On** • 8601 S Sepulveda Blvd • 310-645-2323

Post Offices

- **US Post Office** • 7381 La Tijera Blvd
- **US Post Office** • 9029 Airport Blvd

Schools

- **98th St Elementary** • 5431 W 98th St
- **Amino Leadership High** • 1155 Arbor Vitae St
- **B'Nai Tikvah Nursery & Kindergarten** • 5820 W Manchester Ave
- **Cowan Ave Elementary** • 7615 Cowan Ave
- **Escuela de Montessori** • 8820 Sepulveda Eastway
- **Kentwood EEC** • 8376 Dunbarton Ave
- **Kentwood Elementary** • 8401 Emerson Ave
- **La Tijera United Methodist** • 7400 Osage Ave
- **Living World Christian Academy** • 6520 Arizona Ave
- **Los Angeles Open Charter** • 5540 W 77th St
- **Orville Wright Middle** • 6550 W 80th St
- **Playa del Rey Elementary** • 12221 Juniette St
- **St Jerome** • 5580 Thornburn St
- **University of West Los Angeles** • 1155 W Arbor Vitae St
- **Visitation Elementary** • 8740 Emerson Ave
- **Westchester Lutheran Middle** • 7831 S Sepulveda Blvd
- **Westchester Neighborhood** • 5520 Arbor Vitae
- **Westport Heights Elementary** • 6011 W 79th St

Supermarkets

- **Albertsons** • 5750 Mesmer Ave
- **Ralphs** • 8824 S Sepulveda Blvd
- **Trader Joe's** • 8645 S Sepulveda Blvd
- **Vons** • 6571 W 80th St
- **Vons** • 6921 La Tijera Blvd

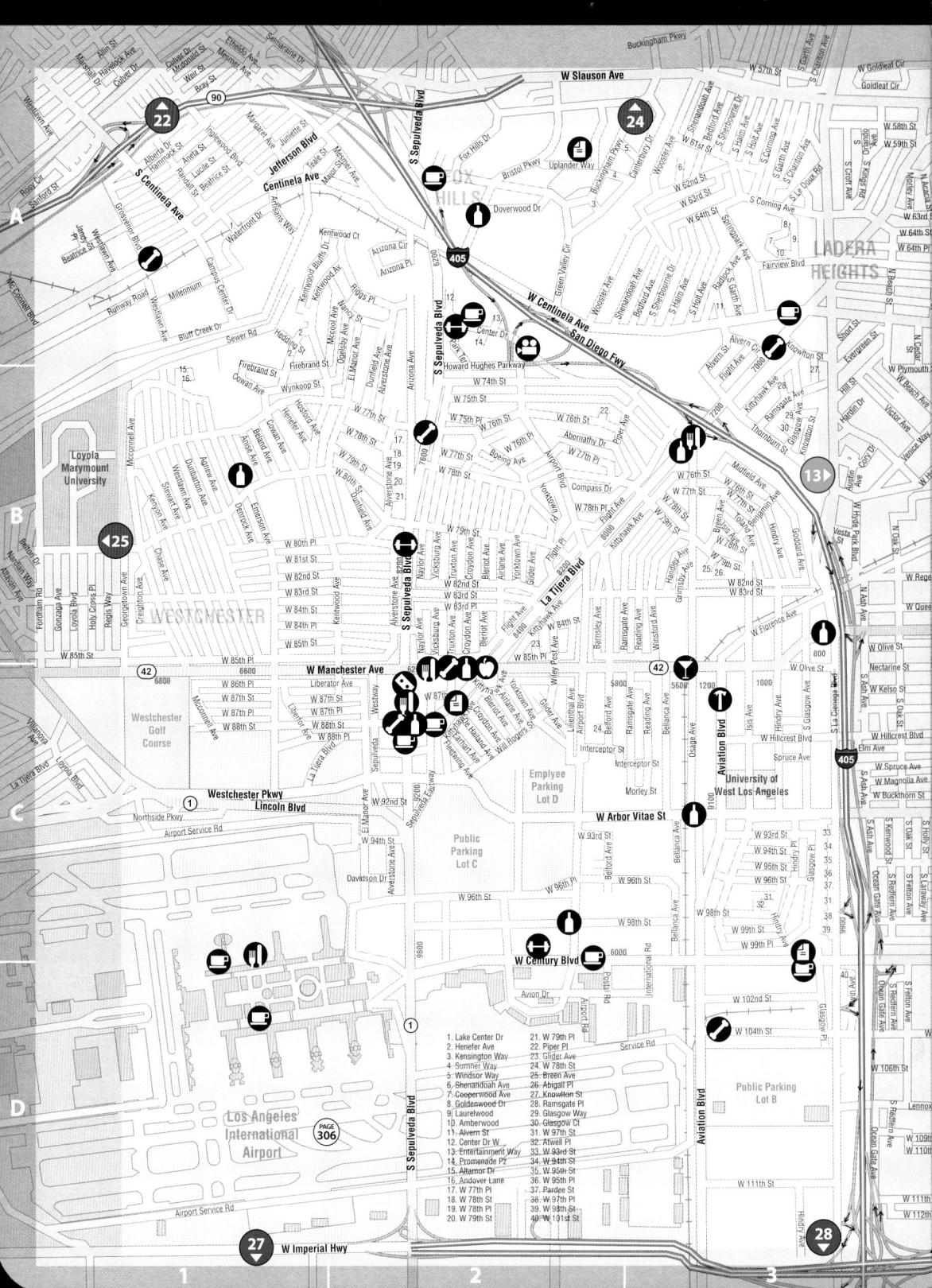

Map 26 • Westchester / Fox Hills / Ladera Heights / LAX

1. Lake Center Dr
2. Henefer Ave
3. Kensington Way
4. Summer Way
5. Windsor Way
6. Shenandoah Ave
7. Cooperwood Ave
8. Goldenwood Dr
9. Laurelwood
10. Amberwood
11. Alvern St
12. Center Dr W
13. Entertainment Way
14. Promenade Pz
15. Altamor Dr
16. Andover Lane
17. W 77th Pl
18. W 78th St
19. W 78th Pl
20. W 79th St
21. W 79th Pl
22. Piper Pl
23. Glider Way
24. W 78th St
25. Breen Ave
26. Abigail Pl
27. Knowlton St
28. Ramsgate Pl
29. Glasgow Way
30. Glasgow Ct
31. W 91st St
32. Atwell Pl
33. W 93rd St
34. W 94th St
35. W 95th St
36. W 95th Pl
37. Pardee St
38. W 97th Pl
39. W 98th St
40. W 101st St

Aah, LAX—the airport that inspired a television show and strives to inspire travelers with the technicolor and surreal "Kinetic Light Towers" at the very colorful price of $112 million. Maybe next year the improvement vote will funnel funds into taming the chaotic baggage claim areas, the long security lines, and the ever-present traffic circling through the airport. But, hey, at least it looks fabulous.

 Coffee

- **Coffee Co** • 8751 La Tijera Blvd
- **Eurotal** • 380 World Wy
- **Eurotal** • 500 World Wy
- **Java Java** • 300 World Wy
- **LAX Café** • 5250 W Century Blvd
- **Starbucks** • 294 Fox Hills Mall
- **Starbucks** • 5301 Centinela Ave
- **Starbucks** • 5855 W Century Blvd
- **Starbucks** • 6081 Center Dr
- **Starbucks** • 8817 S Sepulveda Blvd
- **Starbucks (LAX)** • 201 World Wy

Copy Centers

- **Fox Hills Printing Center** • 5815 Uplander Wy • 310-649-2867
- **Kinko's** • 5855 W Century Blvd • 310-665-5955
- **LA Quick Print** • 5250 W Century Blvd • 310-215-9506
- **Office Depot** • 8900 S Sepulveda Blvd • 310-568-0600
- **The Printing Spot** • 8711 La Tijera Blvd • 310-670-7075
- **Staples** • 8704 S Sepulveda Blvd • 310-342-5113
- **UPS Store** • 8939 S Sepulveda Blvd • 310-216-1324

 Farmer's Markets

- **Westchester** • W 87th St & Truxton Ave

Gyms

- **24-Hour Fitness** • 5959 W Century Blvd • 310-410-9909
- **Curves** • 5839 Green Valley Cir • 310-348-8727
- **Curves** • 6204 W Manchester Ave • 310-337-0810
- **Spectrum Club** • 6833 Park Ter • 310-216-3060
- **Westchester Family YMCA** • 8015 S Sepulveda Blvd • 310-670-4316

 Hardware Stores

- **Southland Lumber & Supply** • 8710 Aviation Blvd • 323-776-3530

Liquor Stores

- **A&A Liquors** • 6200 W Manchester Ave
- **Kentwood Mini Market** • 7923 Emerson Ave
- **Purdy Liquor** • 5919 W 98th St
- **Regal Liquor** • 6295 Bristol Pkwy
- **Sear's Liquor** • 5206 Arbor Vitae St
- **Stan's Liquor** • 842 W Manchester Blvd
- **Stewart's Liquor** • 7411 La Tijera Blvd

 Movie Theaters

- **The Bridge: Cinema de Lux** • 6081 Center Dr • 310-568-3375

Nightlife

- **Westchester Sports Grill** • 5630 W Manchester Ave • 310-670-2366

Pet Stores

- **Centinela Feed & Pet Supplies** • 7600 S Sepulveda Blvd • 310-216-9261
- **Eco-Pet** • 6955 La Tijera Blvd • 310-645-8892
- **Petco** • 8801 S Sepulveda Blvd • 310-645-7198
- **Sea Dwelling Creatures** • 5515 W 104th St • 310-676-9697

Restaurants

- **Buggy Whip** • 7420 La Tijera Blvd • 310-645-7131
- **Encounter** • 209 World Wy • 310-215-5151
- **In-N-Out Burger** • 9149 S Sepulveda Blvd • 800-786-1000
- **Paco's Tacos** • 6212 W Manchester Ave • 310-645-8692
- **Panera Bread** • 8647 S Sepulveda Blvd • 310-641-9200

Video Rental

- **Blockbuster** • 5325 W Centinela Ave • 310-645-8211
- **Blockbuster** • 8813 S Sepulveda Blvd • 310-649-3699

Map 27 • **El Segundo / Manhattan Beach**

Los Angeles International Airport

PAGE 306

Airport Service Rd

Glenn Anderson Fwy

25

26

105

Aviation/ LAX

W Imperial Hwy
W Imperial Ave
W Acacia Ave
W Walnut Ave
W Sycamore Ave

E Acacia Ave
E Walnut Ave
E Sycamore Ave

E Maple Ave

EL SEGUNDO

Mariposa

W Maple Ave
W Oak Ave
W Palm Ave
W Elm Ave
W Mariposa Ave

E Oak Ave
E Palm Ave
E Elm Ave
E Mariposa Ave
E Pine Ave

Library

W Pine Ave

El Segundo
Recreation
Park

E Pine Ave
E Holly Ave
Grand Ave

Continental Blvd

E Holly Ave

Grand Ave
W Franklin Ave

El Segundo

E El Segundo Blvd
E El Segundo Blvd

W El Segundo Blvd

Binder Pl

Dockweiler State Beach

Pershing Dr

Vista Del Mar

11400

12200

12600

600

290

El Segundo Beach

B

Chevron Oil Refinery

The Lakes at El Segundo Golf Course

S Hughes Way
Allied Way

Utah Ave

Alaska Ave

Douglas St

28

1. E Elsey Pl
2. Bridgeport
3. Chatham
4. Stratford
5. Cambridge
6. Santa Cruz Ct
7. San Miguel Ct
8. Evergreen Ln
9. Grenada Ct
10. Catalina Ct
11. Laguna Ct
12. Malaga Pl
13. Malaga Wy
14. Gateway Dr
15. Bermuda Ct
16. Dover Pl
17. Nantucket Pl

18. Cayman Ct
19. Coronado Ct
20. Monterey Ct
21. Marin Ct
22. Tiburon Ct
23. Bryant Pl
24. Villa Escuela
25. Arbolado Ct
26. Center Pl
27. Deegan Pl
28. Church St
29. Fisher Ave
30. Railroad Pl
31. La Carlita Pl
32. Braeholm Pl
33. Hermosa View Dr

EL PORTO

Rosecrans Ave
Rosecrans Ave

Park View Ave

Plaza Golf Course

Continental Way
N Nash St
S Douglas St

N Aviation Blvd

MANHATTAN BEACH

Pacific Ocean

Manhattan County Beach

PAGE 269

Manhattan Beach Pier

Live Oak Park

The Strand

Highland Ave

N Valley Dr
N Ardmore Ave

Marine Ave

Marine Ave Sport Park

Manhattan Beach Blvd
Manhattan Beach Blvd

Carlton
Village Cir

1

PAGE 269

N Valley Dr
N Ardmore Ave

N Sepulveda Blvd

Duncan Ave
Duncan Ave
Longfellow Ave
Boundary Pl

Valley Park
Gould Ave

29

Gates Ave
Curtis Ave
Voorhees Ave

Ruhland Ave
Nelson Ave
Mathews Ave

C

D

1   2   3

The area continues to grow, and has hit the big time with the opening of Raleigh Studios Manhattan Beach, where shows like *CSI: Miami* and *The OC* now film. Traffic on the 405 used to lighten up just past LAX, but the new businesses that have opened along El Segundo Boulevard and Rosecrans Avenue have, unfortunately, extended the congestion farther south.

$ Banks

- **Bank of America** · 1200 Highland Ave
- **Bank of America** · 3016 Sepulveda Blvd
- **Bank of America** · 835 N Sepulveda Blvd
- **Bank of the West** · 3500 Aviation Blvd
- **Citibank** · 2710 Sepulveda Blvd
- **Comerica** · 2321 Rosecrans Ave
- **First Coastal** · 1800 N Sepulveda Blvd
- **First Coastal** · 275 Main St
- **Union** · 2910 N Sepulveda Blvd
- **Union** · 400 Manhattan Beach Blvd
- **US** · 3300 N Sepulveda Blvd
- **Washington Mutual** · 130 E Grand Ave
- **Washington Mutual** · 201 Manhattan Beach Blvd
- **Washington Mutual** · 550 N Sepulveda Blvd
- **Washington Mutual** · 700 S Sepulveda Blvd
- **Wells Fargo** · 3110 N Sepulveda Blvd
- **Wells Fargo** · 500 N Sepulveda Blvd

Car Rental

- **Discovery Rent A Car** · 525 N Sepulveda Blvd
- **Manhattan Beach Toyota Rent A Car** · 1500 N Sepulveda Blvd
- **Penske Truck Rental** · 1910 S Hughes Wy

Car Washes

- **Auto Spa Self Service Car Wash** · 118 E Imperial Ave
- **Manhattan Car Wash** · 300 S Sepulveda Blvd
- **Red Carpet Hand Wash** · 2414 N Sepulveda Blvd

Gas Stations

- **76** · 2121 Highland Ave
- **76** · 603 N Sepulveda Blvd
- **76** · 770 N Sepulveda Blvd
- **Arco** · 1002 Manhattan Beach Blvd
- **Chevron** · 101 S Sepulveda Blvd
- **Chevron** · 2301 N Aviation Blvd
- **Chevron** · 232 Main St
- **Chevron** · 3633 N Sepulveda Blvd
- **Chevron** · 601 Vista Del Mar
- **Manhattan Beach Fuel** · 1100 Manhattan Beach Blvd
- **Mobil** · 1865 Manhattan Beach Blvd
- **Mobil** · 765 N Sepulveda Blvd
- **Shell** · 1129 N Sepulveda Blvd

Landmarks

- **Chevron Oil Refinery** · east of Sepulveda Blvd, north of Rosecrans Ave
- **Manhattan Beach Pier** · west of Manhattan Beach Blvd

Libraries

- **El Segundo Public Library** · 111 W Mariposa Ave · 310-524-2722
- **Manhattan Beach** · 1320 Highland Ave · 310-545-8595

Pharmacies

- **Longs Drugs** · 1570 S Rosecrans Ave · 310-536-9255
- **Ralphs** · 500 N Sepulveda Blvd · 310-615-0537
- **Rite-Aid** · 220 E Grand Ave · 310-640-2715
- **Sav-On** · 2900 Sepulveda Blvd · 310-546-3481

Police

- **El Segundo City Police Dept** · 348 Main St · 310-524-2200
- **Manhattan Beach Police Dept** · 1501 N Peck Ave · 310-802-5100

Post Offices

- **US Post Office** · 1007 N Sepulveda Blvd
- **US Post Office** · 200 Main St
- **US Post Office** · 2130 E Mariposa Ave
- **US Post Office** · 425 15th St

Schools

- **American Martyrs** · 1701 Laurel Ave
- **Arena High** · 630 Arena St
- **Aurelia Pennekamp Elementary** · 110 S Rowell Ave
- **Center St Elementary** · 700 Center St
- **El Segundo High** · 640 Main St
- **El Segundo Middle** · 332 Center St
- **Explorers In Learning Academy** · 1852 6th St
- **Grand View Elementary** · 455 25th St
- **Manhattan Beach Middle** · 1501 Redondo Ave
- **Meadows Ave Elementary** · 1200 N Meadows Ave
- **Mira Costa High** · 701 S Peck Ave
- **Montessori** · 315 S Peck Ave
- **Opal Robinson Elementary** · 80 Morningside Dr
- **Pacific Elementary** · 1214 Pacific Ave
- **Richard Henry Dana Intermediate** · 13500 Aviation Blvd
- **Richmond St Elementary** · 615 Richmond St
- **St Anthony** · 233 Lomita St
- **Via Pacifica** · 1700 Manhattan Beach Blvd
- **Vistamar** · 737 Hawaii St

Supermarkets

- **Bristol Farms** · 1570 Rosecrans Ave
- **Ralphs** · 2700 N Sepulveda Blvd
- **Ralphs** · 500 N Sepulveda Blvd
- **Trader Joe's** · 1800 Rosecrans Ave
- **Trader Joe's** · 1821 Manhattan Beach Blvd
- **Vons** · 410 Manhattan Beach Blvd

25

105   26

Glenn Anderson Fwy

Aviation/
LAX

Los Angeles
International Airport

Airport Service Rd

W Imperial Hwy

N Sepulveda Blvd

W Imperial Ave

W Acacia Ave

W Walnut Ave

W Sycamore Ave

W Oak Ave

W Palm Ave

W Elm Ave

W Mariposa Ave

W Pine Ave

W Holly

Grand

W Franklin

W El Segundo Blvd

Binder
Pl

E Acacia Ave

E Walnut Ave

E Sycamore Ave

E Maple Ave

E Oak Ave

E Palm Ave

E Mariposa Ave

E Pine Ave

E Holly Ave

Grand Ave

E El Segundo Blvd

E Maple Ave

Washington
Park

EL SEGUNDO

Mariposa

Continental Blvd

1

El Segundo

El Segundo
Recreation
Park

Library
Park

Pershing Dr

Vista Del Mar

Dockweiler
State
Beach

11400

12200

12600

600

El Segundo
Beach

200

The Lakes at
El Segundo
Golf Course

S Sepulveda Blvd

N Sepulveda Blvd

Utah Ave

Alaska Ave

Douglas   28

Pacific
Ocean

Manhattan
County
Beach

EL PORTO

MANHATTAN
BEACH

Rosecrans Ave

Park View Ave

Plaza
Golf
Course

Marine Ave
Sport Park

Marine Ave

Douglas St

N Aviation Blvd

Polliwog
Park

Manhattan Beach Blvd

PAGE
269

S Sepulveda Blvd

1

29

Valle
Park

1. E Elsey Pl	18. Cayman Ct
2. Bridgeport	19. Coronado Ct
3. Chatham	20. Monterey Ct
4. Strafford	21. Marin Ct
5. Cambridge	22. Tiburon Ct
6. Santa Cruz Ct	23. Bryant Pl
7. San Miguel Ct	24. Villa Escuela
8. Evergreen Ln	25. Arbolado Ct
9. Grenada Ct	26. Center Pl
10. Catalina Ct	27. Deegan Pl
11. Laguna Ct	28. Church St
12. Malaga Pl	29. Fisher Ave
13. Malaga Wy	30. Railroad Pl
14. Gateway Dr	31. La Carlita Pl
15. Bermuda Ct	32. Braeholm Pl
16. Dover Pl	33. Hermosa View Dr
17. Nantucket Pl	

A

B

C

D

1   2   3

It would be very easy to survive for an indefinite time without ever leaving Rosecrans Avenue, which boasts several supermarkets, movie theaters, and a camping/wilderness store. But make your way closer to the ocean in Manhattan Beach, and you'll find much quirkier shops and restaurants that all have a personality of their own.

Coffee

- **Blue Butterfly Coffee** • 351 Main St
- **Coffee Bean & Tea Leaf** • 3008 N Sepulveda Blvd
- **Latte Lover** • 321 Manhattan Beach Blvd
- **Manhattan Coffee** • 350 N Sepulveda Blvd
- **Our Daily Grind** • 503 Main St
- **Peet's Coffee & Tea** • 328 Manhattan Beach Blvd
- **Starbucks** • 2231 Rosecrans Ave
- **Starbucks** • 233 Manhattan Beach Blvd
- **Starbucks** • 530 N Sepulveda Blvd
- **Starbucks (Target)** • 1200 N Sepulveda Blvd

Copy Centers

- **Copy Shop** • 309 S Sepulveda Blvd • 310-374-5844
- **Dial Instant Printers** • 2313 N Sepulveda Blvd • 310-546-4679
- **Kinko's** • 630 N Sepulveda Blvd • 310-322-9141
- **Office Depot** • 1700 Rosencrans Ave • 310-536-9969
- **Pip Printing** • 116 W Grand Ave • 310-322-7441
- **Pip Printing** • 3201 N Sepulveda Blvd • 310-545-5617
- **UPS Store** • 1601 N Sepulveda Blvd • 310-545-1260
- **UPS Store** • 214 Main St • 310-640-8589

Farmer's Markets

- **El Segundo** • Grand Ave & Eucalyptus Dr
- **Farmers' Market–El Segundo** • Main St at City Hall

Gyms

- **24-Hour Fitness** • 1500 Rosecrans Ave • 310-536-9300
- **Bodysmart on Main** • 505 Main St • 310-414-1400
- **Club at Pacific Corporate Towers** • 200 N Sepulveda Blvd • 310-563-1442
- **Curves** • 433 Main St • 310-414-0004
- **Gorilla Sports** • 3701 Highland Ave • 310-545-4982
- **Spectrum Club** • 2250 Park Pl • 310-643-6878

Hardware Stores

- **Ace** • 203 E Grand Ave • 310-322-4545
- **Manhattan True Value** • 1005 N Aviation Blvd • 310-372-2402

Liquor Stores

- **Bacchus** • 1000 Manhattan Ave
- **Dan's Liquor** • 3232 Manhattan Ave
- **El Porto Market & Deli** • 4103 Highland Ave
- **Jon's Liquor** • 3508 Aviation Blvd
- **Leonard's Liquor** • 630 N Sepulveda Blvd
- **Lindy's Liquor & Deli** • 11720 Aviation Blvd
- **Moon's Market** • 3307 Highland Ave
- **Mr D's Liquor** • 1100 N Sepulveda Blvd
- **Players Liquor** • 3804 Highland Ave
- **Sepulveda Wine** • 917 N Sepulveda Blvd
- **Village Liquor** • 506 Center St

Movie Theaters

- **Old Town Music Hall** • 140 Richmond St • 310-322-2592
- **Pacific Beach Cities 16** • 831 N Nash St • 310-607-0007
- **Pacific Manhattan Village** • 3560 N Sepulveda Blvd • 310-640-1075

Nightlife

- **Beaches** • 117 Manhattan Beach Blvd • 310-545-2523
- **Shark's Cove** • 309 Manhattan Beach Blvd • 310-545-2683

Pet Stores

- **Buster & Sullivan** • 451 Manhattan Beach Blvd • 310-802-1410
- **Critter Corral Pet Shop** • 118 W Grand Ave • 310-322-3077
- **Jim's Exotic Fish** • 630 N Sepulveda Blvd • 310-322-3474
- **Paws a While** • 930 Manhattan Beach Blvd • 310-318-3996
- **We Love Pets** • 815 Manhattan Ave • 310-372-1212

Restaurants

- **Cozymel's** • 2171 Rosecrans Ave • 310-606-5464
- **Good Stuff** • 1300 Highland Ave • 310-545-4775
- **Houston's** • 1550 Rosecrans Ave • 310-643-7211
- **Il Fornaio** • 1800 Rosecrans Ave • 310-725-9555
- **Local Yolk** • 3414 Highland Ave • 310-546-4407
- **Michi Restaurant & Bar** • 903 Manhattan Ave • 310-376-0613
- **North End Café** • 3421 Highland Ave • 310-546-4782
- **Rock'n Fish** • 120 Manhattan Beach Blvd • 310-379-9900
- **The Spot** • 110 2nd St • 310-376-2355
- **Towne** • 1142 Manhattan Ave • 310-545-5405
- **Uncle Bill's Pancake House** • 1305 Highland Ave • 310-545-5177

Shopping

- **Fry's Electronics** • 3600 Sepulveda Blvd • 310-364-3797
- **GeoDecor** • 113 Shelton St • 310-322-4043
- **Growing Wild** • 1201 Highland Ave • 310-545-4432
- **Magpie** • 1141 Highland Ave • 310-546-5132

Video Rental

- **Blockbuster** • 1130 Sepulveda Blvd • 310-545-8659
- **Blockbuster** • 2200 N Sepulveda Blvd • 310-545-0202
- **Blockbuster** • 231 W Grand Ave • 310-414-9194
- **Main Street Video** • 235 Main St • 310-322-8700

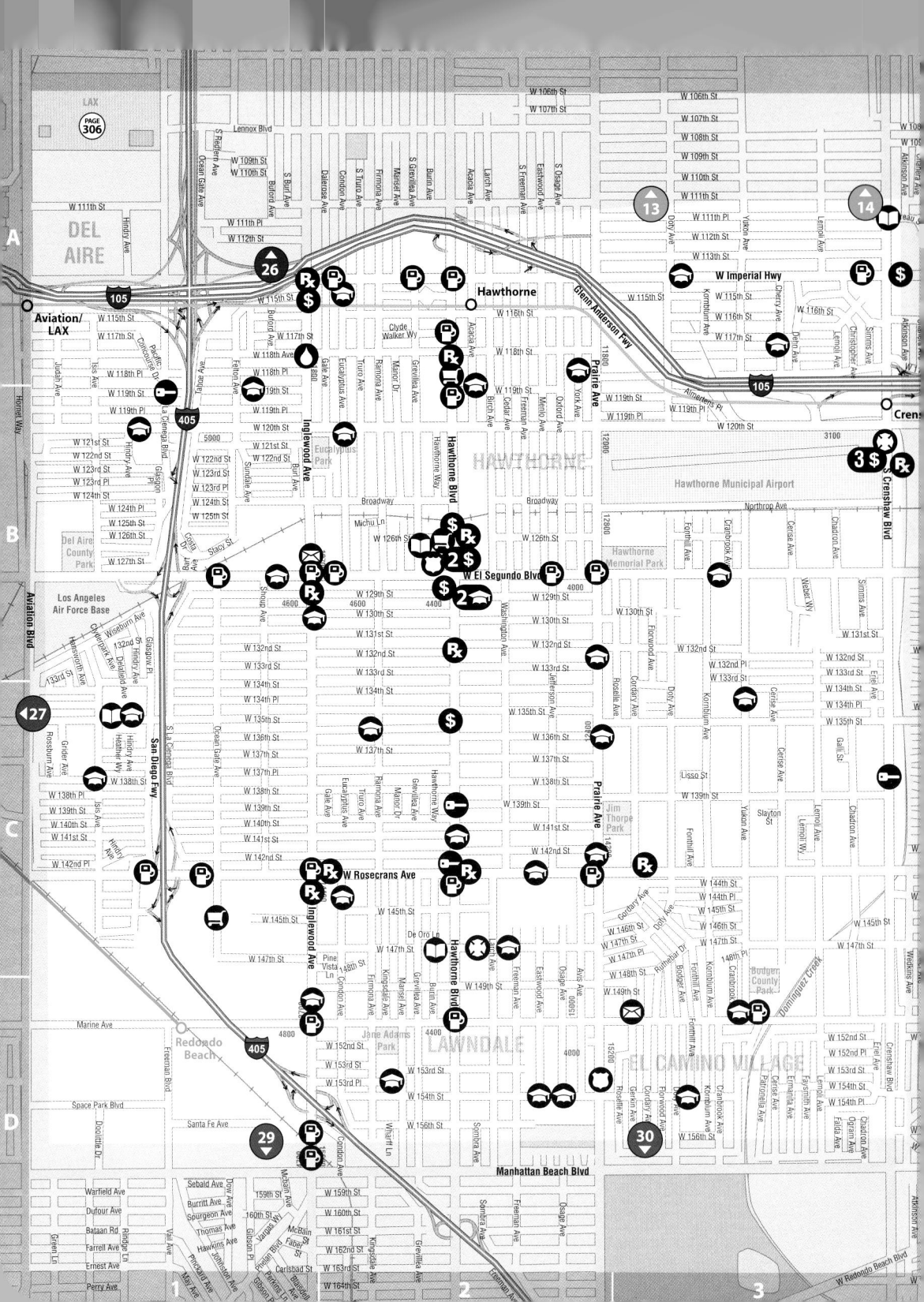

Encompassing six square miles, ensconced by three major freeways—the 405, 105, and 110—Hawthorne calls itself the "hub of the South Bay." Hawthorne's municipal airport, also known as Jack Northrop Field, is home to the Western Museum of Flight. The museum's collection is mainly devoted to one of Hawthorne's largest businesses, Northrop Grumman, which helped boost the city's reputation as the "cradle of aviation."

# Banks

- **Bank of America** · 11525 Crenshaw Blvd
- **Bank of America** · 12547 S Hawthorne Blvd
- **Citibank** · 12710 Hawthorne Blvd
- **Citibank** · 2940 W Imperial Hwy
- **Union** · 12801 Hawthorne Blvd
- **Washington Mutual** · 12645 Hawthorne Blvd
- **Wells Fargo** · 11305 S Crenshaw Blvd
- **Wells Fargo** · 13545 Hawthorne Blvd
- **Wells Fargo** · 4001 Inglewood Ave

Car Rental

- **Eagle Rider** · 11860 S La Cienega Blvd
- **Enterprise** · 13901 Hawthorne Blvd
- **Rent 4 Less** · 15312 Hawthorne Blvd
- **Town Rent-a-Car** · 13815 Crenshaw Blvd

Car Washes

- **E-Z Self Service Car Wash** · 11817 Inglewood Ave

Gas Stations

- **76** · 12806 S Prairie Ave
- **76** · 3101 W Imperial Hwy
- **76** · 4008 W Rosecrans Ave
- **76** · 5105 W Rosecrans Ave
- **Arco** · 11402 Hawthorne Blvd
- **Arco** · 2730 Marine Ave
- **Arco** · 4009 W Rosecrans Ave
- **Arco** · 4015 W El Segundo Blvd
- **Chevron** · 12801 Inglewood Ave
- **Chevron** · 14305 Hawthorne Blvd
- **Independent** · 4773 W El Segundo Blvd
- **Shell** · 11741 Hawthorne Blvd
- **Shell** · 15106 Hawthorne Blvd
- **Shell** · 15606 Inglewood Ave
- **Shell** · 4750 W Rosecrans Ave
- **Shell** · 4755 W Imperial Hwy
- **Thrifty** · 11890 S Hawthorne Blvd
- **Thrifty** · 5038 W El Segundo Blvd
- **Thrifty** · 5230 Rosecrans Ave

Libraries

- **Crenshaw-Imperial Branch** · 11141 Crenshaw Blvd · 310-412-5403
- **Hawthorne** · 12700 Grevillea Ave · 310-679-8193
- **Lawndale Library** · 14615 Burin Ave · 310-676-0177
- **Wiseburn** · 5335 W 135th St · 310-643-8880

Pharmacies

- **CVS (24 hrs)** · 4775 W Rosecrans Ave · 310-263-7330
- **Rite-Aid** · 11340 Crenshaw Blvd · 323-757-2811
- **Rite-Aid** · 13141 Hawthorne Blvd · 310-675-9322
- **Sav-On** · 11831 Hawthorne Blvd · 310-973-6723
- **Sav-On** · 14441 S Inglewood Ave · 310-973-0812
- **Sav-On** · 15103 S Hawthorne Blvd · 310-679-7619
- **Sav-On** · 3880 W Rosecrans Blvd · 310-675-4221
- **Sav-On (Albertsons)** · 12630 S Hawthorne Blvd · 310-675-9494
- **The Medicine Shoppe** · 12816 Inglewood Ave · 310-644-6810
- **Vons** · 4001 Inglewood Ave · 310-349-0863

# Police

- **Hawthorne Police Dept** · 4440 W 126th St · 310-970-7976
- **Lawndale Sheriff Service Center** · 15331 Prairie Ave · 310-219-2750

# Post Offices

- **US Post Office** · 12700 Inglewood Ave
- **US Post Office** · 4320 Marine Ave · 310-679-980

# Schools

- **Al-Huda Islamic** · 12209 Hawthorne Wy
- **Bennett-Kew Elementary** · 11710 Cherry Ave
- **Billy Mitchell Elementary** · 14429 Condon Ave
- **Bud Carlson Middle** · 13838 Yukon Ave
- **Del Aire Day Care** · 4955 W 119th St
- **Environmental Charter** · 4234 W 147th St
- **Eucalyptus Elementary** · 12044 Eucalyptus Ave
- **Hawthorne Academy** · 12500 Ramona Ave
- **Hawthorne High** · 4859 W El Segundo Blvd
- **Hawthorne Mathematics & Science Academy** · 14120 S Hawthorne Blvd
- **Hawthorne Middle** · 4366 W 129th St
- **Jane Addams Elementary** · 4535 W 153rd Pl
- **Jefferson Elementary** · 4091 W 139th St
- **Juan Cabrillo Elementary** · 5309 W 135th St
- **Juan de Anza Elementary** · 5234 W 120th St
- **Kornblum Elementary** · 3630 W El Segundo Blvd
- **Lawndale High** · 14901 Inglewood Ave
- **Leuzinger High** · 4118 W Rosecrans Ave
- **Light and Life Christian** · 14204 Prairie Av
- **Mark Twain Elementary** · 3728 W 154th St
- **Mt Cavalry Christian Academy** · 13253 S Hawthorne Blvd
- **Peter Burnett Elementary** · 5403 W 138th St
- **Prairie Vista Middle** · 13600 Prairie Ave
- **Ramona Elementary** · 4617 W 136th St
- **RK Lloyde High** · 14901 Inglewood Ave
- **Roosevelt Elementary** · 3533 Marine Ave
- **South Bay Lutheran High** · 3600 W Imperial Hwy
- **St Joseph's Elementary** · 11886 Acacia Ave
- **Trinity Lutheran** · 4783 W 130th St
- **Vine Christian Academy** · 3210 W 155th St
- **Washington Elementary** · 4339 W 129th St
- **Will Rogers Middle** · 4110 W 154th St
- **William Anderson Elementary** · 4110 W 154th St
- **Williams Elementary** · 13434 Yukon Ave
- **York Elementary** · 11838 York Ave
- **Zela Davis Elementary** · 13435 S Yukon Ave

Supermarkets

- **Albertsons** · 12630 Hawthorne Blvd
- **Food 4 Less** · 14500 Ocean Gate Ave
- **Ralphs** · 11873 Hawthorne Blvd
- **Vons** · 4001 Inglewood Ave

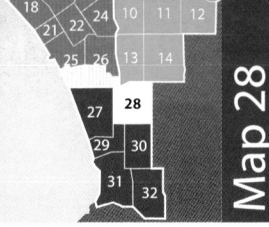
Rising South Bay real estate prices and an active city council have pushed this older, blue collar-flavored municipality to spruce up. New and revamped recreational facilities and the Larry Guidi Skateboard park make it attractive for suburbanite families. Hawthorne is home to Blue Bird Liquor, the luckiest place in LA to buy a lottery ticket. There's a line around the block when the jackpot gets big!

Coffee

- **Coffee Attic** · 3901 Inglewood Ave
- **Starbucks** · 12770 Hawthorne Blvd
- **Starbucks** · 5030 W Rosecrans Ave
- **Starbucks** · 5378 W Rosecrans Ave
- **White's Bakery** · 12215 Hawthorne Blvd

Copy Centers

- **A&H Printing Services** · 14027 Hawthorne Blvd · 310-644-4975
- **Expresso Courier & Printing** · 11344 Crenshaw Blvd · 323-755-0222
- **Kinko's** · 5201 W Rosecrans Ave · 310-297-6850
- **Office Depot** · 14501 Ocean Gate Ave · 310-970-0226
- **Staples** · 14401 Hindry Ave · 310-297-0815
- **UPS Store** · 15228 Hawthorne Blvd · 310-973-7500

Gyms

- **24-Hour Fitness** · 2831 W 120th St · 323-756-2466
- **Bally Total Fitness** · 5001 El Segundo Blvd · 310-263-7520
- **Curves** · 5261 W Rosecrans Ave · 310-727-9958
- **Gold's Gym** · 4949 W 147th St · 310-263-2900

Hardware Stores

- **Hawthorne True Value** · 13532 Hawthorne Blvd · 310-676-2253
- **Home Depot** · 14603 Ocean Gate Ave · 310-644-9600
- **Lowe's** · 2800 120th St · 323-327-4000
- **True Value** · 3856 W El Segundo Blvd · 310-676-5497

Liquor Stores

- **Art's Rite Liquor** · 14000 Inglewood Ave
- **Avenue Liquor** · 13305 Inglewood Ave
- **Blue Bird Liquor** · 13746 Hawthorne Blvd
- **BMW Liquor** · 4533 W Imperial Hwy
- **Bob's Liquor & Deli** · 3127 W Imperial Hwy
- **Coast Liquor Store** · 11935 Inglewood Ave
- **Frank's Liquor** · 12329 Prairie Ave
- **G&G Liquors** · 14989 Prairie Ave
- **Mel & Leo's Liquor** · 14245 Hawthorne Blvd
- **Mr B's Mini Mart** · 3500 W Rosecrans Ave

- **Plaza Liquor** · 11601 Inglewood Ave
- **Pound Penny Liquor & Market** · 13353 Prairie Ave
- **Ramp West Market & Liquor** · 5241 W Rosecrans Ave
- **S&D Liquor** · 3910 W Rosecrans Ave
- **S&P Liquor Store** · 13007 Prairie Ave
- **SK Liquor** · 15202 Prairie Ave
- **Snappy Food Mart** · 4172 W Imperial Hwy
- **South Bay Market Liquor** · 12726 Crenshaw Blvd
- **Ted's Liquor** · 14609 Hawthorne Blvd
- **Variety Liquor** · 4669 W Imperial Hwy
- **Young's Liquor** · 3800 W El Segundo Blvd

Pet Stores

- **Petco** · 3901 Inglewood Ave · 310-355-1370
- **Su Aquarium** · 12625 Hawthorne Blvd · 310-675-8652

Restaurants

- **Daphne's** · 3901 Inglewood Ave · 310-676-9165
- **El Pollo Inka** · 15400 Hawthorne Blvd
- **Guru Palace** · 4850 W Rosecrans Ave · 310-675-5533
- **In-N-Out Burger** · 3801 Inglewood Ave · 800-786-1000
- **Piggies** · 4601 W Rosecrans Ave · 310-679-6326

Video Rental

- **Blockbuster** · 3909 W Rosecrans Ave · 310-644-1970
- **Cali Games** · 14401 Hawthorne Blvd · 310-978-0880
- **Hollywood Video** · 11344 Crenshaw Blvd · 323-756-1750
- **Hollywood Video** · 12750 Hawthorne Blvd · 310-679-5797
- **L&B Video** · 14408 Hawthorne Blvd · 310-644-6844
- **Movie Time** · 13731 Inglewood Ave · 310-973-0750
- **Video Town** · 12404 Inglewood Ave · 310-675-5747
- **Videomax** · 11911 Hawthorne Blvd · 310-644-7345

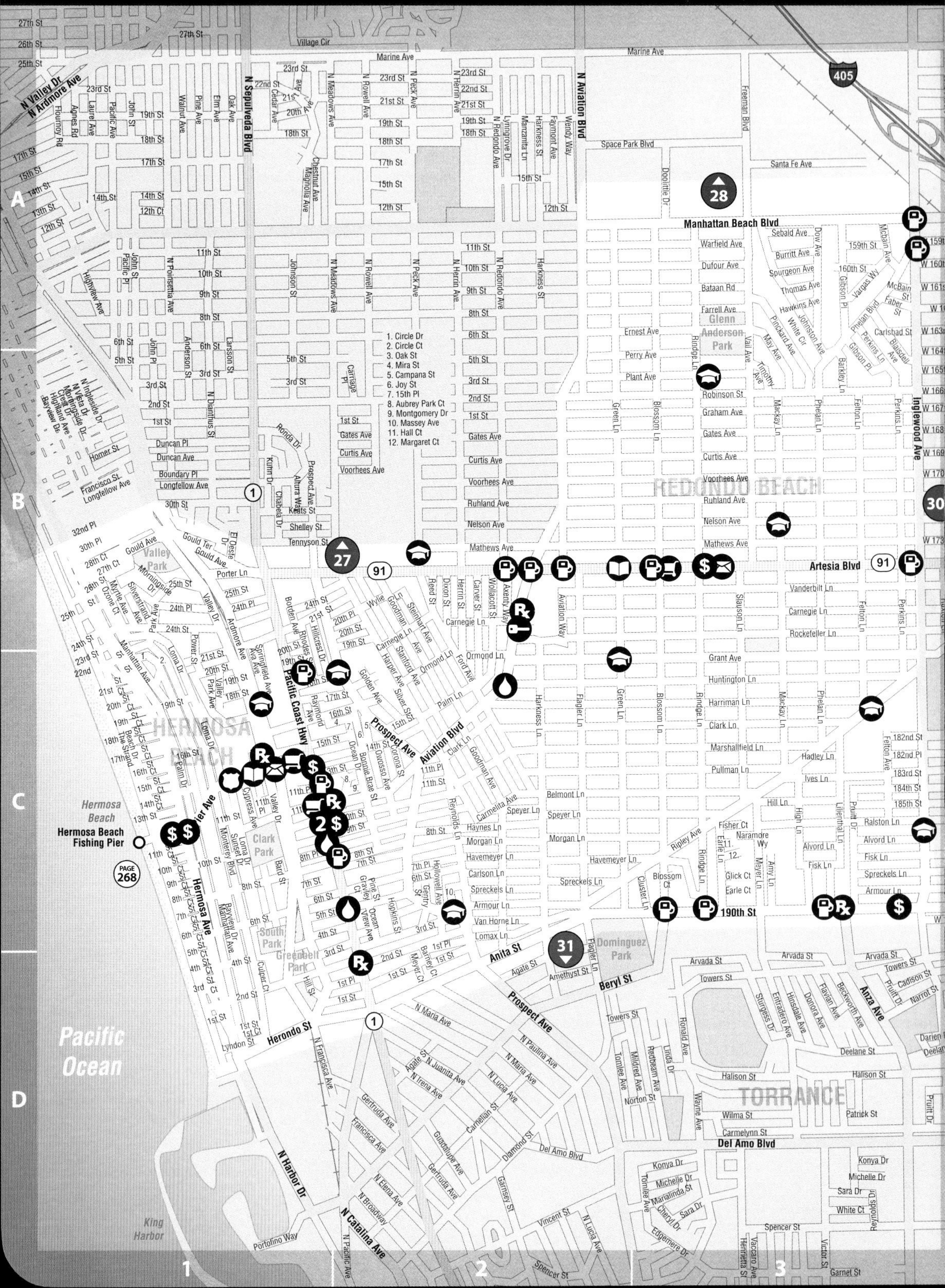

Map 29 · Hermosa Beach / Redondo Beach North

1. Circle Dr
2. Circle Ct
3. Oak St
4. Mira St
5. Campana St
6. Joy St
7. 15th Pl
8. Aubrey Park Ct
9. Montgomery Dr
10. Massey Ave
11. Hall St
12. Margaret Ct

Pacific Ocean

HERMOSA BEACH

REDONDO BEACH

TORRANCE

Hermosa Beach

Hermosa Beach Fishing Pier

King Harbor

PAGE 268

Part quaint beach town, part post-college town, Hermosa Beach is an unusual combination of homey and hoppin'. You'll know you're there when you begin to notice the street signs, which are brown with an almost antique typeface. Hermosa is anything but outdated, however. Whether you want to stroll through an art gallery with a latte, blade on the Strand, or catch the sunset during happy hour, you'll find somewhere to do it near the cross streets of Pier and Hermosa Avenues.

Banks

- **Bank of America** · 90 Pier Ave
- **Citibank** · 81 Pier Ave
- **First Federal** · 1100 Pacific Coast Hwy
- **First Federal** · 2233 Artesia Blvd
- **Wells Fargo** · 1501 Pacific Coast Hwy

Car Rental

- **Hertz** · 1740-B Aviation Blvd

Car Washes

- **Auto Spa Self Service Car Wash** ·
  620 Pacific Coast Hwy
- **Aviation Auto Spa** · 1616 Aviation Blvd
- **Hermosa Beach Car Wash** · 1000 Pacific Coast Hwy

Gas Stations

- **76** · 3601 Inglewood
- **76** · 5404 W 190th St
- **Arco** · 1131 Pacific Coast Hwy
- **Arco** · 15922 Inglewood Ave
- **Arco** · 1800 W Artesia Blvd
- **Arco** · 1890 Pacific Coast Hwy
- **Chevron** · 2118 Artesia Blvd
- **Mobil** · 2714 Artesia Blvd
- **Mobil** · 931 Pacific Coast Hwy
- **Shell** · 1700 Artesia Blvd

Landmarks

- **Hermosa Beach Fishing Pier** · end of Pier Ave

Libraries

- **Hermosa Beach Public Library** · 550 Pier Ave ·
  310-379-8475
- **Redondo Beach North Branch** · 2000 Artesia Blvd ·
  310-318-0677

Pharmacies

- **Ralphs** · 1100 Pacific Coast Hwy · 310-374-2435
- **Rite-Aid** · 1720 Aviation Blvd · 310-376-4460
- **Sav-On** · 155 Pacific Coast Hwy · 310-372-4345
- **Sav-On** · 711 Pier Ave · 310-372-9975
- **Sav-On (24 hrs)** · 5020 W 190th St · 310-370-5607

Police

- **Hermosa Beach Police Dept** · 540 Pier Ave ·
  310-318-0360

Post Offices

- **US Post Office** · 2215 Artesia Blvd
- **US Post Office** · 565 Pier Ave

Schools

- **Adams Middle** · 2600 Ripley Ave
- **Birney Elementary** · 1600 Green Ln
- **Coast Christian** · 850 Inglewood Ave
- **Hermosa Valley Elementary** · 1645 Valley Dr
- **Hermosa View Elementary** · 1800 Prospect Ave
- **Jefferson Elementary** · 600 Harkness Ln
- **Lincoln Elementary** · 2223 Plant Ave
- **Madison Elementary** · 2200 Mackay Ln
- **Our Lady of Guadalupe** · 340 Massey Ave
- **St Lawerence Martyr Elementary** ·
  1950 S Prospect Ave
- **Washington Elementary** · 1100 Lilienthal Ln

Supermarkets

- **Albertsons** · 2115 Artesia Blvd
- **Albertsons** · 2510 Pacific Coast Hwy
- **Ralphs** · 1100 Pacific Coast Hwy
- **Vons** · 715 Pier Ave

Map 29 • Hermosa Beach / Redondo Beach North

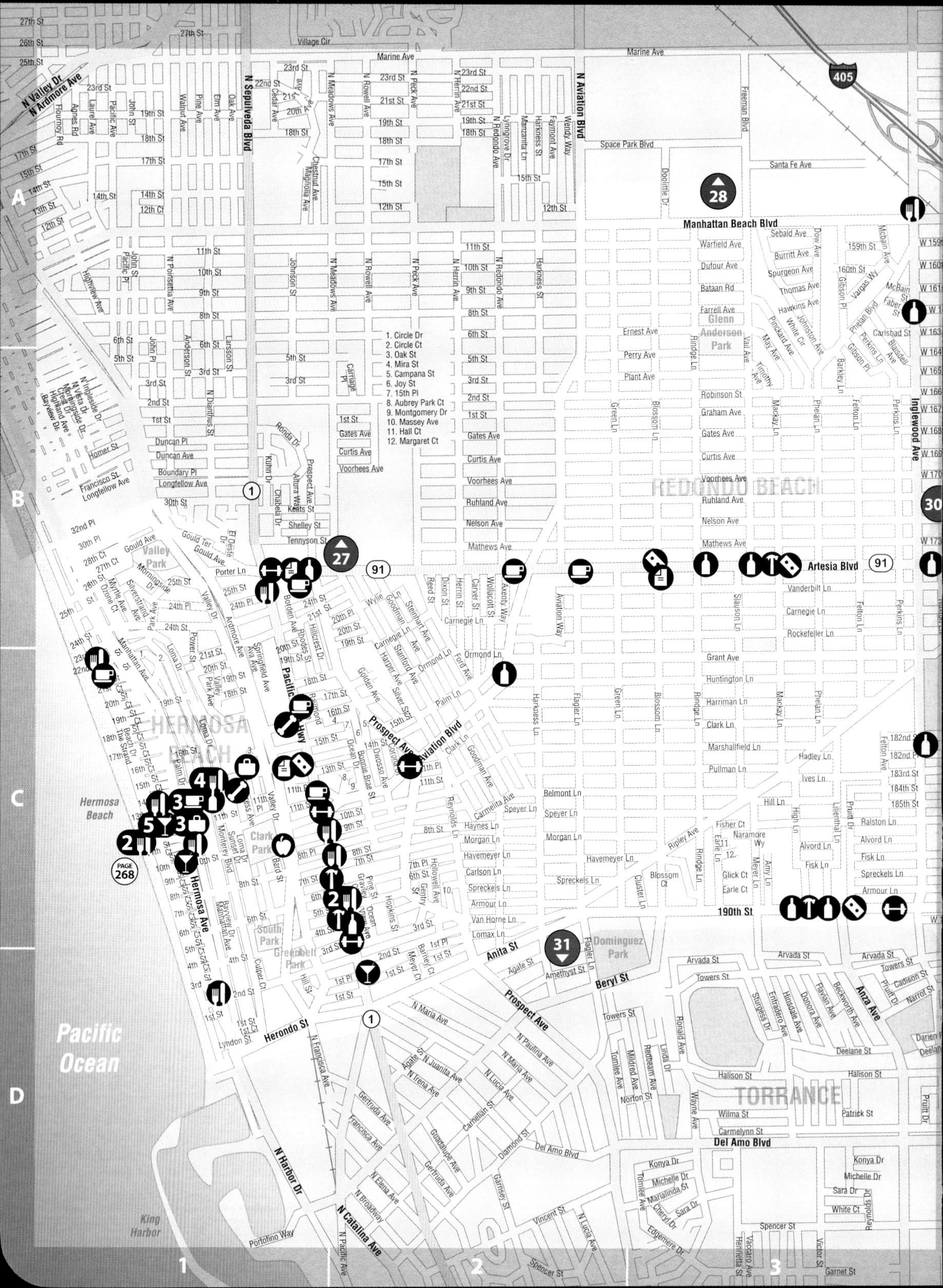

N

Pacific Ocean

HERMOSA BEACH

Hermosa Beach

REDONDO BEACH

TORRANCE

King Harbor

Valley Park

Clark Park

South Park

Greenbelt Park

Glenn Anderson Park

Dominguez Park

1. Circle Dr
2. Circle Ct
3. Oak St
4. Mira St
5. Campana St
6. Joy St
7. 15th Pl
8. Aubrey Park Ct
9. Montgomery Dr
10. Massey Ave
11. Hall St
12. Margaret Ct

405

28

27

30

31

91

91

1

PAGE 268

Street labels (selection):
27th St, 26th St, 25th St, 23rd St, 19th St, 17th St, 15th St, 14th St, 12th Ct, 11th St, 10th St, 9th St, 8th St, 6th St, 5th St, 3rd St, 2nd St, 1st St

N Valley Dr, N Ardmore Ave, N Sepulveda Blvd, Pacific Ave, Walnut Ave, Elm Ave, Oak Ave, Cedar Ave, Magnolia Ave, Chestnut Ave, N Meadows Ave, N Rowell Ave, N Peck Ave, N Herrin Ave, N Redondo Ave, Manzanita St, Harkness St, Fairmont Ave, Wendy Way, N Aviation Blvd, Freeman Ave

Village Cir, Marine Ave, Manhattan Beach Blvd, Space Park Blvd, Santa Fe Ave, Doolittle Dr

Warfield Ave, Dufour Ave, Bataan Rd, Farrell Ave, Ernest Ave, Perry Ave, Plant Ave, Robinson Ave, Graham Ave, Gates Ave, Curtis Ave, Voorhees Ave, Ruhland Ave, Nelson Ave, Mathews Ave, Artesia Blvd, Carnegie Ln, Rockefeller Ln, Grant Ave, Huntington Ln, Harriman Ln, Clark Ln, Marshallfield Ln, Pullman Ln, Belmont Ln, Speyer Ln, Morgan Ln, Havemeyer Ln, Carlson Ln, Spreckels Ln, Armour Ln, Van Horne Ln, Lomax Ln, 190th St

Sebald Ave, Burritt Ave, Spurgeon Ave, Thomas Ave, Hawkins Ave, 159th St, 160th St, W 159th, W 160th, W 161st, W 162nd, Carlsbad St, W 163rd, W 164th, W 165th, W 166th, W 167th, W 168th, W 169th, W 170th, W 173rd, Vanderbilt Ln, Inglewood Ave, Slauson Ln, Rindge Ln, Green Ln, Blossom Ln, Flagler Ln, Phelan Ln, Mackay Ln, Hadley Ln, Ives Ln, 182nd St, 183rd St, 184th St, 185th St, Hill Ln, Fisher Ct, Naramore Wy, Alvord Ln, Fisk Ln, Spreckels Ln, Armour Ln

Anza Ave, Amethyst St, Beryl St, Agate St, Anita St, Prospect Ave, Herondo St, Towers St, Arvada St, Arvada St, Del Amo Blvd, Halison St, Wilma St, Patrick St, Carmelynn St

Konya Dr, Michelle Dr, Sara Dr, White Ct, Spencer St, Garnet St

N Harbor Dr, N Catalina Ave, Portofino Way, N Pacific Ave, N Francisca Ave, N Maria Ave, N Lucia Ave, N Elena Ave, N Broadway, Gertruda Ave, Guadalupe Ave, Carnetian Ave, Diamond Ave, Emerald St, Garnet St

No matter what your scene, Pier Avenue is the place to go for a night out. Young and loud Aloha Sharkeez is a Hermosa staple, but for a more laid-back vibe and a shorter line, try Fat Face Fenner's across the way.

 Coffee

- **Coffee Bean & Tea Leaf** • 1133 Artesia Blvd
- **Coffee Bean & Tea Leaf** • 1227 Hermosa Ave
- **Coffee Bean & Tea Leaf** • 1617 Pacific Coast Hwy
- **Fox Hollow Café** • 1700 Artesia Blvd
- **Java Man** • 157 Pier Ave
- **Starbucks** • 1100 Pacific Coast Hwy
- **Starbucks** • 1303 Hermosa Ave
- **Starbucks** • 1904 Artesia Blvd
- **Starbucks** • 5050 190th St

Copy Centers

- **Kinko's** • 1139 Artesia Blvd • 310-379-7433
- **UPS Store** • 2110 Artesia Blvd • 310-318-3000
- **UPS Store** • 703 Pier Ave • 310-374-4420

Farmer's Markets

- **Farmer's Market** • Valley Dr b/w 10th St & 8th St

Gyms

- **24-Hour Fitness** • 1100 Pacific Coast Hwy • 310-374-4524
- **Bally Total Fitness** • 1133 Artesia Blvd • 310-372-0068
- **Curves** • 1147 Aviation Blvd • 310-372-2440
- **Gorgeous! Women's Fitness Center** • 4850 190th St • 310-542-7741
- **The Gym** • 339 Pacific Coast Hwy • 310-379-7141

Hardware Stores

- **Ace** • 403 Pacific Coast Hwy • 310-372-2414
- **Anza True Value** • 2441 190th St • 310-376-0852
- **Kurt True Value** • 2404 Artesia Blvd • 310-376-3494
- **Learned Lumber** • 635 Pacific Coast Hwy • 310-374-3406

 Liquor Stores

- **Abe's Liquor** • 240 Pier Ave
- **B&K Liquor** • 16210 Inglewood Ave
- **Coast Liquor** • 400 Pacific Coast Hwy
- **M&C Liquor** • 1320 Inglewood Ave
- **Manhattan Liquors** • 1157 Artesia Blvd
- **McNamara's Liquor** • 4703 Artesia Blvd
- **Mr B's Liquor** • 2433 190th St
- **Number One Liquor** • 1520 Aviation Blvd
- **Paul's Liquor** • 2218 Artesia Blvd
- **Quick Stop** • 2301 Artesia Blvd
- **Robert's Liquor** • 74 Pier Ave
- **Three Kings Liquor** • 5126 190th St

Nightlife

- **Aloha Sharkeez** • 52 Pier Ave • 310-374-7823
- **Comedy & Magic Club** • 1018 Hermosa Ave • 310-372-1193
- **Dragon** • 22 Pier Ave • 310-372-4462
- **Fat Face Fenner's Fishack** • 53 Pier Ave, 2nd Floor • 310-379-5550
- **The Lighthouse Café** • 30 Pier Ave • 310-372-6911
- **Patrick Molloy's** • 50-A Pier Ave • 310-798-9762
- **The Pitcherhouse** • 142 Pacific Coast Hwy • 310-374-0626

Pet Stores

- **Bow Wow Boutique** • 433 Pier Ave • 310-372-7722
- **The Petcare Company-Store** • 1630 Pacific Coast Hwy • 310-372-1980

Restaurants

- **Back on the Beach** • 445 Pacific Coast Hwy • 310-393-8282
- **Blue Pacific Restaurant** • 201 Hermosa Ave • 310-406-8986
- **Buona Vita** • 439 Pier Ave • 310-379-7626
- **Créme de la Crepe** • 424 Pier Ave • 310-937-2822
- **El Burrito Jr** • 919 Pacific Coast Hwy • 310-316-5058
- **Fritto Misto** • 316 Pier Ave • 310-318-6098
- **Havana Mania** • 3615 Inglewood Ave • 310-725-9075
- **Hennessey's Tavern** • 8 Pier Ave • 310-372-5759
- **Il Boccaccio** • 39 Pier Ave • 310-376-0211
- **Le Beaujolais** • 522 Pacific Coast Hwy • 310-543-5100
- **Martha's 22nd Street Grill** • 25 22nd St • 301-376-7786
- **Mediterraneo** • 73 Pier Ave • 310-318-2666
- **Paisano's** • 1132 Hermosa Ave • 310-376-9883
- **Ragin' Cajun Café** • 422 Pier Ave • 310-376-7878

Shopping

- **Re:Style** • 138 Pier Ave • 310-379-1706
- **Splash Bath & Body** • 132 Pier Ave • 310-376-7270
- **Star's Antique Market** • 526 Pier Ave • 310-318-2800
- **Yak & Yeti** • 116 Pier Ave • 310-406-2890

Video Rental

- **Blockbuster** • 5050 190th St • 310-793-9802
- **Blockbuster** • 709 Pier Ave • 310-379-1834
- **Disc Is It** • 2301 Artesia Blvd • 310-921-9993
- **Hollywood Video** • 2101 Artesia Blvd • 310-921-3102

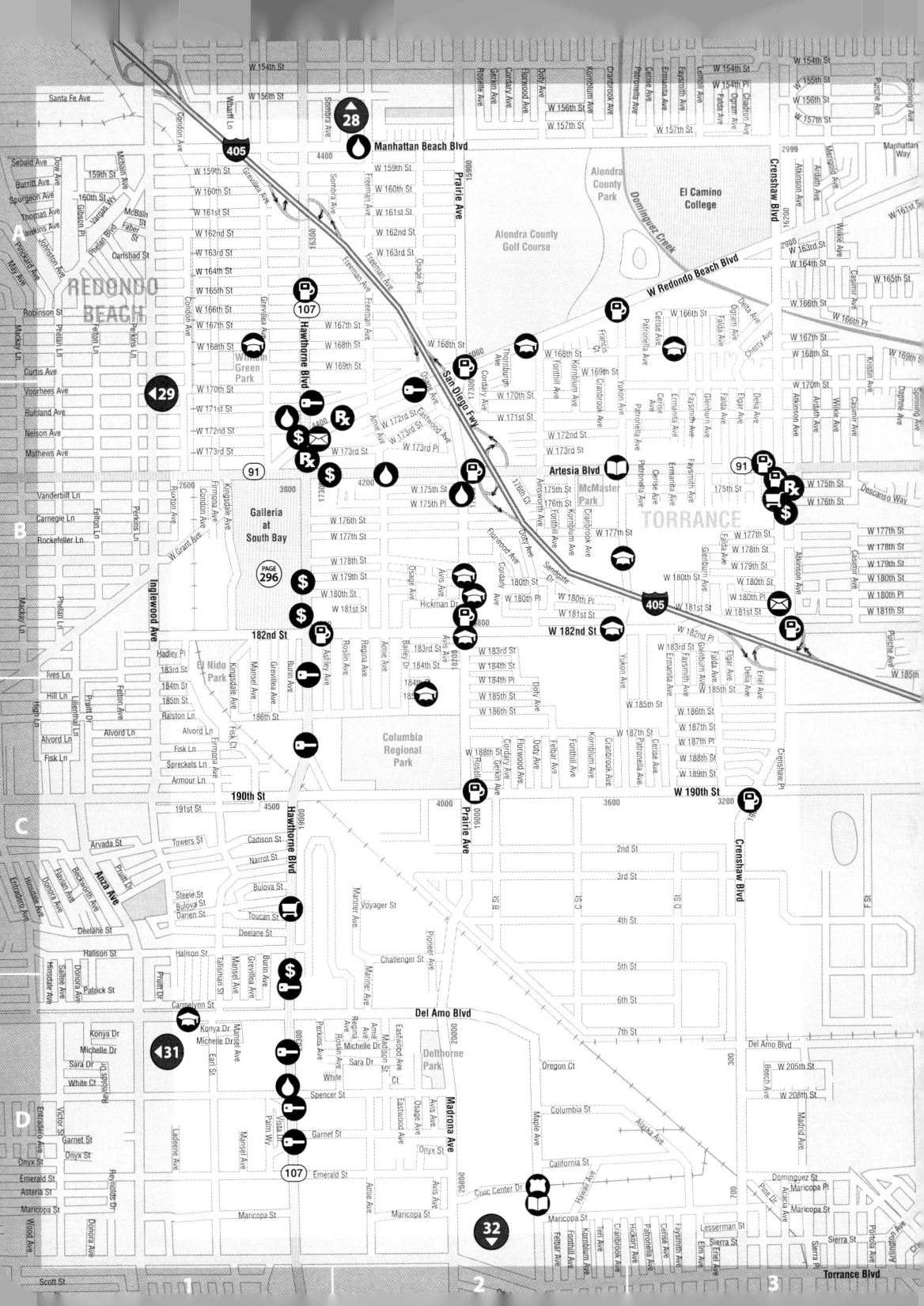

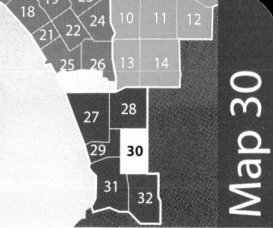
This is primarily a suburban area characterized by tract homes and large chain stores. The main social hub of this area is the South Bay Galleria, which is decidedly more upscale than neighboring Del Amo Mall. The local community college, El Camino, is also worth a gander for recent North High grads or those wishing to rejoin the educational world.

$ Banks

- **Bank of America** · 1603 Hawthorne Blvd
- **Bank of America** · 17512 Crenshaw Blvd
- **First Bank & Trust** · 20016 Hawthorne Blvd
- **Union** · 1413 Hawthorne Blvd
- **Washington Mutual** · 17200 Hawthorne Blvd
- **Washington Mutual** · 4840 190th St
- **Wells Fargo** · 4340 Artesia Blvd

Car Rental

- **Budget** · 20522 Hawthorne Blvd
- **Dollar** · 20125 Hawthorne Blvd
- **Enterprise** · 18800 Hawthorne Blvd
- **Enterprise** · 20340 Hawthorne Blvd
- **Enterprise** · 20625 Hawthorne Blvd
- **Hertz** · 18409 Hawthorne Blvd
- **Rent 4 Less** · 4111 W Redondo Beach Blvd

Car Washes

- **AAA Galleria Hand Car Wash** · 4641 Artesia Blvd
- **Artesian Car Wash** · 17500 Prairie Ave
- **Bay Cities Carwash** · 4457 Manhattan Beach Blvd
- **Del Amo Car Wash** · 20505 Hawthorne Blvd
- **Lawndale Car Wash** · 17111 Hawthorne Blvd

Gas Stations

- **76** · 3975 W 190th St
- **76** · 4373 W 182nd St
- **Arco** · 16518 Hawthorne Blvd
- **Arco** · 18180 Prairie Ave
- **Arco** · 3015 W 182nd St
- **Chevron** · 17405 Crenshaw Blvd
- **Chevron** · 3962 Artesia Blvd
- **Independent** · 4000 Redondo Beach Blvd
- **Mobil** · 16926 Hawthorne Blvd
- **Mobil** · 19009 Crenshaw Blvd
- **Shell** · 3101 Artesia Blvd

Libraries

- **LA County Law Library** · 825 Maple Ave · 310-222-8816
- **North Torrance Branch** · 3604 Artesia Blvd · 310-323-7200

Pharmacies

- **Ralphs** · 1413 Hawthorne Blvd · 310-370-8784
- **Ralphs** · 17500 Crenshaw Blvd · 310-327-0675
- **Sav-On** · 4320 Redondo Beach Blvd · 310-542-7327

Police

- **Torrance Police Dept** · 3300 Civic Center Dr · 310-328-3456

Post Offices

- **US Post Office** · 18080 Crenshaw Blvd
- **US Post Office** · 1815 Hawthorne Blvd

Schools

- **ABC Playhouse** · 18213 Prairie St
- **Ascension Luthern Elementary** · 17910 S Prairie Ave
- **Crenshaw Children's Center** · 18909 Crenshaw Blvd
- **Edison Elementary** · 3800 W 182nd St
- **El Camino College** · 16007 Crenshaw Blvd
- **Evelyn Carr Elementary** · 3404 W 168th St
- **North High** · 3620 W 182nd St
- **Philip Magruder Middle** · 4100 W 185th St
- **School of Life** · 18090 Prairie Ave
- **South Bay Junior Academy** · 4400 Del Amo Blvd
- **St Catherine's Laboure** · 3846 Redondo Beach Blvd
- **William Green Elementary** · 4520 W 168th St
- **Yukon Elementary** · 17815 Yukon Ave

Supermarkets

- **Ralphs** · 1413 Hawthorne Blvd
- **Ralphs** · 17500 Crenshaw Blvd
- **Trader Joe's** · 19720 Hawthorne Blvd

Map 30 · Torrance North

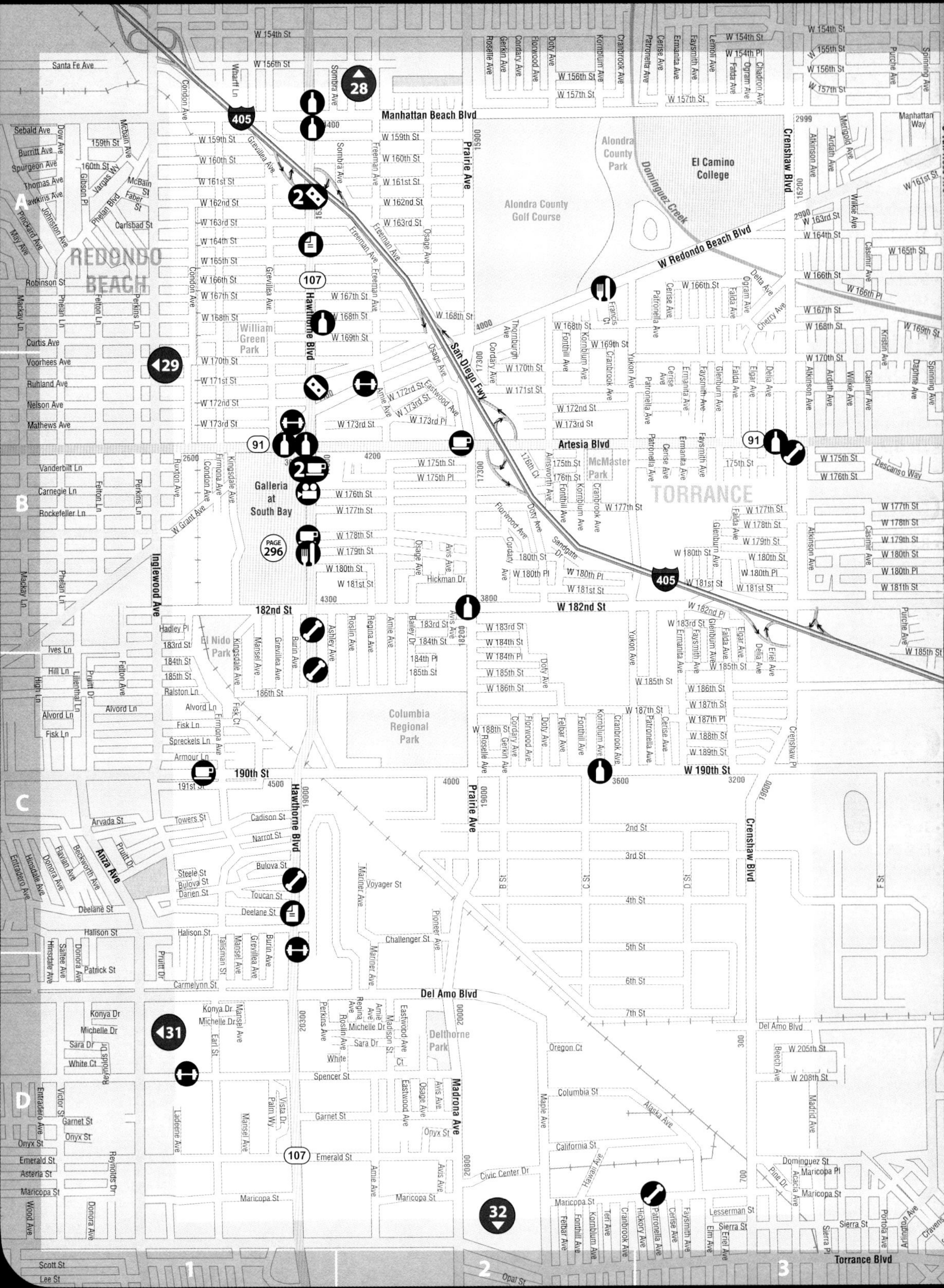

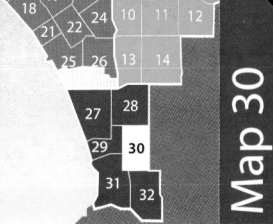
The South Bay Galleria couldn't be more opposite from its neighbor down the road, Del Amo. While Del Amo is the larger mall, it's big and gloomy and unremarkable. The Galleria, because of its glass roof, feels airier and brighter, and the variety of vendors makes for an infinitely more pleasurable shopping experience. Columbia Regional Park, just around the corner, hosts youth and soccer tournaments throughout the year.

Coffee

- **Boba Loca** · 1815 Hawthorne Blvd
- **Starbucks** · 1450 190th St
- **Starbucks** · 17400 Hawthorne Blvd
- **Starbucks** · 1815 Hawthorne Blvd
- **Starbucks** · 3931 W Artesia Blvd

Copy Centers

- **Copier Fax Land** · 16402 Hawthorne Blvd · 310-214-4636
- **Office Depot** · 19800 Hawthorne Blvd · 310-214-9179
- **Sir Speedy** · 21213 Hawthorne Blvd · 310-543-5114

Gyms

- **Bally Total Fitness** · 20040 Hawthorne Blvd · 310-542-3511
- **Curves** · 4230 Redondo Beach Blvd · 310-371-1122
- **Ladies Workout Express** · 4447 Redondo Beach Blvd · 310-921-6332
- **West End Racquet & Health Club** · 4343 Spencer St · 310-542-7373

Liquor Stores

- **ABC Liquors** · 3709 W 190th St
- **J's Liquor** · 3133 Artesia Blvd
- **Jug's Liquor Mart** · 15814 Hawthorne Blvd
- **M&M Liquor** · 4015 W 182nd St
- **Mr J's Liquor** · 15734 Hawthorne Blvd

Movie Theaters

- **AMC Galleria - South Bay Cinema 16** · 1815 Hawthorne Blvd · 310-793-7477
- **Redondo Beach Cinema 3** · 1509 Hawthorne Blvd · 310-370-8588

Pet Stores

- **Centinela Feed & Pet Supplies** · 22840 Hawthorne Blvd · 310-373-4437
- **Centinela Feed & Pet Supplies (Mega Store)** · 2727 Maricopa St · 310-212-1030
- **Pet City** · 18305 Hawthorne Blvd · 310-542-6442
- **Pets Plus** · 17440 Crenshaw Blvd · 310-719-7088

Restaurants

- **Flossie's Restaurant** · 3566 W Redondo Beach Blvd · 310-352-4037

Video Rental

- **Blockbuster** · 17124 Hawthorne Blvd · 310-371-5498
- **Red Hot Video** · 16129 Hawthorne Blvd · 310-214-0856
- **Video Entertainment Center** · 16216 Hawthorne Blvd · 310-371-6306

Map 31 • Redondo Beach

Pacific Ocean

REDONDO BEACH

King Harbor

Portofino Marina

Redondo Beach Marina

PAGE 277

Redondo Beach Pier

Redondo County Beach

PAGE 270

Malaga Cove

TORRANCE

HOLLYWOOD RIVIERA

Palos Verdes Golf Club

Del Amo Fashion Center

PAGE 295

Paradise Park

El Retiro Park

Alta Vista Park

Dominguez Park

Entradero Park

Walteria Park

1. Francisca Ave
2. Helberta Ave
3. Harkness Ln
4. Deelane St
5. Cadison St
6. Flavian Ave
7. Bartlett Dr
8. Halison Pl
9. Jeffrey Dr
10. Felker Dr
11. Maricopa St
12. Colony Ct
13. Talisman St
14. Evalyn Ave
15. Cathann Pl
16. Elmo Ave
17. Tiffany Ct
18. Audrey Ave
19. 228th Pl
20. 229th St
21. 230th St
22. Blak Ct
23. Paul Ave
24. Bernice Ave
25. Dewey Ave
26. Charlotte St
27. Lupine Dr
28. Rockview Dr
29. Crosshill Ave
30. Massena Ave
31. Albert Ave
32. Glenn Pl
33. Barbara St
34. Scannel Ave
35. Sierra Vista Dr
36. Vista Del Mar
37. Via El Prado
38. S Camino De La Costa
39. S Elena Ave
40. Via Estrellita
41. Via Bonita
42. Via Del Puente
43. Paseo De Los Reyes
44. Avd De Jose
45. Calle De Castellana
46. Via Los Miradores
47. Via Los Miradores
48. Paseo De Las Estrellas
49. Calle cabrillo
50. El Chico
51. Via Los Miradores
52. Greenmeadows St
53. Highgrove St
54. Via Las Vegas
55. Via Ardilla
56. Via Adarme
57. Vista Del Vegas
58. Harrlee Ln
59. Nancylee Ln
60. Theo Ave
61. Mayor Dr
62. Meadow Park Ln
63. Los Codona Ave
64. Walnut St
65. Cl De Primera

It's hard to beat living, working, or playing by the beach. A solid school district, many parks, and areas such as the Redondo Beach Pier/King Harbor (a typical beach boardwalk experience) and the Hollywood Riviera, with its cool boutiques and hip restaurants, ensure that there is something for everyone.

$ Banks

- **Bank of America** · 1601 S Pacific Coast Hwy
- **Bank of America** · 21700 Hawthorne Blvd
- **Bank of America** · 22 Malaga Cove Plz
- **Bank of America** · 222 N Catalina Ave
- **Bank of America** · 4206 Pacific Coast Hwy
- **Bank of the West** · 23865 Hawthorne Blvd
- **Bay Cities National** ·
  1333 S Pacific Coast Hwy
- **Bay Cities National** · 23550 Hawthorne Blvd
- **Bay Cities National** · 811 N Catalina Ave
- **California Bank & Trust** ·
  21515 Hawthorne Blvd
- **California Credit Union** ·
  22733 Hawthorne Blvd
- **California National** · 24020 Hawthorne Blvd
- **Cathay** · 23226 Hawthorne Blvd
- **Chinatrust** · 22939 Hawthorne Blvd
- **Comerica** · 21535 Hawthorne Blvd
- **Downey Savings & Loan** · 4350 W Pacific
  Coast Hwy
- **East West** · 23670 Hawthorne Blvd
- **Farmers & Merchants** · 22400 Hawthorne Blvd
- **Fremont Investment & Loan** ·
  21842 Hawthorne Blvd
- **Hanmi** · 21838 Hawthorne Blvd
- **Malaga** · 2514 Via Tejon
- **Union** · 1401 Pacific Coast Hwy
- **Union** · 21201 Hawthorne Blvd
- **Union** · 24030 Hawthorne Blvd
- **United Commercial** · 23211 Hawthorne Blvd
- **US** · 1217 N Catalina Ave
- **Washington Mutual** · 1600 S Pacific Coast Hwy
- **Washington Mutual** · 21660 Hawthorne Blvd
- **Wells Fargo** · 1701 S Elena Ave
- **Wells Fargo** · 21323 Hawthorne Blvd
- **Wells Fargo** · 301 S Pacific Coast Hwy
- **Western Financial** · 21705 Hawthorne Blvd

 Car Rental

- **Enterprise** · 816 N Irena
- **Sakura Rent-a-Car** · 530 N Pacific Coast Hwy
- **U-Haul** · 24091 Hawthorne Blvd

Car Washes

- **Hollywood Riviera Car Wash** ·
  1500 S Pacific Coast Hwy

Gas Stations

- **76** · 21190 Hawthorne Blvd
- **76** · 247 S Pacific Coast Hwy
- **Arco** · 300 Torrance Blvd
- **Arco** · 3900 Sepulveda Blvd
- **Arco** · 4205 Pacific Coast Hwy
- **Chevron** · 1500 S Pacific Coast Hwy
- **Chevron** · 1630 S Elena Ave
- **Chevron** · 4135 Pacific Coast Hwy
- **Chevron** · 5230 Sepulveda Blvd
- **Mobil** · 20306 Anza Ave
- **Mobil** · 246 S Pacific Coast Hwy
- **Mobil** · 4202 Pacific Coast Hwy
- **Shell** · 1200 Beryl St
- **Shell** · 20305 Anza Ave
- **Shell** · 23140 Hawthorne Blvd
- **Shell** · 4530 Torrance Blvd
- **Thrifty** · 4925 Torrance Blvd

 Hospitals

- **Little Company of Mary** · 4101 Torrance Blvd

Libraries

- **El Retiro Branch** · 126 Vista Del Parque ·
  310-375-0922
- **Henderson Branch** · 4805 Emerald St ·
  310-371-2075
- **Malaga Cove Library** · 2400 Via Campesina
  · 310-377-9584
- **Redondo Beach Public Library** ·
  303 N Pacific Coast Hwy · 310-318-0675
- **Walteria Branch** · 3815 W 242nd St ·
  310-375-8418

Pharmacies

- **Longs Drugs** · 1880 S Pacific Coast Hwy ·
  310-316-6492
- **Ralphs** · 5035 Pacific Coast Hwy ·
  310-378-5214
- **Rite-Aid** · 3860 Sepulveda Blvd ·
  310-373-5884
- **Rite-Aid** · 401 N Pacific Coast Hwy ·
  310-372-9029
- **Sav-On** · 4235 Pacific Coast Hwy ·
  310-373-6847
- **Sav-On** · 4625 Torrance Blvd · 310-370-7919
- **Sav-On (Albertsons)** ·
  21035 Hawthorne Blvd · 310-540-6807
- **Walgreens** · 535 S Pacific Coast Hwy ·
  310-540-6122

 Police

- **Redondo Beach Police Dept Main Station** ·
  401 Diamond St · 310-379-2477

 Post Offices

- **US Post Office** · 1201 N Catalina Ave
- **US Post Office** · 2516 Via Tejon
- **US Post Office** · 4216 Pacific Coast Hwy

Schools

- **Alta Vista Elementary** · 815 Knob Hill Ave
- **Anza Elementary** · 21400 Ellenwood Dr
- **Bert M Lynn Middle** · 5038 Halison St
- **Beryl Heights** · 920 Beryl St
- **Bishop Montgomery High** ·
  5430 Torrance Blvd
- **Bishop Mora Salesian High** · 960 S Soto St
- **Calle Mayor Middle** · 4800 Calle Mayor
- **Carden Dominion** · 320 Knob Hill
- **Jefferson Middle** · 21717 Talisman St
- **Joseph Arnold Elementary** ·
  4100 W 227th St
- **Menorah Community Day** ·
  1101 Camino Real
- **Nick G Parras Middle** · 200 N Lucia
- **Redondo Shores High** · 1000 Del Amo St
- **Redondo Union High** · 631 Vincent Park
- **Richardson Middle** · 23751 Nancy Lee Ln
- **Riveria Hall Lutheran** · 330 Palos Verdes Blvd
- **Riviera Elementary** · 365 Paseo De Arena
- **Seaside Elementary** · 4651 Sharynne Ln
- **Sigma** · 23800 Hawthorne Blvd
- **South Bay High** · 4025 W 226th St
- **South High** · 4801 Pacific Coast Hwy
- **St James Elementary** · 4625 Garnet St
- **Towers Elementary** · 5600 Towers St
- **Tulita Elementary** · 1520 S Prospect Ave
- **Victor Elementary** · 4820 Spencer St
- **West High** · 20401 Victor St

Supermarkets

- **Albertsons** · 1516 S Pacific Coast Hwy
- **Albertsons** · 21035 Hawthorne Blvd
- **Albertsons** · 615 N Pacific Coast Hwy
- **Bristol Farms** · 1700 Pacific Coast Hwy
- **Pavilions** · 4705 Torrance Blvd
- **Ralphs** · 5035 Pacific Coast Hwy
- **Smart & Final** · 332 S Pacific Coast Hwy
- **Trader Joe's** · 1761 S Elena Ave
- **Vons** · 1212 Beryl St
- **Vons** · 245 Palos Verdes Blvd
- **Whole Foods Market** ·
  405 N Pacific Coast Hwy

Map 31 · **Redondo Beach**

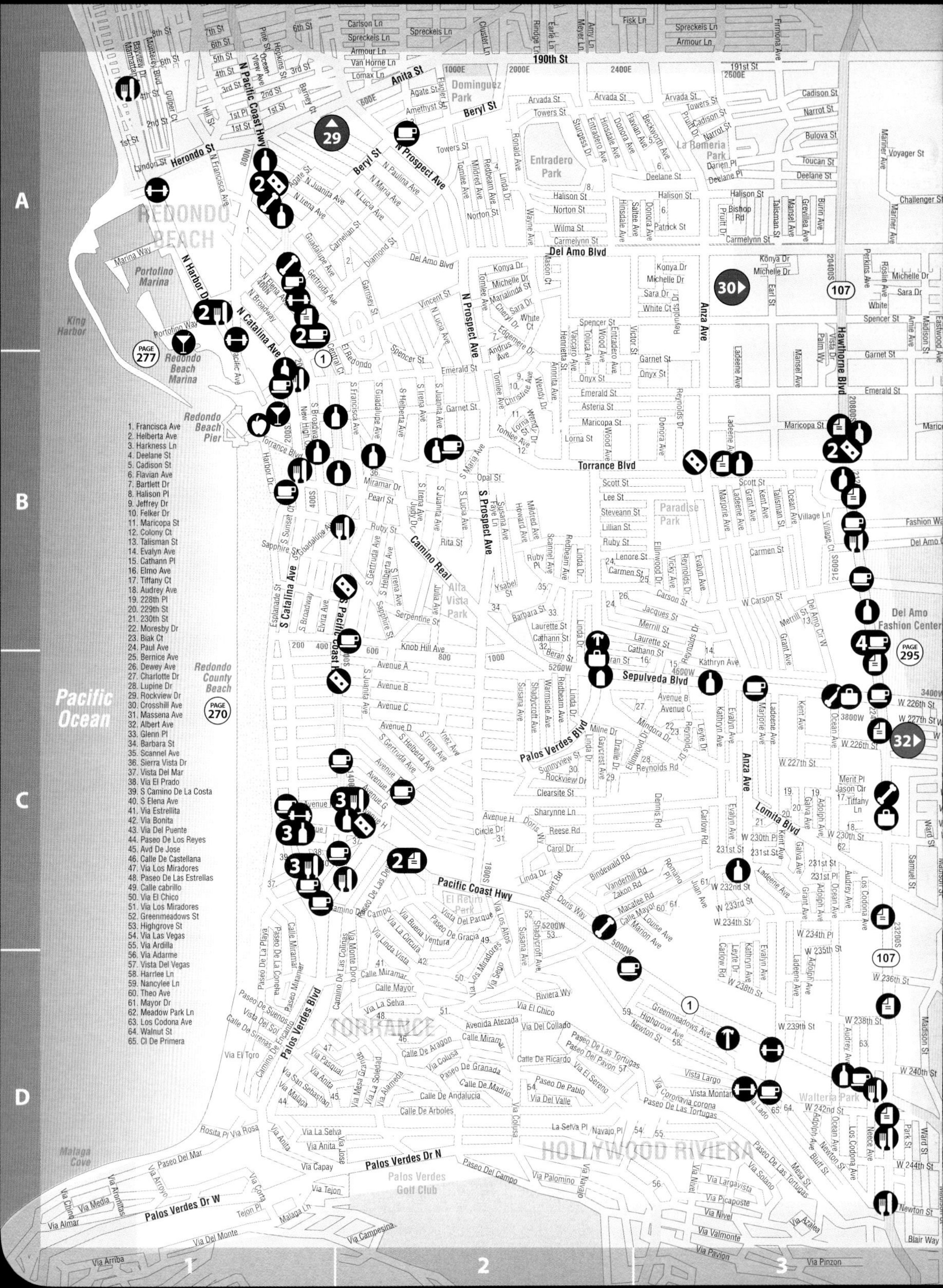

A

B

C

D

1

2

3

Pacific
Ocean

King
Harbor

Portofino Marina

REDONDO
BEACH

Marina Way

PAGE
277

Redondo
Beach
Marina

Redondo
Beach Pier

Redondo
County
Beach

PAGE
270

Malaga
Cove

1. Francisca Ave
2. Helberta Ave
3. Harkness Ln
4. Deelane St
5. Cadison St
6. Flavian Ave
7. Bartlett Dr
8. Halison Pl
9. Jeffrey Dr
10. Felker Dr
11. Maricopa Dr
12. Colony Ct
13. Talisman Dr
14. Evalyn Ave
15. Cathann Pl
16. Elmo Ave
17. Tiffany Ct
18. Audrey Ave
19. 228th Pl
20. 229th St
21. 230th St
22. Moresby Dr
23. Biak Ct
24. Paul Ave
25. Bernice Ave
26. Dewey Ave
27. Charlotte Dr
28. Lupine Ave
29. Rockview Ave
30. Crosshill Ave
31. Massena Ave
32. Albert Ave
33. Glenn Pl
34. Barbara St
35. Scannel Ave
36. Sierra Vista Dr
37. Vista Del Mar
38. Via El Prado
39. S Camino De La Costa
40. S Elena Ave
41. Via Estrellita
42. Via Bonita
43. Via Del Puente
44. Paseo De Los Reyes
45. Avd De Jose
46. Calle De Castellana
47. Via Los Miradores
48. Paseo De Las Estrellas
49. Calle cabrillo
50. Via El Chico
51. Via Los Miradores
52. Greenmeadows St
53. Highgrove St
54. Via Las Vegas
55. Via Ardilla
56. Via Adarme
57. Vista Del Vegas
58. Harrlee Ln
59. Nancylee Ln
60. Theo Ave
61. Mayor Dr
62. Meadow Park Ln
63. Los Codona Ave
64. Walnut St
65. CI De Primera

TORRANCE

HOLLYWOOD RIVIERA

Palos Verdes
Golf Club

Palos Verdes Dr N

Palos Verdes Dr W

At last count, Redondo Beach featured fourteen parks, some of which are even designed for camping. Even better, however, the city enjoys consistent "Grade A" beaches—a rarity considering the filth that has polluted the Southern California surf in recent years.

Coffee

- **Carissimo Bakery** • 1611 S Catalina Ave
- **Catalina Coffee Company** • 126 N Catalina Ave
- **Coffee Bean & Tea Leaf** • 21300 Hawthorne Blvd
- **Coffee Cartel** • 1820 S Catalina Ave
- **Collet Tea** • 320 S Catalina Ave
- **Gloria Jean's Gourmet Coffees** • 275 Del Amo Fashion Ctr
- **Green Patio Café** • 24002 Vista Montana
- **It's a Grind Coffee House** • 1218 Beryl St
- **Kelly's Coffee & Fudge** • 223 Del Amo Fashion Sq
- **La Caffita** • 420 N Pacific Coast Hwy
- **Lizzie's Cup of Joe** • 800 Torrance Blvd
- **Lucky Monkey Espresso Bar** • 1408 S Pacific Coast Hwy
- **Maggie's General Store** • 22244 Palos Verdes Blvd
- **Starbucks** • 1516 S Pacific Coast Hwy
- **Starbucks** • 1749 S Elena Ave
- **Starbucks** • 21209A Hawthorne Blvd
- **Starbucks** • 300 N Pacific Coast Hwy
- **Starbucks** • 3737 Pacific Coast Hwy
- **Starbucks** • 5005 Pacific Coast Hwy
- **Starbucks** • 6 Del Amo Fashion Center
- **Starbucks (Albertsons)** • 21035 Hawthorne Blvd
- **Via Dolce** • 407 N Pacific Coast Hwy

Copy Centers

- **Acro Printing** • 23780 Hawthorne Blvd • 310-791-2651
- **Custom Copy Central** • 22529 Hawthorne Blvd • 310-378-1616
- **Kinko's** • 1770 S Pacific Coast Hwy • 310-792-8635
- **Kinko's** • 23325 Hawthorne Blvd • 310-373-2530
- **Mail Boxes Etc** • 21143 Hawthorne Blvd • 310-540-1370
- **Postal Solutions** • 4455 Torrance Blvd • 310-316-0527
- **Pro Print** • 24205 Hawthorne Blvd • 310-378-8518
- **Staples** • 22025 Hawthorne Blvd • 310-540-3093
- **UPS Store** • 1874 S Pacific Coast Hwy • 310-792-1747
- **UPS Store** • 409 N Pacific Coast Hwy • 310-798-3013
- **UPS Store** • 800 S Pacific Coast Hwy • 310-540-6323

Farmer's Markets

- **Redondo Beach–Harbor Dr** • South of King Harbor Pier
- **Redondo Pier** • Torrance Blvd South of Redondo Pier

Gyms

- **Bally Total Fitness** • 4230 Pacific Coast Hwy • 310-375-9612
- **Curves** • 409 N Pacific Coast Hwy • 310-379-6588
- **Gold's Gym** • 200 N Harbor Dr • 310-374-5522
- **Ladies Workout Express** • 1611 S Catalina Ave • 310-540-5239
- **Sportcenter Fitness** • 819 N Harbor Dr • 310-376-9443

Hardware Stores

- **Ace** • 22217 Palos Verdes Blvd • 310-540-5355
- **Orchard Supply Hardware** • 4340 Pacific Coast Hwy • 310-375-3077

Liquor Stores

- **Beverages & More!** • 21301 Hawthorne Blvd
- **Catalina Liquor & Deli** • 144 N Catalina Ave
- **Chateau Liquor Store** • 4545 Sepulveda Blvd
- **House of Cigars & Liquor** • 400 S Pacific Coast Hwy
- **King's Liquor & Gourmet** • 4435 Torrance Blvd
- **Liquor Depot** • 801 Torrance Blvd
- **Mr S Liquor** • 3885 Pacific Coast Hwy
- **Nick's Liquor Store** • 510 N Pacific Coast Hwy
- **Okay Liquor** • 22216 Palos Verdes Blvd
- **Party House Liquor** • 1817 S Catalina Ave
- **Pierside Liquors** • 310 Torrance Blvd
- **Pony Square Liquors** • 1882 S Pacific Coast Hwy
- **Prince Liquor** • 4425 Calle Mayor
- **Red Eye Liquor Store** • 21186 Hawthorne Blvd
- **Riviera Wine Cellar** • 1708 S Catalina Ave
- **Ruby's Liquor** • 443 S Pacific Coast Hwy
- **Sea Breeze Spirits & Deli** • 715 N Pacific Coast Hwy
- **Village Spirit Liquors** • 1711 S Catalina Ave
- **VIP Liquor & Market** • 604 Torrance Blvd
- **Walteria Country Liquor** • 24212 Hawthorne Blvd
- **Wine Connoisseur** • 201 Torrance Blvd

Nightlife

- **Portofino Hotel & Yacht Club** • 260 Portofino Wy • 310-379-8481
- **Starboard Attitude** • 202 The Pier • 310-379-5144

Pet Stores

- **Animal Lovers Pet Shop** • 5141 Calle Mayor • 310-378-3052
- **Centinela Feed & Pet** • 413 N Pacific Coast Hwy • 310-318-2653
- **Petco** • 537 N Pacific Coast Hwy • 310-374-7969
- **Petsmart** • 3855 Sepulveda Blvd • 310-316-9047

Restaurants

- **The Banyan Water Garden Café** • 600 S Pacific Coast Hwy • 310-316-0316
- **Bluewater Grill** • 665 N Harbor Dr • 310-318-3474
- **The Bull Pen** • 314 Ave I • 310-375-7797
- **Captain Kidd's** • 209 N Harbor Dr • 310-372-7703
- **Catalina Coffee Company** • 126 N Catalina Ave • 310-318-2499
- **Chez Melange** • 1716 S Pacific Coast Hwy • 310-540-1222
- **Christine** • 24530 Hawthorne Blvd • 310-373-1952
- **Collet Tea** • 320 S Catalina Ave • 310-372-0348
- **El Torito Grill** • 21321 Hawthorne Blvd • 310-543-1896
- **Gine Lee's Bistro** • 211 Palos Verdes Blvd • 310-375-4462
- **Hennessey's Tavern** • 1712 S Catalina Ave • 310-540-8443
- **HT Grill** • 1710 S Catalina Ave • 310-316-6658
- **The Original Pancake House** • 1756 S Pacific Coast Hwy • 310-543-9875
- **Riviera Mexican Grill** • 1615 S Pacific Coast Hwy • 310-540-2501
- **Splash** • 300 N Harbor Dr • 310-798-5348
- **Zazou** • 1810 S Catalina Ave • 310-540-4884

Shopping

- **Cookin Stuff** • 22217 Palos Verdes Blvd • 310-371-2220
- **Cost Plus World Market** • 22929 Hawthorne Blvd • 310-378-8331
- **Lindbergh Nutrition** • 3804 Sepulveda Blvd • 310-378-9490

Video Rental

- **20-20 Video** • 705 N Pacific Coast Hwy • 310-376-2020
- **Blockbuster** • 1900 S Pacific Coast Hwy • 310-316-8957
- **Blockbuster** • 21841 Hawthorne Blvd • 310-540-6373
- **Blockbuster** • 417 N Pacific Coast Hwy • 310-798-2833
- **Hollywood Video** • 21149 Hawthorne Blvd • 310-316-9306
- **Movies N You** • 4641 Torrance Blvd • 310-370-8280
- **Premieres Video** • 725 S Pacific Coast Hwy • 310-316-9336
- **Video Out-Takes** • 1014 S Pacific Coast Hwy • 310-540-8913

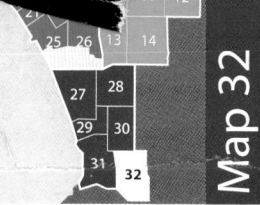
Considering its humble beginnings as a mostly bland residential area, Torrance has morphed into quite a diverse community. Torrance boasts several fine restaurants, a good farmer's market, and many cultural events throughout the year. UCLA-Harbor General Hospital, one of the state's premier teaching hospitals, serves the oft-neglected economically challenged, and Torrance Memorial ranks among California's top medical establishments.

Banks

- **Bank of America** · 25435 Crenshaw Blvd
- **California Center** ·
  2742 W Sepulveda Blvd
- **Citibank** · 2700 Pacific Coast Hwy
- **City National** · 3424 W Carson St
- **Downey Savings & Loan** ·
  1770 Carson St
- **First Federal** · 2177 Pacific Coast Hwy
- **First Federal** · 23415 Crenshaw Blvd
- **First Federal** · 3422 W Carson St
- **Nara** · 3030 Sepulveda Blvd
- **Preferred** · 3501 Sepulveda Blvd
- **Union** · 25345 Crenshaw Blvd
- **US** · 2270 Pacific Coast Hwy
- **US** · 2860 Sepulveda Blvd
- **Washington Mutual** ·
  2121 Torrance Blvd
- **Washington Mutual** ·
  2750 Pacific Coast Hwy
- **Wells Fargo** · 1403 Sartori Ave
- **Wells Fargo** · 24325 Crenshaw Blvd
- **Wells Fargo** · 24439 Crenshaw Blvd

Car Rental

- **Avis** · 2814 Sepulveda Blvd
- **Enterprise** · 21176 S Western Ave
- **Enterprise** · 2230 Pacific Coast Hwy
- **Exclusive Car Rentals** ·
  2020 Lomita Blvd # 6
- **Hertz** · 3635 Fashion Wy
- **U-Haul** · 21707 S Western Ave

Car Washes

- **Bubble Bath Hand Wash** ·
  1831 Torrance Blvd
- **Madrona Car Wash** ·
  3405 Sepulveda Blvd
- **Torrance Auto Spa** ·
  1751 Crenshaw Blvd
- **Torrance Car Wash** ·
  2476 Sepulveda Blvd

Gas Stations

- **76** · 2476 Sepulveda Blvd
- **Arco** · 1210 Crenshaw Blvd
- **Arco** · 22620 Western Ave
- **Arco** · 23510 Crenshaw Blvd
- **Arco** · 2380 Lomita Blvd
- **Chevron** · 23420 Crenshaw Blvd
- **Chevron** · 2761 Cabrillo Ave
- **Chevron** · 3405 Sepulveda Blvd
- **Exxon** · 1886 Lomita Blvd

- **Exxon** · 3401 Torrance Blvd
- **Independent** · 24650 Crenshaw Blvd
- **Independent** · 25001 Western Ave
- **Mobil** · 1640 Crenshaw Blvd
- **Mobil** · 25808 Narbonne Ave
- **Mobil** · 3006 Sepulveda Blvd
- **Mobil** · 3328 W Carson St
- **Shell** · 2477 Lomita Blvd
- **Shell** · 2504 Torrance Blvd

Hospitals

- **Torrance Memorial** · 3330 Lomita Blvd

Libraries

- **Lomita** · 24200 Narbonne Ave ·
  310-539-4515
- **Southeast Branch** ·
  23115 Arlington Ave · 310-530-5044
- **Torrance Public Library** ·
  3301 Torrance Blvd · 310-618-5959

Pharmacies

- **Longs Drugs** · 24663 Crenshaw Blvd ·
  310-784-0395
- **Ralphs** · 1770 Carson St ·
  310-787-8861
- **Rite-Aid** · 2545 Pacific Coast Hwy ·
  310-325-8420
- **Rite-Aid (24 hrs)** · 2240 W Sepulveda
  Blvd · 310-325-0868
- **Sav-On** · 3020 Sepulveda Blvd ·
  310-534-1264
- **Target** · 3433 Sepulveda Blvd ·
  310-370-1021
- **Vons** · 24325 Crenshaw Blvd ·
  310-784-1025
- **Walgreens** · 2205 Sepulveda Blvd ·
  310-320-0993
- **Walgreens** · 2690 Pacific Coast Hwy ·
  310-517-0351
- **Walgreens** · 2967 Sepulveda Blvd ·
  310-534-0063

Post Offices

- **US Post Office** · 1433 Marcelina Ave
- **US Post Office** · 2510 Monterey St
- **US Post Office** · 25131 Narbonne Ave
- **US Post Office** · 291 Del Amo Fashion Sq

Schools

- **Chabad of South Bay** ·
  24412 Narbonne Ave
- **Fern Elementary** · 1314 Fern Ave
- **First Lutheran** · 2900 W Carson St
- **Fleming Middle** · 25425 Walnut St
- **Francisco Bravo Medical Magnet
  High** · 1200 N Cornwell St
- **Harbour Church** · 1716 W 254th St
- **Hickory Elementary** · 2800 W 227th St
- **Hickory Tree** · 21720 Madrona Ave
- **Howard Wood Elementary** ·
  2250 W 235th St
- **Hull Middle** · 2080 W 231st St
- **John Adams Elementary** ·
  2121 W 238th St
- **Kurt T Shery High** · 2600 Vine St
- **Lomita Elementary** · 2211 247th St
- **Madrona Middle** · 21364 Madrona Ave
- **Nativity** · 2371 W Carson St
- **Pacific Coast Montessori** ·
  2342 Pacific Coast Hwy
- **St Margaret Mary** · 25515 Eshelman Ave
- **Switzer Center** · 1110 Satori Ave
- **Torrance Elementary** · 2125 Lincoln Ave
- **Torrance High** · 2200 Carson St
- **Walteria Elementary** ·
  24456 Madison St

Supermarkets

- **Albertsons** · 2130 Pacific Coast Hwy
- **Albertsons** · 2515 Torrance Blvd
- **Ralphs** · 1770 Carson St
- **Ralphs** · 24911 Western Ave
- **Ralphs** · 3455 Sepulveda Blvd
- **Smart & Final** · 2775 Pacific Coast Hwy
- **Trader Joe's** · 2545 Pacific Coast Hwy
- **Vons** · 24325 Crenshaw Blvd
- **Whole Foods Market** · 2655 Pacific
  Coast Hwy

Map 32 · Torrance South

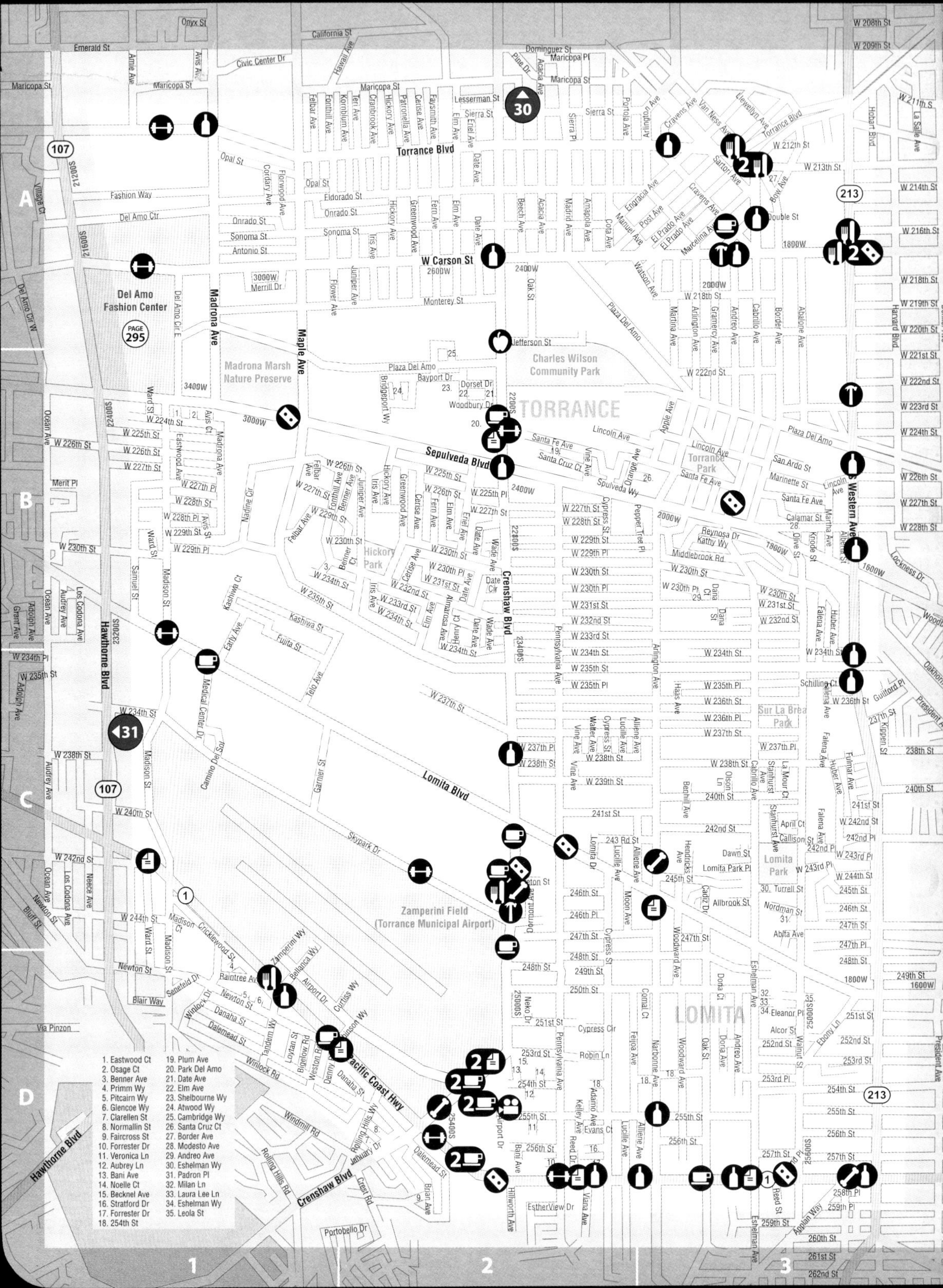

Torrance is home to an annual Oktoberfest, which is held at the Alpine Village on Torrance Boulevard every autumn. There you can enjoy Bavarian pretzels, sausage and, after some really good German beer, a chorus or two of the Chicken Dance. Enjoy!

Coffee

- **Coffee Bean & Tea Leaf** · 25345 Crenshaw Blvd
- **Hot Bagels** · 24200 Crenshaw Blvd
- **Kelly's Coffee & Fudge** · 2595 Airport Dr
- **Krispy Kreme Doughnuts** · 2795 Pacific Coast Hwy
- **Starbucks** · 2104 Pacific Coast Hwy
- **Starbucks** · 2370 Crenshaw Blvd
- **Starbucks** · 24427 Crenshaw Blvd
- **Starbucks** · 25348 Crenshaw Blvd
- **Starbucks (Albertsons)** · 2130 Pacific Coast Hwy
- **Starbucks (Vons)** · 24325 Crenshaw Blvd
- **Tormed Bistro** · 3400 Lomita Blvd
- **Torrance Bakery** · 1341 El Prado Ave

Copy Centers

- **A Blueprint Service & Supply** · 24648 Narbonne Ave · 310-325-3403
- **Copy Rite** · 1962 Pacific Coast Hwy · 310-530-7282
- **Copymax** · 3665 Pacific Coast Hwy · 310-791-0097
- **Lomita Blueprint Service** · 2359 Pacific Coast Hwy · 310-326-7491
- **Office Depot** · 24313 Crenshaw Blvd · 310-326-3291
- **Postal Annex** · 24325 Crenshaw Blvd · 310-326-3498
- **UPS Store** · 2390 Crenshaw Blvd · 310-787-9564
- **UPS Store** · 2785 Pacific Coast Hwy · 310-530-8411

Farmer's Markets

- **Wilson Park** · Crenshaw Blvd & Jefferson St

Gyms

- **24-Hour Fitness** · 2685 Pacific Coast Hwy · 310-534-5100
- **Curves** · 2366 Pacific Coast Hwy · 310-326-6777
- **Curves** · 3535 Torrance Blvd · 310-540-0083
- **LA Fitness Sports Club** · 3550 W Carson St · 310-921-9890
- **Ladies Workout Express** · 2370 Crenshaw Blvd · 310-328-9348
- **Rolling Hills Athletic Club** · 3601 Lomita Blvd · 310-791-2700
- **South End Racquet & Health Club** · 2800 Skypark Dr · 310-530-0630

Hardware Stores

- **Home Depot** · 24451 Crenshaw Blvd · 310-325-9600
- **Lovelady Hardware** · 1967 W Carson St · 310-328-4274
- **Lowe's** · 22255 S Western Ave · 310-787-1469

Liquor Stores

- **Ace Hi Liquors** · 25511 Narbonne Ave
- **Bottle Shop** · 2087 Torrance Blvd
- **Brite Spot Liquor** · 1725 Pacific Coast Hwy
- **Cory's Liquor** · 1954 W Carson St
- **El Dorado Liquor** · 23421 S Western Ave
- **Frank's Liquor** · 1601 Cabrillo Ave
- **International Liquor Store** · 2515 W Carson St
- **J&S Liquor** · 23804 Crenshaw Blvd
- **Lomita Liquor & Deli** · 2022 Pacific Coast Hwy
- **McCowan Liquor** · 22802 S Western Ave
- **Moran's Liquor** · 2354 Pacific Coast Hwy
- **Mr K's Liquor** · 3405 Torrance Blvd
- **One Stop Liquor & Market** · 22540 S Western Ave
- **Royal Liquor** · 3114 Pacific Coast Hwy
- **Town Pump Wine & Spirits** · 22505 Crenshaw Blvd

Pet Stores

- **Lomita Feed Store** · 24403 Narbonne Ave · 310-326-4738
- **Petco** · 24413 Crenshaw Blvd · 310-530-5945
- **Wild Birds Unlimited** · 25416 Crenshaw Blvd · 310-326-2473

Restaurants

- **Aioli** · 1261 Cabrillo Ave · 310-320-9200
- **Beijing Islamic** · 3160 Pacific Coast Hwy · 310-784-0846
- **Breadstix** · 1261 Cabrillo Ave · 310-320-9500
- **Depot** · 1250 Cabrillo Ave · 310-787-7501
- **In-N-Out Burger** · 24445 Crenshaw Blvd · 800-786-1000
- **Koji BBQ Buffet** · 1725 W Carson St · 310-787-1820
- **Mishima** · 21605 S Western Ave · 310-320-2089

Video Rental

- **Blockbuster** · 1929 Pacific Coast Hwy · 310-534-2933
- **Blockbuster** · 24329 Crenshaw Blvd · 310-325-0757
- **Hollywood Video** · 2549 Pacific Coast Hwy · 310-539-5508
- **K Video** · 3030 Sepulveda Blvd · 310-539-1112
- **Sakura Video (Japanese)** · 2383 Lomita Blvd · 310-325-0306
- **Tri-Video** · 1658 W Carson St · 310-212-5358
- **Video Japan Number 2 (Japanese)** · 1735 W Carson St · 310-787-1131

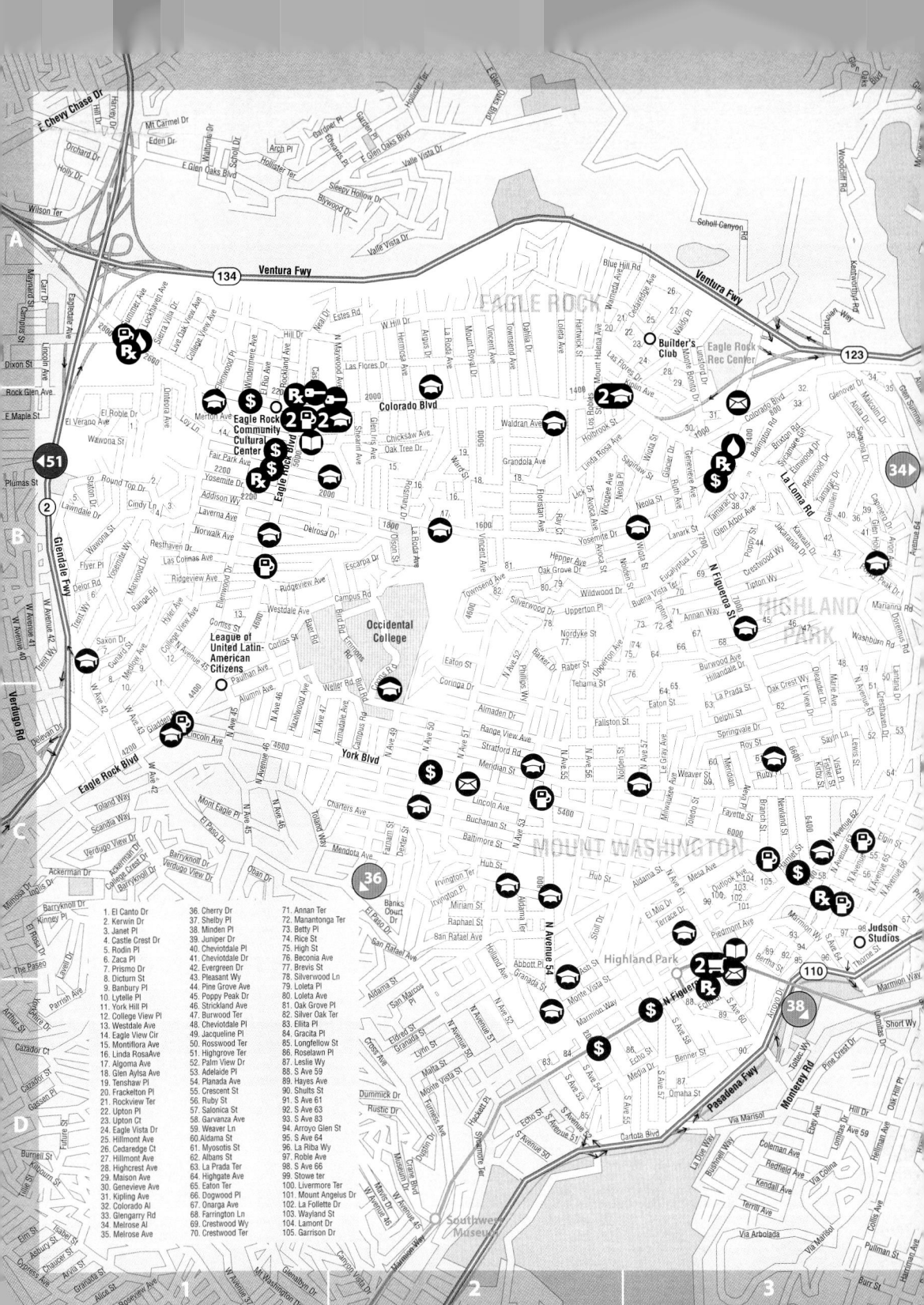

Map legend / street index:

1. El Canto Dr
2. Kerwin Dr
3. Janet Pl
4. Castle Crest Dr
5. Rodin Pl
6. Zaca Pl
7. Prismo Dr
8. Dicturn St
9. Banbury Pl
10. Lytelle Pl
11. York Hill Pl
12. College View Pl
13. Westdale Ave
14. Eagle View Cir
15. Montiflora Ave
16. Linda RosaAve
17. Algoma Ave
18. Glen Aylsa Ave
19. Tenshaw Pl
20. Frackelton Pl
21. Rockview Ter
22. Upton Pl
23. Upton Ct
24. Eagle Vista Dr
25. Hillmont Ave
26. Cedaredge Ct
27. Hillmont Ave
28. Highcrest Ave
29. Maison Ave
30. Geneveve Ave
31. Kipling Ave
32. Colorado Al
33. Glengarry Rd
34. Melrose Al
35. Melrose Ave
36. Cherry Pl
37. Shelby Pl
38. Minden Pl
39. Juniper Dr
40. Cheviotdale Pl
41. Cheviotdale Dr
42. Evergreen Dr
43. Pleasant Wy
44. Pine Grove Ave
45. Strickland Ave
46. Poppy Peak Dr
47. Burwood Ter
48. Cheviotdale Pl
49. Jacqueline Pl
50. Rosswood Ter
51. Highgrove Ter
52. Palm View Dr
53. Adelaide Pl
54. Planada Ave
55. Crescent St
56. Ruby St
57. Salonica St
58. Garvanza Ave
59. Weaver Ln
60. Aldama St
61. Myosotis St
62. Albans St
63. La Prada Ter
64. Highgate Ave
65. Eaton Ter
66. Dogwood Pl
67. Onarga Ave
68. Farrington Ln
69. Crestwood Wy
70. Crestwood Ter
71. Annan Ter
72. Manantonga Ter
73. Betty Pl
74. Rice St
75. High St
76. Beconia Ave
77. Brevis St
78. Silverwood Ln
79. Loleta Pl
80. Loleta Ave
81. Oak Grove Pl
82. Silver Oak Ter
83. Elita Pl
84. Gracita Pl
85. Longfellow St
86. Roselawn Pl
87. Leslie Wy
88. S Ave 59
89. Hayes Ave
90. Shults St
91. S Ave 61
92. S Ave 63
93. S Ave 63
94. Arroyo Glen St
95. S Ave 64
96. La Riba Wy
97. Roble Ave
98. S Ave 66
99. Stowe ter
100. Livermore Ter
101. Mount Angelus Dr
102. La Follette Dr
103. Wayland St
104. Lamont Dr
105. Garrison Dr

Map labels:
E Chevy Chase Dr
Ventura Fwy 134
Ventura Fwy
EAGLE ROCK
Builder's Club
Eagle Rock Rec Center
Colorado Blvd
Eagle Rock Community Cultural Center
Eagle Rock Blvd
Glendale Fwy
Occidental College
League of United Latin-American Citizens
HIGHLAND PARK
N Figueroa St
York Blvd
MOUNT WASHINGTON
Highland Park
Judson Studios
Pasadena Fwy
Monterey Rd
Southwest Museum
Glendale Fwy 2
51
34
36
110
38
123

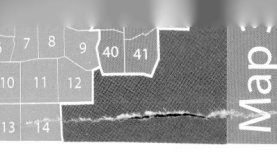

The rock really does look like an eagle, and you can best see it from the 134 heading east as you approach the Figueroa Boulevard exit. There are, in fact, two Eagle Rocks: "north of the boulevard" (Colorado Blvd, to be exact) and "south of the boulevard." The difference? The houses are pricier to the north, but the south is home to some classic local institutions—the All Star Bowling Lanes and Casa Bianca Pizza, to name just two.

 Banks

- **Bank of America** · 2263 Colorado Blvd
- **Bank of America** · 5515 N Figueroa St
- **Citibank** · 5015 Eagle Rock Blvd
- **Citibank** · 5053 York Blvd
- **Union** · 6301 N Figueroa St
- **Washington Mutual** · 4945 Eagle Rock Blvd
- **Washington Mutual** · 5700 N Figueroa St
- **Wells Fargo** · 7311 N Figueroa St

 Car Rental

- **Rent 4 Less** · 2161 Colorado Blvd
- **Rent-a-Wreck** · 2161 Colorado Blvd

 Car Washes

- **Glen-Rock Car Wash** · 2711 Colorado Blvd
- **JJ's Hand Car Wash** · 7320 N Figueroa St

Gas Stations

- **76** · 2711 Colorado Blvd
- **76** · 4755 Eagle Rock Blvd
- **Chevron** · 6405 York Blvd
- **Independent** · 405 N Ave 64
- **Mobil** · 2207 Colorado Blvd
- **Mobil** · 6174 York Blvd
- **Shell** · 2200 Colorado Blvd
- **Shell** · 5404 York Blvd

Landmarks

- **Builder's Club** · 1269 Hill Dr
- **Eagle Rock Community Cultural Center** · 2225 Colorado Blvd
- **Judson Studios** · 200 S Ave 66
- **League of United Latin-American Citizens** · 4512 Eagle Rock Blvd

 Libraries

- **Arroyo Seco Regional** · 6145 N Figueroa St · 323-255-0537
- **Eagle Rock** · 5027 Caspar Ave · 323-258-8078

Pharmacies

- **Rite-Aid** · 6305 York Blvd · 323-550-1317
- **Sav-On** · 2240 Fair Park Ave · 323-254-7346
- **Sav-On** · 5944 N Figueroa Ave · 323-478-8310
- **Target** · 2626 Colorado Blvd · 323-258-5101
- **Vons** · 7311 N Figueroa St · 323-254-7241
- **Walgreens** · 2222 Colorado Blvd · 323-254-4593

Post Offices

- **US Post Office** · 5132 York Blvd · 323-257-1356
- **US Post Office** · 5930 N Figueroa St
- **US Post Office** · 7435 N Figueroa St

Schools

- **ABC Child Development** · 5443 Ash St
- **American Montessori** · 4817 Eagle Rock Blvd
- **Annandale Elementary** · 6125 Poppy Peak Dr
- **Benjamin Franklin Senior High** · 820 N Ave 54
- **Buchanan St Elementary** · 5024 Buchanan St
- **Central High** · 1500 N Ave 53
- **Dahlia Heights Elementary** · 5063 Floristan Ave
- **Delevan Dr Elementary** · 4168 W Ave 42
- **Eagle Rock Elementary** · 2057 Fair Park Ave
- **Eagle Rock Junior-Senior High** · 1750 Yosemite Dr
- **Eagle Rock Montessori** · 1443 Colorado Blvd
- **Eagle Rock Montessori (second location)** · 1439 Colorado Blvd
- **Garvanza Elementary** · 317 N Ave 62
- **Good Shepherd Lutheran** · 6338 N Figueroa St
- **Harvest Christian Academy** · 5066 Ellenwood Dr
- **Highland Park Continuation** · 928 N Ave 53
- **Luther Burbank Middle** · 6460 N Figueroa St
- **Meridian Early Education Center** · 6124 Ruby Pl
- **Monte Vista EEC** · 5509 Ash St
- **Monte Vista St Elementary** · 5423 Monte Vista St
- **Montessori Children's World** · 4371 Eagle Rock Blvd
- **Occidental College** · 1600 Campus Rd
- **Optimist High** · 6957 N Figueroa St
- **Renaissance Arts Academy** · 1800 Colorado Blvd
- **Renaissance Arts Academy** · 2109 Merton Ave
- **Riordan PC** · 5531 Monte Vista St
- **Rockdale Elementary** · 1303 Yosemite Dr
- **St Dominic Elementary** · 2005 Merton Ave
- **St Ignatius Elementary** · 6025 Monte Vista St
- **Westminster Academy** · 1495 Colorado Blvd
- **Yorkdale Elementary** · 5657 Meridian St

Supermarkets

- **Albertsons** · 5944 N Figueroa St
- **Albertsons** · 4211 Eagle Rock Blvd
- **Smart & Final** · 6060 N Figueroa St
- **Super A Foods** · 2245 Yosemite Dr
- **Super A Foods** · 5250 York Blvd
- **Trader Joe's** · 1566 Colorado Blvd
- **Vons** · 7311 N Figueroa St

1. El Canto Dr
2. Kerwin Dr
3. Janet Pl
4. Castle Crest Dr
5. Rodin Pl
6. Zaca Pl
7. Prismo Dr
8. Dicturn St
9. Banbury Pl
10. Lytelle Pl
11. York Hill Pl
12. College View Pl
13. Westdale Ave
14. Eagle View Cir
15. Montiflora Ave
16. Linda RosaAve
17. Algoma Ave
18. Glen Aylsa Ave
19. Tenshaw Pl
20. Frackelton Pl
21. Rockview Ter
22. Upton Pl
23. Upton Ct
24. Eagle Vista Dr
25. Hillmont Ave
26. Cedaredge Ct
27. Hillmont Ave
28. Highcrest Ave
29. Maison Ave
30. Genevieve Ave
31. Kipling Ave
32. Colorado Al
33. Glengarry Rd
34. Melrose Al
35. Melrose Ave

36. Cherry Dr
37. Shelby Pl
38. Minden Pl
39. Juniper Dr
40. Cheviotdale Pl
41. Cheviotdale Dr
42. Evergreen Dr
43. Pleasant Wy
44. Pine Grove Ave
45. Poppy Peak Dr
46. Strickland Ave
47. Burwood Ter
48. Chevlotdale Pl
49. Jacqueline Pl
50. Rosswood Ter
51. Highgrove Ter
52. Adelaide Pl
53. Crescent St
54. Palm View Dr
55. Ruby St
56. Salonica St
57. Garvanza Ave
58. Aldama St
59. Weaver Ln
60.Aldama St
61. Myosotis St
62. Albans St
63. La Prada Ter
64. Highgate Ave
65. Eaton Ter
66. Dogwood Pl
67. Onarga Ave
68. Farrington Ln
69. Crestwood Wy
70. Crestwood Ter

71. Annan Ter
72. Manantonga Ter
73. Betty Pl
74. Rice St
75. High St
76. Beconia Ave
77. Brevis St
78. Silverwood Ln
79. Loleta Pl
80. Loleta Ave
81. Oak Grove Pl
82. Silver Oak Ter
83. Elitta Pl
84. Gracita Pl
85. Longfellow St
86. Roselawn Pl
87. Leslie Wy
88. S Ave 59
89. Hayes Ave
90. Shults St
91. S Ave 61
92. S Ave 63
93. S Ave 83
94. Arroyo Glen St
95. S Ave 64
96. La Riba Wy
97. Roble Ave
98. S Ave 66
99. Stowe ter
100. Livermore Ter
101. Mount Angelus St
102. La Follette Dr
103. Wayland St
104. Lamont St
105. Garrison Dr

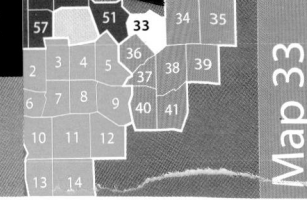
It's entirely possible that on any given day, Eagle Rock will boast the highest temperatures in Los Angeles County. Real estate folks will tell you it's the other kind of hot, too. Despite the area's popularity, and the arrival of a big Target, Colorado Boulevard has hung on to its blue-collar, greasy-spoon roots. There are new cafes cheek to jowl with those old muffler shops, and a healthy mix of ages and interests mingling together to match.

Coffee
- **Beaujolais Boulangerie** · 1661 Colorado Blvd
- **Coffee Table** · 1958 Colorado Blvd
- **Mocha Express** · 2700 Colorado Blvd
- **Oxy Café** · 4862 Eagle Rock Blvd
- **Pat and Lorraine's Coffee Shop** · 4720 Eagle Rock Blvd
- **Starbucks** · 2218 Colorado Blvd
- **Swork Coffee** · 2160 Colorado Blvd

Copy Centers
- **Super Copy** · 2256 Colorado Blvd · 323-255-5800

Farmer's Markets
- **Eagle Rock Farmer's Market** · 2100 Merton Ave

Gyms
- **Curves** · 1414 W Colorado Blvd · 626-796-1667
- **Curves** · 4870 Eagle Rock Blvd · 323-259-5800
- **Dee's New Image** · 1551 Colorado Blvd · 323-254-7071

Hardware Stores
- **Do It Best Hardware** · 5040 York Blvd · 323-254-6843
- **Eagle Rock Lumber & Hardware** · 2223 Fair Park Ave · 323-255-1451
- **Garvanza Hardware** · 6324 York Blvd · 323-256-3211
- **Tritch True Value** · 1620 Colorado Blvd · 323-255-8222

Liquor Stores
- **Amigos Liquor** · 5611 N Figueroa St
- **Bert's Liquor** · 4604 York Blvd
- **Cal's Liquor** · 5326 York Blvd
- **Eagle Rock Market** · 4729 Eagle Rock Blvd
- **Liquor Azteca de Oro** · 5049 York Blvd
- **Mario's Liquor** · 5421 York Blvd
- **One's Liquor** · 1664 Colorado Blvd
- **York Square Liquors** · 6312 York Blvd

Movie Theaters
- **Highland Theater** · 5604 N Figueroa St · 323-256-6383

Nightlife
- **All Star Lanes** · 4459 Eagle Rock Blvd · 323-254-2579
- **The Chalet** · 1630 Colorado Blvd · 323-258-8800
- **Little Cave** · 5922 N Figueroa St · 323-255-6871
- **Mr T's Bowl** · 5621 1/2 N Figueroa St · 323-256-4850

Pet Stores
- **Birdman Pet Shop** · 5926 N Figueroa St · 323-344-0696
- **KB Aquarium & Pets** · 2108 Colorado Blvd · 323-255-7372
- **Verdugo Pet Shop** · 5022 York Blvd · 323-255-2327

Restaurants
- **Auntie Em's Kitchen** · 4616 Eagle Rock Blvd · 323-255-0800
- **Blue Hen Vietnamese Kitchen** · 1743 Colorado Blvd · 323-982-9900
- **Café Beaujolais** · 1712 Colorado Blvd · 323-255-5111
- **Capri Restaurant** · 4604 Eagle Rock Blvd · 323-257-3225
- **Casa Bianca** · 1650 Colorado Blvd · 323-256-9617
- **Classic Thai Restaurant** · 1708 Colorado Blvd · 323-478-0530
- **The Coffee Table** · 1958 Colorado Blvd · 323-810-2898
- **Colombo's** · 1833 Colorado Blvd · 323-254-9138
- **Dante's BBQ Chicken & Ribs** · 2004 Colorado Blvd · 323-257-47247
- **Eagle Rock Italian Bakery & Deli** · 1726 Colorado Blvd · 323-255-8224É
- **El Arco Iris** · 5684 York Blvd · 323-254-3401
- **El Huarache Azteca** · 5225 York Blvd · 323-478-9572
- **Fatty's & Co** · 1627 Colorado Blvd · 323-254-8804
- **Original Tommy's** · 1717 Colorado Blvd · 323-982-1746
- **Pete's Blue Chip** · 1701 Colorado Blvd · 323-478-9022
- **Señor Fish** · 4803 Eagle Rock Blvd · 323-257-7167
- **Sicha Siam** · 4403 Eagle Rock Blvd · 323-344-8285
- **Villa Sombrero** · 6101 York Blvd · 323-256-9784

Shopping
- **Colorado Wine Company** · 2114 Colorado Blvd · 323-478-1985
- **Galco's Soda Pop Stop** · 5702 York Blvd · 323-255-7115
- **Mini-Melt Too** · 1613 Colorado Blvd · 323-258-2300

Video Rental
- **Best Video** · 6473 N Figueroa St · 323-257-8586
- **Blockbuster** · 2175 Colorado Blvd · 323-255-2445
- **Blockbuster** · 6312 N Figueroa St · 323-259-5980
- **Planet Video** · 5445 N Figueroa St · 323-982-9064
- **Video 808** · 1608 Colorado Blvd · 323-259-8282
- **Video Street 56** · 5544 York Blvd · 323-349-0622
- **York Video** · 5044 York Blvd · 323-256-0882

Map 34 • Pasadena

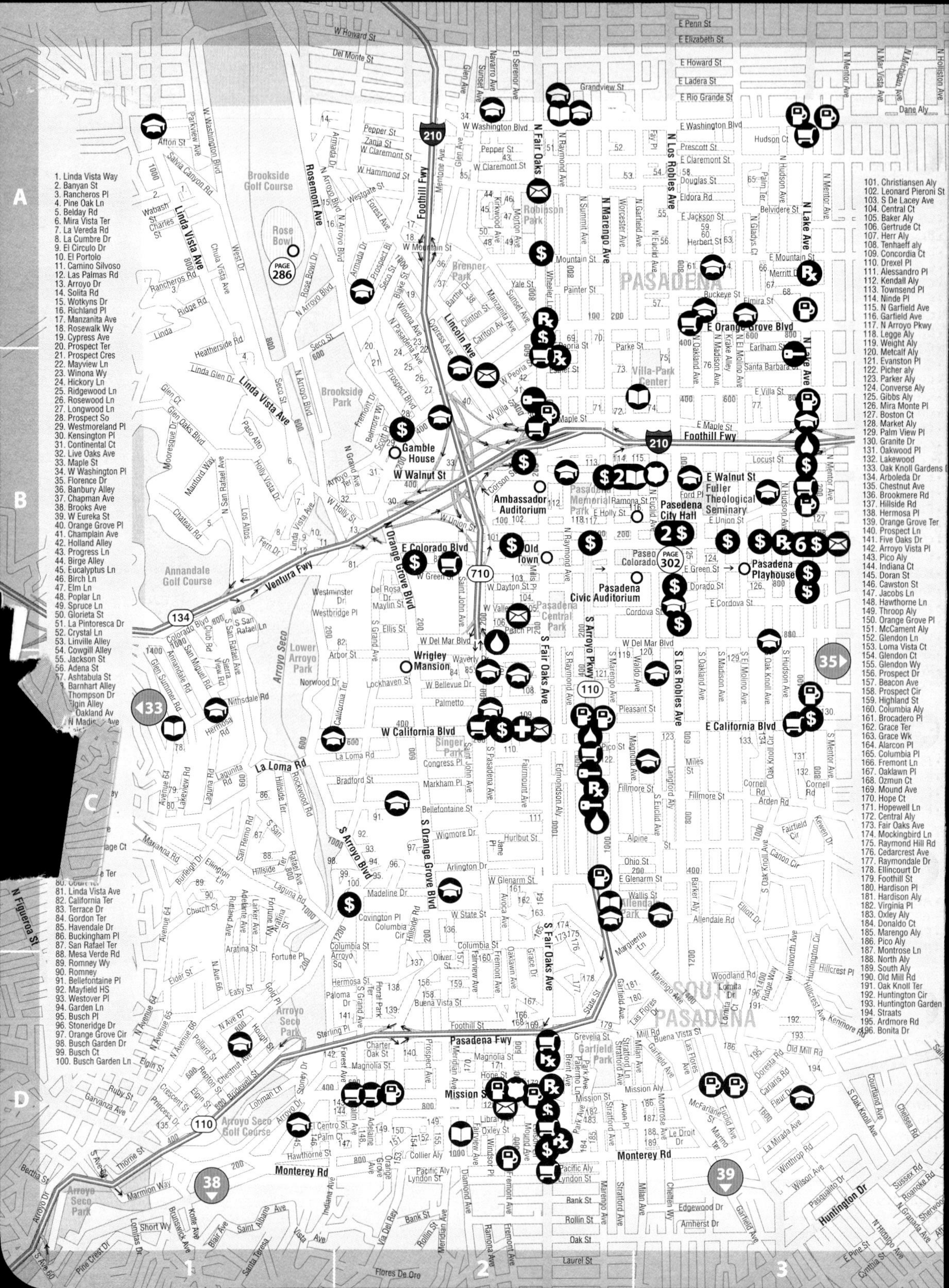

1. Linda Vista Way
2. Banyan St
3. Rancheros Pl
4. Pine Oak Ln
5. Belday Rd
6. Mira Vista Ter
7. La Vereda Rd
8. La Cumbre Dr
9. El Circulo Dr
10. El Portolo
11. Camino Silvoso
12. Las Palmas Rd
13. Arroyo Dr
14. Solita Rd
15. Wotkyns Dr
16. Richland Pl
17. Manzanita Ave
18. Rosewalk Wy
19. Cypress Ave
20. Prospect Ter
21. Prospect Cres
22. Mayview Ln
23. Winona Wy
24. Hickory Ln
25. Ridgewood Ln
26. Rosewood Ln
27. Longwood Ln
28. Prospect So
29. Westmoreland Pl
30. Kensington Pl
31. Continental Ct
32. Live Oaks Ave
33. Maple St
34. W Washington Pl
35. Florence Dr
36. Banbury Alley
37. Chapman Ave
38. Progress Ln
39. W Eureka St
40. Orange Grove Pl
41. Champlain Ave
42. Holland Alley
43. Birge Alley
44. Eucalyptus Ln
45. Birch Ln
46. Poplar Ln
47. Elm Ln
48. Spruce Ln
49. Glorieta Ct
50. La Pintoresca Dr
51. Crystal Ln
52. Linville Alley
53. Cowgill Alley
54. Jackson St
56. Adena St
57. Ashtabula St
58. Barnhart Alley
59. Thompson Dr
60. Elgin Alley
61. N Madison Ave

80. Cobbi Ct
81. Linda Vista Ave
82. California Ter
83. Terrace Dr
84. Gordon Ter
85. Havendale Dr
86. Buckingham Pl
87. San Rafael Ter
88. Mesa Verde Rd
89. Romney Wy
90. Romney
91. Bellefontaine Pl
92. Mayfield HS
93. Westover Pl
94. Garden Ln
95. Busch Pl
96. Stoneridge Dr
97. Orange Grove Cir
98. Busch Garden Cir
99. Busch Ct
100. Busch Garden Ln

101. Christiansen Aly
102. Leonard Pieroni St
103. S De Lacey Ave
104. Central Ct
105. Baker Aly
106. Gertrude Ct
107. Herr Aly
108. Concordia Ct
109. Concordia Ct
110. Drexel Pl
111. Alessandro Pl
112. Kendall Aly
113. Townsend Pl
114. Ninde Pl
115. N Garfield Ave
116. N Garfield Ave
117. N Arroyo Pkwy
118. Legge Aly
119. Weight Aly
120. Metcalf Aly
121. Evanston Pl
122. Picher Aly
123. Parker Aly
124. Converse Aly
125. Gibbs Aly
126. Mira Monte Pl
127. Boston Ct
128. Market Aly
129. Palm View Pl
130. Granite Dr
131. Oakwood Pl
132. Lakewood
133. Oak Knoll Gardens
134. Arboleda Dr
135. Chestnut Ave
136. Brookmere Rd
137. Hillside Rd
138. Hermosa Pl
139. Orange Grove Ter
140. Prospect Ln
141. Five Oaks Dr
142. Arroyo Vista Pl
143. Pico Aly
144. Indiana Ct
145. Doran St
146. Cawston St
147. Jacobs Ln
148. Hawthorne Ln
149. Throop Aly
150. Orange Grove Pl
151. McCament Aly
152. Glendon Ln
153. Loma Vista Ct
154. Glendon Ct
155. Glendon Wy
156. Prospect Dr
157. Beacon Ave
158. Prospect Cir
159. Highland Ave
160. Columbia Aly
161. Brocadero Pl
162. Grace Ter
163. Grace Wk
164. Alarcon Pl
165. Columbia Pl
166. Fremont Ln
167. Oaklawn Pl
168. Ozmun Ct
169. Mound Ave
170. Hope Ct
171. Hopewell Ln
172. Central Aly
173. Fair Oaks Ave
174. Mockingbird Ln
175. Raymond Hill Rd
176. Cedarcrest Ave
177. Raymondale Dr
178. Ellincourt Dr
179. Foothill St
180. Hardison Pl
181. Hardison Rd
182. Virginia Rd
183. Oxley Aly
184. Donaldo Ct
185. Marengo Aly
186. Pico Aly
187. Montrose Ln
188. North Aly
189. South Aly
190. Old Mill Rd
191. Oak Knoll Ter
192. Huntington Cir
193. Huntington Garden
194. Straats
195. Ardmore Rd
196. Bonita Dr

PAGE 286

PAGE 302

PASADENA

SOUTH PASADENA

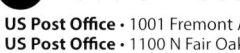

Pasadena has been blessed with a bounty of resources, both natural and human. Among other things, it has preternaturally sunny weather, leafy streets, remarkable architecture, and a large number of startlingly intelligent bipeds. You will find evidence of the latter at the Fuller Theological Seminary, Art Center, the Jet Propulsion Lab, and Vroman's Books on Colorado Boulevard. Should you find all this smarty-pants stuff oppressive, you are free to go completely, shamelessly bonkers every November at the Doo-Dah Parade.

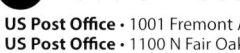
Map

$ Banks

- **Bank of America** · 145 W California Blvd
- **Bank of America** · 399 E Colorado Blvd
- **Bank of America** · 880 E Colorado Blvd
- **Bank of America** · 929 Fair Oaks Ave
- **Bank of the West** · 587 E Colorado Blvd
- **California Credit Union** · 95 S Lake Ave
- **California National** · 102 S Lake Ave
- **California National** · 1153 Fair Oaks Ave
- **Citibank** · 161 W California Blvd
- **Citibank** · 201 N Garfield Ave
- **Citibank** · 285 S Lake Ave
- **Citibank** · 315 E Colorado Blvd
- **Citizens Business** · 225 E Colorado Blvd
- **Citizens Business** · 901 Fair Oaks Ave
- **City National** · 215 N Marengo Ave
- **Comerica** · 35 N Lake Ave
- **Community** · 505 E Colorado Blvd
- **Community** · 790 E Colorado Blvd
- **East West** · 1001 Fair Oaks Ave
- **Far East National** · 301 N Lake Ave
- **Pacific Western** · 150 S Los Robles Ave
- **Union** · 70 S Lake Ave
- **United Commercial** · 199 S Los Robles Ave
- **US** · 720 E Colorado Blvd
- **Washington Mutual** · 860 E Colorado Blvd
- **Wells Fargo** · 1000 Fair Oaks Ave
- **Wells Fargo** · 350 W Colorado Blvd
- **Wells Fargo** · 46 W Colorado Blvd
- **Wells Fargo** · 600 S Lake Ave
- **Wells Fargo** · 655 N Fair Oaks Ave
- **Wells Fargo** · 82 S Lake Ave

Car Rental

- **Avis** · 570 N Lake Ave
- **Budget** · 750 S Arroyo Parkway
- **Enterprise** · 425 N Fair Oaks Ave
- **Pasadena Rent-a-Car** · 665 S Arroyo Pkwy

Car Washes

- **Arroyo-California Car Wash** ·
  605 S Arroyo Pkwy
- **Pasadena Auto Wash** · 164 W Del Mar Blvd
- **Royal Hand Wash** · 850 S Arroyo Pkwy

Gas Stations

- **76** · 122 N Lake Ave
- **76** · 155 E Glenarm St
- **76** · 675 N Lake Ave
- **76** · 911 E Washington Blvd
- **Arco** · 445 E Walnut St
- **Arco** · 736 Mission St
- **Chevron** · 1200 Fair Oaks Ave
- **Chevron** · 160 E California Blvd
- **Garo Gas** · 960 E Washington Blvd
- **Independent** · 2601 Mission St
- **Mobil** · 2507 Mission St
- **Mobil** · 290 S Arroyo Pkwy
- **Mobil** · 392 N Lake Ave
- **Mobil** · 400 N Fair Oaks Ave
- **Mobil** · 474 S Lake Ave
- **Shell** · 1400 Mission St
- **Shell** · 200 N Fair Oaks Ave
- **Shell** · 631 N Garfield Ave

Hospitals

- **Huntington Memorial** · 100 W California Blvd

Landmarks

- **Ambassador Auditorium** ·
  131 S Saint John Ave
- **Gamble House** · 4 Westmoreland Pl
- **Old Town** · Fair Oaks Ave & Colorado Blvd
- **Pasadena City Hall** · 100 N Garfield Ave
- **Pasadena Civic Auditorium** · 300 E Green St
- **Pasadena Playhouse** · 37 S El Molino Ave
- **Rose Bowl** · 991 Rosemont Ave
- **Wrigley Mansion** · 391 S Orange Grove Blvd

Libraries

- **Allendale Branch** · 1130 S Marengo Ave ·
  626-744-7260
- **LA County Law Library–Pasadena** ·
  300 E Walnut St · 626-356-5253
- **La Pintoresca Branch** · 1355 N Raymond Ave
  · 626-744-7268
- **Pasadena Central** · 285 E Walnut St ·
  626-744-4052
- **San Rafael Branch** · 1240 Nithsdale Rd ·
  626-744-7270
- **South Pasadena Library** · 1100 Oxley St ·
  626-403-7330
- **Villa Parke Community Center Branch** ·
  363 E Villa St · 626-744-6510

Rx Pharmacies

- **The Medicine Shoppe** · 711 Fair Oaks Ave ·
  626-403-0728
- **Pavilions** · 1213 Fair Oaks Ave · 626-799-4156
- **Rite-Aid** · 914 Fair Oaks Ave · 626-441-3702
- **Sav-On** · 20 E Orange Grove Blvd ·
  626-795-6609
- **Sav-On** · 727 S Arroyo Pkwy · 626-795-3810
- **Sav-On** · 900 N Lake Ave · 626-794-4418
- **Target** · 777 E Colorado Blvd · 626-795-5472
- **Vons** · 155 W California Blvd · 626-577-2594
- **Vons** · 655 N Fair Oaks Ave · 626-578-1336

Police

- **Pasadena Police Dept** · 207 N Garfield Ave ·
  626-744-4501
- **South Pasadena Police Dept** ·
  1422 Mission St · 626-403-7270

Post Offices

- **US Post Office** · 1001 Fremont Ave
- **US Post Office** · 1100 N Fair Oaks Ave
- **US Post Office** · 1355 N Mentor Ave
- **US Post Office** · 600 Lincoln Ave
- **US Post Office** · 870 S Raymond Ave
- **US Post Office** · 99 W California Blvd

Schools

- **Allendale Elementary** · 1135 S Euclid Ave
- **Aria Montessori** · 693 S Euclid Ave
- **Arroyo Vista Elementary** · 335 El Centro St
- **Blair High** · 1201 S Marengo Ave
- **Chandler** · 1005 Armada Dr
- **Fuller Theological Seminary** ·
  135 N Oakland Ave
- **Hillsides Education Center** · 940 Ave 64
- **Lake Ave Christian** · 393 N Lake Ave
- **Linda Vista Elementary** ·
  1259 Linda Vista Ave
- **Madison Elementary** · 515 E Ashtabula St
- **Mayfield Junior** · 405 S Euclid Ave
- **Mayfield Senior** · 500 Bellefontaine St
- **New Horizon** · 626 Cypress Ave
- **New Horizon (second location)** ·
  651 N Orange Grove Blvd
- **Oak Knoll Montessori** · 1200 N Lake Ave
- **Omowale Ujamaa** · 1415 N Raymond Ave
- **Options for Youth** · 199 S Los Robles Ave
- **Pacific Oaks** · 714 W California Blvd
- **Roosevelt Elementary** · 315 N Pasadena Ave
- **Rose City High** · 325 S Oak Knoll Ave
- **San Pascual Ave Elementary** ·
  815 San Pascual Ave
- **San Rafael Elementary** · 1090 Nithsdale Rd
- **Sankofa Academy** · 1374 Navarro Ave
- **Sequoyah** · 535 S Pasadena Ave
- **Southwestern Academy** · 2800 Monterey Rd
- **St Andrew's Elementary** · 42 Chestnut St
- **The Sycamores Community** ·
  851 N Oakland Ave
- **Waverly** · 396 S Pasadena Ave
- **Waverly (second location)** · 67 W Bellevue Dr
- **Westridge School for Girls** · 324 Madeline Dr

Supermarkets

- **Bristol Farms** · 606 Fair Oaks Ave
- **Farm Fresh Ranch Market** ·
  475 E Orange Grove Blvd
- **Food 4 Less** · 1329 N Lake Ave
- **Gelson's Markets** · 245 E Green St
- **Pavilions** · 1213 Fair Oaks Ave
- **Pavilions** · 845 E California Blvd
- **Ralphs** · 160 N Lake Ave
- **Ralphs** · 320 W Colorado Blvd
- **Smart & Final** · 401 N Fair Oaks Ave
- **Trader Joe's** · 610 S Arroyo Pkwy
- **Trader Joe's** · 613 Mission St
- **Vons** · 1129 Fair Oaks Ave
- **Vons** · 155 W California Blvd
- **Vons** · 655 N Fair Oaks Ave
- **Wild Oats** · 603 S Lake Ave

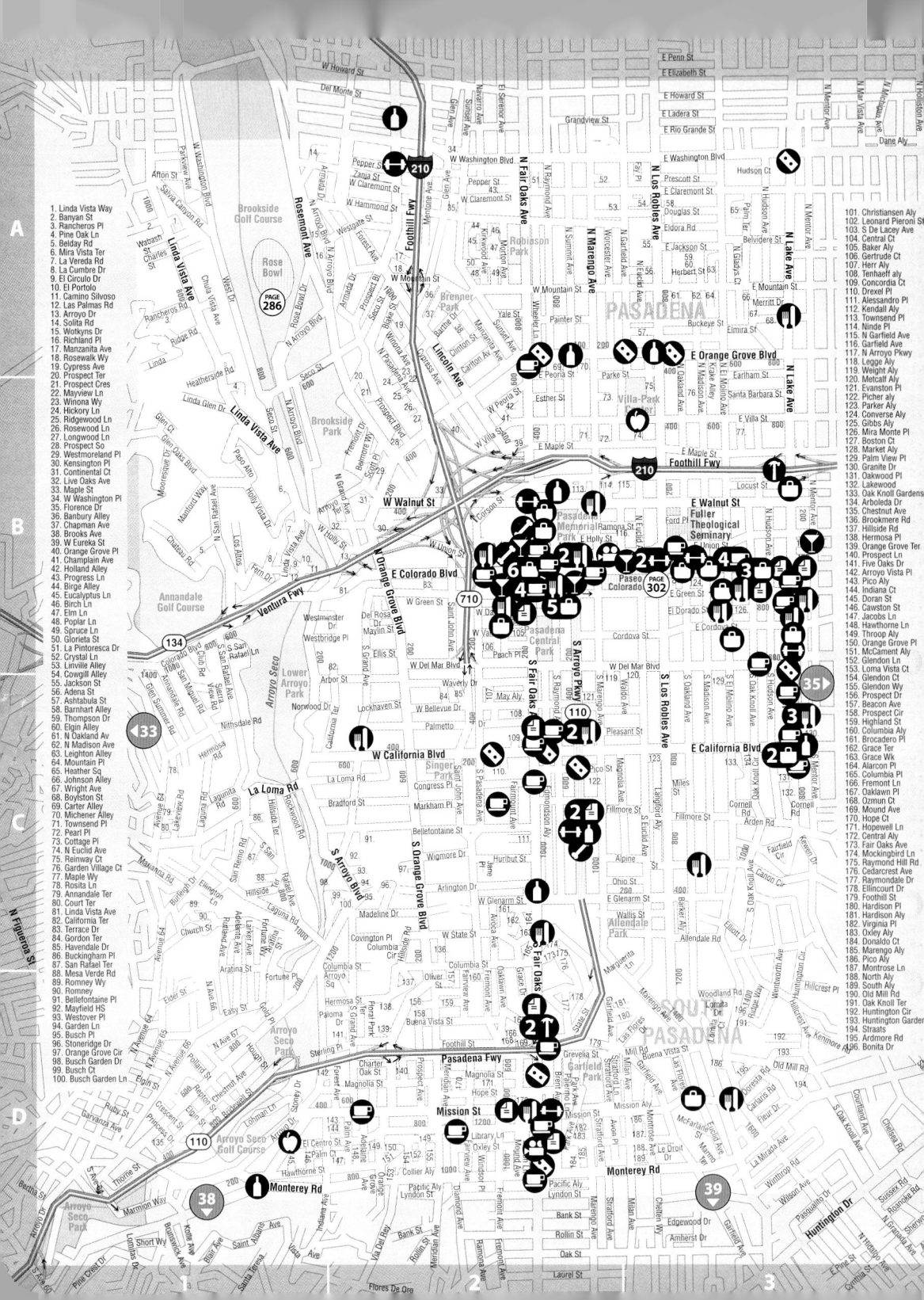

1. Linda Vista Way
2. Banyan St
3. Rancheros Pl
4. Pine Oak Ln
5. Belday Rd
6. Mira Vista Ter
7. La Vereda Rd
8. La Cumbre Dr
9. El Circulo Dr
10. El Portolo
11. Camino Silvoso
12. Las Palmas Rd
13. Arroyo Dr
14. Solita Rd
15. Wolkyns Dr
16. Richland Pl
17. Manzanita Ave
18. Rosewalk Wy
19. Cypress Ave
20. Prospect Ter
21. Prospect Cres
22. Mayview Ln
23. Winona Wy
24. Hickory Ln
25. Ridgewood Ln
26. Rosewood Ln
27. Longwood Ln
28. Prospect So
29. Westmoreland Pl
30. Kensington Pl
31. Continental Ct
32. Live Oaks Ave
33. Maple St
34. W Washington Pl
35. Florence Dr
36. Banbury Alley
37. Chapman Ave
38. Brooks Ave
39. W Eureka St
40. Orange Grove Pl
41. Champlain Ave
42. Holland Alley
43. Progress Ln
44. Birge Alley
45. Eucalyptus Ln
46. Birch Ln
47. Elm Ln
48. Poplar Ln
49. Spruce Ln
50. Glorieta St
51. La Pintoresca Dr
52. Crystal Ln
53. Linvile Alley
54. Cowgill Alley
55. Jackson St
56. Adena St
57. Ashtabula St
58. Barnhart Alley
59. Thompson Dr
60. Elgin Alley
61. N Oakland Ave
62. N Madison Ave
63. Leighton Alley
64. Mountain Pl
65. Heather Sq
66. Johnson Alley
67. Wright Ave
68. Boylston St
69. Carter Alley
70. Michener Alley
71. Townsend Ct
72. Pearl Pl
73. Cottage Pl
74. E Euclid Ave
75. Reinway Ct
76. Garden Village Ct
77. Maple Wy
78. Rosita Ln
79. Annandale Ter
80. Court Ter
81. Linda Vista Ave
82. California Ter
83. Terrace Dr
84. Gordon Ter
85. Havendale Dr
86. Buckingham Pl
87. San Rafael Ter
88. Mesa Verde Rd
89. Romney Wy
90. Romney
91. Bellefontaine Pl
92. Mayfield HS
93. Westover Pl
94. Garden Ln
95. Busch Pl
96. Stoneridge Dr
97. Orange Grove Cir
98. Busch Garden Dr
99. Busch Garden Ln
100. Busch Garden Ln

101. Christiansen Aly
102. Leonard Pieroni Sr
103. S De Lacey Ave
104. Central Ct
105. Baker Aly
106. Gertrude Dr
107. Herr Aly
108. Tenhaeff aly
109. Concordia Dr
110. Drexel Pl
111. Alessandro Pl
112. Kendall Aly
113. Townsend Pl
114. Ninde Pl
115. N Garfield Ave
116. N Garfield Ave
117. N Arroyo Pkwy
118. Legge Aly
119. Weight Aly
120. Metcalf Aly
121. Evanston Pl
122. Picher aly
123. Parker Aly
124. Converse Aly
125. Gibbs Aly
126. Mira Monte Pl
127. Boston Ct
128. Market Aly
129. Palm View Ct
130. Granite Dr
131. Oakwood Pl
132. Lakewood
133. Oak Knoll Gardens
134. Arboleda Dr
135. Chestnut Aly
136. Brookmere Rd
137. Hillside Rd
138. Hermosa Pl
139. Orange Grove Ter
140. Prospect Ln
141. Five Oaks Dr
142. Arroyo Vista Pl
143. Pico Pl
144. Indiana Ct
145. Doran St
146. Cawston St
147. Jacobs Ln
148. Hawthorne Ln
149. Throop Aly
150. Orange Grove Pl
151. McCament Aly
152. Glendon Ln
153. Loma Vista Ct
154. Glendon Ct
155. Glendon Wy
156. Prospect Dr
157. Beacon Ave
158. Prospect Cir
159. Highland Ct
160. Columbia Aly
161. Brocadero Pl
162. Grace Ter
163. Grace Wk
164. Alarcon Pl
165. Columbia Pl
166. Fremont Ln
167. Oaklawn Pl
168. Ozmun Ct
169. Mound Ave
170. Hope Ct
171. Hopewell Ln
172. Central Aly
173. Fair Oaks Ave
174. Mockingbird Ln
175. Raymond Hill Rd
176. Cedarcrest Ave
177. Raymondale Dr
178. Ellincourt Dr
179. Foothill St
180. Hardison Pl
181. Hardison Aly
182. Virginia Pl
183. Oxley Aly
184. Donaldo Ct
185. Marengo Aly
186. Pico Aly
187. Montrose Ln
188. North Aly
189. South Aly
190. Old Mill Rd
191. Oak Knoll Ter
192. Huntington Cir
193. Huntington Garden
194. Straats
195. Ardmore Rd
196. Bonita St

Pedestrian-friendly Old Town Pasadena, with its shops, restaurants, and prime Rose Parade seating, gets a lot of play. It also gets crowded on weekends. So don't forget that South Lake Avenue, the Playhouse District (whose epicenter is, ahem, the Pasadena Playhouse), and South Pasadena around Fair Oaks and Mission St are all pleasant places to walk, stroll, shop, and people-watch. Also note: the rightly famous Rose Bowl Flea Market is the second Sunday of each month. Come early.

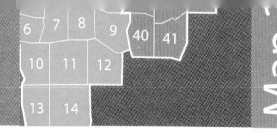
☕Coffee
- **Café Atlantic** • 53 E Union St
- **Café Latte** • 55 S Lake Ave
- **Coffee Bean & Tea Leaf** • 18 S Fair Oaks Ave
- **Coffee Bean & Tea Leaf** • 415 S Lake Ave
- **Coffee Bean & Tea Leaf** • 700 S Fair Oaks Ave
- **Coffee Tree** • 696 E Colorado Blvd
- **Equator Coffee House** • 22 Mills Pl
- **Hey That's Amore** • 27 E Holly St
- **House of Coffee** • 620 Mission St
- **Joan's Coffee Roasters** • 537 S Raymond Ave
- **Just Joe** • 109 E Union St
- **Kaldi Coffee & Tea** • 1019 El Centro St
- **La Luce Café & Deli** • 62 W Union St
- **Lake Coffee & Tea** • 146 S Lake Ave
- **Peet's Coffee & Tea** • 605 S Lake Ave
- **Plaza Café** • 802 Fairmount Ave
- **Second Cup Café** • 84 S Fair Oaks Ave
- **Starbucks** • 1000 Fair Oaks Ave
- **Starbucks** • 117 W Colorado Blvd
- **Starbucks** • 408 E Colorado Blvd
- **Starbucks** • 454 N Fair Oaks Ave
- **Starbucks** • 556 S Fair Oaks Ave
- **Starbucks** • 575 S Lake Ave
- **Starbucks** • 671 N Fair Oaks Ave
- **Starbucks** • 82 S Lake Ave
- **Starbucks (Target)** • 777 E Colorado Blvd
- **Starbucks (Vons)** • 1213 Fair Oaks Ave
- **Tiffany's Coffee** • 263 E Colorado Blvd
- **Zeli Coffee Bar** • 695 E Colorado Blvd
- **Zona Rosa** • 15 S El Molino Ave

🖨Copy Centers
- **Cantu Graphics** • 1421 Mission St • 626-441-5631
- **Copy Rite** • 908 E Colorado Blvd • 626-405-9800
- **Image Quest Plus** • 780 S Arroyo Pkwy • 626-744-1333
- **Kinko's** • 460 Fair Oaks Ave • 626-403-6690
- **Kinko's** • 855 E Colorado Blvd • 626-793-6336
- **Print X-Press & Copy Center** • 718 E Green St • 626-440-9472
- **Reliable Graphics** • 61 Valley St • 626-449-6555
- **Staples** • 875 S Arroyo Pwy • 626-578-3490
- **UPS Store** • 1107 Fair Oaks Ave • 626-799-4589
- **UPS Store** • 556 S Fair Oaks Ave • 626-564-0690

🍎Farmer's Markets
- **Pasadena** • 363 E Villa St
- **South Pasadena** • Meridian Ave & El Centro

🏋Gyms
- **24-Hour Fitness** • 525 E Colorado Blvd • 626-229-9784
- **Bally Total Fitness** • 45 S Arroyo Pkwy • 626-577-8588
- **Bodies In Motion** • 900 S Arroyo Pkwy • 626-577-2211
- **Curves** • 1260 Lincoln Ave • 626-797-5890
- **Curves** • 906 Fair Oaks Ave • 626-403-9615
- **Equinox** • 260 E Colorado Blvd • 626-685-4800
- **High Energy Fitness** • 95 N Arroyo Pkwy • 626-356-0005
- **LA Fitness Sports Club** • 201 S Lake Ave • 626-568-3598
- **Pasadena Athletic Club** • 25 W Walnut St • 626-793-8161

🔧Hardware Stores
- **Orchard Supply Hardware** • 452 Fair Oaks Ave • 626-403-8115
- **True Value** • 409 N Fair Oaks Ave • 626-792-2196

🍾Liquor Stores
- **Andy's Liquors** • 124 E Orange Grove Blvd
- **Chronicle Wine Celler** • 913 E California Blvd
- **Foremost Liquor** • 301 Monterey Rd
- **Gerlach's Drive in Liquors** • 1075 S Fair Oaks Ave
- **Heritage Wine Company** • 155 N Raymond Ave
- **Liquor Box** • 1445 Lincoln Ave
- **Milt's Liquor** • 400 E Orange Grove Blvd

😊Movie Theaters
- **Laemmle One Colorado Cinemas** • 42 Miller Aly • 626-744-1224
- **Laemmle Playhouse 7** • 673 E Colorado Blvd • 626-844-6500
- **Landmark Rialto Theatre** • 1023 Fair Oaks Ave • 626-799-9567
- **Pacific Paseo Stadium 14** • 336 E Colorado Blvd • 626-568-9690

🍸Nightlife
- **Bodega Wine Bar** • 260 E Colorado Blvd • 626-793-4300
- **De Lacey's Club 41** • 41 S De Lacey Ave • 626-795-4141
- **Freddie's 35er Bar** • 12 E Colorado Blvd • 626-356-9315
- **Ice House Comedy Club** • 24 N Mentor Ave • 626-577-1894
- **Jake's Billiards** • 38 W Colorado Blvd • 626-568-1602
- **McMurphy's** • 72 Fair Oaks Ave • 626-666-1445
- **The Muse** • 54 E Colorado Blvd • 626-793-0608

🐾Pet Stores
- **Pet's Delight** • 725 Fair Oaks Ave • 626-799-2935
- **Petco** • 845 S Arroyo Pkwy • 626-577-2600
- **Three Dog Bakery** • 24 Smith Aly • 626-440-0443

🍴Restaurants
- **Akbar** • 44 N Fair Oaks Ave • 626-577-9916
- **Arroyo Chop House** • 536 S Arroyo Pkwy • 626-577-7463
- **Bar Celona** • 46 E Colorado Blvd • 626-405-1000
- **Burger Continental** • 535 S Lake Ave • 626-792-6634
- **Café Atlantic** • 53 E Union St • 626-796-7350
- **Café Bizou** • 91 N Raymond Ave • 626-792-9923
- **Café Santorini** • 64 W Union St • 626-564-4200
- **Celestino** • 141 S Lake Ave • 626-795-4006
- **De Lacey's Club 41** • 41 S De Lacey Ave • 626-795-4141
- **Five Sixty-One** • 561 E Green St • 626-405-1561
- **Gordon Biersch** • 41 Hugus Aly • 626-449-0052
- **Hop Li** • 526 Alpine St • 213-680-3939
- **Julienne** • 2649 Mission St • 626-441-2299
- **Maison Akira** • 713 E Green St • 626-796-9501
- **Marston's** • 151 E Walnut St • 626-796-2459
- **Parkway Grill** • 510 S Arroyo Pkwy • 626-795-1001
- **Pho 79** • 29 S Garfield Ave • 626-289-0239
- **Pie 'N Burger** • 913 E California Blvd • 626-795-1123
- **Radhika's** • 140 Shoppers Ln • 626-744-0994
- **The Raymond** • 1250 S Fair Oaks Ave • 626-441-3136
- **Roscoe's House of Chicken 'n Waffles** • 830 N Lake Ave • 626-791-4890
- **Shiro** • 1505 Mission St • 626-799-4774
- **Twin Palms** • 101 W Green St • 626-577-2567
- **Xiomara** • 69 N Raymond Ave • 626-796-2520
- **Yujean Kang's** • 67 N Raymond Ave • 626-585-0855

🛍Shopping
- **Angels School Supply** • 600 E Colorado Blvd • 626-584-0855
- **The Art Store** • 44 S Raymond Ave • 626-795-4985
- **Assistance League of Pasadena** • 820 N E California Blvd • 626-449-6590
- **Bungalow News** • 746 E Colorado Blvd • 626-795-9456
- **Cannyon Beachwear** • 34 Hugus Aly • 626-564-0752
- **Canterbury Record Shop** • 805 E Colorado Blvd • 626-792-7184
- **Carroll & Co** • 146 S Lake Ave • 626-396-7060
- **CP Shades** • 20 S Raymond Ave • 626-564-9304
- **Dreams of Tibet** • 20 E Holly St • 626-585-8100
- **Elisa B** • 12 Douglas Aly • 626-792-4746
- **Essence of France** • 275 S El Molino Ave • 626-449-4019
- **Fine Kicks** • 88 E Colorado Blvd • 626-744-0656
- **Heritage Wine Co** • 155 N Raymond Ave • 800-630-WINE
- **Jacob Maarse Florists** • 655 E Green St • 626-449-0246
- **Lather** • 106 W Colorado Blvd • 626-397-9050
- **Lush** • 24 E Colorado Blvd • 626-792-0901
- **Messarian Oriental Rugs** • 493 Colorado Blvd • 626-792-9858
- **Paperwhites** • 2491 Mission St • 626-441-2196
- **Pasadena Antique Mall** • 35 S Raymond Ave • 626-304-9886
- **Pasadena Stone & Tile** • 175 S Fair Oaks Ave • 626-793-3773
- **room 107** • 174 S De Lacey Ave • 626-432-4867
- **Rose Tree Cottage** • 828 E California Blvd • 626-793-3337
- **Run with Us** • 235 N Lake Ave • 626-568-3331
- **Stats** • 170 S Raymond Ave • 626-795-9308
- **Target** • 777 E Colorado Blvd • 626-584-1606
- **Three Dog Bakery** • 24 Smith Aly • 626-440-0443
- **Z Gallerie** • 42 W Colorado Blvd • 626-578-1538

📼Video Rental
- **Blockbuster** • 1100 Fair Oaks Ave • 626-441-8112
- **Blockbuster** • 151 W California Blvd • 626-440-7074
- **Blockbuster** • 320 S Lake Ave • 626-568-9874
- **Five Star Video** • 633 S Arroyo Pkwy • 626-792-7090
- **Hollywood Video** • 25 E California Blvd • 626-304-9340
- **Ito Video** • 41 E Orange Grove Blvd • 626-683-9503
- **Pasadena Video** • 453 E Orange Grove Blvd • 626-744-9498
- **Pepe's Video Store** • 313 E Orange Grove Blvd • 626-792-7127
- **Q Video** • 1279 N Lake Ave • 626-398-8686

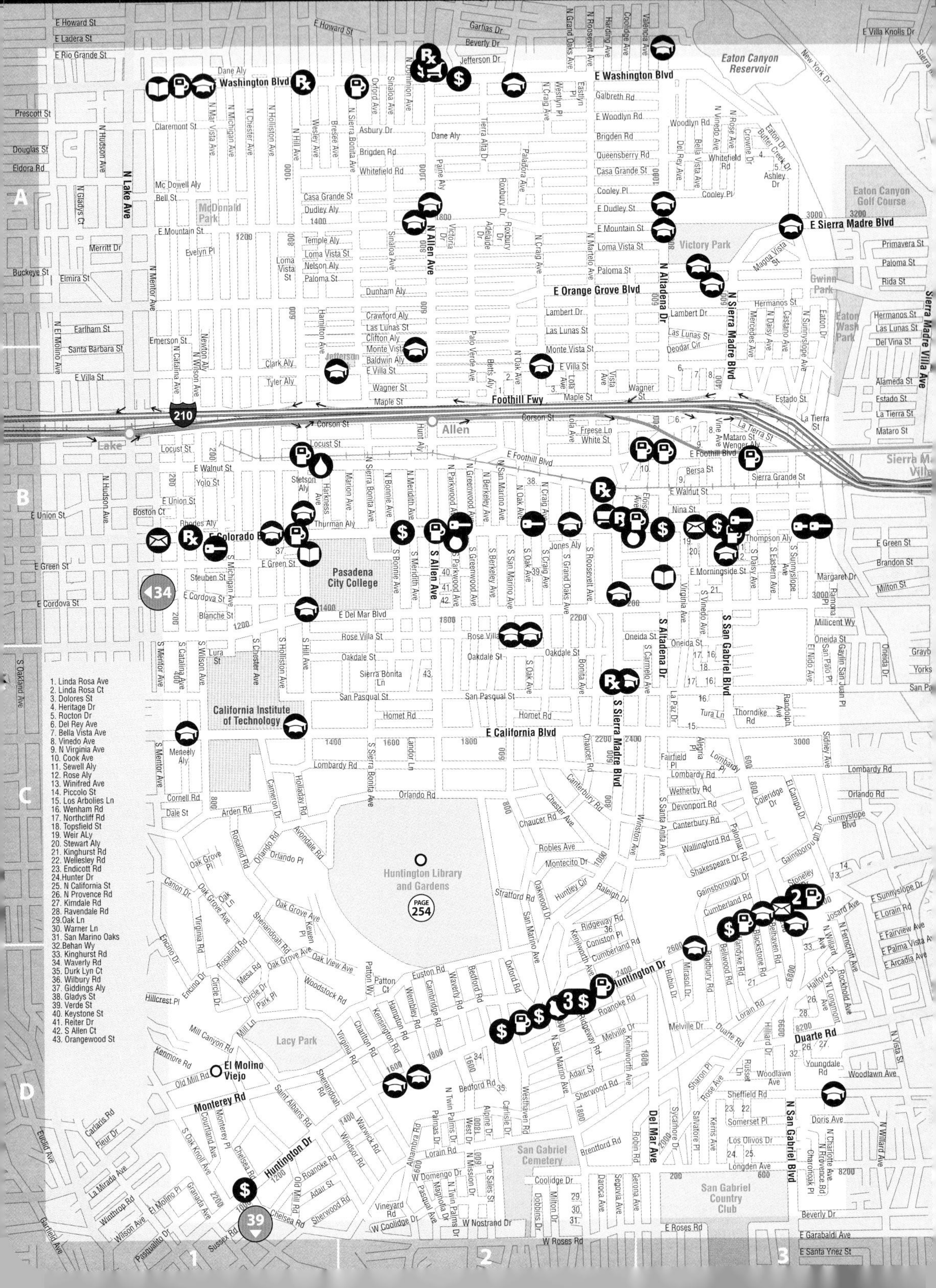

Map 35 • Pas
N

1. Linda Rosa Ave
2. Linda Rosa Ct
3. Dolores St
4. Heritage Dr
5. Rocton Dr
6. Del Rey Ave
7. Bella Vista Ave
8. Vinedo Ave
9. N Virginia Ave
10. Cook Ave
11. Sewell Aly
12. Rose Aly
13. Winifred Ave
14. Piccolo St
15. Los Arbolles Ln
16. Wenham Rd
17. Northcliff Rd
18. Topsfield St
19. Weir Aly
20. Stewart Aly
21. Kinghurst Rd
22. Wellesley Rd
23. Endicott Rd
24. Hunter Dr
25. N California St
26. N Provence Rd
27. Kimdale Rd
28. Ravendale Rd
29. Oak Ln
30. Warner Ln
31. San Marino Oaks
32. Behan Wy
33. Kinghurst Rd
34. Waverly Rd
35. Durk Lyn Ct
36. Wilbury Rd
37. Giddings Aly
38. Gladys St
39. Verde St
40. Keystone St
41. Reiter Dr
42. S Allen Ct
43. Orangewood St

Colorado Boulevard changes its tune east of Lake Avenue, and the shiny chain stores of Old Town are replaced by the matte-finish of auto repair shops, motels, and hardware stores. South of Colorado Boulevard, you will find two venerable institutions of the San Gabriel Valley: Cal Tech (to which Southern California turns for seismic expertise whenever the ground shakes) and award-winning public radio station KPCC, which makes its home at Pasadena City College.

$ Banks

- **Bank of America** · 1687 E Colorado Blvd
- **Bank of America** · 2180 Huntington Dr
- **Bank of the West** · 2395 Huntington Dr
- **Bank of the West** · 2500 E Colorado Blvd
- **Chinatrust** · 2956 Huntington Dr
- **Citizens Business** · 980 Huntington Dr
- **United National** · 2090 Huntington Dr
- **Washington Mutual** · 1845 E Washington Blvd
- **Washington Mutual** · 2270 Huntington Dr
- **Washington Mutual** · 2670 E Colorado Blvd
- **Wells Fargo** · 1390 N Allen Ave
- **Wells Fargo** · 2355 Huntington Dr

Car Rental

- **All-Rite Rent-a-Car** · 1150 E Colorado Blvd
- **Enterprise** · 1890 E Colorado Blvd
- **Enterprise** · 2982 E Colorado Blvd
- **Hertz** · 2738 E Colorado Blvd
- **Thrifty** · 2965 E Colorado Blvd
- **Value Rent-a-Car** · 2106 E Colorado Blvd

Car Washes

- **Chevron Car Wash** · 1400 E Colorado Blvd
- **Sparkle Car Wash** · 2400 E Colorado Blvd
- **Walnut-Hill Hand Car Wash** · 1465 E Walnut St

Gas Stations

- **76** · 200 N Hill Ave
- **76** · 2390 Huntington Dr
- **Arco** · 2800 E Foothill Blvd
- **Chevron** · 1400 E Colorado Blvd
- **Chevron** · 233 N Altadena Dr
- **Exxon** · 2995 Huntington Dr
- **Independent** · 2400 E Colorado Blvd
- **Mobil** · 1813 E Colorado Blvd
- **Mobil** · 210 N Sierra Madre Blvd
- **Price Savers** · 1010 E Washington Blvd
- **Shell** · 2716 E Colorado Blvd
- **Shell** · 8204 Huntington Dr
- **Texaco** · 1600 E Washington Blvd
- **Texaco** · 8204 Huntington Dr
- **Valero** · 2155 Huntington Dr

Landmarks

- **El Molino Viejo** · 1120 Old Mill Rd
- **Huntington Library and Gardens** · 1151 Oxford Rd

Libraries

- **Hill Avenue Branch** · 55 S Hill Ave · 626-744-7264
- **Lamanda Park Branch** · 140 S Altadena Dr · 626-744-7266
- **Santa Catalina Branch** · 999 E Washington Blvd · 626-744-7272

Pharmacies

- **Rite-Aid** · 1038 E Colorado Blvd · 626-796-5539
- **Rite-Aid** · 1421 E Washington Blvd · 626-296-0245
- **Rite-Aid** · 2330 E Walnut St · 626-304-2725
- **Sav-On** · 451 S Sierra Madre Blvd · 626-564-8840
- **Vons** · 1390 N Allen Ave · 626-798-0764
- **Vons** · 2355 E Colorado Blvd · 626-449-4110

Police

- **San Marino Police Dept** · 2200 Huntington Dr · 626-300-0720

Post Offices

- **US Post Office** · 2609 E Colorado Blvd
- **US Post Office** · 2960 Huntington Dr
- **US Post Office** · 967 E Colorado Blvd

Schools

- **Assumption Elementary** · 2660 E Orange Grove Blvd
- **California Academy for Liberal Studies** · 3838 Eagle Rock Blvd
- **California Institute of Technology** · 1200 E California Blvd
- **Carver Elementary** · 3100 Huntington Dr
- **Chaim Weizmann Community Day** · 1434 N Altadena Dr
- **Frosting Center of Education Therapy** · 971 N Altadena Dr
- **Grace Christian** · 73 N Hill Ave
- **Hamilton Elementary** · 2089 Rose Villa St
- **Huntington Middle** · 1700 Huntington Dr
- **International Montessori Academy** · 1788 Monte Vista St
- **Jefferson Elementary** · 1500 E Villa St
- **Living Way Christian Academy** · 2495 E Mountain St
- **Longfellow Elementary** · 1065 E Washington Blvd
- **Marshall Fundamental** · 990 N Allen Ave
- **Merryland** · 1305 E Colorado Blvd
- **Norma Coombs Elementary** · 2600 Paloma St
- **Oddessy Charter** · 1555 E Colorado Blvd
- **Our School** · 1800 E Mountain St
- **Pasadena City College** · 1570 E Colorado Blvd
- **Pasadena High** · 2925 E Sierra Madre Blvd
- **Pasadena Progressive Monessori** · 615 S Catalina Ave
- **Pasadena Towne Country** · 200 S Sierra Madre Blvd
- **Polytechnic** · 1030 E California Blvd
- **San Marino High** · 2701 Huntington Dr
- **San Marino Montessori** · 444 S Sierra Madre Blvd
- **St Gregory** · 2215 E Colorado Blvd
- **St Philip the Apostle** · 161 S Hill Ave
- **Sts Felicita & Perpetua** · 2955 Huntington Dr
- **Valentine Elementary** · 1650 Huntington Dr
- **Villa Esperanza** · 2116 E Villa St
- **Walden** · 74 S San Gabriel Blvd
- **Washington Elementary** · 300 N San Marino Ave
- **Webster Elementary** · 2101 E Washington Blvd
- **Woodrow Wilson Elementary** · 8317 Sheffield Rd

Supermarkets

- **Vons** · 1390 N Allen Ave
- **Vons** · 2355 E Colorado Blvd

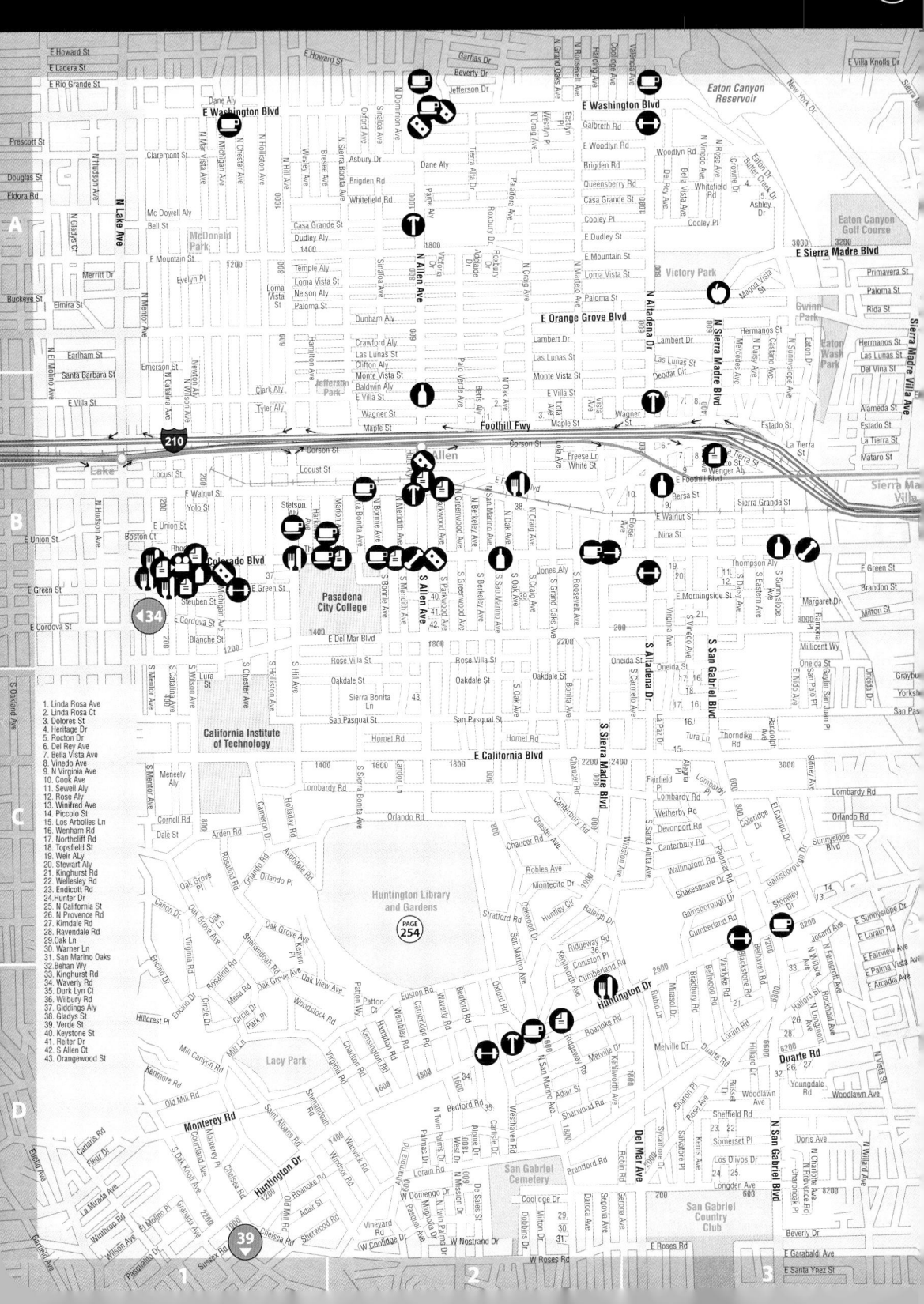

Nestled amongst the two-million-dollar "starter homes" of San Marino are the 150 acres of the Huntington Library and Gardens, with enough perennials, annuals, Shakespeare folios, and cheerful docents to make even the most hardened misanthrope rediscover his or her humanity. Lacy Park in San Marino offers a wonderful display of Sousa-worthy 4th of July fireworks. Arrive early with a blanket to stake out your place on the grass.

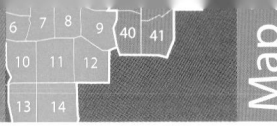

Coffee

- **Café Kulture** • 1359 N Altadena Dr
- **Coffee Beanery** • 1225 E Washington Blvd
- **Coffee Club** • 12 Harkness Ave
- **Lollicup** • 1491 E Colorado Blvd
- **Pasadena Coffee** • 1625 E Walnut St
- **Ragtime Gourmet Tea Coffee** • 975 E Green St
- **Starbucks** • 161 N Hill Ave
- **Starbucks** • 1687 E Colorado Blvd
- **Starbucks** • 1830 E Washington Blvd
- **Starbucks** • 2265 Huntington Dr
- **Starbucks** • 3007 Huntington Dr
- **Starbucks (Vons)** • 1390 N Allen Ave
- **Starbucks (Vons)** • 2355 E Colorado Blvd

Copy Centers

- **Baughman Printing Company** • 1842 E Walnut St • 626-793-0753
- **Book Mart & Copy Center** • 1535 E Colorado Blvd • 626-683-3391
- **Copy Store** • 30 S Wilson Ave • 626-796-1395
- **Econoprint Printing & Graphics Center** • 1765 E Colorado Blvd • 626-795-1000
- **Office Depot** • 1130 E Colorado Blvd • 626-666-6900
- **Office Depot** • 325 N Altadena Dr • 626-792-5800
- **Print Stop** • 300 N Allen Ave • 626-577-0510
- **Printcraft Copy Center** • 985 E Colorado Blvd • 626-584-6971
- **UPS Store** • 1443 E Washington Blvd • 626-529-0325
- **UPS Store** • 2275 Huntington Dr • 626-795-1999

Farmer's Markets

- **Pasadena High School Market** • Paloma St & Sierra Madre Blvd

Gyms

- **Curves** • 1250 E Green St • 626-793-9711
- **Curves** • 1311 N Altadena Dr • 626-794-5294
- **Curves** • 2920 Huntington Dr • 626-287-1513
- **Evolution Fitness** • 2370 E Colorado Blvd • 626-793-5353
- **Gold's Gym** • 39 S Altadena Dr • 626-304-1133
- **Women's World Fitness Center** • 2000 Huntington Dr • 626-284-7741

Hardware Stores

- **Berg Hardware** • 495 N Altadena Dr • 626-793-6161
- **Crown City Hardware** • 1047 N Allen Ave • 626-794-1188
- **Davis Lumber** • 1787 E Walnut St • 626-792-7104
- **San Marino Hardware** • 2134 Huntington Dr • 626-282-6536

Liquor Stores

- **Allen Villa Beverage** • 490 N Allen Ave
- **Foothill Liquor** • 2547 E Foothill Blvd
- **Golden Liquor** • 2897 E Colorado Blvd
- **Liquor Mart** • 2044 E Colorado Blvd
- **Mission Liquor** • 1801 E Washington Blvd
- **Pat's Liquors** • 1072 E Colorado Blvd

Movie Theaters

- **Academy 6** • 1003 E Colorado Blvd • 626-229-9400

Pet Stores

- **Dog's Best Friend** • 1776 E Colorado Blvd • 626-793-5938
- **Pasadena Tropical Fish** • 2982 E Colorado Blvd • 626-449-4987

Restaurants

- **Bistro 45** • 45 S Mentor Ave • 626-795-2478
- **Europane** • 950 E Colorado Blvd • 626-577-1828
- **Halie** • 1030 E Green St • 626-440-7067
- **In-N-Out Burger** • 2114 E Foothill Blvd • 800-786-1000
- **Sushi Bar Yoshida** • 2026 Huntington Dr • 626-281-9292
- **Zankou Chicken** • 1415 E Colorado Blvd • 818-244-1937

Video Rental

- **Blockbuster** • 1830 E Washington Blvd • 626-345-9136
- **LaserLibrary dot com** • 1190 E Colorado Blvd • 626-577-7035
- **Plaza Video** • 1832 E Colorado Blvd • 626-793-2451
- **Star Video** • 1878 E Washington Blvd • 626-791-9708
- **Video Grand** • 376 N Allen Ave • 626-578-1640

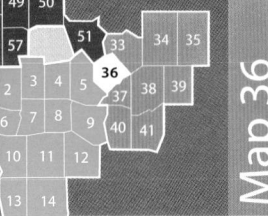
Los Angeles' outrageous housing prices have pushed young first-time home-buyers east to areas like Mt. Washington. As they discover its off-the-beaten-path charms, the neighborhoods are on the upswing and new businesses are popping up every day. ("The place is really turning around!" is the realtor's line.) Sure, gang and graffiti trouble still linger, but the hilly landscape's upper areas offer some of the best views of downtown you'll ever see. In addition, Mt Washington is home to the arresting river rock home built by the hands of eccentric journalist Charles Lummis after he walked from Ohio to California.

Car Rental

- **Enterprise** · 4442 York Blvd

Car Washes

- **Highland Car Wash** · 5128 N Figueroa St

Gas Stations

- **76** · 2250 N Figueroa St
- **Arco** · 105 N Ave 52
- **Arco** · 2135 San Fernando Rd
- **Arco** · 2251 N Figueroa St
- **Arco** · 4380 Eagle Rock Blvd
- **Chevron** · 2600 N Figueroa St
- **Chevron** · 2601 N Figueroa St
- **Chevron** · 4005 Eagle Rock Blvd
- **Shell** · 4236 Eagle Rock Blvd
- **Shell** · 5137 N Figueroa St

○ Landmarks

- **The Lummis Home** · 200 E Ave 43
- **Mount Washington Hotel/Self-Realization** · 3880 San Rafael Ave
- **Southwest Museum** · 234 Museum Dr

Libraries

- **Cypress Park Branch** · 1150 Cypress Ave · 323-224-0039

Pharmacies

- **Rite-Aid** · 4044 Eagle Rock Blvd · 323-254-8642
- **Sav-On (Albertsons)** · 133 W Ave 45 · 323-222-0121

Post Offices

- **US Post Office** · 3950 Eagle Rock Blvd ·

Schools

- **Aldama Elementary** · 632 N Ave 50
- **Aragon Ave Elementary** · 1118 Aragon Ave
- **Arroyo Seco** · 4805 Sycamore Ter
- **Divine Saviour** · 624 Cypress Ave
- **Dorris Pl Elementary** · 2225 Dorris Pl
- **Florence Nightingale Middle** · 3311 N Figueroa St
- **Glassell Park Elementary** · 2211 W Ave 30
- **Loreto St Elementary** · 3408 Arroyo Seco Ave
- **Milagro Charter Elementary** · 3420 Verdugo Rd
- **Mount Washington Elementary** · 3981 San Rafael Ave
- **Ribet Academy** · 2911 San Fernando Rd
- **St Bernard Elementary** · 3254 Verdugo Rd
- **Sycamore Grove** · 4900 N Figueroa St
- **Toland Way EEC** · 4505 Toland Wy
- **Toland Way Elementary** · 4545 Toland Wy

Supermarkets

- **Albertsons** · 133 W Ave 45
- **Food 4 Less** · 5100 N Figueroa St
- **Super A Foods** · 2925 Division St

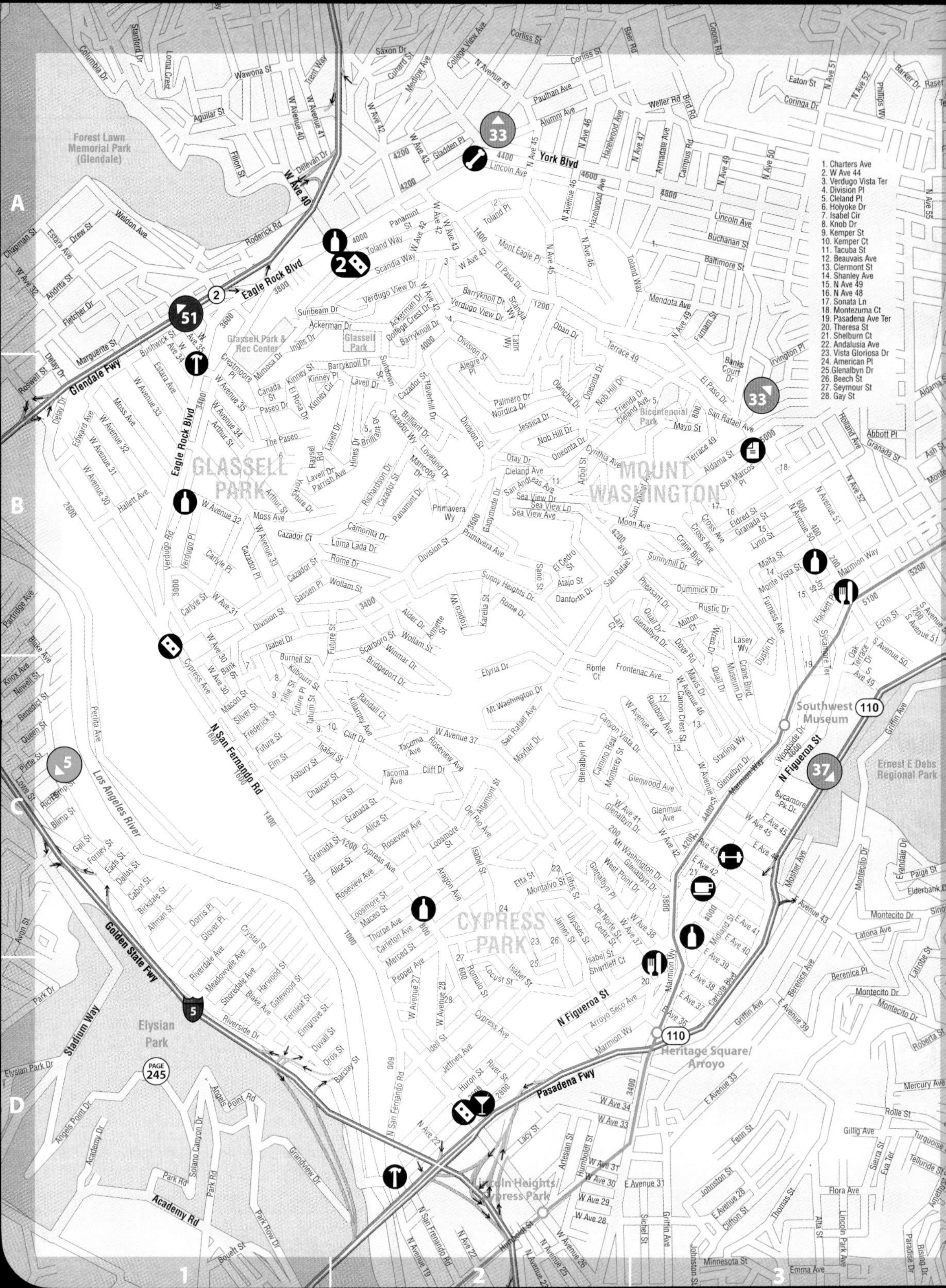

Map 36 · **Mt Washington**

Forest Lawn
Memorial Park
(Glendale)

GLASSELL
PARK

Glassell Park &
Rec Center

Glassell
Park

MOUNT
WASHINGTON

CYPRESS
PARK

Southwest
Museum

Ernest E Debs
Regional Park

Elysian
Park

PAGE
245

Heritage Square/
Arroyo

Lincoln Heights/
Cypress Park

1. Charters Ave
2. W Ave 44
3. Verdugo Vista Ter
4. Division Pl
5. Cleland Pl
6. Holyoke Dr
7. Isabel Cir
8. Knob Dr
9. Kemper St
10. Kemper Ct
11. Tacuba St
12. Beauvais Ave
13. Clermont St
14. Shanley Ave
15. N Ave 49
16. N Ave 48
17. Sonata Ln
18. Montezuma Ct
19. Pasadena Ave Ter
20. Theresa St
21. Shelburn Ct
22. Andalusia Ave
23. Vista Gloriosa Dr
24. American Pl
25. Glenalbyn Dr
26. Beech St
27. Seymour St
28. Gay St

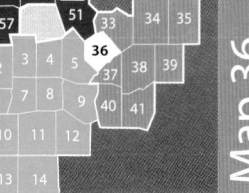

Map 36

Don't come to Mt. Washington for chain shops, restaurants, or supermarkets. Local businesses largely rule here, offering many surprises if you know where to look (ask that young couple who just bought a house in the area to give you the 411). But if you need, say, a Gap fix, any mass-produced item anyone could ever want is a quick trip away in neighboring Pasadena or Glendale.

Coffee
- **Rock Rose Café** · 4108 N Figueroa St

Copy Centers
- **The Copierman** · 720 N Ave 50 · 323-255-8606

Gyms
- **Curves** · 4319 N Figueroa St · 323-224-0044

Hardware Stores
- **Home Depot** · 2055 N Figueroa St · 323-441-1310
- **Verdugo True Value** · 3516 Eagle Rock Blvd · 323-255-5191

Liquor Stores
- **Barney's Liquors** · 5001 Monte Vista St
- **Golden Liquor** · 3924 N Figueroa St
- **L&M Liquor** · 4010 Eagle Rock Blvd
- **Mike's Liquor** · 3192 Verdugo Rd
- **S&J Liquor** · 925 Cypress Ave

Nightlife
- **Footsie's Café** · 2640 N Figueroa St · 323-221-7357

Pet Stores
- **Hal's Eagle Rock Pet Shop** · 4374 Eagle Rock Blvd · 323-255-5714

Restaurants
- **Chico's** · 100 N Ave 50 · 323-254-2445
- **La Abeja** · 3700 N Figueroa St · 323-221-0474

Video Rental
- **21 Video** · 2211 N San Fernando Rd · 323-221-1793
- **Landmark Video (Filipino)** · 3756 W Ave 40 · 323-256-0969
- **Video Club of LA** · 3756 W Ave 40 · 323-255-9883

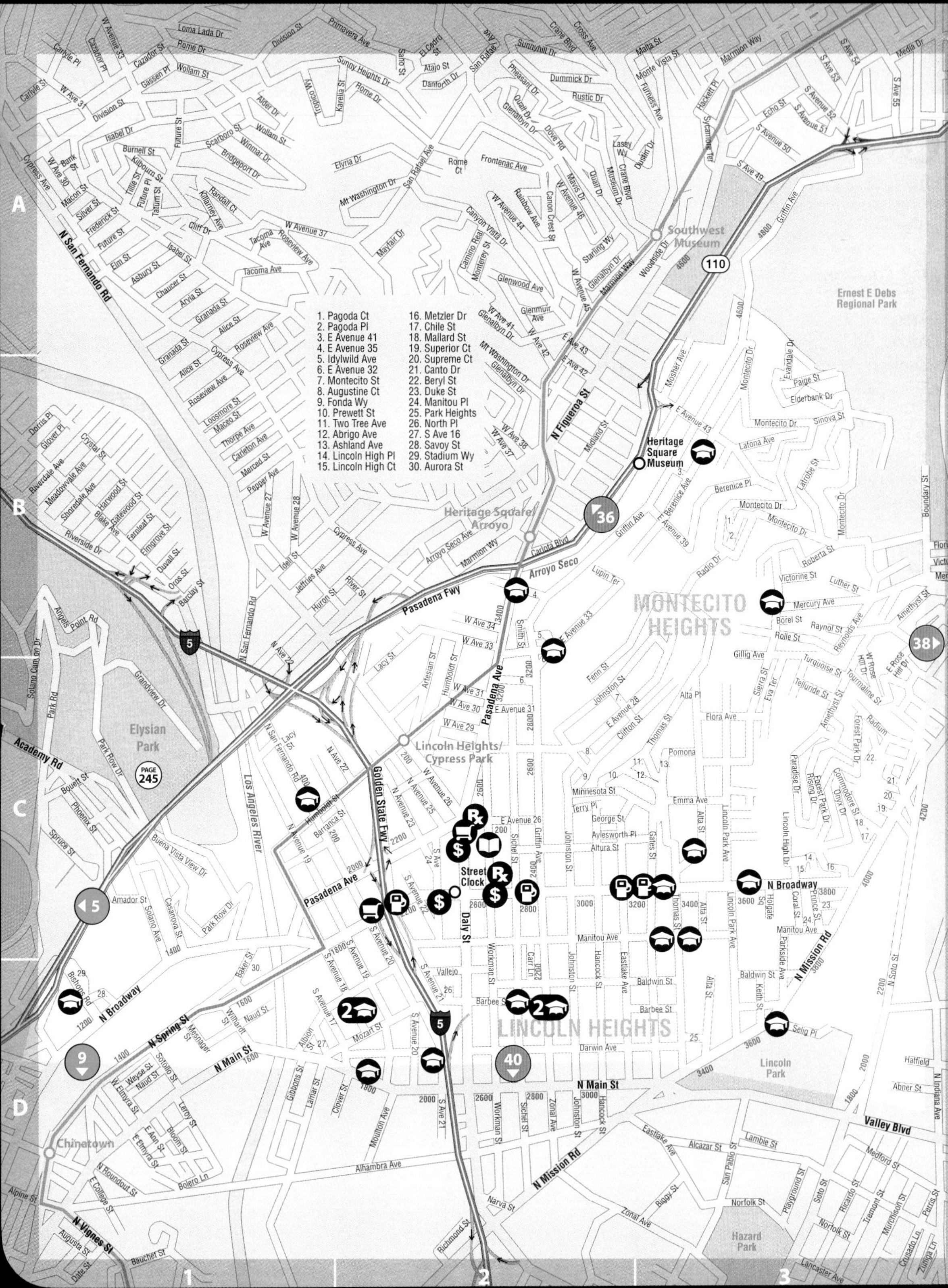

Map 37 · **Lincoln Heights**

1. Pagoda Ct
2. Pagoda Pl
3. E Avenue 41
4. E Avenue 35
5. Idylwild Ave
6. E Avenue 32
7. Montecito St
8. Augustine Ct
9. Fonda Wy
10. Prewett St
11. Two Tree Ave
12. Abrigo Ave
13. Ashland Ave
14. Lincoln High Pl
15. Lincoln High Ct
16. Metzler Dr
17. Chile St
18. Mallard St
19. Superior Ct
20. Supreme Ct
21. Canto St
22. Beryl St
23. Duke St
24. Manitou Pl
25. Park Heights
26. North Pl
27. S Ave 16
28. Savoy St
29. Stadium Wy
30. Aurora St

Montecito Heights: birdwatcher's paradise. The area is home to a chorus of songbirds, numerous hawks, and the occasional Great White Owl. So vast is the local avian population that the Audubon Society is considering the creation of a bird sanctuary in Ernest E. Debs Regional Park.

Banks

- **Bank of America** • 2400 N Broadway
- **East West** • 2601 N Broadway
- **Wells Fargo** • 2511 Daly St

Gas Stations

- **Arco** • 2214 N Broadway
- **Arco** • 2829 N Broadway
- **Shell** • 3130 N Broadway
- **Shell** • 3200 N Broadway

o Landmarks

- **Heritage Square Museum** • 3800 N Homer St
- **Street Clock** • 2423 Broadway

Libraries

- **Lincoln Heights Branch** • 2530 Workman St • 323-226-1692

Pharmacies

- **Rite-Aid** • 111 E Ave 26 • 323-222-8876
- **Sav-On** • 2419 Workman St • 323-223-9059

Schools

- **Abraham Lincoln Senior High** • 3501 N Broadway
- **Albion EEC** • 348 S Ave 18
- **Albion Street Elementary** • 322 S Ave 18
- **Boyle Heights Continuation** • 544 S Mathews St
- **Cathedral High** • 1253 Bishop Rd
- **Crittenton High** • 234 E Ave 33
- **Gates EEC** • 2306 Thomas St
- **Gates St Elementary** • 3333 Manitou Ave
- **Glen Alta Elementary** • 3410 Sierra St
- **Goodwill High** • 342 N San Fernando Rd
- **Griffin Elementary** • 2025 Griffin Ave
- **Hillside Elementary** • 120 E Ave 35
- **Jardin De Ninos EEC** • 3921 Selig Pl
- **Kipp LA College Prep** • 1855 N Main St
- **Latona Ave Elementary** • 4312 Berenice Ave
- **Little Flower Missionary House** • 2434 Gates St
- **Our Lady Help of Christians** • 2024 Darwin Ave
- **Pubelo de Los Angeles Continuation** • 2506 Alta St
- **Sacred Heart Elementary** • 2109 Sichel St
- **Sacred Heart High** • 2111 Griffin Ave

Supermarkets

- **Smart & Final** • 2019 Pasadena Ave
- **Vons** • 2511 Daly St

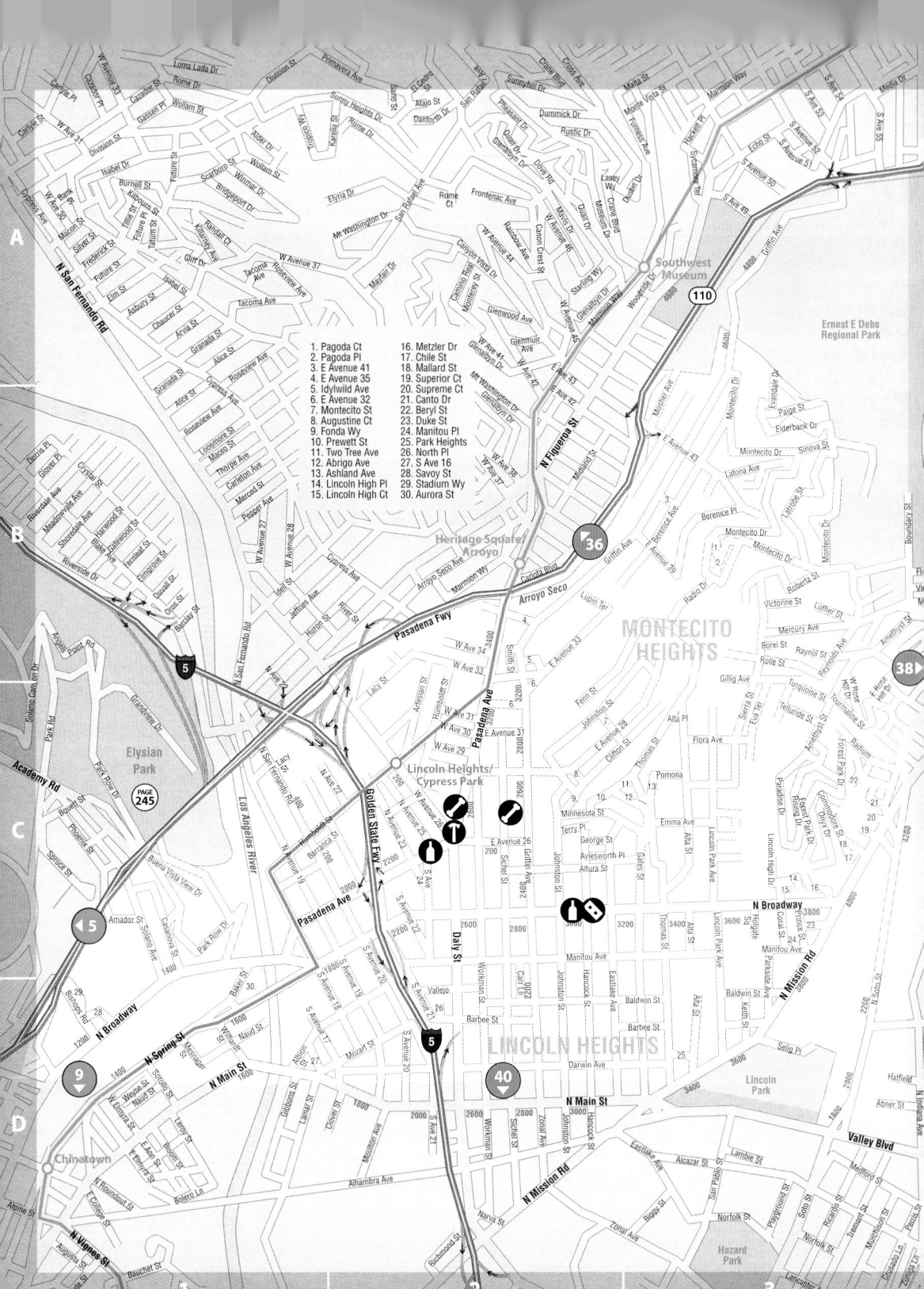

1. Pagoda Ct
2. Pagoda Pl
3. E Avenue 41
4. E Avenue 35
5. Idylwild Ave
6. E Avenue 32
7. Montecito St
8. Augustine Ct
9. Fonda Wy
10. Prewett St
11. Two Tree Ave
12. Abrigo Ave
13. Ashland Ave
14. Lincoln High Pl
15. Lincoln High Ct
16. Metzler Dr
17. Chile St
18. Mallard St
19. Superior Ct
20. Supreme Ct
21. Canto Dr
22. Beryl St
23. Duke St
24. Manitou Pl
25. Park Heights
26. North Pl
27. S Ave 16
28. Savoy St
29. Stadium Wy
30. Aurora St

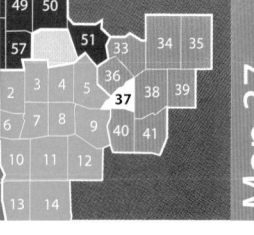
Lincoln Heights is home to the San Antonio Winery, Los Angeles' last remaining winery. Tours are available, along with dinner at the winery's restaurant and live music on the weekends. Also in this area is The Brewery—the world's largest artist community, living and working in a converted Pabst Blue Ribbon brewery. Twice yearly, the 500 or so artists open their studios over the weekend to the public during the ArtWalk.

 Hardware Stores

• **5 Points Hardware** • 2615 Pasadena Ave •
  323-225-6423

 Liquor Stores

• **Mandala Liquor** • 2920 N Broadway
• **Royal Liquor** • 2501 Pasadena Ave

 Pet Stores

• **Jack's Pet Shop** • 2634 Pasadena Ave • 323-225-6315

 Video Rental

• **Hollywood Video** • 3030 N Broadway • 323-221-3201

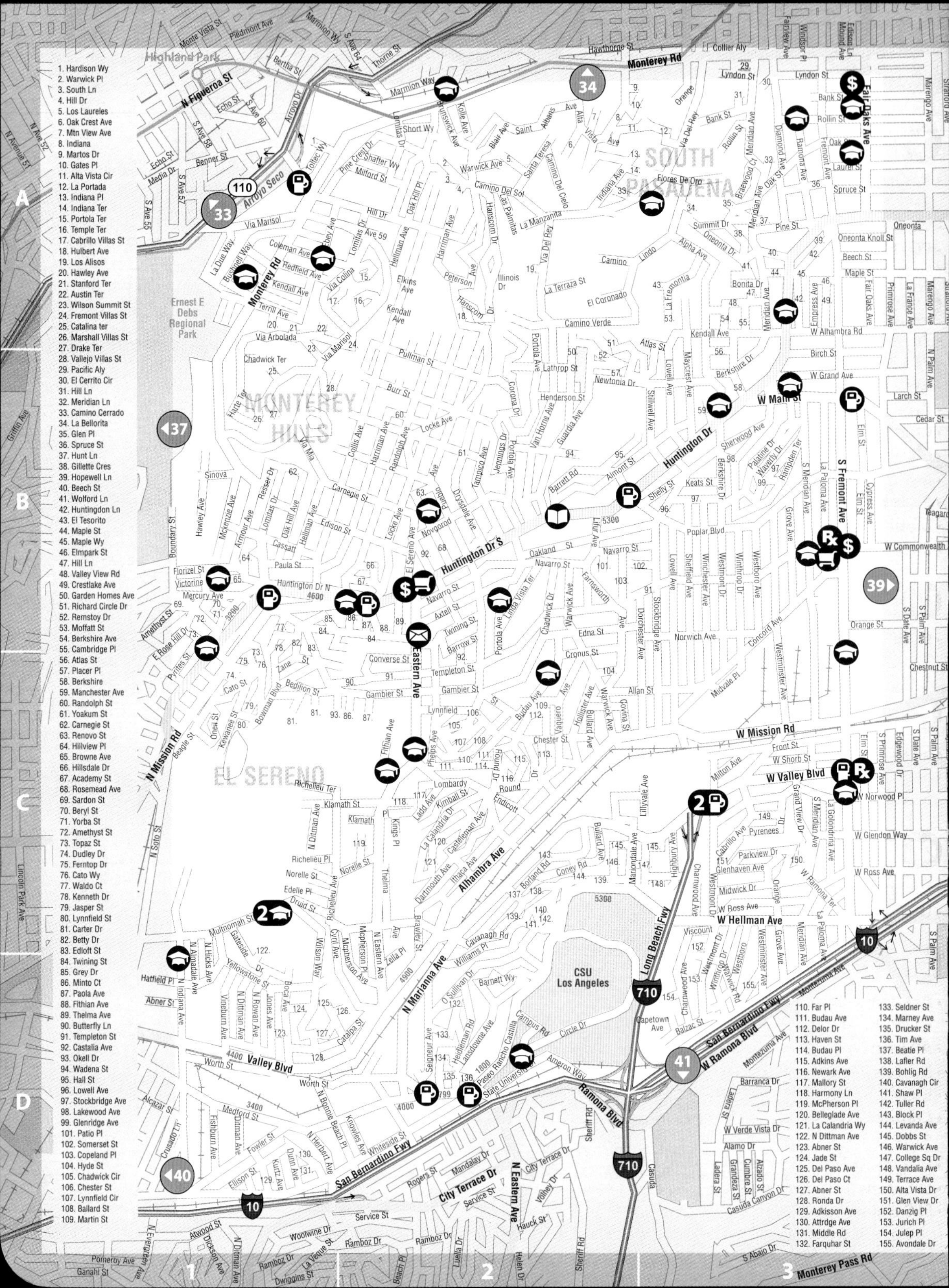

Map 38 • El Sereno

1. Hardison Wy
2. Warwick Pl
3. South Ln
4. Hill Dr
5. Los Laureles
6. Oak Crest Ave
7. Mtn View Ave
8. Indiana
9. Martos Dr
10. Gates Pl
11. Alta Vista Cir
12. La Portada
13. Indiana Pl
14. Indiana Ter
15. Portola Ter
16. Temple Ter
17. Cabrillo Villas St
18. Hulbert Ave
19. Los Alisos
20. Hawley Ave
21. Stanford Ter
22. Austin Ter
23. Wilson Summit St
24. Fremont Villas St
25. Catalina ter
26. Marshall Villas St
27. Drake Ter
28. Vallejo Villas St
29. Pacific Aly
30. El Cerrito Cir
31. Hill Ln
32. Meridian Ln
33. Camino Cerrado
34. La Bellorita
35. Glen Pl
36. Spruce St
37. Hunt Ln
38. Gillette Cres
39. Hopewell Ln
40. Beech St
41. Wolford Ln
42. Huntingdon Ln
43. El Tesorito
44. Maple St
45. Maple Wy
46. Elmpark St
47. Hill Ln
48. Valley View Rd
49. Crestlake Ave
50. Garden Homes Ave
51. Richard Circle Dr
52. Remstoy Dr
53. Moffatt St
54. Berkshire Ave
55. Cambridge Pl
56. Atlas St
57. Placer Pl
58. Berkshire
59. Manchester Ave
60. Randolph St
61. Yoakum St
62. Carnegie St
63. Renovo St
64. Hillview Pl
65. Browne Ave
66. Hillsdale Dr
67. Academy St
68. Rosemead Ave
69. Sardon St
70. Beryl St
71. Yorba St
72. Amethyst St
73. Topaz St
74. Dudley Dr
75. Ferntop Dr
76. Cato Wy
77. Waldo St
78. Kenneth Dr
79. Jasper St
80. Lynnfield St
81. Carter Dr
82. Betty Dr
83. Edloft St
84. Twining St
85. Grey Dr
86. Minto Ct
87. Paola Ave
88. Fithian Ave
89. Thelma Ave
90. Butterfly Ln
91. Templeton St
92. Castalia Ave
93. Okell Dr
94. Wadena St
95. Hall St
96. Lowell Ave
97. Stockbridge Ave
98. Lakewood Ave
99. Glenridge Ave
101. Patio Pl
102. Somerset St
103. Copeland Pl
104. Hyde St
105. Chadwick Cir
106. Chester St
107. Lynnfield Cir
108. Ballard St
109. Martin St
110. Far Pl
111. Budau Ave
112. Delor Dr
113. Haven St
114. Budau Pl
115. Adkins Ave
116. Newark Ave
117. Mallory St
118. Harmony Ln
119. McPherson Pl
120. Belleglade Ave
121. La Calandria Wy
122. N Dittman Ave
123. Abner St
124. Jade St
125. Del Paso Ave
126. Del Paso Ct
127. Abner St
128. Ronda Dr
129. Adkisson Ave
130. Attrdge Ave
131. Middle Rd
132. Farquhar St
133. Seldner St
134. Marney Ave
135. Drucker St
136. Tim Ave
137. Beatie Pl
138. Lafler Rd
139. Bohlig Rd
140. Cavanagh Cir
141. Shaw Pl
142. Tuller Rd
143. Block Pl
144. Levanda Ave
145. Dobbs St
146. Warwick Ave
147. College Sq Dr
148. Vandalia Ave
149. Terrace Ave
150. Alta Vista Dr
151. Glen View Dr
152. Danzig Pl
153. Jurich Pl
154. Julep Pl
155. Avondale Dr

SOUTH PASADENA

MONTEREY HILLS

EL SERENO

Ernest E Debs Regional Park

CSU Los Angeles

It should come as no surprise that in 1997, Cal State LA—located at the intersection of two major freeways, the 10 and 710, in one of the most car-oriented cities in the nation—brought home the gold for its student-built, solar-powered car in Sunrayce 97, a famed North American solar car race.

$ Banks

- **Bank of America (Albertsons)** ·
  2400 W Commonwealth Ave
- **Washington Mutual** · 1305 Fair Oaks Ave
- **Washington Mutual** · 4887 Huntington Dr N

Gas Stations

- **76** · 475 S Ave 60
- **76** · 5376 Huntington Dr
- **Arco** · 3201 W Valley Blvd
- **Arco** · 4860 S Huntington Dr
- **Chevron** · 1535 N Eastern Ave
- **Chevron** · 2600 W Valley Blvd
- **Independent** · 3200 W Valley Blvd
- **Mobil** · 1600 N Eastern Ave
- **Mobil** · 2601 W Main St
- **Shell** · 4590 Huntington Dr

Libraries

- **El Sereno Branch** · 5226 Huntington Dr S ·
  323-255-9201

Pharmacies

- **Sav-On** · 2532 W Valley Blvd · 626-308-1001
- **Sav-On (Albertsons)** · 2400 W Commonwealth Ave ·
  626-293-7100

Post Offices

- **US Post Office** · 3316 N Eastern Ave
- **US Post Office** · 4875 Huntington Dr

Schools

- **Academia Semillas Del Pueblo Charter School 2202**
  · 4736 Huntington Dr S
- **All Saints** · 3420 Portola Ave
- **Bushnell Way Elementary** · 5507 Bushnell Wy
- **Busy Bees Wonderland** · 1851 W Imperial Hwy
- **California State University–Los Angeles** ·
  5151 State University Dr
- **El Sereno EEC** · 3802 Pueblo Ave
- **El Sereno Elementary** · 3838 Rosemead Ave
- **El Sereno Middle** · 2839 N Eastern Ave

- **Emery Park Elementary** ·
  2821 W Commonwealth Ave
- **Farmdale Elementary** · 2660 Ruth Swiggett Dr
- **Fremont Elementary** · 2001 S Elm St
- **Holy Family Elementary** · 1301 Rollin St
- **Huntington Dr Elementary** · 4435 Huntington Dr N
- **Institute for Redesign of Learning** ·
  1137 Huntington Dr
- **John C Fremont Elementary** · 3320 Las Palmas Ave
- **Kingston** · 4555 Multnomah St
- **LA County High School for the Arts** ·
  5151 State University Dr
- **Monterey Hills Elementary** · 1624 Via del Rey
- **Multnomah St Elementary** · 2101 N Indiana St
- **Our Lady of Guadalupe** · 4522 Browne Ave
- **Pacific Christian High** · 625 Coleman Ave
- **SEEDS** · 1101 Arroyo Verde Rd
- **Sherman** · 1000 S Fremont Ave
- **Sierra Park Elementary** · 3170 Budau Ave
- **Sierra Vista Elementary** · 4342 Alpha St
- **South Pasadena Middle** · 1600 Oak St
- **South Pasadena Senior High** · 1401 Fremont Ave
- **Sugar Cone Castle Educational Center** ·
  3044 W Main St
- **Woodrow Wilson Senior High** · 4500 Multnomah St

Supermarkets

- **Albertsons** · 2400 W Commonwealth Ave
- **Food 4 Less** · 4910 Huntington Dr S

157

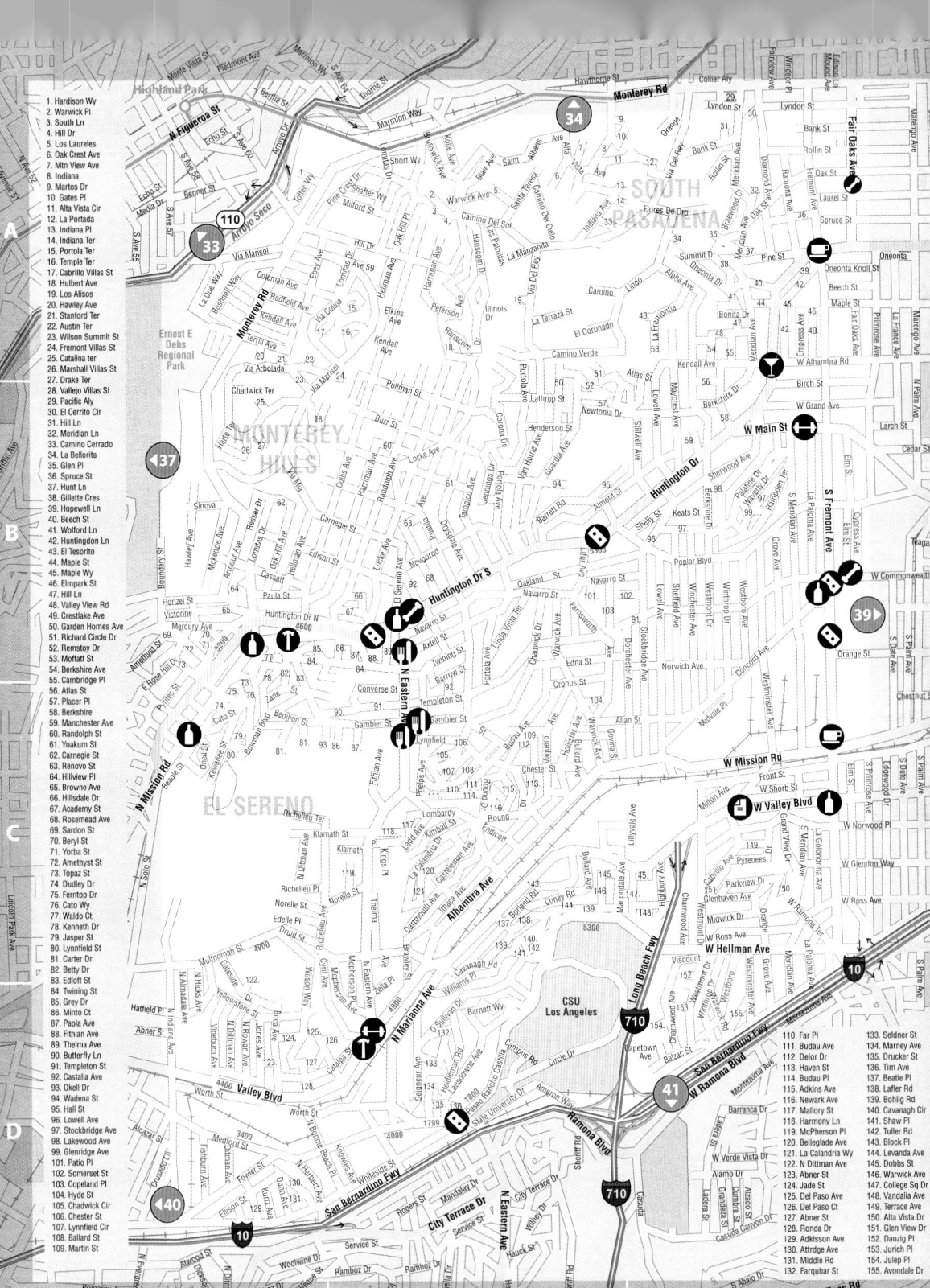

SOUTH
PASADENA

MONTEREY
HILLS

Ernest E
Debs Regional
Park

EL SERENO

CSU
Los Angeles

Monterey Rd

Huntington Dr

Huntington Dr S

W Main St

W Mission Rd

W Valley Blvd

W Hellman Ave

W Ramona Blvd

San Bernardino Fwy

Valley Blvd

Alhambra Ave

Ramona Blvd

Monterey Pass Rd

N Figueroa St

Monterey Rd

N Mission Rd

N Eastern Ave

Fair Oaks Ave

S Fremont Ave

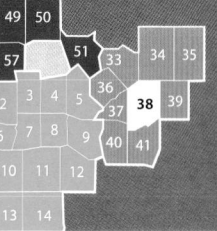
Among the eclectic group of alumni who have passed through the gates of Cal State University Los Angeles (CSULA) are Los Angeles District Attorney Steve Cooley, Billie Jean King, and Joseph Wambaugh. Check out a live performance at the fabulous Luckman Center.

Coffee

- **Starbucks** · 1190 S Fremont Ave
- **Starbucks** · 1318 Huntington Dr

Copy Centers

- **Sharp Image Copier** · 2960 W Valley Blvd · 626-458-8000

Gyms

- **Curves** · 2718 W Main St · 626-284-2744
- **Curves** · 4815 Valley Blvd · 323-223-4348

Hardware Stores

- **Newland True Value** · 4938 Huntington Dr S · 323-227-1933
- **Valley Hardware** · 4757 Valley Blvd · 323-222-9670

Liquor Stores

- **Mickey's Liquor** · 4904 Huntington Dr S
- **Nate's Friendly Liquor** · 4412 Huntington Dr S
- **Pete's Liquor** · 2639 W Valley Blvd
- **Tropic Liquor** · 210 N Huntington Dr

Nightlife

- **The Derby** · 233 Huntington Dr · 626-447-8174

Pet Stores

- **David's Pet Shop** · 4913 Huntington Dr N · 323-226-9007
- **Petsmart** · 2568 W Commonwealth Ave · 626-284-3390

Restaurants

- **Tamale Man** · 3320 N Eastern Ave · 323-221-5954
- **Taqueria Gudalupana** · 3100 N Eastern Blvd · 323-441-1036

Video Rental

- **Blockbuster** · 2581 W Commonwealth Ave · 626-576-4550
- **Legend Entertainment** · 4960 Huntington Dr S · 323-225-9833
- **Neighborhood Video of Alhambra** · 2146 S Fremont Ave · 626-282-6146
- **Rene's Video** · 5380 Huntington Dr S · 323-221-7771
- **Videostory** · 1689 N Eastern Ave · 323-262-8850

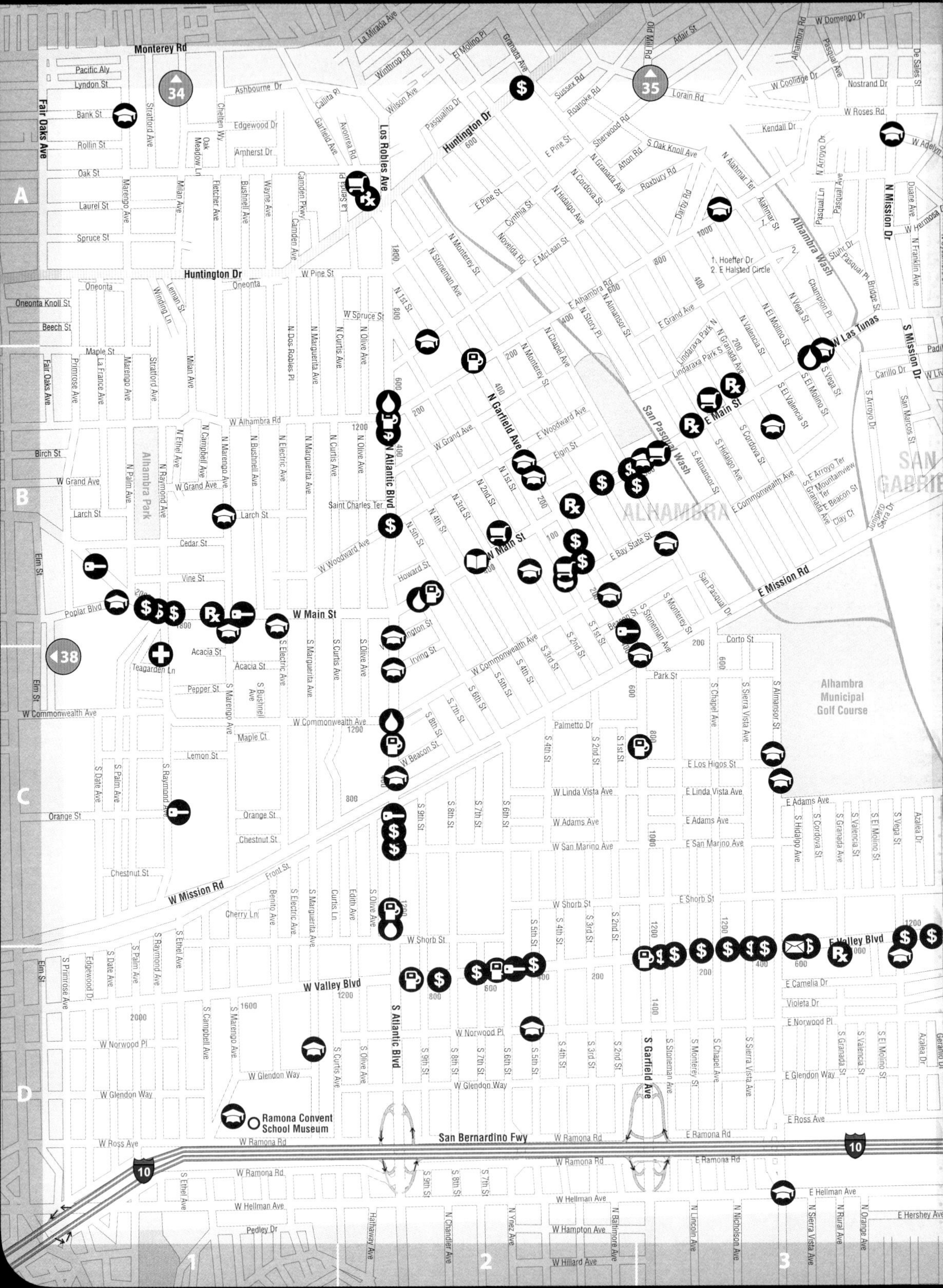
N
Monterey Rd
Pacific Aly
Lyndon St
Bank St
Rollin St
Oak St
Laurel St
Spruce St
Fair Oaks Ave
34
35
Ashbourne Dr
Edgewood Dr
Amherst Dr
Huntington Dr
Los Robles Ave
La Mirada Ave
Winthrop Rd
El Molino Pl
Granada Ave
Old Mill Rd
Adair St
Sussex Rd
Roanoke Rd
Lorain Rd
Sherwood Rd
Afton Rd
S Oak Knoll Ave
Roxbury Rd
Darby Rd
N Alhambra Ter
Alhambra Wash
W Domengo Dr
W Coolidge Dr
Nostrand Dr
W Roses Rd
Kendall Dr
W Adelyn
N Mission Dr
Pasqual Ave
De Sales St
Hoeffer Dr
E Halsted Circle
Stuhr Dr
Champion Pl
Bridge St
N Franklin Ave
W Las Tunas
S Mission Dr
Carillo Dr
Oneonta
Oneonta Knoll St
Beech St
Maple St
W Spruce St
W Pine St
Birch St
W Grand Ave
Larch St
Cedar St
Vine St
Poplar Blvd
W Main St
Acacia St
Teagarden Ln
Pepper St
W Commonwealth Ave
Maple Ct
Lemon St
Orange St
Chestnut St
W Mission Rd
Front St
Cherry Ln
W Shorb St
W Valley Blvd
W Norwood Pl
W Glendon Way
W Ross Ave
W Ramona Rd
W Hellman Ave
Pedley Dr
Alhambra Park
W Alhambra Rd
N Atlantic Blvd
S Atlantic Blvd
Saint Charles Ter
W Woodward Ave
Howard St
Irving St
W Beacon St
N Garfield Ave
S Garfield Ave
E Woodward Ave
Elgin St
W Main St
E Main St
San Pasqual Wash
E Bay State St
E Mission Rd
E Commonwealth Ave
San Pasqual Dr
ALHAMBRA
SAN GABRIEL
Corto St
Park St
Palmetto Dr
E Los Higos St
W Linda Vista Ave
E Linda Vista Ave
W Adams Ave
E Adams Ave
W San Marino Ave
E San Marino Ave
E Shorb St
E Valley Blvd
E Camelia Dr
Violeta Dr
E Norwood Pl
E Glendon Way
E Ross Ave
E Ramona Rd
E Hellman Ave
E Hershey Ave
W Hampton Ave
W Hilliard Ave
San Bernardino Fwy
10
38
Alhambra Municipal Golf Course
Ramona Convent School Museum
A
B
C
D
1
2
3

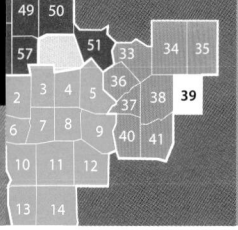
Alhambra is considered the "Gateway to the San Gabriel Valley." The city is essentially a subdivision, having once been part of a massive ranch belonging to Don Benito Wilson. The rest of Wilson's humble abode included Pasadena, South Pasadena, and San Marino.

$ Banks

- **Bank of America** · 160 E Main St
- **Bank of America** · 300 N Atlantic Blvd
- **Bank of America** · 444 E Valley Blvd
- **Bank of the West** · 100 S Garfield Ave
- **Bank of the West** · 1833 N Atlantic Blvd
- **Bank of the West** · 331 N Atlantic Blvd
- **Bank of the West** · 855 W Valley Blvd
- **California Bank & Trust** ·
  230 E Valley Blvd
- **Cathay** · 43 E Valley Blvd
- **Cathay** · 601 N Atlantic Blvd
- **Cathay** · 701 S Atlantic Blvd
- **Citibank** · 1 W Bay State St
- **East West** · 1881 W Main St
- **East West** · 403 W Valley Blvd
- **East West** · 805 Huntington Dr
- **Far East National** · 105 E Valley Blvd
- **Far East National** · 809 S Atlantic Blvd
- **International Bank of California** ·
  711 W Valley Blvd
- **Preferred** · 325 E Valley Blvd
- **United Commercial** · 1211 E Valley Blvd
- **Washington Mutual** · 401 E Valley Blvd
- **Wells Fargo** · 123 S Chapel Ave
- **Wells Fargo** · 1910 W Main St
- **Wells Fargo** · 345 E Main St
- **Wells Fargo** · 726 E Valley Blvd
- **World Savings & Loan** ·
  1300 E Valley Blvd

 Car Rental

- **Avis** · 330 S Garfield Ave
- **Budget** · 539 W Valley Blvd
- **Dollar** · 1601 W Main St
- **Enterprise** · 2201 W Main St
- **U-Haul** · 552 S Raymond Ave
- **U-Haul** · 657 S Atlantic Blvd

Car Washes

- **Alhambra Car Wash** · 707 W Main St
- **Atlantic Self-Serve Car Wash** ·
  1271 S Atlantic Blvd
- **Boulevard Hand Car Wash** ·
  389 S Atlantic Blvd
- **Butch's Beauty Shine** · 1200 E Main St
- **Monterey Park Car Wash** ·
  521 N Atlantic Blvd

Gas Stations

- **76** · 1201 S Atlantic Blvd
- **76** · 525 N Atlantic Blvd
- **76** · 601 W Valley Blvd
- **76** · 707 W Main St
- **76** · 848 S Garfield Ave
- **Chevron** · 300 S Atlantic Blvd
- **Exxon** · 600 N Garfield Ave
- **Mobil** · 1000 W Valley Blvd
- **Shell** · 1401 S Garfield Ave

Hospitals

- **Alhambra** · 100 S Raymond Ave

Landmarks

- **Ramona Convent School Museum** ·
  1701 W Ramona Rd

Libraries

- **Alhambra Library** · 410 W Main St ·
  626-570-5008
- **San Marino Public Library** ·
  1890 Huntington Dr · 626-300-0777

Pharmacies

- **CVS** · 816 E Main St · 626-293-5750
- **The Medicine Shoppe** ·
  1711 W Main St · 626-289-3190
- **Ralphs** · 1745 Garfield Ave ·
  626-799-2926
- **Rite-Aid** · 69 E Main St · 626-300-8049
- **Rite-Aid** · 920 E Valley Blvd ·
  626-281-8422
- **Sav-On** · 401 E Main St · 626-284-9490

Police

- **Alhambra Police Dept** · 211 S 1st St ·
  626-570-5107

Post Offices

- **US Post Office** · 1603 W Valley Blvd ·

Schools

- **Alhambra High** · 101 S 2nd St
- **All Souls** · 29 S Electric Ave
- **Calvin Coolidge Elementary** ·
  421 N Mission Dr
- **Century High** · 20 S Marengo Ave
- **Children Montessori Center** ·
  150 N Garfield Ave
- **Childtime Child Care** · 1418 S Vega St
- **Dr Sun Yatsen Chinese** ·
  225 S Atlantic Blvd
- **Emmaus Lutheran** · 840 S Almansor St
- **First Baptist Church Alhambra** ·
  101 S Atlantic Blvd
- **Garfield Elementary** ·
  110 W McLean St
- **Granada Elementary** ·
  100 S Granada Ave
- **Independence High** ·
  217 N Garfield Ave
- **Kumon Math & Reading Center** ·
  330 S Garfield Ave
- **Leeway** · 9 N Almansor Ave
- **Marengo Elementary** ·
  1400 Marengo Ave
- **Marguerita Elementary** ·
  1603 S Marguerita Ave
- **Mark Keppel High** · 501 E Hellman Ave
- **Martha Baldwin Elementary** ·
  900 S Almansor Ave
- **Oneonta Montessori** · 2221 Poplar Blvd
- **Options for Youth** · 1300 E Main St
- **Park Elementary** · 301 N Marengo Ave
- **Payke Gymnastics Academy** ·
  107 S Garfield Ave
- **Ramona Convent Secondary** ·
  1701 W Ramona Rd
- **Ramona Elementary** ·
  509 W Norwood Pl
- **St Therese** · 1106 E Alhambra Rd
- **Triumph Education Center** ·
  29 N Garfield Center
- **UCLA Education Center** ·
  210 E Main St
- **William Northrup Elementary** ·
  409 S Atlantic Blvd

Supermarkets

- **Ralphs** · 1745 Garfield Ave
- **Ralphs** · 345 E Main St
- **Smart & Final** · 725 E Main St
- **Super A Foods** · 300 W Main St

161

Map 39 · Alhambra

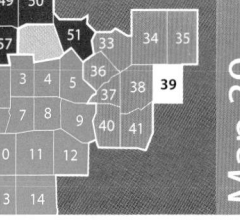

Map 39

Downtown Alhambra has undergone a major renovation. The former bedroom community has woken up to a thriving Main Street featuring theaters, eateries, clubs, and unique shopping. And of course, Fosselman's Ice Cream Parlor—the old staple of high-fat heaven—is still in business.

Coffee

- **Coffee Bean & Tea Leaf** · 9 E Main St
- **I Browse Coffee** · 11 W Main St
- **Lollicup** · 228 W Valley Blvd
- **Starbucks** · 1 East Valley Blvd
- **Starbucks** · 101 W Main St
- **Starbucks** · 141 N Atlantic Blvd
- **Valley Tea & Coffee** · 1101 W Valley Blvd

Copy Centers

- **Alhambra Blueprint** · 17 N 1st St · 626-289-4455
- **John-Henry Printing & Copying** · 1143 W Valley Blvd · 213-381-1301
- **Office Depot** · 1200 W Valley Blvd · 626-943-0900
- **Sal Aguilar Printing** · 718 S Date Ave · 626-570-6746
- **Staples** · 610 E Valley Blvd · 626-281-6900
- **UPS Store** · 560 W Main St · 626-284-8298

Farmer's Markets

- **Alhambra** · S Monterey St b/w E Main St & E Bay State St

Gyms

- **Curves** · 244 E Main St · 626-282-2999
- **LA Fitness Sports Clubs** · 412 E Main St · 626-299-5980

Hardware Stores

- **Home Depot** · 500 S Marengo Ave · 626-458-9800

Liquor Stores

- **Lee's Liquor** · 1152 W Valley Blvd
- **Marengo Liquor** · 1700 W Valley Blvd
- **Ocean Liquor** · 2005 Huntington Dr
- **Super Store** · 320 W Alhambra Rd

Movie Theaters

- **Edwards Atlantic Cinemas** · 700 W Main St · 626-458-8663
- **Edwards Renaissance Stadium 14** · 1 E Main St · 626-300-8312

Nightlife

- **Azul Bar and Nightclub** · 129 W Main St · 626-282-6320
- **California Brewing Co** · 100 W Main St · 626-943-8430
- **The Granada** · 17 S 1st St · 626-227-2572
- **Havana House** · 133 W Main St · 626-576-0547
- **Jay-dee Café** · 1843 W Main St · 626-281-6887
- **Lucky Baldwin's** · 17 S Raymond Ave · 626-795-0652
- **Nonya** · 61 N Raymond Ave · 626-583-8428

Pet Stores

- **Atlantic Aquarium** · 1419 S 9th St · 626-576-0028
- **McCormick's Pet Emporium** · 644 E Main St · 626-289-4393

Restaurants

- **Angelo's Italian Restaurant** · 1540 W Valley Blvd · 626-282-0153
- **Charlie's Trio Café** · 47 W Main St · 626-284-4943
- **Cuban Bistro** · 28 W Main St · 626-308-3350
- **Del Taco** · 1410 S Atlantic Blvd · 626-282-2891
- **El Ranchero Restaurant** · 511 S Garfield Ave · 626-281-3452
- **Fosselman's Ice Cream Parlor** · 1824 W Main St · 626-282-6533
- **The Hat** · 1 W Valley Blvd · 626-282-0140
- **Hiro Sushi Restaurant** · 120 S Monterey St · 626-282-3557
- **Indo Kitchen** · 5 N 4th St · 626-282-1676
- **Little London Fish & Chips** · 19 S Garfield Ave · 626-282-4477
- **Mahan Indian Restaurant** · 2 S Garfield Ave · 626-458-6299
- **Mission 261** · 261 S Mission St · 626-588-1666
- **MPV Seafood** · 1412 S Garfield Ave · 626-289-3018
- **OK Café** · 301 E Valley Blvd · 626-282-8899
- **Perfectly Sweet** · 126 W Main St · 626-282-9400
- **Pho 79** · 29 S Garfield Ave · 626-289-0239
- **Rick's Drive In & Out** · 132 W Main St · 626-576-8519
- **Sam Woo Barbeque** · 514 W Valley Blvd · 626-281-0038
- **Señor Fish** · 115 W Main St · 626-299-7550
- **Wahib's Middle East** · 910 E Main St · 626-576-1048
- **Yazmin Malaysian Restaurant** · 27 E Main St · 626-308-2036

Shopping

- **Mi Casita Rustica** · 135 West Main St · 626-576-8143
- **Penny Lane** · 110 W Main St · 626-457-5787
- **Shades of Blue** · 112 W Main St · 626-457-6255

Video Rental

- **Blockbuster** · 1334 W Valley Blvd · 626-289-3829
- **Hollywood Video** · 701 E Main St · 626-308-3427
- **Video 101** · 1100 W Commonwealth Ave · 626-308-3883

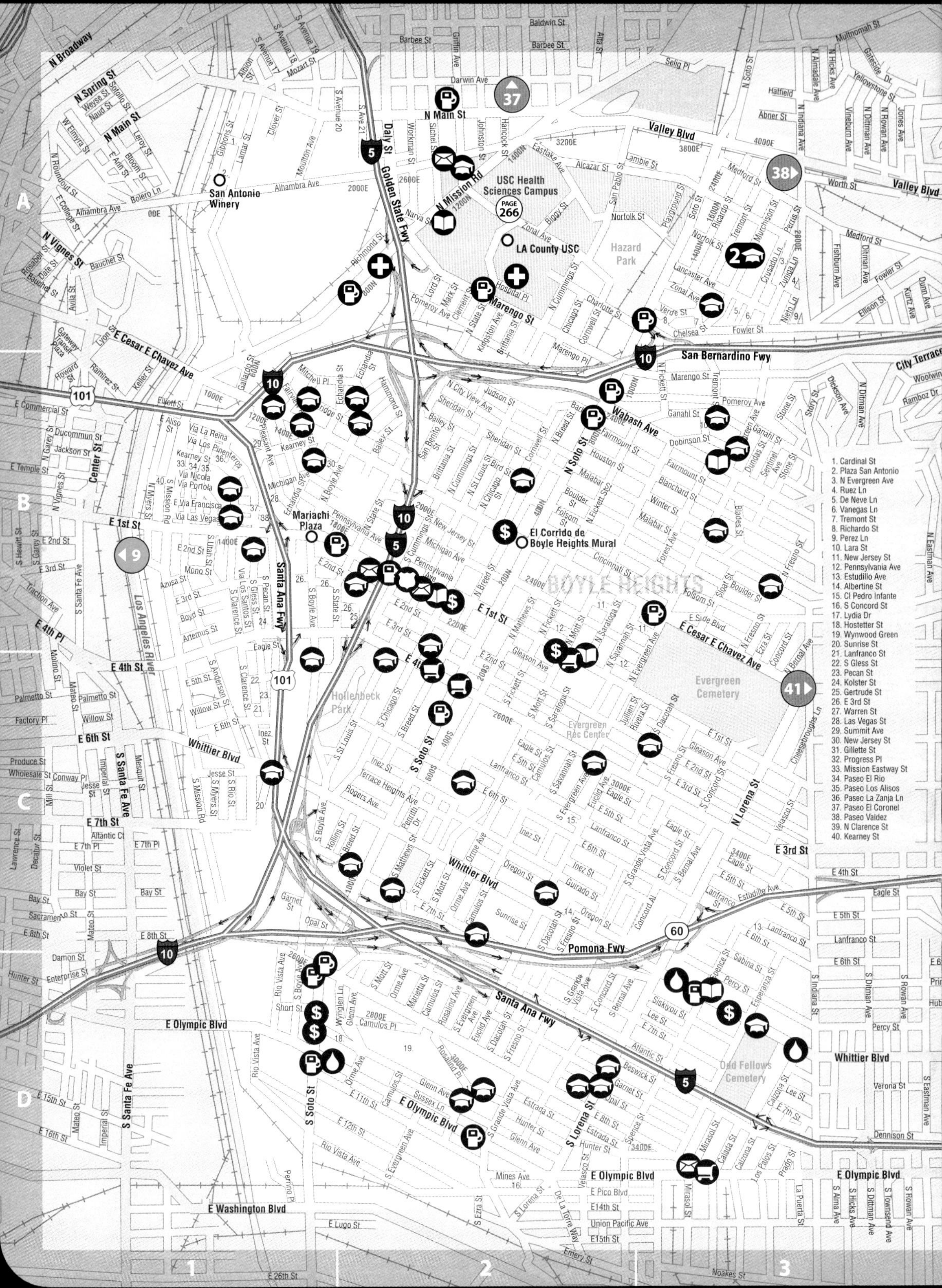

Map 40 · **Boyle Heights**

1. Cardinal St
2. Plaza San Antonio
3. N Evergreen Ave
4. Ruez Ln
5. De Neve Ln
6. Vanegas Ln
7. Tremont St
8. Richardo St
9. Perez Ln
10. Lara St
11. New Jersey St
12. Pennsylvania St
13. Estudillo Ave
14. Albertine St
15. Ct Pedro Infante
16. S. Concord St
17. Lydia Dr
18. Hostetter St
19. Wynwood Green
20. Sunrise St
21. Lanfranco St
22. S Gless St
23. Pecan St
24. Kolster St
25. Gertrude St
26. E 3rd St
27. Warren St
28. Las Vegas St
29. Summit Ave
30. New Jersey St
31. Gillette St
32. Progress Pl
33. Mission Eastway St
34. Paseo El Rio
35. Paseo Los Alisos
36. Paseo La Zanja Ln
37. Paseo El Coronel
38. Paseo Valdez
39. N Clarence St
40. Kearney St

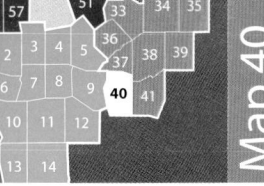
Mariachi Plaza is exactly what its name implies: a public gathering place where mariachis can show off their stuff and book future performances. This is the place to come if you're looking for authentic entertainment from the other Americas. Check out some of the murals near the corner of Cesar E Chavez Avenue and Soto Street, while soaking in the vibrant and social nature of the neighborhood.

$ Banks

- **Bank of America** · 1308 S Soto St
- **Bank of America** · 2305 E Cesar E Chavez Ave
- **Bank of America** · 3475 Whittier Blvd
- **US** · 2708 E 1st St
- **Washington Mutual** · 1350 S Soto St
- **Washington Mutual** · 2301 E 1st St

Car Washes

- **Bob's Hand Car Wash** · 3629 Whittier Blvd
- **Olympic Car Wash** · 2740 E Olympic Blvd
- **Tio Car Wash** · 3442 Whittier Blvd

Gas Stations

- **76** · 1171 S Soto St
- **76** · 1800 E 4th St
- **76** · 1848 Marengo St
- **Arco** · 3401 Whittier Blvd
- **Arco** · 401 S Soto St
- **Arco** · 918 N Soto St
- **Chevron** · 1101 N Mission Rd
- **Exxon** · 2740 E Olympic Blvd
- **Exxon** · 2925 E Cesar E Chavez Ave
- **Independent** · 2829 N Main St
- **Independent** · 3154 E Olympic Blvd
- **Mobil** · 1010 N Soto St
- **Mobil** · 1166 S Soto St
- **Shell** · 1203 N Soto St
- **Shell** · 1410 S Soto St
- **Shell** · 2005 E 4th St

Hospitals

- **LA County USC Medical Center** · 1200 N State St
- **LA County Women's** · 1240 N Mission Rd

Landmarks

- **El Corrido de Boyle Heights Mural** · 2336 E Cesar E Chavez Ave
- **LA County USC** · 1200 N State St
- **Mariachi Plaza** · Boyle Ave & 1st St
- **San Antonio Winery** · 737 Lamar St

Libraries

- **Benjamin Franklin Branch** · 2200 E 1st St · 323-263-6901
- **Hinomoto Library** · 129 N Saratoga St · 323-261-3300
- **Malabar Branch** · 2801 Wabash Ave · 323-263-1497
- **Nursing Library** · 1237 N Mission Rd · 323-226-6521
- **Robert Louis Stevenson Branch** · 803 Spence St · 323-268-4710

Police

- **Los Angeles Police Dept** · 2111 E 1st St · 213-485-2942

Post Offices

- **US Post Office** · 2016 E 1st St
- **US Post Office** · 2425 Alhambra Ave
- **US Post Office** · 3641 E 8th St

Schools

- **1st St Elementary** · 2820 E 1st St
- **2nd St Elementary** · 1942 E 2nd St
- **Assumption** · 3016 Winter St
- **Breed St Elementary** · 2226 E 3rd St
- **Bridge EEC** · 648 Echandia St
- **Bridge St Elementary** · 605 N Boyle Ave
- **Christopher Dena Elementary** · 1314 Dacotah St
- **Cristio Viene Ministries Chris** · 3607 Whittier Blvd
- **Dacotah St Combination** · 3142 Lydia Dr
- **Dolores Mission Elementary** · 170 S Gless St
- **East Los Angeles College** · 1301 E Cesar E Chavez Ave
- **Euclid Ave Elementary** · 806 Euclid Ave
- **Evergreen Ave Elementary** · 2730 Ganahl St
- **Evergreen EEC** · 1027 N Evergreen Ave
- **Hollenbeck Middle** · 2510 E 6th St
- **LAC+USC Employees Children's** · 1401 N Mission Rd
- **Lane Elementary** · 1500 Cesar E Chavez Ave
- **Light and Life** · 207 Dacotah St
- **Lorena St Elementary** · 1015 S Lorena St
- **Malabar St Elementary** · 3200 Malabar St
- **Murchison EEC** · 1537 Murchison St
- **Murchison St Elementary** · 1501 Murchison St
- **Oscar Dela Hoya Amino Charter High** · 1114 S Lorena St
- **Our Lady of the Rosary of Talp** · 411 S Evergreen Ave
- **Puente Charter** · 501 S Boyle Ave
- **Resurrection** · 3360 E Opal St
- **San Antonio de Padua** · 1500 Bridge St
- **Santa Isabel Elementary** · 2424 Whittier Blvd
- **Santa Teresita** · 2646 Zonal Ave
- **Sheridan St Elementary** · 416 Cornwell St
- **Soto St Elementary** · 1020 S Soto St
- **Soto Street Children's Center** · 2616 E 7th St
- **St Mary** · 416 S St Louis St
- **Sunrise Elementary** · 2821 E 7th St
- **Theodore Roosevelt Senior High** · 456 S Mathews St
- **Utah EEC** · 1367 Via Las Vegas
- **Utah St Elementary** · 255 N Clarence St
- **White Memorial Adventist** · 1605 New Jersey St

Supermarkets

- **Food 4 Less** · 2750 E 1st St
- **Food 4 Less** · 3654 E Olympic Blvd
- **Smart & Final** · 2308 E 4th St
- **Super A Foods** · 425 S Soto St

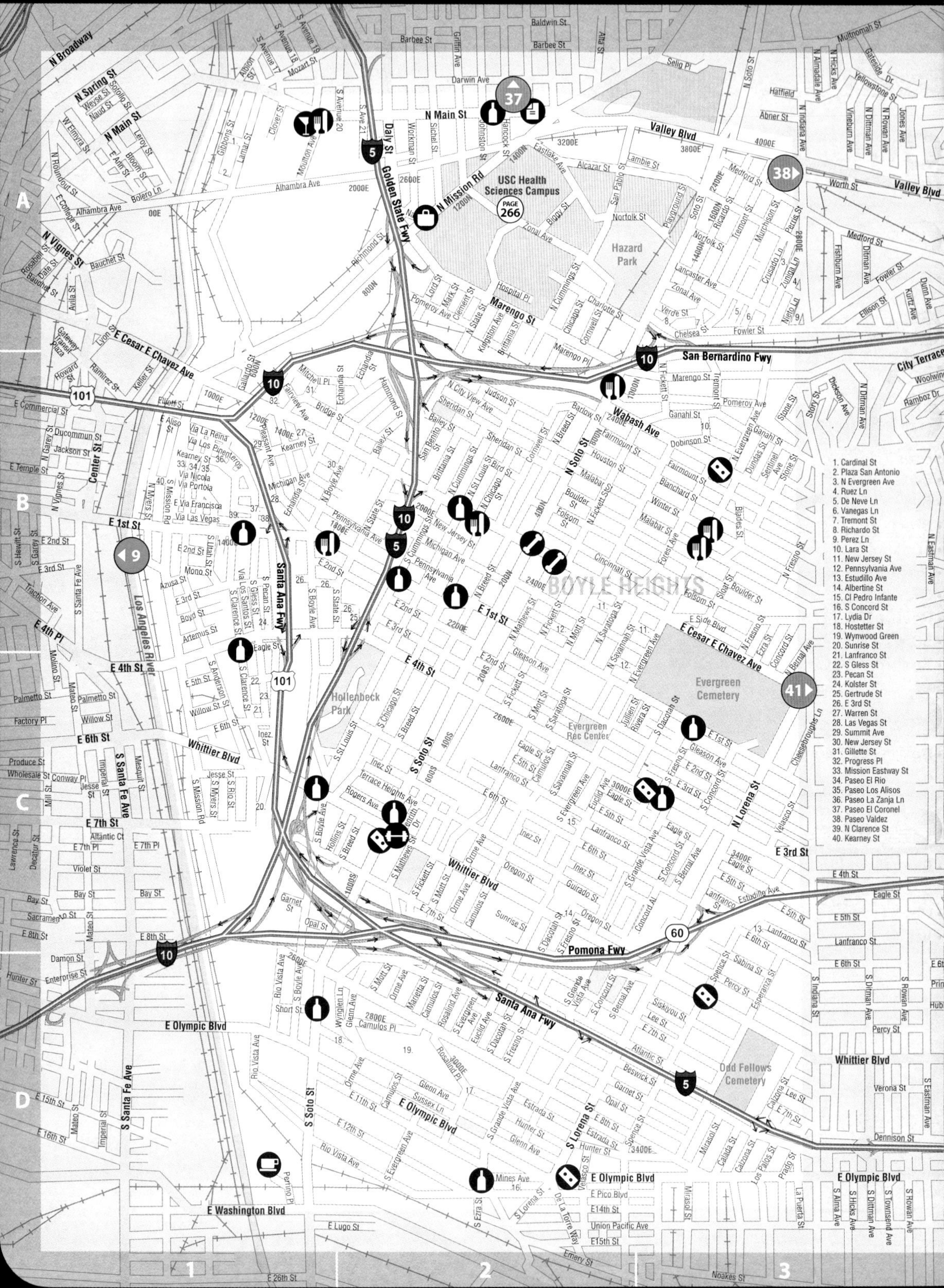

Map 40 · **Boyle Heights**

1. Cardinal St
2. Plaza San Antonio
3. N Evergreen Ave
4. Ruez Ln
5. De Neve Ln
6. Vanegas Ln
7. Tremont St
8. Richardo St
9. Perez Ln
10. Lara St
11. New Jersey St
12. Pennsylvania St
13. Estudillo Ave
14. Albertine St
15. Ol Pedro Infante
16. S Concord St
17. Lydia Dr
18. Hostetter St
19. Wynwood Green
20. Sunrise St
21. Lanfranco St
22. S Gless St
23. Pecan St
24. Kolster St
25. Gertrude St
26. E 3rd St
27. Warren St
28. Las Vegas St
29. Summit Ave
30. New Jersey St
31. Gillette St
32. Progress Pl
33. Mission Eastway St
34. Paseo El Rio
35. Paseo Los Alisos
36. Paseo La Zanja Ln
37. Paseo El Coronel
38. Paseo Valdez
39. N Clarence St
40. Kearney St

There may be no better area for Mexican food in all of LA. Be sure to visit some of the local bakeries for pan dulce, pop into any of the local taquerias for some soft tacos, and treat yourself to a sumptuous dinner at La Serenata de Garibaldi, which offers some of the finest fish dishes in California.

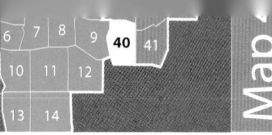

Coffee
- **Bradford Coffee** • 1607 Perrino Pl

Copy Centers
- **Davis Blue Print Co** • 3205 N Main St • 323-225-4703

Gyms
- **Curves** • 2421 Whittier Blvd • 323-263-1311

Liquor Stores
- **Amigos Liquor** • 3124 E 4th St
- **B&G Liquors** • 1529 E 1st St
- **Beverage Center** • 6033 Whittier Blvd
- **Brooklyn Liquor** • 2101 E Cesar E Chavez Ave
- **JT Ramirez Market** • 736 S Soto St
- **Major Liquor** • 2335 E 1st St
- **Ole Dad Davis Liquor** • 1462 S Grande Vista Ave
- **Regency Liquor** • 1260 S Soto St
- **S&M Liquor Store** • 3000 N Main St
- **Xochitl** • 3200 E 1st St

Nightlife
- **Barbara's at the Brewery Complex** • 620 Moulton Ave • 323-221-9204

Pet Stores
- **Elias Pet Shop** • 2500 E Cesar E Chavez Ave • 323-263-3138
- **Happy Pets** • 2011 E 1st St • 323-265-3614
- **VIP Pet Shop** • 305 N Soto St • 323-266-1166

Restaurants
- **Barbara's at the Brewery** • Brewery Art Complex, 620 Moulton Ave • 323-221-9204
- **Ciro's** • 705 N Evergreen St • 323-267-8637
- **El Tepeyac** • 812 N Evergreen Ave • 323-267-8668
- **La Parrilla** • 2126 E Cesar E Chavez Ave • 323-262-3434
- **La Serenata de Garibaldi** • 1842 E 1st St • 323-265-2887
- **Taqueria Guadalupana** • 1000 N Soto St • 323-441-1036

Shopping
- **Skeletons in the Closet** • 1104 N Mission Road • 323-343-0760

Video Rental
- **Joyce's Videos** • 2830 Wabash Ave • 323-261-5385
- **S&S Video (Spanish)** • 3358 E Olympic Blvd • 323-780-3981
- **Video Century** • 919 S Soto St • 323-262-5003

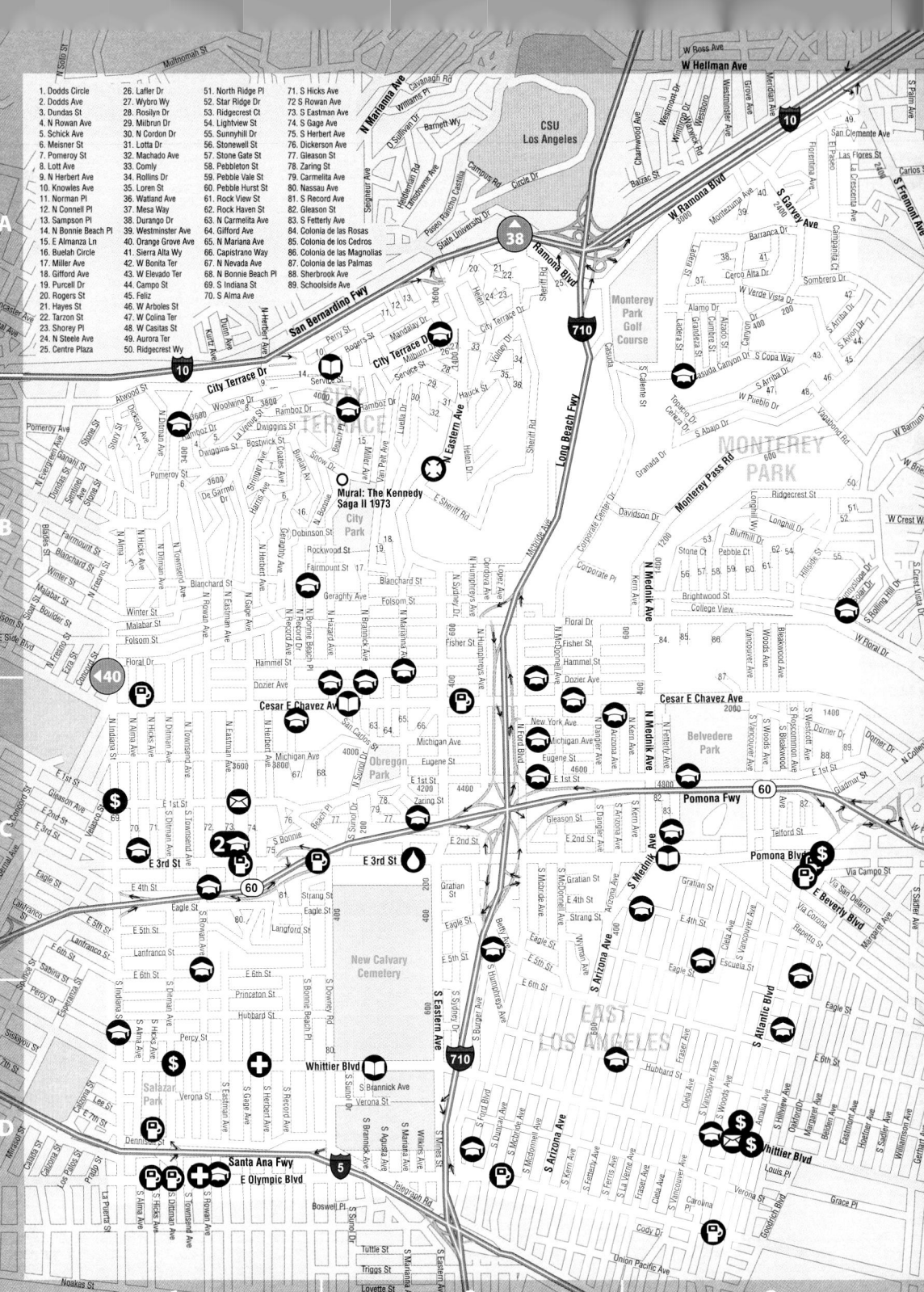

1. Dodds Circle
2. Dodds Ave
3. Dundas St
4. N Rowan Ave
5. Schick Ave
6. Meisner St
7. Pomeroy St
8. Lott Ave
9. N Herbert Ave
10. Knowles Ave
11. Norman Pl
12. N Connell Pl
13. Sampson Pl
14. N Bonnie Beach Pl
15. E Almanza Ln
16. Buelah Circle
17. Miller Ave
18. Gifford Ave
19. Purcell Dr
20. Rogers St
21. Hayes St
22. Tarzon St
23. Shorey Pl
24. N Steele Ave
25. Centre Plaza

26. Lafler Dr
27. Wybro Wy
28. Rosilyn Dr
29. Milbrun Dr
30. N Cordon Dr
31. Lotta Dr
32. Machado Ave
33. Comly
34. Rollins Dr
35. Loren St
36. Watland Ave
37. Mesa Way
38. Durango Dr
39. Westminster Ave
40. Orange Grove Ave
41. Sierra Alta Wy
42. W Bonita Ter
43. W Elevado Ter
44. Campo St
45. Feliz
46. W Arboles St
47. W Colina Ter
48. W Casitas St
49. Aurora Ter
50. Ridgecrest Wy

51. North Ridge Pl
52. Star Ridge Dr
53. Ridgecrest Ct
54. Lightview St
55. Sunnyhill Dr
56. Stonewall St
57. Stone Gate St
58. Pebbleton St
59. Pebble Vale St
60. Pebble Hurst St
61. Rock View St
62. Rock Haven St
63. N Carmelita Ave
64. Gifford Ave
65. N Mariana Ave
66. Capistrano Way
67. N Nevada Ave
68. N Bonnie Beach Pl
69. S Indiana St
70. S Alma Ave

71. S Hicks Ave
72. S Rowan Ave
73. S Eastman Ave
74. S Gage Ave
75. S Herbert Ave
76. S Dickerson Ave
77. Zaring St
78. Carmelita Ave
79. Nassau Ave
80. S Record Ave
81. S Record Ave
82. Gleason St
83. S Fetterly Ave
84. Colonia de las Rosas
85. Colonia de los Cedros
86. Colonia de las Magnolias
87. Colonia de las Palmas
88. Sherbrook Ave
89. Schoolside Ave

Since before the famed Zoot Suit Riots of 1943, East LA has been the heart of the Chicano population in Los Angeles and it remains so to this day. Tour the neighborhood for myriad colorful murals, home-style restaurants (whether home is Zacatecas or Michoacan), cultural centers, and unique art and icon shops along Whittier Boulevard.

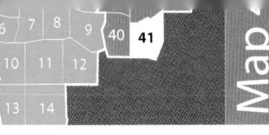

$ Banks

- **Bank of America** · 941 S Atlantic Blvd
- **Cathay** · 250 S Atlantic Blvd
- **Citibank** · 3479 E 1st St
- **Washington Mutual** · 5301 Whittier Blvd
- **Wells Fargo** · 3800 Whittier Blvd

Car Washes

- **Ricky's Hand Car Wash** · 4247 E 3rd St

Gas Stations

- **76** · 1141 S Ditman Ave
- **76** · 300 S Atlantic Blvd
- **76** · 3860 E 3rd St
- **76** · 3915 E Olympic Blvd
- **Arco** · 3541 E Cesar E Chavez Ave
- **Arco** · 3834 E 3rd St
- **Arco** · 3949 E Dennison Ave
- **Chevron** · 250 S Atlantic Blvd
- **Exxon** · 5050 E Olympic Blvd
- **Independent** · 4625 E Olympic Blvd
- **Mobil** · 301 S Atlantic Blvd
- **Shell** · 4357 E Cesar E Chavez Ave

Hospitals

- **East LA Doctors** · 4060 Whittier Blvd
- **Los Angeles Community** · 4081 E Olympic Blvd

Landmarks

- **Mural: The Kennedy Saga II 1973 (City Terrace Park)**
  · 1126 N Hazard Ave

Libraries

- **Anthony Quinn** · 3965 E Cesar E Chavez Ave ·
  323-264-7715
- **City Terrace** · 4025 City Terrace Dr · 323-261-0295
- **East Los Angeles** · 4801 E 3rd St · 323-264-0155
- **El Camino Real** · 4264 Whittier Blvd · 323-269-8102

Post Offices

- **US Post Office** · 3729 E 1st St
- **US Post Office** · 975 S Atlantic Blvd

Schools

- **4th St Elementary** · 420 Amalia Ave
- **Apostolic Christian Academy** · 4818 E Hubbard St
- **Belvedere EEC** · 221 S Eastman Ave
- **Belvedere Elementary** · 3724 E 1st St
- **Belvedere Middle** · 312 N Record Ave
- **Brightwood Elementary** · 1701 Brightwood St
- **Brooklyn Ave Elementary** · 4620 E Cesar E Chavez Ave
- **Brooklyn EEC** · 329 N Arizona Ave
- **City Terrace Elementary** · 4350 City Terrace Dr
- **Cornerstone Learning Academy** ·
  2421 W Jefferson Blvd
- **David Wark Griffith Middle** · 4765 E 4th St
- **De La Hoya Animo Senior High** · 5156 Whittier Blvd
- **Eastman Ave Elementary** · 4112 E Olympic Blvd
- **Ford Blvd Elementary** · 1112 S Ford Blvd
- **Garfield Community Adult** · 831 N Bonnie Beach Pl
- **Hammel EEC** · 452 N Marianna Ave
- **Hammel St Elementary** · 438 N Brannick Ave
- **Harrison St Elementary** · 3529 City Terrace Dr
- **Humphreys Ave Elementary** · 500 S Humphreys Ave
- **James A Garfield Senior High** · 5101 E 6th St
- **Marianna Ave Elementary** · 4215 Gleason St
- **Monterey Continuation** · 466 S Fraser St
- **Monterey Highlands Elementary** ·
  400 Casuda Canyon Dr
- **Morris K Hamasaki Elementary** · 4865 E 1st St
- **Our Lady of Guadalupe** · 436 N Hazard Ave
- **Our Lady of Lourdes** · 315 S Eastman Ave
- **Our Lady of Soledad** · 4545 Dozier St
- **Perez Special Ed Center** · 4540 Michigan Ave
- **Perez Special Education Center** · 4535 E 1st St
- **Ramona High** · 231 S Alma Ave
- **Robert F Kennedy Elementary** · 4010 E Ramboz Dr
- **Robert Louis Stevenson Middle** · 725 S Indiana St
- **Rowan Ave Elementary** · 600 S Rowan Ave
- **Soledad Enrichment Action** · 3763 E 4th St
- **St Alphonsus** · 552 Amalia Ave

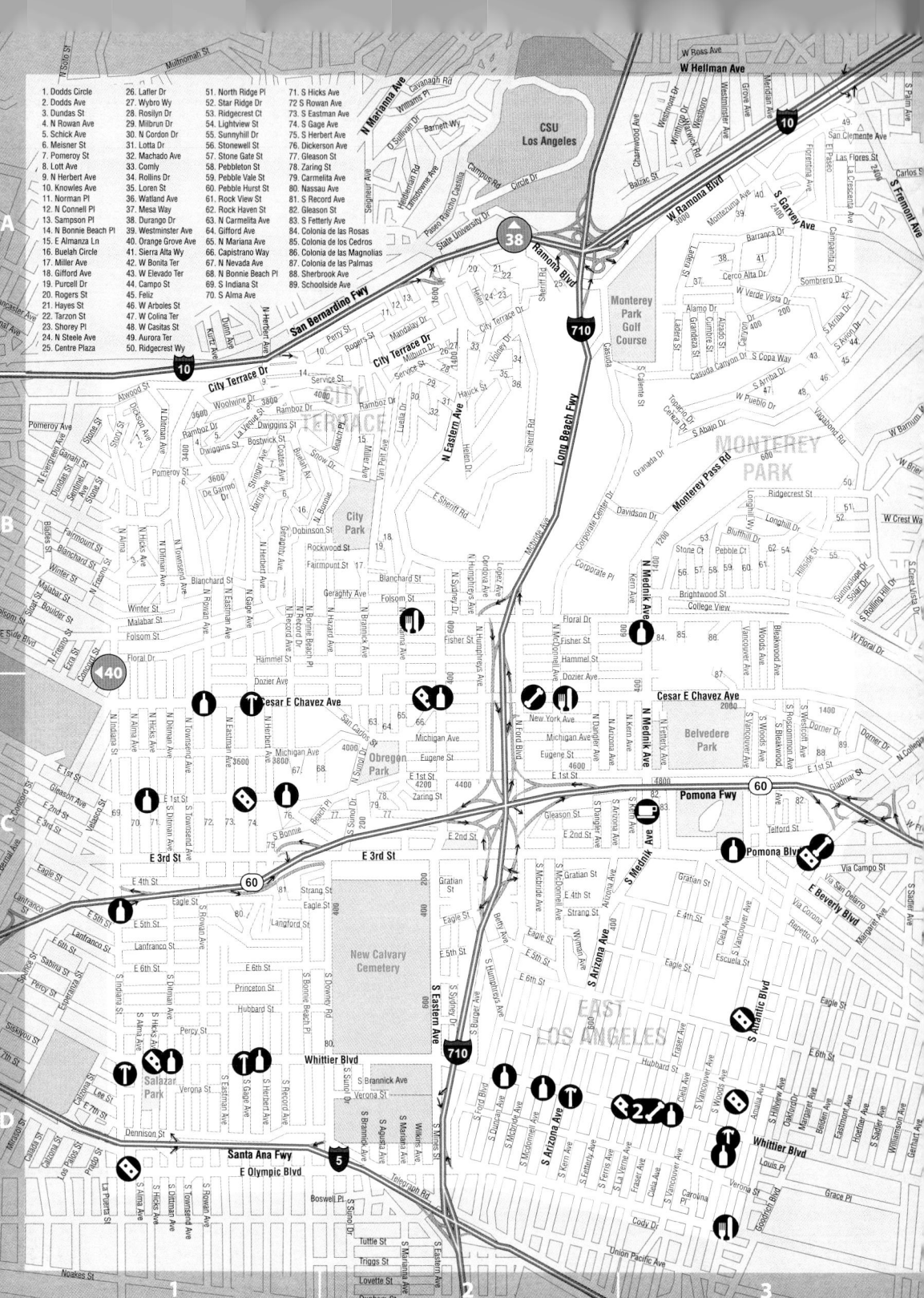

1. Dodds Circle
2. Dodds Ave
3. Dundas St
4. N Rowan Ave
5. Schick Ave
6. Meisner St
7. Pomeroy St
8. Lott Ave
9. N Herbert Ave
10. Knowles Ave
11. Norman Pl
12. N Connell Pl
13. Sampson Pl
14. N Bonnie Beach Pl
15. E Almanza Ln
16. Buelah Circle
17. Miller Ave
18. Gifford Ave
19. Purcell Dr
20. Rogers St
21. Hayes St
22. Tarzon St
23. Shorey Pl
24. N Steele Ave
25. Centre Plaza

26. Lafler Dr
27. Wybro Wy
28. Rosilyn Dr
29. Milbrun Dr
30. N Cordon Dr
31. Lotta Dr
32. Machado Ave
33. Comly
34. Rollins Dr
35. Loren St
36. Watland Ave
37. Mesa Way
38. Durango Dr
39. Westminster Ave
40. Orange Grove Ave
41. Sierra Alta Wy
42. W Bonita Ter
43. W Elevado Ter
44. Campo St
45. Feliz
46. W Arboles St
47. W Colina Ter
48. W Casitas St
49. Aurora Ter
50. Ridgecrest Wy

51. North Ridge Pl
52. Star Ridge Dr
53. Ridgecrest Ct
54. Lightview St
55. Sunnyhill Dr
56. Stonewell St
57. Stone Gate St
58. Pebbleton St
59. Pebble Vale St
60. Pebble Hurst St
61. Rock View St
62. Rock Haven St
63. N Carmelita Ave
64. Gifford Ave
65. N Nevada St
66. N Mariana Ave
67. Capistrano Way
68. N Bonnie Beach Pl
69. S Indiana St
70. S Alma Ave

71. S Hicks Ave
72. S Rowan Ave
73. S Eastman Ave
74. S Gage Ave
75. S Herbert Ave
76. Dickerson Ave
77. Gleason St
78. Zaring St
79. Carmelita Ave
80. Nassau Ave
81. S Record Ave
82. Gleason St
83. S Fetterly Ave
84. Colonia de las Rosas
85. Colonia de los Cedros
86. Colonia de las Magnolias
87. Colonia de las Palmas
88. Sherbrook St
89. Schoolside Ave

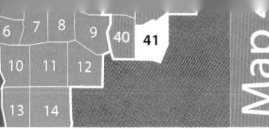

Feel like goin' fishin'? Look no further than the pond at Belvedere Park, located just north of Pomona Boulevard on Vancouver Avenue.

Coffee

• **Coffee Bean & Tea Leaf** • 209 S Mednik Ave

Hardware Stores

• **Brooklyn Hardware** • 3734 E Cesar E Chavez Ave • 323-264-6260
• **Eddie Dillen True Value** • 4615 Whittier Blvd • 323-269-3126
• **Indiana Home Supply** • 944 S Indiana St • 323-265-2008
• **Laguna Park Hardware** • 3948 Whittier Blvd • 323-263-1044
• **Marce's** • 1012 S Atlantic Blvd • 323-269-8375

Liquor Stores

• **Andy's Liquors** • 4312 E Cesar E Chavez Ave
• **Atlantic Liquors** • 1010 S Atlantic Blvd
• **Ayutla Liquor** • 3548 E 1st St
• **Eddie's Drive-In Liquor Store** • 5024 Whittier Blvd
• **Green Mill Liquor** • 3812 Whittier Blvd
• **John's Liquor** • 405 S Indiana St
• **Lim Fung Liquor** • 3563 E Cesar E Chavez Ave
• **Paco's Liquor** • 5048 E 3rd St
• **Pueblo Liquor** • 4600 Whittier Blvd
• **Safety Liquor** • 4635 Whittier Blvd
• **Salud Market** • 625 N Mednik Ave
• **Sam's Liquor** • 3984 Whittier Blvd
• **Victoria's Liquor** • 3882 E 1st St

Pet Stores

• **Bob's Tropical Fish** • 234 S Atlantic Blvd • 323-261-6675
• **Jesse's Pet Shop** • 3875 Whittier Blvd • 323-262-7947
• **Pet Shop Casa Galleros** • 4516 E Cesar E Chavez Ave • 323-780-5811

Restaurants

• **Juanito's** • 4214 E Floral Dr • 323-268-2365
• **Tamales Lilianas** • 4619 E Cesar E Chavez Ave • 323-780-7265
• **Tamayo** • 5300 E Olympic Blvd • 323-260-4700

Video Rental

• **20-20 Video** • 4975 Whittier Blvd • 323-266-0202
• **Ecumex Video** • 3757 E 1st St • 323-269-2972
• **JC Video Superstore** • 283 S Atlantic Blvd • 323-266-1055
• **Nancy's Video** • 715 1/2 S Atlantic Blvd • 323-268-5849
• **Sonia's Fashions & Video Rents** • 4308 E Cesar E Chavez Ave • 323-268-5785
• **Videoland** • 3857 Whittier Blvd • 323-266-2553
• **Videopolis** • 3918 E Olympic Blvd • 323-264-0366

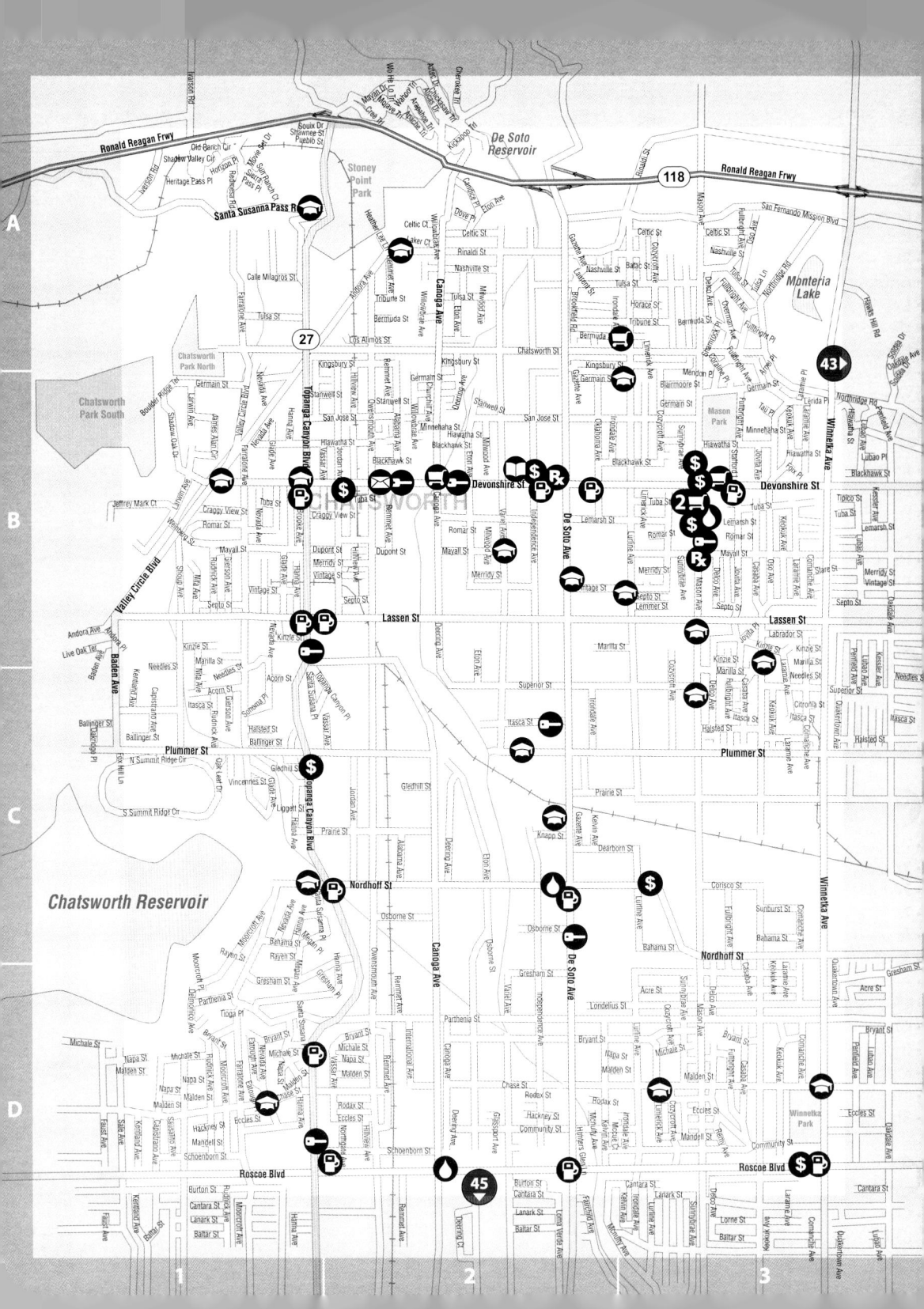

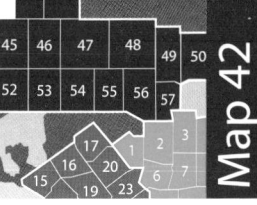
Chatsworth has long been the wilder fringe of the San Fernando Valley, flanked on the north and west by mounds of rock unlike any other geological feature in the Valley. The hills above Chatsworth were the site of rocket testing during World War II. This community on the northern rim of Los Angeles County occasionally sees an unsettling visitor from the wilds in the form of a bear settling into a neighborhood swimming pool for a nice soak.

$ Banks

- **Bank of America** · 20118 Roscoe Blvd
- **Bank of America** · 20699 Nordhoff St
- **Bank of America** · 21001 Devonshire St
- **Citibank** · 20520 Devonshire St
- **City National** · 9400 Topanga Canyon Blvd
- **Union** · 21821 Devonshire St
- **Washington Mutual** · 10370 Mason Ave
- **Wells Fargo** · 10230 Mason Ave

Car Rental

- **Enterprise** · 8364 Topanga Canyon Blvd
- **Enterprise** · 9800 Topanga Canyon Blvd
- **Hertz** · 10170 Mason Ave
- **Hertz** · 20944 Itasca St
- **Hertz** · 21510 Devonshire St
- **Penske Truck Rental** · 8921 De Soto Ave
- **U-Haul** · 21326 Devonshire Ave

Car Washes

- **Chatsworth Car Wash** · 10241 Mason Ave
- **M&S Professional Detail** · 20914 Nordhoff St
- **West Hills Car Wash** · 8301 Canoga Ave

Gas Stations

- **76** · 13455 Osborne St
- **76** · 20841 Devonshire St
- **76** · 21930 Lassen St
- **76** · 8308 De Soto Ave
- **Arco** · 10259 Topanga Canyon Blvd
- **Arco** · 20455 Devonshire St
- **Arco** · 9110 Topanga Canyon Blvd
- **Chevron** · 20904 Devonshire St
- **Chevron** · 21935 Roscoe Blvd
- **Independent** · 9061 De Soto Ave
- **Mobil** · 20101 Roscoe Blvd
- **Mobil** · 9906 Topanga Canyon Blvd
- **Shell** · 20850 Devonshire St

Libraries

- **Chatsworth Branch** · 21052 Devonshire St · 818-341-4276

Pharmacies

- **Rite-Aid** · 10120 Mason Ave · 818-349-7213
- **Walgreens** · 20901 Devonshire St · 818-341-4102

Post Offices

- **US Post Office** · 21606 Devonshire St

Schools

- **Aggeler Opportunity High** · 21050 Plummer St
- **Ark Christian Academy** · 9823 Mason Ave
- **Chatsworth Hills Academy** · 21523 Rinaldi St
- **Chatsworth Park Elementary** · 22005 Devonshire St
- **Chatsworth Senior High** · 10027 Lurline Ave
- **Elan International** · 22001 Nordhoff St
- **Ernest Lawrence Middle** · 10100 Variel Ave
- **Germain St Elementary** · 20730 Germain St
- **Leap HS** · 20920 Knapp St
- **Limerick Ave Elementary** · 8530 Limerick Ave
- **Meraj** · 11070 Old Santa Susana Pass Rd
- **Nevada Ave Elementary** · 22120 Chase St
- **Our Redeemer Lutheran** · 8520 Winnetka Ave
- **Santa Susana** · 22280 Devonshire St
- **St John Eudes Elementary** · 9925 Mason Ave
- **Stoney Point Continuation** · 10010 De Soto Ave
- **Superior St Elementary** · 9756 Oso Ave

Supermarkets

- **Ralphs** · 21431 Devonshire St
- **Smart & Final** · 10340 Mason Ave
- **Trader Joe's** · 10330 Mason Ave
- **Vons** · 18135 Sherman Wy
- **Vons** · 20440 Devonshire St

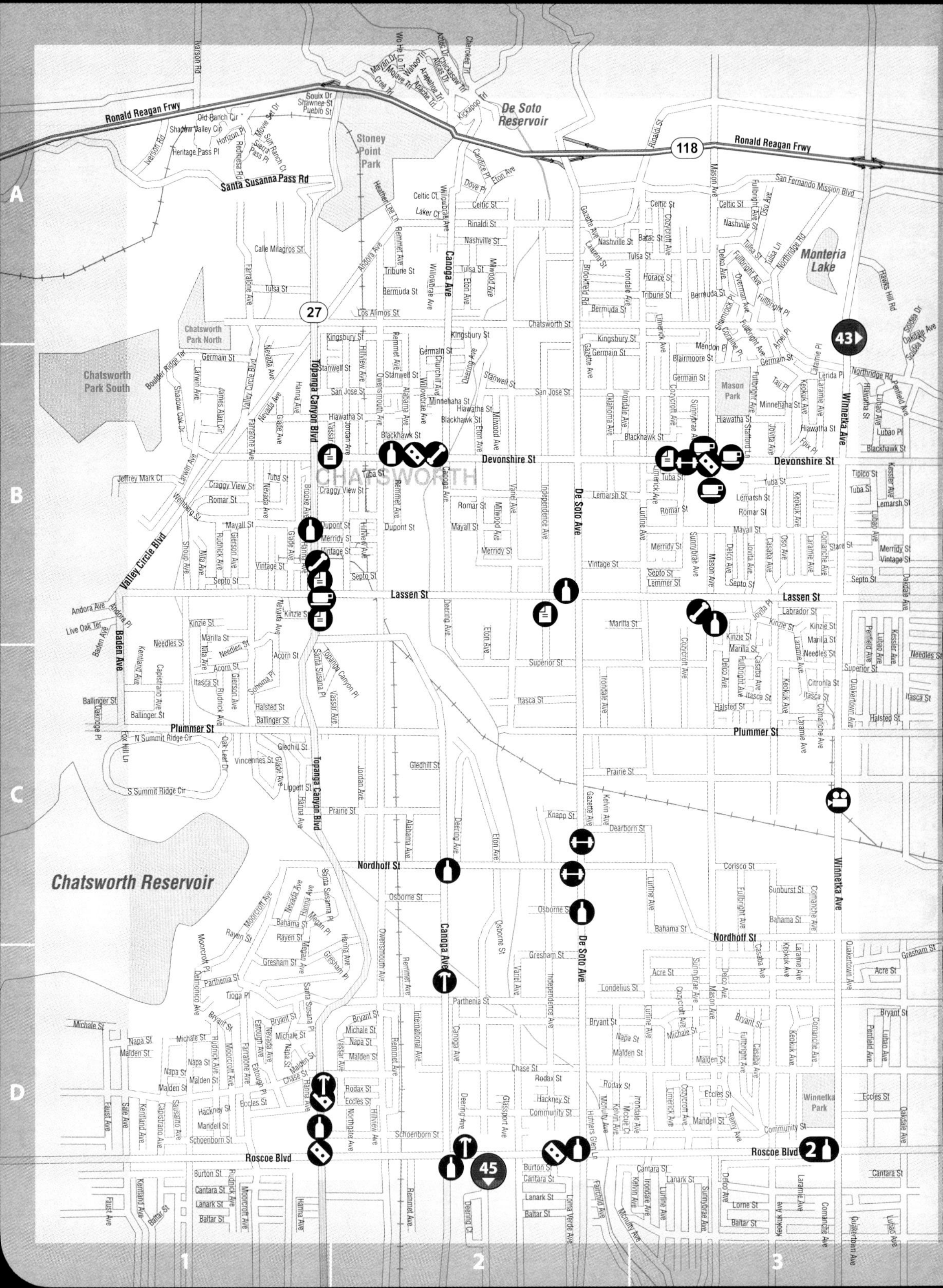

Map 42 · **Chatsworth**

N

Ronald Reagan Frwy

De Soto Reservoir

Ronald Reagan Frwy

118

Stoney Point Park

Santa Susanna Pass Rd

Monteria Lake

27

Chatsworth Park North

Chatsworth Park South

43

Chatsworth St

Devonshire St

Devonshire St

CHATSWORTH

Lassen St

Lassen St

Plummer St

Plummer St

Chatsworth Reservoir

Nordhoff St

Nordhoff St

Osborne St

45

Roscoe Blvd

Winnetka Park

21

Roscoe Blvd

To casual observers, Chatsworth may appear to be interchangeable with any other of LA's Valley suburbs. But sleepy little Chatsworth has one dubious distinction—it's the epicenter of the porn industry, home to countless production companies, video distributors, and the industry bible, *Adult Video News*. Or so we've been told. Aside from adult merchandise, shoppers can choose from an array of stores scattered about, but no central malls to speak of.

| 52 | 53 | 54 | 55 | 56 | 57 |

Map

Coffee

- **Lollicup** · 10224 Mason Ave
- **Starbucks** · 20516 Devonshire St
- **Starbucks** · 9935 Topanga Canyon Blvd
- **Starbucks (Vons)** · 20440 Devonshire St

Copy Centers

- **All Valley Printing** · 9721 Canoga Ave · 818-709-8734
- **Dot Copy & Print** · 21901 Devonshire St · 818-882-2232
- **Postnet** · 9909 Topanga Canyon Blvd · 818-349-1099
- **Unlimited Printing** · 9829 Independence Ave · 818-882-1212
- **UPS Store** · 20555 Devonshire St · 818-349-2584
- **UPS Store** · 9800 Topanga Canyon Blvd · 818-709-1858

Gyms

- **Bally Total Fitness** · 9143 De Soto Ave · 818-882-5912
- **Curves** · 20521 Devonshire St · 818-341-2643
- **Powerhouse Gym** · 20914 Nordhoff St · 818-775-0300

Hardware Stores

- **Home Depot** · 21218 Roscoe Blvd · 818-348-9400
- **Lowe's** · 8383 Topanga Canyon Blvd · 818-610-1960
- **Plumbing City True Value** · 8751 Canoga Ave · 818-341-1622

Liquor Stores

- **AMS Liquor** · 20930 Lassen St
- **Chatsworth Liquor** · 21615 Devonshire St
- **City Market** · 21400 Nordhoff St
- **De Soto Plaza Liquor** · 8935 De Soto Ave
- **Dorose Liquor** · 9857 Mason Ave
- **Duke of Bourbon** · 20908 Roscoe Blvd
- **Imperial Liquor** · 20152 Roscoe Blvd
- **Jon's Market** · 20151 Roscoe Blvd
- **Liquid Wines & Spirits** · 10100 Topanga Canyon Blvd
- **Papa Mac's Liquor** · 8219 Canoga Ave
- **Tally-Ho Liquor** · 8356 Topanga Canyon Blvd

Movie Theaters

- **Pacific Winnetka 21 Theaters** · 9201 Winnetka Ave · 818-501-5121

Pet Stores

- **Exotic Life Fish & Reptiles** · 9919 Topanga Canyon Blvd · 818-341-1007
- **Pacific Aquatics West** · 21413 Devonshire St · 818-886-6083
- **Reptile Depot** · 9859 Mason Ave · 818-576-1508

Video Rental

- **Blockbuster** · 20516 Devonshire St · 818-727-7166
- **Hollywood Video** · 8301 Topanga Canyon Blvd · 818-713-0591
- **M&K Video** · 20942 Roscoe Blvd · 818-773-9454
- **Star Light Video** · 8382 Topanga Canyon Blvd · 818-346-4348
- **Video House** · 21511 Devonshire St · 818-341-2280

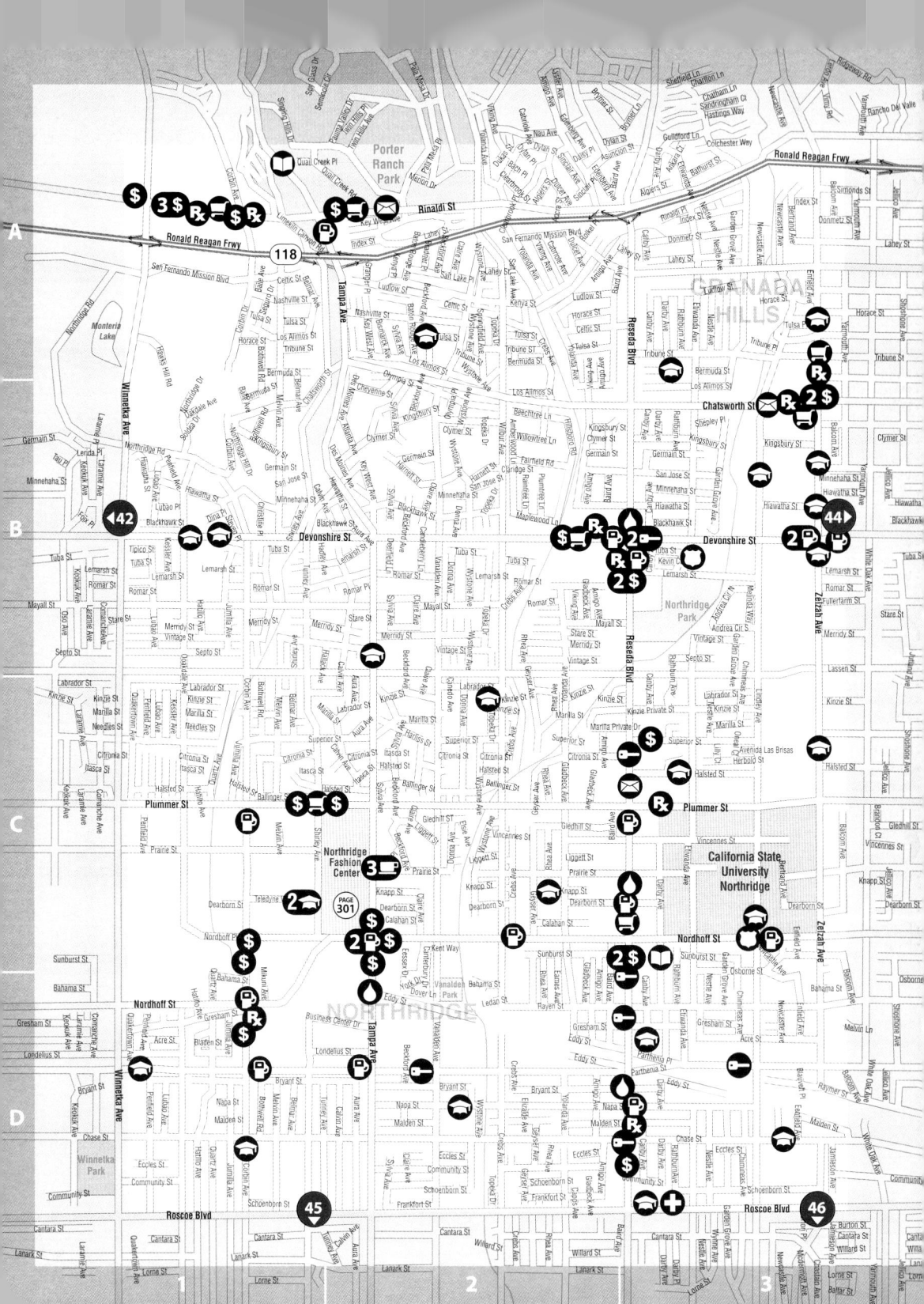

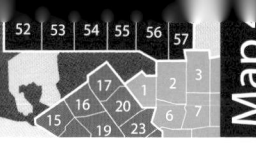
Granada Hills was named to honor its sister city across the pond, Granada, Spain, which shares many of the same climatic conditions as the San Fernando Valley. While little evidence remains, in the 1940s and 1950s, James Cagney owned a ranch here. Just south of Granada Hills is California State University Northridge, where some 33,000 students work toward undergraduate and graduate degrees.

$ Banks

- **Bank of America** · 10200 Reseda Blvd
- **Bank of America** · 19240 Nordhoff St
- **Bank of America** · 19789 Rinaldi St
- **Bank of the West** · 19953 Rinaldi St
- **California Center** · 10147 Reseda Blvd
- **California National** · 19450 Plummer St
- **Cathay** · 9045 Corbin Ave
- **Citibank** · 19350 Rinaldi Ave
- **Citibank** · 9051 Tampa Ave
- **Union** · 19781 Rinaldi St
- **Union** · 19921 Rinaldi St
- **Union** · 9110 Tampa Ave
- **Washington Mutual** · 17900 Chatsworth St
- **Washington Mutual** · 18601 Devonshire St
- **Washington Mutual** · 19500 Plummer St
- **Washington Mutual** · 19837 Rinaldi St
- **Washington Mutual** · 9055 Reseda Blvd
- **Washington Mutual** · 9111 Corbin Ave
- **Wells Fargo** · 18010 Chatsworth St
- **Wells Fargo** · 8812 Corbin Ave
- **Wilshire State** · 8401 Reseda Blvd
- **World Savings & Loan** · 9036 Reseda Blvd

Car Rental

- **Advantage Rent-a-Car** · 8834 Reseda Blvd
- **Avis** · 9545 Reseda Blvd
- **Dollar** · 18473 Devonshire St
- **Enterprise** · 8438 Reseda Blvd
- **Penny's Rent-a-Car** · 9003 Reseda Blvd
- **Ryder Truck Rental** · 19133 Parthenia St
- **Thrifty** · 18501 Devonshire St
- **U-Haul** · 18160 Parthenia

Car Washes

- **Buena Vista Self-Service Car Wash** · 8639 Reseda Blvd
- **Classic Car Wash** · 18470 Devonshire St
- **Cruisers Car Wash** · 8870 Tampa Ave
- **Northridge Car Wash** · 9240 Reseda Blvd

Gas Stations

- **76** · 11240 Tampa Ave
- **76** · 17919 Devonshire St
- **76** · 18050 Nordhoff St
- **76** · 19301 Nordhoff St
- **76** · 9455 Reseda Blvd
- **Arco** · 18473 Devonshire St
- **Arco** · 18855 Nordhoff St
- **Arco** · 8606 Reseda Blvd
- **Arco** · 9454 Corbin Ave
- **Chevron** · 19260 Nordhoff St
- **Chevron** · 8900 Corbin Ave
- **Exxon** · 9240 Reseda Blvd
- **Mobil** · 17836 Devonshire St
- **Mobil** · 18501 Devonshire St
- **Mobil** · 19655 Parthenia St
- **Shell** · 17915 Devonshire St
- **Shell** · 19301 Parthenia St

Hospitals

- **Northridge - Roscoe Campus** · 18300 Roscoe Blvd

Libraries

- **Northridge Branch** · 9051 Darby Ave · 818-886-3640
- **Porter Ranch Branch** · 11371 Tampa Ave · 818-360-5706

Rx Pharmacies

- **Longs Drugs** · 18020 Chatsworth St · 818-831-4152
- **Longs Drugs** · 19783 Rinaldi St · 818-368-6279
- **Ralphs** · 19781 Rinaldi St · 818-832-3156
- **Rite-Aid** · 10811 Zelzah Ave · 818-360-8411
- **Rite-Aid** · 18444 Plummer St · 818-349-6267
- **Sav-On (24 hrs)** · 10181 Reseda Blvd · 818-993-4125
- **Sav-On (Albertsons)** · 8530 Reseda Blvd · 818-341-7104
- **Target** · 8840 Corbin Ave · 818-739-0043
- **Walgreens (24 hrs)** · 18515 Devonshire St · 818-363-1288

Police

- **CSU Northridge Police Dept** · 18111 Nordhoff St · 818-677-2111
- **Los Angeles Police Dept** · 10250 Etiwanda Ave · 818-832-0633

Post Offices

- **US Post Office** · 18039 Chatsworth St
- **US Post Office** · 19300 Rinaldi St
- **US Post Office** · 9534 Reseda Blvd

Schools

- **Alfred Bernhard Nobel Middle** · 9950 Tampa Ave
- **Beckford Ave Elementary** · 19130 Tulsa St
- **Calahan St Elementary** · 18722 Knapp St
- **California State University Northridge** · 18111 Nordhoff St
- **Chaminade College Preparatory Middle** · 19800 Devonshire St
- **Child & Family Studies Center** · 18330 Halsted St
- **Chime Charter** · 20040 Parthenia St
- **Countryside Preparatory** · 8756 Canby Ave
- **Darby Ave Elementary** · 10818 Darby Ave
- **Egremont** · 19850 Devonshire St
- **First Lutheran Elementary** · 18355 Roscoe Blvd
- **First Presbyterian** · 10400 Zelzah St
- **Granada Hills Baptist Elementary** · 10949 Zelzah Ave
- **Granada Hills Charter High** · 10535 Zelzah Ave
- **Kidsville USA** · 8464 Corbin Ave
- **Kirk Douglas Continuation** · 10500 Lindley Ave
- **Napa St Elementary** · 19010 Napa St
- **Northpoint** · 9650 Zelzah Ave
- **Northridge Middle** · 17960 Chase St
- **Our Lady of Lourdes** · 18437 Superior St
- **Topeka Dr Elementary** · 9815 Topeka Dr

Supermarkets

- **Albertsons** · 18555 Devonshire St
- **Gelson's Supermarket** · 19500 Plummer St
- **Ralphs** · 10823 Zelzah Ave
- **Ralphs** · 18010 Chatsworth St
- **Ralphs** · 19781 Rinaldi St
- **Vons** · 9119 Reseda Blvd
- **Whole Foods Market** · 19340 Rinaldi Northridge

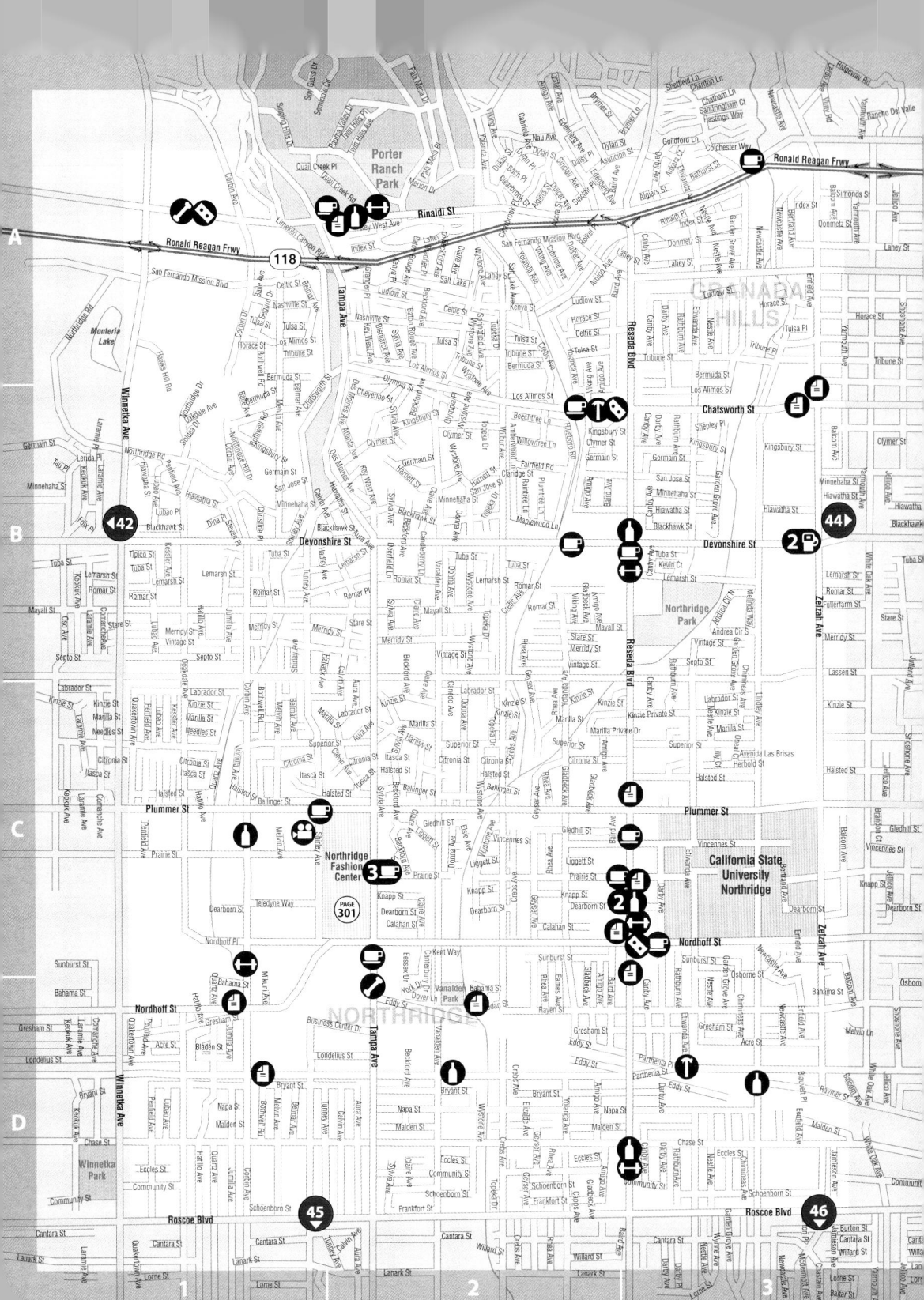

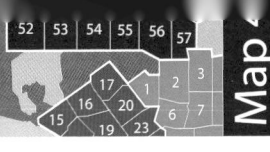

How do we know Northridge has made a full recovery from the eponymous earthquake of 1994? The Northridge Fashion Center, which suffered a partial collapse during the temblor, has emerged trendier than ever and now counts one of LA's few Apple Computer Stores among its tenants. Northridge boasts an outpost of almost every retail chain the marketplace offers. In short: wear comfortable shoes.

Coffee

- **Barclays Coffee & Tea** · 8976 Tampa Ave
- **Big Apple Deli Daily Grind** · 9301 Tampa Ave
- **Café Donut** · 19362 Rinaldi St
- **Coffee Bean & Tea Leaf** · 18705 Devonshire St
- **Gloria Jeans Coffee** · 9301 Tampa Ave
- **Kellys Coffee & Fudge** · 9301 Tampa Ave
- **Lollicup** · 18429 Nordhoff St
- **Muddhouse Coffee** · 9255 Reseda Blvd
- **Starbucks** · 10235 Reseda Blvd
- **Starbucks** · 18100 Chatsworth St
- **Starbucks** · 19500 Plummer St
- **Starbucks** · 19759 Rinaldi St
- **Starbucks** · 9420 Reseda Blvd

Copy Centers

- **ASAP Copy & Print** · 9250 Reseda Blvd · 818-700-7999
- **Kinko's** · 10725 Zelzah Ave · 818-366-3761
- **Minuteman Press** · 19709 Nordhoff St · 818-341-1003
- **Northridge Printing & Copy Center** · 9130 Reseda Blvd · 818-775-0255
- **Office Depot** · 19611 Parthenia St · 818-727-7090
- **Precision Instant Printing** · 8959 Reseda Blvd · 818-993-6010
- **Sun Star Copy** · 9514 Reseda Blvd · 818-718-6151
- **UPS Store** · 17939 Chatsworth St · 818-360-6144
- **UPS Store** · 19360 Rinaldi St · 818-360-0144

Gyms

- **Bally Total Fitness** · 8948 Corbin Ave · 818-885-7417
- **Bodies In Motion** · 10155 Reseda Blvd · 818-700-4900
- **Curves** · 19300 Rinaldi St · 818-368-3811
- **Curves** · 8458 Reseda Blvd · 818-773-7342
- **Gold's Gym** · 9150 B Reseda Blvd · 818-772-1400

Hardware Stores

- **Orchard Supply Hardware** · 18060 Chatsworth St · 818-363-7557
- **Stock Building Supply** · 18300 Parthenia St · 818-885-6322

Liquor Stores

- **International Liquor & Jr Market** · 9250 Reseda Blvd
- **Jolly Jug Liquor** · 8464 Reseda Blvd
- **King Arthur Liquors** · 9348 Corbin Ave
- **Lorenzo's Liquor** · 19061 Parthenia St
- **Northridge Liquor** · 9157 Reseda Blvd
- **Porter Plaza Liquor** · 19344 Rinaldi St
- **Village Liquor** · 8642 Lindley Ave
- **Wines & Spirits of the World** · 10318 Reseda Blvd

Movie Theaters

- **Pacific Fashion Center 10** · 9400 Shirley Ave · 818-501-5121

Pet Stores

- **Petco** · 19869 Rinaldi St · 818-368-3062
- **Petco** · 8800 Tampa Ave · 818-993-1871

Video Rental

- **Blockbuster** · 17945 Chatsworth St · 818-363-7094
- **Blockbuster** · 18497 Nordhoff Blvd · 818-700-9949
- **Blockbuster** · 19767 Rinaldi St · 818-363-9617

Map 44 • Mis

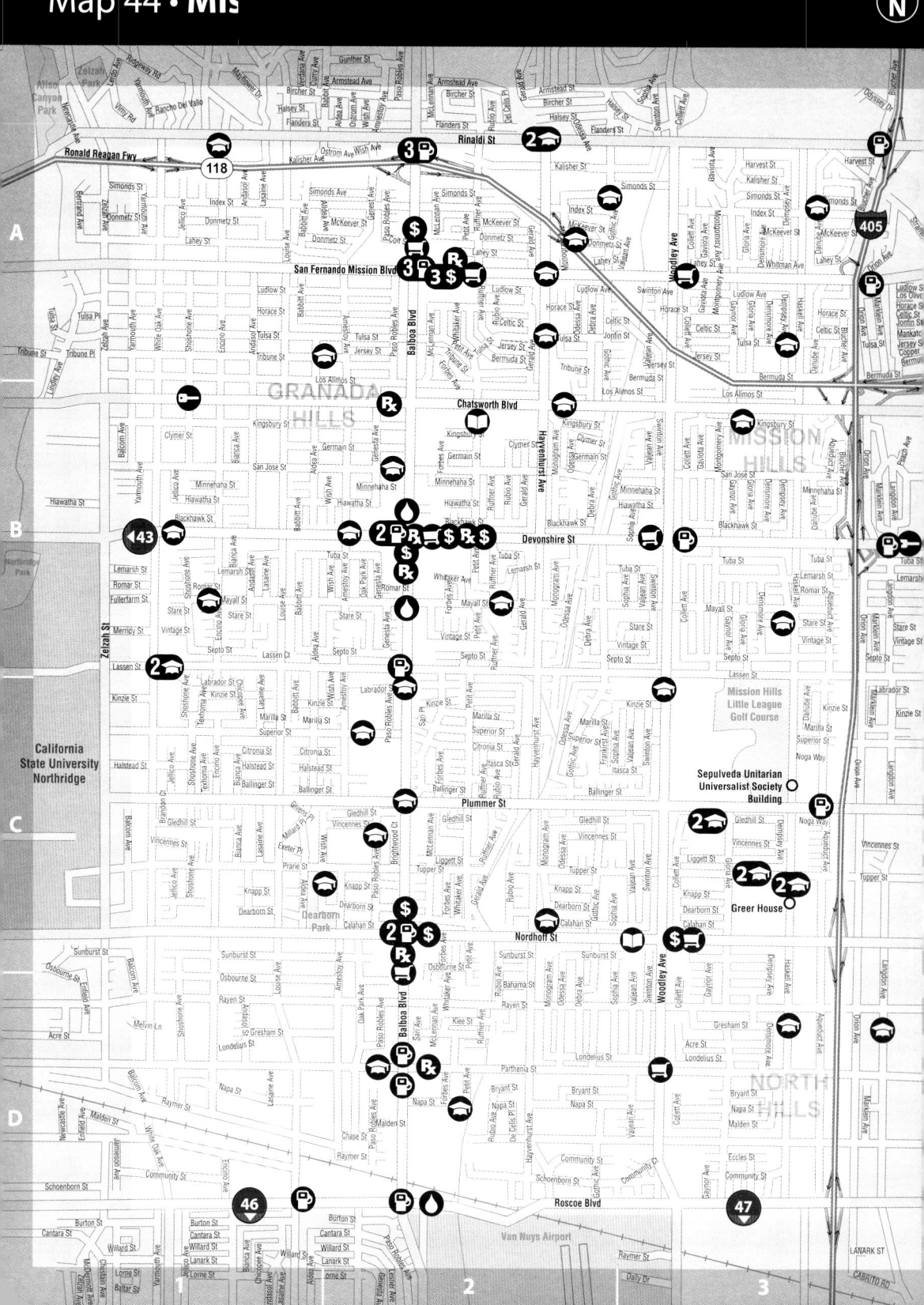

North Hills' Haskell Avenue is home to two of the community's most distinctive buildings—Frank Lloyd Wright Jr's Greer House, and the Sepulveda Unitarian Universalist Society Building, which locals have dubbed "the Onion" for its oddly bulb-like shape. Larger and dearer to the hearts of those more interested in brew than in architecture is the Budweiser Brewery on Roscoe. And for the more spiritually inclined, there is the Mission of San Fernando, for which Mission Hills is named.

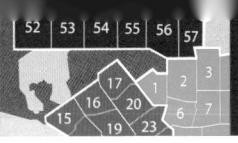

Map

$ Banks

- **Bank of America** · 16944 San Fernando Mission Blvd
- **Bank of America** · 8720 Balboa Blvd
- **Bank of the West** · 16900 Nordhoff St
- **Citibank** · 16152 Nordhoff St
- **Citibank** · 16800 Devonshire St
- **Downey Savings & Loan** · 16940 Devonshire St
- **Washington Mutual** · 11160 Balboa Blvd
- **Wells Fargo** · 10225 Balboa Blvd
- **Wells Fargo** · 16830 San Fernando Mission Blvd
- **World Savings & Loan** · 16844 San Fernando Mission Blvd

Car Rental

- **Enterprise** · 15439 Devonshire St
- **Enterprise** · 17602 Chatsworth St

Car Washes

- **Balboa Car Wash** · 10125 Balboa Blvd
- **Great American Carwash** · 16919 Roscoe Blvd
- **North Hills Car Wash** · 10315 Balboa Blvd

Gas Stations

- **76** · 11062 Balboa Blvd
- **76** · 17000 Rinaldi St
- **76** · 8658 Balboa Blvd
- **Arco** · 11454 Balboa Blvd
- **Arco** · 15508 Devonshire St
- **Arco** · 15544 San Fernando Mission Blvd
- **Arco** · 15705 Nordhoff St
- **Arco** · 17000 Devonshire St
- **Arco** · 8700 Balboa Blvd
- **Chevron** · 16156 Devonshire St
- **Chevron** · 17009 Rinaldi St
- **Chevron** · 17011 Devonshire St
- **Chevron** · 17255 Roscoe Blvd
- **Chevron** · 9106 Balboa Blvd
- **Mobil** · 16955 San Fernando Mission Blvd
- **Mobil** · 16958 Nordhoff St
- **Mobil** · 17011 Lassen St
- **Shell** · 11105 Balboa Blvd
- **Shell** · 15540 Rinaldi St
- **Shell** · 17000 Roscoe Blvd

o Landmarks

- **Greer House** · 9200 Haskell Ave
- **Sepulveda Unitarian Universalist Society Building** · 9550 Haskell Ave

Libraries

- **Granada Hills Branch** · 10640 Petit Ave · 818-368-5687
- **Mid-Valley Regional Branch Library** · 16244 Nordhoff St · 818-895-3650

Rx Pharmacies

- **The Medicine Shoppe** · 16915 Devonshire St · 818-366-8857
- **Ralphs** · 16940 Devonshire St · 818-831-4962
- **Rite-Aid** · 16930 Parthenia St · 818-895-2724
- **Sav-On** · 10208 Balboa Blvd · 818-363-8184
- **Sav-On** · 9038 Balboa Blvd · 818-891-0956
- **Vons** · 16830 San Fernando Mission Blvd · 818-831-5059
- **Walgreens** · 17010 Chatsworth St · 818-360-0496

Schools

- **Abraham Joshua Heschel** · 17701 Devonshire St
- **Andasol Ave Elementary** · 10126 Encino Ave
- **Balboa Gifted / High Ability Magnet Elementary** · 17020 Labrador St
- **Casa Montessori** · 17633 Lassen St
- **Centers of Learning** · 8854 Haskell Ave
- **Danube Ave Elementary** · 11220 Danube Ave
- **De La Salle Elementary** · 16535 Chatsworth St
- **Dearborn St Elementary** · 9240 Wish Ave
- **Einstein HS** · 15938 Tupper St
- **Elam EEC** · 15950 Tupper St
- **George K Porter Middle** · 15960 Kingsbury St
- **Gledhill EEC** · 16058 Gledhill St
- **Gledhill Elementary** · 16030 Gledhill St
- **Granada Elementary** · 17170 Tribune St
- **Haskell Elementary** · 15850 Tulsa St
- **Highland Hall Waldorf** · 17100 Superior St
- **Hillcrest Christian** · 17531 Rinaldi St
- **Imagine Academy** · 16601 Rinaldi St
- **Jane Addams Continuation** · 16341 Donmetz St

- **John F Kennedy High** · 11254 Gothic Ave
- **Knollwood Kindergarten** · 17034 Parthenia St
- **Langdon Elementary** · 8817 Langdon Ave
- **Los Angeles Baptist High** · 9825 Woodley Ave
- **Mayall Elementary** · 16701 Mayall St
- **Monroe SH** · 9229 Haskell Ave
- **N Valley Jewish Community Center** · 16601 Rinaldi St
- **Oliver Wendell Holmes Middle** · 9351 Paso Robles Ave
- **Our Savior First Lutheran** · 16603 San Fernando Mission Blvd
- **Parthenia Elementary** · 16825 Napa St
- **Patrick Henry Middle** · 17340 San Jose St
- **Pinecrest** · 17081 Devonshire St
- **San Fernando Valley Academy** · 17601 Lassen St
- **St Nicholas** · 9501 Balboa St
- **Tulsa St Elementary** · 10900 Hayvenhurst Ave
- **Valley Community Charter** · 16514 Nordhoff St
- **Valley Presbyterian** · 9240 Haskell Ave
- **Vintage Math/Science Magnet** · 15848 Stare St

Supermarkets

- **Albertsons** · 16201 San Fernando Mission Blvd
- **Albertsons** · 9022 Balboa Blvd
- **Food 4 Less** · 16208 Parthenia St
- **Ralphs** · 16940 Devonshire St
- **Smart & Final** · 16210 Devonshire St
- **Trader Joe's** · 11114 Balboa Blvd
- **Vons** · 16130 Nordhoff St
- **Vons** · 16830 San Fernando Mission Blvd

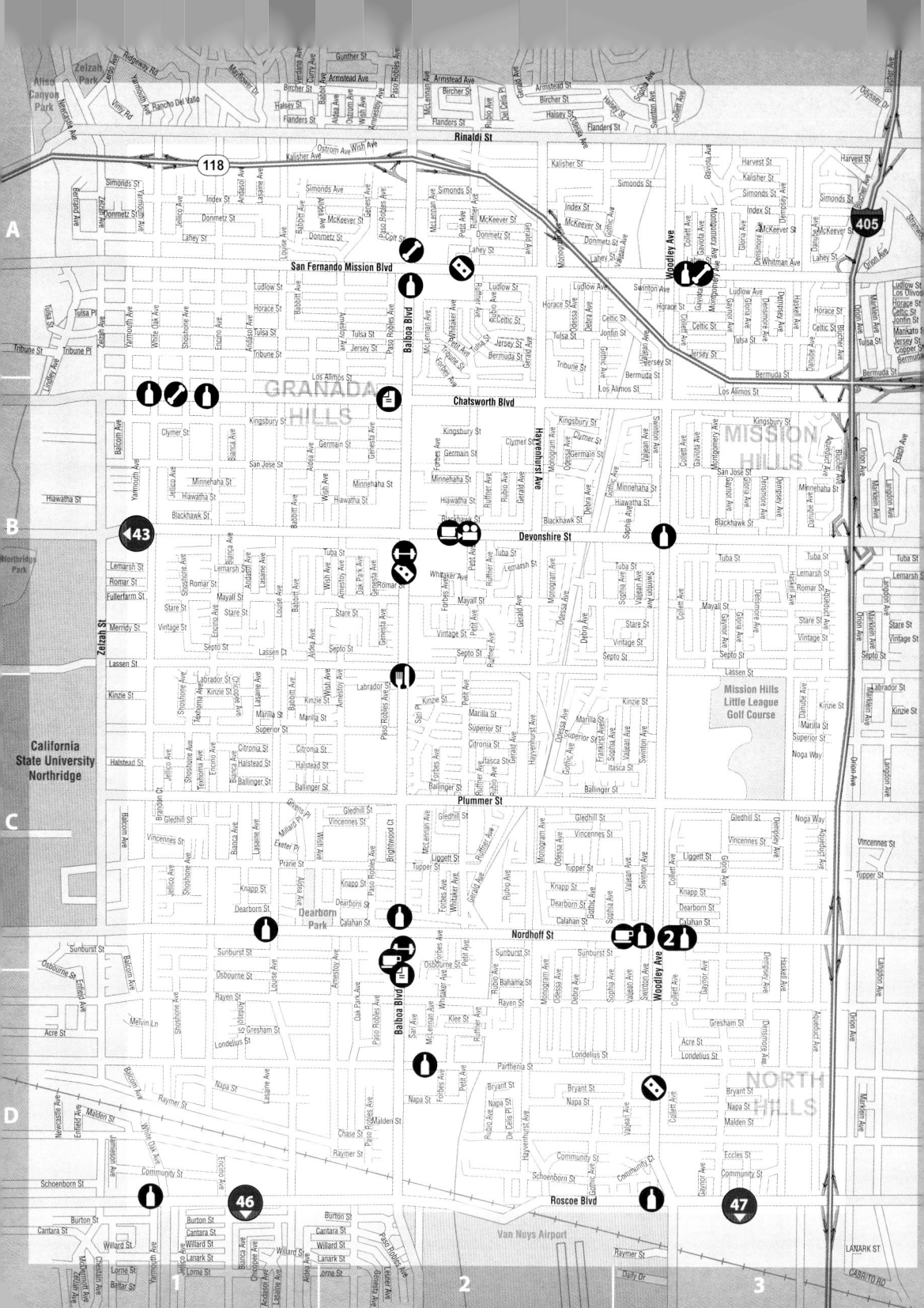

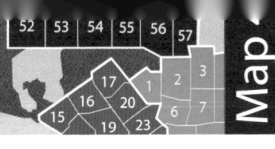

While shoppers must go a bit further afield for their power shopping trips, North Hills does boast a farmer's market each Saturday. Los Angeles Mission College serves the North Hills area, while the Andres Pico Adobe, located near the mission, preserves a slice of the area's history, circa 1830.

 Coffee

- **Perks** • 9028 Balboa Blvd
- **Starbucks** • 16222 Nordhoff St
- **Starbucks** • 16848 Devonshire Blvd

Copy Centers

- **Staples** • 17020 Chatsworth St • 818-831-8095
- **UPS Store** • 9018 Balboa Blvd • 818-894-4993

Gyms

- **Curves** • 9024 Balboa Ave • 818-920-7205
- **Northridge Athletic Club** • 10211 Balboa Blvd • 818-993-3696

Liquor Stores

- **A&A Liquor** • 17311 Roscoe Blvd
- **Alda Liquors** • 16151 Roscoe Blvd
- **Balboa Liquor** • 16904 Parthenia St
- **Cheers Liquor** • 16205 Devonshire St
- **Continental Liquor** • 9114 Balboa Blvd
- **Country Club Liquor & Delicatessen** • 11067 Balboa Blvd
- **Frank's Liquor & Deli** • 16210 Nordhoff St
- **Highland Liquor** • 16163 San Fernando Mason Blvd
- **Joe's Liquor** • 16151 Nordhoff St
- **Party Pantry** • 16145 Parthenia St
- **Safeway Liquor** • 17702 Chatsworth St
- **Stardust Liquor** • 17503 Chatsworth St
- **Wagon Wheel Liquor** • 17724 Roscoe Blvd

Movie Theaters

- **Mann Granada Hills 9** • 16830 Devonshire St • 818-363-0549

Pet Stores

- **All Pet Headquarters** • 11130 Balboa Blvd • 818-368-0269
- **Fumi's Tropical Fish** • 17606 Chatsworth St • 818-363-3710
- **Pat's Bird Connection** • 16156 San Fernando Mission Blvd • 818-363-8034

Restaurants

- **In-N-Out Burger** • 9858 Balboa Blvd • 800-786-1000

Video Rental

- **Hollywood Video** • 10207 Balboa Blvd • 818-700-8931
- **Hollywood Video** • 8635 Woodley Ave • 818-830-7489
- **Video Allstars** • 16848 San Fernando Mission Blvd • 818-360-6988

Map 45 · Car

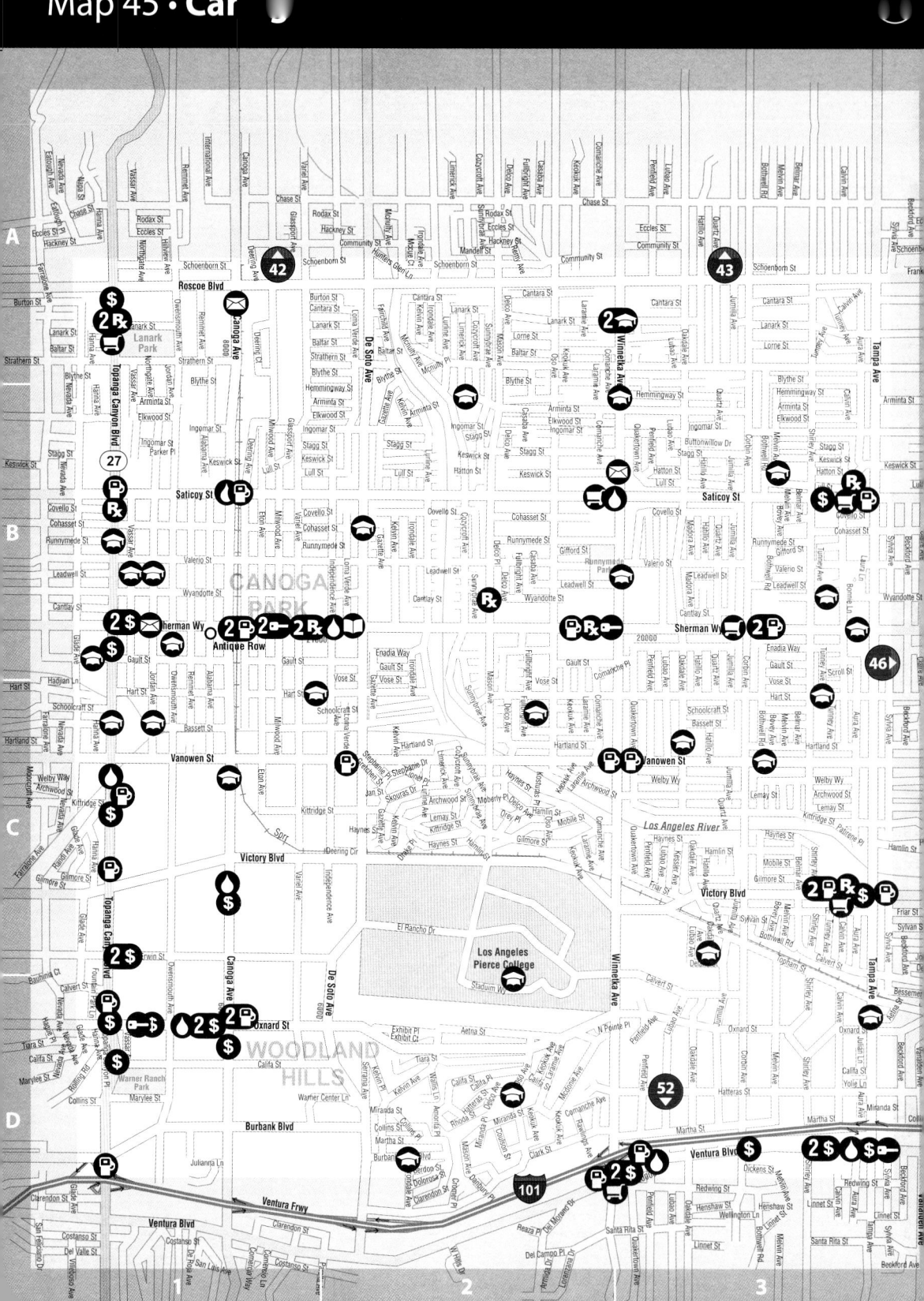

Warner Center, a sprawling industrial park that houses mega-corporations like Blue Cross and Northrop Grumman, sits on what used to be the ranch of movie legend Jack Warner. Though we lament the over-development of the area, at least it comes with air conditioning—Woodland Hills always seems to be five to ten degrees hotter than any other part of the San Fernando Valley.

Banks

- **Bank of the West** • 19858 Ventura Blvd
- **California National** • 19500 Ventura Blvd
- **California National** • 21919 Erwin St
- **Citibank** • 19255 Ventura Blvd
- **Citibank** • 21945 Erwin Sr
- **Citibank** • 7119 Topanga Canyon Blvd
- **City National** • 21800 Oxnard St
- **Comerica** • 21530 Oxnard St
- **Downey Savings & Loan** •
  20060 Ventura Blvd
- **First Bank & Trust** • 5939 Canoga Ave
- **First Bank & Trust** • 6300 Canoga Ave
- **Manufacturers** • 21550 Oxnard St
- **Union** • 5855 Topanga Canyon Blvd
- **Washington Mutual** • 21901 Sherman Wy
  • 19315 Saticoy St   • 19323 Victory Blvd
  • 19436 Ventura Blvd • 20040 Ventura Blvd
  • 6633 Topanga Canyon Blvd
- **Wells Fargo** • 21834 Sherman Wy
- **Wells Fargo** • 6001 Topanga Canyon Blvd
- **Wells Fargo** • 8201 Topanga Canyon Blvd

Car Rental

- **Budget** • 21339 Sherman Wy
- **Enterprise** • 19228 Ventura Blvd
- **Enterprise** • 21330 Sherman Wy
- **Hertz** • 21850 Oxnard St
- **Point Car Rental-Sales** •
  20112 Sherman Wy
- **Rent-It** • 7552 Canoga Ave

Car Washes

- **Boulevard Hand Car Wash** •
  20021 Ventura Blvd
- **Canoga Park Car Wash** •
  21004 Sherman Wy
- **Fiesta Car Wash** • 21403 Saticoy St
- **Marv's Car Wash** • 20238 Saticoy St
- **Red Carpet Car Wash** •
  6760 Topanga Canyon Blvd
- **Steve's Detailing & Hand Car Wash** •
  6326 Canoga Ave
- **Tarzana Car Wash** • 19348 Ventura Blvd
- **Topanga Car Wash** •
  6829 Topanga Canyon Blvd
- **Warner Center Auto Detail** •
  21600 Oxnard St

Gas Stations

- **76** • 20105 Vanowen St
- **76** • 5601 Topanga Canyon Blvd
- **76** • 6760 Topanga Canyon Blvd
- **Arco** • 20055 Vanowen St
- **Arco** • 20250 Sherman Wy
- **Arco** • 6000 Canoga Ave
- **Chevron** • 19156 Ventura Blvd
- **Chevron** • 19650 Sherman Wy
- **Chevron** • 19660 Sherman Wy
- **Chevron** • 21403 Sherman Wy
- **Chevron** • 5960 Canoga Ave
- **Chevron** • 6061 Topanga Canyon Blvd
- **Mobil** • 19248 Victory Blvd
- **Mobil** • 19304 Saticoy St
- **Mobil** • 20101 Ventura Blvd
- **Mobil** • 20910 Vanowen St
- **Mobil** • 21403 Saticoy St
- **Mobil** • 6423 Topanga Canyon Blvd
- **Shell** • 20021 Ventura Blvd
- **Shell** • 21404 Sherman Wy
- **Shell** • 22001 Vanowen St
- **Shell** • 7601 Topanga Canyon Blvd

Landmarks

- **Antique Row** • 21500 block of Sherman Wy

Libraries

- **Canoga Park Branch** • 20939 Sherman Wy • 818-887-0320
- **West Valley Regional** • 19036 Vanowen St • 818-345-9806

Pharmacies

- **The Medicine Shoppe** • 21115 Sherman Wy • 818-883-2321
- **Rite-Aid** • 20141 Sherman Wy • 818-888-0202
- **Rite-Aid** • 8230 Topanga Canyon Blvd • 818-348-5126
- **Sav-On** • 19353 Victory Blvd • 818-996-4814
- **Sav-On** • 21051 Sherman Wy • 818-348-3646
- **Sav-On** • 8201 Topanga Canyon Blvd • 818-340-3458
- **Sav-On (Albertsons)** • 19307 Saticoy St • 818-885-1525
- **Sav-On (Albertsons)** • 7224 Mason Ave • 818-346-8785
- **Walgreens** • 20505 Sherman Wy • 818-719-9144
- **Walgreens** • 7560 Topanga Canyon Blvd • 818-340-2454

Police

- **Los Angeles Police Dept** •
  19020 Vanowen St • 818-756-8542

Post Offices

- **US Post Office** • 21801 Sherman Wy
- **US Post Office** • 7655 Winnetka Ave
- **US Post Office** • 8201 Canoga Ave

Schools

- **Agbu Manoogian-Demirdjian** •
  6844 Oakdale Ave
- **Blythe St Elementary** • 18730 Blythe St
- **Buonora Child Development Center** •
  19325 Sherman Wy
- **Calvert St Elementary** • 19850 Delano St
- **Canoga Park EEC** • 7355 Vassar Ave
- **Canoga Park Elementary** •
  7438 Topanga Canyon Blvd
- **Canoga Park Lutheran** • 7357 Jordan Ave
- **Canoga Park Senior High** •
  6850 Topanga Canyon Blvd
- **Coutin** • 7119 Owensmouth Ave
- **Diane S Leichman Special Education Center** • 19034 Gault St
- **Francis Parkman Middle** •
  20800 Burbank Blvd
- **Fullbright Ave Elementary** •
  6940 Fullbright Ave
- **Green Gables** • 8217 Winnetka Ave
- **Grover Cleaveland High** •
  8140 Vanalden Ave
- **Hart St Elementary** • 21040 Hart St
- **John A Sutter Middle** •
  7330 Winnetka Ave
- **Kirk of the Valley** • 19620 Vanowen St
- **Los Angeles Pierce College** •
  6201 Winnetka Ave
- **Lycee International** • 5754 Oso Ave
- **Melvin Ave Elementary** • 7700 Melvin Ave
- **Multicultural Learning Center** •
  7510 De Soto Ave
- **Our Lady of the Valley** • 22041 Gault St
- **Owensmouth Continuation** •
  6921 Jordan Ave
- **Prime Preschool/Kindergarten** •
  6739 Corbin Ave
- **Shirley Ave Elementary** • 19452 Hart St
- **St Joseph the Worker** • 19812 Cantlay St
- **Sunny Brae Ave Elementary** •
  20620 Arminta St
- **Sven Lokrantz Special Education Center** • 19451 Wyandotte St
- **Vanalden Ave Elementary** •
  19019 Delano St
- **West Valley Christian Academy** •
  7911 Winnetka Ave
- **Winnetka Ave Elementary** •
  8240 Winnetka Ave
- **Woodcrest** • 6043 Tampa Ave
- **Wooden HS** • 18741 Elkwood St

Supermarkets

- **Albertsons** • 19307 Saticoy St
- **Albertsons** • 7224 Mason Ave
- **Food 4 Less** • 20155 Saticoy St
- **Ralphs** • 20060 Ventura Blvd
- **Smart & Final** • 19718 Sherman Wy
- **Vons** • 19333 Victory Blvd
- **Vons** • 8201 Topanga Canyon Blvd

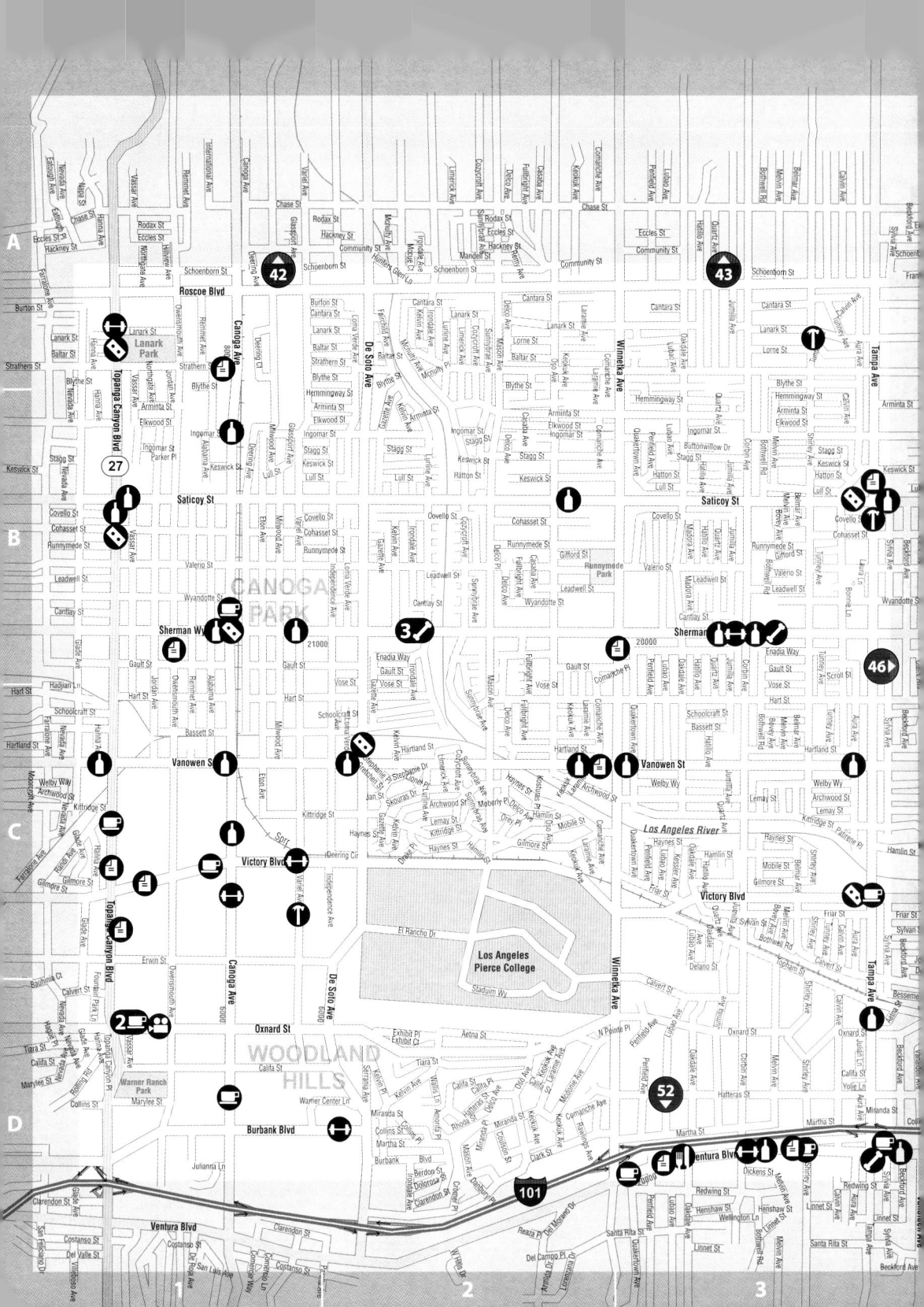

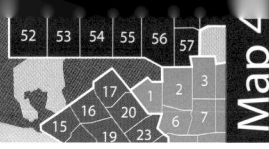

Map 4

The Promenade at Woodland Hills, on Topanga Canyon, is a shopper's, diner's, and moviegoer's paradise. The 21500 block of Sherman Way is the unlikely home to Canoga Park's Antique Row, where vintage furniture and jewelry aficionados can browse while escaping the higher prices found in hipper neighborhoods like West Hollywood or Santa Monica.

Coffee

- **Coffee Bean & Tea Leaf** · 21801 Oxnard St
- **Coffee Bean & Tea Leaf** · 5780 Canoga Ave
- **Coffee Junction** · 19221 Ventura Blvd
- **Rocky Roaster** · 7239 Canoga Ave
- **Starbucks** · 19313 Victory Blvd
- **Starbucks** · 19522 Ventura Blvd
- **Starbucks** · 20054 Ventura Blvd
- **Starbucks** · 21504 Victory Blvd
- **Starbucks** · 6600 Topanga Canyon Blvd
- **Starbucks (Marriott)** · 21850 Oxnard St

Copy Centers

- **A Woodland Printing & Copy** · 7124 Owensmouth Ave · 818-999-2679
- **Copies Plus Printing** · 19911 Ventura Blvd · 818-346-1919
- **Copy Center** · 20113 Vanowen St · 818-883-6283
- **Kinko's** · 21816 Victory Blvd · 818-884-4465
- **Mail Boxes Etc** · 19528 Ventura Blvd · 818-343-4377
- **Office Depot** · 6227 Topanga Canyon Blvd · 818-716-7770
- **Sir Speedy** · 21430 Strathern St · 818-346-2280
- **Universal Copy** · 7141 Winnetka Ave · 818-887-2559
- **UPS Store** · 6433 Topanga Canyon Blvd · 818-704-5808
- **VIP Prints** · 7630 Tampa Ave · 818-609-1013

Gyms

- **Curves** · 19710 Ventura Blvd · 818-340-9614
- **Curves** · 19762 Sherman Wy · 818-264-1313
- **Curves** · 21151 Victory Blvd · 818-702-0230
- **Curves** · 8201 Topanga Canyon Blvd · 818-888-4770
- **LA Fitness Sports Club** · 6336 Canoga Ave · 818-884-1100
- **LA Workout** · 20971 Burbank Blvd · 818-226-3890

Hardware Stores

- **Home Depot** · 6345 Variel Ave · 818-716-9141
- **Tampa Hardware** · 7543 Tampa Ave · 818-709-0354

Liquor Stores

- **Alcon Cut-Rate Liquor** · 21315 Saticoy St
- **Amber Liquor** · 20263 Saticoy St
- **Aria Liquors** · 22015 Vanowen St
- **Beverages & More** · 6520 Canoga Ave
- **Bottle Bin Liquor** · 20915 Vanowen St
- **Corbin Liquor** · 19661 Ventura Blvd
- **J&J Liquor** · 6042 Tampa Ave
- **King's Delight** · 21925 Saticoy St
- **Knight Life Liquor** · 19245 Saticoy St
- **Kwik-Stop Liquor** · 19663 Sherman Wy
- **Ladin's Liquor & Deli** · 20857 Sherman Wy
- **Liquor Mart** · 7547 Topanga Canyon Blvd
- **Liquor Works** · 19200 Ventura Blvd
- **Lucky 7 Liquor** · 19322 Vanowen St
- **Mustang Liquor** · 21121 Sherman Wy
- **Portofino Liquor** · 19756 Sherman Wy
- **Rocket Liquor** · 21413 Vanowen St
- **Star's Cork 'n' Bottle Shop** · 7801 Canoga Ave
- **Super Store** · 20043 Vanowen St
- **US Liquor** · 20127 Vanowen St
- **West End Liquor** · 21500 Sherman Wy

Movie Theaters

- **AMC Promenade 16** · 21801 Oxnard St · 818-883-2262

Pet Stores

- **Aquarium City** · 21723 Sherman Wy · 818-887-7460
- **C&C Aquatics** · 21724 Sherman Wy · 818-340-9923
- **C&C's Pet Food for Less** · 21720 Sherman Wy · 818-348-3018
- **Discount Bird & Pet Supplies** · 19640 Sherman Wy · 818-343-1040
- **Parrots Naturally** · 19224 Ventura Blvd · 818-708-7277

Restaurants

- **In-N-Out Burger** · 19902 Ventura Blvd · 800-786-1000

Video Rental

- **20-20 Video** · 19371 Saticoy St · 818-885-0202
- **Blockbuster** · 19339 Victory Blvd · 818-708-2887
- **Blockbuster** · 8201 Topanga Canyon Blvd · 818-348-7196
- **Mega Value Video** · 6842 De Soto Ave · 818-598-1475
- **Sunshine Groceries (Indian Only)** · 7518 Topanga Canyon Blvd · 818-887-6917
- **Video Stage** · 21418 Sherman Wy · 818-887-4234

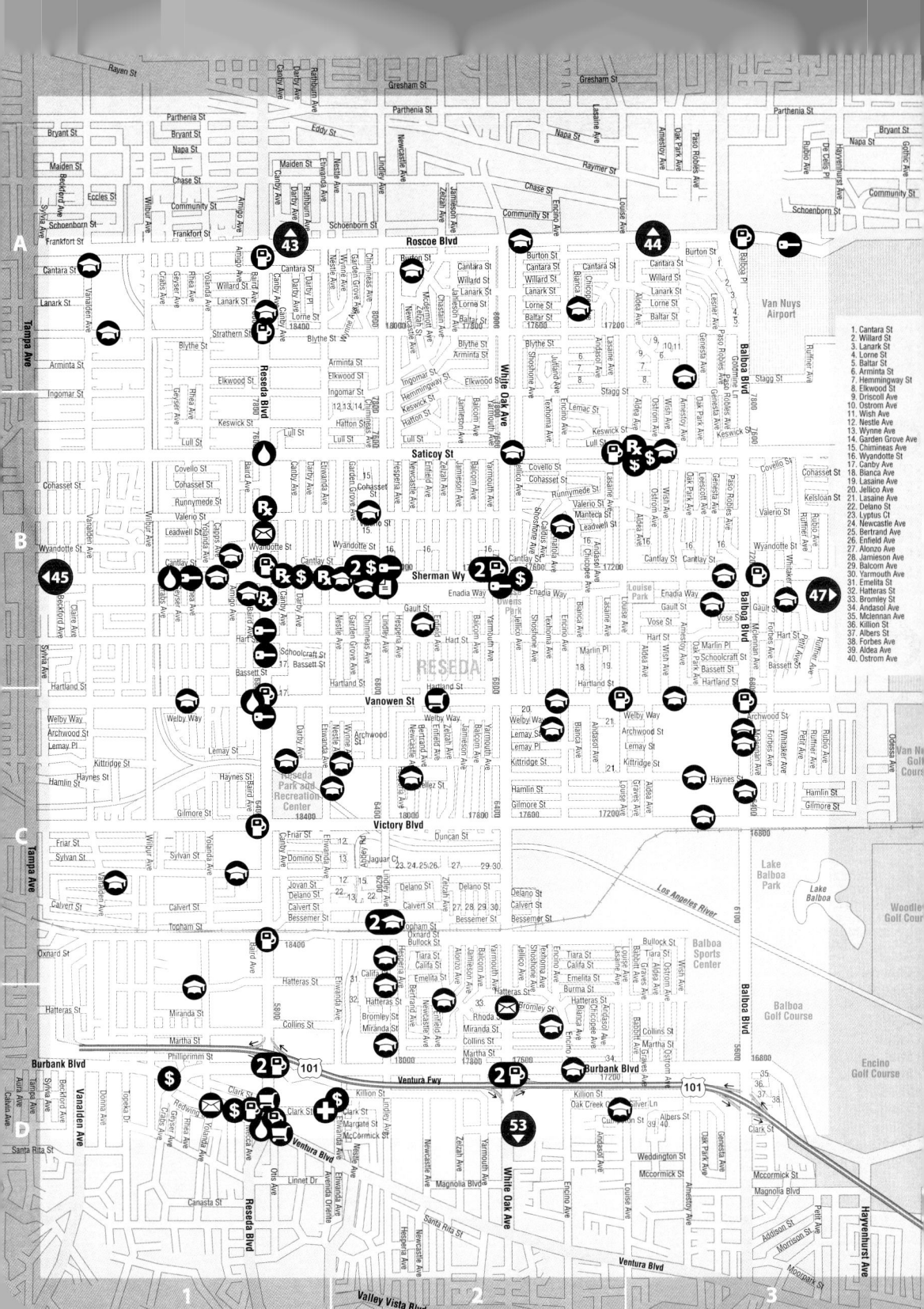

Essentials

42 43 44
45 46 47 48 49 50
52 53 54 55 56 57

17 1 2 3
16 20 6 7
15 19 23

Map 46

Reseda lies in the heart of the San Fernando Valley and was one of its first suburbs. Tom Petty sang of the neighborhood in "Free Fallin'," its biggest claim to fame and what most endears it to the locals—at least, those locals who listen to classic rock. It's also known as the locale for a number of the scenes in *Boogie Nights*.

$ Banks

- **Bank of America** · 18120 Sherman Wy
- **Citibank** · 18260 Sherman Wy
- **Downey Savings & Loan** · 17250 Saticoy St
- **First Federal** · 18585 Ventura Blvd
- **Nara** · 17639 Sherman Wy
- **Pacific Western** · 5525 Etiwanda Ave
- **Washington Mutual** · 17204 Saticoy St
- **Wells Fargo** · 18400 Sherman Wy
- **Wells Fargo** · 18801 Ventura Blvd

Car Rental

- **Discount Rent-a-Car** · 7002 Reseda Blvd
- **Enterprise** · 6933 Reseda Blvd
- **Hertz** · 16700 Roscoe Blvd
- **Hertz** · 6728 Reseda Blvd
- **Rent 4 Less** · 7142 White Oak Ave
- **Rent-a-Wreck** · 18738 Sherman Wy
- **Sark Affordable Rentals** · 18128 Sherman Wy

Car Washes

- **Coast Motor Detailing** · 18500 Ventura Blvd
- **Reseda Center Car Wash** · 7601 Reseda Blvd
- **Sherman Car Wash** · 18815 Sherman Wy
- **Vanowen Car Wash** · 18514 Vanowen St

Gas Stations

- **76** · 17300 Vanowen St
- **76** · 17704 Sherman Wy
- **76** · 18524 Ventura Blvd
- **76** · 8247 Reseda Blvd
- **Arco** · 16851 Sherman Wy
- **Arco** · 6039 Reseda Blvd
- **Arco** · 6801 Reseda Blvd
- **Chevron** · 7208 Reseda Blvd
- **Exxon** · 5605 Reseda Blvd
- **Mobil** · 18468 Burbank Blvd
- **Mobil** · 18510 Victory Blvd
- **Mobil** · 5553 White Oak Ave
- **Shell** · 17660 Burbank Blvd
- **Shell** · 17707 Sherman Wy
- **Shell** · 18500 Ventura Blvd
- **Shell** · 6801 Balboa Blvd
- **Shell** · 8000 Reseda Blvd
- **Texaco** · 16930 Roscoe Blvd
- **Texaco** · 17301 Saticoy St

Hospitals

- **Encino-Tarzana Regional Medical Center–Tarzana Campus** · 18321 Clark St

Rx Pharmacies

- **CVS (24 hrs)** · 7400 Reseda Blvd · 818-776-2600
- **The Medicine Shoppe** · 7111 Reseda Blvd · 818-345-5397
- **Rite-Aid** · 17266 Saticoy St · 818-345-1543
- **Sav-On** · 18247 Sherman Wy · 818-345-9640
- **Walgreens** · 18430 Sherman Wy · 818-343-1680

Post Offices

- **US Post Office** · 5609 Yolanda Ave
- **US Post Office** · 5805 White Oak Ave
- **US Post Office** · 7320 Reseda Blvd

Schools

- **American Hebrew Academy** · 6134 Lindley Ave
- **Anatola Ave Elementary** · 7364 Anatola Ave
- **Bert Corona Charter** · 16922 Sherman Wy
- **Bertrand Ave Elementary** · 7021 Bertrand Ave
- **Bethel Lutheran Elementary** · 17500 Burbank Blvd
- **Beverly Christian** · 345 S Woods Ave
- **Birmingham Senior High** · 17000 Haynes St
- **Cantara St Elementary** · 17950 Cantara St
- **Child's World** · 6100 Lindley Ave
- **Cleveland EEC** · 19031 Strathern St
- **Community** · 17216 Saticoy St
- **Emelita Elementary** · 17931 Hatteras St
- **Fred E Lull Special Education** · 17551 Miranda St
- **The French American** · 5657 Lindley Ave
- **Garden Grove Elementary** · 18141 Valerio St
- **Gault St Elementary** · 17000 Gault St
- **High Tech HS** · 17111 Victory Blvd
- **Independence Continuation** · 6501 Balboa Blvd
- **Lemay EEC** · 17553 Lemay St
- **Lemay St Elementary** · 17520 Vanowen St
- **Lindley Academy** · 5901 Lindley Ave
- **Lorne St Elementary** · 17440 Lorne St
- **Magnolia Science Academy** · 18238 Sherman Wy

- **Meritor Academy** · 5933 Lindley Ave
- **Miller HS** · 8218 Vanalden Ave
- **Miss Tuula's Preschool/Kindergarten** · 18740 Vanowen St
- **New Horizon Christian** · 8055 Reseda Blvd
- **Newcastle Elementary** · 6520 Newcastle Ave
- **Oak Meadow** · 17645 Saticoy St
- **Pinecrest School–Whiteoak** · 17643 Roscoe Blvd
- **Playmates of Reseda** · 7119 Baird Ave
- **Reseda Baptist** · 18644 Sherman Wy
- **Reseda Elementary** · 7265 Amigo Ave
- **Reseda Senior High** · 18230 Kittridge St
- **Sherman Oaks Center for Enriched Students** · 18605 Erwin St
- **St Bridget of Sweden** · 7120 Whitaker Ave
- **St Catherine of Siena** · 18125 Sherman Wy
- **Stagg St Elementary** · 7839 Amestoy Ave
- **Tierra Montessori** · 18706 Hatteras St
- **Trinity Lutheran High** · 18425 Kittridge St
- **Valley Magnet** · 6701 Balboa Blvd
- **Vanalden EEC** · 6212 Vanalden Ave
- **West Valley** · 6649 Balboa Blvd
- **Westmark** · 5461 Louise Ave
- **William Mulholland Middle** · 17120 Vanowen St
- **Zane Grey Continuation** · 6510 Etiwanda Ave

Supermarkets

- **Gelson's Supermarket** · 5500 Reseda Blvd
- **Ralphs** · 17250 Saticoy St
- **Ralphs** · 18300 Vanowen St
- **Trader Joe's** · 17640 Burbank Blvd
- **Vons** · 18439 Ventura Blvd

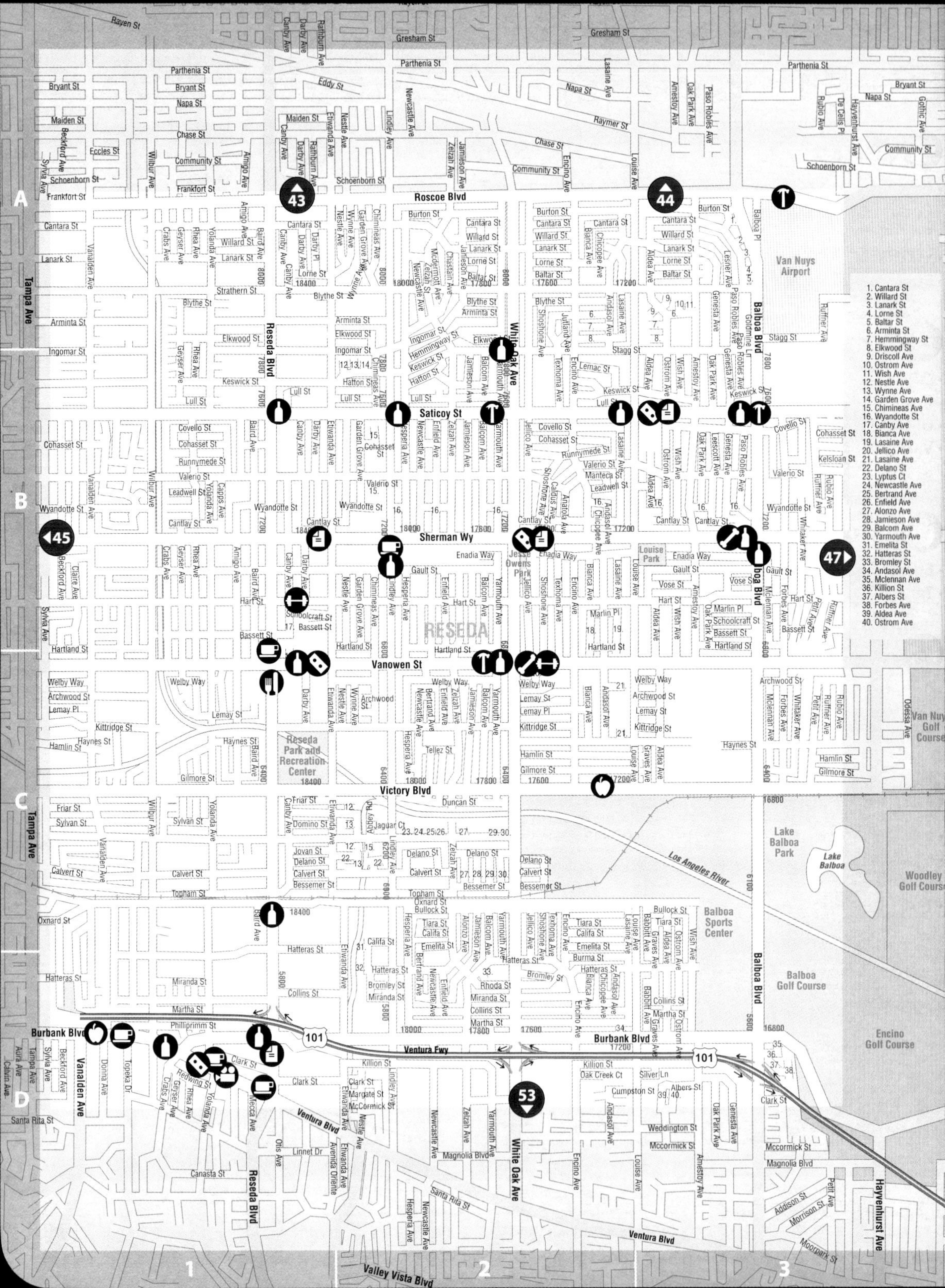
N
Roscoe Blvd
Saticoy St
Sherman Wy
Vanowen St
Victory Blvd
Burbank Blvd
Ventura Fwy
Ventura Blvd
Valley Vista Blvd
Reseda Blvd
White Oak Ave
Balboa Blvd
Tampa Ave
Haynehurst Ave
Van Nuys Airport
RESEDA
Reseda Park and Recreation Center
Jesse Owens Park
Louise Park
Lake Balboa Park
Lake Balboa
Balboa Sports Center
Balboa Golf Course
Encino Golf Course
Woodley Golf Course
Van Nuys Golf Course
Los Angeles River
101
43
44
45
47
53
A
B
C
D
1
2
3
1. Cantara St
2. Willard St
3. Lanark St
4. Lorne St
5. Baltar St
6. Arminta St
7. Hemmingway St
8. Elkwood St
9. Driscoll Ave
10. Ostrom Ave
11. Wish Ave
12. Nestle Ave
13. Wynne Ave
14. Garden Grove Ave
15. Chimineas Ave
16. Wyandotte St
17. Canby Ave
18. Bianca Ave
19. Lasaine Ave
20. Jellico Ave
21. Lasaine Ave
22. Delano St
23. Lyptus Ct
24. Newcastle Ave
25. Bertrand Ave
26. Enfield Ave
27. Alonzo Ave
28. Jamieson Ave
29. Balcom Ave
30. Yarmouth Ave
31. Emelita St
32. Hatteras St
33. Bromley St
34. Andasol Ave
35. Mclennan Ave
36. Killion St
37. Albers St
38. Forbes Ave
39. Aldea Ave
40. Ostrom Ave

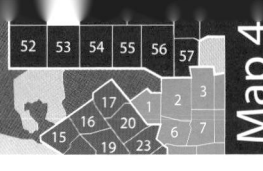

Map 4

Lake Balboa Park is a lovely place to spend a weekend day. Rent a paddleboat and work your way across the lake, or grab a fishing rod—the lake is stocked regularly by the Department of Fish and Game. The park is surrounded by three golf courses and is home to the Valley Jazz Festival.

☕ Coffee

- **Café Donuts** · 7161 Lindley Ave
- **Coffee Bean & Tea Leaf** · 18505 Ventura Blvd
- **Peet's Coffee & Tea** · 18973 Ventura Blvd
- **Starbucks** · 18668 Ventura Blvd
- **Starbucks** · 6840 Reseda Blvd

📋 Copy Centers

- **Office Depot** · 5530 Reseda Blvd · 818-708-7587
- **Printed Image** · 18334 Sherman Wy · 818-705-9390
- **UPS Store** · 17216 Saticoy St · 818-774-9095
- **Variety Printing & Graphics** · 17618 Sherman Wy · 818-705-4422

🍎 Farmer's Markets

- **Encino** · 17400 Victory Blvd
- **Tarzana** · 19130 Ventura Blvd

🏋 Gyms

- **Curves** · 17624 Sherman Wy · 818-668-8433
- **Mid Valley Racquetball Club** · 18420 Hart St · 818-705-6500

🔨 Hardware Stores

- **Home Depot** · 16800 Roscoe Blvd · 818-786-9600
- **M&M Tools** · 7544 Balboa Blvd · 818-989-7514
- **Reseda Hardware** · 17729 Vanowen St · 818-345-6467
- **Tool Depot** · 17746 Saticoy St · 818-881-0146

🍾 Liquor Stores

- **A&S** · 7143 Balboa Blvd
- **Al's Drive-In Liquor** · 18444 Saticoy St
- **Antidote** · 17705 Vanowen St
- **Bob's Liquor** · 17315 Saticoy St
- **Farm Boy's Liquor** · 6026 Reseda Blvd
- **L&M Liquor** · 18400 Vanowen St
- **Lindley Liquor** · 7137 Lindley Ave
- **Party House Liquor & Wine** · 18839 Ventura Blvd
- **Rainbow Liquor** · 18033 Saticoy St
- **Spirits World** · 18523 Burbank Blvd
- **Valli-Ho** · 16925 Sherman Wy
- **Wine & Liquor Depot** · 16938 Saticoy St

🎥 Movie Theaters

- **Mann Valley West 9** · 18632 Ventura Blvd · 818-996-8029

🦴 Pet Stores

- **Quality Pet Shop** · 16929 Sherman Wy · 818-343-7211
- **Tams Pet Food & Supplies** · 17635 Vanowen St · 818-343-6873

🍴 Restaurants

- **Amber's Chicken Kitchen** · 16900 Burbank Blvd · 818-995-3200
- **Melody's Mexican Kitchen** · 6747 Reseda Blvd · 818-609-9062

🎲 Video Rental

- **Blockbuster** · 17288 Saticoy St · 818-342-8835
- **Hollywood Video** · 18346 Vanowen St · 818-344-1890
- **Hollywood Video** · 18705 Ventura Blvd · 818-344-1850
- **Western Video (Korean)** · 17639 Sherman Wy · 818-708-2496

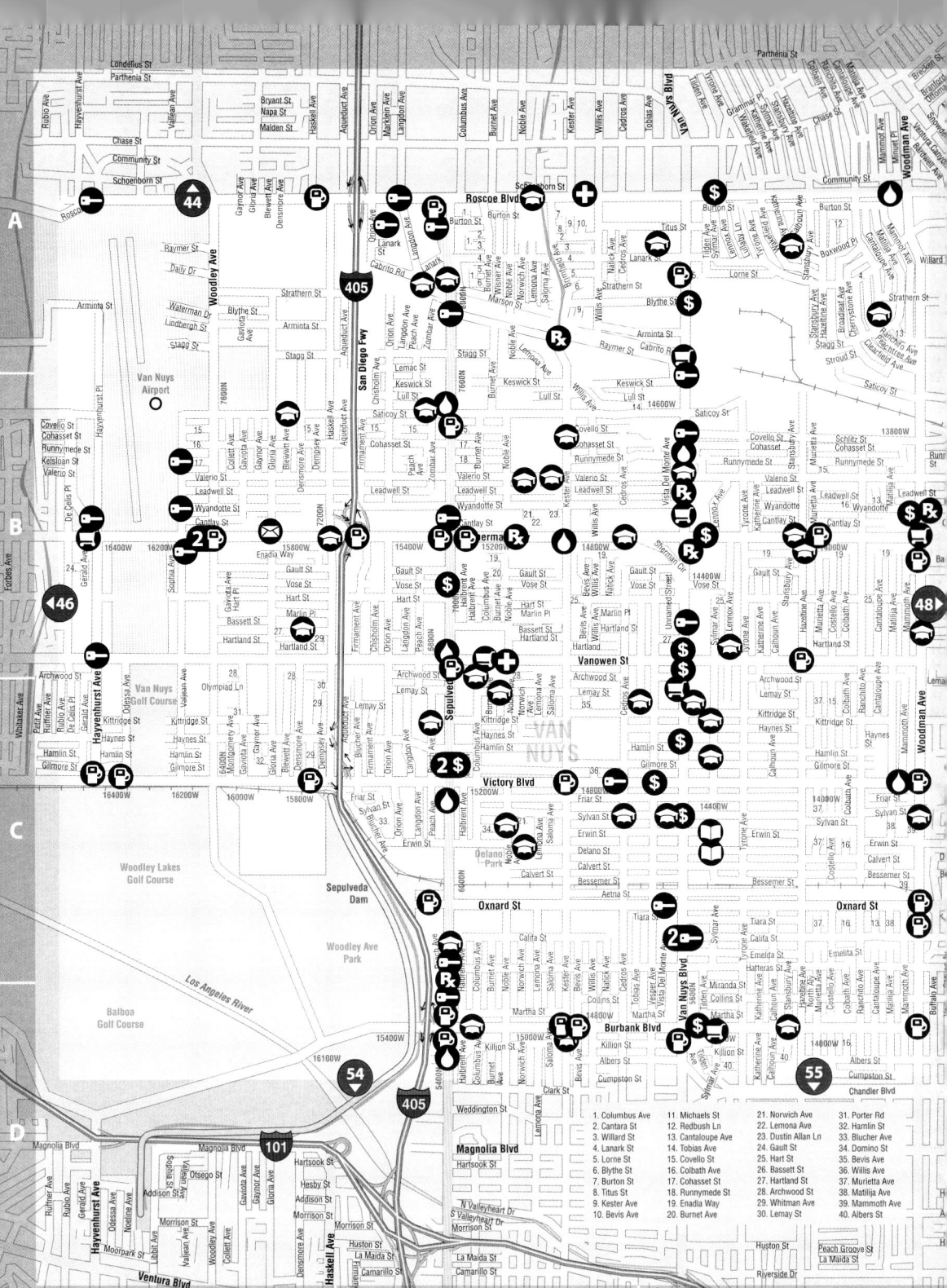

1. Columbus Ave
2. Cantara St
3. Willard St
4. Lorne St
5. Blythe St
6. Burton St
7. Titus St
8. Kester Ave
9. Bevis Ave
10. Bevis Ave
11. Michaels Ave
12. Redbush Ln
13. Cantaloupe Ave
14. Tobias Ave
15. Lanark St
16. Colbath Ave
17. Cohasset St
18. Runnymede St
19. Enadia Way
20. Burnet Ave
21. Norwich Ave
22. Lemona Ave
23. Dustin Allan Ln
24. Gault St
25. Hart St
26. Bassett St
27. Hartland St
28. Archwood St
29. Whitman Ave
30. Lemay St
31. Porter Rd
32. Hamlin St
33. Blucher Ave
34. Domino St
35. Bevis Ave
36. Willis Ave
37. Murietta Ave
38. Matilija Ave
39. Mammoth Ave
40. Albers St

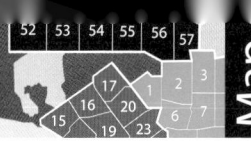
Back in the day, Van Nuys Boulevard was the main drag for teenagers who loved to cruise in their hot rods. Now, Van Nuys is more popular with aviators, some of whom may be aware that Van Nuys airport served as the location for the final scene in *Casablanca*. The airport is a major facility for private jets and small planes. Within the city is the Sepulveda Dam, which marks the official origins of the Los Angeles River.

$ Banks

- **Bank of America** · 6551 Van Nuys Blvd
- **Bank of America** · 7060 Sepulveda Blvd
- **Bank of America** · 7255 Woodman Ave
- **California National** · 14545 Victory Blvd
- **Citibank** · 6750 Van Nuys Blvd
- **Downey Savings & Loan** · 14440 Burbank Blvd
- **East West** · 6450 Sepulveda Blvd
- **Hanmi** · 14427 Sherman Wy
- **Union** · 14360 Roscoe Blvd
- **United Commercial** · 6440 Sepulveda Blvd
- **Washington Mutual** · 6300 Van Nuys Blvd
- **Washington Mutual** · 7950 Van Nuys Blvd
- **Wells Fargo** · 6800 Van Nuys Blvd

Car Rental

- **699 Rent-a-Car** · 14627 Victory Blvd
- **Advantage Rent-a-Car** · 5951 Van Nuys Blvd
- **Economy Rent-a-Car** · 7256 Sepulveda Blvd
- **Enterprise** · 5845 Sepulveda Blvd
- **Enterprise** · 6915 Van Nuys Blvd
- **Enterprise** · 8230 Sepulveda Blvd
- **Excel Rent-a-Car** · 16506 Vanowen St
- **Galpin** · 15505 Roscoe Blvd
- **Hertz** · 16644 Roscoe Blvd
- **Hertz** · 5858 Van Nuys Blvd
- **Hertz** · 7155 Valjean Ave
- **Hertz** · 7277 Valjean Ave
- **Hertz** · 7435 Valjean Ave
- **Hertz** · 7724 Van Nuys Blvd
- **Hertz** · 8244 Orion Ave
- **Midway Car Rental** · 7240 Hayvenhurst Ave
- **U-Haul** · 7610 Van Nuys Blvd
- **United Rentals** · 14540 Oxnard St

Car Washes

- **Auto Hand Wash** · 13716 Victory Blvd
- **Buena Vista Self-Service Car Wash** · 14900 Sherman Wy
- **Buena Vista Self-Service Car Wash** · 15311 Saticoy St
- **Panorama Car Wash** · 13800 Roscoe Blvd
- **Sherman Oaks Auto Resort** · 5546 Sepulveda Blvd
- **Tri Star Car Wash** · 6344 Sepulveda Blvd
- **Valley Car Wash** · 7530 Van Nuys Blvd
- **Wash World** · 6810 Sepulveda Blvd

Gas Stations

- **76** · 14903 Burbank Blvd
- **76** · 15650 Sherman Wy
- **76** · 16505 Victory Blvd
- **76** · 6003 Woodman Ave
- **Arco** · 14114 Vanowen St
- **Arco** · 14903 Victory Blvd
- **Arco** · 15711 Victory Blvd
- **Arco** · 7557 Sepulveda Blvd
- **Arco** · 8050 Van Nuys Blvd
- **Chevron** · 14850 Burbank Blvd
- **Chevron** · 15255 Sherman Wy
- **Chevron** · 15359 Oxnard St
- **Chevron** · 5600 Sepulveda Blvd
- **Chevron** · 7200 Woodman Ave
- **Exxon** · 8250 Sepulveda Blvd
- **Independent** · 14053 Sherman Wy
- **Independent** · 16103 Sherman Wy
- **Mobil** · 15303 Sherman Wy
- **Mobil** · 16106 Sherman Wy
- **Mobil** · 16455 Victory Blvd
- **Mobil** · 5560 Van Nuys Blvd
- **Mobil** · 5955 Woodman Ave
- **Shell** · 13703 Victory Blvd
- **Shell** · 14106 Burbank Blvd
- **Shell** · 15710 Roscoe Blvd
- **Shell** · 15805 Roscoe Blvd
- **Shell** · 5556 Sepulveda Blvd
- **Shell** · 5600 Woodman Ave
- **Thrifty** · 6810 Sepulveda Blvd

Hospitals

- **Mission Community** · 14850 Roscoe Blvd
- **Valley Presbyterian** · 15107 Vanowen St

Landmarks

- **Van Nuys Airport** · 16461 Sherman Wy

Libraries

- **LA County Law Library** · 6230 Sylmar Ave · 818-374-2499
- **Van Nuys Branch** · 6250 Sylmar Ave · 818-756-8453

Pharmacies

- **CVS (24 hrs)** · 15232 Sherman Wy · 818-374-3480
- **Rite-Aid** · 7239 Woodman Ave · 818-781-7127
- **Sav-On** · 6201 N Sepulveda Blvd · 818-373-5005
- **Sav-On (Albertsons)** · 7227 Van Nuys Blvd · 818-787-8081
- **Target** · 14920 Raymer St · 818-922-1002
- **Target** · 5711 Sepulveda Blvd · 818-779-0321
- **Walgreens (24 hrs)** · 7155 Van Nuys Blvd · 818-989-2384

Police

- **Los Angeles Police Dept** · 6240 Sylmar Ave · 818-756-8343

Post Offices

- **US Post Office** · 15701 Sherman Wy
- **US Post Office** · 6200 Van Nuys Blvd

Schools

- **ABC Little** · 14926 Burbank Blvd
- **ABC Little** · 6447 Woodman Ave
- **Advocate School Van Nuys Campus** · 7533 Van Nuys Blvd
- **Bassett St Elementary** · 15756 Bassett St
- **Bridges Academy** · 15223 Burbank Blvd
- **Burton St Elementary** · 8141 Calhoun Ave
- **Children's Community** · 14702 Sylvan St
- **Clairmont Academy** · 8021 Langdon Ave
- **Cohassett St Elementary** · 15810 Saticoy St
- **Columbus Ave Academy** · 6700 Columbus Ave
- **Crawford Academy** · 14530 Sylvan St
- **Crossroads** · 6843 Lennox Ave
- **East Valley Area New Middle** · 15040 Roscoe Blvd
- **East Valley New Continuation HS** · 14630 Lanark St
- **Erikson High** · 6305 Woodman Ave
- **First Lutheran Elementary** · 6952 Van Nuys Blvd
- **Foundations Community** · 14646 Sherman Wy
- **Grace Christian Academy** · 6510 Peach Ave
- **Hazeltine Ave Elementary** · 7150 Hazeltine Ave
- **Kindergarten Learning Center** · 6555 Sylmar Ave
- **Los Angeles Hebrew High** · 5900 Sepulveda Blvd
- **Montclair** · 8071 Sepulveda Blvd
- **Montessori House of Children** · 6252 Woodman Ave
- **New School** · 15339 Saticoy St
- **Pinecrest** · 14111 Sherman Wy
- **Ranchito Ave Elementary** · 7940 Ranchito Ave
- **Robert Fulton Middle** · 7477 Kester Ave
- **Serendipity Early Care** · 14125 Burbank Blvd
- **St Elisabeth Elementary** · 6635 Tobias Ave
- **Sylvan Park EEC** · 15011 Delano St
- **Sylvan Park Elementary** · 6238 Noble Ave
- **Valerio Primary Center** · 14935 Valerio St
- **Valerio St Elementary** · 15035 Valerio St
- **Valley** · 15700 Sherman Wy
- **Valley High** · 6650 Van Nuys Blvd
- **Van Nuys Elementary** · 6464 Sylmar Ave
- **Van Nuys Middle** · 5435 Vesper Ave
- **Van Nuys Senior High** · 6535 Cedros Ave
- **Will Rogers Continuation** · 15141 Lemay St

Supermarkets

- **Albertsons** · 7227 Van Nuys Blvd
- **Food 4 Less** · 16530 Sherman Wy
- **Jons Marketplace** · 6655 Van Nuys Blvd
- **Ralphs** · 14440 Burbank Blvd
- **Ralphs** · 15230 Vanowen St
- **Ralphs** · 7225 Woodman Ave
- **Smart & Final** · 7815 Van Nuys Blvd

1. Columbus Ave
2. Cantara St
3. Willard St
4. Lanark St
5. Lorne St
6. Blythe St
7. Burton St
8. Titus St
9. Kester Ave
10. Bevis Ave
11. Michaels St
12. Redbush Ln
13. Cantaloupe Ave
14. Tobias Ave
15. Covello St
16. Colbath Ave
17. Cohasset St
18. Runnymede St
19. Enadia Way
20. Burnet Ave
21. Norwich Ave
22. Lemona Ave
23. Dustin Allan Ln
24. Gault St
25. Hart St
26. Bassett St
27. Hartland St
28. Archwood St
29. Whitman Ave
30. Lemay St
31. Porter Rd
32. Hamlin St
33. Blucher Ave
34. Domino St
35. Bevis Ave
36. Willis Ave
37. Murietta Ave
38. Matilija Ave
39. Mammoth Ave
40. Albers St

One of the most convenient areas for shopping is The Plant, at 7800 Van Nuys Boulevard, a former General Motors assembly plant, which now houses a Home Depot, a Babies R Us, a 16-screen movie theater, and more. Woodley Avenue Park includes a Japanese Tea Garden and two golf courses, along with numerous sports fields.

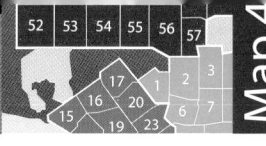
Map 4

Coffee

- **Boba Loca** · 6411 Sepulveda Blvd
- **Krispy Kreme Doughnuts** · 7249 Van Nuys Blvd
- **Lollicup** · 13752 Roscoe Blvd
- **Starbucks** · 14431 Burbank Blvd
- **Starbucks** · 15355 Sherman Wy
- **Starbucks** · 15430 Roscoe Blvd
- **Starbucks (Albertsons)** · 7227 Van Nuys Blvd
- **Won's Coffee Shop** · 14440 Gilmore St

Copy Centers

- **Ford Graphics** · 6920 Hayvenhurst Ave · 818-781-0513
- **Kinko's** · 5810 Sepulveda Blvd · 818-780-2123
- **Kopy-Rite** · 6325 Van Nuys Blvd · 818-787-1667
- **Laminating Services** · 14923 Oxnard St · 818-781-1209
- **Office Depot** · 6440 S Sepulveda Blvd · 818-780-9916
- **Priorty Graphics** · 6961 Valjean Ave · 818-908-2700
- **Staples** · 6104 Sepulveda Blvd · 818-908-2360
- **UPS Store** · 6311 Van Nuys Blvd · 818-781-9000
- **VIP Printing** · 14619 Victory Blvd · 818-994-2216
- **Valley Instant Press** · 14806 Oxnard St · 818-786-5793

Gyms

- **Curves** · 5512 Van Nuys Blvd · 818-782-8783
- **Curves** · 7135 Kester Ave · 818-902-2100
- **Curves** · 8205 Woodman Ave · 818-781-0101
- **LA Fitness Sports Clubs** · 5990 Sepulveda Blvd · 818-988-7411

Hardware Stores

- **CWH** · 7910 Sepulveda Blvd · 818-787-0525
- **Handiman Hardware** · 7730 Burnet Ave · 818-988-0700
- **Home Depot** · 7870 E Van Nuys Blvd · 818-373-0046
- **Orchard Supply Hardware** · 5960 Sepulveda Blvd · 818-779-7292
- **Peterson Lumber & Supply** · 7610 Woodman Ave · 818-782-9320

Liquor Stores

- **Adam's Liquor** · 14556 Vanowen St
- **Allan's Liquor** · 16060 Vanowen St
- **At Express Liquor** · 5658 Sepulveda Blvd
- **Beverages & More** · 5820 Sepulveda Blvd
- **Casino Liquors** · 14900 Victory Blvd
- **Confetti Liquors** · 13674 Oxnard St
- **D&K Liquor** · 15245 Saticoy St
- **F&R Liquor** · 14040 Burbank Blvd
- **George's Liquor** · 14102 Oxnard St
- **Gigi's Liquor** · 14038 Victory Blvd
- **Harvest Markets** · 14055 Burbank Blvd

- **In & Out Liquor Mart & Deli** · 7650 Woodman Ave
- **Jons Market** · 6655 Van Nuys Blvd
- **Lloyd's Liquor Market** · 7219 Kester Ave
- **Louie's Liquors** · 16461 Vanowen St
- **Michael's Liquor** · 7510 Woodman Pl
- **One Stop Liquor & Market** · 14521 Sherman Wy
- **Pat's Liquors** · 6020 Kester Ave
- **Sam's Liquor** · 15717 Vanowen St
- **Sherman Liquors & Jr Market** · 16045 Sherman Wy
- **Short Stop 25** · 14411 Victory Blvd
- **Tori Liquor & Jr Market** · 7300 Sepulveda Blvd
- **Triangle Liquors** · 8120 Sepulveda Blvd
- **Valley Liquor** · 7357 Van Nuys Blvd
- **Woodley Liquors** · 7550 Woodley Ave

Movie Theaters

- **Plant 16** · 7876 Van Nuys Blvd · 818-779-0323

Pet Stores

- **Birds Plus** · 14041 Burbank Blvd · 818-901-1187
- **Petco** · 5850 Sepulveda Blvd · 818-346-9397
- **Poodle Puff** · 14046 Burbank Blvd · 818-780-1600

Restaurants

- **Dr Hogly Wogly's BBQ** · 8136 Sepulveda Blvd · 818-780-6701
- **In-N-Out Burger** · 7930 Van Nuys Blvd · 800-786-1000
- **Krispy Kreme** · 7249 Van Nuys Blvd · 818-908-9113
- **Sam Woo Barbeque** · 6450 Sepulveda Blvd · 818-988-6813
- **Zankou Chicken** · 5658 Sepulveda Blvd · 818-781-0615

Shopping

- **The Plant** · 7800 Van Nuys Blvd

Video Rental

- **20-20 Video** · 6440 Sepulveda Blvd · 818-780-2020
- **Blockbuster** · 13722 Sherman Wy · 818-781-9734
- **Hollywood Video** · 7221 Van Nuys Blvd · 818-997-0706
- **Prael (Thai)** · 8205 Woodman Ave · 818-376-1976
- **Speed Video** · 16065 Vanowen St · 818-785-3051
- **Video City** · 8245 Woodman Ave · 818-786-4950
- **Video Japan (Japanese)** · 15355 Sherman Wy · 818-786-0850
- **Video Rose** · 14655 Victory Blvd · 818-989-4050
- **Video Supermart Valley (Korean)** · 7130 Van Nuys Blvd · 818-997-7410
- **Videomen** · 14522 Vanowen St · 818-786-3561

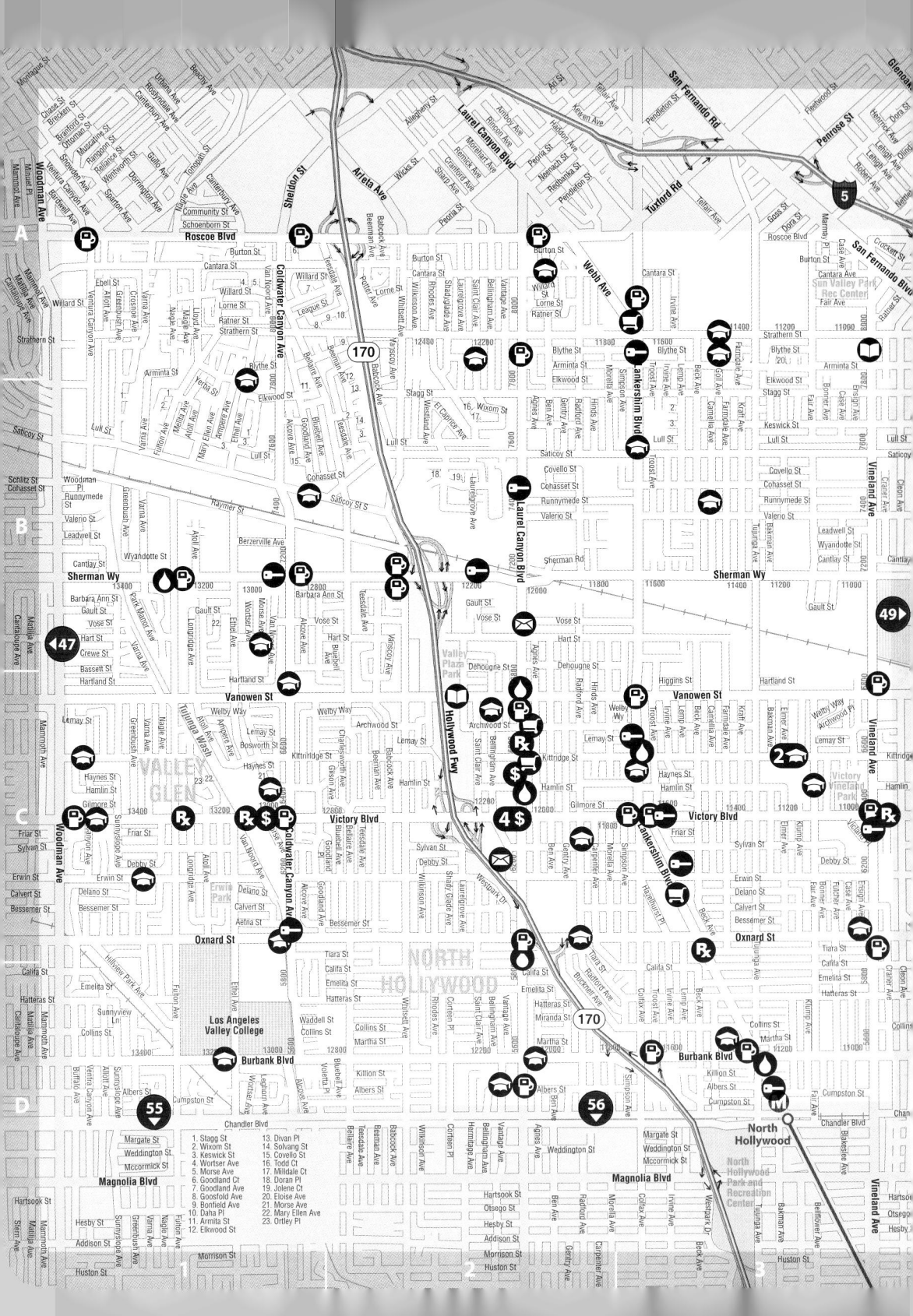

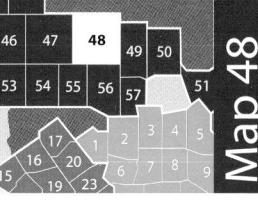
North Hollywood has come a long way in its bid to entertain as well as to produce entertainment. The northern terminus of LA's subway system has made NoHo's offerings more accessible to those venturing "over the hill" by riding "under the hill." More than thirty live theatres are dotted about the area, along with an array of restaurants and stores that prove you don't have to go into the city to have a good time.

$ Banks

- **Bank of America** •
  6600 Laurel Canyon Blvd
- **California National** •
  6350 Laurel Canyon Blvd
- **Citibank** • 13003 Victory Blvd
- **Washington Mutual** •
  6400 Laurel Canyon Blvd
- **Wells Fargo** • 12160 Victory Blvd

Car Rental

- **Enterprise** • 12959 Sherman Wy
- **Enterprise** • 5500 Lankershim Blvd
- **Enterprise** • 6343 Vineland Ave
- **Enterprise** • 7441 Laurel Canyon Blvd
- **Hertz** • 12311 Sherman Wy
- **Hertz** • 7918 Lankershim Blvd
- **Horizon** • 6644 Lankershim Blvd
- **Rent 4 Less** • 6051 Vineland Ave
- **Studio Self Storage** •
  6200 Lankershim Blvd
- **U-Haul** • 11666 Victory Blvd

Car Washes

- **Buena Vista Self-Service Car Wash** •
  6809 Laurel Canyon Blvd
- **J&R Car Wash** •
  5950 Laurel Canyon Blvd
- **Lankershim Car Wash** •
  6622 Lankershim Blvd
- **Plaza Car Wash** •
  6462 Laurel Canyon Blvd
- **Sherman Way Car Wash** •
  13310 Sherman Wy
- **Tujunga Car Wash** • 5553 Tujunga Ave

Gas Stations

- **76** • 11407 Burbank Blvd
- **76** • 11705 Victory Blvd
- **76** • 12856 Sherman Wy
- **76** • 5969 Laurel Canyon Blvd
- **76** • 7955 Laurel Canyon Blvd
- **Arco** • 12050 Roscoe Blvd
- **Arco** • 13260 Sherman Wy
- **Arco** • 13605 Roscoe Blvd
- **Arco** • 6757 Laurel Canyon Blvd
- **Arco** • 6800 Lankershim Blvd
- **Arco** • 6804 Vineland Ave
- **Arco** • 8004 Lankershim Blvd
- **Chevron** • 11000 Victory Blvd
- **Chevron** • 12950 Victory Blvd
- **Chevron** • 5544 Laurel Canyon Blvd
- **Chevron** • 7214 Whitsett Ave
- **Independent** • 13666 Victory Blvd
- **Mobil** • 11680 Burbank Blvd
- **Mobil** • 12500 Sherman Wy
- **Mobil** • 7004 Laurel Canyon Blvd
- **Shell** • 11680 Victory Blvd
- **Shell** • 12858 Roscoe Blvd
- **Shell** • 5957 Vineland Ave

Libraries

- **Sun Valley Branch** • 7935 Vineland Ave
  • 818-764-1338
- **Valley Plaza Branch** • 12311 Vanowen
  St • 818-765-0805

Pharmacies

- **CVS (24 hrs)** • 10945 Victory Blvd •
  818-487-0119
- **Rite-Aid** • 6639 Laurel Canyon Blvd •
  818-982-0695
- **Sav-On** • 13021 Victory Blvd •
  818-760-2986
- **Sav-On** • 5969 Lankershim Blvd •
  818-761-4235
- **Walgreens** • 13231 Victory Blvd •
  818-623-9358

Police

- **Los Angeles Police Dept** • 11640
  Burbank Blvd • 818-623-4016

Post Offices

- **US Post Office** • 6242 Vantage Ave
- **US Post Office** • 6535 Lankershim Blvd
- **US Post Office** •
  7035 Laurel Canyon Blvd

Schools

- **Adat Ari El** • 12020 Burbank Blvd
- **Arminta EEC** • 7911 Goll Ave
- **Arminta St Elementary** •
  11530 Strathern St
- **Bellingham PC** • 6728 Bellingham Ave
- **Burbank Blvd Elementary** •
  12215 Albers St
- **Camellia Ave Elementary** •
  7451 Camellia Ave
- **Charles Leroy Lowman Elementary** •
  12827 Saticoy St
- **Coldwater Canyon Ave Elementary** •
  6850 Coldwater Canyon Ave
- **Erwin St Elementary** • 13400 Erwin St
- **Fair Ave Elementary** • 6501 Fair Ave
- **Fair EEC** • 11300 Kittridge St
- **James Madison Middle** •
  13000 Hart St
- **John B Monlux Elementary** •
  6051 Bellaire Ave
- **Kiddie Academy** •
  6543 Lankershim Blvd
- **Kittridge St Elementary** •
  13619 Kittridge St
- **Laurel Hall** • 11919 Oxnard St
- **Laurence 2000** • 13639 Victory Blvd
- **London Continuation** •
  12924 Oxnard St
- **Los Angeles Valley College** •
  5800 Fulton Ave
- **Maud Booth Family Center** •
  11243 Kitteridge St
- **Messiah Lutheran** • 12020 Cantara St
- **Montessori Academy** • 6000 Ensign Ave
- **New School for Child Development** •
  13130 Burbank Blvd
- **North Hollywood Christian** •
  5616 Farmdale Ave
- **Princeton College Preparatory** •
  13440 Crewe St
- **Saticoy Elementary** • 7850 Ethel Ave
- **St Jane Frances de Chantal** •
  12950 Hamlin St
- **Strathern St Elementary** •
  7939 St Clair Ave
- **Ulysses S Grant Senior High** •
  13000 Oxnard St
- **Via Vera Christian** •
  7615 Lankershim Blvd
- **Victory Blvd Elementary** •
  6315 Radford Ave

Supermarkets

- **Food 4 Less** • 8035 Webb Ave
- **Ralphs** • 6657 Laurel Canyon Blvd
- **Smart & Final** •
  6601 N Laurel Canyon Blvd
- **Vons** • 6140 Lankershim Blvd

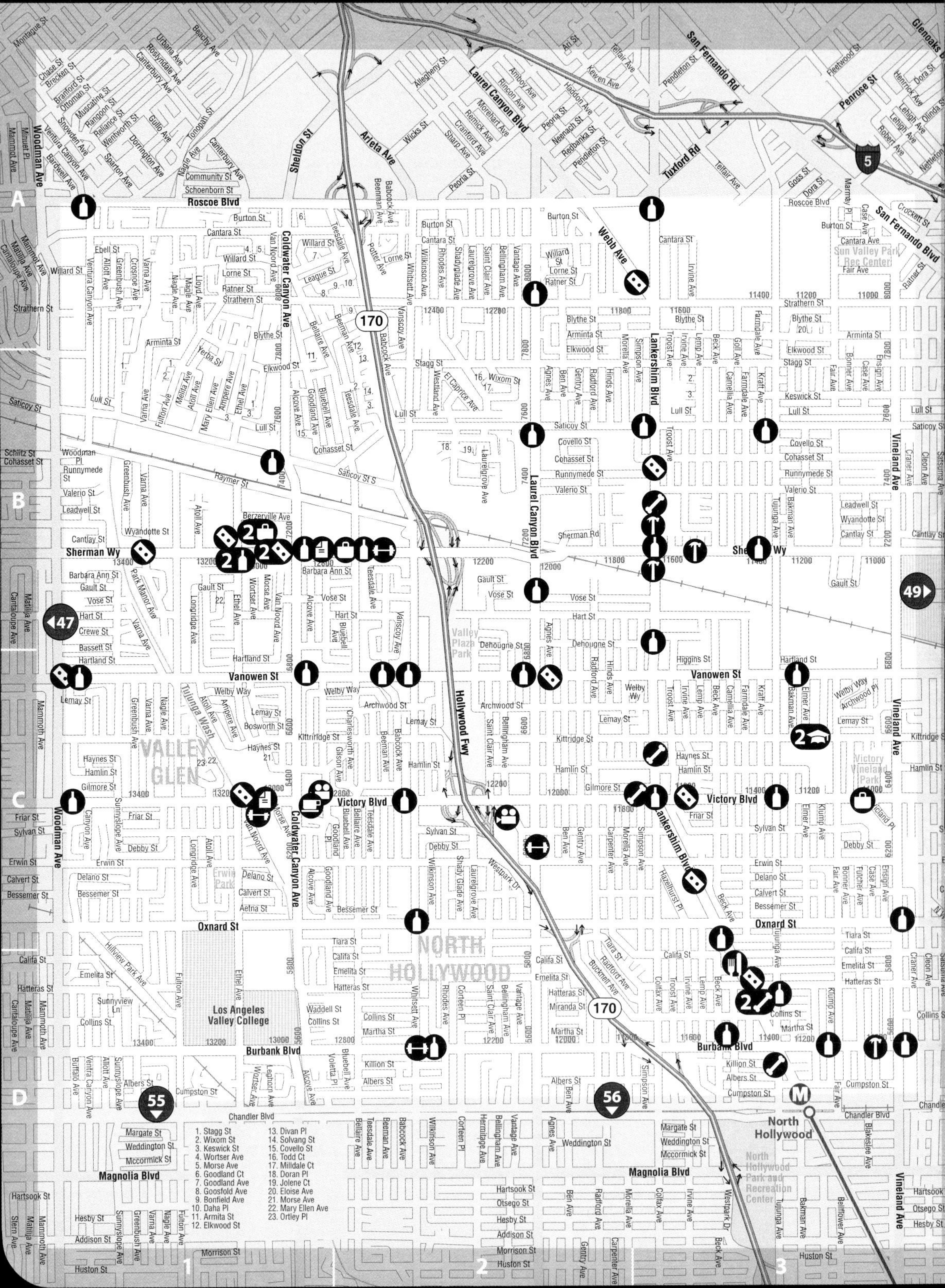

Map 48 · North Hollywood

1. Stagg St
2. Wixom St
3. Keswick St
4. Wortser Ave
5. Morse Ave
6. Goodland Ave
7. Goodland Ave
8. Goosfold Ave
9. Bonfield Ave
10. Daha Pl
11. Armita St
12. Elkwood St
13. Divan Pl
14. Solvang St
15. Covello St
16. Todd Ct
17. Mildale Ct
18. Doran St
19. Jolene Ct
20. Eloise Ave
21. Morse Ave
22. Mary Ellen Ave
23. Ortley Pl

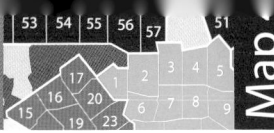

While NoHo will never be accused of being posh, it excels in the interesting and offbeat. Its generous supply of used-clothing stores are treasure chests offering clothing worn in TV shows and movies.

Coffee
- **Starbucks** · 12848 Victory Blvd

Copy Centers
- **Staples** · 12807 Sherman Wy · 818-503-7960
- **UPS Store** · 13029 Victory Blvd · 818-623-9988

Gyms
- **Bally Total Fitness** · 13069 Victory Blvd · 818-506-4208
- **Curves** · 12501 Burbank Blvd · 818-762-2295
- **Curves** · 12650 Sherman Wy · 818-764-9282
- **Gold's Gym** · 6233 Laurel Canyon Blvd · 818-506-4600

Hardware Stores
- **CWH** · 7303 Lankershim Blvd · 818-982-2121
- **Home Depot** · 11600 Sherman Wy · 818-764-9600
- **Stock Building Supply** · 7151 Lankershim Blvd · 818-982-6046
- **True Value** · 11000 Burbank Blvd · 818-769-4421

Liquor Stores
- **7&7 Liquor Junior Mart** · 13654 Victory Blvd
- **A&S Liquors** · 5745 Tujunga Ave
- **Arrow Liquor** · 12521 Vanowen St
- **Ash Dod Market** · 12650 Sherman Wy
- **Brothers Market** · 7050 Laurel Canyon Blvd
- **Carmel Liquor** · 12516 Vanowen St
- **Circus Liquor** · 5600 Vineland Ave
- **Circus Liquors** · 6417 Lankershim Blvd
- **D&R Liquors** · 6917 Lankershim Blvd
- **Dale's Junior Liquor Store** · 12500 Oxnard St
- **Danny's Liquor & Market** · 7202 Lankershim Blvd
- **Dorose Liquors** · 13560 Roscoe Blvd
- **Fair House Liquor** · 12903 Sherman Wy
- **Gigi's Liquor 2** · 12114 Vanowen St
- **Gip Liquor** · 13100 Sherman Wy
- **Handy Mart Liquors** · 8012 Laurel Canyon Blvd
- **Imperial Liquor** · 13324 Vanowen St
- **Joe's Liquor** · 12521 Victory Blvd
- **Joe's Liquor & Deli** · 11228 Burbank Blvd
- **K-1 Liquor** · 13056 Sherman Wy
- **Kim's Liquor** · 5940 Lankershim Blvd
- **Ladd Liquor** · 13646 Vanowen St
- **Ladd Liquors** · 11336 Vanowen St
- **Metro Liquor** · 6400 Tujunga Ave
- **Phil's Liquor & Deli** · 11510 Burbank Blvd
- **Roy's Liquors** · 12441 Burbank Blvd
- **Sal's Liquor** · 7552 Laurel Canyon Blvd
- **Saticoy Liquor** · 11415 Saticoy St
- **Southern Wine & Spirits** · 11428 Sherman Wy

- **Sunrise Liquors** · 12931 Saticoy St
- **Tom's Liquor** · 12861 Vanowen St
- **Urban Liquors** · 8323 Lankershim Blvd
- **Valley Liquor** · 11723 Saticoy St
- **Vineland Wine Cellar** · 6012 Vineland Ave

Movie Theaters
- **Century North Hollywood** · 12827 Victory Blvd · 818-508-6004
- **United Artists Valley Plaza 6** · 6355 Bellingham Ave · 818-766-4317

Nightlife
- **Rawhide** · 10937 Burbank Blvd · 818-760-9798

Pet Stores
- **Aquarium Village** · 11734 Victory Blvd · 818-985-3813
- **Bird House** · 5742 Lankershim Blvd · 818-766-4269
- **Deep Sea Aquarium** · 7355 Lankershim Blvd · 818-764-0875
- **Dog House** · 5742 Lankershim Blvd · 818-753-4325
- **Dragon Aquarium** · 6507 Lankershim Blvd · 818-508-9611
- **Pet Stop** · 5505 1/2 Tujunga Ave · 818-760-7387

Restaurants
- **In-N-Out Burger** · 5864 Lankershim Blvd · 800-786-1000

Shopping
- **99 Cents Store** · 12711 Sherman Wy · 818-764-9991
- **Big Lots** · 13005 Sherman Wy · 818-982-1687
- **K-Mart** · 13007 Sherman Wy · 818-764-0250

Video Rental
- **Blockbuster** · 6112 Lankershim Blvd · 818-487-6929
- **Hollywood Video** · 8065 Webb Ave · 818-504-6438
- **Planet Video** · 13041 Victory Blvd · 818-508-9429
- **SK Video (Thai only)** · 13124 Sherman Wy · 818-764-1666
- **Video 9 (Thai only)** · 12980 Sherman Wy · 818-765-8106
- **Video Center** · 5751 Lankershim Blvd · 818-760-4722
- **Video Citi** · 11650 Victory Blvd · 818-980-1505
- **Video Citi** · 12051 Vanowen St · 818-982-0414
- **Video Hut** · 13648 Vanowen St · 818-994-5878
- **Video Market** · 13434 Sherman Wy · 818-982-8488
- **Video Swan** · 7455 Lankershim Blvd · 818-982-2243
- **Video Universe** · 12937 Sherman Wy · 818-764-8842

199

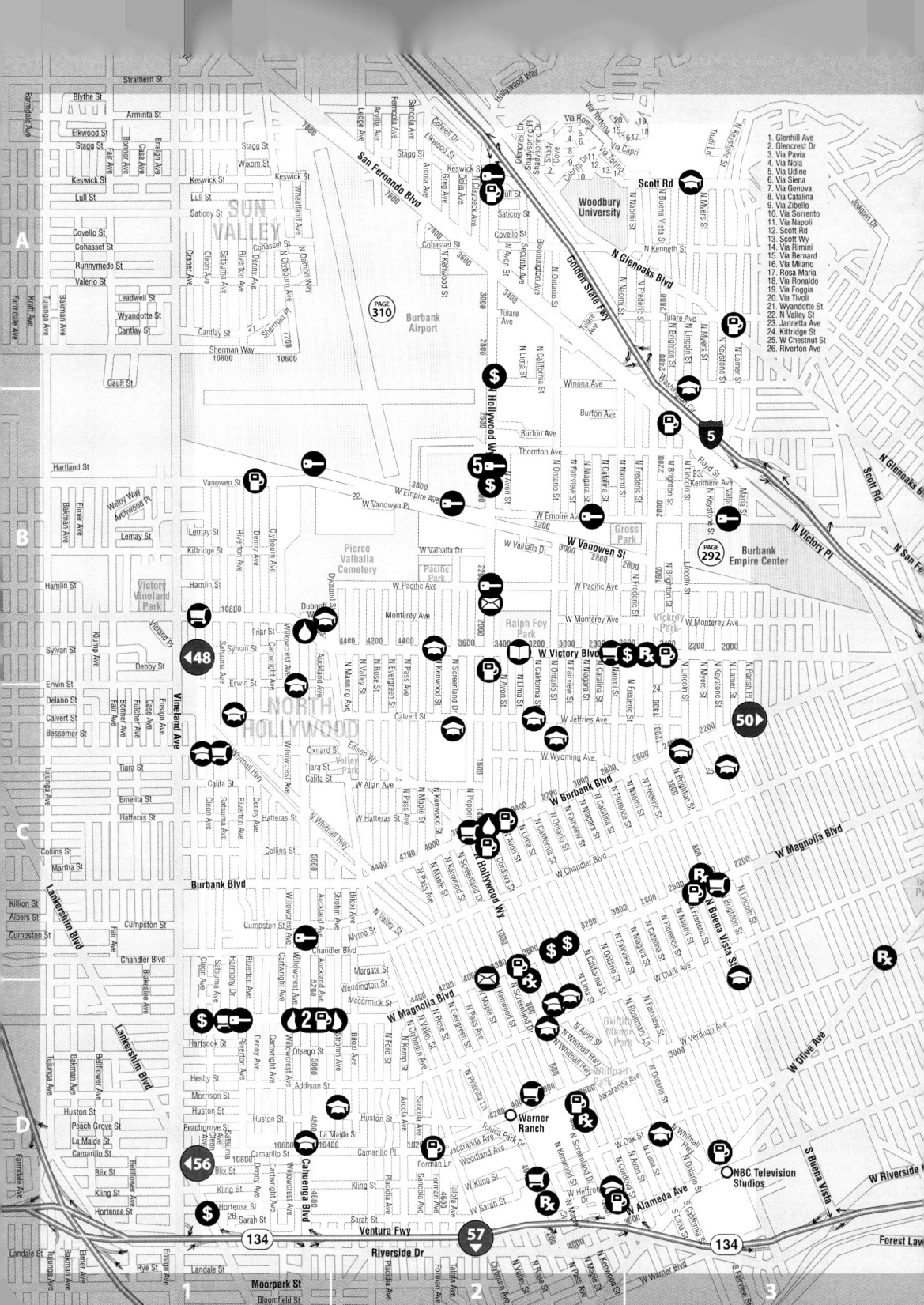

Burbank is something of a company town, though contrary to what non-residents may think, that company is not IKEA. Disney and Warners are also here. Burbank's World War II-era factory-town (in this case, Lockheed) days are gone, but enough long-established locksmiths, car dealers, and regular-Joe bars are around to remind you of the past. The Bob Hope (aka Burbank) Airport is a welcome—and, depending on where you live, potentially life-changing—alternative to the black hole that is LAX.

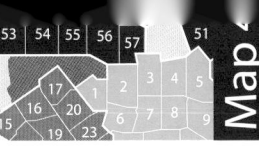

$ Banks

- **Bank of America** · 3400 W Magnolia Blvd
- **City National** · 4605 Lankershim Blvd
- **Community** · 2800 N Hollywood Wy
- **Downey Savings & Loan** · 2600 W Victory Blvd
- **Lockheed Federal Credit Union** · 2340 Hollywood Wy
- **Washington Mutual** · 3521 W Magnolia Blvd
- **Wells Fargo** · 10900 Magnolia Blvd

Car Rental

- **Advantage Rent-a-Car** · 2890 W Empire Ave
- **Alamo** · 2626 Hollywood Wy
- **Avis** · 2627 Hollywood Wy
- **Budget** · 2220 N Hollywood Wy
- **Burbank Airport Rent-A-Car** · 5424 Cahuenga Blvd
- **Enterprise** · 2612 N Hollywood Wy
- **Hertz** · 2100 W Empire Ave
- **Hertz** · 2627 Hollywood Wy
- **Hertz** · 3750 Empire Ave
- **Hertz** · 4531 W Empire Ave
- **National** · 2627 Hollywood Wy
- **Rent-a-Wreck** · 10860 Burbank Blvd
- **U-Haul** · 7721 Hollywood Wy

Car Washes

- **HWB Car Wash** · 3600 W Burbank Blvd
- **In-N-Out Car Wash** · 10505 Victory Blvd
- **Toluca Lake Car Wash** · 10515 Magnolia Blvd
- **Zeavy Car Wash** · 10605 Burbank Blvd

Gas Stations

- **76** · 1401 N Hollywood Wy
- **76** · 200 N Hollywood Wy
- **76** · 2421 W Victory Blvd
- **Arco** · 10601 Magnolia Blvd
- **Exxon** · 2417 N San Fernando Blvd
- **Gallactic Fuel** · 2616 N Glenoaks Blvd
- **Independent** · 10740 Vanowen St
- **Independent** · 3701 W Magnolia Blvd
- **Mobil** · 1951 N Hollywood Wy
- **Mobil** · 2500 W Magnolia Blvd
- **Mobil** · 3020 W Olive Ave
- **Mobil** · 3600 W Burbank Blvd
- **Shell** · 550 N Hollywood Wy
- **Shell** · 7710 N Hollywood Wy

○ Landmarks

- **NBC Television Studios** · 3000 W Alameda Ave
- **Warner Ranch** · Verdugo Ave & Pass Ave

Libraries

- **Northwest Branch** · 3323 W Victory Blvd · 818-238-5640

Pharmacies

- **Dana Drug Store & Boutique** · 317 N Pass Ave · 818-562-1177
- **Rite-Aid** · 935 N Hollywood Wy · 818-841-5336
- **Sav-On** · 1615 W Verdugo Ave · 818-845-9332
- **Sav-On** · 2500 W Victory Blvd · 818-955-8200
- **Sav-On (24 hrs)** · 511 Hollywood Wy · 818-841-0710
- **Walgreens** · 2501 W Magnolia Blvd · 818-841-1685

Post Offices

- **US Post Office** · 2140 N Hollywood Wy
- **US Post Office** · 3810 W Magnolia Blvd

Schools

- **American Lutheran Elementary** · 755 N Whitnall Hwy
- **Bret Harte Children's Center** · 1421 N Ontario St
- **Bret Harte Elementary** · 3200 W Jeffries Ave
- **Burbank Montessori Academy** · 217 N Hollywood Wy
- **Burlington** · 242 N Burlington Ave
- **Dubnoff Elementary** · 10526 Dubnoff Wy
- **George Washington Elementary** · 2322 N Lincoln St
- **The Learning Academy** · 510 N Buena Vista St
- **Luther Burbank Middle** · 3700 W Jeffries Ave
- **Magnolia Park (Special Ed)** · 827 N Avon St
- **Monterey High** · 1915 W Monterey Ave
- **Options for Youth Burbank Charter** · 2309 W Burbank Blvd
- **Oxnard St Elementary** · 10912 Oxnard St
- **Partners In Learning** · 3821 W Victory Blvd
- **Providencia Elementary** · 1919 N Ontario St
- **Robert Louis Stevenson Elementary** · 3333 W Oak St
- **St Francis Xavier** · 3601 Scott Rd
- **St Patrick** · 10626 Erwin St
- **Theodore Roosevelt Elementary** · 850 N Cordova St
- **Thomas Edison Elementary** · 2110 W Chestnut St
- **Toluca Crossroads** · 4814 Cahugena Blvd
- **Toluca Lake EEC** · 4915 Strohm Ave
- **Toluca Lake Elementary** · 4840 Cahuenga Blvd
- **Valley Montessori** · 10816 Calvert St
- **Woodbury University** · 7500 Glenoaks Blvd

Supermarkets

- **Albertsons** · 3830 W Verdugo Ave
- **Handy Market** · 2514 W Magnolia Blvd
- **Ralphs** · 10900 Magnolia Blvd
- **Ralphs** · 10911 Victory Blvd
- **Ralphs** · 2600 W Victory Blvd
- **Smart & Final** · 3708 W Burbank Blvd
- **Vallarta Supermarket** · 10859 Oxnard St
- **Vons** · 301 N Pass Ave

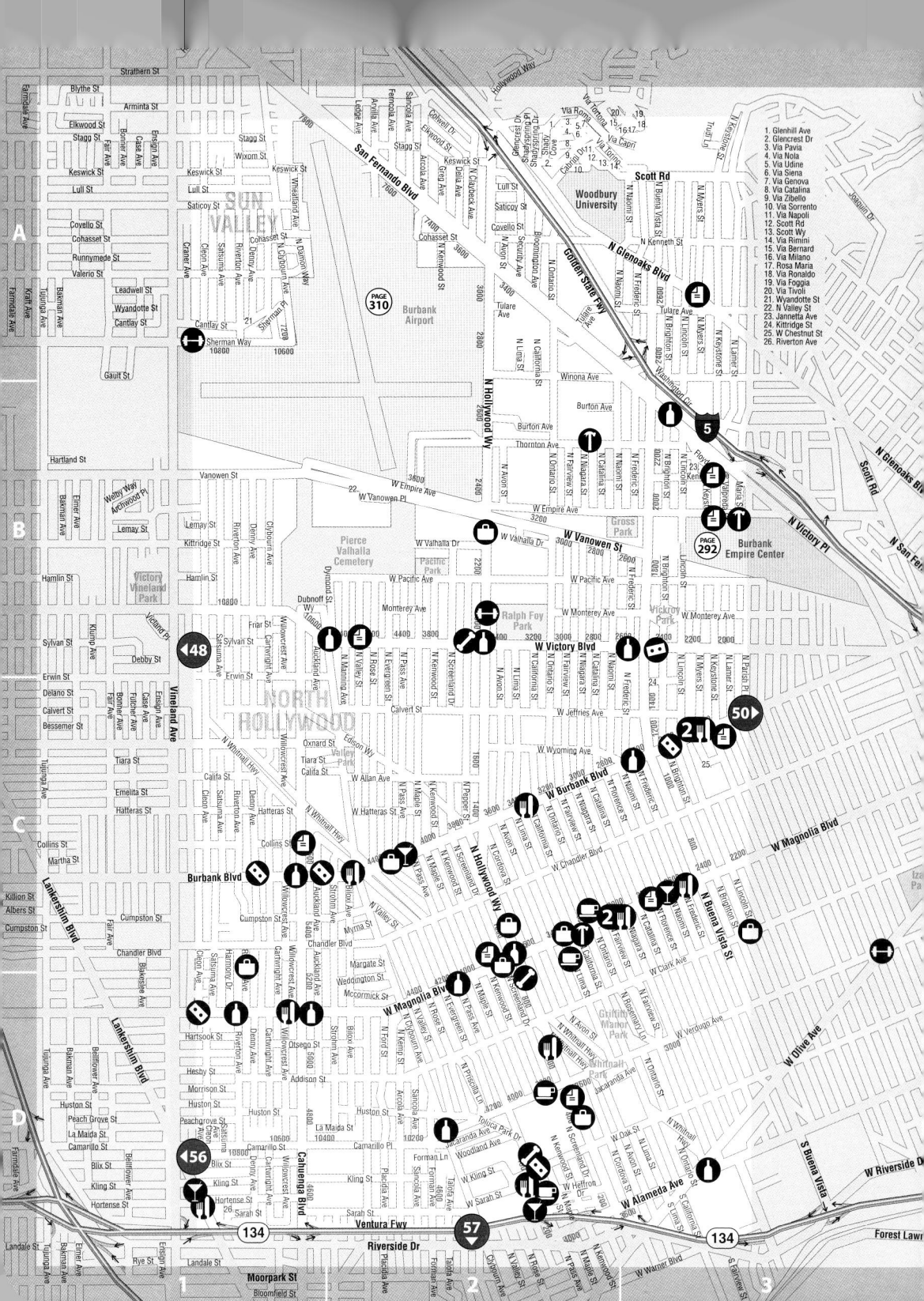

PAGE
310

PAGE
292

Woodbury
University

Burbank
Airport

SUN
VALLEY

NORTH
HOLLYWOOD

Pierce
Valhalla
Cemetery

Pacific
Park

Gross
Park

Ralph Foy
Park

Vickroy
Park

Valley
Park

Victory
Vineland
Park

Griffith
Manor
Park

Whitnall
Park

Burbank
Empire Center

◄48

50▶

50

◄56

57
▼

134

134

57
▼

Golden State Fwy

Ventura Fwy

Riverside Dr

Moorpark St

Bloomfield St

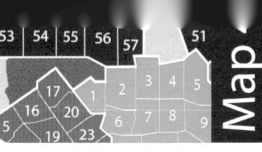
As in many other neighborhoods this side of the hill, Burbank's (relatively) affordable homes and quiet streets are attracting a lot of attention from folks priced out of other areas. The town supports both big box retail (see the Empire Center), and small-scale local businesses. In the latter category, a stroll along Magnolia Boulevard offers something of a hometown flavor, with groovy hair salons, small antique stores, junk stores, and old-school restaurants where "carb" isn't a dirty word.

Coffee

- **Romancing the Bean** • 3208 1/2 W Magnolia Blvd
- **Simply Coffee & Boutique** • 940 N Lima St
- **Starbucks** • 347 N Pass Ave
- **Starbucks (Albertsons)** • 3830 W Verdugo Ave

Copy Centers

- **A Express** • 531 N Hollywood Wy • 818-566-8542
- **Concepts Printing & Copying** • 5668 Cahuenga Blvd • 818-752-8330
- **Copy & Mail** • 2829 N Glenoaks Blvd • 818-843-1010
- **Hayes & Company Printing** • 2817 W Magnolia Blvd • 818-843-7723
- **Image Copy** • 1909 W Burbank Blvd • 818-955-9444
- **Nonstop Printing** • 3820 W Magnolia Blvd • 818-846-3864
- **Pip Printing** • 2111 Kenmere Ave • 818-845-2474
- **Staples** • 2080 Empire Ave • 818-238-2928
- **Turbo Graphics** • 4300 W Victory Blvd • 818-563-5278

Gyms

- **Miami Fitness** • 1611 W Verdugo Ave • 818-566-7547
- **Valley Powerhouse Gym & Fitness Center** • 10950 Sherman Wy • 818-565-5533
- **World Gym** • 2010 N Hollywood Wy • 818-563-4203

Hardware Stores

- **Do It Center** • 3221 W Magnolia Blvd • 818-845-8301
- **Lowe's** • 2000 Empire Ave • 818-557-2300
- **Reno Hardware & Supply** • 2901 Thornton Ave • 818-842-3667

Liquor Stores

- **A&O Liquors** • 3117 W Olive Ave
- **Aero Liquor Store** • 2527 W Burbank Blvd
- **Bamford Liquor & Deli** • 10575 Magnolia Blvd
- **Hermawam Meiling** • 2415 N San Fernando Blvd
- **La Paz Liquor** • 4101 W Magnolia Blvd
- **Magnolia Liquor** • 3801 W Magnolia Blvd
- **Nelson's Liquor** • 4420 W Victory Blvd
- **Prestige Wines & Spirits** • 10101 Camarillo St
- **Riverton Liquors** • 10800 Magnolia Blvd
- **Royal Liquor** • 5600 Cahuenga Blvd
- **Starlite Liquor** • 3510 W Victory Blvd
- **Tip Top Liquor** • 2501 W Victory Blvd

Nightlife

- **Champs Sports Pub** • 4103 W Burbank Blvd • 818-840-9493
- **Dimples** • 3413 W Olive Ave • 818-842-2336
- **Match** • 4657 Lankershim Blvd • 818-766-0116
- **Sardos** • 259 N Pass Ave • 818-846-8126
- **Tinhorn Flats** • 2623 Magnolia Blvd • 818-567-2470

Pet Stores

- **Peggy Woods Pet Emporium** • 923 N Hollywood Wy • 818-848-0123
- **Pet Mania** • 353 N Pass Ave • 818-848-5512
- **Petco** • 3525 W Victory Blvd • 818-566-8528

Restaurants

- **Buchanan Arms** • 2013 W Burbank Blvd • 818-845-0692
- **Chili John's** • 2108 Burbank Blvd • 818-846-3611
- **Coral Café** • 3321 W Burbank Blvd • 818-566-9725
- **Full of Life** • 2515 Magnolia Blvd • 818-845-7411
- **Le Petit Chateau** • 4615 Lankershim Blvd • 818-769-1812
- **Mucho Mas** • 10405 Burbank Blvd • 818-980-0300
- **Pinocchio's** • 3103 Magnolia Blvd • 818-845-3517
- **Poquito Mas** • 10651 Magnolia Blvd • 818-994-8226
- **Santa Fe Tacos** • 353 N Pass Ave • 818-563-4324
- **Tony's Bella Vista** • 3116 W Magnolia Blvd • 818-843-0164

Shopping

- **Arte de Mexico** • 5356 Riverton Ave • 818-769-5090
- **Atomic Records** • 3812 W Magnolia Blvd • 818-848-7090
- **Dark Delicacies Bookstore** • 4213 W Burbank Blvd • 818-556-6660
- **Fry's Electronics** • 2311 N Hollywood Wy • 818-526-8100
- **It's a Wrap** • 3315 W Magnolia Blvd • 818-567-7366
- **Monte Carlo** • 3103 Magnolia Blvd • 818-845-3517
- **Otto's Import Store & Delicatessen** • 2320 W Clark Ave • 818-845-0433
- **The Train Shack** • 1030 N Hollywood Wy • 818-842-3330
- **Western Bagel** • 513 N Hollywood Wy • 818-567-0413

Video Rental

- **Blockbuster** • 2420 W Burbank Blvd • 818-566-1193
- **Hollywood Video** • 10930 Magnolia Blvd • 818-763-4866
- **Hollywood Video** • 2484 W Victory Blvd • 818-559-2560
- **Lakeside Video** • 353 N Pass Ave • 818-848-2001
- **Twisted Video** • 10530 Burbank Blvd • 818-508-0559
- **Video 91** • 10723 Burbank Blvd • 818-766-0684

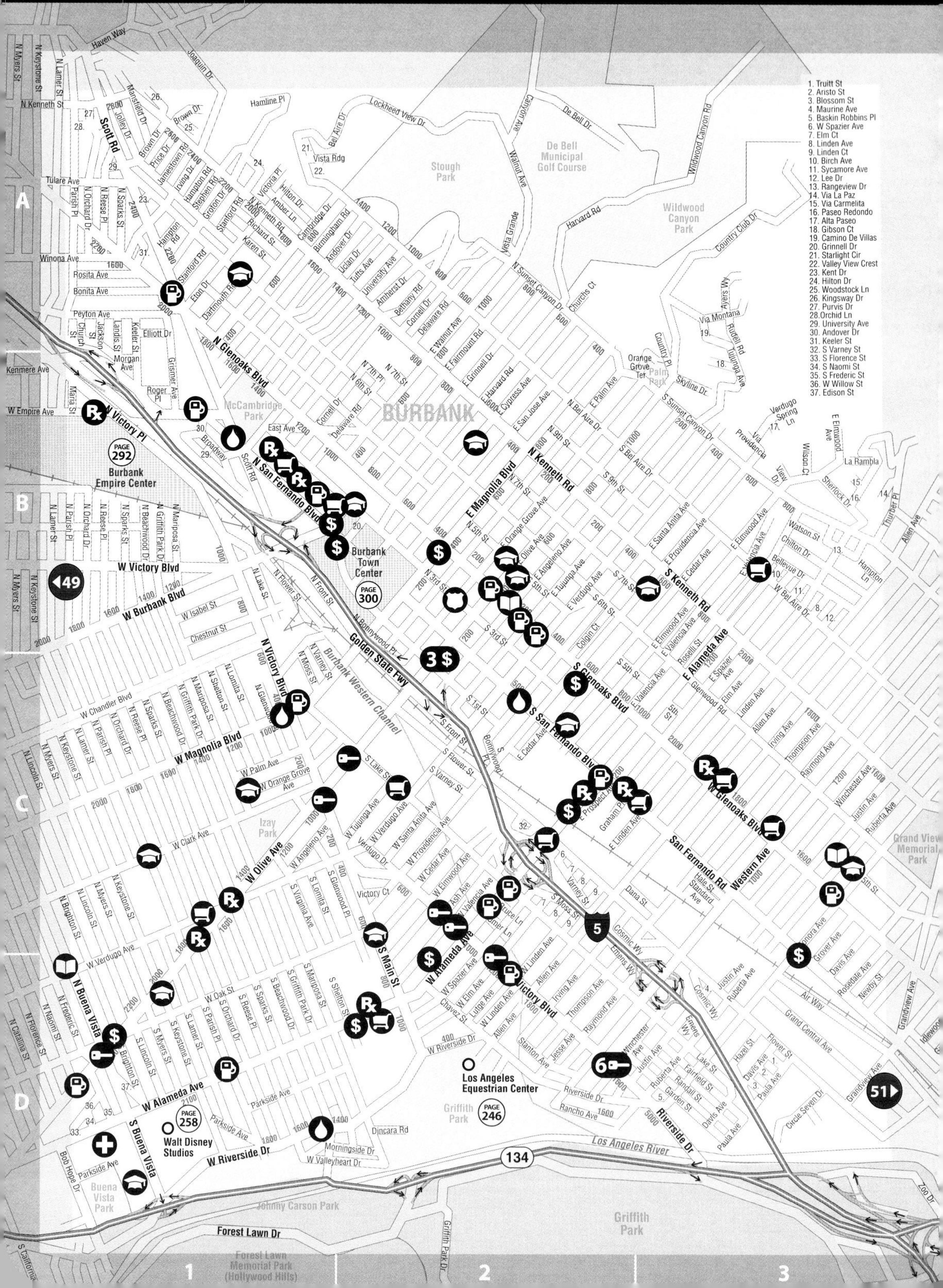
1. Truitt St
2. Aristo St
3. Blossom St
4. Maurine Ave
5. Baskin Robbins Pl
6. W Spazier Ave
7. Elm Ct
8. Linden Ave
9. Linden Ct
10. Birch Ave
11. Sycamore Ave
12. Lee Dr
13. Rangeview Dr
14. Via La Paz
15. Via Carmelita
16. Paseo Redondo
17. Alta Paseo
18. Gibson Ct
19. Camino De Villas
20. Grinnell Dr
21. Starlight Cir
22. Valley View Crest
23. Kent Dr
24. Hilton Dr
25. Woodstock Ln
26. Kingsway Dr
27. Purvis Dr
28. Orchid Ln
29. University Ave
30. Andover Dr
31. Keeler St
32. S Varney St
33. S Florence St
34. S Naomi St
35. S Frederic St
36. W Willow St
37. Edison St
BURBANK
De Bell Municipal Golf Course
Stough Park
Wildwood Canyon Park
McCambridge Park
Burbank Empire Center
Burbank Town Center
Izay Park
Los Angeles Equestrian Center
Griffith Park
Walt Disney Studios
Buena Vista Park
Johnny Carson Park
Forest Lawn Memorial Park (Hollywood Hills)
Grand View Memorial Park
Los Angeles River
Golden State Fwy
Burbank Western Channel
N Glenoaks Blvd
S Glenoaks Blvd
N San Fernando Blvd
S San Fernando Blvd
San Fernando Rd
W Victory Blvd
Victory Blvd
W Burbank Blvd
W Magnolia Blvd
E Magnolia Blvd
W Olive Ave
W Alameda Ave
E Alameda Ave
W Riverside Dr
Riverside Dr
N Buena Vista
S Buena Vista
S Main St
N Kenneth Rd
S Kenneth Rd
W Glenoaks Blvd
Western Ave
Forest Lawn Dr
Scott Rd
Country Club Dr
Wildwood Canyon Rd
N Sunset Canyon Dr
S Sunset Canyon Dr
Lockheed View Dr
PAGE 292
PAGE 300
PAGE 258
PAGE 246
49
51
5
134
A
B
C
D
1
2
3

The area surrounding the equestrian center on Riverside Drive is a great place to spend the day. Within a city block, there's a bowling alley where you can bowl to black lights and rock-and-roll, an ice skating rink that offers lessons and public skating hours, and trail rides that end with a relaxing margarita when you get to the bottom of the hill. Just across the street is Griffith Park, LA's largest green space.

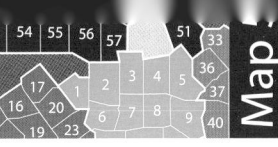

$ Banks

- **Bank of America** · 142 E Olive Ave
- **Bank of America** ·
  6400 San Fernando Rd
- **California National** ·
  240 N San Fernando Blvd
- **Citibank** · 360 E Magnolia Blvd
- **Downey Savings & Loan** ·
  1750 W Olive Ave
- **Downey Savings & Loan** ·
  25 E Alameda Ave
- **Union** · 601 S Glenoaks Blvd
- **Vista Credit Union** · 2411 W Olive Ave
- **Washington Mutual** · 100 N 1st St
- **Washington Mutual** ·
  1110 W Alameda Ave
- **Washington Mutual** ·
  840 N San Fernando Blvd
- **Wells Fargo** · 116 E Olive Ave
- **Wells Fargo** · 900 N San Fernando Blvd

Car Rental

- **Ace Rent-a-Truck** · 1633 W Victory Blvd
- **All-Rite Rent-a-Car** · 810 S Victory Blvd
- **Apple Rent-a-Car** · 1633 Victory Blvd
- **Avis** · 2509 W Olive Ave
- **Enterprise** · 110 S Victory Blvd
- **EZ Rent-a-Car** · 1633 Victory Blvd
- **Penske Truck Rental** ·
  1633 Victory Blvd
- **Rollie's Rent-a-Car** ·
  1633 S Victory Blvd
- **Ryder Rentals** · 1633 Victory Blvd
- **Thrifty Rentals** · 1655 Victory Blvd
- **U-Haul** · 924 S Victory Blvd
- **United Rentals** · 203 W Olive Ave

Car Washes

- **Burbank Pitstop** ·
  1420 N San Fernando Blvd
- **Classic Hand Car Wash** ·
  506 S San Fernando Blvd
- **Magnolia Car Wash** ·
  910 W Magnolia Blvd
- **Sonora Car Wash** · 1521 Riverside Dr

Gas Stations

- **76** · 901 N San Fernando Blvd
- **Arco** · 201 W Alameda Ave
- **Arco** · 250 S Glenoaks Blvd
- **Chevron** · 100 S Glenoaks Blvd
- **Chevron** · 140 E Alameda Ave
- **Chevron** · 1501 W Glenoaks Blvd
- **Chevron** · 1655 Victory Blvd
- **Chevron** · 2501 W Olive Ave
- **Chevron** · 439 W Alameda Blvd
- **Mobil** · 2005 N Glenoaks Blvd
- **Mobil** · 349 S Glenoaks Blvd
- **Sevan** · 1638 N San Fernando Blvd
- **Shell** · 181 W Alameda Ave
- **Shell** · 1919 W Alameda Ave
- **Shell** · 400 N Victory Blvd

Hospitals

- **Providence St Joseph Medical** ·
  501 S Buena Vista St

Landmarks

- **Los Angeles Equestrian Center** ·
  480 Riverside Dr
- **Walt Disney Studios** · 500 S Buena Vista

Libraries

- **Buena Vista Branch** · 300 N Buena
  Vista St · 818-238-5620
- **Burbank Central Library** · 110 N
  Glenoaks Blvd · 818-238-5600
- **Grandview Library** · 1535 5th St ·
  818-548-2049

Pharmacies

- **Pavilions** · 1110 W Alameda Ave ·
  818-567-0257
- **Ralphs** · 1100 N San Fernando Blvd ·
  818-845-5112
- **Rite-Aid** · 1505 W Olive Ave ·
  818-846-7843
- **Sav-On** · 101 E Alameda Ave ·
  818-563-2910
- **Sav-On** · 1015 N San Fernando Blvd ·
  818-841-0800
- **Sav-On (Albertsons)** ·
  1855 W Glenoaks Blvd · 818-244-8485
- **Target** · 1800 W Empire Ave ·
  818-238-0239
- **Walgreens** · 1028 S San Fernando Blvd
  · 818-729-8500

Police

- **Burbank Police Dept** · 200 N 3rd St ·
  818-238-3333

Post Offices

- **US Post Office** · 135 E Olive Ave
- **US Post Office** ·
  1634 N San Fernando Blvd
- **US Post Office** · 6444 San Fernando Rd

Schools

- **Alternative School of California** ·
  704 S Main St
- **Balboa Elementary** · 1844 Bel Aire Dr
- **Bellarmine-Jefferson High** ·
  465 E Olive Ave
- **Benjamin Franklin Elementary** ·
  1610 Lake St
- **Burbank High** · 902 N 3rd St
- **Burroughs High** · 1920 Clark Ave
- **Clearview** · 1930 W Glenoaks Blvd
- **David Starr Jordan Middle** ·
  420 S Mariposa St
- **First Lutheran** · 1001 S Glenoaks Blvd
- **Jefferson Elementary** · 1540 5th St
- **Joaquin Miller Elementary** ·
  720 E Providencia Ave
- **Little Angels Art** ·
  721 S San Fernando Blvd
- **Providence High** · 511 S Buena Vista St
- **Ralph Waldo Emerson Elementary** ·
  720 E Cypress Ave
- **St Finbar** · 2120 W Olive Ave
- **St Robert Bellarmine** · 154 N 5th St
- **Thomas Jefferson Elementary** ·
  1900 N 6th St
- **Walt Disney Elementary** ·
  1220 W Orange Grove Ave
- **William McKinley Elementary** ·
  349 W Valencia Ave

Supermarkets

- **Albertsons** · 1855 W Glenoaks Blvd
- **Pavilions** · 1110 W Alameda Ave
- **Ralphs** · 1100 N San Fernando Blvd
- **Ralphs** · 25 E Alameda Ave
- **Smart & Final** · 6850 San Fernando Rd
- **Trader Joe's** · 216 E Alameda Ave
- **Trader Joe's** · 345 S Lake Blvd
- **Vons** · 1011 N San Fernando Blvd
- **Vons** · 1820 W Verdugo Ave

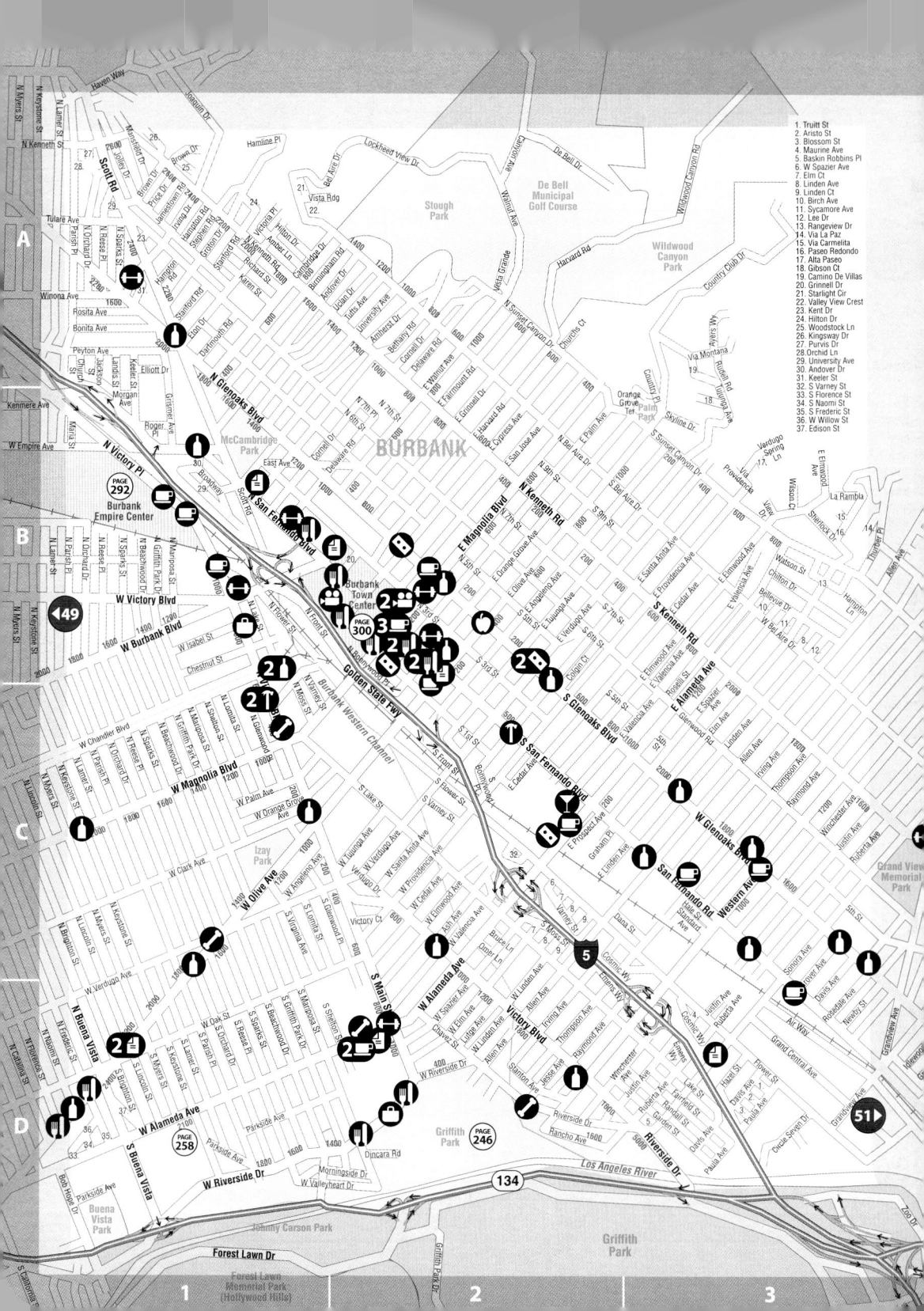

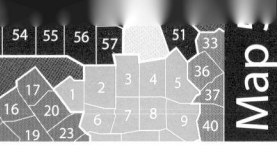
Though the Burbank Town Center remains the area's main destination for dinner and a movie, those looking to improve, re-do, or otherwise tart up the old homestead are to be found at the Empire Center, with its Lowe's, Target, and Great Indoors. We must agree that it is mighty convenient to find building supplies, as well as Krispy Kreme donuts and cases of soda (from Costco) for the construction crew, all in such handy proximity.

Coffee

- **Café Chalet** · 150 E Olive Ave
- **Coffee Bean & Tea Leaf** · 340 N San Fernando Blvd
- **Kelly's Coffee & Fudge** · 201 E Magnolia Blvd
- **Krispy Kreme Doughnuts** · 1521 N Victory Pl
- **Patrick's Café** · 6320 San Fernando Rd
- **San Marco Coffee Roasting** · 401 N Glenoaks Blvd
- **Starbucks** · 113 E Alameda Ave
- **Starbucks** · 1190 Alameda Ave
- **Starbucks** · 1703 W Glenoaks Blvd
- **Starbucks** · 1711 N Victory Pl
- **Starbucks** · 300 N San Fernando Blvd
- **Starbucks (The Great Indoors)** · 1301 N Victory Pl
- **Starbucks (Vons)** · 1110 W Alameda Ave
- **Stardust Café** · 6720 San Fernando Rd

Copy Centers

- **Color Images Copy and Print** · 2320 W Olive Ave · 818-567-2900
- **Copy Central** · 2300 W Olive Ave · 818-841-8800
- **Ford Graphics** · 608 Sonora Ave · 818-841-4338
- **Kinko's** · 101 N San Fernando Blvd · 818-558-3900
- **Mail Boxes Etc** · 1317 N San Fernando Blvd · 818-845-3332
- **Office Depot** · 228 E Burbank Blvd · 818-848-2591
- **Staples** · 1060 W Almeda Dr · 818-558-3350

Farmer's Markets

- **Burbank** · W Olive Ave & S Glenoaks Blvd

Gyms

- **Burbank YMCA** · 321 E Magnolia Blvd · 818-845-8551
- **Curves** · 1090 N San Fernando Blvd · 818-842-1007
- **Curves** · 1416 Kenneth Rd · 818-551-1600
- **Curves** · 940 W Alameda Ave · 818-558-3591
- **Los Angeles Lifting Club** · 1031 N Victory Pl · 818-846-5438
- **World Gym** · 226 E Palm Ave · 818-954-0021

Hardware Stores

- **Burbank Paint** · 548 S San Fernando Blvd · 818-845-2684
- **Orchard Supply Hardware** · 641 N Victory Blvd · 818-557-2755
- **Stock Building Supply** · 640 N Victory Blvd · 818-842-2177

Liquor Stores

- **ABC Liquor & Deli** · 2112 W Magnolia Blvd
- **Ace Liquors** · 1740 Victory Blvd
- **Alameda Liquor** · 929 S Victory Blvd
- **Burbank Liquor** · 500 S Glenoaks Blvd
- **Castle Liquors** · 6808 San Fernando Rd
- **Favorite Liquor & Deli** · 533 S Victory Blvd
- **Glenmar Liquors** · 2000 N Glenoaks Blvd
- **Jons Market** · 1717 W Glenoaks Blvd
- **K&K Liquor** · 515 N Victory Blvd
- **Legacy Liquor** · 1800 W Olive Ave
- **M&M Liquors** · 1951 W Glenoaks Blvd
- **Prime Liquor Jr Market** · 101 N Victory Blvd
- **Roy's Liquor** · 1627 N San Fernando Blvd
- **Selene Liquor Market** · 1427 N Glenoaks Blvd
- **Thirst Quencher Liquors** · 440 N Glenoaks Blvd
- **UM Liquor** · 401 N Victory Blvd
- **Village Liquor** · 211 E Olive Ave
- **Village Market** · 2713 W Olive Ave

Movie Theaters

- **AMC Burbank 16** · 125 E Palm Ave · 818-953-9800
- **AMC Media Center 8** · 201 E Magnolia Blvd · 818-953-9800
- **AMC Media Center North 6** · 770 N 1st St · 818-953-9800

Nightlife

- **The Blue Room** · 916 S San Fernando Blvd · 323-849-2779

Pet Stores

- **Burbank Pet Plaza** · 1080 W Alameda Ave · 818-557-0144
- **Millennium Pets** · 409 N Victory Blvd · 818-845-7305
- **Pets R Us** · 839 W Glenoaks Blvd · 818-553-8060
- **Scales 'N' Tails** · 1720 W Verdugo Ave · 818-842-6496
- **Stephens Hay & Grain** · 1840 Riverside Dr · 818-242-4540

Restaurants

- **Gordon Biersch Brewing** · 145 S San Fernando Blvd · 818-569-5240
- **Harry's Family Restaurant** · 920 N San Fernando Blvd · 818-842-8755
- **In-N-Out Burger** · 761 1st St · 800-786-1000
- **Knight Restaurant** · 138 N San Fernando Blvd · 818-845-4516
- **Market City Caffe** · 164 E Palm Ave · 818-840-7036
- **Mi Piace** · 801 N San Fernando Blvd · 818-843-1111
- **Picanha Churrascaria** · 269 E Palm Ave · 818-972-2111
- **Poquito Mas** · 2635 W Olive Ave · 818-563-2252
- **Ribs USA** · 2711 W Olive Ave · 818-841-8872
- **Riverside Café** · 1221 W Riverside Dr · 818-563-3567
- **Romano's Macaroni Grill** · 102 E Magnolia Blvd · 818-729-9405
- **Viva Fresh** · 900 W Riverside Dr · 818-845-2425

Shopping

- **Pickwick Center** · 1001 Riverside Dr · 818-845-5300
- **Valley Dealer Exchange** · 825 N Victory Blvd · 818-845-4090

Video Rental

- **20-20 Video** · 600 S Glenoaks Blvd · 818-559-2300
- **Blockbuster** · 324 S Glenoaks Blvd · 818-972-9292
- **Goodtime Video** · 520 N Glenoaks Blvd · 818-558-5618
- **Hollywood Video** · 105 E Alameda Ave · 818-845-0553

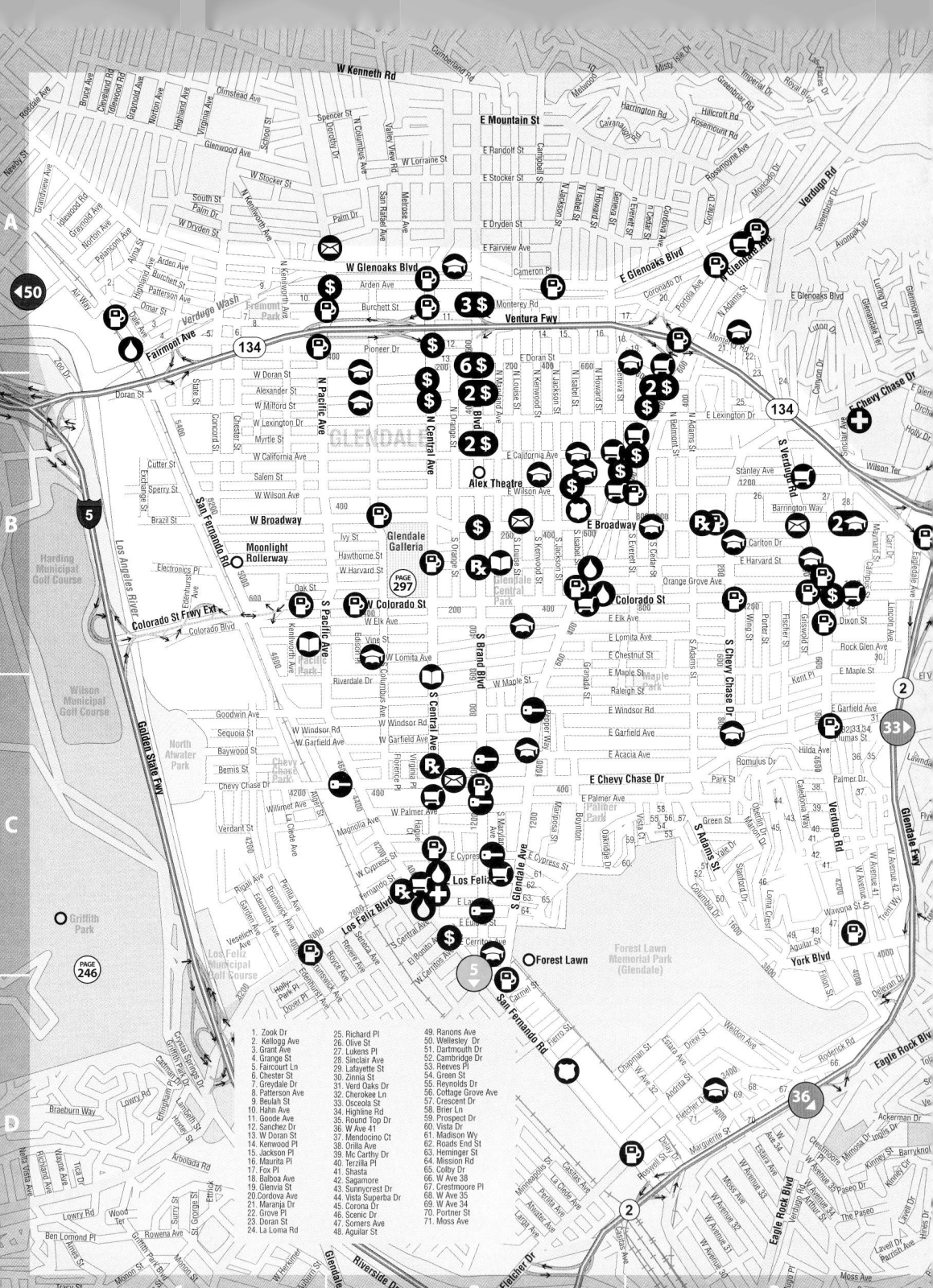

To non-residents, Glendale adds up to little more than the location of Forest Lawn Memorial Park. And that's just not fair. Glendale is a good place for the living, of all ages. Particularly nice are the twisting residential streets named for colleges, just east of Forest Lawn, and Glendale's eminently walkable and interesting downtown.

 Banks

- **Bank of America** · 203 N Glendale Ave
- **Bank of America** · 345 N Brand Blvd
- **Bank of America** · 3812 San Fernando Rd
- **Bank of the West** · 400 N Glendale Ave
- **California Credit Union** · 701 N Brand Blvd
- **California National** · 600 N Brand Blvd
- **Citibank** · 414 N Central Ave
- **Citibank** · 700 N Brand Blvd
- **City National** · 550 N Brand Blvd
- **Community** · 100 N Brand Blvd
- **Downey Savings & Loan** · 211 N Glendale Ave
- **East West** · 520 N Central Ave
- **First Regional** · 655 N Central Ave
- **Jackson Federal** · 500 N Brand Blvd
- **Nara** · 831 N Pacific Ave
- **National Bank of California** · 520 N Brand Blvd
- **Pacific Western** · 400 N Brand Blvd
- **Union** · 330 N Brand Blvd
- **US** · 311 W Los Feliz Rd
- **US** · 561 N Glendale Ave
- **US** · 701 N Brand Blvd
- **Washington Mutual** · 500 N Glendale Ave
- **Washington Mutual** · 620 N Brand Blvd
- **Wells Fargo** · 1416 E Colorado St
- **Wells Fargo** · 535 N Brand Blvd
- **Western Financial** · 611 E Wilson Ave

 Car Rental

- **Advantage Rent-a-Car** · 511 W Chevy Chase Dr
- **Budget** · 1124 S Brand Blvd
- **Enterprise** · 1510 S Brand Blvd
- **Enterprise** · 1820 S Brand Blvd
- **Enterprise** · 827 S Glendale Ave
- **Hertz** · 1001 S Brand Blvd
- **U-Haul** · 1313 S Brand Blvd

Car Washes

- **Antique Car Wash** · 236 S Glendale Ave
- **Broadway Car Wash** · 361 W Broadway
- **California Car Wash** · 3940 San Fernando Rd
- **California Car Wash Detail** · 1411 S Central Ave
- **Galleria Car Wash** · 5720 San Fernando Rd
- **Glendale Car Wash** · 725 E Colorado St

Gas Stations

- **76** · 200 N Glendale Ave
- **76** · 200 S Central Ave
- **76** · 475 W Colorado St
- **76** · 901 N Central Ave
- **76** · 901 N Glendale Ave
- **Arco** · 1118 N Glendale Ave
- **Arco** · 144 N Verdugo Rd
- **Arco** · 3680 San Fernando Rd
- **Arco** · 4103 Verdugo Rd
- **Arco** · 501 W Colorado St

- **Arco** · 5800 San Fernando Rd
- **Chevron** · 1101 E Colorado Blvd
- **Chevron** · 2960 W Broadway
- **Chevron** · 3100 N San Fernando Rd
- **Chevron** · 466 W Broadway
- **Chevron** · 501 E Glenoaks Blvd
- **Mobil** · 1028 S Brand Blvd
- **Mobil** · 1324 S Central Ave
- **Mobil** · 250 S Glendale Ave
- **Mobil** · 301 S Verdugo Rd
- **Mobil** · 700 N Glendale Ave
- **Mobil** · 800 N Pacific Ave
- **Mobil** · 825 N Central Ave
- **Shell** · 1401 E Colorado St
- **Shell** · 625 N Pacific Ave
- **Texaco** · 925 S Verdugo Rd

 Hospitals

- **Glendale Adventist** · 1509 Chevy Chase Dr
- **Glendale Memorial** · 1420 S Central Ave

○ Landmarks

- **Alex Theatre** · 216 N Brand Blvd
- **Forest Lawn Memorial Park** · 1712 S Glendale Ave
- **Griffith Park** · 4730 Crystal Springs Dr
- **Moonlight Rollerway** · 5110 San Fernando Road

Libraries

- **Glendale Central Library** · 222 E Harvard St · 818-548-2030
- **Pacific Park Branch** · 501 S Pacific Ave · 818-548-3760
- **Sons of the Revolution Library** · 600 S Central Ave · 818-240-1775

Pharmacies

- **Longs Drugs** · 221 Glendale Ave · 818-247-7218
- **Rite-Aid** · 216 S Brand Blvd · 818-243-1126
- **Rite-Aid (24 hrs)** · 531 N Glendale Ave · 818-241-9770
- **Sav-On (24 hrs)** · 1122 E Broadway · 818-547-0891
- **Sav-On (Albertsons)** · 1000 S Central Ave · 818-246-5679
- **Vons** · 311 W Los Feliz Rd · 818-246-5399

 Police

- **Glendale Police Dept** · 131 N Isabel St · 818-548-4840
- **Los Angeles Police Dept** · 3353 N San Fernando Rd · 213-485-2563

 Post Offices

- **US Post Office** · 1009 N Pacific Ave
- **US Post Office** · 101 N Verdugo Rd
- **US Post Office** · 120 E Chevy Chase Dr
- **US Post Office** · 313 E Broadway

Schools

- **A Adventist Children's Center** · 234 N Isabel St
- **Allan F Daily High** · 220 N Kenwood Pl
- **Cerritos Elementary** · 120 E Cerritos Ave
- **Columbus Elementary** · 425 W Milford St
- **First Lutheran Art Academy** · 1300 E Colorado St
- **Fletcher Dr Elementary** · 3350 Fletcher Dr
- **Glendale Kindergarten** · 225 S Verdugo Rd
- **Glendale Montessori** · 413 W Doran St
- **Glendale Senior High** · 1440 E Broadway
- **Holy Family Elementary** · 400 S Louise St
- **Holy Family High** · 400 E Lamita Ave
- **Horace Mann Elementary** · 501 E Acacia Ave
- **Hoskins Center** · 1479 E Broadway
- **Incarnation Elementary** · 123 W Glenoaks Blvd
- **John Marshall Elementary** · 1201 E Broadway
- **John Muir Elementary** · 912 S Chevy Chase Dr
- **RD White Elementary** · 744 E Doran St
- **St Anne Montessori** · 1479 E Broadway
- **St Mary's Armenian Tufenkian** · 1200 Carlton Dr
- **Theodore Roosevelt Middle** · 1017 S Glendale Ave
- **Thomas Edison Elementary** · 440 W Lomita Ave
- **Tobinworld** · 920 E Broadway
- **Washington Irving Middle** · 3010 Estara Ave
- **Woodrow Wilson Middle** · 1221 Monterey Rd
- **Zion Lutheran** · 301 N Isabel St

Supermarkets

- **Albertsons** · 1000 S Central Ave
- **Jons Marketplace** · 600 E Colorado St
- **Ralphs** · 1010 N Glendale Ave
- **Ralphs** · 1416 E Colorado Ave
- **Ralphs** · 211 N Glendale Ave
- **Smart & Final** · 210 N Verdugo Rd
- **Trader Joe's** · 130 N Glendale Ave
- **Vons** · 311 W Los Feliz Rd
- **Vons** · 561 N Glendale Ave
- **Whole Foods Market** · 331 N Glendale Ave

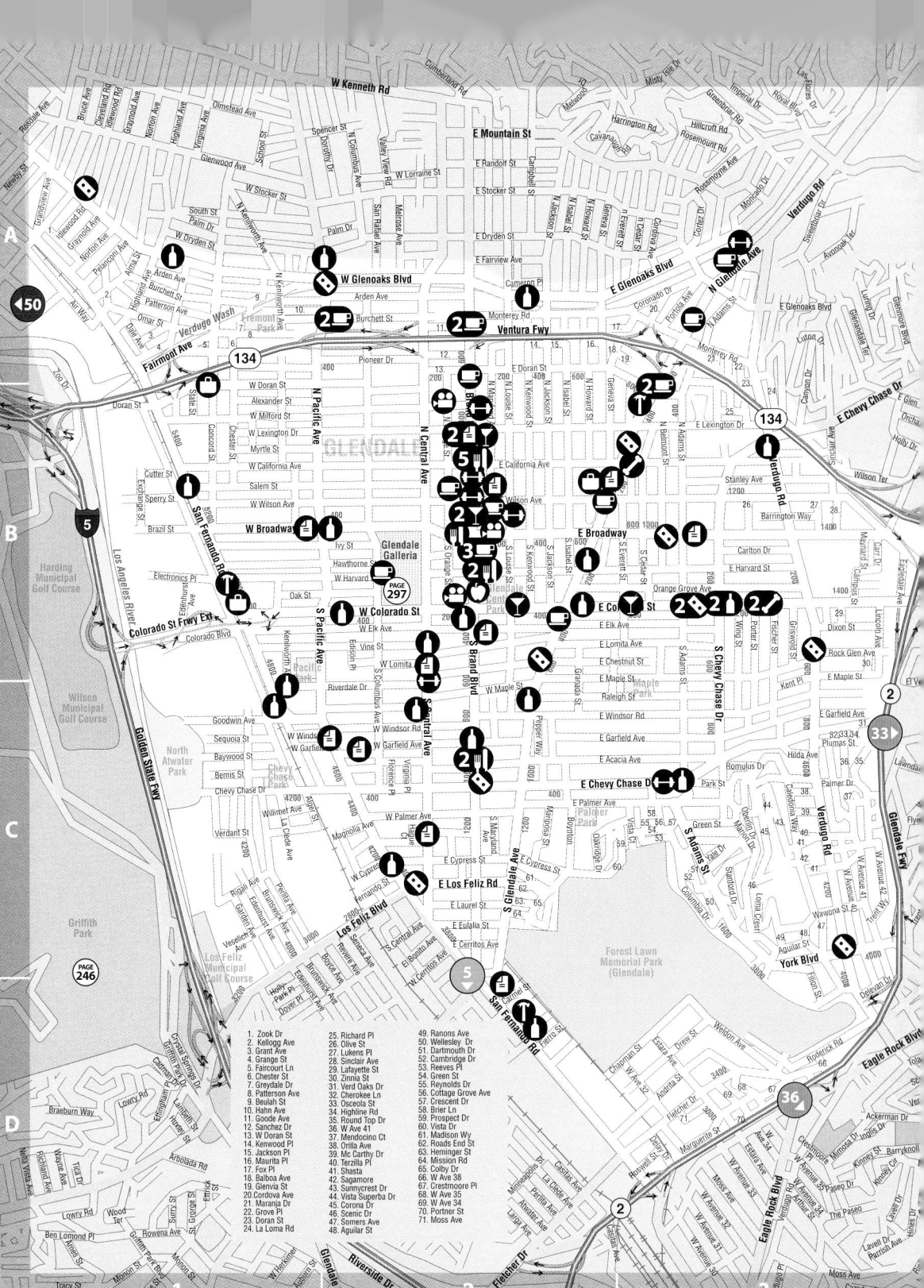

W Kenneth Rd

E Mountain St

W Glenoaks Blvd

Ventura Fwy

134

GLENDALE

W Broadway

Glendale Galleria

PAGE
297

W Colorado St

E Broadway

E Colorado St

E Chevy Chase Dr

E Los Feliz Rd

York Blvd

PAGE
246

Griffith Park

Harding Municipal Golf Course

Wilson Municipal Golf Course

North Atwater Park

Chevy Chase Park

Los Feliz Municipal Golf Course

Forest Lawn Memorial Park (Glendale)

Palmer Park

Glendale Central Park

Maple Park

Fremont Park

1. Zook Dr
2. Kellogg Ave
3. Grant Ave
4. Grange St
5. Faircourt Ln
6. Chester St
7. Greydale Dr
8. Patterson Ave
9. Beulah St
10. Hahn Ave
11. Goode Ave
12. Sanchez Dr
13. W Doran St
14. Kenwood Pl
15. Jackson Pl
16. Maurita Pl
17. Fox Pl
18. Balboa Ave
19. Glenvia St
20. Cordova Ave
21. Maranja Dr
22. Grove Pl
23. Doran St
24. La Loma Rd

25. Richard Pl
26. Olive St
27. Lukens Pl
28. Sinclair Ave
29. Lafayette St
30. Zinnia St
31. Verd Oaks Dr
32. Cherokee Ln
33. Osceola St
34. Highline Rd
35. Round Top Dr
36. W Ave 41
37. Mendocino Ct
38. Orilla Ave
39. Mc Carthy Dr
40. Terzilla Pl
41. Shasta
42. Sagamore
43. Sunnycrest Dr
44. Vista Superba Dr
45. Corona Dr
46. Scenic Dr
47. Somers Ave
48. Aguilar St

49. Ranons Ave
50. Wellesley Dr
51. Dartmouth Dr
52. Cambridge Dr
53. Reeves Pl
54. Green St
55. Reynolds Dr
56. Cottage Grove Ave
57. Crescent Dr
58. Brier Ln
59. Prospect Dr
60. Vista Dr
61. Madison Wy
62. Roads End St
63. Heminger St
64. Mission Rd
65. Colby Dr
66. W Ave 38
67. Crestmoore Pl
68. W Ave 35
69. W Ave 34
70. Portner St
71. Moss Ave

Brand Boulevard changes its stripes several times over on its trip north toward the 134. Past the auto row portion of the journey, you hit downtown Glendale itself, a charming mix of old and new (see the Alex Theater for both live and cinematic events) and a big monster mall within spitting distance. Serial decorators and home-fixers are wise to go San Fernando Road for hardware, statuary, tile, and the like.

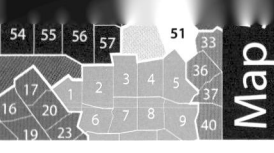

Coffee

- **Brand Coffee** · 701 N Brand Blvd
- **Coffee Cup of Glendale** · 535 N Brand Blvd
- **Coffee Express** · 742 N Glendale Ave
- **Edna's Coffee & Grocery** · 420 S Glendale Ave
- **Favorite Place** · 115 W Wilson Ave
- **Java Time** · 525 N Glendale Ave
- **Just Coffee** · 1010 N Glendale Ave
- **Kelly's Coffee & Fudge** · 2217 Glendale Galleria
- **La Goccia Espresso Bar** · 101 N Brand Blvd
- **Lady Gourmet** · 700 N Brand Blvd
- **Lollicup** · 118 S Brand Blvd
- **Starbucks** · 114 N Brand Blvd
- **Starbucks** · 130 S Brand Blvd
- **Starbucks** · 203 N Glendale Ave
- **Starbucks** · 469 Burchett St
- **Starbucks (Vons)** · 561 N Glendale Ave
- **Tiffany's Coffee** · 900 N Pacific Ave
- **Urartu Coffee** · 119 N Maryland Ave

Copy Centers

- **BJ's Printing Emporium** · 323 N Brand Blvd · 818-551-7840
- **Copy Central** · 330 N Brand Blvd · 818-502-0100
- **JRT Business Supplies** · 445 W Garfield Ave · 818-547-6001
- **K&K Copy** · 1220 S Central Ave · 818-507-7636
- **Kinko's** · 225 N Brand Blvd · 818-500-1811
- **Mail Boxes Etc** · 1125 E Broadway · 818-242-4270
- **Mail Boxes Etc** · 249 N Brand Blvd · 818-244-4448
- **Mercury Blue Print** · 414 S Brand Blvd · 818-243-8722
- **Minuteman Press** · 446 S Central Ave · 818-500-1620
- **Office Depot** · 515 W Broadway · 818-242-2582
- **Pip Printing** · 4614 San Fernando Rd · 818-956-0912
- **Staples** · 213 N Glendale Ave · 818-240-2133
- **Staples** · 3360 N San Fernando Rd · 323-256-2409

Farmer's Markets

- **Farmers' Market–Glendale** · 100 N Brand Blvd

Gyms

- **24-Hour Fitness** · 240 N Brand Blvd · 818-240-5111
- **24-Hour Fitness** · 450 N Brand Blvd · 818-247-4334
- **Bally Total Fitness** · 623 S Central Ave · 818-240-2425
- **Curves** · 1010 Glendale Ave · 818-551-1600
- **Curves** · 1022 E Chevy Chase Dr · 818-242-4553

- **Total Woman** · 601 N Brand Blvd · 818-552-2027
- **World Gym** · 1001 E Colorado Blvd · 818-243-1600
- **YMCA** · 140 N Louise St · 818-240-4130

Hardware Stores

- **Home Depot** · 5040 San Fernando Rd · 818-246-9600
- **Stock Building Supply** · 3250 N San Fernando Rd · 323-478-2200
- **Virgil's Hardware** · 520 N Glendale Ave · 626-449-3461

Liquor Stores

- **A-1 Liquor** · 1145 E Colorado St
- **Adam's Square Liquor** · 1021 E Chevy Chase Dr
- **B&C Liquor** · 102 W Colorado St
- **Broadway Liquors** · 465 W Broadway
- **Cavalier Liquor** · 1307 W Glenoaks Blvd
- **Colorado Liquor** · 468 W Colorado St
- **Eco Wines & Spirits** · 3235 N San Fernando Rd
- **Esquire Liquor** · 5300 San Fernando Rd
- **Glendale House of Liquor** · 420 S Glendale Ave
- **Gourmet Liquors** · 715 S Central Ave
- **House of Liquor** · 1008 E Colorado St
- **Jons Market** · 600 E Colorado St
- **Liquor Zone** · 424 S Central Ave
- **Mitchall's Liquor** · 333 N Verdugo Rd
- **Old Green Mill Liquor House** · 4520 San Fernando Rd
- **Pacific Food Mart** · 1008 N Pacific Ave
- **Red Carpet Wines & Spirits** · 400 E Glenoaks Blvd
- **Rodeo Liquor & Deli** · 205 S Glendale Ave
- **Topline Wine & Spirit** · 556 Riverdale Dr
- **Topline Wines & Spirits** · 7418 San Fernando Rd
- **Vens Liquors** · 825 W Glenoaks Blvd
- **Windsor Liquor** · 801 S Glendale Ave
- **Wine Vault** · 929 S Brand Blvd

Movie Theaters

- **Mann Glendale Exchange 10** · 128 N Maryland Ave · 818-549-0045
- **Mann Glendale Marketplace 4** · 144 S Brand Blvd · 818-241-2784

Nightlife

- **Duffy's Pub** · 204 N Brand Blvd · 818-242-3835
- **Jax Bar and Grill** · 339 N Brand Blvd · 818-500-1604
- **Maurizio's** · 135 N Maryland Ave · 818-247-5600
- **The Scene** · 806 Colorado St · 818-241-7029
- **Yard House** · 330 E Colorado St · 626-577-9273

Pet Stores

- **Petco** · 231 N Glendale Ave · 818-548-0411
- **Pretty Bird** · 1303 E Colorado St · 818-265-0566
- **Tropical Imports Unlimited** · 1134 E Colorado St · 818-240-9356

Restaurants

- **Carousel** · 304 N Brand Blvd · 818-246-7775
- **Cinnabar** · 933 S Brand Blvd · 818-551-1155
- **Damon's Steakhouse** · 317 N Brand Blvd · 818-507-1510
- **Eat Well** · 1013 S Brand Blvd · 818-243-5928
- **Ichiban** · 120 S Brand Blvd · 818-242-9966
- **Max's of Manila** · 313 W Broadway · 818-637-7751
- **Porto's Bakery & Café** · 315 N Brand Blvd · 818-956-5996
- **Seoul Grindz** · 136 S Brand Blvd · 818-637-8566

Shopping

- **Cost Plus World Market** · 223 N Glendale Ave · 818-241-2112
- **Glendale Costume** · 746 W Doran St · 818-244-1161
- **Luigi's Pottery & Gardenware** · 5630 San Fernando Road · 818-246-7579

Video Rental

- **20-20 Video** · 1023 S Brand Blvd · 818-240-2020
- **ABC Video (Asian)** · 4108 Verdugo Rd · 323-257-7225
- **Blockbuster** · 306 N Glendale Ave · 818-547-1146
- **Blockbuster** · 900 E Colorado St · 818-549-0801
- **Blockbuster** · 900 N Pacific Ave · 818-507-4392
- **Chaterian** · 1022 E Broadway · 818-242-6928
- **Glendale Videograph** · 620 S Glendale Ave · 818-240-5463
- **Interhome Video** · 519 S Verdugo Rd · 818-956-6031
- **Mundo Latino (Spanish)** · 401 W Los Feliz Rd · 818-241-2263
- **Pop's Video** · 1121 E Colorado St · 818-242-0777
- **Video Station** · 1112 1/2 W Glenoaks Blvd · 818-242-6512

211

Popular lore has it that Tarzana was so named as a tribute to Edgar Rice Burroughs, writer of the legendary Tarzan books. But in reality, Tarzana had its name long before Burroughs put pen to paper, and it was the character that was named for the town, not the other way around.

 Banks

- **Bank of America** · 22004 Sherman Wy
- **Bank of America** · 5440 Topanga Canyon Blvd
- **Bank of America** · 5959 Canoga Ave
- **Citibank** · 22000 Ventura Blvd
- **Washington Mutual** · 22001 Ventura Blvd
- **Wells Fargo** · 20642 Ventura Blvd
- **World Savings & Loan** · 20800 Ventura Blvd

Car Rental

- **Enterprise** · 21118 Ventura Blvd
- **Hertz** · 21301 Ventura Blvd
- **Vista Ford Rent A Car** · 21501 Ventura Blvd

Car Washes

- **Woodland Hills Car Wash** · 20905 Ventura Blvd

Gas Stations

- **76** · 20905 Ventura Blvd
- **76** · 21940 Ventura Blvd
- **Arco** · 22004 Clarendon St
- **Chevron** · 5356 Canoga Ave
- **Shell** · 20900 Ventura Blvd

 Pharmacies

- **Longs Drugs** · 21055 Ventura Blvd · 818-226-9215
- **Rite-Aid (24 hrs)** · 21949 Ventura Blvd · 818-348-5542
- **Sav-On** · 22050 Ventura Blvd · 818-346-2207

Post Offices

- **US Post Office** · 22121 Clarendon St

Schools

- **Chime Charter** · 19722 Collier St
- **Halsey** · 21321 Costanso St
- **Henry David Thoreau Continuation** · 5429 Quakertown Ave
- **Serrania Ave Elementary** · 5014 Serrania Ave
- **St Mel Elementary** · 20874 Ventura Blvd
- **Wilbur Ave Elementary** · 5213 Crebs Ave
- **William Howard Taft Senior High** · 5461 Winnetka Ave

Supermarkets

- **Ralphs** · 21909 Ventura Blvd
- **Vons** · 21821 Ventura Blvd
- **Whole Foods Market** · 21347 Ventura Blvd

213

Map 5

52 | 53 | 54 | 55 | 56 | 57
17 | 1 | 2 | 3
16 | 20
15 | 19 | 23 | 6 | 7

An interesting grassroots campaign has been underway for some time in Woodland Hills. Over 350 people have pledged money to help purchase land at the corner of Ventura Boulevard & Van Alden Avenue (at a retail cost of $1.8 million) to help protect the lot's trees and wisteria. The corner would serve as a Community Cultural Center, and the movement is spearheaded by the Tarzana Community Center Foundation. We wish them luck!

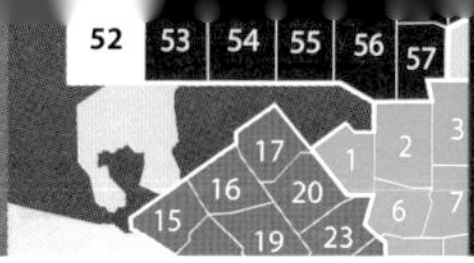

Coffee

- **Mom's Coffee Shop** · 20501 Ventura Blvd
- **Starbucks** · 5422 Topanga Canyon Blvd
- **Starbucks (Target)** · 20801 Ventura Blvd

Copy Centers

- **California Copy & Printing Center** · 21416 Ventura Blvd · 818-703-8686
- **Function Junction** · 20841 Ventura Blvd · 818-710-8841
- **UPS Store** · 20929 Ventura Blvd · 818-702-0456
- **Whitmont Copy** · 21031 Ventura Blvd · 818-340-9200
- **Woodland Hills Printing** · 21602 Ventura Blvd · 818-888-6702

Farmer's Markets

- **Woodland Hills** · 6200 block of Topanga Canyon Blvd

Gyms

- **Curves** · 21800 Ventura Blvd · 818-883-8853

Hardware Stores

- **Ace** · 21142 Ventura Blvd · 818-348-4844
- **Franklin's True Value** · 21936 Ventura Blvd · 818-347-6800

Liquor Stores

- **Carlson's Liquor** · 21900 Ventura Blvd
- **Embassy Liquor** · 4879 Topanga Canyon Blvd
- **Greene's Liquor** · 21056 Ventura Blvd

Nightlife

- **Corbin Bowl** · 19616 Ventura Blvd · 818-996-2695

Pet Stores

- **California Pet Center** · 21906 Ventura Blvd · 818-716-5933
- **Petco** · 21943 Ventura Blvd · 818-346-9397

Video Rental

- **Blockbuster** · 21937 Ventura Blvd · 818-713-9990

1. Green Vista Dr
2. Octavia Pl
3. Rochelle Pl
4. Bosque Dr
5. Shileno Pl
6. Huerta Ct
7. Toquet Dr
8. Corinthian Dr
9. Tarzana St
10. Polora St
11. Sugarman St
12. Greenbrier Ln
13. Marblehead Wy
14. Torrey Pines Ln
15. Green Meadow Ct
16. Deer View Ct
17. Anastasia Dr
18. Lake Vista Ct
19. Avd Puerto Vallarta
20. Weddington St
21. Clark St
22. Shoshone Ave
23. Addison St
24. Hartsook St
25. Forbes Ave
26. Whitaker Ave
27. Saville Ave

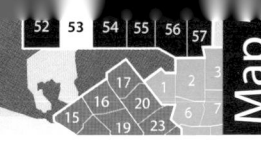

As Sherman Oaks and Studio City become increasingly similar to LA's more urban environs, Encino functions in many ways as the gateway to the 'burbs. The community offers some of the best shopping and dining options for families (even if it's a bit overrun by the chains) and a number of clean, enticing public parks.

$ Banks

- **Bank of America** · 16640 Ventura Blvd
- **Bank of America** · 18337 Ventura Blvd
- **California Credit Union** · 17000 Ventura Blvd
- **California National** · 16830 Ventura Blvd
- **Downey Savings & Loan** · 17250 Ventura Blvd
- **East West** · 18321 Ventura Blvd
- **First Bank & Trust** · 17777 Ventura Blvd
- **First Regional** · 16830 Ventura Blvd
- **Union** · 16633 Ventura Blvd
- **Washington Mutual** · 17107 Ventura Blvd
- **Washington Mutual** · 18421 Ventura Blvd
- **Wells Fargo** · 17232 Ventura Blvd
- **Western Financial** · 17323 Ventura Blvd

Car Rental

- **Enterprise** · 16616 Ventura Blvd

Car Washes

- **Encino Chevron Car Wash** · 18081 Ventura Blvd
- **Premier Car Wash** · 17432 Ventura Blvd

Gas Stations

- **76** · 16900 Ventura Blvd
- **76** · 17849 Ventura Blvd
- **Arco** · 18076 Ventura Blvd
- **Chevron** · 18081 Ventura Blvd
- **Mobil** · 17661 Ventura Blvd
- **Shell** · 16801 Ventura Blvd
- **Shell** · 18101 Ventura Blvd
- **Texaco** · 18101 Ventura Blvd

Landmarks

- **Rancho de los Encinos State Historical Park** · 16756 Moorpark St

Libraries

- **Encino-Tarzana Branch** · 18231 Ventura Blvd · 818-343-1983

Pharmacies

- **Longs Drugs** · 18441 Ventura Blvd · 818-996-1000
- **The Medicine Shoppe** · 17479 Ventura Blvd · 818-995-7283
- **Rite-Aid** · 17864 Ventura Blvd · 818-345-5456
- **Sav-On** · 17320 Ventura Blvd · 818-995-0032

Post Offices

- **US Post Office** · 4930 Balboa Blvd

Schools

- **Crespi Carmelite High** · 5031 Alonzo Ave
- **Encino Elementary** · 16941 Addison St
- **Gaspar de Portola Middle** · 18720 Linnet St
- **Holy Martyrs Elementary & Ferrahian High** · 5300 White Oak Ave
- **Leony Center Foundation** · 16944 Ventura Blvd
- **Los Encinos Elementary** · 17114 Ventura Blvd
- **Nestle Ave Elementary** · 5060 Nestle Ave
- **Our Lady of Grace** · 17720 Ventura Blvd
- **Our Lady of Grace** · 5011 White Oak Ave
- **Sage Academy** · 17730 Magnolia Blvd

Supermarkets

- **Ralphs** · 17840 Ventura Blvd

1. Green Vista Dr
2. Octavia Pl
3. Rochelle Pl
4. Bosque Dr
5. Shileno Pl
6. Huerta Ct
7. Toquet Dr
8. Corinthian Dr
9. Tarzana St
10. Polora St
11. Sugarman St
12. Greenbrier Ln
13. Marblehead Wy
14. Torrey Pines Ln
15. Green Meadow Ct
16. Deer View Ct
17. Anastasia Dr
18. Lake Vista Ct
19. Avd Puerto Vallarta
20. Weddington St
21. Clark St
22. Shoshone Ave
23. Addison St
24. Hartsook St
25. Forbes Ave
26. Whitaker Ave
27. Saville Ave

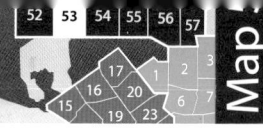

Our new favorite spot for brunch in the Valley: More Than Waffles, tucked away in a corner of the Encino Town Center, at Ventura Boulevard and Louise Avenue. Just across the strip mall is the Laemmle Town Center 5, one of the Valley's only art houses—we can think of no better way to begin a Sunday than a plate of waffles followed by a tasty independent film.

Coffee

- **Café De Gourmets** • 17233 Ventura Blvd
- **Coffee Bean & Tea Leaf** • 17301 Ventura Blvd
- **Coffee Tree** • 18381 Ventura Blvd
- **Nuts Landing** • 17028 Ventura Blvd
- **Starbucks** • 17308 Ventura Blvd
- **Starbucks (Vons)** • 18439 Ventura Blvd

Copy Centers

- **Kinko's** • 16652 Ventura Blvd • 818-788-4243

Gyms

- **Bally Total Fitness** • 17401 Ventura Blvd • 818-382-6060
- **Bodies In Motion** • 17031 Ventura Blvd • 818-995-7700
- **Curves** • 17627 Ventura Blvd • 818-244-3030

Liquor Stores

- **C&C Liquor** • 18089 Ventura Blvd
- **Encino Park Liquor** • 18001 Ventura Blvd

Movie Theaters

- **Laemmle Town Center 5** • 17200 Ventura Blvd • 818-981-9811

Pet Stores

- **Petco** • 17919 Ventura Blvd • 818-343-1124

Restaurants

- **Bagel Nosh Deli & Restaurant** • 17271 Ventura Blvd • 818-995-4545
- **Baklava Factory** • 17145 Ventura Blvd • 818-728-1600
- **Buca di Beppo** • 17500 Ventura Blvd • 818-995-3288
- **California Wok** • 16656 Ventura Blvd • 818-386-0561
- **Catch 21** • 17316 Ventura Blvd • 818-789-3474
- **Cha Cha Cha Encino** • 17499 Ventura Blvd • 818-789-3600
- **Chili My Soul** • 4928 Balboa Blvd • 818-981-7685
- **Jerry's Famous Deli** • 16650 Ventura Blvd • 818-906-1800
- **Jerusalem Pizza** • 17942 Ventura Blvd • 818-758-9595
- **Johnny Rockets** • 16901 Ventura Blvd • 818-981-5900
- **Kaiten Sushi** • 17302 Ventura Blvd • 818-986-7003
- **More Than Waffles** • 17200 Ventura Blvd • 818-789-5937
- **Mulberry Street Pizzeria** • 17040 Ventura Blvd • 818-906-8881
- **Versailles** • 17410 Ventura Blvd • 818-906-0756
- **Vittorio's Italian Cucina** • 17644 Ventura Blvd • 818-986-9074

Shopping

- **A Rodin Art** • 16752 Ventura Blvd • 818-386-9148
- **Antik Shop** • 4909 Genesta Ave • 818-990-5990
- **Encino Newsstand** • 16720 Ventura Blvd •
- **Encino Park & Community Center Map** • 4935 Balboa Blvd • 818-995-1690
- **Herbalogics** • 17200 Ventura Blvd • 818-990-9990
- **Hopscotch** • 16740 Ventura Blvd • 818-783-4080
- **The Knot Garden** • 17200 Ventura Blvd • 818-986-6642
- **Ragg Tatoo** • 17245 Ventura Blvd • 818-990-7244
- **Sneaker Warehouse** • 16736 Ventura Blvd • 818-995-8999

Video Rental

- **Blockbuster** • 18419 Ventura Blvd • 818-342-7618

219

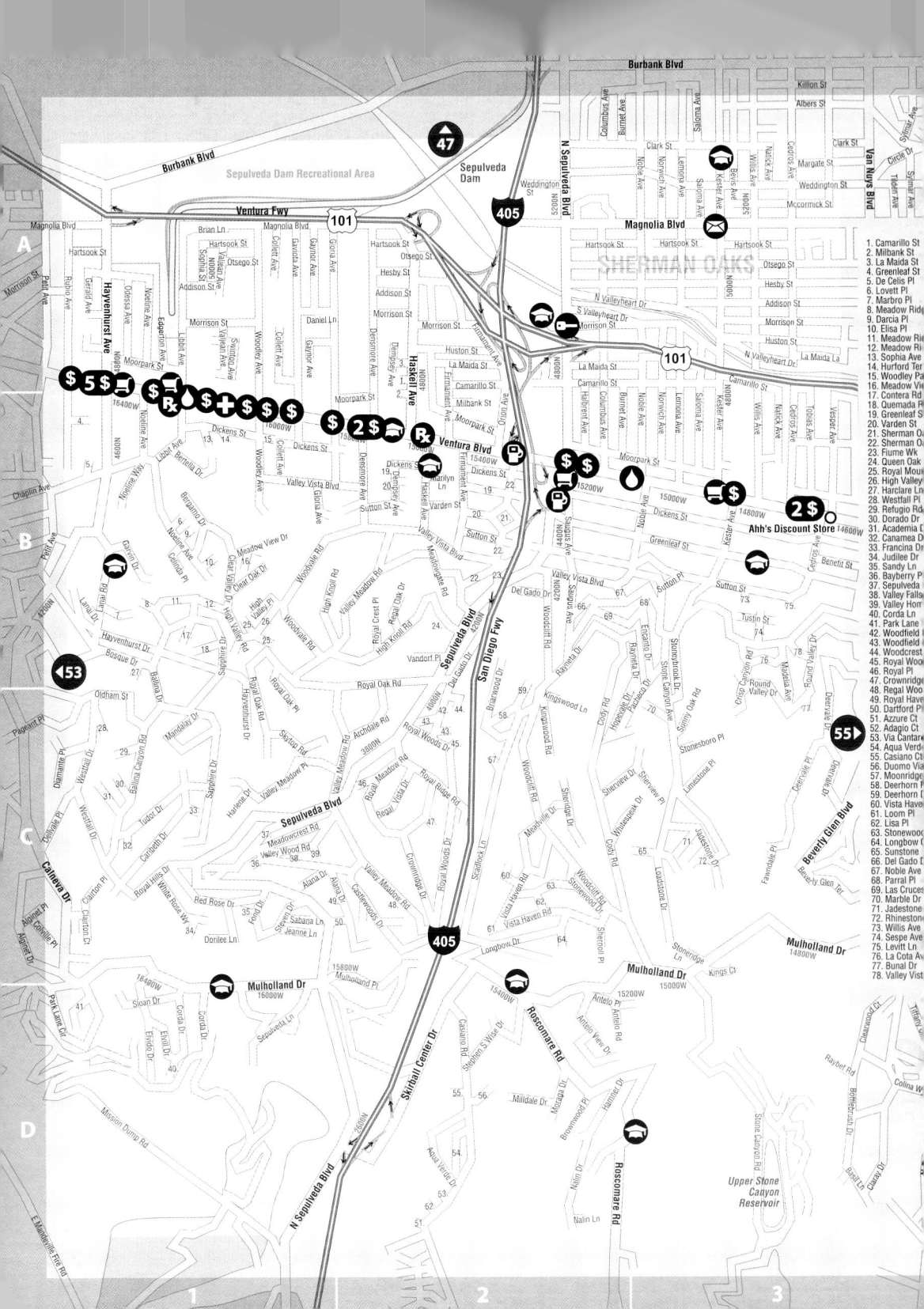

Burbank Blvd

Sepulveda Dam Recreational Area

Burbank Blvd

Ventura Fwy

101

Sepulveda Dam

405

Magnolia Blvd

Magnolia Blvd

SHERMAN OAKS

47

53

55

405

Ahh's Discount Store

Mulholland Dr

Mulholland Dr

Roscomare Rd

Upper Stone Canyon Reservoir

Ventura Blvd

Haskell Ave

Sepulveda Blvd

San Diego Fwy

Skirball Center Dr

N Sepulveda Blvd

N Sepulveda Blvd

Van Nuys Blvd

A

B

C

D

1

2

3

1. Camarillo St
2. Milbank St
3. La Maida St
4. Greenleaf St
5. De Celis Pl
6. Lovett Pl
7. Marbro Pl
8. Meadow Ridge
9. Darcia Pl
10. Elisa Pl
11. Meadow Ri
12. Meadow Ri
13. Sophia Ave
14. Hurford Ter
15. Woodley Pa
16. Meadow Vie
17. Contera Rd
18. Quemada Pl
19. Greenleaf S
20. Varden St
21. Sherman Oa
22. Sherman Oa
23. Fiume Wk
24. Queen Oak
25. Royal Mou
26. High Valley
27. Harclare Ln
28. Westfall Pl
29. Dorado Dr
30. Academia D
32. Canamea D
33. Francina Dr
34. Judilee Dr
35. Sandy Ln
36. Bayberry Pl
37. Sepulveda
38. Valley Falls
39. Valley Mon
40. Corda Ln
41. Park Lane
42. Woodfield
43. Woodfield
44. Woodcrest
45. Royal Woo
46. Royal Pl
47. Crownridge
48. Regal Woo
49. Royal Haven
50. Dartford Pl
51. Azzure Ct
52. Adagio Ct
53. Via Cantara
54. Aqua Verde
55. Casiano Ct
56. Duomo Via
57. Moonridge
58. Deerhorn R
59. Deerhorn C
60. Vista Haven
61. Loom Pl
62. Lisa Pl
63. Stonewood
64. Longbow C
65. Sunstone
66. Del Gado D
67. Noble Ave
68. Parral Pl
69. Las Cruces
70. Marble Dr
71. Rhinestone
72. Willis Ave
73. Sespe Ave
74. Levitt Ln
75. La Cota Av
76. Bunal Dr
77. Bunal Dr
78. Valley Vist

Mulholland Dr

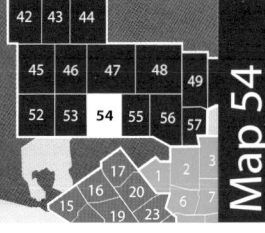
Sherman Oaks can't claim a lot of firsts, but it does have the dubious distinction of being home to the most congested freeway interchange in the nation, the intersection of the 405 and the 101. On any given weekday, over 400,000 cars pass through this interchange, leading to an afternoon "rush hour" that is actually five hours long.

$ Banks

- **Bank Leumi Le Israel** · 16530 Ventura Blvd
- **Bank of America** · 14701 Ventura Blvd
- **Bank of the West** · 15165 Ventura Blvd
- **Bank of the West** · 16027 Ventura Blvd
- **California Bank & Trust** · 16130 Ventura Blvd
- **Citibank** · 15233 Ventura Blvd
- **Citibank** · 16601 Ventura Blvd
- **Citibank** · 3812 Sepulveda Blvd
- **City National** · 15260 Ventura Blvd
- **City National** · 16133 Ventura Blvd
- **Comerica** · 15303 Ventura Blvd
- **Downey Savings & Loan** · 16325 Ventura Blvd
- **First Federal** · 16500 Ventura Blvd
- **Manufacturers** · 16255 Ventura Blvd
- **National Bank of California** · 14724 Ventura Blvd
- **US** · 15910 Ventura Blvd
- **Washington Mutual** · 15260 Ventura Blvd
- **Washington Mutual** · 16437 Ventura Blvd
- **Wells Fargo** · 14855 Ventura Blvd
- **Wells Fargo** · 15760 Ventura Blvd

Car Rental

- **Enterprise** · 4940 S Sepulveda Blvd

Car Washes

- **Encino Auto Wash** · 16300 Ventura Blvd
- **Sherman Oaks Car Wash** · 15150 Ventura Blvd

Gas Stations

- **76** · 15410 Ventura Blvd
- **Mobil** · 4528 Sepulveda Blvd

Hospitals

- **Encino-Tarzana Regional Medical Center–Encino Campus** · 16237 Ventura Blvd

o Landmarks

- **Ahh's Discount Store (former El Reina Theatre)** · 14622 Ventura Blvd

Pharmacies

- **Ralphs** · 16325 Ventura Blvd · 818-728-4515
- **Rite-Aid** · 15630 Ventura Blvd · 818-783-2449

Post Offices

- **US Post Office** · 14900 Magnolia Blvd

Schools

- **Curtis Foundation** · 15871 Mulholland Dr
- **Emek Hebrew Academy** · 15365 Magnolia Blvd
- **Kester Ave Elementary** · 5353 Kester Ave
- **Lanai Rd Elementary** · 4241 Lanai Rd
- **Mirman School for Gifted Children** · 16180 Mulholland Dr
- **Roscomare Rd Elementary** · 2425 Roscomare Rd
- **Sherman Oaks Elementary** · 14755 Greenleaf St
- **St Cyril of Jerusalem** · 4548 Haskell Ave
- **Stephen S Wise Temple Elementary** · 15500 Stephen S Wise Dr
- **Valley Beth Shalom Day** · 15739 Ventura Blvd
- **Westland** · 16200 Mulholland Dr

Supermarkets

- **Gelson's Markets** · 16450 Ventura Blvd
- **Pavilions** · 14845 Ventura Blvd
- **Ralphs** · 16325 Ventura Blvd
- **Whole Foods Market** · 4520 Sepulveda Blvd

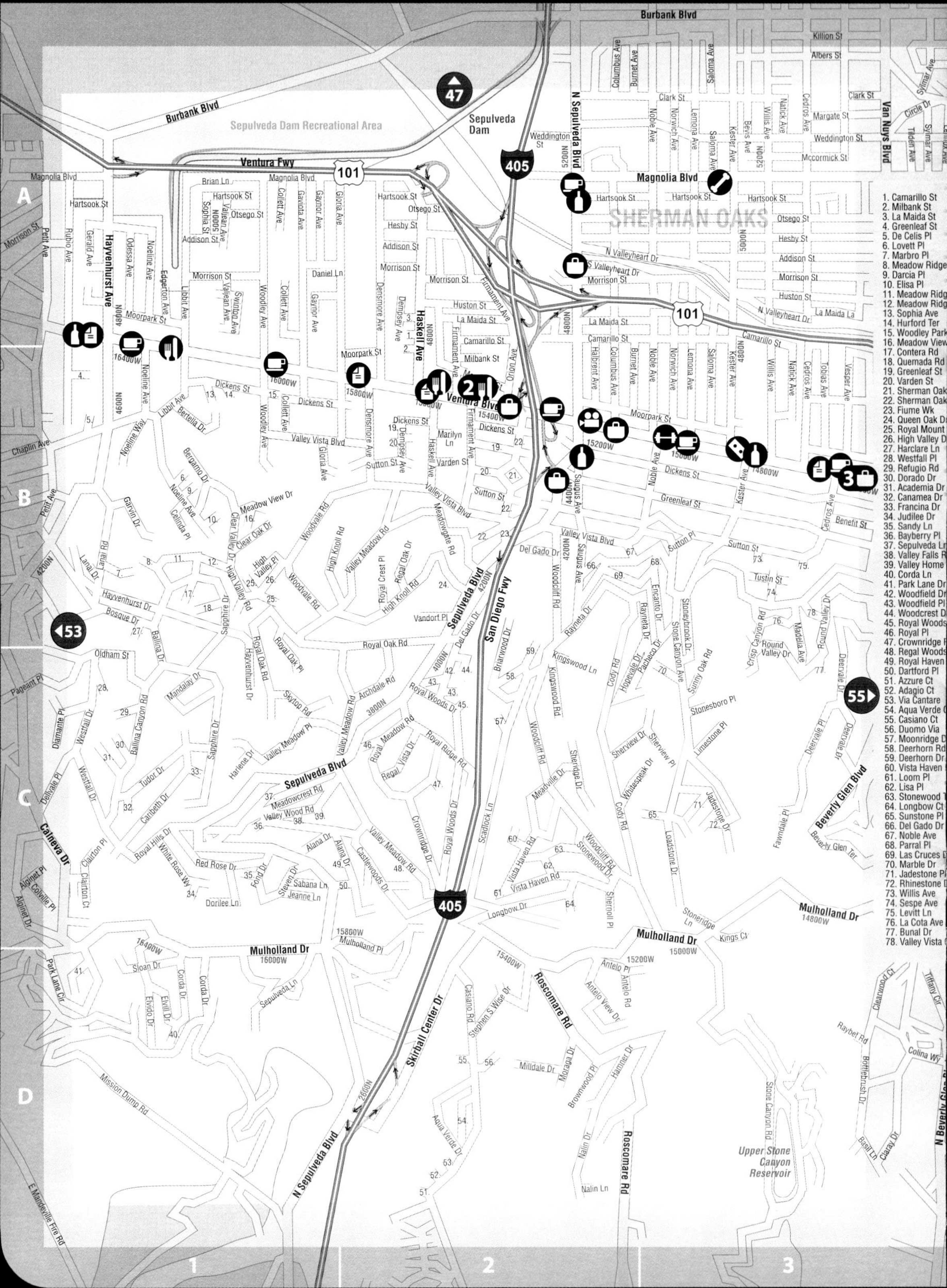

Map 54 • Sherman Oaks West

After you've seen every movie showing at the Galleria multiplex, drive a few blocks north to the Sherman Oaks Castle Park (Sepulveda Boulevard and Valleyhart Drive), home to two miniature golf courses, batting cages, and a large arcade that boasts some of the newest, hippest games (Dance Dance Revolution), and some of the, shall we say, quaintest (Skee Ball).

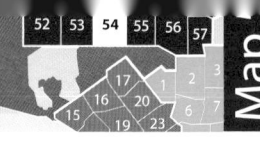

Map

Coffee

Coffee Bean & Tea Leaf · 16101 Ventura Blvd
Miracle Coffee & Pastry · 5150 Sepulveda Blvd
Starbucks · 14622 Ventura Blvd
Starbucks · 15030 Ventura Blvd
Starbucks · 15303 Ventura Blvd
Starbucks · 16461 Ventura Blvd

Copy Centers

All Printing & Graphic Service · 15616 Ventura Blvd · 818-783-0510
Office Depot · 16571 Ventura Blvd · 818-907-1741
Pip Printing · 15826 Ventura Blvd · 818-986-9245
UPS Store · 14622 Ventura Blvd · 818-990-5930

Gyms

24-Hour Fitness · 15301 Ventura Blvd · 818-728-6777
Max Fitness Personal Training Ctr · 15037 Ventura Blvd · 818-501-4436

Liquor Stores

Oak's Liquor · 5148 Sepulveda Blvd
Rubio Liquor & Grocery · 16573 Ventura Blvd
Valley Beverage · 14901 Ventura Blvd
Wines of the World · 4534 Saugus Ave

Movie Theaters

Pacific Galleria Stadium · 15301 Ventura Blvd · 818-501-7033

Pet Stores

· **Animal Affaire** · 14921 Magnolia Blvd · 818-789-3723

Restaurants

· **California Chicken Café** · 15601 Ventura Blvd · 818-789-8056
· **Delmonico's Lobster House** · 16358 Ventura Blvd · 818-986-0777
· **Fuddrucker's** · 15301 Ventura Blvd · 818-995-4552
· **Rubin's Red Hots** · 15322 Ventura Blvd · 818-905-6515

Shopping

· **Buffalo Exchange** · 14621 Ventura Blvd · 818-783-3420
· **Cost Plus World Market** · 15201 Ventura Blvd · 818-205-9620
· **Handmade Galleries** · 14556 Ventura Blvd · 818-382-3444
· **Sherman Oaks Castle Park** · 4989 Sepulveda Blvd · 818-756-9459
· **Tower Records** · 15301 Ventura Blvd · 818-789-0500
· **Ultrazone** · 14622 Ventura Blvd · 818-789-6620

Video Rental

· **Blockbuster** · 14936 Ventura Blvd · 818-788-6162

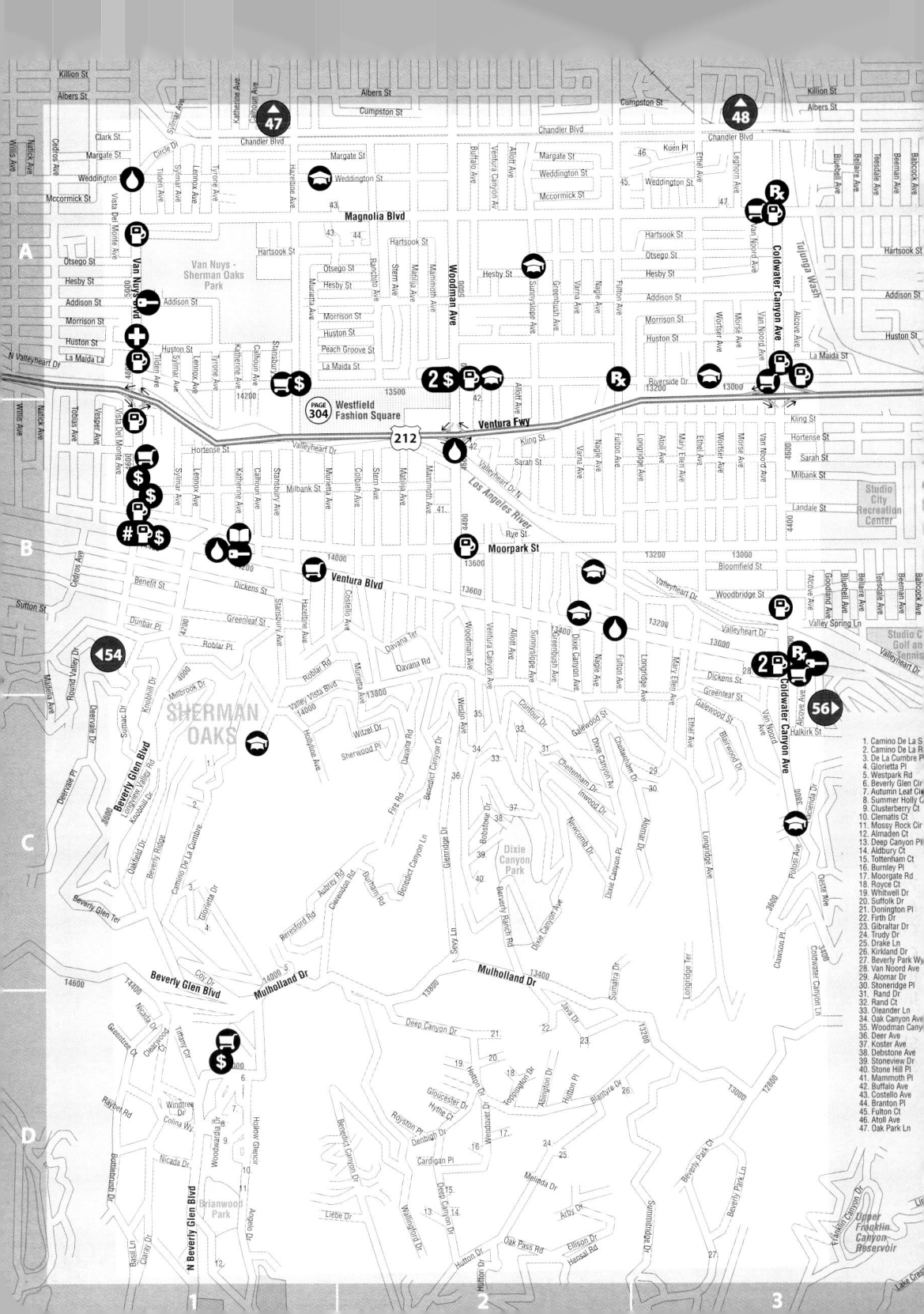

Killion St
Albers St
McCormick St

Clark St
Margate St
Weddington
Mccormick St

Chandler Blvd
Margate St

Magnolia Blvd

Van Nuys - Sherman Oaks Park

Otsego St
Hesby St
Addison St
Morrison St
Huston St
La Maida La

Hartsook St

Otsego St
Hesby St
Morrison St
Huston St
Peach Groove St
La Maida St

14200
13500

PAGE 304

Westfield Fashion Square

2 $

Ventura Fwy

212

Hortense St
Valleyheart Dr

Los Angeles River

Moorpark St
13500

14000
13600

Ventura Blvd

Benefit St

Dickens St

Greenleaf St

Roblar Pl

54

SHERMAN OAKS

Beverly Glen Ter

14600

Beverly Glen Blvd

Mulholland Dr

Mulholland Dr

N Beverly Glen Blvd

Brianwood Park

Upper Franklin Canyon Reservoir

Albers St
Cumpston St
Chandler Blvd

Kuen Pl

Margate St
Weddington St
Mccormick St

Hartsook St

Otsego St
Hesby St
Addison St
Morrison St
Huston St

Riverside Dr
13200

Kling St
Hortense St
Sarah St
Milbank St
Landale St

Studio City Recreation Center

Rx

Coldwater Canyon Ave
Tujunga Wash

Killion St
Albers St
Hartsook St

Addison St
Huston St
La Maida St

Studio City Golf an Tennis

Bloomfield St
Woodbridge St

Valleyheart Dr
Valley Spring Ln

Studio C Golf an Tennis

Dickens St

2

Rx

56

1. Camino De La S
2. Camino De La R
3. De La Cumbre P
4. Glorietta Pl
5. Westpark Rd
6. Beverly Glen Cir
7. Autumn Leaf Cir
8. Summer Holly C
9. Clusterberry Ct
10. Clematis Ct
11. Mossy Rock Cir
12. Almaden Ct
13. Deep Canyon Pl
14. Aldbury Ct
15. Tottenham Ct
16. Burnley Pl
17. Moorgate Rd
18. Royce Ct
19. Whitwell Dr
20. Suffolk Dr
21. Donington Pl
22. Firth Dr
23. Gibraltar Dr
24. Trudy Ct
25. Drake Ln
26. Kirkland Dr
27. Beverly Park Wy
28. Van Noord Ave
29. Alomar Dr
30. Stoneridge Pl
31. Rand Ct
32. Rand Dr
33. Oak Canyon Ave
34. Oak Canyon Ave
35. Woodman Cany
36. Deer Ave
37. Koster Ave
38. Debstone Ave
39. Stoneview Dr
40. Stone Hill Pl
41. Mammoth Ave
42. Buffalo Ave
43. Costello Ave
44. Branton Pl
45. Fulton Ct
46. Atoll Ave
47. Oak Park Ln

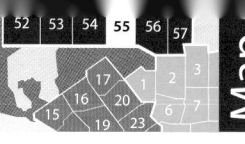

Realtors love to talk up this neighborhood's proximity to the West Side, and they have a point. Beverly Glen Boulevard and Coldwater Canyon are both solid alternatives to the congested 405. But once you make the commitment to a route, you're basically stuck. If they're backed up, Beverly Hills can be almost an hour away.

 Banks

- **Bank of America** • 13700 Riverside Dr
- **California National** • 14475 Ventura Blvd
- **Citibank** • 4464 Van Nuys Blvd
- **Downey Savings & Loan** • 13701 Riverside Dr
- **Downey Savings & Loan** • 4520 Van Nuys Blvd
- **First Federal** • 2920 N Beverly Glen Cir
- **Washington Mutual** • 13949 Ventura Blvd
- **Washington Mutual** • 14111 Riverside Dr

Car Rental

Avis • 12825 Ventura Blvd
Enterprise • 14235 Ventura Blvd
Enterprise • 5005 Van Nuys Blvd

Car Washes

Fashion Square Car Wash • 4625 Woodman Ave
Handy J Car Wash • 14311 Ventura Blvd
Rob's Car Wash • 5300 Van Nuys Blvd
Ventura Car Wash • 13320 Ventura Blvd

Gas Stations

76 • 12863 Ventura Blvd
76 • 12903 Magnolia Blvd
76 • 13650 Riverside Dr
76 • 14478 Ventura Blvd
76 • 4822 Van Nuys Blvd
Arco • 4359 Coldwater Canyon Ave
Chevron • 12860 Riverside Dr
Chevron • 14505 Ventura Blvd
Independent • 4715 Van Nuys Blvd
Independent • 4804 Coldwater Canyon Ave
Mobil • 12904 Ventura Blvd
Shell • 4441 Van Nuys Blvd
Shell • 5161 Van Nuys Blvd

Hospitals

- **Sherman Oaks** • 4929 Van Nuys Blvd

Libraries

- **Sherman Oaks Library** • 14245 Moorpark St • 818-981-7850

Pharmacies

- **Ralphs** • 12842 Ventura Blvd • 818-761-7211
- **Rite-Aid (24 hrs)** • 13333 Riverside Dr • 818-907-1431
- **Walgreens (24 hrs)** • 5224 Coldwater Canyon Ave • 818-487-2537

Schools

- **Buckley** • 3900 Stansbury Ave
- **CE Merdinian Armenian Evangelical Elementary** • 13330 Riverside Dr
- **Chandler Elementary** • 14030 Weddington St
- **Dixie Canyon Ave Elementary** • 4220 Dixie Canyon Ave
- **Harvard-Westlake** • 3700 Coldwater Canyon Ave
- **Notre Dame High** • 13645 Riverside Dr
- **Riverside Dr Elementary** • 13061 Riverside Dr
- **Robert A Millikan Middle** • 5041 Sunnyslope Ave
- **St Francis De Sales Elementary** • 13368 Valleyheart Dr

Supermarkets

- **Gelson's Markets** • 4520 Van Nuys Blvd
- **Ralphs** • 12842 Ventura Blvd
- **Ralphs** • 12921 Magnolia Blvd
- **Ralphs** • 14049 Ventura Blvd
- **Trader Joe's** • 14119 Riverside Dr
- **Whole Foods Market** • 12905 Riverside Dr

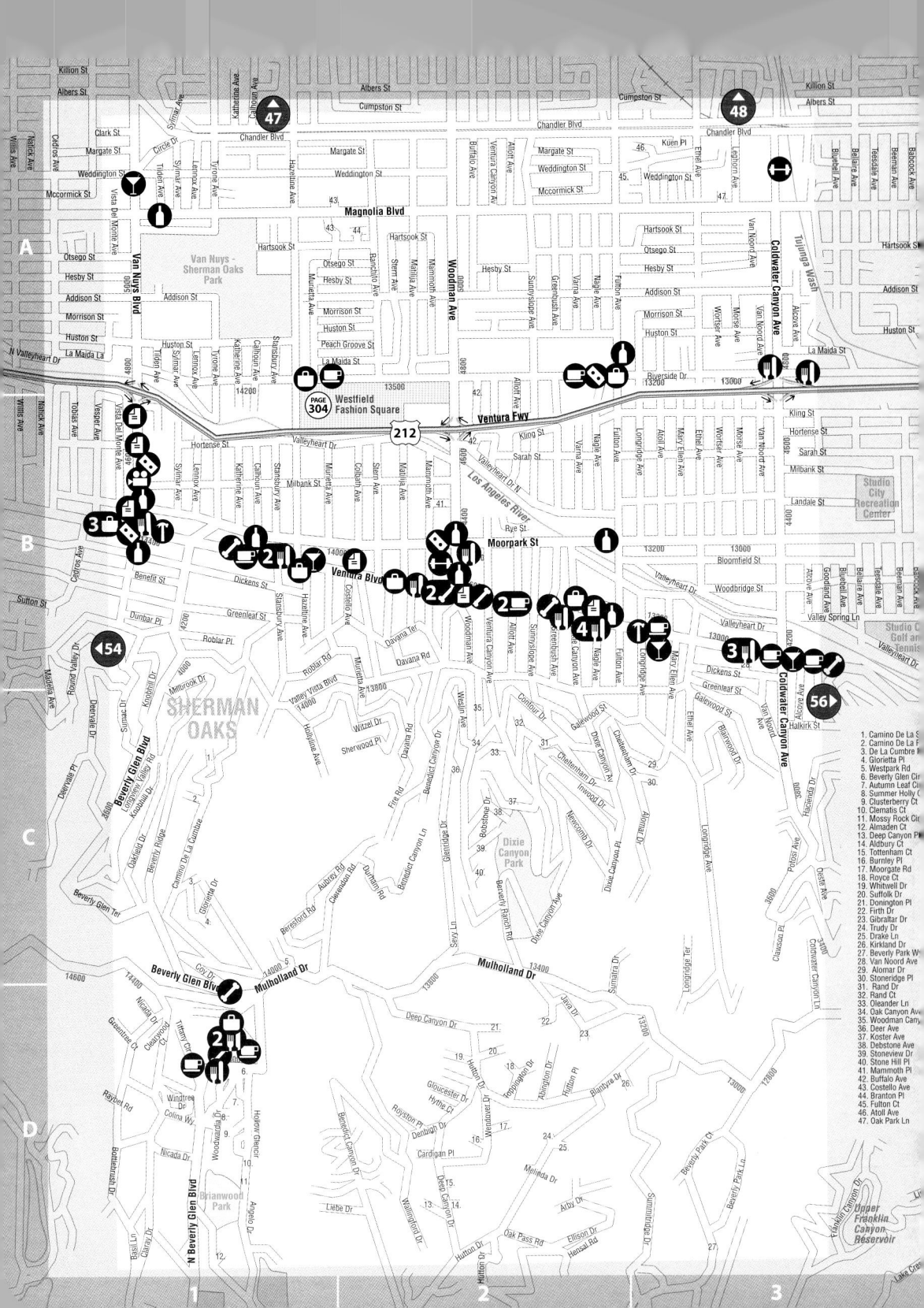

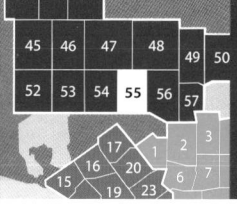

The Van Nuys-Sherman Oaks Park (at Riverside Drive and Hazeltine Avenue) offers one of the San Fernando Valley's most valuable assets in the heat of summer—one of the nicest public pools we've ever used. Admission is $1.50, kids are free, and the pool is clean and well-policed by more lifeguards than there are cops in LA.

Coffee
- **Coffee Bean & Tea Leaf** · 12930 Ventura Blvd
- **Coffee Bean & Tea Leaf** · 14006 Riverside Dr
- **Coffee Roaster** · 13567 Ventura Blvd
- **Grounded Cyberjava** · 14241 Ventura Blvd
- **Lulu's Beehive** · 13203 Ventura Blvd
- **Starbucks** · 12824 Ventura Blvd
- **Starbucks** · 13351 Riverside Dr
- **Starbucks** · 13535 Ventura Blvd
- **Starbucks** · 2952 N Beverly Glen Cir

Copy Centers
- **Alpha Blueprint** · 13346 Ventura Blvd · 818-789-0209
- **Kinko's** · 4556 Van Nuys Blvd · 818-906-2679
- **M&M Quality Printing** · 13946 Ventura Blvd · 818-907-0290
- **Tip Top Printing & Copy Center** · 4454 Van Nuys Blvd · 818-783-0949
- **UPS Store** · 13636 Ventura Blvd · 818-906-3544

Gyms
- **Curves** · 4348 Woodman Ave · 818-981-7985
- **LA Fitness Sports Clubs** · 5300 Coldwater Canyon Ave · 818-505-0772

Hardware Stores
- **Ace Hardware** · 13241 Ventura Blvd · 818-784-6274
- **Checker Paint** · 14434 Ventura Blvd · 818-784-0192

Liquor Stores
F&M Liquors · 14230 Ventura Blvd
Fulton Square Liquors · 4824 Fulton Ave
Metro Liquor · 14431 Magnolia Blvd
Party House Liquors · 13300 Moorpark St
Short Stop 24 · 4344 Woodman Ave
Silver Liquor · 4405 Woodman Ave
Tony's Liquor · 13368 Ventura Blvd
Tropicana Liquors · 4346 Van Nuys Blvd
Wine 'N' Liquor Basket · 4454 Van Nuys Blvd

Movie Theaters
Sherman Oaks 5 · 14424 Millbank St · 818-801-5121

Nightlife
Coda · 5248 Van Nuys Blvd · 818-783-7518
Cozy's · 14058 Ventura Blvd · 818-986-6000
Lulu's Beehive · 13203 Ventura Blvd · 818-986-2233
Muddy Moose Bar & Grill · 12833 Ventura Blvd · 818-755-5000

Pet Stores
- **All Paws** · 13756 Ventura Blvd · 818-788-2797
- **All the Fish U Can Wish** · 13605 Ventura Blvd · 818-783-7199
- **Aquarium Center** · 14255 Ventura Blvd · 818-501-3544
- **Pets Naturally** · 13459 Ventura Blvd · 818-784-1233
- **Pets of Belair** · 2924 Beverly Glen Cir · 310-475-7977
- **Underwater Depot** · 13708 Ventura Blvd · 818-789-7323

Restaurants
- **Bistro Garden at Coldwater** · 12950 Ventura Blvd · 818-501-0202
- **Café Bizou** · 14016 Ventura Blvd · 818-788-3536
- **Carnival Restaurant** · 4356 Woodman Ave · 818-784-3469
- **Casa Vega** · 13301 Ventura Blvd · 818-788-4868
- **The Great Greek** · 13362 Ventura Blvd · 818-905-5250
- **Hugo's** · 12851 Riverside Dr · 818-761-8985
- **In-N-Out Burger** · 4444 Van Nuys Blvd · 800-786-1000
- **Iroha** · 12953 Ventura Blvd · 818-990-9559
- **Jinky's** · 14120 Ventura Blvd · 818-981-2250
- **Le Chine Wok** · 2958 Beverly Glen Cir · 310-475-1146
- **Le Petit Bistro** · 13360 Ventura Blvd · 818-501-7999
- **Maria's Italian Kitchen** · 13353 Ventura Blvd · 818-906-0783
- **Max** · 13355 Ventura Blvd · 818-784-2915
- **Mazzarino's** · 12920 1/2 Riverside Dr · 818-788-5050
- **Mistral Brasserie** · 13422 Ventura Blvd · 818-981-6650
- **Mulholland Grill** · 2932 Beverly Glen Cir · 310-470-6223
- **Pinot Bistro** · 12969 Ventura Blvd · 818-990-0500
- **Rive Gauche** · 14106 Ventura Blvd · 818-990-3573
- **Stanley's** · 13817 Ventura Blvd · 818-986-4623

Shopping
- **Aunt Teek's Collectibles** · 14080 Ventura Blvd · 818-784-3341
- **Baxter Northrup Music** · 14534 Ventura Blvd · 818-788-7510
- **Bel Air Spa** · 2980 Beverly Glen Cir · 310-470-6362
- **Bloomingdale's** · 14060 Riverside Dr · 818-325-2200
- **Doll Shoppe** · 13300 Riverside Dr · 818-784-3655
- **Juvenile Shop** · 13356 Ventura Blvd · 818-986-6214
- **Mark's Garden** · 13838 Ventura Blvd · 818-906-1718
- **Pink Cheeks** · 14562 Ventura Blvd · 818-906-8225
- **Second Spin Records** · 14564 Ventura Blvd · 818-986-6866

Video Rental
- **Blockbuster** · 13303 Riverside Dr · 818-501-8335
- **Blockbuster** · 4560 Van Nuys Blvd · 818-990-1695
- **Hollywood Video** · 14525 Ventura Blvd · 818-986-1874
- **Video Hut** · 13713 Moorpark St · 818-385-0067

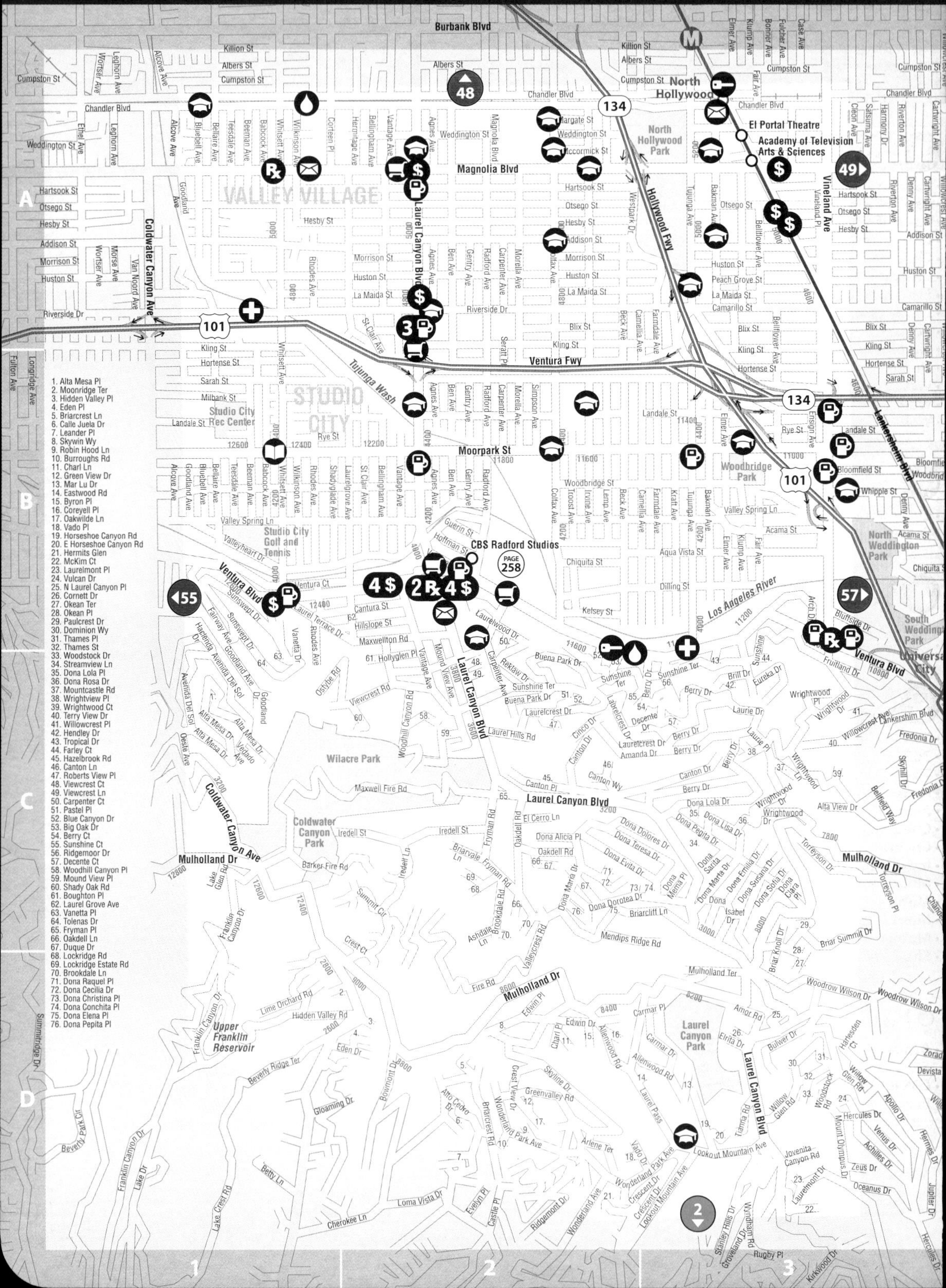

Map 56 · **Studio City / Valley Village**

1. Alta Mesa Pl
2. Moonridge Ter
3. Hidden Valley Pl
4. Eden Pl
5. Briarcrest Ln
6. Calle Juela Dr
7. Leander Pl
8. Skywin Wy
9. Robin Hood Ln
10. Burroughs Rd
11. Charl Ln
12. Green View Dr
13. Mar Lu Dr
14. Eastwood Rd
15. Byron Pl
16. Coreyell Pl
17. Oakwilde Ln
18. Vado Pl
19. Horseshoe Canyon Rd
20. E Horseshoe Canyon Rd
21. Hermits Glen
22. McKim Ct
23. Laurelmont Dr
24. Vulcan Dr
25. N Laurel Canyon Pl
26. Cornett Dr
27. Okean Ter
28. Okean Pl
29. Paulcrest Dr
30. Dominion Wy
31. Thames Pl
32. Thames St
33. Woodstock Dr
34. Streamview Ln
35. Dona Lola Pl
36. Dona Rosa Dr
37. Mountcastle Rd
38. Wrightview Pl
39. Wrightwood Ct
40. Terry View Dr
41. Willowcrest Pl
42. Hendley Dr
43. Tropical Dr
44. Farley Ct
45. Hazelbrook Rd
46. Canton Ln
47. Roberts View Pl
48. Viewcrest Ct
49. Viewcrest Ln
50. Carpenter Ct
51. Pastel Pl
52. Blue Canyon Dr
53. Big Oak Dr
54. Berry Ct
55. Sunshine Ct
56. Ridgemoor Dr
57. Decente Ct
58. Woodhill Canyon Pl
59. Mound View Pl
60. Shady Oak Rd
61. Boughton Pl
62. Laurel Grove Ave
63. Vanetta Pl
64. Tolenas Dr
65. Fryman Pl
66. Oakdell Ln
67. Duque Dr
68. Lockridge Pl
69. Lockridge Estate Rd
70. Brookdale Ln
71. Dona Raquel Pl
72. Dona Cecilia Dr
73. Dona Christina Pl
74. Dona Conchita Pl
75. Dona Elena Pl
76. Dona Pepita Pl

The Studio City Farmer's Market just might be the coolest place in the Valley. This Sunday morning event is a magnet for bleary-eyed locals, as well as for families with small fry, drawn in by pony rides, face-painting, and a bounce-house. Ventura Boulevard is bustling—and seemingly endless—and home to fashionable boutiques, funky coffeehouses, and long-time local businesses. For a tranquil, pedestrian-friendly alternative, head to Tujunga Avenue south of Moorpark Street.

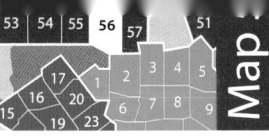

$ Banks

- **Bank of America** · 12223 Ventura Blvd
- **Bank of America** · 5025 Lankershim Blvd
- **Bank of America** · 5201 Laurel Canyon Blvd
- **Citibank** · 12191 Ventura Blvd
- **Citibank** · 4821 Laurel Canyon Blvd
- **Citibank** · 5077 Lankershim Blvd
- **City National** · 12001 Ventura Pl
- **City National** · 12515 Ventura Blvd
- **Comerica** · 12050 Ventura Blvd
- **First Republic** · 12070 Ventura Blvd
- **Union** · 12185 Ventura Blvd
- **Washington Mutual** · 12051 Ventura Blvd
- **Wells Fargo** · 11135 W Magnolia Blvd
- **Wells Fargo** · 12251 Ventura Blvd

Car Rental

- **Enterprise** · 11575 Ventura Blvd
- **Enterprise** · 5401 Lankershim Blvd

Car Washes

- **Galaxy Car Wash** · 12444 Chandler Blvd
- **Studio City Car Wash** · 11514 Ventura Blvd

Gas Stations

- **76** · 10974 Ventura Blvd
- **76** · 10984 Riverside Dr
- **76** · 4654 Laurel Canyon Blvd
- **Arco** · 12500 Ventura Blvd
- **Arco** · 5158 Laurel Canyon Blvd
- **Chevron** · 10960 Moorpark St
- **Chevron** · 4757 Laurel Canyon Blvd
- **Independent** · 4388 Tujunga Ave
- **Mobil** · 11001 Ventura Blvd
- **Mobil** · 4359 Laurel Canyon Blvd
- **Mobil** · 4377 Vineland Ave
- **Mobil** · 4801 Laurel Canyon Blvd
- **Shell** · 12007 Ventura Blvd

Landmarks

- **Academy of Television Arts & Sciences** · 5220 Lankershim Blvd
- **CBS Radford Studios** · 4024 Radford Ave
- **El Portal Theatre** · 5269 Lankershim Blvd

Libraries

- **North Hollywood Regional** · 5211 Tujunga Ave · 818-766-7185
- **Studio City Branch** · 12511 Moorpark St · 818-755-7873

Pharmacies

- **Longs Drugs (24 hours)** · 12100 Ventura Blvd · 818-763-5562
- **Rite-Aid** · 10989 Ventura Blvd · 818-980-1797
- **Rite-Aid** · 12511 Magnolia Blvd · 818-506-8795
- **Sav-On** · 12143 Ventura Blvd · 818-980-1502

Post Offices

- **US Post Office** · 11304 Chandler Blvd
- **US Post Office** · 12450 Magnolia Blvd
- **US Post Office** · 3950 Laurel Canyon Blvd

Schools

- **Amelia Earhart Continuation** · 5355 Colfax Ave
- **Beth Meier** · 11728 Moorpark St
- **Campbell Hall Episcopal** · 4533 Laurel Canyon Blvd
- **Carlson Hospital Home School 1944** · 10952 Whipple St
- **Carpenter Ave Elementary** · 3909 Carpenter Ave
- **Colfax Ave Elementary** · 11724 Addison St
- **Country** · 5243 Laurel Canyon Blvd
- **Emek Hebrew Academy** · 12732 Chandler Blvd
- **Lankershim Elementary** · 5250 Bakman Ave
- **North Hollywood High** · 5231 Colfax Ave
- **Oakwood Elementary** · 11230 Moorpark St
- **Oakwood Secondary** · 11600 Magnolia Blvd
- **San Fernando Valley Professional** · 12034 Riverside Dr
- **St Paul's First Lutheran** · 11330 McCormick St
- **Walter Reed Middle** · 4525 Irvine Ave
- **The Wesley** · 4832 Tujunga Ave
- **Wonderland Ave Elementary** · 8510 Wonderland Ave

Supermarkets

- **Gelson's Markets** · 4738 Laurel Canyon Blvd
- **Jons Marketplace** · 12122 Magnolia Blvd
- **Trader Joe's** · 11976 Ventura Blvd
- **Vons** · 4033 Laurel Canyon Blvd

Map 56 · **Studio City / Valley Village**

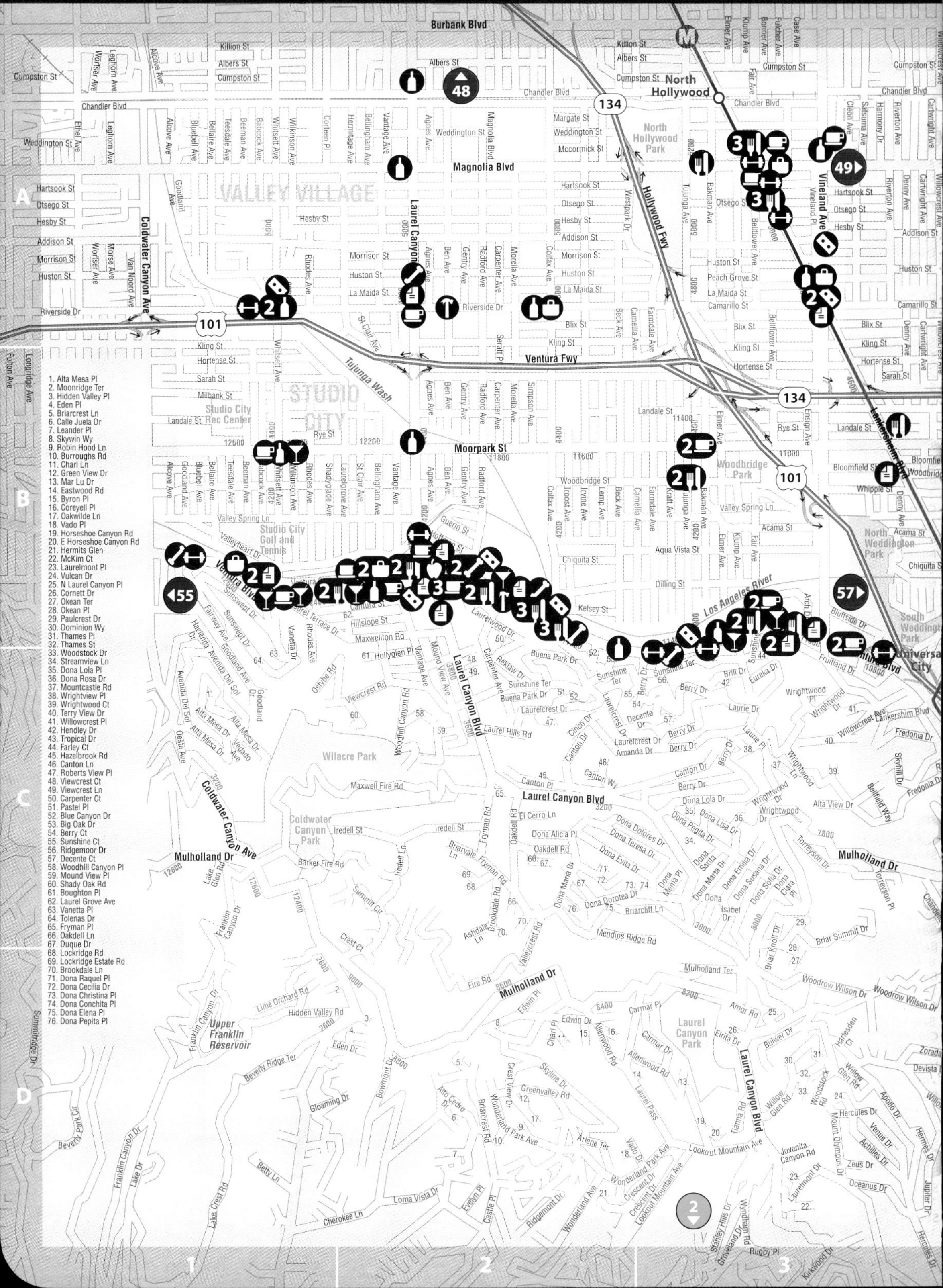

Ⓝ

Ⓜ

Burbank Blvd

Killion St

Albers St

Albers St

Cumpston St

Cumpston St

Chandler Blvd

North Hollywood

134

48

49▶

VALLEY VILLAGE

Magnolia Blvd

Hartsook St

Otsego St

Hesby St

Addison St

Morrison St

Huston St

Coldwater Canyon Ave

Van Noord Ave

101

Kling St

Hortense St

Ventura Fwy

134

101

STUDIO CITY

Moorpark St

Laurel Canyon Blvd

55

2

57▶

Los Angeles River

Universal City

Laurel Canyon Blvd

Mulholland Dr

Mulholland Dr

Upper Franklin Reservoir

Laurel Canyon Park

Mulholland Dr

2

1. Alta Mesa Pl
2. Moonridge Ter
3. Hidden Valley Pl
4. Eden Pl
5. Briarcrest Ln
6. Calle Juela Dr
7. Leander Pl
8. Skywin Wy
9. Robin Hood Ln
10. Burroughs Dr
11. Charl Ln
12. Green View Dr
13. Mar Lu Dr
14. Eastwood Rd
15. Byron Pl
16. Coreyel Pl
17. Oakwilde Ln
18. Vado Pl
19. Horseshoe Canyon Rd
20. E Horseshoe Canyon Rd
21. Hermits Glen
22. McKim Ct
23. Laurelmont Pl
24. Vulcan Dr
25. N Laurel Canyon Pl
26. Cornett Dr
27. Okean Ter
28. Okean Pl
29. Paulcrest Dr
30. Dominion Wy
31. Thames Pl
32. Thames St
33. Woodstock Dr
34. Streamview Ln
35. Dona Lola Pl
36. Dona Rosa Dr
37. Mountcastle Rd
38. Wrightview Dr
39. Wrightwood Ct
40. Terry View Pl
41. Willowcrest Pl
42. Hendley Dr
43. Tropical Dr
44. Farley Ct
45. Hazelbrook Rd
46. Canton Ln
47. Roberts View Pl
48. Viewcrest Ct
49. Viewcrest Ln
50. Carpenter Ct
51. Pastel Pl
52. Blue Canyon Dr
53. Big Oak Dr
54. Berry Ct
55. Sunshine Ct
56. Ridgemoor Dr
57. Decente Ct
58. Woodhall Canyon Pl
59. Mound View Pl
60. Shady Oak Rd
61. Boughton Pl
62. Laurel Grove Ave
63. Vanetta Pl
64. Tolenas Dr
65. Fryman Dr
66. Oakdell Ln
67. Duque Dr
68. Lockridge Rd
69. Lockridge Estate Rd
70. Brookdale Ln
71. Dona Raquel Dr
72. Dona Cecilia Dr
73. Dona Christina Pl
74. Dona Conchita Pl
75. Dona Elena Dr
76. Dona Pepita Pl

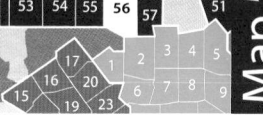

Though officially part of "the Valley," Studio City is becoming less and less distinguishable from the neighborhoods on the other side of the hill. This strip of Ventura Boulevard is brimming with good places to shop and great places to eat and drink, from all-ages (Lala's, Art's Deli, Dupar's) to very grown-up (Firefly, Wine Bistro, The Sapphire).

Coffee

Aroma Café • 4360 Tujunga Ave
Boba Bar • 12044 1/2 Ventura Blvd
Caffe Neo • 11239 Ventura Blvd
Coffee Bean & Tea Leaf • 12501 Ventura Blvd
Coffee Bean & Tea Leaf • 12050 Ventura Blvd
Coffee Fix • 12508 Moorpark St
Dupar's Coffee Shop • 12036 Ventura Blvd
Jennifer's Coffee Connection •
4397 Tujunga Ave
Peet's Coffee & Tea • 12215 Ventura Blvd
Perk U Up Café • 10905 Magnolia Blvd
Starbucks • 10965 Ventura Blvd
Starbucks • 12170 Ventura Blvd
Starbucks • 4800 Laurel Canyon Blvd
Starbucks • 5166 A Lankershim Blvd
Starbucks (Vons) • 4033 Laurel Canyon Blvd
Vivian's Millennium Café • 10968 Ventura Blvd

Copy Centers

Bob the Printer • 4850 Vineland Ave •
818-766-9379
Copies Unlimited • 12548 Ventura Blvd •
818-985-5235
Kinko's • 12101 Ventura Blvd • 818-980-2679
Minuteman Press • 11048 Ventura Blvd •
818-762-7501
NOHO Copy and Printing • 4795 Vineland Ave
• 818-755-4542
Nuprint & Graphics • 3962 Laurel Canyon Blvd
• 818-509-0003
Office Depot • 11211 Ventura Blvd •
818-760-4414
Pink Copy Center • 12080 Ventura Pl •
818-762-8100
Staples • 12605 Ventura Blvd • 818-753-6390
Studio Copy Center • 11839 Ventura Blvd •
818-766-6161
UPS Store • 11271 Ventura Blvd • 818-509-2988
UPS Store • 4804 Laurel Canyon Blvd •
818-509-0802

Farmer's Markets

Studio City Farmer's Market • Ventura Pl b/w
Laurel Canyon Blvd & Ventura Blvd

Gyms

Bally Total Fitness • 11315 Ventura Blvd •
818-760-7800
Body Image • 5077 Lankershim Blvd •
818-761-8840
Cardio Barre • 12530 Riverside Dr •
818-761-4525
Curves • 11440 Ventura Blvd • 818-762-0022
Curves • 5200 Lankershim Blvd • 818-332-1369
North Hollywood Gym • 5126 Lankershim Blvd
• 818-766-8888
Studio City Fitness • 12733 Ventura Blvd •
818-506-1436

Hardware Stores

Steven Nurseries & Hardware •
12000 Riverside Dr • 818-763-6296
Studio City North Hollywood Hardware •
11847 Ventura Blvd • 818-980-2453

Liquor Stores

• **Colfax Liquors** • 11710 Riverside Dr
• **Flask Liquor & Wine** • 12194 Ventura Blvd
• **Hughie's Liquor** • 12121 Magnolia Blvd
• **J&J Wines & Spirits** • 11312 Ventura Blvd
• **Laurel Park Liquors** • 4407 Laurel Canyon Blvd
• **Liquor Center** • 5424 Laurel Canyon Blvd
• **Oasis Liquor** • 4800 Whitsett Ave
• **R&D Liquors** • 10955 Magnolia Blvd
• **Ringside Liquors** • 12500 Moorpark St
• **Sam's Liquor** • 4832 Lankershim Blvd
• **Sauce & Such Liquor** • 4803 Whitsett Ave
• **Valley Liquor** • 11418 Moorpark St
• **Vendome Liquor & Wine** • 11555 Ventura Blvd

Nightlife

• **Aura** • 12215 Ventura Blvd • 818-487-1488
• **Clear** • 11916 Ventura Blvd • 818-980-4811
• **Firefly** • 11720 Ventura Blvd • 818-762-1833
• **Fox & Hounds** • 11100 Ventura Blvd •
818-763-7976
• **La Ve Lee** • 12514 Ventura Blvd • 818-980-8158
• **Oyster House Saloon** • 12446 Moorpark St •
818-761-8686
• **Platinum Live** • 11345 Ventura Blvd •
818-753-1771
• **The Queen Mary** • 12449 Ventura Blvd •
818-506-5619
• **Residuals** • 11042 Ventura Blvd • 818-761-8301
• **The Sapphire** • 11938 Ventura Blvd •
818-506-0777

Pet Stores

• **Kool Kats & Hot Dawgs** • 11440 Ventura Blvd •
818-753-2744
• **Mark's Pet Supplies** • 12077 Ventura Pl •
818-760-4300
• **Mark's Tropical Fish** • 12063 Ventura Pl •
818-762-7700
• **Pam's Pet Palace** • 4841 Laurel Canyon Blvd •
818-762-9035
• **Petco** • 12800 Ventura Blvd • 818-506-6416
• **Sam's Play It to the Bone** • 11736 Ventura Blvd
• 818-763-2904

Restaurants

• **Art's Deli** • 12224 Ventura Blvd • 818-762-1221
• **Caioti** • 4346 Tujunga Ave • 818-761-3588
• **Dupar's** • 12036 Ventura Blvd • 818-766-4437
• **Eclectic Café** • 5156 Lankershim Blvd •
818-760-2233
• **Ernie's Taco House** • 4410 Lankershim Blvd •
818-985-4654
• **Firefly** • 11720 Ventura Blvd • 818-762-1833
• **Good Earth Restaurant & Bakery** •
12345 Ventura Blvd • 818-506-7400
• **Katsu-ya** • 11680 Ventura Blvd • 818-985-6976
• **Killer Shrimp** • 4000 Colfax Ave • 818-508-1570
• **La Loggia** • 11814 Ventura Blvd • 818-985-9222
• **Lala's Argentine Grill** • 11935 Ventura Blvd •
818-623-4477
• **Matsuda** • 11837 Ventura Blvd • 818-760-3917
• **Mexicali** • 12161 Ventura Blvd • 818-985-1744
• **Noosh Deli** • 5118 Lankershim Blvd • 818-769-
1844
• **Panera Bread** • 12131 Ventura Blvd •
818-762-2226

• **Pit Fire Pizza** • 5211 Lankershim Blvd •
818-980-2949
• **Salomi** • 5225 Lankershim Blvd • 818-506-0130
• **Sitton's North Hollywood Diner** •
11329 Magnolia Blvd • 818-761-3341
• **Sushi Dan Rockin' Sushi** • 11056 Ventura Blvd •
818-985-2254
• **Sushi Nozawa** • 11288 Ventura Blvd •
818-508-7017
• **Suzanne's Country Deli** • 11273 Ventura Blvd •
818-762-9494
• **Teru Sushi** • 11940 Ventura Blvd • 818-763-6201
• **Todai** • 11239 Ventura Blvd #2 • 818-762-8311
• **Tokyo Delve's Sushi Bar** • 5239 Lankershim Blvd
• 818-766-3868
• **Vitello's** • 4349 Tujunga Ave • 818-769-0905
• **Wine Bistro** • 11915 Ventura Blvd •
818-766-6233

Shopping

• **Dari** • 12184 Ventura Blvd • 818-762-3274
• **Hamilton Pink** • 4342 1/2 Tujunga Ave •
818-769-1463
• **Hoity Toity** • 4381 Tujunga Ave • 818-766-2503
• **Iliad Bookshop** • 4820 Vineland Ave •
818-509-2665
• **King's Western Wear** • 11450 Ventura Blvd •
818-761-1162
• **La Knitterie Parisienne** • 12642 Ventura Blvd •
818-766-1515
• **Laura's Designer Resale Boutique** •
12426 Ventura Blvd • 818-752-2835
• **Marie et Cie** • 11704 Riverside Dr • 818-508-5049
• **Portrait of a Bookstore** • 4360 Tujunga Ave •
818-769-3853
• **Studio City Camera Exchange** • 12174 Ventura
Blvd • 818-762-4749
• **Suzanne's Resale Boutique** • 4355 Tujunga Ave
• 818-766-8837
• **Tennis Ace** • 12544 Ventura Blvd • 818-762-8751
• **Tuesday Morning** • 11239 Ventura Blvd •
818-508-5334
• **Verona** • 4350 Tujunga Ave • 818-508-6377
• **Village Gourmet** • 4357 Tujunga Ave •
818-487-3807
• **Village Market** • 11653 Moorpark St •
818-761-4848

Video Rental

• **20-20 Video** • 12113 Ventura Blvd •
818-762-2020
• **Blockbuster** • 11978 Ventura Blvd •
818-505-9753
• **Blockbuster** • 4821 Lankershim Blvd •
818-505-1800
• **Eddie Bryant's Saturday Matinee** •
5006 Vineland Ave • 818-506-4242
• **Odyssey Video** • 4810 Vineland Ave •
818-769-2001
• **Red Hot Video** • 11701 Ventura Blvd •
818-753-5323
• **Video Club** • 4811 Whitsett Ave • 818-766-2388
• **Video West** • 11376 Ventura Blvd • 818-760-0096

Map 57 • Universal City / Toluca Lake

N

Hortense St
Denny Ave
Cartwright Ave
Willowcrest Ave
Placidia Ave
Sancola Ave
Forman Ave
Talofa Ave
W Sarah St
W Alameda Ave
S Third St
Bob Hope Dr

Sarah St
Sarah St
Placidia Ave
Forman Ave
10400W

Riverside Dr
10400P
134
49
Bob's Big Boy
2 **$**
N Kenwood St
S California St
S Fairview St
50
W Riverside Dr

Landale St
Landale St
Cartwright Ave
10600N
Moorpark St
Bloomfield St
Woodbridge St
Toluca Lake Ave
Mariola Ave
Ponca Ave
Clybourn Ave
Mc Farlane Ave
N Valley St
N Rose Ave
N Pass Ave
N Maple St
W Olive Ave
W Warner Blvd
S Scioto St
Warner Bros Studios
PAGE 258

Bloomfield St
Whipple St
Bloomfield St
Woodbridge St
Warner Blvd
S Valley St
S Rose Ave
Franklin Ave
Toluca Lake Ave
Hood Ave
$
400S

TOLUCA LAKE

Cahuenga Blvd
Saticoma Ave
Riverton Ave
Denny Ave
Acama St
Aqua Vista St
Chiquita St
Valley Spring Ln
Arcola Ave
Valley Spring Ln
Navajo Ave
Toluca Lake
W Lakeside Dr
Forest Lawn Dr
Forest Lawn Memorial Park

Acama St
Weddington Park North
Brookview Dr
Denny Ave
Cartwright Ave
Valleyheart Ave

Lakeside Country Club

Los Angeles River

N Coyote Canyon Dr
N Knoll Dr

Bluffside Dr
Weddington Park South
Vineland Ave
Bluffside Dr
Universal City
Campo de Cahuenga
Barham Blvd

Dark Canyon Dr

Fruitland Dr
Ventura Blvd
10600W
S Coyote Canyon Dr
Craig Dr
Hinck Dr

Willowcrest Pl
Willowcrest Pl
Terry View Dr
Universal Ctr Plz
2 **$**
Lankershim Blvd
Fredonia Dr
Coral Dr
Universal Center Dr
CityWalk
Troy Dr
Blair Dr
Brady Hollly Dr
Floyd Tr
Ellis Dr
Lake Hollywood Dr
La Suvida Dr
Wonder View Dr

Regal Pl
3600N
Cahuenga Blvd
3400N 16
Oak Glen Dr
101
$
Primera Ave
Lindo St

56
Mulholland Dr
Torteyson Dr
Torteyson Pl
Briar Summit Dr
Skyhill Dr
Fredonia Dr
Mulview Dr
Broadview Dr
Bonnie Hill Dr
Bonnie Hill Dr
Adina Dr
Oakshire Dr
Bennett Dr
Dos Palos Dr
$
Badera Dr
Wonder View Dr
Lake Hollywood Dr
Innsdale Dr
Lake Hollywood

MOUNT OLYMPUS

Woodrow Wilson Dr
Firenze Ave
Scott Dr
Woodrow Wilson Dr
Rue De Valle
Montcalm Ave
Woodrow Wilson Dr
Woodrow Dr
Passmore Dr
Ellington Dr
Valevista Tr
Pacific View Dr
Woody Tr
Vanland Tr
Vista Dr
Treasure Tr
Cahuenga Park Tr
3
Hollywood Reservoir

Woodrow Wilson Dr
Chandelle Rd
Kimdale Ln
N Nichols Canyon
Pacific View Dr
Caverna Dr
Packwood Tr
Sunrise Tr
Sunnydip Tr
Sunnydell Tr

Alta View Dr
Balfour Way
Wrightwood Ln
La Cuesta Dr
Pyramid Pl
Pacific View Dr
Mulholland Dr

MOUNT OLYMPUS
Mount Olympus Dr
Venus Dr
Hercules Dr
Apollo Dr
Achilles Dr
Zeus Dr
Jupiter Dr
Oceanus Dr
Cardwell Pl
Willow Glen Rd
Willow Glen Rd
Zorada Dr
Zorada Dr
Devista Dr
Jalima Wy
Astral Dr
Dresden Dr
Astral Dr

Laurelmont Dr
Mount Olympus Dr
Leaf Ter
Cardwell Pl

Runyon Canyon Park
Lusco Pl
Runyon Canyon Rd
Los Tilos Rd
Malaga Rd
Hillpark Dr
Oporto Dr
Chelan Dr
Castilian Dr
Outpost Dr
Oxford Dr
Oakley Dr
Chelan Dr

Hollywood Fwy
Hollywood Fwy
Lakeridge Dr

2

La Presa Rd
Camrose Dr
Wedgewood Pl

1. Toluca Lake Ln	19. Springlet Tr
2. Velma Dr	20. Sycamore Tr
3. De Witt Dr	21. Goodview Tr
4. Charleston Wy	22. Oak Point Dr
5. Blair Cres	23. Pyramid Dr
6. Winnie Dr	24. Las Alturas St
7. La Sombra Dr	25. Vista Crest Dr
8. La Falda Dr	26. Cahuenga Park Tr
9. Wonder View Pl	27. Park Center Dr
10. Hollycrest Pl	28. Palo Vista Dr
11. Benda Pl	29. Soper Dr
12. Primera Pl	30. Nichols Canyon Rd
13. Wonder View Pz	31. Chandelle Pl
14. Kentucky Dr	32. Flynn Ranch Rd
15. Terry View Dr	33. Firenze Pl
16. Oakley Dr	34. Seattle Pl
17. Carse Dr	35. La Castana Dr
18. Hild Tr	36. Bantam Pl

1 2 3

These neighboring communities couldn't be more different. Universal City amounts to little more than the Studio, the Theme Park, and the hyper-stimulating, always-crowded City Walk. Toluca Lake, on the other hand, has a small-town feel, with a village of neighborhood shops and restaurants on Riverside Drive, as well as a collection of beautiful mansions bordering the Lakeside Country Club and the private lake itself.

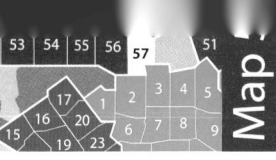

$ Banks

- **Bank of America** · 110 Universal City Plz
- **Bank of America** · 255 N Pass Ave
- **Bank of America** · 4123 W Olive Ave
- **California Credit Union** · 3330 Cahuenga Blvd W
- **Citibank** · 4000 W Alameda Ave
- **Citizens Business** · 4100 W Alameda Ave
- **City National** · 3500 W Olive Ave
- **First Entertainment Credit Union** · 6735 Forest Lawn Dr
- **Union** · 3900 W Alameda Ave
- **Washington Mutual** · 4455 Lankershim Blvd
- **Wells Fargo** · 10225 Riverside Dr
- **World Savings & Loan** · 10064 Riverside Dr

Car Rental

- **Budget** · 4120 Lankershim Blvd
- **Enterprise** · 3550 Cahuenga Blvd W
- **Enterprise** · 3600 Barham Blvd
- **Enterprise** · 4245 Lankershim Blvd
- **Midway Car Rental** · 4201 Lankershim Blvd

Car Washes

- **Lakeside Car Wash** · 3700 W Riverside Dr

Gas Stations

- **Arco** · 3167 Cahuenga Blvd W
- **Arco** · 3704 Cahuenga Blvd
- **Arco** · 4506 Lankershim Blvd
- **Chevron** · 3701 W Riverside Dr
- **Chevron** · 3780 Cahuenga Blvd
- **Mobil** · 10570 Riverside Dr
- **Mobil** · 3240 Cahuenga Blvd W

Landmarks

- **Bob's Big Boy** · 4211 Riverside Dr
- **Campo de Cahuenga** · 3912 Lankershim Blvd
- **CityWalk** · Universal Center Dr
- **Forest Lawn Memorial Park** · 6300 Forest Lawn Dr
- **Hollywood Reservoir** · East of Hwy 101
- **Universal Studios** · 100 Universal Center Dr
- **Warner Brothers Studios** · 4000 Warner Blvd

Police

- **Los Angeles County Sheriff's Dept–Universal Citywalk** · 1000 Universal Studios Blvd · 818-622-9539

Post Offices

- **US Post Office** · 10063 Riverside Dr
- **US Post Office** · 4029 Lankershim Blvd

Schools

- **Rio Vista Elementary** · 4243 Satsuma Ave
- **St Charles Borromeo** · 10850 Moorpark St
- **Valley View Elementary** · 6921 Woodrow Wilson Dr

Supermarkets

- **Ralphs** · 10901 Ventura Blvd
- **Trader Joe's** · 10130 Riverside Dr

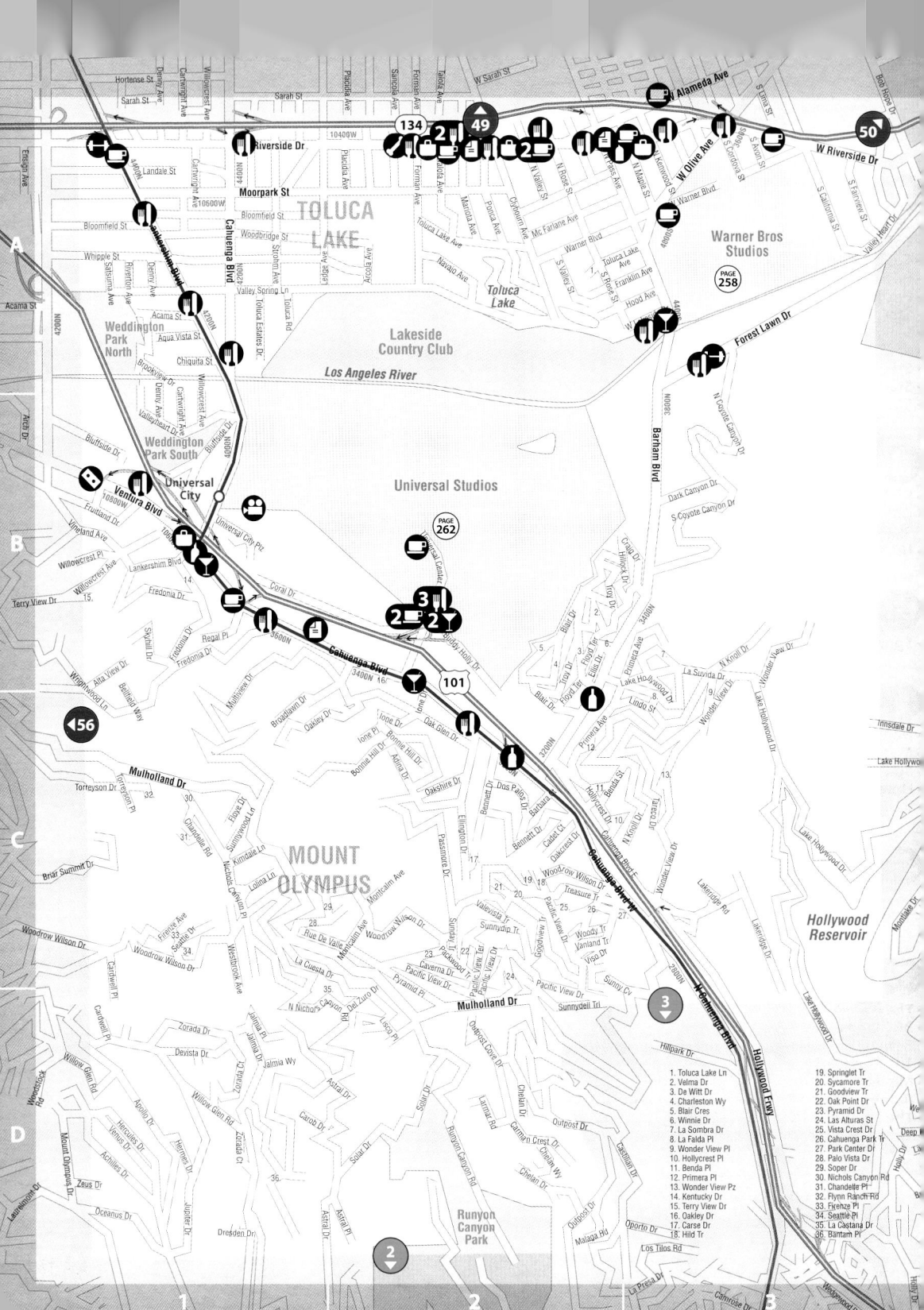

Priscilla's Coffee on Riverside Drive has successfully hung in there against major chains like Coffee Bean & Tea Leaf and Starbucks, which opened an outpost right across the street several years ago. But Priscilla's has its loyalists who appreciate the shop's homey atmosphere—and darned good coffee. Neighbors include the Falcon Theatre, Geographica (which sells maps and travel accessories), and the Italian marketplace Bacco.

53 | 54 | 55 | 56 | 57 | 51

17 | 1 | 2 | 3 | 4 | 5
16 | 20 | 6 | 7 | 8 | 9
15 | 19 | 23

Coffee

- **Cinema Café** · 4444 Lankershim Blvd
- **Coffee Bean & Tea Leaf** · 1000 Universal Studios Blvd
- **Coffee Bean & Tea Leaf** · 10121 Riverside Dr
- **Igloo Café** · 171 N Maple St
- **Priscilla's Coffee Tea & Gifts** · 4150 W Riverside Dr
- **Starbucks** · 100 Universal City Plz
- **Starbucks** · 3400 W Riverside Dr
- **Starbucks** · 3800 W Alameda Ave
- **Starbucks** · 4000 Warner Blvd
- **Starbucks** · 4207 Riverside Dr
- **Starbucks / Café Puccino** · 1000 Universal Studios Blvd

Copy Centers

- **Kinko's** · 4100 W Riverside Dr · 818-567-1044
- **Universal Print & Copy** · 3535 Cahuenga Blvd · 323-876-3500
- **UPS Store** · 10061 Riverside Dr · 818-506-4388

Gyms

- **Sports Center** · 6711 Forest Lawn Dr · 323-851-9376

Liquor Stores

- **House of Ambrose** · 3331 Barham Blvd
- **Maple Liquor** · 4001 W Riverside Dr
- **Spirit Cellar** · 3278 Cahuenga Blvd W
- **Universal Liquors** · 3797 Cahuenga Blvd
- **Vendome Liquor & Wine** · 10600 Riverside Dr

Movie Theaters

- **Loews Universal Citywalk Cinemas and IMAX Theatre** · 100 Universal City Plz · 818-508-0711

Nightlife

- **The Baked Potato** · 3787 Cahuenga Blvd · 818-980-1615
- **BB King's Blues Club** · 100 Universal Center Dr · 818-622-5464
- **The Casting Office** · 3256 Cahuenga Blvd · 323-851-4300
- **Minibar** · 3413 Cahuenga Blvd W · 323-882-6965
- **Rumba Room** · 1000 Universal Center Dr · 818-622-1227
- **The Smoke House** · 4420 W Lakeside Dr · 818-845-3731
- **Timmy Nolan's** · 10111 Riverside Dr · 818-985-3359

Pet Stores

- **Four Paws Only of Toluca Lake** · 10214 Riverside Dr · 818-760-3366

Restaurants

- **Bacco Trattoria** · 3821 Riverside Dr · 818-845-8036
- **Barsac Brasserie** · 4212 Lankershim Blvd · 818-760-7081
- **Buca di Beppo** · 1000 Universal Studios Blvd · 818-509-9463
- **Ca' del Sole** · 4100 Cahuenga Blvd · 818-985-4669
- **California Canteen** · 3311 Cahuenga Blvd · 323-876-1702
- **Chez Nous** · 10550 Riverside Dr · 818-760-0288
- **Dalt's Grill** · 3500 W Olive Ave · 818-953-7750
- **Mardi Gras** · 10151 Riverside Dr · 818-761-4243
- **Miceli's** · 3655 Cahuenga Blvd · 323-851-3345
- **Mo's** · 4301 Riverside Dr · 818-845-3009
- **Paty's** · 10001 Riverside Dr · 818-761-0041
- **Priscilla's Coffee** · 4150 Riverside Dr · 818-843-5707
- **Prosecco Restaurant** · 10144 Riverside Dr · 818-505-0930
- **Smoke House Restaurant** · 4420 W Lakeside Dr · 818-845-3731
- **Steak Joynt** · 4354 Lankershim Blvd · 818-761-9899
- **Taste Buds at the Sports Center** · 6711 Forest Lawn Blvd · 323-874-4006
- **Versailles** · 1000 Universal Center Dr · 818-505-0093
- **Wolfgang Puck Café** · 1000 Universal Center Dr · 818-985-9653
- **Yamakawa** · 10118 Riverside Dr · 818-763-8355
- **Zach's Italian Café** · 10820 Ventura Blvd · 818-762-2445

Shopping

- **Cinema Secrets Beauty Supply** · 4400 W Riverside Dr · 818-846-0579
- **Geographica Map & Book Store** · 4000 W Riverside Dr · 818-848-1414
- **Pergolina** · 10139 Riverside Dr · 818-508-7708
- **Simply Nature Day Spa** · 10067 Riverside Dr · 818-506-8927
- **Steel Casey** · 10624 Ventura Blvd · 818-763-5667
- **Weekendz Only** · 10139 1/2 Riverside Dr · 818-752-3695

Video Rental

- **Blockbuster** · 10911 Ventura Blvd · 818-762-9257

General Information

City of San Pedro Website: www.sanpedro.com
Chamber of Commerce: 310-832-7272;
                        www.sanpedrochamber.com

Overview

Sandwiched between massive Long Beach, highfalutin' Palos Verdes, and Rolling Hills Estates, this fiercely proud community has undergone major renovation in recent years—a revitalization that is ongoing. Hidden delights await San Pedro visitors, from the Mediterranean-style Cabrillo Beach Bathhouse (3800 Stephen M White Dr), built in 1932, to the charming seaside village of Ports O' Call, to the always enlightening Angel's Gate Cultural Center (3601 S Gaffey St, 310-519-0936; www.angelsgateart.org) and the Victorian-era Point Fermin Lighthouse and Park (807 Paseo Del Mar).

Believe it or not, some of the country's foremost tattoo parlors can be found in San Pedro. It also boasts the Warner Grand Theatre (478 W 6th St, 310-548-7672; www.warnergrand.org), an opulent Art Deco venue built in 1931 which is rich in both history and culture. But what defines and distinguishes San Pedro most is the weekly ART Walk. On the first Thursday of every month, art galleries, retail shops, restaurants, and street vendors celebrate creativity by staying open late and offering discounts and specials to patrons. Live entertainment accompanies the action throughout the historic downtown Arts District located between 4th and 8th Streets and Pacific Avenue and Centre Street, a region with terrific vintage shops selling cool and unusual wares. Visit www.1stthursday.com for an extensive list of participating establishments.

How to Get There

From downtown LA, take the Harbor Freeway south (110 S) to Gaffey Street, then head south to San Pedro.

Banks

- **Bank of America** • 800 N Western Ave
- **US** • 1000 N Western Ave
- **US** • 1221 S Gaffey St
- **Washington Mutual** • 1001 S Pacific Ave
- **Washington Mutual** • 980 N Western Ave

○Landmarks

- **Angel's Gate Cultural Center** • 3601 Gaffey St
- **Art Walk** • W 4th St & S Pacific Ave
- **Cabrillo Beach Bathhouse** •
  3800 Stephen M White Dr
- **Catalina Express Terminal** •
  Swinford St & N Harbor Blvd
- **Ports O' Call** • 1100 Nagoy Wy
- **San Pedro Farmer's Market** •
  Mesa St, b/w 6th St and 7th St

Movie Theaters

- **Warner Grand Theater** • 478 W 6th St • 310-833-8333

Nightlife

- **Godmother's** • 302 W 7th St • 310-833-1589
- **June's Bar** • 1100 S Pacific Ave • 310-833-4171
- **Kan Kan** • 104 S Pacific Ave • 310-548-0591

Restaurants

- **6th Street Bistro** • 354 W 6th St • 310-521-8818
- **Ante's Restaurant** • 729 Ante Perkov Wy •
  310-832-5375
- **Beach City Grill** • 376 W 6th St • 310-833-6345
- **Marcello** • 470 W 7th St • 310-519-7100
- **Nam's Red Door** • 2253 S Pacific Ave • 310-832-4120
- **Pacific Diner** • 3821 S Pacific Ave • 310-831-5334
- **Papadakis Taverna** • 301 W 6th St • 310-548-1186
- **Ports O' Call Restaurant** • Berth 76 • 310-833-3553
- **Rex's Café** • 2136 S Pacific Ave • 310-519-7190
- **Think Bistro** • 1420 W 25th St • 310-548-4797
- **Think Bistro** • 302 W 5th St • 310-519-3662
- **The Whale and Ale** • 327 W 7th St • 310-832-0363

Shopping

- **The Antique Shop** • 439 W 6th St • 310-833-2008
- **Coyote Antiques** • 387 W 6th St • 310-547-4222
- **Endangered Species** • 1434 W 8th St • 310-832-7325
- **Office Depot** • 810 N Western Ave • 310-221-0162
- **Ramona Bakery** • 1101 S Pacific Ave • 310-832-0369
- **Sav-On** • 950 N Western Ave • 310-832-7258

General Information

City of Malibu Phone: 310-456-2489
City of Malibu Website: www.ci.malibu.ca.us
Weather/Surf Reports: http://beaches.co.la.ca.us/BandH/
Beaches/main.htm

Overview

When outsiders fantasize about Southern California, it's not the smog-filled sky of downtown LA that runs through their minds. It's the sandy beaches and sunny skies of Malibu and its 21-mile coastline—the city that inspired a coconutty rum and perhaps the most famous Barbie doll ever.

The area's first settlers were the Chumash Indians. The names of some of their villages are still a part of local culture—Ojai, Mugu, and Zuma, to name just a few. But Malibu's current residents are a very different tribe indeed. For instance, The Colony, a gated community, is home to a wide array of celebrities, businessfolk, and anyone else that can spare the $7 million-plus that it takes to buy a parcel of beachfront land.

Depending upon weather and other acts of God (like the fires and mudslides that frequently strike this beautiful stretch of coastline), Malibu lies about 45 minutes from downtown LA, or approximately 35 miles. The best thing about Malibu is definitely its isolation. You feel as though you've left LA and gone somewhere else. The worst thing about Malibu is...its isolation. You feel as though you've left LA and gone somewhere else. Somewhere very far away.

The Beaches

The beaches are the main attraction in Malibu, and you have a number from which to choose. Keep in mind that dogs are not allowed on any public beach, and parking is a big challenge. There are three options: 1) Pay whatever the day's going rate is at parking lots conveniently located at each Malibu beach. 2) Find street parking in Malibu's residential areas—which then requires hiking down to the beach, often with the added challenge of crossing the PCH (Malibu's answer to the video game *Frogger*). 3) Get all of the planets to align just so, allowing you to score that perfect parking spot on the beach side of the PCH, right outside the entrance to

your chosen beach. We grudgingly admit that option #1 may be your best bet.

Many of Malibu's private beaches are accessible to the public via causeways or public gates. Some of Malibu's more popular public beaches are:

- **Topanga State Beach** · Located along the PCH at Topanga Canyon Boulevard. Popular for surfing. Call 310-457-9701 for the northern surf report.
- **Malibu Lagoon State Beach** · Located just west of the Malibu Pier. Also features a bird sanctuary as well as the Malibu Lagoon Museum.
- **Malibu Surfrider Beach** · Home of the Malibu Pier, located along the 23000 block of the PCH. This is one of the most famous surfing beaches in the world.
- **Dan Blocker Beach** · Named for the actor who played "Hoss" on the TV series *Bonanza*. He was one of the original owners of this stretch of beach, along with his co-stars, Lorne Greene and Michael Landon, who donated it to the state after Blocker's death. This beach is on the PCH between Puerco Canyon and Corral Canyon.
- **Point Dume State Beach** · This state-owned beach is accessed from Westward Beach Road. One of the area's most beautiful beaches, it features nearby hiking trails, reefs for scuba diving, and tide pools.
- **Zuma Beach** · This very popular beach is located on the PCH, just west of Heathercliff Drive. It's expansive, is home to a number of volleyball courts, and tends to be very crowded in the summer.
- **Robert H. Meyer Memorial State Beach** · This is actually a grouping of three small beaches—El Pescador, La Piedra, and El Matador. They are located about 10 miles west of Malibu proper.
- **Nicholas Canyon Beach** · Located at 33850 Pacific Coast Highway. Lots of room for lying out in the sun or tossing a Frisbee.

The Adamson House

Located at Malibu Lagoon State Beach, the Adamson House was the home of Merritt Huntley Adamson and his wife Rhoda Rindge Adamson, whose family, the Rindges, once owned the Malibu Spanish Land Grant (as the area was originally known). The house features liberal use of the ceramic tile manufactured by the then-famed Malibu Potteries. The Adamson House and the adjacent

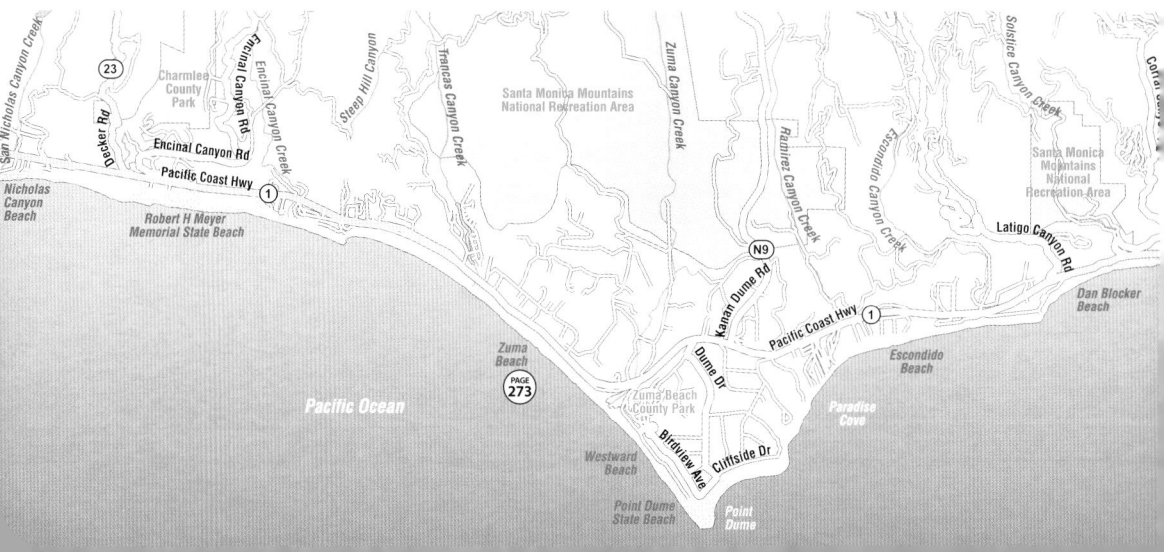

Malibu Lagoon Museum are open Wednesday through Saturday 11 am to 3 pm, while the grounds are open daily from 8 am until sunset. Admission to the adjoining Malibu Lagoon Museum is free and tours of the Adamson House are $5 for adults, $2 for children aged 6-16 years, and nothing for children 5 years and under. The property is also available for weddings and other special events. 310-456-8432; www.adamsonhouse.org.

Malibu Creek State Park

What is now a 7,000-acre state park once belonged to motion picture studio Twentieth Century Fox, which used the park as a double for Korea in the TV series *M*A*S*H*. The park is home to some 30 miles of hiking and riding trails, as well as a campground featuring sixty campsites, barbecues, showers, and bathroom facilities. The park's entrance is located along Las Virgenes/Malibu Canyon Road, just south of Mulholland Highway. 818-880-0367; www.parks.ca.gov/?page_id=614.

Pepperdine University

It's hard to imagine getting any studying done on a campus just a few hundred yards from the ocean, but Pepperdine students manage to pull it off (well…sometimes). The campus may be best known as the location for the 1970s TV spectacular, *The Battle of the Network Stars*, but Pepperdine is represented by 14 NCAA Division I athletic teams in sports ranging from men's water polo to women's golf. The university's Center for the Arts typically hosts an eclectic lineup of events including piano recitals, modern dance, and children's theater. 24255 Pacific Coast Hwy, 310-506-4000; www.pepperdine.edu.

Where to Eat

Malibu relies upon the PCH as its Main Street and most of the town's dining establishments are located along either side. Dining experiences in Malibu tend to be one extreme or the other—either ultra-casual or ultra-pricey. Here are some restaurants that we recommend at both ends of the spectrum:

- **Coogies,** Malibu Colony Plaza, 23755 W Malibu Rd, 310-317-1444. Upscale diner fare. This unpretentious restaurant is healthier than the typical diner and is a great bet for breakfast by the beach.

- **Neptune's Net**, 42505 PCH, 310-457-3095. Seafood. Though it's almost at the Ventura county line, this place is worth the drive. Very "beachy," Neptune's Net serves up a variety of seafood, either steamed or fried.
- **Duke's Malibu**, 21150 PCH, 310-317-0177. California-Hawaiian. Lots of seafood dishes served amidst a fun, surfer theme.
- **Marmalade Café**, 3894 Cross Creek Rd, 310-317-4242. California-style sandwiches and salads. If you want a nice lunch in a nice setting, this is the place to go. Their food also travels well as take-out, and they have a great catering business too.
- **Taverna Tony,** Malibu Country Mart, 23410 Civic Center Wy, 310-317-9667. Greek. Delicious food in a fun, festive setting with live music.
- **Granita,** Malibu Colony Plaza, 23725 W Malibu Rd, 310-456-0488. California-Mediterranean. Wolfgang Puck's restaurant by the beach. The food is good but the décor is better.
- **Geoffrey's,** 27400 PCH, 310-457-1519. California-eclectic. Pronounced "Joffrey's," this restaurant actually serves delicious food that merits the snooty attitude you may occasionally encounter here. This is one of the most beautiful and romantic restaurants in LA.
- **Reel Inn**, 18661 Pacific Coast Hwy, 310- 456-8221. An old Malibu hold-over, the Reel Inn has been a reliable and casual seafood outpost for decades. Fresh snapper, shrimp, and calamari are on the picnic table menu, with requisite cold beer in abundance.

How to Get There

With few exceptions, it's difficult to go anywhere in Malibu without encountering the Pacific Coast Highway for at least some of the trip. From the southern half of LA, the easiest option is to take the 10 Freeway to the PCH and head north. On summer weekends, the PCH becomes a virtual parking lot, but at least you can enjoy the smell and view of the ocean.

From the Valley and points north, your best bet is to hop on the 101 Freeway and head north, toward Ventura. Exit at Las Virgenes and follow the signs for Las Virgenes Road/Malibu Canyon; then take Malibu Canyon Road to the PCH. If you're planning on going even further north into Malibu, you can also exit the 101 at Kanan Road, which becomes Kanan Dume Road and terminates at the PCH.

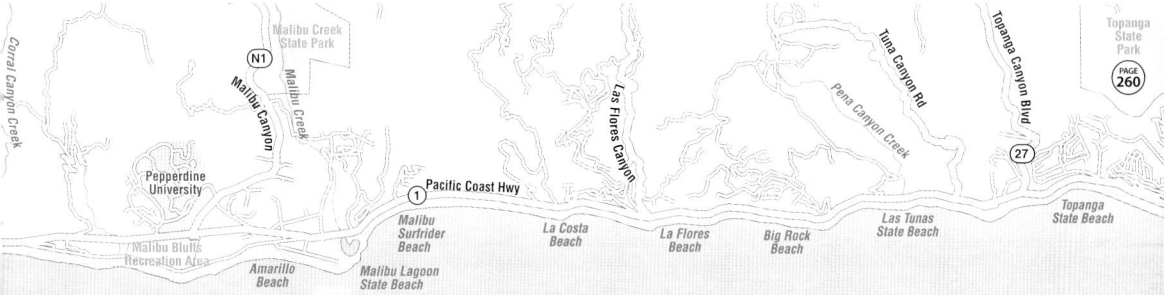

Overview

Long Beach and Hollywood have had a long and symbiotic relationship despite the 25 miles that separate the two cities. The first silent movie studio—Balboa Studios—was located here, and today numerous television shows and feature films continue to be shot in the area. During Hollywood's golden years it was also the favorite destination of celebrities in search of a little sunny R&R. It has managed to successfully retain much of its old charm, as evidenced in the abundance of Art Deco architecture along Ocean Boulevard. Massive downtown revitalization aimed at attracting a young, artsy crowd with new lofts, eclectic cafés, theaters, and the renaissance of an area known as The Pike has helped to develop the metropolis that was named most culturally diverse large city in the country by *USA Today*.

Long Beach is a city of approximately 450,000 people with pocket neighborhoods, each as different as the next. Belmont Shore is the quintessential beach community, with narrow streets and open-minded residents. Belmont Heights and Bluff Park are where the former residents of Belmont Shore go once they have kids and want a yard. North Long Beach is a residential working-class neighborhood near the 405 Freeway. Bixby Knolls is suburbia near the beach, with the usual lineup of ranch homes and minivans. And Shoreline Village is a tourist's paradise with shops and restaurants on the north end of the 11-mile beach.

How to Get There

From Los Angeles, driving to Long Beach couldn't be easier. Find your way to the 405 or the 5 and head south, taking either freeway to the 710 S. The 10 also intersects with the 710 east of downtown LA, so that's a viable option as well.

You can also take the Metro Blue Line to downtown Long Beach from either the 7th Street/Metro Center stop or the Pico Boulevard stop (near the Los Angeles Convention Center) for a round-trip fare of $2.50. The train makes several stops in Long Beach, including one at the Transit Mall on 1st Street, between Pine and Pacific. www.mta.net; 800-COMMUTE.

Once you've arrived, Long Beach Transit (562-591-2301) offers free services, such as the Pine Avenue Link and the Passport, that shuttle visitors all over town, from the Queen Mary to Pine Avenue and Belmont Shore. Another

$ Banks

- **Bank of America** · 101 E Willow St
- **Bank of America** · 150 Long Beach Blvd
- **Bank of America** · 2000 E Anaheim St
- **Bank of America** · 2240 N Bellflower Blvd
- **Bank of America** · 3804 Atlantic Blvd
- **Bank of America** · 5101 E 2nd St
- **Bank of America** · 600 W Willow St
- **Bank of America** · 6351 E Spring St
- **City National** · 6265 E 2nd St
- **Comerica** · 1650 Ximeno Ave
- **Farmers & Merchants** · 2302 N Bellflower Blvd
- **Farmers & Merchants** · 2801 Atlantic Ave
- **Farmers & Merchants** · 3140 E Anaheim St
- **Farmers & Merchants** · 4827 E 2nd St
- **First Bank & Trust** · 3850 Atlantic Ave
- **Union** · 1900 Atlantic Ave
- **Union** · 5430 E 2nd St
- **Washington Mutual** · 3901 Atlantic Ave
- **Washington Mutual** · 4571 E Los Coyotes Diagonal
- **Washington Mutual** · 5200 E 2nd St
- **Washington Mutual** · 6300 E Spring St
- **Wells Fargo** · 1930 N Lakewood Blvd
- **Wells Fargo** · 2096 N Bellflower Blvd
- **Wells Fargo** · 4540 Atlantic Ave
- **Wells Fargo** · 4601 E 2nd St
- **Wells Fargo** · 6290 E Pacific Coast Hwy

○ Landmarks

- **Alexander House** · 5281 El Roble St
- **Art Theater** · 2025 E 4th St
- **California State University at Long Beach** · 1250 N Bellflower Blvd
- **Long Beach Museum of Art** · 2300 E Ocean Blvd

- **Matlock House** · 1560 Ramillo Ave
- **Queen Mary Seaport** · 1126 Queens Hwy
- **Seashell House** · 4325 E 6th St
- **The Skinny House** · 798 Gladys Ave

Movie Theaters

- **AMC Theatres Marina Pacifica 12** · 6346 E Pacific Coast Hwy · 562-435-4262

Nightlife

- **49ers Tavern** · 5660 E Pacific Coast Hwy · 562-494-7670
- **The Belmont Brewing Company** · 2539th Pl · 562-433-3891
- **Fern's Cocktails** · 1253 E 4th St · 562-436-2123
- **Joe Jost's** · 2803 E Anaheim St · 562-439-5446
- **Murphy's Pub** · 4918 E 2nd St · 562-433-6338
- **Portfolio Coffee House** · 2300 E 4th St · 562-434-2486

Restaurants

- **Bono's** · 4901 E 2nd St · 562-434-9501
- **Christy's** · 3937 E Broadway · 562-433-7133
- **Chuck's Coffee Shop** · 4120 E Ocean Blvd · 562-433-9317
- **Enrique's** · 6120 E Pacific Coast Hwy · 562-498-3622
- **La Rizza's** · 1837 E 7th St · 562-599-1080
- **Malvasia** · 5316 E 2nd St · 562-433-5003
- **Open Sesame** · 5215 E 2nd St · 562-621-1698
- **Park Pantry** · 2104 E Broadway · 562-434-0451

Shopping

- **5001** · 5286 E 2nd St · 562-438-3907
- **Olives Gourmet Grocer** · 3510 E Broadway · 562-439-7758

transportation alternative is the AquaBus. This 40-foot-long water taxi costs just $1 and will ferry you to a number of Long Beach's coastal attractions. There are stops at the Aquarium, the Queen Mary, the Catalina Landing, Shoreline Village, Pine Avenue Circle at Dock 7, and the Coast Hotel. The AquaLink water taxi is another option for nautical travel, but while it's faster and bigger than the AquaBus, this boat costs $3 to ride and only makes stops at the Queen Mary and the Aquarium. 800-481-3470; www.lbtransit.com/aqualink.html.

Attractions

Catalina
The Catalina Express ferry service makes regular crossings between mainland California and Catalina Island. The boats leave Long Beach for Catalina from two ports—Catalina Landing (8 times daily) and Queen Mary (3 times on weekends only—and the journey is approximately one hour long. Take sunscreen, a beach towel, and Dramamine—the ride is often a rough one. A round-trip adult ticket costs $49 and reservations are recommended. 800-481-3470; www.catalinaexpress.com.

You can also opt for a quicker route (15 minutes) via helicopter. Island Express offers daily packages at $187 per person that include flight, taxi, and one of two Santa Catalina Island Company Discovery tours. 800-2-AVALON; www.islandexpress.com.

Once you land, you can take advantage of all the leisure activities the island has to offer, from renting a golf cart to snorkeling and parasailing—it's always a pleasant getaway for a day or a weekend. www.catalina.com.

Queen Mary
Once a vessel that first ferried thousands of troops during WWII, then carried movie stars and heads of state across the Atlantic Ocean, the *Queen Mary* is now a floating hotel and museum available for weddings, bar mitzvahs, and rubber stamp conventions. (We kid you not.) In all seriousness, the ship is awesome in scope and historical significance regarding the way we used to travel. There are several restaurants on board the boat as well as other diversions, including the former Russian submarine, *Scorpion*, a "Ghosts & Legends" tour that examines reports that the ship is haunted, and a special tour that covers the *Queen*

Banks
- **Bank of America** • 5253 Long Beach Blvd
- **California Bank & Trust** • 444 W Ocean Blvd
- **Citibank** • 1 World Trade Ctr
- **City National** • 11 Golden Shore St
- **Comerica** • 301 E Ocean Blvd
- **Farmers & Merchants** • 1401 Long Beach Blvd
- **Farmers & Merchants** • 302 Pine Ave
- **First Bank & Trust** • 100 Oceangate
- **International City** • 249 E Ocean Blvd
- **Union** • 400 Oceangate
- **Washington Mutual** • 401 E Ocean Blvd
- **Wells Fargo** • 111 W Ocean Blvd

○ Landmarks
- **Adelaide A Tichenor House** • 852 E Ocean Blvd
- **Aquarium of the Pacific** • 100 Aquarium Wy
- **Catalina Landing** • 330 Golden Shore St
- **Edison Theater** • 213 E Broadway
- **Long Beach Convention & Visitor's Bureau** • 1 World Trade Ctr
- **Museum of Latin-American Art** • 628 Alamitos Ave
- **The Pike at Rainbow Harbor** • Pine Ave & Shoreline Dr
- **Shoreline Village** • 419 Shoreline Village Dr
- **Villa Riviera** • 800 E Ocean Blvd

Movie Theaters
- **AMC Theatres Pine Square 16** • 245 Pine Ave • 562-435-4262
- **Art Theatre** • 2025 E 4th St • 562-438-5435
- **Cinemark at the Pike** • 99 S Pine Ave • 562-435-0353
- **United Artists Long Beach Marketplace 6** •
  6601 E Pacific Coast Hwy •

Nightlife
- **Blue Café** • 210 The Promenade N • 562-983-7111
- **Mariposa** • 135 Pine Ave • 562-951-9711
- **Rock Bottom Brewery** • 1 Pine Ave • 562-308-2255
- **The Sky Room** • 40 S Locust Ave • 562-983-2738
- **V20** • 81 Aquarium Wy • 562-216-2060

Restaurants
- **555 East** • 555 E Ocean Blvd • 562-437-0626
- **Alegria** • 115 Pine Ave • 562-436-3388
- **Cha Cha** • 762 Pacific Ave • 562-495-4242
- **Ego** • 329 Pacific Ave • 562-432-9718
- **Gladstone's** • 330 S Pine Ave • 562-432-8588
- **King's Fish House** • 100 W Broadway • 562-432-7463
- **L'Opera** • 101 Pine Ave • 562-491-0066
- **La Traviata** • 301 Cedar Ave • 562-432-8022
- **Long Beach Café** • 615 E Ocean Blvd • 562-436-6037
- **Madison** • 102 Pine Ave • 562-628-8866
- **Mum's Restaurant** • 144 Pine Ave • 562-437-7700
- **Parker's Lighthouse** • 435 Shoreline Village Dr • 562-432-6500
- **Sky Room** • 40 S Locust Ave • 562-983-2722
- **Uncle Al's Seafood** • 400 E 1st St • 562-436-2553
- **Utopia** • 445 E 1st St • 562-432-6888
- **Wasabi Japanese Restaurant** • 200 Pine Ave • 562-901-0300
- **Yard House** • 401 Shoreline Village Dr • 562-628-0466

Shopping
- **Acres of Books** • 240 Long Beach Blvd • 562-437-6980
- **City Place** • 275 E 4th St • 562-432-8325
- **Crate & Barrel** • 240 Pine Ave • 562-435-6577
- **Mood Swings** • 455 E Ocean Blvd • 562-437-6250
- **Nordstrom Rack** • 300 The Promenade N • 562-733-1223
- **The Pike at Rainbow Harbor** • Pine Ave & Shoreline Dr •
  562-432-8325
- **Z Gallerie** • 230 Pine Ave • 562-491-0766

Mary's WWII troop transportation stint. 562-435-3511; www.queenmary.com.

Admission: A "First Class Passage" that includes admission to all of the attractions costs $29.95 for each adult, $26.95 for seniors and members of the military, and $18.95 for kids 5-11. Smaller packages are also available.

Directions: The *Queen Mary* is located at 1126 Queens Highway, at the south end of the 710 Freeway.

Aquarium of the Pacific

Opened with much fanfare in 1998, the Aquarium of the Pacific's mission is to teach Californians about the wildlife indigenous to the Pacific Ocean, so don't expect to see Atlantic salmon or Maine lobsters. While Sea World, farther south in San Diego, relies heavily upon flashy acts like Shamu to draw visitors, the Aquarium of the Pacific is all about the local animals, focusing on interactive education rather than entertainment.

Admission: Packages start at $18.95 for adults, $10.95 for children 3-11, and $16.95 for seniors. Additional packages include a Behind-The-Scenes tour and an Ocean Experience tour for a few extra bucks. The aquarium is open every day from 9 am until 6 pm. It's closed on Christmas and for the entire weekend of the Toyota Grand Prix, which is usually in April. If you want to avoid lines, online ticketing is available for an additional $1.50 fee per ticket. 562-590-3100; www.aquariumofpacific.org.

Directions: Take the 405 S to the 710 S, and follow the signs to Downtown Long Beach and the Aquarium. The Aquarium is located at 100 Aquarium Way, off Shoreline Drive. Parking is available at a municipal lot located just a few feet from the Aquarium. The cost is $6 with an Aquarium ticket stub, $7 without.

Long Beach Convention & Entertainment Center

Located at 300 East Ocean Boulevard, this complex is home to an eclectic assortment of events. Long Beach's professional hockey team, the Ice Dogs, play its home games at the Long Beach Arena; the Terrace Theater hosts a variety of plays and musical performances; and the Convention Center includes a large ballroom that serves as the site for many a senior prom. 562-436-3636; www.longbeachcc.com.

The Ice Dogs, who play from October until early April, are part of the West Coast Hockey League. Check their schedule at www.icedogs.com. Game tickets are available through Ticketmaster at 213-480-3232 or online at www.ticketmaster.com.

Directions: Take the 405 S to the 710 S and head for the Downtown exits. The 710 turns into Shoreline Drive. Follow this to Linden and turn into the parking lot.

Shoreline Village

Designed to look like an old-fashioned fishing village, Shoreline Village is a collection of shops, restaurants, and amusements that might best be described as "quaint." Don't get us wrong—Skee-ball has its time and place, and sometimes Shoreline Village might prove to be that place. The area also caters to more athletic pursuits such as rollerblading, bike riding, and sailing. Add to this a number of great restaurants and tasty snack shops. 562-435-2668; www.shorelinevillage.com.

Directions: Take the 710 S and follow signs for the Aquarium. Continue past the Aquarium and Pine Avenue, and turn right onto Shoreline Village Drive. Two hours of parking is free with any purchase.

Hours: Shoreline Village is open seven days a week from 10 am until 9 pm, closing an hour later during the summer months.

The Pike at Rainbow Harbor

Constructed more than a hundred years ago, the Pike was a thriving, cheerful place to socialize, with amusement rides and pier, cafés, and movie houses. Over time it fell into disrepair and disrepute, finally closing in 1979. Today, this *new* Pike at Rainbow Harbor includes a gamut of fun—a movie house, Bubba Gump Shrimp Company, GameWorks, The Auld Dubliner, and a footbridge that brings to mind the old Cyclone Racer roller coaster—for teens and families, locals, and visitors. The Pike, covering 18 acres of downtown waterfront, is located smack-dab between the Convention Center and the Aquarium. www.shopthepike.com

Directions: Take the 405 S to the 710 S and head for the Downtown exits. The 710 turns Into Shorline Drive. Park anywhere between Pine and Chestnut Avenues, or in Shoreline Village, and then walk a few steps north.

Toyota Grand Prix

For one weekend every April, Long Beach turns into Daytona Beach and the sound of revving car engines echoes throughout the usually bucolic downtown area. The real draw of the Grand Prix is the Pro/Celebrity Race, where the likes of Sean Astin, Lil' Kim, Laila Ali, and Frankie Muniz get fast and furious with the best of the pros. Tickets are available online at www.longbeachgp.com, or by calling 888-82-SPEED.

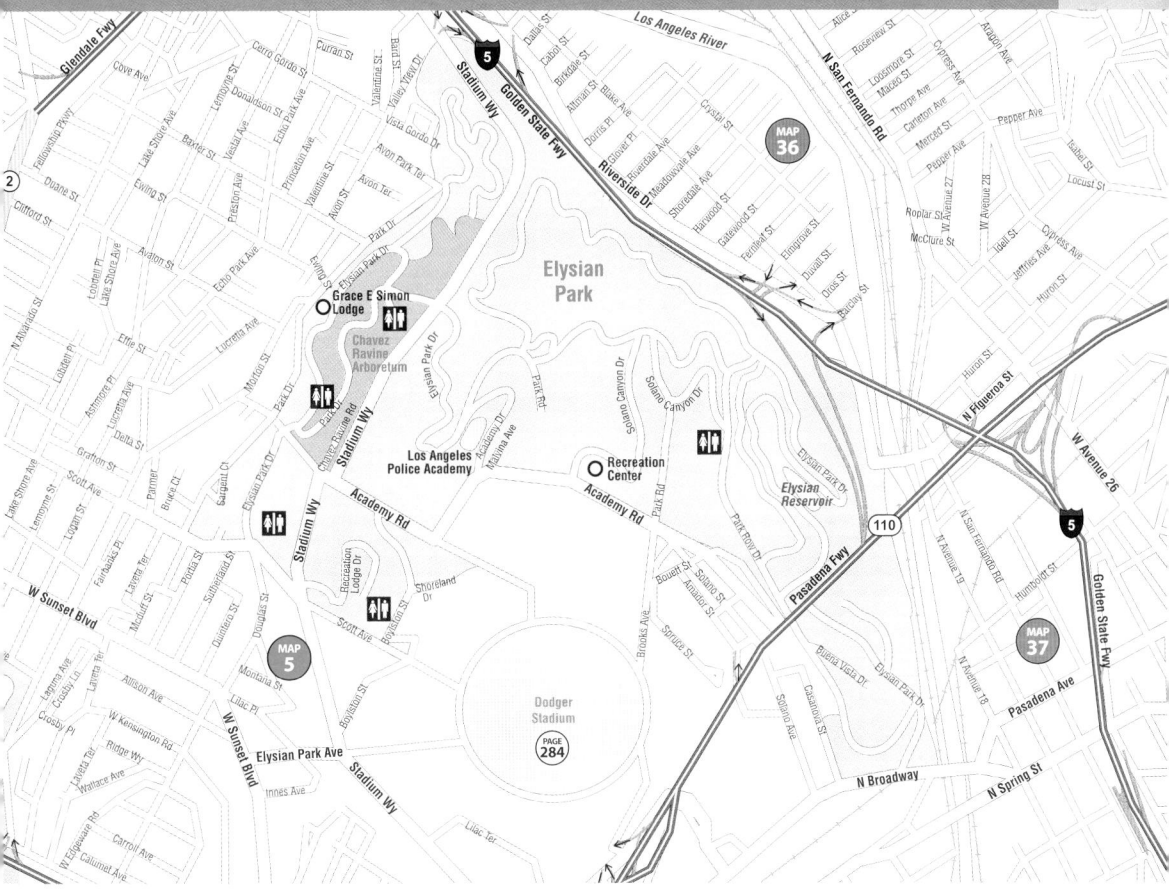

General Information

NFT Maps: 5, 36 & 37
Address: 835 Academy Rd
           Los Angeles, CA 90012
Phone: 213-485-5054
Website: www.laparks.org/dos/parks/facility/elysianPk.htm

Overview

When Los Angeles was founded in 1781, more than 600 acres of parkland was set aside for public use. That allotted land, today known as Elysian Park, is the oldest and second-largest park in the LA area. The majority of the park, which is crisscrossed with hiking trails, has been maintained in its original state since it opened. In 1965, the "Citizens Committee to Save Elysian Park" formed to organize public support to preserve the parkland as public open space. Almost 40 years later, the park has seen none of the planned redevelopment, but the committee continues to "arouse public and official awareness of the value of saving the last of these Pueblo lands set aside two centuries ago." The park actually includes the last large piece of Pueblo land granted to the city by Carlos III, King of Spain, in 1781. Don't let the fault line running underneath the park dissuade you from a relaxing visit.

Practicalities

The central picnic area on Stadium Way has several barbeque pits, a small human-made lake, and a children's play area. A café at the Police Academy is open to the public on weekdays from 6 am until 3 pm. The annual Chinatown Firecracker 10K Run passes through the park every February.

Admission to the park and arboretum is free. Elysian Park is located next to Dodger Stadium and the Police Academy and can be reached from the 5 or 110 Freeways (exit Stadium Way). The Chavez Ravine Arboretum is on the west side of Stadium Way near the Grace E. Simon Lodge.

Chavez Ravine Arboretum

In 1893, the Los Angeles Horticultural Society established the arboretum and extensive botanical gardens in Elysian Park. The Chavez Ravine Arboretum was declared "City Historical-Cultural Monument Number 48" in 1967, and today Los Angeles Beautiful sponsors the arboretum. Many of the trees are the oldest and largest of their kind in California—some even in the United States—and there are over 1,000 tree species from around the world that can be grown in the arboretum's moderate climate. The Los Angeles Beautiful Arbor Day is held annually at the Chavez Ravine Arboretum. 213-485-5054; www.laparks.com/dos/horticulture/chavez.htm.

General Information

NFT Maps: 3, 4, 5, 50, 51 & 57
Address: 4730 Crystal Springs Dr
            Los Angeles, CA 90027
Phone: 213-485-5501 or 323-913-4688
Hours: 5 am-10:30 pm, daily (bridle trails, hiking paths,
            and mountain roads close at sunset).

Overview

In 1896, millionaire Colonel Griffith J. Griffiths gave the city of Los Angeles a pretty sweet Christmas gift: some 3,000 acres that became the core of Griffith Park. The Colonel's only demand was that the land be used as "a place of recreation and rest for the masses, a resort for the rank-and-file, for the plain people." Now the Colonel may not have been the most honorable person (he was, after all, imprisoned for shooting his wife), but when it came to his park, his heart seemed to be in the right place. You'll see people living Griffith's dream today—the park is usually full of families picnicking and couples drinking wine under the oak trees and amongst the wild sage.

The largest municipal park and urban wilderness area in the United States, Griffith Park also houses a zoo, a couple of golf courses, tons of cool hiking trails, and the newly renovated Griffith Observatory. Griffith Park is, hands down, the best place to go in LA that doesn't feel like LA at all.

Practicalities

Located northwest of downtown LA, Griffith Park is easily reached from either I-5 or the 134. From I-5, get off at Los Feliz Boulevard, Griffith Park (direct entry), or Zoo Drive. From 134 eastbound, take either the Forest Lawn Drive or Victory Boulevard exits. From 134 westbound, take Zoo Drive or Forest Lawn Drive. But speed at your own risk: the 25 mph speed limit on all park roads is strictly enforced.

Activities

Located within the park are facilities for golf (Harding, Roosevelt, and Wilson Municipal Golf Courses); swimming (the Plunge Pool is open in summer months); hiking; jogging; horse-riding; tennis (Griffiths Riverside Pay, Vermont Pay, and the free Griffith Park Drive Courts); soccer (John Ferraro Athletic Fields at the northeast corner of the park); and camping and picnicking at one of the five main picnic areas.

Playgrounds are located throughout the park, usually near picnic grounds. Shane's Inspiration, a "boundless playground," is designed to allow children with disabilities to play alongside their able-bodied peers. Bicycles, including tandems, can be rented from Crystal Springs Bike and Skate Rental, located in a shack behind the Crystal Springs Ranger Station.

If you're planning on having a relaxing barbecue in the park, you need to be particularly careful between spring and early fall, when the dry underbrush can easily start a brush fire. Open fires are prohibited, but public barbecue pits are provided free of charge at picnic areas. In case of emergency in the park, call the ranger station at 212-913-4688.

Griffith Park Museums

Griffith Observatory
2800 E Observatory Rd, 323-664-1181; www.griffithobs.org
After closing its doors and shutting down its telescopes in January 2002 for a much-needed renovation, the observatory will be back in business in the spring of 2006—just in time for its 71st anniversary. At first glance, you might not even notice many of the multi-million dollar improvements, since so much care went into retaining the observatory's Art Deco style, and because a majority of the expansion is hidden beneath the front lawn. But with a bigger Hall of Science, a 200-seat presentation theater (called the Leonard Nimoy Event Horizon Theater, for the Trekkies in the house), classrooms, conference rooms, an expanded book store, and just about anything else a stargazer could hope for, the museum will be nearly double in size. The new layout will also highlight many of the perennially popular exhibits, such as the massive Foucault Pendulum and a new, larger Tesla coil (everyone should have one of *these*). Luckily, the price for many of the observatory's offerings hasn't changed: admission will still be free.

Museum of the American West
4700 Western Heritage Wy, 323-667-2000; www.autry-museum.org
Part museum of history, part art gallery, the Museum of the American West is devoted to the stories, the people, the cultures, and the events that have shaped the legacy of the region. Learn about Spanish explorers, discover how the genre of the western evolved through radio, movies, and television, and see paintings by Remington and Russell. Grab a bite at the museum's Golden Spur Café (open for breakfast and lunch). Hours: Tues-Sun: 10 am-5 pm (on Thursdays, the museum is open until 8 pm and admission is free after 4 pm). Admission costs $7.50 for adults, $5 for students and seniors, and $3 for children ages 2-12.

Greek Theatre
2700 N Vermont; 2700 N Vermont Canyon Rd, 323-665-5857; www.greektheatrela.com
Built with funds left to the city by Griffith J. Griffith, LA's outdoor theater has been hosting live music under the stars since 1930. In recent years, the 5,700-seat venue has hosted Sir Paul McCartney, The White Stripes, Tina Turner, Elton John, and the Russian National Ballet, just to name a few. At a ripe old age of 75, the theatre recently underwent a multi-million dollar facelift, which has improved the acoustics and comfort of the outdoor arena. Tickets to performances can be purchased in person at the box office, or through Ticketmaster.

Los Angeles Zoo
5333 Zoo Dr, 323-644-4200; www.lazoo.org
The Los Angeles Zoo is located in Griffith Park at the junction of the Ventura (134) and Golden State (5) Freeways. The most popular attractions are the Red Ape Rainforest, Australia House, and the nearby Botanical Gardens. The zoo is open daily from 10 am until 5 pm (except on Christmas Day) and stays open an hour later during the summer season (July 1-September 3). Note that the zoo puts animals in for the night an hour before closing time. Admission costs $10 for adults, $7 for seniors, and $5 for children ages 2 to 12. Children under two and parking are both free. If you're an AAA member, take your card for a $2 discount for adults and $1 for children (up to two adults and two kids). The LA Zoo has been going through construction and renovation since 2003, including a spiffed up souvenir shop called the International Marketplace.

Travel Town Museum
5200 Zoo Dr, 323-662-5874; www.traveltown.org
Travel Town Museum is an outdoor museum that spotlights the railroad heritage of the western US. The collection includes locomotives, freight cars, passenger cars, and a couple of cabooses, as well as a miniature train ride for kids (one of three in the park). Hours: Mon-Fri: 10 am-4 pm; Sat-Sun: 10 am-5 pm. Admission and parking are free, and a ride on the miniature train costs just $2.

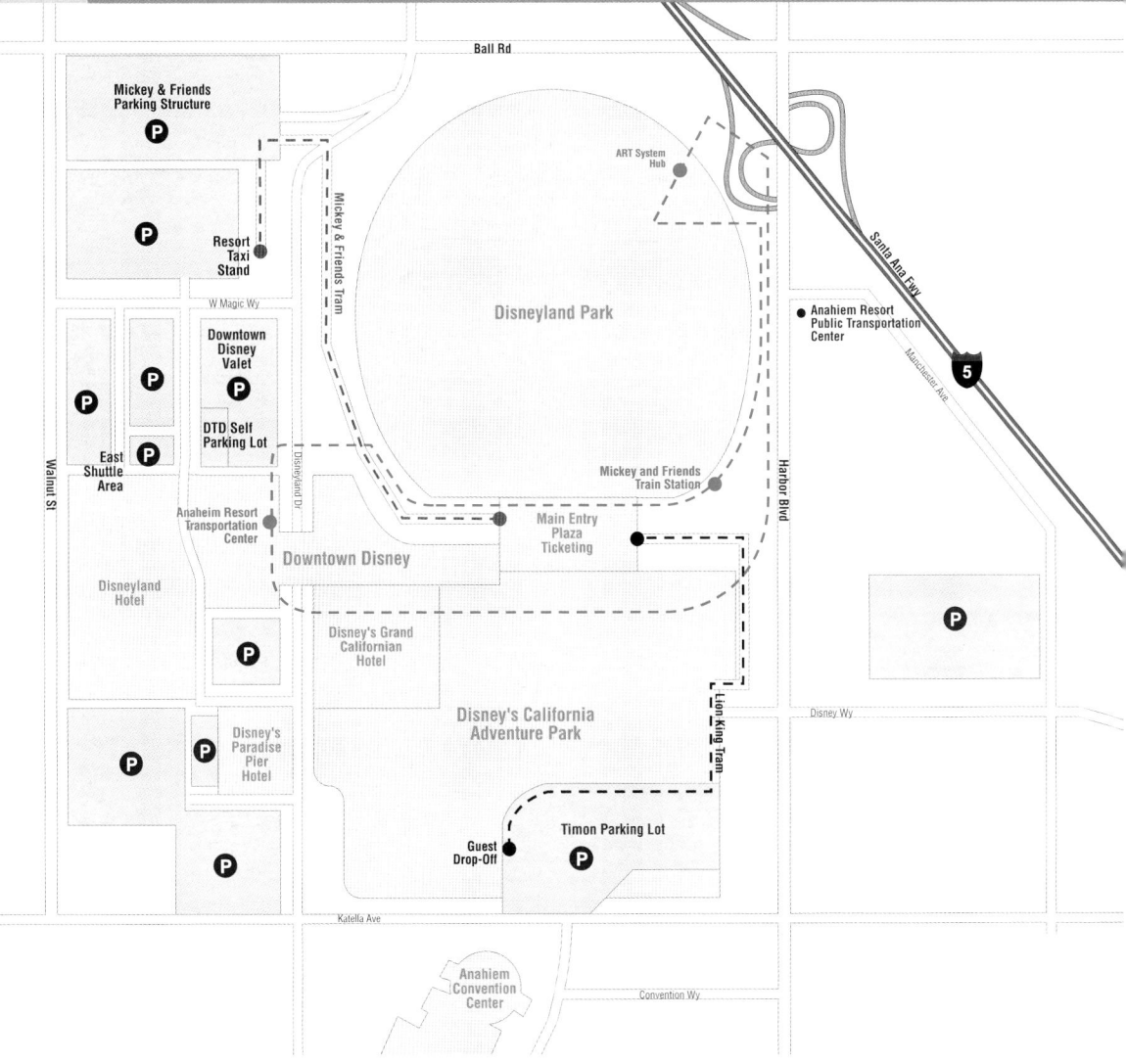

General Information

Address: 1313 S Harbor Blvd
                                      Anaheim, CA 92803
Disneyland Info (recorded):   714-781-4565
Disneyland Info (operator):   714-781-7290
Disneyland Travel Packages: 800-225-2024 or
                                      714-520-5060
Disneyland Resort Hotels: 714-956-6425
Disneyland Ticketing: 714-781-4400
Website: www.disneyland.com

Overview

Sure, you can walk around all day with a chip on your shoulder blaming "The Happiest Place on Earth" for sucking your pocketbook dry at every turn. And, yes, the crowds can be a total pain. But there's something so pleasantly surreal about a visit to the Magic Kingdom. The staff is almost militant about being kind; there's usually some childhood memory running through your head, whether you like it or not; and the second there's a chill in the air—*whammo!*—the hot chocolate carts arrive at your service. It's like…magic!

As for rides, timeless favorites like the Pirates of the Caribbean and the Haunted Mansion never go out of style. And now, thanks to Disneyland's recent 50th anniversary facelift, Sleeping Beauty's Castle has been all dolled up, Main Street is looking better than ever, and the new interactive Buzz Lightyear Astro Blasters ride is truly a blast.

If you're heading to Disneyland with a group of adults, cruise in during the evening or ditch work for shorter lines and more breathing room. If you've got the brood on board, keep an eye out for the Fastpass kiosks near ride entrances. They allow you to take a ticket and return at an appointed time to join the less congested Fastpass queue. If you're on a budget, you'll definitely want to pop out of the park to eat at one of the adjoining Downtown Disney outdoor malls. You'll save more than a few bucks.

The California Adventure Park has never quite lived up to Mickey's mothership. Even with the Tower of Terror, which is really quite frightening, and the Soarin' Over California motion ride, we recommend not wasting your time here— unless the park is offering off-season discount tickets to Southern California residents.

Hours of Operation

The park's hours change depending on the season. During the summer months, school vacations, and holidays, Disneyland is usually open from 8 am until 11 pm, and California Adventure Park is open from 10 am until 10 pm. In the off-season, Disneyland is open from 10 am until 8 pm, and California Adventure Park is open from 10 am until 6 pm. Call the park, or check their website, for more accurate times before heading down. The website is also useful for finding out what rides may be closed for maintenance on any given day. (After all, there's nothing more disappointing than having your Pirates of the Caribbean dreams squashed due to renovations.) The website also lists daily, weekly, and monthly special entertainment events.

Entrance Fees

There are not many places you'll visit where the child admission fee cuts off at 9 years of age—but Disneyland is one of them. One-day general admission tickets to Disneyland or California Adventure Park cost $49.75 for regular admission and $39.75 for children (3-9) (children three and under enter for free). The two-day Park Hopper Ticket costs $98 for regular admission and $78 for children and gains you entry to both parks. Disney sometimes posts special deals on their website, so make sure you check it before you buy tickets—it also saves time waiting in the entrance line. If you plan on becoming a frequent Disneyland guest, you might consider investing in an Annual Passport (rates vary).

Lockers

For tourists on the move, or for visitors who inexplicably brought along valuables to the park, there are lockers located outside the main entrances to Disneyland and California Adventure. Locker rentals cost between $3 and $5 per day.

Package Delivery

If you purchase more mouse ears than you can carry while inside the park, the free Package Express service can have your parcels waiting for pickup on your way out.

Kennels

Traveling with your pooch can create problems, and orchestrating a trip to Disneyland is no exception to this rule. Hotels in the Disneyland Resort do not allow pets, but if you're passing through and plan on staying elsewhere overnight, indoor day kennel facilities, located to the right of the Main Entrance of Disneyland, are available for $10 a day.

How to Get There—Driving

Traveling southbound on I-5 (Golden State/Santa Ana Freeway), exit at Disneyland Drive and turn left (south). Follow the signs to the Mickey & Friends Parking Structure. If you're traveling northbound on I-5 (Santa Ana Freeway), exit on Katella Avenue and turn left (west). Proceed west to Harbor Boulevard. Turn right on Harbor and look for the Mickey & Friends Parking Structure on the left. If you're traveling eastbound or westbound on the 22 (Garden Grove Freeway), you should exit on Harbor Boulevard and head northbound, continuing north on Harbor for approximately four miles. The Mickey & Friends Parking Structure will be on the left, just past Katella Avenue.

Parking

Once in the Mickey & Friends parking lot, head to the escalators, which take you directly to the Mickey & Friends Loading Zone. Trams collect visitors and drop them off at the Mickey & Friends Tram Station, located within walking distance of both theme parks. Parking costs $8 a day for cars, $10 for oversized vehicles, and $15 for buses.

How to Get There—Mass Transit

All of the LA area airports provide shuttle services to the Disneyland Resort. Bus 460 goes somewhere near the park, but we recommend driving a car or taking a shuttle if you can.

W 37th Pl

Watts Wy

W 37th St

Trousdale Pkwy

Childs Wy

University of
Southern
California

PAGE
266

Exposition Blvd

Jesse A
Brewer, Jr
Park

Natural History Museum
of Los Angeles County

MAP
11

Rose Garden

Kinsey Dr

California
Science Center

Wallis
Annenberg
Building

Air & Space
Gallery

P

Parking Lot 3

South Lawn

State Dr

Science
Center
Expansion

California
Science Center

Administration Admin
West   East

California
African
American
Museum

W 39th St

N Coliseum Dr

Museum Dr

IMAX

Vermont Ave

Menlo Ave

Los Angeles
Memorial Coliseum

P

Science Center/African American
Museum Parking Structure

Figueroa St

P

Parking Lot 2

(future
playfield)

N Coliseum Dr

Exposition Park

S Coliseum Dr

Leighton Ave

Playfield

E.P.I.C.C

P

Parking Lot 4

P

Los Angeles
Memorial
Sports Arena

P

Parking Lot 1

(future
community park)

P

Parking Lot 5

S Coliseum Dr

P

Parking Lot 6

W Martin Luther King Jr Blvd

Hoover St

W 40th Pl

W 40th Pl

W 41st St

Overview

NFT Map: 11

Exposition Park is bounded by Figueroa Street to the east, Martin Luther King Jr. Boulevard to the south, Menlo Avenue to the west, and Exposition Boulevard to the north. Originally called Agricultural Park, the area was developed in 1876 as a showground for agricultural and horticultural fairs. In June 1923, the Los Angeles Memorial Coliseum, named in honor of those who died in World War I, was completed. The stadium was enlarged for the 1932 Olympics and also hosted the 1984 Olympics. Today Exposition Park houses the Natural History Museum, Armory Building, IMAX Theatre, Rose Garden, California Museum of Science and Industry, California African American Museum, LA Memorial Coliseum, and the indoor Los Angeles Sports Arena.

Los Angeles Memorial Coliseum & Los Angeles Sports Arena

The history of the Coliseum/Sports Arena complex spans eight decades. It is the only arena in the world to play host to two Olympiads (10th and 23rd), two Super Bowls (1st and 7th), and one World Series (1959). In the past, the complex has played host to the Rams, the Dodgers, and the Lakers, and was the expansion home of the San Diego Chargers and the Kings. Today, the Coliseum is home to the University of Southern California's Trojan football team (call 213-740-GOSC for tickets) and various other special events. Check the website (www.lacoliseum.com) for event details. The main box office switchboard is open from 10 am to 6 pm and can be reached at 213-748-6131.

Rose Garden

The 7.5-acre Rose Garden was completed in 1928 and there were 15,793 roses in full bloom for the opening. Today the sunken garden contains more than 20,000 rose bushes representing 190-plus varieties. In Southern California, roses bloom from March to November. The garden is open daily, is free to the public, and is located within Exposition Park at 701 State Drive (310-548-7675).

Natural History Museum of LA County

The Natural History Museum is located at 900 Exposition Boulevard in Exposition Park, across from the University of Southern California (USC) between Vermont Avenue and Figueroa Street. Parking is available off Menlo Avenue. The fee for parking will run between $5 and $10, depending on events in the Exposition Park area. The museum's opening hours are 9:30 am until 5 pm Monday to Friday and 10 am until 5 pm Saturday and Sunday. Adults can expect to pay $9 for entry, seniors and students are $6.50, and children 5–12 are $2. But if you schedule your visit on the first Tuesday of the month, it won't cost you a cent! Although the museum is open during USC football games, we highly recommend that you avoid the Exposition Park area at all costs on those days unless you're attending the game. 213-763-DINO; www.nhm.org.

California Science Center & IMAX

The Science Center is open daily from 10 am until 5 pm and admission to Science Center exhibition halls is free. The IMAX is open daily and admission is $7.50 adults, $5.50 seniors and students, and $4.50 children. Check the website (www.casciencectr.org) or call 213-744-7400 for show information. Parking is $6 per car, $10 for buses or oversized vehicles, and the entrance to the visitor parking lot is on Figueroa at 39th Street.

California African American Museum

The California African American Museum researches, collects, preserves, and interprets the art, history, and culture of African Americans with emphasis on California and the western United States. The museum is open Wednesdays through Saturdays, from 10 am until 4 pm. Admission is free. 213-744-7432; www.caam.ca.gov.

How to Get There—Driving

From the north, take 101 S to 110 S, exit at Martin Luther King Jr. Boulevard W, and enter on Hoover Street. From the south, take 405 N to 110 N, exit at Martin Luther King Jr. Boulevard W, and enter on Hoover Street. From the west, take 10 E to the 110 S and follow the above directions. From the east, take 10 W to 110 S and follow the above directions.

Parking

There are parking spaces located at various places within the park. Parking rates and availability will vary for special events. Four-hour and two-hour metered parking is available on Figueroa Street and Jefferson Boulevard. There are a number of lots on the streets surrounding the park, and the usual weekly day rate is $3. Rates vary when special events are in progress, and the average cost of parking in a lot is $10.

How to Get There—Mass Transit

If you're taking public transport, take the Metro Rail Red Line or Blue Line to the 7th Street/Metro Center Station then catch the Dash F bus at the corner of Seventh and Flower. The bus will stop in front of the University of Southern California across the street from the Natural History Museum on Exposition Boulevard.

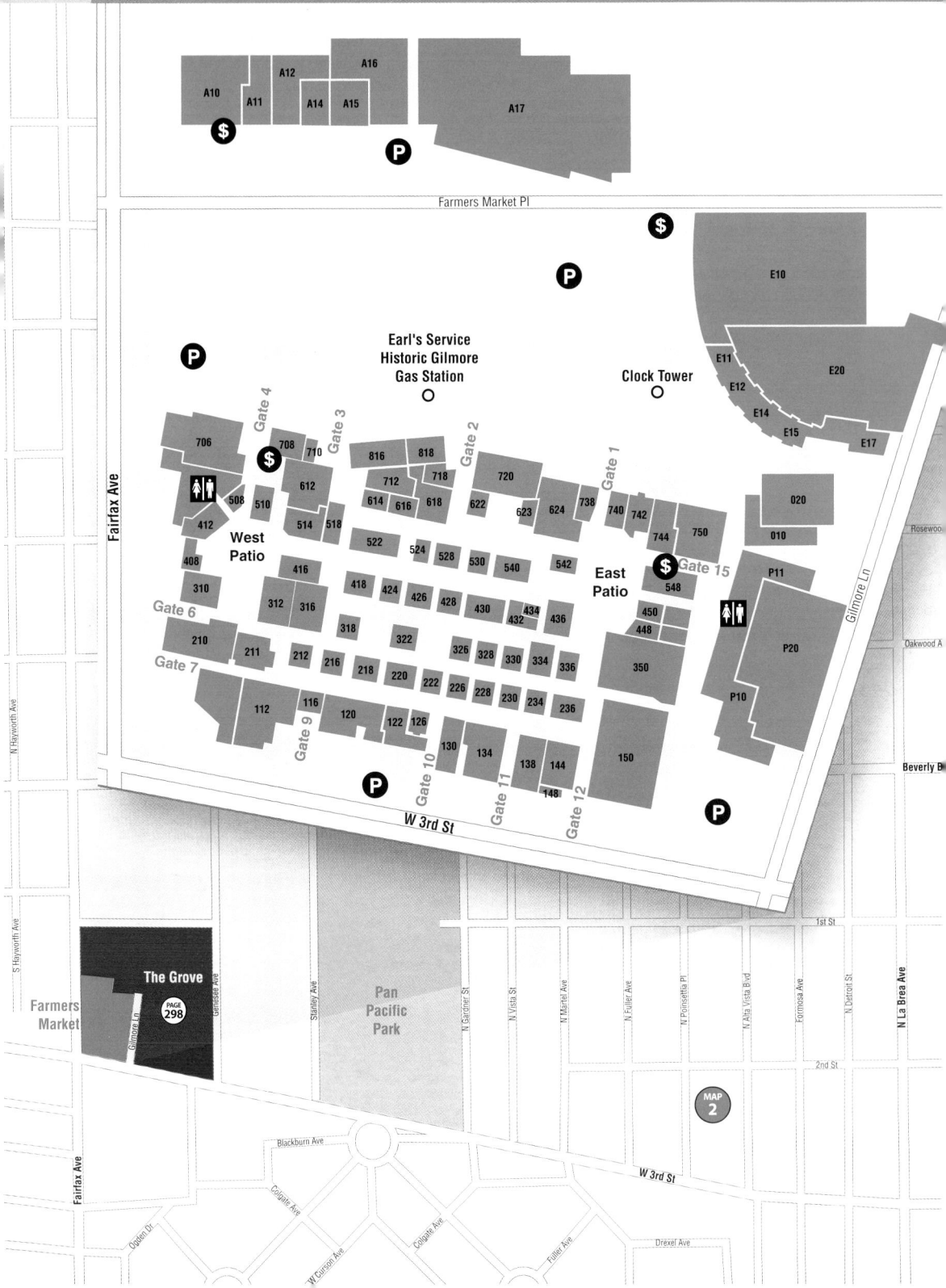

General Information

NFT Map: 2
Address: 6333 W 3rd St
           Los Angeles, CA 90036
Phone: 323-933-9211
Website: www.farmersmarketla.com
Hours: Mon-Fri: 9 am-9 pm; Sat: 9 am-8 pm; Sun: 10 am-7 pm

Overview

The Farmers Market opened in the 1930s as a humble dirt lot where farmers parked their trucks and sold their produce right off their tailgates. Over the years, it's slowly morphed into an occasionally motley crew of souvenir shops and food stalls. In recent years, the Farmers Market has been scaled back considerably—in a move that displaced numerous merchants and angered loyal customers, the north half of the market was razed to make room for The Grove shopping mall. What remains of the market, however, still retains its mid-century aura—from the forest green wooden shopping baskets to the motherly waitresses at Du-par's Restaurant, some things never change.

Where to Shop

There are two kinds of shops at the Farmers Market—the kinds that sell food, and the kinds that don't. It's hard to go wrong with any of the food-sellers. Mr. Marcel Gourmet Market has an extensive selection of imported cheese, and you can watch the whole candy-making process at Littlejohn's English Toffee House. Magee's House of Nuts has been in operation at the Farmers Market since it began and will open your eyes to a world of nut butters that goes far beyond peanuts. And The Fruit Company always offers a wide variety of fruits that are consistently fresher and more reasonably priced than any local supermarket.

The Farmers Market's other businesses are a bit more eclectic, and can be somewhat hit-or-miss. By Candlelight has an impressive selection of candles and Light My Fire sells bottled hot sauce that ranges from mild to downright combustible. There are also many shops that cater to the tourist crowd and sell cheap, Hollywood-themed souvenirs. If you're hoping to do some serious shopping of the mainstream variety, hop on the trolley (or take a short walk) and head over to The Grove.

Where to Eat

There may be no better place for breakfast in all of LA than Kokomo Café, one of the Farmers Market's few sit-down dining establishments. This casual café serves up an eclectic breakfast and lunch menu and, best of all, their egg dishes come with coffeecake. Du-par's has a following of loyal fans, mainly because of the pie and waffles, but the food court may be a better option for some. The Gumbo Pot serves the tastiest Gumbo YaYa this side of the Mississippi, and Bob's Coffee and Doughnuts is considered by many to have the best donuts in all of LA. Some of the finest Mexican dishes west of Alvarado are found at ¡Loteria! Grill. For a more elegant Farmers Market experience, check out the wine bar at Mr. Marcel Pain Vin et Fromage. C'est magnifique.

How to Get There—Driving

To drive to the Farmers Market from almost anywhere south of the Valley or north of LAX, your best bet is to take surface streets. The Grove's opening has made 3rd Street slower going than it used to be, and Beverly Boulevard isn't much better. Take whichever east-west thoroughfare you choose until you hit Fairfax Avenue, and head north. You can't miss the Farmers Market at the corner of 3rd and Fairfax. If you're coming from the Westside or South Bay, you might hop on the 10 Freeway, exit at Fairfax, and head north. Valley residents can hop on the 101 and exit at Highland. Take Highland to 3rd Street and turn right. Continue on 3rd until you reach Fairfax, and the Farmers Market will be on your right.

Parking

Before the opening of The Grove, parking at the Farmers Market was a challenge, but at least it was free. To discourage mall patrons from hogging the smallish parking lot, however, the Farmers Market now charges for parking. With validation, you get two hours of free parking and the third hour is just $1.

A10. Gilmore Bank, 549-2100*
A12. Fazio Cleaners, 800-207-4666
A15. Elements Spa & Salon, 933-0212
A14. South Beach Tan, 933-9211
A16. Beauty Collection Apothecary, 930-0300
A17. Organized Living, 954-8799
E10. Cost Plus World Market, 935-5530
E12. Francesca's Collection, 935-2474
E11. Coffee Bean and Tea Leaf, 857-0461
E14, E15. Jack Gallery, 933-4833
E16. Garden District, 954-2200
E17. Marmalade Café, 954-0088
E20. Party America, 965-0700
P10. Sur La Table, 954-9190
P11. Designer Details, 931-9632
010. Bath & Body Works, 965-1724
020. Maki Maki, 933-4127
112. Starbucks, 965-9594
116. Sheltam's News on Third, 934-1875
120. Kokomo Café, 933-0773
122. Singapore's Banana Leaf, 933-4627
126,130. Farm Fresh Produce II, 936-5917
134. Farmers Market Pharmacy, 938-2737
138. Tusquellas Seafoods, 938-1919
144,150. Mr. Marcel Gourmet Market, 935-9451

148. Mid City West Community Council, 930-1218
148. Police Corner, 954-4225
211. Du-par's Pie Shop, 933-8446
210. Du-par's Restaurant, 933-8446
212. Light My Fire, 930-2484
216. Farmers Market Poultry, 936-8158
218. Magee's House of Nuts, 938-4127
220. Sticker Planet, 939-6933
226. Puritan Poultry, 938-0312
228. Gift Nook, 933-1898
230, 234. Black Orchid Boutique, 932-0071
236. Mr. Marcel Pain Vin et Fromage, 939-7792
310. Deano's Gourmet Pizza, 935-6373
312. The Gumbo Pot, 933-0358
316. Thee's Continental Pastries, 937-1968
318. The French Crepe Company, 934-3113
322. ¡Loteria! Grill, 930-2211
326 Beer & Wine, 549-2156
328. Treasures of the Pacific, 936-9208326.
330. J&T Bread Bin Bakery, 936-0785
334. The Village, 936-9340
336. Moishe's Restaurant, 936-4998
350. Huntington Meats & Sausages,

938-5383
408. E.B.'s Beer & Wine, 549-2157
412. Charlie's Coffee Shop, 933-0616
416. Gill's Old Fashioned Ice Cream, 936-7986
426, 428. By Candlelight, 549-0458
424. The Salad Bar, 933-3204
430. Gift & Gadget Nook, 933-1898
432. Littlejohn's English Toffee House, 936-5379
434. Sushi a Go Go, 930-7874
436. Tusquellas Fish & Oyster Bar, 939-2078
448. Patsy D'Amore's Pizza, 938-4938
450. Bob's Coffee and Doughnuts, 933-8929
508. Peking Kitchen, 936-1949
510. La Korea, 936-3930
524. Essence of Nature, 931-9593
718. Cactus Fashion, 937-1236
514. Marconda's Meats, 938-5131
522,418. Ultimate Nut & Candy Company, 938-1555
528. Gadget Nook Gourmet, 933-1898
530. Country Bakery, 937-1998
540. Phil's Deli & Grill, 936-3704
542. Coffee Corner, 938-0278
548. Bennett's Ice Cream, 939-6786
612, 518. The Fruit Company, 936-6363

614. All Spice, 936-0464
616. Farmers Market Variety Store, 933-1086
618. Pampas Grill, 931-1928
622. The Refresher, 939-6786
623. Sporte Fashion, 932-6454
624. Magee's Kitchen, 938-4127
706. Johnny Rockets, 937-2093
708. Market Optometrix, 936-5140
710. Three Dog Bakery, 935-7512
712. Farmers Market Shoe Repair/Shine, 939-5622
720. Kip's Toyland, 939-8334
738. Weiss Jewelry, 934-1623
740. Bryan's Pit Barbecue, 931-2869
742. Market Grill, 934-0424
744. China Depot, 937-6868
750. Ulysses Voyage Greek Restaurant, 939-9728
816. Farm Fresh Produce, 931-3773
818. Farmers Market Newsstand, 934-0318
818, 116. Lottery Booth, 934-0318

All area codes 323 unless noted

(253)

Directors Dr

N

Median Rd

Orlando Rd

North Rd

N Perimeter

Allen
Gate

Mausoleum N Dr

Orange
Grove

W Perimeter

E Perimeter

Visitor
Parking

Mausoleum

E Mausoleum Dr

MAP
35

Palm Dr

Teaching
Greenhouse

Bing
Children's
Garden

Botanical
Center

Staff
Parking

Head
House

Conservatory

Chinese
Garden
(Phase I)

Deodar Rd

Deodar Rd

Garage Rd

Dorothy Collins
Brown Garden

Munger
Research
Center

Boone
Gallery

North
Vista

Arabella
Gallery

Ikebana Rd

Ginza Dr

Erburu
Gallery

Scott
Galleries
(American Art)

Vista Dr

Library

Visitor
Center

Gift Shop

Friends'
Hall

Oxford
Gate

Shakespeare
Garden

Herb
Garden

Restaurant
& Tea Room

Huntington
Circle

Library Rd

Desert
Conservatory

Japanese
House

Japanese
Garden

Rose
Garden

Huntington Gallery
(British & Continental Art)

Palm
Garden

Oxford Rd

Subtropical
Garden

Jungle
Garden

Zen
Garden

Ombu Ln

Ombu
Circle

Lily
Ponds

Bonsai
Court

Desert Garden Rd

Desert
Garden

Australian
Garden

S Garden Dr

Euston
Gate

Euston Rd

General Information

NFT Map: 35
Address: 1151 Oxford Rd
San Marino, CA 91108
Phone: 626-405-2100
Website: www.huntington.org
Hours: Tues-Fri: 12 pm-4:30 pm; Sat-Sun: 10:30 am-4:30 pm
Admission: adults $15, seniors $12, students $10, youth (ages 5-11) $6, free for children under five. Free first Thursday of each month, and always free for members.

Overview

Part library, part research center, part art gallery, part botanical garden, the Huntington's diverse collection of art and nature rises to the top of its game in every department. The 150 acres of gardens, covered with 14,000 varieties of plants, has the look of a picturesque college campus on steroids. The best way to see the gardens is by joining up with a free group tour—otherwise you risk missing out on the Desert Garden's menacing cacti or the lush canopy of the Jungle Garden. Kids love the new Children's Garden, where a fog grotto and a prism tunnel create a playground for the senses. For a Zen experience, stroll the winding path in the Japanese Garden past the bonsai trees and rock garden and through the bamboo grove. Well-informed docents are permanently stationed in the herb and rose gardens to answer questions. Future exhibits include a classical Chinese garden, touted as the largest of its kind outside of China.

Art Collections

The majestic Huntington is most well-known for its collection of British and French art from the 18th and 19th centuries. Highlights include Admire Gainsborough's celebrated *Blue Boy* and Lawrence's *Pinky*. The Virginia Steele Scott Gallery showcases the works of American painters from the 1730s to the 1930s. This intimate gallery is the perfect place to contemplate masterworks by Sargent, Bellows, and Hopper. In the Library building, the Arabella Huntington Memorial Collection contains 18th-century French furniture, sculpture, and Renaissance paintings.

The Library

The library includes some famous rare books—like a Gutenberg Bible and a world-class edition of Shakespeare's complete works. These famous pieces are on display for the general public, but only professional researchers can gain access to the library's entire collection, which draws scholars from around the globe to this peaceful oasis. The library specializes in 15th-century European books, maritime and scientific history, and Renaissance cartography, among other things. Yeah…we knew we'd scare you back out into the gardens.

Dining and Shopping

Treat your favorite aunt to afternoon tea in the Rose Garden Tea Room for an all-you-can-eat buffet of scones, tea sandwiches, and petit fours. Reservations are required (626-683-8131). For a more casual snack or sandwich, try the adjoining café (although it'll cost you about as much as lunch at the Tea Room). If you're harboring romantic (or thrifty) fantasies of picnicking in the gardens, we will crush them for you right now: the Huntington has a strict "no picnics" policy.

The Huntington's spacious gift shop stocks coffee-table books and scholarly titles relating to its varied collections—it's the perfect place to score Mother's Day presents.

How to Get There—Driving

The Huntington is adjacent to Pasadena in the city of San Marino, about 12 miles northeast of downtown Los Angeles. The Huntington has two entrance gates: one on Oxford Road and one at Allen Avenue, just south of California Boulevard.
From the Harbor or Pasadena Freeways (110): Take the 110 N towards Pasadena where it turns into Arroyo Parkway. Turn right on California Boulevard and continue for about three miles. At Allen Avenue, turn right and proceed two blocks to the Huntington's gates.
Foothill Freeway (210): Traveling westbound on the 210, exit at the Allen Avenue off-ramp in Pasadena. Turn left and drive south for two miles to the Huntington's gates. Traveling eastbound on the 210, exit at Hill Avenue and drive alongside the freeway for about three blocks. Turn right at Allen Avenue and head south for two miles to Huntington's gates.
Santa Monica Monica Freeway (10): Take the 10 E to the 110 N and follow the above directions for the 110.
From San Bernardino Freeway (10): Exit at San Gabriel Boulevard and go north for three miles. Turn left on Huntington Drive and continue for one mile, then make a right on Monterey Road. Bear right onto Oxford Road and continue to the Huntington's gates.

How to Get There—Mass Transit

The Metro Gold Line and a few MTA bus routes stop between one to 1.5 miles from the Huntington. For the most updated routes visit www.mta.net or www.foothiltransit.org.

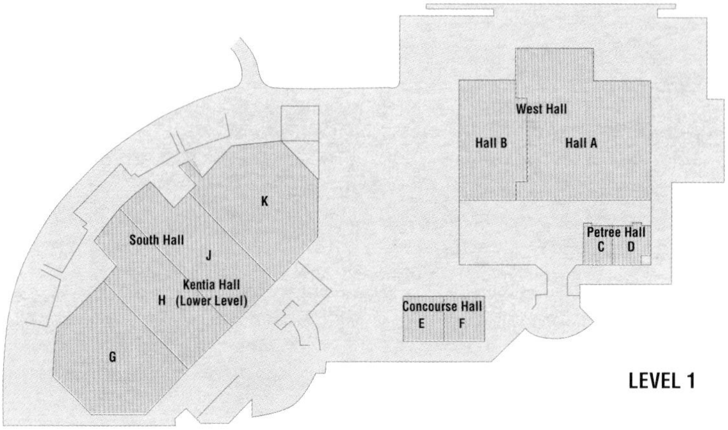

West Hall
Hall B
Hall A
K
South Hall
J
Kentia Hall
H (Lower Level)
G
Petree Hall
C D
Concourse Hall
E F

LEVEL 1

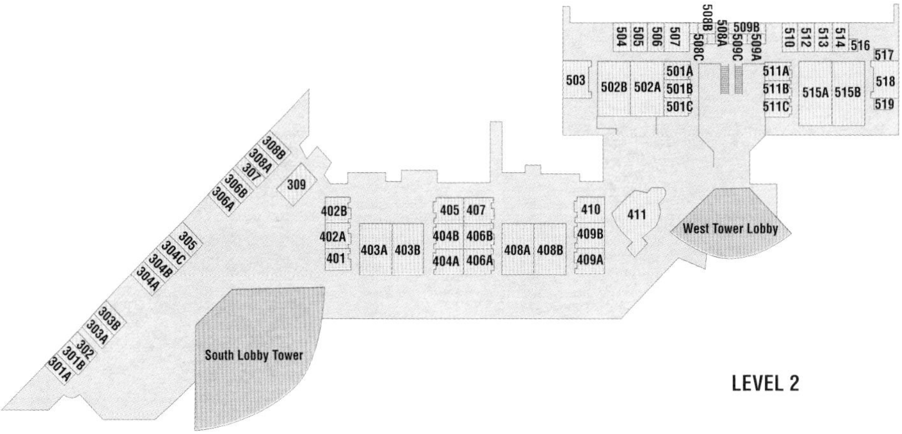

504
505
506
507
508B
508C
508A
509B
509C
509A
510
512
513
514
516
517
503
502B
502A
501A
501B
501C
511A
511B
511C
515A
515B
518
519
308B
308A
307
306B
306A
309
402B
402A
401
403A
403B
405
407
404B
406B
404A
406A
408A
408B
410
409B
409A
411
West Tower Lobby
305
304C
304B
304A
303B
303A
302
301B
301A
South Lobby Tower

LEVEL 2

LA Convention Center
STAPLES Center
PAGE 287
Pico
MAP 8
MAP 9
Federal Reserve
Transamerica Center
W Pico Blvd
Venice Blvd
W Washington Blvd
W Olympic Blvd
S Figueroa St
S Grand Ave
S Broadway
S Main
S Hoover St
W 7th St
W 8th St
W 9th St
W 11th St
W 12th St
W 14th St
E 11th St
E 12th St
S Westlake Ave
Alvarado Ter
Magnolia Ave
Arapahoe St
Wilmot St
S Burlington Ave
S Union Ave
Valencia St
Albany St
Blaine St
Convention Ctr Dr
Gilbert Lindsay Dr
S Flower St
S Hope St
S Olive St
110
10

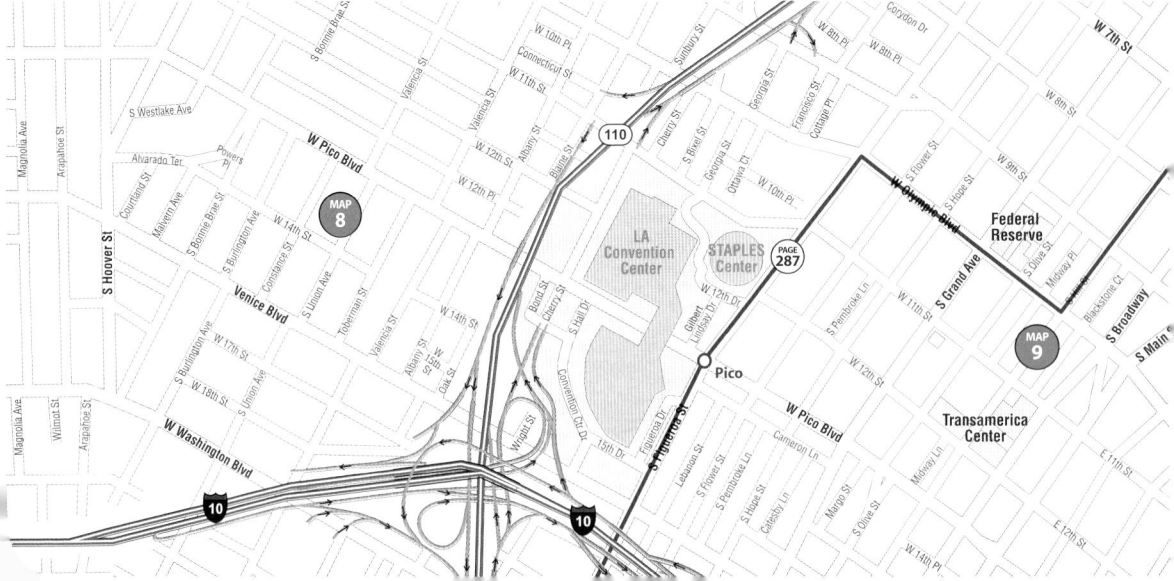

General Information

NFT Maps:	8 & 9
Address:	1201 S Figueroa St
	Los Angeles, CA 90015
Phone:	213-741-1151
Website:	www.lacclink.com

Overview

Given the diverse line-up of events held at the Convention Center, it stands to reason that every Los Angeles resident will most likely find themselves there at least once for one of the various conventions, trade shows, or fairs. In 2006 alone, the Convention Center is scheduled to play host to the 50th Annual LA Boat Show, Wizard World, Erotica LA, and E3 Electronic Entertainment Expo, among many others. From the outside, the imposing building can appear daunting, but, once inside, its halls and facilities are surprisingly user-friendly.

The Convention Center is impossible to miss from the street, and its glass-and-girder exterior is clearly visible from both the 10 and 110 Freeways. The building's design allows for a maximum amount of natural light to flood the lobbies and concourses, in stark contrast to the windowless exhibit halls and meeting rooms, where it's easy to lose track of time. The Convention Center has three major exhibit halls: West Hall, South Hall, and Kentia Hall (located beneath South Hall), as well as fifty-four meeting rooms. It's possible to book anything from a small, intimate gathering for less than twenty people to a large-scale event for over 20,000. The really big exhibitions, like the Auto Show, tend to be held in either the South or West Halls—sometimes even both.

How to Get There—Driving

Located just a stone's throw from STAPLES Center at the intersection of the Santa Monica Freeway (10) and the Harbor Freeway (110), the Los Angeles Convention Center is easily accessible from any part of LA. The simplest option is to exit the 110 at Pico Boulevard and head north. But if you're coming from the West Side or Central Los Angeles area, you may be better off skipping the freeways altogether and using either Olympic or Pico Boulevards to get downtown. The Convention Center's cross street is Figueroa Street.

Parking

There are five parking structures available to patrons of the Convention Center that all charge $10 per day. Parking for the West Hall is located just north of Pico Boulevard. Make a right turn at the intersection of Cherry Street and 12th Street into the parking garage. To park near the South Hall, look for Convention Center Drive just off Venice Boulevard on the center's south side.

How to Get There—Mass Transit

The Metro Blue Line stops on Pico Boulevard for both the Convention Center and STAPLES Center. This is a convenient alternative from the Valley, as well as the South Bay.

Buses 30, 31, 81, 442, 444, 445, 446, 447, 460, 439, LX422, LX423, LX448, and LX419 also stop near the Convention Center.

Where to Eat

The fastest and most convenient way to refuel at the Convention Center is to dine at any one of the restaurants or snack bars. The Galaxy Café, in the lobby of the West Building, is probably the center's nicest. It offers the option of outdoor seating and boasts a full bar, though it's only open for breakfast and lunch. Inside the South Building is the more casual Compass Café, which offers a variety of sandwiches, salads, and beverages. And if you're really on the run, try the concession stands inside both the West and South exhibit halls for hot dogs, sodas, and the usual lunch-counter fare.

If you have time to venture out into the Convention Center's neighborhood, you'll find an eclectic variety of restaurants just a short walk (or cab ride) away. Here are some nearby eateries that are worth a visit:

- **Philippe's the Original**, 1001 N Alameda St, 213-628-3781. Deli fare. They supposedly invented the French Dip sandwich. Would you even think of ordering anything else?
- **Original Pantry Café**, 877 S Figueroa St, 213-972-9279. American/Comfort food. The restaurant never closes. It's an LA landmark, known for good helpings of American classics, cooked from scratch.
- **Langer's**, 704 S Alvarado St, 213-483-8050. Deli menu. Their pastrami sandwich is legendary.
- **Ciudad**, 445 S Figueroa St, 213-486-5171. Latin food. The chefs/owners of Santa Monica's Border Grill take their act downtown. After a long day of meetings and exhibits, check out their rum sampler.
- **Pacific Dining Car**, 1310 W Sixth St, 213-483-6000. Steaks and chops. This meat-and-potatoes restaurant is an LA institution that is open 24 hours. After 11 pm, have your choice of dinner or breakfast.

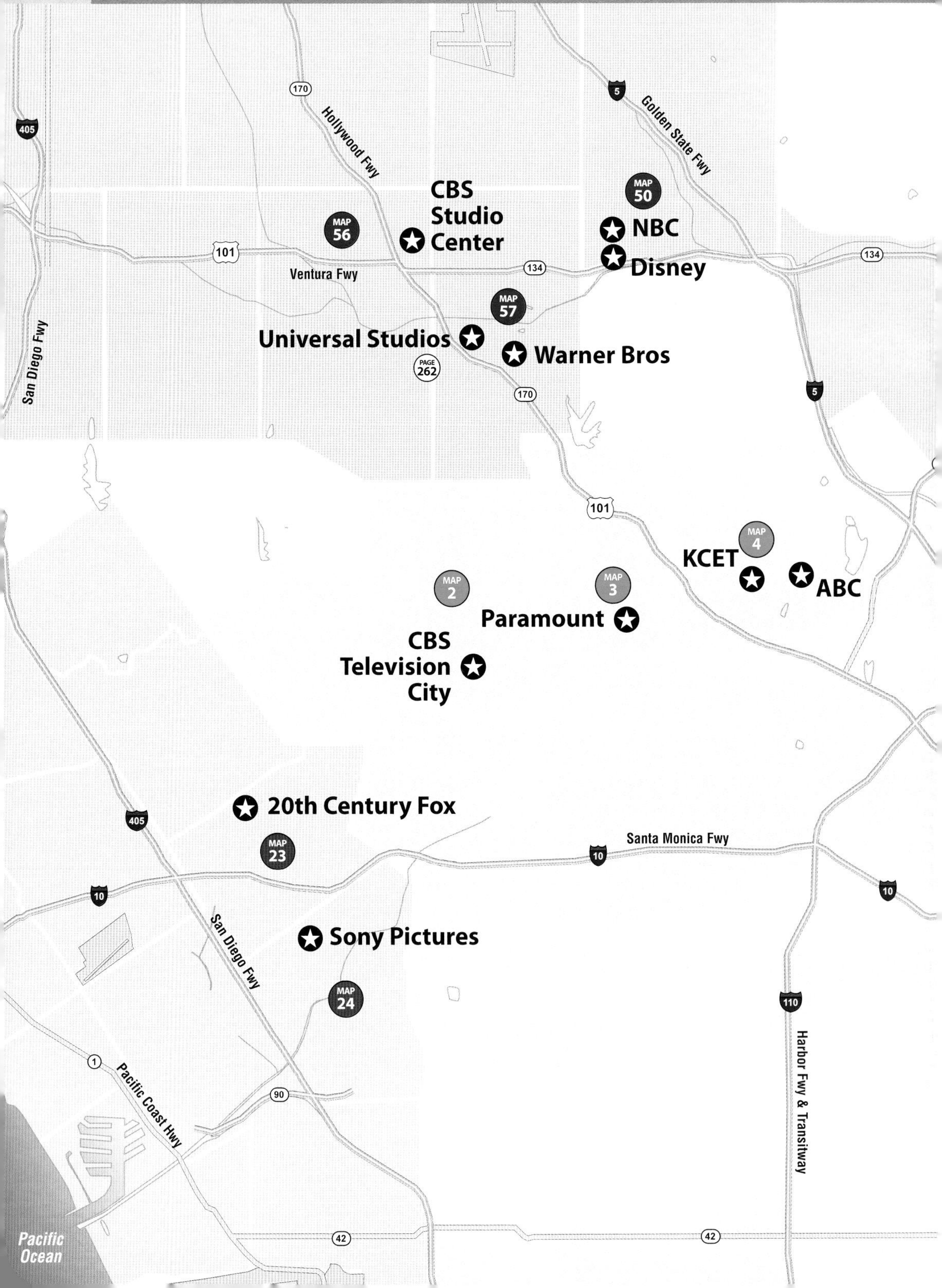

170

Hollywood Fwy

5

Golden State Fwy

405

101

Ventura Fwy

MAP 56

**CBS
Studio
Center**

134

MAP 50

NBC

Disney

134

San Diego Fwy

MAP 57

Universal Studios

PAGE 262

Warner Bros

170

5

101

MAP 4

KCET

ABC

MAP 2

MAP 3

Paramount

**CBS
Television
City**

405

20th Century Fox

MAP 23

10

Santa Monica Fwy

10

10

San Diego Fwy

Sony Pictures

MAP 24

110

1

Pacific Coast Hwy

90

Harbor Fwy & Transitway

*Pacific
Ocean*

42

42

Overview

One of the wonderful things about entertaining guests is that you get to see your own city through a visitor's eyes. And one of the places you might pop in on that you've never visited before are the backstages of the area's TV and movie studios. Many of the major movie studios and some of the television studios offer guided tours. TV studios often need audiences for show tapings, and they give out free tickets to those willing to give up their time. An excellent website for the lowdown on movie and television studios, as well as a host of other "star-related" information, is the Seeing Stars website: www.seeing-stars.com.

Warner Bros. Studio

4000 Warner Blvd, 818-977-8687; www.studio-tour.com
The Warner Bros. Studios tour involves none of the hours of walking required on other tours—they tote you through their lot on a small tram. One of the better studio tours, it is also one of the most expensive. Expect to fork over $39 for this almost three-hour intimate 110-acre back-lot tour. You can take photos when they allow you to, but only stills. Tours are given weekdays between 9 am and 3 pm 'til 4 pm in the summer months. The tours leave every half an hour, and reservations are required. The tour office is located at the studio's Gate 3 entrance. Shows currently taping here include *ER*, *The George Lopez Show*, and *Gilmore Girls*.

Paramount Pictures Studio

5555 Melrose Ave, Hollywood, 323-956-1777; www.paramount.com
Paramount runs two-hour guided walking tours through their storied lot, whose distinctive main gate was immortalized in the Hollywood classic *Sunset Boulevard*. For tour and show taping schedules (presently taping are *Girlfriends*, *Dr. Phil*, and *Judge Judy*), call 323-956-1777.

Sony Pictures Studio

(Columbia/Tristar Pictures)
10202 W Washington Blvd, Culver City, 310-244-4000; www.sonypictures.com
In 1990, Sony Entertainment of Japan purchased the old MGM Studio in Culver City where *The Wizard of Oz* was filmed. More recently, *50 First Dates*, *Monster*, and *Spider-Man* were filmed here. The studio offers two-hour guided walking tours of their working film sets for $24. Tours are offered weekdays at 9:30 am, 11 am, 12 pm, and 2:30 pm, and tickets are available at the Sony Plaza building across from the main gate on Madison Street. Make reservations in advance by calling 323-520-8687. Children under 12 are not allowed on the tour, and all adults must present a photo ID. Cameras are prohibited on the tour. Free parking is available (across from the entrance on Madison Street).

CBS Studio Center

4024 Radford Ave, Studio City, 818-655-5000; www.cbssc.com
The shows currently being shot at the studio are *the CSI series*, *JAG*, and *Two and a Half Men*, as well as the soap opera *The Young & the Restless*. The studio does not offer tours, but if you wish to be an audience member at the taping of a TV show, you can contact Audiences Unlimited (see end of page).

CBS Television City

7800 Beverly Blvd, 818-295-2700; www.cbs.com
Not to be confused with CBS Studio Center, Television City films such gems as *The Price is Right* and *The Late Late Show*. If you want to see a taping and you don't care what show it is, you can walk up to the studio's ticket office (near the corner of Beverly & Fairfax) and pick up tickets. If you're after tickets for a specific show, you'll need to call 323-575-2458 (live) or 323-575-2449 (*The Price is Right* recorded hotline) in advance.

NBC Studios

3000 West Alameda Ave (at Bob Hope Dr), Burbank, 818-840-3537; www.nbc.com
NBC is the only television studio in LA to offer tours. And at $7.50, NBC's is one of the cheapest tours in town. The tour consists of a 70-minute indoor walk through the studios. Tours run every half-hour on weekdays between 9 am and 3 pm and on holiday weekends—call ahead to make reservations and check opening times. If you're interested in seeing a taping of *The Tonight Show with Jay Leno*, tickets are available in-person from the ticket counter on the actual day of taping, or in advance by mail. If you plan on picking up your tickets in person, we recommend phoning first to check availability.

ABC TV

4151 Prospect Ave, 310-557-7777
ABC does not offer public tours, but tickets to some shows can be obtained through Audiences Unlimited, or by calling the ABC Show Ticket Hotline on 310-520-1222. You can also try writing to ABC Guest Services, 4151 Prospect Ave, Los Angeles, CA 90027.

Disney Studios

500 S Buena Vista St, Burbank, 818-560-1000
Not open to the public apart from the taping of such shows as *8 Simple Rules* and *My Wife and Kids*, audiences can secure tickets through Audiences Unlimited (see end of page).

KCET Studio

4401 Sunset Blvd, Hollywood, 323-953-5289; www.kcet.org
KCET, the local public television (PBS) station Channel 28, is a historic studio, where classics like *The Jazz Singer* were filmed. Sadly, they have temporarily suspended free walking tours for security reasons.

Universal Studios

100 Universal City Plz, Universal City, 800-864-8372; www.universalstudios.com
Taking the Universal Studios tour feels like visiting a theme park. Prepare to be attacked by characters from *Jaws* and *King Kong* while riding the tram. (Oops! Did we just ruin the surprise?) Themed rides and staged shows bring to life movie favorites such as *Back to the Future*, *Jurassic Park*, and *Terminator*. The only drawback is that mega-attractions mean long lines and ticket prices in the neighborhood of $45. But most people seem to think that the tour is worth the price. For more information, see page 262.

20th Century Fox

10201 W Pico, Century City; www.fox.com
Tickets for show tapings are available through Audiences Unlimited.

Audiences Unlimited

Audiences Unlimited is an agency that distributes free tickets to the tapings of television shows. Call 818-771-7195, or visit www.audiencesunlimited.com for tickets. Tickets can also be obtained through the mail (include an SASE) by writing to Audiences Unlimited, 100 Universal City Plz, Bldg 153, Universal City, CA 91608. Be sure to specify the name of the show, date, and number of people in your party.

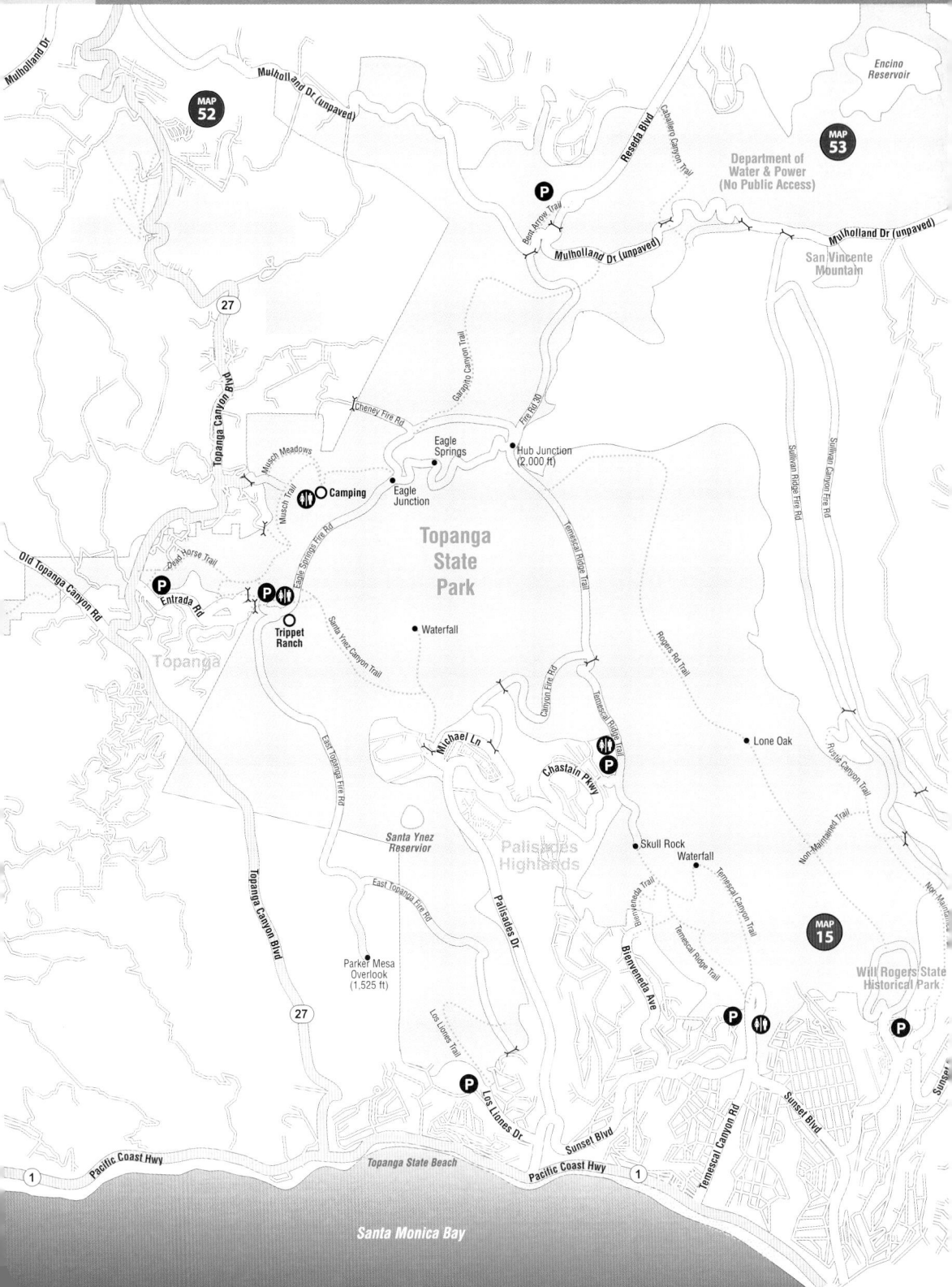

Santa Monica Bay

General Information

NFT Maps:	15, 52 & 53
Address:	20825 Entrada Rd
	Topanga, CA 90290
Phone:	310-455-2465
California State Parks Website:	www.parks.ca.gov

Overview

Depending on which translation you accept, *Topanga* means "the place above," or "the place where the mountains meet the sea," *or* "the place of green water" (and we just thought it meant "really big"). Located entirely within Los Angeles' city limits (although you wouldn't know it by visiting), Topanga State Park's 14,000 acres make it the largest wilderness located within the boundaries of a major city *in the entire universe.*

Bottom line—it's freakin' beautiful; it's *the* place to hit the trails (they've got over 45 miles worth of those), enjoy some nature (check out the bloomin' during the spring), or just chill out away from it all. Topanga offers breathtaking views of the ocean and plenty of fresh air—which you'll need once you actually get out of your car and witness just what Mother Nature has in store for you.

Practicalities

The park is open daily from dawn until dusk (approximately 8 am until 6 pm). Entry into the park is free, but parking costs $4 per vehicle. From Pacific Coast Highway (1), travel north on Topanga Canyon Boulevard, past the post office at the center of "town," then turn right onto Entrada Road. Keep to the left until you reach the park's main parking lot (about one mile). From the Ventura Freeway (101), exit at Topanga Canyon Boulevard, drive south over the crest of the mountains and proceed three miles to Entrada Road and turn left. Follow the above directions from here.

Activities

Topanga is ideal for uninterrupted walking, running, cycling, and horseback riding (although horse rentals are not available at the park). Mountain bikers are supposedly restricted to the fire roads, but often fly down the pedestrian-only paths anyway. Dogs are not allowed on backcountry trails (but the free-range mountain lions are okay; whatever). There are many marked trails for hikers, most of which can be accessed from Trippet Ranch (off Entrada Road), a former "gentleman's ranch" used as a weekend escape from the city back in the day. In addition to the Park Office, Trippet Ranch provides parking facilities, picnic areas, and a great little Visitor's Center that offers guided walking tours on Sunday mornings. If it's relaxation, not activity, that you're after, you might want to try the self-guided nature trail (the trail map costs a quarter and is available at the parking lot) or join one of the Sunday guided walks with experts well-versed in the flora and fauna of the area. Call the park for more information about walk schedules.

Another visual highlight of the park is the blooming flowers that attract thousands of avid gardeners and photographers each year. For information on the different varieties of flowers that grow in the park, call 818-768-3533.

Hiking Trails

Many of the park's trails can be accessed from Trippet Ranch. The Eagle Springs loop begins at the Eagle Junction, just under two miles from Trippet. A climb up the northern section of the loop will afford you a nice panoramic view of the park. At the eastern end of the Eagle Springs loop, you'll come to the Hub Junction, from where you can take the Temescal Ridge Trail south or the fire road north, or simply circle back and complete the Eagle Springs loop to Trippet Ranch.

To reach the unpaved Mullholland Drive, hike north from Hub Junction, and follow the fire road for two miles through chaparral. Heading south on the Temescal Ridge Trail leads you high above the canyons to gorgeous views of sycamore and oak riparian forests below.

Another option from Trippet Ranch is to walk east to the Topanga Fire Road and then north for a short distance to the Santa Ynez Trail. As you descend into the Santa Ynez Canyon, look out for the crumbly sandstone formations with pockets where moisture collects—there are tiny cliff gardens in these areas. Near the bottom of the trail is a short 0.8-mile trail leading to a lovely waterfall that is definitely worth a look.

Shorter hikes can be taken from other parking lots in Topanga State Park. From the Los Liones Drive parking lot, you can complete a 1.7-mile loop hike on the Los Liones Trail. For a longer hike, take the East Topanga Fire Road to the Parker Mesa Overlook for stunning views of the canyon.

If you park in the first lot on Entrada Road (if you hit Trippet Ranch, you've gone too far), you can take the 1.1-mile Dead Horse Trail to Trippet Ranch.

To access the Caballero Canyon Trail or the Bent Arrow Trail, take Reseda Boulevard into the Caballero Canyon Park lot and head out from there.

Camping

Camping facilities are available on a first-come, first-served basis. Your best bet is to follow the Musch Trail to the Musch Trail Campground, but we recommend contacting the park directly for more information before heading out.

Valley Spring Ln

Strohm Ave

Ledge Ave

Toluca Estates Dr

Toluca Rd

Cahuenga Blvd

**Lakeside
Country Club**

Chiquita St

Lankershim Blvd

Denny Ave

Cartwright Ave

Willowcrest Ave

Valleyheart Dr

Bluffside Dr

**Weddington
Park
South**

Backdraft

Lower Lot

Special Effects Stages

Lucy:
A Tribute

Revenge of
The Mummy
The Ride

MAP
57

Jurassic Park
The Ride

**Universal
Studios
Hollywood**

Annual Pass
Processing Center

Animal
Planet
Live!

Back to the Future
The Ride

Flintstones
Carnival Games

Studio
Tour

Terminator 2: 3D

TV Audience
Ticket Booth

Upper Lot

Nickelodeon
Blast Zone

Frankenstein
Parking
(Lower Level)

Hollywood
Globe Theatre

Shrek 4-D

The Blues
Brothers

Van Helsing:
Fortress Dracula

Universal
Amphitheatre

WaterWorld

**Universal
Studios**

Exit

Entrance

Universal
City

Ticket Booths

Universal Hollywood Dr

Curious
George
Parking

Universal Citywalk

10 Universal
City Plaza

Jurassic
Parking

Universal Citywalk

Universal Studios Blvd

Universal City
Hilton Towers

Hotel Dr

Sheraton
Universal

Fredonia Dr

Coral Dr

Skyhill Dr

Regal Pl

Fredonia Dr

Muirview Dr

Cahuenga Blvd

Jane Dr

Buddy Pl

101

Broadlawn Dr

Oakley Dr

Jane Dr

Oak Glen Dr

General Information

NFT Map: 52
Address: 100 Universal City Plz
                  Universal City, CA 91608
Park Information: 800-UNIVERSAL
Special Events: 818-622-3036
Lost & Found: 818-622-3522
Group Sales: 800-959-9688 x2
Website: www.universalstudioshollywood.com

Overview

If you live in Hollywood, you've probably seen a movie being filmed during your daily commute to work, been to a show taping or, heck, even worked as an extra. If that's the case, Universal Studios, with its hissing animatronic Jaws and silly stunt shows, doesn't offer you much beyond nostalgia.

However, if you've got relatives visiting from out-of-state, send them to Universal immediately; it one-ups Disneyland as far as interactivity is concerned, both for kids (*Shrek 4-D*) and adults (the new *Fear Factor Live*). Aunt Mae will flip when she sees Wisteria Lane from *Desperate Housewives* on the studio backlot tour. The park is much more manageable than the Happiest Place on Earth, and rides, such as *Revenge of the Mummy*, are always improving.

Just outside the theme park gates, CityWalk truly embraces the concept of Hollywood hype. Garish storefronts beckon you into knick-knack shops and a variety of restaurants (including mini-versions of LA's best eateries, from Gladstone's to a Dodger Dog stand). Locals can appreciate movies at the 18-screen Universal City Cinemas, including a huge IMAX screen (call 818-508-0588 for movie times), music at B.B. King's Blues Club, a dash of seasonal fun, be it at the wintertime outdoor skating rink, or an, uh, "interactive" fountain which kids just can't resist running through.

Hours of Operation

Universal Studios is open all year (minus Thanksgiving and Christmas), however their operating hours are subject to change without notice, so call the park or check the website before you plan your visit. Typically the park is open from 9 am until 10 pm on weekends during peak times, and 9 am until 8 pm during busy weekdays. During the slower months, it's open from 10 am until 6 pm. But again, check before you go.

Entrance Fees

One-day tickets cost $47 for adults and $43 for those under 48 inches tall. Book tickets online using Universal's Print@Home option to avoid the lines. If money is no object, consider purchasing the Front of Line Pass for $89.95, which allows you to cut the line for rides and snag the best seats in the house for any performance.

If you're a regular, the Premium Annual Pass ($99) provides unlimited year-round entry to the park with a 15% discount on entry for up to 6 friends, discounts on food and merchandise throughout the park, and free parking and front-line access on the Studio Tour. Check the website for other packages and deals.

Lockers

Coin-operated lockers are located just inside the park at varying costs depending on the size you rent. And since they're inside the park, you can keep adding junk as the day goes by.

Package Delivery

If you buy merchandise within the park and you don't feel like schlepping it around, there's a handy delivery service that will have your parcels waiting for you as you leave. The pickup point is located near the exit at Universal Film Co.

Kennels

If you can't bear to leave your pet at home or if you're passing through on a longer journey, Universal provides a complimentary kennel service for park guests. Go to the Guest Services window at the entrance to the park, and your pet will be escorted to the facilities by one of the guest service representatives.

How to Get There—Driving

Universal Studios Hollywood is located between Hollywood and the San Fernando Valley, just off the 101 Hollywood/Ventura Freeway. Exit at Universal Center Drive or Lankershim Boulevard and follow the signs to the parking areas.

Parking

Preferred Parking ($17) is located in the Rocky & Bullwinkle Lot and is one of the closest parking lots to the theme park. If you would prefer to park your car yourself, general parking is located in the Curious George Garage, Jurassic Parking Garage, and the Frankenstein and Woody Woodpecker Lots. All are within walking distance to any Universal destination and cost $10 for the day.

How to Get There—Mass Transit

There is a Red Line Metro rail station at Universal City. MTA Buses 96, 150, 152, 156, 163, 166, 240, and 750 also run to Universal City Station. Shuttles, airport, and charter services are available to and from Universal Studios Hollywood with SuperShuttle. 800-258-3826; www.supershuttle.com.

1. Housing Admin Building
2. NW Auditorium
3. Office of Residential Life
4. Acosta Training Center
5. North Campus Student Center
6. Graduate School of Education and Information Studies Building
7. MacDonald Medical Research Laboratory
8. West Medical Center

General Information

NFT Maps: 17 & 20
Address: 405 Hilgard Ave
                  Los Angeles, CA 90095
Phone: 310-825-4321
Website: www.ucla.edu

Overview

Located on a picturesque campus in Westwood, UCLA is a behemoth public research university that offers 118 undergraduate degree programs and 200 graduate degree programs. Its faculty of nobel prize laureates, MacArthur Grant winners, and National Medal of Science winners has earned UCLA an international reputation for academic excellence. The school has also consistently produced champion sports teams and athletes since it was founded in 1919.

UCLA's Extension Program is extremely popular and offers continuing education for adults in topics ranging from architecture to screenwriting to wine-tasting. The courses, offered quarterly, are popular among people considering career changes, as well as those merely interested in bettering themselves.

Tuition

For the 2005-2006 academic year, living expenses for undergraduate students (including books, registration fees, supplies, room and board, transportation, health insurance, and other personal costs) were estimated by the university to cost $16,949-$22,634 for California residents, and $34,724-$40,454 for students from out of state (costs vary depending on living accomodations).

Facilities

The UCLA campus is like a small city, with its own police department and fire marshal and a range of services including shops, restaurants, post offices, and banks. 11 Parking and Information booths located across the campus will aid visitors in their confusion about where to park. UCLA's circular drive loops around the entire campus and is easy to navigate. If you're just popping in, metered parking is available for 25¢ per eight minutes (bring lots of quarters) or $7 for the entire day. Student parking (granted quarterly through application) is assigned on a need-based point system, which takes into consideration class standing, employment/academic obligations, and commuter distance.

Culture on Campus

UCLA also provides the community with a variety of cultural programs. The university is affiliated with the Geffen Playhouse in Westwood (11301 Wilshire Blvd, 310-208-5454), which has been the LA stop for Broadway plays such as The Weir and Wit. On campus, UCLA LIVE! at Royce Hall (310-825-2101) has hosted a wide variety of music, literary, and dance programs, from the Los Angeles Philharmonic to Laurie Anderson to Phillip Glass. The Fowler Museum of Cultural History holds an impressive collection of art from Africa, Asia, and the Pacific (fowler.ucla.edu, 310-825-4361). The Hammer Museum hosts cutting edge readings, screenings, and music and art celebrations throughout the year (hammer.ucla.edu, 310-443-7078). And each April, UCLA is home to the Los Angeles Times' Festival of Books— the literary event of the year.

Sports

You don't need to be affiliated with the university to appreciate the talents of UCLA's athletes. Their top-ten nationally ranked teams include men's water polo, women's soccer, women's volleyball, and football. For up-to-date information, scores, and schedules, check out the official athletics website at uclabruins.college sports.com. Ticket prices for football and men's basketball games depend on the event. All other sporting events cost $4 with a student ID and $6 without. For tickets, call 310-206-5991.

Department Contact Information

College of Letters & Science 310-825-1805
Graduate Admissions 310-825-3819
Undergraduate Admissions 310-825-3101
Anderson School of Management 310-825-6121
Graduate School of Education
    and Informa tion Studies. 310-825-6774
UCLA Extension (UNEX) 310-826-9971
. . . . or 818-784-7006
School of the Arts & Architecture 310-206-6465
The Henry Samueli School of
    Engineering & Applied Science 310-825-7506
School of Dentistry. 310-825-2337
School of Law. 310-825-4736
School of Medicine. 310-825-6081
School of Nursing 310-825-1755
School of Public Health. 310-825-6381
School of Public Policy &
    Social Research. 310-206-3059
School of Performing Arts 310-825-0964

General Information

NFT Maps: 11,12 & 40
Mailing Address: University Park Campus USC
Los Angeles, CA 90089
Location: University Park, b/w Figueroa St,
Exposition Park & Jefferson Blvd
Phone: 213-740-2311
Website: www.usc.edu

Overview

The University of Southern California opened its doors in 1880 with 53 students when the city of Los Angeles was still in its fledgling frontier stages. Four years later, three of the original 53 became the first class to graduate from the private, non-denominational school (one woman and two men). Enrollment has since jumped to over 31,000, and the school now occupies two main campuses.

The University Park Campus, home to USC's College of Letters, Arts & Sciences, the Graduate School, and 17 professional schools, is located three miles south of downtown Los Angeles. Seven miles from the University Park Campus, the 31-acre Health Sciences Campus houses the medical and pharmaceutical schools, as well as programs in occupational therapy, physical therapy, and nursing. A shuttle bus runs between the two campuses approximately every hour throughout the week.

USC's film school boasts an impressive pedigree. Its founding faculty included Douglas Fairbanks and D.W. Griffith, and it has churned out equally famous alumni, including George Lucas and Robert Zemeckis. USC rejected filmmaker Steven Spielberg's application (oops!); he has since sucked up his pride and now sits on the USC Board of Trustees. At least one USC alumnus has been nominated for an Academy Award every year since the awards ceremony began in 1929.

Tuition

For the 2005-2006 academic year, annual undergraduate tuition and fees total about $32,008 (based on 12-18 units for two semesters). Add on the cost of room, board, books, supplies, and transportation, and your education is going to cost you about $44,582 a year.

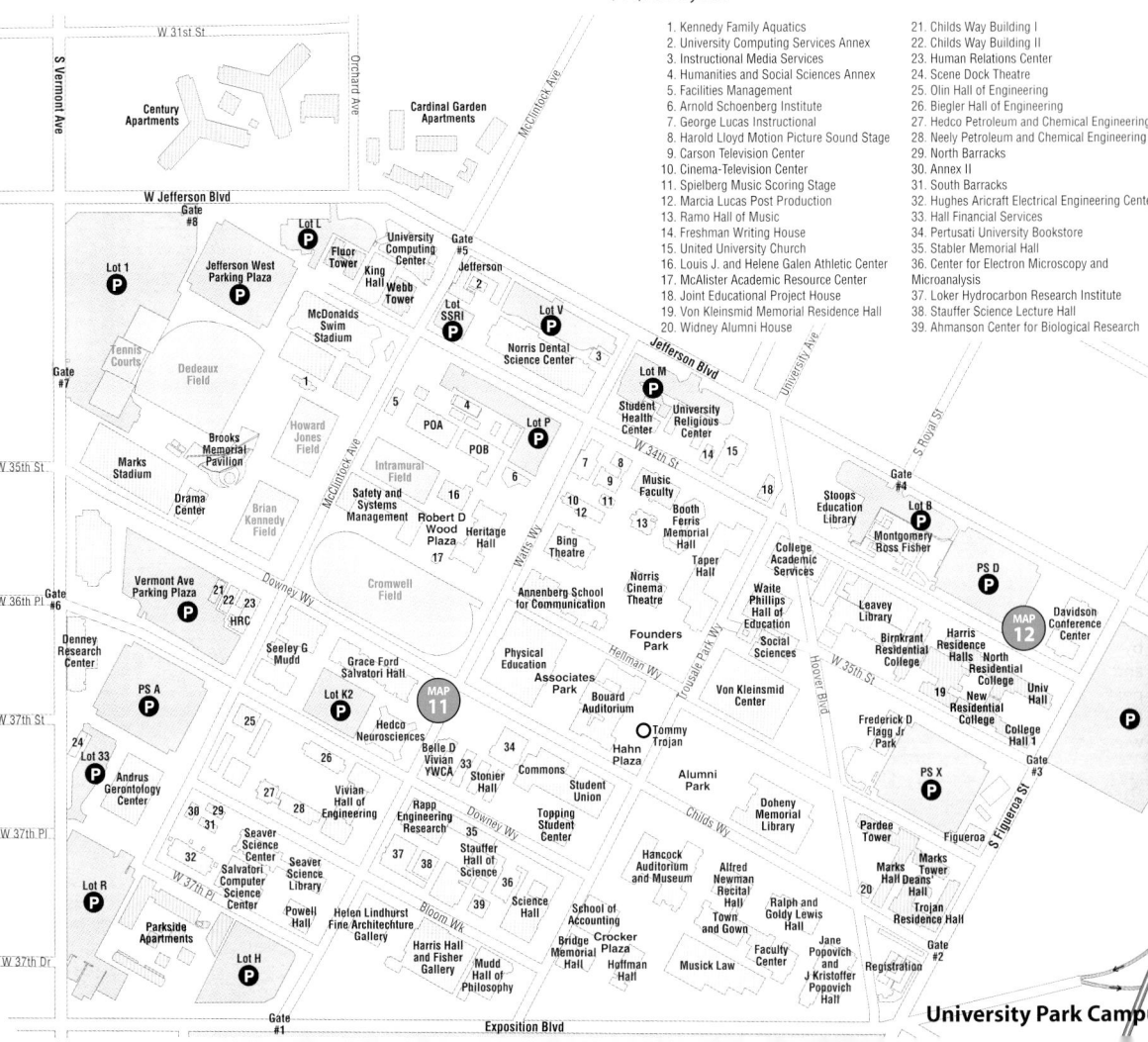

1. Kennedy Family Aquatics
2. University Computing Services Annex
3. Instructional Media Services
4. Humanities and Social Sciences Annex
5. Facilities Management
6. Arnold Schoenberg Institute
7. George Lucas Instructional
8. Harold Lloyd Motion Picture Sound Stage
9. Carson Television Center
10. Cinema-Television Center
11. Spielberg Music Scoring Stage
12. Marcia Lucas Post Production
13. Ramo Hall of Music
14. Freshman Writing House
15. United University Church
16. Louis J. and Helene Galen Athletic Center
17. McAlister Academic Resource Center
18. Joint Educational Project House
19. Von Kleinsmid Memorial Residence Hall
20. Widney Alumni House

21. Childs Way Building I
22. Childs Way Building II
23. Human Relations Center
24. Scene Dock Theatre
25. Olin Hall of Engineering
26. Biegler Hall of Engineering
27. Hedco Petroleum and Chemical Engineering
28. Neely Petroleum and Chemical Engineering
29. North Barracks
30. Annex II
31. South Barracks
32. Hughes Aricraft Electrical Engineering Center
33. Hall Financial Services
34. Pertusati University Bookstore
35. Stabler Memorial Hall
36. Center for Electron Microscopy and Microanalysis
37. Loker Hydrocarbon Research Institute
38. Stauffer Science Lecture Hall
39. Ahmanson Center for Biological Research

University Park Campus

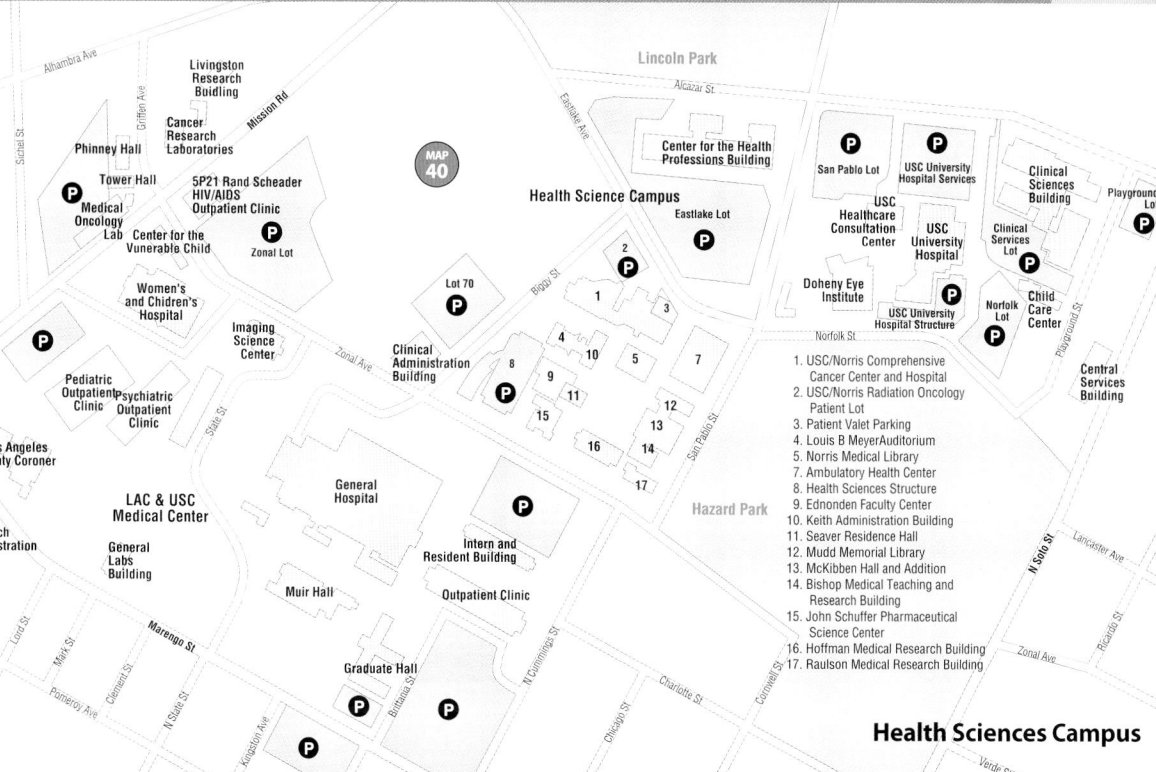

Health Sciences Campus

1. USC/Norris Comprehensive Cancer Center and Hospital
2. USC/Norris Radiation Oncology Patient Lot
3. Patient Valet Parking
4. Louis B Meyer Auditorium
5. Norris Medical Library
6. Ambulatory Health Center
7. Health Sciences Structure
8. Ednonden Faculty Center
9. Edmonden Faculty Center
10. Keith Administration Building
11. Seaver Residence Hall
12. Mudd Memorial Library
13. McKibben Hall and Addition
14. Bishop Medical Teaching and Research Building
15. John Schuffer Pharmaceutical Science Center
16. Hoffman Medical Research Building
17. Raulson Medical Research Building

Parking

Parking on campus costs $6. There are also a small number of one-hour metered parking spaces available. Four-hour and two-hour metered parking is available on Figueroa Street and Jefferson Boulevard. $3- to $5-a-day lots are available Monday through Friday across the street from the campus on Figueroa Street (next to the Sizzler restaurant) and on Jefferson Boulevard (next to the Shrine Auditorium). Parking rates for these lots may vary for special events.

Culture on Campus

Throughout the academic year, USC's prestigious Thornton School of Music, USC Fisher Art Gallery, and the KUSC classical radio station are among the many campus cultural institutions that stage full schedules of arts-related events. For a schedule of performances by the Thornton's symphony, chamber orchestra, wind ensemble, and choir, check out www.usc.edu/music. The USC orchestra also performs regularly at Disney Hall, the home of the LA Philharmonic. (And Frank Gehry, the architect of the famous performance hall, was a USC man himself!)

Sports

USC's top-ten nationally ranked teams include women's volleyball, men's water polo, women's golf, and men's golf. The USC Trojan football team was the back-to-back 2003 and 2004 National Championship winner. For up-to-date information, scores, and schedules, check out the official athletics website at www.usctrojans.com. For tickets, call 213-740-4672.

Department Contact Information

Admissions 213-740-1111
College of Letters, Arts & Sciences 213-740-2531
Leventhal School of Accounting 213-740-4838
School of Architecture 213-740-2723
Marshall School of Business 213-740-6422
School of Cinema-Television 213-740-2804
Annenberg School
for Communication 213-821-6180
School of Dentistry 213-740-1001
Rossier School of Education 213-740-5756
School of Engineering 213-740-7832
School of Fine Arts 213-740-2787
Leonard Davis School of Gerontology 213-740-6060
Independent Health Professions 323-442-2077
The Law School 213-740-7331
Keck School of Medicine 323-442-1842
School of Pharmacy 323-442-1369
School Policy, Planning
& Development 213-740-0350
School of Social Work 213-740-2711
School of Theatre 213-821-2744

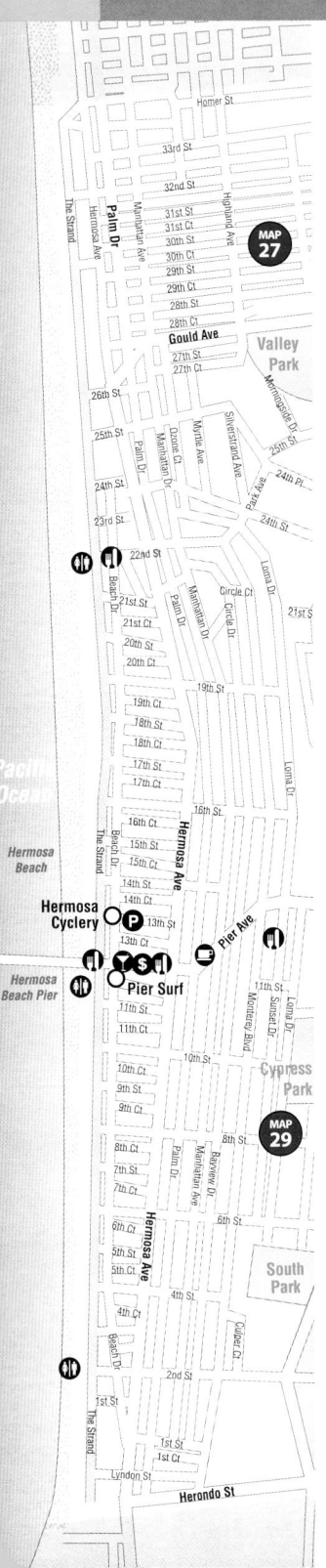

Overview

Hermosa means "beautiful" in Spanish, and it looks quite like the Platonic ideal of a beach town. Hollywood certainly seems to take the place at name-value, filming hits like *The OC*, *CSI*, and *Summerland* on the Pier on a regular basis. But glitz and glamour is an exception here—it's the flips flops, swim trunks, and tans that are the norm. The beach is teeming with surfers, volleyball players, anglers, and sunbathers, while joggers, bikers, skaters, and strollers line the Strand. Visit the City of Hermosa Beach website at www.hermosabch.org, or the Hermosa Beach Chamber of Commerce website at www.hbchamber.net for listings of local events and activities. A summer favorite: movies on the beach at sunset.

If you're a surfing fan, check out the Surfers Walk of Fame. Seven charter members and 16 pioneers are honored with bronze plaques embedded in the Pier (the seven charter members are Bing Copland, Hap Jacobs, Greg Noll, Mike Purpus, Jeff Stoner, Dale Velzy, and Dewey Weber).

Practicalities

Hermosa Beach is open daily from sunrise to sunset. During the summer, parking can be a pain, so come early and bring quarters. There is metered street parking for 25¢ per 15 minutes and a three-story parking lot on 13th Street, which costs $1 per hour, or $16 per day. Hint: If you don't mind walking, there's free 12-hour parking at the Farmer's Market on Valley Drive (between 8th and 10th Streets). Restrooms are located on the new Pier Plaza and at 2nd Street, 11th Street, 14th Street, and 22nd Street.

Sports

It comes as little surprise that TV crews and volleyball players agree to use this beautiful location as one of the sites of nationally televised Pro Beach Volleyball Tournaments. Hermosa's other favorite pastime is honored every year when the the International Surf Festival comes to town (www.surffestival.org). The three-day event, held annually in August, draws lifeguard participants from all over California and as far away as Australia.

Surfing and volleyball lessons are always available right on the beach, as are rental boogie boards, surfboards, or skates. Pier Surf (21 Pier Ave, 310-372-2012), located just up from the Hermosa Beach Pier, rents surfboards for $12 an hour ($35 a day) and boogie boards for $6 an hour ($20 a day).

Hermosa Cyclery (20 13th St, 310-374-7816) provides a good selection of rental bikes, boogie boards, skates, umbrellas, and chairs at affordable prices; rates start at $7 an hour ($21 a day) for bikes and $6 an hour ($18 a day) for rollerblades. Check the Hermosa Cyclery website at www.hermosacyclery.com for a complete list of rental offers.

Hermosa Pier

Nearly a century old, Hermosa Pier is undergoing a much-needed multi-stage renovation project, but the 1,228-foot-long pier will remain open year-round to foot traffic and anglers. Among the expected improvements: fresh pylons, resurfacing, more lights, and a new three-story lifeguard station.

Shopping

From the latest surfer styles to the hottest summer sandals, there are plenty of shopping opportunities within walking distance of the beach along Pier Avenue, Manhattan Avenue, Artesia Boulevard, and the Pacific Coast Highway; the streets are covered with clothing and jewelry boutiques, sunglass huts, antiques showrooms, and souvenir stands. If you're after fresh produce or flowers, the Farmer's Market, located on Valley Drive (between 8th and 10th Streets), is open every Friday from noon until 4 pm, rain or shine.

Restaurants & Cafés

- **Hennessey's Tavern** • 8 Pier Ave • 310-372-5759
- **Il Boccaccio** • 39 Pier Ave • 310-376-0211
- **Martha's 22nd Street Grill** • 25 22nd St • 310-376-7786
- **Ragin' Cajun** • 422 Pier Ave • 310-376-7878
- **Mediterraneo** • 73 Pier Ave • 310-318-2666
- **Blue Pacific Restaurant** • 201 Hermosa Ave • 301-406-8986

Overview

In the town of Manhattan Beach, multi-million dollar condos are as ubiquitous as skyscrapers are in New York City. The beach's upscale accommodations and restaurants attract an affluent clientele, which translates into pricey shopping and dining. There's no shortage of world-class meals served outdoors here. But there's also free fun to be had—the beach is a prime location for surfing, boogie boarding, body surfing, swimming, diving, and fishing.

For information about activities and events in the area, check out the City of Manhattan Beach website at www.ci.manhattan-beach.ca.us, or the Chamber of Commerce website at www.manhattanbeachchamber.net.

Practicalities

Manhattan Beach is open daily from sunrise until midnight. There are six metered parking lots and three free lots within walking distance of the beach. If you want good parking, though, you'd better get there early, as the conveniently located lots fill up fast. A new underground parking facility, located at 1220 Morningside Drive, has 260 long-term meter spots and 200 short-term meter spots. If you're looking to park your Beamer convertible for beach time and you're short on cash, arrive early at Lot 8 off Valley Drive; the lot has 51 free spaces. Metered street parking is available, but one quarter buys you a measley 15 minutes. Note: during the winter season, the city offers free three-hour parking at some meters as its little holiday gift to the diehard beachlovers.

Restrooms

Clean restrooms and showers are located at the end of the pier, as well as at 8th Street, Manhattan Beach Boulevard, Marine Street, and 40th Street.

Sports

Surfers, boogie boarders, and body surfers all find decent breaks at Manhattan Beach. Everyone's happy to share the waves, but you gotta know your place: surfers go to the south of the pier, boogie boarders to the north, and everyone rides the waves in fear of infringing upon the posted swimming areas and enraging the lifeguards. For the land-loving folk, the bike path on the Strand separates the wheels from the pedestrians. There are plenty of volleyball nets (usually occupied by very tanned and toned athletes). The kiddies can enjoy the swing sets scattered along the beach.

Manhattan Pier

Don't be fooled by its "no-frills" atmosphere—the pier at Manhattan Beach is one of LA County's finest. Home to an Oceanographic Teaching Station, Manhattan Pier is equipped with a marine laboratory and aquarium. The Roundhouse Marine Lab & Aquarium is open to the public from 3 pm until sunset during the week and from 10 am until sunset on the weekends. Entry is free, although a $2 per person ($4 per family) donation is suggested (310-379-8117; www.roundhousemb.com). Metered parking is available for $1 per hour. There's a café at the end of the pier, as well as telescopes that offer terrific views of Palos Verdes and Catalina to the left and the northern beaches to the right. If you're lucky, you may even spot a dolphin or two.

Shopping

The streets within walking distance of Manhattan Beach are treasure troves of eclectic shops and boutiques. The Manhattan Village Mall on Sepulveda Boulevard is also just a short and worthwhile drive away.

Restaurants & Bars
- **Cozymel's** • 2171 Rosecrans Ave • 310-606-5505
- **Good Stuff** • 1300 Highland Ave • 310-545-4775
- **Rock'nFish** • 120 Manhattan Beach Blvd • 310-379-9900
- **Soleil** • 1142 Manhattan Ave • 310-545-8654
- **Versailles** • 1000 N Sepulveda Blvd • 310-937-6829
- **Towne** • 1140 Manhattan Ave •310-545-5045

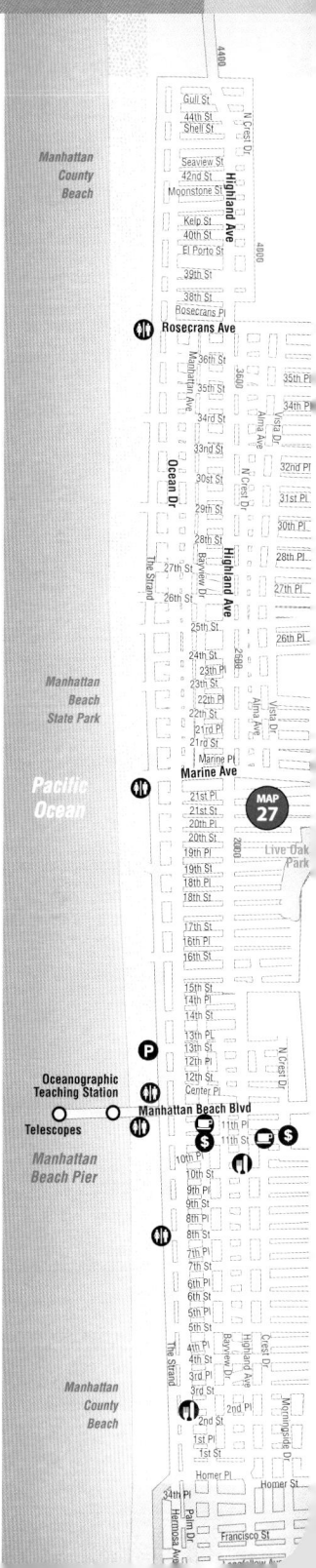

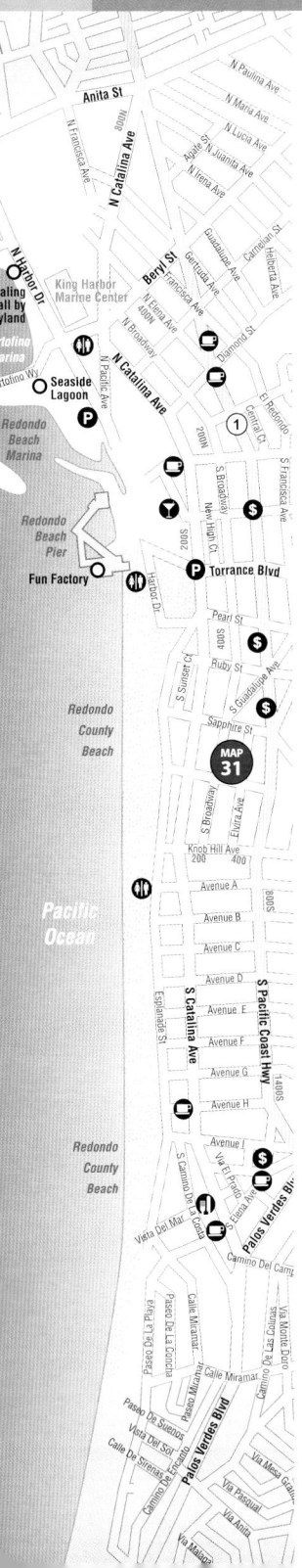

Overview

The Redondo Beach Harbor Enterprise occupies over 150 acres of land and water area, including the beach, parks, pier, boardwalk, and arcade. Redondo Beach may be a historic beach town, but it offers the most modern of amusements, from scuba diving to sport fishing. Because of the vast array of recreational activities it offers, Redondo Beach tends to be the most family-friendly of the South Bay beaches. Famed environmental artist Wyland was so inspired by the natural beauty and sea life here that he created "Whaling Wall 31" in 1991—a spectacular mural that welcomes visitors on North Harbor Drive at Marina Way. From the beach, you get a beautiful view of the Palos Verdes Peninsula, and if you wait around until dusk, you'll be rewarded with a Southern Californian sunset that's so perfect, it might make you sick. For an up-to-date calendar of events, visit www.redondo.org.

Practicalities

Like most of the other South Bay beaches, Redondo is open daily during daylight hours. (You can still walk along the beach after sunset, but swimming is forbidden.) Between the pier parking structure (corner of Pacific Coast Hwy and Torrance Blvd) and the plaza parking structure (N Harbor Dr at Pacific Ave), you should have no trouble finding parking. Lots are open daily 11 am-7 pm, and charge $5 per day on weekdays and $7 per day on weekends during summer months. If you come during winter, you'll find that many things, including parking, are discounted. If you shop along the pier, be sure to validate your parking ticket. Metered street parking is also available. Well-marked restrooms are located throughout the pier (and there's even one on the beach for bathers).

Sports

In addition to the usual beach activities of swimming, skating, and surfing, boating has gained quite a following in Redondo Beach. Whether you're launching your own or riding as a guest on an excursion boat, the Redondo Pier is a good departure point. The double-decked Voyager will take you on a 20-minute cruise of King's Harbor, the Whaling Wall, and the marinas. The Voyager is a good family activity, but the daredevils might prefer the Ocean Racer speedboat for a one-of-a-kind thrill ride. Avid anglers head out into the South Bay's waters for sport fishing opportunities, and cyclists speed to Redondo as a point of origin for LA County's 26-mile bike path that winds up the Pacific coast to Malibu.

Redondo Pier

The pier, boardwalk, and arcade together provide a smorgasbord of entertainment and dining pleasure. The horseshoe-shaped pier holds a couple of upscale restaurants, but for less formal, fresh-from-the-ocean fare, head to any one of the great fish markets in the area (after all, Redondo Beach is known as the "seafood capital" of Southern California, and when in Rome…). Nestled next to the pier, the boardwalk is also stacked with restaurants, bars, and retail stores. Located under the pier, the Fun Factory is open seven days a week and features over 300 arcade and prize-redemption games, as well as a Tilt-A-Whirl and kiddie rides. Hours: Mon-Thurs: 10 am-10 pm; Fri-Sat: 10 am-midnight; Sun: 10 am-10 pm. For more pier info, check out www.redondopier.com, or call 310-318-0631.

Seaside Lagoon

The Seaside Lagoon (200 Portofino Wy) is a heated saltwater lagoon, surrounded by man-made sunbathing beaches, beach volleyball courts, and a snack bar. From 190th Street, go west toward the beach until the street ends, then turn left onto Harbor Drive, and proceed for about one mile. Parking is available at the Redondo Beach Marina and can be validated at the Lagoon. Admission costs $4.50 for adults and $3.25 for children ages 2-17. Hours: 10 am-5:45 pm, daily during the summer months. For more information, call 310-318-0681.

Shopping

When your interest in the shops along the pier and boardwalk begins to flag, check out Riviera Village. In South Redondo, between the Pacific Coast Highway and Catalina Avenue, south of Avenue 1, you'll find a bevy of unique boutiques, galleries, cafés, and restaurants. For a fresh snack, try the Market in front of Veteran's Park (open Thursday mornings from 8 am-1 pm).

Restaurants & Bars

• **Coyote Cantina** • 531 N Pacific Coast Hwy • 310-376-1066
• **El Pollo Inka** • 23705 Hawthorne Blvd • 310-373-0062
• **Gina Lee's Bistro** • 211 Palos Verdes Blvd • 310-375-4462
• **Kincaid's Fish, Chop, & Steakhouse** • 500 The Pier • 310-318-6080
• **Zazou** • 1810 S Catalina Ave • 310-540-4884

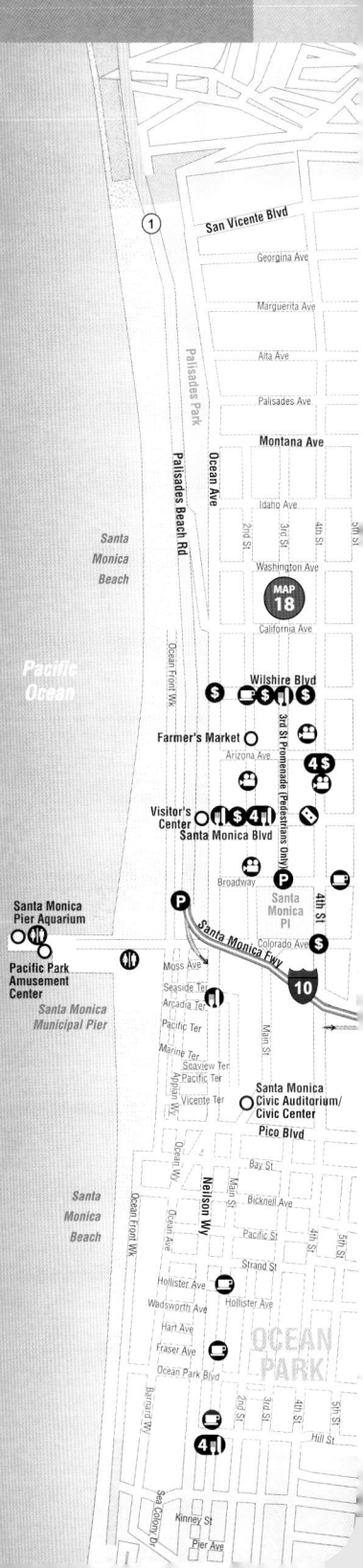

Overview

Santa Monica Beach is the jewel in the crown of Los Angeles beaches. An offshore breakwater assures a gentle surf—perfect for boogie boarders, novice surfers, and even the occasional pro in the everlasting search for that perfect wave. Aside from die-hard beach bums, Santa Monicans tend to stay away from the pier unless they're entertaining visitors. In 1909, the pier opened to an excited public and was a boom town of entertainment until the 1940s, when it experienced a bit of a mid-life crisis. The beloved structure was slated to be torn down after years of deterioration, but local residents rallied and it was rebuilt in 1988. Film crews, photographers, and sun bunnies came flooding back, and today the place is buzzing with activity once again. Check out the Twilight Dance Series concerts on Thursday nights during the summer, featuring popular performers from a wide variety of musical genres. For more information, visit www.santamonicapier.org, www.santamonica.com, or call 310-396-3266.

Amusement Park

Located right on the Santa Monica Pier, Pacific Park Amusement Center is home to the nine-story Ferris Wheel, with a terrific view of the coastline and the city. The famous 1920s vintage carousel was featured in the Paul Newman/Robert Redford movie *The Sting*, and still costs just 25 cents for kids and 50 cents for adults. Other amusements include a rollercoaster, skeeball, air hockey, pinball, and video games. 310-260-8744; www.pacpark.com.

Camera Obscura

1450 Ocean Ave, 310-458-8644. Hours: Mon: 9 am-1 pm; Tues-Fri: 9 am-3 pm; Sat: 12 pm-3 pm; Sun: 11 am-3 pm
Camera Obscura is another popular attraction. Entering the dark room on a sunny day, you can see images from the outside cast onto a table by a long-focus camera lens. The Camera Obscura—essentially a camera the size of a building—is in the Santa Monica Senior Recreation Center. Admission is free, just leave your driver's license at the Rec Center's office in exchange for the key. It may not be as exciting as the nearby roller coaster, or as portable as your sleek, little digital camera, but it's definitely worth popping in.

Santa Monica Pier Aquarium

310-393-6149; www.healthebay.org/smpa. Hours: Sat-Sun: 11 am-5 pm; Tues-Fri: 3 pm-6 pm
At the hands-on marine science aquarium, located underneath the carousel, exhibits focus on local sealife. Sea stars, crabs, snails, and sea urchins populate the touch tanks, but the shark tanks are strictly for eyes only. Suggested donation for admission is $5, but if you have no shame, you can pay as little as $1. Children under 12 enter free with an adult.

Practicalities

The parking lot on the north of the pier at 1550 PCH costs $6 weekdays and $7 weekends during the off-season, and $7 weekdays and $8 weekends during the summer months. There is metered parking along Ocean Avenue north and south of the pier. The visitor information stand is located on the corner of Ocean Avenue and Santa Monica Boulevard. You'll also find some rather grungy restrooms underneath and near the end of the pier.

Shopping

The best shopping in the area is two blocks east of Ocean Avenue along the Third Street Promenade. This three-block pedestrian mall is lined with restaurants, bars, movie theaters, and retail stores including everything from bookstores to swimwear shops. Venture a little south of the pier towards Main Street for more unique boutiques and restaurants. Le Sanctuaire is a fancy culinary boutique frequented by the professionals (2710 Main St, 310-581-8999); Splash Bath & Body sells scented soaps that you can smell a block away (2823 Main St, 310-581-4200); and ZJ Boarding House supplies everything surf-and snowboard- related (2619 Main St, 800-205-7795).

Restaurants & Bars

- **The Lobster** • 1602 Ocean Ave • 310-458-9294
- **Chez Jay** • 1657 Ocean Ave • 310-395-1741
- **Fritto Misto** • 601 Colorado Ave • 310-458-2829
- **Ivy at the Shore** • 1535 Ocean Ave • 310-393-3113
- **Library Alehouse** • 2911 Main St • 310-314-4855
- **Lula Cocina Mexicana** • 2720 Main St • 310-392-5711
- **Ocean Avenue Seafood** • 1401 Ocean Ave • 310-394-5669
- **Ocean Park Omelette Parlor** • 2732 Main St • 310-399-7892
- **Mariasol Cucina Mexicana** • 401 Santa Monica Pier • 310-917-5050
- **Newsroom Café** • 530 Wilshire Blvd • 310-319-9100
- **PF Chang's** • 326 Wilshire Blvd • 310-396-1912
- **Rusty's Surf Ranch** • 256 Santa Monica Pier • 310-393-7437
- **Santa Monica Pier Seafood** • 258 Santa Monica Pier • 310-394-9683
- **Surf View Café** • 330 Santa Monica Pier • 310-394-4231
- **World Café** • 2820 Main St •310-392-1661
- **Ye Olde King's Head** •116 Santa Monica Blvd • 310-451-1402

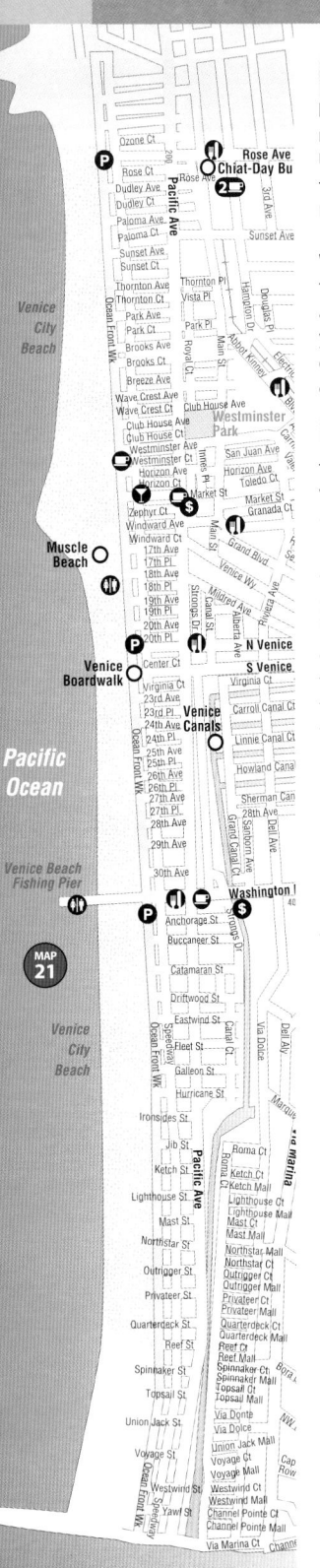

Overview

Funky freaks, hippies, artists, and bohemians have been attracted to this stretch of oceanfront nuttiness since, well, forever. It was at Venice Beach that Jim Morrison and Ray Manzarek—old UCLA buddies—ran into each other in 1965 and decided to form The Doors. Venice Beach is also the famous backdrop of the 1970s roller-disco movie *Xanadu*, and the beach was home to the legendary skateboarding crew, the Z-Boys (as in, the guys in *Lord of Dogtown*).

While some of the shops have acquired better paint jobs since Morrison's day, the attitude of the neighborhood hasn't changed much and remains fiercely eclectic. The boardwalk is always a great place for people-watching, picking up a steal (sometimes literally) from the vendors, and yes, even catching a roller-disco crew every now and then. Just make sure to hit the gym before going, or else the Muscle Beach bodybuilders might leave you questioning your own swimsuit choice. (For slightly less pumped-up sports viewing, check out the paddle tennis courts.)

Practicalities

The beach area is closed nightly from 10 pm until 7 am. The parking lot is located where North Venice intersects with Ocean Front Walk and is open 7 am to 8 pm weekdays ($5) and closes at 9 pm weekends ($6.50). Parking costs $3 before 9 am, but can go up to $10 on holidays. If you're lucky, you might find free parking on the side streets. The area surrounding Venice Beach can get a bit seedy at night, so we don't recommend walking around alone after dark.

Sports

Considering its sunny seaside location, it comes as no surprise that Venice Beach is a hot spot for surfers, skaters, cyclists, and ballers. One of Venice Beach's main sporting attractions is world-famous Muscle Beach, which attracts an international set of weightlifters and spectators. For just five bucks, you can buy a day pass and pump iron with the best of them from 10 am-6 pm (310-399-2775). In addition to the famous free weights section, the Muscle Beach Fitness Center has paddle tennis, handball, and basketball courts. There's also a roller rink, skate park, legal graffiti area, punching bag hookups, rings, parallel bars, and climbing rope—in short, a monkey's paradise. Street vendors along the boardwalk rent out bikes and skates. The Redondo Beach bike path, which runs parallel to Venice Beach, is a perfect place to try out your rented wheels.

Venice Pier

The pier is open daily from 5 am to 10 pm, and the parking lot is located at Washington Boulevard and Ocean Front Walk. A popular spot for anglers, the pier is looking more sturdy than ever after recent renovations. Parking costs $5 weekdays and $6.50 weekends. Restrooms are available on the pier.

Shopping

From cheap t-shirts and sunglasses to fancy surfboards and expensive jewelry, Venice Beach offers a quite a range of shopping opportunities in a unique bohemian environment. In addition to the shops and vendors along the boardwalk, make sure to venture a few blocks inland to Abbot Kinney Boulevard (just north of Venice Boulevard) for a cool stretch of art galleries and hipster shops that would make Melrose jealous.

Restaurants & Cafés

- **Abbots Habit** • 1401 Abbot KinneyBlvd • 310-339-1171
- **Abbot's Pizza** • 1407 Abbot Kinney Blvd • 310-396-7334
- **Canal Club** • 2025 Pacific Ave • 310-823-3878
- **C&O Trattoria** • 31 Washington Blvd • 310-823-9491
- **The Firehouse** • 213 Rose Ave • 310-396-6810
- **Joe's** • 1023 Abbot Kinney Blvd •
- **Rose Café & Market** • 220 Rose Ave • 310-399-5811

Overview

In 1978, idyllic Zuma Beach was the setting for an eponymous made-for-TV-movie starring Suzanne Somers (also featuring Rosanna Arquette and Delta Burke). The premise involved an aging rocker who moved to the beach to try and "get away from it all," but instead became wrapped up in the lives of beach-going teens. Though today old rockers opt to escape behind the high walls of their private beachfront compounds, the clean waters and mile-long stretch of broad, sandy beach still attract Malibu High students and a laid-back, local crowd of surfers, families, young beach bums, and sun-worshipers.

Getting to Zuma means taking a beautifully scenic drive along the Pacific Coast Highway—speaking of rock star compounds, you'll drive by Cher's on the way up. The beach is a 30-minute drive north from Santa Monica on a good day, so avoid the nightmarish weekend traffic on the PCH (especially in the summer) and get an early start.

Practicalities

The parking lot is open from 7 am to 7 pm daily and costs $4.75 to park in the winter, $6 in the summer. The lot has more than 2,000 spaces, but there's also plenty of free parking along the west side of the PCH. Be forewarned that a temperamental marine layer may not burn off until the early afternoon, if at all on some days, and the beach is often windy, so check the weather first and don't forget a cover-up. You may also want to pack some snacks before you head out, though there's a fast food stand near the volleyball courts and a small market across the highway.

Restrooms

Your typical beach-level of cleanliness should be expected in these restrooms, which also have showers.

Sports

The wide, flat stretch of sand between lifeguard towers 6 and 7 features volleyball courts. The waves in this area can be strong enough for body surfing as well as board surfing. In other areas, visitors are allowed to fish and dive, though hopefully not in the same spot. For the kids, there's a swing set too.

Surfing Beaches

Malibu's coast is covered with more than 20 beaches and secret surfing spots. For experienced surfers, body surfers, and body boarders, a couple of good surfing beaches to the north of Zuma include Leo Carrillo and Nicholas Canyon Beach. The latter, known locally as Zero Beach, offers picnic tables, shore fishing, and plenty of parking. To the south, test the waters around Point Dume, or head straight for Surfrider, one of the most famous surfing beaches in the world. Located at the Malibu Pier, this surf spot's no secret, so if everyone's dropping in on your waves during summer months, you may have to hightail it or settle for volleyball.

Restaurants & Cafés

• **The Sunset** • 6800 Westward Beach Rd, 310-589-1007
• **Zooma Sushi** • 29350 W Pacific Coast Hwy, 310-457-4131
• **Hideaway Café** • 6506 Westward Beach Rd, 310-457-2602
• **Spruzzo's** • 29575 Pacific Coast Hwy, 310-457-8282

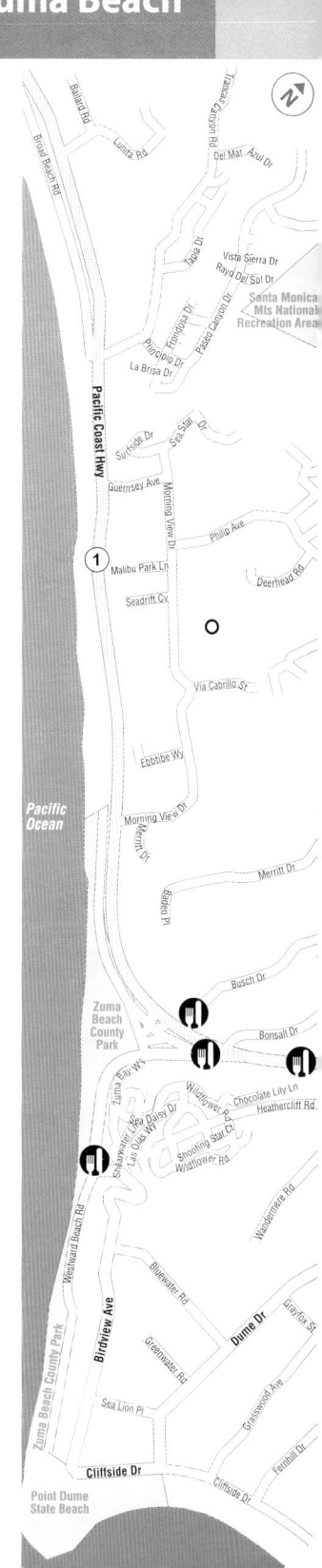

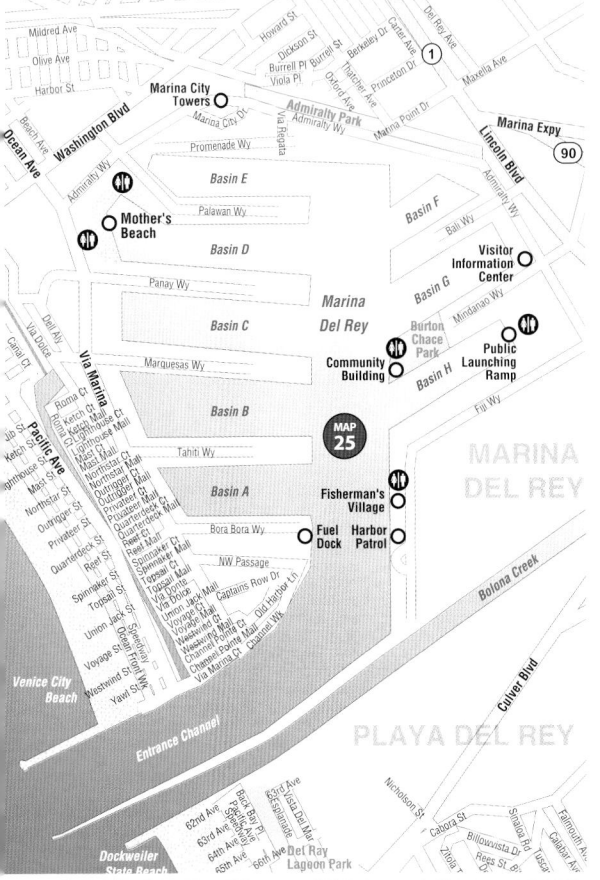

of both jetties are marked with lights that can be distinguished by their color and length between flashes: North Breakwater Light, 1 WHITE flash every six seconds; South Breakwater Light, 2 RED flashes every six seconds; North Jetty Light, 3 WHITE flashes every five seconds; South Jetty Light, 4 RED flashes every four seconds.

Practicalities

Located in the Santa Monica Bay 15 miles southwest of downtown LA, Marina Del Rey can be easily accessed from the 405 and the 90 freeways. Daily parking rates vary in the 15 lots surrounding the marina; however the lowest one can expect to pay is $5 for cars, and $7 for cars with boats in tow. Limited free parking is also available on Dock 52. If you plan on parking overnight, you will need to make arrangements with the harbormaster/sheriff's department beforehand (310-823-7762). There are also 18 metered boat washdown spaces, which cost 50 cents for three minutes (requires quarters). Restrooms are located at Fisherman's Village, near Mother's Beach, and next to the launch ramp.

Launch Ramp & Fuel Dock

Small, hand-carried vessels such as kayaks and tin boats are easily launched at the public beach in Basin D, also known as Mother's Beach because of the absence of surf, making it an ideal swimming beach for children. For larger vessels, there is a public launch ramp at the head of the first finger at Mindanao Way on the east side of the channel. The eight-lane ramp can get very busy, especially on the weekends and during summer months, so be prepared to wait. The fee is $7, and includes one launch, recovery, and 24-hour parking for your car. The fuel dock is located on the west side of the channel just inside the bend.

Guest Slips

The Los Angeles County Department of Beaches and Harbors offers boat slips to guests near Burton Chace Park. There is a free 4-hour tie-up dock between the H and G basins on the east side of the main channel, and overnight docking (for up to 7 days within a 30 day period) can be arranged at the Community Building in the park at a cost of 50 cents per foot per night. To obtain an overnight slip, you will need to produce your registration papers and identification. Overnight facilities include electricity, water, showers, and restrooms. If you are a yacht club member, try contacting the yacht clubs in the area to see if they offer reciprocal guest slips.

Harbor Patrol & Anchorage

The Harbor Patrol is run by the Los Angeles County Sheriff's Department and located on the east side of the main channel. They are on call 24 hours a day and can be reached on Channel 16, with 12 as the working channel (310-823-7762). During storms or other emergencies, anchoring is permitted in the north end of the entrance channel.

No Boat?

If you don't have your own water craft, several commercial boating companies leave from Dock 52 and provide all of the gear you will need for a great day of fishing, including rods, reels, and bait. If pier fishing is more your style, head down Fiji Way to Fisherman's Village and you can throw a line in from the docks.

Overview

Think of Marina Del Rey as Venice Beach's more upstanding sibling. Just east of the weirdest beach in the world, this posh neighborhood and man-made marina (one of the world's largest) can shelter more than 6,000 vessels, and stands as a gateway to the Pacific for recreational and commercial vehicles. Yet, it feels amazingly quaint. In addition to 6,100 boat slips, amenities for boaters include beach-launching for small boats, a launch ramp for trailered boats, a sailing basin for boats and windsurfers, dry dock storage, a Sea Scout base, repair yards, fuel dock, pump-out stations, boat brokerages, and charter businesses. Visit http://beaches.co.la.ca.us or www.visitthemarina.com for more information on what the marina has to offer.

Within the marina, Burton Chace Park is a great spot to pull the car over for a picnic (especially when the weather heats up inland and you want to avoid the beach crowds). Those with deeper pockets can grab dinner at Jer-ne (4375 Admiralty Wy, 310-823-1700) inside The Ritz-Carlton, with an amazing view of the marina. A trip to the Fisherman's Village always makes for a pleasant afternoon. You'll find kayaks, jet skis, and other small vehicles for rent, ice cream, free live music, and if you're there in early December, the annual Holiday Boat Parade.

Harbor Info

The entrance to the marina is situated between two jetties (north and south) that sit inside the breakwater that runs parallel to the shore. The north and south ends of the breakwater and the ends

Overview

The south-facing bay and nearby offshore breakwaters make Long Beach Marina one of the calmest and most popular boat mooring spots in Southern California. The protected enclave and the idyllic boating conditions make sailing the number one recreational activity in Long Beach, home of the Congressional Cup, Transpac, and the Olympic trial races. The 3,800-slip marina is run by the City of Long Beach and includes Alamitos Bay Marina (562-570-3215), Long Beach Shoreline Marina (562-570-4950), and Rainbow Harbor/Rainbow Marina (562-570-8636).

Practicalities

Daily parking is available near the marina. Boaters who wish to park in the launch parking lot for more than 24 hours need to visit the Alamitos Bay office and pay for a parking pass in advance.

Launch Ramps & Fuel Docks

Five separate launch ramps serve the Long Beach Marina population. The **Granada Launch Ramp** (Granada Ave and Ocean Blvd) and the **Claremont Launch Ramp** (Claremont and Ocean Blvds) are sand launches exclusively for small sailing vessels. Water skiers and larger vessels looking to get in the water need look no further than **Marine Stadium** (Appian Wy between 2nd and Colorado Aves). Boats in the stadium must be under 20 feet long, have a reverse gear, and travel counter-clockwise within the stadium. **Davies Ramp**, across from Marine Stadium, is the only launch open 24 hours a day. And last but not least, the **South Shore Launch Ramp** is a small boat launch ramp near the Queen Mary on Queensway Drive. All launch ramps cost $8 and are open year-round, usually from 8 am until dusk. For more information, call 562-570-8636.

Long Beach has two fuel docks—one in Downtown Shoreline Marina (562-436-4430) and one in Alamitos Bay (562-594-0888). The Alamitos fuel dock stocks propane, snacks, beer, ice, and frozen bait, along with gas and diesel fuels. The smaller Downtown Marine fuel dock features gas, CNG, and limited sundries. Both docks accept credit cards or cash. Fuel dock hours (May 31-Labor Day): Mon-Fri: 8 am-5 pm; Sat-Sun: 7 am-6 pm.

Guest Slips

Guest moorings can be rented year-round for 60¢ per foot per night. While it's always best to call ahead, it's only on holiday weekends that reservations are required (with 3,000 slips for rent, you can usually find a spot at short notice on weeknights).

Patrols

The Harbor Patrol looks after the water, while the Marine Patrol guards the land. All Lifeguard/Harbor Patrol boats are run by trained, professional lifeguards and are also equipped for emergencies such as fire, capsized boats, or pump-outs. If you need your boat towed, the Harbor Patrol/Rescue Boats will always oblige, but if it's not an emergency, they'll charge you for the towing.

No Boat?

If you're on a budget but you still want a piece of the action, check out the Belmont Pier at Ocean Boulevard and 39th Place, which offers free public fishing. No license is required as long as you stay on the pier (562-434-6781). If you decide to fish from the beach or the jetties, you'll need a salt-water fishing license. If you get tired of the salt and sand, you might opt for the Belmont Plaza Olympic Pool (4000 Olympic Plaza Dr, 562-438-0389), or grab a pint and a bite at the Belmont Brewing Company (25 39th Pl 562-433-3891) on the pier.

Launch Ramp & Fuel Dock

Run by the LA County Department of Recreation and Parks, the boat ramp is open 24 hours a day and has nearby space for trailer parking and boat washing, as well as restroom facilities. You will find fuel at the Cabrillo Marine Fuel Dock, which is located at Berth 31, 210 Whalers Walk.

Harbor Info

The breakwater entrance to the western end of San Pedro Bay is marked by the Los Angeles Harbor Lighthouse (33°42.5'N-118°15.0' W), also known as Angel's Gate. This marina has a lot of traffic, including huge ships and other commercial vehicles, so boat owners should study their charts in order to navigate the waters appropriately.

Guest Slips

Guest end-ties are available for overnight docking for boats up to 55 feet long for up to three days. Four mooring buoys are offered in the inner harbor for vessels up to 40 feet long, and in the outer harbor 14 mooring buoys are available for boats up to 50 feet long. However, overnight mooring is not permitted.

Harbor Patrol

The Port Warden and staff of the Los Angeles Harbor Department monitor the harbor. They are located at 425 S Palos Verdes Street, San Pedro.

No Boat?

Fishing is permitted from the Cabrillo Pier. During grunion season, the silvery fish emerge twice a month, like clockwork, to lay their eggs under a full or new moon. During part of the season, it is legal to catch these fish—but only by hand! If you want to participate you will need to take a flashlight. If you don't fancy getting wet, it's almost as much fun to watch. The Cabrillo Marine Aquarium (3720 Stephen White Dr), a delightful way to spend a few hours with the kidlets, is nearby and free (with a suggested donation of $5 for adults and $1 for children and seniors). Visit www.cabrilloaq.org or call 310-548-7562 for more information. The beach and bathhouse are also enjoyable playgrounds.

Overview

The wind known as "Hurricane Gulch" coming from Point Fermin into an area just outside the Cabrillo Marina provides first-rate sailing and windsurfing weather year-round. The 885 slips, friendly staff, and abundant amenities make this a pleasant marina to dock for a few days. It's also the closest marina to Catalina (19.4 miles). Check out the marina's website at www.cymcabrillo.com or call the dockmaster at 310-732-2252.

Practicalities

Cabrillo Marina is easy to reach—just a shout from LA Airport. From the 405 or the I-5, take the 110 S and exit at Harbor Boulevard. There is plenty of free parking at the Cabrillo Marina and facilities include restrooms, laundry, water, electricity, showers, and lockers.

Overview

Redondo Beach is the home of four marinas—King Harbor, Port Royal, Portofino, and Redondo Beach—and 1,400 boat slips. The marinas host seasonal activities, such as whale-watching in January, the annual Super Bowl Sunday 10K Run in February (with a beer garden at the finish line), and the Bayou Bash and Crawfish Boil, complete with music straight from New Orleans, in May. Between sailing, kayaking, and enjoying a seafood dinner by the water, let's just say there are worse things in life than having to spend a week at Redondo Beach.

Practicalities

The marina provides several double-spaced parking spots for vehicles with boat trailers. If you're hoping for a space during the summer months, you better head out early—the place gets mobbed. Expect to pay between $3 and $7 per day for parking, depending on the season and location.

Boat Hoist & Fuel Docks

Unlike most other marinas, the Redondo Beach Marina has a boat hoist instead of a launch ramp. Skilled hoist operators launch boats mechanically via slings using two five-ton hoists, which can launch boats up to 10,000 pounds in weight and 30 feet in length. Round-trip hoist fees are $8 for a hand-launch size boat, $18 for personal watercraft, $30 for boats 18-24 feet long, and $40 for boats over 25 feet long. Reservations are not needed. Locals with proof of boat registration can obtain boat hoist coupons from City Hall for $7.50. If you're launching a boat by hand, you'll want to go behind Seaside Lagoon, via the Redondo Beach Marina parking lot, or by Portofino Way.

Fuel docks are located at the commercial basin and across from the Harbor Patrol office.

Boat Hoist Regular Hours: Mon-Fri: 7 am-5 pm; Sat-Sun: 6 am-6 pm. Extended summer hours—6 am-6 pm on weekdays and 6 am-7 pm on weekends—begin Memorial Day weekend. For more information, visit www.rbmarina.com.

…Two If By Sea

If you're coming in from the water, use the lighted buoy to the SSW of the exterior jetty to guide you into the marina. The entrance is at the south end of the harbor, between two lighted jetties.

Guest Slips

King Harbor Marina (208 Yacht Club Wy, 310-376-6926) and the Redondo Beach Yacht Club both offer guest boat slips and docking accommodations. Boat slips come fully equipped with storage lockers, cable TV and phone hook-ups, laundry facilities, and plenty of parking.

Harbor Patrol

The Harbor Patrol office is located at the west end of Marina Way, adjacent to Moonstone Park. Call them if you need them at 310-318-0632.

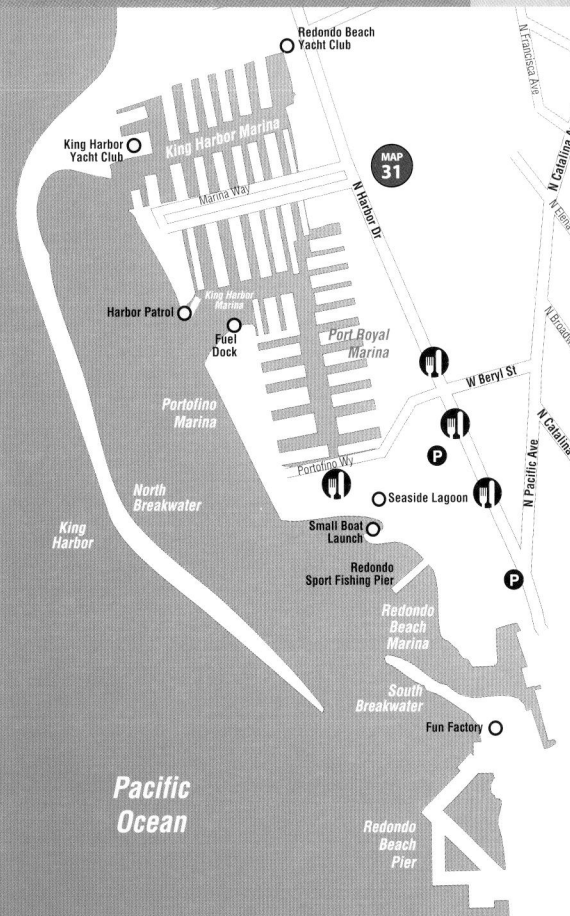

No Boat?

No worries! You can hire fishing rods, tackle, bait, and a salt water fishing license right on the Redondo Sport Fishing Pier. If you prefer being out on the water, fishing trips range from $30 ($25 kids) for a half-day to $650 for a ten-person charter boat for the day. For something a little racier, try sailing classes (310-318-2772) or a high-speed tour of the coast on the Ocean Racer (310-374-3481). For more information about Redondo Beach boating activities, see page [270}.

Restrooms

Restrooms are located in and around the harbor, on the Pier, and along the beach areas.

Restaurants

• **Captain Kidd's Fish Market** • 209 N Harbor Dr • 310-372-7703
• **The Charthouse** • 231 Yacht Club Wy • 310-372-3464
• **Joe's Crab Shack** • 230 Portofino Wy • 310-406-1999
• **The Cheesecake Factory** • 605 N Harbor Dr • 310-376-0466
• **Delzano's By the Sea** • 179 N Harbor Dr • 310-374-7525

Overview

A week of bumper-to-bumper commuting will, no doubt, leave you desperate to escape the concrete jungle of LA. If you can't swing a Polynesian getaway, try a hike in an outdoor recreation area closer to home. Whether it's a jog with your pup in Runyon Canyon or an epic mountain trek in the Angeles National Forest, you should be able to find a hike that fits your ability and fitness level—just try to ignore the traffic on the drive to the trailhead.

An excellent source of information about various trails is *Afoot and Afield in Los Angeles County*, by Jerry Schad (Wilderness Press). If you want to test out new terrain and make new friends, the Sierra Club organizes hikes throughout the city that range in difficulty and cater to a variety of special interests (www.angeles.sierraclub.org). Below, you'll find a handful of hikes that come with our highest endorsement.

West Hollywood

Runyon Canyon Park

This is the perfect early morning or after-work hike, as it's under two miles and can be completed in an less than an hour. If the main path isn't enough of a workout for you, veer left just after the gates near the Vista entrance for a more challenging uphill climb. Runyon Canyon also gets extra points in our book for its off-leash policy for canine hikers. Enter from either Fuller Street or Vista Street, just north of Franklin Avenue. Parking is available on neighboring streets, but check the signs for restrictions. www.runyon-canyon.com, 323-666-5046.

Griffith Park

Fern Dell/Mt Hollywood

The relatively flat terrain of Fern Dell makes it a popular choice for family hikes, and the rich plant life means that the area is almost always bathed in shade. Enter Griffith Park from Los Feliz Boulevard by turning left at Fern Dell Drive. Cross the observatory road and you'll find a path to the top of Mount Hollywood, which offers a lovely view of the Hollywood sign and the downtown smog. Ah, nature. At a brisk pace, the hike should take around two hours.

Mount Lee (aka, the Hollywood Sign)

Drive up Beachwood Canyon to Hollyridge Drive. Hollyridge Trail will take you up to the summit of Mount Lee, where you can look down from behind (and just above) the letters of the 450-foot long Hollywood sign. The round trip is approximately three miles. Parking is free.

Dante's View

Begin this dog-friendly hike in the parking lot for the Griffith Park Observatory, and you will eventually reach Dante's View, a garden planted by Dante Orgolini in 1964 after a failed marriage. Mr. Orgolini has since passed away, and his marital troubles are forgotten, but his garden still blooms and is tended by volunteers. The hike is just 2.25 miles long.

Baldwin Hills

Kenneth Hahn State Recreation Area

Located at 4100 South La Cienega Boulevard, Kenneth Hahn State Recreation Area features seven miles of trails for hiking, from the Bowl Loop (just 0.8 miles) to the 2.6-mile Ridge Trail.

Pacific Palisades

Will Rogers State Park

The most popular walk in this park, located just north of Sunset Boulevard, is to the idyllic Inspiration Point. The hike is easy—almost too easy—and can be completed in one hour round-trip. But the view to Catalina on a clear day is lovely and makes for a nice change of pace. The trails at Will Rogers are open to hikers and horseback riders.

Temescal Canyon

Head north at the intersection of Sunset Boulevard and Temescal Canyon Road, and park at Gateway Park. Once inside, you have two options—Canyon trail or Ridge trail. Be sure to follow the trail markers for the appropriately named Skull Rock, which is this hike's must-see. At approximately four miles round-trip, this hike is considered moderately difficult and takes about 2.5 hours.

Brentwood

Mandeville Canyon

The hike, which can be completed in less than two hours, begins with challenging, hilly terrain, but levels off after a bit. From Sunset Boulevard, go north on Mandeville Canyon until you reach Garden Land Road and find street parking. A fire road takes you to the Nike Missile Site, which has been turned into a park with restrooms and drink machines.

Pasadena/San Gabriel Valley

Chantry Flat/Sturtevant Falls

The waterfalls are breathtaking, close to LA, and just a three-mile hike up a mountain—i.e. totally within reach. The hike to the falls passes private cabins nestled in the woods that look like something out of a fairy tale. Take the 210 to Santa Anita Avenue and head north. Follow the road up the mountain and use the parking lot at Chantry Flat. The whole trip can be completed in 90 minutes.

Eaton Canyon Falls

The Eaton Canyon Falls hike also leads to a waterfall, and it's especially friendly to dogs (on leashes) and kids, because of its relatively flat terrain. The trail crosses over a creek several times during the 3.3-mile round trip, so you may get wet. Dress accordingly. Exit the 210 at Altadena and travel north to the Eaton Canyon Natural Area (just past New York Drive).

Switzer Falls

This is not a difficult hike (four miles round-trip, depending on how far afield you venture), but hopping over rock bridges and fallen logs while wading in the clear, cool waters takes some goat-like maneuvering. At the intersection with Bear Canyon, you can travel up the canyon for awesome views before doubling back. The sound of rushing waterfalls will stay with you long after you've returned to civilization. From the 210 Freeway in La Canada, follow 2 N (Angeles Crest Hwy) for ten miles into the Angeles National Forest. Stop at the Visitor Center at the intersection of Angeles Crest and Angeles Forest Highways to pick up your $5 day pass and map. Then continue on Angeles Crest for about a quarter mile to the Switzer Picnic Area, driving down to the parking lot near the stream. Stop for a sandwich or throw a burger on one of the grills before your trek towards Switzer Falls.

Studio City

Wilacre Park

This short and intense hike (2.7 hilly miles) can be finished in about an hour, and is another great walk to save for the end of the day (especially in the hot summer months) or to do with a canine friend (only if leashed, unfortunately). Park in the gravel lot at the corner of Laurel Canyon Boulevard and Fryman, and travel up the Dearing Mountain Trail. You'll emerge from the canyon in the midst of a residential neighborhood, on Iredell Lane. Follow this street back out to Fryman Road, and turn left to return to the parking lot.

Malibu

Malibu Creek State Park

This 10,000-acre park offers horseback riding, camping, fishing, swimming, and, of course, hiking. The trail will take you on a moderately challenging 3.5-mile hike along gurgling creeks, past swimming holes, and to the spot where M*A*S*H* was filmed. When you reach the fork in the road, hang a left towards the Visitor Center and follow signs to Rock Pool, a swimming hole popular with families and the site of the Planet of the Apes climbing rock. Retrace your steps back to the fork and turn left (away from the Visitor Center) to continue on the wild flower-studded Crags Road trail. When you cross the creek, turn left to explore the marshy Century Lake, or turn right to hike to the M*A*S*H* site—both make good turn-around points and, on the downhill trek back to the parking lot, you can enjoy the craggy mountain vistas, fragrant lavender fields, and chirping wildlife. Summers are hot and dusty, so visit the park after rainfall or in springtime to experience the scenery at its best. From the 101 Freeway, exit at Las Virgenes Road and follow the signs to Malibu Canyon. The entrance to the park is clearly marked just after Mulholland Highway. One bummer when you arrive—there's an $8 day-use fee. Our recommendation: park in the second lot and start at the Crags Road trail that runs past bathrooms to avoid having to use the port-o-lets.

Point Dume State Beach

This is not a long or strenuous hike (four miles round-trip), but the spectacular cliff-side scenery and the semi-isolated beach at the end of the trail makes for a magical day in the great outdoors. From the 101 Freeway, exit at Kanan Road, follow it south for 12 miles, and then make a right on PCH. Turn left on Westward Beach Road and try to find parking before you hit the pay lot. If you can't score a free spot, at least you can drive to the trailhead, located at the far end of the parking lot. The viewing platform is a great place to take a break and to enjoy a marvelous view of the Santa Monica Bay, north Malibu coast, Santa Monica Mountains and, if you're lucky, Catalina Island. Dolphins almost always bob in the waves below, and watch for California gray whales between December and March. On the other side of the bluff, descend a stairway to Paradise Cove, a haven for tide-pool gazers and topless sunbathers. Follow the coast for about a mile to the pier, where you can enjoy a mid-hike meal at the Paradise Cove Beach Café. Check the tide tables before setting out, or this hike may become a swim.

City of LA Tennis Courts

The city of Los Angeles runs two types of public tennis courts: Open Play courts, which are free and available on a first-come, first-served basis, and Reservation/Pay Tennis, where hourly fees apply per court and reservations are required. Courts cost $5 per hour weekdays from 7 am until 4 pm, and $8 per hour all other times. Call 213-625-1010 for Pay Tennis schedules, registration and reservations, or download the tennis card application from www.laparks.org/dos/tennis/permits.htm. Lit courts are open from 7 am to 10 pm. Unlit courts are open from dawn to dusk. Call the City of LA Parks on 323-586-6543 or the County of LA Parks on 213-738-2965.

Reservation/Pay	Address	# of courts	Phone	Map
Griffith-Vermont Canyon*	2715 Vermont Canyon	12	323-664-3521	4
Riverside	3401 Riverside Dr	12	323-661-5318	5
Pacific Palisades	851 Alma Real Dr	8	310-573-1331	15
Westwood	1350 Sepulveda Blvd	8	310-575-8299	19
Cheviot Hills	2551 Motor Ave	14	310-836-8879	23
Westchester	7000 W Manchester Ave	8	310-649-4886	26
Balboa	17015 Burbank Blvd	16	818-995-6570	46
Van Nuys/Sherman Oaks	14201 Huston St	8	818-756-8400	55

Open Play/Free	Address		Phone	Map
Peck Park Community Center	560 N Western Ave		310-548-7580	4
Echo Park Rec	1632 Bellevue Ave		213-250-3578	5
Elysian Park Therapeutic	929 Academy Rd		323-226-1402	5
Queen Anne Rec Center	1240 West Blvd		323-934-0130	7
Lafayette Community Center	625 S Lafayette Pk Pl		213-387-9426	8
Shatto Rec Center	3191 W 4th St		213-386-8877	8
Daniels Field Sports Center	845 W 12th St		310-548-7728	9
Arthur Ashe Center	5001 Rodeo Rd		323-290-3141	10
Jim Gilliam Rec Center	4000 S La Brea Ave		323-291-5928	10
Loren Miller Rec Center	2717 Halldale Ave		323-734-1302	11
Van Ness Rec Center	5720 2nd Ave		323-296-1559	11
Ross Snyder Rec Center	1501 E 41st St		213-847-3255	12
South Park	345 E 51st St		213-847-6746	12
Algin Sutton Rec Center	8800 S Hoover St		323-753-5808	14
Harvard Rec Center	1535 W 62nd St		323-778-2579	14
St Andrews Rec Center	8701 St Andrews Pl		213-485-1751	14
Rustic Canyon Rec Center	601 Latimer Rd		310-454-5734	15
Barrington Rec Center	333 S Barrington Ave		310-476-4866	16
Stoner Rec Center	1835 Stoner Ave		310-479-7200	19
Oakwood Rec Center	767 California St		310-452-7479	21
Penmar Rec Center	1341 Lake St		310-396-8735	21
Glen Alla Park	4601 Alla Rd		N/A	22
Mar Vista Rec Center	11430 Woodbine Ave		310-398-5982	22
Eagle Rock Rec Center*	1100 Eagle Vista Dr		323-257-6948	33
Yosemite Rec Center	1840 Yosemite Dr		213-257-1644	33
Glassell Park Rec Center	3650 Verdugo Rd		323-257-1863	36
Sycamore Grove Park	4702 N Figueroa St		N/A	36
Montecito Heights Rec Center	4545 Homer St		213-485-5148	37
Arroyo Seco Park	5566 Via Marisol St		N/A	38
El Sereno Rec Center	4721 Klamath Pl		323-225-3517	38
Aliso Pico Rec Center	370 S Clarence St		323-264-5261	40
Hazard Rec Center	2230 Norfolk St		213-485-6839	40
Hollenbeck Rec Center	415 S Saint Louis St		323-261-0113	40
Lincoln Park Rec Center	3501 Valley Blvd		213-237-1726	40
Reseda Rec Center	18411 Victory Blvd		818-881-3882	46
Van Nuys Rec Center	14301 Vanowen St		818-756-8131	47
Valley Plaza Rec Center	12240 Archwood St		818-765-5885	48
Victory-Vineland Rec Center	11112 Victory Blvd		818-985-9516	48
Studio City Rec Center	12621 Rye St		818-769-4415	51
Encino Park	16953 Ventura Blvd		818-995-1690	53
North Hollywood Rec Center	5301 Tujunga Ave		818-763-7651	56

* unlit

LA County Tennis Courts	Address		Phone	Map
Ladera Park	6027 Ladera Park Ave		310-217-8361	13
Jesse Owens Park	9651 S Western Ave		310-217-8361	14
Belvedere Park	4914 E Cesar E Chavez Ave		323-260-2342	41
City Terrace Park	1126 N Hazard Ave		323-260-2371	41
Ruben F Salazar Park	3864 Whittier Blvd		323-260-2330	41

Los Angeles is famously dotted with blue swimming pools throughout the county. Even for the unfortunate few without their own private pools, local municipal pools are abundant. The City of Los Angeles operates 35 seasonal (outdoor) pools and 19 year-round (indoor) pools. Individual cities and towns within Los Angeles County also run their own public pools, open to both residents and non-residents (with a discounted fee for residents).

The Aquatics Division of the City's Department of Recreation & Parks maintains all of the pool facilities, with the seasonal pools open during the summer from the third Saturday in June though Labor Day, and the year-round swimming pools open all year for aquatic bliss. Adults (ages 18 through 64) are required to pay a $1.50 admission charge; however, children and seniors can swim for free.

The department also offers Learn to Swim classes for various ages and swimming abilities. The beginning toddler class for children aged 4 to 7 requires that parents participate with their child in the water. Students then progress to Level 1, which involves face-submerging and blowing bubbles, all the way up to Level 7, in which they will learn to complete 500 yards of continuous swimming using various strokes, conduct an in-water rescue, and perform a springboard dive in tuck and pike positions. Most pools also offer team sports, such as inner tube water polo, synchronized swimming, and lifeguard training. Visit your local pool for more information regarding classes and teams.

For public safety, there is an extensive published list of pool rules. Our favorite is "No snapping towels." For a complete list of pool rules and everything Aquatics Division-related, visit www.laparks.com/dos/aquatic/aquatic.htm. Check with the local Recreation & Parks department about municipalities in individual cities and towns.

Seasonal Public Pools

	Address	Phone	Map
Pan Pacific Pool	141 S Gardner St	323-975-4524	2
West Hollywood Pool	647 N San Vicente Blvd, West Hollywood	323-848-6538	2
Hollywood Pool	1122 Cole Ave	323-957-4501	3
Echo Shallow Pool	1632 Bellevue Ave	213-580-3733	5
Griffith Park Pool	3401 Riverside Dr	323-644-6878	5
Van Ness Pool	5720 2nd Ave	323-290-3134	11
Central Pool	1357 E 22nd St	213-765-0565	12
Ross Snyder Pool	1501 E 41st St	213-847-3430	12
South Park Pool	345 E 51st St	323-846-5366	12
Algin Sutton Pool	8800 S Hoover St	323-789-2826	14
Rustic Canyon Pool	601 Latimer Rd, Pacific Palisades	310-230-0137	15
Stoner Park Pool	1835 Stoner Ave	310-575-8286	19
Mar Vista Pool	11655 Palms Blvd	310-390-2016	22
Cheviot Hills Pool	2693 Motor Ave	310-202-2844	23
Westchester Pool	9100 Lincoln Blvd	310-342-3164	25
Highland Park Pool	6150 Piedmont Ave	323-226-1669	33
Yosemite Pool	1840 Yosemite Dr	323-226-1668	33
Robinson Park	1081 N Fair Oaks Ave, Pasadena	626-585-2025	34
Downey Pool	1775 N Spring St	323-226-1671	37
Costello Pool	3121 E Olympic Blvd	323-526-3073	40
Lincoln Park Pool	3501 Valley Blvd	213-847-3382	40
Pecan Pool	120 S Gless St	323-526-3042	40
Lanark Pool	21817 Strathern St, Canoga Park	818-756-9364	42
Reseda Pool	18411 Victory Blvd, Reseda	818-756-9361	46
Valley Plaza Swimming Pool	6715 Laurelgrove Ave, North Hollywood	818-756-9362	48
North Hollywood Pool	5301 Tujunga Ave, North Hollywood	818-755-7654	56

Year-Round Public Pools

	Address	Phone	Map
Echo Lake Pool	751 Echo Park Ave	213-847-8524	5
EG Roberts Indoor Pool	4526 W Pico Blvd	323-936-8483	7
Celes King III Indoor Pool	5001 Rodeo Dr	213-847-3406	10
John C Argue Swim Stadium	3980 S Menlo Ave	213-763-0129	11
Santa Monica Swim Center	2225 16th St, Santa Monica	310-458-8700	18
Venice High School Indoor Pool	2490 Walgrove Ave	310-575-8260	22
Westwood Indoor Pool	1350 Sepulveda Blvd	310-478-7019	32
Glassell Park Pool	3704 Verdugo Rd	323-226-1670	36
Richard Alatorre Indoor Pool	4721 Klamath St	323-276-3042	38
Roosevelt Pool	456 S Matthews St	213-485-7391	40
Van Nuys Sherman Oaks Pool	14201 Huston St, Sherman Oaks	818-783-6721	55

Bowling Alleys

	Address	Phone	Map
Lucky Strike Lanes	6801 Hollywood Blvd, Hollywood	323-467-7776	3
AMF Midtown Lanes	4645 Venice Blvd, Los Angeles	323-933-7171	7
AMF World on Wheels	4645 ½ Venice Blvd, Los Angeles	323-933-5170	7
AMF Bay Shore Lanes	234 Pico Blvd, Santa Monica	310-399-7731	18
AMF Mar Vista Lanes	12125 Venice Blvd, Los Angeles	310-391-5288	22
AMF El Dorado Lanes	8731 Lincoln Blvd, Los Angeles	310-670-0688	25
Gable House Bowl	22501 Hawthorne Blvd, Torrance	310-378-2265	31
AMF Bowl-O-Drome	21915 S Western Ave, Torrance	310-328-3700	32
Palos Verdes Bowl	24600 Crenshaw Blvd, Torrance	310-326-5128	32
Alhambra Bowling Center	1400 E Valley Blvd, Alhambra	626-289-5168	39
Brunswick Matador Bowl	9118 Balboa Blvd, Northridge	818-892-8677	44
AMF Woodlake Lanes	23130 Ventura Blvd, Woodland Hills	818-225-7181	45
Pickwick Bowl	1001 Riverside Dr, Burbank	818-845-5300	50
Jewel City Bowl	135 S Glendale Ave, Glendale	818-243-1188	51
Canoga Park Bowl	20122 Van Owen St, Winnetka	818-340-5190	52
Corbin Bowl	19616 Ventura Blvd, Tarzana	818-996-2695	52
Pinz Bowling Center	12655 Ventura Blvd, Studio City	818-769-7600	56
Jillian's Hi-Life Lanes	1000 Universal Studios Blvd, Universal City	818-985-8234	57

Public Golf Courses

	Address	Phone	Fee	Map
Alhambra Golf Course	630 S Almansor St, Alhambra	626-570-5059	$19.50-$31.50	39
Alondra Park Golf Course	16400 S Prairie Ave, Lawndale	310-217-9919	$21.50-28	30
Arroyo Seco Golf Course	1055 Lohman Ln, S Pasadena	323-255-1506	$12-$14	34
Balboa/Encino Golf Course	16821 Burbank Blvd, Encino	818-995-1170	$7-28.50	42
Chester Washington Golf Course	1930 W 120th St, Los Angeles	323-756-6975	$18-28	25
De Bell Municipal Golf Course	1500 E Walnut Ave, Burbank	818-845-0022	$22-27	50
Los Feliz Golf Course	3207 Los Feliz Blvd, Los Angeles	323-663-7758	$4-5	5
Penmar Golf Course	1233 Rose Ave, Venice	310-396-6228	$11.50-15	21
Rancho Park Golf Course	10460 W Pico Blvd, Los Angeles	310-838-7373	$22-28.50	23
Roosevelt Golf Course	2650 N Vermont Ave, Los Angeles	323-665-2011	$11.50-15	4
Van Nuys Golf Course	6550 Odessa Ave, Van Nuys	818-785-3685	$8-13	47
Westchester Golf Course	6900 Manchester Blvd, Westchester	310-670-5110	$16-21	26
Woodley Golf Course	6331 Woodley Ave, Van Nuys	818-780-6886	$22-28.50	47

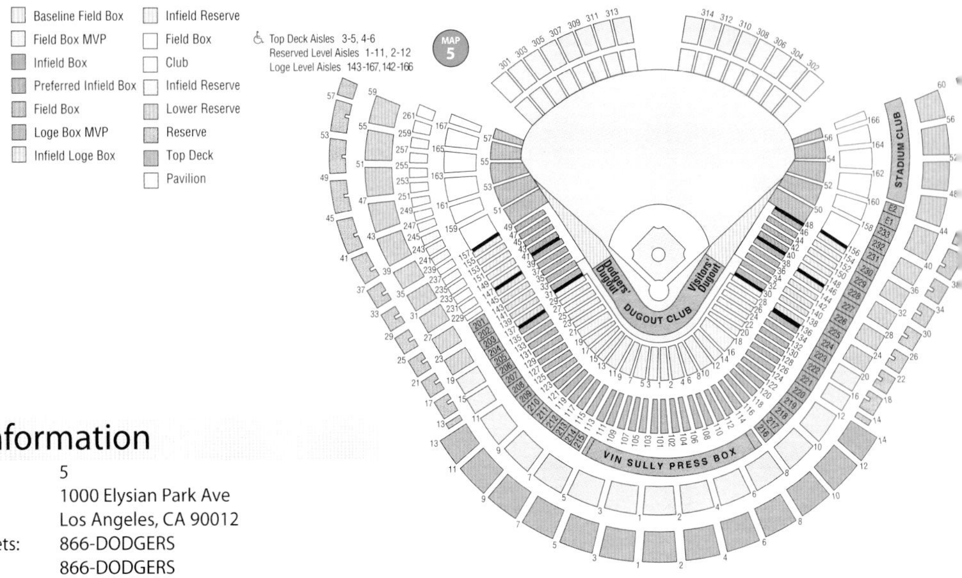

Baseline Field Box
Field Box MVP
Infield Box
Preferred Infield Box
Field Box
Loge Box MVP
Infield Loge Box

Infield Reserve
Field Box
Club
Infield Reserve
Lower Reserve
Reserve
Top Deck
Pavilion

♿ Top Deck Aisles 3-5, 4-6
Reserved Level Aisles 1-11, 2-12
Loge Level Aisles 143-167, 142-166

MAP 5

General Information

NFT Map: 5
Address: 1000 Elysian Park Ave
                            Los Angeles, CA 90012
Information & Tickets: 866-DODGERS
Lost & Found: 866-DODGERS
Blue Crew Fan Club: 323-224-1315
Website: www.dodgers.com

Overview

The Dodgers haven't brought a World Series win to Los Angeles in some 20 years, but they'll always have one thing on their side: great California weather. There's nothing like catching a warm summer night or weekend afternoon game at the hilltop stadium. The view of nearby Chavez Ravine's rolling hills, the taste of an overpriced Dodger Dog (or why not a margarita and a Krispy Kreme doughnut?), and seeing the famous "Think Blue" sign in the distance can excite even the most cynical of Angelenos—even if the team doesn't always come through.

The Dodgers have attracted a bit of heat recently, though, thanks mainly to superstar closing pitcher Eric Gagne who swaggers onto the field to the tune of Guns N' Roses' "Welcome to the Jungle" while "Game Over" graphics blare across the boards. You can't help but appreciate the Hollywood showmanship. On game days, pop into local dive bar, the Short Stop (1455 Sunset Blvd), for drink specials and plenty of folks in blue.

How to Get There—Driving

From the 101, exit at Alvarado, head north, then turn right on Sunset. Go approximately one mile and turn left on Elysian Park Avenue. You will run into Dodger Stadium. From the 110, take the Dodger Stadium exit and follow signs. From the 5 S, exit at Stadium Way, turn left, and follow the signs to Dodger Stadium. From the 5 N, exit at Stadium Way and turn left on Riverside Drive. Turn left onto Stadium Way and follow the signs.

Whenever possible, use surface roads. Sunset Boulevard will take you to Elysian Park Avenue. Beverly Boulevard is often less congested—and more direct—than Sunset Boulevard. Take Beverly to Alvarado, then follow directions above from the 101.

Parking

General parking for cars and motorcycles is $10 and parking is permitted in any unreserved parking area. They've got 16,000 spaces to choose from. Go wild. Parking for large vehicles, including buses, motor homes, limousines, and other oversized vehicles costs $25. Those vehicles are required to park in Lot 7.

How to Get There—Mass Transit

Getting to Dodger Stadium via mass transit once included a three-quarter-mile walk up an incredibly steep hill, but if you're a car-less fan, there is another option: the Roundtripper Station to Stadium Shuttle. Take the Metro to the Chinatown Gold Line Station or to Berth 6 of Union Station and hop on the shuttle. At Dodger Stadium, you'll be dropped off in Lot 13, which is a short walk to Lot 5 and the entrance to all levels of the stadium. Buses leave Union Station every 15 minutes from 5:40 pm to 8 pm, and Chinatown every half-hour. Return service, leaving from Lot 13, begins at the top of the 8th inning and the last bus leaves 60 minutes after the last out or 11 pm, whichever comes first. A $2 round-trip ticket must be purchased at the station before boarding and Metro passes are not accepted. Unfortunately, the shuttle service is not available for all games, so call 866-DODGERS to check schedules.

If you take a cab to the game and you plan to depart from the stadium by cab, a taxi service is available in Lot 3 on the western side of the stadium or at the Union 76 Service Station near Lot 37 beyond the center field wall.

How to Get Tickets

You can order Dodgers tickets by phone, through the box office at Dodger Stadium (Monday through Saturday, 9 am to 5 pm and during all Dodger home games), and online through the Dodgers' website.

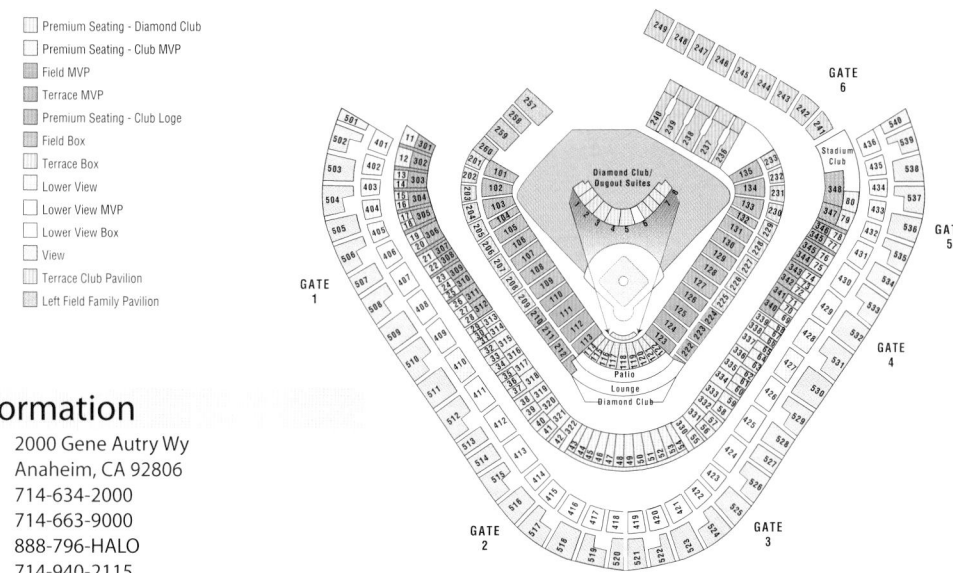

General Information

Address:	2000 Gene Autry Wy
	Anaheim, CA 92806
Box Office:	714-634-2000
Individual Tickets:	714-663-9000
Group Tickets:	888-796-HALO
Lost & Found:	714-940-2115
Website:	http://losangeles.angels.mlb.com

Overview

Fans were finally getting used to calling the place the Angel Stadium of Anaheim (over the horribly corporate Edison International Field of Anaheim), and now *this*? Just as the OC's image was heating up, the Anaheim Angels got slapped with a new moniker in 2005: The Los Angeles Angels of Anaheim. Whatever.

No matter what you call the team or the venue, this stadium is one of the coolest places to catch a game—if you can stand some modern touches and a bit of marketing. The spirit of Disney (the former owner at the time of 1998's $100 million renovation) can still be felt throughout; amenities include three on-site restaurants, family-oriented seating, and a fountain that spouts off when home runs clear the outfield. The energy is palpable at the place, probably because the fans' spirits are still high from the team's 2002 World Series win. No wonder attendance has increased annually by over one million butts in seats since the victory. It's almost enough to have you believing in that dang Rally Monkey...

How to Get There—Driving

From downtown, take 605 S to the CA-91/Artesia Freeway east. Take the I-5/Santa Ana Freeway exit on the right towards Santa Ana. Merge onto I-5 S and take the exit on the right towards Anaheim Boulevard/Haster Street/Katella Avenue. Turn left onto West Freedman Way, turn right onto South Anaheim Boulevard, and turn left onto East Katella Avenue.

Parking

The parking lot opens two-and-a-half hours prior to the start of the scheduled first pitch and, since there are only three entrances to the Angel Stadium parking lot (via Douglass Street, State College Boulevard, and Orangewood Avenue), we suggest you get there early. Parking staff will direct you towards vacancies. Day-of-game parking is $8 and oversized vehicles (greater than 20 feet in length) are $16.

The bus parking lot is located by the Orangewood Avenue entrance. Season ticket holders with parking coupons can use the Express Entry Lane on Orangewood Avenue.

How to Get There—Mass Transit

If you can get yourself to Union Station (Metro Red Line), you can catch the Amtrak Pacific Surfliner bound for San Diego, which stops not too far from the stadium at Anaheim Station. A one-way fare will set you back $10, and the Orange County Transportation Authority has a bus service to the ballpark. Call 800-636-RIDE for more information on bus schedules.

But unless you're watching a pitchers' duel or a complete blowout, the train may not be an option for most night games. The last train back to LA leaves Anaheim just after 10 pm, making an overnight stay in beautiful downtown Anaheim a definite possibility.

Patrons who require a taxi service from Angel Stadium can swing by the Guest Relations Center and ask a concierge to call them a cab.

How to Get Tickets

You can purchase tickets in person at the box office, which is open Monday through Saturday, as well as on Sunday game days, from 9 am to 5:30 pm, or by phoning the box office at 714-634-2000. Online tickets can be purchased through Ticketmaster at www.ticketmaster.com.

General Information

NFT Map: 34
Address: 1001 Rose Bowl Dr
                      Pasadena, CA 91103
Phone: 626-577-3100
Ticketmaster: 213-480-3232
Website: www.rosebowlstadium.com
Rose Parade Grandstand
Tickets: 626-795-4171
UCLA website: uclabruins.collegesports.com
UCLA tickets: 310-825-2916
Flea Market: 323-560-7469

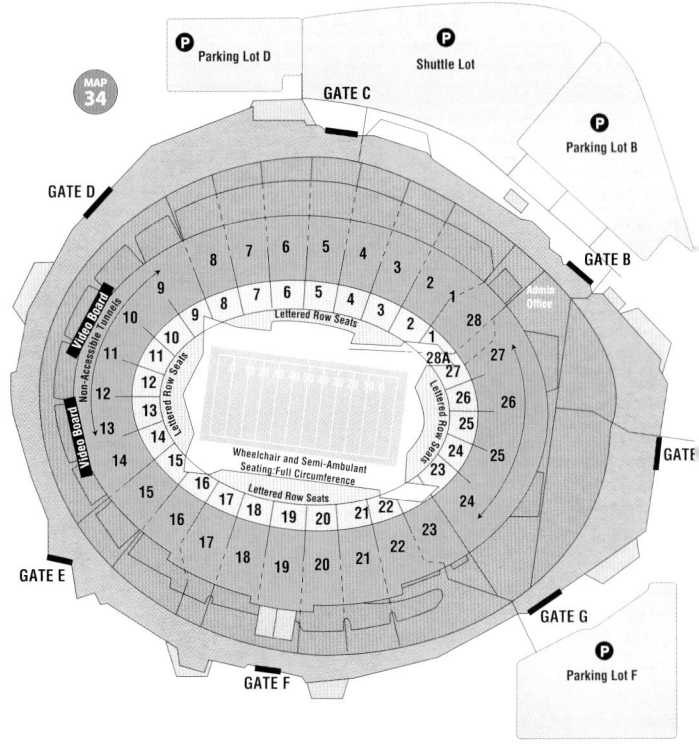

Overview

Everything about the Rose Bowl is big—its size, its reputation, its football games, its flea market, and the concerts it hosts. With seating for 90,000+ screaming fans, it's the largest stadium in Southern California. Every second Sunday of the month, the stadium holds what it claims is the world's largest flea market. And once a year, it's the place to see the game between the Big 10 and Pac 10 champs. The Rose Bowl is home to the UCLA Bruins football team, and has hosted five NFL Super Bowl Games, the 1984 Olympic soccer matches, the 1994 Men's World Cup Soccer, and the 1999 Women's World Cup Soccer.

While the stadium hosts world-class events, there's nothing particularly exceptional about the super-sized structure, except maybe its size. The stadium is moderately accessible by car, and the surrounding area of Pasadena offers good walking and shopping opportunities, with a choice of restaurants and sports bars where you can celebrate your team's victory—or drown out a nasty defeat.

Flea Market

On the second Sunday of each month, the flea market takes over the entire Rose Bowl complex. Inside the gates, you'll find new merchandise next to antique collectibles and vintage clothing, and in the parking lots you'll find the world's most overwhelming garage sale (come with patience, if not cash to burn). Entry into the flea market costs $7 after 9 am. If you want first dibs on the goods, you can gain early entry: admission costs $10 from 8 am to 9 am; $15 from 7 am to 8 am; and $20 from 5 am to 7 am. Serious shoppers arrive at dawn, and few go home empty-handed.

How to Get There—Driving

There is one major consideration you need to take into account when driving to the Rose Bowl—AVOID the 110 Pasadena Freeway at all costs! The best approach to the stadium is the Pasadena 210 Freeway. Take the Mountain/Seco/Arroyo Boulevard/Windsor exit and follow signs to the stadium. If you approach on the 134, exit at Linda Vista and follow signs. A less congested alternative if you're coming from the west is to take 134 to 2 North then take 210 East to Pasadena and exit at Mountain/Seco/Arroyo Boulevard/Windsor.

Parking

Parking for UCLA games costs $5 for cars, $10 for motor homes/limousines, and is free of charge for buses. On Rose Bowl day, parking costs $20 for cars and $40 for motor homes. For the Rose Parade, paid parking is available on a first-come, first-served basis at various lots and parking structures near the parade route, including locations at Boston Court/Mentor, Union/El Molino, Euclid/Union, Raymond/Union, 40 North Mentor/Lake, 465 East Union near Los Robles, 44 South Madison near Green, 462 East Green near Los Robles, and Colorado/Los Robles.

How to Get There—Mass Transit

No city buses or trains stop near the stadium, but on Rose Bowl game day the MTA provides regular bus service from locations throughout the county. Call 800-266-6883 for departure locations. A shuttle is available on UCLA game days from Old Pasadena to the Stadium. The shuttle picks up fans at the Parsons Technology Building (100 W Walnut Ave). Parking costs $5, and the shuttle is free. Service begins four hours prior to the game and continues for one hour after the game.

How to Get Tickets

Tickets to the Rose Bowl, Rose Parade, and UCLA games can be purchased online through Ticketmaster.

General Information

NFT Map:	9
Location:	1111 S Figueroa St
	Los Angeles, CA 90015
Website:	www.staplescenter.com
Box Office:	213-742-7340
Parking:	213-742-7275
LA Sparks (WNBA):	www.lasparks.com; 877-447-7275
LA Lakers (NBA):	www.lakers.com; 310-426-6000
LA Clippers (NBA):	www.clippers.com; 800-462-2849
LA Kings (NHL):	www.lakings.com; 888-546-4752
LA Avengers (AFL):	www.laavengers.com; 888-283-6437

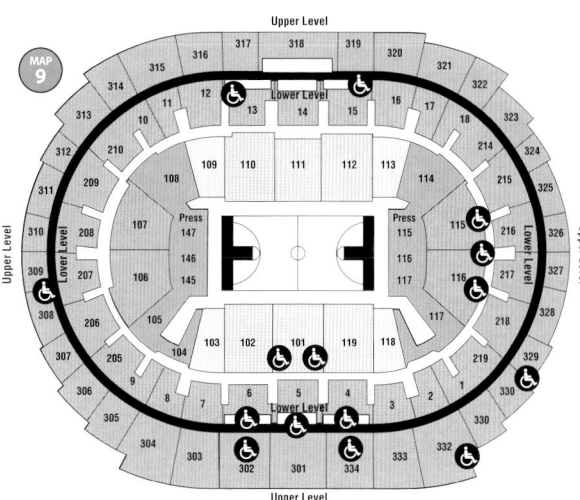

Overview

The revitalization of downtown LA has been slower than molasses. But the STAPLES Center is one of the area's success stories. Built in 1999, it has since become a sports mecca that the Lakers, Clippers, Kings, Sparks, and Avengers all call home. The STAPLES Center hosted the 2000 Democratic National Convention. And whenever, say, Bruce Springsteen or U2 decide to roll through town, this is where they rock out.

In stadium years, the STAPLES Center is no spring chicken, but the place still seems modern, and is more than capable of handling the 19,000+ fans who flood its gates for the 230+ sports and entertainment events held annually. It's the first venue in the country to accommodate three home teams (the Lakers, the Kings, and the Clippers), and it broke naming rights records when office supply superstore Staples jumped on board for $100 million.

With concession stands at every turn, and the Fox Sports Sky Box's rowdy pub for before and after the games, food and booze will never be more than a couple of steps away (but, like all stadium concession stands, they jack up the prices just because they can). Even parking isn't all that bad, given downtown's cramped layout. But just like the city in which it resides, the STAPLES Center caters to the haves, rather than the have-nots. Most of its restaurants are for season ticket holders or VIPs only, good seats for anything worth seeing are hard to get (and are often wickedly expensive), and those luxury sky boxes? Forget it.

Ground broke last year on the Los Angeles Sports and Entertainment District project (LASED). Riding on the coattails of the STAPLES Center's success, the project aims to build an adjacent area filled with $1 billion worth of restaurants, bars, concert theaters, apartments, movie theaters, and an open-air plaza. But STAPLES shouldn't worry about being dwarfed just yet—the project has met with some delays and isn't scheduled for completion until 2014.

How to Get There—Driving

The STAPLES Center is located in downtown Los Angeles, near the intersection of Routes 10 (Santa Monica) and 110 (Harbor). The best advice we can offer is to get off of the freeway as soon as possible and make your way to Olympic Boulevard. If you're coming from the north, take I-5 S (or 101 S) to 110 S (Harbor Freeway/Los Angeles). Exit at Olympic Boulevard and turn left onto 11th Street. Continue past Cherry Street and Georgian Street and the STAPLES Center is on the right. From the south, take the 110 N and exit at Adams Boulevard. Turn left onto Figueroa Street, then make another left at 11th Street.

Parking

Parking at the STAPLES Center is just about as easy as getting your hands on playoff tickets. Lot 2 opens at 8 am for guests visiting the box office, Fox Sports Sky Box, or Team LA store. Lots 1 and 3 open 2.5 hours before the start of an event. The remaining lots open 90 minutes before an event. The lots at STAPLES Center are overpriced (up to $30) and many are available only to VIPs and season ticket holders. If you're willing to arrive a little early for an event and walk a few blocks, there is a fair amount of parking available on neighboring streets. Easy in, easy out, and best of all—it's free!

How to Get There—Mass Transit

The Metro Blue Line to Pico will land you just a block from the stadium. Buses 27, 28, 30, 31, 33, 81, 333, 434, 439, 442, 444, 445, 446, and 447 all stop in the vicinity.

How to Get Tickets

Tickets for Sparks, Lakers, Clippers, Kings, and Avengers games can all be purchased online through Ticketmaster at www.ticketmaster.com, or through the individual websites and phone numbers listed above.

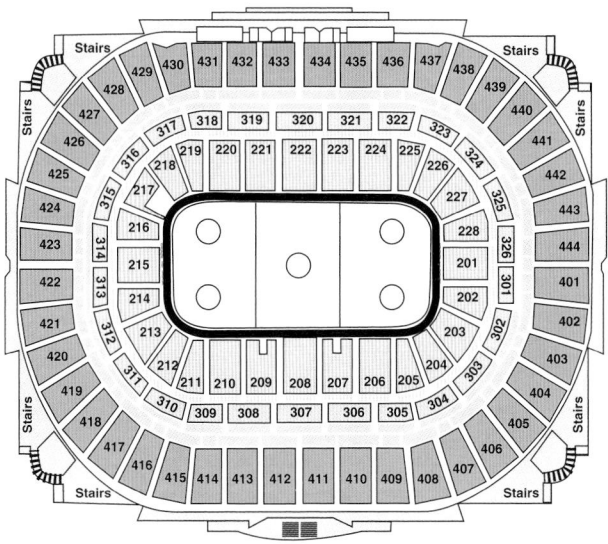

General Information

Location: 2695 East Katella Ave
                                           Anaheim, CA 92806
Admin Phone: 714-704-2400
Box Office Phone: 714-704-2500
Group Sales: 714-704-2420
Website: www.arrowheadpond.com
Mighty Ducks Website (NHL):   www.mightyducks.com

Overview

The man who owns the Arrowhead Pond stadium now owns the team that calls it home. In June 2005, the NHL approved the sale of the Mighty Ducks team to billionaires Henry and Susan Samueli. The Mighty Ducks were previously owned by the Walt Disney Company and have been massive losers in recent years. Perhaps the new management can revive the team that was inspired by a movie.

When the Mighty Ducks aren't duking it out at Arrowhead Pond, the OC's answer to the STAPLES Center is busy accommodating some 17,000+ fans who flock to see Paul McCartney concerts, Tony Hawk's Boom Boom Huckjam, and WWF wrestling tournaments.

Inside, you'll be able to appreciate the Disney World-esque features of the snappy facility: the friendly staff, the easy flow of people traffic, and the edible offerings that will find *you* before you find *them*. Getting to Arrowhead Pond, however, can be a real pain. Because the Pond is right off the always-congested 57 Freeway, traffic is always bad, and parking is worse. If you're coming out for a sold-out event—especially if you're coming from LA proper—you'll want to leave at least an hour and a half to get from inside your home to inside the stadium.

How to Get There—Driving

From Los Angeles, take 405 S to 22 E to 57 N. Exit on Katella Avenue and turn right, then turn left on Douglas Street. If you're approaching on I-5 S, exit on Katella Avenue and turn left, then go left on Douglas Street. From I-10, head east to 57 S and exit on Katella Avenue and turn left, then turn left on Douglas Street.

Parking

Parking for all events at the Pond is $10 for general parking, $15 preferred parking (if available), $20 limos and RVs, and $25 buses (unlimited drop-off and pick-up for an event).

How to Get There—Mass Transit

The Orange County Transit Authority provides transport to Arrowhead Pond. Check www.octa.net for schedules or phone 714-560-6272. In addition to OCTA, Amtrak's station is located within walking distance of the arena, in the parking lot at Angel Stadium. But Amtrak riders beware—the last train back to LA from Anaheim leaves shortly after 10 pm, so unless you're camping out or leaving early, you might want to make other arrangements for getting home after evening events.

How to Get Tickets

Tickets can be purchased in person at the box office, at Ticketmaster outlets, or online at www.ticketmaster.com. The box office is open Monday through Friday, 10 am until 6 pm, and Saturday 10 am until 4 pm. Purchase same-day tickets on Sundays—the box office opens three hours before the scheduled event and sells tickets only to that day's event. A "wristband lottery" for any remaining tickets to popular events takes place the morning of the event, and line-ups begin at 7 am. But even if you're first in line and receive a wristband, obtaining a ticket is no guarantee. 15 minutes before tickets go on sale, one wristband number is drawn randomly and it becomes the starting number for ticket sales.

General Information

Address: 18400 Avalon Blvd
                                  Carson, CA 90746
General Information: 310-630-2200
Stadium Website: www.homedepotcenter.com
LA Galaxy Website: www.lagalaxy.com
LA Galaxy Tickets: 877-342-5299
Group Sales: 866-524-7687
Ticketmaster: 213-480-3232
Parking: 310-630-2060

Overview

While soccer is hardly the most popular sport in LA (or anywhere in the country, for that matter), sports fans will be impressed by the Home Depot Center, the home of LA's soccer team, the Galaxy. Located on the Cal State Dominguez Hills Campus, the Home Depot Center is a mammoth, multi-purpose facility; it boasts a 27,000-seat capacity soccer stadium, an 8,000-seat tennis venue, a track-and-field stadium, a boxing ring, a 3,000-square-foot weight room, 30 tennis courts, nine soccer training fields, and a three-mile jogging trail.

The Home Depot Center is the official training site of the US Track & Field team and the training headquarters of USA cycling, the US Soccer Federation, the US Tennis Association, and the NFL's San Diego Chargers. In 2005, soccer star David Beckham set up his eponymous soccer academy for kids at the Home Depot Center. You, however, will probably just use the main arena to catch a game or Dave Matthews Band concert. The three-year-old stadium still feels brand spankin' new, with plenty of wide gathering areas if you're getting antsy in your seat during a slow game, great views from most seats in the stadium, and so much parking you won't even break a sweat getting into and out of the place.

How to Get There—Driving

A lack of signs makes the Home Depot Center a little difficult to find. Leave time in your travel plans for getting lost.

Approaching on 110 S, exit on 190th Street and make a left. 190th Street becomes Victoria Street. Continue past Avalon Boulevard. For reserved parking, use Gates C or D on your right. For general unreserved parking, head further along and use Gates E or F on your right. From 110 N, take the Del Amo Boulevard exit and make a left on Figueroa Street. Make a right on Del Amo Boulevard and a left on Avalon Boulevard. For reserved parking, continue past University Drive and use Gate B on your right. For general unreserved parking, make a right on University Drive and use Gate I on your left.

From the 405 S, exit on Vermont. At the bottom of the ramp, make a left on 190th Street, which becomes Victoria Street. Follow directions for 110 S. From 405 N, exit on Avalon Boulevard, and make a right. Follow directions for 110 N.

Parking

Parking rates are different for each event. For a Galaxy regular season game, parking costs between $10 and $15 per vehicle. For Galaxy playoffs, or other special events such as concerts, parking costs between $15 and $20 per vehicle. The lot generally opens two hours before game time, but tailgating is prohibited (whatever).

How to Get There—Mass Transit

Take the Metro Blue Line to the Artesia Station. Transfer to Metro Bus 130 and take it to Victoria Street and Avalon Boulevard.

How to Get Tickets

Tickets for all events can be purchased at the box office (Avalon and 184th St), through any Ticketmaster retail location, or online at www.ticketmaster.com. The box office is open days of events only, three hours before game time.

Overview

From the old geezer skating on the Venice Boardwalk to the loose-limbed ingénue posing on her yoga mat, Angelenos love their exercise. All the fun options, not to mention the year-round sunshine, make it easy to join the city's tanned and toned without becoming a gym drone.

League Sports

Work up a sweat, make friends, and get soaked in Gatorade after leading your team to victory. The LA Department of Recreation & Parks offers organized municipal sports leagues for adults ranging from men's basketball to women's flag football. Visit www.laparks.com or call 888-LA-PARKS for more information.

Table Tennis

If you own your own paddle and watch the tournaments on ESPN, stop by the Westside Table Tennis Center (www.alphatabletennis.com) for tips from the pros.

Table Tennis Center	Address	Phone	Map
Olympic Table Tennis Club	1049 S Grand View St	213-387-0200	8
Westside Table Tennis Center	11755 Exposition Blvd	626-584-6377	19
Pasadena Table Tennis Club	85 E Holly St	626-584-6377	34

Horseback Riding

If you are more equine-inclined, check out one of the many companies offering guided trail rides and riding lessons. Looking for a novel way to spend a Friday night? Try one of the Sunset Ranch dinner rides through Griffith Park, which include a stop for margaritas at a restaurant with hitching posts.

Stable	Address	Phone	Map
Sunset Ranch Hollywood Stables	3400 N Beachwood Dr	323-469-5450	3
Traditional Equitation School	480 Riverside Dr	818-569-3666	50
Escape on Horseback	2623 Old Topanga Canyon Rd	818-591-2032	p. 260

Boxing

Train to be the next Oscar De La Hoya—onscreen or in the ring. If you like a bit of history with your blood, sweat, and tears, visit the Broadway Boxing Gym.

Gym	Address	Phone	Map
Hollywood Boxing Gym	1551 N La Brea Ave	323-845-1420	2
Wild Card Gym	1123 Vine St	323-461-4170	3
Broadway Boxing Gym	10730 S Broadway	323-755-9016	14

Yoga

The city's yoga studios could fill a guidebook. Here are some tested yogi favorites:

Studio	Address	Phone	Map
City Yoga	1067 N Fairfax Ave	323-654-2125	2
Golden Bridge	6322 De Longpre Ave	323-936-4172	2
Karuna Yoga	1939 ½ Hillhurst Ave	323-665-6242	4
Silver Lake Yoga	2810 ½ Glendale Blvd	323-953-0496	5
Center for Yoga	230 ½ N Larchmont Blvd	323-464-1276	7
Yoga Circle Downtown	400 S Main St	213-620-1040	9
Brentwood Yoga	11740 San Vicente Blvd	310-442-5900	16
Santa Monica Yoga	1640 Ocean Park Blvd	310-396-4040	18
Sivananda Vedanta Yoga Center	13325 Beach Ave	310-822-9642	22
Yoga Loft	313 11th Pl	310-372-7334	27
Mission Street Yoga	1017 Mission St	626-441-1144	34
Glendale Yoga	746 N Glendale Ave	818-956-1621	51
Black Dog Yoga	4454 Van Nuys Blvd	818-380-0331	55
Angel City Yoga	12408 Ventura Blvd	818-762-8211	56

Skating

Here's your chance to dig those hot pants and leg warmers out of the far reaches of your closet. For the ultimate dance party on wheels, take to the streets of Santa Monica, Hollywood, or Downtown with the Friday Night Skate crew. Visit www.fridaynightskate.org for details.

Rinks & Lessons	Address	Phone	Map
Moonlight Rollerway Roller Skating Rink	5110 San Fernando Rd	818-241-3630	5
World on Wheels	4645 ½ Venice Blvd	323-933-5170	9
California Skate School	multiple locations, www.skateschool.com	888-880-ROLL	n/a
Pedlow Field Skate Park (skateboarding)	17334 Victory Blvd	818-266-6991	53

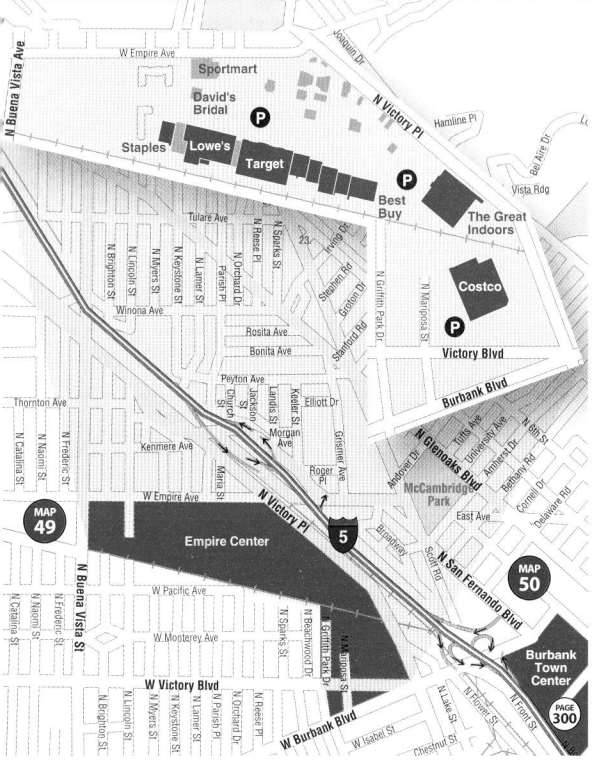

Angeles County where you can buy the bride's dress and the threshold over which the groom will carry her, all in one shopping trip.)

Food

As Homer would say, "Mmmm. Donuts." The arrival of Krispy Kreme was one of the biggest news stories to hit the area in years. (Matched only this spring, when Jet Blue announced direct service from Burbank to New York City.) You can also fuel up for a grueling day of paint-matching and window treatment ordering at either Hometown Buffet or Outback Steakhouse. The Great Indoors has a Starbucks inside the store when shopping for shower curtains wears you down. Should you find yourself longing to be in England when lunchtime is near, be sure to stop by Buchanan Arms (2013 Burbank Blvd, 818-845-0692) for fish and chips and a tall pint of Newcastle in a traditional—and friendly—pub environment.

Drawbacks

True to its name, the place is empire-sized. And in fact, The Great Indoors and Lowe's are at opposite ends of the mall, which can be inconvenient for those on intensive home-improvement missions. The long walk can be especially rough on hot summer days when the heat is shimmering off the parking lot. The Burbank Empire Center is also adjacent to a very busy, very big Costco, which means the intersection of Burbank Boulevard, Victory Place, and Victory Boulevard can tie itself into quite a knot. The good news is that there are long left-turn arrows to ease you through.

How to Get There

From the 5 in either direction, exit at Burbank Boulevard. Head west on Burbank Boulevard to Victory Place and turn right. The Empire Center is about a mile down on your left. Just look for the signs shaped like airplanes and stores the size of airplane hangars. The Great Indoors is at the southern end of the mall, Target and Lowe's are at the northern end. In case you can't smell your way to them, the donuts are to be found on the east side of the mall, where the stand-alone stores are located.

General Information

NFT Map: 49 & 50
Address: 1727 N Victory Pl
              Burbank, CA 91502

Shopping

The Burbank Empire Center is a gift from heaven for home-owners, renovators, redecorators, and spiffer-uppers of all stripes. With Lowe's Home Improvement, Target, The Great Indoors, Best Buy, and Linens 'n Things all in one spot, you can find just about everything you need to go in, on, and around your home. (And the fact that it's just across the freeway from the Burbank IKEA only doubles your fun.) The Great Indoors is not a familiar name to many Angelenos, but one visit will convert any stranger into a fan. A full-service home improvement goldmine, it offers appliances (low- to high-end), bath fixtures, lighting, drapery (custom and off the rack), carpet, blinds, furniture, dishes, towels, sheets, and so on. A handful of clothing stores include Shoe Pavilion, Marshalls, and David's Bridal. (This makes the Burbank Empire Center one of the few places in Los

General Information

NFT Map: 2
Address: 8500 Beverly Blvd
             Los Angeles, CA 90048
Phone: 310-854-0071
Website: www.beverlycenter.com

Shopping

Once upon a time, the Beverly Center was pretty much the ne plus ultra of cool. This was around the time that Guess! jeans were new, drum machines ruled, and the city was still basking in the glow of having hosted the 1984 Summer Olympics. But now, 20+ years down the pike, the Grove is soaking up all the limelight (as well as the weekend crowds), and the shops of nearby Robertson Boulevard are the destinations of choice for the gotta-have-it crowd. While Beverly Center will never be what it once was, its central location will have everyone stopping by once in a while, if only for convenience sake.

Today's Beverly Center is something of a study in contrasts. Stores such as D&G, Louis Vuitton, Furla, Just Cavalli, A/X Armani Exchange, DKNY, and a brightly lit Bloomingdale's cater to 21st-century America's love affair with labels. But there's a distinct middle-of-the-road factor at the Beverly Center, embodied by the presence (persistence?) of GNC, Macy's, Brookstone, Sunglass Hut, and the rest of the chain gang. Shops like Forever XXI, Claire's, and Steve Madden and eateries like the Hard Rock Café and the Grand Lux Café remind us all that the survival of the mall as a species depends on its ability to attract teenage girls and out-of-towners.

Food

Relatively new and surprisingly sophisticated is the Wave Restaurant & Bar, smack-dab in the middle of the mall. It's mainly frequented by moviegoers who stop by to have a cocktail or two before their films begin upstairs. The eighth floor Food Court features all of the usual suspects (Auntie Anne's, Sbarro's, Panda Express, Starbucks, and the like). Patio seating is plentiful and non-smoking, and features an almost panoramic eastern view of the city. For a decidedly less generic feel, head on foot to the Cadillac Café (359 N La Cienega Blvd, near Oakwood) for eclectic food in a cheerful, modern setting.

Drawbacks

This is a fairly popular mall in a busy part of town; it's bordered by another mall (the Beverly Connection) and a huge medical center (Cedars-Sinai). That's why it's a good idea to enter from the San Vicente (westernmost and least-congested) side of the building. And although traffic flows well inside the mall, traffic in the parking lot does not. Stay cool—the good stuff's waiting upstairs. If it's women's clothes you're after, be advised that the Beverly Center best serves those under the age of 30 and smaller than a size 10. The Cineplex Odeon has a lot of screens, but they are all smaller and less luxurious than the mega-theaters with tilt-a-matic stadium seating and boom-around sound that we've come to take for granted.

How to Get There—Driving

From the 10 in either direction, exit at La Cienega Boulevard. Head north on La Cienega for approximately 2.25 miles, and you'll see the behemoth just ahead on your left. Cross 3rd Street and turn left into the mall at the next signal. From the 101 in either direction, exit Highland Boulevard and head south on Highland for approximately two miles until you hit Beverly Boulevard. Turn right onto Beverly, and head west about two miles to La Cienega Boulevard. Make a left onto La Cienega Boulevard, and an immediate right into the mall.

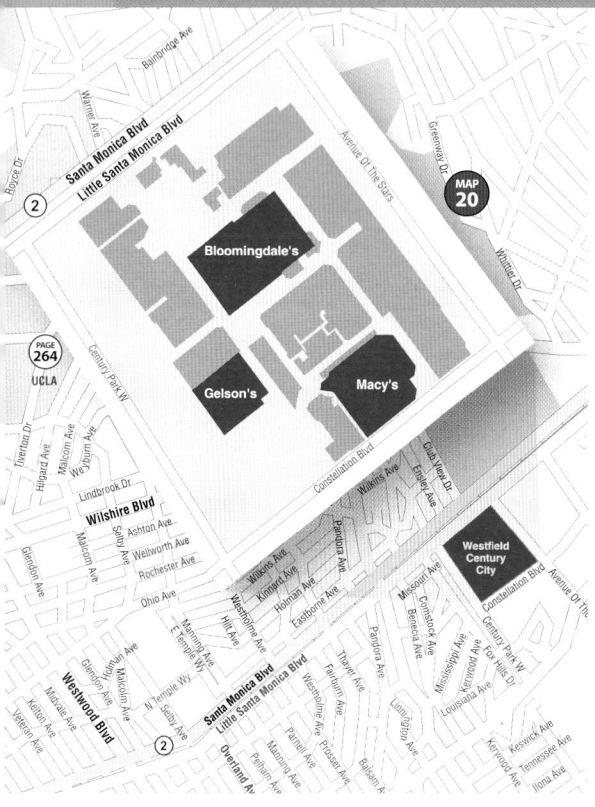

Set around a gleaming Bloomingdale's, the mall is bright, cheerful, and glossy. For months now, Century City has been undergoing a massive make-over, renovation, and overall up-ending. It's still too soon to say (as we go to press) whether or not the overhaul will be worth the hassle, but in the meantime the solid line-up of retail shops still delivers. Between Restoration Hardware, simplehuman, and the Bloomingdale's housewares department, bridal registries are covered. A few other special treats are also on hand in the form of Brentano's Bookstore (thorough, highly browsable, featuring weekly readings and book signings), Wolford (home of fabulous hosiery), and MaxMara (whose lovely coats you need only wear three or four days of the year in LA, but who's counting?).

Food

Lots of outdoor seating and a nice variety of cuisines await you. Gulen's Mediterranean and Tacone Wraps are both good. The teriyaki chicken bowls are always popular at Kisho-an, and Johnny Rockets may be the most reliable, albeit the greasiest, place to take the kids. The coffee cart near the Discovery Channel Store has some tasty coffee and kind service. Houston's is great for a before- or after-movie dinner, but keep an eye on the time (see "Drawbacks" below), as there is often a long wait.

Drawbacks

Construction or no, weekend parking is still a beast. Period. Consider valet parking at Gelson's or on the Santa Monica Boulevard side (free with your receipt if you spend at least $250). Another option is to have your car washed at Abluo Auto Spa while you shop: $16 for standard cars including tip (SUVs cost $18…suckers) and worth every penny (on parking Level A). Once the free parking limit is exceeded (three hours free; four with AMC Theatre validation), the parking fees start racking up quickly and can result in considerable sticker-shock.

How to Get There

From the 405 in either direction, exit Santa Monica Boulevard and head east past Sepulveda. Make a slight jog right onto Little Santa Monica Boulevard, and follow it approximately one-and-a-half miles to the mall. The entrance is on your right just past Century Park. From Olympic Boulevard in either direction, head north on Avenue of the Stars to Constellation. Turn left on Constellation and look for the parking entrance 150 yards down on your right.

General Information

NFT Map: 20
Address: 10250 Santa Monica Blvd
Los Angeles, CA 90067
Phone: 310-277-3898
Website: www.westfield.com/centurycity

Shopping

Though the mall may now be part of a large corporation, in our hearts and minds it will always be the Century City Shopping Center. Regardless of what it's called, Century City is a beacon on the Westside (but not too far west) that seems to say, "Bring me your tired, your hungry, your frazzled masses struggling to get away from fluorescent lighting and the overpowering scent of Cinnabons." In other words, this shopping center is an outdoor, upscale mall blessed with particularly temperate weather, a 14-screen movie theater, and a discerning selection of stores. On a good day, when the Bloomie's sale racks are stocked just-so, and the nice fellow from Gelson's has unloaded the last of your grocery bags into the back of your station wagon, you'd swear that the happiest place on earth is not, in fact, in Orange County, but rather on Santa Monica Boulevard.

General Information

NFT Map: 32
Address: 3 Del Amo Fashion Center
Torrance, CA 90503
Phone: 310-542-8525
Website: www.delamofashioncenter.com

Shopping

It's easy to pick on the Del Amo Fashion Center in Torrance just because it's big and invites comparisons to black holes and all-you-can-eat shrimp specials. But in all fairness, Del Amo offers things other malls don't. Most often, discount retailers such as T.J. Maxx, Marshalls, and Burlington Coat Factory are not found alongside the department stores that sell the same name-brand clothing. Few have Old Navy and the Gap under one roof. But on this scale, the mall illustrates a larger truth: despite the best efforts of retailers, redundancy is inevitable. Though only one has an auto center, Sears and JCPenney actually offer up a fair amount of overlapping product. So do Robinsons-May and Macy's, Forever 21 and Charlotte Russe, and Foot Locker and FootAction USA. But is this sheer volume worth the physical effort and mental concentration required to tap it? Del Amo is best approached with very comfortable shoes, an open mind, and an extra cup of coffee—from whomever you buy it: Dairy Queen/Orange Julius, Starbucks, or Gloria Jean's Coffee. Shoppers seeking a smaller venue should consider the Galleria at South Bay as an alternate venue.

Food

The food court is centrally located, and features Mexican, Mediterranean, and Pacific Rim cuisines in addition to fast food offerings like Chick-fil-A and Hot Dog on a Stick. The area is clean, brightly lit, and well-attended. To break up a long expedition, consider going outside the mall. Black Angus (3405 W Carson St, 310-370-1523) and Lucille's Smokehouse BBQ (21420 Hawthorne Blvd, 310-370-7427), both adjacent to the mall, offer a chance to protein-load in relatively quieter surroundings.

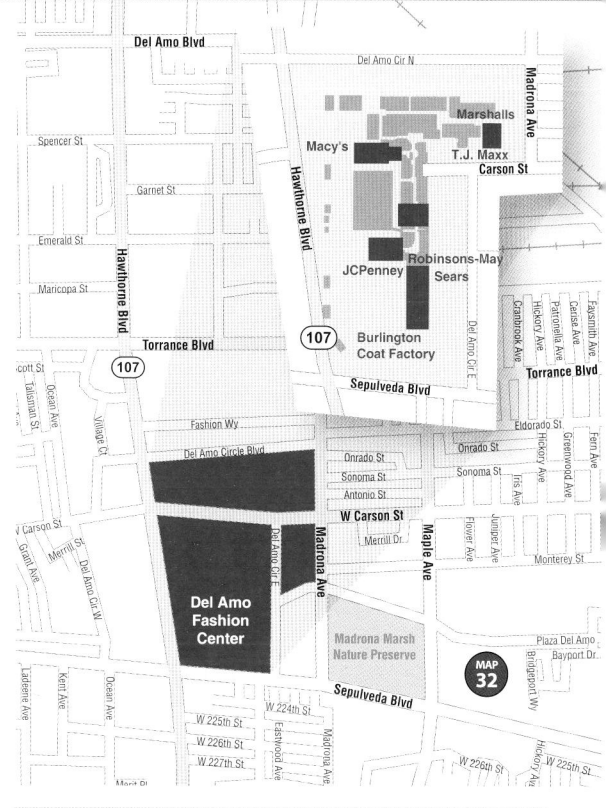

Drawbacks

Even more than its glandular problem, Del Amo suffers from a somewhat labyrinthine floor plan that makes it hard to see what's ahead. An excess of tile and a lack of natural light give some of the corridors a bunker-like feel as well.

How to Get There

From the 405 S, exit Redondo Beach, head east to Prairie Avenue, and take Prairie approximately three miles. Turn right on Carson to enter the parking lot. From the 405 N, exit Artesia Boulevard and head west on Artesia to Prairie Avenue. Make a left at Prairie and continue on Prairie approximately three miles. Turn right on Carson to enter the parking lot. From the 110 in either direction, exit Carson and proceed west three miles on Carson to the Del Amo Fashion Center.

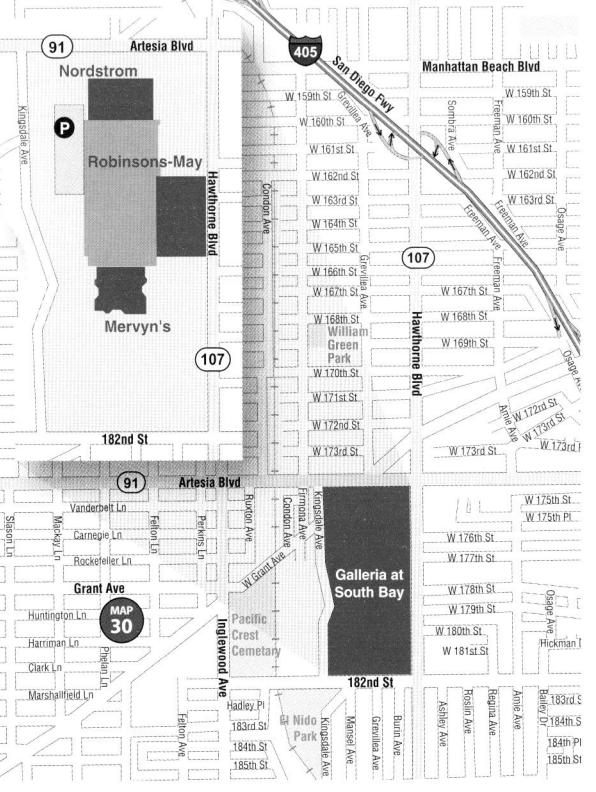

The anchor stores—Mervyn's, Robinsons-May, and Nordstrom—accurately represent the price range available at the Galleria. And among its three levels, the mall manages to strike a nice balance of retail offerings. Ann Taylor, Lane Bryant, Motherhood Maternity, and Forever 21 accommodate women of all different sizes, tastes, and life-stages. Men in need of suits and serious office attire are best served at Nordstrom and Robinsons-May. Between Abercrombie & Fitch and Anchor Blue, young hipsters should have their needs met. Footwear tastes are addressed up and down the spectrum, from Bakers Shoes to Payless. The Eddie Bauer store is a boon, as they are not often easy to find outside of catalog and computer. Rounding out the mix are a good variety of sporting goods and athletic shoe stores, including a Vans store, Champs, and Foot Locker—Kids and Lady FL too.

Food

The Galleria's food court is a winner. Take the express escalator from the main floor and grab a table overlooking the fountain in center court. There's a nice range of food options from Great Khan Mongolian BBQ to Napoli Pizza and Chick-fil-A. The area is clean and well-tended, though located perilously close to K•B Toys. With children generally underfoot during the course of lunch, it can get a little hectic. For table service in a less ricochet-prone setting, try California Pizza Kitchen (CPK) or Red Robin downstairs.

Drawbacks

As with practically everywhere, weekend parking is a big hassle. It's five dollars to park valet and worth every penny. (Valets are near CPK on the east side and adjacent to Nordstrom on the west.) Hot tip: Check with the guest services booth just inside the Galleria; often they have free valet passes stashed behind the counter. A mall this nice cries out for a more serious bookstore than the B. Dalton presently in place. And the already pleasant shopping experience could be made even more so, if water fountains and restrooms were easier to find.

How to Get There

From the 405 S, exit Redondo Boulevard and head west on Redondo three-quarters of a mile to Hawthorne Boulevard. Turn left on Hawthorne; the mall entrance is on your right.

From the 405 N, exit Redondo Boulevard and head west on Artesia approximately three-quarters of a mile to Hawthorne Boulevard. Then follow directions above.

General Information

NFT Map: 30
Address: 1815 Hawthorne Blvd
               Redondo Beach, CA 90278
Phone: 310-371-7546
Website: www.southbaygalleria.com

Shopping

All the malls that bear the name "Galleria" are modeled (in theory at least) on the Galleria Vittorio Emmanuele in Milan, a four-story shopping center with a greenhouse-like roof that floods the space with natural light. The Galleria at South Bay is blessed with just such a glass structure. What's more, both Gallerias are pleasant places to spend time, even if you don't have much shopping to do. But only one of them has a Sharper Image, a Soho Lab, an AMC 16-theater multiplex, and a Dairy Queen/Orange Julius. Along with the high price of transatlantic tickets, these are just a few of the reasons why the Galleria at South Bay is such a solid bet.

General Information

NFT Map:	51
Address:	2148 Glendale Galleria
	Glendale, CA 91210
Phone:	818-240-9481
Website:	www.glendalegalleria.com

Shopping

The Glendale Galleria is a long, L-shaped building anchored by the standard department stores: Robinsons-May, Mervyn's, Macy's, JCPenney, and the always-classy Nordstrom. Coach, Montblanc, and the Apple store represent the high-end of this squarely middle-class temple of consumerism. Boutiques are mostly standard mall fare such as Hot Topic, Foot Locker, and Williams-Sonoma, but some quirky storefronts help break up the monotony. For Love 21 draws crowds with trendy chandelier earrings, boho bags, and sequined scarves at penny candy prices. Metropark offers mall rats a faux urban oasis of hip designer clothing, art books, and live DJs spinning on weekends. Field of Dreams is the place to find a pair of boxing gloves signed by Muhammad Ali or an autographed Kiss poster. A motley crew of kiosks completes the retail landscape, peddling everything from "miracle" face creams to rhinestone encrusted belt buckles.

Food

The Galleria's main food court is on the second level, but you can often smell it from the third. The International Grill is mainly responsible for the smoke. This popular kabob shop serves up steak, lamb chops, Cornish game hen, and a selection of Armenian and American beers. Hot Dog on a Stick adds kitsch factor and McDonald's keeps the happy meals and liver damage coming. The third level has its own selection of fast food restaurants, with Cleo & Cucci offering a more upscale selection of sandwiches, salads, and pastries.

Drawbacks

If malls aren't your thing, the Galleria probably won't change your mind. It is a tunnel-shaped echo chamber where the sound of crying babies and shrieking teenagers rings in your ears. The place is also short on elevators and escalators, meaning you have to walk the length of a proverbial football field just to change floors. On the weekends, you may find yourself swept up in the herds of stroller-pushers, young lovers, and junior high cliques that roam the mall's narrow corridors. Of course to some hard-core shoppers, this is all just part of the fun…

How to Get There

From the 5 in either direction, exit Colorado and take Colorado east about a mile and a half. The entrance to the mall parking lot is at a light on the left a hundred or so yards before you get to the intersection at Central. From the 134 in either direction, exit Central/Brand Boulevard and head south on Brand about a mile and a half. Turn right on Broadway, and head west an eighth of a mile. The entrance to the mall parking lot is at a light on the left about a hundred or so yards after Central. Look for the "Galleria" sign. For Nordstrom's valet service, enter the smaller parking lot on the east side of Central, just south of Broadway.

emphasis here is on high-end specialty stores. NIKEgoddess carries fitness wear for women, while Hawk Skate appeals to the extreme sports enthusiasts. This family-friendly mall also houses the area's only Pottery Barn Kids. The usual suspects—the Gap and its brethren—are well-represented, but The Grove also houses the unexpected—Bodega Chocolates, Amadeus Aveda Spa & Salon, and what might be the mall's most beautifully designed retail store, Anthropologie. If none of these stores fit your mood, there's always Barnes & Noble. They've got something in everyone's size.

Food

We've got good news and bad news. The good news is that the food court doesn't tempt you with typical mall fare. The bad news is that there is no food court—only full-service restaurants, so lunch or dinner at The Grove is going to cost you. The Farm of Beverly Hills offers American comfort food, while the Wood Ranch BBQ & Grill is a carnivore's paradise. Also check out Maggiano's Little Italy (Italian) as well as the handful of specialty kiosks, like Häagen-Dazs and Surf City Squeeze. Our advice: Head for the Farmers Market and its eclectic and far superior food stalls. The Gumbo Pot features the best muffelata this side of N'awlins, ¡Loteria! Grill offers some of the finest Mexican specialties west of Alvarado, and there's no better place for breakfast than Kokomo.

Drawbacks

The lack of affordable places to eat can be a drag, and traffic and parking are always a problem. Third Street gets congested, and the traffic light at Beverly Boulevard and The Grove Drive is so poorly timed that two cars are lucky to advance on a green light.

How to Get There

From the 10 in either direction, exit at Fairfax and head north approximately three miles. Go through the intersection at Third and Fairfax and turn right at Farmers Market Way. Drive past the Farmers Market and enter The Grove's parking structure. From the 101 in either direction, exit at Highland and head south toward Franklin Avenue. Turn right onto Franklin, and continue until you hit La Brea Avenue. Make a left turn and continue south on La Brea to Third Street. Turn right onto Third Street, and continue until you reach The Grove Drive. Make a right turn into the mall. Parking at The Grove is free for the first hour, and $2 per hour for the next 3 hours. Valet parking is also available near each of the main entrances of The Grove's parking structure and costs $5 for the first two hours, and $2 for each block of 30 minutes thereafter.

General Information

NFT Map:	2
Address:	189 The Grove Dr
	Los Angeles, CA 90036
Phone:	323-900-8080
Website:	www.thegrovela.com

Shopping

Many of us were outraged and vowed to boycott when a large section of the historic, 65-year-old Farmers Market was leveled to make way for yet another shopping mall. But when The Grove opened in March 2002, it was beautiful—and many of its most vocal detractors had to sheepishly admit they were wrong, or simply kowtow in light of its widespread acceptance. The Grove is fantastic in that pristine, otherworldly way that only exists in make-believe places like Oz , Disneyland, or Las Vegas, to which it has aptly been compared. The mall offers a little something for everyone—eclectic shops, a 14-screen movie theater, and an old-fashioned trolley linking The Grove to the adjacent Farmers Market. The trolley is mainly for atmosphere, but the kids love it.

The Grove is fairly restrained, with just one anchor store—Nordstrom—and a small one at that. The

General Information

NFT Map:	3
Address:	6801 Hollywood Blvd
	Hollywood, CA 90028
Phone:	323-467-6412
Website:	www.hollywoodandhighland.com

Shopping

Hollywood & Highland opened in late 2001 to much fanfare. Like the Strip in Las Vegas and the "new" Times Square, it's exceptionally clean, well-lit, and family-friendly. The center is most famous for its state-of-the-art Kodak Theatre, which hosts the Academy Awards each year (right across from the Roosevelt Hotel, where the first Academy Awards was held in 1929). It has a very glossy bowling alley serving a whole lotta top-shelf liquor. And once inside the complex—unlike out on Hollywood Boulevard—you aren't likely to be pan-handled.

But let's be honest here: Hollywood & Highland is a gajillion-dollar complex built for the amusement of tourists who come to shop, take pictures of each other, and take pictures of each other shopping. Hollywood & Highland makes little effort to cater to the local set. At this point you have no doubt flipped to the front of this book to confirm that the title is "Not for Tourists." Understandable. We include it here, because eventually we all must entertain our paler friends from the eastern parts of the country who show up to visit in February for what seems to be the express purpose of telling us that California has neither weather nor seasons. But we digress.

Yeah, they've got Build-A-Bear, Mac, Hot Topic, and all of the usual mall rats. But this mall tries to provide a little something else: on Tuesday evenings, there's wine and jazz in the courtyard; every second Sunday, the Children's Museum hosts "Kids Create" at the mall; and the Virgin Megastore west coast flagship store is the biggest of a whole slew of new stores.

Food

Two high-profile local brands raise the meaning of mall food to an unprecedented level: CPK for pizza, and a Wolfgang Puck brasserie, Vert. Koji's Sushi and Shabu-Shabu are also reliable choices for a lunch date. Elixir Tonics & Teas serves up cleansing infusions of something or other and the opportunity to think detached thoughts. The clever (and discreet) visitor might venture up to the Renaissance Marriott's rooftop pool for a spectacular view and a cool drink. On the elevator ride up, be sure to practice your straight face when you tell the guards that you "totally didn't see the 'For Hotel Guests Only' sign."

Drawbacks

The drawbacks of Hollywood & Highland are pretty much the same as those of the Strip in Las Vegas or the "new" Times Square: it's crowded, air-brushed, fabricated out of whole cloth, and devoid of organic materials. Then there's the mind-boggling traffic in the area around the complex. The streets surrounding the place—Highland, Franklin, Orange, and Hollywood—get distressingly backed up on weekends. Also, the entrance to the Mann Chinese 6 Theatres (not to be confused with the Grauman's legendary Chinese Theatre next-door) is not well marked, so be sure to keep your eyes peeled. Parking at Hollywood & Highland costs $2 for up to four hours with validation. For an additional five bucks, you can splurge on valet.

How to Get There

If you're using mass transit, take the Red Line to the Hollywood & Highland station. Exit the station. Thumb your nose at the traffic all around you. From the 101 S, exit at Highland Avenue/Hollywood Bowl and merge onto Cahuenga Boulevard. Cahuenga becomes North Highland Avenue. Stay on Highland until Hollywood Boulevard. From the 101 N, exit at Highland Avenue/Hollywood Bowl and keep right at the fork in the ramp. Merge onto Odin Street, and turn left onto Highland Avenue. From 405 in either direction, exit onto Santa Monica Boulevard. Head east on Santa Monica Boulevard through Beverly Hills, West Hollywood, and into Hollywood. Turn left on Highland.

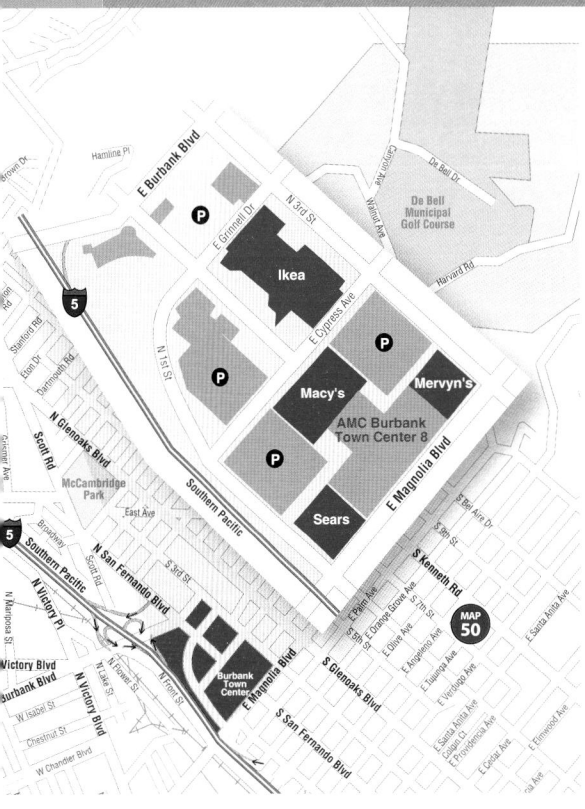

The Burbank Town Center mall itself provides the moderately-priced fare you'd expect from anchors such as Mervyn's, Macy's, and Sears. Sport Chalet is fun and well-stocked, while the newly-minted Bed, Bath & Beyond delivers its reliable supply of home furnishings and gadgetry. Women's clothing outlets (Georgiou, Lane Bryant, Express, and the like) outnumber men's (Corsine, Express Men, etc.) by nearly five to one, while kid magnets like KB Toys and Gameland proliferate like bunnies at Easter. Outside the mall, the Virgin Megastore and Barnes & Noble always provide some quality browsing selections. Exhausted fathers and sons usually seek asylum at Circuit City (particularly on Sundays during football season).

Food

On the Magnolia Boulevard side of the mall's upper level, you'll find all of the standard Food Court fare, while Johnny Rockets, PF Chang's, and Pomodoro Cucina Italiana offer sit-down respites from mall madness. Just outside, along the strollable San Fernando Boulevard, you'll find Market City Caffe (164 E Palm Ave, at San Fernando), specializing in Italian antipasti and inspired martinis; Romano's Macaroni Grill (102 E Magnolia Blvd), serving more Italian standards; Knight Restaurant (138 N San Fernando), offering savory Mediterranean treats, and Picanha Churrascaria (269 E Palm Ave), trotting out abundant quantities of Brazilian meat-on-a-stick fare.

General Information

NFT Map: 50
Address: 201 E Magnolia Blvd
                  Burbank, CA 91501
Phone: 818-566-8556
Website: www.burbanktowncenter.com

Shopping

At some point in the early stages of their assimilation into LA, all new arrivals pass through the portals of IKEA, thus making Burbank Town Center the Ellis Island of Los Angeles. But to see this area only for its prefab Swedish furnishings would be to miss the point entirely. It also has a full-service, mid-range mall (with an oversized chessboard on the first level centercourt), a boatload of movie theaters, and access to a rapidly developing stretch of San Fernando Boulevard, where shoppers can browse movie scripts and used books, migrate toward the peculiar glow emanating from Urban Outfitters, and shoot a game of pool in between all the shopping, eating, and movie-going.

Drawbacks

Three AMC Theatres, with a total of 30 screens, are clustered around Burbank Town Center, including one in in Burbank Town Center. Double-check your movie location before you go, or you'll surely miss the previews in a desperate dash between theatres. Parking gets complicated on weekends. Your best bet is to park in the East Garage on Third between San Jose and Magnolia.

How to Get There

From I-5 in either direction, exit at Burbank Boulevard and head east on Burbank to N 3rd Street. Turn right on 3rd and go four blocks. The East Parking Garage is on your right, the block after IKEA.

General Information

Address: 9301 Tampa Ave
             Northridge, CA 91324
Phone: 818-885-9700
Website: www.northridgefashioncenter.com

Shopping

The Northridge Fashion Center offers an affordable range of retail shops for all ages, all surrounded by a pleasant outdoor pedestrian area. You can find an outpost of Frederick's of Hollywood, engagement rings (McClave Jewelers is very nice, as is Kristof's), formal wear (After Hours Formalwear), and department store bridal registries (Robinsons-May and Macy's). Cost Plus offers more exotic home décor ideas than you can shake a rainstick at. Old Navy, The Children's Place, Gap Kids, and Gymboree are the leaders among the kids' chain stores represented. The only family member who might feel short-changed here is the suit-wearing male who will have better luck at the Fashion Square in Sherman Oaks. With all that Northridge has to offer, including The Apple Store, Borders, and a ten-screen movie theater, it's a shame that it's tucked just far enough out of the way so that you'd never think to go there. However, if you're headed to Sears anyway, for a fridge, new tires, or if you're fairly deep in the West San Fernando Valley, there's no reason not to go check it out. Except, perhaps, for the parking during the summer (see "Drawbacks" below).

Food

The NFC cafés are clean, well lit, and offer outdoor seating. You can choose between a variety of cuisines at restaurants like La Salsa, Sansei, and Surf City Squeeze. The line for Donatello's Pizza is always long, but moves surprisingly fast. Sit-down restaurants in the complex include Topz (hamburgers) and On the Border Mexican Grill. For a break (weather permitting), sit outside on the patio at Wood Ranch BBQ for good food and better people-watching.

Drawbacks

Whether you're coming from the 101 or the 118, the drive along Tampa can be slow. The parking lot fills up quickly too, so in summer you may be in for a long, 100+ degree walk to and from the mall. There is a beautiful Gelson's supermarket nearby—far enough away from the main mall to require moving your car, but close enough to make you feel guilty for doing so.

How to Get There

From the 101 in either direction, exit at Tampa Boulevard and head north on Tampa approximately four miles to Plummer. The mall entrance is on the left. From the 118 in either direction, exit at Tampa Boulevard and head south on Tampa approximately four miles to Plummer. The mall entrance is on the right.

In addition to Macy's, the Paseo features some unexpected offerings for Southern California mall retail: options include Japanese Weekend Maternity Wear, B. Luu, J. Jill, Tommy Bahama, Elements Furniture, and April Cornell. The Bombay Company, Eddie Bauer, Ann Taylor Loft, Brookstone, and KB Toys are all on hand to remind you that, yes, you are in a mall after all. Apart from Macy's, however, the children's clothing options—such as Jacadi—are limited and pricey. As for entertainment (you're still in California), the Pasadena Paseo Theatre shows blockbuster movies on 14 screens.

Food

There isn't one centrally located food court, but there are a variety of good things to eat on the second floor. Sit-down restaurants include Los Angeles favorites, Island's and PF Chang's. It was nothing short of a genius maneuver to put the Cold Stone Creamery within sight of the Pacific Theaters. Summer evenings in Pasadena were made for a post-movie stroll with ice cream cone in hand.

Drawbacks

There is plenty of parking available in the vicinity, though the garage under the Paseo should be avoided at all costs—you're guaranteed to waste time driving in circles, and you'll rarely find a spot. Our directions steer you to a less chaotic option. The restaurants are all on the second floor of the complex, but there isn't one contiguous second floor, which makes finding what you want an up-and-down-the-stairs project. Check the shopping directory before you head up.

How to Get There

From the 134 in either direction, exit at Marengo Avenue and head south on Marengo for a half-mile until you hit Colorado Boulevard. Parking is available in the structure on the right, just past Colorado.

From the 110 N, exit Fair Oaks Boulevard and head north on Fair Oaks to Colorado Boulevard. Turn right and head approximately a half-mile to Marengo Avenue. Turn right at Marengo Avenue to enter parking. There is also parking on the Green Street side of the Paseo. Don't forget to validate your parking ticket!

General Information

NFT Map: 34
Address: 280 E Colorado Blvd
              Pasadena, CA 91101
Phone: 626-795-8891
Website: www.paseocoloradopasadena.com

Shopping

Paseo Colorado, located in the heart of downtown Pasadena, might be peeved to be included in the "malls" section of this book. For the Paseo likes to call itself an "urban village," where people live, work, and shop, all in one stop. Its layout and architecture, designed to encourage pedestrian use of outdoor space, echo both colonial Mexican and classic California craftsman styles. The Paseo Colorado, which stands at the center of the revitalization of downtown Pasadena, presents a relaxing alternative to Old Town (just west on Colorado Boulevard), which often pushes maximum capacity during peak hours.

General Information

NFT Map:	18
Address:	395 Santa Monica Pl
	Santa Monica, CA 90401
Phone:	310-394-1049
Website:	www.santamonicaplace.com

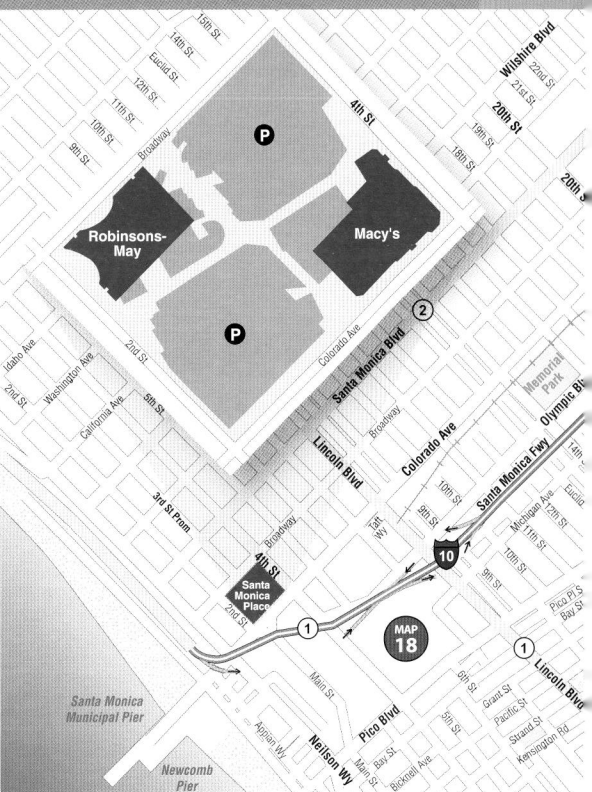

Shopping

Santa Monica Place is a perfectly average mall in a spectacular location. Adjacent to the 3rd Street Promenade, the mall, designed by Frank Gehry in 1980, is barely a quarter-mile from the beach. The location, combined with the usual line-up of unincredible store offerings, make it hard to justify a visit. There are simply better places in the neighborhood to be. Better places, of course, unless it's raining. The typical mall shops serve the local Santa Monica community well for last-minute gifts and clothing necessities. Unless you know that what you're looking for is in one of the stores (Victoria's Secret, Brookstone, Williams-Sonoma, etc.), your best bet is to stroll around and take the mall on its own terms. Santa Monica Place caters to the young, so take your teen-aged niece to the Macy's Junior Department, and then to Wet Seal and Forever 21. Or better still, leave the kids at home and go to Frederick's of Hollywood. (You'll have all the fun without having to brave Hollywood Boulevard.) If you've arrived at the beach unprepared, you can buy bathing suits at Pacific Sunwear or Speedo, and then find some new shades at Sun Shade or Sunglass Hut. (Both have good sales, making it worth at least a drive-by.)

Much to the dismay of local Santa Monicans, proposals are currently underway to renovate Santa Monica Place into a new development that includes office space, residential units, public parks, restaurants, and retail space, in conjunction with the Promenade, the Pier, and the Civic Center (more information about the project is available at www.reimagine-santamonicaplace.com). When the changes will begin to take place remains undecided, but until then, the mall will continue to operate as normal.

Food

The food court is bustling and cacophonous. Hot Dog on a Stick and Charlie Burgers will put you in a good-time mood if you're one of the lucky ones to snag a table, but more likely you'll have to place those orders "to go." For quieter, less greasy dining and waited-on tables, take a stroll down the Promenade to any number of cafés and restaurants, both with indoor and outdoor dining, while watching the street entertainment. Monsoon (1212 3rd Street Promenade) has a daily happy hour, along with sushi and potsticker deals, and Yankee Doodle's (1410 3rd Street Promenade) features 39 screens for sports watching and several pool tables on two levels. Or sample fresh produce at the Farmers' Market on Wednesday and Saturday mornings.

Drawbacks

This particular area of Santa Monica gets particularly congested on the weekends. Pedestrians, some on roller blades or skateboards, will wear out your patience. Once inside the mall, the clientele consists mostly of teens and tourists.

How to Get There

From 10 W, head north on Lincoln Boulevard for a quarter-mile until you hit Colorado Avenue. Head west on Colorado Avenue and enter the parking lot from that side.

From PCH heading east, exit at Ocean Avenue. Turn left on Ocean and then right on Colorado Avenue.

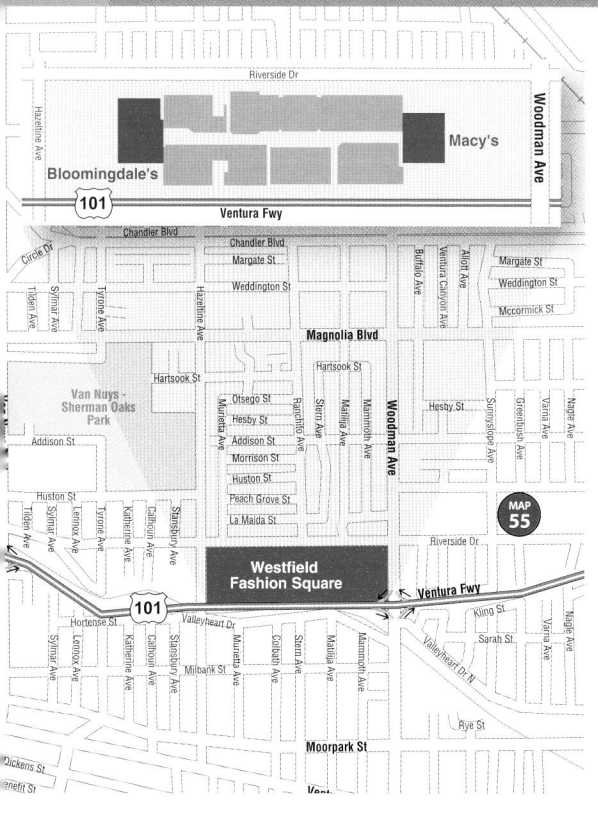

General Information

NFT Map: 55
Address: 14006 Riverside Dr
                   Sherman Oaks, CA 91423
Phone: 818-783-0550
Website: www.westfield.com/fashionsquare

Shopping

A whole spectrum of demographic changes is but one of the interesting side-effects of California's real estate boom. This is particularly true of the Valley, long treated by its southern neighbors "over the hill" like a slightly backward cousin wearing a slutty dress to Buffy and Chip's country club wedding. This perception has yet to catch up with the reality, which is a bit more complicated, and possessed of better taste than "they" might think. Truth is, as home prices spiral out of orbit entirely, more and more young cosmopolitan sorts are moving their families to the Valley. And as if in response, the Fashion Square has taken a more aggressive stance at courting them. In addition to the $55 baby sweaters at the Gap, the mall offers Janie & Jack, Naartjie, Brook's Shoes for Kids, and Kids Footlocker. The source of the high-pitched shrieking you hear is the new kiddie playground at the west end of the mall (lots of plastic surfaces there, folks, so don't forget to pack your Purell). Plus-sized shoppers have options as well—both Bloomingdale's and Macy's have excellent "Woman" departments, and there is also a well-stocked Lane Bryant. (This Macy's, by the way, is famous for its shoe section—epic, busy, thorough, and not for the shrinking violet.) Home décor and any wedding registry needs are pretty much in the bag courtesy of Restoration Hardware, Williams-Sonoma, Z Gallerie, The Verci, The Bombay Company, Pottery Barn Design Studio, and the housewares sections at both department stores. Should the quality family time get to be a bit de trop, you can escape to the Kriza-Aveda Lifestyle Salon and Spa to decompress in an aromatherapeutically correct environment.

Food

The Garden Café Food Court features mall standards—Sbarro, Subway, Great Steak & Potato—but places like California Crisp and Massis Kabob are a nice reminder that you're in LA. Nearby tables are consistently full, so follow the signs upstairs to the additional seating. The line for the Coffee Bean & Tea Leaf is always long—the "Ice Blended" seems to be the official beverage of the Fashion Square. And 59th & Lex, the café on Bloomingdale's third floor, is a good get-away-from-it-all, even if the food isn't great value for the dollar.

Drawbacks

Weekends, the parking lot traffic is deceptively crowded and hostile. Once shoppers are out of their cars and inside the mall, both aggression and density drop dramatically. So don't let the megalomaniacs in the 10 mpg land-barges and the dive bombers in the convertibles deter you. Also, the Fashion Square has neither a movie theater nor a grocery store (though there is a Trader Joe's at the corner of Hazeltine and Riverside).

How to Get There

From the 101 in either direction, exit Woodman. Head north on Woodman one block, and go left onto Riverside. The parking lot can be accessed on both the Riverside and the Hazeltine sides of the mall, though Bloomingdale's shoppers will want to enter on Hazeltine.

General Information

NFT Map: 23
Address: 10800 W Pico Blvd
                Los Angeles, CA 90064
Phone: 310-474-6255
Website: www.westsidepavilion.com

Shopping

The Westside Pavilion is often overshadowed by the more upscale Beverly Center or the outdoor action at The Grove, but this mall holds a few surprises up its escalator. The basics are all here: sizeable anchor stores (Nordstrom and Robinsons-May) and the usual suspects (Banana Republic, Gap, Victoria's Secret, EB Games). There's even a new 51,000-square-foot Macy's Furniture Gallery for more permanent purchases. But the great thing about the Westside Pavilion is that even during the week before Christmas, it hardly feels crowded. Maybe it's the skylights or a genius trick in the layout, but traffic is always comfortably moving along—quite an achievement in LA.

If you're tired of hauling kids around while you go on a shopping spree, plan your trip to the mall during the first or third Wednesday of each month, when Westside Pavilion Kids Club activities offer free recreation. And while a mall is the last place you'd think to check for non-blockbuster flicks, the Westside Pavilion Cinemas specializes in just that—they show indie and foreign films on a tiny screen. Who knows, maybe after watching a depressing French film, buyer's remorse will seem like small potatoes.

Food

All of the major food groups and cuisines are available in the immaculate food court. Not to be missed is Hot Dog on a Stick, serving up fresh lemonade by the best-dressed counter staff on the planet. The best food, however, is just outside the mall: the Apple Pan (10801 W Pico Blvd) is a Los Angeles institution. The small shack serves affordable old-school hickory burgers in a lunch-counter setting.

Drawbacks

Navigating the Westside Pavilion's parking lot basically requires a PhD. Our advice: just rush to the top level and avoid the labyrinth altogether. The Pavilion's location is no help, either. Since it's so close to both the 405 and 10 freeways, making your way around the surrounding streets (especially the biggies like Pico and Westwood) can be a slow-moving pain.

How to Get There

From the Valley, take 405 S and exit at the Pico/Olympic offramp. Make a left to reach Pico Boulevard, and then another left. Continue east on Pico. Westside Pavilion extends from Westwood Boulevard to Overland Avenue. From the South Bay and Orange County, take 405 N, exit at National Boulevard and turn right. Make a left at Westwood Boulevard and travel north until you reach Pico Boulevard. From downtown LA, take 10 W and exit at Overland Avenue. Take a right on Overland Avenue heading north to Pico Boulevard. Westside Pavilion extends west from Overland Avenue to Westwood Boulevard. From Santa Monica, take 10 E and exit at National/Overland. Turn right on National and another right on Overland Avenue. Head north on Overland Avenue to Pico Boulevard.

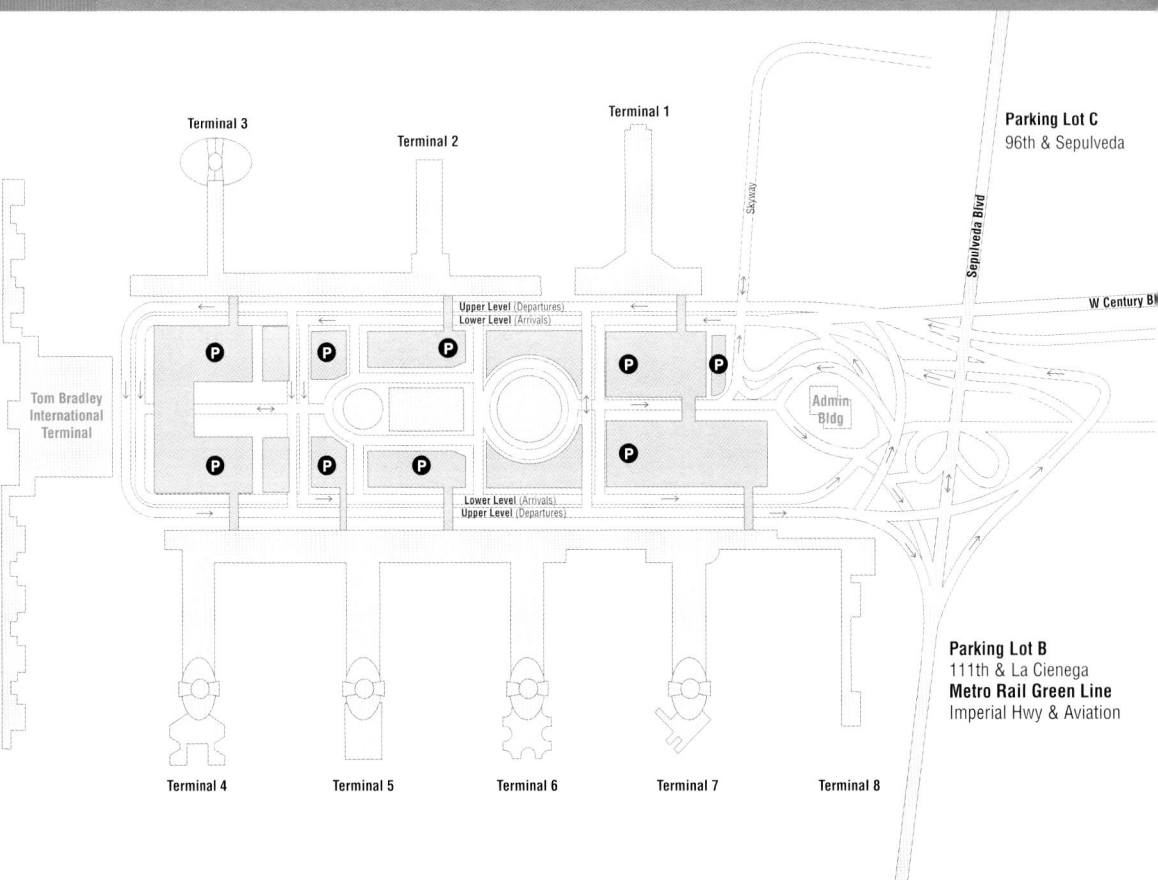

Airline	Terminal	Airline	Terminal	Airline	Terminal
Aer Lingus	TBIT	Champion Air	2	Midwest Express Airlines	3
AeroCalifornia	TBIT	China Airlines	TBIT	Northwest Airlines	2
Aeroflot	TBIT	China Eastern	TBIT	Omni Air International	5
Aerolitoral	5	China Southern Airlines	5	Philippine Airlines	TBIT
Aeromexico	5	Continental Airlines	6	Qantas	TBIT
Air Canada	2	Copa Airlines	6, TBIT	Singapore Airlines	TBIT
Air China	2	Delta Air Lines	5	Song	5
Air France	5, TBIT	El Al	TBIT	Southwest Airlines	1
Air India	TBIT	EVA Air	TBIT	Spirit Airlines	5
Air Jamaica	5	Frontier Airlines	3	Sun Country Airlines	5
Air Mobility Command (AMC)	2	Hawaiian Airlines	2	Swiss Int'l Air Lines	TBIT
Air New Zealand	2	Horizon Air	3	TACA Int'l Airlines	2
Air Pacific	TBIT	Independence Air	3	Ted Airlines	7, 8
Air Tahiti Nui	TBIT	Japan Airlines	TBIT	Thai Airways	TBIT
AirTran Airways	3	KLM Royal Dutch Airlines	2	United Air Lines	6, 7, 8
Alaska Airlines	3, TBIT	Korean Air	TBIT	United Express	7, 8
All Nippon Airways (ANA)	TBIT	LACSA Airlines	2	US Airways	1
America West Airlines	1	LAN Chile	TBIT	Varig Brazilian Airlines	TBIT
American Airlines	4	LAN Peru	TBIT	Virgin Atlantic Airways	2
American Eagle	4	LTU International Airways	TBIT	WestJet	3
American Trans Air (ATA)	2	Lufthansa	TBIT	World Airways	2
Asiana Airlines	TBIT	Malaysia Airlines	TBIT		
Aviacsa Airlines	2	Mesa Airlines	1	*TBIT = Tom Bradley International Terminal*	
British Airways	TBIT	Mexicana Airlines	TBIT		
Cathay Pacific	TBIT	Miami Air	2		

General Information

Address:	1 World Wy
	Los Angeles, CA 90045
Phone:	310-646-5252
Baggage Storage:	310-646-0222
Lost & Found:	310-417-0440
Police:	310-646-7911
First Aid:	310-215-6000
Customs Information:	310-215-2415
Los Angeles MTA:	800-266-6883
Website:	www.lawa.org

Overview

Los Angeles International Airport is one of the busiest airports in the world. But as long as you start out correctly (take the upper ramp for departures, the lower one for arrivals) you'll be just fine. You can't get lost, because it's a big circle—yes, a circle filled with honking traffic, overzealous parking cops, and a hustler or two looking to take advantage of lost tourists. But it's a circle nonetheless.

Give yourself plenty of time to get through the check-in and security lines. Good thing is, once you're through all of the hassle, each terminal offers a variety of places to grab a bite, pick up a magazine, or pep up with a coffee (Starbucks, of course). If you want to avoid eating airline food, try the Wolfgang Puck Café or the Gordon Biersch Brewery. But since security is so tight, you're forced to deal pretty much with whatever is in your airline's terminal.

How to Get There—Driving

The most direct route to LAX is unfortunately not the fastest. The San Diego Freeway (405) to the Century Freeway (105) leads right into the airport. But the 405 is almost always congested. As cab drivers know, surface roads are the preferable way to access LAX whenever possible. From the northern beach cities (Santa Monica, etc.), take Lincoln Boulevard south until it joins Sepulveda Boulevard. This will lead you right to LAX, but be prepared to make a sudden right turn into the airport. From the South Bay, Sepulveda is also the preferred route, but this time the airport will be on your left. The quickest route to LAX from Central LA is La Cienega Boulevard. South of Rodeo, La Cienega becomes a mini-freeway that rarely becomes congested. Take La Cienega to La Tijera Boulevard and go east on La Tijera until you reach Sepulveda. Hang a left onto Sepulveda and drive just a few blocks south until you hit the airport.

How to Get There—Mass Transit

In a word: Don't. Though many buses will take you to LAX, the trip may last longer than your actual flight. Sure, you're getting a lot of bang out of your $1.35 fare, but this is the way to go only if you have time for a "leisurely" ride to the airport. City buses deposit passengers at the LAX Transit Center, where a free shuttle travels to each of the airport's terminals. Another free shuttle connects LAX to the Metro Green Line Aviation Station, where LA's Light Rail system ferries travelers to outlying areas like Redondo Beach (to the south) and Norwalk (to the east).

How to Get There—Really

If you're at all clever, convince a friend to drive you. If that's not an option, car services and taxis are truly the best way to go. Super Shuttle's rates start at under $20 and increase with distance from LAX (800-258-3826; www.supershuttle.com). Most local cab companies also offer a flat rate to LAX that can be economical for parites of two or more. Average cost for a one-way trip from Redondo Beach to LAX is $16; from Santa Monica it's $18; from downtown it's $27; from Van Nuys it's $40 and from Pasadena it's $50. Some taxi services are: Beverly Hills Cab Co. (310-273-6611), Taxi Coop (213-627-7000), and Valley Town Car Service (818-787-1900).

Parking

Two-hour metered parking is available on LAX's Lower/Arrival area opposite Terminals 1, 2A, 2B, 3, 4, 6, and 7. Fifteen minutes costs 25 cents. These spaces can be hard to spot, and you may find yourself in one of the pricier structures opposite each of the terminals. Parking in these lots costs $4 for up to two hours, and $30 maximum. For long-term parking, it's best to use Lots B and C, but be sure to allow an extra half-hour in your schedule for dealing with the parking lot shuttle bus. Lot C is at Sepulveda Boulevard and 96th Street, and rates are $10 for each 24 hours. Lot B is further away, at La Cienega and 111th Street, but less expensive at just $8 per day.

Car Rental

Advantage	310-671-0503
Alamo	800-462-5266
Avis	310-342-9200
Budget	310-215-6854
Dollar	800-800-4000
Enterprise	310-215-6856
Fox/Payless	310-341-3838
Hertz	800-654-3838
National	310-665-1344
Thrifty	310-645-1880

Hotels

Best Western • 640 W Manchester Blvd • 800-233-8060
Comfort Inn • 850 N Sepulveda Blvd • 310-318-1020
Days Inn • 901 W Manchester Blvd • 310-649-0800
Hilton Garden Inn • 21 E Mariposa Blvd •310-726-0100
Marriott Hotel • 5855 W Century Blvd • 310-410-4000
Motel 6 • 5101 W Century Blvd •310-419-1234
Sheraton Gateway • 6101 W Century Blvd • 310-642-1111
Travelodge • 5547 W Century Blvd •310-649-4000

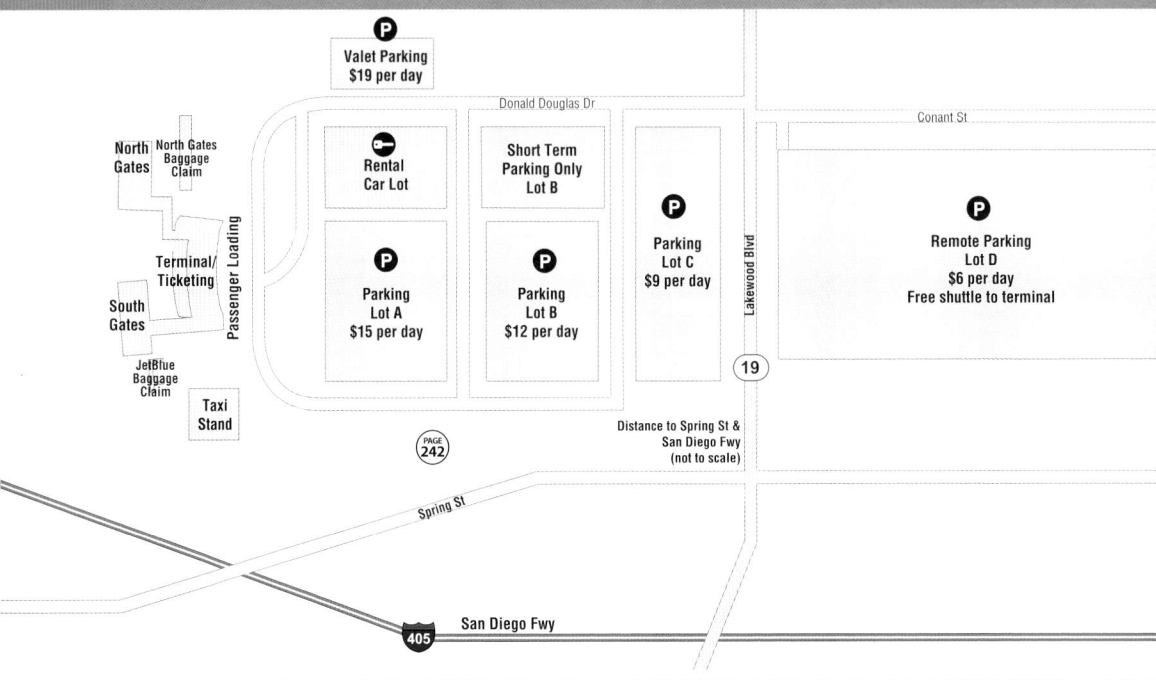

General Information

Address: 4100 Donald Douglas Dr,
Long Beach, CA 90808
Phone: 562-570-2619
Website: www.lgb.org

Overview

What the Long Beach Airport (LGB) lacks in amenities, it makes up for with efficiency. The television show *Wings* comes to mind when popping into the quaint terminal (yes, that's *one* terminal) with its Art Deco style and historical aviation pictures. With a handful of carriers, including the cool and still-inexpensive JetBlue, checking in is a snap. Retrieving your luggage is even easier. And flying in to LGB sure beats the sensory overload of walking out into LAX's smog-ridden, traffic-choked arrivals area.

The best way to get there is by taking a shuttle service. Let someone else deal with the 405 while you read, nap, or crank up the iPod. Oh, and be sure to eat before you go, since your only options are a questionable-at-best snack bar and stuffy upstairs restaurant. A proposed expansion will undoubtedly change the dynamic to some degree, so enjoy it while you can.

How to Get There—Driving

Long Beach Airport can be reached easily from just about anywhere in the Los Angeles basin. From the 405, take the Lakewood Boulevard exit northbound. Proceed past Spring Street to the next stop light, which is Donald Douglas Drive. From the 91, take the Lakewood Boulevard exit and proceed southbound approximately four miles. Make a right at Donald Douglas Drive into the main airport entrance.

How to Get There—Mass Transit

For 90 cents the Long Beach Transit Bus Route 111 runs from Broadway to South Street via Lakewood Boulevard and makes a stop right at the airport (www.lbtransit.com; 562-591-2301). You can take the Blue Line train from downtown LA to the Transit Mall station in Long Beach to connect with the Route 111 bus (www.mta.net; 800-COMMUTE).

Taking a taxi, the best bet is a Long Beach Yellow Cab (562-435-6111). Alternatively, a number of van and limousine services are available including Advantage Ground Transportation (800-752-5211), SuperShuttle (800-BLUE-VAN), Airport Express Limousine (866-800-0700), and Diva Limousine (800-427-DIVA).

Parking

The first twenty minutes in all lots is free. Each hour after that will clock up $1. The maximum daily rate in the long-term parking lots is $15. There is also a $9 per day "Park & Walk" lot at the main airport entrance on the corner of Donald Douglas Drive and Lakewood Boulevard, as well as a $6 per day remote off-site lot at Lakewood Boulevard and Conant Street with a free shuttle to the airport. Valet parking is $19 per day. Short-term parking has a two-hour limit.

Hotels

Holiday Inn • 2640 N Lakewood Blvd, 562-597-4401
Marriott • 4700 Airport Plaza Dr, 562-425-5210
Residence Inn by Marriott • 4111 E Willow St, 562-595-0909

Airlines

Alaska Airlines (North Gates)
America West Airlines
(North Gates)
American Airlines (North Gates)
JetBlue Airways (South Gates)

Car Rental

Avis	800-331-1212
Budget	800-527-0700
Enterprise	800-736-8222
Hertz	800-654-3131
National	800-227-7368

General Information

Address: 18601 Airport Wy
Santa Ana, CA 92707
Phone: 949-252-5200
Lost & Found: 949-252-5000
Website: www.ocair.com

Overview

Though most of us typically associate John Wayne with dusty Hollywood Westerns rather than aviation, Orange County has seen fit to name its only commercial airport after the leather-chapped actor, who was a longtime OC resident. They've even erected an impressive nine-foot bronze statue out front honoring the The Duke in mid-swagger, complete with cowboy hat and spurs. Located well behind the "Orange Curtain," John Wayne Airport (SNA) is quite a trek from LA (approximately fifty miles), but airlines can sometimes make the commute worth your while with lower fares. Aesthetically, the airport makes a solid effort, featuring rotating art exhibits displayed on the Departure level at each end of the terminal. Probably the best thing we can say about John Wayne Airport is that it isn't LAX.

How to Get There—Driving

Driving yourself or tapping that buddy who owes you really big are definitely your best means of transportation to the airport. Sadly, most paths from LA County to John Wayne Airport at some point lead to the 405 Freeway—one of LA's more congested routes. But the 405 will bring you closest to John Wayne, which lies just a short distance from the MacArthur Boulevard exit (CA-73). From downtown or the eastern part of Los Angeles, however, there is another option. Take the Santa Ana Freeway (5 S) to the Costa Mesa Freeway (55 S), exiting at the ramp marked "I-405 S to San Diego/John Wayne Airport" and follow the signs from there.

How to Get There—Mass Transit

From LA? You've got to be kidding. If you're dead-set on taking this course, you'd better have a LOT of free time. Several hours, in fact, as there are no direct bus routes that connect Los Angeles County with John Wayne Airport. However, for only $2.25 the MTA can get you as far as Disneyland on the 460. After the over-two-hour bus ride from downtown LA, get out and stretch your legs with a few rides on Space Mountain, then board Bus 43 heading south toward Costa Mesa, and take this

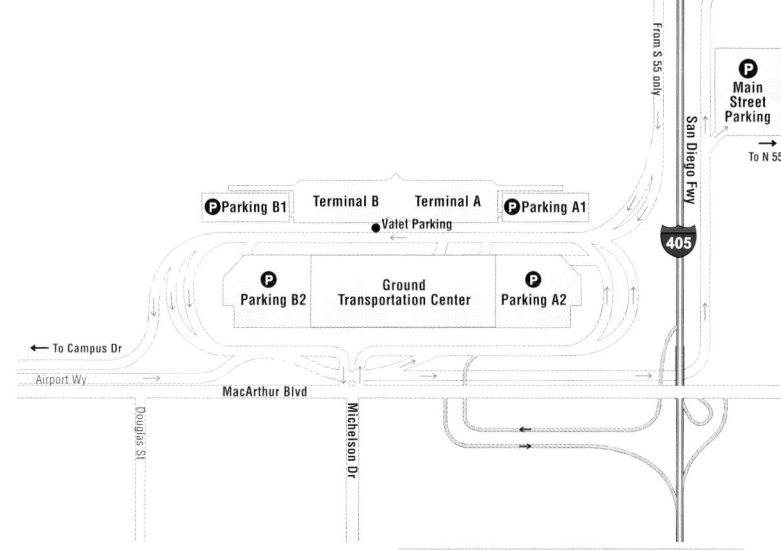

to the corner of Harbor and MacArthur Boulevards. Are we there yet? Hardly. THEN transfer to Bus 76 heading east toward Newport Beach, which will take you right by the airport. All-in-all, you sure saved a bundle going the thrifty route for a grand total of $4.75, but what's that? You say you missed your flight?

How to Get There—Ground Transportation

A taxi ride from Los Angeles to John Wayne Airport starts at about $80. Some companies to consider are Taxi Co-op, (213-627-7000) and the Beverly Hills Cab Company (310-273-6611). Leaving the airport, the John Wayne Airport Yellow Cab Service (800-535-2211) is the only company authorized to pick up fares. They'll charge around $90 from the airport to downtown. Compared to those prices, SuperShuttle (800-258-3826) is a veritable bargain at $65 from downtown LA to John Wayne.

Parking

Short-term lots (A1, A2, B1, and B2) charge $1 per hour, with a $17 maximum per day. The Main Street long-term lot is also $1 per hour, but only $12 per day with a courtesy shuttle to the terminal available every 15 minutes. Selected parking spaces are available in Lots A1 and B1 for a two-hour maximum, and are ideal for dropping people off and picking up, but you still have to fork over that $1. Valet parking costs $23 per day.

Car Rental

On-Site:

Alamo	800-327-9633
Avis	800-230-4898
Budget	800-527-0700
Enterprise	800-736-8222
Hertz	800-654-3131
National	800-227-7368
Thrifty	800-847-4389

Off-Site:

Advantage	800-777-5500
Fox	800-225-4369
Stop-Then-Go	888-704-7867
U-Save	888-757-7687

Hotels

Best Western · 2700 Hotel Terrace Dr,
714-432-8888
Embassy Suites · 1325 E Dyer Rd,
714-241-3800
Holiday Inn · 2726 S Grand Ave,
800-888-5540
Quality Suites · 2701 Hotel Terrace Dr,
714-957-9200
Travelodge · 1400 SE Bristol St,
714-557-8700

Airlines

	Terminal
Alaska Airlines	A
Aloha Airlines	B
America West / America West Express	B
American Airlines / American Eagle	A
Continental Airlines	A
Delta Air Lines / Delta Connection	A
Frontier Airlines	B
Northwest Airlines	B
Southwest Airlines	B
United Air Lines / United Express	B

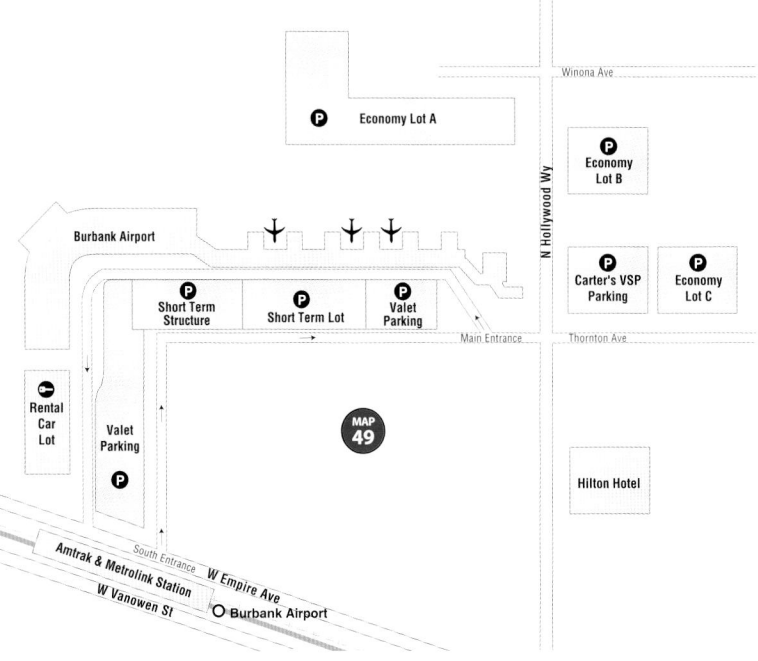

Coach Service to the San Joaquin trains in Bakersfield stops nearby as well. 800-USA-RAIL; www.amtrak.com.

MTA buses are slower but cheaper. Numbers 94, 163, 165, and 394 all make stops at Burbank Airport. 800-COMMUTE; www.mta.net.

Parking

Short-term parking is located in the four-story garage across the entry road from the terminal. It can be pricey if you stick around for more than an hour or two; $2 for the first hour, $4 for the second, $6 for the third, $12 for the fourth, up to a $24 daily maximum. Economy (uncovered) parking in lots A, B, and C is $7 per day. A number of companies also offer covered long-term parking in locations adjacent to the airport. Got more money than time? Valet parking is $17 per day and located a scant 30 yards from the terminal.

Airlines

Alaska Airlines
American Airlines
America West Airlines
Delta Air Lines
JetBlue Airways
Southwest Airlines
United Air Lines

Car Rental

On-Site:
Alamo   800-327-9633
Avis   800-331-1212
Hertz   800-654-3131
National   800-227-7368

Off-Site:
Advantage   800-777-5500
Budget   800-527-0700
Dollar   800-800-4000
Horizon   800-472-8661

Hotels

• Anabelle Hotel • 2011 W Olive Ave, 818-845-7800
• Hilton • 2500 N Hollywood Wy, 818-843-6000
• Hilton • 555 Universal Hollywood Dr, 800-727-7110
• Ramada Inn • 2900 N San Fernando Blvd, 818-843-5955
• Safari Inn • 1911 W Olive Ave, 818-845-8586
• Sheraton • 333 Universal Hollywood Dr, 818-980-1212
• Travelodge • 1112 N Hollywood Wy, 818-845-2408

General Information

NFT Map: 49
Address: 2627 Hollywood Wy
                      Burbank, CA 91505
Phone: 818-840-8840
Parking Information: 818-840-8837
Website: www.bur.com

Overview

Burbank (BUR)—also known as the Bob Hope Airport (LA sure loves naming airports after old celebrities)—is a small, low-key, alternative to LAX, and a must if you live east of La Brea or in the San Fernando or San Gabriel Valleys. (This goes double if you fly Southwest with any regularity, as BUR's short and speedy curb-side check-in and security lines put Terminal 1 at LAX to shame.) When JetBlue announced the inauguration of their Burbank-JFK service this spring, cries of joy could be heard throughout the 213, 323, and 818.

How to Get There—Driving

The airport is just off I-5, so if you're approaching from the north or south, take I-5 and exit at Lincoln Street/Burbank Airport. Head north on San Fernando Boulevard, then turn left onto N Lincoln Street, make a right onto Thornton Avenue. From 101 N, take the Vineland Avenue exit, go north on Vineland for 2.7 miles, turn right onto Victory Boulevard, and then make a left onto N Hollywood Way. From 101 S, take CA-134 E, then take the Vineland Avenue exit and follow the above directions. From the east, take CA-134 west to I-5 and follow the directions given for I-5 above.

It's also possible, and often preferable, to drive to Burbank Airport from parts of the Valley by taking any number of surface roads. Sherman Way is a fairly direct route to the airport from the western end of the Valley. From all other directions, it's best to choose your favorite non-freeway route to Hollywood Way and take that straight into the airport.

How to Get There—Mass Transit

Similar to the rail systems in Europe and Japan, Metrolink and Amtrak trains both go right to the airport—well almost. The terminals are just a short walk or free shuttle bus away.

The Burbank Airport station is on the Ventura County (yellow) Metrolink line and, depending on where you're coming from, during peak hours it will cost between $4.75 one-way (same zone) and $11.75 (if you're starting from the very end of the Orange County Line). Off-peak you can expect to pay between $3.50 and $8.75. 800-371-LINK; www.metrolinktrains.com.

Amtrak's Pacific Surfliner Train (which runs from San Diego to Paso Robles) also makes a stop at the Burbank Airport Rail Station and Amtrak's Motor

Airline	Phone	LAX	John Wayne	Burbank	Long Beach
Aer Lingus	800-474-7424	■			
AeroCalifornia	800-237-6225	■			
Aeroflot	888-340-6400	■			
Aerolitoral	800-237-6639	■			
Aeromexico	800-237-6639	■			
Air Canada	888-247-2262	■			
Air China	800-882-8122	■			
Air France	800-237-2747	■			
Air India	800-223-7776	■			
Air Jamaica	800-523-5585	■			
Air Mobility Command (AMC)	800-851-3144	■			
Air New Zealand	800-262-1234	■			
Air Pacific	800-227-4446	■			
Air Tahiti Nui	877-824-4846	■			
AirTran Airways	800-247-8726	■			
Alaska Airlines	800-426-0333	■	■	■	■
All Nippon Airways (ANA)	800-235-9262	■			
Aloha Airlines	800-367-5250			■	
America West Airlines	800-235-9292	■	■	■	■
American Airlines	800-433-7300	■	■	■	■
American Eagle	800-433-7300	■	■		
American Trans Air	800-225-2995	■			
Asiana Airlines	800-227-4262	■			
Aviacsa Airlines	888-528-4227	■			
British Airways	800-247-9297	■			
Cathay Pacific Airways	800-233-2742	■			
Champion Air	800-922-2606	■			
China Airlines	800-227-5118	■			
China Eastern	626-583-1500	■			
China Southern Airlines	888-338-8988	■			
Continental Airlines	800-525-0280	■	■		
Copa Airlines (Panama)	800-359-2672	■			
Delta Air Lines	800-221-1212	■	■	■	
El Al	800-352-5747	■			
EVA Air	800-695-1188	■			
Frontier Airlines	800-432-1359	■	■		
Hawaiian Airlines	800-367-5320	■			
Horizon Air	800-547-9308	■			
Independence Air	800-359-3594	■			
Japan Airlines	800-525-3663	■			
JetBlue Airways	800-538-2583			■	■
KLM Royal Dutch Airlines	800-225-2525	■			
Korean Air	800-438-5000	■			
LACSA Airlines	800-225-2272	■			
LAN Chile	866-435-9526	■			
LAN Peru	866-435-9526	■			
LTU International Airways	866-266-5588	■			
Lufthansa	800-645-3880	■			
Malaysia Airlines	800-552-9264	■			
Mesa Airlines	800-235-9292	■			
Mexicana Airlines	800-531-7921	■			
Miami Air	305-871-8001	■			
Midwest Express Airlines	800-452-2022	■			
Northwest Airlines	800-225-2525	■	■		
Omni Air International	800-441-5393	■			
Philippine Airlines	800-435-9725	■			
Qantas	800-227-4500	■			
Singapore Airlines	800-742-3333	■			
Song	800-359-7664	■			
Southwest Airlines	800-435-9792	■		■	■
Spirit Airlines	800-772-7117	■			
Sun Country Airlines	800-359-6786	■			
Swiss International Air Lines	877-359-7947	■			
TACA International Airlines	800-535-8780	■			
Ted Airlines	800-225-5833	■			
Thai Airways	800-426-5204	■			
United Air Lines	800-241-6522	■	■	■	
United Express	800-241-6522	■			
US Airways	800-428-4322	■			
Varig Brazilian Airlines	800-468-2744	■			
Virgin Atlantic Airways	800-862-8621	■			
WestJet	888-937-8538	■			
World Airways	800-967-5395	■			

Overview

Driving in Los Angeles is not for the faint of heart. But in a city where geography is destiny, and viable mass transportation options are still thin on the ground (or under it, for that matter), we do what we must. Features peculiar to Los Angeles' motor landscape include: "Sigalerts"(warnings of unusual or hazardous freeway conditions that generally mean the traffic has come to a stand-still), and a rush hour that goes from 7 am to 10 am, and then picks up again at 3 pm and lasts until after 8 pm. Even as gas prices soar to more than $2.50 a gallon, and commutes get longer and longer, no one seems to be driving any less, or any better, and people are still coming to the city in droves. Here are a few NFTsuggestions for surviving the LA roads:

The Ground Rules

1. The best offense is a good defense.

When the law says you have the right of way, don't be so presumptuous as to expect it will be yielded to you. Open your eyes, and pretend you are invisible. Doing so will not make you wimpy, nor does it mean you have admitted defeat: it's just common sense. Judging by the sense of urgency Los Angeles drivers often exhibit, you'd think they were all carrying transplant organs or plasma for the trauma ward in their back seats. But no, they are just completely self-absorbed. So keep your guard up. Knowing that the other guy was in the wrong is not going to make the call to your insurance company any sweeter.

2. Plan a route. And then prepare to abandon it.

For any given drive, there is the logical route—the shortest distance between two points, the freeway, whatever. But, much like the mythical beast that is "right of way," logic doesn't necessarily prevail. Accidents, fallen palm fronds, roadwork, Academy Award festivities—all can wreak havoc on your route of choice. Just as flight attendants instruct you to locate the emergency exit nearest you, we warn you to be aware of where you are at all times, as you may need to bail out quite suddenly.

3. Keep your Thomas Guide within reach.

The Thomas Guide is indispensable, particularly if you ever drive in the hills.

4. Make your left turns, do not let the left turns make you.

Nothing can mess up your progress across town quite like waiting to make a left. Two problems here: not enough left turn arrows to go around (on some kind of endangered species list, apparently), and the major thoroughfares are functioning at 110% capacity (with no arrow, you ain't getting across). How many thousands of hours are lost collectively every day by drivers in Los Angeles waiting to go left onto Third Street from Normandie? From Fairfax onto Wilshire (and that's *with* an arrow)? From Cahuenga onto Sunset? We may never know.

Take control of the turns by taking advantage of other traffic lights. For example: say you're heading west on Sixth Street and need to make the left onto La Brea. This is a sad task, particularly in the morning. But knowing there are traffic lights to assist you, you could instead make a left on Sycamore (one block before La Brea), cross Wilshire at the light, turn right on Eighth Street, and then make your left onto La Brea with the aid

of yet another light. By not trying to wait out La Brea and Sixth, you have also avoided having to pass through the dense mass of vehicles at La Brea and Wilshire. Repeat this often enough and you will find yourself early to appointments and with more free time than you know what to do with.

5. Mind those yellow lights going red.

Simple, but true. First, there's the obvious risk of injury or death to you or your vehicle. But even worse, these days, your chances of getting caught by the law are increasing. More and more intersections are monitored by cameras, which take surprisingly clear photos of you smiling like the cat that caught the canary. The ticket arrives in the mail a few days later, and the fine varies depending upon which city's law you've violated. Consider the photo a "free gift with purchase."

6. You're never really lost in LA.

As long as you know where the hills are, you'll always be able to orient yourself and drive in the right direction. If you're in the Valley, the hills can always be found to the south. On the LA side of Mulholland, the hills are always to your north.

7. All bets are off when it rains.

A mere sprinkle sends LA drivers into a tailspin, leaving accidents in its wake and taking the lead story on the nightly news. Proceed with extreme caution.

Shortcuts

Everybody has discovered at least one shortcut, of which they're extremely proud. Often, they keep these shortcuts even from their children and spouses. But the fact of the matter is that, like knowing where the traffic lights are, there is no way to function in LA without them. Here are a few recommendations:

Downtown

- Avoid the most congested part of the 110: Beaudry to the west and Figueroa to the east offer good alternatives.

- When heading east into downtown, try a more peripheral approach via Second Street or Olympic Boulevard.

Across Town

- Pico is better than Wilshire. Olympic is better than Pico. Venice is better than Olympic. And Washington trumps all of them.

- Strangely, when going through Hollywood, Hollywood Boulevard itself is preferable to Sunset, and can be preferable to Franklin, which backs up at Highland.

- Wilshire Boulevard through Beverly Hills into Westwood can coagulate badly. San Vicente-to-Sunset, and Burton-to-Little Santa Monica to Beverly Glen work well as alternates.

- Though Santa Monica Boulevard is actually a highway (the 2), it is not for cross-town trips, particularly through Hollywood/West Hollywood. Years ago, when asked what advice she had for young actors in Hollywood, Bette Davis is said to have replied, "Take Fountain, dahhling." And what do you know? She's still right—even with the stopsigns and the zig-zag around LeConte Junior High.

North-South

- Normandie moves pretty well between Koreatown and Los Feliz, as does Hillhurst/Virgil.

- Hauser and Cochran move way faster than La Brea, Fairfax, and Crescent Heights.

- Robertson is preferable to La Cienega. Just about everything is preferable to La Cienega.

Westside/Santa Monica

- 23rd Street morphs into Walgrove, getting you to Venice and points south in no time.

- Heading south from Beverly Hills, Beverwil to Castle Heights to Palms to Walgrove comes in handy.

- National Boulevard is a strange and beautiful thing. Almost as strange as San Vicente. If you figure it out, drop us a note.

The Valley

- Moorpark and Riverside can pull through for you when the 101 and Ventura Boulevard fail you (and they will).

- The Hollywood Freeway (the 170) can also help you, particularly if the 101/134 split is heavy.

Getting To and From the Valley

There are several options when traveling between the San Fernando Valley and points south, and none of them are especially attractive.

- The 405 too often turns into a parking lot. You might try Sepulveda Boulevard instead. Nice slalom effect on light days.

- The 101 can be a terror in its own right. If you get on at Highland, as is the case when coming from Hollywood, Hancock Park, and the surrounding areas, you find yourself in the left hand lane—with the rest of traffic moving at the speed of the Autobahn. If Burbank is your destination, you suddenly find yourself with only about 500 yards to cross no less than five lanes of traffic to exit at Barham Boulevard—a true test of one's driving mettle. Screenwriter/playwright Roger Kumble wrote in his play, *Pay or Play*, that there are two kinds of Angelenos, "101 People" and "Cahuenga People." Cahuenga people shy away from this act of bravado and prefer to drive the service road over the hill.

- Canyons: Laurel Canyon becomes less viable daily. Coldwater Canyon backs up just about as easily. Benedict Canyon requires a little finessing. Beverly Glen is the user-friendliest of the four. Head south on Tyrone in Sherman Oaks to get to it.

The Freeways

When the freeway is moving and the weather is dry, Los Angeles is a beautiful place, and you never want to leave. The other 90% of the time, you fantasize about moving to San Francisco. Or about hurting someone.

Here's the thing: all freeways are not created equal, and the 405 is the most unequal of all. Avoid it whenever possible, at least within a ten-mile radius of LAX. If it's at all convenient, La Cienega Boulevard is preferable as a north-south route.

Heading south from Hollywood, La Cienega will actually lead you directly onto the 405, south of the airport, allowing you to overshoot the most common delays.

The 101 is also confusing. It's a north/south road, because its ultimate destination is Northern California, yet it crosses the San Fernando Valley in an east/west direction. The 101 is known as the Hollywood Freeway, at least while you're in Hollywood and Downtown. But once you reach the Valley, the 101 splits off, heading toward Santa Barbara and becomes the Ventura Freeway. If you want to continue on the Hollywood Freeway, you must opt for the 170. Confused yet? Meanwhile, the 134 is known as the Ventura Freeway between I. 5 and I. 2, until it hooks up with the 101, which then becomes the Ventura Freeway. This is the best illustration we know for why the names of freeways are relatively meaningless here in LA.

Though not technically a freeway, the Pacific Coast Highway deserves special mention here. It's one of the most picturesque thoroughfares in LA, running—as its name implies—alongside the Pacific Coast. But this road is plagued by mudslides, brushfires, and floods during the rainy season; and the PCH is often closed to traffic, stranding Malibu residents or forcing them to backtrack inland to pick up the 101. We guess that's the price you pay for beachfront property. (Speaking of beach: the shortest distance between Hollywood and Malibu is the 101 to Malibu Canyon. Period.)

Depending on where you are starting from and where you are going, the 2 and 210 Freeways may save you a lot of time by keeping you out of more congested parts of the city. Just beware of the 2 as it crawls through Echo Park on Alvarado Street.

DMV Locations

800-777-0133; www.dmv.ca.gov; Hours: Mon-Tues: 8 am-5 pm; Wed: 9 am-5 pm; Thurs-Fri: 8 am-5 pm. All DMV offices are open on the third Saturday of every month.

The Department of Motor Vehicles in California handles vehicle registrations and driving records; identification cards and everything to do with driver's licenses; as well as a whole lot of other logistical, vehicle-related things, almost equally as fascinating as the ones listed here. And thanks to our complete dependency on our vehicles, the department manages to dredge up a whopping $5.9 billion in revenue every year. (Maybe we're in the wrong business…)

Office Location	Address	Map
Inglewood	621 N La Brea Ave, Inglewood	2
Hollywood	803 N Cole Ave, Hollywood	3
Hollywood Vine	1600 Vine St, Hollywood	3
Los Angeles	3615 S Hope St, Los Angeles	12
Santa Monica	2235 Colorado Ave, Santa Monica	18
Culver City	11400 Washington Blvd, Los Angeles	24
Hawthorne	3700 W El Segundo Blvd, Hawthorne	28
Torrance	1785 W 220th St, Torrance	32
Lincoln Park	3529 N Mission Rd, Los Angeles	37
Van Nuys	14920 Vanowen St, Van Nuys	43
Glendale	1335 W Glenoaks Blvd, Glendale	49

Overview

9.8 million people live in the 4,061 square-miles of Los Angeles County. And while a railway system does exist, it is buses that make up the majority of LA's public transport network. Most, but not all, of the 300 bus routes through the city are run by the Metropolitan Transportation Authority (MTA). Fares and procedures vary between services. The websites for the services are excellent resources for route and schedule information, as well as trip planning. Fares for seniors, the disabled, and students can be as low as 25% of the full fare, and differ for each service. Monthly passes offer regular riders a smaller discount. Children under the age of five ride free on all services. Most buses don't give change, so be sure to carry exact change when boarding a bus. Fare machines take $1 bills, but they don't give change. If you're planning a multi-stage trip that involves bus, rail, and even Amtrak travel, the Metro Trip Planner website will tell you how to get from point A to point B, and it will conveniently detail times, fares, and directions (for details, see the Metro Trip Planner section on the next page).

Metropolitan Transportation Authority (MTA)

800-266-6883; www.mta.net

MTA buses are distinguished by their white color and distinctive orange and red stripes. Bus stops have a big orange M on a white, rectangular sign. A single fare on an MTA bus costs $1.25 (45¢ for seniors/disabled). A transfer to a municipal bus costs 25¢ (10¢ for seniors/disabled)—ask your driver for one when you board. If you're changing buses again, buy another transfer from the driver when you hand in the first transfer. Transfers are good for an hour after you receive them. If you plan to switch to the Metro Rail, however, you'll have to pay $1.25 again, but at this point, it might be cheaper to purchase a Day Pass, which allows you to board unlimited times for $3. Metro bus night fares (9 pm-5 am) cost 75¢ and 35¢ for seniors/disabled.

Frequent riders can save money by purchasing bags of ten tokens at local stores or supermarkets for $11 (which brings down your per-trip cost to $1.10). If you're a regular bus commuter, you might consider buying a weekly pass ($14), a semi-monthly pass ($27), or regular monthly pass ($52, and $12 for seniors/disabled). You can't just buy the semi-monthly and monthly passes anytime, though. They begin on the 25th or the 11th of each month and can be purchased in person from Metro Customer Centers, or ordered through the mail and delivered to your home or office. MTA passes are valid on Commuter Express, DASH Downtown LA, Community Connection Routes 142, 147, 203, 208, and all Metro MTA rail and bus routes. LADOT passes are not valid on MTA services.

Los Angeles Department of Transportation (LADOT)

818-808-2273; www.ladottransit.com

DASH (Downtown Area Short Hop) shuttle system operates buses A, B, C, D, E, and F throughout downtown LA. The reliable service runs every five to 12 minutes, depending on the time of day and route, and costs only 25¢. The buses service downtown and also stop at the city's major landmark sites, including Union Station, the Convention Center, USC, Exposition Park, and the Garment District. DASH also runs services to many parts of west LA, including Venice, Hollywood, West Hollywood, Beverly Hills, Studio City and Watts, Wilmington, Northridge, Chatsworth, and Crenshaw.

The **Commuter Express** is mainly a commuter service for people living in suburbs such as Culver City, Westwood, Brentwood, Encino, Glendale, Burbank, Redondo Beach, the San Fernando Valley, who work in downtown LA. The fare costs between 90¢ and $3.10. Seniors/disabled pay half the regular fare.

Community Connection serves the needs of city neighborhoods, including San Pedro, Terminal Island, Long Beach Transit Mall, Griffith Park, and Beachwood Canyon. LADOT also operates a battery-powered trolley in San Pedro, which departs every 15 minutes. A one-way fare on the regular bus routes costs 90¢, and 45¢ for seniors/disabled, and the electric trolley costs 25¢ per ride.

Municipal Buses

Santa Monica Bus Lines serve Santa Monica, Malibu, and Venice, and cost 75¢ to race between the beach towns. They also operate an express bus (Line 10) to downtown LA that costs $1.75 (25¢ seniors and disabled). If you buy a "Little Blue Card," you'll save a couple of pennies per ride. The big blue buses are instantly recognizable, and the stops are identified by a blue triangle on a light pole marked "Big Blue Bus." Even Paris Hilton, if she ever rode the bus, could figure this one out. www.bigbluebus.com, 310-451-5444.

The **West Hollywood CityLine** is a shuttle service that covers 18 locations in West Hollywood and costs 25¢ per ride. **West Hollywood Dollar Line** is a free shuttle service available only to seniors and the disabled, 800-447-2189.

Foothill Transit serves primarily the San Gabriel and Pomona Valleys, and fares cost between $1.10 for local trips and $3.75 for express service. Monthly passes cost between $45 for a local pass and up to $133 for a joint Foothills/MTA pass on the most expensive express route; www.foothilltransit.org, 626-967-3147.

Culver CityBus costs 75¢ (50¢ for students, 35¢ for seniors/disabled) and travels between Culver City, Venice, Mar Vista, LAX, and Westwood/UCLA.

Orange County Transit Authority (OCTA)
www.octa.net, 714-636-7433 for Central and North Orange County, 800-636-7433 for South Orange County, Riverside, and Corona.
Regular fare on OCTA buses costs $1.25; senior and disability fares are a mere 50¢. A day pass entitles you to unlimited use of all local routes (excluding express routes 701 & 721) on the day it is purchased and costs $3 ($1 for seniors/disabled). A local monthly pass for OCTA services costs $45 ($15 for seniors/disabled). The express monthly pass (includes daily service to Los Angeles aboard routes 701 and 721) costs $128. Individual journeys on the 701 and 721 express routes to LA cost $3.75 and $2.50 if you have a day pass. (Metrolink monthly passes are now valid on local OCTA services.)

Ventura Intercity Service Transit Authority (VISTA)
www.goventura.org, 800-438-1112
Fixed bus routes will set you back $1 per ride (50¢ for seniors/disabled). Santa Paula and Fillmore dial-a-rides cost $1.50 (75¢ senior/disability), and the Conejo Connection/Coastal Express is $2 ($1 senior/disability). Monthly passes vary between $40 and $75, depending on the routes included in your package.

Metro Trip Planner
Search Engine: mtaweb6.mta.net

The search engine website is one of the best public transport facilities we've ever seen. It covers more than 45 of Southern California's transport networks including MTA buses and trains, OCTA and VISTA buses, Amtrak, Metrolink, MAX, and dozens of municipal services across Southern California.

The search facility prompts you to enter your start point, end point, the day you'd like to travel, the time you need to arrive at your destination, fare category, and special accommodations, such as wheelchairs and bicycles. What you get in return is a detailed itinerary, including the type of transport, where it leaves from, the times it departs and arrives, the fare for each sector, and where you need to transfer. For example, if you were going from Universal Studios to Disneyland, leaving your departure point at noon, you would take the Red Metro Line at Universal City Station (12:16 pm—$1.25, get MTA transfer), get off at 7th Street Metro Center and exit at Figueroa (12:37 pm) and take MTA Bus 460 Anaheim/Disneyland (12:43 pm, show driver transfer and pay $2.25). Get off at Disneyland at 2:39 pm and the entire journey will have cost you $3.50.

Start and end points can be addresses (including residential), intersections, or landmarks, and you can also decide whether you want the fastest itinerary, fewest transfers, or shortest walking distance. It's a good idea to try all three, as the travel times are often similar, and the cost difference is significant. If it doesn't recognize an intersection, reversing the street names sometimes helps. All in all, it's terrific resource for public transportation users—it's more clever and efficient, in fact, than the public transport system it tries to decode.

Union Station

Union Station, built in 1939, is located in downtown Los Angeles on 800 N Alameda Street, between the Santa Ana Freeway (US 101) and Cesar E. Chavez Avenue. Melding Art Deco, Spanish Colonial, and Post-Modern architecture, Union Station is an impressive piece of Los Angeles history. The station services three rail networks—the local Metro Rail Red Line, Amtrak (including the Pacific Sunliner and Coast Starlight Lines), and Southern California's Metrolink. Union Station is also home to the elegant Traxx Restaurant—a good spot to go for lunch, if you want to sample the food and the atmosphere without shelling out big bucks.

Amtrak

800-872-7245; www.amtrak.com

Amtrak, i.e. what passes for a reliable national rail network in this country, runs five major lines into LA's Union Station. The Pacific Surfliner (formerly the San Diegans) runs between San Diego, LA, and Santa Barbara, and on to San Luis Obispo and Paso Robles. You're not guaranteed to arrive on time, but at least you'll have beautiful ocean views to stare at if you're delayed. A one-way trip from San Diego to LA will set you back $30 and will (hopefully) get you there in under three hours. Traveling the length of the line costs around $65. Since the Desert Wind line closed down, Amtrak no longer offers transportation to Las Vegas via train, but they do provide a bus service, which takes between five and six hours, and costs just under $40.

Shuttle service to Bakersfield connects the Pacific Surfliner with the San Joaquin trains, which run from Bakersfield through Fresno to Oakland. The Coast Starlight runs the length of the coast from LA through Oakland, and up to Portland and Seattle. The LA-to-Oakland fare costs between $49 and $70 one-way (buying round-trip is no less expensive than buying two one-way tickets), and if you're traveling all the way to Seattle, you'll be paying between $163 and $195. If you're trying to get to San Francisco, take the train to Oakland and then Amtrak's motor connection to San Francisco, which takes roughly an hour ($74). If you're heading east, the Sunset Limited line will be your train of choice. It runs from LA through Tucson, Phoenix, San Antonio, Houston, New Orleans, Jacksonville, and Orlando. The Texas Eagle has a similar first leg and covers Los Angeles, Tucson, San Antonio, Dallas, Little Rock, St. Louis, and Chicago. The Southwest Chief goes from LA to Kansas City to Chicago. Check the Amtrak website or call to check schedules on the days you wish to travel.

Metrolink

800-371-5465; www.metrolinktrains.com

Not to be confused with the MTA's Metro Rail, Metrolink is an above-ground rail network which serves Southern California, including Los Angeles County, Ventura County, San Bernadino County, Orange County, Riverside County, and San Diego County. The lines run as far south as Oceanside in San Diego County, and as far north as Montalvo in Ventura County and Lancaster in LA County. Fares are calculated according to the number of zones traversed. A one-way fare costs between $4.50 and $11.25 during peak times, and it is always cheaper to purchase a round-trip ticket ($7 peak, one zone) at the beginning of your journey rather than two one-way fares. At $29.50 for one zone ($2.95 per fare) and up to $100.25 for seven zones, the ten-trip pass is a good deal for frequent riders. Discounts are available at all times for senior and disabled riders, and during off-peak hours for youth. Monthly passes are also available at varying rates.

Metro Rail

800-266-6883; www.mta.net

The Metro Rail network is ever-expanding as the city of LA realizes the importance of having an effective rail network, and residents are finally coming around to the idea that taking the Metro Rail is much faster than riding in cars or buses. The Gold Line out to Pasadena opened last year. The Orange Line from North Hollywood to Van Nuys is presently under construction.

It takes a lot to get LA residents out of their cars, but Metro Rail is becoming a popular alternative, particularly for people heading to destinations like the Wiltern, the STAPLES Center, or Universal City—all of which are located just steps from a subway stop.

Police check tickets onboard trains, and if you fail to produce a valid ticket, you'll receive a fine a whole lot higher than the fare. Metro Rail sells monthly metro cards, which cost a little over $50, on their website.

Bikes are allowed onboard the trains only with permits. Call 800-266-6883 and ask for Metro Cycle Express to obtain a permit application. Bicycles are allowed onboard Metro Rail trains during non-peak times and are excluded from boarding weekdays 6 pm-9 am and 3 pm-7 pm. Bicycle racks and lockers are available for use at some Metro stations; bicycle racks are available on a first-come, first-served basis, free of charge. Lockers may be leased through Cycle Express.

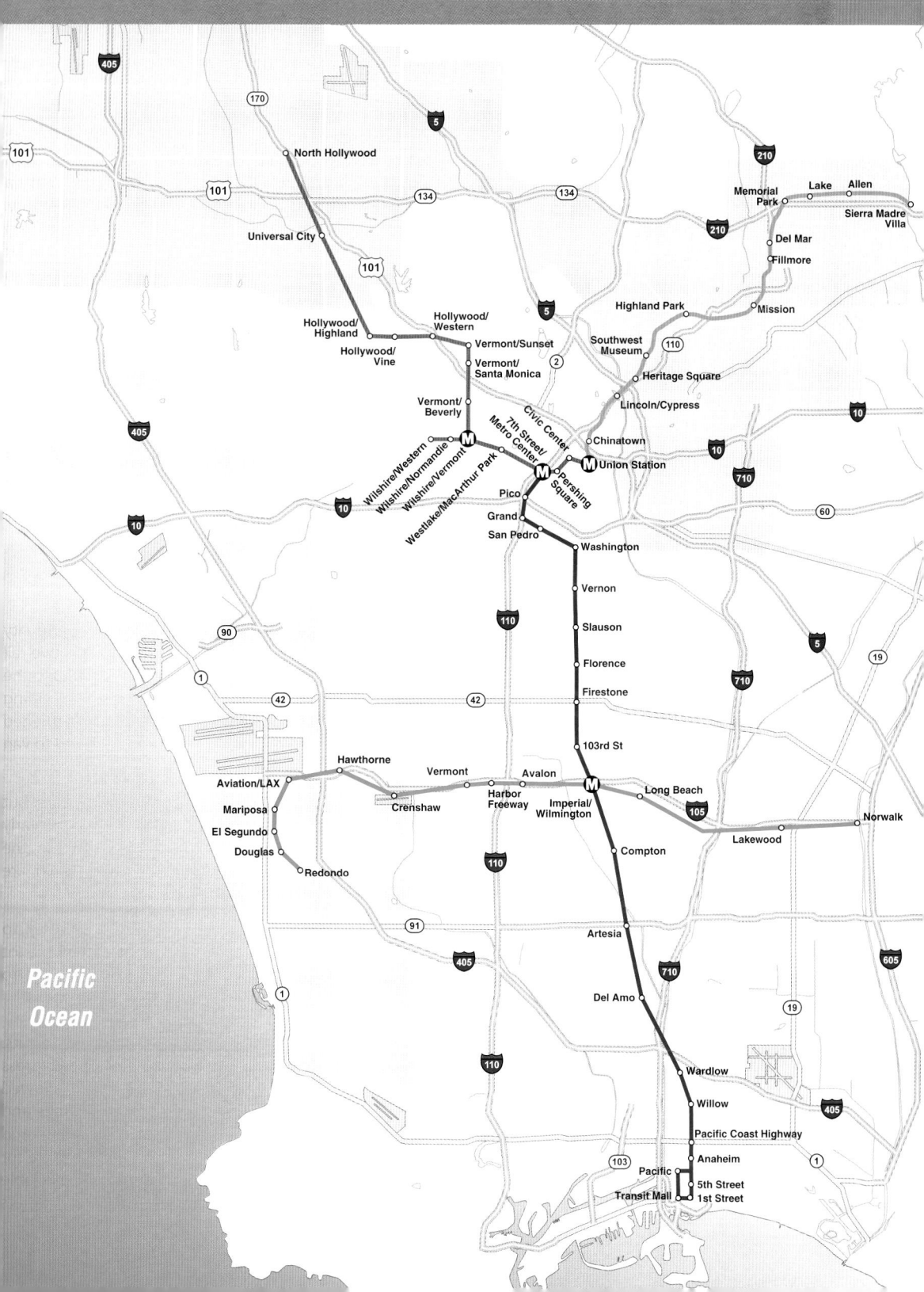

"Turn the world over on its side and everything loose will land in Los Angeles." —Frank Lloyd Wright

Useful Phone Numbers

Emergencies	911
Los Angeles City Hall	213-485-2121
SBC	800-310-2355
CalTrans	213-897-3656
Department of Water & Power	800-342-5397
Southern California Edison	800-655-4555
The Gas Company	800-427-2200

Websites

www.notfortourists.com • The most comprehensive LA site there is. (And no, we weren't paid to say that.)
www.lacity.org • The city's official home on the web.
www.losangeles.com • From buying real estate to planning a night out on the town, this website has it all.
http://trafficinfo.lacity.org • Real-time traffic information.
www.losangelesalmanac.com • It's loaded with everything you could ever want to know about LA.
www.lausd.k12.ca.us • Contact information and report cards for schools in your neighborhood.
www.blacknla.com • Online resource for LA-based African Americans featuring news articles, business listings, and local events.
www.la.com • Online resource for Angeleno luxuries, shopping, events, and nightlife.

Less Practical Information

- Los Angeles averages 329 days of sunshine each year. Yet we still whine about the other 36.
- The longest street in Los Angeles is Sepulveda Boulevard, which runs 76 miles from the San Fernando Valley to Long Beach.
- With few exceptions, LA bars are legally prohibited from serving alcohol between the hours of 2 am and 6 am.
- The Library Tower (633 W Fifth St) is Los Angeles' tallest building (and was spectacularly taken out by aliens in the 1997 blockbuster *Independence Day*).
- The city boasts more stage theaters (80+) and museums (300) than any other city in the US. And New Yorkers say we have no culture.
- There are 527 miles of freeway and 382 miles of conventional highway in Los Angeles County. Bette Midler is determined to clean up all of them.
- Angelenos drive 92 million vehicle miles every day. This gives them ample time to admire the amber hues of our smog-riddled sunsets.
- Annually, LA residents consume over one billion pounds of red meat, over 300 billion pounds of ice cream, and absolutely no carbs whatsoever.

Essential LA Movies

The Big Sleep (1946)
Sunset Boulevard (1950)
Singin' in the Rain (1952)
Rebel Without a Cause (1955)
Chinatown (1974)
Shampoo (1975)
10 (1979)
Blade Runner (1982)
Valley Girl (1983)
Down and Out in Beverly Hills (1986)
Born in East LA (1987)
L.A. Story (1991)
Grand Canyon (1991)
The Player (1992)
Short Cuts (1993)
Pulp Fiction (1994)
Devil in a Blue Dress (1995)
Swingers (1996)
Jackie Brown (1997)
L.A. Confidential (1997)
Volcano (1997)
Laurel Canyon (2002)
Crash (2005)

Essential LA Songs

"Hooray for Hollywood" — Various, written by Johnny Mercer & Richard A. Whiting (1937)
"There's No Business Like Show Business" — Ethel Merman, written by Irving Berlin (1954)
"California Girls" — The Beach Boys (1965)
"Ladies of the Canyon" — Joni Mitchell (1970)
"L.A. Woman" — The Doors (1971)
"I Am, I Said" — Neil Diamond (1971)
"You're So Vain" — Carly Simon (1972)
"Eggs and Sausage" — Tom Waits (1975)
"Hotel California" — The Eagles (1976)
"The Pretender" — Jackson Browne (1976)
"Los Angeles" — X (1980)
"Valley Girl" — Frank and Moon Unit Zappa (1982)
"I Love L.A." — Randy Newman (1983)
"My Life is Good" — Randy Newman (1983)
"Sunset Grill" — Don Henley (1984)
"Paradise City" — Guns N Roses (1987)
"F— Tha Police" — N.W.A. (1988)
"Free Fallin'" — Tom Petty (1989)
"Neighborhood" — Los Lobos (1990)
"All I Wanna Do" — Sheryl Crow (1993)
"California Love" — Tupac Shakur (1995)
"Californication" — Red Hot Chili Peppers (1999)

Los Angeles Timeline—a timeline of significant events in the history of Los Angeles (by no means complete)

1781: El Pueble de Nuestra Senora de la Reina de Los Angeles de Porciuncula—AKA, Los Angeles—is founded.

1822: Los Angeles becomes a Mexican City when Mexico wins its independence from Spain.

1842: Gold rush hits Southern California.

1850: LA County is established, City of LA is incorporated.

1880: USC is founded.

1881: Rail lines between LA and the East Coast are completed.

1881: *The LA Times* begins printing.

1882: Electricity comes to downtown LA.

1890: First Tournament of Roses Parade.

1891: CalTech opens its doors.

1892: Abbott Kinney stakes his claim in Venice.

1894: Labor rioting breaks out in LA during national railroad strike.

1896: Griffith J. Griffith donates land that will become Griffith Park.

1899: LA Stock Exchange opens.

1902: City's first movie theater opens for business.

1909: Construction on LA aqueduct begins.

1910: Alice Stebbins Wells appointed to LA police force as the nation's first female policewoman.

1913: The Los Angeles Aqueduct brings water from the Owens Valley.

1915: Universal Studios opens.

1915: San Fernando Valley annexed by City of LA.

1919: UCLA is formed.

1922: Hollywood Bowl opens.

1923: The Hollywood Sign is erected.

1932: Tenth Olympic Games are held in LA.

1939: Union Station opens.

1940: Pasadena Freeway (later the 110) is LA's first freeway.

1946: KTLA is LA's first commercial television station.

1947: Black Dahlia murder. The case is never solved.

1953: The famed "four-level" opens, linking the 101 and 110 freeways.

1954: Completion of the Watts Towers.

1955: Disneyland opens.

1958: The Dodgers relocate from Brooklyn.

1960: The Lakers leave Minneapolis for LA.

1964: The Music Center opens Downtown.

1965: LACMA opens its door.

1965: The Watts Riots.

1968: Robert Kennedy assassinated at Ambassador Hotel.

1969: Manson Murders.

1971: Sylmar Earthquake.

1974: J. Paul Getty Museum opens in Pacific Palisades.

1980: Screen Actors Guild strike.

1984: The 23rd Olympics are held in LA.

1985: LA Lakers finally beat the Boston Celtics to take out NBA honors after losing nine finals to them previously.

1989: Mayor Tom Bradley elected to an unprecedented fifth term.

1991: Rodney King is beaten by four police officers.

1992: Verdict in King case leads to citywide rioting.

1992: Landers earthquake.

1993: Menendez murder trial #1.

1994: O.J. Simpson arrested after slow-speed chase.

1994: Northridge earthquake.

1995: Menendez murder trial #2.

1995: If it doesn't fit, you must acquit: O.J. found not guilty.

1995: Departure of Rams and Raiders leaves LA without a football team.

1997: The Getty Center opens in Brentwood.

2000: LA Lakers defeat Indiana Pacers for NBA title.

2001: Back-to-back NBA Championships for the LA Lakers.

2001: First championship for the WNBA's LA Sparks.

2002: Three-peat for the LA Lakers and Phil Jackson.

2002: Back-to-back WNBA Championships for the LA Sparks.

2002: Anaheim Angels win their first World Series.

2003: Famed Austrian-bodybuilder-turned-Hollywood-action-star adds another hyphenate. Arnold Schwarzenegger runs for the position of Governor of California during the recall election and wins.

2005: Actor and former child star Robert Blake found not guilty of his wife Bonnie Lee Bakley's murder.

2005: The city elects its first Latino mayor in 130 years.

Living in your car is a way of life for Angelenos. So, like it or not, you probably know your favorite drive time DJs a little too well, thanks to your inevitable commute. The good news is that LA offers some of the most diverse radio programming anywhere, so there's always something to fit your mood—even if it involves a case of road rage.

AM Stations

Station	Format	Noteworthy Programs
570 KLAC	Talk	Lakers games and music so old it's cool.
600 KOGO	Talk	Talk with a conservative slant. Home of Dr. Laura, Art Bell, and, of course, Rush.
640 KFI	Talk	Talk radio that'll push your buttons, from Rush Limbaugh to Matt Drudge.
690 XETRA	Sports/Talk	UCLA basketball and football, as well as the Jim Rome show.
710 KSPN	ESPN Radio	Sports, sports, sports.
740 KBRT	Religious	The Word from Above broadcast from…Catalina Island!
790 KABC	News/Talk	Larry Elder, Bill O'Reilly, et al.
830 KPLS	Spanish	
870 KRLA	Talk	Lots of shows about health.
900 KALI	Spanish/Religious	
930 KHJ	Spanish/News	Regional Mexican music.
980 KFWB	News	Their traffic reports are a must-listen for commuters.
1020 KTNQ	News/Talk (Spanish)	Galaxy soccer games.

Station	Format	Noteworthy Programs
1070 KNX	News	All news, all the time.
1110 KDIS	Radio Disney	Mickey Mouse, squeaky-clean pop tunes, and, of course, death metal.
1150 KXTA	Sports/Talk	Fox's radio affiliate. Dodger games are heard here.
1190 KEZY	Variety/Foreign Language	
1230 KYPA	Korean	Radio Korea.
1260 KJAZ	Jazz	Everyone knows what this is.
1280 KFRN	Religious	"Family Radio."
1300 KAZN	Chinese	
1330 KWKW	Talk (Spanish)	News, talk, sports, and Laker games en español.
1390 KLTX	Spanish/Religious	
1430 KALI	Spanish	
1460 KTYM	Religious/Foreign language	
1510 KSPA	Oldies	Standards.
1540 KMPC	Sports	The Phil Jackson Show, The Sporting News.
1580 KBLA	Korean	Korean-language news, music, and lifestyle programming.
1650 KFOX	Korean	

FM Stations

Station	Format	Noteworthy Programs
88.1 KKJZ	Jazz & Blues	
88.5 KCSN	Classical/BBC	Their diverse line-up includes a Sunday morning commercial-free Beatles show.
88.7 KSPC	Alternative	College radio at its most bizarre.
88.9 KXLU	Eclectic	More college radio. Sample as you like.
89.3 KPCC	Eclectic/NPR	Lots of radio gameshows, and the often-fascinating "AirTalk" with Larry Mantle.
89.9 KCRW	Eclectic/NPR	"Morning Becomes Eclectic" breaks new bands; clever programming gives your brain a workout too.
90.7 KPFK	Eclectic/Political	Talk radio with a very liberal slant.
91.5 KUSC	Classical	Relaxing classical, even in horrible traffic.
92.3 KHHT	R&B Oldies	Legendary Art Leboe knows how to get you in the mood.
92.7 KLIT	Adult Contemporary	
93.1 KCBS	Classic Rock/Pop	Some classic rock and a lotta hits make "Jack FM" a good deal.
93.5 KDAY	Hip-hop/R&B	Old and new hip-hop; features Dr. Dre—both of them!
93.9 KZLA	Country	
94.3 KBUA	Spanish	
94.7 KTWV	Smooth Jazz	"The Wave" is for fans of Kenny G and John Tesh.
95.1 KFRG	Country	"K-Frog" takes its amphibious theme very seriously.
95.5 KLOS	Classic Rock	Mark & Brian in the morning, and old-fashioned rock-and-roll all day.
95.9 KFSH	Contemporary Christian	Ultra clean-cut Christian pop and rock music.
96.3 KXOL	Spanish	Spanish pop and dance music.
96.7 KWIZ	Spanish	Spanish programming.
97.1 KLSX	Talk	Tons of guy chatter, especially when Tom Leykis rules the afternoon.
97.5 KLYY	Spanish Pop/Rock	Modern Spanish hits.

Station	Format	Noteworthy Programs
97.9 KLAX	Mexican	Regional Mexican.
98.3 KRCV	Spanish	
98.7 KYSR	Adult Contemporary	Danny Bonaduce does the morning, adult alternative fills out the rest.
99.1 KGGI	Urban Contemporary	
99.5 KKLA	Religious	Religious talk radio.
99.9 KOLA	Rock Oldies	Plenty of '60s and '70s tunes, plus Beatles Brunch on Sundays.
100.3 KKBT	Urban Contemporary	Steve Harvey handles the morning shift; the mix shows are amazing.
101.1 KRTH	Oldies	It's always a kinder, gentler time on K-Earth.
101.9 KSCA	Spanish	Regional Mexican.
102.3 KJLH	R&B	Owner Stevie Wonder keeps this smooth station on track.
102.7 KIIS	Top 40	Find Ryan Seacrest here, plus more pop than you can handle.
103.1 KDLD	Indie	Totally alternative with the Sex Pistols' Steve Jones and other celeb DJs.
103.5 KOST	Adult Contemporary	Dedications all night with "Love Songs on the KOST."
103.9 KRCD	Spanish	Shares a signal with 98.3 KRCV.
104.3 KBIG	Adult Contemporary	Music from the '70s, '80s, and '90s. And occasionally the '00s.
105.1 KMZT	Classical	"K-Mozart" will have you "air-conducting" in your car.
105.9 KPWR	Dance/Urban	Big Boy's morning show cracks us up; the beats bounce the rest of the day.
106.3 KALI	Vietnamese	
106.7 KROQ	Modern Rock	Heavy on the hard stuff, this influential station breaks new bands all the time.
107.1 KSSE	Spanish	
107.5 KLVE	Spanish	Spanish adult contemporary.
107.9 KWVE	Religious	

January

	Location	Description
› Tournament of Roses Parade	Pasadena. Just follow the crowds.	A Southern California tradition. 117 years and counting. (Jan 2)
› Rose Bowl	The Rose Bowl, of course	"The Granddaddy of All Bowl Games." (Jan 1)
› Japanese New Year "Oshogatsu"	Little Tokyo Celebration	Soothe your New Year's hangover with the sound of Taiko drums. (Jan 1)
› Greater LA Auto Show	LA Convention Center	Cars, cars, and, yes, more cars. (Jan 6-15)
› Golden Globe Awards	Beverly Hilton Hotel	Unlike at the Oscars, the stars are allowed to drink, which leads to occasional embarrassing moments. (Third Sunday in Jan).
› Kingdom Day Parade	Martin Luther King Blvd, at Crenshaw, at Grevillea Park	Parade commemorating the life of MLK, Jr. (Jan 16)
› Chinese New Year	Chinatown & various locations	Features a parade, a street fair, and even a golf tournament. (Jan, Feb, or Mar)
› LA Times Travel Show	Long Beach Convention Center	Get outta town—at least in your head (Jan 27-29)

February

	Location	Description
› Lunar New Year Parade & Festival	Pasadena	Parade along Colorado Blvd. (Feb 9)
› Firecracker Run 5K/10K	N Broadway & College St, Chinatown	Race celebrating Chinese New Year. (Feb 12)
Pan African Film & Arts Festival	Magic Johnson Theaters 3650 Martin Luther King Jr Blvd	One of America's largest festivals of black films and fine arts. (Mid Feb)
› Mardi Gras	El Pueblo Historical Monument, 125 Paseo de la Plaza	Celebrate "Fat Tuesday" on Olvera Street. (Feb 28).
› Brazilian Carnaval	Hollywood Palladium, Sunset & Vine	Samba your way down the Walk of Fame. (Mid-Feb)
› Nissan Open	Riviera Country Club, Pacific Palisades	The PGA championships come to the Westside. (Late Feb)
› Queen Mary Scottish Festival	Long Beach	Relocated from Hollywood, just don't salsa the boat over. (Feb 19-20)
› Ragga Muffins Festival	Long Beach Arena	Bob Marley's b-day celebration. (Feb 19-20)
› Black History Parade & Festival	Jackie Robinson Center, Pasadena	Food, kids' play area, and the Black Inventions Museum. (Mid-Feb)

March

	Location	Description
Academy Awards	Kodak Theatre, Hollywood Blvd & Highland Ave	More revered as an LA holiday than Presidents' Day. (Mar 5)
› Los Angeles Marathon	Throughout LA	The one day a year we choose not to drive. (Mar 5)
› WestWeek	Pacific Design Center, WeHo	An interior design fest! (Last week of Mar).
› Cesar E. Chavez Day	Olvera St	Honors the Mexican American farm labor leader. (Mar 31)
› Big Bunny's Spring Fling	LA Zoo	Kiddie crafts and photo ops with "Big Bunny." (Weekend of Easter Sunday)
Wizard World Convention	LA Convention Center	Wizard's answer to ComiCon equals magical geeks! (Mar 17-19)

April

	Location	Description
Pasadena Cherry Blossom Festival	Rose Bowl	Japanese culture, great food, cool fighting. (first weekend in April)
Blessing of the Animals	Olvera St	Check out the parade of house pets and wild animals. (Saturday before Easter)
Bunka Sai Japanese Cultural Festival	Ken Miller Rec Center, Torrance	Japanese culture, from judo to origami. (Mid-Apr)
Garifuna Street Fest	Avalon Blvd, South Central LA	Celebrates largest Black ethnic group in Central America. (Apr 12)
Jimmy Stewart Relay	Griffith Park	Like running a marathon, but with help. (Apr 23)
Eco Maya Mother Earth Day Festival	Los Angeles City College	Ecology and the cooking of the Largest Tamal in the World (Last week in Apr)
50+ Fitness Jamboree & Health Expo	Griffith Park	Includes 1K and 5K walks with celebrity seniors. (Last week in Apr)
Toyota Grand Prix of Long Beach	Downtown Long Beach	Auto racing. (Apr 7-9)
Los Angeles Times Festival of Books	UCLA campus	The city's biggest and coolest literary event (because we usually have a table). (Apr 29-30)
Blooming of the Roses	Exposition Park Rose Garden	Stop and smell the roses. Literally. (Last week in Apr)
Annual Arbor Day Festival	Cheviot Hills Park & Recreation Center	Trees aren't just for hugging.
Dolo Coker Scholarship Benefit Jazz Concert	Founder's Church, 3281 W 6th St	Supports young jazz hopefuls. (Mid-Apr)
Santa Anita Derby	Santa Anita Racetrack, Arcadia	Big pre-Kentucky Derby race and festival. (Apr 8)
Renaissance Pleasure Faire	Santa Fe Dam Recreation Area, Irwindale	Maidens, meade, and minstrels. (Apr- May)
LA Zoo Earth Day Expo	LA Zoo	Meet Rascal the Recycling Raccoon. (Apr 22-23)
Los Angeles Antiques Show	Santa Monica Air Center, Barker Hangar	Antiques galore. (Apr 28-29)
Indian Film Festival	ArcLight Cinemas, Hollywood	Go beyond Bollywood. (last two weekends of April)

May

	Location	Description
• Fiesta Broadway	Downtown LA	The largest Cinco de Mayo celebration in the world. (May 1)
• Cinco de Mayo Celebration	Olvera St	Celebrate Mexico's victory over the French. Que bueno! (May 5)
• LA Asian Pacific Film & Video Festival	Various locations	Showcases works by Pacific-American and international artists. (late April-early May)
• Revlon Run/Walk for Women	LA Memorial Coliseum, Exposition Park	5K race raises money for women's cancer causes. (May 13)
• Family FunFest and Kodomo-no-Hi Children's Day Celebration	Japanese American Cultural & Community Center, Little Tokyo	Celebrate kids the Japanese way. (mid-May)
• Israeli Festival	Woodley Park, Van Nuys	Annual commemoration of Israel's Independence Day. (May 2)
• NOHO Theater & Arts Festival	Lankershim Blvd & Magnolia, North Hollywood	Performances scattered throughout the NOHO arts district. (mid-May)
• Affaire in the Gardens Art Show	Beverly Gardens Park, Beverly Hills	Art show. (May-20-21 and mid-Oct)
• Venice Artwalk	Victoria Ave & Venice Canals	Community art & architecture on display to benefit Venice Family Clinic. (May 21)
• Huntington Gardens Annual Plant Sale	San Marino	Let your garden grow. (mid-May)
• Festival Dia de Las Madres	Vermont Ave & 8th St Downtown	Mother's Day street fair with food from Mexico, the Caribbean, and Latin America. (May 10)
• E3 Eletronic Entertainment Expo	LA Convention Center	Boys and their toys (okay, some girls, too). (May 10-12)
• Old Pasadena Summer Fest	Rose Bowl	Five fests in one range from eating to sports. (May 29)

June

• Art & Design Walk	West Hollywood	Walk into 300+ showrooms, galleries, and boutiques. (June 3)
• Life Cycle	San Francisco to Los Angeles	585-mile bicycle ride for AIDS-related charities. (June 4-10)
• Kids' Nature Festival	Temescal Gateway Park, Pacific Palisades	Letting kids interact with nature. (mid-June)
• Los Angeles Film Festival	Hollywood	A breath of cinematic fresh air.
• JMP Jazz & Blues Festival	Leimert Park Village	Performances by jazz and blues greats and their protégés.
• Great American Irish Fair & Music Festival	Irvine	St. Patrick's Day in the summer. (mid-June)
• Playboy Jazz Festival	Hollywood Bowl	Almost more jazz than you can handle.
• Mariachi-USA Festival	Hollywood Bowl	Traditional mariachi music, as well as Ballet Foklorico. (mid-June)
• Christopher Street West	West Hollywood Park	Celebrates gay pride. (mid-June)
• ArtWallah Festival of South Asian Arts	Barnsdall Art Park	Art festival of the South Asian Diaspora.
• Long Beach Chili Cook-off	Long Beach Marina Green	The competition really heats up (bad pun intended). (mid-June)

July

• At the Beach, LA Black Pride Festival	Westin Airport Hotel Point Dume Beach in Malibu	Largest annual gathering of African-American lesbians and gay men in the world. (early Jul)
• Mercedes-Benz Cup	LA Tennis Center, UCLA	ATP International Series tennis event. (last week in Jul)
• Outfest	DGA, 7920 Sunset Blvd	Gay and lesbian film festival. (Jul 6-17)
• Lotus Festival	Echo Park Lake	Celebrates Asian and Pacific cultures. (mid-Jul)
• Central Avenue Jazz Festival	Central Ave b/w 42nd & 43rd Sts	Remembers Central Avenue as the hot spot it was in the 1920s-'50s.
• Twilight Dance Series	Santa Monica Pier	Dance away every Thursday in July.

August

• Long Beach Jazz Festival	Long Beach	Jazz by the sea. (mid-Aug)
• Nisei Week Japanese Festival	Little Tokyo	Celebrating Asian culture and community. (Aug 13-21)
• Marcus Garvey Day Parade & Festival	Elegant Manor, 3115 W Adams Blvd	Invites all to celebrate "Africa for the Africans at home or abroad." (mid-Aug)
• Sunset Junction Street Fair	3600 to 4600 Sunset Blvd, LA	One of LA's funkiest neighborhoods puts on a fair. (Late Aug)

September

	Location	Description
• Long Beach Blues Festival	Cal State Long Beach	Spend Labor Day weekend with blues heavyweights. (Sept 4)
• LA International Short Film Festival	ArcLight Cinemas, Hollywood	For movie lovers with short attention spans. (mid-Sept)
• LA Greek Fest	St. Sophia Cathedral	Eat a gyro, break a plate. (Sept 9-11)
• Emmy Awards	Shrine Auditorium	TV's night to shine. (mid-Sept)
• Lobster Festival	Location varies	Great food, good music, family fun, and cheap Maine Lobster. (Sept 22-24)
• Los Angeles City Birthday Celebration	El Pueblo Historical Monument, 125 Paseo de la Plaza	Happy Birthday, dear LA-ay, Happy Birthday to you! (Sept 4)
• Salvadoran Parade & Festival	LA City College	All things Salvadoran. (mid-Sept)
• Mexican Independence Celebration	Olvera St	Traditional Mexican foods and entertainment. (Sept 15-17)
• LA County Fair	Fairplex in Pomona	Livestock, rides, and food on a stick. (Sept-Oct)
• Brazilian Street Carnival	Downtown Long Beach Promenade Theatre	Rio Brazilian fun.
• Thai Cultural Day	Location varies	Day-long celebration of Thailand. (mid-Sept)
• Silver Lake Film Festival	Silver Lake	Thinks it's the coolest film fest in town. (Last week in Sept)
• Taste of Santa Monica	Santa Monica Pier	40 of the area's top restaurants participate. (Sept 17)
• Abbot Kinney Boulevard Festival	Abbot Kinney Blvd, Venice	Over 200 local arts & crafts vendors unite. (Sept 26)

October

	Location	Description
• Asian American Jazz Festival	Luckman Fine Arts Complex, CSULA	Spotlights Asian-American jazz musicians.
• West Hollywood Halloween & Costume Carnival	West Hollywood	Fabu costumes make this the biggest bash in the nation.
• AIDS Walk	West Hollywood Park	10K walkathon raises money for AIDS-related organizations.
• Affaire in the Gardens	Beverly Gardens Park, Beverly Hills	Twice-yearly art show.
• Oktoberfest	Alpine Village, Torrance	German music, German beer, American hangover.
• Feria de los Ninos Celebration	Hollenbeck Park, East LA	Ethnic food and entertainment with an emphasis on family-friendly activities.
• Echo Park Arts Festival	Various	One of LA's artiest communities' time to shine.
• Harvest Festival of the ARTS	Pico Union Alvarado Terrace Park	Raising children's self-esteem through art.
• KTLA KIDS Day LA Celebration	Exposition Park and Recreation Center	Forget the kids. We want to hang out with Jennifer York.
• International Festival of Masks	LA Craft & Folk Art Museum	Celebrates mask-making all around the world.
• Autumn in the Japanese Garden	Japanese Garden, 6100 Woodley Ave, Van Nuys	Learn origami or just stroll through the garden.
• Shipwreck Halloween Terrorfest	Queen Mary, Long Beach	Mazes and monsters on a real haunted boat!
• Fall Festival at the Farmer's Market	Farmer's Market, Los Angeles	Carve a pumpkin, watch the leaves turn.
• Long Beach Marathon	Long Beach	In case the LA Marathon didn't wear you out.
• Day of the Dead	Hollywood Forever Cemetery	A true dead man's party.

November

	Location	Description
• Dia de los Muertos Celebration	Olvera St	Traditional celebration of Mexico's Day of the Dead. (Nov 1-2)
• Arroyo Arts Collective Discovery Tour	Tour begins at Lummis Home, 200 E Ave 43	Local artists kindly open up their homes and studios. (mid-Nov)
• Three Stooges Big Screen Event	Alex Theatre, 216 Brand Blvd, Glendale	Surely this will only interest silly cinephiles. (late-Nov)
• Doo Dah Parade	Colorado Blvd, Pasadena	Irreverent spoof of the more stately Rose Parade. (Nov 25)
• Beverly Hills Flower & Garden Festival	Greystone Estate	Designer gardens, lectures, and tours. (mid-Nov)
• Blockbuster Hollywood Spectacular	Hollywood Blvd, from Grauman's Chinese Theatre to Vine St	We still like to think of it as the Hollywood Christmas Parade. (Thanksgiving weekend)
• Downtown on Ice, Winter Wonderland Skating Rink	Pershing Sq	Pretend you're at a tiny version of Rockefeller Center. (Nov-Dec)
• Griffith Park Holiday Light Festival	Crystal Springs Rd, Griffith Park	Drive-thru tour of impressive lighting displays. (Nov-Dec)

December

	Location	Description
• KROQ Acoustic Christmas	Universal Amphitheatre	Hot alternative bands feel the spirit of the season. (mid-Dec)
• Marina del Rey Holiday Boat Parade	Main Channel, Marina del Rey	Imaginatively lit boats by crazy locals. (mid-Dec)
• Navidad en la Calle Ocho	8th St at Normandie Ave	8th Street's answer to the Hollywood Christmas Parade. (late Dec)
• Las Posadas	Olvera St	Candlelit reenactment of Mary and Joseph's journey to Bethlehem. (Dec 25)
• Reindeer Romp	Los Angeles Zoo	No, seriously, real reindeer. (late Dec)
• Long Beach Christmas Boat Parade of the Thousand Lights	Long Beach Downtown Marina	That's a lotta lights! (Dec 25)

323

From Julia to Gwyneth, or Courtney to Denise, these days the LA chic are more likely to have a child in tow than a Louis Vuitton Murakami bag. Just when you think you've learned to navigate LA in your previously unencumbered form, you suddenly find yourself stumbling through a new maze of baby Gaps, Mommy & Mes, and indoor gyms. There are two awesome things about parenting in LA: We drive almost everywhere, so there's no need to figure out how to fit your Combi Twin Savvy Double Stroller down the narrow aisle of a public bus. And even better—no snowsuits or mittens. Ever. That alone makes dealing with the smog that much more bearable. We'd need an entire book to point out every store or playground to make your rugrat's life richer, but here's a sampling of information that will hopefully make your life a little easier.

Essentials

Kids come into the world with nothing, yet by their first birthday their stuff fills up at least half the rooms in your house. Where does all of this accoutrement come from? Well, we can name a few of the culprits. Here are some of our favorite places for both the necessities and the more frivolous (but no less fun) purchases.

Map	Store	Address	Phone	Description
1	Auntie Barbara's	238 S Beverly Dr, Beverly Hills	310-285-0873	Vintage children's furnishings.
2	Wound & Wound Toy Co	7374 Melrose Ave	323-656-4656	All things wind-up.
7	Flicka	204 N Larchmont Blvd	323-466-5822	Upscale kids' clothes.
13	Sid & Me	8338 Lincoln Blvd, Westchester	323-874-1787	Everything for baby's room.
15	Littlebits	15301 Antioch St, Pacific Palisades	310-459-0011	Fancy children's apparel.
15	Ivy Greene for Kids	1020 Swarthmore Ave, Pacific Palisades	310-230-0301	Kids' formal wear.
15	Palisades Playthings	1041 Swarthmore Ave, Pacific Palisades	310-454-8648	Toys galore.
16	Bellini Juvenile Designer Furniture	114 S Beverley Ct, Brentwood	310-447-5407	Nursery furniture.
18	The Acorn Store	1220 5th St, Santa Monica	310-451-5845	Wooden toys.
18	The Pump Station	2415 Wilshire Blvd, Santa Monica	310-998-1981	For nursing moms & tots.
18	Puzzle Zoo	1413 Third St Promenade, Santa Monica	310-393-9201	Awesome toy store.
18	This Little Piggy Wears Cotton	309 Wilshire Blvd, Santa Monica	310-260-2727	Comfy kids' clothes.
18	Every Picture Tells A Story	1311C Montana Ave, Santa Monica	310-451-2700	Art gallery & bookstore.
19	Malina Children's Store	3304 Pico Blvd, Santa Monica	310-395-5965	High-end clothes.
20	Riginals	10250 Santa Monica Blvd #108, Century City	310-557-2532	High-end clothes.
20	Peanut Butter Playground	2042 Westwood Blvd, Westwood	310-475-5354	Upscale clothes & toys.
20	Traveling Tikes	10461 Santa Monica Blvd, Century City	310-234-9554	Strollers, bikes, & more.
23	Needles N' Tees	9223 W Pico Blvd	310-276-2531	Personalized items.
27	Baby A	1108-A Manhattan Ave, Manhattan Beach	310-798-8086	Upscale gifts for tikes.
27	Babystyle	3200 Sepulveda Blvd, #C5, Manhattan Beach	310-802-0224	Website comes to life.
31	Little Moon	1813 S Catalina Ave, Redondo Beach	310-373-3766	Fancy frocks & the like.
35	Saturday's Child	2529 Mission St, San Marino	626-441-8888	High-end kids' stuff.
51	Moms The Word	12182 1/2 Ventura Blvd, Studio City	818-760-7192	Maternity & nursing wear.
52	Gregory's Toys	16101 Ventura Blvd, Encino	818-906-2212	Toys, toys, toys.
52	Harry Harris Children's Shoes	16744 Ventura Blvd, Encino	818-981-2641	First footwear.
52	Hopscotch Kids	16740 Ventura Blvd, Encino	818-783-4080	Kids' clothing.
52	Encino Kid	17157 Ventura Blvd, Encino	818-990-4510	Kids' clothing.
53	A Mother's Haven	15928 Ventura Blvd, Encino	818-380-3111	Nursing products & support.
54	Juvenile Shop	13356 Ventura Blvd, Sherman Oaks	818-986-6214	One-stop baby shopping.
55	Doll Shoppe	13300 Riverside Dr, Sherman Oaks	818-784-3655	Dolls & their accessories.
56	Safer Baby	12420 Ventura Blvd, Studio City	818-784-6628	One-stop baby-proofing.
56	Storyopolis	12348 Ventura Blvd, Studio City	818-509-5600	Children's literature & art.
56	M Fredric Kids	10282 Ventura Blvd, Studio City	818-985-9445	Cute & comfy clothes.

The Bestest of the Best

★ **Most Kid-Friendly Mall:** The Grove, 189 The Grove Dr, 888-315-8883 (Map 10). They've got a trolley, a musical water fountain, and events for children such as puppet shows, arts, and crafts every Thursday morning at 11 am, and a petting zoo. There's even a huge central lawn where you can watch a live act with an ice cream. Oh, and there are shops and restaurants for parents too.

★ **Coolest Bookstore:** Storyopolis, 12348 Ventura Blvd, Studio City, 818-509-5600 (Map 56). Looking for the Bill Clinton biography? Look somewhere else. This store sells only the most beautiful and beloved children's books, along with the artwork found within. Go for the story time, everyday at 11 am.

★ **Best Playground:** Shane's Inspiration, Griffith Park (Map 5). The playground was designed to allow handicapped children to play alongside their able-bodied peers on equipment that is colorful, innovative, and appealing to all. For a similar playground, check out Aidan's Place in Westwood Park, on Sepulveda Boulevard just south of Wilshire Boulevard.

★ **Restaurant Most Welcoming to Kids:** Angeli Café, 7274 Melrose Ave, 323-936-9086 (Map 2). Sure, you could go to Shakey's or Chuck E. Cheese, but would you want to if you didn't have kids? Angeli Café is moderately priced, serves delicious pizzas and pastas, and provides young diners with their own ball of pizza dough to mold, shape, or fling at each other.

★ **Most Surprising Place For Parents To Network:** Petting Zoo, Studio City Farmer's Market, Ventura Pl b/w Laurel Canyon & Ventura Blvd; Sundays, 8 am-1 pm (Map 56). Overall, the Studio City Farmers Market is a kids' paradise on Sunday mornings. It features pony rides, a moon bounce, face painting, and a small train. But stand in the petting zoo long enough and you will encounter every person you have ever met in LA who has a child under the age of five. The animals are docile and the pen is kept as clean as is realistically possible. And the pig loves to have his belly rubbed.

★ **Best Resource for New Mothers:** The Pump Station, 2415 Wilshire Blvd, Santa Monica, 310-998-1981 (Map 18). From breast pumps to nursing bras to high-end baby clothes, the Pump Station carries everything you need to get through the first few months of mommyhood. Even more useful, however, are the new mother support groups, where lactation consultants/RNs can talk any nervous new mother down from their ledge.

★ **Most Enjoyable Rainy Day Activity:** Boone Children's Gallery at LACMA West, 5905 Wilshire Blvd, 323-857-6000 (Map 6). This exhibit, which changes annually, introduces kids to art by letting them do what kids do best: climb, feel, mold, and explore. Wear them out here, then take them next door to see the Hockneys. Gallery hours vary by season, so you should check the website before planning your visit. Children under 17 years of age get in free.

★ **Handiest Phone Number:** The Babysitters' Guild, 818-552-2274. Give them 24-hours notice, and they'll send you a competent, CPR-trained sitter with at least one year's experience working in childcare.

Parks for Playing

What makes for an excellent public park? In our opinion, any combination of the following: ample shade, well-maintained (and appealing or innovative) equipment, and an indefinable, overall good vibe. Most LA neighborhood parks feature at least a strip of grass and a slide or two, but these are some of the parks that are worth venturing out of your own neighborhood to explore:

• **Coldwater Canyon Park**, Coldwater Canyon Dr & N Beverly Dr, Beverly Hills (Map 1). The signs may say "No wading," but on any given day, dozens of kids splash through the man-made stream that runs through this park.
• **Roxbury Park**, Olympic Blvd & Roxbury Dr, Beverly Hills (Map 1). Not one, but two sizeable playgrounds with a wide variety of obstacles to climb on or slide down. Steam emanates from the dinosaur area every ten minutes or so.
• **West Hollywood Park**, San Vicente Blvd b/w Melrose Ave & Santa Monica Blvd, West Hollywood (Map 2). Run of the mill equipment, but a shady canopy covers the toddler play area. Great weekday "Tiny Tots" program.
• **Shane's Inspiration**, Griffith Park (Map 4). This colorful playground was designed to accommodate handicapped and able-bodied children alike.
• **Echo Park**, b/w Glendale Blvd & Echo Park Ave, just south of Sunset Blvd (Map 5). Lively crowds and a small lake, with paddleboats available for rent.
• **La Cienega Park**, La Cienega Blvd & Olympic Blvd (Map 6). Excellent music and dance classes for the smallest kids; colorful playground and chess players almost all day.
• **MacArthur Park**, 6th St & Alvarado St (Map 8). Small lake with paddleboats, as well as the chance to visit the park that inspired the epic '60s song.
• **Kenneth Hahn State Recreational Area**, La Cienega Blvd south of Rodeo Rd (Map 10). Hiking trails and a terrific play area for kids.
• **Douglas Park**, Wilshire Blvd & 25th St, Santa Monica (Map 19). Lots of grass and a water area that is home to several ducks.

- **Westwood Park**, Sepulveda Blvd b/w Wilshire Blvd & Santa Monica Blvd (Map 20). Features Aidan's Place, a playground designed to accommodate both handicapped and able-bodied children.
- **Penmar Playground**, Marine St & 16th St, Santa Monica (Map 21). Brand new playground and piñata pole, great for kids' birthday parties.
  Culver City Park, Jefferson Blvd & Duquesne Ave (Map 24). Features a 5000-square-foot skateboard park. Helmets required.
- **Polliwog Park**, Redondo Ave & Manhattan Beach Blvd (Map 27). Park contains a pond, as well as a playground area featuring a large, wooden, sunken galleon.
- **Seaside Lagoon**, 200 Portofino Wy, Redondo Beach (Map 31). Beach playground with a large, heated, saltwater swimming pool.
- **Garfield Park**, Stratford Ave & Mission Ave, South Pasadena (Map 34). Lots of shade and rolling green hills.
  Lacey Park, Monterey Rd & Virginia Rd, San Marino (Map 35). Includes a stroller/bicycle loop for fitness-minded moms and traveling tykes.
- **Lake Balboa Park**, Balboa Blvd & Victory Blvd (Map 46). Ducks to feed, a lake to walk around, and a great playground to boot.
- **Johnny Carson Park**, 400 S Bob Hope Dr & Riverside Dr (Map 49). Picturesque park home to numerous community events and festivals.
- **Encino Park**, Ventura Blvd & Genesta Ave (Map 53). Two shady playgrounds, at least one of which keeps the little ones fenced in.
- **Studio City Recreation Center (AKA Beeman Park)**, Beeman Ave & Rye St (Map 56). Play in some sand, swing on a swing, and stop by the park office to meet Beeman the Bunny.

Rainy Day Activities— Indoor Playgrounds

Because wet weather is such an anomaly in Southern California, LA parents tend to lose it a little when forced to seek shelter indoors with the kids for a day or two. The kids, however, are perfectly happy, especially with a trip to some of LA's indoor playgrounds, where the temperature is always a pleasant 72 degrees and there's plenty of padding and cushions to break their fall.

- **Bright Child**, 1315 4th St, Santa Monica, 310-393-4844 (Map 18)
- **Child's Play**, 2299 Westwood Blvd, Westwood, 310-470-4997 (Map 23)
- **Gymboree Play & Music**, Westside Pavilion, 10850 W Pico Blvd, West LA, 310-470-7780 (Map 19)
- **Gymboree Play & Music**, 14801 Ventura Blvd, Sherman Oaks, 818-905-6225 (Map 53)
- **Gymboree Play & Music**, 443 E Irving Dr, Suite F, Burbank, 818-955-8964 (Map 43)

- **Gymboree Play & Music**, 435 S Fair Oaks Ave, South Pasadena, 626-445-1122 (Map 34)
- **Under the Sea**, 2424 W Victory Blvd, Burbank, 818-567-9945 (Map 49)

Classes

Most of the play facilities listed above emphasize open play, allowing for parental spontaneity and the fickle nature of young children. But with a little planning and structure (as counterintuitive as that might be), LA kids have a variety of classes available to them rivaling those of most Ivy League universities.

- **My Gym**, numerous locations around the LA area. Visit www.my-gym.com for addresses. Gymnastics, circle time, and other traditionally kid-like activities.
- **Creative Space**, 6325 Santa Monica Blvd, Hollywood, 323-462-4600 (Map 23). An eclectic line-up of classes that includes Storybook Cooking for toddlers, knitting and breakdancing for the 'tweens, and yoga and scrapbooking for adults.
- **Creative Kids**, 11301 W Olympic Blvd, West LA, 310-473-6090 (Map 34). Their diverse schedule includes art classes for toddlers, dance and cooking for slightly older kids, and children's theater for ages 3-18.
- **Dance & Jingle**, 1900 W Mountain St, Glendale 818-845-3925. Highly sought after music and movement class.
- **LA Zoo**, Zoo Dr, Griffith Park, 323-644-4200 (Map 5). The zoo's classes range from "Toddler Totes," which involves singing, an animal guest, and a backpack filled with educational goodies, to "Wild Planet," a more sophisticated program for adolescent zookeepers-in-training.
- **Music Together**, numerous locations around LA. Visit www.musictogether.com for more information. Teaches young children the fundamentals of rhythm and music through the modeling of parents and caregivers, while exposing them to a wide array of music from diverse cultures and time periods.
- **Family Gallery Kits**, Skirball Cultural Center, 2701 N Sepulveda Blvd, 310-440-4500. Along with the center's on going arts and cultural exhibition, the organization provides an interactive kit packed with games, puzzles, and activities for 4-8 year olds.

Where to Go for More Information

Where to go for additional information:
- www.gocitykids.com
- www.at-la.com/@la-kid.htm
- http://local.thedaisychain.com/Los_Angeles__CA/
- *Fun and Educational Places to Go With Kids and Adults in Southern California*, by Susan Peterson, Sunbelt Publications, 2001.

For the seriously ill or the terminally addicted to cosmetic surgery, Los Angeles boasts some of the most sought after physicians and medical centers in the United States. The UCLA Medical Center and Cedar's Sinai are two of the best treatment facilities in the world. Of course, if you're experiencing a medical emergency, we advise you to go straight to the nearest hospital.

Hospital	Address	Phone	Map
Alhambra	100 S Raymond Ave	626-570-1606	39
Brotman	3828 Delmas Ter	310-836-7000	24
California Hospital Medical	1338 S Hope St	213-742-5555	9
Cedars-Sinai Medical Center	8700 Beverly Blvd	310-423-8780	2
Centinela	555 E Hardy St	310-673-4660	13
Children's	4650 W Sunset Blvd	323-660-2450	4
City of Angels	1711 W Temple St	213-989-6100	9
Daniel Freeman Memorial	333 N Prairie Ave	310-674-7050	13
East LA Doctors Hospital	4060 Whittier Blvd	323-268-5514	41
Encino-Tarzana Regional Medical Center - Encino Campus	16237 Ventura Blvd	818-995-5000	54
Encino-Tarzana Regional Medical Center - Tarzana Campus	18321 Clark St	818-881-0800	46
Glendale Adventist	1509 Chevy Chase Dr	818-409-8000	51
Glendale Memorial	1420 S Central Ave	818-502-1900	51
Good Samaritan	1225 Wilshire Blvd	213-977-2121	9
Hollywood Presbyterian	1300 N Vermont Ave	213-413-3000	4
Huntington Memorial	100 W California Blvd	626-397-5000	34
Kaiser Foundation	4867 W Sunset Blvd	323-783-4011	4
Kaiser Foundation	6041 Cadillac Ave	323-857-2201	6
LA County USC Medical Center	1200 N State St	323-226-2622	40
LA County Women's	1240 N Mission Rd	323-226-3054	40
Little Co of Mary	4101 Torrance Blvd	310-540-7676	31
Los Angeles Community	4081 E Olympic Blvd	323-267-0477	41
Mission Community	14850 Roscoe Blvd	818-787-2222	47
Northridge - Roscoe Campus	18300 Roscoe Blvd	818-885-8500	43
Olympic Medical Center	5900 W Olympic Blvd	310-553-6211	6
Pacific Alliance	531 W College St	213-624-8411	9
Providence St Joseph Medical	501 S Buena Vista St	818-843-5111	50
Sherman Oaks	4929 Van Nuys Blvd	818-981-7111	55
St John's	2130 Santa Monica Blvd	310-829-5511	18
Torrance Memorial	3330 Lomita Blvd	310-325-9110	32
UCLA Medical Center	10833 Le Conte Ave	310-825-7271	20
Valley Presbyterian	15107 Vanowen St	818-782-6600	47

Maybe Google-ing information has replaced the faithful research trip to the library for most high school and college kids, but there are still plenty of reasons to keep your LA County library card on hand. The **Los Angeles Central Library** boasts the Annenberg Gallery, with its permanent exhibit of the city's rich history. You can dig further back in time at the **Sons of the Revolution Library**, founded in 1893, and containing everything you ever need to know about Colonial America.

Overall, most of the libraries have pleasant sitting grounds, and some truly gorgeous gardens, which offer a lovely, quiet respite from the hectic LA lifestyle (especially if you take a trip to one in a swankier part of town). Sometimes it's just nice to relax and read a good book—and not have to be sitting in a Starbucks or Barnes & Noble to do it.

Library	Address	Phone	Map
Alhambra Library	410 W Main St	626-570-5008	39
Allendale Branch	1130 S Marengo Ave	626-744-7260	34
Angeles Mesa	2700 W 52nd St	323-292-4328	11
Anthony Quinn	3965 E Cesar E Chavez Ave	323-264-7715	41
Arroyo Seco Regional	6145 N Figueroa St	323-255-0537	33
Atwater Branch	3379 Glendale Blvd	323-664-1353	5
Baldwin Hills Branch	2906 S La Brea Ave	323-733-1196	10
Benjamin Franklin Branch	2200 E 1st St	323-263-6901	40
Beverly Hills Public Library	444 N Rexford Dr	310-288-2220	1
Buena Vista Branch	300 N Buena Vista St	818-238-5620	50
Burbank Central Library	110 N Glenoaks Blvd	818-238-5600	50
Cahuenga Branch	4591 Santa Monica Blvd	323-664-6418	4
Canoga Park Branch	20939 Sherman Wy	818-887-0320	45
Chatsworth Branch	21052 Devonshire St	818-341-4276	42
Chinatown Branch	639 N Hill St	213-620-0925	9
City Terrace	4025 City Terrace Dr	323-261-0295	41
Crenshaw-Imperial Branch	11141 Crenshaw Blvd	310-412-5403	28
Culver City Julian Dixon	4975 Overland Ave	310-559-1676	24
Cypress Park Branch	1150 Cypress Ave	323-224-0039	36
Donald Bruce Kaufman	11820 San Vicente Blvd	310-575-8273	16
Eagle Rock	5027 Caspar Ave	323-258-8078	33
East Los Angeles	4801 E 3rd St	323-264-0155	41
Echo Park Library	1410 W Temple St	213-250-7808	9
Edendale Branch	2011 W Sunset Blvd	213-207-3000	5
El Camino Real	4264 Whittier Blvd	323-269-8102	41
El Retiro Branch	126 Vista Del Parque	310-375-0922	31
El Segundo Public Library	111 W Mariposa Ave	310-524-2722	27
El Sereno Branch	5226 Huntington Dr S	323-255-9201	38
Encino-Tarzana Branch	18231 Ventura Blvd	818-343-1983	53
Exposition Park Branch	3665 S Vermont Ave	323-732-0169	11
Fairfax Branch Library	161 S Gardner St	323-936-6191	2
Felipe De Neve Branch	2820 W 6th St	213-384-7676	8
Franklin D Murphy Library (Temporarily Closed)	244 S San Pedro St	213-628-2725	9
Glendale Central Library	222 E Harvard St	818-548-2030	51
Goethe Institute-Los Angeles	5750 Wilshire Blvd	323-525-3388	6
Granada Hills Branch	10640 Petit Ave	818-368-5687	44
Grandview Library	1535 5th St	818-548-2049	50
Hawthorne	12700 Grevillea Ave	310-679-8193	28
Henderson Branch	4805 Emerald St	310-371-2075	31
Hermosa Beach Public Library	550 Pier Ave	310-379-8475	29
Hill Avenue Branch	55 S Hill Ave	626-744-7264	35
Hinomoto Library	129 N Saratoga St	323-261-3300	40
Hyde Park-Miriam Matthews Branch	2205 W Florence Ave	323-750-7241	14
Inglewood Public Library	101 W Manchester Blvd	310-412-5380	13
Jefferson Branch	2211 W Jefferson Blvd	323-734-8573	11
John C Fremont Branch	6145 Melrose Ave	323-962-3521	3
John Muir Branch	1005 W 64th St	323-789-4800	14
Junipero Serra Branch	4607 S Main St	323-234-1685	12
LA County Law Library	301 W 1st St	213-629-3531	9
LA County Law Library	825 Maple Ave	310-222-8816	30
LA County Law Library	6230 Sylmar Ave	818-374-2499	47
LA County Law Library-Pasadena	300 E Walnut St	626-356-5253	34
LA County Law Library-Santa Monica	1725 Main St	310-260-3644	18
La Pintoresca Branch	1355 N Raymond Ave	626-744-7268	34
LACMA Visual Resource Center	5905 Wilshire Blvd	323-857-6116	6
Lamanda Park Branch	140 S Altadena Dr	626-744-7266	35
Lawndale Library	14615 Burin Ave	310-676-0177	28

Library	Address	Phone	Map
Lennox	4359 Lennox Blvd	310-674-0385	13
Lincoln Heights Branch	2530 Workman St	323-226-1692	37
Little Tokyo Branch	244 S Alameda St	213-612-0525	9
Lloyd Taber	4533 Admiralty Wy	310-821-3415	25
Lomita	24200 Narbonne Ave	310-539-4515	32
Los Angeles Central Library	630 W 5th St	213-228-7000	9
Los Angeles Main Branch-Braille Institute Library	741 N Vermont Ave	800-808-2555	4
Los Feliz Branch	1874 Hillhurst Ave	323-913-4710	4
Malabar Branch	2801 Wabash Ave	323-263-1497	40
Malaga Cove Library	2400 Via Campesina	310-377-9584	31
Manhattan Beach	1320 Highland Ave	310-545-8595	27
Mar Vista Branch	12006 Venice Blvd	310-390-3454	22
Mark Twain Branch	9621 S Figueroa St	323-755-4088	14
Memorial Branch	4625 W Olympic Blvd	323-938-2732	7
Mid-Valley Regional Branch Library	16244 Nordhoff St	818-895-3650	44
Morningside Park Branch	3202 W 85th St	310-412-5400	14
MTA Library	1 Gateway Plz	213-922-4859	9
North Hollywood Regional	5211 Tujunga Ave	818-766-7185	56
North Torrance Branch	3604 Artesia Blvd	310-323-7200	30
Northridge Branch	9051 Darby Ave	818-886-3640	43
Northwest Branch	3323 W Victory Blvd	818-238-5640	49
Nursing Library	1237 N Mission Rd	323-226-6521	40
Pacific Palisades Branch	861 Alma Real Dr	310-459-2754	15
Pacific Park Branch	501 S Pacific Ave	818-548-3760	51
Palms-Rancho Park Branch	2920 Overland Ave	310-840-2142	23
Pasadena Central	285 E Walnut St	626-744-4052	34
Pico Union Branch	1030 S Alvarado St	213-368-7545	8
Pio Pico Koreatown Branch	694 S Oxford Ave	213-368-7647	8
Playa Vista Branch	6400 Playa Vista Dr	310-437-6680	25
Porter Ranch Branch	11371 Tampa Ave	818-360-5706	43
Redondo Beach North Branch	2000 Artesia Blvd	310-318-0677	29
Redondo Beach Public Library	303 N Pacific Coast Hwy	310-318-0675	31
Robert Louis Stevenson Branch	803 Spence St	323-268-4710	40
Robertson Branch	1719 S Robertson Blvd	310-840-2147	6
San Marino Public Library	1890 Huntington Dr	626-300-0777	39
San Rafael Branch	1240 Nithsdale Rd	626-744-7270	34
Santa Catalina Branch	999 E Washington Blvd	626-744-7272	35
Santa Monica Fairview Branch	2101 Ocean Park Blvd	310-450-0443	18
Santa Monica Montana Avenue Branch	1704 Montana Ave	310-829-7081	18
Santa Monica Ocean Park Branch	2601 Main St	310-392-3804	18
Santa Monica Public Library (Temporarily Closed)	1343 6th St	310-458-8600	18
Santa Monica Public Main Library (Temporary Location)	1324 5th St	315-458-8600	18
Sherman Oaks Library	14245 Moorpark St	818-981-7850	55
Sons of the Revolution Library	600 S Central Ave	818-240-1775	51
South Pasadena Library	1100 Oxley St	626-403-7330	34
Southeast Branch	23115 Arlington Ave	310-530-5044	32
Studio City Branch	12511 Moorpark St	818-755-7873	56
Sun Valley Branch	7935 Vineland Ave	818-764-1338	48
Torrance Public Library	3301 Torrance Blvd	310-618-5959	32
Valley Plaza Branch	12311 Vanowen St	818-765-0805	48
Van Nuys Branch	6250 Sylmar Ave	818-756-8453	47
Venice Branch	501 S Venice Blvd	310-821-1769	21
Vermont Square Branch	1201 W 48th St	323-290-7405	11
Vernon Branch	4504 S Central Ave	323-234-9106	12
View Park	3854 W 54th St	323-293-5371	10
Villa Parke Community Center Branch	363 E Villa St	626-744-6510	34
Walteria Branch	3815 W 242nd St	310-375-8418	31
Washington Irving Branch	4117 W Washington Blvd	323-734-6303	7
Water & Power Library	111 N Hope St	213-367-1995	9
West Hollywood	715 N San Vicente Blvd	310-652-5340	2
West Los Angeles Regional	11360 Santa Monica Blvd	310-575-8323	19
West Valley Regional	19036 Vanowen St	818-345-9806	45
Westchester Branch	7114 W Manchester Ave	310-348-1096	25
Westwood Branch	1246 Glendon Ave	310-474-1739	20
Will & Ariel Durant Branch	7140 W Sunset Blvd	323-876-2741	2
Wilshire Library	149 N St Andrews Pl	323-957-4550	7
Wiseburn	5335 W 135th St	310-643-8880	28
Woodcrest	1340 W 106th St	323-757-9373	14

Here's the deal in LA. The West Hollywood/pretty boy crowd converges on **The Abbey**. Places further east down Santa Monica Boulevard, like **FuBar** and **Parlour Club**, are the closest LA gets to fun New York bars. Fubar is a little daker and more intimate. Parlour's hot on Saturdays with Hot Dog Mario Diaz's sexy boy party. And on Sundays, there's always Club Chubb, for those who like their men a little meatier. The further east you go, the more mellow (aka less WeHo-ish) the vibe gets, with **Akbar** for cute, normal-bodied boys, and the **Faultline** for that hot leather daddy moment we all need from time to time.

Hot Girl Action tends to be a little mixed in with the predominantly male scene in LA. So places like The Abbey, Beige at **The Falcon**, and Parlour Club are also good places to meet the cute lipstick lesbian or sporty girl of your dreams. Like all of LA, the LGBT scene here is image-conscious, stylish, and physically fit. But there is diversity to be had—you might just have to drive a bit further east and south of WeHo to find it.

Websites

- **LA Gay & Lesbian Center · www.laglc.org**
  LA Gay and Lesbian Center is a community resource offering legal, medical, outreach, and educational services, among many others.
- **Circuit Noize · www.circuitnoize.com**
  The premier source of circuit party information, parties, events, music, tickets, gay travel, and dancing.
- **Gay.com · www.gay.com**
  If you're looking for love online, this is the place to visit. Gay.com has hundreds of chat rooms for people around the country, with eight devoted to LA, two to Long Beach, and two to Orange County.
- **Gay Los Angeles · www.gaylosangeles.com**
  Lesbian and gay directory for gay-owned and gay-friendly places in Los Angeles (bars, clubs, saunas, restaurants, and more).
- **West Hollywood · www.westhollywood.com**
  Comprehensive online guide to gay West Hollywood, featuring music, arts, videos, nightlife, circuits, classifieds, buzz, photos, and shopping.
- **QV Magazine · www.qvmagazine.com**
  Online edition of LA's gay Latino magazine.
- **Power Up · www.power-up.net**
  A group dedicated to promoting the visibility of gay women in film, entertainment, and media.
- **Los Angeles Tennis Association · www.lataweb.com**
  With more than 400 members, this is the largest gay and lesbian tennis club in the world. All skill levels welcome.

- **Greater Los Angeles Softball Association · www.lagaysoftball.com**
  This exclusively gay and lesbian league has more than 30 teams participating in their men's and women's divisions.
- **Gay Men's Chorus of Los Angeles · www.gmcla.com**
  Check out their site for performance dates and a rehearsal schedule.
- **Metropolitan Community Church · www.mccla.org**
  This popular church is gay- and lesbian-friendly and offers multi-denominational services.

Bookstores

- **A Different Light Bookstore** · 8853 Santa Monica Blvd (at San Vicente Blvd), West Hollywood · 310-854-6601 · www.adlbooks.com · Hours: 10 am-midnight, daily.
- **Circus of Books** (two locations) · 8230 Santa Monica Blvd (b/w Harper & LaJolla Aves), West Hollywood · 323-656-6533; and 4001 Sunset Blvd (at Sanborn Ave), Silver Lake · 323-666-1304 · www.circusofbooks.com · Hours: 6 am-2 am, daily.

Health Center & Support Organizations

LA Gay & Lesbian Center (LAGLC) McDonald Wright Building · 1625 N Schrader Blvd, Los Angeles, CA 90028 · 323-993-7400 · www.laglc.org
LAGLC offers the following services:
- Pedro Zamora Youth HIV Program · 323-993-7440
- Jeffrey Goodman Special Care Clinic · 323-993-7500
- Counseling services including general, addiction recovery, domestic violence, and HIV/AIDS · 323-993-7640
- HIV Testing · 323-993-7500
- Audre Lorde Lesbian Health Clinic · 323-860-7311
- Sexual Health Program · 323-860-5855

AIDS Project Los Angeles · 213-201-1600 · www.apla.org · Assistance and information hotline for people living with AIDS.

HIV LA · www.hivla.org
An online resource in English and Spanish that helps people with HIV/AIDS find services available in Los Angeles County.

GLAAD Los Angeles · 5455 Wilshire Blvd #1500, Los Angeles, CA 90036 · 323-933-2240 · wwwglaad.org

Gay & Lesbian Youth Talkline · 800-246-77433

Publications

From local news headlines to club listings, these LGBT publications bring you all the news that's gay. Most of these publications can be found in gay-friendly bookstores, cafes, bars, and various shops.

- **Circuit Noize** • 818-769-9390 • www.circuitnoize.com
- **Frontiers** • 323-930-3220 • www.frontiersnewsmagazine.com
- **QV Magazine** • 702-341-6346 • www.qvmagazine.com
- **The Lesbian News** • 800-458-9888 • www.lesbiannews.com
- **The Advocate** • 323-871-1225 • www.advocate.com

Venues—Gay

- **AD** • 836 N Highland Ave • Los Angeles • 323-467-3000
- **Akbar** • 4356 W Sunset Blvd • Silver Lake • 323-665-6810
- **Apache Territory** • 11608 Ventura Blvd & Laurel Canyon • Studio City • 818-506-0404
- **Arena** • 6655 Santa Monica Blvd • West Hollywood • 323-462-0714
- **Banana's Bar & Nightclub** • 7026 Reseda Blvd • Reseda • 818-996-2976
- **The Bullet** • 10522 Burbank Blvd & Cahuenga Blvd • North Hollywood • 818-762-8890
- **Club 7969** • 7969 Santa Monica Blvd (b/w Fairfax & Crescent Heights) • West Hollywood • 323-654-0280
- **Cuff's Bar** • 1941 Hyperion Ave • Silver Lake • 323-660-2649
- **The Factory** • 652 N La Peer Dr (at Robertson) • West Hollywood • 310-659-4551
- **Faultline** • 4216 Melrose Ave • Silver Lake • 323-660-0889
- **Friendship** • 112 W Channel Rd • Santa Monica • 310-454-6024
- **FuBar** • 7994 Santa Monica Blvd • West Hollywood • 323-654-0396
- **Gauntlet II** • 4219 Santa Monica Blvd • Silver Lake • 323-669-9472
- **Here** • 696 N Robertson Blvd • West Hollywood • 310-360-8455
- **House of Blues** • 8430 Sunset Blvd • West Hollywood • 323-848-5100
- **Micky's** • 8857 Santa Monica Blvd • West Hollywood • 310-657-1176
- **MJ's** • 2810 Hyperion Ave • Silver Lake • 323-660-1503
- **Mother Lode** • 8944 Santa Monica Blvd (at San Vicente) • West Hollywood • 310-659-9700
- **Numbers** • 8741 Santa Monica Blvd • West Hollywood • 310-652-7700

- **Oil Can Harry's** • 11502 Ventura Blvd • Studio City • 818-760-9749
- **Parlour Club** • 7702 Santa Monica Blvd (at Stanley) • West Hollywood • 323-650-7968
- **Rage** • 8911 Santa Monica Blvd (b/w Larrabee & San Vicente) • West Hollywood • 310-652-7055
- **Revolver** • 8851 Santa Monica Blvd (at Larrabee) • West Hollywood • 213-659-8851
- **Roosterfish** • 1302 Abbot Kinney Blvd • Venice Beach • 310-392-2123
- **Spike** • 7746 Santa Monica Blvd (at Ogden Dr) • West Hollywood • 323-656-9343
- **Ultra Suede** • 661 N Robertson Blvd (at Melrose Ave) • West Hollywood • 310-659-4551
- **Wonder Bar** • 2692 S La Cienega Ave • Los Angeles • 310-837-7443

Venues—Lesbian

- **Club 7969** (Michelle's XXX Review Tuesday) • 7969 Santa Monica Blvd (b/w Fairfax & Crescent Heights) • West Hollywood • 323-654-0280
- **The Echo** • ("Milk" Thursday) • 1822 W Sunset Blvd • Echo Park • 213-413-8200
- **Here** • (Fuse Thursday) • 696 N Robertson Blvd • 310-360-8455
- **Jewels Catch One** • 4067 W Pico Blvd (at Norton Ave) • Mid-City • 323-734-8849
- **Normandie Room** • 8737 Santa Monica Blvd (at Hancock Ave) • West Hollywood • 310-659-6204
- **The Factory** (Girl Bar Friday) • 652 N La Peer Dr (at Robertson) • West Hollywood • 310-659-4551
- **The Palms** • 8572 Santa Monica Blvd (at La Cienega) • West Hollywood • 310-652-6188

Venues—Both

- **The Abbey** • 692 N Robertson Blvd • 310-289-8410
- **Dream Discotheque** • 1717 Silver Lake Blvd • Los Angeles • 323-661-4380
- **The Echo** • 1822 W Sunset Blvd • Echo Park • 213-413-8200
- **The Falcon** (Beige, Tuesdays) • 7213 Sunset Blvd • Hollywood • 323-850-5350
- **JJ's Pub** • 2692 S La Cienega Blvd • Los Angeles • 310-837-7443
- **Marix Tex-Mex Café** • 1108 N Flores St • West Hollywood • 323-656-8800
- **Parlour Club** • 7702 Santa Monica Blvd (at Stanley) • West Hollywood • 323-650-7968
- **Red Bar** • 2218 E First St • Los Angeles • 323-263-2995

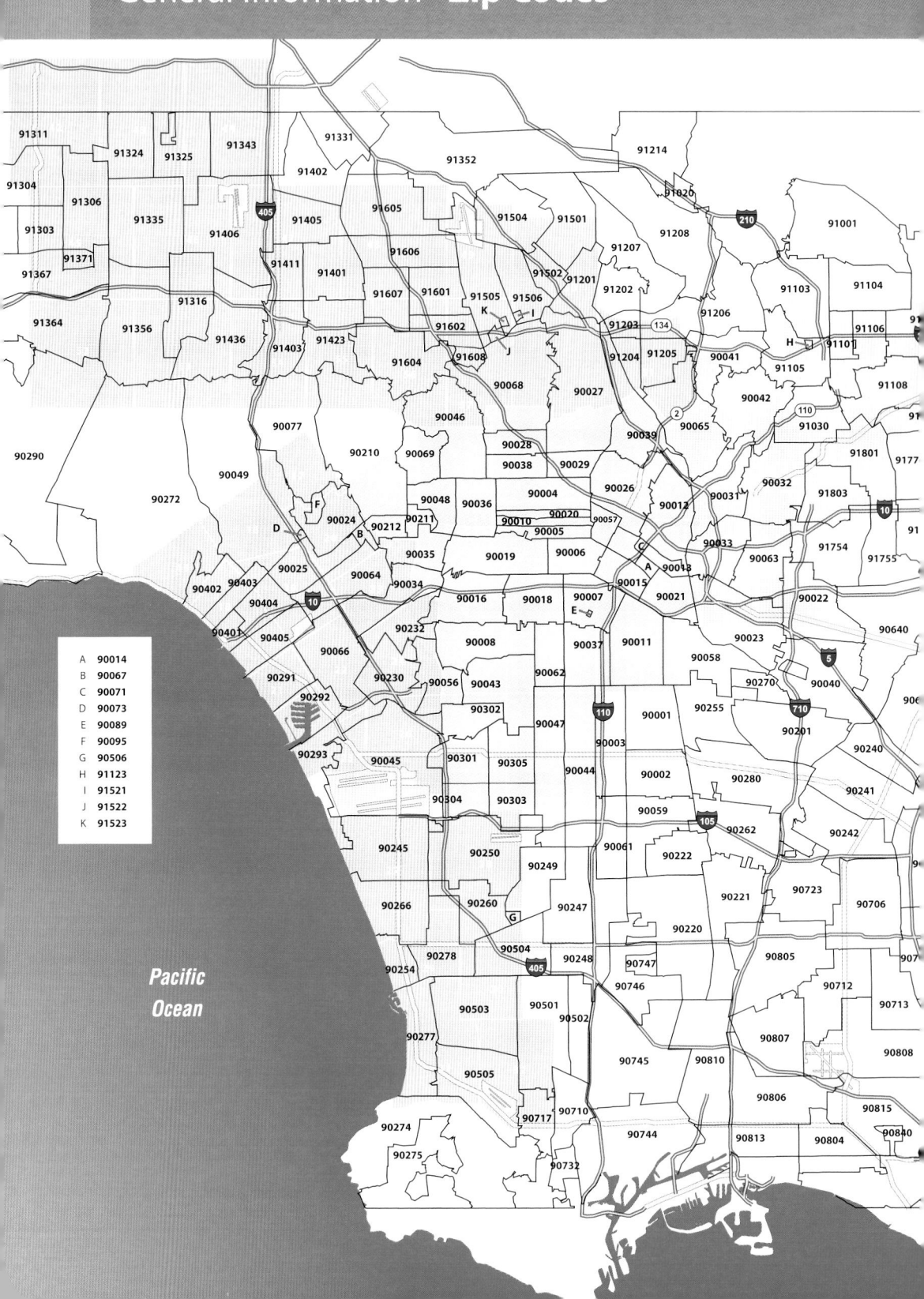

Map	Address	Zip	Map	Address	Zip	Map	Address	Zip
1	325 N Maple Dr	90210	16	200 S Barrington Ave	90049	35	967 E Colorado Blvd	91106
	323 N Crescent Dr	90210	18	1248 5th St	90401		2609 E Colorado Blvd	91107
	312 S Beverly Dr	90212		1025 Colorado Ave	90401		2960 Huntington Dr	91108
2	1125 N Fairfax Ave	90046		1217 Wilshire Blvd	90403	36	3950 Eagle Rock Blvd	90065
	7610 Beverly Blvd	90048		2720 Neilson Wy	90405	38	3316 N Eastern Ave	90032
	820 N San Vicente Blvd	90069	19	11420 Santa Monica Blvd	90025		4875 Huntington Dr	90032
3	1615 Wilcox Ave	90028		11270 Exposition Blvd	90064	39	1603 W Valley Blvd	91803
	1425 N Cherokee Ave	90028		11301 Wilshire Blvd	90073	40	3641 E 8th St	90023
	6457 Santa Monica Blvd	90038	20	11000 Wilshire Blvd	90024		2425 Alhambra Ave	90031
4	1825 N Vermont Ave	90027	21	313 Grand Blvd	90291		2016 E 1st St	90033
5	1525 N Alvarado St	90026		1601 Main St	90291	41	975 S Atlantic Blvd	90022
	3370 Glendale Blvd	90039	22	3826 Grand View Blvd	90066		3729 E 1st St	90063
6	4960 W Washington Blvd	90016	23	3751 Motor Ave	90034	42	21606 Devonshire St	91311
	1270 S Alfred St	90035		9911 W Pico Blvd	90035	43	9534 Reseda Blvd	91324
	5350 Wilshire Blvd	90036		10850 W Pico Blvd	90064		19300 Rinaldi St	91326
	8383 Wilshire Blvd	90211	24	11111 Jefferson Blvd	90230		18039 Chatsworth St	91344
7	4040 W Washington Blvd	90018		9942 Culver Blvd	90232	45	21801 Sherman Wy	91303
8	265 S Western Ave	90004	25	4766 Admiralty Wy	90292		8201 Canoga Ave	91304
	2390 W Pico Blvd	90006		215 Culver Blvd	90293		7655 Winnetka Ave	91306
	3450 Wilshire Blvd	90010		13031 W Jefferson Blvd	90311	46	5805 White Oak Ave	91316
	3751 W 6th St	90020	26	9029 Airport Blvd	90009		7320 Reseda Blvd	91335
9	300 N Los Angeles St	90012		7381 La Tijera Blvd	90045		5609 Yolanda Ave	91356
	1055 N Vignes St	90012	27	200 Main St	90245	47	6200 Van Nuys Blvd	91401
	508 S Spring St	90013		2130 E Mariposa Ave	90245		15701 Sherman Wy	91406
	100 W Olympic Blvd	90015		425 15th St	90266	48	7035 Laurel Canyon Blvd	91605
	1660 Beverly Blvd	90015		1007 N Sepulveda Blvd	90266		6535 Lankershim Blvd	91606
	1122 E 7th St	90021	28	12700 Inglewood Ave	90250		6242 Vantage Ave	91606
	1808 W 7th St	90057		4320 Marine Ave	90260	49	2140 N Hollywood Wy	91505
	2005 W 6th St	90057	29	565 Pier Ave	90254		3810 W Magnolia Blvd	91505
	505 S Flower St	90071		2215 Artesia Blvd	90504	50	6444 San Fernando Rd	91201
	350 S Grand Ave	90071	30	1815 Hawthorne Blvd	90278		135 E Olive Ave	91502
10	3894 Crenshaw Blvd	90008		18080 Crenshaw Blvd	90504		1634 N San Fernando Blvd	91504
	3650 W Martin Luther	90008	31	2516 Via Tejon	90274	51	1009 N Pacific Ave	91202
	King Jr Blvd			1201 N Catalina Ave	90277		313 E Broadway	91205
11	3585 S Vermont Ave	90007		4216 Pacific Coast Hwy	90505		120 E Chevy Chase Dr	91205
	5472 Crenshaw Blvd	90043	32	1433 Marcelina Ave	90501		101 N Verdugo Rd	91206
	1515 W Vernon Ave	90062		2510 Monterey St	90503	52	22121 Clarendon St	91367
12	819 W Washington Blvd	90015		291 Del Amo Fashion Sq	90503	53	4930 Balboa Blvd	91316
13	300 E Hillcrest Blvd	90301		25131 Narbonne Ave	90717	54	14900 Magnolia Blvd	91403
	811 N La Brea Ave	90302	33	7435 N Figueroa St	90041	56	11304 Chandler Blvd	91601
	4443 Lennox Blvd	90304		5132 York Blvd	90042		3950 Laurel Canyon Blvd	91604
14	8200 S Vermont Ave	90044		5930 N Figueroa St	90042		12450 Magnolia Blvd	91607
	2200 W Century Blvd	90047	34	1001 Fremont Ave	91030	57	10063 Riverside Dr	91602
	3212 W 85th St	90305		1100 N Fair Oaks Ave	91103		4029 Lankershim Blvd	91604
15	15243 La Cruz Dr	90272		1355 N Mentor Ave	91104			
	15209 W Sunset Blvd	90272		99 W California Blvd	91105			
				870 S Raymond Ave	91105			
				600 Lincoln Ave	91109			

** Last pick-up time, pm*

Map 1 • Beverly Hills

		*
FedEx Staffed	9201 W Sunset Blvd	6:00
FedEx Staffed	9680 Santa Monica Blvd	6:00
Drop Box	9100 Wilshire Blvd	5:30
Drop Box	9440 Santa Monica Blvd	5:30
FedEx Staffed	9334 Wilshire Blvd	5:30
Mail Box Times	9461 Charleville Blvd	5:30
Drop Box	312 S Beverly Dr	5:00
Drop Box	325 N Maple Dr	5:00
Drop Box	345 N Maple Dr	5:00
Drop Box	421 N Rodeo Dr	5:00
Drop Box	9171 Wilshire Blvd	5:00
Drop Box	9220 W Sunset Blvd	5:00
Drop Box	9300 Wilshire Blvd	5:00
Drop Box	9301 Wilshire Blvd	5:00
Drop Box	9401 Wilshire Blvd	5:00
Drop Box	9454 Wilshire Blvd	5:00
Drop Box	9460 Wilshire Blvd	5:00
Drop Box	9465 Wilshire Blvd	5:00
Drop Box	9595 Wilshire Blvd	5:00
Drop Box	9601 Wilshire Blvd	5:00
Drop Box	9665 Wilshire Blvd	5:00
Drop Box	9701 Wilshire Blvd	5:00
Drop Box	9720 Wilshire Blvd	5:00
Drop Box	9777 Wilshire Blvd	5:00
Mail Boxes Etc	269 S Beverly Dr	5:00
Mail Boxes Etc	9663 Santa Monica Blvd	5:00
Mailbox & Services	9190 W Olympic Blvd	5:00
Drop Box	301 N Canon Dr	4:45
Drop Box	9229 W Sunset Blvd	4:45
Drop Box	9255 W Sunset Blvd	4:45
Drop Box	9560 Wilshire Blvd	4:45
Beverly Hills Mail Box	9903 Santa Monica Blvd	4:30
Drop Box	433 N Camden Dr	4:30
Drop Box	100 N Crescent Dr	4:00
Drop Box	9292 Civic Center Dr	4:00
Drop Box	9350 Wilshire Blvd	4:00

Map 2 • West Hollywood

		*
Drop Box	7551 W Sunset Blvd	5:30
Mail & More On Hollywood	7095 Hollywood Blvd Ste 104	5:30
Drop Box	7610 Beverly Blvd	5:15
Drop Box	7753 Santa Monica Blvd	5:15
Drop Box	8265 W Sunset Blvd	5:15
Mister Mail	7510 W Sunset Blvd	5:15
Box 2 Go	901 N Fairfax Ave	5:00
Box & Ship Hollywood	8172 W Sunset Blvd	5:00
Boxes & More	8491 W Sunset Blvd	5:00
Drop Box	116 N Robertson Blvd	5:00
Drop Box	145 S Fairfax Ave	5:00
Drop Box	7060 Hollywood Blvd	5:00
Drop Box	7080 Hollywood Blvd	5:00
Drop Box	7250 Beverly Blvd	5:00
Drop Box	7920 W Sunset Blvd	5:00
Drop Box	8060 Melrose Ave	5:00
Drop Box	8075 W 3rd St	5:00
Drop Box	8439 W Sunset Blvd	5:00
Drop Box	8500 Melrose Ave	5:00
Drop Box	8635 W 3rd St	5:00
Drop Box	8687 Melrose Ave	5:00
Drop Box	8899 Beverly Blvd	5:00
Drop Box	8981 W Sunset Blvd	5:00
Drop Box	9000 W Sunset Blvd	5:00
Drop Box	9060 Santa Monica Blvd	5:00
FedEx Staffed	7630 W Sunset Blvd	5:00
FedEx Staffed	8471 Beverly Blvd	5:00
Mail Boxes Pmb	7336 Santa Monica Blvd	5:00
Mail Boxes & Things	8424 Santa Monica Blvd Ste A	5:00
Mailrose Shipping	7215 Melrose Ave	5:00
Postal Center & More	8205 Santa Monica Blvd	5:00
Postal Plus	836 N La Cienega Blvd	5:00
The Box Depot	119 N Fairfax Ave	5:00
West Hollywood Mail & Msg	7985 Santa Monica Blvd Ste 109	5:00
Drop Box	1011 N Fuller Ave	4:45
Drop Box	200 N Robertson Blvd	4:45
Drop Box	250 N Robertson Blvd	4:45
Drop Box	444 S San Vicente Blvd	4:45
Mail Boxes Etc	8581 Santa Monica Blvd	4:45
Box Brothers	8365 Santa Monica Blvd	4:30
Drop Box	110 S Fairfax Ave	4:30
Drop Box	189 The Grove Dr	4:30
Drop Box	820 N San Vicente Blvd	4:30
Drop Box	8730 W Sunset Blvd	4:30
Mail Boxes Etc	8391 Beverly Blvd	4:30
Miracle Mail	5850 W 3rd St	4:30
Russian Universal	1123 N Fairfax Ave	4:30
Banner Packaging	8231 W 3rd St	4:00
Beverly Hills Us Mailbox	311 N Robertson Blvd	4:00
Beverly Place	7162 Beverly Blvd	4:00
Box and Ship	7304 Beverly Blvd	4:00
Drop Box	8436 W 3rd St	4:00
E and G Mail Boxes	8023 Beverly Blvd	4:00
Mail Service Center	8721 Santa Monica Blvd	3:45
Hybrid	8936 Santa Monica Blvd	3:30

Map 3 • Hollywood

		*
FedEx Staffed	6255 W Sunset Blvd	6:00
FedEx Staffed	6666 Lexington Ave	6:00
Drop Box	1040 N Las Palmas Ave	5:45
Drop Box	6464 W Sunset Blvd	5:30
Drop Box	6922 Hollywood Blvd	5:30
Drop Box	1680 Vine St	5:15
Drop Box	6450 W Sunset Blvd	5:15
Drop Box	6671 W Sunset Blvd	5:15
Drop Box	846 N Cahuenga Blvd	5:15
Rex Mail Company	1608 N Cahuenga Blvd	5:15
Village Mail Call	419 N Larchmont Blvd	5:15
Drop Box	5300 Melrose Ave	5:00
Drop Box	6430 W Sunset Blvd	5:00
Drop Box	6525 W Sunset Blvd	5:00
Drop Box	6565 W Sunset Blvd	5:00
Drop Box	6801 Hollywood Blvd	5:00
FedEx Staffed	1440 Vine St	5:00
Highland Postal Center	1304 N Highland Ave	5:00
Ship & More	6767 W Sunset Blvd	5:00
Drop Box	1615 Wilcox Ave	4:30
Shipping and Mailboxes	6660 W Sunset Blvd	4:30
Drop Box	306 N Larchmont Blvd	4:00

Map 4 • Los Feliz

		*
Box Brothers	1954 Hillhurst Ave	5:00
Drop Box	1825 N Vermont Ave	5:00
Drop Box	4021 Rosewood Ave	5:00
Drop Box	1300 N Vermont Ave	4:30
Copycat/ Pack'n'fly	2046 Hillhurst Ave	4:00
Kingston Mail & Gift Mart	1555 N Vermont Ave	4:00

Map 5 • Silver Lake/Echo Park/Atwater

		*
Drop Box	1525 N Alvarado St	5:00
Drop Box	1910 W Sunset Blvd	5:00
Postalworks	2658 Griffith Park Blvd	5:00
Drop Box	2512 Hyperion Ave	4:45
Drop Box	3370 Glendale Blvd	4:30
Box and Ship	2590 Glendale Blvd	4:15
Box Brothers	3108 Glendale Blvd	4:00
Speedco Fax & Pack	3371 Glendale Blvd	4:00

Map 6 • Miracle Mile/Mid-City

		*
FedEx Staffed	8950 W Olympic Blvd	6:00
FedEx Staffed	5500 Wilshire Blvd	5:45
Drop Box	5670 Wilshire Blvd	5:30
Drop Box	8383 Wilshire Blvd	5:30
Drop Box	8484 Wilshire Blvd	5:30
Drop Box	9033 Wilshire Blvd	5:30
Digital Express Etc	6404 Wilshire Blvd	5:15
Drop Box	5900 Wilshire Blvd	5:15
Drop Box	8920 Wilshire Blvd	5:15
Drop Box	1833 S La Cienega Blvd	5:00
Drop Box	195 S Robertson Blvd	5:00
Drop Box	5350 Wilshire Blvd	5:00
Drop Box	5700 Wilshire Blvd	5:00
Drop Box	5750 Wilshire Blvd	5:00
Drop Box	5757 Wilshire Blvd	5:00
Drop Box	6100 Wilshire Blvd	5:00
Drop Box	6300 Wilshire Blvd	5:00
Drop Box	6500 Wilshire Blvd	5:00
Drop Box	8500 Wilshire Blvd	5:00
Drop Box	8730 Wilshire Blvd	5:00
Drop Box	9107 Wilshire Blvd	5:00
Mail Boxes Etc	5482 Wilshire Blvd	5:00
Mailbox Depot	6230-A Wilshire Blvd	5:00
Mailcom Services	5939 W Pico Blvd	5:00
The Box Store	5657 Wilshire Blvd	5:00
Drop Box	640 S San Vicente Blvd	4:45
Drop Box	1270 S Alfred St	4:30
Drop Box	6310 San Vicente Blvd	4:30
The Box Store	8918 W Pico Blvd	4:30
Adore Freight/ shipping	1494 S Robertson Blvd	4:00
Mail Box Exchange	369 S Doheny Dr	4:00
Postal Connection	287 S Robertson Blvd	4:00
Coast To Coast	1109 S La Cienega Blvd	4:00
United Mail Boxes	264 S La Cienega Blvd	4:00
Drop Box	50 N La Cienega Blvd	3:45
Beverly Hills Postal Center	8306 Wilshire Blvd	3:30

Map 7 • Hancock Park

		*
Drop Box	4055 Wilshire Blvd	5:00
Drop Box	4201 Wilshire Blvd	5:00
Drop Box	4221 Wilshire Blvd	5:00
Drop Box	4751 Wilshire Blvd	5:00
Drop Box	4929 Wilshire Blvd	5:00
Drop Box	5055 Wilshire Blvd	5:00
The Mail Shoppe	137 N Larchmont Blvd	5:00
Wilshire Mail Boxes	5042 Wilshire Blvd	5:00
Drop Box	4601 Wilshire Blvd	4:30
Charlie Chan Printing	3974 Wilshire Blvd	4:20

Map 8 • Korea Town

		*
FedEx Staffed	3345 Wilshire Blvd	6:00
Drop Box	672 S La Fayette Park Pl	5:30
Drop Box	2500 Wilshire Blvd	5:00
Drop Box	3055 Wilshire Blvd	5:00
Drop Box	3200 Wilshire Blvd	5:00
Drop Box	3250 Wilshire Blvd	5:00
Drop Box	3255 Wilshire Blvd	5:00
Drop Box	3435 Wilshire Blvd	5:00
Drop Box	3450 Wilshire Blvd	5:00
Drop Box	3530 Wilshire Blvd	5:00
Drop Box	3550 Wilshire Blvd	5:00
Drop Box	3600 Wilshire Blvd	5:00
Drop Box	3660 Wilshire Blvd	5:00
Drop Box	3699 Wilshire Blvd	5:00
Drop Box	3700 Wilshire Blvd	5:00
Drop Box	3731 Wilshire Blvd	5:00
Drop Box	3751 W 6th St	5:00
Drop Box	3780 Wilshire Blvd	5:00
Drop Box	520 S La Fayette Park Pl	5:00
Drop Box	520 S Virgil Ave	5:00
Joy Express	139 N Western Ave	5:00
Kebson Group	3540 Wilshire Blvd	5:00
Mail Plus	269 S Western Ave	4:45
Copy Express La	3321 Wilshire Blvd	4:00
Kenmore Express	550 S Kenmore Ave	3:30

Map 9 • Downtown

		*
FedEx Staffed	330 S Hope St	6:15
FedEx Staffed	554 S Grand Ave	6:00
FedEx Staffed	735 S Figueroa St	6:00
FedEx Staffed	110 E 9th St	5:45
FedEx Staffed	835 Wilshire Blvd	5:45
Drop Box	1010 Wilshire Blvd	5:30
Drop Box	1200 W 7th St	5:30
Drop Box	333 S Hope St	5:30
Drop Box	444 S Flower St	5:30
Drop Box	555 W 5th St	5:30
Drop Box	601 S Figueroa St	5:30
Drop Box	707 Wilshire Blvd	5:30
Drop Box	1055 Wilshire Blvd	5:15
Drop Box	112 W 9th St	5:15
Drop Box	1150 S Olive St	5:15
Drop Box	117 W 9th St	5:15
Drop Box	1201 S Figueroa St	5:15
Drop Box	2010 Wilshire Blvd	5:15
Drop Box	300 N Los Angeles St	5:15
Drop Box	315 W 9th St	5:15
Drop Box	350 S Figueroa St	5:15
Drop Box	600 Wilshire Blvd	5:15
Drop Box	624 S Grand Ave	5:15
Drop Box	660 S Figueroa St	5:15
Drop Box	750 W 7th St	5:15
Drop Box	800 E 12th St	5:15
Drop Box	800 W 6th St	5:15

Last pick-up time, pm

Drop Box	911 Wilshire Blvd	5:15
Drop Box	207 S Broadway	5:10
Drop Box	312 N Spring St	5:10
Drop Box	700 S Flower St	5:10
Drop Box	1545 Wilshire Blvd	5:05
City Business & Shipping	225 E 9th St	5:00
Drop Box	1000 W Temple St	5:00
Drop Box	1000 Wilshire Blvd	5:00
Drop Box	1055 W 7th St	5:00
Drop Box	1100 S San Pedro St	5:00
Drop Box	1127 Wilshire Blvd	5:00
Drop Box	1200 Santee St	5:00
Drop Box	1200 Wilshire Blvd	5:00
Drop Box	1601 E Olympic Blvd	5:00
Drop Box	1625 W Olympic Blvd	5:00
Drop Box	201 N Figueroa St	5:00
Drop Box	255 E Temple St	5:00
Drop Box	261 S Figueroa St	5:00
Drop Box	350 S Grand Ave	5:00
Drop Box	420 E 3rd St	5:00
Drop Box	445 S Figueroa St	5:00
Drop Box	510 W 6th St	5:00
Drop Box	515 S Figueroa St	5:00
Drop Box	550 S Hope St	5:00
Drop Box	601 W 5th St	5:00
Drop Box	606 S Olive St	5:00
Drop Box	627 S Central Ave	5:00
Drop Box	650 S Hill St	5:00
Drop Box	714 W Olympic Blvd	5:00
Drop Box	800 N Alameda St	5:00
Drop Box	801 S Figueroa St	5:00
Drop Box	801 S Grand Ave	5:00
Drop Box	810 N Alameda St	5:00
Drop Box	818 W 7th St	5:00
Drop Box	819 Santee St	5:00
Drop Box	860 S Los Angeles St	5:00
Drop Box	865 S Figueroa St	5:00
Drop Box	888 S Figueroa St	5:00
Drop Box	900 Wilshire Blvd	5:00
Lecs USA	608 E 1st St	5:00
Mail America	952 S Broadway	5:00
Mail Boxes and More	655 S Flower St	5:00
Drop Box	626 Wilshire Blvd	4:50
Drop Box	333 S Beaudry Ave	4:45
Drop Box	420 Boyd St	4:45
Drop Box	633 W 5th St	4:45
Drop Box	800 S Figueroa St	4:45
Drop Box	800 Wilshire Blvd	4:45
Drop Box	811 W 7th St	4:45
Drop Box	977 N Broadway	4:45
Drop Box	1201 W 5th St	4:30
Drop Box	634 S Spring St	4:30
Drop Box	800 W 1st St	4:30

Map 10 • Baldwin Hills *

Drop Box	8985 Venice Blvd	5:30
Drop Box	3650 W Martin Luther King Jr Blvd	5:00
Drop Box	3870 Crenshaw Blvd	5:00
Drop Box	5100 W Goldleaf Cir	5:00
Drop Box	5120 W Goldleaf Cir	5:00
My Mailbox	3717 S La Brea Ave	4:30
Mailboxes Depot	5786 Rodeo Rd	3:30

Map 11 • South Central West *

Drop Box	900 Exposition Blvd	5:00
Drop Box	4401 Crenshaw Blvd	4:00
Drop Box	840 Childs Wy	4:00
Echo Int'l Co	2701 W Western Ave	4:00

Map 12 • South Central East *

FedEx Staffed	3333 S Grand Ave	6:00
Drop Box	1701 S Figueroa St	5:15
Drop Box	2723 S Figueroa St	5:15
Drop Box	1631 S Alameda St	5:00
Drop Box	1933 S Broadway	5:00

Map 13 • Inglewood *

Drop Box	101 N La Brea Ave	5:30
Drop Box	111 N La Brea Ave	5:30
Drop Box	300 E Hillcrest Blvd	5:00
Drop Box	333 N Prairie Ave	5:00
Drop Box	401 S Prairie Ave	5:00

The Mail Connection	6709 La Tijera Blvd	5:00
Drop Box	811 N La Brea Ave	4:30
Drop Box	1050 S Prairie Ave	4:30
One Stop Shipping & Supplies	724 N La Brea Ave	4:00
Postal Plus	309 E Hillcrest Blvd	4:00

Map 14 • Inglewood East *

Drop Box	2200 W Century Blvd	4:45
One-Stop Post Parcel Center	2107 W Manchester Ave	4:00

Map 15 • Pacific Palisades *

Drop Box	15209 W Sunset Blvd	4:01
Drop Box	860 Via de la Paz	4:01
Drop Box	881 Alma Real Dr	4:01
Mail Boxes Etc	15332 Antioch St	4:01
The Office Supplier	15237 W Sunset Blvd	3:46
Palisadus Letter Shop	865 Via de la Paz	3:31

Map 16 • Brentwood *

Drop Box	200 S Barrington Ave	5:16
Drop Box	11611 San Vicente Blvd	5:01
Drop Box	11661 San Vicente Blvd	5:01
Drop Box	11726 San Vicente Blvd	5:01
Drop Box	11812 San Vicente Blvd	5:01
Drop Box	11911 San Vicente Blvd	5:01
Mail Boxes Etc #1577	149 S Barrington Ave	5:00
Drop Box	11777 San Vicente Blvd	4:46
Brentwood Mail Box	11693 San Vicente Blvd	4:31
Drop Box	12011 San Vicente Blvd	4:11
Drop Box	11999 San Vicente Blvd	4:06
Brentwood Shipping & Mail	212 26th St	4:01

Map 17 • Bel Air/Holmby Hills *

Drop Box	612 N Sepulveda Blvd	4:31

Map 18 • Santa Monica *

FedEx Staffed	925 Wilshire Blvd	6:00
Drop Box	100 Wilshire Blvd	5:31
Drop Box	1250 4th St	5:31
Drop Box	1401 Ocean Ave	5:31
Ocean Park Mail & Bus	171 Pier Ave	5:31
Drop Box	1437 7th St	5:15
Drop Box	1248 5th St	5:16
Drop Box	501 Santa Monica Blvd	5:05
Drop Box	120 Broadway	5:01
Drop Box	1245 16th St	5:01
Drop Box	1250 6th St	5:01
Drop Box	1299 Ocean Ave	5:01
Drop Box	1601 Cloverfield Blvd	5:01
Drop Box	1630 17th St	5:01
Drop Box	1640 5th St	5:01
Drop Box	1661 Lincoln Blvd	5:01
Drop Box	1717 4th St	5:01
Drop Box	1821 Wilshire Blvd	5:01
Drop Box	1919 Santa Monica Blvd	5:01
Drop Box	2001 Wilshire Blvd	5:01
Drop Box	2020 Santa Monica Blvd	5:01
Drop Box	233 Wilshire Blvd	5:01
Drop Box	2415 Main St	5:01
Drop Box	2425 Colorado Ave	5:01
Drop Box	2450 Colorado Ave	5:01
Drop Box	2720 Neilson Wy	5:01
Drop Box	401 Wilshire Blvd	5:01
Drop Box	429 Santa Monica Blvd	5:01
Drop Box	501 Colorado Ave	5:01
Drop Box	520 Broadway	5:01
Drop Box	725 Arizona Ave	5:01
Drop Box	902 Colorado Ave	5:01
FedEx Staffed	601 Wilshire Blvd	5:01
Drop Box	201 Wilshire Blvd	4:46
Drop Box	2120 Colorado Ave	4:46
Drop Box	530 Wilshire Blvd	4:46
Box Brothers	2113 Wilshire Blvd	4:35
Aim Mail Centers #4	2461 Santa Monica Blvd	4:31
Drop Box	1422 2nd St # 24	4:31
Drop Box	1542 15th St	4:31

Drop Box	1750 Ocean Park Blvd	4:31
Drop Box	2001 Santa Monica Blvd	4:31
Drop Box	2040 Broadway	4:31
Drop Box	2121 16th St	4:31
Drop Box	221 Hampton Dr	4:31
Drop Box	2444 Wilshire Blvd	4:31
The Mail House	1247 Lincoln Blvd	4:31
Posttel Business Center	2118 Wilshire Blvd	4:30
Box Brothers	825 Wilshire Blvd	4:01
Mail & Photo	1112 Montana Ave	3:46
Lowels Santa Monica Hotel	1700 Ocean Ave	3:31
Delta Instant Press	828 Pico Blvd	3:30

Map 19 • West LA/Santa Monica East *

Drop Box	11420 Santa Monica Blvd	5:31
Drop Box	11601 Wilshire Blvd	5:31
FedEx Staffed	11819 Wilshire Blvd	5:31
Drop Box	11620 Wilshire Blvd	5:16
Drop Box	11859 Wilshire Blvd	5:16
Mail Boxes Etc	1158 26th St	5:05
National Shipping Center	11664 National Blvd	5:05
Boxes Plus	11209 National Blvd	5:01
Drop Box	11111 Santa Monica Blvd	5:01
Drop Box	11150 Santa Monica Blvd	5:01
Drop Box	11150 W Olympic Blvd	5:01
Drop Box	11340 W Olympic Blvd	5:01
Drop Box	11377 W Olympic Blvd	5:01
Drop Box	11400 W Olympic Blvd	5:01
Drop Box	11500 W Olympic Blvd	5:01
Drop Box	11755 Wilshire Blvd	5:01
Drop Box	11766 Wilshire Blvd	5:01
Drop Box	11845 W Olympic Blvd	5:01
Drop Box	11900 W Olympic Blvd	5:01
Drop Box	12100 Wilshire Blvd	5:01
Drop Box	12121 Wilshire Blvd	5:01
Drop Box	12233 W Olympic Blvd	5:01
Drop Box	12300 Wilshire Blvd	5:01
Drop Box	12301 Wilshire Blvd	5:01
Drop Box	12304 Santa Monica Blvd	5:01
Drop Box	12400 Wilshire Blvd	5:01
Drop Box	12424 Wilshire Blvd	5:01
Drop Box	1640 S Sepulveda Blvd	5:01
Drop Box	1815 Centinela Ave	5:01
Drop Box	1849 Sawtelle Blvd	5:01
Drop Box	1950 Sawtelle Blvd	5:01
Drop Box	1990 S Bundy Dr	5:01
Drop Box	2001 S Barrington Ave	5:01
Drop Box	2052 S Bundy Dr	5:01
Drop Box	2400 S Barrington Ave	5:01
Drop Box	2425 Olympic Blvd	5:01
Drop Box	2716 Ocean Park Blvd	5:01
Drop Box	2730 Wilshire Blvd	5:01
Drop Box	2800 28th St	5:01
Drop Box	2811 Wilshire Blvd	5:01
Drop Box	3000 Olympic Blvd	5:01
Drop Box	3130 Wilshire Blvd	5:01
Drop Box	3223 Donald Douglas Loop S	5:01
National Mailbox	2801 Ocean Park Blvd	5:01
Drop Box	1620 26th St	4:46
Drop Box	2525 Michigan Ave	4:46
Drop Box	2530 Wilshire Blvd	4:46
FedEx Staffed	2139 S Bundy Dr	4:46
VIP Postal Services	12335 Santa Monica Blvd	4:46
Box Brothers	11701 Wilshire Blvd	4:45
Boxes & More	11901 Santa Monica Blvd	4:31
Drop Box	11628 Santa Monica Blvd	4:31
Drop Box	12200 W Olympic Blvd	4:31
Drop Box	2440 S Sepulveda Blvd	4:31
Drop Box	3210 Ocean Park Blvd	4:31
Packaging Store	2510 Wilshire Blvd	4:31
Drop Box	2100 Sawtelle Blvd	4:16
Save On Box	2215 S Sepulveda Blvd	4:05
Drop Box	2701 Ocean Park Blvd	4:01

Last pick-up time, pm

Map 20 • Westwood/Century City

		*
FedEx Staffed	1925 Century Park E	6:30
FedEx Staffed	1520 Westwood Blvd	5:46
Drop Box	1900 Ave of The Stars	5:36
Drop Box	10100 Santa Monica Blvd	5:31
Drop Box	10250 Santa Monica Blvd	5:31
Drop Box	1801 Century Park E	5:31
Drop Box	2080 Century Park E	5:31
Drop Box	2121 Ave of The Stars	5:31
FedEx Staffed	10924 Weyburn Ave	5:31
Drop Box	10880 Wilshire Blvd	5:16
Drop Box	11000 Wilshire Blvd	5:15
Drop Box	924 Westwood Blvd	5:15
Mail Boxes Box & Ship	11041 Santa Monica Blvd	5:15
Mail Boxes Etc	914 Westwood Blvd	5:10
Box Brothers	1351 Westwood Blvd	5:01
Drop Box	10351 Santa Monica Blvd	5:01
Drop Box	10390 Santa Monica Blvd	5:01
Drop Box	10474 Santa Monica Blvd	5:01
Drop Box	10585 Santa Monica Blvd	5:01
Drop Box	10635 Santa Monica Blvd	5:01
Drop Box	10850 Wilshire Blvd	5:01
Drop Box	10877 Wilshire Blvd	5:01
Drop Box	10920 Wilshire Blvd	5:01
Drop Box	10940 Wilshire Blvd	5:01
Drop Box	10990 Wilshire Blvd	5:01
Drop Box	1100 Glendon Ave	5:01
Drop Box	11050 Santa Monica Blvd	5:01
Drop Box	1800 Ave of The Stars	5:01
Drop Box	1840 Century Park E	5:01
Drop Box	1880 Century Park E	5:01
Drop Box	1888 Century Park E	5:01
Drop Box	1901 Ave of The Stars	5:01
Drop Box	1999 Ave of The Stars	5:01
Drop Box	2029 Century Park E	5:01
Drop Box	2049 Century Park E	5:01
Mail Boxes Etc	1875 Century Park E	5:01
Box & Ship	2180 Westwood Blvd	4:50
Box City	2056 Westwood Blvd	4:46
Drop Box	10780 Santa Monica Blvd	4:46
Mail & More In LA	2331 Westwood Blvd	4:45
Drop Box	1000 Veteran Ave	4:31
Drop Box	10866 Wilshire Blvd	4:31
Drop Box	308 Westwood Plz	4:31
Drop Box	500 S Sepulveda Blvd	4:31
Plaza Printers	2025 Ave of The Stars	4:31
Print Run	950 Gayley Ave	3:30
Westwood Services Center	1414 Westwood Blvd	3:30

Map 21 • Venice

		*
Aim Mail Center	13400 Washington Blvd	4:05
Drop Box	1501 Lincoln Blvd	5:01
Drop Box	1601 Main St	5:01
Drop Box	330 Washington Blvd	5:01
Drop Box	636b Venice Blvd	5:01
USA Mail & Business Center	520 Washington Blvd	4:31

Map 22 • Mar Vista

		*
Drop Box	12910 Culver Blvd	5:31
Drop Box	3826 Grand View Blvd	5:31
Drop Box	4501 Glencoe Ave	5:31
Drop Box	4551 Glencoe Ave	5:16
Drop Box	11965 Venice Blvd	5:01
Drop Box	6060 Center Dr	5:00
Drop Box	13323 W Washington Blvd	4:46

Map 23 • Rancho Park/Palms

		*
Drop Box	10801 National Blvd	5:16
Drop Box	11270 Exposition Blvd	5:16
Drop Box	10951 W Pico Blvd	5:01
Drop Box	2566 Overland Ave	5:01
Drop Box	1180 S Beverly Dr	5:00
Drop Box	3415 S Sepulveda Blvd	5:00
Drop Box	3751 Motor Ave	5:00
Drop Box	9911 W Pico Blvd	5:00
Osg Print & Copy	10665 W Pico Blvd	4:16
24/7 Postal Center	10008 National Blvd	4:00
Mailboxes and More 24/7	3500 Overland Ave	4:00
Us 24-7 Postal Center	9854 National Blvd	4:00
West Side LA	3728 Overland Ave	4:00

Map 24 • Culver City

		*
FedEx Staffed	5575 Sepulveda Blvd	6:00
Drop Box	5701 W Slauson Ave	5:15
Drop Box	100 Corporate Pointe	5:00
Drop Box	11111 Jefferson Blvd	5:00
Drop Box	11144 Washington Blvd	5:00
Drop Box	301 Corporate Pointe	5:00
Drop Box	400 Corporate Pointe	5:00
Drop Box	5601 W Slauson Ave	5:00
Drop Box	9696 Culver Blvd	5:00
Drop Box	9942 Culver Blvd	5:00
Culver Mail Box	10866 Washington Blvd	4:30
Drop Box	3851 Overland Ave	4:30
Drop Box	600 Corporate Pointe	4:15

Map 25 • Marina Del Rey

		*
FedEx Staffed	4170 Del Rey Ave	6:30
Drop Box	13160 Mindanao Wy	6:01
Drop Box	4333 Admiralty Wy	5:16
Drop Box	4640 Admiralty Wy	5:01
Drop Box	4676 Admiralty Wy	5:01
Drop Box	4720 Lincoln Blvd	5:01
Drop Box	5419 McConnell Ave	5:01
FedEx Staffed	4350 Lincoln Blvd	5:01
Drop Box	7001 World Wy W	4:45
Box and Ship	4242 Lincoln Blvd	4:31
Box City 36	4220 Lincoln Blvd	4:31
Drop Box	7301 World Wy W	4:30
Drop Box	8055 W Manchester Ave	4:30
Drop Box	322 1/2 Culver Blvd	4:00
Playa Postal Center	8117 W Manchester Ave	4:00

Map 26 • Westchester/Fox Hills

		*
FedEx Staffed	11221 Hindry Ave	6:45
Drop Box	11222 S La Cienega Blvd	5:30
Drop Box	5757 W Century Blvd	5:30
Drop Box	9800 S La Cienega Blvd	5:30
Drop Box	9920 S La Cienega Blvd	5:30
Drop Box	5777 W Century Blvd	5:15
Drop Box	5933 W Century Blvd	5:15
Drop Box	5959 W Century Blvd	5:15
Drop Box	6167 Bristol Pkwy	5:15
Drop Box	6701 Center Dr W	5:15
Drop Box	9841 Airport Blvd	5:15
Drop Box	12555 W Jefferson Blvd	5:01
Drop Box	419 Hindry Ave	5:00
Drop Box	420 Hindry Ave	5:00
Drop Box	5200 W Century Blvd	5:00
Drop Box	5250 W Century Blvd	5:00
Drop Box	6053 W Century Blvd	5:00
Drop Box	6080 Center Dr	5:00
Drop Box	6101 W Centinela Ave	5:00
Drop Box	6133 Bristol Pkwy	5:00
Drop Box	6151 W Century Blvd	5:00
Drop Box	6225 W Century Blvd	5:00
Drop Box	7381 La Tijera Blvd	5:00
Drop Box	8901 S La Cienega Blvd	5:00
Drop Box	8939 S Sepulveda Blvd	5:00
Drop Box	9029 Airport Blvd	5:00
Drop Box	9133 S La Cienega Blvd	5:00
FedEx Staffed	5855 W Century Blvd	5:00
Mail Call	8726 S Sepulveda Blvd	4:45
Drop Box	6100 Center Dr	4:30
Drop Box	8704 S Sepulveda Blvd	4:30

Map 27 • El Segundo/Manhattan Beach*

Drop Box	1334 Park View Ave	5:45
Drop Box	300 Continental Blvd	5:45
Drop Box	300 N Sepulveda Blvd	5:45
Drop Box	100 N Sepulveda Blvd	5:30
Drop Box	1960 E Grand Ave	5:30
Drop Box	2101 Rosecrans Ave	5:30
Drop Box	2121 Park Pl	5:30
Drop Box	2141 Rosecrans Ave	5:30
Drop Box	222 N Sepulveda Blvd	5:30
Drop Box	2221 Rosecrans Ave	5:30
Drop Box	2250 E Imperial Hwy	5:30
Drop Box	831 S Douglas St	5:30
Drop Box	840 Apollo St	5:30
Drop Box	880 Apollo St	5:30
Drop Box	2221 Park Pl	5:15
Drop Box	225 S Sepulveda Blvd	5:15
Drop Box	101 Continental Blvd	5:15
Drop Box	1230 Rosecrans Ave	5:15
Drop Box	130 E Grand Ave	5:15
Drop Box	3601 N Aviation Blvd	5:15
Drop Box	1 Hornet Wy	5:00
Drop Box	1007 N Sepulveda Blvd	5:00
Drop Box	2041 Rosecrans Ave	5:00
Drop Box	2361 Rosecrans Ave	5:00
Drop Box	2401 E El Segundo Blvd	5:00
Drop Box	505 N Sepulveda Blvd	5:00
Drop Box	601 N Nash St	5:00
Drop Box	645 S Allied Wy	5:00
FedEx Staffed	630 N Sepulveda Blvd	5:00
Drop Box	201 N Douglas St	4:45
Drop Box	1600 Rosecrans Ave	4:30
Drop Box	425 15th St	4:30
Mail Stop Plus	1116 8th St Ste A	4:30
The Mailbox	531 Main St	4:30
Drop Box	818 Manhattan Beach Blvd	4:15
Current Events	1140 Highland Ave	4:00
Drop Box	1700 E Walnut Ave	4:00
Drop Box	898 N Sepulveda Blvd	4:00
Manhattan Postal Center	2905a N Sepulveda Blvd	4:00

Map 28 • Hawthorne

		*
FedEx Staffed	12600 Prairie Ave	6:45
FedEx Staffed	5201 W Rosecrans Ave	6:00
Drop Box	3690 Redondo Beach Ave	5:30
Drop Box	1 Northrop Ave	5:00
Drop Box	5220 Pacific Concourse Dr	5:00
Drop Box	5230 Pacific Concourse Dr	5:00
Drop Box	5245 Pacific Concourse Dr	5:00
Mail Box and Stuff	14402 Hawthorne Blvd	4:30
Postal Page	3918 W Rosecrans Ave	4:30
Vons Shopping Center	4001 Inglewood Ave	4:00

Map 29 • Hermosa Beach

		*
Drop Box	1102 Aviation Blvd	5:00
Drop Box	2200 Pacific Coast Hwy	5:00
Drop Box	2601 Manhattan Beach Blvd	5:00
Drop Box	565 Pier Ave	5:00
Drop Box	1426 Aviation Blvd	4:45
Drop Box	1620 Aviation Blvd	4:45
Drop Box	2215 Artesia Blvd	4:45
Beach Mail Box	2629 Manhattan Ave	4:30
Drop Box	1139 Artesia Blvd	4:30
Effective Express	2613 Manhattan Beach Blvd	4:30
Box Brothers	2302 Artesia Blvd	4:00
Metech Copier & Ship Center	3407 Inglewood Ave	4:00

Map 30 • Torrance North

		*
Drop Box	18080 Crenshaw Blvd	5:00
Drop Box	18411 Crenshaw Blvd	5:00
Drop Box	205th St & Beech Ave	5:00
Drop Box	2908 Oregon Ct	5:30
Drop Box	3547 Voyager Wy	5:00
Drop Box	3625 Del Amo Blvd	5:30
Drop Box	3880 Del Amo Blvd #3914	5:00
Postal Boxes Etc	17252 Hawthorne Blvd	4:45
Pit Stop Packaging	15900 Crenshaw Blvd	4:30
Postal Plus	17528 Hawthorne Blvd	4:30
Mj Express Mail	3025 Artesia Blvd	4:15

Map 31 • Redondo Beach

		*
FedEx Staffed	21023 Hawthorne Blvd	6:00
Drop Box	21250 Hawthorne Blvd	5:30
Drop Box	21535 Hawthorne Blvd	5:30
Drop Box	23326 Hawthorne Blvd	5:30
Drop Box	23456 Hawthorne Blvd	5:30
FedEx Staffed	23325 Hawthorne Blvd	5:30
Drop Box	21307 Hawthorne Blvd	5:15
Drop Box	3838 W Carson St	5:15
Drop Box	200 S Pacific Coast Hwy	5:00
Drop Box	22750 Hawthorne Blvd	5:00
Drop Box	23430 Hawthorne Blvd	5:00
Drop Box	24 Malaga Cove Plz	5:00
Drop Box	4216 Pacific Coast Hwy	5:00
Mail Boxes Etc	21143 Hawthorne Blvd	5:00
Postal Solutions	4455 Torrance Blvd	5:00
Drop Box	1201 N Catalina Ave	4:30
Drop Box	1611 S Catalina Ave	4:30
Drop Box	1611 S Pacific Coast Hwy	4:30
FedEx Staffed	1770 S Pacific Coast Hwy	4:30
Mail Stop Extra	817 Torrance Blvd	4:30
Drop Box	811 N Catalina Ave	4:15

* Last pick-up time, pm

Packaging Store	1207 S Pacific Coast Hwy	4:15
Post Net	217 Palos Verdes Blvd	4:15
Postal Annex Rb	553 N Pacific Coast Hwy	4:00
Drop Box	119 W Torrance Blvd	3:30

Map 32 • Torrance South *

Drop Box	23545 Crenshaw Blvd	5:30
Drop Box	2501 W 237th St	5:30
Drop Box	2535 W 237th St	5:30
Drop Box	3305 Fujita St	5:30
Drop Box	1919 Torrance Blvd	5:15
Drop Box	21171 S Western Ave	5:15
Drop Box	Telo Ave & Fujita St	5:15
Box Brothers Lomita	1827 1/2 Pacific Coast Hwy	5:00
Drop Box	1433 Marcelina Ave	5:00
Drop Box	1815 W 213th St	5:00
Drop Box	1820 W Carson St	5:00
Drop Box	2377 Crenshaw Blvd	5:00
Drop Box	2510 Monterey St	5:00
Drop Box	25131 Narbonne Ave	5:00
Drop Box	2601 Airport Dr	5:00
Drop Box	2780 Skypark Dr	5:00
Drop Box	3400 Torrance Blvd	5:00
Drop Box	3424 W Carson St	5:00
Drop Box	3440 Lomita Blvd	5:00
Drop Box	3528 Torrance Blvd	5:00
Postal Center	1658 W Carson St	5:00
Drop Box	2720 Monterey St	4:45
Mail Boxes Galore	1880 W Carson St	4:45
The Postal Mart	2537 Pacific Coast Hwy	4:45
Aim Mail Center 107	24631 Crenshaw Blvd	4:30
Drop Box	21081 S Western Ave	4:30
Drop Box	3665 Pacific Coast Hwy	4:30
Lomita Mail Car	2017 Lomita Blvd	4:30
Postal Annex	24325 Crenshaw Blvd	4:30

Map 33 • Highland Park *

Drop Box	7435 N Figueroa St	4:30
Eaglerock Mailing Center	2272 Colorado Blvd	4:00

Map 34 • Pasadena *

FedEx Staffed	135 N Los Robles Ave	5:45
FedEx Staffed	855 E Colorado Blvd	5:30
Drop Box	150 S Los Robles Ave	5:15
Drop Box	210 S De Lacey Ave	5:15
Drop Box	46 Smith Aly	5:15
Drop Box	1001 Fremont Ave	5:00
Drop Box	101 S Marengo Ave	5:00
Drop Box	1111 S Arroyo Pkwy	5:00
Drop Box	145 Pasadena Ave	5:00
Drop Box	150 E Colorado Blvd	5:00
Drop Box	155 N Lake Ave	5:00
Drop Box	199 S Los Robles Ave	5:00
Drop Box	2 N Lake Ave	5:00
Drop Box	200 S Los Robles Ave	5:00
Drop Box	201 S Lake Ave	5:00
Drop Box	221 E Walnut St	5:00
Drop Box	273 S Lake Ave	5:00
Drop Box	300 N Lake Ave	5:00
Drop Box	301 N Lake Ave	5:00
Drop Box	35 N Lake Ave	5:00
Drop Box	35 S Raymond Ave	5:00
Drop Box	350 W Colorado Blvd	5:00
Drop Box	55 S Lake Ave	5:00
Drop Box	600 S Lake Ave	5:00
Drop Box	625 Fair Oaks Ave	5:00
Drop Box	719 Mission St	5:00
Drop Box	800 E Colorado Blvd	5:00
Drop Box	937 E Green St	5:00
Drop Box	99 W California Blvd	5:00
Drop Box	117 E Colorado Blvd	4:45
Drop Box	123 S Marengo Ave	4:45
Drop Box	200 E Del Mar Blvd	4:45
FedEx Staffed	460 Fair Oaks Ave	4:45
Drop Box	130 N Marengo Ave	4:30
Drop Box	140 S Lake Ave	4:30
Drop Box	2600 Mission St	4:30
Drop Box	281 E Colorado Blvd	4:30
Drop Box	600 Lincoln Ave	4:30
Drop Box	70 S Lake Ave	4:30
Mailbox Planet	530 S Lake Ave	4:30
Post Pack & Ship	115 W California Blvd	4:30
Post & Package	920 E Colorado Blvd	4:30
Box and Ship	319 S Arroyo Pkwy	4:00
Cal Oaks Box & Ship	422 S Pasadena Ave	4:00
Drop Box	125 S Grand Ave	4:00

Drop Box	721 E Colorado Blvd	4:00
Mail Box Plus	235 E Colorado Blvd	4:00

Map 35 • Pasadena East/San Marino *

Drop Box	1010 E Union St	5:00
Drop Box	1224 E Green St	5:00
Drop Box	2500 E Foothill Blvd	5:00
Drop Box	2540 Huntington Dr	5:00
Drop Box	2960 Huntington Dr	5:00
Drop Box	967 E Colorado Blvd	5:00
Drop Box	2060 Huntington Dr	4:45
The Postmaster	2245 E Colorado Blvd	4:45
Drop Box	2609 E Colorado Blvd	4:30
Drop Box	1055 E Colorado Blvd	4:00
Box City #5	2650 E Colorado Blvd	3:00

Map 36 • Mt Washington *

FedEx Staffed	2000 N San Fernando Rd	6:00
Boxes Express	4302 N Figueroa St	4:00

Map 37 • Lincoln Heights *

Drop Box	1900 N Main St	5:00

Map 38 • El Sereno *

Mail Depot	200 N Huntington Dr	4:00
TBS- Tax & Bus Svcs	5902 Monterey Rd	4:00

Map 39 • Alhambra *

Drop Box	1603 W Valley Blvd	5:15
Box-All Parcel Center	2107 W Commonwealth Ave	5:00
Drop Box	801 S Garfield Ave	5:00
Drop Box	10 W Bay State St	4:45
Drop Box	610 E Valley Blvd	4:30
Broad Solutions	630 E Main St	4:00

Map 40 • Boyle Heights *

Drop Box	1200 N State St	5:00
Drop Box	1240 N Mission Rd	4:45
Drop Box	2010 Zonal Ave	4:45

Map 41 • City Terrace/East LA *

Drop Box	1000 Corporate Center Dr	5:00
Drop Box	1255 Corporate Center Dr	5:00
Drop Box	2540 Corporate Pl	5:00

Map 42 • Chatsworth *

Drop Box	9430 Topanga Canyon Blvd	5:00
Drop Box	9592 Topanga Canyon Blvd	5:00
Mail & Box Depot	21911 Devonshire St	4:45
PostNet	9909 Topanga Canyon Blvd	4:45
Chatsworth Postal Center	21704 Devonshire St	4:30
Drop Box	21606 Devonshire St	4:30
Drop Box	21610 Lassen St	4:30
Mail America	20863 Lassen St	4:00
Mail Boxes & Beyond	10200 Mason Ave	3:30

Map 43 • Granada Hills/Northridge *

Box Brothers	8925 Reseda Blvd	5:00
Drop Box	19215 Parthenia St	5:00
Drop Box	19809 Prarie St	5:00
Drop Box	19850 Plummer St	5:00
Drop Box	19900 Plummer St	5:00
Drop Box	20001 Prairie St	5:00
Drop Box	9003 Reseda Blvd	5:00
Drop Box	9200 Oakdale Ave	5:00
Drop Box	9401 Oakdale Ave	5:00
Drop Box	9451 Corbin Ave	5:00
FedEx Staffed	10725 Zelzah Ave	5:00
FedEx Staffed	9000 Tampa Ave	5:00
Mail Boxes Etc	9420 Reseda Blvd	5:00
Mail Depot	18533 Roscoe Blvd	5:00
PostNet	9135 Reseda Blvd	5:00
Drop Box	9301 Corbin Ave	4:30
Drop Box	9301 Oakdale Ave	4:30
Drop Box	9401 Corbin Ave	4:30
Mail Box World	18543 Devonshire St	4:30
Drop Box	18039 Chatsworth St	4:00
Drop Box	18050 Chatsworth St	4:00
Injet-max	18110 Nordhoff St	4:00
US Mail Etc	9250 Reseda Blvd	4:00
Drop Box	11145 Tampa Ave	3:30

Map 44 • Mission Hills/North Hills *

FedEx Staffed	16633 Schoenborn St	5:45
Drop Box	16800 Devonshire St	4:45
Drop Box	8550 Balboa Blvd	4:45
Drop Box	15545 Devonshire St	4:00
Drop Box	15650 Devonshire St	4:00
Postal Plus	11024 Balboa Blvd	4:00

Map 45 • Canoga Park/Woodland Hills *

FedEx Staffed	21300 Vanowen St	6:00
Drop Box	19303 Ventura Blvd	5:00
Drop Box	20301 Ventura Blvd	5:00
Drop Box	21111 Erwin St	5:00
Drop Box	21271 Burbank Blvd	5:00
Drop Box	21300 Victory Blvd	5:00
Drop Box	21550 Oxnard St	5:00
Drop Box	21600 Oxnard St	5:00
Drop Box	21700 Oxnard St	5:00
Drop Box	21800 Burbank Blvd	5:00
Drop Box	21820 Burbank Blvd	5:00
Drop Box	21900 Burbank Blvd	5:00
Drop Box	5500 Canoga Ave	5:00
Drop Box	5550 Topanga Canyon Blvd	5:00
Drop Box	5850 Canoga Ave	5:00
Drop Box	5855 Topanga Canyon Blvd	5:00
Drop Box	5959 Topanga Canyon Blvd	5:00
Drop Box	6301 Owensmouth Ave	5:00
Drop Box	6320 Canoga Ave	5:00
Drop Box	6355 Topanga Canyon Blvd	5:00
Drop Box	6400 Canoga Ave	5:00
FedEx Staffed	21816 Victory Blvd	5:00
Drop Box	21800 Oxnard St	4:45
Drop Box	6351 Owensmouth Ave	4:45
Aim Mail Center	19301 Saticoy St	4:30
Drop Box	20121 Ventura Blvd	4:30
Drop Box	20501 Ventura Blvd	4:30
Drop Box	21201 Victory Blvd	4:30
Drop Box	21301 Burbank Blvd	4:30
Drop Box	21650 Oxnard St	4:30
Drop Box	5530 Corbin Ave	4:30
Drop Box	22120 Clarendon St	4:15
Box Brothers	19714 Ventura Blvd	4:00
Drop Box	20201 Sherman Wy	4:00
Drop Box	21333 Oxnard St	4:00
Drop Box	21801 Sherman Wy	4:00
Drop Box	22020 Clarendon St	4:00
Drop Box	22121 Clarendon St	4:00
Box City #17	7008 Topanga Canyon Blvd	3:30
Drop Box	6430 Independence Ave	4:00
Express Pack & Ship	7657 Winnetka Ave	4:30
Let's Talk Today	7140 Topanga Canyon Blvd	4:00
Mail Boxes Etc	19528 Ventura Blvd	4:30

Map 46 • Reseda *

Drop Box	17750 Sherman Wy	5:00
Drop Box	18840 Ventura Blvd	4:45
Drop Box	18401 Burbank Blvd	4:30
Drop Box	18425 Burbank Blvd	4:30
Drop Box	18455 Burbank Blvd	4:30
Drop Box	18757 Burbank Blvd	4:30
Drop Box	18801 Ventura Blvd	4:30
Drop Box	5535 Balboa Blvd	4:30
Drop Box	5805 White Oak Ave	4:30
Drop Box	6345 Balboa Blvd	4:30
Drop Box	6914 Canby Ave	4:30
Drop Box	5609 Yolanda Ave	4:00
Drop Box	7320 Reseda Blvd	4:00
Reseda	18349 Sherman Wy	4:00
Wall Street Connection	18663 Ventura Blvd	4:00

General Information • FedEx Locations

Last pick-up time, pm

Map 47 • Van Nuys

		*
FedEx Staffed	5810 Sepulveda Blvd	5:45
Drop Box	16380 Roscoe Blvd	5:15
Drop Box	15701 Sherman Wy	5:00
Drop Box	16461 Sherman Wy	5:00
Drop Box	16600 Sherman Wy	5:00
Drop Box	5990 Sepulveda Blvd	5:00
Drop Box	7120 Hayvenhurst Ave	5:00
Drop Box	14141 Covello St	4:45
Drop Box	6200 Van Nuys Blvd	4:45
Drop Box	7100 Hayvenhurst Ave	4:45
Box City	16113 Sherman Wy	4:30
Drop Box	5805 Sepulveda Blvd	4:30
Drop Box	6230 Van Nuys Blvd	4:30
Drop Box	15107 Vanowen St	4:15
Drop Box	6454 Van Nuys Blvd	4:15
B&E Postal Center	5632 Van Nuys Blvd	4:00
Box Brothers	16227 Victory Blvd	4:00
Civi Center Legal Service	14425 Sylvan St	4:00

Map 48 • North Hollywood

		*
Drop Box	11340 Sherman Wy	5:45
Drop Box	6400 Laurel Canyon Blvd	5:00
Drop Box	6180 Laurel Canyon Blvd	4:45
Drop Box	12807 Sherman Wy	4:30
Drop Box	7254 Bellaire Ave	4:30
Armati Printing	12901 Sherman Wy	4:00
Box City #2	12800 Victory Blvd	4:00
Smart Mailbox 2	12450 Burbank Blvd	4:00
Valley Box Office	12828 Victory Blvd	4:00
West Coast Mail Centers	13659 Victory Blvd	4:00

Map 49 • Burbank

		*
Drop Box	4605 Lankershim Blvd	5:30
Drop Box	4640 Lankershim Blvd	5:30
Drop Box	2140 N Hollywood Wy	5:15
Drop Box	2500 N Hollywood Wy	5:15
Drop Box	2627 N Hollywood Wy	5:15
Drop Box	5503 Cahuenga Blvd	5:15
Drop Box	4116 W Magnolia Blvd	5:00
Copy & Mail	2829 N Glenoaks Blvd	4:45
Drop Box	2255 N Ontario St	4:45
Drop Box	2740 W Magnolia Blvd	4:45
ASAP American Pack & Ship	3727 W Magnolia Blvd	4:30
Global Pack & Mail	1020 N Hollywood Wy	4:30
Drop Box	2924 W Magnolia Blvd	4:15
Abs Zone	3106 W Magnolia Blvd	4:00
In & Out Mailbox	10907 Magnolia Blvd	4:00
Mail Boxes & Accessories	859 N Hollywood Wy	4:15

Map 50 • Burbank East/Glendale West

		*
FedEx Staffed	101 N San Fernando Blvd	5:30
Drop Box	100 N 1st St	5:15
Box Brothers	1806 W Olive Ave	5:00
Drop Box	1700 Victory Blvd	5:00
Drop Box	1918 W Magnolia Blvd	5:00
Drop Box	2300 W Olive Ave	5:00
Drop Box	303 N Glenoaks Blvd	5:00
Drop Box	601 S Glenoaks Blvd	5:00
Mail Boxes Etc	1317 N San Fernando Blvd	5:00
Boxes & Accessories	263 W Olive Ave	4:45
Drop Box	101 S 1st St	4:45
Drop Box	1213 Flower St	4:45
Drop Box	333 N Glenoaks Blvd	4:45
Central Pak & Mail	145 S Glenoaks Blvd	4:30
Drop Box	217 E Alameda Ave	4:30
Drop Box	221 W Alameda Ave	4:30
Drop Box	1060 W Alameda Ave	4:00
Jenny's Postal Center	1436 W Glenoaks Blvd	4:00
Smart Mailbox	101 N Victory Blvd Ste L	3:30

Map 51 • Glendale South

		*
Drop Box	100 W Broadway	5:00
Drop Box	101 N Brand Blvd	5:00
Drop Box	1400 S Central Ave	5:00
Drop Box	144 N Glendale Ave	5:00
Drop Box	230 N Maryland Ave	5:00
Drop Box	315 Arden Ave	5:00
Drop Box	330 N Brand Blvd # B	5:00
Drop Box	425 E Colorado St	5:00
Drop Box	425 W Broadway	5:00
Drop Box	4820 San Fernando Rd	5:00
Drop Box	500 N Brand Blvd	5:00
Drop Box	500 N Central Ave	5:00
Drop Box	505 N Brand Blvd	5:00
Drop Box	550 N Brand Blvd	5:00
Drop Box	700 N Brand Blvd	5:00
Drop Box	700 N Central Ave	5:00
Drop Box	801 N Brand Blvd	5:00
FedEx Staffed	225 N Brand Blvd	5:00
Drop Box	517 E Wilson Ave	4:45
Drop Box	101 N Verdugo Rd	4:30
Drop Box	1010 N Central Ave	4:30
Drop Box	130 N Brand Blvd	4:30
Drop Box	300 W Glenoaks Blvd	4:30
ABC Mailbox	501 W Glenoaks Blvd	4:00
Drop Box	655 N Central Ave	4:00
Mail Boxes Etc	1125 E Broadway	4:00
Mail Boxes Etc	249 N Brand Blvd	4:00

Map 52 • Tarzana/Woodland Hills

		*
Drop Box	20700 Ventura Blvd	5:00
Drop Box	20750 Ventura Blvd	5:00
Drop Box	20969 Ventura Blvd	5:00
Drop Box	21031 Ventura Blvd	5:00
Drop Box	21241 Ventura Blvd	5:00
Function Junction	20841 Ventura Blvd	4:00
Mailbox International	4872 Topanga Canyon Blvd	4:00

Map 53 • Encino

		*
Drop Box	16633 Ventura Blvd	5:00
Drop Box	16830 Ventura Blvd	5:00
Drop Box	17000 Ventura Blvd	5:00
Drop Box	17337 Ventura Blvd	5:00
Drop Box	17547 Ventura Blvd	5:00
Drop Box	18321 Ventura Blvd	5:00
Encino Mail Boxes	4924 Balboa Blvd	5:00
Drop Box	4930 Balboa Blvd	4:45
Mail Boxes Etc	18034 Ventura Blvd	4:45
Drop Box	17200 Ventura Blvd	4:30
PostNet	17328 Ventura Blvd	4:30
FedEx Staffed	16652 Ventura Blvd	4:00
Mailboxes Int'l	18375 Ventura Blvd	4:00

Map 54 • Sherman Oaks West

		*
FedEx Staffed	15720 Ventura Blvd	6:00
Drop Box	15165 Ventura Blvd	5:15
Drop Box	15233 Ventura Blvd	5:15
Drop Box	15303 Ventura Blvd	5:15
Drop Box	16530 Ventura Blvd	5:15
Drop Box	14724 Ventura Blvd	5:00
Drop Box	14900 Ventura Blvd	5:00
Drop Box	15250 Ventura Blvd	5:00
Drop Box	15760 Ventura Blvd	5:00
Drop Box	15821 Ventura Blvd	5:00
Drop Box	15910 Ventura Blvd	5:00
Drop Box	15915 Ventura Blvd	5:00
Drop Box	16000 Ventura Blvd	5:00
Drop Box	16027 Ventura Blvd	5:00
Drop Box	16030 Ventura Blvd	5:00
Drop Box	16055 Ventura Blvd	5:00
Drop Box	16130 Ventura Blvd	5:00
Drop Box	16133 Ventura Blvd	5:00
Drop Box	16200 Ventura Blvd	5:00
Drop Box	16311 Ventura Blvd	5:00
Drop Box	16400 Ventura Blvd	5:00
Drop Box	16501 Ventura Blvd	5:00
Drop Box	15000 Ventura Blvd	4:45
Drop Box	16255 Ventura Blvd	4:45
All Boxed Inn	16161 Ventura Blvd	4:30
Drop Box	15060 Ventura Blvd	4:30
Drop Box	15206 Ventura Blvd	4:30
Drop Box	15300 Ventura Blvd	4:30
Drop Box	15315 Magnolia Blvd	4:30
Drop Box	15456 Ventura Blvd	4:30
Drop Box	15928 Ventura Blvd	4:30
Bizzy Box	16060 Ventura Blvd	4:00
Blvd Postal Stop N Service	15030 Ventura Blvd	4:00

Map 55 • Sherman Oaks East

		*
Drop Box	13400 Riverside Dr	5:15
Drop Box	13701 Riverside Dr	5:15
Drop Box	4400 Coldwater Canyon Ave	5:15
Box Brothers	13824 Ventura Blvd	5:00
Drop Box	5000 Van Nuys Blvd	5:00
FedEx Staffed	4556 Van Nuys Blvd	5:00
Drop Box	4730 Woodman Ave	4:45
Dickens Box	4335 Van Nuys Blvd	4:30
Drop Box	14011 Ventura Blvd	4:30
Drop Box	14140 Ventura Blvd	4:30
Federal Mailbox Center	4570 Van Nuys Blvd	4:30
Mail Boxes & Things	12930 Ventura Blvd	4:30
Around The Clock	4327 Woodman Ave	4:00
Mail Box Service Plus	14431 Ventura Blvd	4:00
Mail Boxes N More	14320 Ventura Blvd	4:00
Personally Yours Mailbox	13547 Ventura Blvd	4:00
Post Masters	13351 Riverside Dr	4:00

Map 56 • Studio City/Valley Village

		*
FedEx Staffed	12101 Ventura Blvd	5:30
American Post and Parcel	11333 Moorpark St	5:15
Drop Box	5200 Lankershim Blvd	5:15
Drop Box	12001 Ventura Pl	5:00
Drop Box	12711 Ventura Blvd	5:00
Drop Box	4370 Tujunga Ave	5:00
Drop Box	11304 Chandler Blvd	4:45
Drop Box	11846 Ventura Blvd	4:45
Drop Box	12605 Ventura Blvd	4:45
Pack N Mail	11054 Ventura Blvd	4:45
Drop Box	12450 Magnolia Blvd	4:30
Drop Box	12650 Riverside Dr	4:30
Drop Box	5161 Lankershim Blvd	4:30
EZ Pack & Ship	5424 Laurel Canyon Blvd	4:30
Postal & Packing Emporium	11288 Ventura Blvd	4:30
Postal Stop	12115 Magnolia Blvd	4:30
Studio Postal Service	4388 Tujunga Ave	4:30
Universal Mail & Business	12400 Ventura Blvd	4:30
Express Mailboxes	5062 Lankershim Blvd	4:00
Mailbox & Photo	4821 Lankershim Blvd	4:00
Studio City Postal Center	3940 Laurel Canyon Blvd	4:00

Map 57 • Universal City/Toluca Lake

		*
FedEx Staffed	3575 Cahuenga Blvd W	6:00
Drop Box	10 Universal City Plz	5:30
Drop Box	3500 W Olive Ave	5:30
Drop Box	3817 W Riverside Dr	5:30
FedEx Staffed	3817 W Riverside Dr	5:30
Drop Box	3151 Cahuenga Blvd W	5:15
Drop Box	3365 Barham Blvd	5:15
FedEx Staffed	4100 W Riverside Dr	5:15
Drop Box	3400 W Riverside Dr	5:00
Drop Box	3900 W Alameda Ave	5:00
Drop Box	4100 W Alameda Ave	5:00
Drop Box	4450 W Lakeside Dr	5:00
Drop Box	6711 Forest Lawn Dr	5:00
Drop Box	6735 Forest Lawn Dr	5:00
Drop Box	6767 Forest Lawn Dr	5:00
The Mail Box	10153 1/2 Riverside Dr	4:15
Packaging Store	10218 Riverside Dr	4:00

Important Phone Numbers

Life-Threatening Emergencies:	911
Citywide Services Directory:	311
Non-Emergency Information Line:	877-ASK-LAPD
	(275-5273)
Rape Victims Hotline:	626-793-3385
Suicide Hotline:	213-381-5111
Crime Victims Hotline:	213-485-6976
Domestic Violence Hotline:	800-978-3600
Missing Persons Unit:	213-485-5381
Sex Crimes Report Line:	213-485-2883
Legal Aid:	213-385-2202
Lights & Noise Complaints:	888-524-2845
California Highway Patrol:	323- 906-3434
Terrorist Threats:	877-A-THREAT
	(284-7328)
Website:	www.lapdonline.org

Statistics

	2004	2003	2002	2001
Homicide	515	517	647	605
Rapes	1,073	1,162	1,246	1,314
Robberies	13,990	16,484	17,072	17,065
Felony Assaults	15,295	17,557	18,940	18,965
Burglaries	22,637	24,862	24,893	25,442
Child/Spousal Abuse	11,031	12,786	13,432	13,930
Grand Theft Auto	28,260	32,033	32,370	30,428

Police Stations

	Address	Phone	Map
Alhambra Police Dept	211 S 1st St	626-570-5107	39
Beverly Hills Police	464 N Rexford Dr	310-550-4951	1
Burbank Police Dept	200 N 3rd St	818-238-3333	50
CSU Northridge Police Dept	18111 Nordhoff St	818-677-2111	43
Culver City Police Dept	4040 Duquesne Ave	310-837-1221	24
El Segundo City Police Dept	348 Main St	310-524-2200	27
Glendale Police Dept	131 N Isabel St	818-548-4840	51
Hawthorne Police Dept	4440 W 126th St	310-970-7976	28
Hermosa Beach Police Dept	540 Pier Ave	310-318-0360	29
Inglewood Police Dept	1 W Manchester Blvd	310-412-5111	13
Lawndale Sheriff Service Center	15331 Prairie Ave	310-219-2750	28
Los Angeles County Sheriff's Department:			
Marina del Rey Station	13851 Fiji Wy	310-823-7762	25
Universal Citywalk	1000 Universal Studios Blvd	818-622-9539	57
Lennox Station	4331 W Lennox Blvd	310-617-7531	13
West Hollywood Station	720 N San Vicente Blvd	310-855-8850	2
Los Angeles Police Department:			
Administrative Office	150 N Los Angeles St	213-485-3205	9
	1358 Wilcox Ave	213-972-2971	3
	4861 W Venice Blvd	213-473-0476	7
	4849 W Venice Blvd	213-473-0277	7
	2710 W Temple St	213-485-4061	8
	251 E 6th St	213-485-3294	9
	1546 W Martin Luther King Jr Blvd	213-485-2582	11
	3400 S Central Ave	323-846-6524	12
	1663 Butler Ave	310-575-8402	19
	12312 Culver Blvd	310-482-6334	22
	2111 E 1st St	213-485-2942	40
	10250 Etiwanda Ave	818-832-0633	43
	19020 Vanowen St	818-756-8542	45
	6240 Sylmar Ave	818-756-8343	47
	11640 Burbank Blvd	818-623-4016	48
	3353 N San Fernando Rd	213-485-2563	51
Manhattan Beach Police Dept	1501 N Peck Ave	310-802-5100	27
Pasadena Police Dept	207 N Garfield Ave	626-744-4501	34
Redondo Beach Police Dept Main Station	401 Diamond St	310-379-2477	31
San Marino Police Dept	2200 Huntington Dr	626-300-0720	35
Santa Monica Police Headquarters	1685 Main St	310-395-9931	18
South Pasadena Police Dept	1422 Mission St	626-403-7270	34
Torrance Police Dept	3300 Civic Center Dr	310-328-3456	30

Many of Los Angeles' landmarks double as a tangible history of the city. From the Mexican-influenced architecture to the ubiquitous and confusion-inducing billboards of Angelyne, a cruise around Los Angeles is more educational—and much cheaper—than a day spent at Disneyland.

Suggested itineraries for playing tourist in your own town are: mural sightings in Echo Park and East LA; rediscovering the stars on Hollywood Boulevard and a drink at the historical and newly refurbished **Pig 'n Whistle**; an afternoon of browsing in the downtown **LA Central Library** and a stroll in the surrounding Maguire Gardens, topped off with a bite at **Clifton's Cafeteria**; or a train ride in **Griffith Park**, followed by a golf lesson at one of the four unpretentious courses where novices are welcome.

Historical LA

Grand Central Market in downtown Los Angeles has been operating since 1917 and is still a great place to buy meat, produce, and ice cream. Just across the street is **Angel's Flight**, a relic from old LA's ancient trolley system. If beach-going is your idea of a good time, be sure to ride the Ferris Wheel at **Santa Monica Pier** after a day of surf and sand**.** Just south of Santa Monica, the remaining four **Venice Canals** (between Venice Boulevard and Sherman Canal Court) give you a sense of Abbot Kinney's original 1904 Italian vision for this beach community.

Buildings

Hollywood's cylindrical **Capital Records Building** is evocative of a pile of vinyl on a spindle. In the same 'hood, **Grauman's Chinese Theatre**, which opened in 1927, recently reverted back to its original name after a 30-year stint as Mann's Chinese Theatre. The green **Wiltern LG**, named for the intersection where it sits at Wilshire and Western, is a great example of Art Deco architecture. Downtown Los Angeles is home to a bevy of historical landmarks, among them the grand **Union Station**, built in 1939 in the Spanish mission style. The Persian-inspired **Shrine Auditorium**, formerly of Oscar fame, now hosts concerts. As a convergence of the holy and the post-modern, there is the impressive strength and serenity of the **Our Lady of the Angels Cathedral**, strategically placed to overlook one of the city's busiest freeway interchanges.

Outdoor Spaces

For all its freeways and urban sprawl, Los Angeles is home to some terrific places to have a picnic, go for a hike, hear music, cheer for your team, or just laze in the sunshine. The athletic flock to **Pan Pacific Park** in West Hollywood for softball and basketball; families, hikers, golfers, and horseback riders recreate in **Griffith Park**; golfers and sun seekers head to the vast **Rancho Park** in Cheviot Hills; and those seeking a refreshing hike in the hills visit the **Hollywood Reservoir**. There is absolutely nothing that can match an outdoor summertime concert at the **Hollywood Bowl** or the **Greek Theatre**—both boast awesome acoustics and make for a lovely evening of food, wine, and music. Much cherished by Angelenos and a fine example of mid-century modern architecture, **Dodger Stadium** opened in 1962 and still remains free of the ubiquitous corporate sponsor moniker. An enduring celebration of LA's Mexican heritage and always a great place to see traditional dancing while eating authentic Mexican food is **Olvera Street**, off Cesar Chavez downtown.

Architecture

Always a forward thinking city, Los Angeles has been attracting the funky and the innovative with its municipal reputation for starting trends. The results are evident in the colorful shapes of the **Pacific Design Center**, housing furniture, art galleries, and design offices. Two famous Frank Lloyd Wright-designed homes near Hollywood—the ailing **Ennis-Brown House** and the **Hollyhock House**—offer tours daily. The most recent architectural wonder in Los Angeles is, of course, Frank Gehry's **Walt Disney Concert Hall**—resembling a carefully wadded crumple of metal, the building is quite impressive both inside and out. Running a close second to Gehry's LA opus is the new, expressively modern **Caltrans District 7 Headquarters** in downtown.

Lowbrow Landmarks

Nobody did lowbrow better than the late great drunken saint of Los Angeles: Charles Bukowski. To relive the poetic debauchery, drop a few bucks and bet on the ponies at **Hollywood Park** near LAX; afterwards, take your winnings to tip the dancers at the seedy (yet historic) **Jumbo's Clown Room** in Hollywood, where the performers gyrate to Tom Waits and The Clash. **Whisky A Go-Go** is a distinct musical landmark surrounded by the garish cultural wasteland of the Sunset Strip. Once the home of legendary rock bands like The Doors, Love, Van Halen, and X, the Whiskey has since lost its luster to a never ending line-up of wanna-be bands. However, it's still worth a look, for posterity's sake.

Lame, Bad, & Overrated Landmarks

If **Rock Walk** doesn't prove as rockin' as you had hoped, cross the street and head to El Compadre for a kick-ass margarita to tame those blues. Further down Sunset you'll find the **Sunset Strip**. Crowded with hordes of suburban drunk kids, gridlocked traffic, and cops at every corner, the Strip is best done once and left to the tourists thereafter. Many of the tourist traps on Hollywood Boulevard are a waste of traveler's checks; avoid the **Hollywood Wax Museum** and the sterile, new **Hollywood & Highland Mall**. Also terribly overrated are the **La Brea Tar Pits**—smelly and boring, they've lost the arresting appeal they once possessed thousands of years ago.

Underrated Landmarks

The **Silent Movie Theatre** on Fairfax was silenced for a number of years following the murder of its second owner, Lawrence Austin, in 1997, but now it's up and running again and definitely worth a visit. Continuing in the macabre vein of the dead and the silent, the **Hollywood Forever Cemetery** is the final resting place of Douglas Fairbanks, the Talmadge sisters, and Charlie Chaplin. Old films are frequently shown al fresco in the graveyard—check www.cinespia.org for details. For a little more Hollyweird, check out the **Magic Castle**—you can book a room here or go for dinner and a show put on by some of the world's premiere smoke-and-mirror masters. Sticking with the weirdly metaphysical, head on over to the **Museum of Jurassic Technology** on Venice Boulevard for a peek into a cabinet of curiosities that will surely leave you dumbstruck.

Map 1 • Beverly Hills

Academy of Motion Pictures Arts & Sciences	8949 Wilshire Blvd • 310-278-8990	Brake for red carpets and klieg lights! Many premieres are held here.
Beverly Hills Civic Center	Rexford Dr & Santa Monica Blvd • 310-550-4654	Infrastructure for the rich and famous.
Beverly Hills Hotel	9641 Sunset Blvd • 310-276-2251	Legends have stayed at the Pink Palace.
Greystone Park	905 Loma Vista Dr • 310-786-1000	Formerly the Doheny Mansion, now a lovely public park.
Museum of Television and Radio	465 N Beverly Dr • 310-786-1000	Where reruns of old sitcoms are considered art.
Prada Store	469 N Rodeo Dr • 310-385-5959	Architect Rem Koolhaas gives BH something to look at.
Regent Beverly Wilshire Hotel	9500 Wilshire Blvd • 310-275-5200	Pretty Woman stayed here.
The Witch's House	516 Walden Dr	Fairytale haunt straight out of Hansel and Gretel.

Map 2 • West Hollywood

Case Study House #22 (Stahl House)	1636 Woods Dr	Pierre Koenig's architectural triumph that sums up the whole spirit of late twentieth-century architecture.
CBS Television City	Beverly Blvd & N Fairfax Ave • 323-852-2624	Wanna be on Price is Right? Come on down.
Chateau Marmont	8221 Sunset Blvd • 323-656-1010	Home to Hollywood stars and notoriety through the ages.
Pacific Design Center	Melrose Ave & San Vicente Blvd • 310-657-0800	Nicknamed "The Blue Whale" for obvious reasons.
Pan Pacific Park	7600 Beverly Blvd • 323-939-8874	It's a storm drain! We mean, it's a park!
Rock Walk	7435 Sunset Blvd • 323-874-1060	Grauman's Chinese has John Wayne, the Rock Walk has Slash.
Runyon Canyon Park	Franklin Ave & Fuller Dr	Once Errol Flynn's estate, now an off-leash hiking trail.
Santa Monica Blvd	b/w La Cienega Blvd & Robertson Blvd	The heart of gay West Hollywood.
Schindler House	833 N Kings Rd • 323-651-1510	A desert camp inspired this creation by architect Rudolph Schindler.
Silent Movie Theatre	611 N Fairfax Ave • 323-655-2520	Only the ticket prices will remind you that it's the 21st century.
Sunset Strip	Sunset Blvd b/w N Doheny Dr & N Fairfax Ave	Its clubs and restaurants are still the center of LA's nightlife.
Tail O' the Pup	329 N San Vicente Blvd • 310-652-4517	The only place you can buy a hot dog from a hot-dog-shaped building.
Whiskey A Go Go	8901 Sunset Blvd • 310-652-4202	Music venue for legendary bands of yore.

Map 3 • Hollywood

Capitol Records Building	1750 N Vine St • 323-462-6252	Designed to look like a stack of records.
Crossroads of the World	6671 Sunset Blvd	Former 1930s shopping center with a nautical theme deemed a cultural landmark.
Egyptian Theater	6712 Hollywood Blvd • 323-466-3456	Historic movie palace and home of American Cinematheque.
The Erotic Museum	6741 Hollywood Blvd • 323-463-7684	One serving of smut for every three servings of art.
Frederick's of Hollywood Lingerie Museum	6608 Hollywood Blvd	Two words: Madonna's panties.
Grauman's Chinese Theatre	6925 Hollywood Blvd • 323-464-8111	See how your shoe size measures up against Sylvester Stallone's.
Hollywood Bowl	2301 N Highland Ave • 323-850-2000	Eclectic music and picnicking under the stars.
Hollywood Forever Cemetery	6000 Santa Monica Blvd • 323-469-1181	The only place in LA where you can still see Douglas Fairbanks and Tyrone Power.
Hollywood & Highland Mall	6801 Hollywood Blvd • 323-467-6412	Sterile, touristy mall.
Hollywood Roosevelt Hotel	7000 Hollywood Blvd • 323-466-7000	Rumored to be haunted by Marilyn & other lingering spirits.
Hollywood Walk of Fame	Hollywood Blvd from N Gower St to La Brea Ter • 323-469-8311	Tourists love this shrine to often mediocre celebs.
Hollywood Wax Museum	6767 Hollywood Blvd • 323-462-5991	Celebrities in wax. Greeeat.
Magic Castle of Hollywood	7025 Franklin Ave • 323-851-0800	Spend the night or catch a show.
Pantages Theatre	6233 Hollywood Blvd • 323-410-1062	Go for the big Broadway shows.
Paramount Studios	5555 Melrose Ave • 323-956-5575	The last movie studio actually in Hollywood.
Pig 'n Whistle	6714 Hollywood Blvd • 323-463-0000	Hollywood watering hole and restaurant dating back to the golden era.
Ripley's Believe It or Not	6780 Hollywood Blvd • 323-466-6335	More oddities, less exhausting than Guinness Book.

Map 4 • Los Feliz

American Film Institute	2021 N Western Ave • 323-856-7600	The next David Lynch might be honing his craft here right now. Or not.
Ennis-Brown House (Frank Lloyd Wright)	2607 Glendower Ave • 323-660-0607	Frank Lloyd Wright's version of a Mayan temple.
Greek Theatre	2700 N Vermont Ave • 323-468-1767	A more intimate alternative to the Hollywood Bowl.
Hollyhock House (Frank Lloyd Wright)	4800 Hollywood Blvd • 323-485-4580	Another Frank Lloyd Wright design, open for public tours.
Jumbo's Clown Room	5153 Hollywood Blvd • 323-666-1187	The seediest little joint in Hollywood.
Silverlake Conservatory of Music	3920 Sunset Blvd • 323-665-3363	Neighborhood music school and hang-out courtesy of Chili Pepper Flea.

341

Map 5 · Silver Lake/Echo Park/Atwater

Angelus Temple	1100 Glendale Blvd	Founder claimed the Lord led her to the site.
Dodger Stadium	1000 Elysian Park Ave · 323-224-1400	With a view like this, who needs luxury boxes?
Echo Park	Glendale Blvd & Park Ave	The paddle boats alone are worth a trip.
Richard Neutra Houses	2200 Silver Lake Blvd	A don't-miss for architecture buffs.
Rowena Reservoir	Corner of Hyperion Ave & Rowena Ave	This strategically landscaped reservoir contains 10 million gallons of water and cost a few more million to build.
Silver Lake Reservoir	Silverlake Blvd & Duane St	Take a jog, a stroll, and a dog! There is an off-leash dog park at the reservoir's base.

Map 6 · Miracle Mile/Mid-City

Craft & Folk Art Museum	5800 Wilshire Blvd · 323-937-5544	If you like that sort of thing…
George C Page Museum of La Brea Discoveries	5801 Wilshire Blvd · 323-936-2230	Don't miss the La Brea Woman exhibit.
La Brea Tar Pits	Wilshire Blvd & S Curson Ave · 323-934-7243	It's just a big pool of tar, yet it continues to fascinate us.
LA County Museum of Art	5905 Wilshire Blvd · 328-857-6000	From King Tut to Jasper Johns, this museum covers it all.
LACMA West (former May Co Building)	6067 Wilshire Blvd · 323-933-4510	This art deco building used to be home to the May Co. Department Store.
Lula Washington Dance Theatre	5041 W Pico Blvd · 323-936-6519	Renowned African-American dance company with classes and residencies.
Petersen Automotive Museum	6060 Wilshire Blvd · 323-930-2277	Like you don't see enough cars in LA.

Map 7 · Hancock Park

Getty House (Mayor's official residence)	605 S Irving Blvd · 323-930-6430	The home that LA's mayors use to par-tay.
Los Altos Apartments	4121 Wilshire Blvd · 323-464-0600	There is a waiting list for apartments in this historic Spanish-style building.
Wilshire Ebell Theatre & Club	4401 W 8th St · 323-939-1128	Renaissance-style buildings used mainly for private events.
Wiltern LG	3780 Wilshire Blvd · 323-380-5005	Cool art deco building attracts equally cool, eclectic musical acts.

Map 8 · Korea Town

MacArthur Park	Wilshire Blvd & S Alvarado St	No longer the safest of public parks, but definitely one of the oldest.
Southwestern Law School	3050 Wilshire Blvd · 213-738-6700	Art Deco department store turned law school.

Map 9 · Downtown

Angel's Flight	W 4th St & Hill St · 213-626-1901	Due to a tragic accident, funicular is now simply a walkway.
Angeleno Heights	Carroll/Kellam/W Kensington Aves	Enclave of Victorian homes. Some lavished with astonishing TLC, some not.
Bradbury Building	304 S Broadway	Eclectic and dramatic Victorian masterpiece that was featured in *Blade Runner*.
Caltrans District 7 Headquarters	100 S Main St	A solar behemoth that is as energy efficient as it is commanding.
Chinatown	700-1000 N Broadway	It may not sound like much, but the slippery shrimp at Yang Chow can't be missed.
City Hall	200 N Spring St · 213-485-2121	Got a gripe? Here's the place to start.
Coca-Cola Building	1334 S Central Ave	LA historic monument, looks like a luxury cruise ship.
Clifton's Cafeteria	648 S Broadway · 213-627-1673	Tri-level cafeteria with a woodsy theme and fake animals since 1931.
Eastern Columbia Buildings	849 S Broadway	Do not leave these off of your tour of LA's Art Deco gems.
Garfield Building	403 W 8th St	Another Art Deco monument from LA's past. Check out the lobby.
Grand Central Market	317 S Broadway · 213-624-2378	Mexican specialties and more.
Instituto Cultural Mexicano	125 Paseo de la Plz · 213-624-3660	Dedicated to cultural exchange between American and Mexican cultures.
Japanese American National Museum	369 E 1st St · 213-625-0414	Chronicling the Japanese experience in the US.
LA Central Library	630 W 5th St · 213-228-7000	Grand downtown library.
LA Convention Center	1201 S Figueroa St · 213-741-1151	The building's green glass exterior is visible for miles.
Mayan Theater	1038 S Hill St · 213-239-0799	Spooky and cool. Check out the lobby if you can.
MOCA	250 S Grand Ave · 213-626-6222	Received much well-deserved attention for its wildly popular Andy Warhol retrospective.
MOCA at the Geffen Contemporary	152 N Central Ave · 213-626-6222	Formerly known as the "Temporary Contemporary," the museum is still going strong.
Museum of Neon Art	501 W Olympic Blvd · 213-489-9918	It's electric.
Music Center	135 N Grand Ave · 213-972-7211	Four music venues in one.
Olvera Street	Olvera St	An authentic Mexican marketplace in the heart of downtown L.A.

Our Lady of the Angels Cathedral	555 W Temple St	Architectural Catholicism for the post-Y2K generation.
Oviatt Building	617 S Olive St	Art Deco treasure. Be sure to sneak a peek inside.
STAPLES Center	1111 S Figueroa St • 213-742-7333	If the Staples folk could find a way to play baseball inside the arena, they'd lure the Dodgers too.
Union Station	800 N Alameda St • 213-625-5865	Makes you wish people still traveled by train.
Walt Disney Concert Hall	141 S Grand Ave • 323-850-2000	Gehry's architectural masterpiece.
World Trade Center	350 S Figueroa St • 213-489-3337	Far less impressive than its former NY namesake, but a vital part of Downtown nonetheless.

Map 10 • Baldwin Hills

Baldwin Hills Village Oil Wells	East of La Cienega Blvd	There's really oil in LA?
Kenneth Hahn State Recreation Area	4100 S La Cienega Blvd • 323-298-3660	Most people only think of this park as they're driving to LAX. That's a mistake.

Map 11 • South Central West

Exposition Park	Menlo Ave & S Park Dr • 213-765-5369	Forget the Coliseum and check out the Rose Garden. Or not.
LA County Museum of Natural History	900 Exposition Blvd • 213-744-3466	Kids just love the dinosaur fossils.
Museum of Science & Industry	700 State Dr • 213-744-7400	The IMAX theatre is the best part of the museum experience.

Map 12 • South Central East

LA Memorial Coliseum	3911 S Figueroa St • 213-747-7111	We're still waiting for that LA football team…
Shrine Auditorium	665 W Jefferson Blvd • 213-748-5116	The mosque design makes it one of the neighborhood's most visible buildings.
Sports Arena	3939 S Figueroa St • 213-748-6131	It's been pretty lonely here since the Clippers left.

Map 13 • Inglewood

Great Western Forum	Manchester Ave & Prairie Ave • 213-419-3100	The Lakers' and Kings' former home is now the Faithful Central Bible Church. There's irony for you.
Hollywood Park	1050 S Prairie Ave • 213-419-1500	When you've just got to play the ponies…
Randy's Donuts	805 W Manchester Blvd • 310-645-4747	Giant donut perched on top of this loved donut stop.

Map 15 • Pacific Palisades

Santa Monica Steps	4th St & Adelaide Dr	Climbing these is the most LA workout you can ever hope to have.
Self Realization Fellowship Lake Shrine Temple	Sunset Blvd near Palisades Dr • 310-454-4114	Stunning gardens.
Will Rogers Historic State Park	Sunset Blvd • 310-454-8282	Hiking, picnicking, and polo. Yes, polo.

Map 16 • Brentwood

Getty Center	1200 Getty Center Dr • 310-440-7300	Richard Meier designed with panoramic views.

Map 17 • Bel Air/Holmby Hills

Beverly Hillbillies' House	700 Bel Air Rd	Former Clampett stomping ground.

Map 18 • Santa Monica

3rd Street Promenade	3rd St b/w Broadway & Wilshire	Day or night, there's always something going on.
Heritage Square	Main St & Ocean Park Blvd • 310-392-8537	A taste of 19th century life amidst Starbucks and bagel shops.
Santa Monica Civic Auditorium/ Civic Center	1855 Main St • 310-393-9961	Bizarre mix of cool rock concerts and antique sales.
Santa Monica Pier	Ocean Ave & Colorado Ave • 310-458-8900	The merry-go-round, the chocolate-dipped bananas, and the view from the ferris wheel make it worth a trip.

Map 19 • West LA/Santa Monica East

Bergamot Station	2525 Michigan Ave • 310-829-5854	The best one-stop art experience you can have in L.A.
Museum of Flying	2772 Donald Douglas Loop N • 310-392-8822	Learn the history of the airport.
Santa Monica Municipal Airport	3223 Donald Douglas Loop S • 310-458-8591	Home to lots of small planes and private jets. And an annual Barneys N.Y. sale.
Veteran's Administration	Federal Ave & S Sepulveda Blvd • 213-809-7229	Non-veterans may wind up parking here when the UCLA lots are full.

Map 20 • Westwood/Century City

Federal Building	Wilshire Blvd & Sepulveda Blvd	Picketers of any and all causes seem magnetically drawn to this building.
Fox Plaza (AKA the "Die Hard" building)	2121 Ave of the Stars • 310-277-2121	Known to locals as "the Die Hard Building" for its role in the Bruce Willis actioner of the same name.

Map 20 • Westwood/Century City

Mormon Temple	10777 Santa Monica Blvd • 310-474-1549	Always one of the more festively lit buildings at Christmastime.
Playboy Mansion	10236 Charing Cross Rd	We'd tell you all about it if only Hef would send us an invitation.
UCLA Hammer Museum	10889 Wilshire Blvd • 310-443-7000	Cutting edge art museum with largely contemporary exhibits.
Wadsworth Theater	11000 Wilshire Blvd • 310-478-7578	They offer free jazz concerts on the first Sunday of every month.
Westwood Memorial Cemetery	1218 Glendon Ave • 310-272-2484	Marilyn Monroe and Natalie Wood are among the famous residents.

Map 21 • Venice

Chiat-Day Building	340 Main St • 310-305-5000	Frank Gehry's design features a large statue of binoculars marking its entrance.
Muscle Beach	1817 Ocean Front Wk • 310-578-6131	Don't forget to oil up first.
Venice Boardwalk	Ocean Front Wk	A freak show to some, while others thrive on the eclectic crowds that are drawn here.
Venice Canals	Venice Blvd & Pacific Ave	There used to be more than six, but they were deemed impractical and turned into roads.
Venice Pier	Far west end of Washington Blvd	It's been a casualty to weather conditions at least twice.
Windward Circle	Main St & Windward Ave	A great meeting place for those looking to spend the day at the beach.

Map 23 • Rancho Park/Palms

20th Century Fox Studios	10201 Pico Blvd • 310-277-2121	Check out the Star Wars mural. It's way cool.
Museum of Tolerance	9786 W Pico Blvd • 310-553-8403	A humbling experience that is worth a visit.
Rancho Park	W Pico Blvd & S Beverly Glen Blvd • 310-838-7373	Good, but crowded, municipal golf course.
Westside Pavilion	10800 W Pico Blvd • 310-474-6255	We defy you to find your car at the end of any shopping expedition.

Map 24 • Culver City

Culver Hotel	9400 Culver Blvd	Home to many a munchkin during the shooting of *The Wizard of Oz*.
Helm's Bakery Building	3233 Helms Ave	They used to make bread, now they sell furniture.
Museum of Jurassic Technology	9341 Venice Blvd • 310-836-6131	The coolest. Check out Mary Davis' horn.
Sony Pictures Studios	10202 W Washington Blvd • 310-244-4000	No tours, no trams, just Sony's foothold in the entertainment business.

Map 25 • Marina Del Rey/Westchester West

Ballona Wetlands	Around Ballona Creek	The city is encroaching upon these Wetlands, so their days may sadly be numbered.
Fisherman's Village	13755 Fiji Wy • 310-823-5411	"Quaint" shopping and dining are geared to resemble an East Coast fishing town.
Marina City Towers	4333 Admiralty Wy • 310-822-0611	Massive condo complex that has even turned up on shows like *Melrose Place*.

Map 26 • Westchester/Fox Hills/Ladera Heights/LAX

Pann's Restaurant	6710 La Tijera Blvd • 323-776-3770	Mid-century modern diner designed by Armet & Davis.

Map 27 • El Segundo/Manhattan Beach

Chevron Oil Refinery	East of Sepulveda Blvd, north of Rosecrans Ave	It ain't pretty, but it's definitely noticeable.
Manhattan Beach Pier	West of Manhattan Beach Blvd	Don't miss the Roundhouse Marine Studies Lab and Aquarium at the end of the pier!

Map 29 • Hermosa Beach/Redondo Beach North

Hermosa Beach Fishing Pier	End of Pier Ave	Just bring your pole. There are bait and tackle shops right on the pier.

Map 33 • Eagle Rock/Highland Park

Builder's Club	1269 Hill Dr	A kiwanis community service club.
Eagle Rock Community Cultural Center	2225 Colorado Blvd • 323-226-1617	Classes, performances, and exhibitions for the local community.
Judson Studios	200 S Ave 66 • 323-255-0131	Stained glass like you've never seen before.
League of United Latin American Citizens	4512 Eagle Rock Blvd • 202-833-6130	Helps to improve conditions for Latin-American Citizens nationally.

Map 34 • Pasadena

Ambassador Auditorium	131 S Saint John Ave	Operated by the Worldwide Church of God.

Gamble House	4 Westmoreland Pl · 626-793-3334	Pasadena's Craftsman style, at its best.
Old Town	Fair Oaks Ave & Colorado Blvd	A fine example of urban regentrification at work.
Pasadena City Hall	100 N Garfield Ave · 626-744-4000	A lovely building with even lovelier gardens.
Pasadena Civic Auditorium	300 E Green St · 626-793-2122	Home to both the Pasadena Symphony and the People's Choice Awards.
Pasadena Playhouse	37 S El Molino Ave · 626-356-7529	Back in the day, the Playhouse's now defunct acting school turned out many a movie star.
Rose Bowl	991 Rosemont Ave · 626-577-3100	UCLA football and a swap meet every month.
Wrigley Mansion	391 S Orange Grove Blvd · 626-449-7673	Check out the Mission-style architecture.

Map 35 · Pasadena East/San Marino

El Molino Viejo	1120 Old Mill Rd · 626-449-5450	Southern California's first water-powered gristmill. Who needs Disney's California Adventure?
Huntington Library and Gardens	1151 Oxford Rd · 626-405-2100	A perfect place to take relatives from out-of-town.

Map 36 · Mt Washington

The Lummis Home	200 E Ave 43 · 323-222-0546	An original home conceived by an original man.
Mount Washington Hotel/ Self-Realization	3880 San Rafael Ave · 323-225-2471	Beautiful gardens, which are open to the public.
Southwest Museum	234 Museum Dr · 323-221-2164	An underrated collection of Native American art.

Map 37 · Lincoln Heights

Heritage Square Museum	3800 N Homer St · 626-449-0193	A cluster of buildings that have been saved from demolition through relocation to Heritage Square.
Street Clock	2423 Broadway	Art Deco timepiece.

Map 39 · Alhambra

Ramona Convent School Museum	1701 W Ramona Rd · 626-282-4151	Some of the campus' buildings have been here since the 19th century.

Map 40 · Boyle Heights

El Corrido de Boyle Heights Mural	2336 E Cesar E Chavez Ave	Public art at its most colorful.
LA County USC	1200 N State St · 323-226-2622	The façade may look familiar to viewers of TV's *General Hospital*.
Mariachi Plaza	Boyle Ave & 1st St	Need a mariachi? Look no further!
San Antonio Winery	737 Lamar St · 323-223-1401	The last remaining winery along the LA river basin-- check out the killer tasting room.

Map 41 · City Terrace/East LA

Mural: The Kennedy Saga II 1973 (City Terrace Park)	1126 N Hazard Ave	Located inside the City Terrace Park social hall.

Map 44 · Mission Hills/North Hills

Greer House	9200 Haskell Ave	Frank Lloyd Wright Jr. crawled out from under his father's shadow and built a house.
Sepulveda Unitarian Universalist Society Building	9550 Haskell Ave · 818-894-9251	A church shaped like an onion—only in LA.

Map 45 · Canoga Park/Woodland Hills

Antique Row	21500 block of Sherman Wy	It is what it is.

Map 47 · Van Nuys

Van Nuys Airport	16461 Sherman Wy · 818-785-8838	The world's busiest general aviation airport.

Map 49 · Burbank

NBC Television Studios	3000 W Alameda Ave · 818-840-4444	The line forms early for crowds hoping to view the daily *Tonight Show* taping.
Warner Ranch	Verdugo Ave & Pass Ave · 818-954-6000	That NY fountain where TV's *Friends* dance in the opening credits? Right here on the ranch.

Map 50 · Burbank East/Glendale West

Los Angeles Equestrian Center	480 Riverside Dr · 818-840-9066	Polo, dressage, and the Los Angeles Gay Rodeo.
Walt Disney Studios	500 S Buena Vista · 818-560-1000	The quirkiest architecture of all of the major motion picture studios.

Map 51 · Glendale South

Alex Theatre	216 N Brand Blvd · 818-243-2539	Former Vaudeville house opened in 1925.
Forest Lawn Memorial Park	1712 S Glendale Ave · 800-204-3131	The Ponderosa of LA cemeteries.
Griffith Park	4730 Crystal Springs Dr · 323-913-4688	Ride the carousel.
Moonlight Rollerway	5110 San Fernando Road · 818-241-3630	Time stands still at Glendale's premier roller-boogie spot.

Map 53 • Encino

Rancho de los Encinos State Historical Park	16756 Moorpark St • 818-784-4849	The rancho was damaged in the Northridge quake, but the park is still open.

Map 54 • Sherman Oaks West

Ahh's Discount Store (formerly El Reina Theatre)	14622 Ventura Blvd • 818-990-2951	Once glamorous movie palace turned novelty store.

Map 56 • Studio City/Valley Village

Academy of Television Arts & Sciences	5220 Lankershim Blvd • 818-754-2825	Where else can you see a 20-foot tall Emmy award?
CBS Radford Studios	4024 Radford Ave • 818-655-5000	*Seinfeld*'s NY sensibilities were actually found here, in the heart of the Valley.
El Portal Theatre	5269 Lankershim Blvd • 818-508-4234	Former Vaudeville/Silent Movie house now anchors the NoHo Arts District.

Map 57 • Universal City/Toluca Lake

Bob's Big Boy	4211 Riverside Dr • 818-843-9334	The original Bob's Big Boy, as if the giant "Big Boy" out front didn't tip you off.
Campo de Cahuenga	3912 Lankershim Blvd • 818-763-7651	This historic park is not regularly open to the public.
City Walk	Universal Center Dr • 818-622-4455	High volume/low culture LA in miniature.
Forest Lawn Memorial Park	6300 Forest Lawn Dr • 800-204-3131	It's the Disneyland of cemeteries.
Hollywood Reservoir	East of Hwy 101	Jog or stroll around lovely "Lake Hollywood."
Universal Studios	100 Universal Center Dr • 818-777-1000	New Yorkers scoff at the Studio's diminutive "tower." Entering City Walk is like walking through the glitzy gates of mega franchise hell.
Warner Brothers Studios	4000 Warner Blvd • 818-954-1744	The studio's water tower serves as a beacon for much of downtown Burbank.

Long Beach

Adelaide A Tichenor House	852 E Ocean Blvd	Historic Greene & Greene house.
Alexander House	5281 El Roble St	Red brick modernist house by famed architect John Lautner.
Aquarium of the Pacific	100 Aquarium Wy • 562-590-3100	See, learn, touch marine life! Interactive entertainment.
Art Theater	2025 E 4th St • 562-438-5435	One of the last Art Deco movie theaters standing in Long Beach.
California State University at Long Beach	1250 N Bellflower Blvd • 562-985-5761	One of the top state colleges, athletically and scholastically.
Catalina Landing	330 Golden Shore	Go to and come back from Catalina Islandl
Edison Theater	213 E Broadway	This place has stories and ghosts in every wall panel.
Long Beach Convention & Visitor's Bureau	1 World Trade Ctr • 562-800-452-7829	It ain't just "Iowa by the Sea" anymore.
Long Beach Museum of Art	2300 E Ocean Blvd	Fine collection inside, lovely grounds outside.
Matlock House	1560 Ramillo Ave	Beautiful pitched-roof house from Richard Neutra.
Museum of Latin American Art	628 Alamitos Ave • 562-437-1689	Nationally reputable; bevy of time periods and artists featured.
Oil Drilling Islands	Off shore in Long Beach	Manmade oil-drilling islands decorated with loads of fake nature.
The Pike at Rainbow Harbor	Pine Ave & Shoreline Dr	Former seaside playland reinterpreted as a concept mall.
Queen Mary Seaport	1126 Queens Hwy • 800-437-2934	This dame shuttled soldiers and ferried the uber-rich.
Seashell House	4325 E 6th St	A piece of 1920s folk art made from crushed sea shells.
Shoreline Village	419 Shoreline Village Dr • 562-435-2668	Buy a hat, grab a snack and fly a kite 100 yards away.
The Skinny House	798 Gladys Ave	Deemed the nation's narrowest home.
Villa Riviera	800 E Ocean Blvd	Gothic wonder and former residence of Charlie Chaplin and Norma Talmadge.
York Rite Masonic Temple	835 Locust Ave	Grand Masonic temple.

San Pedro

Angel's Gate Cultural Center	3601 South Gaffey St • 310-519-0936	Don't miss this historical site.
Art Walk	W 4th St & S Pacific Ave	This is Who We Are, say San Pedro-ites.
Cabrillo Beach Bathhouse	3800 Stephen M White Dr • 310-548-7554	Renovated and worth a gander.
Catalina Express Terminal	Swingford St & N Harbor Blvd • 800-481-3470	Departs for and embarks from Catalina Island.
Ports O' Call	1100 Nagoy Wy	Ole touristy standby, still a pleasant afternoon.
San Pedro Farmer's Market	Mesa St, b/w 6th and 7th Sts	Avoid the traffic on Aviation to beach cities.

Los Angeles offers just a few too many hotel choices—so many, in fact, that it can easily induce a case of option paralysis. We offer this cheat-sheet to aid your decision-making. **Chateau Marmont**: legendary, low-key, timeless. The **Four Seasons**: beautiful rooftop pool, and with press junkets held year-round here, you never know who you might encounter on the elevator. Need a place to hide out while you recover from a "procedure?" The **Peninsula**, definitely. **Maison 140** and the **Avalon Hotel** are stylish, sexy, and lighter-hearted than the more Baroque stuff you'd otherwise find in Beverly Hills. (Similarly style-conscious and opening this year is their sibling property, the **Chamberlain** in West Hollywood.) The **Sunset Marquis** has a famously fabulous scene at the Whiskey Bar on-premises—though you must be a hotel guest, or a bold-faced name, to belly-up.

Feeling architecturally significant? Art Deco gem, the **Argyle**, is back in business after extensive renovations, and offers a substantially lower profile than Sunset Boulevard ball-hogs, the **Standard** and the **Mondrian**. Out at the beach, within sight of the Santa Monica Pier, but far from the maddening crowd is the delicious **Hotel Casa Del Mar**. If you are planning to spend a longish evening in Hollywood, book a room at the **Roosevelt**—a landmark within stumbling distance of all of clubland. And finally, when headed downtown, say, for an oversized night at the STAPLES Center, or for your company's Christmas blow-out, book one of the Moroccan Suites at the **Figueroa Hotel**. It's a quirky, mysterious beauty, and once you've time-traveled through the lobby, and sat down for a nightcap by the pool, you will wonder why it took you so long to find the place.

As with so many things, the best rates are always found online. Check out Tablet Hotels ("hotels for global nomads") for au courant, cool-design options; Luxury Link for the high-end stuff; Hotels.com, Hotwire, and Travelzoo, to cast a wider net.

Map 1 • Beverly Hills

			Average price	Rating
Avalon Hotel Of Beverly Hills	9400 W Olympic Blvd	310-277-5221	219	★★★★
Beverly Crescent Hotel	403 N Crescent Dr	310-247-0505	165	
Beverly Hills Hotel	9641 Sunset Blvd	310-276-2251	395	★★★★★
Beverly Hills Reeves Hotel	120 S Reeves Dr	310-271-3006	89	★★
Beverly Hilton	9876 Wilshire Blvd	310-274-7777	239	★★★★★
Beverly Pavilion Hotel	9360 Wilshire Blvd	310-273-1400	189	★★★
Four Seasons Hotel	300 S Doheny Dr	310-273-2222	455	★★★★★
Hotel Del Flores	409 N Crescent Dr	310-274-5115	85	
L'Ermitage Hotel	9291 Burton Wy	310-278-3344	498	★★★★★
Maison 140	140 Lasky Dr	310-281-4000		
Mosaic Hotel	125 S Spalding Dr	310-275-0303	275	
Peninsula Beverly Hills	9882 Santa Monica Blvd	310-551-2888	425	★★★★★
Regent Beverly Wilshire Hotel	9500 Wilshire Blvd	310-275-5200	425	★★★★
Summit Hotel Rodeo Drive	360 N Rodeo Dr	310-273-0300	209	★★★

Map 2 • West Hollywood

Argyle	8358 Sunset Blvd	323-654-7100	199	★★★★
Bel Age	1020 N San Vicente Blvd	310-854-1111	189	★★★★
Beverly Inn	7701 Beverly Blvd	323-931-8108	60	
Beverly Laurel Motor Hotel	8018 Beverly Blvd	323-651-2441	94	★
Beverly Terrace Motor Hotel	469 N Doheny Dr	310-274-8141	110	★★
Bevonshire Lodge Motel	7575 Beverly Blvd	323-936-6154	60	
Chamberlain Hotel	1000 Westmount Dr	310-657-7400	179	★★★★
Chateau Marmont	8221 W Sunset Blvd	323-656-1010	315	
Days Inn	7023 W Sunset Blvd	323-464-8344	99	★★★
Elan Hotel Modern	8435 Beverly Blvd	323-658-6663	170	★★★
Fairfax Motel	913 N Fairfax Ave	323-654-5570	29	
Farmer's Daughter Hotel	115 S Fairfax Ave	323-937-3930	124	
Grafton on Sunset	8462 Sunset Blvd	323-654-4600	169	★★★
Guest House Inn	7721 Beverly Blvd	323-692-1777	69	
Highland Gardens Hotel	7047 Franklin Ave	323-850-0536	99	
Holiday Inn Express	1520 N La Brea Ave	323-464-3243	119	★★★
Hollywood Seven Star Motel	1730 N La Brea Ave	323-876-2714	60	
Hollywood-La Brea Motel	7110 Hollywood Blvd	323-876-8000	56	
Hotel Sofitel	8555 Beverly Blvd	310-278-5444	249	★★★
Hyatt on Sunset	8401 Sunset Blvd	323-656-1234	189	★★★★
Le Meridien At Beverly Hills	465 S La Cienega Blvd	310-247-0400	219	★★★★
Le Parc	733 N W Knoll Dr	310-855-8888	185	★★★
Mondrian	8440 Sunset Blvd	323-650-8999	315	
Orbit Hotel	7950 Melrose Ave	323-655-1510	64	
The Orlando	8384 W 3rd St	323-658-6600	189	★★★★
Park Plaza Lodge	6001 W 3rd St	323-931-1501	95	
Ramada	8585 Santa Monica Blvd	310-652-6400	169	★★★
Saharan Motel	7212 W Sunset Blvd	323-874-6700	60	
San Vicente Inn	845 N San Vicente Blvd	310-854-6915	149	
Standard	8300 Sunset Blvd	323-650-9090	145	
Sunset Marquis Hotel	1200 N Alta Loma Rd	310-657-1333	299	★★★★
Travel Inn Hollywood	7370 W Sunset Blvd	323-876-0330	49	
Travelodge	7051 W Sunset Blvd	323-462-0905	85	

Map 3 • Hollywood

		Average price	Rating	
Best Inn	1822 N Cahuenga Blvd	323-467-2252	50	
Budget Inn	6826 W Sunset Blvd	323-465-7186	60	
Comfort Inn & Suites	2010 N Highland Ave	323-874-4300	109	★★★
Dunes Sunset Motel & Coffee	5625 W Sunset Blvd	323-467-5171	78	★★
Econo Lodge Hollywood	777 Vine St	323-463-5671	59	
French Cottage	6757 W Sunset Blvd	323-464-9144	50	
Guest House international Inn	6700 W Sunset Blvd	323-467-6137	79	★★
Holiday Inn	2005 N Highland Ave	323-850-5811	129	
Hollywood Celebrity Hotel	1775 Orchid Ave	323-850-6464	95	
Hollywood Center Motel	6720 W Sunset Blvd	323-462-6051	52	
Hollywood Downtowner Motel	5601 Hollywood Blvd	323-464-7193	69	
Hollywood Hills Hotel	6141 Franklin Ave	323-464-5181	109	★★★
Hollywood International Hotel	1921 N Highland Ave	323-876-6544	59	
Hollywood International Youth Hostel	6820 Hollywood Blvd	323-463-0797	40 private, 19 dorm	
Hollywood Metropolitan Hotel	5825 W Sunset Blvd	323-962-5800	89	★★
Hollywood Orchid Suites	1753 Orchid Ave	323-874-9678	99	★★½
Hollywood Plaza Inn	2011 N Highland Ave	323-851-1800	89	
Hollywood Roosevelt Hotel	7000 Hollywood Blvd	323-466-7000	149	★★★★
Hotel Mark Twain	1622 Wilcox Ave	323-463-2111	45	
La Mirage Inn	6020 Franklin Ave	323-464-1824	65	
Las Palmas Hotel	1738 N Las Palmas Ave	323-464-9236	35	
Liberty Hotel	1770 Orchid Ave	323-962-1788	75	
Magic Castle of Hollywood	7025 Franklin Ave	323-851-0800	139	★★★
Motel 6 Hollywood	1738 Whitley Ave	323-464-6006	60	
Renaissance Hollywood Hotel	1755 N Highland Ave	323-856-1200	249	★★★★★
St Moritz Hotel	5849 W Sunset Blvd	323-467-2174	45	
Trylon Hotel	6515 Franklin Ave	323-851-7036	50	
Vagabond Inn	1133 Vine St	323-466-7501	79	★★
Vine Lodge Hotel	1818 Vine St	323-464-9661	45	
Vista Hotel	1611 Vista Del Mar St	323-460-6000	45	
Western Plaza Motel	1066 N Wilton Pl	323-871-1126	55	

Map 4 • Los Feliz

Bon-Air Motel	1727 N Western Ave	323-464-4154	55	
College Hotel	4620 Santa Monica Blvd	323-666-3785	500/month	
Comfort Inn	321 N Vermont Ave	323-665-0344	70	★★★
Days Inn	5410 Hollywood Blvd	323-463-7171	65	★★★½
Economy Inn	5308 W Sunset Blvd	323-466-9191	52	
Gerschwin Hotel	5533 Hollywood Blvd	323-464-1131	42	
Harvard House Motel	5251 Hollywood Blvd	323-463-3238	85	
Holiday Inn Express	250 Silver Lake Blvd	213-387-5737	119	★★★
Hollywood Inn Express	5131 Hollywood Blvd	323-663-1243	53	
Hollywood Premiere Motel	5333 Hollywood Blvd	323-466-1691	55	
Hollywood Stars Inn	5435 W Sunset Blvd	323-462-0062	55	
Ramada Hollywood	1160 N Vermont Ave	323-660-1788	89	
Super 8 Motel	1536 N Western Ave	323-467-3131	64	
Travelodge	1401 N Vermont Ave	323-665-5735	75	★★
Tropicana Inn Motel	5444 Fountain Ave	323-469-4999	60	
Value Inn	5200 W Sunset Blvd	323-666-0692	55	

Map 5 • Silver Lake/Echo Park/Atwater

Comfort Inn	2717 W Sunset Blvd	213-413-8222	70	★★★
Holiday Lodge Motel	811 N Alvarado St	213-413-0050	65	
Los Feliz Motel	3101 Los Feliz Blvd	323-667-2567	79	★★★
Olive Motel	2751 W Sunset Blvd	213-413-0300	39	
Super 8 Motel	1341 W Sunset Blvd	213-250-2233	67	

Map 6 • Miracle Mile/Mid-City

Annes Motel	1755 S La Cienega Blvd	310-837-5173	60	
Best Motel	5350 W Olympic Blvd	323-936-6966	55	
Carlyle Inn	1119 S Robertson Blvd	310-275-4445	129	★★★
Cinema Motel	5274 W Washington Blvd	323-935-1526	35	
Gem Motel	4930 W Washington Blvd	323-934-3027	55	
Grand Motel	1479 S La Cienega Blvd	310-652-3644	40	
La Cienega Motel	1725 S La Cienega Blvd	310-559-1570	45	
Mansfield Motel	5000 W Washington Blvd	323-935-4060	48	
Olympic Motor Lodge	5850 W Olympic Blvd	323-936-1625	67	

Park Cienega Motor Hotel	1777 S La Cienega Blvd	310-837-5366	45	
Relax Inn Motel	1269 S La Brea Ave	323-939-3772	60	
Reno Motel	5136 W Washington Blvd	323-932-8251	45	
Royal Hawaiian Motel	1632 S La Brea Ave	323-937-2049	55	
Sea Way Motel	5961 Venice Blvd	323-933-2467	53	
Wilshire Crest Hotel	6301 Orange St	323-936-5131	98	
Wilshire Orange Hotel	6060 W 8th St	323-931-9533	65	

Map 7 · Hancock Park

Dunes Wilshire Motor Hotel	4300 Wilshire Blvd	323-938-3616	78	★
Friendship Motor Inn	1148 Crenshaw Blvd	323-937-1600	50	
Ramada Inn	3900 Wilshire Blvd	213-736-5222	85	★★★
Rotex Hotel	3411 W Olympic Blvd	323-734-7373	93	

Map 8 · Korea Town

Alexandria Motel	300 S Alexandria Ave	213-385-6015	75	
Alvarado Inn Towner Motel	1212 S Alvarado St	213-383-4774	45	
Alvarado Palms Motel	931 S Alvarado St	213-480-8867	50	
Best Western Mid-Wilshire Plaza Hotel	603 S New Hampshire Ave	213-385-4444	80	★★
Catalina 8 Inn	812 S Catalina St	213-739-8681	65	
Coronado Inn	682 S Coronado St	213-388-5277	50	
Days Inn	457 S Mariposa Ave	213-380-6910	62	★★
East West Hotel	3206 W 8th St	213-389-6711	60	
Garden Suites Hotel	681 S Western Ave	213-383-3344	91	
JJ Grand Hotel	620 S Harvard Blvd	213-383-3000	98	
LA Hamilton Tourist Hotel	3160 W 8th St	213-384-7768	65	
Mariposa Motel	518 S Mariposa Ave	213-388-1433	45	
Motel Inn	2787 W 8th St	213-487-0197	50	
New Seoul Hotel	2666 W Olympic Blvd	213-381-6262	84	
Oasis Motel	2200 W Olympic Blvd	213-385-4191	55	
Oxford Palace Hotel	745 S Oxford Ave	213-389-8000	103	★★★
Quality Inn & Suites Downtown	1901 W Olympic Blvd	213-385-7141	79	
Radisson Wilshire Plaza Hotel	3515 Wilshire Blvd	213-381-7411	149	★★★
Vermont Motel	1717 S Vermont Ave	323-730-1578	55	
Western Inn	921 S Western Ave	323-733-5166	69	
Westwood Inn	906 S Alvarado St	213-388-3137	60	★★
Wilshire Inn	3400 W 3rd St	213-385-0061	60	

Map 9 · Downtown

Alexandria Hotel	501 S Spring St	213-626-7484	141/week	
Baltimore Hotel	501 S Los Angeles St	213-627-5941	102/week	
Barclay Hotel	103 W 4th St	213-626-5231	30 w/bathroom	
Best Western Dragon Gate Inn	818 N Hill St	213-617-3077	119	★★★
Best Western Mayfair Hotel	1256 W 7th St	213-484-9789	89	★★
Bixby Hotel	433 Wall St	213-620-1374	25	
City Center Motel	1135 W 7th St	213-628-7141	45	
Daimaru Hotel	345 E 1st St	213-972-9208	45	
Delux Inn	355 S Alvarado St	213-484-1883	45	
Figueroa Hotel	939 S Figueroa St	213-627-8971	124	
Holiday Inn	1020 S Figueroa St	213-748-1291	109	★★★
Hollywood Inn Express	141 N Alvarado St	213-413-6699	50	
Hyatt Hotels & Resorts	711 S Hope St	213-683-1234	149	★★★
Jerry's Motel	285 Lucas Ave	213-481-8181	65	
Kawada Hotel	200 S Hill St	213-621-4455	90	★★★
Little Tokyo Hotel	327 1/2 E 1st St	213-617-0128	40	
Madison Hotel	423 E 7th St	213-622-1508	20	
Marriott Hotels & Resorts	333 S Figueroa St	213-617-1133	199	★★★
Metro Plaza Hotel	711 N Main St	213-680-0200	75	
Millennium Biltmore Hotel	506 S Grand Ave	213-624-1011	179	★★★★
Milner Hotel	813 S Flower St	213-627-6981	79	★★
Miyako Inn & Spa	328 E 1st St	213-617-2000	145	★★★
Motel de Ville	1123 W 7th St	213-624-8474	48	
New Otani Hotel & Garden	120 S Los Angeles St	213-629-1200	150	★★★★
Nutel Hotel	1906 W 3rd St	213-483-6681	45	
Olive Hotel	750 S Olive St	213-972-8931	40	
Omni Los Angeles Hotel	251 S Olive St	213-617-3300	229	★★★★
Paradise Motel	1116 W Sunset Blvd	213-250-9094	65	
Prince Hotel LA	1255 W Temple St	213-250-8925	59	
Ramada Inn	611 S Westlake Ave	213-483-8606	95	★★
Rosslyn Hotel	112 W 5th St	213-624-3311	40	

Map 9 • Downtown—continued

			Average price	Rating
Royal Pagoda Motel	995 N Broadway	323-223-3381	52	
Royal Viking Motel	2025 W 3rd St	213-353-0619	50	
Standard Hotel	550 S Flower St	213-892-8080	99	
The New Cecil Hotel	640 S Main St	213-624-4545	37	
Westin Bonaventure Hotel	404 S Figueroa St	213-624-1000	139	★★★★
Wilshire Grand Hotel & Centre	930 Wilshire Blvd	213-688-7777	149	★★★★
Wyndham Checkers Hotel	535 S Grand Ave	213-624-0000	249	★★★

Map 10 • Baldwin Hills

Adams Motel	4905 W Adams Blvd	323-731-2165	45	
Baldwin Hills Motor Inn	3020 S La Brea Ave	323-732-0864	65	
Expo Inn	4523 Exposition Blvd	323-731-9293	45	
Jet Inn Motor Hotel	4542 W Slauson Ave	323-295-2544	45	
Universal Inn	3930 W Slauson Ave	323-299-7741	45	

Map 11 • South Central West

Best Value Inn	4122 S Western Ave	323-294-5200	69	★★★
Harvard Motor Inn	1574 W Martin Luther King Jr Blvd	323-298-1018	65	
Mustang Motel	4121 S Western Ave	323-298-0351	65	
Raymona Motel	3211 W Jefferson Blvd	323-735-9077	48	
Santa Barbara Motel	1758 W Martin Luther King Jr Blvd	323-296-2576	55	
Snooty Fox Motor Inn	4120 S Western Ave	323-294-0083	75	
Y-Tell Motel	5501 S Western Ave	323-290-3563	55	

Map 12 • South Central East

Broadway Motel	301 W 49th St	323-231-4303	50	
City Motel	4731 S Figueroa St	323-232-4200	45	
King Junior Hotel	1194 E 35th St	323-233-5574	170/week	
Radisson Hotel Midtown	3540 S Figueroa St	213-748-4141	159	★★★
Sandpiper Motel	4112 S Central Ave	323-231-0249	60	
Vagabond Inn	3101 S Figueroa St	213-746-1531	89	

Map 13 • Inglewood

Airport Motel	4054 W Century Blvd	310-671-0104	45	
Airport Park View Hotel	3900 W Century Blvd	310-677-8899	51	
American Inn	11025 S Prairie Ave	310-412-7100	55	
Best Western Air Park Hotel	640 W Manchester Blvd	310-677-7378	89	★★★
Best Western Airport Plaza Inn	1730 Centinela Ave	310-568-0071	79	★★
Best Western Suites Hotel	5005 W Century Blvd	310-677-7733	109	★★★
Comfort Inn & Suites	4922 W Century Blvd	310-671-7213	79	★★★
Econo Lodge	4123 W Century Blvd	310-672-7285	57	
Econo Lodge	439 W Manchester Blvd	310-674-8596	65	
Geneva Budget Motel	321 W Manchester Blvd	310-677-9171	50	
Holly Crest Hotel	4027 W Century Blvd	310-673-8612	30	
LA Adventurer All Suite Hotel	4200 W Century Blvd	310-419-0999	55	
La Brea Hotel	524 N La Brea Ave	310-672-1333	35	
Lotus Motel	437 W Manchester Blvd	310-672-5586	57	
Marletta's Motel	4849 W Century Blvd	310-677-7500	40	
Motel 6	5101 W Century Blvd	310-419-1234	55	
Ramada Limited	4300 W Century Blvd	310-419-1011	58	★★★
Rodeway Inn	3940 W Century Blvd	310-672-4570	55	
Royal Century Hotel	4330 W Century Blvd	310-673-2400	45	
Sea Breeze Inn	4307 W Century Blvd	310-674-5444	45	
Super 8 Motel	4238 W Century Blvd	310-672-0740	54	
Tivoli Motor Hotel	4861 W Century Blvd	310-677-9181	65	
Topper Motel	4331 W Century Blvd	310-671-0424	45	
Westfield Inn	4652 W Century Blvd	310-671-6161	40	

Map 14 • Inglewood East/Morningside Park

Anand Motel	10210 S Western Ave	323-418-8488	45	
Atlas Motel	7322 S Western Ave	323-752-7542	45	
Celestial Motel	7410 S Vermont Ave	323-778-3117	45	
Cornett Motel	6345 Crenshaw Blvd	323-751-3227	55	
El Paso Inn	3220 W Florence Ave	323-751-4527	55	
Hoover Motel	9710 S Hoover St	323-755-9272	50	
Hyde Park Motel	6340 Crenshaw Blvd	323-752-0355	50	
Look Motor Inn	7827 Crenshaw Blvd	323-759-1623	50	
Western Motel	10411 S Vermont Ave	323-755-2596	55	

Map 15 • Pacific Palisades

Channel Road Inn	219 W Channel Rd	310-459-1920	195	★★★

Map 16 • Brentwood

Brentwood Motor Hotel	12200 W Sunset Blvd	310-476-9981	139	★★
Holiday Inn	170 N Church Ln	310-476-6411	129	★★★★
Luxe Summit	11461 W Sunset Blvd	310-476-6571	149	★★★★

Map 17 • Bel Air/Holmby Hills

Hotel Bel Air	701 Stone Canyon Rd	310-472-1211	395	★★★★★

Map 18 • Santa Monica

The Ambrose	1255 20th St	310-315-1555	175	
American Motel	1243 Lincoln Blvd	310-458-1411	68	
Bayside Hotel	2001 Ocean Ave	310-396-6000	99	
Best Western Ocean View	1447 Ocean Ave	310-458-4888	169	★★
Cal Mar Hotel Suites	220 California Ave	310-395-5555	139	★★★
Doubletree Guest Suites	1707 4th St	310-395-3332	309	★★★★
Fairmont Miramar	101 Wilshire Blvd	310-576-7777	339	★★★★
Four Point Sheraton	530 Pico W Blvd	310-399-9344	309	★★★
Georgian Hotel	1415 Ocean Ave	310-395-9945	240	★★★1/2
Holiday Inn	120 Colorado Ave	310-451-0676	189	★★★★
Holiday Motel	1102 Pico Blvd	310-450-9666	60	
Hotel California	1670 Ocean Ave	310-393-2363	179	★★
Hotel Carmel	201 Broadway	310-451-2469	129	★★
Hotel Casa Del Mar	1910 Ocean Wy	310-581-5533	420	★★★★
Hotel Ocenana	849 Ocean Ave	310-393-0486	285	★★★
Le Merigot Santa Monica Beach	1740 Ocean Ave	310-395-9700	299	★★★★
Loews Santa Monica Beach Hotel	1700 Ocean Ave	310-458-6700	329	★★★★
Ocean Lodge	1667 Ocean Ave	310-451-4146	150	
Ocean Park Inn	2452 Lincoln Blvd	310-392-3966	70	
Pacific Sands Motel	1515 Ocean Ave	310-395-6133	85	
Palm Motel	2020 14th St	310-452-3861	70	
Radisson Hotel Huntley	1111 2nd St	310-394-5454	249	★★★★
Rest Haven Motel	815 Grant St	310-452-3977	65	
Santa Monica Gateway Hotel	1920 Santa Monica Blvd	310-829-9100	119	★★★
Santa Monica Motel	2102 Lincoln Blvd	310-392-6806	60	
Sea Shore Motel & Apartments	2637 Main St	310-392-2787	90	
Seaview Motel	1760 Ocean Ave	310-393-6711	65	
Shangri-La Hotel	1301 Ocean Ave	310-394-2791	170	★★★
Shutters on the Beach	1 Pico Blvd	310-458-0030	445	★★★★★
Travelodge	1525 Ocean Ave	310-451-0761	135	
Viceroy	1819 Ocean Ave	310-260-7500	359	★★★★

Map 19 • West LA/Santa Monica East

Best Western Royal Palace & Suites	2528 S Sepulveda Blvd	310-477-9066	99	★★★
Best Western Westwood Pacific Hotel	11250 Santa Monica Blvd	310-478-1400	119	★★★
Brooks Hotel	1541 Sawtelle Blvd	310-479-9404	25	
Comfort Inn	2815 Santa Monica Blvd	310-828-5517	99	★★
Days Inn	3007 Santa Monica Blvd	310-829-6333	95	★★★★★
Pavilions Motel	2338 Ocean Park Blvd	310-450-4044	60	
Travelodge	3102 Pico Blvd	310-450-5766	80	
Village Motel	2624 Santa Monica Blvd	310-828-0515	75	
West End Hotel	1538 Sawtelle Blvd	310-444-8990	175/week	
Wilshire Motel	12023 Wilshire Blvd	310-478-3545	80	

Map 20 • Westwood/Century City

Beverly Hills Plaza Hotel	10300 Wilshire Blvd	310-275-5575	135	★★★★
Century Plaza Hotel	2025 Ave of the Stars	310-551-3334	299	★★★★
Century Wilshire Hotel	10776 Wilshire Blvd	310-474-4506	99	★★★
Courtyard By Marriott	10320 N Olympic Blvd	310-556-2777	149	★★★
Courtyard LA/Century City/Beverly Hills	10320 W Olympic Blvd	800-321-2211	149	★★★
Doubletree Hotel	10740 Wilshire Blvd	310-475-8711	174	★★★
Hilgard House Hotel	927 Hilgard Ave	310-208-3945	144	
Holiday Inn Express Hotels	10330 W Olympic Blvd	866-270-5110	109	
Hotel Claremont	1044 Tiverton Ave	310-208-5957	60	
Park Hyatt Los Angeles	2151 Ave of the Stars	310-277-1234	275	★★★★
Royal Palace Westwood	1052 Tiverton Ave	310-208-6677	99	
Royal Santa Monica Motel	10811 Santa Monica Blvd	310-475-3536	60	

Map 20 • Westwood/Century City—*continued*

			Average price	Rating
Stars Inn	10269 Santa Monica Blvd	310-556-3076	65	
Travelodge	10740 Santa Monica Blvd	310-474-4576	97	
W Hotel	930 Hilgard Ave	310-208-8765	299	
Westwood Motel	10604 Santa Monica Blvd	310-475-4422	55	

Map 21 • Venice

Cadillac Hotel	8 Dudley Ave	310-399-8876	99	
Encore Motel	13432 Washington Blvd	310-823-5066	50	
Golden Star Motel	710 Rose Ave	310-399-1208	70	
Holiday Inn	737 Washington Blvd	310-821-4455	99	
Inn at Venice Beach	327 Washington Blvd	310-821-2557	199	★★★
Jolly Roger Hotel	2904 Washington Blvd	310-822-2904	90	★★★
Lincoln Inn	2447 Lincoln Blvd	310-822-0686	75	★★
Marina Pacific Hotel & Suites	1697 Pacific Ave	310-452-1111	199	★★★
Ramada Inn	3130 Washington Blvd	310-821-5086	109	
Rose Inn	2435 Lincoln Blvd	310-301-7073	79	
Venice Beach Hotel	1515 Pacific Ave	310-452-3052	64 private, 25 share	
Venice Beach Hotel	25 Windward Ave	310-399-7649	60 private, 30 dorm	
Venice Beach House	15 30th Ave	310-823-1966	170	
Venice Beach Suites	1305 Ocean Front Wk	310-396-4559	119	

Map 22 • Mar Vista

Baldwin Motel	12823 W Washington Blvd	310-301-0687	50	
Culver Motel	11162 Culver Blvd	310-558-9769	40	
Econo Lodge	11933 W Washington Blvd	310-398-1651	72	★★
Paradise Motel	11750 W Washington Blvd	310-390-4044	58	
Sunbay Motels	12841 W Washington Blvd	310-306-7081	69	
Super 8 Motel	12664 W Washington Blvd	310-306-8243	75	★★
Villa Brasil Motel	11740 W Washington Blvd	310-636-0141	60	

Map 23 • Rancho Park/Palms

Crown Plaza Hotel	1150 S Beverly Dr	310-553-6561	229	★★★
Loews Beverly Hills	1224 S Beverwil Dr	310-277-2800	209	★★★★
Marriott Residence Inn	1177 S Beverly Dr	310-277-4427	179	★★★
Royal Westwood	2352 Westwood Blvd	310-475-4551	45	

Map 24 • Culver City

Astro Motel	3850 Sepulveda Blvd	310-398-3815	45	
Circle K Motel	5329 Sepulveda Blvd	310-391-9309	40	
Culver Hotel	9400 Culver Blvd	310-838-7963	89	
Deano's Motel	3868 Sepulveda Blvd	310-390-3511	50	
Half Moon Motel	3958 Sepulveda Blvd	310-391-5279	44	
Lindblade Hotel	8925 Lindblade St	310-839-1856	550/month	
Metro Motel	8846 National Blvd	310-838-4554	55	
Ramada Inn	3930 Sepulveda Blvd	310-390-2189	85	★★
Sunburst Motel	3900 Sepulveda Blvd	310-398-7523	79	
Travelodge	11180 Washington Pl	310-839-1111	89	★★★
Vista Motel	4900 Sepulveda Blvd	310-390-2014	55	
Westchester Hotel	5630 Sawtelle Blvd	310-390-6534	225/week	

Map 25 • Marina Del Rey/Westchester West

Foghorn Beachfront Hotel	4140 Via Marina	310-823-4626	129	★★
Furama Hotel	8601 Lincoln Blvd	310-670-8111	69	★★★
Inn at Playa Del Rey	435 Culver Blvd	310-574-1920	145	★★★
Jamaica Bay Inn	4175 Admiralty Wy	310-823-5333	199	★★★
Marina Beach Marriott Resort	4100 Admiralty Wy	310-301-3000	249	★★★★
Marina Del Rey Courtyard	13480 Maxella Ave	310-822-8555	189	★★★
Marina Del Rey Hotel	13534 Bali Wy	310-301-1000	129	★★★
Marina International Hotel	4200 Admiralty Wy	310-301-2000	109	★★★
Ritz Carlton Hotel	4375 Admiralty Wy	310-823-1700	309	★★★★★

Map 26 • Westchester/Fox Hills/Ladera Heights/LAX

Courtyard by Marriott LAX	6161 W Century Blvd	310-649-1400	169	★★★
Crowne Plaza Los Angeles Arprt	5985 W Century Blvd	310-642-7500	179	★★★★
Days Inn	901 W Manchester Blvd	310-649-0800	75	
Embassy Suites Hotel	9801 Airport Blvd	310-215-1000	159	★★★
Extended Stayamerica	6531 S Sepulveda Blvd	310-568-9337	99	

Four Points Barcelo Hotel	5990 Green Valley Cir	310-641-7740	109	
Four Points Hotel By Sheraton	9750 Airport Blvd	310-645-4600	129	★★★
Hampton Inn	10300 S La Cienega Blvd	310-846-3200	85	★★★★
Holiday Inn	9901 S La Cienega Blvd	310-649-5151	129	★★★
Howard Johnson Hotel LAX	8620 Airport Blvd	310-645-7700	85	★★★
Marriott Los Angeles Airport	5855 W Century Blvd	310-641-5700	199	
Quality Hotel	5249 W Century Blvd	310-645-2200	79	★★★
Radisson Hotel	6225 W Century Blvd	310-670-9000	189	★★★
Radisson Hotel Los Angeles West	6161 W Centinela Ave	310-649-1776	129	★★★
Renaissance Los Angeles Hotel	9620 Airport Blvd	310-337-2800	179	★★★
Sandman Motel	850 W Manchester Blvd	310-649-6500	49	
Sheraton	6101 W Century Blvd	310-642-1111	189	★★★
Super 8 Motel	9250 Airport Blvd	310-670-2900	65	★★
Travelodge	5547 W Century Blvd	310-649-4000	70	
Westin Los Angeles Airport	5400 W Century Blvd	310-216-5858	209	★★★

Map 27 • El Segundo/Manhattan Beach

The Belmar	3501 N Sepulveda Blvd	310-750-0300	139	★★★★
Comfort Inn	850 N Sepulveda Blvd	310-318-1020	85	★★★
Concord Hotel	221 Concord St	310-322-6116	125/week	
Courtyard By Marriott	2000 E Mariposa Ave	310-322-0700	179	★★★
Doubletree Hotel	1985 E Grand Ave	310-322-0999	119	★★★
Embassy Suites Hotel	1440 E Imperial Ave	310-640-3600	149	★★★
Hacienda Hotel – LA Airport	525 N Sepulveda Blvd	310-615-0015	79	★★★
Hi View Motel	100 S Sepulveda Blvd	310-374-4608	69	
Hilton Garden Inn LAX	2100 E Mariposa Ave	310-726-0100	119	★★★
Homestead Studio Suites Hotel	1910 E Mariposa Ave	310-607-4000	109	★★★
LAX Suites Motel	11838 Aviation Blvd	310-643-9905	62	
Marriott Manhattan Beach	1400 Park View Ave	310-546-7511	229	★★★
Marriott Residence Inn	2135 E El Segundo Blvd	310-333-0888	169	★★★
Residence Inn	1700 N Sepulveda Blvd	310-546-7627	159	★★★
Sea View Inn	3400 Highland Ave	310-545-1504	105	★★★
Seahorse Inn	233 N Sepulveda Blvd	310-376-7951	62	
Spring Hill Suites Marriott	14620 Aviation Blvd	310-727-9595	129	★★★
Summerfield Suites El Segundo	810 S Douglas St	310-725-0100	159	★★★
Travelodge–LAX South	1804 E Sycamore Ave	310-615-1073	74	
Twin Towers Motel	11706 Aviation Blvd	310-643-5384	50	

Map 28 • Hawthorne

Acacia Inn	4307 W Imperial Hwy	310-674-3110	50	
Best Western South Bay Hotel	15000 Hawthorne Blvd	310-973-0998	86	
Budget Inn Motel	14815 Hawthorne Blvd	310-675-8523	50	
Colonial Inn	4210 W El Segundo Blvd	310-355-1178	40	
Days Inn	15636 Hawthorne Blvd	310-676-7378	69	
Del Aire Inn	4610 W Imperial Hwy	310-673-4141	55	
Deluxe Motel	13640 Hawthorne Blvd	310-644-1154	65	
Diamond Inn	3735 W Imperial Hwy	310-674-1278	51	
Dream Inn	3201 W Imperial Hwy	310-412-0912	50	
El Rancho Inn	3900 W El Segundo Blvd	310-973-3522	50	
El Segundo Inn	4930 W El Segundo Blvd	310-644-4944	61	
Hawthorne Plaza Inn	12043 Hawthorne Blvd	310-973-3432	65	
Holiday Inn	14814 Hawthorne Blvd	310-676-1111	89	★★★
Imperial Motel	4709 W Imperial Hwy	310-671-7700	50	
Kings Motel	3501 W Imperial Hwy	310-674-2196	50	
La Mirage Inn	4501 W Imperial Hwy	310-671-6017	57	
Manor Motel	4191 W El Segundo Blvd	310-675-9179	45	
Palm Hotel	4207 W El Segundo Blvd	310-644-2346	40	
Prairie Motel	15125 Prairie Ave	310-679-6850	50	
Ramada Inn	5250 W El Segundo Blvd	310-536-9800	69	★★★
Tourist Lodge	3649 W Imperial Hwy	310-677-0112	60	
Travelers Inn	14808 Hawthorne Blvd	310-675-5228	55	

Map 29 • Hermosa Beach/Redondo Beach North

Beach House Inn at Hermosa	1300 The Strand	310-374-3001	232	
Best Western Galleria Inn	2740 Artesia Blvd	310-370-4353	79	★★
Grand View Motor Hotel	55 14th St	310-374-8981	119	
Hampton Inn & Suites	1530 Pacific Coast Hwy	310-318-7800	125	★★★
Holiday Inn Express Hotel & Suites	125 Pacific Coast Hwy	888-303-1753	109	
Hotel Hermosa	2515 Pacific Coast Hwy	310-318-6000	89	★★★

Map 29 • Hermosa Beach/Redondo Beach North—*continued*

			Average price	Rating
Quality Inn & Suites	901 Aviation Blvd	310-374-2666	90	★★★
Sea Side Motel	1935 Artesia Blvd	310-376-0430	55	
Sea Sprite Ocean Front Motel	216 The Strand	310-376-6933	99	

Map 30 • Torrance North

Del Amo Inn	20534 Hawthorne Blvd	310-542-9417	65	
Summerfield Suites	19901 Prairie Ave	310-371-8525	176	★★★

Map 31 • Redondo Beach

Best Western Redondo Beach Inn	1850 S Pacific Coast Hwy	310-540-3700	99	★★★
Crowne Plaza	300 N Harbor Dr	310-318-8888	209	★★★★
Days Inn	4111 Pacific Coast Hwy	310-378-8511	69	★★★★
Driftwood Motel	3960 Pacific Coast Hwy	310-375-0511	50	
Moonlite Inn	625 S Pacific Coast Hwy	310-540-4058	50	
Palos Verdes Inn	1700 S Pacific Coast Hwy	310-316-4211	98	★★★★
The Portofino Hotel & Yacht Club	260 Portofino Wy	310-379-8481	169	★★★½
Ramada Unlimited	435 S Pacific Coast Hwy	310-540-5998	69	★★½
Redondo Motel	711 S Pacific Coast Hwy	310-540-1888	59	
Redondo Pier Lodge	206 S Pacific Coast Hwy	310-318-1811	74	★★
Starlite Motel	716 S Pacific Coast Hwy	310-316-4314	52	
Torrance Hilton at South Bay	21333 Hawthorne Blvd	310-540-0500	189	★★★

Map 32 • Torrance South

Bartlett Motel	2364 Pacific Coast Hwy	310-325-0302	45	
Bestall Inn	2065 Pacific Coast Hwy	310-326-8288	48	
Courtyard By Marriott	2633 Sepulveda Blvd	310-533-8000	149	★★★
Eldorado Coast Hotel	2037 Pacific Coast Hwy	310-534-0700	55	
Extended Stayamerica	3525 Torrance Blvd	310-540-5442	84	
Leo's Motel	1879 Lomita Blvd	310-326-0445	45	
Lomita Motel	2237 Pacific Coast Hwy	310-326-7530	50	
Plaza Hotel	1720 Cabrillo Ave	310-328-4671	52	
Pride Hotel	1806 Cabrillo Ave	310-533-9747	130/week	
Ramada Inn	2880 Pacific Coast Hwy	310-325-0660	65	★★
Ramada Inn	3673 Torrance Blvd	310-316-5570	85	
Residence Inn	3701 Torrance Blvd	310-543-4566	179	★★★
Torrance Marriott	3635 Fashion Wy	310-316-3636	194	★★★
Travelodge Torrance	2448 Sepulveda Blvd	310-326-1888	75	★★

Map 33 • Eagle Rock/Highland Park

Casa Lu-An Motel	1045 Colorado Blvd	323-257-6341	51	
Comfort Inn	2300 W Colorado Blvd	323-256-1199	77	★★
Eagle Rock Motel	7041 N Figueroa St	323-256-5106	50	
Islander Motel	1460 Colorado Blvd	323-257-8926	55	
Regency Inn	2378 Colorado Blvd	323-257-8168	55	
Rose Bowl Motel	1533 Colorado Blvd	323-258-8033	45	
Welcome Inn	1840 Colorado Blvd	323-256-1673	53	

Map 34 • Pasadena

Bissell House Bed & Breakfast	201 Orange Grove Ave	626-441-3535	150	★★★
Hilton Pasadena	168 S Los Robles Ave	626-577-1000	159	★★★
Livingstone Hotel & Apartments	139 S Los Robles Ave	626-795-3311	65	
Pasadena Courtyard By Marriot	180 N Fair Oaks Ave	626-403-7600	189	★★★
Pasadena Inn	400 S Arroyo Pkwy	626-795-8401	89	★★½
Ritz Carlton Huntington Hotel	1401 S Oak Knoll Ave	626-568-3900	315	★★★★
Sheraton Pasadena Hotel	303 Cordova St	626-449-4000	189	★★★
Westin Pasadena Hotel	191 N Los Robles Ave	626-792-2727	189	★★★

Map 35 • Pasadena East/San Marino

Best Western Inn	2156 E Colorado Blvd	626-793-9339	67	
Comfort Inn	2462 E Colorado Blvd	626-405-0811	83	★★★
Econo Lodge	2860 E Colorado Blvd	626-792-3700	49	
Saga Motor Hotel	1633 E Colorado Blvd	626-795-0431	84	
Siesta Inn	2855 E Colorado Blvd	626-795-2017	39	
Super 8 Motel	2863 E Colorado Blvd	626-449-3020	66	
Swiss Lodge	2800 E Colorado Blvd	626-449-1122	45	
Travelodge	2131 E Colorado Blvd	626-796-3121	65	
Vagabond Inn	1203 E Colorado Blvd	626-449-3170	69	

Westway Inn – Pasadena	1599 E Colorado Blvd	626-304-9678	63	

Map 36 · Mt. Washington

			Average price	*Rating*
Triangle Motel	3951 Eagle Rock Blvd	323-255-2109	45	

Map 38 · El Sereno

Ambassador Inn	2720 W Valley Blvd	626-308-1638	55	
Huntington Premiere Inn	5533 Huntington Dr N	323-221-8828	50	
Super 8 Motel	5350 Huntington Dr S	323-225-2310	59	★★

Map 39 · Alhambra

Days Inn	15 N 1st St	626-308-0014	79	
Fremont Inn	2221 W Commonwealth Ave	626-300-0003	86	
Lanai Motel	1749 W Valley Blvd	626-282-8421	40	

Map 40 · Boyle Heights

Hotel Antonio	229 N Soto St	323-264-5574	40	
Marengo Inn	2050 Marengo St	323-223-2080	60	
Soto Hotel	402 N Soto St	323-264-3388	85	

Map 41 · City Terrace/East LA

Com-On Inn	1560 Monterey Pass Rd	323-263-9888	50	
Vista Motel	4180 City Terrace Dr	323-260-7880	50	

Map 42 · Chatsworth

7-Star Suites Hotels LA – Chatsworth	21603 Devonshire St	818-998-8888	89	
Paradise Lodge	20128 Roscoe Blvd	818-341-7200	62	
Radisson Hotel Chatsworth	9777 Topanga Canyon Blvd	818-709-7054	150	★★★
Summerfield Suites By Wyndham	21902 Lassen St	818-773-0707	150	

Map 44 · Mission Hills/North Hills

Granada Motel	15543 Rinaldi St	818-366-5901	73	

Map 45 · Canoga Park/Woodland Hills

Best Western Canoga Park Motor	20122 Vanowen St	818-883-1200	84	★★★
Canoga House Motor Hotel	7435 Winnetka Ave	818-341-9700	55	
Holiday Inn Hotels	21101 Ventura Blvd	818-883-6110	99	★★★
Motel 6	7132 De Soto Ave	818-346-5400	55	
Movieland Motel	19335 Ventura Blvd	818-344-5886	60	
St George Motor Inn	19454 Ventura Blvd	818-345-6911	77	★★

Map 46 · Reseda

Chalet Lodge of Tarzana	19170 Ventura Blvd	818-345-9410	89	★★★

Map 47 · Van Nuys

Airtel Plaza Hotel	7277 Valjean Ave	818-997-7676	179	★★★★
Best Western Carriage Inn	5525 Sepulveda Blvd	818-787-2300	129	★★★
Cabana Motel	5764 Sepulveda Blvd	818-780-8413	65	
Cinema Motel	6242 Sepulveda Blvd	818-786-3606	48	
Holiday Inn	8244 Orion Ave	818-989-5010	119	★★★
Hyland Motel	7041 Sepulveda Blvd	818-781-2780	50	
Le Rendezvous Motel	6501 Sepulveda Blvd	818-786-1564	45	
Motel 6	15711 Roscoe Blvd	818-894-9343	47	
Panorama Motel	8209 Sepulveda Blvd	818-786-4434	60	
Starlight Cottage	5450 Sepulveda Blvd	818-786-4722	60	
Tangiers Motel	7615 Sepulveda Blvd	818-994-8547	45	
Town House Motel	6957 Sepulveda Blvd	818-782-8800	55	
Travelodge	6909 Sepulveda Blvd	818-787-5400	60	
Voyager Motor Inn	6500 Sepulveda Blvd	818-780-1142	51	

Map 48 · North Hollywood

Camino Motel & Apartments	13561 Sherman Wy	818-780-0558	63	
Pepper Tree Motel	5909 Lankershim Blvd	818-763-6959	57	
Ritz Motel	6021 Lankershim Blvd	818-769-7520	55	
Silver Saddle Motel	6235 Lankershim Blvd	818-766-5285	55	
Studio Lodge	11254 Vanowen St	818-760-1194	35	
Super 8 Motel	7541 Laurel Canyon Blvd	818-765-9800	61	
Village Inn Motel	7833 Lankershim Blvd	818-764-6007	45	

Map 49 • Burbank

Courtyard Los Angeles – Burbank Airport	2100 W Empire Ave	800-321-2211	179	★★★
Extended Stayamerica	2200 W Empire Ave	818-567-0952	99	
The Graciela	322 N Pass Ave	818-842-8887	224	★★★★
Hilton	2500 N Hollywood Wy	818-843-6000	179	★★★
Quality Inn	2255 N Buena Vista St	818-848-1680	69	★★★
Ramada Inn	2900 N San Fernando Blvd	818-843-5955	75	★★★
Travelodge	1112 N Hollywood Wy	818-845-2408	79	

Map 50 • Burbank East/Glendale West

Anabelle Hotel	2011 W Olive Ave	818-845-7800	149	★★★
Burbank Inn & Suites	180 W Alameda Ave	818-842-1114	95	★★★
Glen Capri Motel	6700 San Fernando Rd	818-244-8434	60	
Holiday Inn	150 E Angeleno Ave	818-841-4770	149	
Homestead Studio Suites Hotel	1377 W Glenoaks Blvd	818-956-6665	109	★★★
Olive Manor Motel	924 W Olive Ave	818-842-5215	56	
Providencia Motels	108 E Providencia Ave	818-842-6974	50	
Safari Inn	1911 W Olive Ave	818-845-8586	122	★★★

Map 51 • Glendale South

Astro Glendale Motel	326 E Colorado St	818-246-7401	55	
Best Western Inn	123 W Colorado St	818-247-0111	109	★★★
Best Western Inn	2911 Colorado Blvd	323-256-7711	83	★★★
Brentwood Hotel	339 1/2 N Brand Blvd	818-244-3820	72	
Chariot Inn Motel	1118 E Colorado St	818-507-9600	62	
Days Inn	450 W Pioneer Dr	818-956-0202	87	★★★★
Econo Lodge	1437 E Colorado St	818-246-8367	64	★★
El Rio Motel	1515 E Colorado St	818-243-3157	45	
Glendale Lodge	1510 E Colorado St	818-507-6688	79	
Hilton	100 W Glenoaks Blvd	818-956-5466	199	★★★★
Motel Sakura – Glendale	1500 E Colorado St	818-243-8999	58	
Rodeway Inn	200 W Colorado St	818-246-7331	64	
Tropico Motel	401 W Chevy Chase Dr	818-242-5098	44	
Vagabond Inn	120 W Colorado St	818-240-1700	79	

Map 52 • Tarzana/Woodland Hills

Best Western AKU Motel	21830 Ventura Blvd	818-340-1000	53	
Comfort Inn Woodland Hills	20157 Ventura Blvd	818-347-8080	79	
Hilton & Towers Woodland Hills	6360 Canoga Ave	818-595-1000	179	★★★
Marriott Hotels Resorts Suites	21850 Oxnard St	818-887-4800	209	★★★
Super 8 Canoga Park	7631 Topanga Canyon Blvd	818-883-8888	61	
Warner Center Hilton & Tower	6320 Canoga Ave	818-596-4500	179	★★★★
Warner Gardens Motel	21706 Ventura Blvd	818-992-4426	60	

Map 53 • Encino

Tokyo Princess Inn	17448 Ventura Blvd	818-788-3820	70	

Map 54 • Sherman Oaks West

777 Motor Inn	4781 Sepulveda Blvd	818-788-3200	74	
Courtyard by Marriott	15433 Ventura Blvd	818-981-5400	179	★★★

Map 55 • Sherman Oaks East

Days Inn	12933 Ventura Blvd	818-789-6900	79	★★
Park Motel	12963 Ventura Blvd	818-501-9292	60	
Sportsmen's Lodge Hotel	12825 Ventura Blvd	818-769-4700	144	★★★

Map 56 • Studio City/Valley Village

Best Western Inn	12600 Riverside Dr	818-763-9141	119	★★
Beverly Garland's Holiday Inn	4222 Vineland Ave	818-980-8000	120	★★★
Carlton Motor Lodge	11811 Ventura Blvd	818-763-3515	60	
Colony Inn	4917 Vineland Ave	818-763-2787	92	
El Patio Inn	11466 Ventura Blvd	818-508-5828	69	
Studio City Inn	11733 Ventura Blvd	818-766-9599	55	

Map 57 • Universal City/Toluca Lake

Best Western	3910 W Riverside Dr	818-239-3433	134	★★★
Holiday Inn Express Hotels	3241 Cahuenga Blvd W	866-270-5110	119	
Holiday Lodge Motel	3901 W Riverside Dr	818-843-1121	79	
Nite Inn	10612 Ventura Blvd	818-508-8022	70	
Sheraton Universal Hotel	333 Universal Hollywood Dr	818-980-1212	189	★★★

Overview

Given the large size of Los Angeles, the number of designated dog-friendly parks in the city is embarrassingly small. Only a handful of parks and beaches in the greater LA area allocate space exclusively for dogs, and volunteer groups have long been lobbying for increased pooch playgrounds. Below you'll find our list of dog parks, all of which prohibit aggressive dogs, dogs without inoculations, and dogs in heat. Some parks prohibit toys, such as balls and Frisbees, and most of them require you to "clean up" after your pets (read: scoop the poop). Each park has a different set of rules, so read the posted signs before you enter. A great website to check out is www.dogfriendly.com, which provides loads of information on dog-friendly parks, accommodations, attractions, restaurants, and even retail stores.

Laurel Canyon Park

8260 Mulholland Dr (near Laurel Canyon Blvd), Studio City

Laurel Canyon Park features three acres of off-leash space in a fenced area. Dogs must be leashed between 10 am and 3 pm, but can run free between 6 am and 10 am, and again from 3 pm until dusk. Other amenities include free parking, a small fenced-in children's play area, and a hot dog stand! (Sometimes life just gives you lemonade…)

This is a fairly spacious dog park, but it does have drainage problems, so be prepared for your dog to come home fairly filthy. Laurel Canyon Park remains a popular place for dog lovers, nonetheless, and attracts lots of celebrity pet owners. You're more likely to have a star sighting here than at Moomba.

Silver Lake Recreation Center

1850 W Silver Lake Dr, Los Angeles, 323-644-3946

Open from 6 am until 10 pm, the Rec Center features 1.25 acres of off-leash running room. The only parking available is street parking. Silver Lake Recreation Center is a well-renowned meeting place for pooch owners, so if you're new to town and looking to make new friends, take your dog down for a run.

Runyon Canyon Park

2001 N Fuller Ave (north of Franklin Ave), Hollywood, 323-666-5046

Located in Hollywood, Runyon Canyon Park is almost completely undeveloped. While it doesn't have a fenced-in dog play area, dogs are permitted to walk the hiking trails unleashed with their owners. Of the 160-acre park, 90 acres are designated as off-leash areas. Runyon Canyon also has several hiking trails of varying difficulty, so you and your pooch can break a sweat together.

Westminster Senior Citizens Center

1234 Pacific Ave, Venice, 310-392-5566

This park features a little under an acre of off-leash space and a fenced-in area (50' x 25') for small dogs only. Open from 6 am until 10 pm, the center has limited on-site parking.

Sepulveda Basin Off-Leash Dog Park

17550 Victory Blvd, Encino

Featuring a five-acre off-leash area with half an acre for small pooches, Sepulveda Basin Dog Park is open daily from sunrise to sunset, except Friday mornings when it opens at 11 am. On-site parking can accommodate up to 100 cars. Whatever you do, avoid parking on White Oak Avenue or Victory Boulevard at all times, as ticketing agents here are eagle-eyed and vigilant. (Getting a ticket is a matter of "when," not "if.") Check out Randy's Sepulveda Basin Dog Park page at www.dog-park.com.

Griffith Park

North end of John Ferraro Soccer Field on North Zoo Drive, Los Angeles, 323-913-4688

There are various places within Griffith Park that allow dogs to roam off-leash. The trails across from the observatory are dog-friendly, and you can even take your dog to the roof of the observatory via the outside stairs (here the dog's got to be on a leash). The one-mile train ride off Crystal Springs allows dogs onboard (accompanied by an adult, of course). We suggest that you pick up a map at the Ranger's Station (Crystal Spring and Griffith Park Drive) to check which trails allow dogs.

Beaches

While dogs, leashed or not, are prohibited from places like Venice Beach and the Ocean Front Walk, there are still some dog-friendly beaches and a core group of volunteers fighting hard to keep it that way. Huntington Dog Beach (PCH and Golden West Street) is a beautiful one-mile stretch of beach that allows dogs on leashes, so long as their owners pick up after them. The only place dogs are allowed off-leash is in the water, under supervision. Leo Carillo State Beach (PCH 30 miles north of Malibu) also allows leashed dogs, but there are restrictions about where dogs can play—check the signs carefully before embarking on a beach adventure with your dog. Redondo Beach Dog Park is located away from the foreshore next to Dominguez Park (Flagler Lane and 190th Street). A fenced area, Redondo Beach Dog Park has play spaces for large and small dogs. Long Beach Dog Park, an off-leash dog run, is located at 7th Street and Federation Drive behind the Casting Pond.

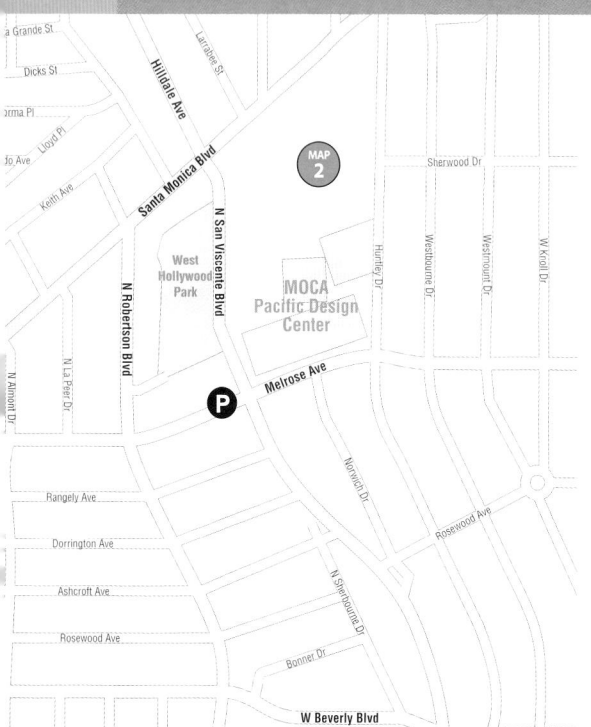

of the '00s that built reputations in places like the adjacent Chinatown art scene, and those experimenting with interactive and digital media.

The entrance plaza of MOCA at Grand Avenue sports a massive sculpture by Nancy Rubins, comprised mainly of airplane parts and pieces of stainless steel statically exploding into space. You can't miss it. Down below, MOCA's main location is a sprawling, subterranean maze that features exhibits culled from its more than 5,000 permanent works, including paintings by Frank Stella and Ed Ruscha, sculpture by Dan Flavin and Donald Judd, photography by Lee Friedlander and Cindy Sherman, and video and multimedia installations by Tracy Emin and Steve McQueen.

It's also host to larger, traveling exhibitions, many of which include pieces loaned by the museum. MOCA has gained a reputation for mounting innovative retrospectives on contemporary artists and movements that have rarely been explored in such depth. Highlights include 2005's *Visual Music*, a look at the cross-stimulation of visual and aural senses through painting, film, music and projections, and 2004's *A Minimal Future?*, one of the first comprehensive looks at the Minimalism movement.

This location hosts numerous art lectures (free with the price of admission) given by the museum's curators, noted art theorists, as well as exhibited artists (a benefit of focusing on contemporary art). The museum store here is also worth checking out, for everything from Freitag bags and designer stationary to limited edition artworks.

MOCA at the Geffen Contemporary

152 Central Ave, 213-621-1741
Hours & Admission same as Grand Avenue location.
MOCA at the Geffen Contemporary—once known as the "Temporary Contemporary" until a donation by namesake David Geffen made it permanent—is a cavernous former police car garage in the heart of Little Tokyo. Past shows have included a 30-year retrospective on installation art, in which many of the installations inhabited room-sized areas, and Gregor Schneider's *Dead House Ur*, in which the artist reconstructed the entire interior of his childhood home. MOCA also uses this space in collaboration with other arts organizations to host gala events; in 2005 it co-hosted the GenArt independent designer runway shows that kicked off LA's Fashion Week.

During the summer of '05, the space went through a major renovation. The revamped facility opened with a new exhibit entitled *Ecstasy: In and About Altered States* that included Tom Friedman's Play-Doh pills and Roxy Paine's polymer psychedelic mushrooms scattered across the floor. Awesome.

General Information

NFT Maps: 2 & 9
Main Address: 250 S Grand Ave
            Los Angeles, CA 90012
Phone: 213-626-6222
Website: www.moca.org
Hours: Mon & Fri: 11 am-5 pm; Thurs: 11 pm-8 pm; Sat & Sun: 11 am-6 pm; closed Tuesdays Wednesdays, and major holidays
Admission: adults: $8; seniors & students: $5; children under 12: free; Thursdays after 5 pm: free

Overview

Located downtown on an expansive stretch of Grand Avenue, the Museum of Contemporary Art (MOCA) sits catty-corner from Frank Gehry's Walt Disney Concert Hall and features an exhaustive exhibition on the architect's future projects, as well as the concert hall, in honor of its opening in 2003. This main building houses the impressive permanent collection, while the two satellite locations—one in Little Tokyo and one in West Hollywood—display large installations and design-focused exhibits, respectively.

Founded in 1979, this is the only LA museum devoted exclusively to contemporary art (American and European works dating from the 1940s onward). Between its three locations, the MOCA offers an in-depth look at the art that shaped the latter half of the 20th century, as well as artists

MOCA at the Pacific Design Center

8687 Melrose Ave, 310-657-0800

Hours: *Tues, Wed, & Fri: 11 am-5 pm; Thurs: 11 am-8 pm, Sat & Sun: 11 am-6 pm; closed Mondays & major holidays*

Admission: *free*

This smaller satellite location in West Hollywood opened in 2001, and is mainly used for exhibits that focus on one artist, architect, designer, or art collective at a time. The museum's lot at the Pacific Design Center is a separate structure that's set away from the PDC's home décor shops and across an expansive plaza where MOCA loves to throw its big fundraiser parties. This little, gallery-like space allows you to cruise through its two floors in about 20 minutes.

How to Get There—Driving

MOCA Grand Avenue: From the 110, exit at 4th Street. Turn left on Grand Avenue. The museum will be on your right.

MOCA at Geffen Contemporary: From the 101, exit at Los Angeles Street. Turn right on Los Angeles Street, then turn left on 1st Street. The museum will be on your left.

MOCA at the Pacific Design Center: From the 10, exit at Robertson Boulevard going north. Turn right on Melrose Avenue, then turn left on San Vicente Boulevard. The Design Center will be on your right. From the 101, exit west on Melrose Avenue. Turn right on San Vicente Boulevard. The Design Center will be on your right.

Parking

MOCA Grand Avenue: Parking is available for $8 in the Walt Disney Concert Hall parking garage on Grand Avenue. On the weekends, museum members can park for free in the California Plaza parking garage on Olive Street. Metered street parking is also available on Grand Avenue, 3rd Street, and Hope Street, but you'll only have two hours, max.

MOCA at Geffen Contemporary: Parking is available at the Advanced Parking Systems garage on Central Aveue for a daily flat rate of $4.25.

MOCA at the Pacific Design Center: Parking is available in the Pacific Design Center's lot on Melrose. The first 30 minutes are free, then it's $1 for each block of 30 minutes thereafter with an $8 maximum charge.

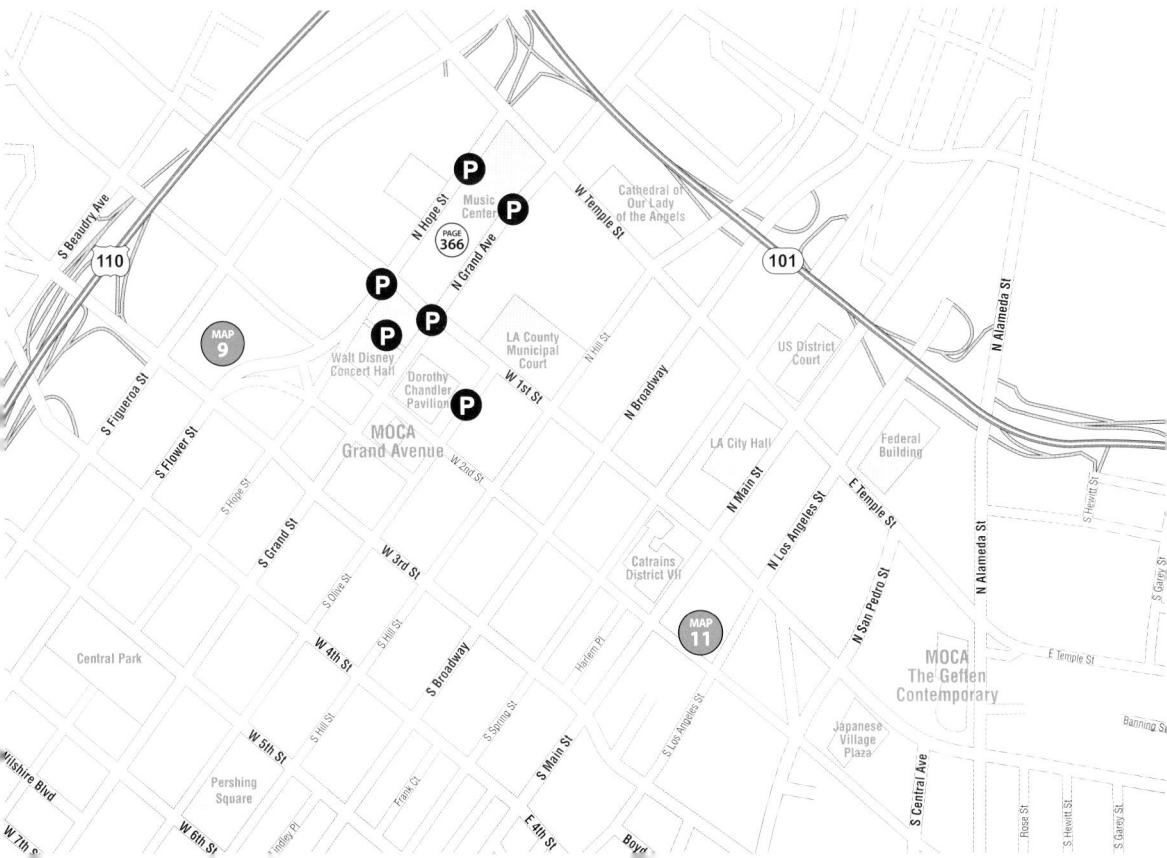

General Information

NFT Maps: 2 & 6
Address: 5905 Wilshire Blvd
    Los Angeles, CA 90036
Phone: 323-857-6000
Website: www.lacma.org
Hours: Mon, Tues, Thurs: 12 pm–8 pm
    Fri: 12 pm–9 pm
    Sat, Sun: 11 am–8 pm
    Wed: Closed
Admission: adults: $9 adults, seniors & students: $5
    children 17 & under: free
    After 5 pm every day and
    second Tues of the month: free
Annual Membership: $75

Overview

The Los Angeles County Museum of Art is like that old sweater hanging in the back of your closet. You forget that it's there, sometimes for years at a time, but when you do finally put it on again, you wonder why it's been so long. A return visit to LACMA almost always triggers this reaction, if only because there's just so much there to do. In addition to the Art Museum, the LACMA grounds are also home to a lovely park, the Page Museum, and the rather anticlimactic La Brea Tar Pits.

In 2001, plans were announced to tear down LACMA's four main buildings—the last of which was only opened in 1986—and replace them with a single building designed by superstar architect, Rem Koolhaas. But public outrage over the destruction of perfectly good buildings, coupled with fiscal concerns, recently sent LACMA in a new direction; in late 2004, the board announced that a proposed design by Italian architect Renzo Piano would unify, rather than demolish, the existing buildings. Philanthropist Eli Broad has chipped in $60 million towards the project—$50 million to build the tentatively named "Broad Contemporary Art Museum at LACMA" and $10 million for art acquisition. Under the new plan, the only structure pegged for demolition is the parking garage, which will be replaced by the Eli Broad building; construction of an underground parking garage will accommodate visitors to the museum. Now if only the city would extend the red line to Wilshire and Fairfax to alleviate some of the area's horrific traffic problems.

LACMA East

The museum's collection is housed mainly in four buildings. The Anderson Building is home to LACMA's collection of modern and contemporary art. The permanent collection includes David Hockney's *Mulholland Drive; The Road to the Studio*, one of the most "LA" paintings that we know. Inside the Ahmanson Gallery, you'll find European paintings and sculpture from the 12th to 20th centuries, as well as American art from the colonial period to World War II. The Hammer Building tends to hold temporary exhibitions, while the Pavilion for Japanese Art is a freestanding building that holds Japanese works from 3000 B.C. to the 20th century.

LACMA is also a great destination on weekend evenings. On Fridays, the museum is open late—until 9 pm—and there's live jazz in the Times Mirror Central Court from 5:30 pm until 8:30 pm. You can also hear live chamber music every Sunday at 6 pm in the Bing Theater. Both of these weekly concerts are free. The Bing Theater is also home to regular screenings of classic films, occasionally with a guest speaker. Movie tickets include admission to all of the galleries and cost $9 for the public and $6 for members, seniors, and students. Screenings are every Friday and Saturday at 7:30 pm.

LACMA West

In 1998, the Art Deco May Company department store reopened as LACMA West. The building has hosted special exhibits, like 1999's Van Gogh show, but LACMA West is now the place in LA to view Latin American art. The building houses the Bernard and Edith Lewin Latin American Art Galleries, a collection dominated by Mexican modern masters. The collection rotates, but Diego Rivera and David Alfaro Siqueiros are among the artists whose work has been displayed here. Young art enthusiasts may enjoy the Boone Children's Gallery, which frequently incorporates works from the main museum's permanent collection. Admission is included along with your regular museum ticket.

The George C. Page Museum

Located just east of LACMA, the Page Museum is best known as the home of the La Brea Tar Pits. Almost everyone who moves to Los Angeles has heard of the Tar Pits in some context, and most make a pilgrimage at some point, hoping to see something dynamic, something bubbling, something interesting. What you end up seeing, however, is a large pool of tar. It's about as anticlimactic as it gets. The Tar Pits become exponentially more interesting, during an eight to ten-week period, usually in July and August, when excavation takes place. It's during this time that museum-goers can watch paleontologists sift through the tar. The process is painstaking and oddly fascinating, even if it's hard to escape the feeling that everything cool has already been unearthed.

Inside the Page Museum, it's possible to view over one million specimens of fossils recovered from the Tar Pits. Among them are saber-toothed cats and mammoths. Sadly, there are no dinosaurs; but many a child has been riveted by the exhibit of the 9000-year old La Brea Woman, whose fossil is still the only human remains ever found in the Tar Pits.

Open Monday through Friday from 9:30 am until 5 pm, and from 10 am until 5 pm on Saturdays and Sundays. Adults $7, seniors and students $4.50, and children 5-12, $2. Admission is free on the first Tuesday of every month. 323-934-PAGE; www.tarpits.org.

How to Get There—Driving

From the 10, exit at Fairfax Avenue and drive north. Turn right at Wilshire Boulevard. The museum will be on your left. From the 101 S, exit at Highland and head south to Franklin. Turn right and take Franklin to La Brea. Make a left onto La Brea, and continue south to Wilshire Boulevard. Turn right on Wilshire, and the museum will be on your right.

Parking

There are parking lots on Wilshire, just across from the museum at Spaulding Avenue and at Ogden Drive. You have to pay for parking during the day, but the lots are free after 7 pm. If you're lucky, you'll nab one of the metered spots behind the museum (along 6th Street) that allow 4-hour parking from 8 am until 6 pm. Take lots of quarters with you.

How to Get There—Mass Transit

MTA buses 20, 21, 217, and 720 all stop near the museum, on either Wilshire Boulevard or Fairfax Avenue.

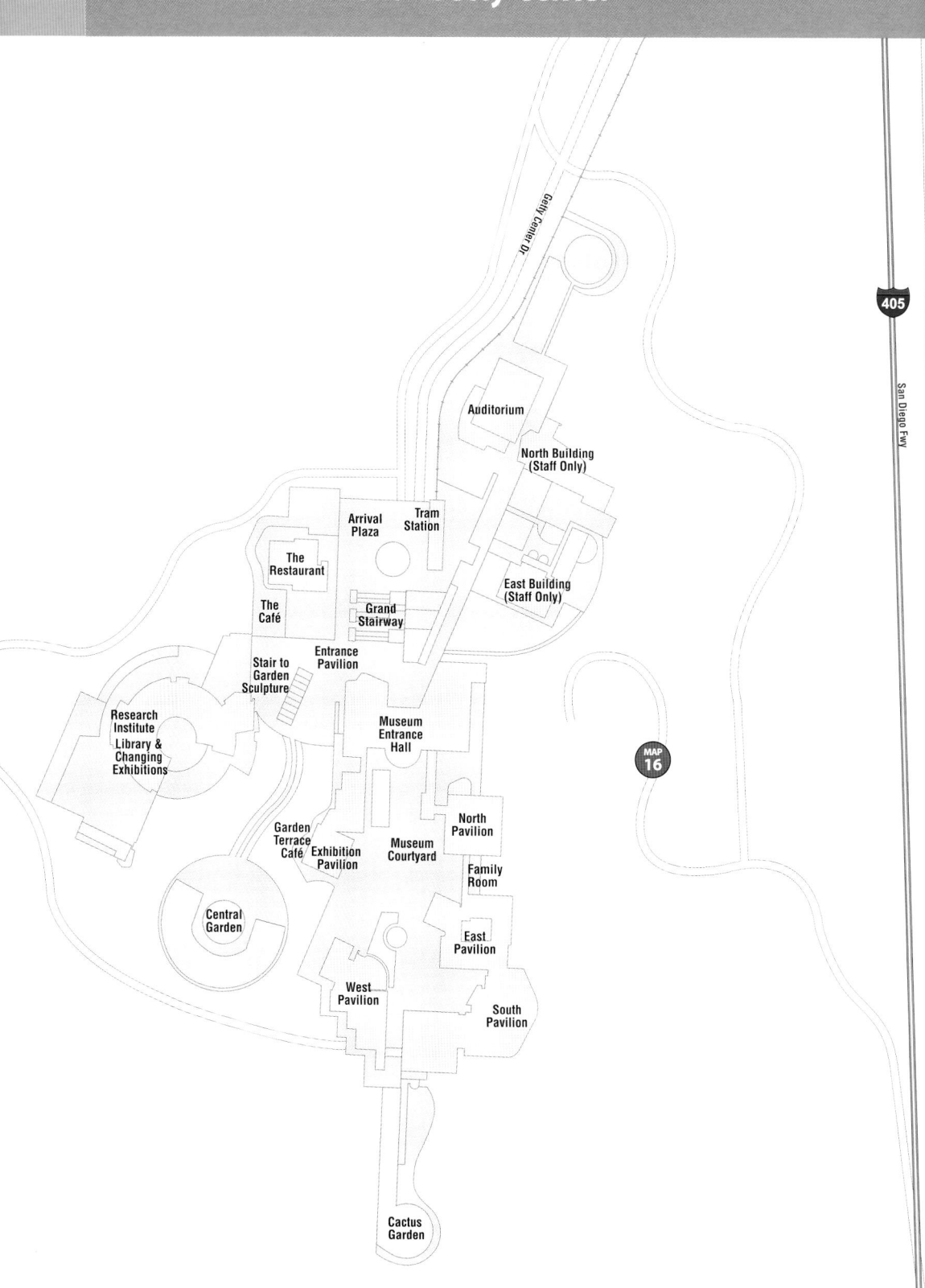

405

San Diego Fwy

Getty Center Dr.

Auditorium

North Building
(Staff Only)

Tram
Station

Arrival
Plaza

The
Restaurant

East Building
(Staff Only)

The
Café

Grand
Stairway

Stair to
Garden
Sculpture

Entrance
Pavilion

Research
Institute
Library &
Changing
Exhibitions

Museum
Entrance
Hall

MAP
16

North
Pavilion

Garden
Terrace
Café

Exhibition
Pavilion

Museum
Courtyard

Family
Room

Central
Garden

East
Pavilion

West
Pavilion

South
Pavilion

Cactus
Garden

General Information

NFT Map: 16
Address: 1200 Getty Center Dr
Los Angeles, CA 90049
Phone: 310-440-7300
Website: www.getty.edu
Hours: Tues-Thurs & Sun: 10 am-6 pm
Fri & Sat: 10 am-9 pm
Closed Mondays and major holidays
Admission: free, but parking is $5

Overview

One of the biggest misconceptions about the Getty is that it's still hard to get in. That simply isn't the case. Parking reservations are not required anymore, but parking is based on availability, so it's best to get there somewhat early.

The Getty Center is so cool that you can visit and come away completely satisfied, even if you never enter the museum and look at the art. Designed by Richard Meier, the J. Paul Getty Center sits high atop the Santa Monica Mountains. Though best known for the museum, there is so much more to the complex than that; the Getty is a multi-sensory experience, from the feel of the building's travertine marble façade, to the sound of water flowing through the garden, to the taste of the food served in the Getty's restaurant, fresh from that day's farmers market.

What to See

Oh, and there's art, too. The original Getty Museum began as a place for oilman J. Paul Getty to hang his large collection of art. Most art critics agree that although Getty's collection habits proved prolific, his purchases were somewhat naïve. Though he never lived to see the museum, he left behind a staggering trust fund that has allowed the Getty to aggressively add to the collection over the years. The permanent collection includes several Van Goghs, including what might be the Getty's highest profile acquisition, *Irises*. There are also Rembrandts, Cezannes, and a rare collaboration between Rubens and Brueghel. In addition to the mostly pre-20th-century paintings, the Getty boasts an impressive collection of photography from the late 1830s to the present. The ever changing special exhibitions are a highlight of any visit to the Getty Center.

It may be impossible to see the entire collection in one visit—three hours is the absolute minimum you should plan on spending at the museum—and then there is the rest of the Getty Center. The Central Garden, designed by Robert Irwin, is intended to be (and most definitely is) a work of art on its own. The garden's benches and chairs invite visitors to relax and enjoy the view, which includes the entire Santa Monica Bay. Meier's building design is also worth much more than a cursory look. The travertine marble used in the construction comes from the same source as the Coliseum

in Rome and, if you look closely, you can sometimes spot fossils that are trapped inside the stone. Both highly trained aesthetes and novice admirers of beauty and design will notice and appreciate the lovely sparseness and order of Meier's main buildings in contrast to Irwin's controlled chaos in the garden which he re-landscapes seasonally.

Where to Eat

The remote location means that you're basically limited to the Getty Center's dining facilities, but luckily the options here are many and all quite good. At the high end, The Restaurant is open for lunch every day and serves dinner from 5 pm until 9 pm on Fridays and Saturdays. Their menu is market-driven, so it changes frequently, but serves healthy, California-style fare. Reservations are suggested and can be made by email or by calling 310-440-6810. Same-day reservations are sometimes available through the Visitor Information Desk.

The Café is run by the same management as The Restaurant, making the same high-quality food available in a more casual self-service setting. The Café is open on weekdays from 11:30 am until 3:30 pm, and on Friday and Saturday evenings until 8:30 pm. Additionally, the Garden Terrace Café is a seasonal self-serve dining facility that overlooks the Central Garden.

There are also several coffee carts around the complex that carry lunch items and snacks. Should you opt to brown bag it, a picnic area is located at the lower tram station and is open until 30 minutes before closing time.

How to Get There—Driving

The easiest way to get to the Getty is to make your way to the 405 and exit at Getty Center Drive. Follow the signs into the parking garage. Parking is $5. Elevators for the parking garage are all color-coded, making it easy to remember where you've parked.

Once you park your car, you have two options for getting to the Getty Center. You can take the tram, which runs frequently, or you can walk to the top of the hill. But bear in mind that the walk is about a mile and at a very steep incline.

How to Get There—Mass Transit

MTA Bus 761 will drop you off right at the Getty's entrance on Sepulveda Boulevard.

General Information

NFT Map:	4
Address	2700 N Vermont Ave
	(in Griffith Park)
	Los Angeles, CA 90027
Hotline:	323-665-1927
Administration::	323-665-5857
Ticketmaster:	213-480-3232
	or 714-740-2000
Website:	www.greektheatrela.
com	

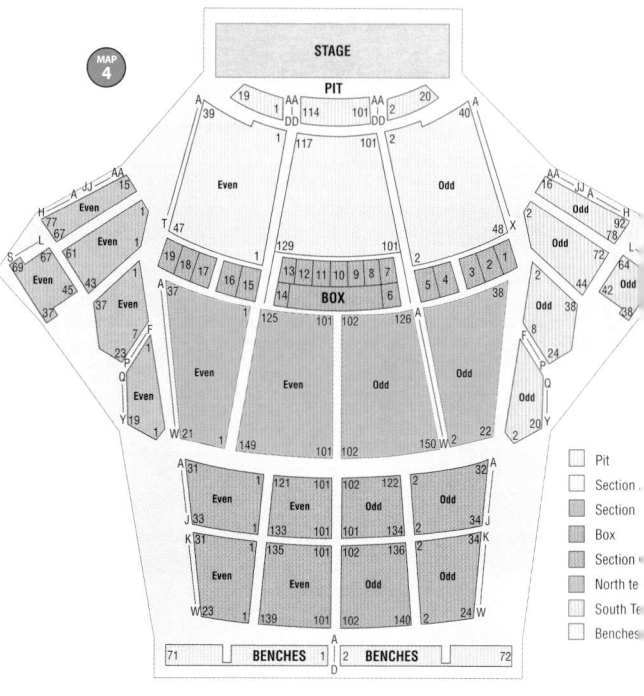

Overview

Sure, a majority of the acts that play the Greek are, shall we say, more *experienced* than most. But if you're feeling a bit nostalgic or ironic—or you're just on a date with your mom—this is *the* place to see the Moody Blues, a '70s-era soul fest, or Daryl Hall & John Oates, when the old folks' home lets them out so they can tour for the summer.

Next to the Hollywood Bowl, the Greek Theatre is LA's only other outdoor venue, and it's gorgeous. Nestled up in Griffith Park, it always feels cooler and less smoggy than the rest of the city. The Greek Theatre is about a third of the size of the Bowl, so you'll be hard pressed to find a bad seat. And if the weather's right, the sky can be so clear that you'll forget that you're in LA all together. No wonder some young 'uns are getting hip to the place (or is that the other way around?). The White Stripes, the Yeah Yeah Yeahs, and the Mars Volta homeboys all decided to go Greek during recent tours. And they haven't trashed the place—yet.

How to Get There—Driving

From the 10, exit at Vermont and drive north to Griffith Park. From the 101 heading north, exit at Vermont Avenue. Turn right onto Vermont and follow it into Griffith Park. From the 101 heading south, exit at Vine Street. Go straight under the underpass, and you will be going east on Franklin Avenue. When you reach Western Avenue, turn left. Western will curve to the right and turn into Los Feliz Boulevard. Turn left at Vermont, and follow it into Griffith Park.

Parking

$10 at the Greek Theatre will buy you the stacked parking option (read: you can't leave until everyone around you does). For $40, you can get valet, which allows you to leave whenever the heck you want. Call 323-665-5857 to make advance reservations. (Yes, reservations for parking. We know, it sounds ridiculous) The reservations office is open 10 am to 6 pm Monday through Friday, and 10 am until 2 pm the day of the show. All major credit cards are accepted. If you're really sly (or just lucky), you can score parallel parking along the many side roads around the Greek. You just have to hope the attendant directs you that way (it may be an option after stacked parking is full, we've never quite figured it out). This option also costs $10, and you can also leave whenever you want. Free shuttles will take you from your parking spot to the venue.

How to Get Tickets

The Greek Theatre's box office only sells tickets in person. Tickets to all events are available through Ticketmaster: www.ticketmaster.com, 213-480-3232.

General Information

NFT Map: 3
Address: 2301 N Highland Ave
Hollywood, CA 90078
General Information: 323-850-2000
Website: www.hollywoodbowl.org
Ticketmaster Arts Line: 213-365-3500

Overview

Visiting the Hollywood Bowl is like back-country camping: getting there takes preparation and perseverance, but once you've arrived, opened the cooler, and looked up at the stars twinkling overhead, you sigh and think, "This is the life, baby." But unlike camping, (with the exception of Yosemite during July 4th weekend), you are surrounded by about 18,000 other people who are also sighing, opening coolers, and "living the life."

Since it opened in 1922, the Hollywood Bowl has presented music, theater, and dance on its stage, and hosted everybody who has been anybody in the performing arts over the past 80+ years (Ella Fitzgerald, Judy Garland, Sinatra, Baryshnikov, The Beatles, Simon and Garfunkel, and Stravinsky, to name a few). One of the world's largest natural amphitheaters, the Hollywood Bowl hosts one million visitors during its season (late June through mid-September). Performances run the gamut from Garrison Keillor to Bjork, with entire series devoted to classical, jazz, and world music. Both the Los Angeles Philharmonic and the pops-oriented Hollywood Bowl Orchestra play weekly, and every weekend brings a "fireworks spectacular" to light up the sky above Bolton Canyon.

Last year the Bowl unveiled its new shell, rebuilt to improve the transistor radio-style acoustics and to increase the stage size by 30%. In addition, four huge projection screens hang above the crowd, so people in the nosebleeds can now examine the sweat beads on Yo-Yo Ma's brow.

How to Get There—Driving

The Hollywood Bowl is located on Highland Avenue, just north of Franklin Avenue. From the 10, exit at La Brea, and drive north. Turn right at Franklin Avenue, and head east until you reach Highland Avenue. Make a left turn, and the Bowl will be just ahead on your left. From the 101, exit at Highland Avenue and follow the signs to the Bowl.

Parking

There are a stingy 2,800 on-site parking spaces for an 18,000-seat amphitheater. If that doesn't stop you from wanting to park, you have your choice of pricey stacked parking lots operated by the Bowl. Pre-purchased parking is available through the box office in the Lower Terrace lot ($12), Upper Terrace lot ($11), and Odin Street lot ($11). Night-of parking, if available, costs $13 in the Terrace lots, $12 in Odin, and $12 in the Fairfield lots, located across Highland Avenue from the Bowl's main entrance. There are many privately run lots open for business when there's a concert. One option is to park in the Hollywood & Highland lot, validate your ticket at mall customer service, and walk up the hill with your picnic basket. It's usually cheaper, less difficult to leave, and a little exercise never killed anyone.

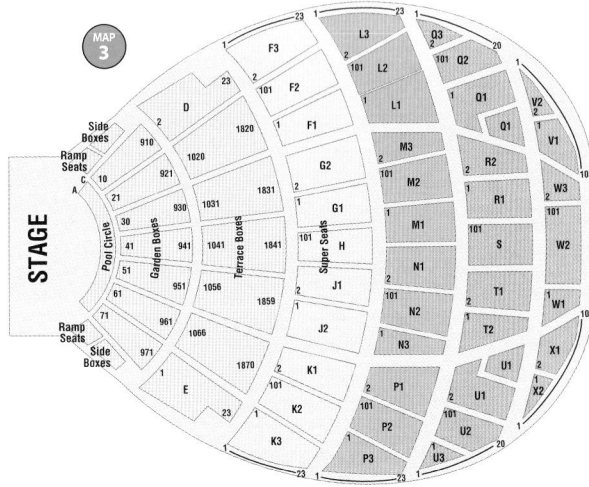

How to Get There—Mass Transit

The Park & Ride service, available for all "LA Phil Presents" concerts, lets you park at one of 15 lots around town and ride a shuttle to the Bowl for $5, round-trip. The BowlBus shuttle service offers free parking at three different locations and a $3 round-trip shuttle every 15 minutes or so starting 2.5 hours before show time. For Park & Ride and BowlBus information, visit the "Getting to the Bowl" section of www.hollywoodbowl.org.

The MTA Hollywood Bowl Shuttle (line 163) offers non-stop service to and from the Bowl when there's a concert. Catch the bus at Hollywood and Argyle, steps away from the Hollywood/Vine Metro Rail Red Line stop. The shuttle is free with a round-trip Metro Rail ticket. 800-266-6883; visit www.mta.net.

Where to Eat

Fill your basket with Trader Joe's camembert, dry salami, and a bottle of two-buck-Chuck, and join the thousands munching *en plein air* before the concert. If DIY is not your thing, the Hollywood Bowl offers a variety of overpriced dining choices, all owned and operated by Patina at the Bowl, part of chef Joachim Splichal's catering and restaurant empire. Whether it's lobster and Veuve Clicquot at the exclusive Pool Circle, or popcorn from a concession stand, you will find something to simultaneously ease your hunger pains and the weight of your wallet. The Rooftop Grill offers sit-down service pre-concert, and the two Marketplace outlets sell sushi and other foodie nibbles to go.

Tickets

Subscription series go on sale earlier than individual seats for all "LA Phil Presents" concerts, and subscribers can add individual tickets to their orders before the general public. Individual tickets go on sale in May. Prices in those coveted box seats can approach $100 per person most nights, but the Bowl still offers their famous $1 seats for many concerts. Call the box office at 323-850-2000 or visit www.hollywoodbowl.com. Tickets are also available through Ticketmaster.

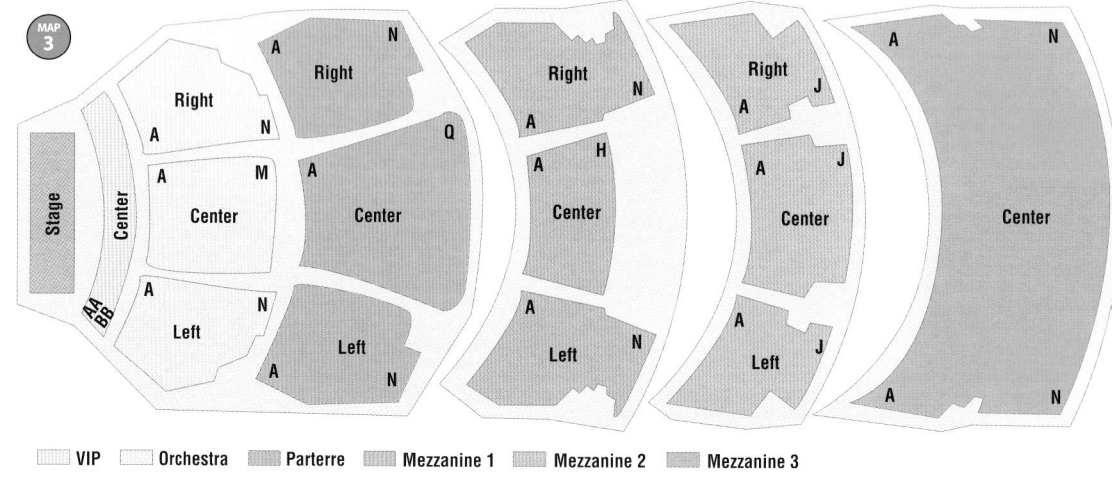

VIP | Orchestra | Parterre | Mezzanine 1 | Mezzanine 2 | Mezzanine 3

General Information

NFT Map: 3
Address: 6801 Hollywood Blvd
Hollywood, CA 90028
Box Office: 323-308-6363
Ticketmaster: 213-480-3232
Website: www.kodaktheatre.com

Overview

The Kodak Theatre has been the home of the Academy Awards since 2001, its grand entrance lined with the names of every Best Picture winner to date. But not everything that takes place on its hallowed stage is Oscar-worthy. Just last year Val Kilmer couldn't get a good word regarding his performance as Moses in *Jesus Christ Superstar*. But that's the Kodak: lots of hits and plenty of misses.

The Kodak is the perfect venue for an awards show or taking in a performance of the *Nutcracker*. Drawbacks that lessen the venue's cred include seats in the upper levels (the only ones that you can usually afford) raked at an alarmingly high angle and the fact that the red carpet for the Academy Awards actually rolls out through a mall. Maybe taking one of the place's guided tours (adults $15, students & seniors $10) to see where recent nominees sat and gain access to the exclusive VIP room is money better spent when you're looking for some Hollywood magic.

The good news? The Hollywood & Highland entertainment complex, which houses the Kodak, is slowly improving with more affordable, if chain, eateries. If you want to balance a night of theater with a little trashiness, there's always Hooters across the street...

How to Get There—Driving

The Kodak Theatre is part of the Hollywood & Highland complex, which—surprise!—can be found at the corner of Hollywood & Highland. From most parts of Los Angeles, the easiest way to reach this behemoth is via the 101 Freeway. Exit the freeway at Highland Avenue and head south. Enter the parking garage via Highland, next to the Renaissance Hollywood Hotel. From the south, you may want to avoid significant traffic downtown by taking the 10 to La Brea Avenue and heading north. Take La Brea all the way up to Franklin Avenue and turn right, then make another right onto Highland Avenue. Drive south until you reach the entrance for the parking garage.

Parking

The closest parking facility for the Kodak is the Hollywood & Highland parking garage. Escalators from said garage will deliver you virtually to the Kodak Theatre's doorstep, and any merchant in the mall will validate your parking, making it a bargain at just $2 for four hours. (Valet parking is also available for an additional $5.) But as you circle lower and lower into the parking garage, journeying ever closer to the Earth's core, you become increasingly aware of what a colossal bummer it would be to get stuck in this garage in the event of an earthquake. That said, when you're late for *Sesame Street Live* and the kids are screaming in the backseat for Elmo, you may want to let Fate roll the dice.

If you've got a little extra time, however, there are several lots that can be entered from Hollywood Boulevard that cater to the tourists who have come to see the Walk of Fame. Rates vary but are relatively inexpensive, rarely setting you back more than $6 for the evening.

How to Get There—Mass Transit

The Metro Red Line stops at the Hollywood/Highland Station. This may actually be the easiest option for people coming from the Valley, especially when Highland Avenue backs up during Hollywood Bowl season. The 156, 212, 217, 312, and 717 buses also stop in the immediate vicinity of the Kodak.

How to Get Tickets

The box office at the Kodak Theatre, located on level one of the Hollywood & Highland center, is open Monday through Saturday from 10 am to 6 pm, and on Sundays from 10 am until 2:30 pm. Tickets are also available through Ticketmaster.

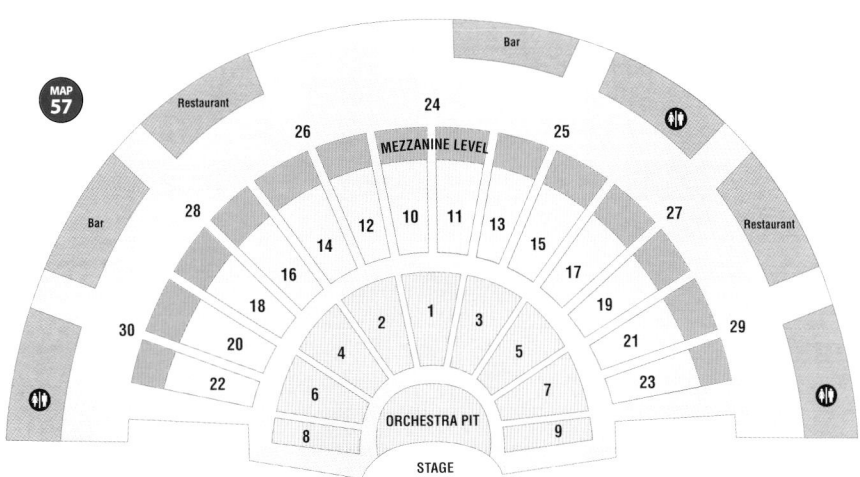

General Information

NFT Map:	57
Address:	100 Universal City Plz
	Universal City, CA 91608
Box Office:	818-622-4440
Ticketmaster:	213-480-3232
Website:	www.hob.com/venues/concerts/gibson

Overview

Last year we said this place lacked personality. Well, either somebody listened or there was some multimillion-dollar corporate branding deal in the works, because the former Universal Amphitheatre is getting a face-lift. Now officially known as the "Gibson Amphitheatre at Universal CityWalk" (we want to be the first to anoint it "The Gibby"), this 6,000-seat venue is not only getting fancy new signs and snazzy new uniforms for employees, but also a Gibson Guitar Garden with guitar sculptures and real axes on display.

At its heart, the Gibby (see, it works) is essentially the same great place to see bands on the rise who haven't quite hit the arena market yet, annual radio concerts, and popular comedians. Everyone from Madonna to Pope John Paul II (in a closed-circuit teleconference) have appeared on its stage—how's that for karmic balance? The adjoining Universal CityWalk is bigger than ever, offering plenty of places to eat and drink beforehand, making that whole dinner-and-a-show thing all the easier.

How to Get There—Driving

The Gibson Amphitheatre is located right outside the gates of the Universal Studios Hollywood theme park, just off the 101 Freeway. If you are coming from the north, take the 101 S and exit at Lankershim Boulevard. Turn left onto Cahuenga Boulevard and make a left onto Universal Center Drive. From there, head up the hill to the parking facilities. From the south, take the 101 N and exit at Universal Center Drive. Turn right at the first traffic light and drive up the hill to the parking facilities.

Parking

Parking at Universal Studios Hollywood costs $8 for the general parking lots and $13 for preferred parking. If you're happy to pay someone else to park your car, validated valet parking costs $5 for the first two hours and $2.50 per half hour thereafter. Without validation, valet parking is $7.50 for the first half hour and $2.50 for each half hour after that. Restaurants at Universal CityWalk provide validation for parking, but concession stands inside the Amphitheatre do not.

How to Get There—Mass Transit

The Universal City Metro Red Line stop is located just across Lankershim Boulevard from the Universal Studios entrance. If you cross the street from the subway station, a free shuttle will take you up the hill to the theme park and Amphitheatre.

MTA buses 96, 150, 152, 156, 166, 240, and 750 also run to the Universal City Station.

How to Get Tickets

You can call the box office hotline at 818-622-4440 to hear what shows are playing. Tickets for most events are available through Ticketmaster, the Gibson Amphitheatre Main box office, or the CityWalk box office. The Main box office is open Thursday through Sunday 1 pm-9 pm. The CityWalk Box Office is open daily 1 pm-9 pm. Tickets may also be charged by phone at 213-252-TIXS (8497).

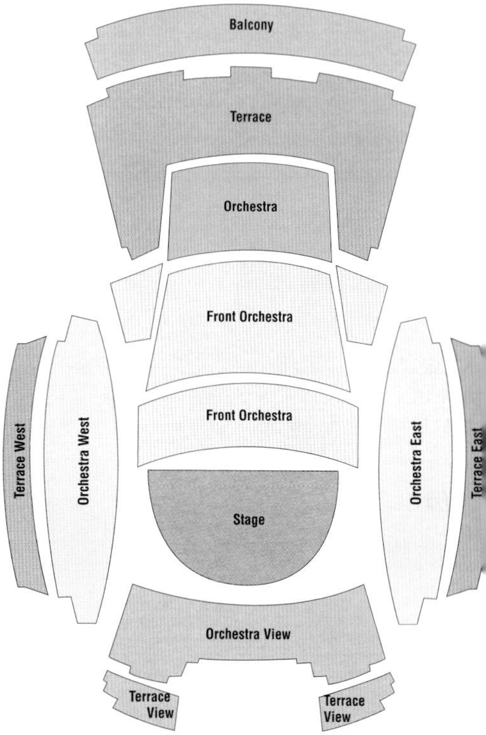

Map

- Pasadena Fwy
- Sunset Blvd
- Cesar E Chavez Ave
- 101 Hollywood Fwy
- Cathedral of Our Lady of the Angels
- Temple St
- Kenneth Hahn Hall of Administration
- 110
- Harbor Fwy
- Figueroa St
- DWP Building
- Hope St
- Ahmanson Theatre
- Mark Taper Forum
- Dorothy Chandler Pavilion
- Grand Ave
- MAP 9
- Stanley Mosk Courthouse
- Hill St
- First St
- Hope St
- Walt Disney Concert Hall
- Flower St
- Second Pl
- (Lower Grand below)
- Second St
- Olive St
- M
- P

Walt Disney Concert Hall

- Balcony
- Terrace
- Orchestra
- Front Orchestra
- Front Orchestra
- Terrace West
- Orchestra West
- Orchestra East
- Terrace East
- Stage
- Orchestra View
- Terrace View
- Terrace View

Walt Disney Concert Hall

Dorothy Chandler Pavilion

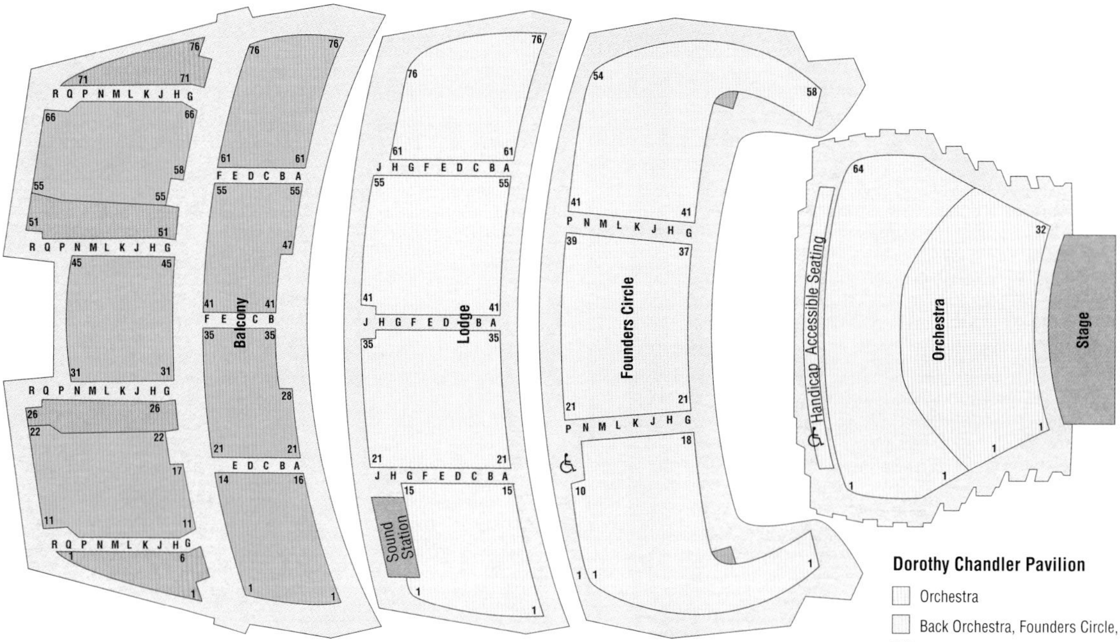

- Balcony
- Lodge
- Founders Circle
- Orchestra
- Stage
- Sound Station
- Handicap Accessible Seating

Dorothy Chandler Pavilion

- Orchestra
- Back Orchestra, Founders Circle, Lo[...]
- Balcony
- Obstructed View

General Information

NFT Map:	9
Address:	135 N Grand Ave
	Los Angeles, CA 90012
Phone:	213-972-7211
Website:	www.musiccenter.org

Overview

The Music Center brings world-renowned actors, dancers, and classical musicians to its four main venues in downtown LA. Whether it's a classic production of *La Bohème,* or a new composition by John Adams, the Music Center's resident companies add much-needed artistic *gravitas* to the city that is mocked for thinking that frozen yogurt constitutes culture.

Walt Disney Concert Hall

Frank Gehry's curving stainless-steel exterior of the Walt Disney Concert Hall made this building an instant landmark when it opened in October 2003. The Los Angeles Philharmonic, led by music director Esa-Pekka Salonen, sells out the acoustically brilliant auditorium. Catching a concert in the state-of-the-art auditorium is something everyone living in LA, or even just passing through, should experience at least once. Steep ticket prices are as convincing an excuse as telling your teacher that your dog ate your homework—$15 can buy you a seat in the choral bench section, where you can look over the musicians' shoulders and follow along with their scores. These cheap seats are available by phone or at the Grand Avenue box office starting at noon on the Tuesday two weeks before the week of the concert. They sell-out within 30 minutes, and are not available for all performances. For more information on the Los Angeles Philharmonic and Walt Disney Concert Hall, including schedules and tickets, visit www.laphil.org, or call 323-850-2000.

Under the baton of musical director Grant Gershon, the Grammy-nominated Los Angeles Master Chorale sings everything from avant-garde opera to the Handel's Messiah (yes, you can sing along) in a hall that gives new meaning to Surround Sound. $10 rush tickets (obstructed view) are available two hours before every performance on a cash-only, two-per-person basis. For Master Chorale schedules and tickets, visit www.lamc.org, or call 213-972-7282.

REDCAT

Short for the Roy and Edna Disney/CalArts Theatre & Gallery, REDCAT is a black box theater and art gallery operated by the California Institute of the Arts, and has a separate entrance under the twisted neon at 2nd Street and Hope Street. REDCAT shows innovative up-and-comers, including cutting-edge performance artists from around the world. $10 student rush tickets are available at the box office 30 minutes before most performances on a cash-only, one-per-person (with ID) basis. For REDCAT schedules and tickets, visit www.redcat.org, or call 213-237-2800.

Dorothy Chandler Pavilion

The 3,197-seat Chandler, located on the southern end of the Music Center plaza, is home to the Los Angeles Opera and Music Center Dance programs. LA Opera, led by Plácido Domingo and music director Kent Nagano, presents the greatest hits, new works, and intimate vocal recitals with stars like Renée Fleming. $20 student and senior rush tickets go on sale 90 minutes before selected performances on a cash-only, one-per-person basis (with valid ID only). Visit www.losangelesopera.com, or call 213-972-8001 for LA Opera tickets and schedules.

Dance at the Music Center is the organization responsible for bringing famed troupes such as the Merce Cunningham Dance Company and the American Ballet Theatre to the Chandler's stage. Student and senior rush tickets priced $10-$15 are available at the Chandler box office two hours prior to curtain on a cash-only, one-per-person basis (with valid ID only). For more information, visit www.musiccenter.org, or call 213-972-0711.

Mark Taper Forum & Ahmanson Theatre

Center Theatre Group produces musicals, dramas, and comedies on the stages of the Mark Taper Forum and Ahmanson Theatre. Purchase tickets for either venue at the Ahmanson's box office, located on the north end of the Music Center plaza, or buy online. $12 rush tickets (balcony level) are available two hours before most performances on a cash-only, two-per-person basis. For more information on Center Theatre Group, including schedules and tickets, visit www.taperahmanson.com or call 213-628-2772.

Where to Eat/Shop

The Patina Group operates all Music Center restaurants and concessions. Kendall's Brasserie & Bar, located on Grand Avenue under the Chandler, has an impressive selection of imported beers and tasty French fare. Both the casual grab-and-go Spotlight Café and the sit-down burger spot Pinot Grill are centrally located between the Dorothy Chandler Pavilion and the Mark Taper Forum. Across First Street, the Walt Disney Concert Hall has both a ho-hum sandwich shop in the lobby and chef Joachim Splichal's fine-dining flagship, Patina. For more information on Patina's restaurants, visit www.patinagroup.com. REDCAT's minimal-yet-cozy bar is independently operated and serves snacks, coffee drinks, and cocktails.

The LAPhil Store is located in the Walt Disney Concert Hall lobby and sells gifts for music aficionados and architecture buffs, including t-shirts, jewelry, music recordings, and books.

How To Get There—Driving

The Music Center is located in downtown Los Angeles near the intersection of the 110 and the 101 freeways.

Chandler/Ahmanson/ Taper (135 N Grand Ave)
110 N and 110 S: Exit Temple, turn left on Temple, right on Grand, and turn right into the Music Center garage
101 N: Exit at Grand, turn right on Grand, and turn right into the Music Center garage
101 S: Exit on Temple, turn left on Temple, right on Grand and turn right into the Music Center garage

Walt Disney Concert Hall (111 S Grand Ave)
From 110 N: Exit on Fourth, continue straight, turn left on lower Grand, pass Kosciuszko, and turn left into the WDCH parking garage.
From 110 S: Exit at Hill, continue past Temple, turn right on First, left on Olive, right on Kosciuszko, right on lower Grand, and left into the WDCH parking garage.
From 101 N: Exit on Grand before the 110 interchange, turn right on Grand, right on Second, and right into the WDCH parking garage.
From 101 S: Exit at Temple, go straight onto Hope, turn left at Second Place, merge onto Kosciuszko from the middle lane, turn left on lower Grand, and turn left into the WDCH parking garage.

Parking

For self-parking at the Chandler, Ahmanson, or Taper, use the Music Center garage located on Grand Avenue between Temple and 1st streets. Daytime parking costs $17 and the evening/event rate (after 4 pm for evening performances and 11 am for matinees) costs $8. Valet parking is available on Hope for $20.

WDCH has two entrances; one on 2nd Street and one on lower Grand Avenue. Valet parking is available on Hope Street for $20.

If you're buying or picking up tickets for any venue, the box office will validate for 30 minutes of free parking.

Additional parking options are within walking distance. County Lot 17 on Olive has parking for $8, DWP charges $5 (enter on Hope Street or 1st Street), or cruise through County Mall Parking VIP-style, with their underground tunnel to the Music Center Garage (enter on Hill Street) for $8.

How To Get There—Mass Transit

The MTA Metro Red Line stops at the Civic Center/Tom Bradley station at First & Hill Streets, two blocks east of the Music Center. Metro Blue, Green, and Gold lines connect with the Red Line.

Many bus lines stop near the center—consult the service providers listed below for routes and schedules.

MTA: 800-266-6883, www.mta.net
Foothill Transit: 800-743-3463, www.foothilltransit.org
Metro Link: 800-371-5465, www.metrolinktrains.com
Big Blue Bus: 310-451-5444, www.bigbluebus.com

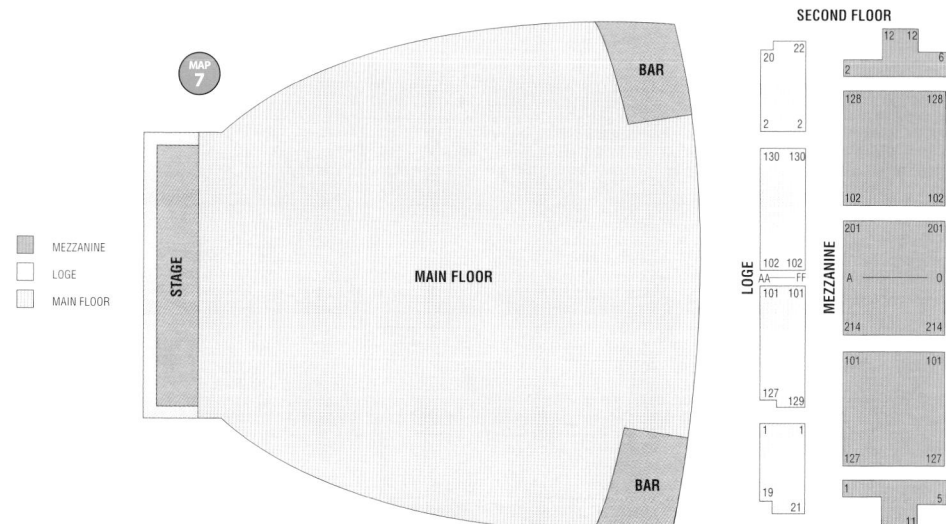

General Information

NFT Map: 7

Address:	3790 Wilshire Blvd
	Los Angeles, CA 90010
Phone:	213-388-1400
Box Office:	213-380-5005
Ticketmaster:	213-480-3232
Website:	www.thewiltern.com

Overview

From the outside, the Wiltern LG looks like the hottest concert venue in town. That's because a recent interior reconfiguration knocked out the lower level's 1,200 permanent seats located closest to the stage to make room for a first-come, first-served general admission area. So when, say, Audioslave or Death Cab for Cutie come to town, you can bet there will be a massive line of concertgoers snaked around the building, waiting to claim a choice spot in the pit. When older acts pop into the venue, it's almost worse: Uncomfortable folding chairs are your only options down front. (However, there is permanent seating available in the back for those who prefer to rock comfortably.)

But enough of the negativity. The building's Art Deco architecture is so snazzy that the place was declared an official City of Los Angeles Historic-Cultural Monument, and its moderate size makes it a great place to catch a band before they hit arena status. Plus, there's a Denny's down the block, which is always a decent post-show destination (well, if you've been drinking a lot…).

How to Get There—Driving

Any number of east-west streets will take you to Western Avenue. The Wiltern LG is at the corner of Western and Wilshire. From the 10, exit at Western Avenue and drive north until you reach Wilshire Boulevard. The venue will be on your right. From the 101, use the Santa Monica Boulevard/Western Avenue exit and take Western south to Wilshire.

Parking

There are a number of parking lots in the area and limited street parking on and around Wilshire Boulevard. A large parking structure is available right behind the theater, which can be accessed from Oxford or Western. Lots generally charge between $5 and $20.

How to Get There—Mass Transit

You can take the Metro Rail Red Line to the Wilshire/Western stop located just across Wilshire from the Wiltern, at Western Avenue. A number of buses also access the theater. Bus 720 runs along Wilshire Boulevard, while buses 207 and 357 run on Western Avenue. Routes 18 and 209 also stop near the theater.

How to Get Tickets

You can purchase tickets in person at the box office three hours prior to show time. Otherwise, you can book tickets online or by phone through Ticketmaster.

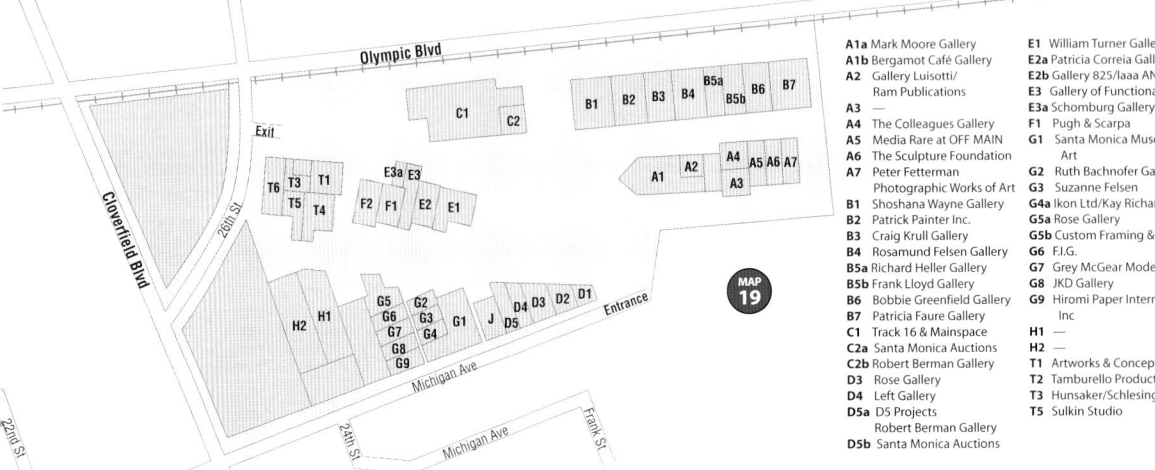

A1a Mark Moore Gallery
A1b Bergamot Café Gallery
A2 Gallery Luisotti/
Ram Publications
A3 —
A4 The Colleagues Gallery
A5 Media Rare at OFF MAIN
A6 The Sculpture Foundation
A7 Peter Fetterman
Photographic Works of Art
B1 Shoshana Wayne Gallery
B2 Patrick Painter Inc.
B3 Craig Krull Gallery
B4 Rosamund Felsen Gallery
B5a Richard Heller Gallery
B5b Frank Lloyd Gallery
B6 Bobbie Greenfield Gallery
B7 Patricia Faure Gallery
C1 Track 16 & Mainspace
C2a Santa Monica Auctions
C2b Robert Berman Gallery
D3 Rose Gallery
D4 Left Gallery
D5a D5 Projects
Robert Berman Gallery
D5b Santa Monica Auctions

E1 William Turner Gallery
E2a Patricia Correia Galle
E2b Gallery 825/Iaaa ANN
E3 Gallery of Functional
E3a Schomburg Gallery
F1 Pugh & Scarpa
G1 Santa Monica Museo
Art
G2 Ruth Bachnofer Gall
G3 Suzanne Felsen
G4a Ikon Ltd/Kay Richarc
G5a Rose Gallery
G5b Custom Framing & C
G6 F.I.G.
G7 Grey McGear Moder
G8 JKD Gallery
G9 Hiromi Paper Interna
Inc
H1 —
H2 —
T1 Artworks & Concepts
T2 Tamburello Productio
T3 Hunsaker/Schlesinge
T5 Sulkin Studio

General Information

NFT Map: 19
Address: 2525 Michigan Ave
                      Santa Monica, CA 90404
Bergamot Website: www.bergamotstation.com
                      (not always operational)
SMMOA Phone: 310-586-6488
SMMOA Website: www.smmoa.org
Hours: Tues-Sat: 11 am-6 pm, Closed Sun & Mon
Admission: free

Overview

Without a doubt, Bergamot Station is the best one-stop art experience you can have in Los Angeles. Originally a stop on the now nonexistent Red Line trolley in the 1800s, Bergamot Station spent most of the last fifty years in a variety of incarnations, from celery-packing facility to ice-making plant. After it was abandoned, the City of Santa Monica wisely saw the area's potential and asked developer Wayne Black to find an artistic use for the property. By 1994, Bergamot Station was up and running as a destination for art lovers who could simply park their cars and spend the day looking at art, rather than driving all over the city from one gallery to the next.

What to See

Bergamot Station is home to almost forty galleries, each of which has its own personality. Rose Gallery deals in photographs and has shown a diverse line-up of artists from Manuel Alvarez Bravo to Wim Wenders. Track 16 focuses on modern and contemporary art and has featured artists like Karen Finley and Man Ray. The Gallery of Functional Art definitely shows art—but that art often doubles as furniture or lighting. Suzanne Felsen's unique jewelry is art by any definition of the word. One of the first Bergamot Galleries, the Shoshana Wayne Gallery, showcases artists such as Yoko Ono and Philip Argent. There is an eclectic variety to be seen at Bergamot Station and our advice is to use the complex as it was intended—park and simply stroll from one gallery to the next. If you keep a brisk pace, you can get through everything in an hour or two. But to get the most out of Bergamot Station, we would suggest spending an entire afternoon there.

In addition to the galleries, Bergamot Station has several other tenants of note, including the Santa Monica Museum of Art. Admission is free and this non-collecting museum always features exhibits like no other museum in LA. Santa Monica Auctions features live art auctions of works by major artists. And Hiromi Paper International is a retail shop that sells just one thing—paper. Hiromi's papers range from offbeat to exquisite and most are so gorgeous that it would be a shame to write on them.

Where to Eat

The Gallery Café remains the complex's only option for breakfast or lunch. It's open Monday from 9 am until 4 pm, Tuesday through Friday from 9 am until 5 pm, and on Saturday from 10 am until 5 pm. They mainly serve sandwiches and salads.

There are also some excellent restaurants in the area for a more leisurely lunch or a post-gallery dinner.

- **Il Moro,** 11400 W Olympic Blvd, 310-575-3530. Delicious pastas and Italian entrees.
- **LA Farm,** 3000 W Olympic Blvd, 310-449-4000. California-style cuisine in a beautiful patio setting.
- **JR Seafood,** 11901 Santa Monica Blvd, 310-268-2463. Your favorite Chinese dishes, with an emphasis on fish and seafood.

How to Get There—Driving

Located on Michigan Avenue in Santa Monica, just east of Cloverfield Boulevard, Bergamot Station is easily accessed from the 10 by exiting at Cloverfield/26th Street. Turn right at the first traffic light, Michigan Avenue, and stay on Michigan until it dead ends. The entrance to Bergamot Station will be on your left.

If you're taking surface streets, Olympic Boulevard is usually the best bet. Take Olympic to Cloverfield and turn left, then turn left again on Michigan Avenue. Bergamot Station is at the end of the street on the left-hand side.

Despite the guppy-short life span of many galleries, LA's art scene is thriving in pedestrian-friendly areas around the city. The Downtown Art Walk, held every second Thursday of the month, is a self-guided introduction to the Downtown galleries. Visit **El Nopal Press**, a publisher of prints and lithographs by artists from Mexico and Los Angeles, or stop by the **Kristi Engle Gallery**, a promising new space in the Spring Arts Tower. **MOCA** and the **Museum of Neon Art** offer free admission during Art Walk.

You can find the Westside's gallery ground zero where Culver City meets Baldwin Hills. **Blum & Poe** boasts an impressive artist roster, including Neo-Pop artist Takashi Murakami, a current art-world superstar. Notable neighbors include the **Anna Helwing Gallery**, focusing on young, risky talent, and **The Project**, a recent transplant from Downtown.

WeHo's busy scene clusters around the Pacific Design Center, and the Miracle Mile's A-list galleries are down the street from LACMA. At Santa Monica's **Bergamot Station,** you can hop through more than thirty galleries without setting a foot outdoors. In Boyle Heights, tour the resident artists' studios at the **Brewery Art Colony** during one of their twice-yearly art walks.

Map 1 • Beverly Hills

Anderson Galleries	354 N Bedford Dr	310-858-1644
Christie's Los Angeles	360 N Camden Dr	310-385-2600
Gagosian Gallery	456 N Camden Dr	310-271-9400
Galerie Michael	430 N Rodeo Dr	310-273-3377
Galerie Yoram Gil	462 N Robertson Blvd	310-275-8130
Latin American Masters	264 N Beverly Dr	310-271-4847
Martin Lawrence Gallery	460 N Rodeo Dr	310-777-0365
MB Fine Art	612 N Almont Dr	310-550-0050
Solaris Gallery	9013 Melrose Ave	310-273-6935

Map 2 • West Hollywood

A+D Museum	8560 W Sunset Blvd	310-659-2445
Adamson-Duvannes	484 S San Vicente Blvd	323-653-1015
Chac Mool Gallery	8920 Melrose Ave	310-550-6792
Couturier Gallery	166 N La Brea Ave	323-933-5557
DiRT	7906 Santa Monica Blvd	323-822-9359
Earl McGrath Gallery	454 N Robertson Blvd	310-657-4257
Edenhurst Gallery	8920 Melrose Ave	310-247-8151
Fahey/Klein Gallery	148 N La Brea Ave	323-934-2250
Forum Gallery Los Angeles	8069 Beverly Blvd	323-655-1550
Gallery 825, LAAA	825 N La Cienega Blvd	310-652-8272
Gallery Saint Germain	300 N Robertson Blvd	310-652-5511
Gemini GEL	8365 Melrose Ave	323-651-0513
George Stern Fine Arts	8920 Melrose Ave	310-276-2600
Glass Garage Fine Art	414 N Robertson Blvd	310-659-5228
Hamilton Selway Fine Art	8678 Melrose Ave	310-657-1711
Herbert Palmer Gallery	9003 Melrose Ave	310-278-6407
Iturralde Gallery	116 S La Brea Ave	323-937-4267
Jack Rutberg Fine Arts	357 N La Brea Ave	323-938-5222
Jan Baum Gallery	170 S La Brea Ave	323-932-0170
Jerry Solomon Art Centre/ ArtTerritory	962 N La Brea Ave	323-512-0124
Johnson Art Collection	8304B Melrose Ave	323-655-5738
Kantor Gallery	7025 Melrose Ave	310-659-5388
Koplin Del Rio Gallery	464 N Robertson Blvd	310-657-9843
Lacy Primitive & Fine Art	8448 Melrose Pl	323-653-1655
Louis Stern Fine Arts	9002 Melrose Ave	310-276-0147
Mak Center for Art & Architecture	835 N Kings Rd	323-651-1510
Manny Silverman Gallery	619 N Almont Dr	310-659-8256
Margo Leavin Gallery	812 N Robertson Blvd	310-273-0603
Michael Hittleman Gallery	8797 Beverly Blvd	323-655-5364
Michael Kohn Gallery	8071 Beverly Blvd	323-658-8088
Morseburg Galleries	9089 Santa Monica Blvd	310-273-5207
Muriel Kretchner Gallery	8908 Melrose Ave	310-858-8566
Pacific Design Center	8687 Melrose Ave	310-657-0800
Papilon Gallery	8010 Melrose Ave	323-655-4468

Regen Projects	633 N Almont Dr	310-276-5424
Riskpress Gallery	8533 Melrose Ave	310-659-4680
Silk Roads Design Gallery	145 N La Brea Ave	310-855-0585
Stephen Cohen Gallery	7358 Beverly Blvd	323-937-5523
Storyopolis	116 N Robertson Blvd	310-358-2509
Tasende Gallery	8808 Melrose Ave	310-276-8686
Tobey C Moss Gallery	7321 Beverly Blvd	323-933-5523
White Room Gallery	8810 Melrose Ave	310-859-2402
William A Karges Fine Art	427 N Canon Dr	310-276-8551

Map 3 • Hollywood

The Advocate Gallery, LA Gay and Lesbian Center	1625 Schrader Blvd	323-993-7400
Los Angeles Contemporary Exhibitions	6522 Hollywood Blvd	323-957-1777
Michael Dawson Gallery	535 N Larchmont Blvd	323-469-2186
Newspace Gallery	5241 Melrose Ave	323-469-9353

Map 4 • Los Feliz

Barnsdall Art Park	4800 Hollywood Blvd	323-644-6269
Clair Obscur Gallery	4310 Melrose Ave	323-913-2513

Map 5 • Silver Lake/Echo Park/Atwater

Black Maria Gallery	3137 Glendale Blvd	323-660-9393
City Gallery	3165 Los Feliz Blvd	323-663-9921
Enisen Gallery	3419 Glendale Blvd	323-660-3789

Map 6 • Miracle Mile/Mid-City

Artbrokering.com	8621 Wilshire Blvd	323-939-3533
Don O'Melveny Gallery	5472 Wilshire Blvd	310-273-7868
Doublevision Gallery	5820 Wilshire Blvd	323-936-1553
Paul Kopeikin Gallery	6150 Wilshire Blvd	323-937-0765

Map 9 • Downtown

626	626 S Spring St	323-394-5363
Acuna-Hansen Gallery	427 Bernard St	323-441-1624
Art Share -Warehouse Gallery	801 E 4th Pl	213-687-4278
Bamboo Lane/Revisited	418 Bamboo Ln	213-620-1188
Bank	400 S Main St	213-621-4055
Bert Green Fine Art	102 W 5th St	213-624-6212
Cirrus Gallery	542 S Alameda St	213-680-3473
Downtown Art Gallery	1611 S Hope St	562-833-6991
El Nopal Press at 5th St	109 W 5th St	323-581-7112

Map 9 • Downtown—*continued*

Fototeka	102 W 5th St	213-250-4686
Infusion	828 S Main St	213-683-8827
Japanese American Cultural	244 S San Pedro St	213-628-2725
and Community Center, George Doizaki Gallery		
Kristi Engle Gallery	453 S Spring St	213-629-2358
LA Artcore	120 Judge John Aiso St	213-617-3274
MJ Higgins Gallery	244 S Main St	213-617-1700
Pharmaka	101 W 5th St	323-954-8499
POST	1904 E 7th Pl	213-488-3379
The Geffen Contemporary	152 N Central Ave	213-626-6222
at MOCA		
Transport Gallery	1308 Factory Pl	213-623-4099
Tropico de Nopal Gallery	1665 Beverly Blvd	213-481-8112
-Art Space		

Map 10 • Baldwin Hills

Anna Helwing Gallery	2766 S La Cienega Blvd	310-202-2213
Billy Shire Fine Art	5790 Washington Blvd	323-297-0600
Blum & Poe	2754 S La Cienega Blvd	310-836-2062
George Billis Gallery	2716 S La Cienega Blvd	310-838-3685
The Project	6086 Corney Ave	323-939-3777
Sandroni Rey	2762 S La Cienega Blvd	310-280-0111
Susanne Vielmeter	5795 Washington Blvd	323-933-2117
Los Angeles Projects		

Map 11 • South Central West

USC Fisher Gallery,	823 Exposition Blvd	213-740-4561
University of Art Galleries		

Map 12 • South Central East

Mixografia	1419 E Adams Blvd	323-232-1158

Map 13 • Inglewood

Harold's Gallery	550 N Oak St	310-680-2444
at INSYNC Media		

Map 15 • Pacific Palisades

Heritage Gallery	1300 Chautauqua Blvd	310-230-4340

Map 16 • Brentwood

Del Mano Gallery	11981 San Vicente Blvd	310-476-8508
J Paul Getty Museum	1200 Getty Center Dr	310-440-7300
at The Getty		
Leslie Sacks Fine Art	11640 San Vicente Blvd	310-820-9448
Mount St Mary's College	12001 Chalon Rd	310-954-4360
- Jose Drudis-Biada Gallery		

Map 18 • Santa Monica

18th Street Arts Complex	1639 18th St	310-453-3711
Angles Gallery	2230 Main St	310-396-5019
Christopher Grimes Gallery	916 Colorado Ave	310-587-3373
Crossroads School	1714 21st St	310-829-7391
For arts and Sciences-Sam Francis Gallery		
Eames Office Gallery	2665 Main St	310-396-5991
& Store		
Hamilton Galleries	1431 Ocean Ave	310-451-9983
LA Foto	806 Pico Blvd	310-664-1563
The Lowe Gallery	2034 Broadway	310-449-0184
M Hanks Gallery	3008 Main St	310-392-8820
Santa Monica College,	11th St	310-434-3434
Pete & Susan Barrett	& Santa Monica Blvd	
Art Gallery		
Sylvia White Gallery	1013 Pico Blvd	310-452-4000
Terrence Rogers Fine Art	1231 5th St	310-394-4999

Map 19 • West LA/Santa Monica East

Art Source LA	2801 Ocean Park Blvd	310-452-4411
Backstreet Galleries	11618 W Exposition Blvd	310-479-6262
Bergamot Station	2525 Michigan Ave	310-652-8272
Berman Turner Projects	Bergamot Station,	310-315-9506
	2525 Michigan Ave	
Bobbie Greenfield Gallery	Bergamot Station,	310-264-0640
	2525 Michigan Ave	
Ernie Wolfe Gallery	1655 Sawtelle Blvd	310-473-1645
Faure & Light Gallery	Bergamot Station,	310-449-1479
	2525 Michigan Ave	
FIG Gallery	Bergamot Station,	310-829-0345
	2525 Michigan Ave	
Frank Lloyd Gallery	Bergamot Station,	310-264-3866
	2525 Michigan Ave	
Gail Harvey Gallery	Bergamot Station,	310-829-9125
	2525 Michigan Ave	
Gallery 825	Bergamot Station	310-652-8272
	2525 Michigan Ave	
Griffin Contemporary	2902 Nebraska Ave	310-586-6886
Hunsaker/	Bergamot Station,	310-828-1133
Schlesinger Fine Art	2525 Michigan Ave	
JKD Gallery	Bergamot Station,	310-998-5888
	2525 Michigan Ave	
Marylin Pink/Fine Arts	509 Avondale Ave	310-395-1465
Patricia Correia Gallery	Bergamot Station,	310-264-1760
	2525 Michigan Ave	
Patrick Painter	Bergamot Station,	310-264-5988
	2525 Michigan Ave	
Richard Heller Gallery	Bergamot Station,	310-453-9191
	2525 Michigan Ave	
Robert Berman Gallery	Bergamot Station,	310-315-9506
	2525 Michigan Ave	
Rosamund Felsen Gallery	Bergamot Station,	310-828-8488
	2525 Michigan Ave	
Ruth Bachofner Gallery	Bergamot Station,	310-829-3300
	2525 Michigan Ave	
Schomburg Gallery	Bergamot Station,	310-453-5757
	2525 Michigan Ave	
Sherry Frumkin Gallery	3026 Airport Ave	310-397-7493
Shoshana Wayne Gallery	Bergamot Station,	310-453-7535
	2525 Michigan Ave	
TAG, The Artists' Gallery	2903 Santa Monica Blvd	310-829-9556
Track 16 Gallery	Bergamot Station,	310-264-4678
	2525 Michigan Ave	

Map 20 • Westwood/Century City

Italian Culture Institute	1023 Hilgard Ave	310-443-3250
- Spazio Italia		
Jonathan Novak	1880 Century Park E	310-277-4997
Contemporary Art		
UCLA Fowler Museum	UCLA Campus,	310-825-4361
	west of Royce Hall	
UCLA Hammer Museum	10899 Wilshire Blvd	310-443-7000

Map 21 • Venice

Abbot Kinney Gallery	1301 Abbot Kinney Blvd	310-664-9030
Clay	226 Main St	310-399-1416
LA Louver Galleries	45 N Venice Blvd	310-822-4955
Light Space Gallery	1732 Abbot Kinney Blvd	310-301-6969
Off-Rose, The Secret Studio	841 Flower Ave	310-664-8977
-Gallery of Venice		
Soapbox	701 Venice Blvd	310-305-9145
Sparc Art Gallery	685 Venice Blvd	310-822-9560

Map 24 • Culver City

BLK/MRKT Gallery	6009 Washington Blvd	310-837-1989
d.e.n. contemporary art	6023 Washington Blvd	310-559-9355
Duncan Miller Gallery	10959 Venice Blvd	310-838-2440
Fresh Paint Art Advisors	9355 Culver Blvd	310-558-9355
MC	6086 Comey Ave	323-939-3777
West Los Angeles College Art Gallery	9000 Overland Ave	310-287-4200

Map 25 • Marina Del Rey/Westchester West

Ben Maltz Gallery, Otis College of Art and Design	9045 Lincoln Blvd	310-665-6906
Loyola Marymount University - Laband Gallery	7101 W 80th St	310-338-2880

Map 28 • Hawthorne

Soicher Marin Gallery	12824 Cerise Ave	310-679-5000

Map 29 • Hermosa Beach/Redondo Beach North

Cannery Row Studios	604 N Francisca Ave	310-379-6313
Gallery C	1225 Hermosa Ave	310-798-0102

Map 30 • Torrance North

El Camino College Art Gallery	16007 Crenshaw Blvd	310-660-3010
Joslyn Fine Arts Gallery	3320 Civic Center Dr	310-681-6340

Map 33 • Eagle Rock/Highland Park

Eagle Rock Community Cultural Center	2225 Colorado Blvd	323-226-1617
Judson Gallery of Contemporary and Traditional Art	200 S Ave 66	323-255-0131

Map 34 • Pasadena

Armory Northwest	965 N Fair Oaks Ave	626-792-5101
Chouinard School of Art	1020 Mission St	626-799-0826
Kelley Gallery	696 E Colorado Blvd	626-577-5657
Mendenhall Sobieski	40 Mills Pl	626-535-9757
Pasadena Museum of California Art	490 E Union St	626-568-3665
The Folk Tree	217 S Fair Oaks Ave	626-795-8733
The Folk Tree Collection	199 S Fair Oaks Ave	626-795-4828

Map 35 • Pasadena East/San Marino

Absolute Art Gallery	2326 Huntington Dr	626-285-8585
California Art Club Gallery at The Old Mill	1120 Old Mill Rd	626-449-5458
Huntington Library Art Collection	1151 Oxford Rd	626-449-6840
Pasadena City College Art Gallery	1570 E Colorado Blvd	626-568-7412

Map 36 • Mt Washington

LA River Li'l Frogtown	1625 Blake Ave	323-226-0356
Southwest Museum	234 Museum Dr	323-221-2164

Map 37 • Lincoln Heights

La Mano Press	1749 N Main St	323-227-0650
Plaza de la Raza, Boathouse Gallery	3540 N Mission Rd	323-223-2475

Map 38 • El Sereno

Luckman Gallery, Harriet & Charles Luckman Fine Arts Complex, California State University, Los Angeles	5151 State University Dr	323-343-6604

Map 40 • Boyle Heights

At The Brewery Project	676 S Ave 21	323-222-0222
East Los Angeles College, Vincent Price Gallery	1301 E Cesar E Chavez Ave	323-265-8650
Raid Projects Gallery	602 Moulton St	323-441-9553

Map 42 • Chatsworth

The Atelier	21501 Devonshire St	818-576-1545

Map 50 • Burbank East/Glendale West

Creative Arts Center Gallery	1100 W Clark Ave	818-238-5397

Map 51 • Glendale South

Harvest Gallery	938 N Brand Blvd	818-546-1000

Map 52 • Tarzana/Woodland Hills

Joseph Wahl Art Gallery	5305 Topanga Canyon Blvd	818-340-9245

Map 54 • Sherman Oaks West

Skirball Cultural Center	2701 N Sepulveda Blvd	310-440-4500
University of Judaism-Platt and Borstein Galleries	15600 Mulholland Dr	310-476-9777

Map 56 • Studio City/Valley Village

Soho Gallery	12202 Ventura Blvd	818-766-5569

Map 57 • Universal City/Toluca Lake

A Studio Gallery	4260 Lankershim Blvd	818-980-9100
Martin Lawrence Gallery	1000 University Center Dr	818-508-7867

Long Beach

Rio Hondo College Art Gallery	3600 Workman Mill Rd	562-692-0921

Los Angeles, the world's other film capital (we tip our hats to prolific Bollywood with awe and respect), is a movie-goer's paradise, offering a huge assortment of theaters playing old, new, revival, director's cuts, foreign, indie, gay, and silent films (and, of course, the rare gay-foreign-silent trifecta). The sprawling range of genres and theaters that cater to the movie-obsessed ensures that whatever your passion, you're bound to find something in this town to sate your cinematic tastes.

Palaces

Once you make it past the Darth Vader impersonator, **Grauman's Chinese Theatre** really is a thrill—cavernous and elegantly lined with old velvet. The **ArcLight Hollywood** offers real butter on your popcorn, an assigned seat of your choice, and one of the best sound and picture systems in the world (but at a cost: $14 on Friday and Saturday nights; $11 otherwise). **Pacific's The Grove Stadium 14** and **Pacific Paseo Stadium 14** are satisfyingly super-sized, though the Saturday night crowds tend to be, as well. The **Vista Theatre** in Silver Lake has leg-room galore and a beautiful Egyptian theme. The **Loews Magic Johnson Theatre 15** in Baldwin Hills is also pleasingly palatial.

Jewel-boxes

If you are of a certain age, it's possible that your love of film was born in a real theater—not at home in front of the VCR—watching something by Bergman, de Sica, or Renoir. If so, there are a handful of movie houses in LA where you can recapture some of that delicate, old-school thrill—regardless of what contemporary film might be playing. In this category we place **Landmark Theatres Regent**, **NuArt**, **NuWilshire**, and **Rialto**. The **Cecchi Gori Fine Arts Theater,** in particular, may be the quietest and most thoughtful film-going venue ever. The **Laemmle Music Hall 3** and **Royal** theaters, as well as the **Aero Theater** in Santa Monica, are also excellent in that capacity.

Shoe Boxes

At $10 or more per ticket, we felt it irresponsible not to mention that some theaters are inherently disappointing in their size or layout. We cast no aspersions on their programming (most of which is beyond reproach), but want you to be prepared for smallish screens and/or unusual spatial configurations at **Landmark's Westside Pavilion Cinemas**, the **Five Star Theaters Los Feliz 3**, **Laemmle's Sunset 5**, and the **Loews Beverly Center 13**.

Independent

Laemmle and **Landmark** theaters are located throughout the city and can be counted on to play the low-budget, the independent, the foreign, or the controversial film that you've been waiting to see. The **Five Star Theaters Los Feliz 3** on Vermont screens a nice mix of indie and big-budget pictures, with a Wednesday "Mommy and Me" matinee at 10:30 am.

Bargains

The **Academy 6** in Pasadena gives you a second chance to see first-run films you missed a month or so ago, as well as independent/foreign films that you might not have seen at all—tickets are as low as $4 if you go before six o'clock. Seven dollars will buy you admission to a double feature of second-run movies at the **Vine Theatre**; the two films are often oddly paired, though—an R-rated thriller and a G-rated animated feature, for instance. Also billing double features—although this movie match-up is strictly revival—is the **New Beverly Cinema**, where for $6 you can see two by Godard, or a couple of spaghetti westerns.

Specialty

Every summer, the Los Angeles Conservancy presents classic films (*Ninotchka*, anyone? *To Have and Have Not*?) in the historic theaters downtown on Broadway as part of their "Last Remaining Seats" program (on the web at www.laconservancy.org). For art films, with or without a narrative, check out the current listings at **REDCAT** in the Disney Hall. Frequently showing films that correspond with one of the current exhibits is the **Bing Theater** at LACMA—the museum also hosts the occasional film series, as well as talks with legendary actors and directors.

The **Egyptian Theater** has been carefully restored to its 1922 grandeur by the folks of American Cinematheque, who also call this famous landmark their home; the theater features a veritable feast of film geek favorites—director's cuts, anniversary specials, and films not on video. Graveyard screenings at **Hollywood Forever Cemetery** allow film buffs to actually sit on the grave of the matinee idol projected on the screen (check www.cinespia.org for details). While not technically a theater, **Cinespace**, a bar and restaurant in Hollywood, shows films nightly. **Pacific's El Capitan** theater across from Grauman's is owned by Disney and presents Disney films exclusively. Last, but certainly not least, is the historic **Silent Movie Theatre** on Fairfax, where both the bill of pre-talkie films and the murderous legend of the theater draws a curious audience.

Movie Theater	Address	Phone	Map
Academy 6	1003 E Colorado Blvd	626-229-9400	35
Aero Theater	1328 Montana Ave	310-260-1528	18
AMC Avco Center Cinemas	10840 Wilshire Blvd	310-475-0711	20
AMC Burbank 16	125 E Palm Ave	818-953-9800	50
AMC Century 14	10250 Santa Monica Blvd	310-553-8900	20
AMC Galleria - South Bay Cinema 16	1815 Hawthorne Blvd	310-793-7477	30
AMC Media Center 8	201 E Magnolia Blvd	818-953-9800	50
AMC Media Center North 6	770 N 1st St	818-953-9800	50
AMC Promenade 16	21801 Oxnard St	818-883-2262	45
AMC Santa Monica 7 Plex	1310 Third St Promenade	310-395-3030	18
AMC Theatres Marina Pacifica 12	6346 E Pacific Coast Hwy	562-435-4262	p 240
AMC Theatres Pine Square 16	245 Pine Ave	562-435-4262	p 240
ArcLight Hollywood/Cinerama Dome	6360 W Sunset Blvd	323-464-1465	3

Movie Theater	Address	Phone	Map
Art Theatre	2025 E 4th St	562-438-5435	p 240
Bing Theater at LACMA	5905 Wilshire Blvd	323-857-6000	6
The Bridge: Cinema de Lux	6081 Center Dr	310-568-3375	26
California Science Center IMAX	700 State Dr	213-748-6321	11
Campus Movie Theatre	1020 N Vermont Ave	323-665-5881	4
Century North Hollywood	12827 Victory Blvd	818-508-6004	48
Cinemark at the Pike	99 S Pine Ave	562-435-0353	p 240
Cinespace	6356 Hollywood Blvd	323-817-3456	3
Edwards Atlantic Cinemas	700 W Main St	626-458-8663	39
Edwards Renaissance Stadium 14	1 E Main St	626-300-8312	39
Egyptian Theater	6712 Hollywood Blvd	323-466-3456	3
Five Star Theaters Los Feliz 3	1822 N Vermont Ave	323-668-9004	4
Flagship University Village 3	3323 S Hoover St	213-748-6321	12
Glendale Cinema	501 N Orange St	818-549-9950	51
Grauman's Chinese Theatre	6925 Hollywood Blvd	323-464-6266	3
Highland Theater	5604 N Figueroa St	323-256-6383	33
Laemmle Fairfax 3	7907 Beverly Blvd	323-655-4010	2
Laemmle Grande 4	349 S Figueroa St	213-617-0268	9
Laemmle Monica 4	1332 2nd St	310-394-9741	18
Laemmle Music Hall 3	9036 Wilshire Blvd	310-274-6869	6
Laemmle One Colorado Cinemas	42 Miller Aly	626-744-1224	34
Laemmle Playhouse 7	673 E Colorado Blvd	626-844-6500	34
Laemmle Royal	11523 Santa Monica Blvd	310-478-1041	19
Laemmle Sunset 5	8000 W Sunset Blvd	323-848-3500	2
Laemmle Town Center 5	17200 Ventura Blvd	818-981-9811	53
Landmark Cecchi Gori Fine Arts Theatre	8556 Wilshire Blvd	310-281-8223	6
Landmark NuArt Theatre	11272 Santa Monica Blvd	310-478-6379	19
Landmark NuWilshire Theatre	1314 Wilshire Blvd	310-394-8099	18
Landmark Regent Theatre	1045 Broxton Ave	310-208-3259	20
Landmark Rialto Theatre	1023 Fair Oaks Ave	626-799-9567	34
Landmark Westside Pavilion Cinemas	10800 W Pico Blvd	310-475-0202	23
Loews Beverly Center 13	8522 Beverly Blvd	310-652-7760	2
Loews Broadway Cinemas 4	1441 Third St Promenade	310-458-3924	18
Loews Magic Johnson Theatre 15	4020 Marlton Ave	323-290-5900	10
Loews Marina Marketplace Cinemas	13455 Maxella Ave	310-827-2883	25
Loews Universal Citywalk Cinemas and IMAX Theatre	100 Universal City Plz	818-508-0711	57
Majestic Crest Theatre	1262 Westwood Blvd	310-474-7866	20
Mann Bruin	948 Broxton Ave	310-208-8998	20
Mann Chinese 6	6801 Hollywood Blvd	323-461-9624	3
Mann Criterion 6	1313 Third St Promenade	310-395-1599	18
Mann Culver Plaza 6	9919 Washington Blvd	310-841-2993	24
Mann Glendale Exchange 10	128 N Maryland Ave	818-549-0045	51
Mann Glendale Marketplace 4	144 S Brand Blvd	818-241-2784	51
Mann Granada Hills 9	16830 Devonshire St	818-363-0549	44
Mann National Theatre	10925 Lindbrook Dr	310-208-4366	20
Mann Valley West 9	18632 Ventura Blvd	818-996-8029	46
Mann Village Theatre Westwood	961 Broxton Ave	310-208-5576	20
New Beverly Cinema	7165 Beverly Blvd	323-938-4038	2
Old Town Music Hall	140 Richmond St	310-322-2592	27
Pacific Beach Cities 16	831 N Nash St	310-607-0007	27
Pacific El Capitan	6838 Hollywood Blvd	323-467-7674	3
Pacific Fashion Center 10	9400 Shirley Ave	818-501-5121	43
Pacific Galleria Stadium	15301 Ventura Blvd	818-501-7033	54
Pacific Manhattan Village	3560 N Sepulveda Blvd	310-640-1075	27
Pacific Paseo Stadium 14	336 E Colorado Blvd	626-568-9690	34
Pacific's The Grove Stadium 14	189 The Grove Dr	323-692-0829	2
Pacific Winnetka 21 Theaters	9201 Winnetka Ave	818-501-5121	42
Plant 16	7876 Van Nuys Blvd	818-779-0323	47
REDCAT	631 W 2nd St	213-237-2800	9
Redondo Beach Cinema 3	1509 Hawthorne Blvd	310-370-8588	30
Regent Showcase Theatre	614 N La Brea Ave	323-934-2944	2
Sherman Oaks 5	14424 Millbank St	818-801-5121	55
Silent Movie Theatre	611 N Fairfax Ave	323-655-2520	2
UCLA Film & TV Archive	1409 Melnitz Bldg	310-206-8422	20
United Artists Long Beach Marketplace 6	6601 E Pacific Coast Hwy		p 240
United Artists Marina del Rey 6	4335 Glencoe Ave	310-823-3959	22
United Artists Valley Plaza 6	6355 Bellingham Ave	818-766-4317	48
Vine Theatre	6321 Hollywood Blvd	323-463-6819	3
Vista Theatre	4473 Sunset Blvd	323-660-6639	4
Warner Grand Theater	478 W 6th St	310-833-8333	p 236

Angelenos are brainwashed to believe that the weather's too nice to stay indoors. Vegetate in front of a *Brady Bunch* marathon one sunny Saturday, and we're bound to feel guilty about the new surfboard or pair of hiking boots stashed in the closet. How to gain absolution without risking premature wrinkles and shark attacks? Pay a visit to one of the city's many museums. Not only will you raise your intellectual spirits and expand your cultural horizons, you'll also keep your skin baby smooth and your limbs firmly attached.

Large/City

At the heart of the Miracle Mile is the **Los Angeles County Museum of Art**, or LACMA, with its comprehensive collection including Renaissance masterpieces, ukiyo-e prints, and African beadwork. The museum hosts weekly jazz and chamber music concerts and its Bing Theater shows documentaries and revival films. The **Page Museum,** part of the LACMA campus, showcases fossils recovered from the La Brea Tar Pits that ooze nearby. In Brentwood, escape the hellish 405 and ascend by computer-operated tram to the **Getty Center**, a heavenly museum complex perched on a hilltop. The permanent collection includes works by Van Gogh, Cézanne, and Rembrandt, but the museum's spectacular views, gardens, and architecture steal the show. The Getty's sister museum, the **Getty Villa** in Malibu, is slated to open in the winter of 2006. Downtown's **Museum of Contemporary Art** (MOCA) owns works by Lichtenstein, Rauschenberg, and Rothko, and hosts hip opening-night parties. The **Museum of the American West** in Griffith Park mounts fascinating exhibits on subjects like the art of rawhide braiding and Jewish life along the Santa Fe Trail. Kids love to visit the creepy-crawly insect zoo at the **Natural History Museum of Los Angeles** in Exposition Park. In San Marino, bask in the glorious gardens at the **Huntington**, but don't miss the institution's world-renowned art and rare manuscript collections.

Small Collections

The **Norton Simon Museum** in Pasadena houses a fine private collection of European, American, and Asian art, including many of the bronze sculptures in Edgar Degas' *Dancer* series. Work by famed Harlem Renaissance artist Palmer C. Hayden is on display at the **Museum of African American Art** in Crenshaw. UCLA's **Hammer Museum** shows this year's cutting-edge artwork alongside last century's masterpieces. For a family field trip, try the **Craft & Folk Art Museum** or the **Zimmer Children's Museum** on Wilshire's Museum Row.

Specialty

Test your beliefs at the **Museum of Tolerance**, where interactive exhibits focus on the Holocaust and the American civil rights movement. The **Japanese American National Museum** in Little Tokyo hosts taiko drummers, sumi-e lessons, and special exhibitions such as the recent Isamu Noguchi retrospective. Indulge your favorite hot-rod historian at the **Petersen Automotive Museum** near LACMA or nurse a beer on the real *Cheers* set at the **Hollywood Entertainment Museum**. The **Los Angeles Police Historical Society** displays bullets older than your grandfather, and the photos at the **African American Firefighter Museum** tell both the history of black firefighters and of Los Angeles.

Oddities

It's not called Hollyweird for nothing—skip the tourist trap wax museums on Hollywood Boulevard and view the electric chair, guillotine, and celebrity photos at the **Museum of Death** instead. As its name suggests, Culver City's **Museum of Jurassic Technology** defies description (but you should give it a shot anyway). Downtown's **Museum of Neon Art**, or MONA, celebrates the medium that makes signs great. While not technically a museum, the LA County Coroner's Gift Shop, Skeletons in the Closet (1104 N Mission Rd, 323-343-0760), is a must-shop experience for the macabre or anyone looking for a chalk body outline beach towel.

Museum	Address	Phone	Map
African American Firefighter Museum	1401 S Central Ave	213-744-1730	51
African American Museum	600 State Dr	213-744-7432	11
Alhambra Historical Society	1550 W Alhambra Rd	626-300-8845	39
Angels Attic	516 Colorado Ave	310-394-8331	18
Armory Center for the Arts	145 N Raymond Ave	626-792-5101	34
Blitzstein Museum of Art	428 N Fairfax Ave	323-852-4830	2
Bonnie Brae House Museum	216 N Bonnie Brae St	213-484-6690	9
California Heritage Museum	2612 Main St	310-392-8537	18

Museum	Address	Phone	Map
Chinese American Museum	425 N Los Angeles St	213-626-5240	9
El Pueblo de Los Angeles Historical Monument	Main St & Cesar E Chavez Ave	213-628-3562	9
Geffen Contemporary	152 N Central Ave	213-621-1741	9
Getty Museum	1200 Getty Center Dr	310-440-7360	16
Grier-Musser Museum	403 S Bonnie Brae St	213-413-1814	9
Hermosa Beach Historical Society Museum	710 Pier Ave	310-318-9421	29
Hollywood Entertainment Museum	7021 Hollywood Blvd	323-465-7900	3
Hollywood Guinness Museum	6764 Hollywood Blvd	323-463-6433	3
The Hollywood Heritage Museum	2100 N Highland Ave	323-874-2276	3
Hollywood History Museum	1660 N Highland Ave	323-464-7776	3
Hollywood Wax Museum	6767 Hollywood Blvd	323-462-5991	3
Holyland Exhibition	2215 Lake View Ave	323-664-3162	5
Huntington	1151 Oxford Rd	626-405-2141	35
Japanese American National Museum	369 E 1st St	213-625-0414	9
Kidspace – An Interactive Museum	480 N Arroyo Blvd	626-449-9144	34
L Ron Hubbard Life Exhibition	6331 Hollywood Blvd	323-960-3511	3
Los Angeles County Museum of Art	5905 Wilshire Blvd	323-857-6000	6
Los Angeles Craft & Folk Art Museum	5814 Wilshire Blvd	323-937-4230	6
Los Angeles Museum of the Holocaust	6435 Wilshire Blvd	323-651-3704	6
Los Angeles Police Historical Society	6045 York Blvd	323-344-9445	33
Mak Center Mackey House	1137 S Cochran Ave	323-939-9420	6
Manhattan Beach Historical Society	1601 Manhattan Beach Blvd	310-374-7575	27
MOCA at the Pacific Design Center	8687 Melrose Ave	310-657-0800	2
Museum In Black	4331 Degnan Blvd	323-292-9528	11
Museum of African American Art (temporarily closed)	4005 Crenshaw Blvd	323-294-7071	10
Museum of Contemporary Art (MOCA)	250 S Grand Ave	213-626-6222	9
Museum of Death	6340 Hollywood Blvd	323-466-8011	3
Museum of Flying (temporarily closed)	2772 Donald Douglas Loop N	310-392-8822	19
Museum of Jurassic Technology	9341 Venice Blvd	310-836-6131	24
Museum of Neon Art	501 W Olympic Blvd	213-489-9918	9
Museum of Television & Radio	465 N Beverly Dr	310-786-1000	1
Museum of Tolerance	9786 W Pico Blvd	310-553-8403	23
Natural History Museum of Los Angeles	900 Exposition Blvd	213-763-3466	11
Norton Simon Museum of Art	411 W Colorado Blvd	626-449-6840	34
Pacific Asia Museum	46 N Los Robles Ave	626-449-2742	34
Page Museum at the La Brea Pits	5801 Wilshire Blvd	323-934-7243	6
Pasadena Historical Museum	470 W Walnut St	626-577-1660	34
Petersen Automotive Museum	6060 Wilshire Blvd	323-930-2277	6
Santa Monica Historical Museum	1539 Euclid St	310-395-2290	18
Santa Monica Museum of Art	2525 Michigan Ave	310-586-6488	19
Skirball Cultural Center	2701 N Sepulveda Blvd	310-440-4500	54
Southwest Museum of the American Indian	234 Museum Dr	323-221-2164	36
Torrance Historical Society	1345 Post Ave	310-328-5392	32
Travel Town Museum	5200 Zoo Dr	323-662-5874	99
UCLA Hammer Museum	10889 Wilshire Blvd	310-443-7000	20
Western Museum of Flight	12016 Prairie Ave	310-332-6228	28
Zimmer Children's Museum	6505 Wilshire Blvd	323-761-8989	6

General New/Used

LA's humongous selection of bookstores makes it easy to blow your grocery money on hard covers, even without a visit to the local **Barnes & Noble**, **Borders**, or **Waldenbooks**.

Vroman's in Pasadena is over a century old, but its collection is as large and current as those at the big chains. **Dutton's**, another major independent, has locations in Brentwood, Beverly Hills, and Valley Village. (The Village store sells used books, too.) **Brand Bookshop** in Glendale lures customers with its eccentric window display (edible insect cookbook, anyone?), and keeps them turning the pages with over 100,000 used and out-of-print titles in every category imaginable.

The mother ship of Southern California bookstores is **Acres of Books** in Long Beach. This airplane hangar-sized store carries over a million used, rare, and out-of-print books. Get lost in the stacks and channel your inner Ray Bradbury or Upton Sinclair, two of the institution's celebrated browsers.

Small New/Used

Skylight Books in Los Feliz has a well-edited collection of literary fiction, travel, local-interest, and film books, a resident kitty cat dozing in the window, and an impressive monthly lineup of literary events. **Small World Books** in Venice combines a fine selection of new titles with an ideal beachfront location. Downtown's **Caravan Bookstore**, the last of the old Bookseller's Row shops, carries rare and out-of-print works.

Specialty

If you're into something, odds are there's a bookshop that'll suit your interests. An intriguing selection of maps, travel guides, and photography books at **Distant Lands** in Pasadena inspires journeys by plane, train, or armchair. **Eso Won Books** in Baldwin Hills specializes in African-American literature and hosts frequent signings. (Bill Clinton visited during his recent book tour.) **Dawson's Book Shop** in Hollywood is the source for antiquarian books on California history, Western Americana, and photography, and its gallery exhibits the likes of Ansel Adams, Edward Weston, and Eadweard Muybridge. The sleek **Equator Books** on Venice's trendy Abbot-Kinney strip specializes in rare and collectible coffee table tomes on surfing, call girls, and circus freaks. **Traveler's Bookcase** is an excellent all-around travel bookstore, and **California Map & Travel** has the best overall collection of maps and atlases in Los Angeles

West Hollywood is a microcosm of LA's literary scene, supporting a mind-boggling range of special interest bookstores. **Cook's Library** on 3rd Street stocks thousands of cookery books for Ferran Adria wannabes. Aromas of herbal tea and incense waft through the **Bodhi Tree Bookstore** on Melrose, purveyor of metaphysical titles, both new and recycled. On Santa Monica, **A Different Light** caters to the area's gay, lesbian, bisexual, and transgender communities. **Storyopolis** on Ventura specializes in children's literature, including rare and collectible titles from the turn of the 20th century. The store's readings, art classes, and sock hops (yes, sock hops!) keep kids and parents coming back for more.

Art/Film Books

LA is where art and entertainment collide, and the city's bookstores gather up the pieces. The eye-popping **Taschen** store in Beverly Hills stocks the iconoclast publisher's brand of luxe art tomes and naughty coffee table books. **MOCA**, **LACMA**, and the **Getty** are some of the many area museums that carry exhibition catalogues and academic art books. **Meltdown** in West Hollywood is famous for comics, but its selection of graphic novels is equally strong. **Book Soup** on the Sunset Strip boasts a celebrity clientele and floor-to-ceiling shelves stocked with art, photography, film, and music-oriented titles. The wonderful **Hennessey + Ingalls** is also a great art

Map 1 • Beverly Hills

Dutton's Beverly Hills	447 N Canon Dr	310-281-0997	Independent.
Taschen Books	354 N Beverly Dr	310-274-4300	Art & photo books.

Map 2 • West Hollywood

A Different Light Bookstore	8853 Santa Monica Blvd	310-854-6601	Gay/lesbian.
Arundel Books	8380 Beverly Blvd	323-852-9852	Art and design books.
Audobon Society Bookstore	7377 Santa Monica Blvd	323-876-0202	Books on nature.
Automobile Books	8980 Santa Monica Blvd	310-657-5278	Books about cars.
Barnes & Noble	189 Grove Dr	323-525-0270	Chain.
Bodhi Tree Bookstore	8585 Melrose Ave	310-659-1733	New Age, spiritual.
Book Soup	8818 W Sunset Blvd	310-659-3110	Great independent bookstore.
Borders	330 S La Cienega Blvd	310-659-4045	Chain.
Brentano's	8500 Beverly Blvd	310-652-8024	Chain owned by Borders.

Circus of Books	8230 Santa Monica Blvd	323-656-6533	Gay/lesbian; general interest art/photo books.
Cook's Library	8373 W 3rd St	323-655-3141	Cookbooks.
Dailey Rare Books	8216 Melrose Ave	323-658-8515	Antiquarian books.
Golden Apple Comics	7711 Melrose Ave	323-658-6047	Comics.
Houle Rare Books & Autographs	7260 Beverly Blvd	323-937-5858	Used and rare.
Interbook	7513 Santa Monica Blvd	323-882-6160	Russian books.
Kovcheg Russian Bookstore	7508 W Sunset Blvd	323-876-2749	Russian books.
Meltdown Comics & Collectibles	7522 Sunset Blvd	323-851-7283	Comics, graphic novels, and art books.
Mystery Pier Books	8826 W Sunset Blvd	310-657-5557	First edition and rare books.
Samuel French Theatre & Film	7623 W Sunset Blvd	323-876-0570	Theater and film books.
Talking Book World	7164 Beverly Blvd	323-932-8111	Audio books.
Traveler's Bookcase	8375 W 3rd St	323-655-0575	Excellent shop for travelers.

Map 3 • Hollywood

A-Z Technical Book Store	1033 N Sycamore Ave	323-464-4322	Technical books.
Book City Collectables	6627 Hollywood Blvd	323-466-0120	Scripts & collectables.
Borders	1501 Vine St	323-463-8519	Chain.
Counterpoint Records & Books	5911 Franklin Ave	323-957-7965	Rare books and records
Daily Planet Book Store	5931 Franklin Ave	323-957-0061	New fiction.
Dawson's Book Shop	535 N Larchmont Blvd	323-469-2186	Rare books on the American West.
Edmund's Bookshop	6644 Hollywood Blvd	323-463-3273	Cinema and theater books.
Hollywood Book City	6627 Hollywood Blvd	323-466-2525	Mostly used.
Hollywood Magic	6614 Hollywood Blvd	323-464-5610	Magic books.

Map 4 • Los Feliz

Aldine Books	4663 Hollywood Blvd	323-666-2690	Used.
Circus of Books	4001 W Sunset Blvd	323-666-1304	Gay books and magazines.
Philosophical Bookstore	3910 Los Feliz Blvd	323-663-2167	Philosophy and spirituality.
Siam Books	5178 Hollywood Blvd	323-665-4236	Thai books.
Skylight Books	1818 N Vermont Ave	323-660-1175	Independent general interest.
Soap Plant	4633 Hollywood Blvd	323-663-0122	Eclectic selection.

Map 5 • Silver Lake/Echo Park/Atwater

33 1/3 Books	1200 N Alvarado St	213-483-3500	Books, art gallery.
CM Bookshop	2388 Glendale Blvd	323-913-9677	General new and used.

Map 6 • Miracle Mile/Mid-City

New Mastodon German Books	5820 Wilshire Blvd	323-525-1948	New and used German books.
The Bookshelf at LACMA	5905 Wilshire Blvd	323-857-6489	Eclectic art books.

Map 7 • Hancock Park

Chevalier's Books	126 N Larchmont Blvd	323-465-1334	General interest, new books.
Educational Bookstore	3959 Wilshire Blvd	213-387-3184	Educational books and school supplies.

Map 8 • Korea Town

ASSI Book City	3525 W 8th St	213-480-5773	Korean books.
California Comic	355 S Western Ave	213-739-2021	Asian comics.
Chong Books	2785 W Olympic Blvd	213-739-8107	Korean books.
Dong-A Book Plaza	3460 W 8th St	213-382-7100	Korean books.
Jeong Eum Sa	928 S Western Ave	213-738-9140	Korean books, some English.
Korea One	170 S Western Ave	213-388-0914	Korean books.
Libreria Hispanoamerica	2502 W 6th St	213-384-6084	Spanish books.
Orange Comics	3500 West 8th St	213-383-5250	Comics.
Seojong Bookstore	3250 W Olympic Blvd	323-735-7374	Koren books.
Springwater Book Imports	3003 W Olympic Blvd	213-380-0212	Korean books.
Student Books	244 S Oxford Ave	213-387-1582	K-7 textbooks.
Sung Ji Books	2837 W Olympic Blvd	213-388-2839	Korean books.
Western Comics	730 S Western Ave	213-385-7025	Korean comics.

Map 9 • Downtown

Asahiya Bookstore	333 S Alameda St	213-626-5650	Japanese books.
B Dalton	201 N Los Angeles St	213-687-3050	Chain.
Caravan Bookstore	550 S Grand Ave	213-626-9944	Out of print books.
China Bookstore	652 N Broadway	213-680-9230	Chinese books.
Great Wall Books & Art	970 N Broadway	213-617-2817	Chinese and medical books.
Hongwanji Place	311 E 1st St	213-680-0364	Asian books.

Map 9 • Downtown—*continued*

Kinokuniya Bookstore	123 Astronaut Onizuka St E	213-687-4480	Japanese books, some English.
Legal Book Store	316 W 2nd St	213-626-2139	Legal books.
Libros Revolucion	312 W 8th St	213-488-1303	Spanish & English books.
The MOCA Store	250 S Grand Ave	213-621-1710	Contemporary art books and magazines.
Niming Books	969 N Hill St	213-687-9817	Chinese books.
Thai Books & Music Dokya	1100 N Main St	323-342-9982	Thai books.
Waldenbooks	700 W 7th St	213-624-5137	Chain.

Map 10 • Baldwin Hills

Eso Won Books	3655 S La Brea Ave	323-294-0324	African-American books.
Waldenbooks	3650 Martin Luther King Blvd	323-295-5905	Chain.

Map 11 • South Central West

Libreria Azteca	1429 W Adams Blvd	323-733-4040	Spanish books.
University of Southern California Bookstore	840 Childs Wy	213-740-5214	Text and trade books.

Map 12 • South Central East

Theosophy	245 W 33rd St	213-748-7244	Theosophy books.

Map 13 • Inglewood

Zarah's Books & Things	900 N La Brea Ave	310-330-1300	African-American books.

Map 14 • Inglewood East/Morningside Park

Bright Lights Children's Books	8461 S Van Ness Ave	323-971-1296	Multicultural children's books—Saturday only.
Express Yourself Books	1425 W Manchester Ave	323-750-4114	General interest books.

Map 15 • Pacific Palisades

Village Books	1049 Swarthmore Ave	310-454-4063	General.

Map 16 • Brentwood

Dutton's Brentwood	11975 San Vicente Blvd	310-476-6263	Great independent bookstore.
The Getty Museum Store	1200 Getty Center Dr	310-440-7300	Getty publications.

Map 17 • Bel Air/Holmby Hills

UCLA BookZone	308 Westwood Plz	310-206-4041	Indie bookstore, no textbooks.

Map 18 • Santa Monica

A&R Textbooks	1703 Pico Blvd	310-314-4361	Textbooks.
Angel City Bookstore & Gallery	218 Pier Ave	310-399-8767	Used art and literature.
Arcana Books on the Arts	1229 3rd St Prom	310-458-1499	Excellent art and architecture. Hard to find.
Barnes & Noble	1201 3rd St Prom	310-260-9110	Chain.
Barry R Levin Science Fiction	720 Santa Monica Blvd	310-458-6111	Science fiction, fantasy, and horror.
Borders	1415 3rd St Prom	310-393-9290	Chain.
Hennessey + Ingalls Art Books	214 Wilshire Blvd	310-458-9074	Superb art and architecture.
HI de Ho Comics & Books With Pictures	525 Santa Monica Blvd	310-394-2820	Comics
Novel Café	212 Pier Ave	310-396-8566	General interest, new, used and donated books.
Wilshire Books	3018 Wilshire Blvd	310-828-3115	Used books.

Map 19 • West LA/Santa Monica East

Alias Books	1650 Sawtelle Blvd	310-473-4442	Rare and out-of-print.
California Map & Travel Center	3312 Pico Blvd	310-396-6277	Map and travel.
Gene de Chene Bookseller	11556 Santa Monica Blvd	310-477-8734	General.
RR News	11203 National Blvd	310-312-0405	News/periodicals.
Sawtelle Books & Music	2105 Sawtelle Blvd	310-477-8686	Japanese books.

Map 20 • Westwood/Century City

Borders	1360 Westwood Blvd	310-475-3444	Chain.
Brentano's	10250 Santa Monica Blvd	310-785-0204	Chain in Century City Mall.
Dehkhoda Persian Bookstore	1387 Westwood Blvd	310-477-0044	Persian books.
East Wind Books & Art	923 Westwood Blvd	310-824-4888	Asian culture books.
Jay & Silent Bob's Secret Stash	1045 Westwood Blvd	310-824-1373	Comics.
Johnny's Used Books	1743 Westwood Blvd	310-996-5558	General used.

Mystery Bookstore	1036 Broxton Ave	310-209-0415	Mystery.
Text Book Plus	927 Westwood Blvd	310-824-1155	College books.

Map 21 • Venice

Beyond Baroque Foundation	681 Venice Blvd	310-822-3006	Literary arts.
Equator Books	1103 Abbot Kinney Blvd	310-399-5544	Rare and collectibles.
Recyclepedia	1707 Lincoln Blvd	310-305-9880	Used and rare.
Small World Books	1407 Ocean Front Wk	310-399-2360	General and mystery.

Map 22 • Mar Vista

Sam Johnson's Bookshop	12310 Venice Blvd	310-391-5047	Rare and out-of-print.

Map 23 • Rancho Park/Palms

Barnes & Noble	10850 W Pico Blvd	310-475-4144	Chain.
Building News Bookstore	10801 National Blvd	310-474-7771	Construction books.
Children's Book World	10850 W Pico Blvd	310-559-2665	Children's books.
Waldenbooks	10800 W Pico Blvd	310-474-6550	Chain.

Map 24 • Culver City

Comic Ink	4267 Overland Ave	310-204-3240	Comic books.
Pepperdine Bookstore	6100 Center Dr	310-568-5741	College textbooks.

Map 25 • Marina Del Rey/Westchester West

Barnes & Noble	13400 Maxella Ave	310-306-3213	Chain.

Map 26 • Westchester/Fox Hills/Ladera Heights/LAX

Book Market	8655 S Sepulveda Blvd	310-216-0836	Bargain books, new.
Borders	6081 Center Dr	310-215-3720	Chain.
Borders Express	124 Fox Hills Mall	310-313-9352	Chain.
Read It Again Sam	6208 W Manchester Ave	310-641-2665	Used general.

Map 27 • El Segundo/Manhattan Beach

Barnes & Noble	1800 Rosecrans Ave	310-725-7025	Chain.
Dave's Old Bookshop	350 N Sepulveda Blvd	310-376-0879	Used indie fiction.
Richard Upton & Son's Book	917 Hillcrest St	310-322-7202	Publishes and sells books on American West. By appointment only.

Map 29 • Hermosa Beach/Redondo Beach North

Book Value	2573 Pacific Coast Hwy	310-530-5343	Japanese books.
Eclectic Collector	1116 Hermosa Ave	310-374-4240	General used.
Read It Again, Sam	1102 Aviation Blvd	310-372-6930	Used general.

Map 30 • Torrance North

B Dalton	1815 Hawthorne Blvd	310-371-8737	Chain.
Kaede Shobo Japanese Bookstore	2147 W 182nd St	310-324-9892	Japanese books.
Nations Travel Store	287 Del Amo Fashion Square	310-921-2242	Travel books and maps.

Map 31 • Redondo Beach

Barnes & Noble	21500 Hawthorne Blvd	310-370-5552	Chain.
Book Again	5039 Torrance Blvd	310-542-1156	Used fiction.
Encore Books	1704 S Pacific Coast Hwy	310-540-1106	Used and rare.
Jimmy B's Audiobooks	1632 S Pacific Coast Hwy	310-792-1718	Audio books.
Psychic Eye Bookshop	3902 Pacific Coast Hwy	310-378-7754	Metaphysical, self-help.
Reiki Metaphysical Bookstore	501 Esplanade	310-265-8005	Metaphysical books. By appointment only.
Sandpiper Books	4665 Torrance Blvd	310-371-2002	Used.

Map 32 • Torrance South

Borders	3700 Torrance Blvd	310-540-7000	Chain.
Third Planet	3631 Pacific Coast Hwy	310-791-6227	Graphic novels and comics.

Map 33 • Eagle Rock/Highland Park

Another World Comics & Books	1615 Colorado Blvd	323-257-7757	Comics, sci-fi.
Appleby Books	1007 N Ave 51	323-478-0655	Children's collectibles.
Imix Books	5052 Eagle Rock Blvd	213-765-0827	Spanish books.
San Rafael Rare Books	178 Malcolm Dr	626-440-9900	Older cookery, science, poetry, and children's books. By appointment only.

Map 34 • Pasadena

Alexandria Metaphysical Bookstore II	567 S Lake Ave	626-792-7885	Metaphysical books.
Barnes & Noble	111 W Colorado Blvd	626-585-0362	Chain.
Book Alley	611 E Colorado Blvd	626-683-8083	Used art, literature, philosophy.
Book 'em Mysteries	1118 Mission St	626-799-9600	Mystery.
Bookhouse	1026 Fair Oaks Ave	626-799-0756	General used.
Borders	475 S Lake Ave	626-304-9773	Chain.
Bungalow News	746 E Colorado Blvd	626-795-9456	Magazines and paperbacks.
Cliff's Books	630 E Colorado Blvd	626-449-9541	Used.
Distant Lands Travel Bookstore & Outfitter	56 S Raymond Ave	626-449-3220	Maps and travel books.
Gamble House Bookstore	4 Westmoreland Pl	626-449-4178	Design, art, and architecture.
Norton Simon Museum of Art	411 W Colorado Blvd	626-449-6840	Museum shop.
Rudolf Steiner Library Bookstore	110 Martin Aly	626-578-7513	Library and small bookstore.
Vroman's Bookstore	695 E Colorado Blvd	626-449-5320	Great independent bookstore.

Map 35 • Pasadena East/San Marino

Archives Bookshop	1396 E Washington Blvd	626-797-4756	Academics, philosophy, religious.
Cal-Gold Enterprises	2569 E Colorado Blvd	626-792-6161	Gold miners.
Comics Factory	1298 E Colorado Blvd	626-585-0618	Comics.
Cook Books	1388 E Washington Blvd	626-296-1638	Cook books.
Crossroads Books	1196 E Walnut St	626-795-8772	Rehab books.
Mitchell Books	1395 E Washington Blvd	626-798-4438	Mystery.
Oriental Book Store	1713 East Colorado Blvd	626-577-2413	Books on the Orient.
Textmania	1308 E Colorado Blvd	626-844-7105	Textbooks.

Map 38 • El Sereno

Legal Books Distributing	4247 Whiteside St	323-526-7110	Legal books warehouse.
Student Book Mart & Copy Center	1725 N Eastern Ave	323-262-5511	Textbooks for Cal-State.

Map 39 • Alhambra

Dragon Books	1436 S Atlantic Blvd	626-282-6980	Chinese books.
Jilie	1283 E Valley Blvd	626-308-1466	Chinese books.
Kingston Culture Plaza	228 W Valley Blvd	626-570-1277	Chinese books.

Map 40 • Boyle Heights

Sears Book Center	2650 E Olympic Blvd	323-265-3153	Spanish books.

Map 42 • Chatsworth

Books 5150	10144 Mason Ave	818-993-7253	Used and rare.

Map 43 • Granada Hills/Northridge

A&S Bargain Books	10821 Zelzah Ave	818-831-6000	Bargain books.
Anime Plus	8937 Reseda Blvd	818-773-7371	Anime.
B Dalton	9301 Tampa Ave	818-773-8255	Chain.
Borders	9301 Tampa Ave	818-886-5443	Chain.
Golden Apple Comics	8967 Reseda Blvd	818-993-7804	Comics.

Map 44 • Mission Hills/North Hills

Bookhouse	17048 Devonshire St	818-832-0976	Children's, biography.
Continental Comics	17032 Devonshire St	818-368-8909	

Map 45 • Canoga Park/Woodland Hills

Builder's Bookstore	8001 Canoga Ave	818-887-7828	Construction books.
The Flip Side	19950 Ventura Blvd	818-883-9550	Comics and videos.
Green Ginger Bookshop	21710 Sherman Way	818-713-1601	Used.

Map 46 • Reseda

Russian Gifts & Books	5424 Reseda Blvd	818-342-1668	Russian books.

Map 47 • Van Nuys

Bargain Books	14426 Friar St	818-782-2782	General used.
Libreria El Quijote	14534 Victory Blvd	818-989-2411	Spanish books.
Musical Literature	16122 Cohasset St	818-994-1902	Books about music.
Russian Books	13757 Victory Blvd	818-781-7533	Russian books.

Map 48 • North Hollywood

Chamber of Comics	13545 Roscoe Blvd	818-780-4551	Comics

Map 49 • Burbank

Aeroplane & Automobile Books	3524 W Magnolia Blvd	323-849-1294	Auto and air.
American Opinion Books & Flags	5653 Cahuenga Blvd	818-769-4019	Political education, history, social.
Autobooks	3524 W Magnolia Blvd	818-845-0707	Trains, planes, and automobiles.
Borders Express	201 E Magnolia Blvd	818-557-0828	Chain.
Dark Delicacies	4213 West Burbank Blvd	818-556-6660	Horror books.
Eros Archives	5708 Cahuenga Blvd	818-760-6463	Vintage and contemporary erotica.
Twice Told Tales	3427 W Magnolia Blvd	818-841-0652	Rare and out-of-print.

Map 50 • Burbank East/Glendale West

A&S Bargain Books	301 N San Fernando Blvd	818-238-0371	Bargain books.
Barnes & Noble	731 N San Fernando Blvd	818-558-1383	Chain.
Best-Seller Bookshop	130 N San Fernando Blvd	818-955-8243	General used.
Psychic Eye Bookshop	1011 W Olive Ave	818-845-8831	Metaphysical, self-help.

Map 51 • Glendale South

Barnes & Noble	245 N Glendale Ave	818-246-4677	Chain.
Berj Armenian Bookstore	422 S Central Ave	818-244-3830	Armenian books.
Bookfellows Fine & Rare Books	238 N Brand Blvd	818-545-0121	Rare books.
Borders	100 S Brand Blvd	818-241-8099	Chain.
Brand Bookshop	231 N Brand Blvd	818-507-5943	Used books.
Legacy Comic Books & Sportscards	123 W Wilson Ave	818-247-8803	Comics.
Sardarabad Books	1111 S Glendale Ave	818-500-0790	Iranian books.
Young Scholar	233 N Central Ave	818-246-7063	Children's and teacher's books.

Map 52 • Tarzana/Woodland Hills

B Dalton	6600 Topanga Canyon Blvd	818-883-8195	Chain.
Barnes & Noble	6100 Topanga Canyon Blvd	818-704-3850	Chain.
Borders	6510 Canoga Ave	818-887-1999	Chain.

Map 54 • Sherman Oaks West

Barnes & Noble	16461 Ventura Blvd	818-380-1636	Chain.
Borders	14651 Ventura Blvd	818-728-6593	Chain.
Earth-2 Comics	15017 Ventura Blvd	818-386-9590	Comics.

Map 55 • Sherman Oaks East

Borders Express	14006 Riverside Dr	818-788-8661	Chain owned by Borders.
Crown Books	4454 Van Nuys Blvd	818-906-0986	General.
Psychic Eye Bookshop	13435 Ventura Blvd	818-906-8263	Metaphysical, self-help.

Map 56 • Studio City/Valley Village

Bookstar	12136 Ventura Blvd	818-505-9528	Owned by B&N—chain.
Comicsmash	11824 Ventura Blvd	818-761-3753	Comic books.
Dutton's Books	5146 Laurel Canyon Blvd	818-769-3866	Great independent bookstore.
Iliad Bookshop	4820 Vineland Ave	818-509-2665	Used literature, cinema, and arts.
Laurel Park Newsstand	4346 Laurel Canyon Blvd	818-769-8583	Magazines.
Paris Bookstore	4820 Laurel Canyon Blvd	818-762-7557	Russian books.
Portrait of a Bookstore	4360 Tujunga Ave	818-769-3853	General interest Indie bookstore.
Raven's Flight	5044 Vineland Ave	818-985-2944	Metaphysical, witchcraft, and herbs.
Samuel French's Theatre & Film	11963 Ventura Blvd	818-762-0535	Theater and film books.
Storyopolis	12348 Ventura Blvd	818-509-5600	Great children's bookstore.

Map 57 • Universal City/Toluca Lake

Geographica Map & Travel	4000 W Riverside Dr	818-848-1414	Maps and travel.
Upstart Crow	1000 Universal Center Dr	818-763-1811	General interest.

Dive Bars

You know you've entered a dive bar in Los Angeles when there's no velvet rope, no schmoozing the bouncer, and the inside smells of sweat and stale beer. Don't you dare order a schmancy Negroni or any rainbow-colored drink here because your request will be met with ironic laughter at best, a disgusted grunt at worst. And a warning to oenophiles: these places stock the worst of the worst in wine, so don't even bother. Best stick to what dive bars do best: beer, shots, pool, and darts. Our favorite dive bar in LA is **White Horse** on the ground floor of Motel 8 on Western Avenue, just north of Sunset Boulevard; its red walls and black leatherette bar stools lend a sense of unpretentiousness, and the owner will pop you a bag of popcorn if you're nice, or tell you to "get lost" if you're not. While the Westside tends to shy away from cracked seats and beer nuts, the Eastside does dives well: a few great ones to check out are the **Red Lion Tavern** in Silver Lake, **The Roost** in Atwater Village, or **Little Joy** and the slightly less ghetto **Short Stop**—conveniently just a block's stumble from one to the other in Echo Park.

Outdoor Spaces

Constant sun and an average temperature at a perfect 72 degrees mean that many LA bars drag their tables outside. And for those of you who enjoy a smoke with your drink, outdoor seating is best option. The tres rive gauche **Figaro Café** on Vermont in Los Feliz lines up round marble tables to squeeze in thirsty hipsters. **Malo** on Sunset has an industrial-looking, yet surprisingly intimate outdoor seating area with heating lamps. A happier Friday was never had than at **Ciudad**'s happy hour at 5th and Fig downtown, where cheap mojitos, delicious tapas, and zesty Latin jazz spice up TGIF. **Blue on Blue** at the Avalon Hotel in Beverly Hills serves chilled martinis poolside (plan ahead and reserve a cabana), while oceanside **Gladstone's** is always jumping. For stargazing through your beer goggles, the rooftop bar at downtown's **The Standard** can't be beat. And Brit expats especially enjoy a pint in **The Cat & Fiddle**'s leafy beer garden, ringing their mates in rainy ol' England to gloat about the balmy stateside summer nights.

Best Beer Selection

There is oh so much more to beer than Bud and MGD, and places like **Father's Office**, with 30 microbrews on tap, and **The Library Ale House**, with 29 on tap, are all the proof you'll need. Los Angeles' own brew, Angel City Brewing beer, is on draft in a number of locations, including the vast and sporty **Hollywood Billiards** and the swanky **Loews Santa Monica Beach Hotel**. For a night in with your favorite rare ale, stock up at Cost Plus World Market, where "Beers of the World" are sold by the 12-pack.

Best Décor

Décor varies greatly among all of the gin joints in this town. Drop by the **Bigfoot Lodge** in Atwater to swig down a few beers while you cozy up to Smokey the Bear. The owner of **Tiki Ti** in Los Feliz is so dedicated to the upkeep of his mini-Polynesian paradise that patrons will find the bar closed when he's in the islands "doing research." The **4100 Club** is like drinking in the belly of a Buddha with draped batiks, Persian lanterns, and intimate booths, yet it manages to keep the hippy vibe at bay. For upscale chic, **Casa del Mar** in Santa Monica delivers with a grand lobby/bar serving drinks with grand price tags, or try **The Bar at the Four Seasons Hotel**. Modish warmth is key to **The Well**'s hip brown and black design and tall leather banquettes, while **The Brig** on Abbot Kinney in Venice is a chic, sleekly illuminated, mod dream.

Best Dancing

Salsa, Hip Hop, Electric Slide, or Shoe Gazing—there is somewhere for everyone to get their groove on in Los Angeles. The **Mayan** downtown is an exclusive salsa club with a strict dress code—be sure to call ahead for details. In Boy's Town, take your pick of a number of gay dance clubs. Some of the most popular are: **The Factory/Ultra Suede** and **The Abbey**. The newly named "Cahuenga Corridor" between Yucca and Fountain is fast replacing former club central, West Hollywood. Check out **La Velvet Margarita Cantina**, **AD**, **Ivar**, or **White Lotus**. For a wild night out on the cheap we recommend **La Plaza** on La Brea, with DJ's spinning ranchero music and fabulous Latino drag queen performances at 10 pm and midnight on the weekends.

Map 1 • Beverly Hills

Bar Noir in Maison 140	140 S Lasky Dr	310-281-4000	Tres petit hotel bar serves mondo martinis.
Belvedere at the Peninsula Hotel	9882 Santa Monica Blvd	310-551-2888	Classy hotel bar.
Blue on Blue	9400 W Olympic Blvd	310-277-5221	Mid-century modern poolside cocktails.
Larry Flynt's Supper Cabaret	424 Beverly Dr	310-275-8511	Burlesque club. Larry loves velvet; a dinner res avoids crowds.
Regent Beverly Wilshire	9500 Wilshire Blvd	310-275-5200	Hotel bar with clubby feel.
Trader Vic's	9876 Wilshire Blvd	310-276-6345	Polynesian LA institution. Virgins sacrificed nightly.
Writer's Bar at L'Ermitage Hotel	9291 Burton Wy	310-278-3344	Sophisticated and elegant, the perfect spot for an intimate rendezvous.

Map 2 • West Hollywood

The Abbey	692 N Robertson Blvd	310-289-8410	Great gay dance club.
The Bar at the Four Seasons Hotel	300 S Doheny Dr	310-273-2222	Elegant hotel bar.
Bar at the Standard	8300 W Sunset Blvd	323-650-9090	Jet setters take off nightly with each other.
Bar Marmont	8221 W Sunset Blvd	323-650-0575	Hollywood elite sip pricey drinks in the beautiful garden.
Barney's Beanery	8447 Santa Monica Blvd	323-654-2287	A low rent (but fun) LA institution.
Bel Age Hotel	1020 N San Vicente Blvd	310-854-1111	Hotel bar.
Bliss	650 N La Cienega Blvd	310-659-0999	Monosyllabically sleek scene for the glamorously succint.
Club 7969	7969 Santa Monica Blvd	323-654-0280	Ravers rejoice! This place is all about the dance.
Dominick's	8715 Beverly Blvd	310-652-2335	Entertainment industry hangout.
El Carmen Tequila & Taco Bar	8138 W 3rd St	323-852-1552	Among the best margaritas in LA.
El Coyote	7312 Beverly Blvd	323-939-2255	Go for the drinks, not the food.
The Factory/Ultra Suede	661 N Robertson Blvd	310-659-4551	Wildly popular gay dance club.
Falcon	7213 W Sunset Blvd	323-850-5350	Design-heavy restaurant with a smooth bar scene.
Fenix Lounge	8385 W Sunset Blvd	323-654-7100	Like an aging starlet still auditioning for the big scene.
Formosa Café	7156 Santa Monica Blvd	323-850-9050	Train car drinks and rooftop bar. Avoid the food.
Garden of Eden	7080 Hollywood Blvd	323-465-3336	And on the weekend G-d made debaucherous clubbers.
Genghis Cohen	740 N Fairfax Ave	323-653-0640	Acoustic music & Chinese food.
Here	696 N Robertson Blvd	310-360-8455	Like an animated Hugo Boss ad, only gayer.
House of Blues	8430 Sunset Blvd	323-848-5100	Venue attracts major musical acts.

Jones	7205 Santa Monica Blvd	323-850-1727	Bathroom has nude pics of unruly patrons.
La Plaza	739 N La Brea Ave	323-939-0703	Drag queens and ranchero music—ay yi yi!
Largo	432 N Fairfax Ave	323-852-1073	Jon Brion on Friday nights: a perfect LA experience.
Lava Lounge	1533 N La Brea Ave	323-876-6612	Mini-mall tiki bar.
Lola's	945 N Fairfax Ave	213-736-5652	Birthplace of the apple martini.
Molly Malone's	575 S Fairfax Ave	323-935-1577	The ultimate neighborhood pub.
Monsieur Marcel	6333 W 3rd St	323-939-7792	Parisian wine bar in the Farmer's Market.
Pearl	665 N Robertson Blvd	310-358-9191	New WeHo hotspot tries for supper club scene. And succeeds.
Prey	643 N La Cienega Blvd	310-652-2012	Party promoters' dream club.
Rage	8911 Santa Monica Blvd	310-652-7055	Hard-bodied boys cram the soft rubber dance floor.
The Rainbow	9015 Sunset Blvd	310-278-4232	Those who rock will be saluted at this hairband hangout.
Roxy	9009 Sunset Blvd	310-276-2222	A bastion of the Sunset Strip.
The Ruby	7070 Hollywood Blvd	323-467-7070	Popular dance club with a young crowd.
Saddle Ranch Chop House	8371 W Sunset Blvd	323-656-2007	Two words: mechanical bull.
The Skybar	8440 W Sunset Blvd	323-650-8999	Excuse me, you're standing on my Manolos…
Snake Pit Ale House	7529 Melrose Ave	323-653-2011	Fairfax District neighborhood bar.
Tower Bar at the Argyle Hotel	8358 Sunset Blvd	323-654-7100	Restaubar in mobster Bugsy Siegel's old pad.
The Troubadour	9081 Santa Monica Blvd	310-276-6168	Legendary club where Tom Waits got his start.
Viper Room	8852 Sunset Blvd	310-358-1880	After Johnny fled to France, scensters say it lost its bite.
Whiskey Bar	1200 N Alta Loma Rd	310-657-0611	Oh show me the way to this exclusive hotel bar.
Whisky A Go Go	8901 Sunset Blvd	310-652-4202	No sitting allowed, beer cups, five bands a night. Good times, bro.

Map 3 · Hollywood

AD	836 N Highland Ave	323-467-3000	Make nice with the bouncer to enter this huge dance club.
ArcLight Café Bar & Balcony	6360 W Sunset Blvd	323-464-1478	Discuss the film over martinis and fried raviolis.
Avalon	1735 Vine St	323-462-8900	Old Palace, now Oakenfold and the Streets.
The Bar	5851 Sunset Blvd	323-468-9154	Formerly Raji's, now rocker bar/lounge.
Beauty Bar	1638 N Cahuenga Blvd	323-464-7676	Girlfriends gather for pre-party manicures and martinis.
Birds	5925 Franklin Ave	323-465-0175	Unpretentious cafe/bar favored by the carefully disheveled.
Blu Monkey	5521 Hollywood Blvd	323-957-9000	Middle Eastern vibes in deep Hollywood.
Boardner's	1642 N Cherokee Ave	323-462-9621	Quiet watering hole becomes dance club.
Burgundy Room	1621 1/2 Cahuenga Blvd	323-465-7530	If Johnny Rotten and Blondie had a kid. And the kid was a bar.
The Cat & Fiddle	6530 Sunset Blvd	323-468-3800	Pub plus patio draws Brits in search of better weather.
Catalina Bar & Grill	6725 Sunset Blvd	323-466-2210	New location, same groovy jazz.
The Cinegrill	7000 Hollywood Blvd	323-466-7000	Cabaret.
Cinespace	6356 Hollywood Blvd	323-817-3456	Movies, music, food, cocktails, and huge smoking room.
Circus Disco	6655 Santa Monica Blvd	323-462-1291	Eclectic Hollywood mega-(supper)club.
Daddy's Bar & Lounge	1610 N Vine St	323-463-7777	Cozy cocktail lounge.
Dragonfly	6510 Santa Monica Blvd	323-466-6111	Alcoholics-in-training dance the night away in one of two rooms.
El Centro	6202 Santa Monica Blvd	323-957-1066	Signless club points to Hollywood's misbehaved.
El Floridita	1253 N Vine St	323-871-8612	Salsa club (with lessons!).
Element	1642 Las Palmas Ave	323-460-4632	Celebs and their publicists, rooftop VIPs.
Forty Deuce	5574 Melrose Ave	323-465-4242	Bourbon, burlesque, and beautiful people.
Frolic Room	6245 Hollywood Blvd	323-462-5890	Where Spacey searched his soul in *LA Confidential*.
Henry Fonda Music Box	6126 Hollywood Blvd	323-464-0808	Great place to see up-and-coming bands.
The Highlands	6801 Hollywood Blvd	323-461-9800	Club within the Hollywood & Highland complex.
Hollywood Athletic Club	6525 Sunset Blvd	323-462-6262	Old-style gym is now a dance hall.
Hollywood Billiards	5750 Hollywood Blvd	323-465-0115	Huge sports bar.
Hollywood Canteen	1006 N Seward St	323-465-0961	Bette Davis' club got a makeover; still hot after all these years.
Hollywood Palladium	6215 W Sunset Blvd	323-962-7600	One of the premier music venues in LA.
The Hotel Café	1623 1/2 N Cahuenga Blvd	323-461-2040	New York-style acoustic club draws a crowd.
The Ivar	6356 Hollywood Blvd	323-465-4827	Ginormous club with industrial interior.
Joseph's	1775 Ivar Ave	323-462-8697	The Olsens and Paris make the rounds.
King King	6555 Hollywood Blvd	323-960-5765	Live music, rotating DJs, very few jerks per capita.
Knitting Factory	7021 Hollywood Blvd	323-463-0204	Eclectic acoustic lineup.
The Larchmont	5657 Melrose Ave	323-467-4068	Deep house grooves and sushi.
La Velvet Margarita Cantina	1612 N Cahuenga Blvd	323-469-2000	Imagine a gothic circus in Tijuana…
Las Palmas	1714 N Las Palmas Ave	323-464-0171	Once a hot club, now favored by suburbanites.
M-Bar	1253 Vine St	323-856-0036	Liberace would have loved the interior.
Montmartre Lounge	6757 Hollywood Blvd	no phone	Hollywood and rock scene playground.
Mood	6623 Hollywood Blvd	323-464-6663	Bali-inspired, go-go dancers in ripped t-shirts.
Musso & Frank Grill Bar	6667 Hollywood Blvd	323-467-5123	Hollywood's oldest bar.
Nacional	1645 Wilcox Ave	323-962-7712	Cuban-themed bar/lounge.
The Room	1626 N Cahuenga Blvd	323-462-7196	Make-out crowd drinks 'til dawn.
Spider Club at the Avalon	1735 Vine St	323-462-8270	The chic VIP hideaway away from packed partygoers.
Star Shoes	6364 Hollywood Blvd	323-462-7827	Vintage shoe salon and cocktails.
Teddy's at the Roosevelt Hotel	7000 Hollywood Blvd	323-466-7000	Swank drinks at the haunted hotel.
Three of Clubs	1123 N Vine St	323-462-6441	Low-key Hollywood hangout.
The Vanguard	6021 Hollywood Blvd	323-463-3331	Fashion and rock shows, electronica, drum n' bass.

Map 3 • Hollywood—continued

Vine	1235 Vine St	323-960-0800	Fondue's gone; just wine, sake, n' booze.
Vine Street Lounge	1708 Vine St	323-464-0404	Tues and Thurs hot celeb nights, white VIP lounge.
The Well	6255 W Sunset Blvd	323-467-9355	Daddy's owners draw up another watering hole.
The White Horse	1532 N Western Ave	323-462-8088	Serious drinking with Bukowski's ghost.
White Lotus	1743 N Cahuenga Ave	323-463-0060	Beware of the silicone bounce on the dance floor.
Xes	1716 N Cahuenga Blvd	323-461-8190	Don your bling and party with the Lakers.

Map 4 • Los Feliz

4100 Club	4100 W Sunset Blvd	323-666-4460	Red bohemian chic enclave where conversing is a reality.
Akbar	4356 W Sunset Blvd	323-665-6810	Your friendly neighborhood homo/hetero hangout.
The Derby	4500 Los Feliz Blvd	323-663-8979	Still swinging with cool cats and foxy felines.
Drawing Room	1800 Hillhurst Ave	323-665-0135	Tiny strip mall dive, no pretense, TV n' locals.
The Dresden Room	1760 N Vermont Ave	323-665-4294	Home of Marty & Elayne's famed lounge act.
Figaro Café	1802 N Vermont Ave	323-662-1587	Great outdoor spot.
Gauntlet II	4219 Santa Monica Blvd	323-669-9472	Lez-be friends and leather pals.
Good Luck Bar	1514 Hillhurst Ave	323-666-3524	Confucius say: hook-ups likely.
Jumbo's Clown Room	5153 Hollywood Blvd	323-666-1187	The seediest little joint in Hollywood.
Little Temple	4519 Santa Monica Blvd	323-660-4540	The temple of boom for local and visiting DJs.
Malo	4326 W Sunset Blvd	323-664-1011	Intimate outdoor seating.
Tangier Lounge	2138 Hillhurst Ave	323-666-8666	Moroccan-themed Los Feliz hot-spot with outdoor patio.
Tantra Bar	3705 W Sunset Blvd	323-663-9090	Hollywood goes Bollywood in this erotically-charged hot-spot.
Tiki Ti	4427 W Sunset Blvd	323-669-9381	Fortify yourself with a famous Blood of the Bull.
Vermont Bar	1714 N Vermont Ave	323-661-6163	Hot DJs & cool cocktails.
Ye Rustic Inn	1831 Hillhurst Ave	323-662-5757	If ye want pink drinks, get thee the hell out.

Map 5 • Silver Lake/Echo Park/Atwater

Bigfoot Lodge	3172 Los Feliz Blvd	323-662-9227	When you feel like enjoying nature but would rather get smashed.
Club Tee Gee	3210 Glendale Blvd	323-669-9631	Dependable watering hole since 1946.
The Echo	1822 W Sunset Blvd	213-413-8200	Eastside hipster haven for DJ electronica and dancing.
Gold Room	1558 W Sunset Blvd	213-482-5259	Looks scarier from the outside than it is.
Johnny's Bar	2939 W Sunset Blvd	323-660-2276	Soju cocktails and pinup paintings.
Little Joy	1477 W Sunset Blvd	213-250-3417	Locals and hipsters mix at this Echo Park dive.
Mixville Bar	2838 Rowena Ave	323-666-2000	Casual bar with outdoor seating adjacent to Edendale Grill.
Red Lion Tavern	2366 Glendale Blvd	323-662-5337	Year-round Oktoberfest, plus schnitzel.
The Roost	3100 Los Feliz Blvd	323-664-7272	Cheap drinks, free popcorn, no frills.
Rudolpho's	2500 Riverside Dr	323-669-1226	Mexican by day, salsa dancing and cross-dressing by night.
Short Stop	1455 W Sunset Blvd	213-482-4942	Cool dive bar, seasonally packed with Dodger fans.
Silverlake Lounge	2906 Sunset Blvd	323-666-2407	Silver Lake's holy church of rock'n'roll salvation.
Spaceland	1717 Silver Lake Blvd	323-661-4380	Smokin' alt. music venue.
The Tam O'Shanter	2980 Los Feliz Blvd	323-664-0228	Me want prime rib and beer. Grrr.

Map 6 • Miracle Mile/Mid-City

Conga Room	5364 Wilshire Blvd	323-938-1696	Latin music, dining, and dancing.
El Rey	5515 Wilshire Blvd	323-936-4790	Diverse musical lineup.
The Joint	8771 W Pico Blvd	310-275-2619	Jazz bar.
The Mint	6010 Pico Blvd	323-954-9630	Casual acoustic venue with smoking sound system.
Tom Bergin's	840 S Fairfax Ave	323-936-7151	Guinness and fifty years of paper shamrocks.

Map 7 • Hancock Park

Jewel's Catch One	4067 W Pico Blvd	323-737-1159	Think Madonna's "Material Girl" days.
Mixed Nuts Comedy Club	4000 W Washington Blvd	323-735-6622	Basic comedy club featuring unknowns and 2-drink minimum.

Map 8 • Korea Town

Barcade	4366 2nd St	no phone	Tuesdays only, best arcade drinking in town.
Brass Monkey	659 Mariposa Ave	213-381-7047	One of the best of K-town karaoke, enter in back.
HMS Bounty	3357 Wilshire Blvd	213-385-7275	Nautical-themed old-man bar patronized by the new kids.
La Fonda De Los Camperos	2501 Wilshire Blvd	213-380-5055	Traditional Latin music.
Orchid Karaoke Club	3900 W 6th St, 2nd Fl	213-251-8886	Sing and swill in your own private room.
The Prince	3198 7th St	213-389-1586	Smokin' waitresses, undercover celebs, cool.

Map 9 • Downtown

Bonaventure Brewing Co at the Bonaventure Hotel	404 Figueroa St	213-236-0802	Secret microbrewery, packed happy hour.
BonaVista at the Bonaventure Hotel	404 Figueroa St	213-624-1000	You're not drunk, this rooftop room really is spinning.
Ciudad	445 S Figueroa St	213-486-5171	Best mojitos in LA, and a shockingly cheap feliz hour.
Gallery Bar at the Millennium Biltmore Hotel	506 S Grand Ave	213-624-1011	Specialty drink is the Black Dahlia: champagne + Guinness.
The Golden Gopher	417 W 8th St	213-614-2001	Outdoor smoking alley, chandeliers, gold gopher lamps.
Hop Louie	950 Mei Ling Wy	213-628-4244	Popular w/ the art crowd, cheap bevs.
Little Pedro's	901 E 1st St	213-687-3766	LA's 2nd-oldest bar gets 2nd wind w/ hip crowd.
Mayan	1040 S Hill St	213-746-4287	Salsa club with strict dress code, call for required attire.

Mountain Bar	473 Ging Ling Wy	213-625-7500	Art bar, Jorge Pardo did the bloody décor.
Oiwake	122 Japanese Village Plz Mall	213-628-2678	Karaoke restaubar with a serious songbook.
Pete's Café & Bar	400 S Main St	213-617-1000	The Downtown Martini has bleu cheese-stuffed olives.
Point Moorea Lounge (Wilshire Grand Hotel)	930 Wilshire Blvd	213-833-5100	Get Bali Hai on Polynesian libations.
Roof Bar at the Standard Downtown	550 S Flower St	213-892-8080	Make an entrance upstairs, then stumble to your room.
The Smell	247 S Main St	no phone	All ages, no booze, but underground music.
Stock Exchange	618 S Spring St	213-489-3877	Upscale Art Deco dance club.

Map 10 • Baldwin Hills

Café Club Fais Do-Do	5257 W Adams Blvd	323-954-8080	Cajun food, eclectic music.
The Living Room	2636 Crenshaw Blvd	323-735-8748	Blues bar.

Map 11 • South Central West

Babe's Ricky Inn	4339 Leimert Blvd	323-295-9112	Blues music.

Map 15 • Pacific Palisades

Pearl Dragon	15229 Sunset Blvd	310-459-9790	Cocktail lounge from Voda owners, full liquor license.

Map 17 • Bel Air/Holmby Hills

Hotel Bel Air Lounge	701 Stone Canyon Rd	310-472-1211	Where golddiggers and grandpas meet.

Map 18 • Santa Monica

14 Below	1348 14th St	310-451-5040	Pay-to-play rock 'n' roll bar.
Bar Copa	2810 Main St	310-452-2445	Low-lit, packed hip-hop beachside haven.
Big Dean's Café	1615 Ocean Front Wk	310-393-2666	Straight off the beach, fried locals.
Cameo Bar at The Viceroy Hotel	1819 Ocean Ave	310-451-8711	Chic hotel bar surrounding two swimming pools.
Casa del Mar	1910 Ocean Wy	310-581-5533	High-end hotel bar.
Circle Bar	2926 Main St	310-450-0508	Once divey, now trendy.
Cock N' Bull Pub	2947 Lincoln Blvd	310-399-9696	Irish pub.
Fairmont Miramar Hotel/ Grill Restaurant	101 Wilshire Blvd	310-576-7777	Hotel deluxe, waterfall included.
Father's Office	1018 Montana Ave	310-393-2337	No Bud Light here, it's all about the microbrew.
Harvelle's	1432 4th St	310-395-1676	You like your clubs dark and sexy.
The Library Ale House	2911 Main St	310-314-4855	No books, lots of beer.
Loews Santa Monica Beach Hotel	1700 Ocean Ave	310-458-6700	Swanky.
Lounge 217	217 Broadway	310-394-6336	Weekends packed with perfect 10s and tans.
O'Brien's	2941 Main St	310-396-4725	Neighborhood Irish pub.
Renee's Courtyard	522 Wilshire Blvd	310-451-9341	Spacious for an alleyway, hot staff.
The Room SM	1323 Santa Monica Blvd	310-458-0707	Westside station of Hollywood spot.
Rusty's Surf Ranch	256 Santa Monica Pier	310-393-7437	Surfboards, margs at sunset.
Shutters	1 Pico Blvd	310-458-0030	One of the "beachiest" Santa Monica hotel bars.
Sugar	814 Broadway	310-899-1989	Hip Westside dance spot.
Temple Bar	1026 Wilshire Blvd	310-393-6611	Food, martinis, and good local music.
Voda	1449 2nd St	310-394-9774	Means "water" in Russian; translates to "lots of vodka" in English.
Ye Olde King's Head	116 Santa Monica Blvd	310-451-1402	Traditional English fare and beer.
Zanzibar	1301 5th St	310-451-2221	Grooves spun by KCRW's Garth Trinidad & Jason Bentley.

Map 19 • West LA/Santa Monica East

Liquid Kitty	11780 W Pico Blvd	310-473-3707	Westside DJ club.
McCabe's	3101 Pico Blvd	310-828-4403	Famed LA haunt for live acoustic music.
Plan B	11637 W Pico Blvd	310-312-3633	The Ladies Man would hang at this after-2 am cigar lounge.
Q's Billiards	11835 Wilshire Blvd	310-477-7550	Pool, pool, beer, and pool.
Sonny McLean's	2615 Wilshire Blvd	310-828-9839	Boston bar, go Sox, go Pats!
The Arsenal	12012 W Pico Blvd	310-575-5511	'60s era cool at this quite-metro-for-the-Westside bar.
The Joker	2827 Pico Blvd	310-828-9235	Dive bar with chic clientele.
The Shack	2518 Santa Monica Blvd	310-449-1171	Philly phans rejoice, get a cheesesteak, watch the Flyers.

Map 20 • Westwood/Century City

The Century Club	10131 Constellation Blvd	310-553-6000	Upscale rock club for the VH1 set.
Westwood Brewing Company	1097 Glendon Ave	310-209-2739	Microbrewery with comedy upstairs.
Whiskey Blue (W Hotel)	930 Hilgard Ave	310-208-8765	Modern, trendy hotel bar.

Map 21 • Venice

Baja Cantina	311 Washington Blvd	310-821-2252	Free chips 'n' salsa with your margs.
The Brig	1515 Abbot Kinney Blvd	310-399-7537	Artsy neighborhood's trendy bar.
Firehouse	213 Rose Ave	310-396-6810	Neighborhood bar.
James' Beach	60 Venice Blvd	310-823-5396	Outdoor patio bar with ocean view.
Red Garter	2536 Lincoln Blvd	310-306-8300	Serving since the '60s.
Roosterfish	1302 Abbot Kinney Blvd	310-392-2123	Friendly gay oasis in dude-ridden beach area.

Map 21 • Venice—*continued*

The Town House	52 Windward Ave	310-392-4040	Oldest bar in Venice, trap door leads to bands.
Venice Whaler Bar & Grill	10 Washington Blvd	310-821-8737	Take out-of-town friends for buckets of beer, sunsets.

Map 22 • Mar Vista

Dear John's	11208 Culver Blvd	310-397-0276	Old school piano bar.
Good Hurt	12249 Venice Blvd	310-390-1076	Medical-themed beer and wine remedies.

Map 23 • Rancho Park/Palms

Zabumba	10717 Venice Blvd	310-841-6525	Brazilian themed, Brazilian dancing, Brazilian live music.

Map 24 • Culver City

Jazz Bakery	3238 Helms Ave	310-271-9039	Live theatre-style jazz and yes, dessert.

Map 25 • Marina Del Rey/Westchester West

Brennan's	4089 Lincoln Blvd	310-821-6622	Irish pub with turtle racing.
Marina Lounge at the Furama Hotel	8601 Lincoln Blvd	310-670-8111	Hotel bar near LAX.

Map 26 • Westchester/Fox Hills/Ladera Heights/LAX

Westchester Sports Grill	5630 W Manchester Ave	310-670-2366	All things sports.

Map 27 • El Segundo/Manhattan Beach

Beaches	117 Manhattan Beach Blvd	310-545-2523	Drink, dance, and sweat. Expect a line on weekends.
Shark's Cove	309 Manhattan Beach Blvd	310-545-2683	Sports bar with nightly specials.

Map 29 • Hermosa Beach/Redondo Beach North

Aloha Sharkeez	52 Pier Ave	310-374-7823	Proving anytime is a good time for a beer.
Comedy & Magic Club	1018 Hermosa Ave	310-372-1193	Off-Hollywood club with an all-star lineup.
Dragon	22 Pier Ave	310-372-4462	Hit the dance floor at this Hermosa hot-spot.
Fat Face Fenner's Fishack	53 Pier Ave, 2nd Floor	310-379-5550	A local hangout: more bar, less nightclub.
The Lighthouse Café	30 Pier Ave	310-372-6911	Jazz by the beach.
Patrick Molloy's	50-A Pier Ave	310-798-9762	Good brews on tap inside and a shorter line outside.
The Pitcherhouse	142 Pacific Coast Hwy	310-374-0626	Rock 'n' roll bar with 50 years of history.

Map 31 • Redondo Beach

Portofino Hotel & Yacht Club	260 Portofino Wy	310-379-8481	Jazz nights. On the water, great view, solid wine list.
Starboard Attitude	202 The Pier	310-379-5144	South Bay's oldest blues bar.

Map 33 • Eagle Rock/Highland Park

All Star Lanes	4459 Eagle Rock Blvd	323-254-2579	Bowling? Ha! Locals flock for cheap drinks and wild karaoke.
The Chalet	1630 Colorado Blvd	323-258-8800	Alpine-themed bar high atop Eagle Rock.
Little Cave	5922 N Figueroa St	323-255-6871	Watch for the stalagtites while sipping Bat-tinis.
Mr T's Bowl	5621 1/2 N Figueroa St	323-256-4850	Bowling alley turned rock club.

Map 34 • Pasadena

Bodega Wine Bar	260 E Colorado Blvd	626-793-4300	Ideal for chilled wines on warm nights.
De Lacey's Club 41	41 S De Lacey Ave	626-795-4141	Rat Pack steakhouse serves swank bevs.
Freddie's 35er Bar	12 E Colorado Blvd	626-356-9315	Neighborhood bar.
Ice House Comedy Club	24 N Mentor Ave	626-577-1894	Stand-up comedy, improv, booze.
Jake's Billiards	38 W Colorado Blvd	626-568-1602	Pool hall and bar.
McMurphy's	72 Fair Oaks Ave	626-666-1445	Irish pub in Old Town.
The Muse	54 E Colorado Blvd	626-793-0608	Dance club with Salsa Thursdays.

Map 36 • Mt Washington

Footsie's Café	2640 N Figueroa St	323-221-7357	The destination for DJ karaoke and no fuss.

Map 38 • El Sereno

The Derby	233 Huntington Dr	626-447-8174	Seabiscuit's racing memorabilia.

Map 39 • Alhambra

Azul Bar and Nightclub	129 W Main St	626-282-6320	Dance and drink your blues away.
California Brewing Co	100 W Main St	626-943-8430	Get some food with your beer.
The Granada	17 S 1st St	626-227-2572	Offers lessons and three dance floors to practice on.
Havana House	133 W Main St	626-576-0547	Dress-code-enforced cigar lounge.
Jay-dee Café	1843 W Main St	626-281-6887	Great dive bar.
Lucky Baldwin's	17 S Raymond Ave	626-795-0652	Expat Brits, imported ales, high tea.
Nonya	61 N Raymond Ave	626-583-8428	Thai, elegant for the after-work set.

Map 40 • Boyle Heights

Barbara's at the Brewery Complex	620 Moulton Ave	323-221-9204	Rub elbows with artists in old Pabst brewery.

Map 48 • North Hollywood

Rawhide	10937 Burbank Blvd	818-760-9798	Gay bar features country music and line dancing.

Map 49 • Burbank

Champs Sports Pub	4103 W Burbank Blvd	818-840-9493	Burgers, brews, big-screens, plus pool, darts, shuffleboard.
Dimples	3413 W Olive Ave	818-842-2336	Claims to be the "first karaoke club in America."
Match	4657 Lankershim Blvd	818-766-0116	Formerly NoHo's Thunderbird Saloon; no signage.
Sardos	259 N Pass Ave	818-846-8126	Great karaoke.
Tinhorn Flats	2623 Magnolia Blvd	818-567-2470	Karaoke Thursday nights.

Map 50 • Burbank East/Glendale West

The Blue Room	916 S San Fernando Blvd	323-849-2779	Somewhat upscale neighborhood bar.

Map 51 • Glendale South

Duffy's Pub	204 N Brand Blvd	818-242-3835	More polished than an actual dive.
Jax Bar and Grill	339 N Brand Blvd	818-500-1604	Jazz club.
Maurizio's	135 N Maryland Ave	818-247-5600	Sports bar and karaoke.
The Scene	806 Colorado St	818-241-7029	Eastside hipsters and the DJs they love.
Yard House	330 E Colorado St	626-577-9273	More than 200 beers on tap.

Map 52 • Tarzana/Woodland Hills

Corbin Bowl	19616 Ventura Blvd	818-996-2695	Ain't no Lucky Strike; serious bowlers abound.

Map 55 • Sherman Oaks East

Coda	5248 Van Nuys Blvd	818-783-7518	NYC-style lounge w/ dress code.
Cozy's	14058 Ventura Blvd	818-986-6000	Ventura Blvd. blues club.
Lulu's Beehive	13203 Ventura Blvd	818-986-2233	A coffee bar with music, comedy, and open mike.
Muddy Moose Bar & Grill	12833 Ventura Blvd	818-755-5000	Sports bar with jazz music.

Map 56 • Studio City/Valley Village

Aura	12215 Ventura Blvd	818-487-1488	Supperclub brings glitz to the Valley.
Clear	11916 Ventura Blvd	818-980-4811	Transparent décor, trendy crowd.
Firefly	11720 Ventura Blvd	818-762-1833	Good food, excellent cocktails.
Fox & Hounds	11100 Ventura Blvd	818-763-7976	English pub.
La Ve Lee	12514 Ventura Blvd	818-980-8158	Brazilian, jazz, R&B, plus Middle Eastern food.
Oyster House Saloon	12446 Moorpark St	818-761-8686	Stellar bartenders sling drinks like pros.
Platinum Live	11345 Ventura Blvd	818-753-1771	Elegant hot nightclub with live music and TV events too.
Residuals	11042 Ventura Blvd	818-761-8301	Low-key entertainment industry hangout.
The Queen Mary	12449 Ventura Blvd	818-506-5619	Female impersonator shows.
The Sapphire	11938 Ventura Blvd	818-506-0777	Trendy club for the jr studio exec.

Map 57 • Universal City/Toluca Lake

The Baked Potato	3787 Cahuenga Blvd	818-980-1615	Jazz club.
BB King's Blues Club	100 Universal Center Dr	818-622-5464	Nightly blues lineup and Sunday gospel brunch. Amen!
The Casting Office	3256 Cahuenga Blvd	323-851-4300	Divey neighborhood strip mall bar.
Minibar	3413 Cahuenga Blvd W	323-882-6965	Libations and white leather mod up Universal City.
Rumba Room	1000 Universal Center Dr	818-622-1227	City Walk Salsa club.
The Smoke House	4420 W Lakeside Dr	818-845-3731	Keyboards Tues, Thurs, bands Fri & Sat.
Timmy Nolan's	10111 Riverside Dr	818-985-3359	Irish pub.

Long Beach

49ers Tavern	5660 E Pacific Coast Hwy	562-494-7670	Nearly a landmark in itself; real tavern atmosphere.
The Belmont Brewing Company	25 - 39th Pl	562-433-3891	Try the Strawberry Blonde. Food's spectacular too.
Blue Café	210 The Promenade N	562-983-7111	Variety of bands, brews, pool tables upstairs, lotsa hipsters.
Fern's Cocktails	1253 E 4th St	562-436-2123	
Joe Jost's	2803 E Anaheim St	562-439-5446	Opened in 1924 as a barbershop. Try the pickled eggs!
Mariposa	135 Pine Ave	562-951-9711	Decent food, trendy crowd, lotsa dancing.
Murphy's Pub	4918 E 2nd St	562-433-6338	Fun patio bar, great sandwishes. Don't spit on those walking below.
Portfolio Coffee House	2300 E 4th St	562-434-2486	TV shows film here; unbeatable atmosphere.
Rock Bottom Brewery	1 Pine Ave	562-308-2255	
The Sky Room	40 S Locust Ave	562-983-2738	Swanky Suppah Club, located atop The Breakers; 360-degree view.
V20	81 Aquarium Wy	562-216-2060	New joint in The Pike; upscale trendy revelers.

San Pedro

Godmother's	302 W 7th St	310-833-1589	Part of the Art Walk scene.
June's Bar	1100 S Pacific Ave	310-833-4171	Warm, literally and figuratively.
Kan Kan	104 S Pacific Ave	310-548-0591	Kan you dig it?

Eating Old

Taix on Sunset in Echo Park has been serving up French country cuisine at peasant prices to Angelenos since 1927. Grab a tray and grin at all the stuffed woodsy creatures at **Clifton's** downtown, where Jell-O and brisket have been on the menu since 1931. **Philippe, the Original** still serves their famous French dip sandwiches at long tables on the sawdust-covered dining room floor. During the exodus from a STAPLES Center event, don't pass up **The Original Pantry Café**, a 24-hour diner that claims to have never closed its doors since its opening more than 80 years ago, a feat that includes moving locations. **Musso & Frank Grill** has been operating since Hollywood was an infant in 1919, serving steaks, burgers, and other industry standards. Legend has it that Orson Welles once ate 18 hot dogs in one sitting at **Pink's** on La Brea—hundreds line up daily to challenge the portly actor's record.

Eating Cheap

Why make a run for the border when there are so many independent taquerias throughout LA? Many starving actors kill the hunger pangs at a number of ethnic hole-in-the-wall restaurants. Some of our favorite taco stands are the orange **Benito's** throughout the city where $3 will buy you 5 "rolled tacos" or a burrito the size of a Chihuahua; also *delicioso* are the **Loteria Grill** and **Poquito Mas**. If you are so stuffed that you think you're not seeing the bill correctly following a filling, yet inexpensive meal, you're most likely at one of the five **Versailles** restaurants serving up authentic Cuban food. But our hands-down favorite for cheap eats is **Zankou Chicken**, an Armenian, cash-only mini-chain with the most delectable poultry you will ever taste, served with garlic sauce and pita.

Eating Hip

If any city does hip, it's Los Angeles, though unfortunately it does so to the detriment of the food on occasion. Recommended here are restaurants that are both hip *and* delicious. Head to **Café Stella** in Silver Lake to enjoy scrumptious and hearty French food with an extensive wine list. **A.O.C.** on Third Street has so many tiny menu items to sample, along with at least 12 wines by the glass, that you may have to unbutton your Gucci slacks at the end of the meal. Often, "hip" is defined by scruffy-yet-sophisticated 20- and 30-somethings bobbling about a glass of wine while they tell you of their planned trajectory to fame and fortune. **Kate Mantilini**'s on Wilshire is where you'll find those Westside hipsters eating steak sandwiches, while on the Eastside they tend to favor the outdoor patio at **Malo**, the petite quarters of **Blair's**, and the heat-lamp-aided **Edendale Grill** (a recent hotspot for low-key celebs who've escaped Hollywood). Also fashionably yummy is **Luna Park**—a San Francisco transplant that is as loud as the food is good.

Eating Late

Heaven knows that after a night of sweaty dancing, passionate lovemaking, or just heavy drinking, a person can get ravenous. Fortunately LA has a number of places open until the wee hours where you can fill up or sober up. **Fred 62** on Vermont serves starving hipsters burgers, Asian noodles, gooey desserts, and great coffee 24 hours a day. For a late-night diner experience, head to the pop-art fabulous **Swingers** on Beverly Boulevard or the historic **Canter's Deli** on Fairfax, where you can also pick up bagels for the morning after. If you've just returned from Paris and are used to eating bistro-style at midnight, drive over the hill to Studio City's **Firefly** for *tres magnifique*, if pricey, food and a lovely outdoor seating area. We'd be remiss to not mention the **Brite Spot Family Restaurant** in Echo Park; it's open until 4 am Thursday through Sunday and serves cheap diner favorites like grilled cheese and heaping plates of seasoned french fries with featured DJ nights.

Eating Ethnic

Often, but not always, the best ethnic restaurants are situated in the corresponding ethnic neighborhoods. A wealth of Ethiopian restaurants line Fairfax, just south of Olympic Boulevard; our favorite is **Nyala Ethiopian Cuisine**, where dishes like doro wat and injera can be sampled for less than $7 during the daily lunch buffet. The affordable four-course dinner at Armenian restaurant **Carousel** in East Hollywood is not to be missed. South Los Angeles is home to some of the city's best soul and Cajun food; for finger-licking gumbo try **Harold & Belle's** on Jefferson. Our tummies rumble just thinking about Koreatown. For an interactive and highly satisfying group dining experience, try one of the many Korean barbecue restaurants—we like **Soot Bull Jeep** on the cheap side and **Dong Il Jang** on the posh end. Don't worry if you can't read Korean, the menus have pictures that you can point to for ordering ease.

Eating Meat

From duck to filet mignon, from foie gras to consommé, we love to eat meat in the US of A. While California is supposed to be a national leader in the natural foods and vegetarian movement, you would never know from the assortment of restaurants serving every piece of the animal anatomy. For steaks, try **Arroyo Chop House** in Pasadena, **Mastro** in Beverly Hills, or the **Tam O' Shanter** in Silver Lake for prime rib. A variety of sausages are served at **Pink's** and **Tail O' the Pup**. And for German-style brats, give the **Red Lion Tavern** in Silver Lake a try. Let's not forget fish—downtown LA's **Water Grill** is an upscale seafood destination, as is **Crustacean** in Beverly Hills. And **Killer Shrimp** in Venice serves exactly what the restaurant's name states. **Chloe** in Playa del Rey, although off the beaten path, is a new culinary destination because of their fresh-from-the-farmers' market menu and assortment of meat, steak, and fish that they grill up swimmingly.

Eating Meatless

We appreciate a non-animal-based meal from time to time, and for this crunchy dining experience we'll head to **Real Food Daily**, a chain of organic, vegan restaurants serving tempeh, tofu, and interesting noodle salads. Also of note is the **Urth Caffé**, another chain of organic eateries—although meat is on the menu, they offer a wide selection of homemade soups, salads, and veggie sandwiches. **A Votre Sante** in Brentwood has been dishing up vegetarian specialties since the 1980s, and they've managed to plump their menu without resorting to imitation meat products. To really own your veggie roots at **Home** in Los Feliz, order the yogurt, fruit, and granola concoction titled "My Sister the Tree Hugger."

Editor's Favorites

When we have a few Ben Franklins to blow, the aforementioned **A.O.C.** is the place we treat ourselves. Be sure to request the banquette when making a reservation and swoon over the small plate menu with a group of foodie friends. Often we find ourselves stopping at Trader Joe's for a bottle of 2 Buck Chuck and then grabbing a table at **The Kitchen** on Fountain and Sunset, where we can sample one of the ever-changing creative comfort-food specials. One of the benefits of LA weather is the endless supply of outdoor brunch spots. Two of our favorites are Silver Lake's **Cliff's Edge**, whose hidden patio sits under an old tree's sprawling branches, and **Home** in Los Feliz, where the fountain reminds us that they serve one of the few alcohol-enabled brunches on the Eastside.

Key: $: Under $10 / $$: $10–$20 / $$$: $20–$30 / $$$$: $30+; * : Does not accept credit cards / † : Accepts only American Express.

Map 1 • Beverly Hills

Baja Fresh	475 N Beverly Dr	310-858-6690	$	Cheap, reliable Mexican.
Barney Greengrass	9570 Wilshire Blvd	310-777-5877	$$$	An LA icon.
Basic Bites	443 N Beverly Blvd	310-247-9673	$	Fresh sandwiches and salads.
The Belvedere	9882 Little Santa Monica Blvd	310-788-2306	$$$$	Upscale hotel dining.
Blowfish Sushi	9229 Sunset Blvd	310-887-3848	$$$	Sushi to die for.
Blue on Blue	9400 W Olympic Blvd	310-277-5221	$$$$	Poolside cocktails—very LA.
BOE	403 N Crescent Dr	310-247-0505	$$	Small plates and casual atmosphere.
Brighton Coffee Shop	9600 Brighton Wy	310-276-7732	$$	Comfort food.
Café Talesai	9198 W Olympic Blvd	310-271-9345	$	Thai specialties with a twist.
Crustacean	9646 Little Santa Monica Blvd	310-205-8990	$$$$	High-end Vietnamese.
Da Pasquale	9749 Little Santa Monica Blvd	310-859-3884	$$$	Neighborhood Italian.
Dan Tana's	9071 Santa Monica Blvd	310-275-9444	$$$$	Old H'wood glamour—if you can get a table.
El Torito Grill	9595 Wilshire Blvd	310-550-1599	$$	Okay food, better drinks.
Farm of Beverly Hills	439 N Beverly Dr	310-273-5578	$$$	Yeehaw darlings! Farm fresh salads and entrees.
Ginza Sushi-Ko	218 N Rodeo Dr	310-247-8939	$$$$	Very high-end sushi.
The Grill	9560 Dayton Wy	310-276-0615	$$$$	Hollywood power lunch spot.
Joss	9255 Sunset Blvd	310-276-1886	$$	Haute Chinese cuisine.
Kate Mantilini	9101 Wilshire Blvd	310-278-3699	$$	Boxing-themed upscale bistro with knockout desserts.
La Scala	434 N Canon Dr	310-275-0579	$$$$	Classic Italian.
Le Pain Quotidien	9630 Little Santa Monica Blvd	310-859-1100	$$	Classy French sandwich shop.
Maple Drive	345 N Maple Dr	310-274-9800	$$$$	Comfort food for the entertainment industry.
Mastro	246 N Canon Dr	310-888-8782	$$$$	Great steaks; don't miss the upstairs piano bar.
Mulberry Street Pizzeria	240 S Beverly Dr	310-247-8100	$$	Thin-crust pizza.
Mulberry Street Pizzeria	347 N Canon Dr	310-247-8998	$$	Thin-crust pizza.
Nate 'n Al's	414 N Beverly Dr	310-274-0101	$$	New York-style deli.
Nic's	453 N Canon Dr	310-550-5707	$$$$	Oysters and martinis, need we say more?
Polo Lounge	9641 Sunset Blvd	310-276-2251	$$$$	The Grande Dame of hotel dining.
Real Food Daily	242 S Beverly Dr	310-858-0880	$$	Tofu burgers with tempeh bacon, for the adventurous vegan.
Regent Beverly Wilshire	9500 Wilshire Blvd	310-275-5200	$$$$	For the "Pretty Woman" in us all.
Trader Vic's	9876 Wilshire Blvd	310-276-6345	$$$$	Old-school Polynesian-themed restaurant; fruity drinks and fried appetizers.
Xi'an	362 N Canon Dr	310-275-3345	$$$	Healthy and delicious Chinese in a BH atmosphere.

Map 2 • West Hollywood

AOC	8022 W 3rd St	323-653-6359	$$$$	Little plates, big wine selection and savvy servers.
Ago	8478 Melrose Ave	323-655-6333	$$$$	High-end Italian.
Amalfi	143 N La Brea Ave	323-938-2504	$$$	Rustic, authentic Italian, good for groups.
Angeli Caffe	7274 Melrose Ave	323-936-9086	$$$	Starch-tastic bread and tasty pastas.
Angelini Osteria	7313 Beverly Blvd	323-297-0070	$$$	Upscale Italian.
Authentic Café	7605 Beverly Blvd	323-939-4626	$$$	Eclectic.
Balboa	The Grafton Hotel, 8462 W Sunset Blvd	323-650-8383	$$$$	Steaks on the Sunset Strip.
Barefoot Bar & Grill	8722 W 3rd St	310-276-6223	$$$	The California cuisine always draws crowds.
Basix Café	8333 Santa Monica Blvd	323-848-2460	$$	Popular breakfast spot.
Benito's Taco Shop	7912 Beverly Blvd	323-938-7427	$*	$3 burritos the size of your Chihuahua.
Bistro 21	846 N La Cienega Blvd	310-967-0021	$$$$	French-Asian bistro with a cult following.
Bossa Nova	685 N Robertson Blvd	310-657-5070	$	Paradise for meat lovers.
Café Angelino	8735 W 3rd St	310-246-1177	$$	Flaky thin crust pizzas.
Café Med	8615 Sunset Blvd	310-652-0445	$$	Low-key Sunset Plaza Italian.
Campanile	624 S La Brea Ave	323-938-1447	$$$$	Romantic Mediterranean.
Canter's Deli	419 N Fairfax Ave	323-651-2030	$$	Classic deli with swinging lounge attached.
Chameau	339 N Fairfax Ave	323-951-0039	$$$	BYOB Moroccan.
Chateau Marmont	8221 W Sunset Blvd	323-656-1010	$$$$	Celeb-heavy scene, cuisine-light menu.
Chaya Brasserie	8741 Alden Dr	310-859-8833	$$$$	Great food in a schmoozy setting.
Cheebo	7533 W Sunset Blvd	323-850-7070	$$	Organic gourmet pizza and sandwiches.
Chipotle	121 N La Cienega Blvd	310-855-0371	$*	Good 'n' fresh.
Cynthia's	8370 W 3rd St	323-658-7851	$$$	American favorites. Order the cobbler—trust us.
Daily Grill	100 N La Cienega Blvd	310-659-3100	$$$	Steak and fries chain.
Dolce Enoteca	8284 Melrose Ave	323-852-7174	$$$$	Ashton's Italian endeavor, still going strong.
Doughboys	8136 W 3rd St	323-651-4202	$	An anti-Atkins indulgence spot.
East India Grill	345 N La Brea Ter	323-936-8844	$	Indian with a California twist.
Eat Well	8252 Santa Monica Blvd	323-656-1383	$*	Hip chain for cheap comfort food.
Ed's Coffee Shop	460 N Robertson Blvd	310-659-8625	$	Home-cookin'.
El Compadre	7408 Sunset Blvd	323-874-7924	$$	Tasty Mexican with flaming, kick ass margaritas.
Farm of Beverly Hills	189 The Grove Dr	323-525-1699	$$$	Yeehaw darlings! Farm fresh salads and entrees.
Fish Grill	7226 Beverly Blvd	323-937-7162	$*	No-frills, super-fresh fish.

Arts & Entertainment • **Restaurants**

Key: $: Under $10 / $$: $10–$20 / $$$: $20–$30 / $$$$: $30+; * : Does not accept credit cards / † : Accepts only American Express.

Map 2 • West Hollywood—*continued*

Flora Kitchen	460 S La Brea Ave	323-931-9900	$$	A café in a flower shop. Delicious and fragrant.
French Quarter Market Place	7985 Santa Monica Blvd	323-654-0898	$$	Food for everyone, especially night owls.
Genghis Cohen	740 N Fairfax Ave	323-653-0640	$$$	Chinese with live music.
Gumbo Pot	6333 W 3rd St	323-933-0358	$$	Best Cajun in LA.
Hirozen	8385 Beverly Blvd	323-653-0470	$$$	Great mini-mall sushi.
House of Blues	8430 Sunset Blvd	323-848-5100	$$$	Saucy Cajun. Try Sunday's Gospel Brunch.
Hugo's	8401 Santa Monica Blvd	323-654-3993	$$	Power brunches.
In-N-Out Burger	7009 W Sunset Blvd	800-786-1000	$*	Top California burger joint.
The Ivy	113 N Robertson Blvd	310-274-8303	$$$$	Broker a deal over traditional American fare.
JAR	8225 Beverly Blvd	323-655-6566	$$$$	Upscale comfort food.
King's Road Café	8361 Beverly Blvd	323-655-9044	$$	Strongest coffee you'll ever drink.
Kokomo	Inside Farmer's Market, 3rd St & Fairfax Ave	323-933-0773	$$	Standard American fare.
Le Pain Quotidien	8607 Melrose Ave	310-854-3700	$$	Classy French sandwich shop.
Loteria Grill	6333 W 3rd St	323-930-2211	$	Muy fresicita.
Lucques	8474 Melrose Ave	323-655-6277	$$$$	Chez Panisse-style cooking in LA.
Mandarette	8386 Beverly Blvd	323-655-6115	$$	Chinese fusion.
Newsroom Café	120 N Robertson Blvd	310-652-4444	$$	Star-laden vegetarian.
Noura Café	8479 Melrose Ave	323-651-4581	$$	Middle Eastern with belly dancing.
The Pig	612 N La Brea Ave	323-935-1116	$$	Messy southern BBQ joint. Yum.
Pink's Famous Chili Dogs	709 N La Brea Ave	323-931-4223	$*	A line around the block; it's that famous.
Quality Food & Beverage	8030 W 3rd St	323-658-5959	$*	Dog-friendly brunch hangout.
Real Food Daily	414 N La Cienega Blvd	310-289-9910	$$	One of the healthiest tasting restaurants in town.
Saddle Ranch Chop House	8371 Sunset Blvd	323-656-2007	$$$	Chophouse with a mechanical bull.
The Standard	8300 Sunset Blvd	323-650-9090	$$	Late night star watching.
Surya India	8048 W 3rd St	323-653-5151	$$$	Tasty with a breezy interior.
Susina	7122 Beverly Blvd	323-934-7900	$	French bakery and café.
Sweet Lady Jane	8360 Melrose Ave	323-653-7145	$$	Decadent desserts to die for.
Swingers	8020 Beverly Blvd	323-653-5858	$	Classic late-night diner.
Tail O' the Pup	329 N San Vicente Blvd	310-652-4517	$*	LA's other famous hot dog stand.
Trattoria Amici	469 N Doheny Dr	310-858-0271	$$$	Pacific Italian chain.
Urth Caffé	8565 Melrose Ave	310-659-0628	$$	All organic lunch place, plus coffee and sweets.
Yabu	521 N La Cienega Blvd	310-854-0400	$$$	Hip sushi and noodles.

Map 3 • Hollywood

Ammo	1155 N Highland Ave	323-871-2666	$$$	Trendy California comfort food.
Astro Burger	5601 Melrose Ave	323-469-1924	$*	Tasty meat-free burgers.
Benito's Taco Shop	6751 Santa Monica Blvd	323-466-9333	$*	$3 burritos the size of your Chihuahua.
California Chicken Café	6805 Melrose Ave	323-935-5877	$$$	Popular cop hangout: the safest chicken in town.
Chan Dara	310 N Larchmont Blvd	323-467-1052	$$$	Huge Thai portions served by tiny Thai women.
Cinespace	6356 Hollywood Blvd	323-817-3456	$$$$	Check that the kitchen is open before you go.
Fabiolus Café	5255 Melrose Ave	323-464-5857	$$	Dine in, deliver, or take-away Italian.
Fabiolus Café	6270 W Sunset Blvd	323-467-2882	$$	Dine in, deliver, or take-away Italian.
Geisha House	6633 Hollywood Blvd	323-460-6300	$$$$	Celebrities' Asian persuasion.
Hola Fresh Mexican Grill	1807 N Cahuenga Blvd	323-466-0000	$	Muy cheap Mexican eats with free delivery.
Hollywood and Vine	6263 Hollywood Blvd	323-464-2345	$$$	Californian cuisine in a dressed-up 1940's Hollywood diner.
La Buca	5210 Melrose Ave	323-462-1900	$$	Sophia Loren would eat at this tiny Italian ristorante.
La Poubelle	5907 Franklin Ave	323-465-0807	$$$	Gallic gourmet dining and '80s music.
Larchmont Deli	5210 Beverly Blvd	323-466-1193	$	Try the pastrami.
Miceli's	1646 N Las Palmas Ave	323-466-3438	$$	Classic Hollywood Italian since 1949 (warning for the easily annoyed: singing waiters here).
Musso & Frank Grill	6667 Hollywood Blvd	323-467-7788	$$$$	Old fashioned American.
Off Vine	6263 Leland Wy	323-962-1900	$$$$	Romantic Californian.
Patina	Walt Disney Concert Hall, 141 S Grand Ave	213-972-3331	$$$$	French-Californian fusion.
Pig 'n Whistle	6714 Hollywood Blvd	323-463-0000	$$$	Dine in "bed" or people-watch from a comfy booth.
Roscoe's House of Chicken n' Waffles	1514 N Gower St	323-466-7453	$$	Southern-fried bonanza.
Xiomara	6101 Melrose Ave	323-461-0601	$$$$	Upscale Cuban with revolutionary mojitos.
Yamakasa	1900 N Highland Ave	323-882-6524	$$	Sushi; good for groups.
Yamashiro	1999 N Sycamore Ave	323-466-5125	$$$$	Romantic Japanese with a view.

Map 4 • Los Feliz

Alcove Bakery & Café	1929 Hillhurst Ave	323-644-0100	$	Brunch, lunch, gourmet food market, beautiful patio out front.

Name	Address	Phone	Price	Description
Alegria on Sunset	3510 W Sunset Blvd	323-913-1422	$$*	Lively Mexican food made with home-style finesse.
Café Los Feliz	2081 N Hillhurst Ave	323-664-7111	$	Neighborhoody gem. Exquisite tarts and cinnamon rolls.
Café Stella	3932 Sunset Blvd	323-666-0265	$$$$	Trendy French bistro and wine bar.
Casbah Café	3900 W Sunset Blvd	323-664-7000	$$	Mint tea, pointy slippers, excellent local hang.
Cha Cha Cha	656 N Virgil Ave	323-664-7723	$$$	Caribbean food and sangria.
Cliff's Edge	3626 W Sunset Blvd	323-666-6116	$$	Cal-Euro tapas, upscale bohemian digs and Silver Lake's swankiest patio.
Cobras and Matadors	4655 Hollywood Blvd	323-669-3922	$$$	C&M tapas now on the Eastside too.
Eat Well	3916 E Sunset Blvd	323-664-1624	$	Hip chain for cheap comfort food.
El Conquistador	3701 Sunset Blvd	323-666-5136	$$	Mole olé!
Electric Lotus	4656 Franklin Ave	323-953-0040	$$	Hip Indian disco.
Farfalla Trattoria	1978 Hillhurst Ave	323-661-7365	$$$	Inexpensive, reliable Italian.
Fred 62	1850 N Vermont Ave	323-667-0062	$$	Retro-styled diner with surprising menu.
Home	1760 Hillhurst Ave	323-669-0211	$$	No place like this outdoor eatery. Try the waffle fries.
House of Pies	1869 N Vermont Ave	323-666-9961	$	Perfect pancakes and pecan pie—life's good.
The Kitchen	4348 Fountain Ave	323-664-3663	$$	Late night comfort food.
La Belle Epoque	2129 Hillhurst Ave	323-669-7640	$$	Bakery, brunch, sidewalk seating.
Madame Matisse	3536 W Sunset Blvd	323-662-4862	$$	Matchbox-sized and mellow French café packed with regulars. B.Y.O.B.
Malo	4326 W Sunset Blvd	323-664-1011	$$$	Yummy Mexican for the hipster cheapskate.
Mexico City	2121 Hillhurst Ave	323-661-7227	$$$	Arty Tex-Mex cantina.
Millie's	3524 Sunset Blvd	323-664-0404	$*	The Devil's Mess is the best reason to be bad.
Mustard Seed Café	1948 Hillhurst Ave	323-660-0670	$$	Tasty and laid-back; may take awhile to get the check!
Palermo	1858 N Vermont Ave	323-663-1178	$$	Uninspired, gooey, popular.
Paru's	5140 W Sunset Blvd	323-661-7600	$$	Delicious South Indian food with lots of happy-smiley service.
Prasadam	3818 W Sunset Blvd	323-644-0068	$	Groovy neighborhood juice bar and café.
Shin	1972 Hillhurst Ave	323-664-1891	$$	Japanese food, sushi, good salads.
Tantra	3705 W Sunset Blvd	323-663-8268	$$$$	Ultra-sexy Indian, with lounge.
Vermont	1714 N Vermont Ave	323-661-6163	$$$$	Dine in style before heading to the punk show.
Vida	1930 Hillhurst Ave	323-662-1248	$$$	Hip, creative Californian.
Yuca's	2056 Hillhurst Ave	323-662-1214	$*	A busy shack serving luscious Yucatan-style burritos and tacos.
Zankou Chicken	5065 W Sunset Blvd	323-665-7845	$*	Palm-licking, Beck-serenaded chicken.

Map 5 • Silver Lake/Echo Park/Atwater

Name	Address	Phone	Price	Description
Astro Family Restaurant	2300 Fletcher Dr	323-663-9241	$	Relaxed '50s modern diner.
Baracoa Cuban Café	3175 Glendale Blvd	323-665-9590	$	Home-style Cuban cooking.
Blair's	2903 Rowena Ave	323-660-1882	$$$$	Silver Lake's premier eatery.
Brite Spot Family Restaurant	1918 W Sunset Blvd	213-484-9800	$	Late night diner.
Café Tropical	2900 W Sunset Blvd	323-661-8391	$*	Latin bakery and coffee house.
Caffe Capri	2547 Hyperion Ave	323-644-7906	$$	Low-key and tasty Italian.
The Downbeat Café	1202 N Alvarado St	213-483-3955	$$*	Jazz café for neighborhood politicos.
Dusty's	3200 W Sunset Blvd	323-906-1018	$$$	Eclectic French bistro.
Edendale Grill	2838 Rowena Ave	323-666-2000	$$$$	Former fire station serves American favorites—dine in or dine out.
Gingergrass	2396 Glendale Blvd	323-644-1600	$$	Upscale Vietnamese food for a gringo palate.
Hard Times Pizza Co	2664 Griffith Park Blvd	323-661-5656	$$	Sicilian- and Neopolitan-style pies to take out or eat in.
India Sweets and Spices	3126 Los Feliz Blvd	323-345-0360	$$	Vegetarian delicacies, Indian groceries, and Bollywood hits under one roof.
La Parrilla	3129 W Sunset Blvd	323-661-8055	$$	Authentic Mexican, order the molcajete azteca.
Leela Thai	1737 Silver Lake Blvd	323-660-6100	$$*	Inexpensive, delicious, friendly.
Mae Ploy	2606 W Sunset Blvd	213-353-9635	$$	Home-style Thai food served with a smile.
Masa	1800 W Sunset Blvd	213-989-1558	$	Neighborhood bakery and pizza house run by Patina vets.
Michelangelo Pizzeria	1637 Silver Lake Blvd	323-660-4843	$$	Italian fare with old-world flair.
Mimi's Café	2925 Los Feliz Blvd	323-668-1715	$$	Average TGIF-style family restaurant.
Netty's	1700 Silver Lake Blvd	323-662-8655	$$$	Funky local fave since before Silver Lake was cool.
Nicky D's Wood-Fired Pizza	2764 Rowena Ave	323-664-3333	$$	Friendly local spot for NYC-style pies. Try the Garlic Clam pizza.
Osteria Nonni	3219 Glendale Blvd	323-666-7133	$$	Tasty Italian in a pleasant room.
Pho' Café	2841 W Sunset Blvd	213-413-0888	$$*	Vietnamese noodle shop with hipster flavor.
Police Academy Café	1880 Academy Dr	323-221-5222	$	Dine with the cadets.
Rambutan Thai	2835 W Sunset Blvd	213-273-8424	$$	Trendy but good Thai favorites.
Red Lion Tavern	2366 Glendale Blvd	323-662-5337	$$	Go for the German brats.
Taix	1911 W Sunset Blvd	213-484-1265	$$	Say "Tex" and check out "Two-fer Tuesdays" for double the wine at this French standard.
Tam O'Shanter	2980 Los Feliz Blvd	323-664-0228	$$$$	Scottish-English pub.
Thai Mix Grill	2728 Fletcher Dr	323-664-1812	$$*	The usual pad-thai in unusual surroundings.

Key: $: Under $10 / $$: $10–$20 / $$$: $20–$30 / $$$$: $30+; * : Does not accept credit cards / † : Accepts only American Express.

Map 6 • Miracle Mile/Mid-City

Benito's Taco Shop	1544 S La Cienega Blvd	310-360-7386	$*	$3 burritos the size of your Chihuahua.
Black Dog Coffee	5657 Wilshire Blvd	323-933-1976	$	Friendly and tasty. Breakfast, lunch, coffee, dog biscuits.
Caffé Latte	6254 Wilshire Blvd	323-936-5213	$$	California-style coffee and breakfast shop.
Cobra Lily	8442 Wilshire Blvd	323-651-5051	$$	Get bitten by delicious tapas.
Crazy Fish	9105 W Olympic Blvd	310-550-8547	$$$	Insanely popular sushi joint.
La Boca del Conga Room	5364 Wilshire Blvd	323-938-1696	$$$$	Next to the Conga Room: eat Cuban before heading next door for Salsa.
Lucy's	1371 S La Brea Ave	323-938-4337	$	A 24-hour drive through taco stand that also sells chili dogs, burgers, and anything else bad for you.
Luna Park	672 S La Brea Ave	323-934-2110	$$$	Cocktails, tasty food, lively scene. LA outpost of San Francisco original.
Natalee Thai	998 S Robertson Blvd	310-855-9380	$$	Popular Thai food.
Nyala Ethiopian Cuisine	1076 S Fairfax Ave	323-936-5918	$$	Ethiopian serving unbeatable vegetarian $5.95 lunch buffet.
Rosalind's	1044 S Fairfax Ave	323-936-2486	$$	Local favorite, Ethiopian.
Roscoe's Chicken & Waffles	5006 W Pico Blvd	323-934-4405	$$	Cheap Southern soul food chain.
Versailles	1415 S La Cienega Blvd	310-289-0392	$$	Cheap Cuban chain.
Wi Jammin	5103 Pico Blvd	323-965-9809	$	A tiny hole in the wall Caribbean restaurant where the local hairdressers hang out.

Map 7 • Hancock Park

Girasole	225 1/2 N Larchmont Blvd	323-464-6978	$$	Tiny, cozy, delicious osso buco.
Kiku Sushi	246 N Larchmont Blvd	323-464-1200	$$	All-you-can-eat sushi.
La Bottega Marino	203 N Larchmont Blvd	323-962-1325	$$	Italian café/deli serving especially nice brunch.
La Luna	113 N Larchmont Blvd	323-962-2130	$$$	Casual Italian trattoria.
Larchmont Village Pizzeria	131 N Larchmont Blvd	323-465-5566	$*	Might be LA's best NY-style pizza.
Le Petit Greek	127 N Larchmont Blvd	323-464-5160	$$	Gyros, anyone?
Prado	244 N Larchmont Blvd	323-467-3871	$$$	Spicy Latin-Caribbean.
Z Pizza	123 N Larchmont Blvd	323-466-6969	$$	Thin-crust deliciousness. A handful of sidewalk and indoor tables.

Map 8 • Korea Town

Dong Il Jang	3455 W 8th St	213-383-5757	$$	Upscale Korean barbecue, also serving sushi.
El Cholo	1121 S Western Ave	323-734-2773	$$	Long time favorite Mexican chain.
El Farolito	2737 W Pico Blvd	323-731-4329	$	Chicken enchiladas.
M Grill	3832 Wilshire Blvd	213-389-2770	$$$	Authentic Brazilian, sleek interior.
Soot Bull Jeep	3136 W 8th St	213-387-3865	$$$	Korean BBQ.
Taylor's Prime Steaks	3361 W 8th St	213-382-8449	$$$	Old fashioned steak house.
Tommy's	2575 Beverly Blvd	213-389-9060	$	Their burgers are renowned.

Map 9 • Downtown

Brooklyn Bagel	2217 Beverly Blvd	213-413-4114	$*	Five decade old authentic bagelry.
Café Pinot	700 W 5th St	213-239-6500	$$$$	Downtown's classy French bistro.
California Roll & Sushi Fish	727 W 7th St	213-489-0238	$	Good Japanese, including bento box lunches and sushi combination plates.
Checkers	535 S Grand Ave	213-624-0000	$$$$	Upscale downtown pre-theater dining.
Cicada	617 S Olive St	213-488-9488	$$$$	Californian-Italian.
Ciudad	445 S Figueroa St	213-486-5171	$$$$	Mod interior, killer mojitos, and eclectic pan-Latin menu.
Clifton's Cafeteria	648 S Broadway	213-627-1673	$	Tri-level cafeteria with a woodsy theme and fake animals since 1931.
Emerson's	606 S Olive St	213-623-3006	$*	Specialty salads, sandwiches, and coffees.
Emerson's	862 S Los Angeles St	213-623-8807	$*	Specialty salads, sandwiches, and coffees.
Empress Pavillion	988 N Hill St	213-617-9898	$$	Specialty salads, sandwiches, and coffees.
Engine Co No 28	644 S Figueroa St	213-624-6996	$$$$	Good firehouse-inspired eats. Go after 8 pm.
Mrs Beasley's	735 S Figueroa St	213-228-0227	$	Baked goods, soups, sandwiches, coffee—also does gift baskets.
Nick & Stef's Steakhouse	330 S Hope St	213-680-0330	$$$$	Old fashioned steaks in an ultra modern downtown setting.
Noe	251 S Olive St	213-356-4100	$$$$	Omni Hotel's upscale Japanese-American.
NY Pizza	518 W 6th St	213-614-1100	$	Best pizza in the neighborhood.
Original Pantry Café	877 S Figueroa St	213-972-9279	$*	All American diner open 24 hours since 1924.
Pacific Dining Car	1310 W 6th St	213-483-6000	$$$$	Steak all day, all night.
Pete's Café & Bar	400 S Main St	213-617-1000	$$$	Great bar, big drinks, tasty American fare.
Philippe, the Original	1001 N Alameda St	213-628-3781	$*	The best French dips in town.
Plum Tree Inn	937 N Hill St	213-613-1819	$$	Delicious Chinese.
R-23	923 E 2nd St	213-687-7178	$$$$	Stylish sushi in the LA arts district.
Seoul Jung Korean	930 Wilshire Blvd	213-688-7880	$$$$	Upscale Korean BBQ with fresh meat, fish, and veggies.

Soul Folks Café	613 Imperial St	213-613-0381 $$	Great Southern food that's considerate of vegetarians.
The Standard Downtown Restaurant & Lounge	550 S Flower St	213-892-8080 $$$	24-hour diner menu, post-party or in your room.
Water Grill	544 S Grand Ave	213-891-0900 $$$	Expense-account dining to impress. And it's delicious.
Yang Chow	819 N Broadway	213-625-0811 $$	Popular Chinese chain.

Map 10 • Baldwin Hills

Stevie's Creole Café	3403 Crenshaw Blvd	323-734-6975 $$*	Sonuvva gun, have big fun at this authentic Cajun.
Tasty Q	2959 Crenshaw Blvd	323-735-8325 $	Fried birds--from whole turkeys to drumsticks.

Map 11 • South Central West

Harold & Belle's	2920 W Jefferson Blvd	323-735-3376 $$$	Great Cajun food.
La Barca	2414 S Vermont Ave	323-735-6567 $$	Mexican.
Phillip's Barbecue	4307 Leimert Blvd	323-292-7613 $$	Southern-style ribs in southern LA.

Map 12 • South Central East

29th Street Café	2827 S Hoover St	213-746-2929 $$	The spot in South Central for brunch.
Chano's Drive-In	3000 S Figueroa St	213-747-3944 $	Drive-in to dive into authentic Mexican food.
Pasta Roma	2827 S Figueroa St	213-742-0303 $	University student hangout for cheap Italian.

Map 13 • Inglewood

Caribbean Treehouse	1226 Centinela Ave	310-330-1170 $	Casual cuisine from Trinidad and Tobago.

Map 15 • Pacific Palisades

A La Tarte Bistrot	1037 Swarthmore Ave	310-459-6635 $$	French.
Dante Palisades Restaurant	1032 Swarthmore Ave	310-459-7561 $$	Italian food (closed from 3-5 pm).
Giorgio Baldi	114 W Channel Rd	310-573-1660 $$$$	Memorable Tuscan cooking.
Kay 'n Dave's	15246 W Sunset Blvd	310-459-8118 $$	Mexican food.
Marix Tex Mex Café	118 Entrada Dr	310-459-8596 $$$	Perfect for post-beach margaritas and tacos. Sandy patrons OK.
Mort's Deli	1035 Swarthmore Ave	310-454-5511 $$	Breakfast, lunch, dinner, sandwiches $8, Mexican food.
Patrick's Roadhouse	106 Entrada Dr	310-459-4544 $$	Quintessential place for breakfast at the beach.
Pure Energy Café	17383 W Sunset Blvd	310-573-4105 $	Health-conscious Mexican food.
Robek's Juice	15280 Antioch St	310-230-3991 $	Juice, salads, sandwiches.
Terry's	1028 Swarthmore Ave	310-454-6467 $$	Breakfast, lunch, dinner, sandwiches, salads, omelettes.

Map 16 • Brentwood

A Votre Sante	13016 San Vicente Blvd	310-451-1813 $$	Vegetarian health food.
Cheesecake Factory	11647 San Vicente Blvd	310-826-7111 $$*	American comfort food—and, of course, cheesecake.
Chin Chin	11740 San Vicente Blvd	310-826-2525 $$	Chinese chain.
Daily Grill	11677 San Vicente Blvd	310-442-0044 $$$	Home cooking.
Gaucho Grill	11754 San Vicente Blvd	310-447-7898 $$	Argentine cuisine with lots of meat.
La Scala Presto	11740 San Vicente Blvd	310-826-6100 $$$	Classic Italian.
Le Pain Quotidien	11702 Barrington Ct	310-476-0969 $$	Classy French sandwich shop.
Pizzicotto	11758 San Vicente Blvd	310-442-7188 $$$	Pizza and pasta.
Reddi Chick BBQ	225 26th St	310-393-5238 $*	Chicken with a cult following.
The Brentwood	148 S Barrington Ave	310-476-3511 $$$$	California-style comfort food.
Toscana	11633 San Vicente Blvd	310-820-2448 $$$$	Tuscan with great pizzas.
Vincenti	11930 San Vicente Blvd	310-207-0127 $$$$	Fine Italian food & wine.

Map 17 • Bel Air/Holmby Hills

Bel Air Bar & Grill	662 N Sepulveda Blvd	310-440-5544 $$$$	Californian with quick Getty access.
Four Oaks	2181 N Beverly Glen Blvd	310-470-2265 $$$$	Intimate spot with excellent food and plenty of star sightings.
Hotel Bel Air Dining Room	701 Stone Canyon Rd	310-472-1211 $$$$	Excellent nouvelle Cal-French for when you're feeling rich. Swanky bar.

Map 18 • Santa Monica

17th Street Café	1610 Montana Ave	310-453-2771 $$$	California casual.
Babalu	1002 Montana Ave	310-395-2500 $$$	Caribbean, don't skip dessert.
Blueberry	510 Santa Monica Blvd	310-394-7766 $$	Cheap home cooking.
Border Grill	1445 4th St	310-451-1655 $$$	Mexican restaurant run by popular TV chefs.
Broadway Deli	1457 3rd St Prom	310-451-0616 $$	Overpriced but popular deli food.
Buffalo Club	1520 Olympic Blvd	310-450-8600 $$$$	Exclusive clubby dining.
Café Montana	1534 Montana Ave	310-829-3990 $$$	A neighborhood staple.
California Chicken Café	2401 Wilshire Blvd	310-453-0477 $	Good rotisserie chicken and sides. Cheap and fast.
Cha Cha Chicken	1906 Ocean Ave	310-581-1684 $$	Caribbean chicken.
Chaya Venice	110 Navy St	310-396-1179 $$$$	Slightly upscale place to meet.
Chez Jay	1657 Ocean Ave	310-395-1741 $$$	Californian seafood.

Key: $: Under $10 / $$: $10–$20 / $$$: $20–$30 / $$$$: $30+; * : Does not accept credit cards / † : Accepts only American Express.

Map 18 • Santa Monica—continued

Chinois on Main	2709 Main St	310-392-9025	$$$$	Wolfgang Puck does Chinese brilliantly.
Dhaba	2104 Main St	310-399-9452	$$	Visit India with a Dhaba Dinner.
El Cholo	1025 Wilshire Blvd	310-899-1106	$$	Popular Mexican chain.
Falafel King	1315 3rd St Prom	310-587-2551	$	One of the cheapest, best meals on the Promenade.
Finn McCool's	2702 Main St	310-452-1734	$$	Neighborhood comfort food.
Fritto Misto	601 Colorado Ave	310-458-2829	$$	Inexpensive Californian-Italian.
Fromin's Delicatessen	1832 Wilshire Blvd	310-829-5443	$	Old-school deli and diner.
Library Ale House	2911 Main St	310-314-4855	$$	Beer and classy pub fare.
The Lobster	1602 Ocean Ave	310-458-9294	$$$$	Definitely order the lobster.
Lula	2720 Main St	310-392-5711	$$	Inexpenisve Mexican with strong margaritas.
Mani's	2507 Main St	310-396-7700	$	Bakery, café, juices, sugarless cookies—oh my!
Michael D's Café & Catering	234 Pico Blvd	310-452-8737	$	Next to bowling alley: scarf 'n' score!
Newsroom Café	530 Wilshire Blvd	310-319-9100	$$	Popular vegetarian lunch spot.
Ocean Ave Seafood	1401 Ocean Ave	310-394-5669	$$$$	Upscale seafood by the beach.
Ocean Park Omelette Parlor	2732 Main St	310-399-7892	$	Home of well-stuffed, three-egg omelettes.
Sushi Roku	1401 Ocean Ave	310-458-4771	$$$	Sushi by the beach.
Trastavere	1360 3rd St Prom	310-319-1985	$$$	Their gnocchi and olive dip rate a trip.
Tudor House	1403 2nd St	310-451-4107	$	Lovely afternoon tea.
World Café	2820 Main St	310-392-1661	$$	Outdoor people-watching.
Ye Olde King's Head	116 Santa Monica Blvd	310-451-1402	$$	Traditional English fare and beer.
Yu Restaurant and Lounge	1323 Montana Ave	310-395-4727	$$$$	Chic chef, pan-Asian bites.

Map 19 • West LA/Santa Monica East

Asakuma	11701 Wilshire Blvd	310-826-0013	$$$	More than just sushi.
Bandera	11700 Wilshire Blvd	310-477-3524	$$$	Dimly-lit; yuppy-ish. Reliable New-American cuisine.
Benito's Taco Shop	11614 Santa Monica Blvd	310-442-9924	$*	$3 burritos the size of your Chihuahua.
Bombay Café	12021 W Pico Blvd	310-473-3388	$$$	Inspired Indian Cuisine.
Chez Mimi	246 26th St	310-393-0558	$$$$	Onion soup and other French staples.
Hide Sushi	2040 Sawtelle Blvd	310-477-7242	$$$*	Not for the sushi-phobic.
Il Forno	2901 Ocean Park Blvd	310-450-1241	$$$	Northern Italian cuisine. Great pastas and NYC-style pizzas.
Il Moro	11400 W Olympic Blvd	310-575-3530	$$$$	Creative Italian specialties.
Javan	11500 Santa Monica Blvd	310-207-5555	$$	Persian cuisine. Huge portions of tasty charbroiled meats.
Josie Restaurant	2424 Pico Blvd	310-581-9888	$$$$	Reputable chef. Great interior. New-American cuisine.
Kay 'n Dave's	262 26th St	310-260-1355	$$	Healthy Mexican with a family-friendly atmosphere.
La Bottega Marino	11363 Santa Monica Blvd	310-477-7777	$$	Italian deli-restaurant. Affordable. Charming setting.
Lares	2909 Pico Blvd	310-829-4550	$$	Rich, authentic Mexican meals and potent margaritas.
Le Saigon	11611 Santa Monica Blvd	310-312-2929	$$*	Great Korean food.
Rae's Restaurant	2901 Pico Blvd	310-828-7937	$*	Neighborhood hangout—they line up for breakfast!
Royal Star Seafood	3001 Wilshire Blvd	310-828-8812	$$	Dim sum and then some seafood.
Sushi Sasabune	11300 Nebraska Ave	310-268-8380	$$	No California Roll, no menu. Trust the chef.
Tlapazola Grill	11676 Gateway Blvd	310-477-1577	$$$	Southern Mexican.
Typhoon	3221 Donald Douglas Loop S	310-390-6565	$$$	Eclectic Pan-Asian. Aviation motif. Cool & chic.
Valentino	3115 Pico Blvd	310-829-4313	$$$$	Classy Italian. Flawless. Dazzling wine list.
Vito	2807 Ocean Park Blvd	310-450-4999	$$$	Reliable Italian.
Yabu	11820 W Pico Blvd	310-473-9757	$$$	Hip sushi and noodles.
Zabies	3003 Ocean Park Blvd	310-392-9036	$	Neighborhood café. Friendly. Cheap. Good breakfast & lunch.

Map 20 • Westwood/Century City

Big Chill	10850 Olympic Blvd	310-441-0643	$*	Best frozen yogurt in LA!
Clementine	1751 Ensley Ave	310-552-1080	$$	True American cuisine with a modern flare.
Diddy Riese Cookies	926 Broxton Ave	310-208-0448	$*	25¢ cookies and ice cream sandwiches.
Earth, Wind & Flour	1776 Westwood Blvd	310-470-2499	$$	"Boston-style" pizzas and pastas.
Falafel King	1059 Broxton Ave	310-208-4444	$	Fast food Middle Eastern.
Gardens on Glendon	1139 Glendon Ave	310-824-1818	$$$$	Californian favorites.
In-N-Out Burger	922 Gayley Ave	800-786-1000	$*	Top California burger joint.
Johnnie's NY Pizzeria	10251 Santa Monica Blvd	310-553-1188	$$	New York-style pizza.
La Bruschetta	1621 Westwood Blvd	310-477-1052	$$$$	Classic Italian. Their bruschetta is delicious.
La Cachette	10506 Santa Monica Blvd	310-470-4992	$$$$	High-end French.
Matteo's Hoboken	2323 Westwood Blvd	310-474-1109	$$	Southern Italian fare with a Jersey flair?
Napa Valley Grille	1100 Glendon Ave	310-824-3322	$$$$	Upscale dining.
Stan's Donuts	10948 Weyburn Ave	310-208-8660	$*	Try a Reese's Peanut Butter Cup donut.
Tengu	10853 Lindbrook Dr	310-209-0071	$$$$	Hip Asian fare.

Map 21 • Venice

Abbot's Pizza	1407 Abbot Kinney Blvd	310-396-7334	$	Bagel crust pizza.
Amuse Café	796 Main St	310-450-1956	$$	Bright lil' American bistro.

Baja Cantina Restaurant	311 Washington Blvd	310-821-2252 $$	Mexican with seafood specialties and sizeable margaritas.
Beechwood	822 Washington Blvd	310-448-8884 $$$$	Big décor, Amuse Café entrees.
The Brick House	826 Hampton Dr	310-581-1639 $$	Definitely a local hangout. Lunch & breakfast only.
C&O Trattoria	3016 Washington Blvd	310-301-7278 $$	C&O Trattoria's sibling is more diverse but just as filling.
C&O Trattoria	31 Washington Blvd	310-823-9491 $$	Cheap Italian.
Café 50's	838 Lincoln Blvd	310-399-1955 $$*	All-American food without pretense.
Canal Club	2025 Pacific Ave	310-823-3878 $$$	Chinese-Cuban fusion.
Casablanca	220 Lincoln Blvd	310-392-5751 $$$	Nice evening out, guaranteed.
Figtree's Café	429 Ocean Front Wk	310-392-4937 $$	Great service, take in the ocean view!
Hal's Bar & Grill	1349 Abbot Kinney Blvd	310-396-3105 $$$	Pub food.
Hama Sushi	213 Windward Ave	310-396-8783 $$$$	Hip Japanese.
Jer-ne	4375 Admiralty Wy	323-574-4333 $$$$	The Ritz Carlton's restaurant; amazing views.
Jin Patisserie	1202 Abbot Kinney Blvd	310-399-8801 $	Fabulous pastries and a soothing tea garden.
Joe's	1023 Abbot Kinney Blvd	310-399-5811 $$$$	Nouveau Californian.
Killer Shrimp	523 Washington Blvd	310-578-2293 $$	An exotic option to seafood dining.
La Cabana Restaurant and Bar	738 Rose Ave	310-392-7973 $$	Very festive atmosphere and diverse meeting place.
Rose Café	220 Rose Ave	310-399-0711 $$	Trendy eclectic Californian.
Tony P's Dockside Grill	4445 Admiralty Wy	310-823-4534 $$	Kick-back tavern with a nice breeze.
Wabi-Sabi	1635 Abbot Kinney Blvd	310-314-2229 $$$	Sushi.

Map 22 • Mar Vista

Aunt Kizzy's Back Porch	4325 Glencoe Ave	310-578-1005 $$	Southern comfort food.
Empanada's Place	3811 Sawtelle Blvd	310-391-0888 $*	The name says it all.
Paco's Tacos	4141 Centinela Ave	310-391-9616 $	Cheap Tex-Mex.
Pepy's Galley	12125 Venice Blvd	310-390-0577 $*	Unpretentious bowling alley diner.
Venus of Venice	12034 Venice Blvd	310-391-7674 $	Tex-Mex vegan.

Map 23 • Rancho Park/Palms

Apple Pan	10801 W Pico Blvd	310-475-3585 $*	Hamburger joint.
Bourbon Street Shrimp	10928 W Pico Blvd	310-474-0007 $$	Cajun and seafood.
Delmonico's Seafood Grille	9320 W Pico Blvd	310-550-7737 $$$$	Dependable old school seafood.
Factor's Famous Deli	9420 W Pico Blvd	310-278-9175 $$	A little bit of Brooklyn in West LA, including charmingly rude servers.
Guelaguetza	11127 Palms Blvd	310-837-1153 $$	Authentic Oaxacan dishes.
Gyu-kaku	10925 W Pico Blvd	310-234-8641 $$$	Japanese-style Korean BBQ.
Hop Li	10974 W Pico Blvd	310-441-3708 $$	Cantonese cuisine.
Jack Sprat's	10668 W Pico Blvd	310-837-6662 $$	Healthy.
John O'Groat's	10516 W Pico Blvd	310-204-0692 $$	Breakfast hang-out.
Junior's Deli	2379 Westwood Blvd	310-475-5771 $$	New York diner/deli.
La Serenata Gourmet	10924 W Pico Blvd	310-441-9667 $$$	Mexican with seafood specialties.
Lot 1224	1224 S Beverlywil Dr	310-277-2800 $$$	Inventive hotel dining, locals swear by the Thai fried calamari.
Milky Way	9108 W Pico Blvd	310-859-0004 $$$	Kosher dairy restaurant.
Overland Café	3601 Overland Ave	310-559-9999 $$	Truly a casual California eatery.

Map 24 • Culver City

Bamboo	10835 Venice Blvd	310-287-0668 $$$	Caribbean.
Café Brasil	10831 Venice Blvd	310-837-8957 $$	The fresh-squeezed juices are amazing!
Conservatory for Coffee	10117 Washington Blvd	310-558-0436 $	They roast their own and serve it up graciously.
In-N-Out Burger	9245 W Venice Blvd	800-786-1000 $*	Top California burger joint.
Johnnie's Pastrami	4017 Sepulveda Blvd	310-397-6654 $*	The best dang dip in town.
Natalee Thai	10101 Venice Blvd	310-202-7003 $$	Popular Pad Thai and curries.
Petrelli's Steakhouse	5615 S Sepulveda Blvd	310-397-1438 $$$	Meat and potato lovers' paradise.
S&W Country Diner	9748 Washington Blvd	310-204-5136 $*	Yee-haw! Breakfast's on.
Tito's Tacos	11222 Washington Pl	310-391-5780 $*	Cheap taco stand.
Versailles	10319 Venice Blvd	310-558-3168 $	Cuban fusion.

Map 25 • Marina Del Rey/Westchester West

Alejo's	4002 Lincoln Blvd	310-822-0095 $$	Italian for bargain hunters.
Alejo's	8343 Lincoln Blvd	310-670-6677 $$	Classic cheap Italian.
Antica Pizzeria	13455 Maxella Ave	310-577-8182 $$	Classic Neapolitan pizzas and pastas.
Ballona Fish Market	13455 Maxella Ave	310-822-8979 $$$	Hans Rockenwagner does fish.
Café Del Rey	4451 Admiralty Wy	310-823-6395 $$$$	Eclectic seafood.
Caffe Pinguini	6935 Pacific Ave	310-306-0117 $$$	Italian on the beach.
Casa Escobar	14160 Palawan Wy	310-822-2199 $$	Great quesadillas and chimichangas!
Chan Dara	13490 Maxella Ave	310-301-1004 $$	Trendy Thai.
Chloe	333 Culver Blvd	310-305-4505 $$$$	Yummy New American with evolving menu.
Shanghai Red's	13813 Fiji Wy	310-823-4522 $$$	Lovely Victorian-style restaurant; incredible brunch.
The Shack	185 Culver Blvd	310-823-6222 $$	Cheap burgers and more.
The Warehouse	4499 Admiralty Wy	310-823-5451 $$$	Romantic enough to ask someone to marry you.

Key: $: Under $10 / $$: $10–$20 / $$$: $20–$30 / $$$$: $30+; * : Does not accept credit cards / † : Accepts only American Express.

Map 26 · Westchester/Fox Hills/Ladera Heights/LAX

Buggy Whip	7420 La Tijera Blvd	310-645-7131	$$$$	Go for the piano bar more than the food.
Encounter	209 World Wy	310-215-5151	$$$	Pre-flight futuristic meals.
In-N-Out Burger	9149 S Sepulveda Blvd	800-786-1000	$*	Top California burger joint.
Paco's Tacos	6212 W Manchester Ave	310-645-8692	$	Inexpensive Tex-Mex.
Panera Bread	8647 S Sepulveda Blvd	310-641-9200	$	Excellent soup, coffee, sandwiches and pastries.

Map 27 · El Segundo/Manhattan Beach

Cozymel's	2171 Rosecrans Ave	310-606-5464	$$	Tex-Mex.
Good Stuff	1300 Highland Ave	310-545-4775	$$	California favorites and all around good stuff.
Houston's	1550 Rosecrans Ave	310-643-7211	$$$	Casual, upscale American favorites.
Il Fornaio	1800 Rosecrans Ave	310-725-9555	$$$	Tuscan chain.
Local Yolk	3414 Highland Ave	310-546-4407	$	Get breakfast here after you drop Aunt Mira off at the airport.
Michi Restaurant & Bar	903 Manhattan Ave	310-376-0613	$$$$	Martinis + sushi happy hour from 5:30-7pm.
North End Café	3421 Highland Ave	310-546-4782	$*	Sandwiches, salads, and fries with four dipping sauces.
Rock'n Fish	120 Manhattan Beach Blvd	310-379-9900	$$	Always packed. Lunch and dinner from the sea.
The Spot	110 2nd St	310-376-2355	$$*	Vegetarian specialties.
Towne	1142 Manhattan Ave	310-545-5405	$$$	Upscale surf & turf.
Uncle Bill's Pancake House	1305 Highland Ave	310-545-5177	$$	Breakfast by the beach.

Map 28 · Hawthorne

Daphne's	3901 Inglewood Ave	310-676-9165	$	Excellent Baklava!
El Pollo Inka	15400 Hawthorne Blvd	310-676-6665	$$	Chicken fit for Virococha.
Guru Palace	4850 W Rosecrans Ave	310-675-5533	$$	Good vegetarian choices and great Naan!
In-N-Out Burger	3801 Inglewood Ave	800-786-1000	$*	Top California burger joint.
Piggies	4601 W Rosecrans Ave	310-679-6326	$*	Older style Greek coffee shop.

Map 29 · Hermosa Beach/Redondo Beach North

Back on the Beach	445 Pacific Coast Hwy	310-393-8282	$$	California food, California beach, California experience.
Blue Pacific Restaurant	201 Hermosa Ave	310-406-8986	$$	Japanese. Elegant. Sushi. Patio dining.
Buona Vita	439 Pier Ave	310-379-7626	$$	Best Italian in town. BYO vino.
Crème de la Crepe	424 Pier Ave	310-937-2822	$$	Savory or sweet. How do you say yum in French?
El Burrito Jr	919 Pacific Coast Hwy	310-316-5058	$*	Always a line outside this amazingly authentic Mexican food stand.
Fritto Misto	316 Pier Ave	310-318-6098	$$	Create your own pasta combo or choose a house special.
Havana Mania	3615 Inglewood Ave	310-725-9075	$$	Cuban cuisine at its finest!
Hennessey's Tavern	8 Pier Ave	310-372-5759	$$	Californian favorites.
Il Boccaccio	39 Pier Ave	310-376-0211	$$$$	Authentic Italian.
Le Beaujolais	522 Pacific Coast Hwy	310-543-5100	$$$	Quality French food served with a very French attitude to boot.
Martha's 22nd Street Grill	25 22nd St	301-376-7786	$$	American fusion.
Mediterraneo	73 Pier Ave	310-318-2666	$$	Try tapas on the patio.
Paisano's	1132 Hermosa Ave	310-376-9883	$	Pizza straight from New York.
Ragin' Cajun Café	422 Pier Ave	310-376-7878	$$	Blackened catfish is a favorite.

Map 30 · Torrance North

Flossie's Restaurant	3566 W Redondo Beach Blvd	310-352-4037	$*	The fried chicken is legendary.

Map 31 · Redondo Beach

The Banyan Water Garden Café	600 S Pacific Coast Hwy	310-316-0316	$$	Authentic Indonesian cuisine without having to board a plane!
Bluewater Grill	665 N Harbor Dr	310-318-3474	$$$	Fresh fish and seafood specialties.
The Bull Pen	314 Ave I	310-375-7797	$$	Good old-school steak joint.
Captain Kidd's	209 N Harbor Dr	310-372-7703	$$	Seafood dinners run from $7.99 to $22 for a whole lobster!
Catalina Coffee Company	126 N Catalina Ave	310-318-2499	$	Homier than Starbucks. Breakfast, sandwiches, and, of course, coffee.
Chez Melange	1716 S Pacific Coast Hwy	310-540-1222	$$$$	Foodies from all over L.A. flock to the eclectic, continental menu.
Christine	24530 Hawthorne Blvd	310-373-1952	$$$$	Eclectic California-Mediterranean food.
Collet Tea	320 S Catalina Ave	310-372-0348	$$	Not-so-traditional English tea: feather boa provided.
El Torito Grill	21321 Hawthorne Blvd	310-543-1896	$$	Good food, better margaritas.
Gina Lee's Bistro	211 Palos Verdes Blvd	310-375-4462	$$*	Neighborhood Cal-Asian bistro food.
Hennessey's Tavern	1712 S Catalina Ave	310-540-8443	$	Bar food at its finest, a great place to watch the game and drink hearty.
HT Grill	1710 S Catalina Ave	310-316-6658	$$	Innovative, eclectic bistro food at reasonable prices.
The Original Pancake House	1756 S Pacific Coast Hwy	310-543-9875	$*	Line up with the weekend breakfast crowd.

Riviera Mexican Grill	1615 S Pacific Coast Hwy	310-540-2501 $$	Casual; yummy quesadillas.
Splash	300 N Harbor Dr	310-798-5348 $$$	Mediterrean bistro.
Zazou	1810 S Catalina Ave	310-540-4884 $$$$	Mediterranian-Italian fusion.

Map 32 • Torrance South

Aioli	1261 Cabrillo Ave	310-320-9200 $$$	Bistro features eclectic global dishes and tapas.
Beijing Islamic	3160 Pacific Coast Hwy	310-784-0846 $$	Delicious, quality Chinese food at bargain prices.
Breadstix	1261 Cabrillo Ave	310-320-9500 $	Fresh-baked breads, excellent sandwiches, salads, and other goodies.
Depot	1250 Cabrillo Ave	310-787-7501 $$$$	Broad range of chef Michael Shafer's culinary creations.
In-N-Out Burger	24445 Crenshaw Blvd	800-786-1000 $*	Top California burger joint.
Koji BBQ Buffet	1725 W Carson St	310-787-1820 $$	Cook your own Korean-style BBQ, over 100 menu items.
Mishima	21605 S Western Ave	310-320-2089 $$	Noodle paradise.

Map 33 • Eagle Rock/Highland Park

Auntie Em's Kitchen	4616 Eagle Rock Blvd	323-255-0800 $	Homemade, unique goodness.
Blue Hen Vietnamese Kitchen	1743 Colorado Blvd	323-982-9900 $$	Family recipes with an organic update.
Café Beaujolais	1712 Colorado Blvd	323-255-5111 $$	Delicious French romanticism, but for dinner only.
Capri Restaurant	4604 Eagle Rock Blvd	323-257-3225 $	Twin Italian bros serve up a warm neighborhood spot.
Casa Bianca	1650 Colorado Blvd	323-256-9617 $$*	Legendary pizza with atmosphere to spare.
Classic Thai Restaurant	1708 Colorado Blvd	323-478-0530 $	Bustling Thai with a home-y feel.
The Coffee Table	1958 Colorado Blvd	323-810-2898 $	Spacious and satisfying bistro, bearable even on Sundays.
Colombo's	1833 Colorado Blvd	323-254-9138 $$	Incredible Continental cuisine at reasonable prices.
Dante's BBQ Chicken & Ribs	2004 Colorado Blvd	323-257-4742 $$	Name says it all, hot as the Inferno.
Eagle Rock Italian Bakery & Deli	1726 Colorado Blvd	323-255-8224 $	Famous rum cake and amazing deli sandwiches.
El Arco Iris	5684 York Blvd	323-254-3401 $	Mexican.
El Huarache Azteca	5225 York Blvd	323-478-9572 $*	The best tacos, huaraches, tortas, and sopes in town.
Fatty's & Co	1627 Colorado Blvd	323-254-8804 $*	Eat a "Fat Elvis" for breakfast.
Original Tommy's	1717 Colorado Blvd	323-982-1746 $	The chain's legendary chili burgers offer gassy goodness.
Pete's Blue Chip	1701 Colorado Blvd	323-478-9022 $*	Greasy burgers and everything else.
Señor Fish	4803 Eagle Rock Blvd	323-257-7167 $	Amazing fish tacos and other hot stuff.
Sicha Siam	4403 Eagle Rock Blvd	323-344-8285 $$	Thai.
Villa Sombrero	6101 York Blvd	323-256-9784 $$	Mexican.

Map 34 • Pasadena

Akbar	44 N Fair Oaks Ave	626-577-9916 $$$	Creative Indian cooking.
Arroyo Chop House	536 S Arroyo Pkwy	626-577-7463 $$$$	Take your father for steaks.
Bar Celona	46 E Colorado Blvd	626-405-1000 $$	Tapas by the plate and hipsters by the glass.
Burger Continental	535 S Lake Ave	626-792-6634 $$	Burgers and more.
Café Atlantic	53 E Union St	626-796-7350 $$	Inexpensive and mouthwatering Cuban.
Café Bizou	91 N Raymond Ave	626-792-9923 $$$	BYOB French bistro.
Café Santorini	64 W Union St	626-564-4200 $$$	Mediterranean magic on the rooftop terrace.
Celestino	141 S Lake Ave	626-795-4006 $$$$	Italian.
De Lacey's Club 41	41 S De Lacey Ave	626-795-4141 $$$	For carnivores and cocktail connoisseurs.
Five Sixty-One	561 E Green St	626-405-1561 $$$	Culinary Arts students show off their stuff.
Gordon Biersch	41 Hugus Aly	626-449-0052 $$$	Basic American brewpub.
Hop Li	526 Alpine St	213-680-3939 $$	Inexpensive Chinese.
Julienne	2649 Mission St	626-441-2299 $$	Californian/French/bistro.
Maison Akira	713 E Green St	626-796-9501 $$$$	Light, French-Japanese cooking.
Marston's	151 E Walnut St	626-796-2459 $$	Awesome breakfasts and traditional American dinners.
Parkway Grill	510 S Arroyo Pkwy	626-795-1001 $$$$	Pasadena's perennial upscale favorite; live music in the bar.
Pho 79	29 S Garfield Ave	626-289-0239 $*	Cheap Vietnamese noodle shop.
Pie 'N Burger	913 E California Blvd	626-795-1123 $*	Juicy burgers, homey pies.
Radhika's	140 Shoppers Ln	626-744-0994 $$$	Tikka Masala and live jazz.
Roscoe's House of Chicken n' Waffles	830 N Lake Ave	626-791-4890 $$	Cheap Southern chain.
Shiro	1505 Mission St	626-799-4774 $$$$	Low-key interior, sublime fusion cuisine.
The Raymond	1250 S Fair Oaks Ave	626-441-3136 $$$$	Romantic, special occasion dining.
Twin Palms	101 W Green St	626-577-2567 $$$$	Hip, casual Californian.
Xiomara	69 N Raymond Ave	626-796-2520 $$$	Cuban continental, killer mojitos.
Yujean Kang's	67 N Raymond Ave	626-585-0855 $$$$	Chinese fusion.

Map 35 • Pasadena East/San Marino

Bistro 45	45 S Mentor Ave	626-795-2478 $$$$	High-end gourmet food and wine.
Europane	950 E Colorado Blvd	626-577-1828 $	Sophisticated pastries for subtle palates.
Halie	1030 E Green St	626-440-7067 $$$$	Reasonably priced gourmet California-French food.

Arts & Entertainment • **Restaurants**

Key: $: Under $10 / $$: $10–$20 / $$$: $20–$30 / $$$$: $30+; * : Does not accept credit cards / † : Accepts only American Express.

Map 35 • Pasadena East/San Marino—continued

In-N-Out Burger	2114 E Foothill Blvd	800-786-1000	$*	Top California burger joint.
Sushi Bar Yoshida	2026 Huntington Dr	626-281-9292	$$$	San Marino's only place for raw fish and dim sum.
Zankou Chicken	1415 E Colorado Blvd	818-244-1937	$*	Cheap Armenian chain.

Map 36 • Mt Washington

Chico's	100 N Ave 50	323-254-2445	$	Mexican seafood.
La Abeja	3700 N Figueroa St	323-221-0474	$*	Mexican.

Map 38 • El Sereno

Tamale Man	3320 N Eastern Ave	323-221-5954	$*	From sweet to savory, this man knows tamales.
Taqueria Gudalupana	3100 N Eastern Blvd	323-441-1036	$*	East LA does carne asada right.

Map 39 • Alhambra

Angelo's Italian Restaurant	1540 W Valley Blvd	626-282-0153	$$	Pizza worth the wait.
Charlie's Trio Café	47 W Main St	626-284-4943	$$	Solid Italian.
Cuban Bistro	28 W Main St	626-308-3350	$$$	Cuban comfort food and unorthodox cocktails that would make Fidel want to defect.
Del Taco	1410 S Atlantic Blvd	626-282-2891	$$	Our favorite taco joint in the area.
El Ranchero Restaurant	511 S Garfield Ave	626-281-3452	$	Mexican flavors in a friendly neighborhood setting.
Hiro Sushi Restaurant	120 S Monterey St	626-282-3557	$$	Good value sushi.
Indo Kitchen	5 N 4th St	626-282-1676	$$	Padang-style cooking.
Little London Fish & Chips	19 S Garfield Ave	626-282-4477	$	Eat fish and chips like the Brits.
Mahan Indian Restaurant	2 S Garfield Ave	626-458-6299	$$	Friendly family Indian.
Mission 261	261 S Mission Dr	626-588-1666	$	Chinese fare from dim sum to dinner served in Spanish mission-style former city hall.
MPV Seafood	1412 S Garfield Ave	626-289-3018	$$*	Seafood with an Asian twist.
OK Cafe	301 E Valley Blvd	626-282-8899	$$	The name says it all—the American/Asian food is just OK.
Perfectly Sweet	126 W Main St	626-282-9400	$*	Decadent and deadly desserts.
Pho 79	29 S Garfield Ave	626-289-0239	$	Go for the noodle soup and dessert drinks.
Rick's Drive In & Out	132 W Main St	626-576-8519	$	Fast food at its best.
Fosselman's Ice Cream Parlor	1824 W Main St	626-282-6533	$*	Treats and novelties.
Sam Woo Barbeque	514 W Valley Blvd	626-281-0038	$	Chinese fast food.
Señor Fish	115 W Main St	626-299-7550	$$	Eat Mexican seafood with Caltech students.
The Hat	1 W Valley Blvd	626-282-0140	$	Best burgers for miles.
Yazmin Malaysian Restaurant	27 E Main St	626-308-2036	$$	Go for the curry.
Wahib's Middle East	910 E Main St	626-576-1048	$$	Very traditional Middle Eastern cooking.

Map 40 • Boyle Heights

Barbara's at the Brewery	Brewery Art Complex, 620 Moulton Ave	323-221-9204	$$	Bar food and drinks for the art crowd.
Ciro's	705 N Evergreen St	323-267-8637	$	Family fave for flautas.
El Tepeyac	812 N Evergreen Ave	323-267-8668	$$*	Famous hole-in-the-wall Mexican.
La Parrilla	2126 E Cesar E Chavez Ave	323-262-3434	$$	Better than average Mexican chain.
La Serenata de Garibaldi	1842 E 1st St	323-265-2887	$$	Creative Mexican seafood.
Taqueria Guadalupana	1000 N Soto St	323-441-1036	$*	East LA does carne asada right.

Map 41 • City Terrace/East LA

Juanito's	4214 E Floral Dr	323-268-2365	$	Tender tamales by the dozen.
Tamales Lilianas	4619 E Cesar E Chavez Ave	323-780-7265	$*	The most famous tamales in LA.
Tamayo	5300 E Olympic Blvd	323-260-4700	$$	Mexican.

Map 44 • Mission Hills/North Hills

In-N-Out Burger	9858 Balboa Blvd	800-786-1000	$*	Top California burger joint.

Map 45 • Canoga Park/Woodland Hills

In-N-Out Burger	19902 Ventura Blvd	800-786-1000	$*	Top California burger joint.

Map 46 • Reseda

Amber's Chicken Kitchen	16900 Burbank Blvd	818-995-3200	$$	Chicken! Donuts and bagels for breakfast.
Melody's Mexican Kitchen	6747 Reseda Blvd	818-609-9062	$$*	Great Mexican in a casual, artsy atmosphere.

Map 47 • Van Nuys

Dr Hogly Wogly's BBQ	8136 Sepulveda Blvd	818-780-6701	$$	Texas BBQ.

In-N-Out Burger	7930 Van Nuys Blvd	800-786-1000	$*	Top California burger joint.
Krispy Kreme	7249 Van Nuys Blvd	818-908-9113	$	Hot donut chain.
Sam Woo Barbeque	6450 Sepulveda Blvd	818-988-6813	$*	Peking duck to go or stay, Chinatown-style.
Zankou Chicken	5658 Sepulveda Blvd	818-781-0615	$*	Palm-licking, Beck-serenaded chicken.

Map 48 • North Hollywood

In-N-Out Burger	5864 Lankershim Blvd	800-786-1000	$*	Top California burger joint.

Map 49 • Burbank

Buchanan Arms	2013 W Burbank Blvd	818-845-0692	$$	Sample British eats seated 'neath a portrait of the Queen.
Chili John's	2108 Burbank Blvd	818-846-3611	$*	Best chili this side of the Mississippi.
Coral Café	3321 W Burbank Blvd	818-566-9725	$	Burbank landmark serves breakfast 24/7, along with wholesome American favorites.
Full of Life	2515 Magnolia Blvd	818-845-7411	$	Health food store/restaurant.
Le Petit Chateau	4615 Lankershim Blvd	818-769-1812	$$$	Romantic little French bistro.
Mucho Mas	10405 Burbank Blvd	818-980-0300	$	Mexican standards on the patio or in a cozy cavern.
Pinocchio's	3103 Magnolia Blvd	818-845-3517	$	Super cheap, great Italian deli.
Poquito Mas	10651 Magnolia Blvd	818-994-8226	$	Cheap, fresh Mexican chain.
Santa Fe Tacos	353 N Pass Ave	818-563-4324	$	Great cheap Mexican.
Tony's Bella Vista	3116 W Magnolia Blvd	818-843-0164	$	Italian standards in a friendly, straw-covered-Chianti-bottle setting.

Map 50 • Burbank East/Glendale West

Gordon Biersch Brewing	145 S San Fernando Blvd	818-569-5240	$$$	Basic American brewpub.
Harry's Family Restaurant	920 N San Fernando Blvd	818-842-8755	$	American diner fare; open 24/7.
In-N-Out Burger	761 1st St	800-786-1000	$*	Top California burger joint.
Knight Restaurant	138 N San Fernando Blvd	818-845-4516	$	Savory Greek & Mediterranean dishes.
Market City Caffe	164 E Palm Ave	818-840-7036	$$	Inexpensive Italian chain.
Mi Piace	801 N San Fernando Blvd	818-843-1111	$$$	Italian chain with outdoor tables.
Picanha Churrascaria	269 E Palm Ave	818-972-2111	$$	Tasty Brazilian all-you-can-eat meat-on-a-stick.
Poquito Mas	2635 W Olive Ave	818-563-2252	$	Cheap, fresh, Mexican chain.
Ribs USA	2711 W Olive Ave	818-841-8872	$$	Cheap casual BBQ.
Riverside Café	1221 W Riverside Dr	818-563-3567	$$*	Casual dining with a British flair.
Romano's Macaroni Grill	102 E Magnolia Blvd	818-729-9405	$$	Standard Italian food and drink and plenty of it.
Viva Fresh	900 W Riverside Dr	818-845-2425	$$	Mexican restaurant/lounge.

Map 51 • Glendale South

Carousel	304 N Brand Blvd	818-246-7775	$$$	Delicious Armenian food, BYO liquor.
Cinnabar	933 S Brand Blvd	818-551-1155	$$$$	Pacific rim cuisine in an industrial setting.
Damon's Steakhouse	317 N Brand Blvd	818-507-1510	$$	Lots of red meat and cheesy tropical drinks.
Eat Well	1013 S Brand Blvd	818-243-5928	$	Comfort food, great breakfasts.
Ichiban	120 S Brand Blvd	818-242-9966	$$	Affordable, fresh sushi.
Max's of Manila	313 W Broadway	818-637-7751	$	Famous Filipino fried chicken.
Porto's Bakery & Café	315 N Brand Blvd	818-956-5996	$*	To-die-for Cuban pastries and cakes.
Seoul Grindz	136 S Brand Blvd	818-637-8566	$$	Korean/Hawaiian BBQ and yummy boba drinks.

Map 53 • Encino

Bagel Nosh Deli & Restaurant	17271 Ventura Blvd	818-995-4545	$	Bagels, sandwiches, salads, hamburgers.
Baklava Factory	17145 Ventura Blvd	818-728-1600	$	European and Eastern pastries.
Buca di Beppo	17500 Ventura Blvd	818-995-3288	$$	Lively, traditional Italian chain, dinner only.
California Wok	16656 Ventura Blvd	818-386-0561	$$	Healthy Chinese food.
Catch 21	17316 Ventura Blvd	818-789-3474	$	Seafood, chicken, ribs, salads.
Cha Cha Cha Encino	17499 Ventura Blvd	818-789-3600	$$$	Caribbean party atmosphere.
Chili My Soul	4928 Balboa Blvd	818-981-7685	$	Chili.
Jerry's Famous Deli	16650 Ventura Blvd	818-906-1800	$$	Everything from pizza to salads, Mexican to Jewish food.
Jerusalem Pizza	17942 Ventura Blvd	818-758-9595	$	Pizza!
Johnny Rockets	16901 Ventura Blvd	818-981-5900	$$	'50s-style family diner.
Kaiten Sushi	17302 Ventura Blvd	818-986-7003	$	Sushi.
More Than Waffles	17200 Ventura Blvd	818-789-5937	$	They don't lie: Belgian waffles and more.
Mulberry Street Pizzeria	17040 Ventura Blvd	818-906-8881	$$	Thin-crust NY-style pizza.
Versailles	17410 Ventura Blvd	818-906-0756	$$	Cuban food.
Vittorio's Italian Cucina	17644 Ventura Blvd	818-986-9074	$$	Pasta, chicken, seafood.

Map 54 • Sherman Oaks West

California Chicken Café	15601 Ventura Blvd	818-789-8056	$	Cheap, fresh, chicken in every way.
Delmonico's Lobster House	16358 Ventura Blvd	818-986-0777	$$$$	Upscale seafood.
Fuddrucker's	15301 Ventura Blvd	818-995-4552	$$	Build your own burger joint.
Rubin's Red Hots	15322 Ventura Blvd	818-905-6515	$	Best Chicago style franks around. Classic hot dog stand.

Key: $: Under $10 / $$: $10–$20 / $$$: $20–$30 / $$$$: $30+; * : Does not accept credit cards / † : Accepts only American Express.

Map 55 · Sherman Oaks East

Bistro Garden at Coldwater	12950 Ventura Blvd	818-501-0202	$$$$	Longtime Studio City favorite. Take your parents!
Café Bizou	14016 Ventura Blvd	818-788-3536	$$$	Popular French bistro.
Carnival Restaurant	4356 Woodman Ave	818-784-3469	$$	Lebanese Food.
Casa Vega	13301 Ventura Blvd	818-788-4868	$$	Very popular restaurant and bar. Good food, even better margaritas.
The Great Greek	13362 Ventura Blvd	818-905-5250	$$$	Lively, fun Greek.
Hugo's	12851 Riverside Dr	818-761-8985	$$	Neighborhood restaurant and tea house, good food.
In-N-Out Burger	4444 Van Nuys Blvd	800-786-1000	$*	Top California burger joint.
Iroha	12953 Ventura Blvd	818-990-9559	$$$$	Great sushi and ambience.
Jinky's	14120 Ventura Blvd	818-981-2250	$$	Neighborhood diner known for breakfast.
Le Chine Wok	2958 Beverly Glen Cir	310-475-1146	$$	Fancy Chinese.
Le Petit Bistro	13360 Ventura Blvd	818-501-7999	$$$$	Busy French bistro.
Maria's Italian Kitchen	13353 Ventura Blvd	818-906-0783	$$	Casual family Italian.
Max	13355 Ventura Blvd	818-784-2915	$$$$	Eclectic California bistro menu.
Mazzarino's	12920 1/2 Riverside Dr	818-788-5050	$$	Southern Italian pizza and more.
Mistral Brasserie	13422 Ventura Blvd	818-981-6650	$$$$	French bistro with cozy atmosphere.
Mulholland Grill	2932 Beverly Glen Cir	310-470-6223	$$$	Neighborhood Northern Italian.
Pinot Bistro	12969 Ventura Blvd	818-990-0500	$$$$	Creative California-French bistro.
Rive Gauche	14106 Ventura Blvd	818-990-3573	$$$$	French bistro with courtyard setting.
Stanley's	13817 Ventura Blvd	818-986-4623	$$	Excellent salads, casual neighborhood restaurant and bar.

Map 56 · Studio City/Valley Village

Art's Deli	12224 Ventura Blvd	818-762-1221	$$	New York-style deli.
Caioti	4346 Tujunga Ave	818-761-3588	$$	Trendy, creative Italian.
Dupar's	12036 Ventura Blvd	818-766-4437	$$	Cheap breakfast joint.
Eclectic Café	5156 Lankershim Blvd	818-760-2233	$$	California cuisine and art—it's in the name.
Ernie's Taco House	4410 Lankershim Blvd	818-985-4654	$*	Legendary, old-school Mexican eats and drinks, for 50+ years.
Firefly	11720 Ventura Blvd	818-762-1833	$$$$	Gourmet French bistro with a cozy, clubby atmosphere.
Good Earth Restaurant & Bakery	12345 Ventura Blvd	818-506-7400	$	Healthy meals served against a backdrop of soothing fountains.
Katsu-ya	11680 Ventura Blvd	818-985-6976	$$$$	Great Sushi; gets crowded on weekends. Try the baked crab roll in soy paper.
Killer Shrimp	4000 Colfax Ave	818-508-1570	$$	Inexpensive shrimp only.
La Loggia	11814 Ventura Blvd	818-985-9222	$$$$	Homestyle Italian.
Lala's Argentine Grill	11935 Ventura Blvd	818-623-4477	$$$	Empanadas, chorizo, steak, and more. Trendy casual.
Matsuda	11837 Ventura Blvd	818-760-3917	$$$	Yet another decent mini-mall sushi experience.
Mexicali	12161 Ventura Blvd	818-985-1744	$$	Lively California-Mexican.
Noosh Deli	5118 Lankershim Blvd	818-769-1844	$*	Satisfying, inexpensive Mediterranean fare.
Panera Bread	12131 Ventura Blvd	818-762-2226	$*	Freshly baked bread and tasty sandwiches; laptop-friendly.
Pit Fire Pizza	5211 Lankershim Blvd	818-980-2949	$$	Trendy, crowded California-style pizza establishment. Great patio.
Salomi	5225 Lankershim Blvd	818-506-0130	$$	Vegetarian-Indian cuisine with heat that's not for wimps.
Sitton's North Hollywood Diner	11329 Magnolia Blvd	818-761-3341	$	Basic American diner fare; open all night.
Sushi Dan Rockin' Sushi	11056 Ventura Blvd	818-985-2254	$$	Excellent Sushi on a budget. Fun atmosphere
Sushi Nozawa	11288 Ventura Blvd	818-508-7017	$$$$	Extreme sushi storefront.
Suzanne's Country Deli	11273 Ventura Blvd	818-762-9494	$	Great salads and sandwiches—bright and cheery.
Teru Sushi	11940 Ventura Blvd	818-763-6201	$$$$	Basic—but delicious—sushi.
Todai	11239 Ventura Blvd #2	818-762-8311	$$$	All-u-can-eat sushi. Japanese & Asian. Great value.
Tokyo Delve's Sushi Bar	5239 Lankershim Blvd	818-766-3868	$$$$	Sushi.
Vitello's	4349 Tujunga Ave	818-769-0905	$$	Robert Blake's favorite Italian.
Wine Bistro	11915 Ventura Blvd	818-766-6233	$$$	Romantic, traditional menu.

Map 57 · Universal City/Toluca Lake

Bacco Trattoria	3821 Riverside Dr	818-845-8036	$$	Italian trattoria, wine bar, and marketplace.
Barsac Brasserie	4212 Lankershim Blvd	818-760-7081	$$$$	French-Californian.
Buca di Beppo	1000 Universal Studios Blvd	818-509-9463	$$	Lively traditional Italian chain, dinner only.
Ca' del Sole	4100 Cahuenga Blvd	818-985-4669	$$$$	Italian with garden tables.
California Canteen	3311 Cahuenga Blvd	323-876-1702	$$	French.
Chez Nous	10550 Riverside Dr	818-760-0288	$$$	Big salads, pizza, eggs benedict, and nightly music too.
Dalt's Grill	3500 W Olive Ave	818-953-7750	$	American favorites.
Mardi Gras	10151 Riverside Dr	818-761-4243	$$	N'awlins fare served in a festive atmosphere.
Miceli's	3655 Cahuenga Blvd	323-851-3345	$$	Lively, fun Italian known for its singing waiters.
Mo's	4301 Riverside Dr	818-845-3009	$$	Hamburger haven.

Paty's	10001 Riverside Dr	818-761-0041	$$	American classics.
Priscilla's Coffee	4150 Riverside Dr	818-843-5707	$	All sorts of coffee.
Prosecco Restaurant	10144 Riverside Dr	818-505-0930	$$$	Northern Italian.
Smoke House Restaurant	4420 W Lakeside Dr	818-845-3731	$$$	Steakhouse.
Steak Joynt	4354 Lankershim Blvd	818-761-9899	$$$	Steak and martinis the old fashioned way.
Taste Buds at the Sports Center	6711 Forest Lawn Blvd	323-874-4006	$$	40-love, dining tennis courtside. Closed weekends.
Versailles	1000 Universal Center Dr	818-505-0093	$$	Cheap Cuban fast-food chain.
Wolfgang Puck Café	1000 Universal Center Dr	818-985-9653	$$	Casual California chic.
Yamakawa	10118 Riverside Dr	818-763-8355	$$	Across the board Japanese.
Zach's Italian Café	10820 Ventura Blvd	818-762-2445	$$	Satisfying Italian, with one of the city's best courtyards.

Long Beach

555 East	555 E Ocean Blvd	562-437-0626	$$$$	High-end steakhouse, extensive wine list.
Alegria	115 Pine Ave	562-436-3388	$$$	Terrific tapas, flamenco music, sangria…ooh la la!
Bono's	4901 E 2nd St	562-434-9501	$$$	That would be Chastity, the owner. Quality over quantity here.
Cha Cha	762 Pacific Ave	562-495-4242	$$	What is "Caribbean fusion"? Pipe down and eatcher jerk chicken.
Christy's	3937 E Broadway	562-433-7133	$$$	Owned by Sonny Bono's eldest daughter; superb Italian cuisine.
Chuck's Coffee Shop	4120 E Ocean Blvd	562-433-9317	$*	Fun breakfast joint. Order the Weasel and greet Chuck himself.
Ego	329 Pacific Ave	562-432-9718	$$	Fresh, delicious Italian.
Enrique's	6120 E Pacific Coast Hwy	562-498-3622	$$	Unrivaled, authentic Mexican food. Prepare to fight over the appetizers.
Gladstone's	330 S Pine Ave	562-432-8588	$$$	Scrumptious fish, lovely waterfront view.
King's Fish House	100 W Broadway	562-432-7463	$$$	Point to your preferred lobster (in tank); extensive fish selection.
L'Opera	101 Pine Ave	562-491-0066	$$$$	Even people born in Italy are impressed with the menu.
La Rizza's	1837 E 7th St	562-599-1080	$	Cheerful gingham curtains, saucy Italian food.
La Traviata	301 Cedar Ave	562-432-8022	$$$$	Diverse entrees, from French-Asian to Italian, each worth tasting.
Long Beach Café	615 E Ocean Blvd	562-436-6037	$$	Hidden amidst office buildings; it's a major find. Big portions.
Madison	102 Pine Ave	562-628-8866	$$$$	Lavish décor, varied menu, unremarkable food.
Malvasia	5316 E 2nd St	562-433-5003	$$	Divine Mediterranean cuisine; sunny, breezy location.
Mum's Restaurant	144 Pine Ave	562-437-7700	$$$$	Watch the chef work (open kitchen); exquisite sushi bar.
Open Sesame	5215 E 2nd St	562-621-1698	$	This Lebanese food will blow your mind, it's that good.
Park Pantry	2104 E Broadway	562-434-0451	$	The original. Meatloaf and octegenarians and honest American food.
Parker's Lighthouse	435 Shoreline Village Dr	562-432-6500	$$$	Great for galas, receptions, and other celebrations.
Sky Room	40 S Locust Ave	562-983-2722	$$$$	Continental.
Uncle Al's Seafood	400 E 1st St	562-436-2553	$$	Fresh fish with Cajun and West African influences.
Utopia	445 E 1st St	562-432-6888	$$$	A cosmopolitan menu; accompanied by jazz music on weekends.
Wasabi Japanese Restaurant	200 Pine Ave	562-901-0300	$$$	Dine or just people-watch; the place is always packed.
Yard House	401 Shoreline Village Dr	562-628-0466	$$$	World's largest selection of draft beer; decent food, too.

San Pedro

6th Street Bistro	354 W 6th St	310-521-8818	$$	Flamenco dancing, first Thursday of every month!
Ante's Restaurant	729 Ante Perkov Wy	310-832-5375	$$	Delicious Croatian food, homey atmosphere.
Beach City Grill	376 W 6th St	310-833-6345	$	Funky and eclectic—the food and the surroundings.
Marcello	470 W 7th St	310-519-7100	$$	Choose this one when you're craving Italian.
Nam's Red Door	2253 S Pacific Ave	310-832-4120	$$	Secret jewel of a Vietnamese restaurant.
Pacific Diner	3821 S Pacific Ave	310-831-5334	$$	The best place for a great breakfast.
Papadakis Taverna	301 W 6th St	310-548-1186	$$$	Greek food, family owned, fun experience.
Ports O' Call Restaurant	Berth 76	310-833-3553	$$	Eat outdoors and take in the view.
Rex's Café	2136 S Pacific Ave		$	Breakfast and lunch only; you can't go wrong with either.
Think Bistro	1420 W 25th St	310-548-4797	$$	Thought: If one Think is good, two are better.
Think Bistro	302 W 5th St	310-519-3662	$$	Continental cuisine, cosy atmosphere.
The Whale and Ale	327 W 7th St	310-832-0363	$$$	Delightful, hugely popular British pub.

Shopping is a major Los Angeles pre-occupation—ranking in the top four along with 1) being waitlisted for a Toyota Prius, 2) weekend box office grosses, and 3) carb-avoidance. Because so many entertainment professionals live and work Los Angeles, retail operates at an accelerated speed and under intense media scrutiny. To that end, a number of monthlies—*In Style*, *Lucky*, and the prosaically named *Shop*—do a good job of covering the latest must-have and must-go in local retail. Consult your newsstand for timely recommendations. Shop on.

Shopping Districts

Los Angeles has wonderful shopping malls, but thankfully that is not a credit card-wielder's only option. In fact, LA has a surprising number of neighborhood shopping drags that feature lively, locally-owned businesses should the whole "United States of Generica" thing be getting you down.

Downtown: Whether you're looking for flowers, textiles, or jewelry, downtown has a district devoted to whatever your pleasure may be (even if the "district" turns out to be only one city block). The LA Fashion District (formerly called the "Garment District") is home to more than Santee Alley's knock-off handbags and shoes. You'll also find a huge assortment of fabrics for fashion or home design, flowers, produce, and housewares. This huge area is located between 6th Street to the north, the 10 Freeway to the south, Main Street to the west, and San Pedro Street to the east.

Melrose Avenue, between Gardner Street and Fairfax, offers clothes, funky tees, this week's jewelry, and more for everyone from the 'tweens to the Harley riders. It is accessibly priced, for the most part, though west of Fairfax, Melrose changes its tune—and price point—making a definite upscale swing.

Larchmont Boulevard, between Beverly and 1st Streets, is Hancock Park's friendly, low-key commercial area. A perfectly delightful place to shop for books, gifts, wine, and women's clothing, it is made all the more pleasant by the number of restaurants offering sidewalk seating. Not to be missed, the Farmers Market on Sundays always draws a crowd.

Similarly inclined, but farther to the west, is **Montana Avenue** in Santa Monica. The blocks between 7th and 17th Streets feature upscale boutiques selling sweaters, chic clothes for men and women, children's apparel, and jewelry.

For an artsy and laid back shopping day, head to **Abbot Kinney** in Venice where fancy furniture stores vie with surf shops and galleries for your attention and your dollar.

Over the hill in **Studio City**, Tujunga Avenue south of Moorpark keeps it real and local; it's another good spot for shoes, gifts, cards, and lazy weekend meals. This district is an altogether more pleasant daytime alternative to the **Beachwood** area of Franklin Avenue in Hollywood, with infinitely easier parking.

Los Feliz Village is the square mile-or-so delineated by Los Feliz Boulevard, Hillhurst Avenue, Vermont Avenue, and Hollywood Boulevard. In recent years, a rash of press excitement turned it from "America's hippest neighborhood" into its most-hyped. The din has died down a bit, though new cafés and boutiques open with stunning regularity. In the meantime, there are still enough family-owned restaurants and beloved local landmarks to keep it grounded.

East on **Sunset Boulevard** from Los Feliz (especially once you've passed Maltman, and head on into Echo Park), a flotilla of furniture stores has begun to form. The options range from proper antiques to vintage to just plain old junk, but prices are still better than what you'd find in similarly-themed venues west of there (for example, La Brea). Like everywhere else in this city and others, neighborhood die-hards wail a lot about gentrification and homogenization (to be fair, the rents are going up), but let's be honest: even with a Starbucks, this is no Montana Avenue.

Clothing

Fred Segal (with stores on Melrose and on Broadway in Santa Monica) is, for many, the *arbiter dicta* of Los Angeles style. Even those who don't wear their high-end threads have to admit that their cosmetics and apothecary departments are exceptional. Paris, Lindsay, Nicole, and other members of the gotta-have-it crowd find what they're looking to wear on 3rd Street between Crescent Heights and La Cienega, on Robertson Boulevard south of Beverly, and on Melrose west of Fairfax. (Over at the mall, **Bloomingdale's** also offers similar labels, low-rises, and boot-cuts for this set.) For a change of pace, check out the stores on Rowena in Silver Lake, on Echo Park Boulevard, and on La Brea (**Jet Rag**, **American Rag**, etc.).

Housewares

Serious home restoration and décor are a way of life in Los Angeles. And as there is not one dominant style in architecture—or interior design—finding stuff that looks like "you" isn't too difficult a task. Finding it at a reasonable price is another matter entirely. Those with big wallets will enjoy their visit to **H.D. Buttercup** at the Helms Bakery. They've got tens of thousands of square feet filled with beautiful furniture and other elegant household items from the kind people who brought you ABC Carpet in New York. **Berbere Imports**, also in the neighborhood, is a one-stop shop for teak furniture, Moroccan lamps, stone Buddhas, and terra cotta urns. On La Brea, between Melrose and Wilshire, are funky yet elegant furniture shops such as **Futurama, Maison Midi**, and **Pom Pom**. The folks at **Liz's Antique Hardware** can locate or recreate any doorknob or hinge you show them. **Koontz Hardware** in West Hollywood has everything from dish towels to chainsaws packed into their Santa Monica Boulevard store. **Eames Office** in Santa Monica carries mid-century modern chairs and more.

Music

The enormous **Amoeba Music** on Sunset and Cahuenga has two floors of every type of music you can imagine—and with twenty clerks working the registers, you can grab the newest Radiohead import and be on your way in no time. Just around the corner is the smaller **Aron's Records**, which has incredible parking lot sales twice a year with 30,000 CDs priced at less than a dollar. **Canterbury Records** in Pasadena and Silver Lake's **Rockaway Records** also offer inspired browsing along the new-used continuum. And let's not forget the excellent retail outlet, **Rhino Records**.

Food

Surfas in West LA has an impressive wholesale stock of imported gourmet food and restaurant supplies that is open to the public (but let's just keep that between us, got it?). Wildly popular and tasty is the French-style take-home deli and catering at **Joan's on Third**. East-siders can roll down the hill to **Picholine** on 1st Street for superb take-out sandwiches and the like. Despite the prevailing low-carb-mania, good cheese can be hard to find. Fortunately, **Say Cheese**, the **Cheese Store of Silver Lake**, and the **Cheese Store of Beverly Hills** carry everything from Abbaye to Humboldt Fog, along with wine and other gourmet foods. For those exalted occasions when Two Buck Chuck simply will not do, **Silverlake Wine** and **Larchmont Village Wines & Spirits** are invaluable resources for good grape. (Speaking of Chuck: For those born yesterday, it is only fair that we mention **Trader Joe's**, a Southern California institution where each and every item on the shelf is handpicked, sampled, and sold at more than reasonable prices because the chain buys in bulk and doesn't rent out their shelf space to manufacturers like other grocery chains.) Last, but certainly not least, is downtown's **Grand Central Market**, located on Broadway near 4th Street, which has been bustling with a diverse crowd ever since they opened in 1917.

Map 1 • Beverly Hills

Anthropologie	320 N Beverly Dr	310-385-7390	Unique, super-feminine clothes and accessories.
Barney's New York	9570 Wilshire Blvd	310-276-4400	Upscale department store.
Cheese Store of Beverly Hills	419 N Beverly Dr	310-278-2855	High quality cheese, even better olives.
Geary's of Beverly Hills	351 N Beverly Dr	310-273-4741	The place for wedding gifts and now wedding rings.
Mrs Beasley's/ Miss Grace Lemon Cake Co	255 1/2 S Beverly Dr	310-276-6516	How most Hollywood assistants' holiday weight is gained.
Prada Epicenter	343 N Rodeo Dr	310-278-8661	The conceptual Rem Koolhaas-designed store.
Saks Fifth Avenue	9600 Wilshire Blvd	310-275-4211	Chi-chi department store.
The Taschen Store	354 N Beverly Dr	310-274-4300	For all your art and fetish needs.

Map 2 • West Hollywood

Aardvark's Odd Ark	7579 Melrose Ave	323-655-6769	Score the pièce de résistance of your vintage Hawaiian shirt collection.
Agent Provocateur	7961 Melrose Ave	323-653-0229	Sexy undies annually contribute to Hollywood's baby boom.
American Apparel	104 N Robertson Blvd	310-274-6292	Simple clothing made sweatshop-free.
American Rag	150 S La Brea Ave	323-935-3154	Trend-setting designer and vintage looks at a price.
Apple Store	189 The Grove Dr	323-965-8400	iParadise for Mac fanatics.
The Bodhi Tree	8585 Melrose Ave	310-659-1733	New-age bookshop and West Hollywood fixture.
Book Soup	8818 Sunset Blvd	310-659-3110	One of LA's coolest bookstores.
Button Store	8344 W 3rd St	323-658-5473	Every button you could possibly need.
Centerfold Newsstand	716 N Fairfax Ave	323-651-4822	A terrific selection of magazines and papers.
Chado Tea Room	8422 1/2 W 3rd St	323-655-2056	Where tea lovers go when they die.
Chateau Marmutt	8128 W 3rd St	323-653-2062	If you love your pet and money is no object.
The Cook's Library	8373 W 3rd St	310-655-3141	Books on food for amateur chefs and professional eaters.
Cost Plus World Market	6333 W 3rd St	323-935-5530	An "everything" superstore.
Denim Doctor	8044 W 3rd St	323-852-0171	They'll sell you vintage jeans or fix ones you've already got.
Doggie Bag	8568 1/2 Melrose Ave	310-855-9990	Great, mostly casual, handbags.
Ethel	8235 1/2 W 3rd St	323-658-8602	Great women's clothing, indie brands.
Flight 001	8235 3rd St	323-966-0001	Luxe luggage tags soothe pre-flight jitters, really.
Fred Segal	8100 Melrose Ave	323-651-4129	The place to shop in LA for trendy clothes and accessories.
Futurama	446 N La Brea Ave	323-937-4522	Get your boomerang couch and chairs here.
Golden Apple	7711 Melrose Ave	323-658-6047	Shangri-la for comic book lovers.
Guitar Center	7425 Sunset Blvd	323-874-1060	Their walk of fame alone is worth the trip.
I Martin	8330 Beverly Blvd	323-653-6900	Catering to riders from serious racers to the training wheels crowd.
Jet Rag	825 N La Brea Ave	323-939-0528	Vintage; Sunday is $1 sale day in the parking lot.
Joan's on Third	8350 W 3rd St	323-655-2285	French-style take-home deli and catering.
Koontz Hardware	8914 Santa Monica Blvd	310-652-0123	If they don't carry it, it probably doesn't exist.
Liz's Antique Hardware	453 S La Brea Ave	323-939-4403	Search for doorknobs, hinges, nuts, and bolts in the overcrowded store.
Maison Midi	148 S La Brea Ave	323-935-3157	Home wares central for the Euro-trash set.
Mani's Bakery	519 S Fairfax Ave	323-938-8800	Desserts so delicious you'll never know they're sweetened with fruit juice.
Marc Jacobs	8400 Melrose Pl	323-653-5100	Marc Jacobs has arrived. Say "hi" to Winona if you see her.
Marc Jacobs Accessories	8401 Melrose Pl	323-653-0100	Marc by Marc Jacobs, two Marcs are better than one!
Mr Marcel's	6333 W 3rd St, Farmers Market	323-935-9451	Gourmet French cheeses and wine bar.
Plastica	8405 W 3rd St	323-655-1051	All things trendy and plastic. So LA.
Pleasure Chest	7733 Santa Monica Blvd	323-650-1022	Popular sex shop with something for everyone, in a discreet setting.
Pulp	452 S La Brea Ave	323-937-3505	For people who still write letters (or wish they did).
Restoration Hardware	131 N La Cienega Blvd	310-360-9651	Simply traditional home goods.
Room Service	8115 3rd St	323-653-4242	It's a mod, mod interior world.
Sam Ash Music	8000 Sunset Blvd	323-654-4922	Like the nearby Guitar Center, but far less intimidating.
Samy's Camera	431 S Fairfax Ave	323-938-4400	The only place to go to for cameras in LA.
Satine	8117 3rd St	323-655-2142	Coveted de$igners: Chloé, Tsumori Chisato, et al.
Solomon's	447 N Fairfax Ave	323-653-9045	Everything from seder plates to menorahs.
Soolip	8646 Melrose Ave	310-360-0545	Cards, wrapping paper, and gifts you'd like to give to yourself.
Splash Bath & Body	8934 Santa Monica Blvd	877-664-7627	Their soaps and bath bombs turn your tub into your own personal spa.
Storyopolis	116 N Robertson Blvd	310-358-2500	You can get lost in here for hours amidst the Dr. Seuss and Maurice Sendak books.
Susina bakery	7122 Beverly Blvd	323-934-7900	Not just a bakery—yummy chocolates, focaccia sandwiches, and beautiful cakes.
Tower Records	8801 W Sunset Blvd	310-657-7300	The store where celebs buy their tunes.
Trashy Lingerie	402 La Cienega Blvd	310-652-4543	Trashy, but they also sell high quality custom-fitted lingerie.
Traveler's Bookcase	8375 W 3rd St	310-665-0575	A must-visit before any trip.
Twentieth	8057 Beverly Blvd	323-904-1200	Modern furnishings and design.
Virgin Megastore	8000 W Sunset Blvd	323-650-8666	Hours of endless music-buying fun—if you can find parking!
Zipper	8316 W 3rd St	323-951-0620	Upscale gifts and funky home furnishings.

Map 3 • Hollywood

Amoeba Music	6400 Sunset Blvd	310-245-6400	Cavernous music store—used CDs, DVDs too.
Aron's Records	1150 N Highland Ave	323-469-4700	Legendary parking lot sales and great staff recommendations.
Cahuenga World News	1652 N Cahuenga Blvd	323-465-4357	If this place doesn't carry it, chances are it's not in circulation.
Conservatory Florist	1900 N Highland Ave	323-851-6290	Gorgeous, minimalist floral creations.
Counterpoint Records and Books	5911 Franklin Ave	323-957-7965	Wide selection of gently used books and music.
Espiritu de Vida	5913 Franklin Ave	323-463-0281	Funky imported jewelry, lotions, candles, and toys. Open late.
Half-Off Clothing	660 N Larchmont Blvd	323-463-6613	Discount designer duds.
Hollywood Hills Beauty Center and Spa	1915 N Highland Ave	323-874-5159	Deceptively large, unassuming spot offers cheap good massages.
Larry Edmunds Cinema and Theater Bookshop	6644 Hollywood Blvd	323-463-3273	Need to find a movie still from the 30's? It's here.
Pom Pom	6819 Melrose Ave	323-938-6286	Rustic dining tables and vintage garden furniture.
Ray the Retoucher	1330 N Highland Ave	323-463-0555	Headshot help.
Vine American Party Store	5969 Melrose Ave	323-467-7124	Decorations and party favors for parties from New Year's to Hanukkah.

Map 4 • Los Feliz

American Apparel	4665 Hollywood Blvd	323-661-1407	Sweatshop-free clothing made in downtown LA.
Atmosphere	1728 N Vermont Blvd	323-666-8420	Co-ed hipster boutique for the fashion forward.
The Bicycle Kitchen	706 N Heliotrope Dr	323-NO-CARRO	Non-profit community bicycle workshop.
Blue Rooster Art Supplies	1718 N Vermont Ave	323-661-9471	Everything for the starving artist, except food.
Camille Hudson	4685 Hollywood Blvd	323-953-0377	Lurvely shoes for the ladies.
Casbah Café	3900 W Sunset Blvd	323-664-7000	Café featuring gifts and home décor stuff a la Marocaine.
Cheese Store of Silver Lake	3926 W Sunset Blvd	323-644-7511	High quality cheese and a great selection of cured meats, olives, and gourmet teas.
Eastside Records	1813 Hillhurst Ave	323-913-7461	Lots of used vinyl, hard-to-find music.
Glory	4659 Hollywood Blvd	323-644-5679	'50s Americana, cycles, and oddities.
Golden Needle Tailoring	2044 Hillhurst Ave	323-666-3365	Excellent spot for major alterations and custom tailoring when you got a few to spend.
Gypsy	3915 W Sunset Blvd	323-660-2556	Ponchos, Che tees, Mexican silver and assorted funkiness.
Half-Off Clothing	1748 N Vermont Ave	323-665-1526	Discount designer duds.
LS	2120 Hillhurst Ave	323-913-1444	One of a kind necklaces, bracelets, and earrings made of eclectic gemstones.
Mishka	3820 W Sunset Blvd	323-664-8778	Clothing, soaps, lookin' good, smellin' fine.
Moss House	1936 Hillhurst Ave		New neighborhood favorite for gifts and home accessories.
Naturemart & Bulk Bin	2080 Hillhurst Ave	323-667-1677	Neighborhood health food store.
Oou	1764 N Vermont Ave	323-665-6263	Pretty things for pretty girls.
Ozzie Dots	4641 Hollywood Blvd	323-663-2867	Vintage clothes, costume rentals, loads o' fun.
Rosetta Stone	1958 Hillhurst Ave	323-913-0369	Interior décor and design services.
Serifos	3814 W Sunset Blvd	323-660-7467	"Gifts for everyone, including yourself." Especially if "yourself" is a Volvo-driving Silverlake mom.
Skylight Books	1818 Vermont Ave	323-660-1175	Neighborhood fave, readings, mags, cat in the window.
Squaresville	1800 N Vermont Ave	323-669-8464	An awesome collection of vintage clothing, including high-end labels like Gucci and Pucci.
Steinberg & Sons	4712 Franklin Ave	323-660-0294	A slice of fashionista a la Nolita in old Los Angeles.
Uncle Jer's	4459 W Sunset Blvd	323-662-6710	They sell everything from funky clothes to incense.
Village Gourmet	1927 Hillhurst Ave	323-660-3803	Cheese, spreads, cornichons, etc, adjacent to Alcove Café.
Wacko	4633 Hollywood Blvd	323-663-0122	Books, tchotchkes, party favors, and obscure tees.
White Trash Charms	1951 Hillhurst Ave	323-666-9585	More charming than trashy, indie clothes n' jewelry.
Y Que Trading Post	1770 Vermont Ave	323-664-0021	Gifts, trinkets, "Free Martha Stewart" t-shirts.
Zoe & Sage	2134 Hillhurst Ave	323-906-1874	Cutie-pie clothes and jewelry and such for local hipsters.

Map 5 • Silver Lake/Echo Park/Atwater

American Apparel	2111 W Sunset Blvd	213-484-6464	Simple clothing made sweatshop-free.
Bittersweet Butterfly	1406 Micheltorena St	323-660-4303	Flowers and lingerie to really butter 'er up.
Edna Harte & Fay	2941 Rowena Blvd	323-661-4070	Gifts, clothes, bags, cards, jewels from "the Queen of Silver Lake."
Grometville	2876 Rowena Ave	323-665-5524	For the baby punk rocker and her hipster mama.
Island LS	3038 Rowena Blvd	323-665-7454	Liza Shtromberg's jewelry, plus ethnic and unusual gifts and clothes.
The Kids Are Alright	2201 W Sunset Blvd	213-413-4104	Designer names for the Eastside set.
Le Pink	1545 Echo Park Ave	213-250-0265	Girly gifts, olde time candy treats.
mini MELT	3151 Los Feliz Blvd	323-668-1212	Cutesy toys, comic books, and Japanese collectibles.
Panty Raid	2378 Glendale Blvd	323-668-1888	Tell your boyfriend/girlfriend about their frequent lingerie sales.
Pot-ted	3158 Los Feliz Blvd	323-665-3801	Tiles, fountains, wrought-iron furniture, enthusiastic advice from "exterior decorators."
Rockaway Records	2395 Glendale Blvd	323-664-3232	5000 square feet of used vinyl and CDs.
Say Cheese	2800 Hyperion Ave	323-665-0545	Great smelly cheese tastings.

Sea Level Records	1716 W Sunset Blvd	213-989-0146	Surprisingly well-stocked indie music shop.
Show Pony	1543 Echo Park Ave	213-482-7676	Hip, handmade clothing, unpretentious.
Silverlake Wine	2395 Glendale Blvd	323-662-9024	Snacks and hors d'oeuvres served with tastings at this convivial wine store.
Video Journeys	2730 Griffith Park Blvd	323-663-5857	Rentals and sales for film lovers, not film snobs.

Map 6 • Miracle Mile/Mid-City

99 Cent Store	6121 Wilshire Blvd	323-939-9991	99 cent cell phone charger or a half gallon of soy milk.
Ace Gallery	5514 Wilshire Blvd	323-935-4411	Established in 1940, this up and down gallery showcases mostly local Los Angeles artists.
Albertson Wedding Chapel	5318 Wilshire Blvd	323-937-4919	Wanna get married NOW? Civil and Catholic services available.
Bang a Drum	1255 S La Brea Ave	800-495-1109	Hand drums, from Native American to Middle Eastern.
City Spa	5325 Pico Blvd	323-933-5954	Body wraps, massages, and steam rooms galore.
Feldmar Watch	9000 W Pico Blvd	310-274-8016	From Timex to Rolex, they've got it all.
Hansen's Cakes	1072 S Fairfax Ave	323-936-4332	Wedding cake central and imaginative birthday creations.
Kitson	115 S Robertson Blvd	310-859-2652	It's the place to shop for the person who has everything.
Marinello Beauty School	6111 Wilshire Blvd	323-938-2005	A full-service beauty school with facials at half the going rate.
Miauhaus	1201 S La Brea Ave	323-933-6150	Art gallery spotlighting emerging and contemporary artists.
Oh My Nappy Hair!	805 S La Brea Ave	323-939-3999	Specializes in braids, locks, and extensions.
Pearl Art and Craft Supplies	1250 S La Cienega Blvd	310-854-4900	Art supplies for everyone from the career artist to the scrapbook hobbyist.
Tom Bergin's	840 S Fairfax Ave	323-936-7151	Guinness and fifty years of paper shamrocks.
Up Health Merchants	6051 San Vicente Blvd	323-935-3020	Vitamins, holistic remedies, and other crunchy stuff.

Map 7 • Hancock Park

Absolute Tickets	144 N Larchmont Blvd	323-957-6699	Tickets to just about everything, if you've got a few bucks to spend.
Center for Yoga	230-1/2 N Larchmont Blvd	323-464-1276	Classes, clothing, books, incense, sticky mats, and deep breaths.
Cottage Antiques	107 N Larchmont Blvd	323-469-6444	Pricey, but lovely old things for home and garden.
Earl Jean	141-1/2 N Larchmont Blvd	323-463-1556	When you must have your hip-hugging, fetish-wash, flares.
Hans Custom Optik	212 N Larchmont Blvd	323-462-5195	Great selection of frames.
Kicks Sole Provider	143 N Larchmont Blvd	323-468-9794	Lots of stylin' sneaks.
Landis Department Store	138 N Larchmont Blvd	323-465-7998	A little bit of EVERYTHING. The stationery department is especially good.
Larchmont Beauty Center	208 N Larchmont Blvd	323-461-0162	Arguably the best beauty supply store in the city.
Larchmont News Stand	230 N Larchmont Blvd		Good selection of newspapers and magazines.
Larchmont Village Wine & Cheese	223 N Larchmont Blvd	323-856-8699	When Two-Buck Chuck just won't do. Amateurs are just as welcome as oenophiles.
Leonidas Belgian Chocolates	201 N Larchmont Blvd	323-860-7966	Fine and finely wrapped cocoa lusciousness.
Picket Fences	214 N Larchmont	323-467-2140	Juicy Couture, Cosa Bella undies, Kaminski hats, cute gifts.

Map 8 • Korea Town

Beautiful Tonight Lingerie	928 S Western Ave	213-736-5844	Make him think you are beautiful tonight.
Picholine	3360 W 1st	213-252-8722	French foodie heaven at a really unlikely intersection. Delicious sandwiches, take-out, gourmet groceries. Superb!

Map 9 • Downtown

7 + Fig at Ernst & Young Plaza	735 S Figueroa St	213-955-7150	Downtown's only real shopping mall.
American Apparel	374 E 2nd St	213-687-0467	Simple clothing made sweatshop-free.
California Market Center	110 E 9th St	213-630-3600	Gift and home accent showrooms, as well as nine restaurants.
Grand Central Market	317 S Broadway	213-625-5006	An LA legend since 1917 with produce, fish, meat, ice cream all under one roof.
LA Flower Market	766 Wall St	213-622-1966	Say it with flowers-cheaply.
MOCA Store	250 S Grand Ave	213-621-1710	Museum store's a haven for design.
Moskatel's	733 San Julian St	213-689-4590	They carry everything you need for a party, except for the guests.
Munky King	441 Gin Ling Wy	213-620-8787	Chinatown art scene + designer action figures.
Santee Alley	midway b/w Santee St & Maple Ave, from 12th St to Olympic Blvd	213-488-1153	The perfect place to find convincing "Kate Spate" or "Prado" handbags.

Map 10 • Baldwin Hills

Bebere Imports	3049 La Cienega Blvd	310-842-3842	Beautiful, old world furniture, textiles, accessories, statuary, lighting from all corners of the Mediterranean.
Graphaids	3030 S La Cienega Blvd	310-204-1212	If you're not an artist, this store will make you wish you were.
Normandie Pate	3022 S Cochran Ave	323-939-5528	A Parisian oasis.

409

Map 14 • Inglewood East/Morningside Park

Costco	3560 W Century Blvd	310-242-2774	Buy it in bulk.

Map 15 • Pacific Palisades

Benton's Sporting Goods	1038 Swarthmore Ave	310-459-8451	Beach clothing and equipment.
Gelson's Market	15424 Sunset Blvd	310-459-4483	Fancy groceries.
Gift Garden Antiques	15266 Antioch St	310-459-4114	Fine gifts.
Ivy Greene for Kids	1020 Swarthmore Ave	310-230-0301	Kids' clothes.
Palisades Playthings	1041 Swarthmore Ave	310-454-8648	Toy store.
The Prince's Table	1051 Swarthmore Ave	310-573-3667	Gifts.
Village Books	1049 Swarthmore Ave	310-454-4063	Books.
Vivian's Boutique	970 Monument St	310-573-1326	Clothing.
Whispers	1013 Swarthmore Ave	310-454-5582	Women's clothing.

Map 16 • Brentwood

Dutton's Brentwood	11975 San Vicente Blvd	310-476-6263	Fantastic collection of books, outdoor reading area.
Falconhead	11911 San Vicente Blvd	310-471-7075	Cowboy's one-stop-boots, buckles, and belts.
PJ London	11661 San Vicente Blvd	310-826-4649	Women's fashions, mostly resale.
Porta Bella	11715 San Vicente Blvd	310-820-2550	Antique wood furniture—armchairs to armoirs.
Terra Cotta	11922 San Vicente Blvd	310-826-7878	Furniture in warm earthen colors.
Whole Foods Market	11737 San Vicente Blvd	310-826-4433	Fresh produce and groceries—Brentwood's hippie corner.

Map 18 • Santa Monica

Acorn Store	1220 5th St	310-451-5845	Unique toy store, handmade dolls and puppets.
Apple Store	1248 3rd St Prom	310-576-1011	iParadise for Mac fanatics.
Continental Shop	1619 Wilshire Blvd	310-453-8655	One stop shopping for everything from AbFab tapes to tea cozies.
Eames Office	2665 Main St	310-396-5991	Who'd think that a desk chair could be fun?
Fred Segal	500 Broadway	310-393-3940	LA institution and celebrity-spotter's paradise. All the fun of the one on Melrose, minus the parking nightmares.
Hear Music	1429 3rd St Prom	310-319-9527	Knowledgable staff that lets you listen before you buy.
Helen's Cycles	2501 Broadway	310-829-1836	Bikes sold by people who know what they're talking about.
Herb King	2305 Main St	310-399-4470	One stop for herbs and homeopathic remedies.
Horizons West	2011 Main St	310-392-1122	Everything for the surf and skate crowd.
Kiehl's	1516 Montana Ave	310-255-0055	No more mail-order. NY-fave beauty products.
Le Sanctuaire	2710 Main St	310-581-8999	Kitchen and dining boutique for Food Network fans.
London Sole	1331 Montana Ave	310-255-0937	Chic but comfortable flat-soled shoes.
Midnight Special Bookstore	1318 3rd St Prom	310-393-2923	Get lost for hours reading about any and everything.
Number One Beauty Supply	1426 Montana Ave	310-394-6968	High-end Montana Ave selection at un-Montana Ave prices.
One Life Natural Foods	3001 Main St	310-392-4501	Produce, groceries, herbs, everything organic.
Palmetto	1034 Montana Ave	310-395-6687	Bath supplies, soap, natural beauty products.
Pump Station	2415 Wilshire Blvd	310-826-5774	Where new mothers turn for helpful advice and swell baby products.
Puzzle Zoo	1413 3rd St Prom	310-393-9201	Toy store caters to the sci-fi geek and child within us all.
Santa Monica Farms	2015 Main St	310-396-4069	Organic produce, groceries, juices, sandwiches to go.
Splash Bath & Body	2823 Main St	310-581-4200	Creatively scented soaps and bath goods that are fun to use.
Step!	1004 Montana Ave	310-899-4409	Luxury and comfort in footware.
Tao Healing Arts Center	2309 Main St	310-396-4877	Learn to give a massage or just have one yourself.
Tiffany & Jax	1244 3rd St Prom	310-260-8656	Here's to tasteful clothes for the ladies who lunch.
Tudor House	1403 2nd St	310-451-4107	British souvenirs and afternoon tea.

Map 19 • West LA/Santa Monica East

Any Occasion Balloons	12009 W Pico Blvd	310-473-9963	Every size balloon, in every shape and color imaginable.
California Map & Travel	3312 Pico Blvd	310-396-6277	Great map warehouse.
Graphaids	12400 Santa Monica Blvd	310-820-0445	They appeal to both serious artists and doodlers.
Hiromi Paper International	Bergamot Station, 2525 Michigan Ave	310-998-0098	Handcrafted paper so gorgeous you won't want to write on it.
McCabe's Guitar Shop	3101 Pico Blvd	310-828-4497	Geared more toward the fledgling Bob Dylan than Eddie Van Halen.
Musicians' Supply Shop	12010 Ohio Ave	310-478-7836	Huge selection of sheet music.
Record Surplus	11609 W Pico Blvd	310-478-4217	No glitz, no pizzazz. For serious music lovers only.
Utrecht Arts Supplies	11677 Santa Monica Blvd	310-478-5775	All manner of stuff for the artsy and the craftsy, and helpful service.

Map 20 • Westwood/Century City

Bristol Farms	1515 Westwood Blvd	310-481-0100	Upscale grocery. Newest and biggest of it's kind.
Cost Plus World Market	10860 Santa Monica Blvd	310-441-5115	An "everything" superstore.
Restoration Hardware	10250 Santa Monica Blvd	310-551-4995	All the beautiful unique furniture you can imagine!
Rhino Records	2028 Westwood Blvd	310-474-8685	Unique new and used record store. Don't miss the parking lot sales.
The Writer's Store	2040 Westwood Blvd	310-441-5151	Seminars, books, and computer software for writing.

Map 21 • Venice

Brick Lane	1132 Abbot Kinney Blvd	310-392-2525	Pricey imported UK duds.

Cabana Joe's	1415 Abbot Kinney Blvd	310-452-2343	Retro home wares.
Daisy Arts	1312 Abbot Kinney Blvd	310-396-8463	Luxurious Italian leather items. Open only occasionally and by appointment.
DNA	411 Rose Ave	310-399-0341	Shhh—this tiny designer outlet is a big secret.
Green House Smoke Shop	1428 Abbot Kinney Blvd	310-450-6420	Tools for those high on life.
Helen's Cycles	2472 Lincoln Blvd	310-306-7843	One of the best bike stores in the area.
Hydro Lab	1140 Abbot Kinney Blvd	310-450-7221	Skater/surfer duds.
Johnny B Wood	1108 Abbot Kinney Blvd	310-709-4189	Vintage and collectible furniture.
Samy's Camera	585 Venice Blvd	310-450-4551	The only place to go to for cameras in LA.
The Starting Line	114 Washington Blvd	310-827-3035	If you are a serious walker or runner, this place is for you. Super-smart staff is very service-oriented. They host free Fun Runs.
Venice Bike & Skate	21 Washington Blvd	310-301-4011	Rentals.
Waraku	1225 Abbot Kinney Blvd	310-452-5300	Specializing in custom sneakers and other cool clothes.

Map 22 • Mar Vista

A Mano Yarn Center	12808 Venice Blvd	310-397-7170	Yarn, classes, conversation, community.
Prebica Coffee	4325 Glencoe Ave	310-823-4446	They mainly supply fine restaurants, but here they can supply you.
The Los Angeles Wine Company	4935 McConnell Ave	310-306-9463	Stemware, gift bag, and wine accessories too.
Vanity Room	13217 Washington Blvd	310-306-3336	Anthropologie-like boutique, but affordable.

Map 23 • Rancho Park/Palms

Adventure 16	11161 Pico Blvd	310-473-4574	Camping supplies that make city slickers want to commune with nature.
Delmarus Lox	9340 W Pico Blvd	310-273-3004	If only LA had a bagel that measured up to their lox.

Map 24 • Culver City

Allied Model Trains	4411 Sepulveda Blvd	310-313-9353	It's so much more than just Lionel.
Civilization	8884 Venice Blvd	310-202-8883	Trendy and offbeat furniture that manages to look homey.
Culver City Home Brewing Supply	4358 1/2 Sepulveda Blvd	310-397-3453	Literally everything you need to brew beer.
Dovetail	8918 Venice Blvd	310-559-9431	Solid pine furniture for every room of your house.
HD Buttercup	3225 Helms Ave	310-558-8900	Interior design mecca in Helms Bakery building.
Last Chance	8712 Washington Blvd	310-287-2333	Discount women's clothing from major brands.
Surfas	8825 National Blvd	310-559-4770	For those who own a restaurant or just wish they did.

Map 27 • El Segundo/Manhattan Beach

Fry's Electronics	3600 Sepulveda Blvd	310-364-3797	Polynesian-themed electronic superstore.
GeoDecor	113 Shelton St	310-322-4043	Fossils. This unusual store is open only by appointment.
Growing Wild	1201 Highland Ave	310-545-4432	Great floral creations.
Magpie	1141 Highland Ave	310-546-5132	Classy, conversation-starting home décor.

Map 29 • Hermosa Beach/Redondo Beach North

Re:Style	138 Pier Ave	310-379-1706	For your more alternative attire.
Splash Bath & Body	132 Pier Ave	310-376-7270	Fizzy bath boms, funky soaps, and rubber duckies.
Star's Antique Market	526 Pier Ave	310-318-2800	Grandma's barn in a beach town.
Yak & Yeti	116 Pier Ave	310-406-2890	Boho chic.

Map 31 • Redondo Beach

Cookin Stuff	22217 Palos Verdes Blvd	310-371-2220	Possibly the largest selection of cooking supplies for the layperson in all of LA County.
Cost Plus World Market	22929 Hawthorne Blvd	310-378-8331	An "everything" superstore.
Lindbergh Nutrition	3804 Sepulveda Blvd	310-378-9490	A mecca for bodybuilders and others wishing to "keep in the pink."

Map 33 • Eagle Rock/Highland Park

Colorado Wine Company	2114 Colorado Blvd	323-478-1985	Helpful owners and numerous tastings keep you "Sideways."
Galco's Soda Pop Stop	5702 York Blvd	323-255-7115	Who knew there were so many different brands of root beer?
Mini-Melt Too	1613 Colorado Blvd	323-258-2300	Second sibling of cool comics 'n' more store, Meltdown.

Map 34 • Pasadena

Angels School Supply	600 E Colorado Blvd	626-584-0855	Back to school isn't so bad after all.
Assistance League of Pasadena	820 E California Blvd	626-449-6590	Charity gift shop featuring all hand-crafted items. Great for baby gifts.
Bungalow News	746 E Colorado Blvd	626-795-9456	Monster newsstand.
Canyon Beachwear	34 Hugus Aly	626-564-0752	Bathing suit-a-rama.
Canterbury Record Shop	805 E Colorado Blvd	626-792-7184	New and used, plus DVD and video. Great jazz, blues, and classical.
Carroll & Co	146 S Lake Ave	626-396-7060	Classic men's clothier.
CP Shades	20 S Raymond Ave	626-564-9304	Everybody's favorite pre-faded super soft clothing.
Dreams of Tibet	20 E Holly St	626-585-8100	Folk arts, flags, and all manner of items to get you on the right side of the issue.
Elisa B	12 Douglas Aly	626-792-4746	Contemporary clothing for women.
Essence of France	275 S El Molino Ave	626-449-4019	French antiques.

Map 34 • Pasadena—*continued*

Fine Kicks	88 E Colorado Blvd	626-744-0656	Great shoe selection.
Heritage Wine Co	155 N Raymond Ave	800-630-WINE	Tastings and sales of California wines.
Jacob Maarse Florists	655 E Green St	626-449-0246	Fabulous floral arrangements.
Lather	106 W Colorado Blvd	626-397-9050	"Modern apothecary" products that smell good and feel good.
Lush	24 E Colorado Blvd	626-792-0901	Super-fresh beauty and bath products.
Messarian Oriental Rugs	493 Colorado Blvd	626-792-9858	Beautiful rugs from the Near and Middle East.
Paperwhites	2491 Mission St	626-441-2196	Packaged cards, as well as custom invitations and announcements.
Pasadena Antique Mall	35 S Raymond Ave	626-304-9886	Dozens of dealers under one roof.
Pasadena Stone & Tile	175 S Fair Oaks Ave	626-793-3773	Must-visit for your next home improvement project.
room 107	174 S De Lacey Ave	626-432-4867	Home décor and decorating services.
Rose Tree Cottage	828 E California Blvd	626-793-3337	English tea room and gift shop.
Run with Us	235 N Lake Ave	626-568-3331	For those who still have knees enough to run.
Stats	170 S Raymond Ave	626-795-9308	Every imaginable supply and bauble for your décor, floral, crafting projects.
Target	777 E Colorado Blvd	626-584-1606	Perfect-sized, not too big, two story, very manageable.
The Art Store	44 S Raymond Ave	626-795-4985	Art supplies for every métier.
Three Dog Bakery	24 Smith Aly	626-440-0443	Fancy biscuits you'd be proud to offer man's best friend.
Z Gallerie	42 W Colorado Blvd	626-578-1538	Unique home items.

Map 39 • Alhambra

Mi Casita Rustica	135 West Main St	626-576-8143	Everything Mexican for your rustic home.
Penny Lane	110 W Main St	626-457-5787	Music, movies, games.
Shades of Blue	112 W Main St	626-457-6255	Scent-ual shop for candles and bath products.

Map 40 • Boyle Heights

Skeletons in the Closet	1104 N Mission Road	323-343-0760	County Coroner's gift shop stocks chalk outline beach towels and post-its.

Map 47 • Van Nuys

The Plant	7800 Van Nuys Blvd		A mall in a former Ford factory.

Map 48 • North Hollywood

99 Cents Store	12711 Sherman Wy	818-764-9991	Plus tax!
Big Lots	13005 Sherman Wy	818-982-1687	Monster close-out store. Always something surprising and marked way, way down.
K-Mart	13007 Sherman Wy	818-764-0250	Welcome, shoppers…

Map 49 • Burbank

Arte de Mexico	5356 Riverton Ave	818-769-5090	Furniture and crafts with a Mexican flair.
Atomic Records	3812 W Magnolia Blvd	818-848-7090	Used records. An eclectic inventory at reasonable prices.
Dark Delicacies Bookstore	4213 W Burbank Blvd	818-556-6660	Everything for your D&D/goth/horror/fantasy friend (we all have one).
Fry's Electronics	2311 N Hollywood Wy	818-526-8100	Huge electronics store with a B-movie, spaceship-themed exterior.
It's a Wrap	3315 W Magnolia Blvd	818-567-7366	Clothes previously worn by your favorite TV stars.
Monte Carlo	3103 Magnolia Blvd	818-845-3517	Authentic Italian market.
Otto's Import Store & Delicatessen	2320 W Clark Ave	818-845-0433	All manner of Hungarian delicacies and deliciousness.
The Train Shack	1030 N Hollywood Wy	818-842-3330	Fun model train store.
Western Bagel	513 N Hollywood Wy	818-567-0413	Local favorite.

Map 50 • Burbank East/Glendale West

Pickwick Center	1001 Riverside Dr	818-845-5300	Bowling alley, ice rink, often hosts antique or art fairs.
Valley Dealer Exchange	825 N Victory Blvd	818-845-4090	One of the most painless used car-buying experiences you will ever have.

Map 51 • Glendale South

Cost Plus World Market	223 N Glendale Ave	818-241-2112	An "everything" superstore.
Glendale Costume	746 W Doran St	818-244-1161	Amazing costume rental house.
Luigi's Pottery & Gardenware	5630 San Fernando Road	818-246-7579	Fountains, tiles, heavy stuff to sit out in the garden.

Map 53 • Encino

A Rodin Art	16752 Ventura Blvd	818-386-9148	Bronze statues, paintings.
Antik Shop	4909 Genesta Ave	818-990-5990	Funky antiques.
Encino Newsstand	16720 Ventura Blvd		Foreign and domestic mags.
Encino Park & Community Center Map	4935 Balboa Blvd	818-995-1690	Playground, picnic tables, tennis courts, grass and trees.
Herbalogics	17200 Ventura Blvd	818-990-9990	Herb store and acupuncture.
Hopscotch	16740 Ventura Blvd	818-783-4080	Kids clothing.
Ragg Tatoo	17245 Ventura Blvd	818-990-7244	Funky clothing.
Sneaker Warehouse	16736 Ventura Blvd	818-995-8999	Shoes galore!
The Knot Garden	17200 Ventura Blvd	818-986-6642	A knitter's paradise.

Map 54 • Sherman Oaks West

Buffalo Exchange	14621 Ventura Blvd	818-783-3420	Revolving door of used clothing. Buy, sell, trade.
Cost Plus World Market	15201 Ventura Blvd	818-205-9620	An "everything" superstore.
Handmade Galleries	14556 Ventura Blvd	818-382-3444	Gifts and home stuff made by hand. From "huh?" to "wow."
Sherman Oaks Castle Park	4989 Sepulveda Blvd	818-756-9459	Excellent batting cages and miniature golf.
Tower Records	15301 Ventura Blvd	818-789-0500	Giant music store.
Ultrazone	14622 Ventura Blvd	818-789-6620	The laser tag capital of the San Fernando Valley.

Map 55 • Sherman Oaks East

Aunt Teek's Collectibles	14080 Ventura Blvd	818-784-3341	Antique furniture and collectables on consignment.
Baxter Northrup Music	14534 Ventura Blvd	818-788-7510	Great selection of sheet music. Also instrument sales.
Bel Air Spa	2980 Beverly Glen Cir	310-470-6362	Well known day spa frequented by ladies who lunch, as well as celebrities.
Bloomingdale's	14060 Riverside Dr	818-325-2200	Quieter than the Century City location. Especially good shoes, kids, and Women's departments.
Doll Shoppe	13300 Riverside Dr	818-784-3655	A leading source for dolls, miniatures, and doll houses, as well as a "doll hospital."
Juvenile Shop	13356 Ventura Blvd	818-986-6214	A civilized alternative to Babies R Us.
Mark's Garden	13838 Ventura Blvd	818-906-1718	Florist.
Pink Cheeks	14562 Ventura Blvd	818-906-8225	Spa. Claims to have invented the famous 'playboy' bikini wax.
Second Spin Records	14564 Ventura Blvd	818-986-6866	Reasonably priced used CDs.

Map 56 • Studio City/Valley Village

Dari	12184 Ventura Blvd	818-762-3274	One of the Valley's outposts for trendy women's clothes.
Hamilton Pink	4342 1/2 Tujunga Ave	818-769-1463	Trendy boutique.
Hoity Toity	4381 Tujunga Ave	818-766-2503	Upscale women's clothing boutique.
Iliad Bookshop	4820 Vineland Ave	818-509-2665	Used and new books; specializing in literature and art.
King's Western Wear	11450 Ventura Blvd	818-761-1162	Everything to "ride 'em cowboy" here.
La Knitterie Parisienne	12642 Ventura Blvd	818-766-1515	The best knitting store around.
Laura's Designer Resale Boutique	12426 Ventura Blvd	818-752-2835	Used celebrity clothes and more.
Marie et Cie	11704 Riverside Dr	818-508-5049	Coffee, home furnishings, and gifts all in one.
Portrait of a Bookstore	4360 Tujunga Ave	818-769-3853	A very social bookstore, with great gifts too.
Studio City Camera Exchange	12174 Ventura Blvd	818-762-4749	Great local camera store. Very knowledgeable staff.
Suzanne's Resale Boutique	4355 Tujunga Ave	818-766-8837	Designer used clothes.
Tennis Ace	12544 Ventura Blvd	818-762-8751	Everything Tennis! Clothes, shoes, balls, etc.
Tuesday Morning	11239 Ventura Blvd	818-508-5334	Home and housewares at a big discount.
Verona	4350 Tujunga Ave	818-508-6377	Shoe boutique. Handbags too.
Village Gourmet	4357 Tujunga Ave	818-487-3807	Great gifts for the foodie in your life.
Village Market	11653 Moorpark St	818-761-4848	Old style, family-owned local market. Good deli.

Map 57 • Universal City/Toluca Lake

Cinema Secrets Beauty Supply	4400 W Riverside Dr	818-846-0579	Fabulous selection, including film makeup.
Geographica Map & Book Store	4000 W Riverside Dr	818-848-1414	This is an amazing travel store. They've thought of everything.
Pergolina	10139 Riverside Dr	818-508-7708	Gifts and items for home.
Simply Nature Day Spa	10067 Riverside Dr	818-506-8927	Unpretentious pampering spot.
Steel Casey	10624 Ventura Blvd	818-763-5667	Popular seller of retro office furniture.
Weekendz Only	10139 1/2 Riverside Dr	818-752-3695	Trendy boutique, great handbags and tees.

Long Beach

5001	5286 E 2nd St	562-438-3907	A smaller, kitschier, more clever Z Gallerie.
Acres of Books	240 Long Beach Blvd	562-437-6980	Huge family-owned used bookstore.
City Place	275 E 4th St	562-432-8325	Eight-block urban retail development, with some actual cool shops!
Crate & Barrel	240 Pine Ave	562-435-6577	All forward-thinking cities need one of these. They're reassuring.
Mood Swings	455 E Ocean Blvd	562-437-6250	Unique designs, vintage jewelry, truly beautiful stuff.
Nordstrom Rack	300 The Promenade N	562-733-1223	Somehow this boosts Long Beach's cachet.
Olives Gourmet Grocer	3510 E Broadway	562-439-7758	This gourmet shop has no equal anywhere within 30 miles.
The Pike at Rainbow Harbor	Pine Ave & Shoreline Dr	562-432-8325	Entertainment available for every member of the family.
Z Gallerie	230 Pine Ave	562-491-0766	Unique home items.

San Pedro

Coyote Antiques	387 W 6th St	310-547-4222	A must, as you amble the ArtWalk.
Endangered Species	1434 W 8th St	310-832-7325	A mix of antiques—prints, dishware, furniture.
Office Depot	810 N Western Ave	310-221-0162	Getcher office supplies here.
Ramona Bakery	1101 S Pacific Ave	310-832-0369	People travel for miles for the fresh strawberry cake.
Sav-On	950 N Western Ave	310-832-7258	Drugstore.
The Antique Shop	439 W 6th St	310-833-2008	American antiques, part of the ArtWalk.

The film industry in Los Angeles has spawned a culture of acting, and the dozens of theaters in this city are home to both thespians who've yet to gain their screen close-up and successful film stars who want to get back on the stage. A number of small theaters line Santa Monica Boulevard, east and west of Highland; check out the **Actor's Gang, Black Box, Elephant Asylum Theater,** and **The Complex**.

The **Pantages Theater** in Hollywood hosts off-Broadway productions. So do the **Mark Taper Forum** and the **Ahmanson Theater**—both downtown at the Music Center. These two theaters routinely show works by both local and internationally famous playwrights. Also downtown, the **REDCAT** at the Disney Hall has an interesting and varied line-up of plays throughout the year.

Actors and directors experiment at **Odyssey Theatre Ensemble** in West LA and something good is always cooking at the **Playwright Kitchen** at the **Coronet Theatre**.

Theater	Address	Phone	Map
2100 Square Feet	5615 San Vicente Blvd	323-936-6818	6
24th Street Theatre	1117 W 24th St	213-745-6516	11
2nd Stage Theater	6500 Santa Monica Blvd	323-882-8065	3
ACME Comedy Theatre	135 N La Brea Ave	323-525-0202	2
Action Reaction Theater	12443 Chandler Blvd	818-786-1045	56
Actor's Co-op	1760 N Gower St	323-462-8460	3
Actor's Gang	9070 Venice Blvd	310-838-4264	24
Actor's Playpen	1514 N Gardner St	310-713-9322	2
Actors Circle Theater School	7313 Santa Monica Blvd	323-882-8043	2
Actors Forum Theater	10655 Magnolia Blvd	818-506-0600	49
Ahmanson Theater	135 N Grand Ave	213-972-7401	34
Alex Theatre	216 N Brand Blvd	818-243-2539	51
American Renegade Theater	11136 Magnolia Blvd	818-763-4430	56
Ark Theater	1647 S La Cienega Blvd	323-969-1707	6
Attic Theater	5429 W Washington Blvd	323-525-0600	6
Attic Theatre Center	8663 Chalmers Dr	323-467-6850	6
Avery Schreiber Theater	11050 Magnolia Blvd	866-811-4111	56
Bang Improv Studio	457 N Fairfax Ave	323-653-6886	2
Beverly Hills Playhouse	254 S Robertson Blvd	310-855-1556	6
Black Box	12420 Santa Monica Blvd	310-979-7078	19
Black Dahlia Theatre	5453 W Pico Blvd	323-525-0070	6
Boston Court Theater	70 N Mentor Ave	626-683-6883	35
Brick Box Theater	1608 Cosmo St	323-960-7721	3
Canon Theatre Box Office	205 N Canon Dr	310-859-2830	1
Celebration Theater	7051 Santa Monica Blvd	323-957-1884	3
Celtic Arts Center	4843 Laurel Canyon Blvd	818-760-8322	56
Century City Playhouse	10508 W Pico Blvd	310-204-4440	23
City Garage	1340 1/2 4th St	310-319-9939	18
Civic Light Opera of South Bay Cities	2224 Artesia Blvd	310-372-4477	29
Civic Light Opera-South Bay	710 Pier Ave	310-379-1979	29
Coast Playhouse	8325 Santa Monica Blvd	323-650-8507	2
Colony Theater	555 N 3rd St	818-558-7000	50
Company of Angels Theater	2106 Hyperion Ave	323-666-6789	5
The Complex	6470 Santa Monica Blvd	323-668-0071	3
Coronet Theatre	366 N La Cienega Blvd	310-652-9955	2
Court Theatre	722 N La Cienega Blvd	310-652-4035	2
David Henry Hwang Theater	120 Judge John Aiso St	213-625-7000	9
Deaf West Theatre	5112 Lankershim Blvd	818-762-2998	56
Ebell Theatre	4401 W 8th St	323-939-0126	7
Egyptian Arena Theater	1625 N Las Palmas Ave	323-650-3100	3
Electric Lodge	1416 Electric Ave	310-306-1854	21
Elephant Asylum Theater	6320 Santa Monica Blvd	877-642-0227	3
Empty Stage Theater	2374 Veteran Ave	310-560-1185	23
The Evidence Room Theater	2220 Beverly Blvd	213-381-7118	9
The Fake Gallery	4319 Melrose Ave	323-661-0786	4
Falcon Theatre Box Office	4252 W Riverside Dr	818-955-8101	57
Ford Amphitheater	2580 Cahuenga Blvd E	323-461-3673	3
Fountain Theater	5060 Fountain Ave	323-663-1525	4
Fremont Center Theater	1000 Fremont Ave	626-441-5977	34
Frida Kahlo Theater	2332 W 4th St	213-382-8133	8
Gascon Center Theatre Live	8737 Washington Blvd	310-204-3126	24
Geffen Playhouse	11301 Wilshire Blvd	310-208-6500	16
Gene Bua Acting for Life Theatre	3435 Magnolia Blvd	818-547-3810	49
GGC Theater	6468 Santa Monica Blvd	800-595-4849	3
Glendale Center Theatre	324 N Orange St	818-244-8481	51
Globe Playhouse	1107 N King's Rd	323-960-7863	2
Greenway Arts Alliance	544 N Fairfax Ave	323-655-7679	2
Groundling Theater	7307 Melrose Ave	323-934-9700	2
Harry Mastrogeorge Theater @ the Brewery Art Colony	600 Moulton Ave	323-227-5410	40
Highways	1651 18th St	310-453-1755	18

Theater	Address	Phone	Map
Hollywood Fight Club Theater	6767 W Sunset Blvd	323-465-0800	3
Hudson Avenue Theater	6539 Santa Monica Blvd	323-769-5858	3
Improv Olympic West	6366 Hollywood Blvd	323-962-7560	3
International City Theater	300 E Ocean Blvd	562-436-4610	p 240
Ivar Theatre	1605 Ivar Ave	323-461-7300	3
Kirk Douglas Theatre	9820 Washington Blvd	213-628-2772	24
Knightsbridge Theatre	1944 Riverside Dr	626-440-0821	5
LA Repertory Company	6560 Hollywood Blvd	323-464-8542	3
Lee Strasberg Creative Center	7936 Santa Monica Blvd	323-960-4412	2
Lex Theater	6760 Lexington Ave	323-957-5782	3
Lillian Theater	1076 Lillian Wy	323-692-2652	3
Lost Studio	130 S La Brea Ave	323-960-5563	2
Madrid Theatre	21622 Sherman Wy	818-347-9419	52
Magicopolis	1418 4th St	310-451-2241	18
Mark Taper Auditorium	630 W 5th St	213-228-7025	9
Mark Taper Forum	135 N Grand Ave	213-972-0700	9
Masquer's Cabaret	8334 W 3rd St	323-653-4848	2
McCadden Place Theater	1157 N McCadden Pl	323-463-2942	3
Met Theatre	1089 N Oxford Ave	323-957-1741	4
Meta Theater	7801 Melrose Ave	866-649-9048	2
Morgan Theatre	2627 Pico Blvd	310-828-7519	19
Moving Arts	514 S Spring St	213-622-8906	9
National Comedy Theater	733 Seward St	323-871-1193	3
New Place Theater	4900 Vineland Ave	866-811-4111	56
NoHo Actor's Studio	5215 Lankershim Blvd		56
Odyssey Theatre	2055 S Sepulveda Blvd	310-477-2055	19
Open Fist Theatre Co	1625 N La Brea Ave	323-882-6912	2
Pacific Resident Theater	703 Venice Blvd	310-301-3917	9
Pantages Theater	6233 Hollywood Blvd	323-468-1770	3
Pasadena Center	300 E Green St	626-793-2122	34
Pasadena Playhouse State Theater	39 S El Molino Ave	626-792-8672	34
Pilot Light Theater	6902 Santa Monica Blvd	323-960-1054	2
Playhouse West School and Repertory Theater	4250 Lankershim Blvd	818-971-7191	57
Playwright Kitchen	366 N La Cienega Blvd	310-652-9602	2
Powerhouse Theater	3116 2nd St	310-396-3680	18
Promenade Playhouse	1404 Third St Promenade	323-960-7846	18
Rachel Rosenthal Co	2847 S Robertson Blvd	310-839-0661	23
Raven Playhouse	5233 Lankershim Blvd	818-509-9519	56
REDCAT	631 W 2nd St	213-237-2800	9
Redondo Beach Performing Arts	1935 Manhattan Beach Blvd	310-937-6607	27
Riprap Studio Theater	5755 Lankershim Blvd	818-990-7498	48
Sacred Fools Theater	660 N Heliotrope Dr	310-281-8337	4
Sanford Meisner Theater	5124 Lankershim Blvd	818-509-9651	56
Santa Monica Playhouse & Group	1211 4th St	310-394-9779	18
Secret Rose Theater	11246 Magnolia Blvd	818-766-3691	56
Shakespeare Festival LA	1238 W 1st St	213-481-2273	9
Sidewalk Studio Theater	4150 Riverside Dr	818-846-3403	57
Sierra Madre Playhouse	87 S Sierra Madre Blvd	626-256-3809	35
Sierra Stage Theater	1444 N Sierra Bonita Ave	310-226-6148	2
Skirball Cultural Center	2701 N Sepulveda Blvd	310-440-4500	54
Stage 52	5299 W Washington Blvd	323-549-9026	6
Stella Adler Academy of Acting	6773 Hollywood Blvd	323-465-4446	3
Studio/Stage	520 N Western Ave	323-860-6503	4
Tamarind Theater	5919 Franklin Ave	323-465-7980	3
Theater 68	5419 W Sunset Blvd	323-467-6688	4
Theater Banchy	3435 W Magnolia Blvd	818-628-0688	49
The Theater District	804 N El Centro Ave	323-957-2343	3
Theater of NOTE	1517 N Cahuenga Blvd	323-856-8611	3
Theater West	3333 Cahuenga Blvd W	323-851-7977	57
Theatre Palisades	941 Temescal Canyon Rd	310-454-1970	15
Third Stage	2811 W Magnolia Blvd	818-842-4755	49
Torrance Cultural Arts Center	3330 Civic Center Dr N	310-781-7150	30
Tre Stage	1523 N La Brea Ave	323-850-7827	2
Two Roads Theater	4348 Tujunga Ave	866-811-4111	56
Victory Theatres	3326 W Victory Blvd	818-843-9253	49
West Valley Playhouse	7242 Owensmouth Ave	818-884-1907	52
Westchester Playhouse	8301 Hindry Ave	310-645-5156	26
Whitfire Theater	13500 Ventura Blvd	818-990-2324	55
Whitmore Lindley Theatre Center	11006 Magnolia Blvd	818-761-0704	56
Working Stage	1516 N Gardner St	323-851-2603	2
Works Theater	6569 Santa Monica Blvd	323-874-8205	3
Zephyr Theater	7456 Melrose Ave	323-852-9111	2

Founded in 1918, Otis prepares diverse students of art and design to enrich our world through their creativity, their skill, and their vision.

Architecture/Landscape/Interiors

Communication Arts
Graphic Design/Illustration/Advertising

Digital Media
Motion Graphics/Broadcast Design/Animation/Visual Effects/Game Design

Fashion Design

Fine Arts
Painting/Photography/Sculpture and New Genres

Interactive Product Design

Toy Design

Otis College of Art + Design
9045 Lincoln Blvd LA 90045
800.527.OTIS (6847) 310.665.6820
www.otis.edu

KCRW To Go!

Now Podcasting >

@KCRW.com >>

**Never miss your favorite
KCRW radio shows again.**

Hear programs like *To the Point,
The Treatment, Bookworm,
Left, Right & Center* when you
want to and where you want to.

Podcasts are automatically
downloaded to your computer
or your MP3 player. **Free.**

Just go to KCRW.com and click
on keyword "Podcast."

RELOAD
BAGGAGE

custom handmade
MESSENGER BAGS
+
ACCESSORIES

+
rare
BIKES
PARTS
+
CLOTHING

RELOADBAGS.COM

Your ad here

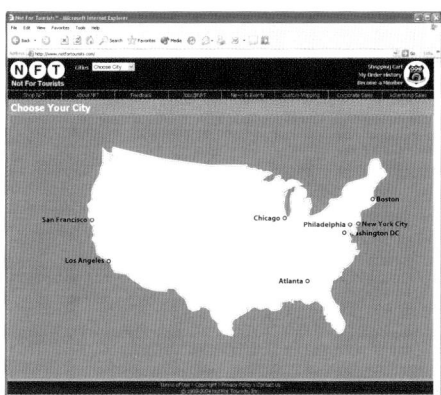

or here.

We offer half- and full-page advertising options inside each of the **Not For Tourists**™ Guidebooks, including multi-city packages for national companies and organizations, as well as space on our website. Advertising in **NFT**™ means that the city dwellers who rely on our indispensable guidebooks everyday will literally have your business information right at their fingertips wherever they go. Come on. Everybody's doing it.

Street Index

Street Index

Street Index

Street Index

Street	City	Page	Grid
Addison St			
(10400-10799)	NH	49	D1/D2
(11500-11699)	NH	56	A2
(11700-12799)	NH/SC	56	A1/A2
(12800-12899)	NH/SC	55	A3
(12900-14599)	SO/VN	55	A1/A2/A3
(14600-14999)	SO/VN	54	A3
(15700-16299)	EN/VN	54	A1/A2
(16600-17299)	EN/VN	53	A3
Addison Way	LA	33	B1/B2
Adelaide Dr			
(100-699)	SM	15	C2/C3
(832-901)	PA	35	A2
Adelaide Pl			
(700-899)	SM	18	A2
(6300-6399)	LA	33	C3
Adelaine Aly	SP	34	D1
Adelaine Ave	SP	34	D1/D2
Adelante Ave	LA	34	C1
Adelbert Ave	LA	5	B2
Adele Ct	WH	52	B2
Adele Dr	WH	52	B2
Adelyn Dr	SG	39	A3
Adena St	PA	34	A3
Aderno Way	PP	15	B1/C1
Adina Dr	LA	57	C2
Adkins Ave	LA	38	C2
Adkisson Ave	LA	38	D1
Adlon Pl	EN/VN	53	B3
Adlon Rd	EN/VN	53	B3
Admiral Ave			
(12500-12999)	LA	22	C2
(13200-13236)	MA/VE	25	A2
Admiralty Way	MA/VE	25	A1/A2
Adobe St	LA	9	A2
Adolph Ave	TO	31	C3/D3
Adona Dr	LO	32	C3
Adrian St	LA	4	D3
Aerick St	IN	13	B2
Aero Way	TO	32	D1
Aetna St			
(12900-13399)	SO/VN	48	C1
(14100-14899)	SO/VN	47	C2/C3
(19200-19299)	TZ	45	D3
(20241-20699)	WH	45	D2
Afton Pl	LA	3	C2
Afton Rd	PA	39	A1
Afton St	PA	34	A1
Agate St	RB	31	A1
Agatha St	LA	9	C2
Agnes Ave			
(4200-5449)	NH/SC	56	A2/B2
(5450-5999)	NH/SC	48	D2
(6200-8299)	NH	48	A2/B2/C2
Agnes Rd	MB	27	C2
Agnew Ave	LA	26	B1
Aguilar St	LA	51	C3
Aguilar Way	LA	51	C3
Aiglon St	PP	15	B1
Aiken Ave	LA	23	B1
Ainsworth Ave	TO	30	A2/B2
Aintree Ln	LA	40	D2
Air Way	GL	51	A1
Airdrome St			
(5500-9224)	LA	6	C1/C2
(9225-9399)	LA	23	B3
Airlane Ave	LA	26	B2/C2
Airole Way	LA	17	B2
Airport Ave	LA	19	D2
(2300-3499)	SM	19	D1/D2
Airport Blvd	LA	26	B2/C2/D2
Airport Dr	TO	32	C1/D1/D2
Akron St	PP	15	B1
Alabama Ave			
(6800-7999)	CP	45	B1/C1
(9100-10699)	CH	42	A2/B2/C2
Alabama St	SG	35	D3
Aladdin St	LA	10	B1
Alahmar St	AL	39	A3
N Alahmar St	AL	39	A3
Alahmar Ter	SG	39	A3
Alameda Ave	GL	50	B3/C3
E Alameda Ave	BU	50	B3/C2/C3
W Alameda Ave			
(1-2849)	BU	50	C2/D1/D2
(2850-3799)	BU	49	D2/D3
(3800-4299)	BU	57	A2/A3
N Alameda St	LA	9	B3
S Alameda St			
(100-1451)	LA	9	C3/D3
(1452-5899)	LA	12	B3/C3/D3
Alamo Dr	MP	41	A3
Alamo St	WH	52	B1
Alana Dr	SO/VN	54	C1
Alandele Ave			
(400-599)	LA	2	D2/D3
(800-999)	LA	6	B2
Alarcon Pl	PA	34	C2
Alaska Ave			
(400-699)	TO	30	D3
(2301-2399)	ES	27	B3
Alatar Dr	WH	52	B1
Alba St	LA	12	D3
Albany St			
(900-1349)	LA	9	B1/C1
(1350-1599)	LA	8	D3
Albata St	LA	16	B3/C3
Albers Pl	SO/VN	48	D1
Albers St			
(11400-11599)	NH	48	D3
(11700-12899)	NH/SC	48	D1/D2
(12900-13674)	SO/VN	48	D1
(13675-16399)	SO/VN	47	D2/D3
(16800-17299)	EN/VN	46	D3
Albert Ave	TO	31	C2
Alberta Ave	MA/VE	21	C2
Alberta Dr	CU	26	A1
Alberta St	TO	32	B3
Albertine St	LA	40	C2
Albion St	LA	37	D1/D2
Albright Ave	LA	22	B3
Albright St	PP	15	B2
Alcazar St	LA	40	A2/A3
Alcima Ave	PP	15	B1
Alcor St	LO	32	D3
Alcott St			
(6000-9124)	LA	6	B1
(9125-9799)	LA	23	A3
Alcove Ave			
(3900-5412)	NH/SC	55	A3/B3
(5413-5999)	NH/SC	48	C1/D1
(6000-8299)	NH	48	A1/B1/C1
Alcyona Dr	LA	3	A2
Aldama St			
(4800-5156)	LA	36	B3
(5157-6699)	LA	33	C2/C3
Aldama Ter	LA	33	C2
Aldbury Ct	BH	55	D2
Aldea Ave			
(5000-5414)	EN/VN	53	A3
(5415-6099)	EN/VN	46	C3/D3
(6400-8199)	VN	46	A3/B3/C3
(9100-10299)	NR	44	B2/C1/C2
(10300-11299)	GH	44	A2/B2
Alden Dr			
(8600-9199)	LA	2	C1
(9150-9299)	BH	1	C3
Alder Dr	LA	36	B2
Alegre Pl	LA	36	B2
Alegria Pl	PA	35	C3
Aleman Dr	TZ	52	B3
Alerion Pl	WH	52	A2
Alesandro Pl	PA	34	C2
Aletta Ave	CU	24	C1
Alexander St	GL	51	B1
N Alexandria Ave			
(100-249)	LA	8	A1
(250-2099)	LA	4	B2/C2/D2
S Alexandria Ave	LA	8	A2/B2
Alexandria Pl	LA	4	D2
Alfarena Pl	TZ	52	B3
N Alfred St	LA	2	B1/C1
S Alfred St	LA	6	B1
Alger St	LA	51	C1
Algiers St	NR	43	A2/A3
Alginet Dr	EN/VN	53	C3
Alginet Pl	EN/VN	53	C3
Algodon Ct	LA	57	D1
Algoma Ave	LA	33	B2
Alhama Dr	WH	52	A1/B1
Alhambra Ave			
(1000-1199)	LA	9	B3
(1200-3199)	LA	40	A1/A2
(5000-5699)	LA	38	C2/C3
Alhambra Ct	MA/VE	21	C2
Alhambra Rd			
(300-1399)	SG	39	A3
(543-799)	SG	35	D2
(1300-2273)	SP	39	B1
(1394-2131)	AL	39	B1
(1800-1999)	PA	35	D2
(2274-2899)	AL	38	A3
E Alhambra Rd			
(1-1183)	AL	39	A2/A3/B2
(1184-1299)	PA	39	A3
W Alhambra Rd	AL	39	B1/B2
Alice St	LA	36	C2
Alisal Ct	SM	15	C3
Alisal Ln	SM	15	C3
Aliso St			
(300-699)	LA	9	B2
(700-799)	LA	40	B1
Alizondo Dr	WH	52	B1
Alla Rd	LA	25	B3
(3900-5499)	LA	22	C1/C2/D2
Allan St	LA	38	C3
Allandale Dr	TZ	52	C3
Allaseba Dr	LA	22	A1
Allbrook St	LO	32	C3
Allegheney Ct	LA	24	D3
Allen Ave	GL	50	B3/C3/D2
N Allen Ave	PA	35	A2/B2
S Allen Ave	PA	35	B2/C2
W Allen Ave	BU	49	C2
Allen Ct	PA	35	B2
Allendale Rd	PA	34	C3
Allenford Ave	LA	16	C1
Allentown Dr	WH	52	A2
Allentown Pl	WH	52	A2
Allenwood Rd	LA	56	D2/D3
Allesandro St	LA	5	B2/C2/D1
Allesandro Way	LA	5	C2
S Allied Way	ES	27	B3
Alliene Ave			
(23700-23799)	TO	32	C2
(24100-25599)	LO	32	C2/D2
Allin St			
(11700-12399)	CU	22	C3
(12400-12599)	LA	22	C2/C3
Allison Ave	LA	5	D2
Allott Ave			
(4100-5449)	SO/VN	55	A2/B2
(5450-6799)	SO/VN	48	C1/D1
(7100-8349)	VN	48	A1/B1
E Allview Ter	LA	3	A3
W Allview Ter	LA	3	A2
Alma Ave	MB	27	C2
N Alma Ave	LA	41	B1/C1
S Alma Ave	LA	41	C1/D1
Alma St	GL	51	A1
Alma Real Dr	PP	15	B2/C2
Almadale St	LA	38	D1
Almaden Ct	LA	55	D1
Almaden Dr	LA	33	C2
N Almansor St	AL	39	A2/B3
S Almansor St			
(1-1989)	AL	39	B3/C3/D3
(1990-2099)	MP	39	D3
E Almanza Ln	LA	41	B2
Almar Ave	PP	15	B1/C1
Almar Plz	PP	15	C1
Almarosa Ave	TO	32	B2
Almayo Ave	LA	23	B1/B2
Almazan Rd	WH	52	B1
Almertens Pl	IN	28	B3
Almoloya Pl	PP	15	C2
N Almont Dr			
(100-399)	BH	2	D1
(100-699)	LA	2	C1
S Almont Dr			
(100-499)	BH	6	A1/B1
(100-399)	LA	2	C1
Almont St	LA	38	B2/B3
Aloha Dr	PP	15	C1
Aloha St	LA	Griffith Park	
Alomar Dr	SO/VN	55	C2/C3
Alonzo Ave			
(3700-5799)	EN/VN	53	A2/B2/C2
(5800-6335)	EN/VN	46	C2
Alonzo Pl	EN/VN	53	B2
Alpha St			
(900-999)	IN	13	A3
(1800-2099)	SP	38	A3
(4300-4599)	LA	38	B3
Alpine Dr	PA	35	D2
N Alpine Dr	BH	1	A2/B2/C2/C3
Alpine St			
(100-1199)	LA	9	A2/B2/B3
(201-699)	PA	34	C2/C3
Alsace Ave			
(1800-2499)	LA	6	C3/D3
(2500-5899)	LA	10	A2/B2/D3
Alta Ave			
(100-2449)	SM	18	A1/A2/A3
(2450-2599)	SM	19	A1
Alta Dr	TP	52	D1
N Alta Dr	BH	1	A3/B3
Alta St	LA	37	C3/D3
Alta Loma Rd	LA	2	B1
Alta Loma Ter	LA	3	A1
Alta Mesa Dr	NH/SC	56	C1
Alta Mesa Pl	NH/SC	56	C1
Alta Mura Rd	PP	16	C1
Alta Paseo	BU	50	B3
Alta View Dr			
(10800-10932)	NH/SC	57	B1
(10933-10999)	NH/SC	56	C3
Alta Vista Ave	SP	38	A2
N Alta Vista Ave	LA	2	A1
N Alta Vista Blvd	LA	2	B3/C3
S Alta Vista Blvd	LA	2	D3
Alta Vista Cir	SP	38	A3
Alta Vista Dr			
(600-799)	GL	51	C2
(1700-1999)	AL	38	C3
N Altadena Dr	PA	35	A3/B3
S Altadena Dr	PA	35	B3
Altair Dr	LA	16	B2
Altair Pl	MA/VE	21	C2
Altamont St	LA	36	C2
Altamor Dr	LA	26	B1
Altaridge Dr	TP	52	D1
Altata Dr	PP	15	C2
Altavan Ave	LA	25	B3
Altivo Way	LA	5	C2
Altman Ave	LA	23	B3
Altman St	LA	36	C1
Alto Cedro Dr	BH	56	D2
Alto Oak Dr	LA	3	A3
Altura St	LA	37	C2/C3
Altura Walk	LA	37	C2
Altura Way	MB	27	D3
Alumni Ave	LA	33	B1/C1
Alva Dr	PP	15	C2
N Alvarado St			
(100-510)	LA	9	A1
(511-2499)	LA	5	C2/D1/D2
S Alvarado St			
(100-624)	LA	9	A1/B1
(625-1399)	LA	8	B3/C3
Alvarado Ter	LA	8	D3
Alvern Cir	LA	26	A3
Alvern St	LA	26	A3
Alverstone Ave	LA	26	A2/B2/C2
Alvira St			
(1000-2624)	LA	6	B1/B2/C1
(2625-2699)	LA	24	A3
Alviso Ave			
(1500-1599)	IN	13	A2
(5400-5874)	LA	10	D3
(5875-6399)	LA	13	A2
Alvord Ln			
(2400-2699)	RB	29	C3
(2700-2799)	RB	30	C1
Alzado St	MP	41	A3
Amabel St	LA	36	D2
Amador Pl	LA	5	D3
Amador St			
(500-610)	LA	37	C1
(611-799)	LA	5	D3
Amalfi Ct	SM	15	C3
Amalfi Dr			
(100-399)	SM	15	C2/C3
(400-1549)	PP	15	B3
(1550-1699)	PP	16	C1
Amalia Ave	LA	41	C3/D3
Amanda Dr	NH/SC	56	C2
Amapola Ave	TO	32	A2
Amapola Ln	LA	17	C3
Ambar Dr	WH	52	B1/C1
Ambassador Ave	BH	1	B1
Ambassador St	LA	23	A2
Ambazac Way	LA	17	C2
Amber Ln	BU	50	A1
Amber Pl	LA	38	B1
Amberly Dr	IN	13	C3
Amberwood Dr	SP	34	C3
W Amberwood Dr	IN	26	A3
Amberwood Ln	NR	43	B2
Amboy Ave	SV	48	A2
Ambrose Ave	LA	4	B1/B2/B3
W Ambrose Ave	LA	4	B2
Ambrose Ter	LA	4	B3
Amby Pl	HB	27	D2
American Pl	LA	36	C2
Ameron Way	MP	41	A2
Ames St	LA	4	A3/B3
Amesbury Rd	LA	4	A3

Street Index

Street	Code	Pg	Grid
Burton St			
(11000-11199)	SV	48	A3
(11900-13299)	NH	48	A1/A2
(13300-13499)	VN	48	A1
(13800-15299)	VN	47	A2/A3
(17000-17299)	VN	46	A3
(17300-17699)	NR	46	A2
(17700-18099)	EN/RE/TZ	46	A2
(20900-22299)	CP	45	A1
Burton Way			
(8500-9149)	LA	2	D1
(8800-9177)	BH	2	D1
(9146-9399)	BH	1	C2/C3
Burwood Ave	LA	33	B3
Burwood Ter	LA	33	B3
Busch Pl	PA	34	C2
Busch Garden Ct	PA	34	C1
Busch Garden Dr	PA	34	C1
Busch Garden Ln	PA	34	C1
Bush Way	CU	24	D2
Bushnell Ave	SP	39	A1
N Bushnell Ave	AL	39	A1/B1
S Bushnell Ave	AL	39	C1/D1
Bushnell Way	LA	38	A1
Bushwick St	LA	36	A1/B1
Business Center Dr	NR	43	D2
Butler Ave			
(1400-3274)	LA	19	B3/C3/D3
(3275-3799)	LA	22	A2/B2
Butter Creek Dr	PA	35	A3
Butterfield Ct	CU	24	C2
Butterfield Rd	LA	23	B1/B2/C1
Butterfly Ln	LA	38	C2
Buttonwillow Dr	CP	45	B3
Byrd Ave	IN	14	B1/C1
Byrd St	VN	47	A1
Byron Pl	LA	56	D2
C St	CU	24	C2
Cable Pl	IN	13	B2
Cabora Dr	LA	25	B3
	LA	26	A1
(8100-8325)	MA/VE	25	B2
Cabot St	LA	36	C1
Cabrillo Ave			
(1100-1699)	MA/VE	21	C1/C2
(1200-23999)	TO	32	A3/B3/C3
(1400-1899)	AL	38	C3
Cabrillo Blvd	LA	22	B1
Cabrillo Dr	BH	1	A2
Cabrillo Villas St	LA	38	A2
Cabrini Dr	BU	49	A2/A3
E Cabrini Dr	BU	49	A3
W Cabrini Dr	BU	49	A3
Cabriole Ave	NR	43	A2
Cabrito Rd	VN	47	A2/A3
Cachalote St	WH	52	B1
Cactus Ave	CH	42	B1
Cadet Ct	LA	57	C2
Cadillac Ave	LA	6	C1/D1
Cadison St			
(4500-4749)	TO	30	C1
(4750-5199)	TO	31	A3
Cadiz Dr	LO	32	C3
Cadman Dr	LA		Griffith Park
Cahill Ave	TZ	46	A1
Cahuenga Blvd			
(3700-4527)	NH/SC	57	A1/B1
(4528-4799)	NH/SC	49	D1
(4800-6399)	NH	49	B1/C1/D1
Cahuenga Blvd E			
(2300-2812)	LA	3	A1
(2813-2919)	LA	52	C3
(2920-3299)	LA	57	C2
Cahuenga Blvd W			
(2500-2758)	LA	3	A1
(2759-3699)	LA	57	B1/B2/C2
N Cahuenga Blvd	LA	3	—
Cahuenga Ter	LA	3	A1/A2
Cahuenga Access Rd	LA	57	C2
Cahuenga Park Trl	LA	57	C2
Cairo Walk	SO/VN	55	C1
Calabar Ave	MA/VE	25	B2
Calada St	LA	40	D3
Caladero St	TZ	52	B3
Calahan St			
(16000-16999)	NO/NR	44	C2/C3
(17000-17199)	NR	44	C2
(18600-19299)	NR	43	C2
Calamar Ave	TO	32	B3
Calatrana Dr			
(5000-5345)	WH	52	A1/B1
(5346-5399)	WH	45	D1
Caldus Ave	VN	46	B2
W Caldwell St	LA	40	D1
Caledonia Way	LA	51	C3
Calhoun Ave			
(4300-5449)	SO/VN	55	A1/B1
(5450-6499)	SO/VN	47	C3/D3
(6700-8199)	VN	47	A3/B3/C3
Califa Pl	WH	45	D2
Califa St			
(10400-10914)	NH	49	C1
(10915-11699)	NH	48	D3
(11700-12799)	NH/SC	48	D1/D2
(13500-13664)	SO/VN	48	D1
(13665-15299)	SO/VN	47	C2/C3
(17300-17999)	EN/VN	46	C2
(18100-18899)	TZ	46	C1/C2
(19200-19299)	TZ	45	D3
(19900-20299)	CP	45	A3
(20300-22199)	WH	45	D1/D2
California Ave			
(100-2464)	SM	18	B1/B2/B3
(500-1099)	MA/VE	21	B2/C2
(2465-2999)	SM	19	B1
E California Ave	GL	51	B2/B3
W California Ave	GL	51	B1/B2
E California Blvd			
(1-981)	PA	34	C2/C3
(982-3041)	PA	35	C1/C2/C3
W California Blvd	PA	34	C1/C2
California Ct	MA/VE	21	B2
California Pl N	SM	18	B3
California St			
(200-1099)	ES	27	A2
(2600-2999)	TO	30	D2
N California St			
(100-3299)	BU	49	—
(400-799)	SG	35	D3
S California St			
(100-305)	VN	49	D3
(306-499)	BU	57	A3
California Ter	PA	34	B1/C1
California Incline	SM	18	B1
Calimali Rd	WH	52	B1
Callada Pl	TZ	53	B3
Callado Way	TP	52	C1
Calle Cabrillo	RB	31	D1/D2
Calle De Andalucia	RB	31	D2
Calle De Aragon	RB	31	D2
Calle De Arboles			
(100-899)	RB	31	D1/D2
(4900-5699)	TO	31	D2
Calle De Castellana	RB	31	D2
Calle De Felipe	TO	31	D2
Calle De Madrid	RB	31	D2
Calle De Primera	TO	31	D3
Calle De Ricardo	TO	31	D2
Calle De Sirenas	RB	31	D1
Calle Juela Dr	BH	56	D2
Calle Mayor			
(1-599)	RB	31	D1/D2
(4200-5699)	TO	31	C2/C3/D2
Calle Miramar	RB	31	C1/D1/D2
S Calle Miramar	RB	31	C1
Calle Pedro Infante	LA	40	C2
Calle Vista Dr	BH	1	A2
Callison St	LO	32	C3
Callita Pl	PA	39	A1
Calmar Ct	LA	20	C2
Calneva Dr	EN/VN	53	C3
Calumet Ave	LA	5	D2
Calvert St			
(10700-10899)	NH	49	C1
(10929-12399)	NH	48	C2/C3
(12900-13499)	SO/VN	48	C1
(13700-15099)	SO/VN	47	C2
(17600-18099)	EN/VN	46	C2
(18100-19153)	EN/RE/TZ	46	C1/C2
(19154-19599)	EN/RE/TZ	45	C3/D3
(19700-22199)	WH	45	C3/D1/D3
Calvin Ave			
(4900-5239)	TZ	52	A3/B3
(5300-6099)	TZ	45	D3
(6200-8199)	EN/RE/TZ	45	A3/B3/C3
(8300-10399)	NR	43	B1/B2/C2/D2
(10200-10399)	LA	20	C3
Calzadilla Pl	TZ	52	B3
Calzona St	LA	40	D3
Camarillo St	NH/SC	49	D2
Camarillo St			
(10100-10602)	NH/SC	56	A3
(10603-11399)	NH/SC	49	D2
(14500-15499)	SO/VN	54	A2/A3/B2/B3
(15500-15799)	EN/VN	54	A2/B2
Camarosa Dr	PP	15	C2
Cambria St	LA	9	B1
Cambridge	MB	27	C3
Cambridge Dr			
(400-999)	BU	50	A1
(1300-1399)	GL	51	C3
Cambridge Pl	SP	38	A3
Cambridge Rd	PA	35	D2
Cambridge St	LA	8	D1
Cambridge Way			
(2100-2199)	TO	32	B2
(5600-5699)	CU	24	D3
Camden Ave	LA	23	B1
(1400-2399)	SP	39	A1
(1710-1899)	SP	39	A1
N Camden Dr	BH	1	B1/C1/C2
S Camden Dr	LA	23	A3
(100-424)	BH	1	D2
(425-499)	BH	20	C3
(1100-1299)	LA	20	C3
Camden Pkwy	SP	39	A1
Camelia Dr	AL	39	D3
E Camelia Dr	AL	39	D3
Camellia Ave			
(4000-4799)	NH/SC	56	A3/B2/B3
(5400-7799)	NH	48	B3/C3/D3
(9900-22299)	CP	45	A1/A2/A3
Camello Rd	WH	52	B1
Camerford Ave	LA	3	D2
Camero Ave	LA	4	B2/B3
Cameron Dr	PA	35	C1
Cameron Ln	LA	9	C1
Cameron Pl	GL	51	A2
Caminito Pl	TZ	52	B3
Camino Cerrado	SP	38	A3
Camino De Encanto	RB	31	D1
Camino De La Costa	RB	31	C1/D1
Camino De La Cumbre	SO/VN	55	B1/C1
Camino De La Cumbre Pl	SO/VN	55	C1
Camino De La Solana	SO/VN	55	C1
Camino De Las Colinas	RB	31	C1/C2/D1
Camino De Villas	BU	50	B3
Camino Del Campo	RB	31	C1/C2
Camino Del Cielo	SP	38	A2
Camino Del Sol			
(200-399)	SP	38	A2
(23700-23799)	TO	32	C1
Camino Lindo	SP	38	A3
Camino Palmero St	LA	2	A3
Camino Real			
(358-1199)	RB	31	B2
(4000-4299)	LA	36	C2
Camino Silvoso	PA	34	B1
Camino Verde	SP	38	A2
Camorilla Dr	LA	36	B2
Campana Rd	WH	52	B1
Campana St	HB	29	C2
Campanita Ct	MP	41	A3
N Campbell Ave	AL	39	D1
S Campbell Ave	AL	39	D1
Campbell Dr			
(4200-4499)	LA	22	C2
(4700-4799)	CU	22	C3
Campdell St	MA/VE	25	C2
Campion Dr	LA	25	B3
Campo Rd	WH	52	A1/B1
Campo St	MP	41	A3
Campus Rd	LA	41	A2
(1400-1999)	LA	33	B1/B2/C1/C2
(1800-1999)	LA	38	D2
(1801-1899)	MP	38	D2
Campus St	GL	51	B3
Camrose Dr	LA	3	A1/B1
Camulos Pl	LA	40	D1/D2
Camulos St	LA	40	C2/D1/D2
Canada St	LA	36	C2
Canal Ct	MA/VE	25	A1
Canal St	MA/VE	21	C2
Cananea Dr	EN/VN	54	C1
Canasta St	TZ	53	A1
Canby Ave			
(6119-8199)	EN/RE/TZ	46	A1/B1/C1
(8400-11299)	NR	43	A3/B3/C3/D3
Candace Pl	LA	33	A3
Candice Pl	CH	42	A2
Candleberry Ln	NR	43	B2
Canedo Ave	NR	43	C2
S Canfield Ave	CU	24	A2
(1400-1752)	LA	6	B1/C1
(1753-3809)	LA	23	B3/C3
Canna Rd	LA	16	A2
Canoga Ave			
(4200-5399)	WH	52	A1/B1
(5400-6499)	WH	45	C1/D1
(6500-8122)	CP	45	B1/C1
(8009-9099)	CP	42	C2/D2
(9100-11199)	CH	42	A2/B2/C2
Canoga Dr	WH	52	B1
Canon Dr			
(700-1099)	PA	34	C3
(21600-22099)	TP	52	C1/D1
N Canon Dr	BH	1	B1/B2/C2
S Canon Dr	BH	1	C3
Canon Crest St	LA	36	C3
Cantaloupe Ave			
(5500-5999)	SO/VN	47	C3/D3
(6600-8443)	VN	47	A3/B3/C3
Cantara St			
(11010-11515)	SV	48	A1/A3
(11516-13299)	NH	48	A1/A2/A3
(13300-13664)	VN	48	A1
(13665-15299)	VN	47	A2
(17000-17299)	VN	46	A2
(17300-17699)	NR	46	A2
(17800-19199)	EN/RE/TZ	46	A1/A2
(19200-19699)	EN/RE/TZ	45	A3
(19900-22299)	CP	45	A1/A2/A3
Cantata Dr	LA	2	A3
Canterbury Ave	NH	48	A1
Canterbury Dr			
(1-99)	NR	43	C2/D2
(5600-5949)	CU	24	D3
(5950-6299)	CU	26	A2/A3
Canterbury Rd	PA	35	C2/C3
Canterbury St	GL	51	C3
Cantlay St			
(10700-10899)	SV	49	A1
(10931-11199)	SV	48	B3
(11500-11699)	NH	48	B3
(13500-13699)	VN	48	B1
(13700-16199)	VN	47	B1/B2/B3
(16600-17699)	VN	46	B2/B3
(18200-19049)	EN/RE/TZ	46	B1
(19700-22199)	CP	45	B1/B2/B3
Canto Dr	LA	37	C3
Canton Dr	NH/SC	56	C2/C3
Canton Ln	NH/SC	56	C2
Canton Pl	NH/SC	56	C2
Canton Way	NH/SC	56	C2
Cantura St	NH/SC	56	B1/B2
Canyon Cv	LA	3	A3
Canyon Dr			
(400-517)	GL	51	B3
(1540-2799)	LA	3	A3/B3
(2800-3299)	LA		Griffith Park
Canyon Ter	LA	3	A3
Canyon Heights Ln	LA	3	A3
Canyon Lake Dr	LA		Griffith Park
Canyon Oak Dr	LA	3	A3
N Canyon View Dr	LA	16	C2
S Canyon View Dr	LA	16	C2
Canyon Vista Dr	LA	36	C2/C3
Capello Way	LA	17	B2
Capetown Ave	AL	38	D3
Capinero Dr	PA	33	B3
Capistrano Ave			
(8200-8599)	CP	42	D1
(9500-9599)	CH	42	C1
Capistrano Way			
(650-799)	LA	6	A2
(4200-4299)	LA	41	C2
Capps Ave			
(6400-7599)	EN/RE/TZ	46	B1/C1
(8300-8399)	NR	43	D2
Capri Dr			
(1200-1447)	PP	15	B3
(1448-1699)	PP	16	C1
Caprino Pl	VN	46	B2
Captains Row	MA/VE	25	B1
Caravana Rd	WH	52	B1
Carcassone Rd	LA	17	C2
Cardenas Ave	WH	52	B1
Cardiff Ave			
(1100-3799)	LA	23	A3/B3/C3
(3800-3899)	CU	24	A2
Cardigan Pl	BH	55	D2
Cardinal St			
(1300-1598)	LA	9	B3
(1700-1799)	LA	40	A1
Cardwell St	LA	57	C1
Carellen St	TO	32	D2
Carey St	PP	15	B2
Caribeth Dr	EN/VN	54	C1
Caribou Ln	LA	17	A2

Street	Area	Pg	Grid
Fiske St	PP	15	B2
Fitch Dr	LA	3	B1
Fithian Ave	LA	38	B2/C2
Flag St	LA	3	A3
Flagler Ln			
(1-45)	TO	31	A2
(46-337)	RB	31	A2
(338-1999)	RB	29	B2/C2
Flagmoor Pl	LA		Griffith Park
Flanders St	GH	44	A2
Flavian Ave	TO	31	A2
Flax Pl	LA	25	C3
Flaxton St	CU	24	C2
Fleet St	MA/VE	25	A1
Fleetwing Ave	LA	26	C2
Flemish Ln	LA	4	C1
Fletcher Ave	SP	39	A1
Fletcher Dr			
(2300-2992)	LA	5	A2/B2
(2951-3085)	LA	51	D2
(3086-3899)	LA	47	D3
(3900-3999)	LA	36	A1
Fleur Dr	PA	34	D3
Flicker Way	LA	2	B1
Flight Ave	LA	26	A3/B2/B3
Flight Pl	LA	26	B2
Flint Ave	LA	23	C3
Flora Ave	LA	37	C3
Flora Dr	IN	13	B1
Floral Ave	LA	2	A2
Floral Dr			
(3300-4999)	LA	41	B1/B2/B3
(4848-4868)	MP	41	B3
W Floral Dr	MP	41	B3
Floral Park Ter	SP	34	D2
E Florence Ave	IN	13	A3/B2/B3
W Florence Ave			
(100-793)	IN	13	B1/B2
(400-3599)	LA	14	B1/B2/B3
(794-1199)	IN	26	B3/C3
Florence Dr	PA	34	A2
Florence Pl	GL	51	C2
N Florence St	BU	49	C2/C3/D3
S Florence St	BU	50	D1
Florentina Ave	AL	41	A3
Flores Ave	LA	13	A1
N Flores St	LA	2	B2/C2
S Flores St	LA	2	C2
Flores De Oro	SP	38	A3
Floresta Ave	LA	11	D1
Floresta Way	LA	10	D3
Florida St	LA	9	C1
Floristan Ave	LA	33	B2
Florizel St	LA	38	B1
Florwood Ave			
(1300-1599)	TO	32	A1
(12900-15099)	HA	28	B3/D3
(15100-15699)	LW	28	D3
(17800-18999)	TO	30	B2/C2
Flournoy Rd	ES	27	B2
(1800-3699)	MB	27	C2
Flower Ave			
(600-999)	MA/VE	21	B2
(1600-1799)	TO	32	A1
Flower Ct	MA/VE	21	B2
Flower Dr	LA	12	B1
Flower St			
(700-949)	GL	51	A1
(950-1999)	GL	50	C2/C3/D3
N Flower St			
(300-399)	LA	9	B2
(400-499)	IN	13	B2
(700-999)	BU	50	B1
S Flower St			
(100-1399)	BU	50	C2
(200-1699)	LA	9	B2/C1
(500-1299)	IN	13	C2/D2
(1700-5799)	LA	12	A1/B1/C1/D1
(5867-9999)	LA	14	A3/B3/C3
Floyd St	BU	49	A2/B3
Floyd Ter	LA	57	B2/C2
Floye Dr	LA	57	C1
Flume Walk	SO/VN	54	B2
Flynn Ranch Rd	LA	57	C1
Foix Pl	CH	42	B3
Folsom St			
(2300-3286)	LA	40	B2/B3
(3287-4499)	LA	41	B1/B2
Fond Dr	EN/VN	54	C1
Fonda Way	LA	37	C2
Fontenelle Way	LA	17	B2

Street	Area	Pg	Grid
Fonthill Ave			
(800-23099)	TO	32	A1/B1
(12500-15099)	HA	28	B3/C3
(15100-15399)	LW	28	D3
(16800-18999)	TO	30	A2/B2/C2
E Foothill Blvd	PA	35	B2/B3
Foothill Dr	LA	3	B2/B3
N Foothill Rd	BH	1	B2/C2/C3
Foothill St	SP	34	D2
Forbes Ave			
(5200-5366)	EN/VN	53	A3
(5367-5499)	EN/VN	46	D3
(6400-7599)	VN	46	B3/C3
(8600-10199)	NO/NR	44	B2/C2/B2
(10500-11299)	GH	44	A2/B2
Ford Ave	RB	29	B2/C2
N Ford Blvd	LA	41	B2/C2
S Ford Blvd			
(122-1299)	LA	41	C2/D2
(688-699)	MP	41	B2
Ford Pl	PA	34	B2
N Ford St	BU	49	D2
Fordham Rd	LA	25	B3/C3
Fordyce Rd	LA	16	B3
Forest Ave			
(100-199)	GL	51	C2
(400-999)	LA	40	B2/B3
(600-1199)	SP	34	D1/D2
(1102-1375)	PA	34	A1/A2
Forest St	IN	13	A2
Forest Knoll Dr	LA	2	B1
Forest Lawn Dr	LA	50	D2
(5900-6795)	LA		Griffith Park
(6796-8899)	LA	57	A3
Forest Park Dr	LA	37	C3
Forge Pl	GH	44	B3
Forman Ave			
(4200-4535)	NH/SC	57	A2
(4536-4799)	NH/SC	49	D2
(4800-4999)	NH	49	D2
Forman Ln	NH/SC	49	D2
N Formosa Ave	LA	2	A3/B3/C2
S Formosa Ave	LA	2	D3
Forney St	LA	36	C1
Forrester Dr			
(2300-2499)	LO	32	D2
(2700-2899)	LA	23	B2
Fortuna St	LA	12	D3
Fortune Pl	LA	34	D1
Fortune Way	LA	34	C1/D1
Foster Dr	LA	6	B2
Fountain Ave			
(3836-5574)	LA	4	C1/C2/C3
(5575-7062)	LA	3	C1/C2/C3
(7063-8499)	LA	2	B1/B2/B3
Fountain Pl	GL	51	A2
Fountain Park Ln	WH	45	D1
Fowler St			
(2700-3158)	LA	40	A3
(3159-3699)	LA	38	D1
Fowling St	MA/VE	25	C2
Fox Hill Ln	CH	42	C1
Fox Hills Dr	CU	24	D2
(1800-2343)	LA	20	C3
(2344-2399)	LA	23	B2
(6000-6199)	CU	26	A2
Fox Hills Mall	CU	26	A2
Foxboro Dr	LA	16	C2
Foxtail Dr	SM	18	A2
Frackelton Pl	LA	33	A3
Frances Ave	LA	22	B1/B2/C2
Francina Dr	EN/VN	54	C1
Francis Ave			
(2700-2999)	LA	8	B2
(4200-4499)	LA	7	B2
Francis Ct			
(1100-1199)	GL	50	D3
(16700-16799)	TO	30	A2
Francis Pl			
(10700-10799)	LA	23	D2
(11400-11699)	LA	22	B2
N Francisca Ave	RB	31	A1/B2
S Francisca Ave	RB	31	B1/B2
Francisca Dr	PA	35	A2
Francisco St			
(400-599)	MB	27	D2
(600-999)	LA	9	B1/C1
Frank St	SM	19	C1
Frankfort St	NR	43	D2
Frankirst Ave	NO/NR	44	C2

Street	Area	Pg	Grid
Franklin Ave			
(100-199)	SG	39	A3
(3700-5549)	LA	4	B1/B2/B3
(5550-7043)	LA	3	B1/B2/B3
(7044-8799)	LA	2	A1/A2/A3/B1
(10700-11299)	CU	24	C1/C2
E Franklin Ave	ES	27	A2/B2
W Franklin Ave			
(100-699)	ES	27	A1/A2
(4100-4299)	BU	57	A2
Franklin Ct	GL	51	B2
Franklin Pl	LA	3	B1
Franklin St	SM	19	A1/B1/B2
Franklin Way	LA	2	A1
Franklin Canyon Dr			
(2436-2689)	BH	55	D3
(2690-3099)	BH	56	C1
Fraser Aly	PA	34	B2
Fraser Ave			
(100-199)	SM	18	D1
(300-1299)	LA	41	C3/D2/D3
N Frederic St			
(100-299)	BU	50	D1
(300-3299)	BU	49	A3/B3/C3
S Frederic St	BU	50	D1
Frederick St			
(100-249)	MA/VE	18	D2
(250-1099)	MA/VE	21	B2
(2700-2899)	LA	36	C1
(3100-3199)	SM	18	D2
Fredonia Dr	LA	57	B1
Freeman Ave			
(11400-12799)	HA	28	A2/B2
(14500-15699)	LW	28	C2/D2
(15700-17099)	LW	30	A2/B2
S Freeman Ave			
(10000-11145)	IN	13	D2
(11146-11199)	IN	28	A2
Freeman Blvd			
(2800-2899)	RB	29	B3
(3768-4099)	RB	28	D1
Freemont Villas St	LA	38	A2
Freese Ln	PA	35	B2
Fremont Ave			
(200-1349)	SP	34	B2
(1350-2099)	SP	38	A3
N Fremont Ave			
(1-299)	AL	38	B3
(100-499)	LA	9	B2
S Fremont Ave			
(1-2207)	AL	38	B3/C3
(500-599)	LA	9	B2
(2100-2115)	AL	41	A3
Fremont Dr	PA	34	B2
Fremont Ln	SP	34	D2
Fremont Pl	LA	7	B2/C2
Fremont Pl W	LA	7	B2
Fremont Villas St	LA	38	A2
French Ave	LA	36	D2
Freshman Dr	CU	24	C2
N Fresno St	LA	40	B3/C3
S Fresno St	LA	40	C2/C3/D2
Frey Ave	MA/VE	21	C2
Friar St			
(10600-10699)	NH	49	B1
(11500-12899)	NH	48	C1/C3
(13300-13499)	SO/VN	48	C1
(13700-15599)	SO/VN	47	C2/C3
(18200-19199)	EN/VN	46	C1/C2
(19200-19699)	EN/RE/TZ	45	C3
(19700-20099)	WH	45	C3
Frieda Dr	LA	36	B2
Friends St	PP	15	C1/C2
Front St			
(600-2349)	AL	39	C1/C2/D1
(2350-3299)	AL	38	C3
N Front St	BU	50	B1/B2
S Front St	BU	50	C2
W Front St	AL	38	C3
Frontenac Ave	LA	36	C2/C3
Frontera Dr	PP	15	C2
Frontier Pl	CH	42	A1
Fruitdale St	LA	5	B2
Fruitland Dr			
(10800-10949)	NH/SC	57	B1
(10950-11099)	NH/SC	56	B3
Fryman Pl	NH/SC	56	C2
Fryman Rd	NH/SC	56	C2
Fujita St	TO	32	B1/C1
Fulcher Ave	NH	48	C3/D3
Fullbright Ave			
(6900-7799)	CP	45	B2/C2
(8300-8899)	CP	42	D3

Street	Area	Pg	Grid
(8900-11099)	CH	42	A3/B3/C3
Fullbright Pl	CH	42	A3
N Fuller Ave	LA	2	A3/B3/C2
S Fuller Ave	LA	2	D3
FullerFarm St	NR	44	B1
Fulmar Ave			
(23800-23999)	TO	32	C3
(24000-24199)	LO	32	C3
Fulton Ave			
(4100-5419)	SO/VN	55	A2/B2
(5420-6799)	SO/VN	48	C1/D1
(6800-8099)	NH	48	A1/B1/C1
Fulton Ct	SO/VN	55	A2
Funchal Rd	LA	17	C2
Furness Ave	LA	36	B3
Future Pl	LA	36	C1
Future St	LA	36	B1/C1
Fyler Pl	LA	33	B1
Gable Dr	EN/VN	53	B1
N Gage Ave	LA	41	B1/C1
S Gage Ave	LA	41	C1/D1
W Gage Ave	LA	14	A2/A3
Gail St	LA	36	C1
Gainsborough Ave	LA	4	A2
Gainsborough Dr	PA	35	C3
Galaxy Way	LA	20	C3
Galbreth Rd	PA	35	A2
Gale Ave	HA	28	A2/B2/C2
N Gale Dr	BH	2	D2
S Gale Dr	BH	6	A1
Gale Pl	SM	18	A2/A3
Galena St	LA	38	B1
Galendo St	WH	52	B1
Galer Pl	GL	51	A3/B3
Galewood St			
(4200-13099)	NH/SC	55	B3/C3
(4300-13499)	SO/VN	55	B3/C2
Gallardo St	LA	40	B1
Gallaudet Pl	PP	15	B2
Galleon St	MA/VE	25	A1
Galli St	HA	28	C3
Galloway St	PP	15	B2
Galva Ave	TO	31	C3
Galveston St	LA	5	D2
Galvez St	WH	52	A1
Galvin St	CU	24	C2
Gambier St	LA	38	C2
Ganahl St			
(2500-3149)	LA	40	B3
(3150-3399)	LA	41	B1
Ganymede Dr	LA	36	B2
Gaona St	WH	52	B1
Garcia Walk	LA	5	C1
Garden Ave			
(3100-4049)	LA	5	A2/B2
(4050-4199)	LA	51	C1
Garden Ln	LA	20	C3
(500-699)	PA	34	C2
Garden St	GL	50	D2/D3
Garden Grove Ave			
(4900-5499)	TZ	53	A1
(6800-8299)	EN/RE/TZ	46	A2/B2
(8300-11299)	NR	43	A3/B3/D3
Garden Homes Ave	LA	38	B2
Garden Land Rd	LA	53	D3
Gardena Ave			
(1300-1399)	GL	51	C2
(1400-1999)	GL	5	A2
Gardenside Ln	LA	5	A1
N Gardner St	LA	2	A3/B3/C2
S Gardner St	LA	2	D3
N Garey St	LA	9	B3
S Garey St	LA	9	C3
Garfield Ave			
(300-1199)	SP	34	D2/D3
(900-1199)	MA/VE	21	B3/C3
(1200-1298)	AL	39	A2
(1200-1332)	PA	34	D3
(1333-1799)	PA	39	A2
(1701-1799)	SP	39	A2
(10700-11299)	CU	24	B1/C1
E Garfield Ave	GL	51	C2/C3
N Garfield Ave			
(1-1199)	AL	39	A2/B2
(1-1475)	PA	34	A3/B2
(600-699)	MP	39	D3
S Garfield Ave			
(1-1299)	AL	39	B2/C3/D2
(1-78)	PA	34	B2
W Garfield Ave	GL	51	C1/C2
Garfield Pl	LA	3	B3
Garland Ave	LA	9	B1

Street	Range	City	Pg	Grid
Huntington Dr	(301-829)	PA	39	A2
	(302-1994)	AL	39	A1/A2
	(830-3198)	PA	35	C3/D1/D2/D3
	(1100-1513)	SP	38	A3
	(1501-2199)	SP	39	A1/A2
	(8200-8482)	SG	35	C3
Huntington Dr N	(4200-4279)	LA	37	C3
	(4276-5799)	LA	38	B1/B2/B3/C1
	(5653-5701)	AL	38	B3
Huntington Dr S		LA	38	B1/B2/B3/C1
Huntington Ln	(1-1399)	SP	38	A3
	(1700-2799)	RB	29	C2/C3
Huntington Ter		LA	38	B1
Huntington Garden Dr		PA	34	D3
Huntley Ave	(4100-4299)	CU	22	B3
	(4300-4699)	CU	24	C1
Huntley Cir		PA	35	C2
Huntley Dr	(300-899)	LA	2	C1
	(1100-1299)	LA	9	B2
Huntley Pl		CU	24	C1
Hurford Ter		EN/VN	54	B1
Hurlbut St		PA	34	C2
Huron Ave		CU	24	B1/C1
Huron St		LA	36	D2
Hurricane St		MA/VE	25	A1
Huston St	(10100-10949)	NH	49	D1/D2
	(10950-11699)	NH	56	A2/A3
	(11700-12699)	NH/SC	56	A1/A2
	(12900-14622)	SO/VN	55	A1/A2/A3
	(14623-15499)	SO/VN	54	A2/A3
	(15500-16299)	EN/VN	54	A1/A2
Hutchison Ave		LA	24	A3
Hutton Dr		BH	55	D2
Hutton Pl		BH	55	D2
Huxley St		LA	5	A1
Hyans St		LA	8	A3
Hyde St		LA	38	C2
Hyde Park Blvd		LA	14	A1/A2
E Hyde Park Blvd		IN	13	A2/A3/B2
W Hyde Park Blvd		IN	13	B1/B2
Hyde Park Pl		IN	13	A2
Hyler Ave		LA	33	B1
Hyperion Ave	(700-2004)	LA	4	C3/D3
	(2005-3399)	LA	5	A1/B1
Hythe Ct		BH	55	D2
Ibanez Ave		WH	52	B1
Ida Ave		LA	22	C1
Ida St		PP	15	B1
Idaho Ave	(100-2499)	SM	18	B1/B2/B3
	(2500-2599)	SM	19	A1
	(11300-12499)	LA	19	B2/B3
Idell St		LA	36	D2
Idlewood Rd		GL	51	A1
Idylwild Ave		LA	37	B2
Iglesia Dr		WH	52	B1
Ignatius Cir		LA	25	B3
Iliff St		PP	15	B2
Illinois Ct		ES	27	A3
Illinois Dr		SP	38	A2
Illinois St		ES	27	A3/B2
Ilona Ave		LA	20	C3
Imlay Ave		CU	24	D1
Imogen Ave		LA	4	D3
E Imperial Ave	(100-1876)	ES	27	A2/A3
	(1877-1898)	ES	26	D3
	(1895-1899)	LA	26	D3
W Imperial Ave		ES	27	A1/A2
Imperial Hwy		IN	28	A2
W Imperial Hwy	(2201-2299)	IN	13	D1
	(2624-4084)	HA	28	A2
	(2700-4799)	IN	28	A1/A2/A3
	(5100-5328)	IN	26	D3
	(5101-5959)	LA	26	D1/D2/D3
	(5600-7099)	LA	27	A1/A2/A3
	(5834-6774)	ES	27	A1/A2
	(5960-6656)	LA	25	D3
	(7034-7098)	MA/VE	27	A1
Imperial St		LA	9	C3
Inadale Ave		LA	10	D2
Inaglen Way		LA	10	D2
Inavale Pl		LA	16	B2
Ince Blvd		CU	24	A2/B2
Independence Ave	(6400-6499)	WH	45	C2
	(6500-7799)	CP	45	B2/C2
	(8300-9099)	CP	42	C2/D2
	(9100-11099)	CH	42	A2/B2/C2
Independencia St		WH	52	B1
Index St	(15600-17799)	GH	44	A1/A2/A3
	(17900-17999)	GH	43	A3
	(18100-19299)	NR	43	A2/A3
India St		LA	5	B2
Indian Wood Rd		CU	24	C2
Indiana Ave	(300-1199)	MA/VE	21	A2/B1/B2
	(900-1205)	SP	34	D1
	(1206-1699)	SP	38	A2
N Indiana Ave		LA	38	D1
Indiana Ct	(500-1099)	MA/VE	21	A2/B2
	(500-599)	SP	34	D1
	(700-799)	ES	27	A3
Indiana Pl		SP	38	A3
Indiana St		ES	27	A3
N Indiana St	(100-699)	LA	41	B1/C1
	(1400-2399)	LA	38	C1/D1
S Indiana St		LA	41	C1/D1
Indiana Ter		SP	38	A2
Indianapolis St		LA	22	A1/A2/B1
Industrial Ave		IN	13	B1
Industrial St		LA	9	C2/C3
Inez St		LA	40	C1/C2
Ingledale Ter		LA	5	A1
Ingleside Dr	(100-699)	MB	27	D2
	(2800-3299)	HB	27	D2
S Ingleside Dr		MB	27	D2
Inglewood Ave	(500-3750)	RB	29	A3/B3/C3
	(3751-4099)	RB	28	D1
	(3801-15649)	LW	28	C1/D1
	(9301-11357)	IN	13	C1/D1
	(11358-11473)	IN	28	A1
	(11400-14799)	HA	28	A1/B1/C1
	(15650-17398)	LW	29	A3/B3
	(19000-19124)	TO	29	C3
	(19125-19376)	TO	31	A3
	(19377-19599)	TO	30	C1
N Inglewood Ave		IN	13	A1/B1
S Inglewood Ave	(100-11254)	IN	13	B1/C1/D1
	(4758-4799)	TO	30	C1
Inglewood Blvd	(3000-3208)	LA	19	D3
	(3209-4499)	LA	22	—
	(4500-5279)	CU	22	C3
	(5280-5599)	CU	26	A1
Inglis St		LA	36	A1
Ingomar St	(17900-19199)	EN/RE/TZ	46	A1/A2/B2
	(19200-19699)	EN/RE/TZ	45	B3
	(19700-22199)	CP	45	B1/B2/B3
Ingraham St		LA	8	B1
	(1000-3849)	LA	9	B1
	(3850-4099)	LA	7	B3
Ingram Ranch Dr		WH	52	C1
Ingrum Way		TO	30	D1
Innes Ave		LA	5	D2
Innes Pl		MA/VE	21	C1
Innsdale Dr		LA	—	Griffith Park
Inskeep Ave		LA	12	D1
Institute Pl		LA	4	D1
Interceptor St		LA	26	C2/C3
International Ave		CP	42	D2
International Rd		LA	26	D2
Internatl Boardwalk		RB	31	B1
Inverness Ave		LA	4	A2
Inwood Dr		SO/VN	55	C2
Inyo St		LA	37	C3
Ione Dr		LA	57	C2
Ione Pl		LA	57	C2
Iowa Ave		LA	19	B2/B3
Iowa St		PA	34	A2
Iowa Trl		TP	52	D1
Iredell Ln		NH/SC	56	C2
Iredell St		NH/SC	56	C1/C2
N Irena Ave		RB	31	A1/A2/B2
S Irena Ave		RB	31	B2/C2
Irene Ct		ES	27	A2
Irene St		LA	23	C2
Iris Ave		TO	32	A2/B2
Iris Cir		LA	3	A2
Iris Dr		LA	3	A2
Iris Pl		LA	3	A2
Irolo St		LA	8	B1/C1
Irondale Ave	(5400-5599)	WH	45	D2
	(6700-8264)	CP	45	A2/B2/C2
	(8265-8499)	CP	42	D2/D3
	(9400-10799)	CH	42	A2/B2/C2
Ironsides St		MA/VE	25	A1
Irvine Ave	(4200-4799)	NH/SC	56	A2/B2
	(4800-5499)	NH	56	A2
	(5600-8199)	NH	48	A3/B3/C3/D3
Irving Ave		GL	50	C2/C3/D2
N Irving Blvd		LA	3	D2
S Irving Blvd		LA	7	A3/B3
Irving Dr		BU	50	A1
Irving Pl		CU	24	B2
Irving St		AL	39	C2
Irvington Pl		LA	33	C2
Irvington Ter		LA	33	C2
Irwin Ave		IN	26	D3
Isabel Dr		LA	36	B1/B2/C1
Isabel St		LA	36	B1/C1/C2/D2
N Isabel St		GL	51	A2/B2
S Isabel St		GL	51	B2
W Isabel St		BU	50	B1
Isadora Ln		LA	17	B2
Isis Ave	(100-899)	IN	26	B3/C3
	(7700-9899)	LA	26	B3/C3
	(11400-11599)	LA	28	A1
	(11800-11999)	IN	28	A1/B1
	(12000-14298)	HA	28	B1/C1
	(14300-14599)	LW	28	C1
Isleta St		LA	16	B3
Itasca St	(16200-16999)	NO/NR	44	C2/C3
	(19200-19499)	NR	43	C1/C2
	(19800-19899)	CH	43	C1
	(20100-22599)	CH	42	C1/C2/C3
Ithaca Ave		LA	38	C2
Ivadel Pl		EN/VN	53	B3
Ivan Ct		LA	5	B1
Ivan Hill Ter		LA	5	B2
Ivanhoe Dr		LA	5	B1/B2
Ivar Ave		LA	3	A2/B2/C2
Ivarene Ave		LA	3	A2
Ivarson Rd		CH	42	A1
Iverson Ln		CH	42	A1
Iverson Rd		CH	42	A1
Ives Ln		RB	29	C3
E Ivy Ave		IN	13	B2
W Ivy Ave		IN	13	B2
Ivy Pl		LA	19	D2/D3
Ivy St	(400-799)	GL	51	B1
	(3100-3199)	LA	23	C3
Ivy Way		CU	24	B3
Ivy Glen Way		LA	23	C2
Ivyside Pl		EN/VN	53	C3
W Jacaranda Ave		BU	49	D2
Jacaranda St		PA	33	B3
Jacaranda Rd		LA	33	B2
Jackson Ave		CU	24	B2
Jackson Pl		GL	51	A2
Jackson St	(600-899)	LA	9	B3
	(1800-1999)	BU	50	A1
E Jackson St		PA	34	A3
N Jackson St		GL	51	A2/B2
S Jackson St		GL	51	B2
Jacob St		CU	24	A3
Jacobs Ln		SP	34	D1
Jacqueline St		LA	33	C3
Jacques St		TO	31	B2
Jade St		LA	38	D1
Jadestone Dr		SO/VN	54	C3
Jadestone St		SO/VN	54	C3
Jaguar Ct		EN/RE/TZ	46	C2
Jalmia Dr		LA	57	D1
Jalmia Pl		LA	57	D1
Jalmia Way		LA	57	D1
James St		LA	36	C2
James Alan Cir		CH	42	B1
James M Wood Blvd	(786-1798)	LA	9	B1/C1
	(1715-3575)	LA	8	C1/C2/C3
Jamestown Rd		BU	50	A1
Jamieson Ave	(5700-6399)	EN/VN	46	C2/D2
	(6370-8299)	EN/RE/TZ	46	A2/B2/C2
	(8300-8499)	NR	43	D3
Jan St		CP	45	C2
Jandy Pl		LA	22	D2
Jane Pl		PA	34	C2
Janet Ln		TO	31	D2/D3
Janet Pl		LA	33	B1
Janice Pl		BH	56	D2
Janisann Ave		CU	24	D2
Jannetta Ave		BU	49	B3
January Dr		TO	32	D2
Japanese Village Plaza Mall		LA	9	C3
Jared Dr		TZ	53	A1
Jarvis St		LA	5	D3
Jasmine Ave	(3300-3799)	LA	23	C2
	(3800-4599)	CU	24	B2/C2
Jason Cir		TO	31	C3
Jasper St		LA	38	C1
Java Ave		IN	13	C2
Java Dr		BH	55	C2/D2
Jean Pl		CU	24	B2
Jeanne Ln		EN/VN	54	C1
Jefferies St		LA	36	D2
Jefferson Ave		HA	28	B2/C2
Jefferson Blvd		CU	22	C3
	(6135-11599)	CU	24	B2/B3/C2/D2
	(11600-12399)	CU	26	A1/A2
E Jefferson Blvd		LA	12	B1/B2/C2
N Jefferson Blvd		CU	22	C3
		CU	24	D2
W Jefferson Blvd		MA/VE	25	B2
	(100-799)	LA	12	B1
	(785-3554)	LA	11	B1/B2/B3
	(3555-5686)	LA	10	A1/A2/A3
	(5515-6134)	LA	24	A3/B3
	(12400-12598)	LA	26	A1
	(12531-13399)	LA	25	B3
Jefferson Dr		PA	35	A2
Jefferson St		TO	32	B2
Jeffery Dr		TO	31	B2
Jeffrey Pl		WH	52	B3
Jeffrey Mark Ct		CH	42	B1
W Jeffries Ave		BU	49	C1/C2/C3
Jellico Ave	(5800-6099)	EN/VN	46	C2
	(6700-7599)	VN	46	B2/C2
	(7600-8299)	NR	46	A2/B2
	(8600-9699)	NR	44	C1/D1
	(10400-11399)	GH	44	A1/B1
Jennings Dr		LA	38	B2
Jenny Ave		LA	26	C2
Jersey St		GH	44	A2/A3
Jesse Ave		GL	50	D2
Jesse St	(1500-1599)	LA	9	C3
	(2171-2399)	LA	40	C1
Jessica Dr		LA	36	B2
Jet Pl		LA	57	D1
Jewel St		LA	5	D1
Jewett Dr		LA	2	A1/A2
Jib St		MA/VE	25	B1
Jill Pl		EN/VN	53	B3
Joanne Pl		CU	24	D2
Joffre St		LA	16	B3
John Pl		MB	27	D2
John St	(200-2499)	MB	27	C2/D2
	(3400-3499)	LA	4	D3
Johnson Aly		PA	34	A3
Johnson St		MB	27	C3/D3
Johnson Ave		RB	29	A3/B3
Johnston St	(1700-1949)	LA	40	A2
	(1950-3399)	LA	37	C2/D2
Jolene Ct		NH	48	B2
Jolley Dr		BU	50	A1
Jon Allan Dr		NH	48	B2
Jones Aly		PA	35	A2
Jones Ave		LA	38	D1
Jonesboro Dr	(1300-1383)	LA	15	B3
	(1384-1499)	LA	16	C1
Jonesboro Pl		LA	15	B3
Jonfin St		GH	44	A2
Jordan Ave	(6800-7999)	CP	45	B1/C1
	(9100-10699)	CH	42	A2/B2/C2
Jordan Way		CU	24	C2
Jorderr Ave		LA	56	D3
Josard Ave		SG	35	C3
Jovan St		EN/RE/TZ	46	C1
Jovenita Canyon Dr		LA	56	D3
Jovita Ave		CH	42	B3/C3

Street Index

Street Index

Street	Abbr	Pg	Grid
Oneal Ct	NR	43	C3
Oneida St	PA	35	C2/C3
Oneonta Aly			
(1550-1999)	AL	39	A1
(1600-1699)	SP	39	A1
Oneonta Dr			
(800-1199)	LA	36	A2/B2
(800-899)	SP	38	A3
Oneonta Knls	SP	38	A3
Onrado St	TO	32	A1
N Ontario St	BU	49	A2/B2/C2/D3
Onteora Way	LA	33	B1
Onyx Dr	LA	37	C3
Onyx St			
(3400-4899)	TO	30	D2
(4900-5399)	TO	31	B2
Opal St			
(600-1299)	RB	31	B2
(2300-3599)	LA	40	C1/D2
(2900-3399)	TO	32	A1
Ophir Dr	LA	20	B1
Oporto Dr	LA	3	A1
Oracle Pl	PP	15	B2
Orange Ave	TO	32	B2
N Orange Dr	LA	3	B1/C1/D1
S Orange Dr			
(100-1029)	LA	7	A1/B1
(1030-2499)	LA	6	B3/C3/D3
(2500-3999)	LA	10	A2/B2
Orange Pl			
(1-92)	PA	34	B2
(5100-5199)	LA	10	B2
Orange St			
(1500-2599)	AL	39	C1
(6100-6699)	LA	6	A1/A2
N Orange St	GL	51	A2/B2
S Orange St	GL	51	B2/C2
Orange Grove Ave			
(200-1299)	SP	34	D2
(300-2399)	AL	38	B3/C3
(600-1599)	GL	51	B2/B3
(2600-2641)	AL	41	A3
E Orange Grove Ave	BU	50	B2/C2
N Orange Grove Ave	LA	2	A2/B2/C2
S Orange Grove Ave			
(300-649)	LA	2	D2/D3
(650-1899)	LA	6	A2/B2/C2
(2000-2099)	AL	38	C3
W Orange Grove Ave	BU	50	C1
E Orange Grove Blvd			
(1-981)	PA	34	A2/A3
(982-3025)	PA	35	A1/A2/A3
N Orange Grove Blvd	PA	34	A2/B2
S Orange Grove Blvd	PA	34	B2/C2
Orange Grove Cir	PA	34	C2
Orange Grove Pl	SP	34	D2
Orange Grove Ter			
(1-99)	BU	50	B3
(700-799)	SP	34	D2
Orangewood St	PA	35	C2
Orchard Ave			
(1300-2099)	LA	8	C2/D2
(2100-4699)	LA	11	A3/B3/C3
(8600-11999)	LA	14	C3
Orchard Dr	IN	13	C2
N Orchard Dr	BU	50	A1/B1/C1
S Orchard Dr	BU	50	C1/D1
Orchid Ave	LA	3	B1
Orchid Dr	LA	10	D2
Orchid Ln	BU	50	A1
Ord St	LA	9	B2/B3
Oregon Ave			
(3100-3199)	LA	40	C2
(10700-10899)	CU	24	B1
Oregon Ct	TO	30	D2
Oregon St			
(100-599)	ES	27	A2/B2
(2700-3299)	LA	40	C2
Oreo Pl	PP	15	B1
Orey Pl	CP	45	C2
Orienta Dr	AL	39	A3
Orilla Ave	LA	51	C3
Orinda Ave	LA	10	D3
Oriole Dr	LA	2	B1
Oriole Ln	LA	2	A1
Oriole Way	LA	2	B1
Orion Ave			
(4600-4999)	SO/VN	54	A2/B2
(6200-6399)	SO/VN	47	C2
(6400-8299)	VN	47	A2/B2/C2
(8300-9899)	NO/NR	44	A3/B3
(9930-11134)	MH	44	B3/B3
N Orlando Ave	LA	2	B2/C2
S Orlando Ave			
(100-599)	LA	2	C2/D2
(1000-1299)	LA	6	B1
(5800-5999)	LA	13	A1
Orlando Pl	PA	35	A1
Orlando Rd	PA	35	C1/C2
Orme Ave	LA	40	C2/D1/D2
Ormond Ln	RB	29	C2
Oros St	LA	36	D1
Ortiz Ln	LA	17	A2
Ortley Pl	SO/VN	48	C1
Orton Ave	LA	20	C3
Orum Rd	LA	17	B1
Orville St	CU	24	D2
Osage Ave			
(7300-8798)	LA	26	B3/C3
(14500-15399)	LW	28	C2/D2
(15700-16999)	LW	30	A2
(16900-20799)	TO	30	B2/C2/D2
N Osage Ave	IN	13	B2
S Osage Ave			
(300-11124)	IN	13	B2/C2/D2
(11125-11277)	IN	28	A2
Osage Ct	TO	32	B1
Osborne St			
(15800-16999)	NO/NR	44	C2/D3
(17000-17699)	NR	44	D1/D2
(17800-18299)	NR	43	D3
(20900-21699)	CP	42	C2
Osceola St	GL	51	C3
Oso Ave			
(5500-5899)	WH	45	D2
(6500-8266)	CP	45	A2/B2/C2
(8267-8899)	CP	42	D3
(8900-11099)	CH	42	A3/B3/C3
Ostrom Ave			
(5300-5999)	EN/VN	46	C3/D3
(7200-7999)	VN	46	A3/B3
Ostybe Rd	NH/SC	56	C1
Oswego St	PA	35	B2
Otay Dr	LA	36	B2
Otis Ave	TZ	46	D1
(5000-5399)	TZ	53	A1
Otsego Ct	EN/VN	53	A3
Otsego St			
(10400-10949)	NH	49	D1/D2
(10950-11699)	NH	56	A2/A3
(11700-12799)	NH/SC	56	A1
(12900-14564)	SO/VN	55	A1/A2/A3
(14565-15299)	SO/VN	54	A2/A3
(15500-16599)	EN/VN	54	A1/A2
(16600-17499)	EN/VN	53	A2/A3
Ottawa Ct	LA	9	C1
Ottone Way	LA	17	B2
Outlook Ave	LA	33	C3
Outpost Cir	LA		Griffith Park
Outpost Dr			
(1842-2162)	LA	2	A3
(2163-2799)	LA	57	D2
Outpost Cove Dr	LA	57	D2
Outrigger	MA/VE	25	B1
Outrigger Mall	MA/VE	25	B1
Outrigger St	MA/VE	25	B1
Ovada Pl	LA	17	C1
Overdale Dr	LA	10	D2
Overhill Dr			
(1300-4999)	IN	13	A2
(5000-5898)	LA	10	D2
(5831-6399)	LA	13	A2
Overland Ave			
(1800-2349)	LA	20	C2
(2350-3799)	LA	23	B1/C1/D2
(3800-11299)	CU	24	B1/B2/C2/D2
Overman Ave	CH	42	A3/B3
Overton St	LA	9	C1
Owen Brown Rd	PP/TP	52	C2/C3
Owensmouth Ave			
(5400-6445)	WH	45	C1/D1
(6446-8249)	CP	45	A1/B1/C1
(8250-9099)	CP	42	C2/D2
(9112-10999)	CH	42	A2/B2/C2
Owosso Ave	HB	29	C2
Oxford Ave			
(600-830)	MA/VE	21	C3
(831-1099)	MA/VE	25	A1/A2
(11400-12799)	HA	28	A2/B2
N Oxford Ave			
(100-2099)	LA	4	B1/C1/D1
(1200-1471)	PA	35	A2
S Oxford Ave	LA	8	A1/B1/C1/D1
Oxford Rd	PA	35	C2/D2
Oxford Way			
(1-99)	NR	43	D2
(900-999)	BH	1	B1
Oxley Aly	SP	34	D2
Oxley St	SP	34	D2/D3
Oxnard St			
(4300-4399)	BU	49	C2
(10400-10914)	NH	49	C1
(10915-12899)	NH	48	C1/C2/C3
(12066-12099)	NH/SC	48	C2
(12900-13672)	SO/VN	48	C1
(13673-15399)	SO/VN	47	C2/C3
(17100-17698)	EN/VN	46	C2/C3
(18270-19190)	TZ	46	C1/C2
(19191-19699)	TZ	45	D3
(19700-22199)	WH	45	D1/D2/D3
Ozeta Ter	LA	2	B1
Ozmun Ct	SP	34	D2
Ozone Ave			
(1-199)	MA/VE	18	D1
(600-1399)	SM	18	D2
Ozone Ct			
(1-199)	MA/VE	21	B1
(2300-2699)	HB	29	B1
Pacheco Dr	SO/VN	54	B3/C2
Pacific Aly	SP	34	D2
Pacific Ave	ES	27	B2
(1-191)	MA/VE	18	D1
(192-3257)	MA/VE	21	B1/C1/C2/D2
(500-3699)	MB	27	C2/D2
(3064-3099)	SM	18	D1
(3258-6999)	MA/VE	25	A1/B1/C1
(11800-12899)	LA	22	B1/B2
N Pacific Ave			
(100-1099)	GL	51	A1/A2/B1
(200-499)	RB	31	A1
S Pacific Ave			
(100-799)	GL	51	B1/B2/C1
(100-149)	RB	31	B1
W Pacific Ave			
(1800-1949)	BU	50	B1
(1950-4499)	BU	49	B1/B2/B3
Pacific Ct	MA/VE	25	A1
Pacific Pl	PP	15	C1
(500-1199)	MB	27	C2/D2
Pacific St	SM	18	C1/C2
Pacific Ter	SM	18	C1
Pacific Coast Hwy			
(35-2810)	HB	29	B1/C1/C2/D2
(1700-2441)	LO	32	D2/D3
(2442-3744)	TO	32	C1/D1/D2
(2700-2808)	MB	29	B1
(2809-3298)	MB	27	D3
(2811-3299)	HB	27	D3
(3651-5999)	TO	31	C2/D2/D3
(14700-14899)	SM	15	C2
(14900-16971)	PP	15	C1
N Pacific Coast Hwy			
(1-34)	HB	29	D2
(100-807)	RB	31	A1
(801-999)	RB	29	D2
S Pacific Coast Hwy	RB	31	B1/C1/C2
Pacific Concourse Dr	LA	28	A1
Pacific Oak Dr	CH	42	B1
Pacific View Dr	LA	57	C2/D2
Pacific View Trl	LA	57	C2/D2
Packard St	LA	6	B1/B2/B3/C2
Packwood Trl	LA	57	C2
Pacoima Ct	NH/SC	56	C2
Padilla Pl	LA	10	C2
Padilla St	SG	39	B3
Padre Ln	LA	2	A2
Padre Ter	LA	3	B2
Padron Pl	LO	32	C3
Padua Pl	MA/VE	21	C2
Pageant Pl	EN/VN	53	C3
Pagoda Ct	LA	37	B3
Pagoda Pl	LA	37	B3
Paige St	LA	37	B3
Paine Aly	PA	35	A2
Painter St	PA	34	A2
Paisley Ln	LA	16	C2
Paiute Ave	CH	42	A1
Pala Mesa Dr	NR	43	A2
Pala Mesa Pl	NR	43	A2
Paladora Ave	PA	35	A2
Palatine Dr	AL	38	B3
Palawan Way	MA/VE	21	C2
(13900-14299)	MA/VE	25	A1
Palencia Ave	WH	52	B1
Palermo Ln	SP	34	D2
Palisade St	PA	34	A2
Palisades Ave	SM	18	A1/A2
Palisades Beach Rd	SM	18	A1/B1
Palisair Pl	PP	15	B1
Palm Ave	ES	27	B2
(800-1199)	LA	2	B1
(900-1099)	SP	34	D1
(1800-3699)	MB	27	C2
E Palm Ave			
(1-1099)	BU	50	B2
(500-1799)	ES	27	A2/A3
N Palm Ave	AL	39	B1
S Palm Ave	AL	39	B1/C1/D1
W Palm Ave			
(100-799)	ES	27	A1/A2
(200-1299)	BU	50	C1
Palm Ct	SP	34	D1
Palm Dr			
(1-2817)	HB	29	B1/C1/D1
(2300-2599)	LA	12	A1
(2818-2999)	HB	27	D2
N Palm Dr	BH	1	B2/B3/C3
S Palm Dr	BH	1	C2
Palm Ln	RB	29	C2
Palm Ter	PA	34	A3
Palm Way	TO	30	D1
S Palm Grove Ave			
(1900-2369)	LA	7	D1
(2400-3099)	LA	10	A3
Palm View Dr	LA	33	C3
Palm View Pl	PA	34	C3
Palmas Dr	PA	35	D2
E Palmer Ave	GL	51	C2/C3
W Palmer Ave	GL	51	C2
Palmer Dr			
(2800-2899)	LA	33	B1
(2900-3299)	LA	51	C3
Palmera Ave	PP	15	B1
Palmero Blvd	LA	10	C3
Palmero Dr	LA	36	A2/B2
Palmerston Pl	LA	4	B2
Palmetto Dr			
(1-399)	AL	39	C2
(1-599)	PA	34	C2
Palmetto St	LA	9	C3
Palms Blvd			
(590-1399)	MA/VE	21	B2/B3/C2
(10000-11274)	LA	23	C2/D1
(11275-13299)	LA	22	A2/B1/B2
Palmwood Dr	LA	10	B3
Palmyra Rd	LA	10	B3
Palo Dr	TZ	52	B3
Palo Alto St	LA	9	A1
Palo Verde Ave	PA	35	A2/B2
Palo Vista Dr	LA	57	C1
Paloma Ave			
(1-199)	MA/VE	21	B1
(5600-5899)	LA	12	D2
Paloma Ct	MA/VE	21	B1
Paloma Dr	SP	34	D1
Paloma St			
(1200-1610)	LA	9	D2
(1400-3025)	PA	35	A1/A2/A3
(1611-4099)	LA	12	A2/A3/B2/C2
Palomar Dr	TZ	52	A3
Palomar Pl	TZ	52	A3
Palomar Rd	PA	35	C3
Palomino Dr	TZ	53	B1
Palora St	LA		
(17300-18099)	EN/VN	53	A2
(18200-18299)	TZ	53	A1
Palos Verdes Blvd			
(100-1999)	RB	31	C1/C2/D1
(5300-22499)	TO	31	D1/D2
Palos Verdes Dr N	PV	31	D1
Palos Verdes Dr W	PV	31	D1
Pamela Dr	BH	1	B1
Pampas Rd	WH	52	B3
Pampas Ricas Blvd	PP	15	C2
Panama St			
(10800-11131)	CU	24	C1
(11132-11185)	CU	22	B3
(11186-12999)	LA	22	B3/C2/C3/D2
Panamint Dr	LA	36	B2
Panamint St	LA	36	A2
Panay Way	MA/VE	25	A1
Pandora Ave	LA	20	C2
Panorama Ter	LA	5	B1
Paola Ave	LA	38	B2/C2
Paradise Dr	LA	37	C3
Paradise Ln	TP	52	D2
Paralta Ave	WH	52	A1
Paramount Dr	LA	3	B1
Pardee St	LA	26	C3

Street	City	Pg	Grid
Randall St			
(1300-1699)	GL	50	D2/D3
(5100-5299)	CU	22	C3
(5300-5599)	CU	26	A1
Randi Ave	CP	45	C1
Randolph Ave			
(500-599)	PA	35	C3
(3600-4499)	LA	38	B2
Randolph St	LA	12	D3
	LA	38	B2
Range Rd	LA	33	B1
Range View Ave	LA	33	C2
Rangely Ave	LA	2	C1
Rangely St	LA	2	C2
Rangeview Dr	GL	50	B3
Ranons Ave			
(3900-3951)	LA	47	D3
(3952-4199)	LA	51	C3
Raphael St	LA	33	C2
Rathburn Ave	NR	43	A3/B3/C3/D3
Ratner St	SV	48	A3
(11900-13399)	NH	48	A1/A2
(13400-13599)	VN	48	A1
Ravendale Rd	SG	35	D3
Ravenswood Ave	IN	13	D2
Ravenwood Ct	LA	55	D1
Ravine Rd	LA	5	C2
Ravoli Dr	PP	15	B3
Rawlings Ave	WH	45	D2
Ray Ct	LA	33	B2
Raybet Rd	LA	55	D1
Rayen St			
(15400-16999)	NO/NR	44	D2/D3
(17000-17814)	NR	44	D1/D2
(17815-18899)	NR	43	D2/D3
(22000-23963)	CP	42	D1
Rayford Dr	LA	25	B3/C3
Raymer St			
(12500-13499)	NH	48	B1/B2
(13500-13699)	VN	48	B1
(14400-16399)	VN	47	A1/A2
(17100-17809)	NR	44	D1/D2
(17810-18099)	NR	43	D3
Raymond Ave			
(200-1599)	GL	50	C3/D2/D3
(400-799)	SM	18	D2
(1600-1699)	HB	29	C1
(1900-2199)	LA	8	D2
(2200-5834)	LA	11	A3/B3/D3
(5835-11599)	LA	14	A2/B2/C2
N Raymond Ave			
(1-599)	AL	39	B1
(1-1461)	PA	34	A2/B2
S Raymond Ave			
(1-2099)	AL	39	B1/C1/D1
(1-1039)	PA	34	B2/C2
(4000-4999)	LA	11	C3/D3
Raymond Ln	SP	34	D2
Raymond Hill Rd	SP	34	C2
Raymondale Dr	SP	34	D2
Rayneta Dr	SO/VN	54	B2
Raynol St	LA	37	B3
Readcrest Dr	BH	1	A2
Reading Ave	LA	26	B3/C3
Reaza Pl	WH	52	A2
N Record Ave	LA	41	B1/C1
S Record Ave	LA	41	C1/D1
Record Dr	LA	41	B1
Rector Pl	LA	4	C3
Red Oak Dr			
(5300-5522)	LA	4	A1
(5521-5599)	LA	3	A3
Red Rose Dr	EN/VN	54	C1
Redbeam Ave	TO	31	A2/B2/C2
Redbridge Ln	TZ	52	C3
Redbush Ln	VN	47	A3
Redcliff St	LA	5	B1/C1
Redesdale Ave	LA	5	C1
N Redfern Ave	IN	13	C1/D1
S Redfern Ave	IN	13	D1
Redfield Ave	LA	38	A1
Redlands St	MA/VE	25	C2
Redmesa Rd	CH	42	A1
N Redondo Ave	SO/VN	55	D3
S Redondo Ave	MB	27	C3/D3
	MB	29	B2
(100-799)	MB	27	D3
E Redondo Blvd	IN	13	A3/B3
S Redondo Blvd			
(1000-2499)	LA	6	B3/C3/D3
(2500-3899)	LA	10	A2/B2
Redondo Beach Ave	RB	29	A3
W Redondo Beach Blvd			
(2900-4398)	TO	30	A2/A3/B2
(3301-4498)	LW	30	A2/A3/B1/B2
Redrock Ct	LA	5	B1
Redwing St			
(18700-18827)	TZ	46	D1
(19200-19699)	TZ	45	D3
(19700-20099)	WH	45	D3
Redwood Ave			
(700-799)	ES	27	A1
(3300-4299)	LA	22	B1/C1
(4300-4399)	MA/VE	22	C1
Redwood Dr	PA	33	B3
Reed Dr	LO	32	D2
Reed St			
(1700-1899)	RB	29	B2
(25800-25899)	LO	32	D3
Reedvale Ln	LA	16	B1
Reef	MA/VE	25	B1
Reef Mall	MA/VE	25	B1
Reef St	MA/VE	25	B1
Rees St	MA/VE	25	B2/C2
N Reese Pl	BU	50	A1/B1/C1
S Reese Pl	BU	50	C1/D1
Reese Rd	TO	31	C2/C3
S Reeves Dr	BH	1	D2
Reeves Pl	GL	51	C3
Reeves St	LA	23	A3
Refugio Rd	EN/VN	54	C1
Regal Pl	LA	57	B1
Regal Oak Dr	EN/VN	54	B2
Regal Vista Dr	SO/VN	54	C2
Regal Woods Pl	SO/VN	54	C2
Regent Cir	IN	13	B2
Regent St			
(8700-11249)	LA	23	C2/C3/D1/D2
(11250-11699)	LA	22	B2
E Regent St	IN	13	B2
W Regent St	IN	13	B1/B2
Regina Ave	TO	30	B2/D2
Regina Ct	LA	14	C3
Regis Way	LA	25	B3
Reid Ave	CU	24	A3
Reinway Ct	PA	34	B3
Reiter Dr	PA	35	B2
Reklaw Dr	NH/SC	56	C2
Remmet Ave			
(6800-8149)	CP	45	B1/C1
(8150-8799)	CP	42	D2
(10100-10999)	CH	42	A2/B2
Remstoy Dr	LA	38	B2
Remy Ave	CP	42	D3
Rendall Pl	LA	5	C1
Renfrew Rd	LA	16	B2
Rennie Ave	MA/VE	21	B1
N Reno St			
(100-399)	LA	8	A3
(400-833)	LA	4	D3
(834-999)	LA	5	C1
S Reno St	LA	8	A3
Renovo St	LA	38	B2
Repetto Ave	LA	41	C3
Reppert Ct	LA	57	D1
Repton St	LA	33	C3
Republic St	LA	9	B3
Reseda Blvd			
(3300-3993)	TZ	52	C3
(4000-5398)	TZ	53	A1/B1/C1
(5318-6099)	TZ	46	C1/D1
(6073-8307)	EN/RE/TZ	46	A1/B1/C1
(8308-11521)	NR	43	A1/B3/C3/D3
Reservoir St	LA	5	C1/D1/D2
Resthaven Dr	LA	33	B1
Revere Aly	PA	35	B2
Revere Ave	LA	5	A1/A2
Revere Pl	CU	24	A2
Revuelta Way	LA	17	C3
Rexford Dr	LA	23	A3
N Rexford Dr	BH	1	B1/B2/C2/C3
S Rexford Dr	BH	1	C3/D3
Reyes Dr	TZ	52	B3
Reynier Ave			
(2500-2899)	LA	23	B3/C3
(5100-5499)	LA	24	D3
Reynolds Ave	LA	37	B3
Reynolds Dr			
(1200-1299)	GL	51	C3
(20400-22699)	TO	31	A3/B3/C3
Reynolds Ln			
(400-1399)	HB	29	C2
(700-899)	RB	29	C2
Reynolds Rd	TO	31	C2/C3
Reynosa Dr	TO	32	B3
Rhea Ave			
(5330-5799)	TZ	46	D1
(6300-8299)	EN/RE/TZ	46	A1/B1/C1
(8300-9999)	NR	43	B2/C2/D2
Rhinestone Dr	SO/VN	54	C3
Rhoda St			
(17500-17899)	EN/VN	46	D2
(20500-20599)	WH	45	D2
Rhoda Way	CU	24	C2
Rhode Island Ave	LA	19	B2
Rhodes Aly	PA	35	B1
Rhodes Ave			
(3800-5418)	NH/SC	56	A1/B1
(5419-5999)	NH/SC	48	C2/D2
(6000-8239)	NH	48	A2/B2/C2
Rhodes St	HB	29	C1
Rial Ln	LA	17	A2
Rialto Ave	MA/VE	21	C2
Rialto Ct	MA/VE	21	B2/C2
Ricardo St	LA	40	A3
Rice St	LA	33	B3
Rich St	LA	5	C2
Richard Cir	LA	38	B3
Richard Dr	LA	38	B2
Richard Pl	GL	51	B3
Richard St	BU	50	A1
Richardson Dr	LA	36	B2
Richelieu Ave	LA	38	C1
Richelieu Pl	LA	38	C1
Richelieu Ter	LA	38	C1
Richland Ave			
(200-299)	GL	51	B3
(2200-2399)	LA	4	A3
(10700-11124)	LA	23	B1/C1
(11125-11699)	LA	19	C3
Richland Pl	PA	34	A1
Richmond St			
(100-699)	ES	27	A2
(500-1199)	LA	40	A2/B1
Richwood Dr	LA	16	B2
Ridge Way			
(1346-1499)	PA	34	D3
(1400-1499)	LA	5	D2
Ridge Oak Dr	LA	3	A3
Ridgecrest Ct	MP	41	B3
Ridgecrest Dr	BH	1	A2
Ridgecrest St	MP	41	B3
Ridgecrest Way	MP	41	B3
Ridgedale Dr	BH	1	B1
S Ridgeley Dr			
(600-2249)	LA	6	A3/B3/C2/C3
(2250-3999)	LA	10	A2/B1
Ridgemont Dr			
(2100-2203)	LA	2	A1
(2204-2299)	LA	56	D2
Ridgemoor Dr	NH/SC	56	C3
Ridgeview Ave	LA	33	B1
Ridgeway Rd			
(1432-2599)	PA	35	C2/D2
(17550-17733)	GH	44	A1
Ridgewood Ln	PA	34	B2
N Ridgewood Pl			
(100-249)	LA	7	A3
(250-1399)	LA	3	C3/D3
S Ridgewood Pl	LA	7	A3
Ridpath Dr	LA	2	A1/A2
Rigali Ave	LA	51	C1
W Riggin St	MP	41	C3
Riggs Pl	LA	26	A2
Rimerton Rd	LA	54	D1/D2
Rimmer Ave	PP	15	B2
Rimmerton Rd	LA	54	D2
S Rimpau Blvd			
(200-2399)	LA	7	A2/B2/C1/D1
(2400-5874)	LA	10	A2/A3/D3
(5875-6399)	LA	13	A3
Rinaldi Pl	NR	43	A3
Rinaldi St	NR	42	A1
(15526-17823)	GH	44	A1/A2/A3
(17824-18099)	GH	43	A3
(18300-19599)	NR	43	A1/A2/A3
(20800-21395)	CH	42	A2/A3
Rinconia Dr	LA	3	A2
Rinconia Pl	LA	3	A2
Rindge Ave	MA/VE	25	C2
Rindge Ln	RB	29	A3/B3/C3
Ringgold Dr	LA	38	B2
Ringling St	TZ	53	A1
Rinzler Pl	NO/NR	44	C2
Rio St	LA	40	C1
S Rio St	LA	40	C1
Rio Vista Ave	LA	40	D1
Rios St	WH	52	B1
Ripley Ave	RB	29	C2/C3
Ripple Pl	LA	5	B2
Ripple St	LA	5	B2
Rising Dr	LA	37	C3
Rising Glen Pl	LA	2	B1
Rising Glen Rd	LA	2	A1/B1
Rita St	RB	31	B2
Rivas Cyn	PP	15	B3
River St			
(400-469)	LA	37	B2
(500-599)	LA	36	D2
Rivera St	LA	40	C2
Riverdale Ave	LA	36	C1
Riverdale Dr	GL	51	C1/C2
Rivers Rd	LA	16	B1
Riverside Dr			
(1000-1773)	LA	36	C1/D1
(1500-1899)	GL	50	D2/D3
(1774-3499)	LA	5	A1/B1/B2
(2501-2503)	BU	50	D1
(6100-6199)	LA	50	D3
(10000-10808)	NH/SC	57	A1/A2
(10809-12899)	NH/SC	56	A1/A2/A3
(12900-14499)	SO/VN	55	A1/A2/A3/B3
W Riverside Dr			
(400-2499)	BU	50	D1/D2
(2500-3147)	BU		Griffith Park
(2906-4499)	BU	57	A2/A3
(3196-3423)	BU	49	D3
(10000-10037)	NH/SC	57	A2
Riverside Pl	LA	5	B2
Riverside Ter	LA	5	B2
Riverton Ave			
(3800-4531)	NH/SC	57	A1/B1
(4540-4699)	NH/SC	49	D1
(4800-6799)	NH	49	B1/C1/D1
(7200-7799)	SV	49	A1
Riverview St	LA	36	C2
Riviera Ave	MA/VE	21	C1/C2
Riviera Way	TO	31	D2
Riviera Ranch Rd	LA	16	C1
Rixford Ave	LW	30	A2
Roads End St	GL	51	C2
Roanoke Rd			
(800-949)	PA	39	A2
(950-2499)	PA	35	D1/D2/D3
Robbins Dr	BH	20	B3
Robert Ln	BH	1	A2
Robert Pl	WH	52	B2
Robert Rd	TO	31	C2
Roberta St	LA	37	B3
Roberto Ln	LA	17	B1/B2
Roberts Ave	CU	24	A3
Roberts View Pl	NH/SC	56	C2
N Robertson Blvd			
(100-352)	BH	6	A1
(100-899)	LA	2	C1/D1
(101-399)	BH	2	D1
S Robertson Blvd			
(100-1113)	BH	6	A1/B1
(800-2393)	LA	6	A1/B1/C1
(2394-3391)	LA	23	B3/C3
(3700-3799)	CU	24	A2
Robertson Pl	LA	23	C3
Robin Dr	LA	2	A1
Robin Ln	LO	32	D2
Robin Rd	PA	35	D2/D3
Robincroft Dr	PA	34	A2
Robinhood Ln	LA	56	D2
Robinson Rd	PA	34	A2
Robinson St			
(100-399)	LA	8	A3
(400-999)	LA	4	D3
(1900-2899)	RB	29	B2/B3
Robinson Way	TO	32	D1
N Robinwood Dr	LA	16	B2
Roblar Pl	SO/VN	55	B1
Roblar Rd	SO/VN	55	B1
Roble Ave	LA	33	C3
Roble Vista Dr	LA	4	A3
Robles Ave	PA	35	C2
Robson Pl	SM	18	D2
Rocca Ct	LA	17	B2
Rocca Pl	LA	17	B2
Rocca Way	LA	17	B2
Rochedale Ln	LA	16	B2
Rochedale Way	LA	16	B2
Rochelle Pl	EN/VN	53	B3
Rochester Ave			
(10201-10999)	LA	20	B2/C1/C2
(11400-12499)	LA	19	B2/B3
Rochester Cir	LA	11	B2
Rock St	LA	5	B1

Street Index

Street	Area	Page	Grid
Wilshire Blvd			
(100-2467)	SM	18	B1/B2/B3
(600-2098)	LA	9	B1/B2/C2
(2001-3798)	LA	8	B1/B2/B3
(2468-3299)	SM	19	B1/B2
(3779-5198)	LA	7	B1/B2/B3
(5176-6699)	LA	6	A2/A3/B3
(8200-9198)	BH	6	A1/A2
(9174-9938)	BH	1	C1/C2/C3
(9934-9999)	BH	20	B3
(10000-11099)	LA	20	B2/B3/C1/C2
(11300-11426)	LA	16	C3
(11427-12499)	LA	19	A2/A3/B2
Wilshire Ct	LA	19	A2
Wilshire Pl	LA	8	B2
Wilson Ave			
(1400-1412)	PA	39	A2
(1413-1599)	PA	34	D3
(1600-1699)	BU	50	B1
(2300-2599)	MA/VE	21	C2
E Wilson Ave	GL	51	B2/B3
N Wilson Ave	PA	35	A1/B1
S Wilson Ave	PA	35	B1/C1
W Wilson Ave	GL	51	B1/B2
Wilson Ct	BU	50	B3
Wilson Pl	SM	18	D2
Wilson St	LA	9	D3
Wilson Ter	GL	51	B3
Wilson Way	LA	38	C1
Wilton Dr	LA	7	A3
Wilton Pl	LA	7	B3/C3
N Wilton Pl			
(100-249)	LA	7	A3
(250-1999)	LA	3	B3/C3/D3
S Wilton Pl			
(100-1899)	LA	7	A3/B3/C3/D3
(3700-5849)	LA	11	B2/C2/D2
(5850-11028)	LA	14	A2/C2/D2
Wimbledon Ln	IN	14	C1
Winans Dr	LA	3	A2
Winchester Ave			
(200-3899)	AL	38	B3/C3
(200-1399)	GL	50	C3/D2/D3
(4300-4399)	LA	38	B3
Windermere Ave	LA	33	A1
Winding Ln	SP	39	A1
Windsor Ave	LA	5	C1
N Windsor Blvd	LA	3	D2
S Windsor Blvd	LA	7	A2/A3/B2/C2
Windsor Pl	SP	34	D2
Windsor Rd	PA	35	D1
E Windsor Rd	GL	51	C2/C3
W Windsor Rd	GL	51	C1/C2
Windsor Way	CU	26	A3
Windtree Dr	LA	55	D1
Windward Ave			
(1-399)	MA/VE	21	C1/C2
(11900-12699)	LA	22	B1/B2
Windward Ct	MA/VE	21	C1
Winford Dr			
(3700-3865)	TZ	52	C3
(3866-3899)	TZ	53	C1
Wing St	GL	51	B3/C3
Winifred Ave	PA	35	C3
Winifred St	TZ	52	A3
Winlock Dr	TO	32	C1/D1
Winlock Rd	TO	32	D1
Winmar Dr	LA	36	B2/C2
Winnetka Ave			
(172-9098)	NR	42	D3
(4300-5349)	WH	52	A2/B2
(5350-6602)	WH	45	C3/D2/D3
(6433-8298)	CP	45	A3/B3/C3
(8215-8899)	CP	42	D3
(8901-10771)	CH	42	A3/B3/C3/D3
(10772-11099)	CH	43	A1
Winnetka Cir	WH	52	B2
Winnetka Ct	WH	52	B2
Winnetka Pl	WH	52	A2
Winnett Pl	SM	18	A2
Winnie Dr	LA	57	B2
Winona Ave			
(700-999)	PA	34	A2
(1600-1949)	BU	50	A1
(1950-3499)	BU	49	B2/B3
Winona Blvd	LA	4	A1/B1
Winona Way	PA	34	B2
Winsford Ave	LA	26	B3
Winslow Dr	LA	4	C3
Winston Ave	PA	35	C2/C3/D2
Winston St	LA	9	C2
Winter St			
(2700-3220)	LA	40	B3
(3221-3599)	LA	41	B1
Winthrop Dr	AL	38	B3/C3/D3
Winthrop Rd	PA	34	D3
Wiota St	LA	33	B3
Wisconsin Pl	LA	11	B3
Wisconsin St	LA	11	B3
Wiseburn Ave	HA	28	B1
Wish Ave			
(5600-6099)	EN/VN	46	C3/D3
(6800-7999)	VN	46	A3/B3
(9100-10299)	NR	44	B2/C2
(10300-11451)	GH	44	A2/B2
Wisner Ave	VN	47	A2
Wit Pl	LA	4	C3
Witmer Pl	LA	9	B1
Witmer St	LA	9	B1
Witzel Dr	SO/VN	55	C2
Wixom St			
(10600-10799)	SV	49	A1
(11300-11399)	SV	48	B3
(11600-13399)	NH	48	B1/B2/B3
Wo He Lo Trl	CH	42	A2
Woking Way	LA	4	A3
Wolfe Pl	WH	52	B1
Wolfe Way	WH	52	B1
Wolford Ln	SP	38	A3
Wollacott St	RB	29	B2/C2
Wollam St	LA	36	B1/B2
Wonder View Dr			
(3200-3577)	LA	52	C3
(3578-3699)	LA	57	B3
Wonder View Pl	LA	52	C3
Wonder View Plz	LA	52	C3
Wonderland Ave			
(8500-8882)	LA	56	D2/D3
(8883-9199)	LA	2	A1
Wonderland Park Ave	LA	56	D2
Wood Ave	TO	31	B2
Wood Ter	LA	4	A3
Woodacres Rd	SM	18	A2
Woodbine St			
(3200-10899)	LA	23	C1/C2
(11400-12628)	LA	22	A2/B1
Woodbridge St			
(10200-10799)	NH/SC	57	A1
(11200-12814)	NH/SC	56	B1/B2/B3
(12815-13099)	NH/SC	55	B3
(13300-13399)	SO/VN	55	B2
N Woodburn Dr	LA	16	B3
S Woodburn Dr	LA	16	B3
Woodbury Dr			
(1200-1299)	GL	51	B3
(2500-2699)	TO	32	B2
Woodbury Rd	GL	51	A3/B3
Woodcliff Rd	SO/VN	54	B2/C2
Woodcrest Dr	SO/VN	54	C2
Woodfield Ct	LA	54	D3
Woodfield Dr	SO/VN	54	C2
Woodfield Pl	SO/VN	54	C2
Woodgreen St	LA	22	B1
Woodhaven Dr	LA	Griffith Park	
Woodhill Canyon Pl	NH/SC	56	C2
Woodhill Canyon Rd	NH/SC	56	C2
W Woodland Ave	BU	49	D2
Woodland Dr	BH	1	A2/B2
Woodland Ln	LA	2	A2
Woodland Rd	PA	34	D3
Woodland Way	LA	3	B1
Woodland Crest Dr	WH	52	B1
Woodlawn Ave			
(500-899)	MA/VE	21	C2/C3
(2800-2999)	PA	35	D3
(3700-5199)	LA	12	B1/C1/D1
(8300-8349)	SG	35	D3
Woodlawn Ct			
(600-899)	MA/VE	21	C3
(3700-3799)	LA	12	B1
Woodley Ave			
(4400-5199)	EN/VN	54	A1/B1
(5600-8299)	VN	47	A1/B1/C1/D1
(8300-10299)	NO/NR	44	B3/C3/D3
(10300-11538)	GH	44	A3/B3
Woodley Pl	NO/NR	44	D3
Woodley Park Ln	EN/VN	54	B1
Woodlyn Rd	PA	35	A2/A3
Woodman Ave			
(4100-5449)	SO/VN	55	A2/B2
(5450-6799)	SO/VN	47	B3/C3/D3
(6800-8399)	VN	47	A3/B3
Woodman Cyn	SO/VN	55	C2
Woodman Pl	VN	48	B1
Woodrow Ave	LA	33	B1
Woodrow Wilson Dr			
(6700-7918)	LA	57	C1/C2
(7919-8099)	LA	56	D3
Woodruff Ave	LA	20	A2/B2/C2
Woods Ave	MP	41	B3/C3
S Woods Ave	LA	41	C3/D3
Woods Dr	LA	2	A2
Woodshill Trl	LA	2	B2
Woodshire Dr	LA	Griffith Park	
Woodside Dr	LA	36	C3
Woodstock Ln	BU	50	A1
Woodstock Rd			
(1300-1399)	PA	35	D1
(2500-2899)	LA	56	D3
Woodvale Rd	EN/VN	54	B1/B2
Woodview Dr	LA	Griffith Park	
Woodward Ave	LO	32	C3/D3
E Woodward Ave	AL	39	A3/B2/B3
W Woodward Ave	AL	39	B1/B2
Woodwardia Dr	LA	55	D1
Woodworth Ave	IN	14	C1/D1
Woodworth Ct	LA	9	C3
Woody Trl	LA	57	C2
Woolford St	CU	24	D2
Woolwine Dr	LA	41	A2/B1
Wooster Ave	LA	26	A2/A3
S Wooster St	LA	6	B1/C1
Worcester Ave	PA	34	A2
Workman St			
(1700-1949)	LA	40	A2
(1950-2999)	LA	37	C2/D2
World Way	LA	26	D1
World Way N	LA	26	D1/D2
World Way S	LA	26	D1/D2
World Way W	LA	26	D1
(6900-7499)	LA	25	D2/D3
Worth St	LA	38	D1/D2
Worthen Ave	LA	5	B2
Wortser Ave			
(4400-4599)	NH/SC	55	B3
(4600-5410)	SO/VN	55	A3/B3
(5411-5599)	SO/VN	48	D1
(7000-8199)	NH	48	A1/B1
Wotkyns Dr	PA	34	A1
Wren Dr	LA	36	B3
Wright Ave	PA	34	A3
Wright St	LA	9	C1
Wright Ter	CU	24	B3
Wrightcrest Dr			
(5800-5867)	CU	10	B1
(5868-7099)	CU	24	B3
Wrightview Dr	NH/SC	56	C3
Wrightview Pl	NH/SC	56	C3
Wrightwood Ct	NH/SC	56	C3
Wrightwood Dr	NH/SC	56	C3
Wrightwood Ln			
(10700-10968)	NH/SC	57	B1
(10969-11099)	NH/SC	56	C3
Wrightwood Pl	NH/SC	56	C3
Wyandotte St			
(11100-11199)	SV	48	B3
(11500-13499)	NH	48	B1/B2/B3
(13500-13649)	VN	48	B1
(13650-16199)	VN	47	B1/B2/B3
(16600-17499)	VN	46	B2/B3
(17700-19213)	EN/RE/TZ	46	B1/B2
(19214-19699)	EN/RE/TZ	45	B3
(20200-22199)	CP	45	B1/B2
Wybro Way	LA	41	A2
Wylie Ln	RB	29	B2
Wyman Ave	LA	41	C2
Wyndham Rd	LA	56	D3
Wynglen Ln	LA	40	C1/D1
Wynkoop St	LA	26	B1
Wynne Ave	EN/RE/TZ	46	A2/B2/C2
Wynola St	PP	15	C1
Wynwood Ln	LA	40	D1/D2
Wyoming Ave	LA	19	B3
W Wyoming Ave	BU	49	C2/C3
Wystone Ave			
(6400-7599)	EN/RE/TZ	46	B1/C1
(8300-11199)	NR	43	A2/B2/C2/D2
Wyton Dr	LA	20	B2
Yacht Club Way	RB	31	A1
Yale Ave	MA/VE	21	C3
Yale Dr	GL	51	C3
Yale St			
(1-199)	PA	34	A2
(700-999)	LA	9	B2
(800-1599)	SM	19	A1/B1
Yarmouth Ave			
(4700-5299)	EN/VN	53	A2
(5300-6335)	EN/VN	46	C2/D2
(6370-8299)	EN/RE/TZ	46	A2/B2/C2
(10300-11599)	GH	44	A1/B1
Yawl St	MA/VE	25	B1
Ybarra Rd	WH	52	B1
Yeager Pl	LA	3	A1
Yellowstone St	LA	38	C1/D1
Yerba St	NH	48	B1
Ynez Ave	RB	31	C2
N Ynez Ave	MP	39	D2
Yoakum St	LA	38	B2
Yolanda Ave			
(5100-5349)	TZ	53	A1
(5350-6035)	TZ	46	C1/D1
(6100-8299)	EN/RE/TZ	46	A1/B1/C1
(8300-11599)	NR	43	A2/B2/C2/D2
Yolie Ln	TZ	45	D3
Yolo St	PA	35	B1
Yonkers Ln	LA	17	B2
Yorba St	LA	38	B1
York Ave	HA	28	A2/B2
S York Ave	IN	28	A2
(11200-11303)	IN	13	D2
York Blvd	LA/SP	34	D1
(3600-4103)	LA	51	C3
(4104-6799)	LA	33	C1/C2/C3
(4429-4524)	LA	36	A2
York Dr	NR	43	D2
York Pl	LA	51	C3
York Hill Pl	LA	33	B1
Yorksboro Ln	WH	52	B2
Yorkshire Ave	SM	19	C2
Yorkshire Dr	LA	36	B1
Yorkshire Rd	PA	35	C3
Yorktown Ave	LA	26	B2/C2
Yorktown Pl	LA	26	B2
Yosemite Dr	LA	33	B1/B2/B3
Yosemite Way	LA	33	B1/C1
Young Dr	BH	20	B3
Youngdale St	SG	35	D3
Youngworth Rd	CU	24	C3
Youngworth St	CU	24	D1
Ysabel St	RB	31	B2
Ysidro Pl	PP	15	C1
Yucatan Ave	WH	52	B1
Yucca Ln	LA	2	A2
Yucca St			
(700-799)	ES	27	A1
(5900-6799)	LA	3	B1/B2/B3
(7000-7199)	LA	2	A3
Yucca Trl	LA	2	A2
Yukon Ave			
(10000-11112)	IN	13	D3
(11113-11999)	IN	28	A3/B3
(12500-15099)	HA	28	B3/C3/D3
(15200-15699)	LW	28	D3
(16600-18999)	TO	30	A3/B3/C3
Yuma Pl	LA	2	A2
Zaca Pl	LA	33	B1
Zakon Rd	TO	31	C2/C3
Zaltana St	CH	42	A1
Zalvidea St			
(400-499)	LA	9	A1
(500-599)	LA	5	D1
Zamora St	LA	12	C2
Zane St	LA	38	C1
Zanja St			
(400-757)	PA	34	A1
(12700-13399)	LA	22	C1/C2
(13333-13358)	MA/VE	22	C1
(13357-13599)	MA/VE	21	B3
Zaring St	LA	41	C2
Zayanta Dr	MA/VE	25	B2
Zella Pl	LA	38	D2
Zelzah Ave			
(4734-5299)	EN/VN	53	A2/B2
(5300-6369)	EN/VN	46	C2/D2
(6370-8299)	EN/RE/TZ	46	A2/B2/C2
(8300-10855)	NR	43	B3/C3/D3
(10500-11603)	GH	43	A3/B3
Zeno Pl	MA/VE	21	C2
Zephyr Ct	MA/VE	21	C1
Zerr Ct	GL	51	B3
Zeus Dr	LA	56	D3
Zinnia Ln	GL	51	B3
Zitola Ter	MA/VE	25	B2/C2
Zombar Ave	VN	47	A2/B2
Zonal Ave	LA	40	A2/A3
Zoo Dr	LA	51	B1
(4752-5399)	LA	Griffith Park	
Zook Dr	GL	51	A1
Zorada Ct	LA	57	D1
Zorada Dr	LA	57	D1
Zuni Ln	TP	52	C1
Zuniga Ln	LA	40	A3